Solaris™ 7 Reference

D1546691

Janice Winsor

Sun Microsystems Press
A Prentice Hall Title

The publisher offers discounts on this book when ordered in bulk quantities.
For more information, contact: Corporate Sales Department, Phone: 800-382-3419;
Fax: 201-236-7141; E-mail: corpsales@prenhall.com; or write: Prentice Hall PTR,
Corp. Sales Dept., One Lake Street, Upper Saddle River, NJ 07458.

Editorial/production supervision: *Faye Gemmellaro*
Cover design director: *Jerry Votta*
Cover design: *Scott Weiss*
Cover illustration: *Anthony Gemmellaro*
Manufacturing manager: *Alexis R. Heydt*
Marketing manager: *Bryan Gambrel*
Acquisitions editor: *Gregory G. Doench*
Technical editor: *Bill Calkins*
Sun Microsystems Press:
Marketing manager: *Michael Llwyd Alread*
Publisher: *Rachel Borden*

10 9 8 7 6 5 4 3 2 1

ISBN 0-13-020048-4

Sun Microsystems Press
A Prentice Hall Title

CONTENTS

E

F

G

M

N

R

S

T

PREFACE

The *Solaris 7 Reference* is your complete guide to all of the manual pages in Section 1, "User Commands," of the online reference documentation (except the FMLI commands).

All documentation references within this guide are to the official Solaris documentation. To access Sun Microsystems, Inc., documentation online, see:

`http://docs.sun.com`.

Audience

This book is for any user of the Solaris system software who needs to refer to any of the Section 1 User Commands in the online manual pages for quick reference or for more detailed information.

Conventions Used in This Book

The following table shows the typographic conventions used in this book.

Typeface or Symbol	Description
`courier`	Indicates a command, file name, object name, method, argument, JavaScript keyword, HTML tag, file content, or code excerpt.

Typeface or Symbol	Description
courier italics	Indicates a variable that you should replace with a valid value.
courier	Indicates text that you type.
italics	Indicates definitions, emphasis, or a book title.

Icons

 Within this guide, any material that is new or revised in the Solaris 7 release is marked with a "New!" icon in the margin.

In addition, the list of commands in the Intro manual page in Chapter I is marked with asterisks to show commands that are changed or revised in this release.

How This Book Is Organized

The Introductory chapter provides a quick-reference to the contents of this book by functional grouping. The commands are grouped alphabetically within their installation package categories and list the number for the first page of each command. Within the "Core Solaris (Usr)" category, the commands are grouped by function.

The rest of the book is a dictionary-style alphabetic reference to the commands.

The Subject Index contains page references for commands both by name and by subject.

ACKNOWLEDGMENTS

Sun Microsystems Press would like to acknowledge the following people for their contributions to this book.

Bill Calkins, Sr. Consultant, Pyramid Design Inc., for acting as a technical reference and providing many of the more complex examples.

Linda Gallops, SQA Product Engineering, Sun Microsystems, Inc., for technical help.

Mary Lautner, Program Manager, Solaris Software Group, Sun Microsystems, Inc., for providing useful information about the Solaris 7 release.

Bridget Burke, RavensWord Communications, for help with FrameMaker and PDF file production issues.

The author would like to acknowledge the following people for their contributions to this book.

The individuals at Sun Microsystems, Inc., who contributed to the Section 1 manual pages.

Rachel Borden of Sun Microsystems Press and Greg Doench of Prentice Hall for their unfailing support and friendship.

Mary Lou Nohr for editing this manuscript with her usual skill and tact.

Camille Trentacoste for book and template designs and for her help in implementing additional design elements.

Her husband, Maris, for his love and support and for the air-conditioned computer room that enabled the author to work through the long, hot, Australian summertime.

INTRODUCTION

The *Solaris 7 Reference* is your complete alphabetic reference to all (except the FMLI comands) of the manual pages in Section 1 of the online reference documentation for the Solaris 7 release.

This chapter provides a quick-reference to the contents of this book by functional grouping. The commands are grouped alphabetically within their installation package categories and list the number for the first page of each command. Within the "Core Solaris (Usr)" category, the commands are grouped by function.

Audio Applications (SUNWaudio)

CCS Tools Bundled with SunOS (SUNWbtool)

Core Solaris (Usr) (SUNWcsu)

Archiving Commands

Communication Commands

File Management Commands

Kerberos Commands

Localization Commands

See also "System Localization (SUNWloc)" on page 17.

Miscellaneous

Shell Programming Commands

System Status Commands

Extended System Utilities (SUNWesu)

LDAP Libraries for Software Development of Dynamically Linked Executables (SUNWlldap)

Network Information System (Usr) (SUNWnisu)

Solaris Documentation Server Lookup (SUNWab2m)

Solaris User Registration (SUNWsregu)

Source Compatibility (Usr) (SUNWscpu)

System Accounting (Usr) (SUNWaccu)

System Localization (SUNWloc)

See also "Localization Commands" on page 4.

TNF Core Components (SUNWtnfc)

UUCP Utilities and Daemon (SUNWbnuu)

Volume Management (Usr) (SUNWvolu)

XCU4 Utilities (SUNWxcu4)

The XCU4 commands are an XPG4 superset of POSIX.1-1990, Solaris 2.4 POSIX.2-1992, and POSIX.2a-1992 containing extensions to POSIX standards from XPG3.

A

acctcom — Search and Print Process Accounting Files

Synopsis

```
/usr/bin/acctcom [-abfhikmqrtv] [-C sec] [-e time] [-E time]
[-g group] [-H factor] [-I chars] [-l line]
[-n pattern] [-o output-file] [-O sec]
[-s time] [-S time] [-u user] [filename...]
```

Description

acctcom is one of the suite of commands that you use with the structured set of tools to build accounting systems. Use the acctcom command to search process accounting files created by acct(4) and to display selected records to standard output.

acctcom reads file names, the standard input, or /var/adm/pacct, in the form described by acct(4) and writes selected records to standard output. Each record represents the execution of one process. The output shows the COMMAND, USER, TTY, START TIME, END TIME, REAL (SEC), CPU (SEC), MEAN SIZE (K), and optionally, F (the fork()/exec() flag: 1 for fork() without exec()), STAT (the system exit status), HOG FACTOR, KCORE MIN, CPU FACTOR, CHARS TRNSFD, and BLOCKS READ (total blocks read and written).

When you execute the command with superuser privileges, a pound sign (#) is prepended to the command name. When a process is not associated with a known terminal, a ? is displayed in the TTY field.

`/var/adm/pacct` is read when you do not specify a file name and when the standard input is associated with a terminal or `/dev/null` (as is the case when using `&` in the shell). Otherwise, the standard input is read.

Any file name arguments are read in their respective order. Each file is normally read forward, that is, in chronological order by process completion time. The file `/var/adm/pacct` is usually the current file to be examined; a busy system may need several such files, of which all but the current file are found in `/var/adm/pacctincr`.

`acctcom` reports only on terminated processes. Use ps(1) for active processes.

Options

`-a`	Show some average statistics about the processes selected. Print the statistics after the output records.
`-b`	Read backward, showing latest commands first. This option has no effect when standard input is read.
`-f`	Print the `fork()`/`exec()` flag and system exit status columns in the output. Display the numeric output in octal.
`-h`	Instead of mean memory size, show the fraction of total available CPU time consumed by the process during its execution. This hog factor is computed as (total CPU time)/(elapsed time).
`-i`	Print columns containing the I/O counts in the output.
`-k`	Instead of memory size, show total kcore-minutes.
`-m`	Show mean core size (the default).
`-q`	Do not print any output records, just print the average statistics, as with the `-a` option.
`-r`	Show CPU factor (user-time/(system-time + user-time)).
`-t`	Show separate system and user CPU times.
`-v`	Exclude column headings from the output.
`-C sec`	Show only processes with total CPU time (system-time + user-time) that exceed `sec` seconds.
`-e time`	Show processes existing at or before `time`.
`-E time`	Show processes ending at or before `time`. Using the same time for both `-S` and `-E`, show the processes that existed at `time`.
`-g group`	Show only processes belonging to `group`. You can designate the group by either the group ID or group name.
`-H factor`	Show only processes that exceed `factor`, where `factor` is the hog factor, as explained in option `-h`, above.
`-I chars`	Show only processes transferring more characters than the cutoff number given by `chars`.
`-l line`	Show only processes belonging to terminal `/dev/term/line`.

-n *pattern* Show only commands matching *pattern* that may be a regular
expression, as in regcmp(3C), except + means one or more
occurrences.

-o *output-file*

Copy selected process records in the input data format to
output-file; suppress printing to standard output.

-O *sec* Show only processes with CPU system time exceeding *sec*
seconds.

-s *time* Show processes existing at or after *time*, given in the format
hr[:*min*[:*sec*]].

-S *time* Show processes starting at or after *time*.

-u *user* Show only processes belonging to *user*. You can specify a user ID,
a login name that is then converted to a user ID, # (which
designates only those processes executed with superuser
privileges), or ? (which designates only those processes associated
with unknown user IDs).

Examples

The following example turns on accounting, lists the contents of the
/var/adm/pacct file by using the acctcom command without any
arguments, and then turns off accounting. Notice that the accton command
used to turn on accounting has a pound sign in front of it because it was run by
superuser.

```
castle% su
castle#/usr/lib/acct/accton /var/adm/pacct
castle# exit
castle% acctcom
COMMAND                             START    END       REAL    CPU      MEAN
NAME       USER     TTYNAME        TIME     TIME    (SECS)  (SECS)  SIZE(K)
#accton    root     pts/3          12:09:16 12:09:16   0.12    0.05   543.20
csh        root     pts/3          12:09:21 12:09:21   0.01    0.01   748.00
ls         root     pts/3          12:09:29 12:09:29   0.03    0.03   548.00
more       root     pts/3          12:09:34 12:09:34   0.03    0.03   537.33
acctcom    root     pts/3          12:09:47 12:09:47   0.08    0.07   689.14
dtfile     winsor   ?              12:09:59 12:09:59   0.03    0.03  2510.67
dtfile     winsor   ?              12:10:02 12:10:02   0.02    0.02  3350.00
uusched    uucp     ?              12:11:00 12:11:00   0.05    0.05   409.60
uuxqt      uucp     ?              12:11:00 12:11:00   0.06    0.05   449.60
uudemon.   uucp     ?              12:11:00 12:11:00   0.15    0.04   489.00
#sh        uucp     ?              12:11:00 12:11:00   0.20    0.06   477.33
dtfile     winsor   ?              12:13:00 12:13:00   0.02    0.02  3298.00
dtfile     winsor   ?              12:13:03 12:13:03   0.02    0.02  3338.00
dtfile     winsor   ?              12:16:00 12:16:00   0.03    0.03  2514.67
dtfile     winsor   ?              12:16:03 12:16:03   0.02    0.02  3212.00
dtfile     winsor   ?              12:19:01 12:19:01   0.03    0.03  2472.00
dtfile     winsor   ?              12:19:04 12:19:04   0.02    0.02  3326.00
accton     winsor   pts/5          12:20:06 12:20:06   0.03    0.03   677.33
castle% su
```

```
castle# /usr/lib/acct/accton
castle# exit
castle%
```

Files

/etc/group System group file.

/etc/passwd

System password file.

/var/adm/pacctincr

Active processes accounting file.

Attributes

See attributes(5) for descriptions of the following attributes:

Attribute Type	Attribute Value
Availability	SUNWcsu
CSI	Enabled

See Also

ps(1), acct(1M), acctcms(1M), acctcon(1M), acctmerg(1M), acctprc(1M), acctsh(1M), fwtmp(1M), runacct(1M), su(1M), acct(2), regcmp(3C), acct(4), utmp(4), attributes(5)
System Administration Guide

adb — General-Purpose Debugger

Synopsis

```
/usr/bin/adb [-k] [-w] [-I dir] [-P prompt] [-V mode]
    [objectfile [corefile [swapfile]]]
```

Description

The adb and kadb tools are available in the Solaris 2.x operating environment They offer the same capabilities as the tools in the SunOS release 4.x. kadb has been enhanced to recognize multiple processors. The processor ID is displayed in the kadb prompt.

dbx and dbxtool are no longer available with the default system software. You can purchase enhanced versions of these tools as the SPARCworks Debugger, which is an unbundled product.

The adb command is an interactive, general-purpose debugger. You can use it to examine files. It also provides a controlled environment for the execution of programs.

To make debugging under the Solaris 2.4 operating environment easier:

- Enable savecore by uncommenting the savecore lines in the /etc/init.d/syssetup file.

- Boot under kadb by typing $c when the system crashes.

- Use adb and crash.

Note — The adb command is platform and release dependent. Examine kernel core dumps on the same platform they were created on.

Bugs

Because no shell is invoked to interpret the arguments of the :r command, the customary wild-card and variable expansions cannot occur.

Because there is little type-checking on addresses, using a source file address in an inappropriate context may lead to unexpected results. The $cparameter-count command is a workaround.

The adb command should be changed to use the new format symbolic information generated by -g.

Options

-k	Perform kernel memory mapping; use when corefile is a system crash dump or /dev/mem, or when using a swapfile.
-w	Create both *objectfile* and *corefile*, if necessary, and open them for reading and writing so that they can be modified with adb.
-I *dir*	Specify a colon-separated list of directories for files to be read with $< or $<< (see below); the default is /usr/platform/*plat-name*/lib/adb:/usr/lib/adb, where *plat-name* is the name of the platform implementation. Use the uname(1) -i option to find *plat-name*.
-P *prompt*	Specify the adb prompt string.
-V *mode*	Specify the disassembly and register display mode. *mode* values are 1 (v8), 2 (generic V9), and 4 (v9 plus Sun UltraSPARC-specific instructions). The default mode is determined by the type of corefile being examined. (SPARC only)

Operands

objectfile	Normally, an executable program file, preferably containing a symbol table. If the file does not contain a symbol table, you can still examine it, but you cannot use the symbolic features of adb. The default for *objectfile* is a.out.
corefile	Assumed to be a core image file produced after the *objectfile* is executed. The default for *corefile* is core.
swapfile	The image of the swap device used. It is valid only when used with the -k option.

Usage

The adb command reads commands from the standard input and displays responses on the standard output. By default, it does not supply a prompt. It ignores the QUIT signal. INTERRUPT invokes the next adb command. adb generally recognizes command input of the form:

[*address*] [, *count*] [*command*] [;]

address and *count* (if supplied) are expressions that result in a new current location and a repetition count. *command* is composed of a verb followed by a modifier or list of modifiers.

The symbol dot (.) represents the current location; it is initially 0. The default count is 1.

Expressions

.	The value of dot.
+	The value of dot incremented by the current increment.
^	The value of dot decremented by the current increment.
&	The last address typed. In older versions of adb, a double quote (") was used.
integer	A number. The prefixes 0o and 0O indicate octal; 0t and 0T, decimal; 0x and 0X, hexadecimal (the default).
int.frac	A floating-point number.
'*cccc*'	ASCII value of up to 4 characters.
<*name*	The value of *name*, which is either a variable name or a register name.
symbol	A symbol in the symbol table.
(*exp*)	The value of *exp*.

Unary Operators

`exp`	The contents of location *`exp`* in corefile.
%*`exp`*	The contents of location *`exp`* in objectfile (In older versions of adb, @ was used).
-*`exp`*	Integer negation.
~*`exp`*	Bitwise complement.
#*`exp`*	Logical negation.

Binary Operators

Binary operators are left-associative and have lower precedence than unary operators.

+	Integer addition.
-	Integer subtraction.
*	Integer multiplication.
%	Integer division.
&	Bitwise conjunction ("AND").
|	Bitwise disjunction ("OR").
#	Left-hand side rounded up to the next multiple of right-hand side.

Variables

Named variables are set initially by adb but are not used subsequently.

0	The last value printed.
1	The last offset part of an instruction source.
2	The previous value of variable 1.
9	The count on the last $< or $<< command.

On entry the following variables are set from the system header in the corefile or objectfile as appropriate.

b	The base address of the data segment.
d	The data segment size.
e	The entry point.
m	The magic number.
t	The text segment size.

Command Verbs

Commands to adb consist of a verb followed by a modifier or list of modifiers.

?	Print locations starting at address in *objectfile*.
/	Print locations starting at address in *corefile*.

=	Print the value of address itself.
:	Manage a subprocess.
>	Assign a value to a variable or register.
>/*modifier*/	Take the quantity specified by *modifier* from the address of the value and assign it to a variable or register. *modifier* can be one of the following:

c	Unsigned char quantity.
s	Unsigned short quantity.
i	Unsigned int quantity.
l	Unsigned long quantity.

Return	Repeat the previous command with a count of 1. Increment dot (.).
!	Shell escape.

?, /, and = Modifiers

The following format modifiers apply to the commands ?, /, and =. To specify a format, follow the command with an optional repeat count and the desired format letter or letters.

{ ?/= } [[*r*] *f* ...]]

where *r* is a decimal repeat count, and *f* is one of the format letters listed below.

o	(. increment: 2) Print 2 bytes in octal.
O	(4) Print 4 bytes in octal.
q	(2) Print in signed octal.
Q	(4) Print long signed octal.
g	(8) Display 8 bytes in signed octal.
G	(8) Display 8 bytes in unsigned octal.
d	(2) Print in decimal.
D	(4) Print long decimal.
e	(8) Display 8 bytes in signed decimal.
E	(8) Display 8 bytes in unsigned decimal.
x	(2) Print 2 bytes in hexadecimal.
X	(4) Print 4 bytes in hexadecimal.
J	(8) Display 8 bytes in hexadecimal.
K	(n) Print pointer or long in hexadecimal (displays 4 bytes for 32-bit programs and 8 bytes for 64-bit programs).
u	(2) Print as an unsigned decimal number.

U	(4) Print long unsigned decimal.
f	(4) Print a single-precision floating-point number.
F	(8) Print a double-precision floating-point number.
b	(1) Print the addressed byte in octal.
c	(1) Print the addressed character.
C	(1) Print the addressed character, using ^ escape convention.
s	(n) Print the addressed string.
S	(n) Print a string, using the ^ escape convention.
y	(8) Print 8 bytes in date format.
Y	(4) Print 4 bytes in date format.
i	(4) Print as machine instructions. (SPARC)
i	(variable) Print as machine instructions. (X86)
a	(0) Print the value of dot (.) in symbolic form.
p	(4) Print the addressed value in symbolic form.
t	(0) Tab to the next appropriate TAB stop.
r	(0) Print a space.
n	(0) Print a newline.
"..."	(0) Print the enclosed string.
^	(0) Decrement dot (.).
+	(0) Increment dot (.).
-	(0) Decrement dot (.) by 1.

? and / Modifiers

`l value mask`

> Apply `mask` and compare for `value`; move dot (.) to matching location.

`L value mask`

> Apply `mask` and compare for 4-byte `value`; move dot (.) to matching location.

`M value mask`

> Apply `mask` and compare for 8-byte `value`; move dot (.) to matching location.

`w value`   Write the 2-byte `value` to address.

`W value`   Write the 4-byte `value` to address.

`Z value`   Write the 8-byte `value` to address.

`m b1 e1 f1[?]`

Map new values for b1, e1, f1. If the ? or / is followed by *, then the second segment (b2, e2, f2) of the address mapping is changed.

v   Like w, but write only bytes at a time.

: Modifiers

Values for : modifiers are listed below. Specify the optional len in decimal; if not specified, it defaults to 1.

b *commands*   Set instruction breakpoint; set dot (.) to address and execute commands when reached.

len w *commands*

Set write watchpoint (data breakpoint); set dot (.) to the affected location and execute commands when any byte in the range [address,address+len) is written.

len a *commands*

Set access watchpoint; set dot (.) to the affected location and execute commands when any byte in the range [address,address+len) is read or written.

len p *commands*

Set execution watchpoint; set dot (.) to the affected location and execute commands when any instruction in the range [address,address+len) is executed.

r   Run *objectfile* as a subprocess.

d   Delete breakpoint at address or watchpoint containing address.

z   Delete all breakpoints and watchpoints.

c*s*   Continue the subprocess with signal *s*.

s*s*   Single-step the subprocess with signal *s*.

e*s*   Single-step but do not step into called functions.

i   Add the signal specified by address to the list of signals passed directly to the subprocess.

t   Remove the signal specified by address from the list implicitly passed to the subprocess.

k   Terminate (kill) the current subprocess, if any.

A   Attach adb to an existing process ID. (For example, 0t1234:A attaches adb to decimal process number 1234.)

R   Release the previously attached process.

$ Modifiers

<*filename*	Read commands from the file *filename*.
<<*filename*	Similar to <, but can be used in a file of commands without closing the file.
>*filename*	Append output to *filename*, and create it if it does not exist.
l	Show the current lightweight process (LWP) ID.
L	Show all the LWP IDs.
P	Specify the adb prompt string.
?	Print process ID, the signal that stopped the subprocess, and the registers.
r	Print the names and contents of the general CPU registers, and the instruction addressed by pc.
x	Print the names and contents of floating-point registers 0 through 15. (SPARC)
X	Print the names and contents of floating-point registers 16 through 31. (SPARC)
x or X	Print the contents of floating-point registers. $x and $X accept a count that determines the precision of the floating-point registers; the default is 25. Using $X produces more verbose output than using $x. (x86)
y	Print the names and contents of floating-point registers 32 through 47. (SPARC)
Y	Print the names and contents of floating-point registers 48 through 63. (SPARC)
b	Print all breakpoints and watchpoints and their associated counts, types, lengths, and commands.
c	Backtrace C stack. On SPARC-based systems, it is impossible for adb to determine how many parameters were passed to a function. The default that adb chooses in a $c command is to show the six parameter registers. You can override this default by appending a hexadecimal number to the $c command, specifying how many parameters to display. For example, the $cf command prints 15 parameters for each function in the stack trace.
C	Same as $c, but in addition, display the frame pointer values.
d	Set the default radix to address and report the new value. Note that address is interpreted in the (old) current radix. Thus, 10$d never changes the default radix.
e	Print the names and values of external variables.
w	Set the page width for output to address (default 80).
s	Set the limit for symbol matches to address (default 255).
o	Regard all integers input as octal.

q	Exit from `adb`.
v	Print all non-zero variables in octal.
m	Print the address map.
f	Print a list of known source file names.
p	(Kernel debugging) Change the current kernel memory mapping to map the designated user structure to the address given by u; this is the address of the user's `proc` structure.
i	Show which signals are passed to the subprocess with the minimum of `adb` interference.
V	Change the current disassembly and register display mode. Values are: 1 (v8), 2 (generic V9), and 4 (v9 plus Sun UltraSPARC specific instructions). When you omit the numeric parameter, print the information on the current disassembly mode. (SPARC)
W	Reopen *objectfile* and *corefile* for writing, as though the −w command-line argument had been given.

Usage

See `largefile`(5) for the description of the behavior of `adb` when encountering files greater than or equal to 2 Gbytes (2**31 bytes).

Diagnostics

When there is no current command or format, `adb` comments about inaccessible files, syntax errors, abnormal termination of commands, and so forth.

Examples

In the following examples, the processor ID is 0.

Debugging a Live Kernel

Use the following command to debug a live kernel.

```
# adb -k
physmem 3dec
```

The following example shows how to use `adb` to find the cause of a system panic by examining program and corefiles. The syntax is:

```
adb program corefile
```

```
# adb -k unix.0 vmcore.0
```

Changing a Tunable Parameter

If you change a tunable parameter in an /etc/systems file, you can use the following command to verify that the change was made.

```
castle% su
Password:
# adb -k /dev/ksyms /dev/mem
physmem 3dec
```

adb replies with a hexadecimal number in 4 kilobytes of physical memory with a line similar to `physmem xxxx`.

No prompt is displayed, but `adb` is running. To check a tunable parameter and display the integer as a decimal, type:

`parameter/D`

To check a tunable parameter and display the integer in hexadecimal, type:

`parameter/X`

For example, to display the `maxusers` setting, type:

```
maxusers/D
maxusers:
maxusers:          61
maxusers/X
maxusers:
maxusers:          3d
```

To display the maximum shared memory segment size, type:

```
shminfo_shmmax/D
shminfo_shmmax:
shminfo_shmmax: 1048576
```

To exit `adb`, type **$q** and press Return.

```
$q

castle#
```

Also note that by substituting **?** for **/** in the above commands, you can see the compiled-in values (usually defaults) in the kernel.

Setting maxusers Value

The following example shows how to change the `maxusers` value to 40 in the kernel on systems running Solaris 2.x.

1. In the `/etc/system` file, add the following line:

```
set maxusers=40
```

2. Reboot the system with `boot -r`.

Warning — Do not indiscriminately change the `maxusers` value. Improper `maxusers` values can have negative effects on the system.

The following example verifies the current `maxusers` value.

```
castle% su
Password
# adb -k /dev/ksyms /dev/mem
physmem3dec
maxusers/D
maxusers:40
$q
#
```

Enabling or Disabling SCSI Options in the /etc/system File

A system may have several SCSI drives, large and small. Recent SCSI drives support 16-bit, or wide SCSI, communication, whereas the older ones do not.

Because older, slow drives do not support the wide SCSI configuration, if you add older drives to a newer system that supports fast wide drives, you need to make a kernel modification to enable the system to boot. The required modification runs all SCSI ports in asynchronous mode. This slower mode fully interlocks all the SCSI data transfer signals and provides for reliable operation of the Extended Storage Module at the end of a SCSI bus. In asynchronous mode, you can reliably run Sun configurations that contain both fast SCSI drives and nonconforming devices on fast SCSI ports.

Note — The slower data rate applies to all SCSI ports on the system. Some applications may run more slowly because of the slower data rate.

The following table shows SCSI hexadecimal option bytes where there is 1 bit per option.

bit=1 means the option is enabled; bit=0 means the option is disabled.

SCSI Option	Value to Set the Corresponding Bit to 1	
Disconnect/reconnect	0x008	(bit3=1, starting with bit 0)
Linked commands	0x010	(bit4=1)
Synchronous transfer	0x020	(bit5=1)
Parity	0x040	(bit6=1)
Tagged queuing	0x080	(bit7=1)
Fast scsi	0x100	(bit8=1, or bit 9 if starting with 1)
Wide scsi	0x200	(bit9=1)

To check the current options settings, as `root`:

```
#adb -k
physmem 1f0d
```

```
scsi_options/X
scsi_options:
scsi_options:    178
$q
#
```

The 0x178 response means that bits 3, 4, 5, 6, and 8 are set to 1; thus, disconnect/reconnect, linked commands, synchronous transfer, parity, and fast SCSI are enabled. Tagged queuing and wide SCSI are set to 0, that is, disabled.

To change to the slower, asynchronous data rate, Sun recommends adding the following line to the /etc/system file:

set scsi_options=0x3f8

The following example shows that the change took effect.

```
#adb -k
physmem 1f0d
scsi_options/X
scsi_options:
scsi_options:    3f8
$q
#
```

To turn synchronous transfer back on at the highest possible speed and enable tagged queueing (if available in the operating system), change the scsi_options line in the /etc/system file to the following:

set scsi_options = 0x1f8

Warning — Perform the above procedures with caution. Improper use of adb can result in a corrupted system that may crash or be unable to reboot.

Exit Status

0	Successful completion.
non-zero	The last command either failed or returned a non-zero status.

Files

/usr/lib/adb
/usr/platform/*platform-name*/lib/adb

> Default directories in which files are to be read with $< and $<<. *platform-name* is the name of the platform implementation and can be found by using uname -i.

name/lib/adb/sparcv8
/usr/lib/adb/sparcv9
/usr/platform/platform-

    Default directories in which files for 64-bit SPARC V9 are to be read with $< and $<<. *platform-name* is the name of the platform implementation and can be found by using uname -i.

a.out   Default name for *objectfile* operand.

core   Default name for *corefile* operand.

/dev/ksyms   Special driver to provide an image of the kernel's symbolic table.

Attributes

See attributes(5) for descriptions of the following attributes:

Attribute Type	Attribute Value
Availability	SUNWcsu (32-bit)
	SUNWcsxu (64-bit)

See Also

uname(1), a.out(4), core(4), proc(4), attributes(5), largefile(5), ksyms(7D)

    Writing Device Drivers

addbib — Create or Extend a Bibliographic Database

Synopsis

/usr/bin/addbib [-a] [-p *promptfile*] *database*

Description

Use the addbib command to create or add entries to a bibliographic database. Once you create the database, you can search, index, sort, and format the database by using the related *bib commands. When you start addbib, you can display instructions by typing **y** at the Instructions? prompt. Typing **n** or Return skips them. addbib then prompts you for various bibliographic fields, reads responses from the terminal, and sends output records to *database*. A null response (just pressing Return) means to leave out that field. A minus sign (-) means to go back to the previous field. A trailing backslash (\) enables you to continue a field on the next line. You can, however, type a multiple-line abstract without using the trailing backslash. The repeating Continue? prompt enables you to resume either by typing **y** or by pressing

Return. To quit the current session, type **n** or **u**. You can edit the database with any system editor such as vi(1), ex(1), or ed(1) by typing the name of the editor at the `Continue?` prompt.

Options

-a   Suppress prompting for an abstract; asking for an abstract is the default. You end abstracts by pressing Control-D.

-p *promptfile*

Use a new prompting skeleton, defined in *promptfile*. This file should contain prompt strings, a Tab, and the key letters to be written to the database.

Usage

The most common bibliography key letters and their meanings are listed below. When you use the addbib command to add entries, the prompts are displayed in English. However, if you later edit the bibliography file, the bibliography key letters are displayed as part of the file.

Key Letter	Description
%A	Author's name.
%B	Book containing article referenced.
%C	City (place of publication).
%D	Date of publication.
%E	Editor of book containing article referenced.
%F	Footnote number or label (supplied by refer).
%G	Government order number.
%H	Header commentary, printed before reference.
%I	Issuer (publisher).
%J	Journal containing article.
%K	Keywords to use in locating reference.
%L	Label field used by -k option of refer.
%M	Bell Labs Memorandum (undefined).
%N	Number within volume.
%O	Other commentary, printed at end of reference.
%P	Page number(s).
%Q	Corporate or foreign author (unreversed).
%R	Report, paper, or thesis (unpublished).
%S	Series title.
%T	Title of article or book.

Key Letter	Description
%V	Volume number.
%X	Abstract—used by roffbib, not by refer.
%Y,Z	Ignored by refer.

Examples

The following example creates a *database* named bibliography, displays the instructions, adds one entry, and then displays the contents of the database by means of the vi editor.

```
castle% addbib bibliography
Instructions? y

Addbib will prompt you for various bibliographic fields.
If you don't need a particular field, just hit Return,
        and that field will not appear in the output file.
If you want to return to previous fields in the skeleton,
        a single minus sign will go back a field at a time.
        (This is the best way to input multiple authors.)
If you have to continue a field or add an unusual field,
        a trailing backslash will allow a temporary escape.
Finally, (without -a) you will be prompted for an abstract
Type in as many lines as you need, and end with a ctrl-d.
To quit, type `q' or `n' when asked if you want to continue.
To edit the database, type `edit', `vi', or `ex' instead.

    Author:    Janice Winsor
     Title:    Opening the Dream Door
   Journal:
    Volume:
     Pages:    153
 Publisher:    Merrill-West Publishing
      City:    Carmel, California
      Date:    1998
     Other:
  Keywords:    dreams, psychic development
  Abstract: (ctrl-d to end)
Not just another dream interpretation book! Opening the Dream Door
is a practical guide to psychic development. Written in a
friendly, personal style, Opening the Dream Door does not
attempt to interpret dream symbology. It is the author's belief
that each person has their own personal myths and symbols that
cannot be deciphered in a collective fashion. By using her own
dreams as an example, Janice Winsor makes practical suggestions
for expanding the subconscious life and connecting to other realms.
Processes for remembering and accessing dreams are taught in an
easy to understand style.
^D
Continue? vi
%A Janice Winsor
```

```
%T Opening the Dream Door
%P 153
%I Merrill-West Publishing
%C Carmel, California
%D 1998
%K dreams, psychic development
%X Not just another dream interpretation book! Opening the Dream Door
is a practical guide to psychic development. Written in a
friendly, personal style, Opening the Dream Door does not
attempt to interpret dream symbology. It is the author's belief
that each person has their own personal myths and symbols that
cannot be deciphered in a collective fashion. By using her own
dreams as an example, Janice Winsor makes practical suggestions
for expanding the subconscious life and connecting to other realms.
Processes for remembering and accessing dreams are taught in an
easy to understand style.
~
~
~
"bibliography" 27 lines, 946 characters
```

Attributes

See attributes(5) for descriptions of the following attributes:

Attribute Type	Attribute Value
Availability	SUNWcsu

See Also

ed(1), ex(1), indxbib(1), lookbib(1), refer(1), roffbib(1), sortbib(1),
vi(1), attributes(5)

---

admin, sccs-admin — Create and Administer SCCS History Files

Synopsis

```
/usr/ccs/bin/admin [-bhnz] [-a username |groupid] ...
    [-d flag] ... [-e username |groupid] ...
    [-f flag [value]] ... [-i [filename]]
    [-m mr-list] [-rrelease] [-t [description-file]]
    [-y[comment]] s.filename ...
```

Description

See sccs-admin(1).

aedplot — Graphics Filters for Various Plotters

Synopsis
```
/usr/ucb/plot [-Tterminal]
```

Description
See plot(1).

alias, unalias — Create or Remove a Pseudonym

Synopsis
```
/usr/bin/alias [alias-name[=string] ...]
/usr/bin/unalias alias-name ...
/usr/bin/unalias -a
```

csh
```
alias [alias-name [def]]
unalias alias-name
```

ksh
```
**
alias [-tx] [alias-name[=value]] ...
unalias alias-name...
```

Description
The alias command enables you to define simple aliases. You specify the name you want to use as the alias and define some text that is substituted by the shell whenever that word is used as a command. For example, because one engineer so consistently mistyped the more command as moer, he created an alias so that when he typed moer, the more command was executed. You can also create aliases to simplify complicated commands. You use the unalias command to remove an alias.

An alias can contain as many words as you want, provided you enclose them in quotation marks. You can also include several commands connected by a pipe.

The /usr/bin directory contains alias and unalias commands. The C and Korn shells also provide built-in alias and unalias commands. The Bourne shell does not provide aliasing capabilities. The syntax for defining aliases is slightly different, depending on the environment.

/usr/bin/alias

To display a list of defined aliases, type `alias` and press Return. An alias definition affects the current shell execution environment and the execution environments of the subshells of the current shell. When used as specified here, the alias definition does not affect the parent process of the current shell nor any command environment invoked by the shell.

/usr/bin/unalias

The `unalias` command removes the definition for each alias name specified. The aliases are removed from the current shell execution environment.

C Shell

To display a list of currently defined aliases on standard output, type **alias** with no arguments and press Return.

To define an alias for the current shell, type **alias** *alias-name def* and press Return. Because they are reserved words, you cannot use the names `alias` or `unalias` for *alias-name*. To include spaces in *def*, enclose the definition in quotes.

To display the definition for a specific alias, type **alias** *alias-name* and press Return.

When defining aliases for the current shell, you must have entered an alias definition on a previous command line before you can use it.

Use the `unalias` command to discard aliases that match *alias-name*. To remove all aliases, type **unalias** * and press Return.

To make your favorite aliases more readily available, include them in your `.cshrc` file.

Korn Shell

The Korn shell comes with a default set of predefined aliases. To display the list on standard output, type **alias** with no arguments and press Return.

To define an alias for the current shell, type **alias** *alias-name=value* and press Return. A trailing space in *value* checks the next word for alias substitution. Because they are reserved words, you cannot use the names `alias` or `unalias` for *alias-name*.

To display the definition for a specific alias, type **alias** *alias-name* and press Return.

Use the `unalias` command to discard aliases that match *alias-name*. To remove all aliases, type **unalias** * and press Return.

To make your favorite aliases more readily available, include them either in the `.profile` file or in your Korn shell ENV file. To create a Korn shell ENV file, create a file named *filename* and put your aliases in it. Then export the environment file with the following command.

ENV=*filename*;export ENV

Options

Korn Shell

The Korn shell provides the following options for the built-in `alias` command.

-t   Create a tracked alias. The Korn shell remembers the full path
            name of the command to enable it to be found more quickly and to
            be issued from any directory. If you supply no *alias-name*
            argument, list all currently tracked aliases.

-x   Export the alias so that it can be used in shell scripts and other
            subshells. If you supply no *alias-name* argument, list all current
            exported aliases.

The following option is supported by `unalias`.

-a   Remove all alias definitions from the current shell execution
            environment.

Operands

The following operand is supported for the `alias` command.

alias-name Write the alias definition to standard output.

The following operands are supported for the `unalias` command:

alias-name The name of an alias to be removed.

alias-name=string

            Assign the value of string to the alias *alias-name*.

When you give no operands, all alias definitions are written to standard
output.

Output

The format for displaying aliases (when no operands or only name operands are
specified) is:

`"%s=%s\n" name, value`

The *value* string is written with appropriate quoting so that it is suitable
for reinput to the shell.

Examples

C Shell

The following example creates an alias for the `alias` command and uses the
alias shortcut to create an alias for the `history` command and to create a `moer`
alias for the `more` command.

```
castle% alias a alias
castle% a h history
castle% a moer more
```

The following example lists aliases that are set in the `.cshrc` file.

```
castle% alias
G3        172.16.8.21
a         alias
c         clear
h         history
mac       172.16.8.20
castle%
```

Korn Shell

The following alias changes `ls` to give a more annotated output in columnar format.

```
alias ls="ls -CF"
```

The following alias creates a simple redo command to repeat previous entries in the command history file.

```
alias r='fc -s'
```

The following alias uses 1-kilobyte units for `du`.

```
alias du="du -k"
```

Alternatively, you can create the alias in the following form, using a backslash to escape the space character and omitting the double quotes around the command.

```
alias du=du\ -k
```

The following alias sets up `nohup` so that it can deal with an argument that is itself an alias name.

```
alias nohup="nohup "
```

The following example lists the default aliases that are set for the Korn shell.

```
$ alias
autoload='typeset -fu'
command='command '
functions='typeset -f'
history='fc -l'
integer='typeset -i'
local=typeset
nohup='nohup '
r='fc -e -'
stop='kill -STOP'
suspend='kill -STOP $$'
$
```

Environment Variables

See environ(5) for descriptions of the following environment variables that affect the execution of alias and unalias: LC_CTYPE, LC_MESSAGES, and NLSPATH.

Exit Status

0   Successful completion.

>0   One of the *alias-name* operands specified did not have an alias definition, or an error occurred.

Attributes

See attributes(5) for descriptions of the following attributes:

Attribute Type	Attribute Value
Availability	SUNWcsu

See Also

csh(1), ksh(1), shell_builtins(1), attributes(5), environ(5)

New! **answerbook2** — Online Documentation System

Synopsis

/usr/dt/bin/answerbook2 [-h]

Description

The answerbook2 command brings up the default Web browser and shows any online documentation installed in the default AnswerBook2 server. If an AnswerBook2 server has not been defined, answerbook2 checks if there is one running on the user's system. If so, it displays that server's information.

To define a default AnswerBook2 server, use the environment variable AB2_DEFAULTSERVER.

This functionality is also accessible through the AnswerBook2 option on the CDE front panel Help menu.

> **Note** — Once the Web browser is opened and you can view the AnswerBook2 library, you can use the online Help system to find out more about the AnswerBook2 product.

Options

    -h   Display a usage statement.

Usage

At startup time, `answerbook2` starts up the default Web browser (for example, HotJava or Netscape) and displays the URL specified for the default AnswerBook2 server. If no default AnswerBook2 server is defined, it looks for `http://localhost:8888`.

Environment Variables

`AB2_DEFAULTSERVER`

                Fully qualified URL that identifies the default AnswerBook2 server to use. For example: `http://imaserver.eng.sun.com:8888/`.

Attributes

See `attributes`(5) for descriptions of the following attributes:

Attribute Type	Attribute Value
Availability	SUNWab2m

See Also

`ab2cd(1M)`, `ab2admin(1M)`, `attributes(5)`

---

appletviewer — View Java Applets

Synopsis

```
/usr/java/bin/appletviewer [-debug][-encoding encoding-name]
    [-J javaoption] urls...
```

Description

Use the `appletviewer` command to run Java applets outside of the context of a World Wide Web browser.

`appletviewer` connects to the document(s) or resource(s) designated by *urls* and displays each applet referenced by that document in its own window. Please note that if the documents referred to by *urls* do not reference any applets with the `APPLET` tag, `appletviewer` does nothing.

Options

-debug   Start the applet viewer in the Java debugger, which debugs
                    applets in the document. (See jdb(1).)

-encoding *encoding-name*

                    Specify the input HTML file-encoding name.

-J *javaoption*

                    Pass the *javaoption* string through as a single argument to
                    java(1), which runs the compiler. The argument should not
                    contain spaces. Begin multiple argument words with the prefix -J,
                    which is stripped. This option is useful for adjusting the execution
                    environment or compiler memory usage.

Examples

The following example lists HTML files that contain applets in a directory on a
CD-ROM and starts one of the applets. The applet window that is displayed is
shown below the appletviewer output. The final line in the output is
displayed when you quit the applet viewer.

```
castle% cd /cdrom/jumpingjavascript/objects/applet
castle% ls
BarChart                Hello.zip               appletParameters.html
Hello.class             applet.html             index.html
Hello.java              appletArchive.html      javaMethods.html
castle% appletviewer appletParameters.html &
[2] 609
castle% myFont = TimesRoman
myString = Change Me, below!

castle%
[2]    Done                 appletviewer appletParameters.html
castle%
```

Attributes

See attributes(5) for descriptions of the following attributes:

Attribute Type	Attribute Value
Availability	SUNWjvrt

See Also

java(1), jdb(1), attributes(5)

---

apropos — Locate Commands by Keyword Lookup

Synopsis

/usr/bin/apropos *keyword*...

Description

apropos displays the manual page name, section number, and a short description for each manual page whose line contains the *keyword*. This information is contained in the /usr/share/man/windex database created by catman(1M). If catman(1M) was not run or was run with the -n option, apropos fails. Each word is considered separately, and the case of letters is ignored. Words that are part of other words are considered; for example, when looking for compile, apropos also finds all instances of compiler.

Note — apropos is actually just the -k option to the man(1) command.

Examples

```
castle% apropos password
d_passwd        d_passwd (4)    - dial-up password file
dialups         dialups (4)     - list of terminal devices requiring a dial-up
   password
endpwent        getpwnam (3c)   - get password entry
endspent        getspnam (3c)   - get password entry
fgetpwent       getpwnam (3c)   - get password entry
fgetpwent_r     getpwnam (3c)   - get password entry
fgetspent       getspnam (3c)   - get password entry
fgetspent_r     getspnam (3c)   - get password entry
getpwent        getpwnam (3c)   - get password entry
getpwent_r      getpwnam (3c)   - get password entry
getpwnam        getpwnam (3c)   - get password entry
getpwnam_r      getpwnam (3c)   - get password entry
getpwuid        getpwnam (3c)   - get password entry
```

```
getpwuid_r        getpwnam (3c)      - get password entry
getspent          getspnam (3c)      - get password entry
getspent_r        getspnam (3c)      - get password entry
getspnam          getspnam (3c)      - get password entry
getspnam_r        getspnam (3c)      - get password entry
grpck             pwck (1m)          - password/group file checkers
lckpwdf           lckpwdf (3c)       - manipulate shadow password database lock file
nispasswd         nispasswd (1)      - change NIS+ password information
nispasswdd        rpc.nispasswdd (1m) - NIS+ password update daemon
...
castle% apropos editor
ed                ed (1)             - text editor
edit              edit (1)           - text editor (variant of ex for casual users)
ex                ex (1)             - text editor
ld                ld (1)             - link-editor for object files
ld                ld (1b)            - link editor, dynamic link editor
red               ed (1)             - text editor
sed               sed (1)            - stream editor
sed               sed (1b)           - stream editor
vedit             vi (1)             - screen-oriented (visual) display editor
                                       based on ex
vi                vi (1)             - screen-oriented (visual) display editor
                                       based on ex
view              vi (1)             - screen-oriented (visual) display editor
                                       based on ex
...
castle% apropos format
COLOR_PAIR        can_change_color (3xc)  - manipulate color information
Intro             Intro (4)          - introduction to file formats
NIS+              nis+ (1)           - a new version of the network information
                                       name service
PAIR_NUMBER       can_change_color (3xc)  - manipulate color information
_lwp_info         _lwp_info (2)      - return the time-accounting information of
                                       a single LWP
a.out             a.out (4)          - Executable and Linking Format (ELF) files
acct              acct (4)           - per-process accounting file format
ar                ar (4)             -  archive file format
asysmem           sysmem (3)         - return physical memory information
audioconvert      audioconvert (1)    - convert audio file formats
audit_control     audit_control (4)   - control information for system audit
                                         daemon
audit_data        audit_data (4)     - current information on audit daemon
can_change_color                     can_change_color (3xc)  - manipulate color
                                       information
catman            catman (1m)        - create the formatted files for the reference
                                       manual
...
```

Files

/usr/share/man/windex

Table of contents and keyword database.

Attributes

See attributes(5) for descriptions of the following attributes:

Attribute Type	Attribute Value
Availability	SUNWdoc
CSI	Enabled

See Also

man(1), whatis(1), catman(1M), attributes(5)

Diagnostics

/usr/share/man/windex: No such file or directory

>This database does not exist. You must run catman(1M) to
>create it.

ar — Maintain Portable Archive or Library

Synopsis

```
/usr/ccs/bin/ar -d [-Vv] archive file...
/usr/ccs/bin/ar -m [-abiVv] [posname] archive file...
/usr/ccs/bin/ar -p [-sVv] archive [file...]
/usr/ccs/bin/ar -q [-cVv] archive file...
/usr/ccs/bin/ar -r [-abciuVv] [posname] archive file...
/usr/ccs/bin/ar -t [-sVv] archive [file...]
/usr/ccs/bin/ar -x [-CsTVv] archive [file...]

/usr/xpg4/bin/ar -d [-Vv] archive file...
/usr/xpg4/bin/ar -m [-abiVv] [posname] archive file...
/usr/xpg4/bin/ar -p [-sVv] archive [file...]
/usr/xpg4/bin/ar -q [-cVv] archive file...
/usr/xpg4/bin/ar -r [-abciuVv] [posname] archive file...
/usr/xpg4/bin/ar -t [-sVv] archive [file...]
/usr/xpg4/bin/ar -x [-CsTVv] archive [file...]
```

Description

The ar command maintains groups of files combined into a single archive file.
Its main use is to create and update library files; however, you can use it for any
similar purpose. The magic string and the file headers used by ar consist of
printable ASCII characters. If an archive is composed of printable files, the
entire archive is printable.

When ar creates an archive, it creates headers in a format that is portable across all machines. The portable archive format and structure are described in detail in ar(4). The archive symbol table (described in ar(4)) is used by the link editor ld to effect multiple passes over libraries of object files in an efficient manner. An archive symbol table is created and maintained by ar only when there is at least one object file in the archive. The archive symbol table is in a specially named file that is always the first file in the archive. This file is never mentioned or accessible to the user. Whenever you use the ar command to create or update the contents of such an archive, the symbol table is rebuilt. You can force the symbol table to be rebuilt by using the -s option.

Note — If you mention the same file twice in an argument list, that file may be put in the archive twice.

By convention, archives are suffixed with the characters .a.

Options

-a
: Position new files in archive after the file named by the *posname* operand.

-b
: Position new files in archive before the file named by the *posname* operand.

-c
: Suppress the diagnostic message that is written to standard error by default when archive is created.

-C
: Prevent extracted files from replacing like-named files in the file system. This option is useful when you also use -T to prevent truncated file names from replacing files with the same prefix.

-d
: Delete one or more files from archive.

-i
: Position new files in archive before the file named by the *posname* operand (equivalent to -b).

-m
: Move files. If you specify -a, -b, or -i with the *posname* operand, move files to the new position; otherwise, move files to the end of archive.

-p
: Print the contents of files in archive to standard output. If you specify no files, write the contents of all files in archive in the order of the archive.

-q
: Quickly append files to the end of archive. Positioning options -a, -b, and -i are invalid. The command does not check whether the added files are already in archive. This option is useful to avoid quadratic behavior when creating a large archive piece-by-piece.

-r   Replace or add files in archive. If archive does not exist, create a
            new archive file and write a diagnostic message to standard error
            (unless you specify the -c option). If no files are specified and the
            archive exists, the results are undefined. Files that replace
            existing files do not change the order of the archive. If you use the
            -u option with the -r, option, then only those files with dates of
            modification later than the archive files are replaced. If you use
            the -a, -b, or -i option, then you must specify the *posname* and
            indicate that new files are to be placed after (-a) or before (-b or
            -i) *posname*; otherwise, the new files are placed at the end.

-s   Force the regeneration of the archive symbol table even if you do
            not invoke ar with an option that modifies the archive contents.
            This command is useful to restore the archive symbol table after
            the strip(1) command is used on the archive.

-t   Print a table of contents of archive. The files specified by the file
            operands are included in the written list. If no file operands are
            specified, include all files in archive in the order of the archive.

-T   Allow file-name truncation of extracted files whose archive names
            are longer than the file system can support. By default, extracting
            a file with a name that is too long is an error; a diagnostic message
            is written and the file is not extracted.

-u   Update older files. When used with the -r option, replace files
            within archive only if the corresponding file has a modification
            time that is at least as new as the modification time of the file
            within archive.

-V   Print version number on standard error.

/usr/bin/ar

-v   Give verbose output. When used with the -d, -r, or -x options,
            write a detailed file-by-file description of the archive creation and
            the constituent files, and maintenance activity.

            When used with -p, write the name of the file to the standard
            output before writing the file itself to the standard output.

            When used with -t, include a long listing of information about the
            files within the archive.

            When used with -x, print the file name preceding each extraction.

            When writing to an archive, write a message to the standard error.

/usr/xpg4/bin/ar

-v   Same as /usr/bin/ar version, except when writing to an archive,
            write no message to the standard error.

-x   Extract the files named by the *file* operands from *archive*. The contents of archive are not changed. If you specify no file operands, extract all files in archive. If the name of a file extracted from *archive* is longer than that supported in the directory to which it is being extracted, the results are undefined. Set the modification time of each file extracted to the time *file* is extracted from *archive*.

Operands:

archive   A path name of the archive file.

file   A path name. Only the last component is used when comparing against the names of files in the archive. If two or more *file* operands have the same last path-name component (basename(1)), the results are unspecified. The implementation's archive format does not truncate valid names of files added to or replaced in the archive.

posname   The name of a file in the archive file, used for relative positioning; see options -m and -r.

Examples

The following example shows how to find which object modules make up the libexample.a archive.

```
castle% ar t libexample.a
```

The following example shows how to extract a module from a shared object. If module.o is part of the archive library libexample.a, you can extract the module with the following command.

```
castle% ar x libexample.a module.o
```

The ranlib command in SunOS 4.x was used to add a table of contents to archive libraries. The ranlib command is now incorporated into /usr/ccs/bin/ar. When ar is archiving object files, it automatically creates a symbol table, as shown in the following example.

```
castle% ar rcv libfoo.a foo.o bar.o
```

The following command forces a rebuild of the symbol table in an archive library.

```
castle% ar ts libfoo.a
```

Environment Variables

See environ(5) for descriptions of the following environment variables that affect the execution of ar: LC_CTYPE, LC_MESSAGES, and NLSPATH.

Exit Status

0	Successful completion.
>0	An error occurred.

Attributes

See attributes(5) for descriptions of the following attributes:

/usr/bin/ar:

Attribute Type	Attribute Value
Availability	SUNWbtool

/usr/xpg4/bin/ar:

Attribute Type	Attribute Value
Availability	SUNWxci4

See Also

basename(1), cpio(1), ld(1), lorder(1), strip(1), tar(1), cc(1B), a.out(4), ar(4), attributes(5), environ(5), XPG4(5)

arch — Display the Architecture of the Current Host

Synopsis

/usr/bin/arch [-k | *archname*]

Description

Systems can be broadly classified by their architectures, which define what executables run on which machines. You can make a distinction between kernel architecture and application architecture (or, commonly, just architecture). Systems that run different kernels because of underlying hardware differences may be able to run the same application programs.

arch displays the application architecture of the current host system. Because of extensive historical use of this command without any options, all SunOS 5.x SPARC-based systems return sun4 as their application architecture.

This command is provided for compatibility with previous releases and its use is discouraged. Instead, use the uname command. See uname(1) for usage information.

Options

-k   Display the kernel architecture, such as sun4m, sun4c, and so forth. This option defines which specific SunOS kernel runs on the system and has implications only for programs such as ps(1) that depend on a specific kernel architecture.

Operands

archname   Use archname to determine whether the application binaries for this application architecture can run on the current host system. The archname must be a valid application architecture, such as sun4, i86pc, and so forth. If application binaries for archname can run on the current host system, return true (0); otherwise, return false (1).

Examples

The following example shows the value the arch command returns on a SPARCstation 10.

```
castle% arch
sun4
castle%
```

Exit Status

0   Successful completion.

>0   An error occurred.

Attributes

See attributes(5) for descriptions of the following attributes:

Attribute Type	Attribute Value
Availability	SUNWcsu

See Also

mach(1), ps(1), uname(1), attributes(5)

as — Assembler

Synopsis

SPARC

```
/usr/ccs/bin/as [-b] [-K PIC] [-L] [-m] [-n] [-o outfile]
    [-P] [-Dname] [-Dname=def] [-Ipath] [-Uname...]
    [-q] [-Q y|n] [-s] [-S[a | b | c | 1 | A | B | C | L]][-T][-V]
    [-xarch=v7 | -xarch=v8 | -xarch=v8a | -xarch=v8plus | -xarch=v8plusa
    | -xarch=v9 | -xarch=v9a][-xF] filename ...
```

New!

x86

```
/usr/ccs/bin/as [-b] [-K PIC] [-L] [-m] [-n] [-o outfile] [-P] [-Dname]
    [-Dname=def] [-Ipath] [-Uname ...] [-Qy | n] [-s] [-S [a | b | c | 1
    | A | B | C | L]] [-T] [-V] filename ...
```

New!

Description

The as command creates object files from assembly language source files.

Note — If you use the -m (invoke the m4(1) macro processor) option,
you cannot use keywords for m4(1) as symbols (variables, functions,
labels) in the input file because m4(1) cannot determine which
keywords are assembler symbols and which keywords are real m4(1)
macros.

Whenever possible, access the assembler through a compilation system
interface program such as cc(1B).
All undefined symbols are treated as global.

Options

The following options for the as command are common to both SPARC and X86.
You can specify the options in any order.

-b	Generate extra symbol table information for the Sun SourceBrowser. *New!*
-Dname -Dname=def	When the -P option is in effect, pass these options to the cpp(1) preprocessor without interpretation by the as command; otherwise, ignore them.
-Ipath	When the -P option is in effect, pass this option to the cpp(1) C preprocessor without interpretation by the as command; otherwise, ignore it.
-K PIC	Generate position-independent code. *New!*
-L	Save all symbolsin the ELF symbol table including temporary labels that are normally discarded to save space. *New!*
-m	Run the m4(1) macro processor on the input to the assembler.

-n	Suppress all the warnings while assembling.
-o *outfile*	Put the output of the assembly in *outfile*. By default, the output file name is formed by removing the .s suffix, if there is one, from the input file name and appending a .o suffix.
-P	Run cpp(1), the C preprocessor, on the files being assembled. The preprocessor is run separately on each input file, not on their concatenation. Pass the preprocessor output to the assembler.
Q y | n	If you specify the n option, produce the assembler version information in the comment section of the output object file. If you specify the y option, suppress the information.
-s	Place all stabs in the .stabs section. By default, put stabs in stabs.excl sections, which are stripped out by the static linker, ld(1), during final execution. When you use the -s option, stabs remain in the final executable because .stab sections are not stripped by the static linker.

New! -S [a | b | c | l | A | B | C | L]

> Produce a disassembly of the emitted code to the standard output. Adding each of the following character to the -S option produces:
>
> a Disassemble with address.
>
> b Disassemble with .bof.
>
> c Disassemble with comments.
>
> l Disassemble with line numbers.
>
> Capital letters turn the switch off for the corresponding option.

New!

-T	Interpret symbol names in 4.x assembly files as 5.x symbol names. This option is for 4.x assembly files to be assembled on 5.x systems.
-U*name*	When the -P option is in effect, pass this option to the cpp(1) preprocessor without interpretation by the as command; otherwise, ignore it.
-V	Write the version number of the assembler being run on the standard error output.

New!

-xF	Generate additional information for performance analysis of the executable, using Sun WorkShop analyzer. If the input file does not contain any stabs (debugging directives), then the assembler generates some default stabs that are needed by the Sun WorkShop analyzer. Also, see the dbx manual page available with Sun WorkShop.

The following options are for SPARC only.

-q	Perform a quick assembly. When you use the -q option, many error checks are not performed. Note: This option disables many error checks. It is recommended that you do not use this option to assemble handwritten assembly language.

-xarch=v7   Instruct the assembler to accept instructions defined in the SPARC version 7 (V7) architecture. The resulting object code is in ELF format.

-xarch=v8   Instruct the assembler to accept instructions defined in the SPARC-V8 architecture, less the quad-precision floating-point instructions. The resulting object code is in ELF format.

-xarch=v8a   Instruct the assembler to accept instructions defined in the SPARC-V8 architecture, less the quad-precision floating-point instructions and less the fsmuld instruction. The resulting object code is in ELF format. This choice is the default of the -xarch=options.

-xarch=v8plus

Instruct the assembler to accept instructions defined in the SPARC-V9 architecture, less the quad-precision floating-point instructions. The resulting object code is in ELF format. It does not execute on a Solaris V8 system (a machine with a V8 processor). It does execute on a Solaris V8+ system.

-xarch=v8plusa

Instruct the assembler to accept instructions defined in the SPARC-V9 architecture, less the quad-precision floating-point instructions, plus the instructions in the Visual Instruction Set (VIS). The resulting object code is in V8+ ELF format. It does not execute on a Solaris V8 system (a machine with a V8 processor). It does execute on a Solaris V8+ system

-xarch=v9   Limit the instruction set to the SPARC-V9 architecture. The resulting .o object files are in 64-bit ELF format and can be linked only with other object files in the same format. The resulting executable can be run only on a 64-bit SPARC processor running 64-bit Solaris with the 64-bit kernel.   *New!*

-xarch=v9a   Limit the instruction set to the SPARC-V9 architecture, adding the Visual Instruction Set (VIS) and extensions specific to UltraSPARC processors. The resulting .o object files are in 64-bit ELF format and can be linked only with other object files in the same format. The resulting executable can be run only on a 64-bit SPARC processor running 64-bit Solaris with the 64-bit kernel.   *New!*

Operands

filename   Assenbly language source file.   *New!*

Examples

The following example performs a quick assembly with no error checking.

```
castle% as -q inputfile
```

The -V option to the compiler is a very important flag. It prints the version number of the compiler so that you know exactly what compiler you are using. If the compiler is patched, the patch information is also displayed.

```
castle% as -V inputfile
```

Environment Variables

TMPDIR   as normally creates temporary files in the directory /tmp. You can specify another directory by setting the environment variable TMPDIR to your chosen directory. (If TMPDIR isn't a valid directory, then as uses /tmp).

Files

By default, as creates its temporary files in /tmp. When you set the TMPDIR environment variable, as creates its files in the directory you specify unless TMPDIR is not a valid directory.

Attributes

See attributes(5) for descriptions of the following attributes:

Attribute Type	Attribute Value
Availability	SUNWsprot

See Also

cc(1B), cpp(1), ld(1), m4(1), nm(1), strip(1), tmpnam(3S), a.out(4), attributes(5)

The dbx manual page available with Sun WorkShop.

asa — Convert FORTRAN Carriage-control Output to Printable Form

Synopsis

```
/usr/bin/asa [-f] [file...]
```

Description

The asa command writes its input files to standard output, mapping carriage-control characters from the text files to line-printer control sequences.

The first character of every line is removed from the input, and the following actions are performed.

When the Character is a:	Then:
space	Output the rest of the line without change.
0	Replace it by a newline control sequence followed by the rest of the input line.
1	Replace it by a newpage control sequence followed by the rest of the input line.
+	Replace it by a control sequence that returns to the first column of the previous line, where the rest of the input line is printed.

For any other character in the first column of an input line, asa skips the character and prints the rest of the line unchanged.

If you call asa without providing a file name, the standard input is used.

Options

-f	Start each file on a new page.

Operands

file	A path name of a text file used for input. If you specify no file operands or specify -, then use the standard input.

Examples

You can use asa as a filter to view the output of FORTRAN programs that use ASA carriage-control characters so that they are displayed in normal form. The following example properly formats and paginates the output and then directs it to a line printer.

```
castle% a.out | asa | lp
```

You can view FORTRAN output previously sent to the file on a terminal screen with the following command.

```
castle% asa output
```

The following program is used in the next two examples.

```
write(*,'(" Blank")')
write(*,'("0Zero ")')
write(*,'("+ Plus ")')
write(*,'("1One ")')
end
```

With actual files.

```
castle% a.out > MyOutputFile asa < MyOutputFile | lp
```

With only pipes.

```
castle% a.out | asa | lp
```

Both of the above examples produce two pages of output.

```
Page 1:
  Blank

  ZeroPlus
Page 2:
  One
```

Environment Variables

See environ(5) for descriptions of the following environment variables that affect the execution of asa: LC_CTYPE, LC_MESSAGES, and NLSPATH.

Exit Status

0	All input files were output successfully.
>0	An error occurred.

Attributes

See attributes(5) for descriptions of the following attributes:

Attribute Type	Attribute Value
Availability	SUNWcsu

See Also

lp(1), environ(5), attributes(5)

at, batch — Execute Commands at a Later Time

Synopsis

```
/usr/bin/at [-c|-k|-s] [-f file] [-m] [-q queuename] -t time
/usr/bin/at [-c|-k|-s] x[-f file] [-m] [-q queuename] timespec...
/usr/bin/at -l [-q queuename] [at-job-id...]
/usr/bin/at -r at-job-id...

/usr/bin/batch
```

Description

at

Use the at command to schedule jobs for later execution. You can queue any command line or shell script. The at command reads commands from standard input and groups them together as an *at-job*, to be executed at a later time.

The *at-job* is executed in a separate invocation of the shell, running in a separate process group with no controlling terminal, except that the environment variables, current working directory, file creation mask (see umask(1)), and system resource limits (for sh and ksh only, see ulimit(1)) in effect when the at command is executed are retained and used when the *at-job* is executed.

When you submit the *at-job*, the system assigns a unique *at-job-id* and displays it when you schedule the *at-job*. The *at-job-id* is an identifier that is a string consisting of alphanumeric characters and the period character. You can also display a list of currently scheduled jobs by using the at -l command.

By default, the results of processing an *at-job* are mailed to the user who submitted the job. You can mail the results to other users by specifying the -m option.

Users are permitted to use at and batch if their name appears in the file /usr/lib/cron/at.allow. If that file does not exist, the file /usr/lib/cron/at.deny is checked to determine if the user should be denied access to at. The at.allow and at.deny files consist of one user name per line. If neither file exists, only a process with the superuser privileges is permitted to submit a job. If only at.deny exists and is empty, global usage is permitted.

Note — Regardless of the queue used, cron has a limit of 100 jobs in execution at any time.

There can be delays in cron at job execution. In some cases, these delays can compound to the point that cron job processing seems to be hung. All jobs are executed eventually. When the delays are excessive, the only workaround is to kill cron and restart it.

batch

The batch command reads commands to be executed at a later time. It is the
equivalent of the command at -q b -m now, where queue b is a special at
queue specifically for batch jobs. Batch jobs are submitted to the batch queue
for immediate execution.

Options

If you do not use the -c, -k, or -s options, the SHELL environment variable
determines which shell is used.

-c	Use C shell, csh(1), to execute the *at-job*.
-k	Use Korn shell, ksh(1), to execute the *at-job*.
-s	Use Bourne shell, sh(1), to execute the *at-job*.
-f *file*	Specify the path of a file to be used as the source of the *at-job*, instead of standard input.
-l	(ell) Report all jobs scheduled for the invoking user if you specify no *at-job-id* operands. If you specify *at-job-id*s, report information only for these jobs.
-m	Send mail to the invoking user after the *at-job* has run, announcing its completion. Mail standard output and standard error produced by the *at-job* to the user as well unless redirected elsewhere. Send mail even if the job produces no output. If you do not use -m, the job's standard output and standard error are mailed to the user unless they are redirected elsewhere; if there is no such output to provide, the user is not notified of the job's completion.

-q *queuename*

Specify the queue to schedule a job for submission. When used
with the -l option, limit the search to that particular queue.
Values for *queuename* are limited to the lowercase letters a
through z. By default, *at-jobs* are scheduled in queue a. In
contrast, queue b is reserved for batch jobs. Because queue c is
reserved for cron jobs, you cannot use it with the -q option.

-r *at-job-id*

Remove the jobs with the specified *at-job-id* operands that were
previously scheduled by the at command.

-t *time*   Submit the job to be run at the time specified by the *time* option
argument, which must have the decimal format
[[*CC*]*YY*]*MMDDhhmm*[.*SS*] where each two-digit pair represent the
following:

MM	The month of the year [01-12].
DD	The day of the month [01-31].
hh	The hour of the day [00-23].

mm	The minute of the hour [00-59].
CC	The first two digits of the year.
YY	The second two digits of the year.
SS	The second of the minute [00-61].

Refer to the touch(1) manual page for more details.

Operands

at_job_id	The identification number for a scheduled *at-job*.
timespec	Submit the job to be run at the date and time specified. All of the *timespec* operands are interpreted as if they were separated by space characters and concatenated. The date and time are interpreted as being in the time zone of the user (as determined by the TZ variable), unless a time zone name appears as part of *time*.

In the C locale, the following describe the three parts of the time specification string. All of the values from the LC_TIME categories in the C locale are case insensitive.

time	You can specify the time as one, two, or four digits. One- and two-digit numbers are interpreted as hours. Four-digit numbers are interpreted as hours and minutes. Alternatively, you can specify the time as two numbers separated by a colon, meaning *hour:minute*. You can indicate an a.m./p.m. value (one of the values from the *am_pm* keywords in the LC_TIME locale category). This value can follow the time. Otherwise, a 24-hour clock time is understood. A time zone name of GMT, UCT, or ZULU (case insensitive) can follow to specify that the time is in Coordinated Universal Time. You can specify other time zones by using the TZ environment variable. The time field can also be one of the following tokens in the C locale:

midnight	Indicates the time 12:00 a.m. (00:00).
noon	Indicates the time 12:00 p.m.
now	Indicate the current day and time. Invoking at now submits an *at-job* for potentially immediate execution (that is, subject only to unspecified scheduling delays).

date   You can specify an optional date as either a month
                     name (one of the values from the mon or abmon
                     keywords in the LC_TIME locale category) followed
                     by a day number (and possibly year number
                     preceded by a comma) or a day of the week (one of
                     the values from the day or abday keywords in the
                     LC_TIME locale category). Two special days are
                     recognized in the C locale:

                     today   The current day.

                     tomorrow   The day following the current
                                    day. If no date is given, today is
                                    assumed if the given time is
                                    greater than the current time,
                                    and tomorrow is assumed if it is
                                    less. If the given month is less
                                    than the current month (and no
                                    year is given), next year is
                                    assumed.

increment   The optional increment is a number preceded by a
                     plus sign (+) and suffixed by one of the following:
                     minutes, hours, days, weeks, months, or years.
                     (The singular forms are also accepted.) The
                     keyword next is equivalent to an increment
                     number of +1. For example, the following are
                     equivalent commands:
                     at 2pm + 1 week
                     at 2pm next week

Usage

The format of the at command line shown here is guaranteed only for the C
locale. Other locales are not supported for midnight, noon, now, mon, abmon,
day, abday, today, tomorrow, minutes, hours, days, weeks, months, years,
and next.

Because the commands run in a separate shell invocation, running in a
separate process group with no controlling terminal results in the loss of open
file descriptors, traps, and priority inherited from the invoking environment.

at Examples

The following two examples produce the same result. The first example uses
the -t option to specify the time to run the script named tryit.

```
castle% at -f /export/home/winsor/bin/tryit -t 08281215
commands will be executed using /bin/csh
job 904277700.a at Fri Aug 28 12:15:00 1998
castle%
```

Note — It is a good idea to use the full path name for scripts scheduled with the at command. Otherwise, like cron, at may not find the script when the time comes to run it.

The next example uses the *timespec* operand to specify the time to run the script named `tryit`.

```
castle% at -f /export/home/winsor/bin/tryit 1230pm
commands will be executed using /bin/csh
job 904278600.a at Fri Aug 28 12:30:00 1998
castle%
```

The following example lists the *at-job-id* for the two scheduled jobs.

```
castle% at -l
904277700.a     Fri Aug 28 12:15:00 1998
904278600.a     Fri Aug 28 12:30:00 1998
castle%
```

You can also schedule multiple at jobs by typing a *timespec* and pressing Return. Put one command on each line and press Return. Then type Control-D when you have scheduled all of the jobs. The following example schedules only one job.

```
castle% at 1230pm
at> tryit
at> Control-D <EOT>
commands will be executed using /bin/csh
job 904278601.a at Fri Aug 28 12:30:00 1998
castle%
```

By default, results of *at-jobs* are e-mailed to the person who scheduled the job. The following screen shot shows the in-box with the results of the previous examples.

You can use the following sequence from a terminal.

```
$ at -m 0730 tomorrow
at> sort < file >outfile
at> Control-D <EOT>
commands will be executed using /bin/sh
```

```
job 904380100.a at Sat Aug 29 07:30:00 1998
$
```

The following sequence demonstrates redirecting standard error to a pipe. It is useful in a command procedure. Note that the sequence of output redirection is significant.

```
$ at now + 5 min
at> <<! diff file1 file2 2>&1 > outfile | mailx mygroup!
at> Control-D <EOT>
commands will be executed using /bin/sh
job 904280212.a at Fri Aug 28 12:56:52 1998
$ at -l
904347000.a     Sat Aug 29 07:30:00 1998
904280100.a     Fri Aug 28 12:55:00 1998
904280212.a     Fri Aug 28 12:56:52 1998
$
```

You can have a job reschedule itself by calling `at` from within the `at-job`. For example, this daily-processing script named `my.daily` runs every day (although `crontab` is a more appropriate vehicle for such work).

```
# my.daily runs every day at now tomorrow < my.daily daily-processing
```

You have quite a bit of flexibility in the spacing of the three portions of the C locale `timespec`, as long as there are no ambiguities. Examples of various times and operand presentations include:

```
at 0815am Jan 24
at 8 :15amjan24
at now "+ 1day"
at 5 pm FRIday
at '17
        utc+
        30minutes'
```

batch Examples

You can use the following sequence at a terminal. Notice that `batch` uses the at prompt and that `batch` job files end with a `.b` suffix.

```
$ batch
at> at> sort <file >outfile
at> Control-D <EOT>
commands will be executed using /bin/sh
job 904280755.b at Fri Aug 28 13:00:55 1998
$
```

The following sequence demonstrates redirecting standard error to a pipe. It is useful in a command procedure. Note that the sequence of output redirection is significant.

```
$ batch
at> <<!
at> diff file1 file2 2>&1 > outfile | mailx mygroup
```

```
at> !
at> Control-D <EOT>
commands will be executed using /bin/sh
job 904280756.b at Fri Aug 28 13:05:55 1998
$
```

Environment Variables

See environ(5) for descriptions of the following environment variables that affect the execution of at and batch: LC_CTYPE, LC_MESSAGES, NLSPATH, and LC_TIME.

SHELL	Determine a name of a command interpreter to be used to invoke the *at-job*. If the variable is unset or null, sh is used. If it is set to a value other than sh, the implementation uses that shell; a warning diagnostic is printed telling which shell is used.
TZ	Determine the time zone. The job is submitted for execution at the time specified by *timespec* or -t *time* relative to the time zone specified by the TZ variable. If *timespec* specifies a time zone, it overrides TZ. If *timespec* does not specify a time zone and TZ is unset or null, an unspecified default time zone is used.
DATEMSK	If the environment variable DATEMSK is set, at uses its value as the full path name of a template file containing format strings. The strings consist of format specifiers and text characters that are used to provide a richer set of allowable date formats in different languages by appropriate settings of the environment variable LANG or LC_TIME. The list of allowable format specifiers is located in the getdate(3C) manual page. The formats described in the Operands section for the *time* and *date* arguments, the special names noon, midnight, now, next, today, tomorrow, and the increment argument are not recognized when DATEMSK is set.

Exit Status

0	The at command successfully submitted, removed, or listed a job or jobs.
>0	An error occurred, and the job is not scheduled.

Files

/usr/lib/cron/at.allow

> Names of users, one per line, who are authorized access to the at and batch commands.

/usr/lib/cron/at.deny

> Names of users, one per line, who are denied access to the at and batch commands.

Attributes

See `attributes`(5) for descriptions of the following attributes:

at

Attribute Type	Attribute Value
Availability	SUNWcsu
CSI	Enabled

batch

Attribute Type	Attribute Value
Availability	SUNWesu
CSI	Enabled

See Also

`crontab(1), csh(1), date(1), ksh(1), sh(1), touch(1), ulimit(1), umask(1), getdate(3C), attributes(5), environ(5)`

atoplot — Graphics Filters for Various Plotters

Synopsis

`/usr/ucb/plot [-Tterminal]`

Description

See `plot`(1).

atq — Display the Jobs Queued to Run at Specified Times

Synopsis

`/usr/bin/atq [-c] [-n] [username...]`

Description

Use the `atq` command to display for the current user *at-jobs* that were created by the `at`(1) command. If you use the command as superuser, `atq` displays all jobs in the queue.

If you use no options, jobs are displayed in chronological order of execution.

When superuser uses the `atq` command without specifying *username*, the entire queue is displayed; when you specify a user name, those jobs belonging only to the named user are displayed.

Options

-c	Display the queued jobs in the order they were created (that is, the time that the `at` command was given).
-n	Display only the total number of jobs currently in the queue.

Examples

The following example shows output from the `atq` command with no arguments. The list shows the jobs only for the current user, `winsor`.

```
castle% atq
 Rank      Execution Date      Owner     Job        Queue   Job Name
  1st   Aug 28, 1998 17:00   winsor   904294800.a     a      tryit
  2nd   Aug 29, 1998 01:00   winsor   904323600.a     a      tryit
  3rd   Aug 29, 1998 07:30   winsor   904347000.a     a      stdin
  4th   Aug 30, 1998 15:00   winsor   904460400.a     a      tryit
```

For comparison, the following example shows the output from the `at -l` command, which also lists `at` and `batch` jobs in the queue.

```
castle% at -l
904347000.a     Sat Aug 29 07:30:00 1998
904294800.a     Fri Aug 28 17:00:00 1998
904323600.a     Sat Aug 29 01:00:00 1998
904460400.a     Sun Aug 30 15:00:00 1998
```

The following example shows the output from the `atq` command when executed as superuser.

```
castle% su
Password:
castle# atq
 Rank      Execution Date      Owner     Job        Queue   Job Name
  1st   Aug 28, 1998 16:00   root     904291200.a     a      tryit
  2nd   Aug 28, 1998 17:00   winsor   904294800.a     a      tryit
  3rd   Aug 28, 1998 18:00   root     904298400.a     a      tryit
  4th   Aug 28, 1998 19:00   ray      904302000.a     a      tryit
  5th   Aug 28, 1998 21:00   ray      904309200.a     a      tryit
  6th   Aug 29, 1998 01:00   winsor   904323600.a     a      tryit
  7th   Aug 29, 1998 07:30   winsor   904347000.a     a      stdin
  8th   Aug 30, 1998 15:00   winsor   904460400.a     a      tryit
```

The following example shows the same example sorted by creation time.

```
castle# atq -c
 Rank      Execution Date      Owner     Job        Queue   Job Name
  1st   Aug 29, 1998 07:30   winsor   904347000.a     a      stdin
  2nd   Aug 28, 1998 17:00   winsor   904294800.a     a      tryit
  3rd   Aug 29, 1998 01:00   winsor   904323600.a     a      tryit
```

```
4th    Aug 30, 1998 15:00   winsor   904460400.a    a    tryit
5th    Aug 28, 1998 16:00   root     904291200.a    a    tryit
6th    Aug 28, 1998 18:00   root     904298400.a    a    tryit
7th    Aug 28, 1998 19:00   ray      904302000.a    a    tryit
8th    Aug 28, 1998 21:00   ray      904309200.a    a    tryit
```

The following example shows the value returned by the `atq -n` command. This option lists only the number of items in the queue.

```
castle# atq -n
8
castle#
```

The following example shows the jobs queued only by user `ray`.

```
castle# atq ray
  Rank      Execution Date    Owner      Job        Queue   Job Name
  1st    Aug 28, 1998 19:00   ray     904302000.a     a     tryit
  2nd    Aug 28, 1998 21:00   ray     904309200.a     a     tryit
castle#
```

Files

`/var/spool/cron/atjobs`

> Spool area for at jobs.

Attributes

See `attributes`(5) for descriptions of the following attributes:

Attribute Type	Attribute Value
Availability	SUNWcsu

See Also

`at`(1), `atrm`(1), `cron`(1M), `attributes`(5)

atrm — Remove Jobs Spooled by at or batch

Synopsis

```
/usr/bin/atrm [-afi] [[job #] [user] ...]
```

Description

Use the `atrm` command to remove delayed-execution jobs created with the at(1) command that have not yet executed. You can display a list of these jobs and associated job numbers by using atq(1).

`atrm` removes each job number you specify and/or all jobs belonging to the *user* you specify, provided that you own the indicated jobs or have superuser privileges.

Options

-a	Remove all unexecuted jobs that were created by the current user. If invoked by superuser, flush the entire queue.
-f	Force suppression of all information regarding the removal of the specified jobs.
-i	Interactively ask if a job should be removed. If you respond with a y, remove the job.

Examples

The following example first lists the jobs in the at queue by using the `atq` command, and then, as superuser, removes jobs queued by user `ray`.

```
castle# atq
 Rank     Execution Date    Owner    Job           Queue   Job Name
 1st   Aug 28, 1998 16:00   root     904291200.a     a      tryit
 2nd   Aug 28, 1998 17:00   winsor   904294800.a     a      tryit
 3rd   Aug 28, 1998 18:00   root     904298400.a     a      tryit
 4th   Aug 28, 1998 19:00   ray      904302000.a     a      tryit
 5th   Aug 28, 1998 21:00   ray      904309200.a     a      tryit
 6th   Aug 29, 1998 01:00   winsor   904323600.a     a      tryit
 7th   Aug 29, 1998 07:30   winsor   904347000.a     a      stdin
 8th   Aug 30, 1998 15:00   winsor   904460400.a     a      tryit
castle# atrm ray
904302000.a: removed
904309200.a: removed
```

If you want to suppress display of the list of removed jobs, use the `atrm -f` option.

The following example removes a job by specifying the *at-job* number.

```
castle# atrm 904291200.a
904291200.a: removed
castle#
```

In the following example, superuser uses the atrm -i option to be prompted to interactively remove individual jobs queued by user winsor.

```
castle# atrm -i winsor
904347000.a:    (owned by winsor) remove it? y
904294800.a:    (owned by winsor) remove it? y
904323600.a:    (owned by winsor) remove it? y
904460400.a:    (owned by winsor) remove it? y
castle#
```

Files

/var/spool/cron/atjobs

Spool area for at jobs.

Attributes

See attributes(5) for descriptions of the following attributes:

Attribute Type	Attribute Value
Availability	SUNWcsu

See Also

at(1), atq(1), cron(1M), attributes(5)

audioconvert — Convert Audio File Formats

Synopsis

/usr/bin/audioconvert [-pF] [-f *outfmt*] [-o *outfile*] [[-i *nfmt*]
  [*file*...]] ...

Description

audioconvert converts audio data between a set of supported audio encodings and file formats. You can use it to compress and decompress audio data, to add audio file headers to raw audio data files, and to convert between standard data encodings, such as ulaw and linear PCM.

If no file names are present, audioconvert reads the data from the standard input stream and writes an audio file to the standard output. Otherwise, input files are processed in order, concatenated, and written to the output file.

Input files are expected to contain audio file headers that identify the audio data format. If the audio data does not contain a recognizable header, you must specify the format with the -i option, using the rate, encoding, and channels keywords to identify the input data format.

The output file format is derived by updating the format of the first input file with the format options in the -f specification. If you do not specify -p, all subsequent input files are converted and concatenated. The output file contains an audio file header, unless you specify format=raw in the output format options.

You can convert input files in place by using the -p option. When -p is in effect, the format of each input file is modified according to the -f option to determine the output format. The existing files are then overwritten with the converted data.

The file(1) command decodes and prints the audio data format of Sun audio files.

The algorithm used for converting multichannel data to single channel is implemented by simply summing the channels. If the input data is perfectly in phase (as would be the case if a mono file is converted to stereo and back to mono), the resulting data may contain some distortion.

Options

-p   In place, convert individual input files to the format specified by the -f option and rewrite them. If a target file is a symbolic link, rewrite the underlying file. You cannot combine the -o and -p options.

-F   Ignore any file header for input files whose format is specified by the -i option. If you do not specify -F, audioconvert ignores the -i option for input files that contain valid audio file headers.

-f *outfmt*   Specify the file format and data encoding of the output file. Derive defaults for unspecified fields from the input file format. Valid keywords and values are listed in the next section.

-o *outfile*   Concatenate all input files, convert to the output format, and write to the named output file. If you do not specify either -o or -p, write the concatenated output to the standard output. You cannot combine the -p and -o options.

-i *infmt*   Specify the data encoding of raw input files. Ordinarily, the input data format is derived from the audio file header. This option is required when converting audio data that is not preceded by a valid audio file header. If you specify -i for an input file that contains an audio file header, the input format string is ignored unless you also use the -F option. The format specification syntax is the same as the -f output file format. You can specify multiple input formats. An input format describes all input files following that specification until a new input format is specified.

file	Concatenate and convert the named audio files to the output format, and write them out. If you specify no file name or if you specify the special file-name dash (-), read audio data from the standard input.
-?	Help: Print a command line usage message.

Format Specification

The syntax for the input and output format is a set of *keyword=value* pairs with no intervening white space.

keyword=value[,keyword=value ...]

If values are unambiguous, you can omit the preceding *keyword=*.

rate	Specify the audio sampling rate in samples per second. If a number is followed by the letter k, it is multiplied by 1000 (for example, 44.1k = 44100). Standard, commonly used sample rates are 8k, 16k, 32k, 44.1k, and 48k.
channels	Specify the number of interleaved channels as an integer. You can also use the words mono or stereo to specify one- or two-channel data.
encoding	Specify the digital audio data representation. Encodings determine precision implicitly (ulaw implies 8-bit precision) or explicitly as part of the name (for example, linear16). Valid encoding values are:

ulaw	CCITT G.711 u-law encoding is an 8-bit format primarily used for telephone-quality speech.
alaw	CCITT G.711 a-law encoding is an 8-bit format primarily used for telephone-quality speech in Europe.
linear8, linear16, linear32	Linear Pulse Code Modulation (PCM) encoding. The name identifies the number of bits of precision. linear16 is typically used for high-quality audio data.
pcm	Same as linear16.
g721	CCITT G.721 compression format uses Adaptive Delta Pulse Code Modulation (ADPCM) with 4-bit precision. Its primary use is to compress u-law voice data with a 2:1 compression ratio.

| | g723 | CCITT G.723 compression format uses Adaptive Delta Pulse Code Modulation (ADPCM) with 3-bit precision. Its primary use is to compress u-law voice data with an 8:3 compression ratio. The audio quality is similar to that of G.721 but may result in lower quality when used for nonspeech data. |

The following encoding values are also accepted as shorthand to set the sample rate, channels, and encoding:

	voice	Equivalent to `encoding=ulaw,rate=8k,channels=mono`.
	cd	Equivalent to `encoding=linear16,rate=44.1k,channels=stereo`
	dat	Equivalent to `encoding=linear16,rate=48k,channels=stereo`.

format		Specify the audio file format. Valid formats are:
	sun	Sun-compatible file format (the default).
	raw	Read or write raw audio data with no audio header or in conjunction with an offset to import a foreign audio file format.
	offset	(`-i` only) Specify a byte offset to locate the start of the audio data. You can use this option to import audio data that contains an unrecognized file header.

Usage

See `largefile`(5) for the description of the behavior of `audioconvert` when encountering files greater than or equal to 2 Gbytes (2**31 bytes).

Examples

The following example records voice data and compresses it before storing it in a file.

```
castle% audiorecord | audioconvert -f g721 > mydata.au
```

The following example uses the `file` command to verify that the `mydata.au` file was converted.

```
castle% file mydata.au
mydata.au:  audio data: compressed (4-bit G.721 ADPCM), mono, 8000 Hz
castle%
```

The following example concatenates two Sun format audio files, regardless of their data format, and outputs an 8-bit u-law, 16 kHz, mono file.

```
% audioconvert -f ulaw,rate=16k,mono -o outfile.au infile1 infile2
```

The following example uses the `file` command to verify that the `outfile.au` file was converted.

```
castle% file outfile.au
outfile.au:        audio data: 8-bit u-law, mono, 16000 Hz
castle%
```

The following example converts a directory containing raw voice data files, in place, to Sun format and adds a file header to each file.

```
castle% audioconvert -p -i voice -f sun *.au
```

The following example uses the `file *` command to verify that both the files in the directory were converted.

```
castle% file *
mydata.au:         audio data: 8-bit u-law, mono, 16000 Hz
outfile.au:        audio data: 8-bit u-law, mono, 16000 Hz
castle%
```

Attributes

See `attributes(5)` for descriptions of the following attributes:

Attribute Type	Attribute Value
Availability	SUNWaudio

See Also

audioplay(1), audiorecord(1), file(1), attributes(5), largefile(5)

audioplay — Play Audio Files

Synopsis

```
/usr/bin/audioplay [-iV] [-v vol] [-b bal] [-p speaker | headphone |
    line][-d dev] [file...]
```

Description

audioplay copies the named audio files (or the standard input if you specify no file names) to the audio device. If you do not specify an input file and standard input is a TTY, the port, volume, and balance settings specified on the command line are applied and the program exits.

The input files must contain a valid audio file header. The encoding information in this header is matched against the capabilities of the audio device and, if the data formats are incompatible, an error message is printed and the file is skipped. Compressed ADPCM (G.721) monaural audio data is automatically uncompressed before playing.

Minor deviations in sampling frequency (that is, less than 1 percent) are ordinarily ignored. For example, data sampled at 8012 Hz can be played on an audio device that only supports 8000 Hz. If you use the -V option, such deviations are flagged with warning messages.

Bugs

audioplay currently supports a limited set of audio format conversions. If the audio file is not in a format supported by the audio device, you must first convert it. For example, to convert to voice format on-the-fly, use the following command.

```
castle% audioconvert -f voice myfile | audioplay
```

The format conversion does not always keep up with the audio output. If this is the case, convert to a temporary file before playing the data.

Options

-i   Immediately exit if the audio device is unavailable (that is, another process currently has write access). audioplay ordinarily waits until it can obtain access to the device. When you use the -i option and the device is busy, print an error message and exit immediately.

-V   Give verbose output on the standard error when waiting for access to the audio device or when sample rate deviations are detected.

-v *vol*   Set the output volume to the specified value before playing begins and reset it to its previous level when audioplay exits. The *vol* argument is an integer value between 0 and 100, inclusive. If you do not specify this argument, leave the output volume at the level most recently set by any process.

-b *bal*   Set the output balance to the specified value before playing begins and reset it to its previous level when audioplay exits. The *bal* argument is an integer value between -100 and 100, inclusive. A value of -100 indicates left balance, 0 middle, and 100 right. If you do not specify this argument, leave the output balance at the level most recently set by any process.

-p speaker | headphone | line

               Select the built-in speaker, (the default), headphone jack, or line out as the destination of the audio output signal. If you do not specify this argument, the output port remains unchanged. Not all audio adapters support all of the output ports. If the named port does not exist, use an appropriate substitute.

-d *dev*	Direct output to an alternate audio device. If you do not specify the -d option, consult the AUDIODEV environment variable. Otherwise, use /dev/audio as the default audio device.
file	Sequentially play audio files named on the command line If no filenames are present, play the standard input stream (if it is not a TTY). It, too, must contain an audio file header. You can use the special file-name dash (-) to read the standard input stream instead of a file. If you supply a relative path name, consult the AUDIOPATH environment variable.
-\?	Print a command-line usage message.

Usage

See largefile(5) for the description of the behavior of audioplay when encountering files greater than or equal to 2 Gbytes (2**31 bytes).

Environment Variables

AUDIODEV	The full path name of the audio device to write to if you supply no -d argument. If the AUDIODEV variable is not set, use /dev/audio.
AUDIOPATH	Specify a colon-separated list of directories to search for audio files whose names are given by relative path names. You can explicitly specify the current directory (.) in the search path. If the AUDIOPATH variable is not set, search only the current directory.

Attributes

See attributes(5) for descriptions of the following attributes:

Attribute Type	Attribute Value
Availability	SUNWaudio

See Also

audioconvert(1), audiorecord(1), attributes(5), largefile(5), audiocs(7D), audio(7I)

SPARC Only

audioamd(7D), dbri(7D)

x86 Only

sbpro(7D)

audiorecord — Record an Audio File

Synopsis

```
/usr/bin/audiorecord [-af] [-v vol] [-b bal] [-m monvol]
    [-p mic | line | internal-cd] [-c channels] [-s rate]
    [-e encoding] [-t time] [-i info][-d dev] [file]
```

Description

audiorecord copies audio data from the audio device to a named audio file (or the standard output if you specify no file name). If you do not specify an output file and standard output is a TTY, the volume, balance, monitor volume, port, and audio format settings specified on the command line are applied and the program exits.

By default, monaural audio data is recorded at 8 kHz and encoded in ulaw format. If the audio device supports additional configurations, you can use the -c, -s, and -e options to specify the data format. The output file is prefixed by an audio file header that identifies the format of the data encoded in the file.

Recording begins immediately and continues until a SIGINT signal (for example, Control-C) is received. If you specify the -t option, audiorecord stops when the specified time expires.

If the audio device is unavailable (that is, another process currently has read access), audiorecord prints an error message and exits immediately.

Options

-a	Append the data onto the end of the named audio file. The audio device must support the audio data format of the existing file.
-f	When you specify the -a flag, the sample rate of the audio device must match the sample rate at which the original file was recorded. If you also specify the -f flag, ignore sample rate differences and print a warning message on the standard error.
-v vol	Set the recording gain to the specified value before recording begins, and reset it to its previous level when audiorecord exits. The vol argument is an integer value between 0 and 100. If you do not specify this argument, leave the input volume at the level most recently set by any process.
-b bal	Set the recording balance to the specified value before recording begins and reset it to its previous level when audiorecord exits. The bal argument is an integer value between -100 and 100. A value of -100 indicates left balance, 0 middle, and 100 right. If you do not specify this argument, leave the input balance at the level most recently set by any process.

-m *monvol* Set the input monitor volume to the specified value before recording begins, and reset it to its previous level when audiorecord exits. The *monvol* argument is an integer value between 0 and 100. A non-zero value allows a directly connected input source to be heard on the output speaker while recording is in progress. If you do not specify this argument, leave the monitor volume at the level most recently set by any process.

-p mic | line | internal-cd

 Select the mic, line, or internal-cd input as the source of the audio output signal. If you do not specify this argument, the input port remains unchanged. Some systems do not support all possible input ports. If the named port does not exist, ignore this option.

-c *channels*

 Specify the number of audio channels (1 or 2). You can specify the value as an integer or as the string mono or stereo. The default value is mono.

-s *rate* Specify the sample rate, in samples per second. If a number is followed by the letter k, it is multiplied by 1000 (for example, 44.1k = 44100). The default sample rate is 8 kHz.

-e *encoding*

 Specify the audio data encoding. This value may be ulaw, alaw, or linear. The default encoding is ulaw.

-t *time* Specify the maximum length of time to record. You can specify time as a floating-point value, indicating the number of seconds, or in the form: *hh:mm:ss.dd*, where the hour and minute specifications are optional.

-i *info* Set the information field of the output file header to the string specified by the *info* argument. You cannot specify this option in conjunction with the -a argument.

-d *dev* Specify an alternate audio device from which to take input. If you do not specify the -d option, consult the AUDIODEV environment variable. Otherwise, use /dev/audio as the default audio device.

file Rewrite or append the named audio file. If you do not specify a file name (and standard output is not a TTY) or if you specify the special file-name dash (-), direct output to the standard output.

-\? Print a command-line usage message.

Usage

See largefile(5) for the description of the behavior of audiorecord when encountering files greater than or equal to 2 Gbytes (2**31 bytes).

Environment Variables

AUDIODEV   The full path name of the audio device to record from if you do not
            supply a -d argument. If the AUDIODEV variable is not set, use
            /dev/audio.

Attributes

See attributes(5) for descriptions of the following attributes:

Attribute Type	Attribute Value
Availability	SUNWaudio

See Also

audioconvert(1),audioplay(1),attributes(5),largefile(5),audiocs(7D),
audio(7I)

SPARC Only
audioamd(7D), dbri(7D)

x86 Only
sbpro(7D)

awk — Pattern Scanning and Processing Language

Synopsis

```
/usr/bin/awk [-f progfile] [-Fc] ['prog'] [parameters]
  [filename...]
/usr/xpg4/bin/awk [-F ERE] [-v assignment ...]
  'program' | -f progfile ... [argument ...]
```

Description

The awk command is a complete programming language that is very useful for
computation and pattern matching. The name awk is an acronym composed of
the last initials of the three developers of the language: Aho, Weinberger, and
Kernighan. The /usr/xpg4/bin/awk command is described on the nawk(1)
manual page. The nawk (new awk) command is a greatly enhanced and
optimized version of awk.

The /usr/bin/awk command scans a list of input files for lines that match
any of a set of patterns specified in prog. The prog string must be enclosed in
single quotes (') to protect it from the shell. For each pattern in prog there may
be an associated action performed when a line of a file name matches the
pattern. The set of pattern-action statements may appear literally as prog or

in a file specified with the -f *progfile* option. Input files are read in order; if there are no files, the standard input is read. The file-name dash (-) means the standard input.

Notes

Input white space is not preserved on output if fields are involved.

There are no explicit conversions between numbers and strings. To force an expression to be treated as a number, add 0 to it; to force it to be treated as a string, concatenate the null string ("") to it.

Options

-f *progfile*   Read the set of patterns from *progfile*.

-F*c*   Use the character *c* as the field separator (FS) character. See the discussion of FS below.

Usage

Input Lines

Each input line is matched against the pattern portion of every pattern-action statement; the associated action is performed for each matched pattern. Any file name of the form *var=value* is treated as an assignment, not a file name, and is executed at the time it would have been opened if it were a file name. Variables assigned in this manner are not available inside a BEGIN rule and are assigned after previously specified files have been read.

An input line is normally made up of fields separated by white spaces. (You can change this default by using the built-in field separator variable, FS, or the -F*c* option.) The default is to ignore leading blanks and to separate fields by blanks and/or Tab characters. However, if FS is assigned a value that does not include any of the white spaces, then leading blanks are not ignored. The fields are denoted $1, $2, ...; $0 refers to the entire line.

Pattern-Action Statements

A pattern-action statement has the form:

pattern {*action*}

You can omit either *pattern* or *action*. If there is no *pattern*, the action is performed on every input line. If there is no *action*, the matching line is printed. Pattern-action statements are separated by newlines or semicolons.

Patterns are arbitrary Boolean combinations (!, | |, &&, and parentheses) of relational expressions and regular expressions. A relational expression is one of the following:

```
expression relop expression
expression matchop regular-expression
```

where a *relop* is any of the six relational operators in C, and a *matchop* is either ~ (contains) or ! ~ (does not contain). An expression is an arithmetic expression, a relational expression, the special expression var in array, or a Boolean combination of these.

Regular expressions are specified as in egrep(1). In patterns you must surround them with slashes. Isolated regular expressions in a pattern apply to the entire line. You can also use regular expressions in relational expressions. A pattern can consist of two patterns separated by a comma; in this case, the action is performed for all lines between the occurrence of the first pattern to the occurrence of the second pattern.

You can use the special patterns BEGIN and END to capture control before the first input line has been read and after the last input line has been read. These keywords do not combine with any other patterns.

Built-in Variables

Built-in variables include:

FILENAME	Name of the current input file.
FS	Input field separator regular expression (default blank and Tab).
NF	Number of fields in the current record.
NR	Ordinal number of the current record.
OFMT	Output format for numbers (default, %.6g).
OFS	Output field separator (default, blank).
ORS	Output record separator (default, newline).
RS	Input record separator (default, newline).

An action is a sequence of statements. A statement can be one of the following:

```
if (expression) statement [else statement]
while (expression) statement
do statement while (expression)
for (expression; expression; expression) statement
for (var in array) statement
break
continue
{[statement]...}
expression # commonly variable = expression
print [expression-list] [>expression]
printf format [, expression-list] [>expression]
next # skip remaining patterns on this input line
exit [expr] # skip the rest of the input; exit status is expr
```

Terminate statements by semicolons, newlines, or right braces. An empty *expression-list* stands for the whole input line. Expressions take on string or numeric values as appropriate and are built using the operators +, -, *, /, %, ^, and concatenation (indicated by a blank). The operators ++, --, +=, -=, *=, /=, %=, ^=, >, >=, <, <=, ==, !=, and ?: are also available in expressions. Variables may be scalars, array elements (denoted x[i]), or fields. Variables are initialized to the null string or 0. Array subscripts can be any string, not necessarily numeric; this syntax allows for a form of associative memory. String constants are quoted (" "), with the usual C escapes recognized within.

The `print` statement prints its arguments on the standard output, or on a file if >*expression* is present, or on a pipe if '|cmd' is present. The output resulting from the `print` statement is terminated by the output record separator with each argument separated by the current output field separator. The `printf` statement formats its expression list according to the format described for `printf` (see `printf`(3S)).

Built-in Functions

The arithmetic functions are as follows:

cos(x)	Return cosine of x, where x is in radians.
sin(x)	Return sine of x, where x is in radians.
exp(x)	Return the exponential function of x.
log(x)	Return the natural logarithm of x.
sqrt(x)	Return the square root of x.
int(x)	Truncate its argument to an integer. It is truncated toward 0 when x > 0.

The string functions are as follows:

index(s, t)

> Return the position in string s where string t first occurs, or 0 if it does not occur at all.

int(s)	Truncate s to an integer value. If s is not specified, use $0.
length(s)	Return the length of its argument taken as a string, or of the whole line if there is no argument.

match(s, re)

> Return the position in string s where the regular expression re occurs, or 0 if it does not occur at all.

split(s, a, fs)

> Split the string s into array elements a[1], a[2], a[n], and return n. The separation is done with the regular expression fs or with the field separator FS if fs is not given.

sprintf(fmt, expr, expr, ...)

> Format the expressions according to the printf(3S) format given by fmt and return the resulting string.

substr(*s*, *m*, *n*)

> Return the *n*-character substring of *s* that begins at position *m*.

The input/output function is as follows:

getline   Set $0 to the next input record from the current input file. getline
               returns 1 for successful input, 0 for end of file, and –1 for an error.

Large File Behavior

See largefile(5) for the description of the behavior of awk when encountering
files greater than or equal to 2 Gbytes (2**31 bytes).

Examples

Make sure awk has a source of input. The following example doesn't do
anything because there is no source of input.

```
castle% awk '{print "Hello, Everyone" }'
```

The following examples uses a file named file1 that contains the following
lines.

```
bill tom willy nikki
kieth harry ed
mary linda
glenda willy neil
```

The following example prints out all lines from a file whose first record
begins with the letter D or greater (in ASCII sorting sequence).

```
castle% awk '$1 > "D" {print $0}' /tmp/file1
kieth karry ed
mary linda
glenda willy neil
castle%
```

You can use the pipe symbol (|) to match two patterns in awk, as shown in
the following example.

```
castle% awk '$1 ~/(glenda|bill)/ {print $0}' file1
bill tom willy nikki
glenda willy neil
castle%
```

Here are some more examples of searching for patterns.

/Chicago/   Match any occurrence of Chicago in the record.

/^Detroit/   Match only when Detroit is at the beginning of the line.

/Chicago|Detroit/

> Match any occurrence of Chicago or Detroit.

```
$2 ~ /Traverse/
```

> The second field in the record matches `Traverse`.

```
$2 !~ /Bill/
```

> The second field does not match `Bill`.

```
$4 > "k"
```
The fourth field follows `k` in alphabetical order.

The following example matches `willy` only when the name is not in the second field.

```
castle% awk '$2 !~/willy/ {print $0}' file1
bill tom willy nikki
kieth karry ed
mary linda
castle%
```

It does not match the line `glenda willy neil`.

The following example matches lines that contain the names `ed` and `mary`.

```
castle% awk '/ed|mary/ {print $0}' file1
kieth harry ed
mary linda
castle%
```

The following example prints the second field in the lines that contain the names `ed` and `mary`.

```
castle% awk '/ed|mary/ {print $2}' file1
harry
linda
castle%
```

Each of the examples above assumes that the fields are separated by a space or Tab. If the field is separated by a colon (`:`), use `-F` as shown in the following example.

```
castle% awk -F: ' /ed|mary/ {print $2}' file1
```

The following example prints lines longer than 72 characters.

```
length > 72
```

The following example prints the first two fields in opposite order.

```
{ print $2, $1 }
```

The following example prints the first two fields in opposite order, with input fields separated by comma and/or blanks and tabs.

```
BEGIN { FS = ",[\t]*|[\t]+" }
{ print $2, $1 }
```

The following example adds up first column, print sum, and average.

```
{ s += $1 }
END { print "sum is", s, " average is", s/NR }
```

The following example prints fields in reverse order.

```
{ for (i = NF; i > 0; --i) print $i }
```

The following example prints all lines between start/stop pairs.

```
/start/, /stop/
```

The following example prints all lines whose first field is different from previous one.

```
$1 != prev { print; prev = $1 }
```

The following example prints a file, filling in page numbers starting at 5.

```
/Page/ { $2 = n++; } { print }
```

Assuming this program is in a file named prog, the following command line prints the file input numbering its pages starting at 5.

```
castle% awk -f prog n=5 input
```

Environment Variables

See environ(5) for descriptions of the following environment variables that affect the execution of awk: LC_CTYPE and LC_MESSAGES.

Attributes

See attributes(5) for descriptions of the following attributes:

/usr/bin/awk

Attribute Type	Attribute Value
Availability	SUNWesu
CSI	Enabled

/usr/xpg4/bin/awk

Attribute Type	Attribute Value
Availability	SUNWxcu4
CSI	Enabled

See Also

egrep(1), grep(1), nawk(1), sed(1), printf(3S), attributes(5), environ(5), largefile(5), XPG4(5)

B

---

banner — Make Posters

Synopsis

`/usr/bin/banner` *strings*

Description

banner prints its arguments in large letters on the standard output, one argument per line, up to a maximum of 10 characters.

Examples

The following example prints happy birthday.

```
castle% banner happy birthday
```

```
castle%
```

In the following example, the word congratulations is 14 characters, so only the first 10 characters are displayed.

```
castle% banner congratulations
```

```
castle%
```

If you want to print the banner, you can pipe the output to a printer, as shown in the following example.

```
castle% banner happy birthday | lp
castle%
```

Attributes

See attributes(5) for descriptions of the following attributes:

Attribute Type	Attribute Value
Availability	SUNWesu

See Also

echo(1), attributes(5)

basename, dirname — Deliver Portions of Path Names

Synopsis
```
/usr/bin/basename string [suffix]
/usr/xpg4/bin/basename string [suffix] dirname string
```

Description
You can use the basename command to strip path names off a file name. For example, if you have an environment variable that contains a complete path name, you might want to extract just the name of the file without the complete path. This command is normally used inside substitution marks (` `` `) within shell procedures.

/usr/bin/basename
The suffix is a pattern defined on the expr(1) manual page.

/usr/xpg4/bin/basename
/usr/xpg4/bin/basename is a POSIX-compliant version of the /usr/bin/basename command. See standards(5).

The suffix is a string with no special significance attached to any of the characters it contains.

Conversely, you can use the dirname command to strip the file name and return the directory that includes all but the last level of the path name in string.

Examples
The following example first shows the complete path for the EDITOR environment variable. Then, it uses the basename command to display the name of the editor and the dirname file to display the path without the file name.
```
castle% env | grep EDITOR
EDITOR=/usr/dt/bin/dtpad
castle% basename $EDITOR
dtpad
castle% dirname $EDITOR
/usr/dt/bin
castle%
```

Environment Variables
See environ(5) for descriptions of the following environment variables that affect the execution of basename and dirname: LC_CTYPE, LC_MESSAGES, and NLSPATH.

Exit Status

0	Successful completion.
>0	An error occurred.

Attributes

See attributes(5) for descriptions of the following attributes:

/usr/bin/basename

Attribute Type	Attribute Value
Availability	SUNWcsu

/usr/xpg4/bin/basename

Attribute Type	Attribute Value
Availability	SUNWxcu4

See Also

expr(1), attributes(5), environ(5), xpg4(5)

batch — Execute Commands at a Later Time

Syntax

/usr/bin/batch

Description

See at(1).

bc — Binary Calculator

Synopsis

/usr/bin/bc [-c] [-l] [*file*...]

Description

bc is both a calculator and a C-like language that you can use to write numerical programs. bc is actually a preprocessor for the dc desktop calculator and uses the dc command to do its work. However, bc contains many more functions than does dc, including named functions, logical operators, and mathematical functions such as sqrt (square root). bc uses an infix notation, where you place operators between the numbers on which they operate. For example, 2 + 2 = 4.

You execute bc from a command line. It can take input from a command line or directly from a file and then from the command. When you use a file name as an argument, bc reads the file, processes its commands, and then switches to the command line for its input. In this way you can store complex commands and functions in a file and use them directly from a command line.

bc automatically displays the results of its calculations for every line. All of the information for a single calculation must be on one line. To exit from bc, type **quit** and press Return, or type **Control-D** to signal end-of-file.

The bc command language resembles the C language.

Notes

The bc command does not recognize the logical operators && and ||. The for statement must have all three expressions.

Options

-c	Compile only. Send the dc command output to the standard output.
-l	Define the math functions and initialize scale to 20, instead of the default 0.

Operands

file	A path name of a text file containing bc program statements. After all cases of *file* have been read, bc reads the standard input.

Usage

The following list describes in more detail the syntax for bc programs:

Letter	A single letter between a and z.
Expression	
	An expression: a mathematical or logical value, an operand that takes a value, or a combination of operands and operators that evaluates to a value.
Statement	A statement.

Comments

Comments are enclosed between /* and */.

Names (Operands)

Letter   Simple one-letter variables.

Letter [*Expression*] (up to BC_DIM_MAX dimensions)

         Array elements.

ibase   Input base.

obase (limited to BC_BASE_MAX)

         Output base.

scale (limited to BC_SCALE_MAX)

         The number of digits to the right of the decimal point that bc retains in its calculations.

Other Operands

- Arbitrarily long numbers with optional sign and decimal point.
- Strings of fewer than BC_STRING_MAX characters between double quotes (").
- (*Expression*).
- sqrt (*Expression*) (Square root).
- length (*Expression*) (Number of significant decimal digits).
- scale (*Expression*) (Number of digits right of decimal point).
- *Letter* (*Expression* , ... , *Expression*).

Operators

- + - * / % ^ (% is remainder; ^ is power.)
- ++ -- (prefix and postfix; apply to names.)
- == <= >= != < >
- = =+ =- =* =/ =% =^

Statements

- *Expression*
- { *Statement* ;... ; *Statement* }
- if (*Expression*) *Statement*
- while (*Expression*) *Statement*
- for (*Expression* ; *Expression* ; *Expression*) *Statement*
- null statement.
- break
- quit
- *string*

Function Definitions

```
define Letter ( Letter ,..., Letter ) {
  auto Letter ,..., Letter
  Statement ;... Statement
  return ( Expression )
}
```

Functions in -l Math Library

s(x)	Sine.
c(x)	Cosine.
e(x)	Exponential.
l(x)	Log.
a(x)	Arctangent.
j(n, x)	Bessel function.

All function arguments are passed by value.

The value of a statement that is an expression is printed unless the main operator is an assignment. You can separate statements with either semicolons or newlines. Assignment to scale influences the number of digits retained on arithmetic operations in the manner of dc. Assignments to ibase or obase set the input and output number radix.

You can simultaneously use the same letter as an array, a function, and a simple variable. All variables are global to the program. auto variables are stacked during function calls. When arrays are used as function arguments or define them as automatic variables, empty square brackets must follow the array name.

Examples

You can use bc for normal arithmetic computations. Type **bc** and press Return. No prompt is displayed. To exit, type **quit** or **Control-D**. The entire calculation must be all on the same line. bc displays the results of each calculation as soon as you press Return.

```
castle% bc
2 + 2
4
Control-D
castle%
```

You can use a minus sign to indicate negative numbers. In the following examples, subtracting by a negative number adds it. Adding a negative number subtracts it.

```
castle% bc
1 + 2 + 3 - -3.12195
9.12195
1 + 2 + 3 + -2.14197
3.85803
```

```
Control-D
castle%
```

You can use the `scale` operator to specify how many digits to the right of the decimal point are retained in your calculations. The scale setting remains in effect for the current session.

```
castle% bc
scale = 3
1.2345/.9876
1.250
Control-D
castle%
```

You can define and use variables by assigning the value to a single letter. In the following example, x is set to 7 and used in the subsequent calculation.

```
castle% bc
x=7
5*7
35
Control-D
castle%
```

In the shell, the following assigns an approximation of the first 10 digits of -?n to the variable x.

```
x=$(printf "%s\n" 'scale = 10; 104348/33215' | bc)
```

The following `example.dc` file defines a function to compute an approximate value of the exponential function and prints approximate values of the exponential function of the first 10 integers.

```
scale = 20
define e(x){
auto a, b, c, i, s
a = 1
b = 1
s = 1
for(i=1; 1==1; i++){
  a = a*x
  b = b*i
  c = a/b
 if(c == 0) return(s)
  s = s+c
}
}
for(i=1; i<=10; i++) e(i)
```

Reading the file into bc produces the following results.

```
castle% bc example.bc
2.71828182845904523526
7.38905609893065022713
```

```
20.08553692318766774083
54.59815003314423907790
148.41315910257660342091
403.42879349273512260821
1096.63315842845859926350
2980.95798704172827474335
8103.08392757538400770974
22026.46579480671651695759
```

After the file is processed, you are still in bc and can perform additional computations, or you can press Control-D, or type **quit** and press Return to exit.

Environment Variables

See environ(5) for descriptions of the following environment variables that affect the execution of bc: LC_CTYPE, LC_MESSAGES, and NLSPATH.

Exit Status

0   All input files were processed successfully.

unspecified

An error occurred.

Files

/usr/lib/lib.b

Mathematical library.

/usr/include/limits.h

Use to define BC_ parameters.

Attributes

See attributes(5) for descriptions of the following attributes:

Attribute Type	Attribute Value
Availability	SUNWesu

See Also

awk(1), dc(1), attributes(5)

bdiff — Big diff

Synopsis

`/usr/bin/bdiff` *filename1 filename2* `[`*n*`]` `[-s]`

Description

`bdiff` is similar to `diff`, except that you can use it to process files that are too large for `diff`. A large file is a regular file whose size is greater than or equal to 2 Gbytes (2**31 bytes). A small file is a regular file whose size is less than 2 Gbytes.

If *filename1* (*filename2*) is -, the standard input is read.

`bdiff` ignores lines common to the beginning of both files, splits the remainder of each file into *n*-line segments, and invokes `diff` on corresponding segments. If both optional arguments are specified, you must use them in the order indicated above.

The output of `bdiff` is exactly that of `diff`, with line numbers adjusted to make it look as if the files had been processed as one. The first part of the `bdiff` output lists the line numbers that differ in the two files, separated by c for changed. Lines from the first file are marked with <, and lines from the second file are marked with >.

Note — Because of the segmenting of the files, `bdiff` does not necessarily find a smallest sufficient set of file differences.

Options

n	Specify the number of line segments. By default, the value of *n* is `3500`. This option is useful in those cases in which 3500-line segments are too large for `diff`, causing it to fail.
-s	Do not print `bdiff` diagnostics (silent option). This option does not suppress possible diagnostic messages from `diff`, which `bdiff` calls.

Usage

See `largefile`(5) for the description of the behavior of `bdiff` when encountering files greater than or equal to 2 Gbytes (2**31 bytes).

Examples

In the following example, two (small) files are first displayed by the `cat` command, and then `bdiff` compares the two files. You can use `bdiff` on small files; however, `diff` has more options available for comparing small files.

```
castle% cat kookaburra1
Kookaburra sits in the old gum tree
```

```
Merry merry king of the bush is he
Laugh, kookaburra, laugh
Gay your life must be.

Kookaburra sits in the old gum tree
Eating all the gumdrops he can see
Laugh, kookaburra, laugh
Leave some there for me.
castle% cat kookaburra2
Kookaburra sits in the old gum tree
Merry merry king of the bush is he
Laugh, kookaburra, laugh
Glad your life must be.

Kookaburra sits in the old gum tree
Eating all the gumdrops he can see
Laugh, kookaburra, laugh
Leave some there for me.
castle% bdiff kookaburra1 kookaburra2
4c4
< Gay your life must be.
---
> Glad your life must be.
castle%
```

Files

/tmp/bd?????

> Temporary file used for comparison.

While bdiff is comparing files, it creates temporary files in the /tmp directory. When the comparison is done, the files are automatically removed. The following example shows two bdiff temporary files.

```
castle% ls /tmp/bd*
bdCg4GX    bdowlVW
castle%
```

Attributes

See attributes(5) for descriptions of the following attributes:

Attribute Type	Attribute Value
Availability	SUNWesu
CSI	Enabled

See Also

diff(1), attributes(5), largefile(5)

Diagnostics

Use help for explanations.

---

bfs — Big File Scanner

Synopsis

`/usr/bin/bfs [-]` *filename*

Description

The `bfs` command is similar to ed(1) except that it is read-only and processes much larger files. Files can be up to 1024 Kbytes and 32-Kbyte lines, with up to 512 characters, including newline, per line (255 for 16-bit machines). `bfs` is usually more efficient than ed(1) for scanning a file because the file is not copied to a buffer. It is most useful for identifying sections of a large file where you can use `csplit`(1) to divide the file into more manageable pieces for editing.

Normally, the size of the file being scanned is printed, as is the size of any file written with the w (write) command. The optional – suppresses printing of sizes. You can turn on prompting for input with * if you type P and press Return, as in ed(1). You can turn prompting off again by typing another P and pressing Return. Note that when prompting is turned on, messages are displayed in response to errors.

All address expressions described under ed(1) are supported. In addition, you can surround regular expressions with two symbols besides / and ?: > indicates downward search without wrap-around, and < indicates upward search without wrap-around.

You can use only the letters a through z for mark names, and all 26 marks are remembered.

bfs Commands

The e, g, v, k, p, q, w, =, !, and `null` commands operate as described under ed(1). Commands such as `---`, `+++-`, `+++=`, `-12`, and `+4p` are accepted. Note that `1,10p` and `1,10` both print the first 10 lines. The f command prints only the name of the file being scanned; there is no remembered file name. The w command is independent of output diversion, truncation, or crunching (see the `xo`, `xt`, and `xc` commands, below). Additional commands that are available are listed below.

: *label*   Position a *label* in a command file. Terminate the *label* by newline, and ignore blanks between the : (colon) and the start of the *label*. You can also use this command to insert comments into a command file, because labels need not be referenced.

(. , .)xb/*regular expression*/*label*

> Jump (either upward or downward) to *label* if the command succeeds. It fails under any of the following conditions:
>
> - Either address is not between 1 and $.
>
> - The second address is less than the first.
>
> - The regular expression does not match at least one line in the specified range, including the first and last lines.
>
> On success, set dot (.) to the line matched and jump to *label*. This command is the only one that does not issue an error message on bad addresses, so it can be used to test whether addresses are bad before other commands are executed. Note that the command xb/^/ *label* is an unconditional jump.
>
> The xb command is allowed only if it is read from someplace other than a terminal. If it is read from a pipe, you can only jump downward.

xbz *label*
xbn *label*

> Test the last saved return code from the execution of a UNIX system command (!*command*) or non-zero value to the specified *label*. The two examples below both search for the next five lines containing the string size.
>
> Example 1:
> ```
> xv55
> : 1
> /size/
> xv5!expr %5 - 1
> !if 0%5 != 0 exit 2
> xbn 1
> ```
> Example 2:
> ```
> xv45
> : 1
> /size/
> xv4!expr %4 - 1
> !if 0%4 = 0 exit 2
> xbz 1
> ```

xc [*switch*]

> If *switch* is 1, crunch output from the p and null commands; if *switch* is 0, don't crunch output. Without an argument, xc reverses *switch*. Initially, *switch* is set for no crunching. Crunched output reduces strings of tabs and blanks to one blank and suppresses blank lines.

xf *file*

> Take further commands from the named file. When an end-of-file is reached, an interrupt signal is received, or an error occurs, resume reading with the file containing the xf. You can nest the xf commands to a depth of 10.

xn

> List the marks currently in use (you set marks with the k command).

xo [*file*] Divert further output from the p and null commands to the named file, which, if necessary, is created mode 666 (readable and writable by everyone), unless your umask setting (see umask(1)) dictates otherwise. If *file* is missing, divert output to the standard output. Note that each diversion causes truncation or creation of the file.

xt *number* Truncate output from the p and null commands to, at most, *number* characters. The initial number is 255.

xv[*digit*][*spaces*][*value*]

Set the variable name to the specified digit following xv. The commands xv5100 or xv5 100 both assign the value 100 to the variable 5. The command xv61,100p assigns the value 1,100p to the variable 6. To reference a variable, put a % in front of the variable name. For example, using the above assignments for variables 5 and 6, the following commands all print the first 100 lines.

1,%5p
1,%5
%6

g/%5/p globally searches for the characters 100 and prints each line containing a match.

To escape the special meaning of %, precede it with a backslash (\). For example, you can use g/".*\%[cds]/p to match and list %c, %d, or %s formats (for example, printf-like statements) of characters, decimal integers, or strings.

Another feature of the xv command is that you can store the first line of output from a UNIX system command in a variable. The only requirement is that the first character of value be an !. For example, the following lines put the current line into variable 35, print it, and increment the variable 36 by 1.

.w junk
xv5!cat junk
!rm junk
!echo "%5"
xv6!expr %6 + 1

To escape the special meaning of ! as the first character of value, precede it with a \. The following statement stores the value !date in variable 7: xv7\!date

Operands.

filename Any file up to 1024 Kbytes and 32-Kbyte lines, with up to 512 characters, including newline, per line (255 for 16-bit machines). *filename* can be a section of a larger file that has been divided into more manageable sections for editing by the use of csplit(1).

Examples

The following example returns the total number of characters in the `core` file and exits with Control-D.

```
castle% bfs core
11890
^D
castle%
```

The following example returns the total number of characters in the `bibliography` file, assigns the value `100` to a variable named 5, prints lines 1–100 of the file, and exits with Control-D. The example shows only the first few of the 100 lines.

```
castle% bfs bibliography
4471
xv5100
1,%5p
%A Janice Winsor
%T Opening the Dream Door
%P 153
%I Merrill-West Publishing
^D
castle%
```

The following example uses the – option to suppress printing of the total number of characters in the `bibliography` file. It then assigns the value `dreams` to the variable 1, displays the value of the variable, searches for all lines in the file that contain the word `dreams`, and exits with Control-D.

```
castle% bfs - bibliography

xv1dreams
!echo "%1"
dreams
g/%1/p
%K dreams, psychic development
dreams as an example, Janice Winsor makes practical suggestions
Processes for remembering and accessing dreams are taught in an
^D
castle%
```

The following example returns the total number of characters in the `bibliography` file, assigns the value `date` to a variable named 7, displays the value of the variable, and exits with Control-D.

```
castle% bfs bibliography
4471
xv7!date
!echo "%7"
Thursday March 18 08:36:52 WST 1999
^D
castle%
```

Exit Status

    0   Successful completion without any file or command errors.

    >0   An error occurred.

Attributes

See attributes(5) for descriptions of the following attributes:

Attribute Type	Attribute Value
Availability	SUNWesu

See Also

csplit(1), ed(1), umask(1), attributes(5)

Diagnostics

Message is ? for errors in commands if prompting is turned off.
Self-explanatory error messages are displayed when prompting is on.

bg — Control Process Execution

Synopsis

/usr/bin/bg [%*job-id* ...]

Description

See jobs(1).

bgplot — Graphics Filters for Various Plotters

Synopsis

/usr/ucb/plot [-T*terminal*]

Description

See plot(1).

biff — Give Notice of Incoming Mail Messages

Synopsis

```
/usr/ucb/biff [y | n]
```

Description

Use biff to turn mail notification on or off for the terminal session. With no arguments, biff displays the current notification status for the terminal. If notification is enabled, the terminal rings the bell and displays the header and the first few lines of each arriving mail message. biff operates asynchronously. For synchronized notices, use the MAIL variable of sh(1) or the mail variable of csh(1).

You can include a biff y command in your ~/.login or ~/.profile file for execution when you log in.

Options.

y	Enable mail notification for the terminal.
n	Disable notification for the terminal.

Examples

The following example turns biff on, displays the current notification status, turns biff off, and displays the current notification status again.

```
castle% biff y
castle% biff
is y
castle% biff n
castle% biff
is n
castle%
```

Files

~/.login	User's login file.
~/.profile	User's profile file.

Attributes

See attributes(5) for descriptions of the following attributes:

Attribute Type	Attribute Value
Availability	SUNWscpu

See Also

    csh(1), mail(1), sh(1), attributes(5)

break, continue — Shell Built-in Functions to Break Out of Loops

Synopsis

sh
    break [n]
    continue [n]

csh
    break
    continue

ksh
    *
    break [n]
    *
    continue [n]

Description

Bourne Shell

break exits from the enclosing for or while loop, if any. If you specify n, break n levels.

    continue resumes the next iteration of the enclosing for or while loop. If you specify n, resume at the n-th enclosing loop.

C Shell

break resumes execution after the end of the nearest enclosing foreach or while loop. The remaining commands on the current line are executed. You can write multilevel breaks as a list of break commands, all on one line.

    continue continues execution of the next iteration of the nearest enclosing while or foreach loop.

Korn Shell

break exits from the enclosed for, while, until, or select loop, if any. If you specify n, then break n levels.

    continue resumes the next iteration of the enclosed for, while, until, or select loop. If you specify n, resume at the n-th enclosed loop.

    ksh(1) commands that are preceded by one or two asterisks (*) are treated specially in the following ways:

- Variable assignment lists preceding the command remain in effect when the command completes.
- I/O redirections are processed after variable assignments.
- Errors abort a script that contains them.
- Words following a command preceded by ** and that are in the format of a variable assignment are expanded with the same rules as a variable assignment. Thus, tilde substitution is performed after the = sign, and word-splitting and file-name generation are not performed.

Examples

In the following C shell example, the script continues running the `while` loop until the user answers Yes (or yes, y, or Y). When the user does answer **yes**, the break terminates the `while` loop and, in this case, exits because there are no additional commands to execute.

```
#!/bin/csh -f
#
while (1)
        echo "Finished yet? \
        set anser = $<
        if ($answer =- [Yy]*) break
end
```

Attributes

See `attributes`(5) for descriptions of the following attributes:

Attribute Type	Attribute Value
Availability	SUNWcsu

See Also

csh(1), exit(1), for(1), foreach(1), ksh(1), select(1), sh(1), until(1), while(1), attributes(5)

C

cal — Display a Calendar

Synopsis

```
/usr/bin/cal [[month] year]
```

Description

The `cal` command writes a Gregorian calendar to standard output. If you specify a four-digit year operand, a calendar for that year is written. If you specify no operands, a calendar for the current month is written. You can display a calendar for any month of any year by specifying the month, as a digit from 1 to 12, followed by any four-digit year up to 9999.

An unusual calendar is printed for September 1752. That is the month 11 days were skipped to make up for lack of leap year adjustments. To see this calendar, type:

```
castle% cal 9 1752
```

The command **cal 83** refers to the year 83, not 1983. The year is always considered to start in January.

Operands

month   Specify the month to be displayed, represented as a decimal integer from 1 (January) to 12 (December). The default is the current month.

year   Specify the year for which the calendar is displayed, represented as a decimal integer from 1 to 9999. The default is the current year.

Examples

The following example uses the `cal` command with no arguments to display the current month.

```
castle% cal
      January 1999
   S   M Tu  W Th   F   S
                    1   2
   3   4   5   6   7   8   9
  10  11  12  13  14  15  16
  17  18  19  20  21  22  23
  24  25  26  27  28  29  30
  31
castle%
```

The following example displays a calendar for the year 2000.

```
castle% cal 2000

                                 2000
           Jan                    Feb                   Mar
 S   M Tu  W Th  F   S    S   M Tu  W Th  F   S    S   M Tu  W Th  F   S
                     1                1   2   3   4   5              1   2   3   4
 2   3   4   5   6   7   8    6   7   8   9  10  11  12    5   6   7   8   9  10  11
 9  10  11  12  13  14  15   13  14  15  16  17  18  19   12  13  14  15  16  17  18
16  17  18  19  20  21  22   20  21  22  23  24  25  26   19  20  21  22  23  24  25
23  24  25  26  27  28  29   27  28  29                   26  27  28  29  30  31
30  31
           Apr                    May                   Jun
 S   M Tu  W Th  F   S    S   M Tu  W Th  F   S    S   M Tu  W Th  F   S
                     1            1   2   3   4   5   6                       1   2   3
 2   3   4   5   6   7   8    7   8   9  10  11  12  13    4   5   6   7   8   9  10
 9  10  11  12  13  14  15   14  15  16  17  18  19  20   11  12  13  14  15  16  17
16  17  18  19  20  21  22   21  22  23  24  25  26  27   18  19  20  21  22  23  24
23  24  25  26  27  28  29   28  29  30  31              25  26  27  28  29  30
30
           Jul                    Aug                   Sep
 S   M Tu  W Th  F   S    S   M Tu  W Th  F   S    S   M Tu  W Th  F   S
                     1            1   2   3   4   5                       1   2
 2   3   4   5   6   7   8    6   7   8   9  10  11  12    3   4   5   6   7   8   9
 9  10  11  12  13  14  15   13  14  15  16  17  18  19   10  11  12  13  14  15  16
16  17  18  19  20  21  22   20  21  22  23  24  25  26   17  18  19  20  21  22  23
23  24  25  26  27  28  29   27  28  29  30  31          24  25  26  27  28  29  30
30  31
```

```
         Oct                      Nov                      Dec
 S  M Tu  W Th  F  S      S  M Tu  W Th  F  S      S  M Tu  W Th  F  S
 1  2  3  4  5  6  7               1  2  3  4                     1  2
 8  9 10 11 12 13 14      5  6  7  8  9 10 11      3  4  5  6  7  8  9
15 16 17 18 19 20 21     12 13 14 15 16 17 18     10 11 12 13 14 15 16
22 23 24 25 26 27 28     19 20 21 22 23 24 25     17 18 19 20 21 22 23
29 30 31                26 27 28 29 30            24 25 26 27 28 29 30
                                                  31
castle%
```

The following example displays a calendar for March 1946.

```
castle% cal 3 1946
    March 1946
 S  M Tu  W Th  F  S
                1  2
 3  4  5  6  7  8  9
10 11 12 13 14 15 16
17 18 19 20 21 22 23
24 25 26 27 28 29 30
31

castle%
```

Environment Variables

See environ(5) for descriptions of the following environment variables that affect the execution of cal: LC_TIME, LC_CTYPE, and NLSPATH.

Exit Status

0	Successful completion.
>0	An error occurred.

Attributes

See attributes(5) for descriptions of the following attributes:

Attribute Type	Attribute Value
Availability	SUNWesu

See Also

calendar(1), attributes(5), environ(5)

calendar — Reminder Service

Synopsis

```
/usr/bin/calendar [-]
```

Description

You can use the `calendar` command as a simple reminder service to record your appointments. The `calendar` command consults a file named `calendar` in the current directory and writes any lines that contain today's or tomorrow's date anywhere in the line to standard output. `calendar` recognizes most reasonable month-day dates such as Aug. 24, august 24, 8/24. It does not recognize date formats such as 24 August or 24/8. On Fridays and weekends, "tomorrow" extends through Monday. You can run `calendar` regularly by using the `crontab`(1) or `at`(1) commands.

When the optional argument - is present, `calendar` does its job for all users who have a `calendar` file in their login directory and sends any positive results by `mail`(1). Normally, this action is done daily by facilities in the UNIX operating system (see `cron`(1M)).

If the environment variable `DATEMSK` is set, `calendar` uses its value as the full path name of a template file containing format strings. The strings consist of conversion specifications and text characters and can provide a richer set of allowable date formats in different languages by appropriate settings of the environment variable `LANG` or `LC_TIME`; see `environ`(5). See `strftime`(3C) for the list of allowable conversion specifications.

Notes

Appropriate lines beginning with white space are not printed.

Your calendar must be public information for you to get reminder service. `calendar`'s extended idea of tomorrow does not account for holidays.

The - argument works only on calendar files that are local; `calendar` is intended not to work on calendar files that are mounted remotely with NFS. Thus, you should run **calendar** - only on diskful machines where home directories exist; running it on a diskless client has no effect.

`calendar` is no longer in the default root `crontab`. Because of the network burden, it is inadvisable to run `calendar` - in an environment running `ypbind` (1M) with a large `passwd` name map. If, however, the usefulness of `calendar` outweighs the network impact, the superuser can run `crontab -e` to edit the root `crontab`. Otherwise, individual users can use `crontab -e` to edit their own `crontab` to have `cron` invoke `calendar` without the - argument, piping output to mail addressed to themselves.

Examples

If there is no `calendar` file in the current directory, an error message is displayed.

```
castle% calendar
/bin/calendar: /export/home/winsor/calendar not found
castle%
```

In the following example, the `calendar` file in the user's home directory has three entries in it: one for today, one for tomorrow, and one for a few weeks from now. As you can see from the example, only the current calendar items are displayed.

```
castle% cat calendar
Sep 15 - Dentist, 4:30
Chiropractic appointment, Sept 16 at 10:00 AM
Monday, September 28. Start new contract
castle%
castle% calendar
Sep 15 - Dentist, 4:30
Chiropractic appointment, Sept 16 at 10:00 AM
castle%
```

You can extend date formats that are recognized by the `calendar` command by using the DATEMSK environment variable. First, create a template file named `datemask`. In that file, put the following template format:

```
%B %eth of the year %Y
```

`%B` represents the full month name, `%e` the day of the month, and `%Y` a four-digit year.

This template recognizes dates of the following format:

```
March 7th of the year 1999 <Reminder>
```

When you set the DATEMSK environment variable to reference the `datemask` file, `calendar` recognizes traditional dates as well as dates with the extended format.

```
castle% setenv DATEMSK datemask
castle% calendar
Chiropractic appointment September 16th of the year 1998.
castle%
```

Environment Variables

See `environ(5)` for descriptions of the following environment variables that affect the execution of `calendar`: LC_CTYPE, LC_TIME, LC_CTYPE, LC_MESSAGES, LC_MESSAGES, and TZ.

Exit Status

0	Successful completion.
>0	An error occurred.

Files

/etc/passwd

System password file.

/tmp/cal*   Temporary files used by calendar.

/usr/lib/calprog

Program used to determine dates for today and tomorrow.

Attributes

See attributes(5) for descriptions of the following attributes:

Attribute Type	**Attribute Value**
Availability	SUNWesu

See Also

at(1), crontab(1), mail(1), cron(1M), ypbind(1M), trftime(3C),
attributes(5), environ(5)

cancel — Cancel Print Request

Synopsis

```
/usr/bin/cancel [request-ID ...] [destination ...]
/usr/bin/cancel -u username ... [destination ...]
```

Description

Use the cancel command to cancel print requests while they are in the queue
or while they are printing. To cancel a specific print request, you need to know
the request ID for the print job. The request ID always includes the name of the
printer, a dash, and the number of the print request. When a request is
submitted from standard input, the request ID is displayed. To find the request
ID, type **lpstat** and press Return. Only the user who submitted the request or
someone logged in as root or lp can cancel a print request.

You can also use the cancel command in the following ways:

- Cancel a specific print job on a specific printer by specifying the *request-ID* and *destination* arguments.
- Cancel all jobs on a specific destination by specifying a *destination* argument.
- Cancel all requests for a specific user by specifying the -u *username* option.
- Cancel all requests for a specific user on a specific printer by specifying the -u *username* and *destination* arguments.

Users can cancel only their own print requests. By default, users can only cancel print requests on the host from which the print request was submitted. If a superuser has set user-equivalence=true in /etc/printers.conf on the print server, users can cancel print requests associated with their user name on any host. Superusers can cancel print requests on the host from which the print request was submitted. Superusers can also cancel print requests from the print server.

Options

-u *username*

> Specify the name of the user for whom print requests are to be canceled.

Operands

destination

> Specify the destination on which the print requests are to be canceled. *destination* is the name of a printer or class of printers (see lpadmin(1M)). If you do not specify *destination*, cancel cancels the requested print request on all destinations.
>
> Specify destination using atomic, POSIX-style (*server:destination*), or Federated Naming Service (FNS) (.../service/printer/...) names.
>
> The print client commands locate destination information in a very specific order. See printers.conf(4) and printers(4) for details.
>
> POSIX-style destination names (*server:destination*) are treated as print requests if *destination* has the same format as an LP-style *request-ID*. See standards(5).

request-ID Specify the ID for the print request to be canceled, using LP-style request IDs (destination-number).

Examples

The following example lists the jobs in the print queue and then cancels them, using the different options and operands.

In the first example, user winsor tries to cancel print jobs owned by user ray. The prompt is returned but the jobs are not removed from the print queue. Notice that when you do not have permission to cancel a job, the cancel command does not display an error message.

```
castle% lpstat
seachild-077      castle!winsor    615    Sep 29 08:30
seachild-078      castle!winsor    615    Sep 29 08:32
seachild-079      castle!winsor    615    Sep 29 08:33
seachild-080      castle!ray       615    Sep 29 08:36
seachild-081      castle!ray       615    Sep 29 08:37
seachild-082      castle!root      615    Sep 29 08:40
castle% whoami
winsor
castle% cancel -u ray
castle%
```

Still as user winsor, the next example removes all winsor's print jobs from the printer destination seachild. Then, user winsor tries to remove a print job owned by root by using the request ID.

```
castle% cancel -u winsor seachild
        seachild-77: canceled
        seachild-78: canceled
        seachild-79: canceled
castle% cancel seachild-82
castle% lpstat
seachild-080      castle!ray       615    Sep 29 08:36
seachild-081      castle!ray       615    Sep 29 08:37
seachild-082      castle!root      615    Sep 29 08:40
castle%
```

In the following example, root removes a print job owned by root, and then removes all print jobs from the printer destination seachild. Notice that when you cancel all of the print jobs for a destination printer, no list of the jobs canceled is displayed, even when there are print jobs listed in the queue.

```
castle% su
Password:
castle# cancel seachild-82
        seachild-82: canceled
castle# cancel seachild
castle# lpstat
castle#
```

Exit Status

0	Successful completion.
non-zero	An error occurred.

Files

`/var/spool/print/*`
>   LP print queue.

`$HOME/.printers`
>   User-configurable printer database.

`/etc/printers.conf`
>   System printer configuration database.

`printers.conf.byname`
>   NIS version of `/etc/printers.conf`.

`fns.ctx_dir.domain`
>   NIS+ version of `/etc/printers.conf`.

Attributes

See `attributes`(5) for descriptions of the following attributes:

Attribute Type	Attribute Value
Availability	SUNWpcu

See Also

`lp(1)`, `lpstat(1)`, `lpq(1B)`, `lpr(1B)`, `lprm(1B)`, `lpadmin(1M)`, `printers(4)`, `printers.conf(4)`, `attributes(5)`, `standards(5)`

---

case, switch, select — Shell Built-in Functions to Choose from a List of Actions

Synopsis

sh
```
case word in [pattern [| pattern]) actions ;;] ... esac
```

csh
```
switch (expression)
 case comparison1:
 actions
 breaksw
 case comparison2:
 actions
 breaksw
 ...
```

```
    default:
endsw
```

ksh

```
case word in [pattern [| pattern] ) actions ;;] ... esac
select identifier [in word ...] ; do list ; done
```

Description

In shell scripts, you may want to take several different types of action depending on the value of a variable or a parameter. You can do so in the Bourne shell by using the `case` statement, in the C shell by using the `case` and `switch` statements, or in the Korn shell by using the `case` and `select` statements.

The value of the variable is successively compared against patterns until a match is found. The commands immediately following the matching pattern are executed until `;;` is found for the Bourne and Korn shells or `breaksw` is found for the C shell. The last test `*)` for the Bourne and Korn shells or `default:` for the C shell is a default action. If no other values match, the shell executes the default action. In many scripts, the default action displays an error message and exits from the shell.

`case` statements can be especially helpful for processing parameters to a function.

Bourne Shell

A `case` command executes the actions associated with the first pattern that matches *word*. The form of the patterns is the same as that used for file-name generation except that a slash, a leading dot, or a dot immediately following a slash need not be matched explicitly.

C Shell

The C shell uses the `switch` statement, in which each comparison is successively matched against the specified expression. The expression is first command and file-name expanded. You can use the file metacharacters `*`, `?` and `[...]` in the `case` comparison, which are variable expanded. If none of the comparisons match before a default comparison is found, execution begins after the default comparison. Position each `case` statement and the default statement at the beginning of a line. The command `breaksw` continues execution after the `endsw`. Otherwise, control falls through subsequent `case` and default statements as with C. If no comparison matches and there is no default, execution continues after the `endsw`.

The following list describes the C shell syntax.

`case comparison:`

>   A compared-expression in a `switch` statement.

`default:`   If none of the preceding comparisons match *expression*, then this is the default case in a `switch` statement. The default should come after all case comparisons. Execute any remaining commands on the command line first.

```
breaksw
```
Exit from a `switch`, resuming after the `endsw`.

Korn Shell

A `case` command executes the actions associated with the first pattern that matches *word*. The form of the patterns is the same as that used for file-name generation (see ksh(1)).

A `select` command prints to standard error (file descriptor 2) the set of words, each preceded by a number. If you omit in *word*..., then the positional parameters are used instead. The PS3 prompt is printed, and a line is read from the standard input. If this line consists of the number of one of the listed words, then the value of the variable identifier is set to the word corresponding to this number. If this line is empty, the selection list is printed again. Otherwise, the value of the variable identifier is set to null. The contents of the line read from standard input is saved in the shell variable REPLY. The list is executed for each selection until the shell finds a `break` or end-of-file. If the REPLY variable is set to null by the execution of *list*, then the selection list is printed before the PS3 prompt is displayed for the next selection.

Examples

The following Bourne and Korn shell example tests for the conditions of a stoplight. This particular example does not use the Korn shell `select` statement.

```
STOPLIGHT=green
case $STOPLIGHT in
        red) echo "STOP" ;;
        orange) echo "Go with caution; prepare to stop" ;;
        green) echo "you may GO" ;;
        blue|brown) echo "invalid stoplight colors" ;;
esac
```

The following C shell example tests for the conditions of a stoplight. Note that in the C shell you must add newline characters.

```
set STOPLIGHT = green
switch ($STOPLIGHT)
        case red:
            echo "STOP"
            breaksw
        case orange:
            echo "Go with caution; prepare to stop"
            breaksw
        case green:
            echo "you may GO"
            endsw
endsw
```

The following Bourne script example sets the terminal type.

```
#!/bin/sh
#
```

```
# Set the terminal type
#
case $TERM in
        tvi???)
                echo $TERM
                echo Probably the system console ;;
        vt[12][02]0)
                echo A VT terminal ;;
        Wyse40 | Wyse 75)
                echo A Wyse terminal ;;
        sun)
                echo Aha!! A Workstation ;;
        *0
                echo surprise! It's a $TERM
esac
```

The following example shows an interactive C shell script to set the terminal type.

```
#!/bin/csh -f
#
# Set the terminal type
#
echo "Do you want to see the present setting? \c"
set input = $<
switch ("$input")
        case [Yy]*:
                echo "term =" $TERM
                breaksw
endsw
echo "Terminal type? \c"
set term - $<
switch ($term)
        case tvi950:
        case vt100:
        case sun:
            setenv TERM $term
            breaksw
        default:
            echo "I don't know that one."
            breaksw
endsw
```

Attributes

See `attributes`(5) for descriptions of the following attributes:

Attribute Type	Attribute Value
Availability	SUNWcsu

See Also

break(1), csh(1), ksh(1), sh(1), attributes(5)

cat — Concatenate and Display Files

Synopsis

/usr/bin/cat [-nbsuvet] [*file*...]

Description

Use the cat command to create short files, to concatenate two files into a third one, to append one file to the end of another, or to display the contents of files in sequence on the standard output.

The following syntax creates a new file named *file*. Everything that you type is written to *file*. cat sends one line at a time to the file after you press Return. You can use the backspace key to correct typos on the current line, but you cannot back up across lines. When you are finished, type **Control-D** on a line by itself to terminate the session and close the file. If the file does not exist, it is created. If it already exists, the contents are overwritten with no warning.

cat > *file*

The following syntax displays the contents of *file* on your terminal.

cat *file*

The following syntax concatenates *file1* and *file2* and writes the results into *file3*. If you give no input file, cat reads from the standard input file.

cat *file1 file2* >*file3*

The following syntax appends the contents of *file1* to the end of *file2*.

cat *file1* >> *file2*

The following syntax displays the contents of *file1*, *file2*, and *file3* in sequence on your terminal.

cat *file1 file2 file3*

Note — Redirecting the output of cat onto one of the files being read overwrites the data originally in the file without any warning message.

Options

-n	Precede each line output with its line number.
-b	Number the lines, as with -n, but omit the line numbers from blank lines.
-s	Be silent about nonexistent files.
-u	Do not buffer the output. (The default is buffered output.)
-v	Display nonprinting characters (with the exception of Tabs, newlines, and formfeeds). ASCII control characters (octal 000–037) are printed as ^n, where n is the corresponding ASCII character in the range octal 100–137 (@) A, B, C, . . ., X, Y, Z, [, \,], ^, and _); the DEL character (octal 0177) is printed ^?. Other nonprintable characters are printed as M-x, where x is the ASCII character specified by the low-order seven bits.

You can combine the following options with the -v option.

-e	Print a $ character at the end of each line (before the newline).
-t	Print Tabs as ^I's and formfeeds as ^L's.

The -e and -t options are ignored if you do not specify the -v option.

Operands

file	A path name of an input file. If no file is specified, use the standard input. If *file* is -, read from the standard input at that point in the sequence. cat does not close and reopen standard input when it is referenced in this way but accepts multiple occurrences of dash (-) as *file*.

Usage

See largefile(5) for the description of the behavior of cat when encountering files greater than or equal to 2 Gbytes (2**31 bytes).

Examples

The following command writes the contents of the file kookaburra to standard output:

```
castle% cat kookaburra
Kookaburra sits in the old gum tree
Merry merry king of the bush is he
Laugh, kookaburra, laugh, kookaburra
Gay your life must be.

Kookaburra sits in the old gum tree
Eating all the gumdrops he can see
Stop, kookaburra, stop, kookaburra
Leave some there for me.
castle%
```

The following example concatenates kookaburra1 and kookaburra2 and writes the result to kookaburra3. It then uses the cat command to display the combined result.

```
castle% cat kookaburra1 kookaburra2 > kookaburra3
castle% cat kookaburra3
Kookaburra sits in the old gum tree
Merry merry king of the bush is he
Laugh, kookaburra, laugh, kookaburra
Gay your life must be.

Kookaburra sits in the old gum tree
Eating all the gumdrops he can see
Stop, kookaburra, stop, kookaburra
Leave some there for me.
Kookaburra sits in the old gum tree
Merry merry king of the bush is he
Laugh, kookaburra, laugh, kookaburra
Glad your life must be.

Kookaburra sits in the old gum tree
Eating all the gumdrops he can see
Stop, kookaburra, stop, kookaburra
Leave some there for me.
castle%
```

The following example uses the -n option to display line numbers for the file kookaburra.

```
castle% cat -n kookaburra
     1  Kookaburra sits in the old gum tree
     2  Merry merry king of the bush is he
     3  Laugh, kookaburra, laugh, kookaburra
     4  Gay your life must be.
     5
     6  Kookaburra sits in the old gum tree
     7  Eating all the gumdrops he can see
     8  Stop, kookaburra, stop, kookaburra
     9  Leave some there for me.
```

The following example uses the -b option to display line numbers, omitting any numbers for blank lines. Compare the results with those for the -n command above.

```
castle% cat -b kookaburra
     1  Kookaburra sits in the old gum tree
     2  Merry merry king of the bush is he
     3  Laugh, kookaburra, laugh, kookaburra
     4  Gay your life must be.

     5  Kookaburra sits in the old gum tree
     6  Eating all the gumdrops he can see
     7  Stop, kookaburra, stop, kookaburra
     8  Leave some there for me.
```

The following example displays the contents of three files, the first two of which do not exist. It then uses the -s option to suppress error messages about nonexistent files.

```
castle% cat file1 file2 kookaburra
cat: cannot open file1
cat: cannot open file2
Kookaburra sits in the old gum tree
Merry merry king of the bush is he
Laugh, kookaburra, laugh, kookaburra
Gay your life must be.

Kookaburra sits in the old gum tree
Eating all the gumdrops he can see
Stop, kookaburra, stop, kookaburra
Leave some there for me.
castle% cat -s file1 file2 kookaburra
Kookaburra sits in the old gum tree
Merry merry king of the bush is he
Laugh, kookaburra, laugh, kookaburra
Gay your life must be.

Kookaburra sits in the old gum tree
Eating all the gumdrops he can see
Stop, kookaburra, stop, kookaburra
Leave some there for me.
```

The following example uses the -vet options to display all nonprinting characters in the file kookaburra. The only nonprinting characters in this file are the newlines at the end of each line, which are displayed as a dollar sign ($).

```
castle% cat -vet kookaburra
Kookaburra sits in the old gum tree$
Merry merry king of the bush is he$
Laugh, kookaburra, laugh, kookaburra$
Gay your life must be.$
$
Kookaburra sits in the old gum tree$
Eating all the gumdrops he can see$
Stop, kookaburra, stop, kookaburra$
Leave some there for me.$
castle%
```

Environment Variables

See environ(5) for descriptions of the following environment variables that affect the execution of cat: LC_CTYPE, LC_MESSAGES, and NLSPATH.

Exit Status

0	All input files were output successfully.
>0	An error occurred.

Attributes

See `attributes`(5) for descriptions of the following attributes:

Attribute Type	Attribute Value
Availability	SUNWcsu
CSI	Enabled

See Also

`touch(1), environ(5), attributes(5), largefile(5)`

---

cc — C Compiler

Synopsis

`/usr/ucb/cc [options]`

Description

`/usr/ucb/cc` is the interface to the BSD Compatibility package C compiler. It is a script that looks for the link `/usr/ccs/bin/ucbcc` to the C compiler. `/usr/ccs/bin/ucbcc` is available only with the SPROcc package, whose default location is `/opt/SUNWspro`. `/usr/ucb/cc` is identical to `/usr/ccs/bin/ucbcc`, except that it uses BSD headers and links BSD libraries before base libraries. The `/opt/SUNWspro/man/man1/acc.1` manual page is available only with the SPROcc package.

Options

`/usr/ucb/cc` accepts the same options as `/usr/ccs/bin/ucbcc`, with the exceptions noted below.

    `-Idir`   Search `dir` for included files whose names do not begin with a slash (`/`) before searching the usual directories. cc searches the directories for multiple `-I` options in the order specified. The preprocessor first searches for `#include` files in the directory containing `sourcefile`, and then in directories named with `-I` options (if any), then `/usr/ucbinclude`, and finally, in `/usr/include`.

    `-Ldir`   Add `dir` to the list of directories searched for libraries by `/usr/ccs/bin/ucbcc`. Pass this option to `/usr/ccs/bin/ld` and `/usr/ccs/lib`. Search directories specified with this option before `/usr/ucblib` and `/usr/lib`.

-Y P, *dir*   Change the default directory used for finding libraries. Note that this option may have unexpected results and should not be used.

Exit Status

0   Successful compilation or link edit.

>0   An error occurred.

Files

/usr/ccs/bin/ld link

> Editor.

/usr/lib/libcC

> Library.

/usr/ucbinclude

> BSD Compatibility directory for header files.

/usr/ucblib

> BSD Compatibility directory for libraries.

/usr/ucblib/libuc

> BSD Compatibility C library.

/usr/lib/libsocket

> Library containing socket routines.

/usr/lib/libnsl

> Library containing network functions.

/usr/lib/libelf

> Library containing routines to process ELF object files.

/usr/lib/libaio

> Library containing asynchronous I/O routines.

Attributes

See attributes(5) for descriptions of the following attributes:

Attribute Type	Attribute Value
Availability	SUNWscpu

See Also

ld(1), a.out(4), attributes(5)

cd, chdir, pushd, popd, dirs — Change Working Directory

Synopsis

```
/usr/bin/cd [directory]
```

sh
```
cd [argument]
chdir [argument]
```

csh
```
cd [dir]
chdir [dir]
pushd [+n | dir]
popd [+n]
dirs [-l]
```

ksh
```
cd [arg]
cd old new
```

Description

You can move between directories by using the cd (change directory) command. Depending on the shell you are using, you may have alternative ways to change directories.

The /usr/bin/cd command changes the working directory of the current shell execution environment. When you use the cd command with no arguments and the HOME environment variable is set, cd changes the new working directory to the directory named in the HOME environment variable.

Bourne Shell

The Bourne shell built-in cd command changes the current directory to *argument*. The shell parameter HOME is the default argument. The shell parameter CDPATH defines the search path for the directory containing *argument*. Separate alternative directory names by a colon (:). The default path is null (specifying the current directory).

Note — The current directory is specified by a null path name, which can appear immediately after the equal sign or between the colon delimiters anywhere else in the path list. If argument begins with /, ., or .., the search path is not used. Otherwise, each directory in the path is searched for *argument*. cd must have execute (search) permission in *argument*. Because a new process is created to execute each command, cd is ineffective if it is written as a normal command; therefore, it is recognized by and is internal to the shell. (See pwd(1), sh(1), and chdir(2)).

chdir is just another way to call cd.

C Shell
If you do not specify *dir*, the C shell built-in cd uses the value of shell parameter HOME as the new working directory.

If *dir* specifies a complete path starting with /, ., or .., *dir* becomes the new working directory. If *dir* does not start with /, ., or .., cd tries to find the designated directory relative to one of the paths specified by the CDPATH shell variable. CDPATH has the same syntax as, and similar semantics to, the PATH shell variable. cd must have execute (search) permission in *dir*. Because a new process is created to execute each command, cd is ineffective if it is written as a normal command; therefore, it is recognized by and is internal to the C shell. (See pwd(1), csh(1), and chdir(2).)

chdir changes the shell's working directory to directory *dir*. If no argument is given, change to the home directory of the user. If *dir* is a relative path name not found in the current directory, check for it in those directories listed in the cdpath variable. If *dir* is the name of a shell variable whose value starts with a /, change to the directory named by that value.

pushd pushes a directory onto the directory stack. With no arguments, it exchanges the top two elements. You can also use the following arguments for pushd.

+n	Rotate the *n*-th entry to the top of the stack and use cd to change to it.
dir	Push the current working directory onto the stack and change to *dir*.

popd pops the directory stack and changes to the new top directory. The elements of the directory stack are numbered from 0 starting at the top. You can use the following arguments for popd.

+n	Discard the *n*-th entry in the stack.
dirs	Print the directory stack, most recent to the left; the first directory shown is the current directory. With the -l argument, produce an unabbreviated printout; suppress use of the ~ notation.

Korn Shell
The Korn shell built-in cd command can be in either of two forms. In the first form, cd changes the current directory to *arg*. If *arg* is -, the directory is changed to the previous directory. The shell variable HOME is the default *arg*. The variable PWD is set to the current directory. The shell variable CDPATH defines the search path for the directory containing *arg*. Separate alternative directory names by a colon (:). The default path is <null> (specifying the current directory). Note that the current directory is specified by a null path name, which can appear immediately after the equal sign or between the colon delimiters anywhere else in the path list. If *arg* begins with a /, ., or .., then the search path is not used. Otherwise, each directory in the path is searched for *arg*.

The second form of `cd` substitutes the string *new* for the string *old* in the current directory name, PWD, and tries to change to this new directory.

The `cd` command may not be executed by `rksh`. Because a new process is created to execute each command, `cd` is ineffective if it is written as a normal command; therefore, it is recognized by and is internal to the Korn shell. (See pwd(1), ksh(1), and chdir(2)).

Operands

directory	An absolute or relative path name of the directory that becomes the new working directory. The interpretation of a relative path name by `cd` depends on the CDPATH environment variable.

Environment Variables

See environ(5) for descriptions of the following environment variables that affect the execution of `cd`: LC_CTYPE, LC_MESSAGES, and NLSPATH.

CDPATH	A colon-separated list of path names that refer to directories. If the directory operand does not begin with a slash (/) character and the first component is not dot or dot-dot, `cd` searches for a directory relative to each directory named in the CDPATH variable, in the order listed. The new working directory is set to the first matching directory found. An empty string in place of a directory path name represents the current directory. If CDPATH is not set, it is treated as if it were an empty string.
	When CDPATH is defined, the `cd` command for the Korn and Bourne shells displays the absolute path name of the new directory to the standard output. If CDPATH is not set, there is no output.
HOME	The name of the home directory, used when no directory operand is specified.
PWD	A path name of the current working directory, set by `cd` after it has changed to that directory.

Exit Status

0	The directory was successfully changed.
>0	An error occurred.

Attributes

See attributes(5) for descriptions of the following attributes:

Attribute Type	Attribute Value
Availability	SUNWcsu

See Also

csh(1), ksh(1), pwd(1), sh(1), chdir(2), attributes(5), environ(5)

---

cdc, sccs-cdc — Change the Delta Commentary of an SCCS Delta

Synopsis

/usr/ccs/bin/cdc -rsid [-mmr-list] [-y [comment]] s.filename ...

Description

See sccs-cdc(1).

---

chdir — Change Working Directory

Synopsis

sh
chdir [argument]

csh
chdir [dir]

Description\

See cd(1).

---

checkeq — Typeset Mathematics Test

Synopsis

/usr/bin/checkeq [file] ...

Description

See eqn(1).

checknr — Check nroff and troff Input Files for Errors

Synopsis

```
/usr/bin/checknr [-fs] [-a x1 .y1 .x2 .y2 ... .xn .yn]
   [-c .x1 .x2 .x3 ... .xn] [filename ...]
```

Description

checknr checks a list of nroff(1) or troff(1) input files for certain kinds of errors involving mismatched opening and closing delimiters and unknown commands. If you specify no files, checknr checks the standard input. Delimiters checked are:

- Font changes using \fx ... \fP.
- Size changes using \sx ... \s0.
- Macros that come in open ... close forms, for example, the .TS and .TE macros which must always come in pairs.

checknr knows about the ms(5) and me(5) macro packages.

Use checknr on documents that are prepared with checknr in mind. It expects a certain document writing style for \f and \s commands, in that each \fx must be terminated with \fP and each \sx must be terminated with \s0. Although it works to go directly into the next font or to explicitly specify the original font or point size (and many existing documents actually do this), such a practice produces complaints from checknr. Because it is probably better to use the \fP and \s0 forms anyway, think of this restriction as a contribution to your document preparation style.

Bugs

You cannot define a one-character macro name by using the -a option.

Options

-f	Ignore \f font changes.
-s	Ignore \s size changes.

-a.x1 .y1...

Add pairs of macros to the list. The pairs of macros are assumed to be those (such as .DS and .DE) that should be checked for balance. Follow the -a option by groups of six characters, each group defining a pair of macros. The six characters are a period, the first macro name, another period, and the second macro name. For example, to define a pair .BS and .ES, use -a.BS.ES

-c .x1...   Define commands that checknr would otherwise complain about as undefined.

Examples

The following example runs the checknr command on the checknr.1 manual page from the /usr/share/man directory.

```
castle% checknr checknr.1
13: Unknown command: .BI
14: Unknown command: .BI
15: Unknown command: .BI
16: Unknown command: .BI
18: Unknown command: .BI
19: Unknown command: .BI
24: Unknown command: .BI
25: Unknown command: .BI
26: Unknown command: .BI
28: Unknown command: .BI
42: Unknown command: .BR
44: Unknown command: .BR
62: Unknown command: .SB
64: Unknown command: .SB
54: Unmatched \f3
54: Unmatched \f2
54: Unmatched \f1
54: Unmatched \f3
54: Unmatched \f1
57: Unmatched \f3
57: Unmatched \f2
57: Unmatched \f1
57: Unmatched \f3
57: Unmatched \f1
70: Unknown command: .BR
72: Unknown command: .BR
84: Unknown command: .BI
88: Unknown command: .BI
90: Unknown command: .BR
96: Unknown command: .BR
116: Unknown command: .BI
120: Unknown command: .SB
122: Unknown command: .BR
131: Unknown command: .SB
133: Unknown command: .BR
135: Unknown command: .RB
137: Unknown command: .BI
144: Unknown command: .BR
156: Unknown command: .BR
157: Unknown command: .BR
158: Unknown command: .BR
159: Unknown command: .BR
160: Unknown command: .BR
161: Unknown command: .BR
137: Unmatched \f1
116: Unmatched \f1
castle%
```

The following example uses the -a option to suppress the Unknown command messages for .BI and .BR.

```
castle% checknr -a.BI.BR checknr.1
62: Unknown command: .SB
64: Unknown command: .SB
54: Unmatched \f3
54: Unmatched \f2
54: Unmatched \f1
54: Unmatched \f3
54: Unmatched \f1
57: Unmatched \f3
57: Unmatched \f2
57: Unmatched \f1
57: Unmatched \f3
57: Unmatched \f1
120: Unknown command: .SB
131: Unknown command: .SB
135: Unknown command: .RB
137: Unmatched \f1
116: Unmatched \f1
castle%
```

Attributes

See attributes(5) for descriptions of the following attributes:

Attribute Type	Attribute Value
Availability	SUNWdoc

See Also

eqn(1), nroff(1), troff(1), attributes(5), me(5), ms(5)

chgrp — Change File Group Ownership

Synopsis

/usr/bin/chgrp [-fhR] *group file*

Description

You can use the chgrp command to change the group that owns a file, provided that you own the file and are a member of the group that owns it. The chgrp command sets the group ID of the file named by each *file* operand to the group ID specified by the *group* operand.

For each file operand, chgrp performs actions equivalent to the chown(2) function, called with the following arguments:

- The *file* operand is used as the path argument.
- The user ID of the file is used as the *owner* argument.
- The specified group ID is used as the *group* argument.

Unless chgrp is invoked by a process with appropriate privileges, the set-user-ID and set-group-ID bits of a regular file are cleared on successful completion; the set-user-ID and set-group-ID bits of other file types may be cleared.

The operating system has a configuration option {_POSIX_CHOWN_RESTRICTED}, to restrict ownership changes. When this option is in effect, the owner of the file can change the group of the file only to a group to which the owner belongs. Only superuser can arbitrarily change owner IDs, regardless of whether this option is in effect. To set this configuration option, include the following line in /etc/system:

```
set rstchown = 1
```

To disable this option, include the following line in /etc/system:

```
set rstchown = 0
```

{_POSIX_CHOWN_RESTRICTED} is enabled by default. See system(4) and fpathconf(2).

Options

-f	Do not report errors.
-h	If the file is a symbolic link, change the group of the symbolic link. Without this option, change the group of the file referenced by the symbolic link.
-R	Recursively descend through the directory and any subdirectories, setting the specified group ID as chgrp proceeds. When chgrp encounters a symbolic link, change the group of the target file (unless you specify the -h option), but do no recursion.

Operands

group	A group name from the group database or a numeric group ID. Either specifies a group ID to be given to each file named by one of the file operands. If a numeric group operand exists in the group database as a group name, the group ID number associated with that group name is used as the group ID.
file	A path name of a file whose group ID is to be modified.

Usage

See largefile(5) for the description of the behavior of chgrp when encountering files greater than or equal to 2 Gbytes (2**31 bytes).

Examples

In the following example, winsor, the owner of the file, changes the group for the file named tryit to other.

```
castle% chgrp other tryit
castle% ls -l tryit
-rw-rw-rw-   1 winsor    other         18 Aug 27 17:45 tryit
castle%
```

In the following example, user ray tries to change the group for the file named tryit back to staff but does not own the file. An error message is displayed.

```
castle% whoami
ray
castle% chgrp staff tryit
chgrp: tryit: Not owner
castle%
```

In the following example, superuser changes the group for the file named tryit back to staff.

```
castle% su
Password:
castle# chgrp staff tryit
castle# ls -l tryit
-rw-rw-rw-   1 winsor    staff         18 Aug 27 17:45 tryit
castle#
```

Environment Variables

See environ(5) for descriptions of the following environment variables that affect the execution of chgrp: LC_CTYPE, LC_MESSAGES, and NLSPATH.

Exit Status

0   The command executed successfully and all requested changes were made.

>0   An error occurred.

Files

/etc/group   Group file.

Attributes

See attributes(5) for descriptions of the following attributes:

Attribute Type	Attribute Value
Availability	SUNWcsu
CSI	Enabled

Note — chgrp is CSI-enabled except for the group name.

See Also

chmod(1), chown(1), id(1M), chown(2), fpathconf(2), group(4), passwd(4), system(4), attributes(5), environ(5), largefile(5)

chkey — Change User's Secure RPC Key Pair

Synopsis

New!   /usr/bin/chkey [-p] [-s nisplus | nis | files] [-m <mechanism>]

Description

Use chkey to change a user's secure RPC public key and secret key pair. chkey prompts for the old secure RPC password and verifies that it is correct by decrypting the secret key. If the user has not already keylogged in, chkey registers the secret key with the local keyserv(1M) daemon. If the secure RPC password does not match the login password, chkey prompts for the login password. chkey uses the login password to encrypt the user's secret Diffie-Hellman (192-bit) cryptographic key.

chkey ensures that the login password and the secure RPC password are kept the same, thus enabling password shadowing (see shadow(4)).

The key pair can be stored in the /etc/publickey file, (see publickey(4)), NIS public key map, or the NIS+ cred.org_dir table. If a new secret key is generated, it is registered with the local keyserv(1M) daemon.

New!   You can change or reencrypt specific mechanisms with the -m option followed by the authentication mechanism name. You can use multiple -m options to change one or more keys. However, only mechanisms configured using nisauthconf(1M) can be changed with chkey.

If you do not specify the source of the public key with the -s option, chkey consults the public key entry in the name service switch configuration file (see nsswitch.conf(4)). If the public key entry specifies one and only one source, then chkey changes the key in the specified name service. However, if multiple

name services are listed, chkey cannot decide which source to update and
displays an error message. Specify the source explicitly with the -s option.
    Non-root users are not allowed to change their key pair in the files
database.

Options

-p   Reencrypt the existing secret key with the user's login password.

-s nisplus   Update the NIS+ database.

-s nis   Update the NIS database.

-s files   Update the files database.

-m *mechanism*

              Change or reencrypt the secret key for the specified mechanism.

Examples

The following example changes the NIS secure RPC key pair for user ray.

```
seachild% chkey -p
Updating nis publickey database.
Reencrypting key for unix.1002@Castle.Abc.COM
Please enter the Secure-RPC password for ray:
Please enter the login password for ray:
Sending key change request to castle...
Seachild%
```

Files

/etc/nsswitch.conf

/etc/publickey

Attributes

See attributes(5) for descriptions of the following attributes:

Attribute Type	Attribute Value
Availability	SUNWcsu

See Also

keylogin(1), keylogout(1), keyserv(1M), newkey(1M), nisaddcred(1M),
nsswitch.conf(4), publickey(4), shadow(4), attributes(5)

chmod — Change the Permissions Mode of a File

Synopsis
```
/usr/bin/chmod [-fR] absolute-mode file...
/usr/bin/chmod [-fR] symbolic-mode-list file...
```

Description
Use the chmod (change mode) command to change the mode of a file. The mode of a file specifies its permissions and other attributes. You can specify the mode in one of two ways: absolute or symbolic.

Absolute Mode
You specify an absolute mode in octal numbers by using the following syntax:
```
chmod nnnn file ...
```

where n is a number from 0 to 7. You construct an absolute mode from the OR of any of the following modes:

4000	Set user ID on execution.
20#0	Set group ID on execution if # is 7, 5, 3, or 1. Enable mandatory locking if # is 6, 4, 2, or 0. For directories, create files with BSD semantics for propagation of the group ID. With this option, files and subdirectories created in the directory inherit the group ID of the directory, instead of of the current process. You can clear the group ID bit only by using symbolic mode.
1000	Turn on sticky bit. See chmod(2).
0400	Allow read by owner.
0200	Allow write by owner.
0100	Allow execute (search in directory) by owner.
0700	Allow read, write, and execute (search) by owner.
0040	Allow read by group.
0020	Allow write by group.
0010	Allow execute (search in directory) by group.
0070	Allow read, write, and execute (search) by group.
0004	Allow read by others.
0002	Allow write by others.
0001	Allow execute (search in directory) by others.
0007	Allow read, write, and execute (search) by others.

Note — You cannot set or clear the setgid bit in absolute mode; you must set (or clear) it in symbolic mode, using g+s (or g-s).

Symbolic mode

You specify a symbolic mode by using the following syntax:

chmod *symbolic-mode-list file*...

where *symbolic-mode-list* is a comma-separated list (with no intervening white space) of symbolic mode expressions of the form:

[*who*] *operator* [*permissions*]

Operations are performed in the order given. Multiple permissions letters following a single operator perform the corresponding operations simultaneously.

The modes for the chmod command are shown below.

who Zero or more of the characters u, g, o, and a, specifying whose permissions are to be changed or assigned.

    u   User's permissions.

    g   Group's permissions.

    o   Others' permissions.

    a   All permissions (user, group, and other).

    If you omit *who*, it defaults to a, but the setting of the file mode creation mask (see umask in sh(1) or csh(1) for more information) is taken into account. When you omit *who*, chmod does not override the restrictions of your user mask.

operator Either +, -, or =, signifying how permissions are to be changed.

    +   Add permissions.

        If you omit *permissions*, nothing is added.

        If you omit *who*, add the file-mode bits represented by *permissions*, except for those with corresponding bits in the file-mode creation mask.

        If you specify *who*, add the file-mode bits represented by the *permissions*.

    -   Take away *permissions*.

        If you omit *permissions*, do nothing.

        If you omit *who*, clear the file-mode bits represented by permissions, except for those with corresponding bits in the file-mode creation mask.

        If you specify *who*, clear the file-mode bits represented by permissions.

=   Assign permissions absolutely.

If you omit *who*, clear all file-mode bits; if you specify *who*, clear the file-mode bits represented by *who*.

If you omit *permissions*, do nothing else.

If you omit *who*, add the file-mode bits represented by *permissions*, except for the those with corresponding bits in the file-mode creation mask.

If you specify *who*, add the file-mode bits represented by *permissions*.

Unlike other symbolic operations, = has an absolute effect in that it resets all other bits represented by *who*. Omitting permissions is useful only with = to take away all permissions.

permissions Any compatible combination of the following letters:

r   Read permission.

w   Write permission.

x   Execute permission.

l   Mandatory locking.

s   User or group set-ID.

t   Sticky bit.

u,g,o   Take permission from the current user, group, or other mode.

Permissions to a file can vary depending on your user identification number (UID) or group identification number (GID). Permissions are described in three sequences, each having three characters. The following example shows the access class for each group of permissions and the permissions themselves. It gives user, group, and others permission to read, write, and execute a given file.

```
User Group Other
rwx   rwx   rwx
```

The letter s is meaningful only with u or g, and t works only with u.

Mandatory file and record locking refers to a file's ability to have its reading or writing permissions locked while a program is accessing that file.

In a directory that has the set-group-ID bit set (reflected as either `-----s---` or `----- l---` in the output of ls -ld), files and subdirectories are created with the group-ID of the parent directory, not that of current process.

You cannot permit group execution and enable a file to be locked on execution at the same time. In addition, you cannot turn on the set-group-ID bit and enable a file to be locked on execution at the same time. The following examples, therefore, are invalid and result in error messages.

```
chmod g+x,+l file
chmod g+s,+l file
```

Only the owner of a file or directory (or the superuser) can change its mode. Only the superuser can set the sticky bit on a nondirectory file. If you are not superuser, chmod masks the sticky bit but does not return an error. To turn on a file's set-group-ID bit, your own group ID must correspond to that of the file and group execution must be set.

Notes

Absolute changes don't work for the set-group-ID bit of a directory. You must use g+s or g-s. chmod permits you to produce useless modes so long as they are not illegal (for instance, making a text file executable). chmod does not check the file type to see if mandatory locking is meaningful.

If the file system is mounted with the nosuid option, setuid execution is not allowed.

Options

-f	Do not complain if chmod fails to change the mode of a file.
-R	Recursively descend through directory arguments, setting the mode for each file as described above. When symbolic links are encountered, change the mode of the target file, but do no recursion.

Operands

mode	The change to be made to the file-mode bits of each file named by one of the file operands.
file	A path name of a file whose file-mode bits are to be modified.

Usage

See largefile(5) for the description of the behavior of chmod when encountering files greater than or equal to 2 Gbytes ($2**31$ bytes).

Examples

The following example denies execute permissions to everyone.

```
castle% chmod a-x file
```

The following example gives everyone only read permission.

```
castle% chmod 444 file
```

The following examples makes a file readable and writable by the group and others.

```
castle% chmod go+rw file
castle% chmod 066 file
```

The following example locks a file during access.

```
castle% chmod +l file
```

The following example enables everyone to read, write, and execute the file and turns on the set group-ID.

```
castle% chmod a=rwx,g+s file
castle% chmod 2777 file
```

Environment Variables

See environ(5) for descriptions of the following environment variables that affect the execution of chmod: LC_CTYPE, LC_MESSAGES, and NLSPATH.

Exit Status

0   Successful completion.

>0   An error occurred.

Attributes

See attributes(5) for descriptions of the following attributes:

Attribute Type	Attribute Value
Availability	SUNWcsu
CSI	Enabled

See Also

ls(1), chmod(2), attributes(5), environ(5), largefile(5)

chown — Change File Ownership

Synopsis

```
/usr/bin/chown [-fhR] owner[:group] file...
```

Description

Use the chown (change owner) command to change the user ID of files that you own. You can also optionally change the group ID with this command. If chown is used by somebody other than the superuser, the setuser-ID bit is cleared.

Only the owner of a file (or the superuser) can change the owner of that file.

The operating system has a configuration option, {_POSIX_CHOWN_RESTRICTED}, to restrict ownership changes. When this option is in effect, even the owner of the file cannot change the owner ID of the file. Only the superuser can arbitrarily change owner IDs regardless of whether this option is in effect. To set the {_POSIX_CHOWN_RESTRICTED} configuration option, include the following line in /etc/system:

```
set rstchown = 1
```

To disable the {_POSIX_CHOWN_RESTRICTED} option, include the following line in /etc/system:

```
set rstchown = 0
```

{_POSIX_CHOWN_RESTRICTED} is enabled by default. See system(4) and fpathconf(2).

Options

-f	Do not report errors.
-h	If the file is a symbolic link, change the owner of the symbolic link. Without this option, the owner of the file referenced by the symbolic link is changed.
-R	Recursively descend through the directory and any subdirectories, setting the ownership ID. When a symbolic link is encountered, change the owner of the target file (unless you specify the -h option), but do no recursion.

Operands

owner[:*group*]

A user ID and optional group ID to be assigned to file. The owner portion of this operand must be a user name from the user database or a numeric user ID. Either specifies a user ID to be given to each file named by *file*. If a numeric owner exists in the user database as a user name, chown uses the user ID number associated with that user name. Similarly, if you use the *group* portion of this operand, it must be a group name from the group database or a numeric group ID. Either specifies a group ID to be given to each file. If a numeric group operand exists in the group database as a group name, chown uses the group ID number associated with that group name as the group ID.

file   A path name of a file whose user ID is to be modified.

Usage

See largefile(5) for the description of the behavior of chown when encountering files greater than or equal to 2 Gbytes (2**31 bytes).

Examples

In the following example, although user winsor owns the file named kookaburra, {_POSIX_CHOWN_RESTRICTED} is enabled (by default) and so the Not owner error message is displayed.

```
castle% ls -l kookaburra
-rw-rw-rw-   1 winsor     staff          242 Oct  1 16:12 kookaburra
castle% chown ray kookaburra
chown: kookaburra: Not owner
castle%
```

In the following example, superuser changes the ownership of the file named kookaburra to ray and the group to other.

```
castle% su
Password:
castle# chown ray kookaburra
castle# ls -l kookaburra
-rw-rw-rw-   1 ray        staff          242 Oct  1 16:12 kookaburra
castle# chown ray:other kookaburra
castle# ls -l kookaburra
-rw-rw-rw-   1 ray        other          242 Oct  1 16:12 kookaburra
castle#
```

Environment Variables

See environ(5) for descriptions of the following environment variables that affect the execution of chown: LC_CTYPE, LC_MESSAGES, and NLSPATH.

Exit Status

0   The command executed successfully and all requested changes were made.

>0   An error occurred.

Files

/etc/passwd

System password file.

Attributes

See attributes(5) for descriptions of the following attributes:

Attribute Type	Attribute Value
Availability	SUNWcsu
CSI	Enabled

> **Note** — chown is CSI-enabled except for the owner and group names.

See Also

chgrp(1), chmod(1), chown(2), fpathconf(2), passwd(4), system(4), attributes(5), environ(5), largefile(5)

cksum — Write File Checksums and Sizes

Synopsis

/usr/bin/cksum [*file*...]

Description

The cksum command calculates and writes to standard output a cyclic redundancy check (CRC) for each input file and also writes to standard output the number of octets in each file.

For each file processed successfully, cksum writes in the following format:

"%u %d %s\n" *checksum*, # *of octets*, *pathname*

If you do not specify a file operand, the path name and its leading space are omitted.

The CRC is based on the polynomial used for CRC error checking in the referenced Ethernet standard.

The encoding for the CRC checksum is defined by the generating polynomial:

G(x) = x32 + x26 + x23 + x22 + x16 + x12 + x11 + x10 + x8 + x7 + x5 + x4 + x2 + x + 1

Mathematically, the CRC value corresponding to a given file is defined by the following procedure:

1. The n bits to be evaluated are considered to be the coefficients of a mod 2 polynomial M(x) of degree n-1. These n bits are the bits from the file; the most significant bit is the most significant bit of the first octet of the file, and the last bit is the least significant bit of the last octet, padded with zero bits (if necessary) to achieve an integral number of octets. The last bit is followed by one or more octets representing the length of the file as a binary value, with least significant octet first. The smallest number of octets capable of representing this integer is used.

2. M(x) is multiplied by x 32 (that is, shifted left 32 bits) and divided by G(x) using mod 2 division, producing a remainder R(x) of degree < 31.

3. The coefficients of R(x) are considered to be a 32-bit sequence.

4. The bit sequence is complemented, and the result is the CRC.

Examples

You can display a checksum for an individual file or directory, for a list of files, or for all of the files in a directory. The following example displays checksums for all the directories and files in the current working directory.

```
castle% cksum *
1583778740    1024    Art
2849654401    512     DeadLetters
4294967295    0       Design.book
3648788112    512     Mail
1811574335    737     bibliography
2131326963    526     commands
3414952850    934     examples
4294967295    0       file
2520900578    12      file1
3048412797    241     file3
599464025     242     kookaburra
3048412797    241     kookaburra1
2464961294    242     kookaburra2
40181032      483     kookaburra3
1589184179    2007    listfile
766785258     124     local.cshrc
1383060028    560     local.profile
50931726      85      mycode
2025597153    3673    permissions
3135107960    4182    printing
1365772283    18      script
1580610504    20      sortfile
1681251586    20      sortoutput
2655897922    23      template
2618551756    84      typescript
2176151109    40020   whtpaper.html
castle%
```

clear — Clear the Terminal Screen

Synopsis

```
/usr/bin/clear
```

Description

The clear command clears your screen or the current shell window if it can. It looks in the environment for the terminal type and then in the terminfo database to figure out how to clear the screen.

Attributes

See attributes(5) for descriptions of the following attributes:

Attribute Type	Attribute Value
Availability	SUNWcsu

See Also

attributes(5)

---

cmp — Compare Two Files

Synopsis

/usr/bin/cmp [-l] [-s] *file1* *file2* [*skip1*] [*skip2*]

Description

Use the cmp command to compare two files. If the files are the same, cmp writes no output. Under default options, if the files differ, cmp writes to standard output the byte and line numbers at which the first difference occurred. Bytes and lines are numbered beginning with 1. If one file is an initial subsequence of the other, that fact is noted. *skip1* and *skip2* are initial byte offsets into *file1* and *file2*, and may be either octal or decimal; a leading 0 denotes octal.

Options

-l	Write the byte number (decimal) and the differing bytes (octal) for each difference.
-s	Write nothing for differing files; return exit statuses only.

Operands

file1	A path name of the first file to be compared. If *file1* is -, use the standard input.
file2	A path name of the second file to be compared. If *file2* is -, use the standard input.

If both *file1* and *file2* refer to standard input or refer to the same FIFO special, block special, or character special file, an error results.

Usage

See largefile(5) for the description of the behavior of cmp when encountering files greater than or equal to 2 Gbytes (2**31 bytes).

Examples

The following example does a byte-for-byte comparison of kookaburra1 and kookaburra2.

```
castle% cmp kookaburra1 kookaburra2
kookaburra1 kookaburra2 differ: char 110, line 4
castle%
```

The following example does a byte-for-byte comparison of kookaburra1 and kookaburra2 and skips the first 64 bytes in kookaburra2 before starting the comparison. Notice that the line and character numbers differ because of the skip offset.

```
castle% cmp kookaburra1 kookaburra2 0 64
kookaburra1 kookaburra2 differ: char 1, line 1
castle%
```

Environment Variables

See environ(5) for descriptions of the following environment variables that affect the execution of cmp: LC_CTYPE, LC_MESSAGES, and NLSPATH.

Exit Status

0	The files are identical.
1	The files are different; this includes the case where one file is identical to the first part of the other.
>1	An error occurred.

Attributes

See attributes(5) for descriptions of the following attributes:

Attribute Type	Attribute Value
Availability	SUNWcsu
CSI	Enabled

See Also

comm(1), diff(1), attributes(5), environ(5), largefile(5)

col — Reverse Linefeeds Filter

Synopsis

    /usr/bin/col [-bfpx]

Description

The col command is a postprocessing filter that handles escape characters and removes reverse linefeeds that are used to handle underlining, superscripts, and subscripts. Use col to convert reverse line motions into single-line combinations of backspaces and characters. col removes superscripts and subscripts from nroff output. It is particularly useful for filtering multicolumn output made with the .rt command of nroff(1) and output resulting from use of the tbl(1) preprocessor.

col reads from the standard input and writes to the standard output. It performs the line overlays implied by reverse linefeeds, and by forward and reverse half-linefeeds. Unless you use the -x option, all blank characters in the input are converted to Tab characters wherever possible.

The ASCII control characters SO and SI are assumed to start and end text in an alternative character set. The character set to which each input character belongs is remembered, and on output SI and SO characters are generated as appropriate to ensure that each character is written in the correct character set.

On input, the only control characters accepted are space, backspace, Tab, Return, and newline characters, SI, SO, VT, reverse linefeed, forward half-line feed and reverse half-line feed. The VT character is an alternative form of full reverse linefeed, included for compatibility with some earlier programs of this type. The only other characters to be copied to the output are those that are printable.

The ASCII codes for the control functions and line-motion sequences mentioned above are shown below. Esc stands for the ASCII escape character, with the octal code 033; Esc- means a sequence of two characters, Esc followed by the character x.

Code	Description
Esc-7	Reverse linefeed
Esc-8	Reverse half-linefeed
Esc-9	Forward half-linefeed
013	Vertical-Tab (VT)
016	Start-of-text (SO)
017	End-of-text (SI)

Notes

The input format accepted by `col` matches the output produced by `nroff` with either the `-T37` or `-Tlp` options. Use `-T37` (and the `-f` option of `col`) if the ultimate disposition of the output of `col` is a device that can interpret half-line motions. Otherwise, use `-Tlp`.

`col` cannot back up more than 128 lines or handle more than 800 characters per line.

Local vertical motions that would result in backing up over the first line of the document are ignored. As a result, the first line must not have any superscripts.

Options

`-b`	Assume that the output device in use is not capable of backspacing. In this case, if two or more characters are to appear in the same place, only the last one read is output.
`-f`	Include forward half-linefeeds (Esc-9) but do not include reverse line motion. Usually half-line input motion is displayed on the next full line.
`-p`	Esc-7.
`-x`	Esc-8.

Examples

The following example runs a file through `tbl` and `nroff` and then displays output on the screen by filtering through `col` and `more`.

```
castle% tbl file | nroff | col | more
```

The following example runs `nroff` output from a VDT through `col`.

```
castle% nroff -cm -rO8 -rW79 document | col
```

The following example removes the ^M's from a DOS text document.

```
castle% cat filename | col output-file
```

Before the `col` command, the file looks like this:

```
The od command copies sequentially each input file to  stan-^M
dard output and transforming the input data according to the^M
output types specified by the -t or -bcCDdFfOoSsvXx options.^M
If  no output type is specified, the default output is as if^M
-t o2 had been specified.  Multiple types can  be  specified^M
by  using  multiple  -bcCDdFfOoSstvXx options.  Output lines^M
are written for each type specified in the  order  in  which^M
the types are specified.  If no file is specified, the stan-^M
dard input is used.  The [offset_string] operand is mutually^M
exclusive from the -A, -j, -N, and -t options.  For the pur-^M
poses of this description, the following terms are used:^M
^M
```

```
^M
^M
^M
^M
```

After the col command, the file looks like this:

```
The od command copies sequentially each input file to  stan-
dard output and transforming the input data according to the
output types specified by the -t or -bcCDdFfOoSsvXx options.
If  no output type is specified, the default output is as if
-t o2 had been specified.  Multiple types can  be  specified
by  using  multiple  -bcCDdFfOoSstvXx options.  Output lines
are written for each type specified in the  order  in  which
the types are specified.  If no file is specified, the stan-
dard input is used.  The [offset_string] operand is mutually
exclusive from the -A, -j, -N, and -t options.  For the pur-
poses of this description, the following terms are used:
```

Alternatively, you can use the dos2unix command for DOS formatted files, as shown below.

```
castle% dos2unix input-file output-file
```

The following example filters reverse line feeds from input to print a manual page without the formatting.

```
castle% man od | col -b lpr
```

Without using the col command, the output looks like this:

```
NAME

     od - octal dump



SYNOPSIS

     /usr/bin/od [ -bcCDdFfOoSsvXx ] [ -] [ _ f_ i_ l_ e ]

        [ _ o_ f_ f_ s_ e_ t__ s_ t_ r_ i_ n_ g ]

     /usr/bin/od [ -bcCDdFfOoSsvXx ] [ -A _ a_ d_ d_ r_ e_ s_ s__ b_ a_
     s_ e ]
          [ -j _ s_ k_ i_ p ] [ -N _ c_ o_ u_ n_ t ] [ -t _ t_ y_ p_ e__
     s_ t_ r_ i_ n_ g ] ...
          [ - ] [ _ f_ i_ l_ e

     /usr/xpg4/bin/od [ -bcCDdFfOoSsvXx ] [ -] [ _ f_ i_ l_ e ]
          [ _ o_ f_ f_ s_ e_ t__ s_ t_ r_ i_ n_ g ]
     /usr/xpg4/bin/od [ -bcCDdFfOoSsvXx ] [ -A _ a_ d_ d_ r_ e_ s_ s__
     b_ a_ s_ e ]
          [ -j _ s_ k_ i_ p ] [ -N _ c_ o_ u_ n_ t ] [ -t _ t_ y_ p_ e__
```

```
s_ t_ r_ i_ n_ g
        [ - ] [ _ f_ i_ l_ e
```

The col command strips out the formatting so that the output is a normal text file like this:

```
NAME

    od - octal dump


SYNOPSIS

    /usr/bin/od [ -bcCDdFfOoSsvXx ] [ -] [ file ]

        [ offset_string ]

    /usr/bin/od [ -bcCDdFfOoSsvXx ] [ -A address_base ]

        [ -j skip ] [-N count ] [ -t type_string ] ...
        [ - ]    [ file

    /usr/xpg4/bin/od [-bcCDdFfOoSsvXx [ -] [ file ]
        [ offset_string ]
    /usr/xpg4/bin/od [-bcCDdFfOoSsvXx [ -A address_base ]
        [ -j skip ] [-N count ] [ -t type_string
        [ - ]    [ file
```

The nroff formatter produces outputs for line printers and CRT displays. To bold characters, it prints the character followed by a backspace and then prints the same character again. Underlining is done by printing an underscore, a backspace, and then the character to be underlined. At times you need to strip these special effects, such as when you want to use the grep command to search formatted manual pages for a particular string. The following example uses col to get rid of these special effects.

castle% **col -b** *nroff-output stripped-output*

Environment Variables

See environ(5) for descriptions of the following environment variables that affect the execution of col: LC_CTYPE, LC_MESSAGES, and NLSPATH.

Exit Status

0	Successful completion.
>0	An error occurred.

Attributes

See attributes(5) for descriptions of the following attributes:

Attribute Type	Attribute Value
Availability	SUNWesu
CSI	Enabled

See Also

nroff(1), tbl(1), ascii(5), attributes(5), environ(5)

comb, sccs-comb — Combine SCCS Deltas

Synopsis

/usr/ccs/bin/comb [-os] [-csid-list] [-psid] s.filename ...

Description

See sccs-comb(1).

comm — Select or Reject Lines Common to Two Files

Synopsis

/usr/bin/comm [-123] file1 file2

Description

Use the comm command to compare lines common to the sorted files or to
display lines unique to each file. comm reads file1 and file2, which should be
ordered in the current collating sequence, and produces three text columns as
output:

1. Lines only in file1.
2. Lines only in file2.
3. Lines in both files.

If the input files were ordered according to the collating sequence of the
current locale, the lines written are in the collating sequence of the original
lines. If not, the results are unspecified.

Options

-1	Suppress the output column of lines unique to *file1*.
-2	Suppress the output column of lines unique to *file2*.
-3	Suppress the output column of lines duplicated in *file1* and *file2*.

By combining these options, you can display specific information. For example:

comm -12 Print only lines that are common to the two files.
comm -13 Print only lines that are unique in *file2*.
comm -23 Print only lines that are unique to *file1*.

Operands

file1	A path name of the first file to be compared. If *file1* is -, use the standard input.
file2	A path name of the second file to be compared. If *file2* is -, use the standard input.

Usage

See largefile(5) for the description of the behavior of comm when encountering files greater than or equal to 2 Gbytes (2**31 bytes).

Examples

The following example compares kookaburra1 with kookaburra2, using none of the options.

```
castle% comm kookaburra1 kookaburra2
                Kookaburra sits in the old gum tree
                Merry merry king of the bush is he
                Laugh, kookaburra, laugh, kookaburra
Gay your life must be.

        Glad your life must be.

                Kookaburra sits in the old gum tree
                Eating all the gumdrops he can see
                Stop, kookaburra, stop, kookaburra
                Leave some there for me.
castle%
```

The following example uses the -12 option to display files that are common to the two files.

```
castle% comm -12 kookaburra1 kookaburra2
Kookaburra sits in the old gum tree
Merry merry king of the bush is he
Laugh, kookaburra, laugh, kookaburra
Kookaburra sits in the old gum tree
```

```
Eating all the gumdrops he can see
Stop, kookaburra, stop, kookaburra
Leave some there for me.
castle%
```

The following example uses the −13 option to display lines that are unique to kookaburra2.

```
castle% comm -13 kookaburra1 kookaburra2
Glad your life must be.

castle%
```

The following example uses the −23 option to display lines that are unique to kookaburra1.

```
castle% comm -23 kookaburra1 kookaburra2
Gay your life must be.

castle%
```

Environment Variables

See environ(5) for descriptions of the following environment variables that affect the execution of comm: LC_COLLATE, LC_CTYPE, LC_MESSAGES, and NLSPATH.

Exit Status

0	All input files were successfully output as specified.
>0	An error occurred.

Attributes

See attributes(5) for descriptions of the following attributes:

Attribute Type	Attribute Value
Availability	SUNWesu
CSI	Enabled

See Also

cmp(1), diff(1), sort(1), uniq(1), attributes(5), environ(5), largefile(5)

command — Execute a Simple Command

Synopsis

```
/usr/bin/command [-p] command-name [argument...]
/usr/bin/command [-v | -V] command-name
```

Description

You can use the command command to escape commands that a shell would otherwise treat as built-in functions. With command, the shell treats the arguments as a simple command,

If the command-name is the same as the name of one of the special built-in commands, the special properties are not used. In every other respect, if command-name is not the name of a function, the effect of command is the same as omitting command.

The command command also provides information concerning how a command name is interpreted by the shell; see -v and -V.

Options

-p   Perform the command search using a default value for PATH that is guaranteed to find all of the standard commands.

-v   Write a string to standard output that indicates the path or command that is used by the shell in the current shell execution environment to invoke command-name.

Write commands, regular built-in commands, command-name including a slash character, and any implementation-provided functions that are found, using the PATH variable as absolute path names.

Write shell functions, special built-in commands, regular built-in commands not associated with a PATH search, and shell reserved words as just their names.

Write an alias as a command line that represents its alias definition.

Otherwise, write no output and return an exit status that reflects that the name was not found.

-V   Write a string to standard output that indicates how the name given in the command-name operand is interpreted by the shell in the current shell execution environment. Although the format of this string is unspecified, it indicates in which of the following categories command-name falls and includes the information stated below.

Identify commands, regular built-in commands, and any implementation-provided functions that are found using the PATH variable and include the absolute path name in the string.

Identify other shell functions.

Identify aliases and include their definitions in the string.

Identify special built-in commands.

Identify regular built-in commands not associated with a PATH search.

Identify shell reserved words.

Operands

argument   One of the strings treated as an argument to *command-name*.

command-name

The name of a command or a special built-in command.

Examples

The following example makes a version of cd that always prints out the new working directory exactly once.

```
cd() {
command cd "$@" >/dev/null
pwd
}
```

The following example starts up a secure shell script in which the script avoids being fooled by its parent.

```
IFS='
'
# The preceding value should be <space><tab><newline>.
# Set IFS to its default value.
\unalias -a
# Unset all possible aliases.
# Note that unalias is escaped to prevent an alias
# being used for unalias.
unset -f command
# Ensure command is not a user function.
PATH="$(command -p getconf _CS_PATH):$PATH"
# Put on a reliable PATH prefix.
# ...
```

At this point, given correct permissions on the directories called by PATH, the script can ensure that any command it calls is the intended one. The script is being very cautious because it assumes that implementation extensions may be present that would allow user functions to exist when it is invoked; this capability is not specified by this document, but it is not prohibited as an extension. For example, the ENV variable precedes the invocation of the script with a user startup script. Such a script could define functions to spoof the application.

Environment Variables

See environ(5) for descriptions of the following environment variables that affect the execution of command: LC_CTYPE, LC_MESSAGES, and NLSPATH.

PATH   Determine the search path used during the command search, except as described under the -p option.

Exit Status

When you use the -v or -V options, the following exit values are returned:

0   Successful completion.

>0   The *command-name* could not be found, or an error occurred.

Otherwise, the following exit values are returned:

126   The command specified by *command-name* was found but could not be invoked.

127   An error occurred in the command command, or the command specified by *command-name* could not be found.

Otherwise, the exit status of command is that of the simple command specified by the arguments to command.

Attributes

See attributes(5) for descriptions of the following attributes:

Attribute Type	Attribute Value
Availability	SUNWcsu

See Also

sh(1), type(1), attributes(5)

compress, uncompress, zcat — Compress, Uncompress Files or Display Expanded Files

Synopsis

```
/usr/bin/compress [-fv] [-b bits] [file...]
/usr/bin/compress [-cfv] [-b bits] [file]
/usr/bin/uncompress [-cfv] [file...]
/usr/bin/zcat [file...]
```

Description

compress

The compress command tries to reduce the size of the named files by using adaptive Lempel-Ziv coding. Except when the output is to the standard output, each file is replaced by one with the extension .Z, while keeping the same ownership modes, change times, and modification times.

If appending the .Z to the file name would make the name exceed 14 bytes, the command fails. If no files are specified, the standard input is compressed to the standard output.

The amount of compression obtained depends on the size of the input, the number of bits per code, and the distribution of common substrings. Typically, text such as source code or English is reduced by 50-60 percent. Compression is generally much better than that achieved by Huffman coding (as used in pack(1)) and takes less time to compute. The bits parameter specified during compression is encoded within the compressed file, along with a magic number to ensure that neither decompression of random data nor recompression of compressed data is subsequently allowed.

> **Note** — Although compressed files are compatible between machines with large memory, use -b 12 for file transfer to architectures with a small process data space (64 kilobytes or less).

uncompress

The uncompress command restores files to their original state after they have been compressed by the compress command. If you specify no files, the standard input is uncompressed to the standard output.

This command supports the uncompressing of any files produced by compress. For files produced by compress on other systems, uncompress supports 9- to 16-bit compression (see -b).

zcat

The zcat command writes to standard output the uncompressed form of files that have been compressed using compress. It is the equivalent of uncompress -c. Input files are not affected.

Options

-c	Write to the standard output; change no files and create no .Z files. The behavior of zcat is identical to that of uncompress -c.
-f	When compressing, force compression of file, even if it does not actually reduce the size of the file or if the corresponding *file*.Z file already exists. If you do not use the -f option and the process is not running in the background, prompt to verify whether to overwrite an existing *file*.Z file. When uncompressing, do not

	prompt for overwriting files. If the standard input is not a terminal and you do not use the -f option, write a diagnostic message to standard error and exit with a status greater than 0.
-v	Write to standard error messages concerning the percentage reduction or expansion of each file.
-b bits	Set the upper limit (in bits) for common substring codes. Bits must be between 9 and 16 (16 is the default). Lowering the number of bits results in larger, less compressed files.

Operands

file	A path name of a file to be compressed. If file is - or if no file is specified, use the standard input.

Examples

The following example compresses and uncompresses a file named testcompress and uses the ls -l command to display the uncompressed and compressed file size. As you can see, the compressed file is about 50 percent smaller than the uncompressed file.

```
castle% ls -l testcompress
-r--r--r--   1 winsor    staff        13054 Dec 30 15:21 testcompress
castle% compress testcompress
castle% ls -l testcompress.Z
-r--r--r--   1 winsor    staff         6486 Dec 30 15:21 testcompress.Z
castle% uncompress testcompress.Z
castle% ls -l testcompress
-r--r--r--   1 winsor    staff        13054 Dec 30 15:21 testcompress
castle%
```

Usage

See largefile(5) for the description of the behavior of compress, uncompress, and zcat when encountering files greater than or equal to 2 Gbytes (2**31 bytes).

Environment Variables

See environ(5) for descriptions of the following environment variables that affect the execution of compress, uncompress, and zcat: LC_CTYPE, LC_MESSAGES, and NLSPATH.

Exit Status

0	Successful completion.
1	An error occurred.
2	One or more files were not compressed because they would have increased in size (and you did not specify the -f option).
>2	An error occurred.

Attributes

See attributes(5) for descriptions of the following attributes:

Attribute Type	**Attribute Value**
Availability	SUNWesu
CSI	Enabled

See Also

ln(1), pack(1), attributes(5), environ(5), largefile(5)

Diagnostics

Usage: compress [-fvc] [-b maxbits] [file...]

> Invalid options were specified on the command line.

Missing maxbits

> maxbits must follow -b, or invalid maxbits, not a numeric value.

file: not in compressed format

> The file specified to uncompress has not been compressed.

file: compressed with xxbits, can only handle yybits

> The file was compressed by a program that could deal with more bits than the compress code on this machine. Recompress the file with smaller bits.

file: already has .Z suffix -- no change

> The file is assumed to be already compressed. Rename the file and try again.

file: already exists; do you wish to overwrite (y or n)?

> Respond y if you want the output file to be replaced; n if not.

uncompress: corrupt input

> A SIGSEGV violation was detected, which usually means that the input file is corrupted.

```
Compression: xx.xx%
```
> Percentage of the input saved by compression. (Relevant only for -v.)

```
-- not a regular file: unchanged
```
> When the input file is not a regular file (such as a directory), it is left unaltered.

```
-- has xx other links: unchanged
```
> The input file has links; it is left unchanged. See ln(1) for more information.

```
-- file unchanged
```
> No savings are achieved by compression. The input remains uncompressed.

```
filename too long to tack on .Z
```
> The path name is too long and the .Z suffix cannot be appended.

continue, break — Shell Built-in Functions

Synopsis

sh
```
continue [n]
```

csh
```
continue
```

ksh
```
*
continue [n]
```

Description
See break(1).

cp — Copy Files

Synopsis

```
/usr/bin/cp [-fip] source-file target-file
/usr/bin/cp [-fip] source-file... target
/usr/bin/cp -r -R [-fip] source-dir... target
/usr/xpg4/bin/cp [-fip] source-file target-file
/usr/xpg4/bin/cp [-fip] source-file... target
/usr/xpg4/bin/cp -r -R [-fip] source-dir... target
```

Description

With the cp command, you can do the following actions:

- Make copies of individual files and assign new names to them.
- Copy one or more files into a different existing directory, keeping the existing file names.
- Recursively copy an entire directory structure to another directory.

When you make a copy of a *source-file*, *target-file* is created if it does not already exist. The *target-file* has the same owner, group, and modes as *source-file*, except that the sticky bit is not set unless the user is superuser.

If *target-file* exists, it is overwritten, but the mode (and access control list (ACL) if applicable), owner, and group associated with it are not changed. The last modification time of *target-file* and the last access time of *source-file* are set to the time the copy was made.

If *target-file* is a link to another file with links, the other links remain and *target-file* becomes a new file.

When files are copied to an existing *target* directory, one or more *source-file*s are copied to the directory specified by target. For each *source-file* specified, a new file with the same mode (and ACL if applicable) is created in *target*; the owner and group are those of the user making the copy.

When an entire directory structure is recursively copied, one or more directories specified by *source-dir* are copied to the directory specified by *target*. If the *target* directory does not exist, cp -r | -R creates it and recursively copies all of the directories and subdirectories, maintaining the same owner, group, and modes as for the *source-dir*.

You can use a double dash (--) to explicitly mark the end of any command-line options to enable cp to recognize file name arguments that begin with a dash (-). If you include both a - and a - on the same command line, the second is interpreted as a file name.

Options

The following options are supported for both /usr/bin/cp and /usr/xpg4/bin/cp.

-f   If a file descriptor for a destination file cannot be obtained, try to unlink the destination file and proceed.

-i   Interactively prompt for confirmation whenever the copy would overwrite an existing *target*. A y answer means proceed with the copy. Any other answer prevents cp from overwriting *target*.

-r   Recursively copy the directory and all its files, including any subdirectories and their files, to *target*.

-R   Same as -r, except replicate pipes.

   The following options are supported for /usr/bin/cp only.

-p   Duplicate not only the contents of *source-file*, but also preserve ID, permissions modes, modification and access time, and ACLs if applicable. Note that the command may fail if you copy ACLs to a file system that does not support them. The command does not fail if unable to preserve modification and access time or permission modes. If unable to preserve owner and group ID, cp does not fail and it clears S_ISUID and S_ISGID bits in the *target*. Print a diagnostic message to standard error and return a non-zero exit status if unable to clear these bits.

            To preserve the owner and group ID, permission modes, and modification and access times, users must have the appropriate file access permissions; this includes being superuser or the same owner ID as the destination file.

   The following option is supported for /usr/xpg4/bin/cp only.

-p   Same as -p, above, except the command fails if unable to duplicate the modification and access time or the permission modes. Print a diagnostic message to standard error and return a non-zero exit status.

Operands

source-file

            A path name of a regular file to be copied.

source-dir

            A path name of a directory to be copied.

target-file

            A path name of an existing or nonexisting file, used for the output when a single file is copied.

target   A path name of a directory to contain the copied files.

Usage

See largefile(5) for the description of the behavior of cp when encountering files greater than or equal to 2 Gbytes (2**31 bytes).

Examples

The following example copies a file.

```
castle% cp goodies goodies.old
castle% ls goodies*
goodies goodies.old
castle%
```

The following example copies all of the files in one directory to a destination directory.

```
castle% cp ~/src/* /tmp
```

The following example copies a directory, first to a new, and then to an existing destination directory.

```
castle% ls ~/bkup
/usr/example/fred/bkup not found
castle% cp -r ~/src ~/bkup
castle% ls -R ~/bkup
x.c y.c z.sh
castle% cp -r ~/src ~/bkup
castle% ls -R ~/bkup
src x.c y.c z.sh
src:
x.c y.c z.sh
castle%
```

Environment Variables

See environ(5) for descriptions of the following environment variables that affect the execution of cp: LC_COLLATE, LC_CTYPE, LC_MESSAGES, and NLSPATH.

Exit Status

0	All files were copied successfully.
>0	An error occurred.

Attributes

See `attributes`(5) for descriptions of the following attributes:

/usr/bin/cp

Attribute Type	Attribute Value
Availability	SUNWcsu
CSI	Enabled

/usr/xpg4/bin/cp

Attribute Type	Attribute Value
Availability	SUNWxcu4
CSI	Enabled

See Also

chmod(1), chown(1), setfacl(1), utime(2), attributes(5), environ(5), largefile(5), xpg4(5)

---

cpio — Copy File Archives In and Out

Synopsis

```
/usr/bin/cpio -i [bBcdfkmPrsStuvV6] [-C bufsize] [-E file]
   [-H header] [-I file [-M message]] [-R id] [pattern ...]
/usr/bin/cpio -o [aABcLPvV] [-C bufsize] [-H header] [-O file
   [-M message]]
/usr/bin/cpio -p [adlLmPuvV] [-R id] directory
```

Description

Use the `cpio` command to copy files, special files (files used to represent peripheral devices attached to a system), and file systems that require multiple tape volumes. `cpio` provides compatibility for copying files from SunOS 5.x systems to SunOS 4.x systems. Advantages of using the `cpio` command are that it packs data onto tape more efficiently than the `tar` command, skips over any bad spots in a tape when restoring files, provides options for writing files with different header formats (`tar`, `ustar`, `crc`, `odc`, `bar`) for portability between different system types, and creates multiple tape volumes.

The `cpio` command, when used to create an archive, takes a list of files or path names from standard input and writes to standard output. The output is almost always redirected to a file or to a device.

You use the -i (copy in), -o (copy out), or -p (pass) option to choose the actions to perform.

Note — cpio assumes 4-byte words. If, when writing to a character device (-o) or reading from a character device (-i), cpio reaches the end of a medium (such as the end of a diskette) and you do not use the -O and -I options, cpio prints the following message: To continue, type device/file name when ready. To continue, you must replace the medium and type the character special device name (/dev/rdiskette, for example) and press Return. You may want to continue by directing cpio to use a different device. For example, if you have two diskette drives, you may want to switch between them so cpio can proceed while you are changing the diskettes. (Simply pressing Return exits cpio.)

Copy-In Mode

cpio -i (copy in) extracts files from the standard input, which is assumed to be the product of a previous cpio -o. Only files with names that match patterns are selected.

Extracted files are conditionally created and copied into the current directory tree, based on the options described below. The permissions of the files are those of the previous cpio -o. Owner and group are the same as the current user unless the current user is superuser. If the user is superuser, owner and group are the same as those resulting from the previous cpio -o. Note that if cpio -i tries to create a file that already exists and the existing file is the same age or younger (newer), cpio outputs a warning message and does not replace the file. (You can use the -u option to unconditionally overwrite the existing file.)

Copy-Out Mode

cpio -o (copy out) reads the standard input to obtain a list of path names and copies those files onto the standard output together with path name and status information. Output is padded to a 512-byte boundary by default, to the block size specified by the -B or -C options, or to some device-dependent block size where necessary (as with the CTC tape).

Pass Mode

cpio -p (pass) reads the standard input to obtain a list of path names of files that are conditionally created and copied into the destination directory tree, based on the options described below.

Notes

Path names are restricted to 256 characters for the binary (the default) and -H odc header formats. Otherwise, path names are restricted to 1024 characters. An error message is output for files whose UID or GID is too large to fit in the selected header format. Use -H crc or -c to create archives that allow all UID or GID values.

Only the superuser can copy special files. Blocks are reported in 512-byte quantities.

If a file has 000 permissions, contains more than 0 characters of data, and the user is not root, the file is not saved or restored.

The inode number stored in the header (/usr/include/archives.h) is an unsigned short, which is 2 bytes. This restriction limits the range of inode numbers from 0 to 65535. Files that are hard-linked must fall in this inode range, which can be a problem when moving cpio archives between different vendors' machines.

When the Volume Management daemon is running, access to diskette devices through the conventional device names (for example, /dev/rdiskette) may not succeed. See vold(1M) for further details.

You must use the same blocking factor when you retrieve or copy files from the tape to the hard disk as you did when you copied files from the hard disk to the tape. Therefore, you must specify the -B option.

Options

-i   Copy in. Extract files from the standard input.

-o   Copy out. Read the standard input to obtain a list of path names and copy those files onto the standard output.

-p   Pass. Read the standard input to obtain a list of path names of files.

You can append the following options in any sequence to the -o, -i, or -p option:

-a   Reset access times of input files after they have been copied. Access times are not reset for linked files when you specify cpio -pla (mutually exclusive with -m).

-A   Append files to an archive. The -A option requires the -O option. Valid only with archives that are files or that are on floppy diskettes or hard disk partitions.

-b   Reverse the order of the bytes within each word. (Use only with the -i option.)

-B   Block input/output 5120 bytes to the record. The default buffer size is 512 bytes when you do not use this and the -C option. -B does not apply to the pass option; -B is meaningful only with data directed to or from a character special device, for example, /dev/rmt/0m.

-c   Read or write header information in ASCII character form for portability. There are no UID or GID restrictions associated with this header format. Use this option between SVR4-based machines, or the -H odc option between unknown machines. The -c option implies the use of expanded device numbers, which are only supported on SVR4-based systems. When transferring files between Solaris 1.x or INTERACTIVE UNIX and Solaris 2.x, use -H odc.

-C *bufsize*   Block input/output *bufsize* bytes to the record, where *bufsize* is replaced by a positive integer. The default buffer size is 512 bytes when you do not use this and the -B option. (-C does not apply to the pass option; -C is meaningful only with data directed to or from a character special device, for example, /dev/rmt/0m.)

-d   Create directories as needed.

-E *file*   Specify an input file (*file*) that contains a list of file names to be extracted from the archive (one file name per line).

-f   Copy in all files except those in *patterns*.

-H *header* Read or write header information in *header* format. Always use this option or the -c option when the origin and the destination machines are different types (mutually exclusive with -c and -6). Available *header* formats are listed below.

      bar   bar head and format. Use only with the -i option (read-only)

      crc|CRC   ASCII header with expanded device numbers and an additional per-file checksum. No UID or GID restrictions are associated with this header format.

      odc   ASCII header with small device numbers. This is the IEEE/P1003 Data Interchange Standard cpio header and format. It has the widest range of portability of any of the header formats. It is the official format for transferring files between POSIX-conforming systems (see standards(5)). Use this format to communicate with Solaris 1.x and INTERACTIVE UNIX. This header format enables UIDs and GIDs up to 262143 to be stored in the header.

      tar|TAR   tar header and format. This header format enables UIDs and GIDs up to 2097151 to be stored in the header.

      ustar|USTAR IEEE/P1003 Data Interchange Standard tar header and format. This header format enables UIDs and GIDs up to 2097151 to be stored in the header.

Files with UIDs and GIDs greater than the limit stated above are archived with the UID and GID of 60001.

-I *file*   Read the contents of *file* as an input archive. If *file* is a character special device and the current medium has been completely read, you should replace the medium and press Return to continue to the next medium. Use this option only with the -i option.

-k   Try to skip corrupted file headers and I/O errors that may be encountered. If you want to copy files from a medium that is corrupted or out of sequence, this option lets you read only those files with good headers. (For cpio archives that contain other cpio archives, if an error is encountered, cpio may terminate prematurely. cpio finds the next good header, which may be one for a smaller archive, and terminates when the smaller archive's trailer is encountered.) Use only with the -i option.

-l   Whenever possible, link files instead of copying them. (Use only with the -p option.)

-L   Follow symbolic links. The default is not to follow symbolic links.

-m   Retain previous file modification time. This option is ineffective on directories that are being copied (mutually exclusive with -a).

-M *message*   Define a *message* to use when switching media. When you use the -O or -I options and specify a character special device, you can use this option to define the message that is printed when you reach the end of the medium. You can put one %d in *message* to print the sequence number of the next medium needed to continue.

-O *file*   Direct the output of cpio to *file*. If *file* is a character special device and the current medium is full, you should replace the medium and press Return to continue to the next medium. Use only with the -o option.

-P   Preserve access control lists (ACLs). If the option is used for output, write existing ACLs along with other attributes to the standard output. ACLs are created as special files with a special file type. If the option is used for input, extract existing ACLs along with other attributes from standard input. The option recognizes the special file type. Note that errors occur if a cpio archive with ACLs is extracted by previous versions of cpio. Do not use this option with the -c option because ACL support may not be present on all systems, and hence is not portable. Use ASCII headers for portability.

-r   Interactively rename files. Use a Return alone to skip the file and a dot (.) to retain the original path name. (Not available with cpio -p.)

-R id	Reassign ownership and group information for each file to user ID (ID must be a valid login ID from /etc/passwd). This option is valid only for the superuser.
-s	Swap bytes within each half-word.
-S	Swap half-words within each word.
-t	Print a table of contents of the input. No files are created (mutually exclusive with -V).
-u	Copy unconditionally (normally, an older file does not replace a newer file with the same name).
-v	Print a list of file names. When you use the verbose option with the -t option, the table of contents looks like the output of an ls -l command.
-V	Print a dot for each file read or written. This special verbose option is useful to assure you that cpio is working without printing out all file names.
-6	Process a UNIX System Sixth Edition archive format file. Use only with the -i option (mutually exclusive with -c and -H).

Operands

directory	A path name of an existing directory to be used as the target of cpio -p.
pattern	Expressions making use of a pattern-matching notation similar to that used by the shell (see sh(1)) for file-name pattern matching and similar to regular expressions. The following metacharacters are defined:

*	Match any string, including the empty string.
?	Match any single character.
[...]	Match any one of the enclosed characters. A pair of characters separated by a dash (-) matches any symbol between the pair (inclusive), as defined by the system default collating sequence. If the first character following the opening [is a !, the results are unspecified.
!	Don't match. (For example, the !abc* pattern excludes all files that begin with abc.)

In patterns, metacharacters ?, *, and [...] match the slash (/) character, and backslash (\) is an escape character. You can specify multiple cases of *pattern* and, if no pattern is specified, the default for *pattern* is * (that is, select all files).

Enclose each pattern in double quotes; otherwise, the name of a file in the current directory might be used.

Usage

See largefile(5) for the description of the behavior of cpio when encountering files greater than or equal to 2 Gbytes (2**31 bytes).

Examples

The following example lists files and pipes the output to cpio -o so it can be directed (>) to a single file (../newfile). The -c option ensures that the file is portable to other machines (as would the -H option).

```
castle% ls | cpio -oc > ../newfile
```

Instead of ls(1), you could use find(1), echo(1), cat(1), and so on, to pipe a list of names to cpio. You could also direct the output to a device instead of to a file.

The following example of cpio -i uses the output file of cpio -o (directed through a pipe with cat in the example below), extracts those files that match the patterns (memo/a1, memo/b*), creates directories below the current directory as needed (-d option), and puts the files in the appropriate directories. Use the -c option if the input file was created with a portable header. If no patterns are given, all files from newfile are put in the directory.

```
castle% cat newfile | cpio -icd "memo/a1" "memo/b*"
```

The following example of cpio -p takes the file names piped to it and copies or links (-1 option) those files to another directory (newdir). The -d option creates directories as needed. The -m option retains the modification time.

```
castle% find . -depth -print | cpio -pdlmv newdir
```

Note — It is important to use the -depth option of find(1) to generate path names for cpio. This option eliminates problems cpio could have trying to create files under read-only directories. The destination directory, newdir, must exist.

When you use cpio in conjunction with find, if you use the -L option with cpio, then you must use the -follow option with find, and vice versa. Otherwise, you will get undesirable results.

For multiple-reel archives, dismount the old volume, mount the new one, and continue to the next tape by typing the name of the next device (probably the same as the first reel). To stop, press Return and cpio exits.

Environment Variables

See environ(5) for descriptions of the following environment variables that affect the execution of cpio: LC_COLLATE, LC_CTYPE, LC_MESSAGES, LC_TIME, TZ, and NLSPATH.

Exit Status

0	Successful completion.
>0	An error occurred.

Attributes

See attributes(5) for descriptions of the following attributes:

Attribute Type	Attribute Value
Availability	SUNWcsu
CSI	Enabled

See Also

ar(1), cat(1), echo(1), find(1), ls(1), setfacl(1), sh(1), tar(1), vold(1M), archives(4), attributes(5), environ(5), largefile(5), standards(5)

cpp — C Language Preprocessor

Synopsis

```
/usr/ccs/lib/cpp [-BCHMpPRT] [-undef] [-Dname] [-Dname=def]
    [-Idirectory] [-Uname] [-Ydirectory] [input-file [output-file]]
```

New!

Description

cpp is the C language preprocessor. It is invoked as the first pass of any C compilation started with the cc(1B) command; however, you can also use cpp as a first-pass preprocessor for other Sun compilers.

> **Note —** Although you can use cpp as a macro processor, it is not normally recommended because its output is designed to be acceptable as input to a compiler's second pass. The preferred way to invoke cpp is through the cc(1B) command or some other compilation command. For general-purpose macro processing, see m4(1), and the chapter on m4 in *Programming Utilities Guide*.

cpp optionally accepts two file names as arguments: *input-file* and *output-file* are the input and output files for the preprocessor. They default to the standard input and the standard output.

Options

-B	Support the C++ comment indicator //. With this indicator, treat everything on the line after the // as a comment.
-C	Pass all comments (except those that appear on cpp directive lines) through the preprocessor. By default, cpp strips out C-style comments.
-H	Print the path names of included files, one per line on the standard error.
-M	Generate a list of makefile dependencies and write them to the standard output. This list indicates that the object file that is generated from the input file depends on the input file as well as the include files referenced.
-p	Use only the first eight characters to distinguish preprocessor symbols, and issue a warning if extra tokens appear at the end of a line containing a directive.
-P	Preprocess the input without producing the line control information used by the next pass of the C compiler.
-R	Allow recursive macros.
-T	Use only the first eight characters for distinguishing different preprocessor names. This option is included for backward compatibility with systems that always use only the first eight characters.
-undef	Remove initial definitions for all predefined symbols.
-Dname	Define name as 1 (one). This option is the same as if you included the -Dname=1 option on the cpp command line, or as if a #define name 1 line is included in the source file that cpp is processing.
-Dname=def	Define name as if by a #define directive. This option is the same as if a #define name def line is included in the source file that cpp is processing. The -D option has lower precedence than the -U option. That is, if the same name is used in both a -U option and a -D option, the name is undefined regardless of the order of the options.
-Idirectory	

Insert *directory* into the search path for #include files with names not beginning with /. *directory* is inserted ahead of the standard list of include directories. Thus, #include files with names enclosed in double quotes (") are searched for first in the directory of the file with the #include line, then in directories named with -I options, and lastly, in directories from the standard list. For #include files with names enclosed in angle brackets (<>), do not search the directory of the file with the #include line.

-U*name*   Remove any initial definition of *name*, where *name* is a symbol that
                     is predefined by a particular preprocessor. The following partial list
                     shows symbols you can predefine, depending on the architecture of
                     the system:

ibm, gcos, os, tss, unix	Operating system.
interdata, pdp11, u370, u3b, u3b2, u3b5, u3b15, u3b20d, vax, ns32000, iAPX286, i386, sparc, sun	Hardware.
RES, RT	UNIX system variant.
lint	The lint command.

The symbols sun, sparc, and unix are defined for all Sun systems.

-Y*directory*

Use *directory* in place of the standard list of directories when
searching for #include files.

Usage

Directives
Start all cpp directives with a hash symbol (#) as the first character on a line.
You can include white space (space or Tab characters) after the initial # for
proper indentation.

#define *name token-string*

Replace subsequent instances of *name* with *token-string*.

#define *name*(*argument* [, *argument*] ...) *token-string*

Leave no space between *name* and the (. Replace subsequent
instances of *name*, followed by a parenthesized list of arguments,
with *token-string*, where each occurrence of an argument in the
token string is replaced by the corresponding token in the
comma-separated list. When a macro with arguments is
expanded, the arguments are placed into the expanded
token-string unchanged. After the entire *token-string* has
been expanded, cpp restarts its scan for names to expand at the
beginning of the newly created token string.

#undef *name*

Remove any definition for the symbol *name*. No additional tokens
are permitted on the directive line after *name*.

```
#include
#include <filename>
```

> Read in the contents of *filename* at this location. This data is processed by cpp as if it were part of the current file. When the *<filename>* notation is used, *filename* is searched for only in the standard include directories. See the -I and -Y options above for more detail. No additional tokens are permitted on the directive line after the final " or >.

`#line` *integer-constant* `"filename"`

> Generate line control information for the next pass of the C compiler. *integer-constant* is interpreted as the line number of the next line, and *filename* is interpreted as the file that contains it. If "*filename*" is not given, the current *filename* is unchanged. No additional tokens are permitted on the directive line after the optional *filename*.

`#if` *constant-expression*

> Include subsequent lines up to the matching #else, #elif, or #endif directive in the output only if *constant-expression* yields a non-zero value. All binary nonassignment C operators, including &&, ||, and , , are legal in *constant-expression*. The ?: operator, and the unary -, !, and ~ operators, are also legal in *constant-expression*.

> The precedence of these operators is the same as that for C. In addition, the defined unary operator can be used in *constant-expression* in these two forms: defined (name) or defined name. This allows the effect of #ifdef and #ifndef directives in the #if directive. Only use these operators, integer constants, and names known by cpp within *constant-expression*. In particular, the size of operator is not available.

`#ifdef` *name*

> Include subsequent lines up to the matching #else, #elif, or #endif in the output only if *name* has been defined either with a #define directive or a -D option, and in the absence of an intervening #undef directive. Additional tokens after *name* on the directive line are silently ignored.

`#ifndef` *name*

> Include subsequent lines up to the matching #else, #elif, or #endif in the output only if *name* has not been defined, or if its definition has been removed with an #undef directive. No additional tokens are permitted on the directive line after *name*.

#elif *constant-expression*

> Any number of #elif directives can appear between an #if, #ifdef, or #ifndef directive and a matching #else or #endif directive. Include the lines following the #elif directive in the output only if *all* of the following conditions hold.
>
> - The constant-expression in the preceding #if directive evaluates to zero, the *name* in the preceding #ifdef is not defined, or the *name* in the preceding #ifndef directive was defined.
> - The *constant-expression* in all intervening #elif directives evaluates to zero.
> - The current *constant-expression* evaluates to non-zero. If the *constant-expression* evaluates to non-zero, ignore subsequent #elif and #else directives up to the matching #endif. Any *constant-expression* allowed in an #if directive is allowed in an #elif directive.

#else

> Invert the sense of the conditional directive otherwise in effect. If the preceding conditional would indicate that lines are to be included, then ignore lines between the #else and the matching #endif. If the preceding conditional indicates that lines are ignored, include subsequent lines in the output. You can nest conditional directives and corresponding #else directives.

#endif

> End a section of lines begun by one of the conditional directives #if, #ifdef, or #ifndef. Each such directive must have a matching #endif.

Because the standard directory for included files may be different in different environments, use the following form of #include directive:

```
#include <file.h>
```

instead of one with an absolute path, like:

```
#include "/usr/include/file.h"
```

cpp warns about the use of the absolute path name.

Note — While the compiler allows 8-bit strings and comments, 8-bits are not allowed anywhere else.

Macros

Formal parameters for macros are recognized in #define directive bodies, even when they occur inside character constants and quoted strings. For instance, the output from:

```
#define abc(a)  |`|a|
abc(xyz)
```

is:

```
# 1 ""
```

`|`|xyz|`

The second line is a newline. The last seven characters are `|`|xyz|` (vertical-bar, backquote, vertical-bar, x, y, z, vertical-bar). Macro names are not recognized within character constants or quoted strings during the regular scan.

Thus:

```
#define abc xyz
printf("abc");
```

does not expand abc in the second line, because it is inside a quoted string that is not part of a #define macro definition.

Macros are not expanded while processing a #define or #undef. Thus:

```
#define abc zingo
#define xyz abc
#undef abc
xyz
```

produces abc. The token appearing immediately after an #ifdef or #ifndef is not expanded.

Macros are not expanded during the scan that determines the actual parameters to another macro call. Thus:

```
#define reverse(first,second)second first
#define greeting hello
reverse(greeting,
#define greeting goodbye
)
```

produces

```
#define hello goodbye hello
```

In some previous versions of cpp, when newline characters were found in argument lists for macros to be expanded, the newline characters were put out as they were found and expanded. The current version of cpp replaces them with space characters.

Output

Output consists of a copy of the input file, with modifications, plus lines of the form:

```
#lineno "filename" "level"
```

indicating the original source line number and *filename* of the following output line and whether this is the first such line after an include file has been entered (level=1), the first such line after an include file has been exited (level=2), or any other such line (level is empty).

Directory Search Order
#include files are searched for in the following order:

1. The directory of the file that contains the #include request (that is, #include is relative to the file being scanned when the request is made).
2. The directories specified by -I options, in left-to-right order.
3. The standard directory(s) (/usr/include on UNIX systems).

Special Names
cpp understands two special names:

- __LINE__ is defined as the current line number (a decimal integer) as known by cpp.
- __FILE__ is defined as the current *filename* (a C string) as known by cpp.

You can use these special names anywhere, including in macros, just as any other defined name.

Newline Characters
A newline character terminates a character constant or quoted string. You can use an escaped newline (that is, a backslash immediately followed by a newline) in the body of a #define statement to continue the definition onto the next line. The escaped newline is not included in the macro value.

Comments
Comments are removed (unless you use the -C option on the command line). Comments are also ignored, except that a comment terminates a token.

Exit Status

0	Successful completion.
non-zero	An error occurred.

Attributes
See attributes(5) for descriptions of the following attributes:

Attribute Type	Attribute Value
Availability	SUNWsprot

See Also

cc(1B), m4(1), attributes(5)
Programming Utilities Guide

Diagnostics

The error messages produced by cpp are intended to be self-explanatory. The line number and *filename* where the error occurred are printed along with the diagnostic.

crontab — User Chronological Table File

Synopsis

/usr/bin/crontab [*filename*]
/usr/bin/crontab [-elr] *username*

Description

Use the crontab command to manage a user's access with cron by copying, creating, listing, and removing crontab files. If invoked without options, crontab copies the specified file, or the standard input if no file is specified, into a directory that holds all users' crontabs.

crontab Access Control

User access to crontab is allowed:

- If the user's name appears in /etc/cron.d/cron.allow.
- If /etc/cron.d/cron.allow does not exist and the user's name is not in /etc/cron.d/cron.deny.

User access to crontab is denied:

- If /etc/cron.d/cron.allow exists and the user's name is not in it.
- If /etc/cron.d/cron.allow does not exist and user's name is in /etc/cron.d/cron.deny.
- If neither file exists.

Note that the rules for allow and deny apply to root only if the allow/deny files exist. The allow/deny files consist of one user name per line.

crontab Entry Format

A crontab file consists of lines of six fields each. The fields are separated by spaces or tabs. The first five fields are integer patterns that specify the following:

- Minute (0-59),
- Hour (0-23),
- Day of the month (1-31),
- Month of the year (1-12),
- Day of the week (0-6 with 0=Sunday).

Each of these patterns may be either an asterisk (meaning all legal values) or a list of elements separated by commas.

An element is either a number or two numbers separated by a dash (meaning an inclusive range). Note that the specification of days may be made by two fields (day of the month and day of the week). Both are adhered to if specified as a list of elements.

The sixth field of a line in a crontab file is a string that is executed by the shell at the specified times. A percent character in this field (unless escaped by \) is translated to a newline character.

Only the first line (up to a percent sign (%) or end of line) of the command field is executed by the shell. Other lines are made available to the command as standard input. Any line beginning with a hash mark (#) is a comment and is ignored. The file should not contain blank lines.

The shell is invoked from your $HOME directory with an arg0 of sh. Users who want to have their .profile executed must explicitly do so in the crontab file. cron supplies a default environment for every shell, defining HOME, LOGNAME, SHELL (=/bin/sh), TZ, and PATH. The default PATH for user cron jobs is /usr/bin; root cron jobs default to /usr/sbin:/usr/bin. You can set the default PATH in /etc/default/cron; see cron(1M).

If you do not redirect the standard output and standard error of your commands, any generated output or errors are e-mailed to you.

Warning — If you inadvertently enter the crontab command with no argument(s), do not use Control-D to get out. This key sequence removes all entries in your crontab file. Instead, exit with Control-C.

If a superuser modifies another user's crontab file, resulting behavior may be unpredictable. Instead, the privileged user should first invoke su(1M) with the other user's login before making any changes to the crontab file.

Options

-e   Edit a copy of the current user's crontab file, or create an empty file to edit if crontab does not exist. When editing is complete, install the file as the user's crontab file. If a *username* is given, edit the specified user's crontab file instead of the current user's crontab file; this action can be done only by a superuser. The environment variable EDITOR determines which editor is invoked with the -e option. The default editor is ed(1). Note that all crontab jobs should be submitted via crontab; you should not add jobs by just editing the crontab file because cron is not aware of changes made in this way.

-l   List the crontab file for the invoking user. Only a superuser can specify a *username* following the -r or -l options to remove or list the crontab file of the specified user.

-r   Remove a user's crontab from the crontab directory.

Examples

The following example cleans up core files every weekday morning at 3:15 a.m.

```
15 3 * * 1-5 find $HOME -name core 2>/dev/null | xargs
rm -f
```

The following example e-mails a birthday greeting.

```
0 12 14 2 * mailx john%Happy Birthday!%Time for lunch.
```

The following example runs a command on the first and fifteenth of each month, as well as on every Monday.

```
0 0 1,15 * 1
```

To specify days by only one field, set the other field to *. The following example runs a command only on Mondays.

```
0 0 * * 1
```

Environment Variables

See environ(5) for descriptions of the following environment variables that affect the execution of crontab: LC_TYPE, LC_CTYPE, and NLSPATH.

EDITOR   Determine the editor to be invoked when the -e option is specified. The default editor is ed(1). If both the EDITOR and VISUAL environment variables are set, the value of the VISUAL variable is used as the editor.

Exit Status

0   Successful completion.

>0   An error occurred.

Files

/etc/cron.d

     Main cron directory.

/etc/cron.d/cron.allow

     List of allowed users.

```
/etc/default/cron
```
> Contains `cron` default settings.

```
/etc/cron.d/cron.deny
```
> List of denied users.

```
/var/cron/log
```
> Accounting information.

```
/var/spool/cron/crontabs
```
> Spool area for `crontab`.

Attributes

See `attributes`(5) for descriptions of the following attributes:

Attribute Type	Attribute Value
Availability	SUNWcsu

See Also

`atq(1)`, `atrm(1)`, `ed(1)`, `sh(1)`, `cron(1M)`, `su(1M)`, `attrbutes(5)`, `environ(5)`

---

crtplot — Graphics Filters for Various Plotters

Synopsis

```
/usr/ucb/plot [-Tterminal]
```

Description

See `plot`(1).

---

crypt — Encode or Decode a File

Synopsis

```
/usr/bin/crypt [password]
```

Description

`crypt` encrypts and decrypts the contents of a file. `crypt` reads from the standard input and writes on the standard output. The password is a key that selects a particular transformation. If no password is given, crypt demands a key from the terminal and turns off printing while the key is being typed in. crypt encrypts and decrypts with the same key, as shown in the following example.

```
castle% crypt key < clear.file > encrypted.file
castle% crypt key < encrypted.file | pr
```

Files encrypted by crypt are compatible with those treated by the editors ed(1), ex(1), and vi(1) in encryption mode.

The security of encrypted files depends on three factors:

- The fundamental method must be hard to solve.
- Direct search of the key space must be infeasible.
- "Sneak paths" by which keys or cleartext can become visible must be minimized.

crypt implements a one-rotor machine designed along the lines of the German Enigma, but with a 256-element rotor. Methods of attack on such machines are widely known; thus, crypt provides minimal security.

The transformation of a key into the internal settings of the machine is deliberately designed to be expensive, that is, to take a substantial fraction of a second to compute. However, if keys are restricted to (say) three lowercase letters, then encrypted files can be read by expending only a substantial fraction of five minutes of machine time.

Because the key is an argument to the crypt command, it is potentially visible to users executing ps(1) or a derivative command. To minimize this possibility, crypt takes care to destroy any record of the key immediately on entry. No doubt the choice of keys and key security are the most vulnerable aspect of crypt.

Files

/dev/tty   For typed key.

Attributes

See attributes(5) for descriptions of the following attributes:

Attribute Type	Attribute Value
Availability	SUNWcsu

See Also

des(1), ed(1), ex(1), makekey(1), ps(1), vi(1), attributes(5)

csh — Shell Command Interpreter with a C-like Syntax

Synopsis
```
/usr/bin/csh [-bcefinstvVxX] [argument...]
```

Description
csh, the C shell, is a command interpreter with a syntax reminiscent of the C language. It provides a number of convenient features for interactive use that are not available with the Bourne shell, including file-name completion, command aliasing, history substitution, job control, and a number of built-in commands. As with the Bourne shell, the C shell provides variable, command and file-name substitution.

> **Note** — Although the C shell is robust enough for general use, adventures into its esoteric periphery may reveal unexpected quirks.

Initialization and Termination
When first started, the C shell normally performs commands from the .cshrc file in your home directory, provided that it is readable and you either own it or your real group ID matches its group ID. If the shell is invoked with a name that starts with a dash (-), as when started by login(1), the shell runs as a login shell.

If the shell is a login shell, it is invoked in the following sequence:

1. Execute commands in /etc/.login.
2. Execute commands from the .cshrc file in your home directory.
3. Execute commands from the .login file in your home directory; the same permission checks as those for .cshrc are applied to this file. Typically, the .login file contains commands to specify the terminal type and environment.

As a login shell terminates, it performs commands from the .logout file in your home directory; the same permission checks as those for .cshrc are applied to this file.

Interactive Operation
After startup processing is complete, an interactive C shell begins reading commands from the terminal, prompting with *hostname*% (or *hostname*# for superuser). The shell then repeatedly performs the following actions:

1. Reads a line of command input and breaks it into words.
2. Puts the sequence of words in the history list and then parses them.
3. Executes each command in the current line.

Noninteractive Operation

When running noninteractively, the shell does not prompt for input from the terminal. A noninteractive C shell can execute a command supplied as an argument on its command line or interpret commands from a file, also known as a script.

Note — When the shell executes a shell script that attempts to execute a nonexistent command interpreter, the shell returns an erroneous diagnostic message that the shell script file does not exist.

Options

-b	Force a "break" from option processing. Do not interpret subsequent command-line arguments as C shell options. This option enables the passing of options to a script without confusion. You must use this option or the shell will not run set-user-ID or set-group-ID scripts.
-c	Execute the first argument (which must be present). Remaining arguments are placed in argv, the argument-list variable, and passed directly to csh.
-e	Exit if a command terminates abnormally or yields a non-zero exit status.
-f	For a fast start, read neither the .cshrc file nor the .login file (if a login shell) on startup.
-i	Force interactive mode. Prompt for command-line input, even if the standard input does not appear to be a terminal (character special device).
-n	Parse (interpret), but do not execute commands. You can use this option to check C shell scripts for syntax errors.
-s	Take commands from the standard input.
-t	Read and execute a single command line. You can use a backslash (\) to escape each newline for continuation of the command line onto subsequent input lines.
-v	Set the verbose predefined variable; echo command input after history substitution (but before other substitutions) and before execution.
-V	Set verbose before reading .cshrc.
-x	Set the echo variable; echo commands after all substitutions and just before execution.
-X	Set echo before reading .cshrc.

Except with the options -c, -i, -s, or -t, take the first nonoption argument to be the name of a command or script. Pass it as argument zero, and add subsequent arguments to the argument list for that command or script.

Usage

File-name Completion

When you enable the file-completion variable, filec, an interactive C shell can complete a partially typed file name or user name. When you type an unambiguous beginning of a file name and press the Escape key, the shell fills in the remaining characters of a matching file name from the working directory.

If you follow a partial file name with the EOF character (usually typed as Control-D), the shell lists all file names that match. It then prompts once again, supplying the incomplete command line typed in so far.

When the last (partial) word begins with a tilde (~), the shell tries to complete with a user name, instead of a file in the working directory.

If there is no match or multiple matches, the terminal bell beeps. You can turn the beep off by setting the nobeep variable. You can exclude files with certain suffixes by listing those suffixes in the fignore variable. If, however, the only possible completion includes a suffix in the list, it is not ignored. fignore does not affect the listing of file names by the EOF character.

Lexical Structure

The shell splits input lines into words at space and Tab characters, except as noted below. The characters &, |, ;, <, >, (, and) form separate words; if paired, the pairs form single words. These shell metacharacters can be made part of other words, and their special meaning can be suppressed by preceding them by a backslash (\). A newline preceded by a \ is equivalent to a space character.

In addition, a string enclosed in matched pairs of single quotes ('), double quotes ("), or backquotes (`), forms a partial word; metacharacters in such a string, including any space or Tab characters, do not form separate words. Within pairs of backquote (`) or double quote (") characters, a newline preceded by a backslash (\) gives a true newline character. Additional functions of each type of quote are described, below, under Variable Substitution, Command Substitution, and File-name Substitution.

When the shell's input is not a terminal, the character # introduces a comment that continues to the end of the input line. Its special meaning is suppressed when preceded by a \ or enclosed in matching quotes.

Note — Words can be no longer than 1,024 bytes. The system limits argument lists to 1,048,576 bytes. However, the maximum number of arguments to a command for which file-name expansion applies is 1,706. Command substitutions may expand to no more characters than are allowed in the argument list. To detect looping, the shell restricts the number of alias substitutions on a single line to 20.

Command-Line Parsing

A simple command is composed of a sequence of words. The first word (that is not part of an I/O redirection) specifies the command to be executed. A simple command, or a set of simple commands separated by | or |& characters, forms a pipeline. With |, the standard output of the preceding command is redirected to the standard input of the command that follows. With |&, both the standard error and the standard output are redirected through the pipeline.

Pipelines can be separated by semicolons (;), in which case they are executed sequentially. Pipelines that are separated by && or || form conditional sequences in which the execution of pipelines on the right depends on the success or failure of the pipeline on the left.

A pipeline or sequence can be enclosed within parentheses ( ) to form a simple command that can be a component in a pipeline or sequence.

A sequence of pipelines can be executed asynchronously or "in the background" by appending an ampersand (&); instead of waiting for the sequence to finish before issuing a prompt, the shell displays the job number (see "Job Control" on page 197) and associated process IDs and prompts immediately.

> **Note** — Quote conventions are confusing. Overriding the escape character to force variable substitutions within double quotes is counterintuitive and inconsistent with the Bourne shell.

History Substitution

History substitution enables you to use words from previous command lines in the command line you are typing. This process simplifies spelling corrections and the repetition of complicated commands or arguments. Command lines are saved in the history list, the size of which is controlled by the `history` variable. The most recent command is retained in any case. A history substitution begins with a ! (although you can change this with the `histchars` variable) and can occur anywhere on the command line; history substitutions do not nest. You can escape the ! with \ to suppress its special meaning.

Input lines containing history substitutions are echoed on the terminal after being expanded but before any other substitutions take place or the command gets executed.

> **Note** — The g (global) flag in history substitutions applies only to the first match in each word, instead of to all matches in all words. The common text editors consistently do the latter when given the g flag in a substitution command.

Refer to `history`(1) for more details.

Event Designators

An event designator is a reference to a command-line entry in the history list.

!	Start a history substitution, except when followed by a space character, Tab, newline, = or (.
!!	Refer to the previous command. By itself, this substitution repeats the previous command.
!n	Refer to command line n.
!-n	Refer to the current command line minus n.
!str	Refer to the most recent command starting with str.
!?str?	Refer to the most recent command containing str.

!?str? additional

Refer to the most recent command containing str, and append additional to that referenced command.

!{command} additional

Refer to the most recent command beginning with command and append additional to that referenced command.

^previous-word^replacement^

Repeat the previous command line, replacing the string previous-word with the string replacement. This is equivalent to the history substitution: !:s/previous-word/replacement/.

To reexecute a specific previous command *and* make such a substitution, say, reexecuting command #6, !:6s/previous-word/replacement/.

Word Designators

A colon (:) separates the event specification from the word designator. You can omit it if the word designator begins with a ^, $, *, or %. If the word is to be selected from the previous command, you can omit the second ! character from the event specification. For instance, !!:1 and !:1 both refer to the first word of the previous command, whereas !!$ and !$ both refer to the last word in the previous command. Word designators include:

#	The entire command line typed so far.
0	The first input word (command).
n	The n-th argument.
^	The first argument, that is, 1.
$	The last argument.
%	The word matched by (the most recent) ?s search.
x-y	A range of words; -y abbreviates 0-y.

*	All the arguments, or a null value if there is just one word in the event.
*x**	Abbreviates *x*-$.
x-	Like *x** but omitting word $.

Modifiers

After the optional word designator, you can add one of the following modifiers, preceded by a colon (:).

h	Remove a trailing path name component, leaving the head.
r	Remove a trailing suffix of the form . *xxx*, leaving the basename.
e	Remove all but the suffix, leaving the extension.
s/*l*/*r*/	Substitute *r* for *l*.
t	Remove all leading path-name components, leaving the tail.
&	Repeat the previous substitution.
g	Apply the change to the first occurrence of a match in each word by prefixing the above (for example, g&).
p	Print the new command but do not execute it.
q	Quote the substituted words, escaping further substitutions.
x	Like q, but break into words at each space character, Tab, or newline.

Note — Although it should be possible to use the : modifiers on the output of command substitution, there are two problems with : modifier usage on variable substitutions: not all of the modifiers are available, and only one modifier per substitution is allowed.

Unless preceded by a g, the modification is applied only to the first string that matches *l*; an error results if no string matches.

The left-hand side of substitutions are not regular expressions, but character strings. You can use any character as the delimiter in place of /. A backslash quotes the delimiter character. The character &, in the right-hand side, is replaced by the text from the left-hand side. You can escape the & with a backslash. A null *l* uses the previous string either from a *l* or from a contextual scan string s from !?s. You can omit the rightmost delimiter if a newline immediately follows *r*; similarly, you can omit the rightmost ? in a context scan.

Without an event specification, a history reference refers either to the previous command or to a previous history reference on the command line (if any).

Quick Substitution

^*l*^*r*^ is equivalent to the history substitution !:s/*l*/*r*/.

Aliases

The C shell maintains a list of aliases that you can create, display, and modify by using the `alias` and `unalias` commands. The shell checks the first word in each command to see if it matches the name of an existing alias. If it does, the command is reprocessed with the alias definition replacing its name; the history substitution mechanism is made available as though that command were the previous input line. History substitutions, escaped with a backslash in the definition, can be replaced with actual command-line arguments when you use the alias. If no history substitution is called for, the arguments remain unchanged.

You can nest aliases. That is, an alias definition can contain the name of another alias. Nested aliases are expanded before any history substitution is applied. This expansion is useful in pipelines such as

```
alias lm 'ls -l \!* | more'
```

which when called, pipes the output of `ls`(1) through `more`(1).

Except for the first word, the name of the alias may not appear in its definition nor in any alias referred to by its definition. Such loops are detected and display an error message.

I/O Redirection

The following metacharacters indicate that the subsequent word is the name of a file to which to redirect the command's standard input, standard output, or standard error; this word is variable, command, and file-name expanded separately from the rest of the command.

`<`	Redirect the standard input.
`<<word`	Read the standard input, up to a line that is identical with *word*, and place the resulting lines in a temporary file. Unless *word* is escaped or quoted, perform variable and command substitutions on these lines. Then, invoke the pipeline with the temporary file as its standard input. *word* is not subjected to variable, file-name, or command substitution, and each line is compared to it before any substitutions are performed by the shell.
`> >! >& >&!`	Redirect the standard output to a file. If the file does not exist, create it. If it does exist, overwrite it; its previous contents are lost.
	When set, the variable `noclobber` prevents destruction of existing files. It also prevents redirection to terminals and `/dev/null`, unless you use one of the `!` forms. The `&` forms redirect both standard output and the standard error (diagnostic output) to the file.
`>> >>& >>! >>&!`	
	Append the standard output. Like `>`, but place output at the end of the file instead of overwriting it. If `noclobber` is set, it is an error

for the file not to exist, unless you use one of the ! forms. The &
forms append both the standard error and standard output to the
file.

Note — Control over terminal output after processes are started is
primitive; use the Sun window system if you need better output
control.

The only way to direct the standard output and standard error
separately is by invoking a subshell, as follows:

```
castle% (command > outfile) >& errorfile
```

Variable Substitution

The C shell maintains a set of variables, each of which is composed of a *name*
and a *value*. A variable name consists of up to 20 letters and digits, and starts
with a letter (the underscore is considered a letter). A variable's value is a
space-separated list of zero or more words.

To refer to a variable's value, precede its name with a dollar sign ($). You can
use certain references (described below) to select specific words from the value
or to display other information about the variable. You can use braces to
insulate the reference from other characters in an input-line word.

Variable substitution takes place after the input line is analyzed, aliases are
resolved, and I/O redirections are applied. Variable references in I/O
redirections and backquoted strings, however, are substituted at the time the
redirection is made.

You can suppress variable substitution by preceding the $ with a \, except
within double quotes where it always occurs. Variable substitution is
suppressed inside of single quotes. A $ is escaped if followed by a space
character, Tab, or newline.

You can use the set and unset commands to create, display, or destroy
variables. Some variables are maintained or used by the shell. For instance, the
argv variable contains an image of the shell's argument list. Of the variables
used by the shell, a number are toggles; the shell does not care what their value
is, only whether they are set or not.

You can operate on numerical values as numbers (as with the @ built-in
command). With numeric operations, an empty value is considered to be 0; the
second and subsequent words of multiword values are ignored. For instance,
when the verbose variable is set to any value (including an empty value),
command input is echoed on the terminal.

Command and file-name substitution is subsequently applied to the words
that result from the variable substitution, except when suppressed by double
quotes, when noglob is set (suppressing file-name substitution), or when you
quote the reference with the :q modifier. Within double quotes, a reference is
expanded to form (a portion of) a quoted string; multiword values are expanded
to a string with embedded space characters. When the :q modifier is applied to

the reference, it is expanded to a list of space-separated words, each of which is quoted to prevent subsequent command or file-name substitutions.

Except as noted below, it is an error to refer to a variable that is not set.

$var   Replace by words from the value of var, each separated by a space
${var}   character. If var is an environment variable, return its value (but
              : modifiers and the other forms given below are not available).

$var[index]
${var[index]}

              Select only the indicated words from the value of var. Variable
              substitution is applied to $index$, which may consist of (or result in)
              either a single number, two numbers separated by a dash (-), or an
              asterisk (*). Words are indexed starting from 1; an asterisk selects
              all words. If you omit the first number of a range (as with
              $argv[-2]), it defaults to 1. If you omit the last number of a range
              (as with $argv[1-]), it defaults to $#var (the word count). It is not
              an error for a range to be empty if you omit the second argument
              (or it is within range).

$#name   Give the number of words in the variable.
${#name}

$0   Substitute the name of the file from which command input is being
              read except for setuid shell scripts. An error occurs if the name is
              not known.

$n   Equivalent to $argv[n].
${n}

$*   Equivalent to $argv[*].

You can apply the modifiers :e, :h, :q, :r, :t, and :x (see "History Substitution" on page 188), :gh, :gt, and :gr. If you use braces ({}), then the modifiers must appear within the braces. The current implementation allows only one such modifier per expansion.

You cannot use : modifiers with the following references.

$?var   Substitute the string 1 if var is set, or 0 if it is not set.
${?var}

$?0   Substitute 1 if the current input file name is known, or 0 if it is not.

$$ Substitute the process number of the (parent) shell.

$<   Substitute a line from the standard input, with no further
              interpretation thereafter. You can use this modifier to read from
              the keyboard in a C shell script.

Command and File-name Substitutions

Command and file-name substitutions are applied selectively to the arguments of built-in commands. Portions of expressions that are not evaluated are not expanded. For non-built-in commands, file-name expansion of the command name is done separately from that of the argument list; expansion occurs in a subshell after I/O redirection is performed.

Command Substitution

A command enclosed by backquotes (` ... `) is performed by a subshell. Its standard output is broken into separate words at each space character, Tab, and newline; null words are discarded. This text replaces the backquoted string on the current command line. Within double quotes, only newline characters force new words; space and Tab characters are preserved. However, a final newline is ignored. It is, therefore, possible for a command substitution to yield a partial word.

File-name Substitution

Unquoted words containing any of the characters *, ?, [, or { or that begin with ~ are expanded (also known as globbing) to an alphabetically sorted list of file names, as follows:

*	Match any (0 or more) characters.
?	Match any single character.
[...]	Match any single character in the enclosed list(s) or range(s). A list is a string of characters. A range is two characters separated by a dash (-) and includes all the characters in between in the ASCII collating sequence (see ascii(5)).

{ *str*, *str*, ... }

Expand to each string (or file-name-matching pattern) in the comma-separated list. Unlike the pattern-matching expressions above, the expansion of this construct is not sorted. For instance, {b,a} expands to b a, (not a b). As special cases, the characters { and }, along with the string { }, are passed undisturbed.

~[*user*]   Your home directory, as indicated by the value of the variable *home*, or that of *user*, as indicated by the password entry for user.

Only the patterns *, ? and [...] imply pattern matching; an error results if no file name matches a pattern that contains them. The dot character (.) must be matched explicitly when it is the first character in a file-name or path-name component. The slash (/) must also be matched explicitly.

Expressions and Operators

A number of C shell built-in commands accept expressions in which the operators are similar to those of C and have the same precedence. These expressions typically appear in the @, exit, if, set, and while commands and are often used to regulate the flow of control for executing commands. Components of an expression are separated by white space.

Null or missing values are considered 0. The result of all expressions is a string, which may represent decimal numbers.

The following C shell operators are grouped in order of precedence:

(. . .)	Grouping.
~	One's complement.
!	Logical negation.
* / %	Multiplication, division, remainder. (These operators are right-associative, which can lead to unexpected results. Group combinations explicitly with parentheses.)
+ -	Addition, subtraction (also right-associative).
<< >>	Bitwise shift left, bitwise shift right.
< > <= >=	Less than, greater than, less than or equal to, greater than or equal to.
== != =~ !~	Equal to, not equal to, file-name-substitution pattern match (described below), file-name-substitution pattern mismatch.
&	Bitwise AND.
^	Bitwise XOR (exclusive OR).
|	Bitwise inclusive OR.
&&	Logical AND.
||	Logical OR.

The operators ==, !=, =~, and !~ compare their arguments as strings; other operators use numbers. The operators =~ and !~ each check whether a string to the left matches a file-name substitution pattern on the right. This checking reduces the need for switch statements when pattern-matching between strings is all that is required.

Also available are file inquiries:

-r *filename*

> Return true, or 1 if the user has read access. Otherwise, return false, or 0.

-w *filename*

> true if the user has write access.

-x *filename*

> true if the user has execute permission (or search permission on a directory).

-e *filename*

> true if *filename* exists.

-o *filename*

> true if the user owns *filename*.

-z *filename*

> true if *filename* is of 0 length (empty).

-f *filename*

> true if *filename* is a plain file.

-d *filename*

> true if *filename* is a directory.

If *filename* does not exist or is inaccessible, then all inquiries return false. An inquiry as to the success of a command is also available:

{*command*}   If *command* runs successfully, the expression evaluates to true, 1. Otherwise, it evaluates to false, 0. (Note: Conversely, *command* itself typically returns 0 when it runs successfully, or some other value if it encounters a problem. If you want to get at the status directly, use the value of the status variable instead of this expression).

Control Flow

The shell contains a number of commands to regulate the flow of control in scripts and, within limits, from the terminal. These commands operate by forcing the shell either to reread input (to loop), or to skip input under certain conditions (to branch).

Each occurrence of a foreach, switch, while, if...then, or else built-in command must appear as the first word on its own input line.

If the shell's input is not seekable and a loop is being read, that input is buffered. The shell performs seeks within the internal buffer to accomplish the rereading implied by the loop. (To the extent that this action allows, backward goto commands succeed on nonseekable inputs.)

> **Note** — Commands within loops, prompted for by ?, are not placed in the history list.

Command Execution

If the command is a C shell built-in command, the shell executes it directly. Otherwise, the shell searches for a file by that name with execute access. If the command name contains a /, the shell takes it as a path name and searches for it. If the command name does not contain a /, the shell attempts to resolve it to a path name, searching each directory in the path variable for the command. To speed the search, the shell uses its hash table (see the rehash built-in command) to eliminate directories that have no applicable files. You can disable this hashing with the -c or -t, options or by using the unhash built-in command.

As a special case, if there is no / in the name of the script and there is an alias for the word shell, the expansion of the shell alias is prepended (without modification) to the command line. The system tries to execute the first word of this special (late-occurring) alias, which should be a full path name. Remaining words of the alias's definition, along with the text of the input line, are treated as arguments.

When a path name is found that has proper execute permissions, the shell forks a new process and passes it, along with its arguments, to the kernel, using the execve() system call (see exec(2)). The kernel then tries to overlay the new process with the desired program. If the file is an executable binary (in a.out(4) format), the kernel succeeds and begins executing the new process. If the file is a text file and the first line begins with #!, the next word is taken to be the path name of a shell (or command) to interpret that script. Subsequent words on the first line are taken as options for that shell. The kernel invokes (overlays) the indicated shell, using the name of the script as an argument.

If neither of the above conditions holds, the kernel cannot overlay the file and the execve() call fails (see exec(2)); the C shell then tries to execute the file by spawning a new shell, as follows:

- If the first character of the file is a #, the file invokes a C shell.
- Otherwise, the file invokes a Bourne shell.

Signal Handling

The shell normally ignores QUIT signals. Background jobs are immune to signals generated from the keyboard, including hangups (HUP). Other signals have the values that the C shell inherited from its environment. You can control the shell's handling of interrupt and terminate signals within scripts by using the onintr built-in command. Login shells catch the TERM signal; otherwise, this signal is passed on to child processes. In no case are interrupts allowed when a login shell is reading the .logout file.

Job Control

The shell associates a numbered job with each command sequence to keep track of those commands that are running in the background or have been stopped with TSTP signals (typically Control-Z). When a command or command sequence in a semicolon-separated list is started in the background by use of the & metacharacter, the shell displays a line with the job number in brackets and a list of associated process numbers, for example:

```
[1] 1234
```

To see the current list of jobs, use the jobs built-in command. The job most recently stopped (or put into the background if none are stopped) is referred to as the current job and is indicated with a +. The previous job is indicated with a –; when the current job is terminated or moved to the foreground, this job takes its place (becomes the new current job).

To manipulate jobs, refer to the bg, fg, kill, stop, and % built-in commands.

A reference to a job begins with a %. By itself, the percent sign refers to the current job.

% %+ %%	The current job.
%-	The previous job.

`%j`	Refer to job j as in `kill -9 %j`. j can be a job number or a string that uniquely specifies the command line that started it; for example, `fg %vi` might bring a stopped `vi` job to the foreground.
`%?string`	Specify the job for which the command line uniquely contains *string*.

A job running in the background stops when it tries to read from the terminal. Background jobs can normally produce output, but you can suppress this output by using the `stty tostop` command.

Status Reporting

While running interactively, the shell tracks the status of each job and reports whenever the job finishes or becomes blocked. To avoid disturbing the appearance of your input, the shell normally displays a message to this effect as it issues a prompt. When set, the `notify` variable indicates that the shell is to report status changes immediately. By default, the `notify` command marks the current process; after starting a background job, type **notify** to mark it.

Built-in Commands

Built-in commands are executed within the C shell. If a built-in command occurs as any component of a pipeline except the last, it is executed in a subshell.

Note — Shell built-in functions are not stoppable/restartable. Command sequences of the form a ; b ; c are also not handled gracefully when stopping is attempted. If you suspend b, the shell never executes c. This problem is especially noticeable if the expansion results from an alias. It can be avoided by placing the sequence in parentheses to force it into a subshell.

It is up to the user to manually remove all duplicate path names accrued from using built-in commands as `set path = `*pathnames* or `setenv PATH `*pathnames* more than once. For example, these duplicates often occur because a shell script or a `.cshrc` file does something like `set path=(/usr/local /usr/hosts $path)` to ensure that the named directories are in the path-name list.

The C shell built-in commands are shown below. For more details, refer to the individual manual page for each built-in command.

`: ` Null command

> Interpret the command but perform no action.

`alias [`*name* `[`*def*`]]`

> Assign *def* to the alias *name*. *def* is a list of words that may contain escaped history-substitution metasyntax. *name* is not allowed to be `alias` or `unalias`. If you omit *def*, display the current definition for

the alias name. If you omit both *name* and *def*, display all aliases with their definitions.

`bg [%job ...]`

Run the current or specified jobs in the background.

`break`   Resume execution after the end of the nearest enclosing `foreach` or `while` loop. Execute the remaining commands on the current line. You can write multilevel breaks as a list of `break` commands, all on one line.

`breaksw`   Break from a switch, resuming after the `endsw`.

`case label:` A label in a `switch` statement.

`cd [dir]`
`chdir [dir]`

Change the shell's working directory to directory *dir*. If no argument is given, change to the home directory of the user. If *dir* is a relative pathname not found in the current directory, check for it in those directories listed in the `cdpath` variable. If *dir* is the name of a shell variable whose value starts with a /, change to the directory named by that value.

`continue`   Continue execution of the next iteration of the nearest enclosing `while` or `foreach` loop.

`default:`   Label the default case in a `switch` statement. The default should come after all case labels. First, execute any remaining commands on the command line.

`dirs [-l]`   Print the directory stack, most recent to the left; the first directory shown is the current directory. With the `-l` argument, produce an unabbreviated printout; suppress use of the ~ notation.

`echo [-n] list`

Write the words in *list* to the shell's standard output, separated by space characters. Terminate the output with a newline unless you use the -n option. `csh`, by default, invokes its built-in `echo` if `echo` is called without the full path name of a UNIX command, regardless of the configuration of your PATH (see `echo(1)`).

`eval argument...`

Read the arguments as input to the shell and execute the resulting command(s). This command is usually used to execute commands generated as the result of command or variable substitution. See `tset(1B)` for an example of how to use `eval`.

`exec command`

Execute *command* in place of the current shell, which terminates.

`exit [(expr)]`

Exit the calling shell or shell script, either with the value of the status variable or with the value specified by the expression *expr*.

`fg [%`*`job`*`]`   Bring the current or specified job into the foreground.

`foreach` *`var`* `(`*`wordlist`*`)`

`...`

`end`

> Successively set the variable *`var`* to each member of *`wordlist`*. Execute the sequence of commands between this command and the matching `end` for each new value of *`var`*. Both `foreach` and `end` must appear alone on separate lines.
>
> You can use the built-in `continue` command to terminate the execution of the current iteration of the loop, and the built-in command `break` to terminate execution of the `foreach` command. When this command is read from the terminal, the loop is read once, prompting with `?` before any statements in the loop are executed.

`glob` *`wordlist`*

> Perform file-name expansion on *`wordlist`*. Like `echo`, but no `\` escapes are recognized. Words are delimited by NULL characters in the output.

`goto` *`label`*   The specified *`label`* is a file name and a command expanded to yield a label. The shell rewinds its input as much as possible and searches for a line of the form *`label`*: possibly preceded by space or Tab characters. Execution continues after the indicated line. It is an error to jump to a label that occurs between a `while` or `for` built-in command and its corresponding `end`.

`hashstat`   Print a statistics line indicating how effective the internal hash table for the path variable has been at locating commands (and avoiding `exec`s). Try an `exec` for each component of the path where the `hash` function indicates a possible hit and in each component that does not begin with a `/`. These statistics reflect only the effectiveness of the `path` variable, not the `cdpath` variable.

`history [-hr] [`*`n`*`]`

> Display the history list; if *n* is given, display only the *n* most recent events.
>
> | | |
> |---|---|
> | `-h` | Display the history list without leading numbers. Use this option to produce files suitable for sourcing, using the `-h` option to source. |
> | `-r` | Reverse the order of printout to be most recent first instead of oldest first. |

`if (`*`expr`*`)` *`command`*

> If the specified expression evaluates to `true`, execute the single command with arguments. Variable substitution on *`command`* happens early, at the same time it does for the rest of the `if` command. *`command`* must be a simple command, not a pipeline, a

	command list, or a parenthesized command list. Note: I/O redirection occurs even if `expr` is `false`, when `command` is not executed (this is a bug).

`if (expr)`
`then`
`...`
`else if`
`(expr2)`
`then`
`...`
`else`
`...`
`endif`
	If `expr` is `true`, execute commands up to the first `else`. Otherwise, if `expr2` is `true`, execute the commands between the `else if` and the second `else`. Otherwise, execute commands between the `else` and the `endif`. Any number of `else if` pairs are allowed, but only one `else`. You need only one `endif`, but it is required. The words `else` and `endif` must be the first nonwhite characters on a line. The `if` must appear alone on its input line or after an `else`.

`jobs [-l]`	List the active jobs under job control.
`-l`	List process IDs, in addition to the normal information.

`kill [-sig] [pid] [%job] ...`

`kill -l`	Send the TERM (terminate) signal, by default, or the signal specified, to the specified process ID, the job indicated, or the current job. Give signals either by number or by name. There is no default. Typing `kill` does not send a signal to the current job. If the signal being sent is TERM (terminate) or HUP (hang up), then the job or process is sent a CONT (continue) signal as well.
`-l`	List the signal names that can be sent.

`limit [-h] [resource [max-use]]`

Limit the consumption by the current process or any process it spawns, each not to exceed `max-use` on the specified resource. If you omit `max-use`, print the current limit; if you omit `resource`, display all limits. (Run the sysdef(1M) command to obtain the maximum possible limits for your system. The values reported are in hexadecimal, but you can translate them into decimal numbers by using the bc(1) command.)

`-h`	Use hard limits instead of the current limits. Hard limits impose a ceiling on the values of the current limits. Only superuser can raise the hard limits.

`resource` can be one of the following values:

`cputime`	Maximum CPU seconds per process.
`filesize`	Largest single file allowed; limited to the size of the file system. See df(1M).
`datasize` `(heapsize)`	Maximum data size (including stack) for the process; the size of your virtual memory. See swap(1M).
`stacksize`	Maximum stack size for the process. See swap(1M).

coredumpsize   Maximum size of a core dump (file); limited to the size of the file system.

descriptors   Maximum number of file descriptors. Run sysdef().

memorysize   Maximum size of virtual memory.

max-use is a number, with an optional scaling factor, as follows:

*n*h   Hours (for cputime).

*n*k v   Kilobytes; the default for all but cputime.

*n*m v   Megabytes or minutes (for cputime).

mm:v   Minutes and seconds (for cputime).

Example of limit: to limit the size of a corefile dump to 0 megabytes, type the following:

```
limit coredumpsize 0M
```

login [*username*| -p]

Terminate a login shell and invoke login(1). Do not process the .logout file. If you omit *username*, prompt for the name of a user.

-p   Preserve the current environment (variables).

logout   Terminate a login shell.

nice [+*n* | -*n*] [*command*]

Increment the process priority value for the shell or for command by *n*. The higher the priority value, the lower the priority of a process and the slower it runs. When given, *command* is always run in a subshell. If command is omitted, nice increments the value for the current shell. If you specify no increment, set the process priority value to 4. The range of process priority values is from -20 to 20. Values of *n* outside this range set the value to the lower, or to the higher boundary, respectively.

+*n*   Increment the process priority value by *n*.

-*n*   Decrement by *n*. This argument can be used only by superuser.

nohup [*command*]

Run command with HUPs ignored. With no arguments, ignore HUPs throughout the remainder of a script. When given, always run *command* in a subshell, and the restrictions placed on commands in simple if statements apply. All processes detached with & are effectively nohup'd.

notify [%*job*] ...

Notify the user asynchronously when the status of the current job or specified jobs changes.

onintr [-| *label*]

>Control the action of the shell on interrupts. With no arguments, restore the default action of the shell on interrupts. (The shell terminates shell scripts and returns to the terminal command input level). With the - argument, the shell ignores all interrupts. With a *label* argument, the shell executes a goto *label* when it receives an interrupt or a child process terminates because it was interrupted.

popd [+*n*]   Pop the directory stack and change to the new top directory. Number the elements of the directory stack from 0, starting at the top. When you specify +*n*, discard the *n*'th entry in the stack.

pushd [+*n* | *dir*]

>Push a directory onto the directory stack. With no arguments, exchange the top two elements. When you specify +*n*, rotate the *n*'th entry to the top of the stack and change to it. With the *dir* argument, push the current working directory onto the stack and change to *dir*.

rehash   Recompute the internal hash table of the contents of directories listed in the path variable to account for new commands added. Recompute the internal hash table of the contents of directories listed in the cdpath variable to account for new directories added.

repeat *count command*

>Repeat *command count* times. *command* is subject to the same restrictions as with the one-line if statement.

set [*var* [= *value*]]

set *var*[*n*]   With no arguments, display the values of all shell variables. Display
= *word*   multiword values as a parenthesized list. With the *var* argument alone, assign an empty (null) value to the variable *var*. With arguments of the form *var* = *value*, assign *value* to *var*, where *value* is one of:

>| | |
>|---|---|
>| *word* | A single word (or quoted string). |
>| (*wordlist*) | A space-separated list of words enclosed in parentheses. |

>Values are command and file-name expanded before being assigned. The form set *var*[*n*] = *word* replaces the *n*'th word in a multiword value with *word*.

setenv [*VAR* [*word*]]

>With no arguments, display all environment variables. With the *VAR* argument, set the environment variable *VAR* to have an empty (null) value. (By convention, environment variables are normally given uppercase names.) With both *VAR* and *VAR arguments*, set the environment variable NAME to the value *word*, which must be either a single word or a quoted string. The most commonly used

environment variables, USER, TERM, and PATH, are automatically imported to and exported from the csh variables user, term, and path; you do not need to use setenv for these. In addition, the shell sets the PWD environment variable from the csh variable cwd whenever the latter changes.

The environment variables LC_CTYPE, LC_MESSAGES, LC_TIME, LC_COLLATE, LC_NUMERIC, and LC_MONETARY take immediate effect when changed within the C shell.

If any of the LC_* variables (LC_CTYPE, LC_MESSAGES, LC_TIME, LC_COLLATE, LC_NUMERIC, and LC_MONETARY) (see environ(5)) are not set in the environment, the operational behavior of csh for each corresponding locale category is determined by the value of the LANG environment variable. If LC_ALL is set, its contents are used to override both the LANG and the other LC_* variables. If none of the above variables are set in the environment, the C (U.S. style) locale determines how csh behaves.

LC_CTYPE   Determine how csh handles characters. When LC_CTYPE is set to a valid value, csh can display and handle text and file names containing valid characters for that locale.

LC_CTYPE   Determine how diagnostic and informative messages are presented. This presentation includes the language and style of the messages and the correct form of affirmative and negative responses. In the C locale, the messages are presented in the default form found in the program itself (in most cases, U.S. English).

LC_NUMERIC   Determine the value of the radix character (decimal point (.) in the C locale) and thousand separator (empty string (" ") in the C locale).

shift [*variable*]

Shift the components of argv or *variable*, if supplied, to the left, discarding the first component. It is an error for the variable not to be set or to have a null value.

source [-h] *name*

Read commands from *name*. You can nest source commands, but if they are nested too deeply, the shell may run out of file descriptors. An error in a sourced file at any level terminates all nested source commands.

-h   Place commands from the file *name* on the history list without executing them.

stop %*jobid* ...

Stop the current or specified background job.

```
stop pid ...
```
> Stop the specified process, *pid*. (see ps(1)). Note that when you restart a command from a stop, the shell prints the directory it started in if this is different from the current directory; this result can be misleading (that is, wrong) as the job may have changed directories internally.

suspend
> Stop the shell in its tracks, much as if it had been sent a stop signal with ^Z. This command is most often used to stop shells started by su.

```
switch
(string)
case label:
...
breaksw
....
default:
...
breaksw
endsw
```
> Successively match each *label* against the specified *string*, which is first command and file-name expanded. You can use the file metacharacters *, ? and [...] in the case labels, which are variable expanded. If none of the labels match before a default *label* is found, begin execution after the default *label*. Each case statement and the default statement must appear at the beginning of a line. The command breaksw continues execution after the endsw. Otherwise, control falls through subsequent case and default statements as with C. If no *label* matches and there is no default, execution continues after the endsw.

```
time [command]
```
> With no argument, print a summary of time used by this C shell and its children. With an optional *command*, execute *command* and print a summary of the time it uses.

> As of this writing, the time built-in command does *not* compute the last six fields of output, erroneously reporting the value 0 for these fields.

> ```
> example% time
> 9.0u 11.0s 3:32 10% 0+0k 0+0io 0pf+0w
> ```

```
umask [value]
```
> Display the file creation mask. With an optional *value*, set the file creation mask. With *value* given in octal, you can turn off any bits, but you cannot turn on bits to allow new permissions. Common values include 077, restricting all permissions from everyone else; 022, giving complete access to the group and read (and directory search) access to others; or 022, giving read (and directory search) but not write permission to the group and others.

```
unalias pattern
```
> Discard aliases that match (file-name substitution) *pattern*. unalias * removes all aliases.

unhash
> Disable the internal hash tables for the path and cdpath variables.

```
unlimit [-h] [resource]
```
> Remove a limitation on *resource*. If you specify no resource, then remove all resource limitations. See the description of the limit command for the list of resource names. Only superuser can use the -h option to remove corresponding hard limits.

```
unset pattern
```
> Remove variables whose names match (file-name substitution) *pattern*. unset * removes all variables, which has noticeably distasteful side effects.

```
unsetenv variable
```
> Remove *variable* from the environment. As with unset, pattern matching is not performed.

```
wait
```
> Wait for background jobs to finish (or for an interrupt) before prompting.

```
while (expr)
...
end
```
> While *expr* is true (evaluates to non-zero), repeat commands between the while and the matching end statement. You can use break and continue to terminate or continue the loop prematurely. The while and end must appear alone on their input lines. If the shell's input is a terminal, it prompts for commands with a question mark until the end command is entered and then performs the commands in the loop.

```
%[job] [&]
```
Bring the current or indicated job to the foreground. With the optional ampersand, continue running job in the background.

```
@ [var =expr]
@ [var[n] =expr]
```
> With no arguments, display the values for all shell variables. With arguments, set the variable *var*, or the *n*-th word in the value of *var*, to the value that *expr* evaluates to. (If you supply [n], both *var* and its *n*-th component must already exist.)

> If the expression contains the characters >, <, &, or |, then at least this part of *expr* must be placed within parentheses.

> The operators *=, +=, and so forth, are available as in C. The space separating the name from the assignment operator is optional. Spaces are, however, mandatory in separating components of *expr* that would otherwise be single words.

> Special postfix operators, ++ and --, increment or decrement *expr*.

Environment Variables and Predefined Shell Variables

Unlike the Bourne shell, the C shell maintains a distinction between environment variables and shell variables. Environment variables are automatically exported to processes the shell invokes. Shell variables are not. Both types of variables are treated similarly under variable substitution. The shell sets the variables `argv`, `cwd`, `home`, `path`, `prompt`, `shell`, and `status` on initialization. The shell copies the environment variable `USER` into the shell variable `user`, `TERM` into `term`, and `HOME` into `home`, and copies each back into the respective environment variable whenever the shell variables are reset. `PATH` and `path` are handled similarly. You need set `path` only once in the `.cshrc` or `.login` file. The environment variable `PWD` is set from `cwd` whenever the latter changes. The shell variables shown below have predefined meanings.

`argv`	The list of command-line arguments supplied to the current invocation of the shell. This variable determines the value of the positional parameters $1, $2, and so on.
`cdpath`	A list of directories to be searched by the cd, chdir, and popd commands if the directory argument each accepts is not a subdirectory of the current directory.
`cwd`	The full path name of the current directory.
`echo`	Echo commands (after substitutions) just before execution.
`fignore`	A list of file-name suffixes to ignore when attempting file-name completion. Typically, the single word .o.
`filec`	Enable file-name completion, in which case the Control-D character EOT and the ESC character have special significance when typed in at the end of a terminal input line.

	`EOT`	Print a list of all file names that start with the preceding string.
	`ESC`	Replace the preceding string with the longest unambiguous extension.

`hardpaths`	Resolve path names in the directory stack to contain no symbolic-link components. Note that symbolic links can fool the shell. Setting the hardpaths variable alleviates this.
`histchars`	A two-character string. The first character replaces ! as the history-substitution character. The second replaces the carat (^) for quick substitutions.
`history`	The number of lines saved in the history list. A very large number can use up all of the C shell's memory. If not set, the C shell saves only the most recent command.
`home`	The user's home directory. The file-name expansion of ~ refers to the value of this variable.
`ignoreeof`	Ignore EOF from terminals. This variable protects against accidentally killing a C shell by typing a Control-D.
`mail`	A list of files that the C shell checks for mail. If the first word of the value is a number, it specifies a mail-checking interval in seconds (default, 5 minutes).

nobeep | Suppress the bell during command completion when asking the C shell to extend an ambiguous file name.

noclobber | Restrict output redirection so that existing files are not destroyed by accident. > redirections can be made only to new files. >> redirections can be made only to existing files.

noglob | Inhibit file-name substitution. This variable is most useful in shell scripts once file names (if any) are obtained and no further expansion is desired.

nonomatch | Returns the file-name substitution pattern, instead of an error, if the pattern is not matched. Malformed patterns still result in errors.

notify | Notify you immediately as jobs are completed, instead of waiting until just before issuing a prompt.

path | The list of directories to search for commands. path is initialized from the environment variable PATH, which the C shell updates whenever path changes. A null word specifies the current directory. The default is typically (/usr/bin .). If path becomes unset, execute only full path names. An interactive C shell normally hashes the contents of the directories listed after reading .cshrc and whenever path is reset. If new commands are added, use the rehash command to update the table.

prompt | The string an interactive C shell prompts with. Noninteractive shells leave the prompt variable unset. Aliases and other commands in the .cshrc file that are useful only interactively can be placed after the following test: 'if ($?prompt == 0) exit', to reduce startup time for noninteractive shells. A ! in the prompt string is replaced by the current event number. The default prompt is *hostname*% for mere mortals, or *hostname*# for superuser.

The setting of $prompt has three values:

$prompt not set

Noninteractive shell, test $? prompt.

$prompt set but == ""

.cshrc called by the which(1) command.

$prompt set and != ""

Normal interactive shell.

savehist | The number of lines from the history list that are saved in ~/.history when the user logs out. Large values for savehist slow down the C shell during startup.

shell | The file in which the C shell resides. This variable is used in forking shells to interpret files that have execute bits set but that are not executable by the system.

status	The status returned by the most recent command. If that command terminated abnormally, 0200 is added to the status. Built-in commands that fail return exit status 1; all other built-in commands set status to 0.
time	Control automatic timing of commands. Can be supplied with one or two values. The first is the reporting threshold in CPU seconds. The second is a string of tags and text indicating which resources to report on. A tag is a percent sign (%) followed by a single, uppercase letter (unrecognized tags print as text):

%D	Average amount, in kilobytes, of unshared data space used.
%E	Elapsed (wall clock) time for the command.
%F	Page faults.
%I	Number of block input operations.
%K	Average amount of unshared stack space used, in kilobytes.
%M	Maximum real memory used during execution of the process.
%O	Number of block output operations.
%P	Total CPU time—U (user) plus S (system) —as a percentage of E (elapsed) time.
%S	Number of seconds of CPU time consumed by the kernel on behalf of the user's process.
%U	Number of seconds of CPU time devoted to the user's process.
%W	Number of swaps.
%X	Average amount of shared memory used, in kilobytes.

The default summary display outputs from the %U, %S, %E, %P, %X, %D, %I, %O, %F, and %W tags, in that order.

verbose	Display each command after history substitution takes place.

Large File Behavior

See largefile(5) for the description of the behavior of csh when encountering files greater than or equal to 2 Gbytes (2**31 bytes).

Files

~/.cshrc	Read at beginning of execution by each shell.
~/.login	Read by login shells after .cshrc at login.
~/.logout	Read by login shells at logout.
~/.history	Saved history for use at next login.

/usr/bin/sh

> The Bourne shell, for shell scripts not starting with a #.

/tmp/sh*   Temporary file for <<.

/etc/passwd

> Source of home directories for ~name.

Attributes

See attributes(5) for descriptions of the following attributes:

Attribute Type	Attribute Value
Availability	SUNWcsu
CSI	Enabled

See Also

bc(1), echo(1), login(1), ls(1), more(1), ps(1), sh(1),
shell_builtins(1), which(1), tset(1B), df(1M), swap(1M), sysdef(1M),
access(2), exec(2), fork(2), pipe(2), a.out(4), environ(4), ascii(5),
attributes(5), environ(5), largefile(5), termio(7I)

Diagnostics

You have stopped jobs.

> You exited the C shell with stopped jobs under job control. An immediate second attempt to exit succeeds, terminating the stopped jobs.

Warnings

The use of setuid shell scripts is strongly discouraged.

csplit — Split Files, Based on Context

Synopsis

/usr/bin/csplit [-ks] [-f prefix] [-n number] file arg1 argn

Description

Use the csplit command to split a file into sections. The csplit command reads the file named by the *file* operand, writes all or part of that file into other files as directed by the *arg* operands, and writes the sizes of the files.

Options

-k   Leave previously created files intact. By default, csplit removes
                created files if an error occurs.

-s   Suppress the output of file size messages.

-f *prefix*   Name the created files *prefix*00, *prefix*01, *prefix*n. The default
                is xx00 ... xxn. If the *prefix* argument would create a file name
                exceeding 14 bytes, an error results; csplit exits with a
                diagnostic message and no files are created.

-n *number*   Specify the *number* of decimal digits used to form file names for the
                file pieces. The default is 2, starting with 00. For example, if you
                specify -n 4, output files are numbered starting with xx0000.

Operands

file   The path name of a text file to be split. If *file* is -, use the standard
                input.

arg1...argn

                The operands *arg1...argn* can be a combination of the following:

/*rexp*/[*offset*]

                                Create a file using the content of the lines from
                                the current line up to, but not including, the line
                                that results from the evaluation of the regular
                                expression with *offset*, if any, applied. The
                                regular expression *rexp* must follow the rules
                                for basic regular expressions. The optional offset
                                must be a positive or negative integer value
                                representing a number of lines. The integer
                                value must be preceded by + or -. If the selection
                                of lines from an offset expression of this type
                                would create a file with zero lines or one with
                                greater than the number of lines left in the
                                input file, the results are unspecified. After the
                                section is created, the current line is set to the
                                line that results from the evaluation of the
                                regular expression with any offset applied. The
                                pattern match of *rexp* is always applied from
                                the current line to the end of the file.

%*rexp*%[*offset*]   This operand is the same as /*rexp*/[*offset*],
                                except create no file for the selected section of
                                the input file.

line-no   Create a file from the current line up to, but not
                                including, the line number *line-no*. Lines in
                                the file are numbered starting at 1. The current
                                line becomes *line-no*. For example, an *in-line*
                                argument of 100 puts 99 lines in each file.

"{*num*}"

Repeat operand. This operand can follow any of the operands described previously. If it follows a *rexp* type operand, that operand is applied *num* more times. If it follows a *line-no* operand, the file are split every *line-no* lines, *num* times, from that point. You must enclose the {*num*} operand in double quotes (" ") or it does not work properly.

csplit reports an error if an operand does not reference a line between the current position and the end of the file.

Usage

See largefile(5) for the description of the behavior of csplit when encountering files greater than or equal to 2 Gbytes (2**31 bytes).

Examples

The following example splits the file named whtpaper.html in two.

```
castle% csplit whtpaper.html 100
4884
35136
castle%
```

The output displays the number of blocks in each file.
The following example creates four files, cobol00...cobol03.

```
castle% csplit -f cobol filename '/procedure division/' /par5./ /par16./
```

After editing the split files, you can recombine them as follows.

```
castle% cat cobol0[0-3] > filename
```

Note — This example overwrites the original file.

The following example splits the file at every 100 lines, up to 10,000 lines. The -k option retains the created files if there are fewer than 10,000 lines; however, an error message is still printed.

```
castle% csplit -k testfile 100 "{99}"
2821
3670
3617
3195
3896
3754
2787
3691
3609
3207
```

```
3760
3849
csplit: {99} - out of range
1780
castle% ls -l xx*
-rw-rw-rw-   1 winsor     staff          2821 Jan   6 12:23 xx00
-rw-rw-rw-   1 winsor     staff          3670 Jan   6 12:23 xx01
-rw-rw-rw-   1 winsor     staff          3617 Jan   6 12:23 xx02
-rw-rw-rw-   1 winsor     staff          3195 Jan   6 12:23 xx03
-rw-rw-rw-   1 winsor     staff          3896 Jan   6 12:23 xx04
-rw-rw-rw-   1 winsor     staff          3754 Jan   6 12:23 xx05
-rw-rw-rw-   1 winsor     staff          2787 Jan   6 12:23 xx06
-rw-rw-rw-   1 winsor     staff          3691 Jan   6 12:23 xx07
-rw-rw-rw-   1 winsor     staff          3609 Jan   6 12:23 xx08
-rw-rw-rw-   1 winsor     staff          3207 Jan   6 12:23 xx09
-rw-rw-rw-   1 winsor     staff          3760 Jan   6 12:23 xx10
-rw-rw-rw-   1 winsor     staff          3849 Jan   6 12:23 xx11
-rw-rw-rw-   1 winsor     staff          1780 Jan   6 12:23 xx12
castle%
```

Note — The online csplit manual page does not show double quotes around the number in curly braces. Without the double quotes, the first output file contains the specified number of lines but subsequent files are not split properly.

If prog.c follows the normal C coding convention (the last line of a routine consists only of a } in the first character position), the following example creates a file for each separate C routine (up to 21) in prog.c.

```
castle% csplit -k prog.c '%main(%' '/^}/+1' "{20}"
```

Environment Variables

See environ(5) for descriptions of the following environment variables that affect the execution of csplit: LC_COLLATE, LC_CTYPE, LC_MESSAGES, and NLSPATH.

Exit Status

0	Successful completion.
>0	An error occurred.

Attributes

See attributes(5) for descriptions of the following attributes:

Attribute Type	Attribute Value
Availability	SUNWcsu
CSI	Enabled

See Also

sed(1), split(1), attributes(5), environ(5), largefile(5)

Diagnostics

The diagnostic messages are self-explanatory, except for the following:

arg out of range

> The given argument did not reference a line between the current
> position and the end of the file.

ct — Spawn Login to a Remote Terminal

Synopsis

/usr/bin/ct [*options*] *telno*...

Description

ct dials the telephone number of a modem that is attached to a terminal and
spawns a login process to that terminal. *telno* is a telephone number, with
equal signs for secondary dial tones and minus signs for delays at appropriate
places. (The set of legal characters for *telno* is 0 through 9, -, =, *, and #. The
maximum length of *telno* is 31 characters). If you specify more than one
telephone number, ct tries each in succession until one answers; this feature is
useful for specifying alternate dialing paths.

ct tries each line listed in the file /etc/uucp/Devices until it finds an
available line with appropriate attributes or until it runs out of entries.

After the user on the destination terminal logs out, two things could occur,
depending on what type of port monitor is monitoring the port. When there is
no port monitor, ct prompts: Reconnect? If the response begins with the
letter n, the line is dropped; otherwise, ttymon is started again and the
login: prompt is printed. When a port monitor is monitoring the port, the port
monitor reissues the login: prompt.

The user should log out properly before disconnecting.

> **Note —** The ct program does not work with a DATAKIT Multiplex
> interface.

For a port that is shared for both dial-in and dial-out, the ttymon program
running on the line must have the -r and -b options specified (see
ttymon(1M)).

Options

-h   Prevent ct from hanging up the current line so that it can be used to answer the incoming call. Also, wait for the termination of the specified ct process before returning control to the user's terminal.

-s*speed*   Set the data rate. *speed* is expressed in baud rates. The default baud rate is 1200.

-v   Send a running narrative to the standard error output stream.

-w*n*   Override the default action of asking if ct should wait if there are no free lines, and if so, specifying how many minutes to wait. *n* specifies the maximum number of minutes that ct should wait for a free line.

-x*n*   Produce a detailed output of the program execution on stderr. *n* specifies the level of detail of debugging information as a single number between 0 and 9. As *n* increases to 9, give more detailed debugging information.

Files

/etc/uucp/Devices

/var/adm/ctlog

Attributes

See attributes(5) for descriptions of the following attributes:

Attribute Type	Attribute Value
Availability	SUNWbnuu

See Also

cu(1C), login(1), uucp(1C), ttymon(1M), attributes(5)

ctags — Create a Tags File for Use with ex and vi

Synopsis

/usr/bin/ctags [-aBFtuvwx] [-f *tagsfile*] *file*...
/usr/xpg4/bin/ctags [-aBFuvwx] [-f *tagsfile*] *file*...

Description

The ctags command makes a tags file for ex(1) from the specified C, C++,
Pascal, FORTRAN, yacc(1), and lex(1) sources. A tags file gives the locations
of specified objects (in this case, functions and typedefs) in a group of files.
Each line of the tags file contains the object name, the file in which it is
defined, and an address specification for the object definition. Functions are
searched with a pattern, typedefs with a line number. Specifiers are given in
separate fields on the line, separated by space or Tab characters. Using the tags
file, ex can quickly find these object definitions.

Normally, ctags places the tag descriptions in a file called tags; you can
override this default by using the -f option.

Files with names ending in .c or .h are assumed to be either C or C++
source files and are searched for C/C++ routine and macro definitions. Files
with names ending in .cc, .C, or .cxx, are assumed to be C++ source files.
Files with names ending in .y are assumed to be yacc source files. Files with
names ending in .l are assumed to be lex files. Others are first examined to
see if they contain any Pascal or FORTRAN routine definitions; if not, they are
processed again, looking for C definitions.

The tag main is treated specially in C or C++ programs. The tag formed is
created by prepending M to file, with a trailing .c , .cc, .C, or .cxx removed,
if any, and leading path-name components also removed. This behavior makes
use of ctags practical in directories with more than one program.

Options

When printing, specify first the -x and -v options, then the remaining options.

-a	Append output to an existing tags file.
-B	Use backward searching patterns (?...?).
-f *tagsfile*	
	Place the tag descriptions in a file called *tagsfile* instead of tags.
-F	Use forward searching patterns (/.../) (default).
-t	Create tags for typedefs. /usr/xpg4/bin/ctags creates tags for typedefs by default.
-u	Update the specified files in tags, that is, delete all references to them, and append the new values to the file. Beware: this option is implemented in a way that is rather slow; it is usually faster to simply rebuild the tags file.
-v	Produce on the standard output an index listing the function name, file name, and page number (assuming 64-line pages). Because the output is sorted into lexicographic order, you may want to run the output through sort -f.
-w	Suppress warning diagnostics.

-x   Produce a list of object names, the line number, and file name on
                 which each is defined, as well as the text of that line and print it on
                 the standard output. This list provides a simple index that can be
                 printed as an off-line readable function index.

Operands

file.c   Treat files with basenames ending with the .c suffix as
                 C-language source code.

file.h   Treat files with basenames ending with the .h suffix as
                 C-language source code header files.

file.f   Treat files with basenames ending with the .f suffix as
                 FORTRAN-language source code.

Usage

The -v option is used mainly with vgrind, which is part of the optional BSD
Compatibility package.

Notes

Recognition of functions, subroutines, and procedures for FORTRAN and
Pascal is done in a simple-minded way. No attempt is made to deal with block
structure; if you have two Pascal procedures in different blocks with the same
name, you lose.

The method of deciding whether to look for C or Pascal and FORTRAN
functions is a hack.

The ctags command does not know about #ifdefs.

The ctags command should know about Pascal types. It relies on the input
being well formed to detect typedefs. Use of -tx shows only the last line of
typedefs.

Examples

Using ctags with the -v option produces entries in an order that may not
always be appropriate for vgrind. To produce results in alphabetical order, you
may want to pipe the output through sort -f, as shown in the following
example.

```
castle% ctags -v filename.c filename.h | sort -f > index
castle% vgrind -x index
```

To build a tags file for C sources in a directory hierarchy rooted at
sourcedir, first create an empty tags file, and then run find(1), as shown in
the following example

```
castle% cd sourcedir ; rm -f tags ; touch tags
castle% find . \( -name SCCS -prune -name '*.c' -o -name '*.h' \) -exec
    ctags -u {} \;
```

Note — Spaces must be entered exactly as shown.

Environment Variables

See environ(5) for descriptions of the following environment variables that affect the execution of ctags: LC_COLLATE, LC_CTYPE, LC_MESSAGES, and NLSPATH.

Exit Status

0	Successful completion.
>0	An error occurred.

Files

tags	Output tags file.

Attributes

See attributes(5) for descriptions of the following attributes:

/usr/bin/ctags

Attribute Type	Attribute Value
Availability	SUNWtoo

/usr/xpg4/bin/ctags

Attribute Type	Attribute Value
Availability	SUNWxcu4

See Also

ex(1), lex(1), vgrind(1), vi(1), yacc(1), attributes(5), environ(5), xpg4(5)

cu — Call Another UNIX System

Synopsis

```
/usr/bin/cu [-c device | -l line] [-s speed][-b bits][-h][-n]
[-t][-d][-o | -e][-L][-C][-H] telno|systemname [local-cmd]
```

Description

cu calls up another UNIX system, a terminal, or possibly a non-UNIX system. It manages an interactive conversation with possible transfers of files. It is convenient to think of cu as operating in two phases. The first phase is the connection phase in which the connection is established. cu then enters the conversation phase. The -d option is the only one that applies to both phases.

Options

The -c, -l, and -s options play a part in selecting the medium; the remaining options are used in configuring the line.

-c *device*   Use entries only in the Type field (the first field in the /etc/uucp/Devices file) that match the user-specified device, usually the name of a local area network.

-l *line*   Specify a device name to use as the communication line. You can use this option to override the search that would otherwise take place for the first available line with the right speed. When you use the -l option without the -s option, the speed of a line is taken from the /etc/uucp/Devices file record in which *line* matches the second field (the Line field). When you use the -l and -s options together, cu searches the /etc/uucp/Devices file to check if the requested speed for the requested line is available. If so, the connection is made at the requested speed; otherwise, an error message is printed and the call is not made. In the general case where a specified device is a directly connected asynchronous line (for instance, /dev/term/a), a telephone number (*telno*) is not required. The specified device need not be in the /dev directory. If the specified device is associated with an autodialer, you must provide a telephone number.

-s *speed*   Specify the transmission speed (300, 1200, 2400, 4800, 9600, 19200, 38400). The default value is Any speed that depends on the order of the lines in the /etc/uucp/Devices file.

-b *bits*   Force *bits* to be the number of bits processed on the line. *bits* is either 7 or 8. This option enables connection between systems with different character sizes. By default, the character size of the line is set to the same as the current local terminal.

-h   Set communication mode to half-duplex. This option emulates local echo to support calls to other computer systems that expect terminals to be set to half-duplex mode.

-n   Request user prompt for telephone number. For added security, this option prompts the user to provide the telephone number to be dialed, instead of taking it from the command line.

-t   Dial a terminal that has been set to autoanswer. Appropriate mapping of Return to Return-linefeed pairs is set.

-d   Print diagnostic traces.

-o	Set an ODD data parity for data sent to the remote system.
-e	Set an EVEN data parity for data sent to the remote system.
-L	Go through the login chat sequence specified in the /etc/uucp/Systems file. For more information about the chat sequence, see *TCP/IP and Data Communications Administration Guide.*
-C	Run the local-cmd specified at the end of the command line instead of entering interactive mode. The standard in and standard out of the command that is run refer to the remote connection.
-H	Ignore one hangup. This option enables the user's system to remain in cu while the remote machine disconnects and places a call back to the local machine. Use this option when connecting to systems with callback or dialback modems. Once the callback occurs, subsequent hangups terminate cu. You can specify this option more than once. For more information about dialback configuration, see remote(4) and *TCP/IP and Data Communications Administration Guide.*

Operands

telno	When using an automatic dialer, specify the telephone number with equal signs for secondary dial tone or minus signs placed appropriately for delays of 4 seconds.
systemname	Specify a uucp system name that can be used instead of a telephone number; in this case, cu obtains an appropriate direct line or telephone number from a system file.

Usage

Connection Phase

cu uses the same mechanism that uucp(1C) does to establish a connection. It uses the uucp control files /etc/uucp/Devices and /etc/uucp/Systems, enabling cu to choose from several different media to establish the connection. The possible media include telephone lines, direct connections, and local area networks (LAN). The /etc/uucp/Devices file contains a list of media available on your system. The /etc/uucp/Systems file contains information for connecting to remote systems, but it is not generally readable.

Note — cu determines which /etc/uucp/Systems and /etc/uucp/Devices files to use based on the name used to invoke cu. In the simple case, this name is cu, but you could also have created a link to cu with another name, such as pppcu, in which case, cu then looks for a `service=pppcu` entry in the `/etc/uucp/Sysfiles` file to determine which `/etc/uucp/Systems` file to use.

The `telno` or `systemname` parameter from the command line tells cu what system you want to connect to. This parameter can be blank, a telephone number, a system name, or a LAN-specific address, as described below.

`telephone number`

> A string consisting of the tone dial characters (the digits 0 through 9, *, and #) plus the special characters = and –. The equal sign designates a secondary dial tone, and the minus sign creates a 4-second delay.

`system name`

> The name of any computer that uucp can call; you can print a list of these names by using the uuname(1C) command.

`LAN address`

> The documentation for your LAN shows the form of the LAN specific address.

If cu's default behavior is invoked (not using the -c or -l options), cu uses the `telno` or `systemname` parameter to determine what medium to use. If you specify a telephone number, cu assumes that you want to use a telephone line and selects an automatic call unit (ACU). Otherwise, cu assumes that the parameter is a system name. cu follows the uucp calling mechanism and uses the `/etc/uucp/Systems` and `/etc/uucp/Devices` files to obtain the best available connection. Because cu chooses a speed that is appropriate for the medium, you may not use the -s option when this parameter is a system name.

You can use the -c and -l options to modify the default behavior. -c is most often used to choose a LAN by specifying a `Type` field from the `/etc/uucp/Devices` file. You must include either a `telno` or `systemname` value when using the -c option. If the connection to `systemname` fails, a connection is attempted, using `systemname` as a LAN-specific address. The -l option is used to specify a device associated with a direct connection. If the connection is truly a direct connection to the remote system, then there is no need to specify a `systemname`. This case is the only one where a `telno` or `systemname` parameter is unnecessary. On the other hand, there may be cases in which the specified device connects to a dialer, so it is valid to specify a telephone number. Do not specify both the -c and -l options on the same command line.

Conversation Phase

After making the connection, cu runs as two processes:

- The transmit process reads data from the standard input and, except for lines beginning with ~, passes it to the remote system.

- The receive process accepts data from the remote system and, except for lines beginning with ~, passes it to the standard output. Normally, an automatic DC3/DC1 protocol controls input from the remote so the buffer is not overrun. Lines beginning with ~ have special meanings.

Commands

The transmit process interprets the following user initiated commands:

~.	Terminate the conversation.
~!	Escape to an interactive shell on the local system.
~%break	Transmit a BREAK to the remote system (can also be specified as ~%b).
~%cd	Change the directory on the local system. Note: ~!cd runs the command in a subshell, probably not what was intended.
~!*cmd*...	Run *cmd* on the local system (by using sh -c).
~$*cmd*...	Run *cmd* locally and send its output to the remote system.
~%debug	Toggle the -d debugging option on or off (can also be specified as ~%d).
~%divert	Allow/disallow unsolicited diversions not specified by ~%take.
~%ifc	Toggle between DC3/DC1 input control protocol and no input control. This command is useful when the remote system does not respond properly to the DC3 and DC1 characters (can also be specified as ~%nostop).
~l	Print the values of the termio structure variables for the remote communication line (useful for debugging).
~~*line*	Send the line ~ *line* to the remote system.
~%nostop	Same as ~%ifc.
~%ofc	Toggle the output flow control setting. When enabled, outgoing data may be flow-controlled by the remote host (can also be specified as ~%nostop).
~%old	Allow/disallow old-style syntax for received diversions.
~%put *from* [*to*]	
	Copy file *from* (on local system) to file *to* on remote system. If you omit *to*, use the *from* argument in both places.
~t	Print the values of the termio structure variables for the user's terminal (useful for debugging).
~%take *from* [*to*]	
	Copy file *from* (on the remote system) to file *to* on the local system. If you omit *to*, use the *from* argument in both places.

The receive process normally copies data from the remote system to the standard output of the local system. It may also direct the output to local files.

The use of ~%put requires stty(1) and cat(1) on the remote side. It also requires that the current erase and kill characters on the remote system be identical to these current control characters on the local system. Backslashes are inserted at appropriate places.

The use of ~%take requires the existence of echo(1) and cat(1) on the remote system, and that the remote system must be using the Bourne shell, sh. Also, Tabs mode (see stty(1)) should be set on the remote system if Tabs are to be copied without expansion to spaces.

When cu is used on system X to connect to system Y and subsequently used on system Y to connect to system Z, commands on system Y can be executed by use of ~~. Executing a tilde command reminds the user of the local system uname. For example, uname can be executed on Z, X, and Y as follows.

```
uname
Z
~[X]!uname
X
~~[Y]!uname
Y
```

In general, ~ executes the command on the original machine. ~~ executes the command on the next machine in the chain.

Notes

The cu command takes the default action on receipt of signals, with the exception of:

SIGHUP	Close the connection and terminate.
SIGINT	Forward to the remote system.
SIGQUIT	Forward to the remote system.
SIGUSR1	Terminate the cu process without the normal connection closing sequence.

The cu command does not do any integrity checking on data it transfers. Data fields with special cu characters may not be transmitted properly. Depending on the interconnection hardware, it may be necessary to use a ~ . to terminate the conversion, even if you use stty 0. Nonprinting characters are not dependably transmitted with either the ~%put or ~%take commands. You cannot use ~%put and ~%take over multiple links. You must move files one link at a time.

cu artificially slows transmission during the ~%put operation so that loss of data is unlikely. Files transferred using ~%take or ~%put must contain a trailing newline; otherwise, the operation hangs. Entering a Control-D command usually clears the hang condition.

Examples

The following example dials a system whose telephone number is 9 1 201 555 1234, using 1200 baud (where dial tone is expected after the 9). If you do not specify a speed, `Any` is the default value.

```
castle% cu -s 1200 9=12015551234
```

The following example logs in to a system connected by a direct line.

```
castle% cu -l /dev/term/b
```

or

```
castle% cu -l term/b
```

The following example dials a system with a specific line and speed.

```
castle% cu -s 1200 -l term/b
```

To connect to a specific system by name, use

```
castle% cu systemname
```

Environment Variables

See `environ`(5) for descriptions of the following environment variables that affect the execution of `cu`: LC_CTYPE, LC_MESSAGES, and NLSPATH.

Exit Status

0	Successful completion.
>0	An error occurred.

Files

/etc/uucp/Devices

        Device file.

/etc/uucp/Sysfiles

        System file.

/etc/uucp/Systems

        System file.

/var/spool/locks/*

        Lock file.

Attributes

See attributes(5) for descriptions of the following attributes:

Attribute Type	Attribute Value
Availability	SUNWbnuu

See Also

cat(1), echo(1), stty(1), uname(1), ct(1C), uucp(1C), uuname(1C),
remote(4), attributes(5), environ(5)
TCP/IP and Data Communications Administration Guide

cut — Cut Out Selected Fields of Each Line of a File

Synopsis

```
/usr/bin/cut -blist [-n] [file ...]
/usr/bin/cut -clist [file ...]
/usr/bin/cut -flist [-ddelim] [-s] [file ...]
```

Description

Use cut to cut out columns from a table or fields from each line of a file; in
database parlance, cut implements the projection of a relation. The fields as
specified by *list* can be fixed length, that is, character positions as on a
punched card (-c option), or the length can vary from line to line and be
marked with a field delimiter character like Tab (-f option). You can use cut as
a filter.

Note — You must specify the -b, -c, or -f option.

Use grep(1) to make horizontal cuts (by context) through a file, or paste(1)
to put files together column-wise (that is, horizontally). To reorder columns in
a table, use cut and paste.

Options

-b*list*	Specify byte positions (for instance, -b1-72 would pass the first 72 bytes of each line). When you use -b and -n together, *list* is adjusted so that no multibyte character is split. If you use -b, the input line should contain 1023 bytes or less.
-c*list*	Specify character positions (for instance, -c1-72 would pass the first 72 characters of each line).

`-d`*delim*	Specify the field delimiter character (`-f` option only). Default is t for Tab. You must quote space or other characters with special meaning to the shell. *delim* can be a multibyte character.
`-f`*list*	Specify list of fields assumed to be separated in the file by a delimiter character (see `-d`); for instance, `-f1,7` copies the first and seventh field only. Lines with no field delimiters are passed through intact (useful for table subheadings), unless you specify `-s`. If you use `-f`, the input line should contain 1023 characters or less.
`-n`	Do not split characters. When you use `-b`*list* and `-n` together, *list* is adjusted so that no multibyte character is split.
`-s`	Suppress lines with no delimiter characters for the `-f` option. Unless specified, lines with no delimiters are passed through untouched.

Operands

file	A path name of an input file. If you specify no *file* operands or if a *file* operand is -, use the standard input.
list	A comma-separated or blank-character-separated list of integer field numbers (in increasing order), with optional - to indicate ranges (for instance, 1,4,7; 1-3,8; -5,10 (short for 1-5,10); or 3 (short for third through last field)).

Usage

See `largefile`(5) for the description of the behavior of `cut` when encountering files greater than or equal to 2 Gbytes ($2^{**}31$ bytes).

Examples

The following example maps user IDs to names.

```
castle% cut -d: -f1,5 /etc/passwd
root:Super-User
daemon:
bin:
sys:
adm:Admin
lp:Line Printer Admin
smtp:Mail Daemon User
uucp:uucp Admin
nuucp:uucp Admin
listen:Network Admin
nobody:Nobody
noaccess:No Access User
nobody4:SunOS 4.x Nobody
winsor:
ray:
des:
```

```
rob:
castle%
```

The following Bourne shell example sets `name` to the current login name.

```
$ name=`who am i | cut -f1 -d' '`
$ echo $name
winsor
$
```

Environment Variables

See `environ`(5) for descriptions of the following environment variables that affect the execution of `cut`: LC_CTYPE, LC_MESSAGES, and NLSPATH.

Exit Status

0	All input files were output successfully.
>0	An error occurred.

Attributes

See `attributes`(5) for descriptions of the following attributes:

Attribute Type	Attribute Value
Availability	SUNWcsu
CSI	Enabled

See Also

grep(1), paste(1), attributes(5), environ(5), largefile(5)

Diagnostics

```
cut: -n may only be used with -b
cut: -d may only be used with -f
cut: -s may only be used with -f
cut: cannot open <file>
```

> Either *file* cannot be read or does not exist. If multiple files are present, processing continues.

```
cut: no delimiter specified
```

> Missing *delim* on -d option.

```
cut: invalid delimiter
cut: no list specified
```

> Missing *list* on -b, -c, or -f, option.

```
cut: invalid range specifier
cut: too many ranges specified
cut: range must be increasing
cut: invalid character in range
cut: internal error processing input
cut: invalid multibyte character
cut: unable to allocate enough memory
```

D

---

date — Write the Date and Time

Synopsis

```
/usr/bin/date [-u][+format]
/usr/bin/date [-a [-]sss.fff]
/usr/bin/date [-u][[mmdd]HHMM | mmddHHMM[cc]yy][.SS]

/usr/xpg4/bin/date [-u][+format]
/usr/xpg4/bin/date [-u][[mmdd]HHMM | mmddHHMM[cc]yy][.SS]
```

Description

The date command writes the date and time to standard output or tries to set the system date and time. By default, the current date and time are written.

Specifications of native language translations of month and weekday names are supported. The month and weekday names used for a language are based on the locale specified by the environment variable LC_TIME; see environ(5).

The following is the default form for the C locale:

```
%a %b %e %T %Z %Y
```

where

%a	Day of the week.
%b	Month.

`%e`	Date.
`%T`	Time.
`%Z`	Time zone.
`%Y`	Year.

For example:

```
Fri Jan  8 13:15:42 WST 1999
```

Note — If you try to set the current date to one of the dates that the standard and alternate time zones change (for example, the date that daylight saving time is starting or ending), and you try to set the time to a time in the interval between the end of standard time and the beginning of the alternate time (or the end of the alternate time and the beginning of standard time), the results are unpredictable.

Options

`-a [-]sss.fff`

Slowly adjust the time by `sss.fff` seconds (`fff` represents fractions of a second). This adjustment can be positive or negative. The system's clock is speeded up or slowed down until it has drifted by the number of seconds specified.

`-u`

Display (or set) the date in Greenwich Mean Time (GMT-universal time), bypassing the normal conversion to (or from) local time.

Operands

`+format`

If the argument begins with +, the output of date is the result of passing `format` and the current time to `strftime()`. date uses the conversion specifications listed on the `strftime`(3C) manual page, with the conversion specification for `%C` determined by whether you use `/usr/bin/date` or `/usr/xpg4/bin/date`:

`/usr/bin/date` — Locale's date and time representation. This is the default output for date.

`/usr/xpg4/bin/date` — Century (a year divided by 100 and truncated to an integer) as a decimal number [`00-99`].

The string is always terminated with a newline. You must quote an argument containing blanks.

mm	You can omit the month, day, year, and century. The current
dd	values are applied as defaults. For example:
HH	
MM	`date 10080045`
SS	
cc	sets the date to Oct 8, 12:45 a.m. Because no year is supplied, the
yy	current year is the default. The system operates in GMT. `date`
	takes care of the conversion to and from local standard and
	daylight time. Only superuser can change the date. After
	successfully setting the date and time, `date` displays the new date
	according to the default format. The `date` command uses `TZ` to
	determine the correct time zone information. See `environ`(5).

Examples

The following command displays the current date and time in a format
different from that of the default.

```
castle% date '+DATE: %m/%d/%y%nTIME: %H:%M:%S'
DATE: 01/08/99
TIME: 13:59:38
castle%
```

The following command sets the current time to 12:34:56.

```
castle% su
Password:
castle# date 1234.56
Fri Jan  8 12:34:56 WST 1999
castle#
```

Environment Variables

See `environ`(5) for descriptions of the following environment variables that
affect the execution of `date`: LC_CTYPE, LC_TIME, LC_MESSAGES, and
NLSPATH.

TZ	Determine the time zone in which the time and date are written,
	unless you specify the -u option. If the TZ variable is not set and
	you do not specify the -u option, the system default time zone is
	used.

Exit Status

0	Successful completion.
>0	An error occurred.

Attributes

See attributes(5) for descriptions of the following attributes:

/usr/bin/date

Attribute Type	Attribute Value
Availability	SUNWcsu
CSI	Enabled

/usr/xpg4/bin/date

Attribute Type	Attribute Value
Availability	SUNWxcu4
CSI	Enabled

See Also

strftime(3C), attributes(5), environ(5), xpg4(5)

Diagnostics

no permission

> You are not the superuser and you tried to change the date.

bad conversion

> The date set is syntactically incorrect.

dc — Desk Calculator

Synopsis

/usr/bin/dc [*filename*]

Description

The dc desktop calculator is an arbitrary-precision arithmetic package. Ordinarily, it operates on decimal integers, but you can specify an input base, output base, and a number of fractional digits to be maintained. The dc command uses postfix notation (so-called reverse Polish). With postfix notation, first you type two numbers, one on each line, and then the operator. To print the results on the screen, you type the **p** command as shown in the following example.

castle% **dc**
2

```
2
+
p
4
q
castle%
```

Type **q** to exit dc.

The dc command also can accept several commands on a single line. You must delimit numbers by white space, but you can run other commands together. For example, you could write the previous example in the following way:

```
castle% dc
2 2+p
4
q
castle%
```

The dc command is stack oriented, which means that all operations take place on a single variable stack. The dc command recognizes the arithmetic operators + (addition), - (subtraction), / (division), * (multiplication), % (remainder), and ^ (exponentiation). Each of these operators pops the top two numbers off the stack, performs the operation, and pushes the result of the operation back onto the stack in place of the two numbers. You use the p (print) command to display the results. Additional special commands enable you to further control operations.

If you give a *filename* argument, dc takes input from that file until its end, then accepts further input from the standard input.

Note — bc is a preprocessor for dc. bc provides infix notation and a C-like syntax that implements functions. bc also provides reasonable control structures for programs. See bc(1).

Usage

The constructions that the dc command recognizes are listed below.

number   Push the value of *number* onto the stack. A number is an unbroken string of the digits 0-9. You can precede *number* by an underscore (_) to input a negative number. Numbers can contain decimal points.

+ - / * % ^

Add (+), subtract (-), multiply (*), divide (/), remainder (%), or exponentiate (^) the top two values onto the stack. Pop the two entries off the stack; push the result onto the stack in their place. Ignore any fractional part of an exponent.

`sx,  Sx`	Pop the top of the stack and store into a register named x, where x can be any character. If you capitalize the S, treat x as a stack and push the value onto it.
`lx,  Lx`	Push the value in register x onto the stack. The register x is not altered. All registers start with zero value. If you capitalize the L, treat register x as a stack and pop its top value onto the main stack.
`d`	Duplicate the top value onto the stack.
`p`	Print the top value onto the stack. The top value remains unchanged.
`P`	Interpret the top of the stack as an ASCII string, remove it, and print it.
`f`	Print all values onto the stack.
`q`	Exit the program. If executing a string, pop the recursion level by 2.
`Q`	Exit the program. Pop the top value onto the stack and pop the string execution level by that value.
`x`	Treat the top element of the stack as a character string and execute it as a string of dc commands.
`X`	Replace the number on the top of the stack with its scale factor.
`[...]`	Put the bracketed ASCII string onto the top of the stack.
`<x  >x  =x`	Pop the top two elements of the stack and compare. Evaluate register x if they obey the stated relation.
`v`	Replace the top element onto the stack by its square root. Take into account any existing fractional part of the argument, but otherwise ignore the scale factor.
`!`	Interpret the rest of the line as a shell command.
`c`	Pop all values onto the stack.
`i`	Pop the top value onto the stack and use as the number radix for further input.
`I`	Push the input base on the top of the stack.
`o`	Pop the top value onto the stack and use as the number radix for further output.
`O`	Push the output base on the top of the stack.
`k`	Pop the top of the stack and use that value as a nonnegative scale factor: print the appropriate number of places on output, and maintain during multiplication, division, and exponentiation. The interaction of scale factor, input base, and output base are reasonable if all are changed together.
`K`	Push the current scale factor on the top of the stack.
`z`	The stack level is pushed on the stack.
`Z`	Replace the number on the top of the stack with its length.

?	Take a line of input from the input source (usually the terminal) and execute it.
Y	Display dc debugging information.
; :	Used by bc(1) for array operations.

Examples

The following example prints the first ten values of n!. First we create a file named examples that contains the following three lines.

```
[la1+dsa*pla10>y]sy
0sa1
1yx
```

When you run the command, the first ten values of n! are displayed.

```
castle% dc examples
1
2
6
24
120
720
5040
40320
362880
3628800
```

Attributes

See attributes(5) for descriptions of the following attributes:

Attribute Type	Attribute Value
Availability	SUNWesu

See Also

bc(1), attributes(5)

Diagnostics

x is unimplemented

        x is an octal number.

out of space The free list is exhausted (too many digits).

out of stack space

        Too many pushes onto the stack (stack overflow).

empty stack Too many pops from the stack (stack underflow).

nesting depth

Too many levels of nested execution.

divide by 0 Division by zero.

sqrt of neg number

Square root of a negative number is not defined (no imaginary numbers).

exp not an integer

dc processes only integer exponentiation.

exp too big The largest exponent allowed is 999.

input base is too large

The input base x: 2<= x <= 16.

input base is too small

The input base x: 2<= x <= 16.

output base is too large

The output base must be no larger than BC_BASE_MAX.

invalid scale factor

Scale factor cannot be less than 1.

scale factor is too large

A scale factor cannot be larger than BC_SCALE_MAX.

symbol table overflow

You have specified too many variables.

invalid index

Index cannot be less than 1.

index is too large

An index cannot be larger than BC_DIM_MAX.

delta, sccs-delta — Make a Delta to an SCCS File

Synopsis

```
/usr/ccs/bin/delta [-dnps][-g sid-list | -gsid-list]
  [-m mr-list | -mmr-list][-r sid | -rsid][-y[comment]]
  s.filename...
/usr/xpg4/bin/delta [-dnps][-g sid-list | -gsid-list]
  [-m mr-list | -mmr-list][-r sid | -rsid][-y[comment]]
  s.filename...
```

Description

See `sccs-delta(1)`

deroff — Remove nroff/troff, tbl, and eqn Constructs

Synopsis

`/usr/bin/deroff [-m [m | s | l] [-w] [-i] [`*filename*`...]`

Description

`deroff` reads each of the file names in sequence; it removes all `troff(1)` requests, macro calls, backslash constructs, `eqn(1)` constructs (between `.EQ` and `.EN` lines and between delimiters), and `tbl(1)` descriptions, perhaps replacing them with white space (blanks and blank lines). Then, `deroff` writes the remainder of the file on the standard output. `deroff` follows chains of included files (`.so` and `.nx troff` commands); if a file has already been included, a `.so` naming that file is ignored and a `.nx` naming that file terminates execution.

If you specify no input file, `deroff` reads the standard input.

> **Note** — `deroff` is not a complete `troff` interpreter, so it can be confused by subtle constructs. Most such errors result in too much instead of too little output.

Options

`-mm | s | l`   You can follow the -m option with an m, s, or l. The –mm option interprets the macros so that only running text is output (that is, no text from macro lines). The –ml option forces the –mm option and also deletes lists associated with the mm macros. Note that the –ml option does not handle nested lists correctly.

`-w`   Output a word list, one word per line, and delete all other characters. In text, a word is any string that contains at least two letters and is composed of letters, digits, ampersands (&), and apostrophes (`'`); in a macro call, however, a word is a string that begins with at least two letters and contains a total of at least three letters. Delimiters are any characters other than letters, digits, apostrophes, and ampersands. Trailing apostrophes and ampersands are removed from words.

`-i`   Ignore `troff` `.so` and `.nx` commands.

Examples

The following example uses the `more` command to display the beginning lines of the `deroff.1` manual page, then uses the `deroff` command to remove formatting constructs.

```
castle% more deroff.1
'\" t
.\" @(#)deroff.1 1.26 97/01/03 SMI;
.\" Copyright 1989 AT&T
.nr X
.TH deroff 1 "14 Sep 1992"
.SH NAME
deroff \- remove nroff/troff, tbl, and eqn constructs
.SH SYNOPSIS
.B deroff
[
.B \-m
[
.B m
\||\|
.B s
\||\|
.B l
][
.B \-w
][
.B \-i
][
.IR filename \|.\|.\|.\|
]
.SH DESCRIPTION
.IX "deroff command" "" "\fLderoff\fP \(em remove \fLnroff\fP,
   \fLtroff\fP, \fLtbl\fP and \fL
eqn\fP constructs"
.IX "nroff utilities" "remove nroff/troff, tbl, and eqn constructs" ""
   "remove \fLnroff\fP, \
fLtroff\fP, \fLtbl\fP and \fLeqn\fP constructs \(em \fLderoff\fP"
.IX "troff utilities" "remove nroff/troff, tbl, and eqn constructs" ""
   "remove \fLnroff\fP, \
fLtroff\fP, \fLtbl\fP and \fLeqn\fP constructs \(em \fLderoff\fP"
.IX "tbl" "remove nroff/troff, tbl, and eqn constructs" "" "remove
   \fLnroff\fP, \fLtroff\fP,
\fLtbl\fP and \fLeqn\fP constructs \(em \fLderoff\fP"
.IX "eqn" "remove nroff/troff, tbl, and eqn constructs" "" "remove
   \fLnroff\fP, \fLtroff\fP,
\fLtbl\fP and \fLeqn\fP constructs \(em \fLderoff\fP"
.IX "document production" "remove nroff/troff, tbl, and eqn constructs"
   "" "remove \fLnroff\f
P, \fLtroff\fP, \fLtbl\fP and \fLeqn\fP constructs \(em \fLderoff\fP"
.B deroff
reads each
of the
.I filenames
in sequence
```

```
and removes all
.BR troff (1)
requests, macro calls, backslash constructs,
.BR eqn (1)
constructs
(between
.B \&.EQ
and
.SM
...
castle% deroff deroff.1

    SMI;
 Copyright  AT&T

 deroff    Sep
 NAME
deroff    remove nroff/troff, tbl, and eqn constructs
 SYNOPSIS
 deroff
[

 [

 |

 |

][

][

][
 filename
]
 DESCRIPTION
 deroff command    deroff    remove  nroff   troff   tbl  and  eqn
   constructs
 nroff utilities remove nroff/troff, tbl, and eqn constructs  remove
   nroff   troff   tbl  and  eqn  constructs    deroff
 troff utilities remove nroff/troff, tbl, and eqn constructs  remove
   nroff   troff   tbl  and  eqn  constructs    deroff
 tbl remove nroff/troff, tbl, and eqn constructs remove nroff  troff
   tbl  and  eqn  constructs    deroff
 eqn remove nroff/troff, tbl, and eqn constructs remove nroff  troff
   tbl  and  eqn  constructs    deroff
 document production remove nroff/troff, tbl, and eqn constructs remove
   nroff   troff   tbl  and  eqn  constructs    deroff
 deroff
reads each
of the
 filenames
in sequence
and removes all
```

```
    troff
requests, macro calls, backslash constructs,
 eqn
constructs
(between

and
...
```

Attributes

See attributes(5) for descriptions of the following attributes:

Attribute Type	Attribute Value
Availability	SUNWdoc

See Also

eqn(1), nroff(1), tbl(1), troff(1), attributes(5)

df — Report Number of Free Disk Blocks and Files

Synopsis

/usr/bin/df [-F *FSType*] [-abegklntV] [-o *FSType-specific-options*]
    [*directory* | *block-device* | *resource*...]
/usr/xpg4/bin/df [-F *FSType*] [-abegklnPtV] [-o *FSType-specific-options*]
    [*directory* | *block-device* | *resource*...]

Description

Use the df command to determine the amount of free space and disk space in use for mounted or unmounted file systems, directories, or mounted resources in each file system.

When you type **df** with no options or operands, df reports on all mounted file systems, as shown in the following example.

```
castle% df
/                      (/dev/dsk/c0t3d0s0 ):  119680 blocks   407239 files
/proc                  (/proc            ):       0 blocks      930 files
/dev/fd                (fd               ):       0 blocks        0 files
/tmp                   (swap             ):  252720 blocks     9771 files
/files                 (/dev/dsk/c0t0d0s2 ):  293656 blocks   236812 files
castle%
```

The columns report file-system location, device name of the file system, the number of free blocks, and number of free inodes.

To display the output in the old SunOS 4.x format, type **df** **-k** and press Return, as shown in the following example.

```
castle% df -k
Filesystem              kbytes      used    avail capacity  Mounted on
/dev/dsk/c0t3d0s0       879079    819239    58375     94%   /
/proc                        0         0        0      0%   /proc
fd                           0         0        0      0%   /dev/fd
swap                    126632       276   126356      1%   /tmp
/dev/dsk/c0t0d0s2       489702    342874   146339     71%   /files
castle%
```

The columns report file-system location, total kilobytes, used kilobytes, available kilobytes, percentage of capacity used, and mount point for local disk partitions.

directory represents a valid directory name. If you specify *directory*, df reports on the file system that contains *directory*. *block-device* represents a block special device (for example, /dev/dsk/c1d0s7); if you specify *block-device*, the corresponding file system need not be mounted. *resource* is an NFS resource name.

Options

-a	Report on all file systems including ones whose entries in /etc/mnttab (see mnttab(4)) have the ignore option set.
-b	Print the total number of kilobytes free.
-e	Print only the number of files free.
-F *FSType*	Specify the *FSType* on which to operate. You need to use this option only if the file system is unmounted. df determines the *FSType* from this option, by matching the *directory*, *block-device*, or *resource* with an entry in the /etc/vfstab table (see vfstab(4)) or by consulting /etc/default/fs. See default_fs(4). This command may not be supported for all *FSTypes*.
-g	Print the entire statvfs(2) structure. Use this option only for mounted file systems. You cannot use it with the -o option. This option overrides the -b, -e, -k, -n, -P, and -t options.
-k	Print the allocation in kilobytes. The output consists of one line of information for each specified file system. This information includes the file-system name, the total space allocated in the file system, the amount of space allocated to existing files, the total amount of space available for the creation of new files by unprivileged users, and the percentage of normally available space that is currently allocated to all files on the file system. This option overrides the -b, -e, -n, and -t options.
-l	Report on local file systems only. Use this option only for mounted file systems. You cannot use it with the -o option.

-n   Print only the *FSType* name. Invoked with no operands, this option prints a list of mounted file system types. Use this option only for mounted file systems. You cannot use it with the -o option.

-o *FSType-specific-options*

            Specify *FSType-specific-options* as a comma-separated list with no intervening spaces.

-P   Same as -k except report in 512-byte units. (/usr/xpg4/bin/df only.)

-t   Print full listings with totals. This option overrides the -b, -e, and -n options.

-V   Echo the complete set of file-system-specific command lines, but do not execute them. The command line is generated by using the options and operands provided by the user and adding to them information derived from /etc/mnttab, /etc/vfstab, or /etc/default/fs. You can use this option to verify and validate the command line.

Operands

directory   A valid directory name. df reports on the file system that contains *directory*.

block-device

            A block special device (for example, /dev/dsk/c1d0s7); the corresponding file system need not be mounted.

resource   An NFS resource name.

Usage

See largefile(5) for the description of the behavior of df when encountering files greater than or equal to 2 Gbytes (2**31 bytes).

Examples

The following example writes portable information about the /usr file system.

```
castle% /usr/xpg4/bin/df -P /usr
Filesystem            512-blocks      Used  Available Capacity  Mounted on
/dev/dsk/c0t3d0s0        1758158    1638478     116750     94%    /
```

    Assuming that /usr/src is part of the /usr file system, the following command is the same as the previous example.

```
castle% /usr/xpg4/bin/df -P /usr/src
Filesystem            512-blocks      Used  Available Capacity  Mounted on
/dev/dsk/c0t3d0s0        1758158    1638478     116750     94%    /
castle%
```

Environment Variables

SYSV3   Override the default behavior of df and provide compatibility with
         INTERACTIVE UNIX System and SCO UNIX installation
         scripts. Do not use this variable in new scripts. (It is provided for
         compatibility only.) When SYSV3 is set, any header that normally
         displays *files* now displays *nodes*.

See environ(5) for descriptions of the following environment variables that
affect the execution of df: LC_CTYPE, LC_MESSAGES, and NLSPATH.

Exit Status

0   Successful completion.

>0   An error occurred.

Files

/dev/dsk/*   Disk devices.

/etc/default/fs

         Default local file system type. Default values can be set for the
         following flags in /etc/default/fs. For example, LOCAL=ufs
         LOCAL: The default partition for a command if you specify no
         FSType.

/etc/mnttab   Mount table.

/etc/vfstab   List of default parameters for each file system.

Attributes

See attributes(5) for descriptions of the following attributes:

/usr/bin/df

Attribute Type	Attribute Value
Availability	SUNWcsu

/usr/xpg4/bin/df

Attribute Type	Attribute Value
Availability	SUNWxcu4

See Also

find(1), mount(1M), statvfs(2), default_fs(4), mnttab(4), vfstab(4),
attributes(5), environ(5), largefile(5), XPG4(5), Manual pages for the
FSType-specific modules of df.

dhcpinfo — Display Value of Parameters Received Through DHCP

Synopsis

```
/sbin/dhcpinfo [-i interface] [-n limit] tag | identifier | name
```

Description

DHCP (Dynamic Host Configuration Protocol) permits a client to establish an endpoint for communication with a network by delivering an IP address of one or more of the client's network interfaces and a "lease" on that address. Use the dhcpinfo command to print the value(s) of the parameter requested on the command line as supplied by the DHCP protocol. If the DHCP parameter implies more than one value (that is, a list of gateways), the values are printed, separated by newline characters. The parameter can be identified either by its numeric value in the DHCP protocol, by its mnemonic identifier, or by its long name. This value is intended to be used in command substitutions in the shell scripts invoked by init(1M) at system boot. init first contacts the DHCP agent daemon dhcpagent(1M) to verify that DHCP has successfully completed. When a particular interface is given with the -i option, the daemon verifies successful DHCP configuration of that specific interface; otherwise, the client verifies that the interface marked as the "primary" has successfully configured and supplies the name of that interface back to dhcpinfo. You should not use parameter values echoed by dhcpinfo without checking the exit status.

See dhcptags(4) for the list of mnemonic identifier codes and names of all DHCP parameters. See *DHCP Options and BOOTP Vendor Extensions* (RFC 2132) for more detail.

Options

-i *interface*

In general, you should need to use this option only on hardware with two or more interfaces configurable by DHCP, and for a parameter that is interface specific.

-n *limit*   When the *tag* is one with a list of values, limit the number printed.

Operands

tag   Numeric value of the parameter (or option) returned to the client by the DHCP protocol.

identifier   Mnemonic symbol of the parameter returned to the client by the DHCP protocol.

name   Long name of the parameter returned to the client by the DHCP protocol.

Exit Status

0   Successful operation.

2   DHCP was not successful. The DHCP agent may not be running, the interface might have failed to configure, or no satisfactory DHCP responses were received.

3   Bad arguments.

4   A timer was set, using wait (see ifconfig(1M)), and the interface had not configured before it expired.

6   Some system error (should never occur).

Attributes
See attributes(5) for descriptions of the following attributes:

Attribute Type	Attribute Value
Availability	SUNWcsr

See Also
dhcpagent(1M), ifconfig(1M), init(1M), dhcptags(4), attributes(5)
Alexander, S., and R. Droms, *DHCP Options and BOOTP Vendor Extensions*, RFC 2132, Silicon Graphics, Inc., Bucknell University, March 1997.

diff — Display Line-by-Line Differences Between Pairs of Text Files

Synopsis
```
/usr/bin/diff [-bitw][-c | -e | -f | -h | -n] file1 file2
/usr/bin/diff [-bitw][-C number] file1 file2
/usr/bin/diff [-bitw][-D string] file1 file2
/usr/bin/diff [-bitw][-c | -e | -f | -h | -n][-l][-r][-s]
    [-S name] file1 file2
```

Description
The diff command compares the contents of *file1* and *file2* line by line and produces a complete index of all of the lines that differ between the two

files, along with their line numbers. It also reports what must be changed to make the files match. No output is produced if the files are identical.

The following example illustrates the diff output for two simple files.

```
castle% diff kookaburra1 kookaburra2
4c4
< Gay your life must be.
---
> Glad your life must be.
castle%
```

Each section of the diff output begins with a code that indicates what kinds of differences the following lines refer to. In the previous example, the differences are marked with the code 4c4. This code tells you that there is a change (c) between line 4 in the first file and line 4 in the second file. Lines containing text found only in the first file begin with <. Lines containing text found only in the second file begin with >. The dashed line separates parts of the output that refer to different sections of the files.

The normal output contains lines of these forms:

```
n1 a n3,n4
n1,n2 d n3
n1,n2 c n3,n4
```

where $n1$ and $n2$ represent lines in *file1* and $n3$ and $n4$ represent lines in *file2*. The a (append) code indicates that a line is added following the line in the first file. The d (delete) code indicates that lines are found in one file but not in the other. The c (change) code indicates that there is a change between the lines in the two files.

These lines resemble ed(1) or vi(1) commands to convert *file1* to *file2*. By exchanging a for d and reading backward, you can convert *file2* to *file1*. As in ed, identical pairs, where $n1=n2$ or $n3=n4$, are abbreviated as a single number.

Following each of these lines come all the lines that are affected in the first file flagged by <, then all the lines that are affected in the second file flagged by >.

Note — Editing scripts produced under the -e or -f options are naive about creating lines consisting of a single period (.).

A missing newline at end-of-file indicates that the last line of the file in question did not have a newline. If the lines are different, they are flagged and output, although the output seems to indicate they are the same.

Options

-b   Ignore trailing blanks (spaces and tabs) and treat other strings of blanks as equivalent.

-i   Ignore the case of letters; for example, compare A equal to a.

-t   Expand Tab characters in output lines. Normal or -c output adds character(s) to the front of each line that may adversely affect the indentation of the original source lines and make the output lines difficult to interpret. This option preserves the original source's indentation.

-w   Ignore all blanks (space and Tab characters) and treat all other strings of blanks as equivalent; for example, if (a == b) compares equal to if(a==b).

Options for the diff command that are mutually exclusive are listed below.

-c   Produce a listing of differences with three lines of context. With this option, output format is modified slightly: output begins with identification of the files involved and their creation dates, then each change is separated by a line with a dozen asterisks. The lines removed from *file1* are marked with –; those added to *file2* are marked +. Lines that are changed from one file to the other are marked in both files with !.

-C *number*   Produce a listing of differences identical to that produced by -c with *number* lines of context.

-e   Produce a script of only a, c, and d commands for the editor ed, which recreates *file2* from *file1*. In connection with -e, the following shell program may help maintain multiple versions of a file. Only an ancestral file ($1) and a chain of version-to version ed scripts ($2,$3,...) made by diff need be on hand. A latest version appears on the standard output.

            (shift; cat $*; echo '1,$p') | ed - $1

            Except in rare circumstances, diff finds a smallest sufficient set of file differences.

-f   Produce a script similar to -e in the opposite order. Not useful with ed.

-h   Do a fast, half-hearted job. This option works only when changed stretches are short and well separated but does work on files of unlimited length. Options -c, -e, -f, and -n are unavailable with -h. diff does not descend into directories with this option.

-n   Produce a script similar to -e, but in the opposite order and with a count of changed lines on each insert or delete command.

-D *string*   Create a merged version of *file1* and *file2* with C preprocessor controls included so that a compilation of the result without defining string is equivalent to compiling *file1*, while defining *string* yields *file2*.

The following options for the diff command are used to compare directories.

-l	Produce output in long format. Before the diff, pipe each text file through pr(1) to paginate it. Remember other differences and summarize them after all text file differences are reported.
-r	Apply diff recursively to common subdirectories encountered.
-s	Report files that are the identical; these would not otherwise be mentioned.
-S name	Start a directory diff in the middle, beginning with the file *name*.

Operands

file1 *file2*	A path name of a file or directory to be compared. If either *file1* or *file2* is -, use the standard input in its place.
directory1 *directory2*	A path name of a directory to be compared.

If only one of *file1* and *file2* is a directory, diff is applied to the nondirectory file and the file contained in the directory file with a file name that is the same as the last component of the nondirectory file.

Usage

See largefile(5) for the description of the behavior of diff when encountering files greater than or equal to 2 Gbytes (2**31 bytes).

Examples

If dir1 is a directory containing a directory named x, dir2 is a directory containing a directory named x, dir1/x and dir2/x both contain files named date.out, and dir2/x contains a file named y, then the command:

```
castle% diff -r dir1 dir2
```

could produce output similar to:

```
Common subdirectories: dir1/x and dir2/x
Only in dir2/x: y
diff -r dir1/x/date.out dir2/x/date.out
1c1
< Mon Jul 2 13:12:16 PDT 1990
---
> Tue Jun 19 21:41:39 PDT 1990
```

The following example shows a comparison between two files. The test1 file was generated by the command deroff deroff.1. The test2 file was generated by the command deroff -mm deroff.1. As you can see from the diff output, the deroff -mm command dropped data from the file.

```
castle% diff test1 test2
6,10d5
<   NAME
< deroff    remove nroff/troff, tbl, and eqn constructs
<   SYNOPSIS
<   deroff
<   [
25,26d19
<   DESCRIPTION
<   deroff command    deroff    remove   nroff    troff    tbl   and   eqn
  constructs
72,73d64
<   OPTIONS
<
140,141d130
<   ATTRIBUTES
< See
145,149d133
< ATTRIBUTE TYPE           ATTRIBUTE VALUE
< =
< Availability  SUNWdoc
<   SEE ALSO
<   eqn
154,160d137
<   NOTES
<   deroff
< is not a complete
<   troff
< interpreter,
< so it can be confused by subtle constructs.
< Most such errors result in too much rather than too little output.
castle%
```

Environment Variables

See environ(5) for descriptions of the following environment variables that affect the execution of diff: LC_CTYPE, LC_MESSAGES, LC_TIME, and NLSPATH.

TZ	Determine the locale for affecting the time zone used for calculating file timestamps written with the -C and -c options.

Exit Status

0	No differences were found.
1	Differences were found.
>1	An error occurred.

Files

/tmp/d?????

    Temporary file used for comparison.

/usr/lib/diffh

    Executable file for -h option.

Attributes

See attributes(5) for descriptions of the following attributes:

Attribute Type	Attribute Value
Availability	SUNWesu
CSI	Enabled

See Also

bdiff(1), cmp(1), comm(1), dircmp(1), ed(1), pr(1), sdiff(1), attributes(5), environ(5), largefile(5)

diff3 — Three-Way Differential File Comparison

Synopsis

/usr/bin/diff3 [-exEX3] *filename1 filename2 filename3*

Description

diff3 compares three versions of a file and publishes disagreeing ranges of text flagged with these codes:

====	All three files differ.
====1	*filename1* is different.
====2	*filename2* is different.
====3	*filename3* is different.

    The type of change in converting a given range of a given file to some other is indicated in one of these ways:

f : n1 a   Text is to be appended after line number n1 in file *f*, where *f* = 1, 2, or 3.

f : n1 , n2 c

    Text is to be changed in the range line n1 to line n2. If n1 = n2, the range may be abbreviated to n1.

The original contents of the range follow immediately after a c (change) indication. When the contents of two files are identical, the contents of the lower-numbered file are suppressed.

The following command applies the resulting script to *filename1*.

```
(cat script; echo '1,$p') | ed - filename1
```

> **Note** — Text lines that consist of a single dot (.) defeat -e. Files longer than 64 Kbytes do not work.

Options

-e
Produce a script for the editor ed(1) that incorporates into *filename1* all changes between *filename2* and *filename3*, that is, the changes that normally would be flagged ==== and ====3.

-x
Produce a script to incorporate only changes flagged ====.

-3
Produce a script to incorporate only changes flagged ====3.

-E
Produce a script that incorporates all changes between *filename2* and *filename3*, but treat overlapping changes (that is, changes that would be flagged with ==== in the normal listing) differently. The overlapping lines from both files are inserted by the edit script, bracketed by <<<<<< and >>>>>> lines.

-X
Produce a script that incorporates only changes flagged ====, but treat these changes in the manner of the -E option.

Examples

The following example compares three files. The test1 file was generated by the command deroff deroff.1. The test2 file was generated by the command deroff -mm deroff.1. The test3 file was generated by the command deroff -ml deroff.1.

```
castle% diff3 test1 test2 test3
====1
1:6,10c
  NAME
  deroff     remove nroff/troff, tbl, and eqn constructs
  SYNOPSIS
  deroff
  [
2:5a
3:5a
====1
1:25,26c
  DESCRIPTION
  deroff command     deroff     remove nroff  troff  tbl  and  eqn
  constructs
2:19a
3:19a
```

```
====1
1:72,73c
    OPTIONS

2:64a
3:64a
====1
1:140,141c
    ATTRIBUTES
  See
2:130a
3:130a
====1
1:145,149c
  ATTRIBUTE TYPE          ATTRIBUTE VALUE
  =
  Availability  SUNWdoc
    SEE ALSO
    eqn
2:133a
3:133a
====1
1:154,160c
    NOTES
  deroff
  is not a complete
   troff
  interpreter,
  so it can be confused by subtle constructs.
  Most such errors result in too much rather than too little output.
2:137a
3:137a
castle%
```

Usage

See largefile(5) for the description of the behavior of diff3 when encountering files greater than or equal to 2 Gbytes (2**31 bytes).

Files

/tmp/d3*

/usr/lib/diff3prog

Attributes

See attributes(5) for descriptions of the following attributes:

Attribute Type	Attribute Value
Availability	SUNWesu
CSI	Enabled

See Also

diff(1), attributes(5), largefile(5)

diffmk — Mark Differences Between Versions of a troff Input File

Synopsis

/usr/bin/diffmk *oldfile newfile markedfile*

Description

diffmk compares two versions of a file and creates a third version that includes "change mark" (.mc) commands for nroff(1) and troff(1). *oldfile* and *newfile* are the old and new versions of the file. diffmk generates *markedfile*, which contains the text from *newfile* with troff(1) "change mark" requests (.mc) inserted where *newfile* differs from *oldfile*. Formatted, changed, or inserted text in *markedfile* shows a | at the right margin of each line. The position of deleted text is shown by a single *.

Usage

See largefile(5) for the description of the behavior of diffmk when encountering files greater than or equal to 2 Gbytes (2**31 bytes).

Examples

You can also use diffmk in conjunction with the proper troff requests to produce program listings with marked changes. In the command line

castle% **diffmk old.c new.c marked.c ; nroff reqs marked.c | pr**

the file reqs contains the following troff requests that eliminate page breaks, adjust the line length, set no-fill mode, ignore escape characters, and turn off hyphenation.

```
.pl 1
.ll 77
```

```
.nf
.eo
.nh
```

If the characters | and * are inappropriate, you might run `markedfile` through sed(1) to globally change them.

Attributes

See `attributes`(5) for descriptions of the following attributes:

Attribute Type	Attribute Value
Availability	SUNWdoc

See Also

`diff(1), nroff(1), sed(1), troff(1), attributes(5), largefile(5)`

Bugs

Aesthetic considerations may dictate manual adjustment of some output. File differences involving only formatting requests may produce undesirable output, that is, replacing `.sp` by `.sp 2` produces a "change mark" on the preceding or following line of output.

dircmp — Directory Comparison

Synopsis

`/usr/bin/dircmp [-ds][-w n] dir1 dir2`

Description

The `dircmp` command compares the contents of two directory structures. It reports on the files from only one directory and uses the `cmp` command to compare the files that appear in both directories. If you want the output to be generated in `diff` format, specify the `-d` option. If you specify no options, `dircmp` generates a list indicating whether the file names common to both directories have the same contents.

Options

-d   Compare the contents of files with the same name in both directories and output a list telling what must be changed in the two files to bring them into agreement. The list format is described in diff(1).

-s   Suppress messages about identical files.

-w *n*   Change the width of the output line to *n* characters. The default width is 72.

Operands

dir1   A path name of directories to be compared.
dir2

Examples

The following example compares the contents of the two directories /export/home/winsor/Audiofiles and /usr/demo/SOUND/sounds.

```
castle% dircmp /export/home/winsor/Audiofiles/ /usr/demo/SOUND/sounds

Jan  8 17:13 1999  /export/home/winsor/Audiofiles/ only and
  /usr/demo/SOUND/sounds only Page 1

./Audiotest
./Audiotest/mydata.au
./Audiotest/outfile.au
./file1

Jan  8 17:13 1999  Comparison of /export/home/winsor/Audiofiles/
  /usr/demo/SOUND/sounds Page 1

directory         .
same              ./bark.au
same              ./bong.au
same              ./bubbles.au
same              ./busy.au
...
castle%
```

Note — The dircmp file generated quite a few extra linefeeds, which have been removed from this example along with a number of the files that were marked same.

Usage

See largefile(5) for the description of the behavior of dircmp when encountering files greater than or equal to 2 Gbytes (2**31 bytes).

Environment Variables

See environ(5) for descriptions of the following environment variables that affect the execution of dircmp: LC_COLLATE, LC_CTYPE, LC_MESSAGES, and NLSPATH.

Exit Status

0	Successful completion.
>0	An error occurred. (Differences in directory contents are not considered errors.)

Attributes

See attributes(5) for descriptions of the following attributes:

Attribute Type	Attribute Value
Availability	SUNWesu

See Also

cmp(1), diff(1), attributes(5), environ(5), largefile(5)

dirname — Deliver Portions of Path Names

Synopsis

/usr/bin/dirname *string*

Description

See basename(1).

dirs — Change Working Directory

Synopsis

csh
dirs [-l]

Description

See cd(1).

dis — Object Code Disassembler

Synopsis

```
/usr/ccs/bin/dis [-C][-o][-V][-L][-d sec][-D sec]
    [-F function][-l string][-t sec] file ...
```

Description

The dis command produces an assembly language listing of *file*, which may
be an object file or an archive of object files. The listing includes assembly
statements and an octal or hexadecimal representation of the binary that
produced those statements.

Options

The options are interpreted by the disassembler. You can specify them in any
order.

-C	Display demangled C++ symbol names in the disassembly.
-d *sec*	Disassemble the named section as data, printing the offset of the data from the beginning of the section.
-D *sec*	Disassemble the named section as data, printing the actual address of the data.
-F *function*	Disassemble only the named function in each object file specified on the command line. You can specify the -F option multiple times on the command line.
-l *string*	Disassemble the archive file specified by *string*. For example, you would issue the command dis -l x -l z to disassemble libx.a and libz.a, which are assumed to be in LIB-DIR.
-L	Invoke a lookup of C-language source labels in the symbol table for subsequent writing to standard output.
-o	Print numbers in octal. The default is hexadecimal.
-t *sec*	Disassemble the named section as text.
-V	Print, on standard error, the version number of the disassembler being executed.

If you specify the -d, -D, or -t options, only those named sections from each
user-supplied file are disassembled. Otherwise, all sections containing text are
disassembled.

On output, a number enclosed in brackets, such as [5], at the beginning of
a line indicates that the break-pointable line number starts with the following
instruction. These line numbers are printed only if the file was compiled with
additional debugging information, for example, the -g option of cc(1B). An
expression such as <40> in the operand field or in the symbolic disassembly,

following a relative displacement for control transfer instructions, is the computed address within the section to which control is transferred. A function name is displayed in the first column, followed by () if the object file contains a symbol table.

Operands

file   A path name of an object file or an archive (see ar(1)) of object files.

Environment Variables

See environ(5) for descriptions of the following environment variables that affect the execution of dis: LC_CTYPE, LC_MESSAGES, and NLSPATH.

New!   LIBDIR   Use this as the path to search for the library. If the variable contains a null value or is not set, search for the library under /usr/lib.

Exit Status

0   Successful completion.

>0   An error occurred.

Files

New!   /usr/lib   Default LIBDIR.

Attributes

See attributes(5) for descriptions of the following attributes:

Attribute Type	Attribute Value
Availability	SUNWbtool

See Also

ar(1), as(1), ld(1), cc(1B), a.out(4), attributes(5), environ(5)

Diagnostics

The self-explanatory diagnostics indicate errors in the command line or problems encountered with the specified files.

---

disable — Disable LP Printers

Synopsis

```
/usr/bin/disable [-c | -W][-r [reason]] printer...
```

Description

See enable(1).

---

dispgid — Display a List of All Valid Group Names

Synopsis

```
/usr/bin/dispgid
```

Description

dispgid displays a list of all group names on the system (one group per line).

Examples

The following example displays the group names for the system castle.

```
castle% dispgid
root
other
bin
sys
adm
uucp
mail
tty
lp
nuucp
staff
daemon
sysadmin
nobody
noaccess
nogroup
castle%
```

Exit Status

0	Successful execution.
1	Cannot read the group file.

Attributes

See `attributes`(5) for descriptions of the following attributes:

Attribute Type	Attribute Value
Availability	SUNWcsu

See Also

`attributes(5)`

dispuid — Display a List of All Valid User Names

Synopsis

`/usr/bin/dispuid`

Description

`dispuid` displays a list of all user names on the system (one line per name).

Examples

The following example displays the user names for the system `castle`.

```
castle% dispuid
root
daemon
bin
sys
adm
lp
smtp
uucp
nuucp
listen
nobody
noaccess
nobody4
winsor
ray
des
rob
castle%
```

Exit Status

0	Successful execution.
1	Cannot read the password file.

Attributes

See attributes(5) for descriptions of the following attributes:

Attribute Type	Attribute Value
Availability	SUNWcsu

See Also

attributes(5)

dos2unix — Convert Text File from DOS Format to ISO Format

Synopsis

/usr/bin/dos2unix [-ascii][-iso][-7] *originalfile convertedfile*

Description

dos2unix converts characters in the DOS extended character set to the corresponding ISO standard characters.

You can invoke this command from either DOS or SunOS. However, the file names must conform to the conventions of the environment in which you invoke the command.

If *originalfile* and *convertedfile* are the same, dos2unix rewrites the original file after converting it.

Options

-ascii	Remove extra Returns and convert end-of-file characters in DOS format text files to conform to SunOS requirements.
-iso	Convert characters in the DOS extended character set to the corresponding ISO standard characters (the default).
-7	Convert 8-bit DOS graphics characters to 7-bit space characters so that SunOS can read the file.

Attributes

See `attributes`(5) for descriptions of the following attributes:

Attribute Type	Attribute Value
Availability	SUNWesu

See Also

`unix2dos(1), attributes(5)`

Diagnostics

`File filename not found, or no read permission`

> The input file you specified does not exist, or you do not have read permission (check with the SunOS `ls -l` command).

`Bad output filename filename, or no write permission`

> The output file you specified is either invalid, or you do not have write permission for that file or the directory that contains it.
>
> Check also that the drive or diskette is not write protected.

`Error while writing to temporary file`

> An error occurred while converting your file, possibly because there is not enough space on the current drive. Check the amount of space on the current drive, using the `DIR` command. Also be certain that the default diskette or drive is write enabled (not write protected). Note that when this error occurs, the original file remains intact.

`Could not rename temporary file to filename`

`Translated temporary file name = filename`

> The command could not perform the final step in converting your file. Your converted file is stored under the name indicated on the second line of this message.

download — Download Host-Resident PostScript Font

Synopsis

```
/usr/lib/lp/postscript/download [-f][-p printer][-m name]
    [-H directory][file...]
/usr/lib/lp/postscript/download
```

Description

`download` prepends host-resident fonts to files and writes the results on the standard output. If you specify no files or if - is one of the input files, `download` reads the standard input. `download` assumes the input files make up a single PostScript job and that requested fonts can be included at the start of each input file.

Requested fonts are named in a comment (marked with `%%DocumentFonts:`) in the input files. Available fonts are the ones listed in the map table selected with the `-m` option.

The map table consists of fontname-file pairs. The fontname is the full name of the PostScript font, exactly as it would appear in a `%%DocumentFonts:` comment. The file is the path name of the host-resident font. A file that begins with a `/` is used as is. Otherwise, the path name is relative to the host font directory. Comments are introduced by `%` (as in PostScript) and extend to the end of the line.

The only candidates for downloading are fonts listed in the map table that points `download` to readable files. A font is downloaded once, at most. Requests for unlisted fonts or inaccessible files are ignored. All requests are ignored if the map table cannot be read.

Note — `download` does not look for `%%PageFonts:` comments and there is no way to force multiple downloads of a particular font.

Using full path names in either map tables or the names of map tables is not recommended.

Options

`-f`	Force a complete scan of each input file. In the absence of an explicit comment pointing `download` to the end of the file, stop the default scan immediately after the PostScript header comments.
`-p printer`	
	Check the list of printer-resident fonts in `/etc/lp/printers/printer/residentfonts` before downloading.

-m *name*   Use *name* as the font map table. A name that begins with / is the full path name of the map table and is used as is. Otherwise, *name* is appended to the path name of the host font directory.

-H *directory*

Use *directory* as the host font directory. The default is /usr/lib/lp/postscript.

Examples

You could use the following map table to control the downloading of the Bookman font family:

```
%
% The first string is the full PostScript font name. The second string
% is the file name - relative to the host font directory unless it begins
% with a /.
%

Bookman-Light          bookman/light
Bookman-LightItalic    bookman/lightitalic
Bookman-Demi           bookman/demi
Bookman-DemiItalic     bookman/demiitalic
```

Using the file myprinter/map (in the default host font directory) as the map table, you could download fonts by issuing the following command.

castle% **download -m myprinter/map file**

Exit Status

0   Successful completion.

non-zero   An error occurred.

Attributes

See attributes(5) for descriptions of the following attributes:

Attribute Type	Attribute Value
Availability	SUNWpsf

See Also

dpost(1), postdaisy(1), postdmd(1), postio(1), postmd(1), postprint(1), posttek(1), attributes(5)

dpost — troff Postprocessor for PostScript Printers

Synopsis

```
/usr/lib/lp/postscript/dpost  [-c num][-e num][-m num][-n num]
    [-o list][-p mode][-w num]  -x num][-y num][-F dir][-H dir]
    [-L file][-O][-T name][file...]
/usr/lib/lp/postscript/dpost
```

Description

dpost translates files created by troff(1) into PostScript and writes the results on the standard output. If you specify no files or if - is one of the input files, the standard input is read.

The files should be prepared by troff. The default font files in /usr/lib/font/devpost produce the best and most efficient output. They assume a resolution of 720 dpi, and you can use them to format files by adding the -Tpost option to the troff call. Older versions of the eqn and pic preprocessors need to know the resolution that troff is using to format the files. If those are the versions installed on your system, use the -r720 option with eqn and -T720 with pic.

dpost makes no assumptions about resolutions. The first x res command sets the resolution used to translate the input files, the DESC.out file, usually /usr/lib/font/devpost/DESC.out, defines the resolution used in the binary font files, and the PostScript prologue is responsible for setting up an appropriate user coordinate system.

Output files often do not conform to the file structuring conventions of Adobe. Piping the output of dpost through postreverse(1) should produce a minimally conforming PostScript file.

Although dpost can handle files formatted for any device, emulation is expensive and can easily double the print time and the size of the output file. No attempt has been made to implement the character sets or fonts available on all devices supported by troff. Missing characters are replaced by white space, and unrecognized fonts usually default to one of the Times fonts (that is, R, I, B, or BI).

An x res command must precede the first x init command, and all the input files should have been prepared for the same output device.

Note — Use of the -T option is not encouraged. Its only purpose is to enable the use of other PostScript font and device description files that, perhaps, use different resolutions, character sets, or fonts.

Although level 0 encoding is the only scheme that has been thoroughly tested, level 2 is fast and may be worth a try.

Options

-c *num*	Print *num* copies of each page. By default, only one copy is printed.
-e *num*	Set the text encoding level to *num*. The recognized values are 0, 1, and 2. The size of the output file and print time should decrease as *num* increases. Level 2 encoding typically is about 20 percent faster than level 0 (the default) and produces output essentially identical to previous versions of dpost.
-m *num*	Magnify each logical page by the factor *num*. Scale pages uniformly about the origin, which is located near the upper-left corner of each page. The default magnification is 1.0.
-n *num*	Print *num* logical pages on each piece of paper, where *num* can be any positive integer. By default, *num* is set to 1.
-o *list*	Print those pages for which numbers are given in the comma-separated list. The list contains single numbers *N* and ranges *N1*-*N2*. A missing *N1* means the lowest numbered page, a missing *N2* means the highest. The page range is an expression of logical pages instead of physical sheets of paper. For example, if you are printing two logical pages to a sheet and you specify a range of 4, then two sheets of paper print, containing four page layouts. If you specified a page range of 3-4 when requesting two logical pages to a sheet, then only page 3 and page 4 layouts print on one physical sheet of paper.
-p *mode*	Print files in either p (portrait) or l (landscape) mode. Only the first character of *mode* is significant. The default mode is portrait.
-w *num*	Set the line width used to implement troff graphics commands to *num* points, where a point is approximately 1/72 of an inch. By default, *num* is set to 0.3 points.
-x *num*	Translate the origin *num* inches along the positive x axis. The default coordinate system has the origin fixed near the upper-left corner of the page, with positive x to the right and positive y down the page. Positive *num* moves everything right. The default offset is 0 inches.
-y *num*	Translate the origin *num* inches along the positive y axis. Positive *num* moves text up the page. The default offset is 0.
-F *dir*	Use *dir* as the font directory. The default *dir* is /usr/lib/font, and dpost reads binary font files from directory /usr/lib/font/devpost.
-H *dir*	Use *dir* as the host-resident font directory. Files in this directory should be complete PostScript font descriptions. They must be assigned a name that corresponds to the appropriate two-character troff font name. Each font file is copied to the output file only when needed and at most once during each job. There is no default directory.

-L *file*	Use *file* as the PostScript prologue. The default is /usr/lib/lp/postscript/dpost.ps.
-O	Disable PostScript picture inclusion. A recommended option when running dpost by a spooler in a networked environment.
-T *name*	Use font files for device *name* as the best description of available PostScript fonts. By default, *name* is set to post, and dpost reads binary files from /usr/lib/font/devpost.

Examples

If the old versions of eqn and pic are installed on your system, you can obtain the best-looking output possible by issuing a command such as the following.

```
castle% pic -T720 file | tbl | eqn -r720 | troff -mm -Tpost | dpost
```

Otherwise, the following command should give the best results.

```
castle% pic file | tbl | eqn | troff -mm -Tpost | dpost
```

Exit Status

0	Successful completion.
non-zero	An error occurred.

Files

/usr/lib/font/devpost/*.out

/usr/lib/font/devpost/charlib/*

/usr/lib/lp/postscript/color.ps

/usr/lib/lp/postscript/draw.ps

/usr/lib/lp/postscript/forms.ps

usr/lib/lp/postscript/ps.requests

/usr/lib/macros/pictures

/usr/lib/macros/color

Attributes

See attributes(5) for descriptions of the following attributes:

Attribute Type	Attribute Value
Availability	SUNWpsf

See Also

download(1), postdaisy(1), postdmd(1), postio(1), postmd(1), postprint(1), postreverse(1), posttek(1), troff(1), attributes(5)

du — Summarize Disk Usage

Synopsis

```
/usr/ucb/du
/usr/ucb/du [-a][-s][filename]
```

Description

The /usr/ucb/du command, provided for BSD compatibility, displays the number of kilobytes contained in all files and, recursively, directories within each specified directory or file name. If you do not specify *filename*, then the current directory (.) is used.

A file that has multiple links is counted only once.

Entries are generated only for each directory in the absence of options. Unless you use the -a option, *filename* arguments that are not directory names are ignored.

Note — If there are too many distinct linked files, du counts the excess files more than once.

Options

-a   Generate an entry for each file.

-s   Display only the grand total for each of the specified file names.

Examples

The following example uses the pwd command to identify the directory, then uses the du command to show the usage of all the subdirectories in that directory. The grand total for the directory, in kilobytes, is the last entry.

```
castle% pwd
/export/home/winsor/Misc
castle% du
5      ./Jokes
33     ./Squash
44     ./Tech.papers/lpr.document
217    ./Tech.papers/new.manager
401    ./Tech.papers
144    ./Memos
80     ./Letters
388    ./Window
93     ./Messages
15     ./Useful.news
1211   .
castle%
```

Environment Variables

If any of the LC_* variables (LC_CTYPE, LC_MESSAGES, LC_TIME, LC_COLLATE, LC_NUMERIC, and LC_MONETARY) (see environ(5)) are not set in the environment, the operational behavior of du for each corresponding locale category is determined by the value of the LANG environment variable. If LC_ALL is set, its contents are used to override both the LANG and the other LC_* variables. If none of the above variables are set in the environment, the C (U.S. style) locale determines how du behaves.

LC_CTYPE   Determine how du handles characters. When LC_CTYPE is set to a valid value, du can display and handle text and file names containing valid characters for that locale. du can display and handle Extended UNIX Code (EUC) characters where any individual character can be 1, 2, or 3 bytes wide. du can also handle EUC characters of 1, 2, or more column widths. In the C locale, only characters from ISO 8859-1 are valid.

LC_MESSAGES

Determine how diagnostic and informative messages are presented, including the language and style of the messages, and the correct form of affirmative and negative responses. In the C locale, the messages are presented in the default form found in the program itself (in most cases, U.S. English).

Attributes

See attributes(5) for descriptions of the following attributes:

Attribute Type	Attribute Value
Availability	SUNWscpu

See Also

pwd(1), df(1M), quot(1M), attributes(5), environ(5)

---

dumbplot — Graphics Filters for Various Plotters

Synopsis

/usr/ucb/plot [-Tterminal]

Description

See plot(1).

dump — Dump Selected Parts of an Object File for Shell Scripts

Synopsis

```
/usr/ccs/bin/dump [-aCcDfghLlorstV][-T index [, indexn]]
    filename ...
/usr/ccs/bin/dump [-afhorstL [v]] filename ...
/usr/ccs/bin/dump [-hsr [-d number [, numbern]]] filename ...
/usr/ccs/bin/dump [-hsrt [-n name]] filename ...
```

Description

The dump command dumps selected parts of each of its object file arguments to the standard output.

New!   The dump command is best suited for use in shell scripts. The elfdump(1) command is recommended for more human-readable output.

Options

The dump command accepts both object files and archives of object files. It processes each file argument according to one or more of the options listed below.

-a	Dump the archive header of each member of an archive.
-c	Dump the string table(s).
-C	Dump decoded C++ symbol table names.
-D	Dump debugging information.
-f	Dump each file header.
-g	Dump the global symbols in the symbol table of an archive.
-h	Dump the section headers.
-l	Dump line number information.
-L	Dump dynamic linking information and static shared library information if available.
-o	Dump each program execution header.
-r	Dump relocation information.
-s	Dump section contents in hexadecimal.
-t	Dump symbol table entries.
-T index -T index1, index2	
	Dump only the indexed symbol table entry defined by index or a range of entries defined by index1, index2.
-V	Print version information.

You can use the following modifiers to modify the capabilities of the options listed above.

Modifier   **Description**

`-d` *number*
`-d` *number1, number2*

Dump the section number indicated by *number* or the range of sections starting at *number1* and ending at *number2*. You can use this modifier with `-h`, `-s`, and `-r`. When you use `-d` with `-h` or `-s`, treat the argument as the number of a section or range of sections. When you use `-d` with `-r`, treat the argument as the number of the section or range of sections to which the relocation applies. For example, to print out all relocation entries associated with the `.text` section, specify the number of the section as the argument to `-d`. If `.text` is section number 2 in the file, `dump -r -d 2` prints all associated entries. To print out a specific relocation section, use `dump -s -n` *name* for raw data output or `dump -sv -n` *name* for interpreted output.

`-n` *name*   Dump information pertaining only to the named entity. You can use this modifier with `-h`, `-s`, `-r`, and `-t`. When you use `-n` with `-h` or `-s`, treat the argument as the name of a section. When you use `-n` with `-t` or `-r`, treat the argument as the name of a symbol. For example, `dump -t -n .text` dumps the symbol table entry associated with the symbol whose name is `.text`, where `dump -h -n .text` dumps the section header information for the `.text` section.

`-p`   Suppress printing of the headings.

`-v`   Dump information in symbolic representation instead of numeric. You can use this modifier with the following options.
                   `-a`   (date, user ID, group ID).
                   `-f`   (class, data, type, machine, version, flags).
                   `-h`   (type, flags).
                   `-o`   (type, flags).
                   `-r`   (name, type).
                   `-s`   (interpret section contents wherever possible).
                   `-t`   (type, bind).
                   `-L`   (value).
                   When you use `-v` with `-s`, all sections that can be interpreted, such as the string table or symbol table, are interpreted. For example, `dump -sv -n .symtab` *filename*... produces the same formatted output as `dump -tv` *filename*..., but `dump -s -n .symtab` *filename*... prints raw data in hexadecimal. Without additional modifiers, `dump -sv` *filename*... dumps all sections in the files, interpreting all those that it can and dumping the rest (such as `.text` or `.data`) as raw data.

The dump command tries to format the information it dumps in a meaningful way, printing certain information in character, hexadecimal, octal, or decimal representation as appropriate.

Examples

The following example shows the first few lines of the section header information for the zipinfo command.

```
castle% /usr/ccs/bin/dump -h /bin/zipinfo

/bin/zipinfo:


        **** SECTION HEADER TABLE ****
[No]    Type    Flags   Addr        Offset      Size        Name
        Link    Info    Adralgn     Entsize

[1]     1       2       0x100d4     0xd4        0x11        .interp
        0       0       0x1         0

[2]     5       2       0x100e8     0xe8        0x64c       .hash
        3       0       0x4         0x4

[3]     11      2       0x10734     0x734       0xbe0       .dynsym
        4       28      0x4         0x10

[4]     3       2       0x11314     0x1314      0xc25       .dynstr
        0       0       0x1         0

[5]     1879048190      2           0x11f3c     0x1f3c      0x20
    .SUNW_version
        4       1       0x4         0
...
```

For contrast, the following example shows the first few lines of the output from the elfdump command for the zipinfo command.

```
castle% /usr/ccs/bin/elfdump -c /bin/zipinfo

Section Header[1]:   sh_name:  .interp
        sh_addr:        0x100d4         sh_flags:     [ SHF_ALLOC ]
        sh_size:        0x11            sh_type:      [ SHT_PROGBITS ]
        sh_offset:      0xd4            sh_entsize: 0
        sh_link:        0               sh_info:      0
        sh_addralign: 0x1

Section Header[2]:   sh_name:  .hash
        sh_addr:        0x100e8         sh_flags:     [ SHF_ALLOC ]
        sh_size:        0x64c           sh_type:      [ SHT_HASH ]
        sh_offset:      0xe8            sh_entsize: 0x4
        sh_link:        3               sh_info:      0
        sh_addralign: 0x4

Section Header[3]:   sh_name:  .dynsym
        sh_addr:        0x10734         sh_flags:     [ SHF_ALLOC ]
```

```
      sh_size:        0xbe0              sh_type:     [ SHT_DYNSYM ]
      sh_offset:      0x734             sh_entsize: 0x10
      sh_link:        4                 sh_info:     28
      sh_addralign: 0x4
...
```

The following example displays the program execution headers for the
zipinfo command.

castle% **/usr/ccs/bin/dump -o /bin/zipinfo**

```
/bin/zipinfo:
 ***** PROGRAM EXECUTION HEADER *****
 Type          Offset        Vaddr        Paddr
 Filesz        Memsz         Flags        Align

 6             0x34          0x10034      0
 0xa0          0xa0          5            0

 3             0xd4          0            0
 0x11          0            4            0

 1             0             0x10000      0
 0x14a5a       0x14a5a       5            0x10000

 1             0x14a5c       0x34a5c      0
 0x4460        0x11858       7            0x10000

 2             0x14d34       0x34d34      0
 0xa8          0            7            0

 castle%
```

Attributes

See attributes(5) for descriptions of the following attributes:

Attribute Type	Attribute Value
Availability	SUNWbtool

See Also

elfdump(1), nm(1), a.out(4), ar(4), attributes(5)

New!

dumpcs — Show Codeset Table for the Current Locale

Synopsis

```
/usr/bin/dumpcs [-0123vw]
```

Description

dumpcs displays a list of printable characters for the user's current locale, along with their hexadecimal code values. The display device is assumed to be capable of displaying characters for a given locale. With no option, dumpcs displays the entire list of printable characters for the current locale.

With one or more numeric options specified, dumpcs shows EUC codeset(s) for the current locale according to the numbers specified, and in order of codeset number. Each nonprintable character is represented by an asterisk (*) and enough ASCII space character(s) to fill that codeset's column width.

Note — dumpcs can handle only EUC locales.

Options

-0	Show ASCII (or EUC primary) codeset.
-1	Show EUC codeset 1 if used for the current locale.
-2	Show EUC codeset 2 if used for the current locale.
-3	Show EUC codeset 3 if used for the current locale.
-v	Verbose. Normally, ranges of nonprintable characters are collapsed into a single line. This option produces one line for each nonprintable character.
-w	Replace code values with corresponding wide character values (process codes).

Examples

The following example first uses the dumpcs command with no arguments, then uses the -0 option. Notice that the output from these two commands is identical.

```
castle% dumpcs
: : : : : : : : : : : : : :
LC_CTYPE:C CS:0
: : : : : : : : : : : : : :
20    ! " # $ % & ' ( ) * + , - . / 0 1 2 3 4 5 6 7 8 9 : ; < = > ?
40  @ A B C D E F G H I J K L M N O P Q R S T U V W X Y Z [ \ ] ^ _
60  ` a b c d e f g h i j k l m n o p q r s t u v w x y z { | } ~*
: : : : : : : : : : : : : :
LC_CTYPE:C CS:1
```

```
: : : : : : : : : : : : : : : :
*
castle% dumpcs -0
: : : : : : : : : : : : : : : :
LC_CTYPE:C CS:0
: : : : : : : : : : : : : : : :
20    ! " # $ % & ' ( ) * + , - . / 0 1 2 3 4 5 6 7 8 9 : ; < = > ?
40    @ A B C D E F G H I J K L M N O P Q R S T U V W X Y Z [ \ ] ^ _
60    ` a b c d e f g h i j k l m n o p q r s t u v w x y z { | } ~*
castle% dumpcs -1
: : : : : : : : : : : : : : : :
LC_CTYPE:C CS:1
: : : : : : : : : : : : : : : :
*
castle%
```

Environment Variables

The environment variables LC_CTYPE and LANG control the character classification throughout dumpcs. On entry to dumpcs, these environment variables are checked in that order, which means that a new setting for LANG does not override the setting of LC_CTYPE. When none of the values are valid, the character classification defaults to the POSIX.1 C locale.

Attributes

See attributes(5) for descriptions of the following attributes:

Attribute Type	Attribute Value
Availability	SUNWcsu

See Also

localedef(1), attributes(5)

dumpkeys — Dump Keyboard Translation Tables

Synopsis

/usr/bin/dumpkeys

Description

See loadkeys(1).

E

---

echo — Write Arguments to Standard Output

Synopsis

```
/usr/bin/echo [string...]
/usr/ucb/echo [-n] [string...]
```

Description

The echo command writes its arguments, separated by blanks and terminated by a newline, to the standard output. If you provide no arguments, only the newline character is written.

echo is useful for producing diagnostics in command files, sending known data into a pipe, and displaying the contents of environment variables.

Note — The C shell, the Korn shell, and the Bourne shell all have echo built-in commands, which, by default, are invoked if you call echo without a full path name. See shell_builtins(1).

Options

/usr/ucb/echo

-n   Do not add the newline to the output.

> **Note** — The -n option is provided for transition for BSD applications and may not be supported in future releases.

The Korn shell's echo command does not have a -n option to suppress displaying the terminating newline. /usr/bin/echo and the Bourne shell echo command have a -n option only if the SYSV3 environment variable is set. If it is, none of the backslashed characters are available. On the other hand, /usr/ucb/echo and the C shell echo command have a -n option but do not understand the backslash escape characters.

Operands

string	A string to be written to standard output. For /usr/bin/echo, if any operand is -n, it is treated as a string, not an option.

/usr/bin/echo
The following character sequences are recognized within any of the arguments:

\a	Alert character.
\b	Backspace.
\c	Print line without newline.
\f	Formfeed.
\n	Newline.
\r	Return.
\t	Tab.
\v	Vertical tab.
\\	Backslash.
\0*n*	Where *n* is the 8-bit character whose ASCII code is the 1-, 2- or 3-digit octal number representing that character.

> **Note** — /usr/bin/echo and the Korn and Bourne shell built-in echo commands understand the backslash escape characters, except that the Bourne shell echo command does not recognize \a as the alert character.

When an 8-bit character is represented by the escape convention \0*n*, the *n* must always be preceded by the digit zero (0).

For example, the following command prints the phrase WARNING: and sounds the bell on your terminal.

```
$ echo 'WARNING:\07'
WARNING:
$
```

The single (or double) quotes (or two backslashes) are required to protect the backslash that precedes the 07.

Following the \0, you can use up to three digits in constructing the octal output character. If, following the \0n, you want to echo additional digits that are not part of the octal representation, you must use the full 3-digit n. For example, if you want to echo ESC 7, you must use the three digits 033 instead of just the two digits 33 after the \0.

The following example shows that using only two digits is incorrect.

```
$ echo "\0337" | od -xc
0000000    df0a
          337  \n
0000002
$
```

The following example shows that the 3-digit syntax produces the correct results.

```
$ echo "\00337" | od -xc
0000000    1b37    0a00
          033   7  \n
0000003
$
```

For the octal equivalents of each character, see ascii(5).

Usage

Portable applications should not use -n (as the first argument) or escape sequences. The printf(1) command can be used portably to emulate any of the traditional behaviors of the echo command as follows.

The Solaris 2.x /usr/bin/echo is equivalent to:

```
printf "%b\n" "$*"
```

The /usr/ucb/echo is equivalent to:

```
if ["X$1" = "X-n"]
then
 shift
 printf "%s" "$*"
else
 printf "%s\n" "$*"
fi
```

New applications are encouraged to use printf instead of echo.

Examples

You can use the echo command to display the value for a variable by preceding the variable name with a dollar sign ($). The following example displays the values for the PATH environment variable.

```
castle% echo $PATH
/usr/openwin/bin:/usr/dt/bin:/bin:/usr/bin:/usr/sbin:/usr/ucb:/etc:/usr
  /proc/bin:/opt/hpnp/bin:/usr/local/games:.
castle%
```

The following example shows how you can use the echo command in combination with the tr and wc commands to determine how many subdirectories are between the root directory (/) and your current directory. The example has the following parts:

- Echo the full path name of your current working directory.

- Pipe the output through tr to translate the path's embedded slash characters into space characters.

- Pipe that output through wc -w for a count of the names in your path.

```
castle% /usr/bin/echo $PWD | tr '/' ' ' | wc -w
       3
castle%
```

See tr(1) and wc(1) for their functionality.

The following examples show the different ways you can echo a string without a newline.

/usr/bin/echo

```
castle% /usr/bin/echo "$USER's current directory is $PWD\c"
winsor's current directory is /export/home/winsorcastle%
```

Bourne and Korn Shells

```
$ /usr/bin/echo "$USER's current directory is $PWD\c"
winsor's current directory is /export/home/winsor$
```

C Shell

```
castle% echo -n /usr/bin/echo "$USER's current directory is $PWD"
/usr/bin/echo winsor's current directory is /export/home/winsorcastle%
```

/usr/ucb/echo

```
castle% /usr/ucb/echo -n "$USER's current directory is $PWD"
winsor's current directory is /export/home/winsorcastle%
```

Environment Variables

SYSV3   Provide compatibility with INTERACIVE UNIX System and SCO UNIX installation scripts. SYSV3 is intended for compatibility only and should not be used in new scripts.

See environ(5) for descriptions of the following environment variables that affect the execution of echo: LC_CTYPE, LC_MESSAGES, and NLSPATH.

Exit Status

0	Successful completion.
>0	An error occurred.

Attributes

See attributes(5) for descriptions of the following attributes:

/usr/bin/echo

Attribute Type	Attribute Value
Availability	SUNWcsu
CSI	Enabled

/usr/ucb/echo

Attribute Type	Attribute Value
Availability	SUNWscpu

See Also

printf(1), shell_builtins(1), tr(1), wc(1), echo(1B), ascii(5), attributes(5), environ(5)

---

ed, red — Text Editor

Synopsis

```
/usr/bin/ed [-s|-] [-p string] [-x] [-C] [file]
/usr/xpg4/bin/ed [-s|-] [-p string] [-x] [-C] [file]
/usr/bin/red [-s|-] [-p string] [-x] [-C] [file]
```

Description

The ed command is the standard text editor. If you specify a file, ed reads the file into ed's buffer so that it can be edited.

Note — Although vi and ex have superseded ed as a line editor, some commands such as diff continue to use ed.

The ed command operates on a copy of the file it is editing; the original file remains unchanged until you issue a w (write) command. The copy of the text being edited resides in a temporary file called the buffer. There is only one buffer.

Unlike the vi and ex commands, ed does not display any of the text in its buffer unless you ask for it. As a result, it can be difficult to keep track of the current contents of the buffer.

The red command is a restricted version of ed. It enables editing of files in the current directory only. It prohibits executing shell commands by using the !shell command. Attempts to bypass these restrictions result in an error message (restricted shell).

Both ed and red support the fspec(4) formatting capability. The default terminal mode is either stty -tabs or stty tab3, where Tab stops are set at eight columns (see stty(1)). If, however, the first line of file contains a format specification, that specification overrides the default mode. The following example of the first line of a file sets Tab stops at 5, 10, and 15, and a maximum line length of 72.

```
<:t5,10,15 s72:>
```

Commands to ed have a simple and regular structure: zero, one, or two addresses followed by a single-character command, possibly followed by parameters to that command. The addresses specify one or more lines in the buffer. Every command that requires addresses has default addresses, so that you can often omit the addresses. In general, you can specify only one command per line.

ed has separate input and command modes. If you enter an invalid command, ed writes the string ?\n (followed by an explanatory message if you have enabled help mode with the H command) to standard output and continues in command mode with the current line number unchanged.

Certain commands allow the input of text. This text is put in the appropriate place in the buffer. While ed is accepting text, it is said to be in input mode. In this mode, ed recognizes no commands; it merely collects all input. You leave input mode by typing a period (.) at the beginning of a line, followed immediately by a Return.

Note — If the editor input is coming from a command file (for example, ed file < ed-cmd-file), the editor exits at the first failure.

---

ed has the following size limitations:

- 512 characters in a line.
- 256 characters in a global command list.
- 255 characters in the path name of a file (counting slashes).

The limit on the number of lines depends on the amount of user memory; each line takes 1 word. When reading a file, ed discards ASCII and null characters.

If a file is not terminated by a newline character, ed adds one and puts out a message explaining what it did.

/usr/bin/ed

If ed executes commands with arguments, it uses the default shell
/usr/bin/sh (see sh(1)).

/usr/xpg4/bin/ed

/usr/xpg4/bin/ed is a POSIX-compliant version of the /usr/bin/ed
command. See standards(5).

If ed executes commands with arguments, it uses /usr/xpg4/bin/sh,
which is equivalent to /usr/bin/ksh (see ksh(1)).

Regular Expressions

The ed command supports a limited form of regular expression notation. You
can use regular expressions in addresses to specify lines and in some
commands (for example, s) to specify portions of a line that are to be
substituted. With ed addressing, at any time there is a current line. Generally,
the current line is the last line affected by a command; the exact effect on the
current line is discussed under the description of each command.

Internationalized Basic Regular Expressions are used for all
system-supplied locales. See regex(5).

If the closing delimiter of an *RE* or of a replacement string (for example, /)
would be the last character before a newline, you can omit that delimiter, in
which case the addressed line is written. The following pairs of commands are
equivalent:

```
s/s1/s2      s/s1/s2/p

g/s1         g/s1/p

?s1          ?s1?
```

ed Commands

Commands may require zero, one, or two addresses. Commands that require no
addresses regard the presence of an address as an error. Commands that accept
one or two addresses assume default addresses when you specify an
insufficient number of addresses; if you specify more addresses than such a
command requires, ed uses the last one(s).

Typically, you separate addresses from each other by a comma (,) or a
semicolon (;). If you use a semicolon separator, the first address is calculated,
the current line (.) is set to that value, and then the second address is
calculated. You can use this feature to determine the starting line for forward
and backward searches. The second address of any two-address sequence must
correspond to a line in the buffer that follows the line corresponding to the first
address.

In the following list of ed commands, the parentheses shown before the
command are not part of the address; instead, they show the default
address(es) for the command.

You can precede each address component by zero or more blank characters.
You can precede the command letter by zero or more blank characters. If you
use a suffix letter (l, n, or p), it must immediately follow the command.

The e, E, f, v, and w commands take an optional file parameter, separated from the command letter by one or more blank characters.

If changes have been made in the buffer since the last w command that wrote the entire buffer, ed warns you if you use either the e or q commands because such use would destroy the buffer. The ed command writes the string: ?\n (followed by an explanatory message if you have used the H command to enable help mode) to standard output and continues in command mode with the current line number unchanged. If you repeat the e or q command with no other intervening command, the buffer is cleared and ed exits.

If an end-of-file is detected on standard input when a command is expected, the ed command acts as if a q command had been entered.

It is generally illegal for more than one command to appear on a line. However, you can suffix any command (except e, f, r, or w) by l, n, or p, in which case the current line is either listed, numbered, or written.

The ed commands are listed below.

(.)a text .	Append zero or more lines of text after the addressed line in the buffer. Leave the current line (.) at the last inserted line, or, if there was none, at the addressed line. Address 0 is legal for this command, placing the appended text at the beginning of the buffer. The maximum number of characters per line is 256, including the newline character.
(.)c text .	Change the addressed lines from the buffer with zero or more lines of text. Leave the current line (.) at the last line input, or, if there was none, at the first line that was not deleted; if the lines deleted were originally at the end of the buffer, set the current line number to the address of the new last line; if no lines remain in the buffer, set the current line number to 0.
C	Assume that all text read in for the e and r commands is encrypted unless a null key is typed in.
(.,.)d	Delete the addressed lines from the buffer. The line after the last line deleted becomes the current line; if the lines deleted were originally at the end of the buffer, the new last line becomes the current line. If no lines remain in the buffer, set the current line number to 0.
e file	Edit by deleting the entire contents of the buffer and then reading the contents of file into the buffer. Set the current line (.) to the last line of the buffer. If you do not specify file, use the currently remembered file name if any (see the f command). Write the number of bytes read to standard output in the following format, unless you specify the -s option: %d\n number of bytes read Remember file for possible use as a default file name in subsequent e, E, r, and w commands. If you replace file with !, take the rest of the line to be a shell command (see sh(1)) whose output is to be read. Such a shell command is not remembered as the current file name. Discard all marks on completion of a

successful e command. If the buffer has changed since the last time the entire buffer was written, you are warned, as described previously.

E *file*   Edit as with the e command but do not check to see if any changes have been made to the buffer since the last w command.

f [*file*]   Change the currently remembered path name to *file* if given. Then, write the (possibly new) currently remembered path name to the standard output in the following format:
                 "%s\n" *pathname*
                 The current line number is unchanged.

(1,$)g/*RE*/*command list*

Make global changes by first marking every line that matches the given *RE*. Then, for every marked line, execute the given command with the current line (.) initially set to that line. When the g command completes, the current line number has the value assigned by the last command in the command list. Leave the line number unchanged if no lines were matched. A single command or the first of a list of commands appears on the same line as the global command. You must end all lines of a multiline list except the last line with a backslash (\); a, i, and c commands and associated input are permitted. If the . terminating input mode would be the last line of the command, you can omit it. An empty command list is equivalent to the p command. The g, G, v, V, and ! commands are not permitted in the command list. You can use any character other than space or newline instead of a slash to delimit *RE*. Within *RE*, you can use the *RE* delimiter itself as a literal character by preceding it with a backslash.

(1,$)G/*RE*/   Make interactive global changes by first marking every line that matches the given *RE*. Then, write each such line to standard output. Change the current line (.) to that line, and you can input any single command except a, c, i, g, G, v, and V. After the execution of that command, write the next marked line, and so on; a newline acts as a null command; an & reexecutes the most recent non-null command within the current invocation of G. The commands input as part of the execution of the G command can address and affect any lines in the buffer. The final value of the current line number is the value set by the last command successfully executed. (Note that the last command successfully executed is the G command itself if a command fails or you specify the null command.) The current line number is not changed if no lines matched. You can terminate the G command by a SIGINT signal, an ASCII DEL, or BREAK. You can use any character other than space or newline instead of a slash to delimit *RE*. Within *RE*, you can use the *RE* delimiter itself as a literal character by preceding it with a backslash. Note that the sequence \n in an *RE* does not match a newline character.

h   Display a short help message that explains the reason for the most
             recent ? diagnostic. The current line number is unchanged.

H   Enter a mode that displays help messages for all subsequent ?
             diagnostics. Explain the previous ? diagnostic if there was one.
             Enter the H command again to exit this mode. The current line
             number is unchanged.

(.)i   Insert zero or more lines of text before the addressed line in the
text   buffer. Leave the current line (.) at the last inserted line, or, if
.   there was none, at the addressed line. This command differs from
             the a command only in the placement of the input text. Address 0
             is not legal for this command. The maximum number of characters
             that you can enter from a terminal is 256 per line (including the
             newline character).

(.,.+1)j   Join contiguous lines by removing the appropriate newline
             characters. If you give exactly one address, do nothing. If lines are
             joined, set the current line number to the address of the joined
             line; otherwise, the current line number is unchanged.

(.)kx   Mark the addressed line with name x, which must be an ASCII
             lowercase letter (a-z). The address 'x then addresses this line; the
             current line (.) is unchanged.

(.,.)l   Write the addressed lines to standard output in a visually
             unambiguous form. Write the characters (\\, \a, \b, \f, \r, \t, \v)
             as the corresponding escape sequence; the \n in that table is not
             applicable. Write nonprintable characters not in the table as one
             3-digit octal number (with a preceding backslash character) for
             each byte in the character (most significant byte first).

             Fold long lines, indicating the point of folding by writing
             backslash/newline character; the length at which folding occurs is
             unspecified but should be appropriate for the output device. Mark
             the end of each line with a $. You can append an l command to any
             command except e, E, f, q, Q, r, w, or !. Set the current line number
             to the address of the last line written.

(.,.)ma   Move the addressed line(s) by repositioning them after the line
             addressed by a. Address 0 is legal for a and moves the addressed
             line(s) to the beginning of the file. It is an error if address a falls
             within the range of moved lines. Leave the current line (.) at the
             last line moved.

(.,.)n   Write the addressed lines, preceding each line by its line number
             and a Tab character. Leave the current line (.) at the last line
             written. You can append the n command to any command except e,
             E, f, q, Q, r, w, or !.

(.,.)p   Print the addressed lines to standard output. Leave the current
             line (.) at the last line written. You can append the p command to
             any command except e, E, f, q, Q, r, w, or !. For example, dp deletes
             the current line and writes the new current line.

P   Prompt with an asterisk (*) (or string, if you specified the -p
                         option) for all subsequent commands. Enter the P command again
                         to exit this mode. By default, the prompt mode is off unless you
                         specify the -p option. The current line is unchanged.

q   Quit ed. If the buffer has changed since the last time the entire
                         buffer was written, display a warning message.

Q   Quit ed without checking if changes have been made in the buffer
                         since the last w command.

($)r *file*   Read the contents of *file* into the buffer. If you do not specify
                         file, use the currently remembered file name if any (see the e and
                         f commands). Leave the currently remembered file name
                         unchanged unless *file* is the very first file name mentioned since
                         ed was invoked. Address 0 is legal for r and reads the file in at the
                         beginning of the buffer. If the read is successful and you did not
                         specify the -s option, write to standard output the number of
                         characters read in the following format.
                         %d\n, <number of bytes read>

                         Set the current line (.) to the last line read. If you replace *file*
                         with !, take the rest of the line to be a shell command (see sh(1))
                         whose output is to be read. For example, $r !ls appends the
                         current directory to the end of the file being edited. Such a shell
                         command is not remembered as the current file name.

(.,.)s/*RE*/*replacement*/
(.,.)s/*RE*/*replacement*/ *count*, *count*=[1-512]
(.,.)s/*RE*/*replacement*/g
(.,.)s/*RE*/*replacement*/l
(.,.)s/*RE*/*replacement*/n
(.,.)s/*RE*/*replacement*/p

                         Substitute by searching each addressed line for an occurrence of
                         the specified *RE*. You can specify zero or more substitution
                         commands. In each line in which a match is found, replace all
                         (nonoverlapped) matched strings by the replacement if you use the
                         global replacement indicator g after the command. If you do not
                         use the global indicator, replace only the first occurrence of the
                         matched string. If you specify a number *count* after the command,
                         replace only the *count*-th occurrence of the matched string on each
                         addressed line. It is an error if the substitution fails on all
                         addressed lines. You can use any character other than space or
                         newline instead of the slash (/) to delimit the *RE* and the
                         replacement. Leave the current line (.) at the last line on which a
                         substitution occurred. Within the *RE*, you can use the *RE* delimiter
                         itself as a literal character by preceding it with a backslash.

Replace an ampersand (&) in the *replacement* with the string matching the *RE* on the current line. You can escape the special meaning of & in this context by preceding it with a backslash. As a more general feature, replace the characters \n, where *n* is a digit, with the text matched by the *n*-th regular subexpression of the specified *RE* enclosed between \(and \). When you use nested parenthesized subexpressions, *n* is determined by counting occurrences of \(starting from the left. When the character % is the only character in the replacement, use the replacement used in the most recent substitute command as the replacement in the current substitute command; if there was no previous substitute command, the use of % in this manner is an error. The % loses its special meaning when it is in a replacement string of more than one character or is preceded by a backslash. For each backslash encountered in scanning replacement from beginning to end, the character following loses its special meaning (if any). It is unspecified what special meaning is given to any character other than &, \, %, or digits.

You can split a line by substituting a newline character into it. You must escape the newline in the replacement by preceding it with a backslash. You cannot do such substitution as part of a g or v command list. Set the current line number to the address of the last line on which a substitution is performed. If no substitution is performed, the current line number is unchanged. If a line is split, a substitution is considered to have been performed on each of the new lines for the purpose of determining the new current line number. A substitution is considered to have been performed even if the replacement string is identical to the string that it replaces.

The substitute command supports the following indicators:

count	Substitute for the *count*-th occurrence only of the *RE* found on each addressed line. *count* must be between 1 and 512, inclusive.
g	Globally substitute for all nonoverlapping instances of the *RE* instead of just the first one. If you specify both g and *count*, the results are unspecified.
l	Write to standard output the final line in which a substitution was made. The line is written in the format specified for the l command.
n	Write to standard output the final line in which a substitution was made. The line is written in the format specified for the n command.
p	Write to standard output the final line in which a substitution was made. The line is written in the format specified for the p command.

(.,.) t a   Copy the addressed lines after address *a* (which may be 0). Leave
                 the current line (.) at the last line copied. This command is similar
                 to the m command.

u   Undo the most recent command that modified anything in the
                 buffer, namely, the most recent a, c, d, g, i, j, m, r, s, t, u, v, G, or V
                 command. Undo all changes made to the buffer by a g, G, v, or V
                 global command as a single change; if the global command made
                 no changes (such as with g/ *RE* /p), the u command has no effect.
                 Set the current line number to the value it had immediately before
                 the command being undone started.

(1,$) v/*RE*/*command list*

                 Make global changes as with the g command, except during the
                 first step, mark the lines that do not match the *RE*.

(1,$) V/*RE*/   Make interactive global changes as with the G command, except
                 during the first step, mark the lines marked that do not match the
                 RE.

(1,$) w *file*   Write the addressed lines into *file*. If *file* does not exist, create
                 it with mode 666 (readable and writable by everyone), unless your
                 file creation mask dictates otherwise; see the description of the
                 umask special command on sh(1). Leave the currently remembered
                 file name unchanged unless *file* is the very first file name
                 mentioned since ed was invoked. If you specify no *file*, use the
                 currently remembered file name if any (see the e and f
                 commands). Leave the current line (.) unchanged. If the command
                 is successful, print the number of characters written, unless you
                 specify the -s option in the following format: "%d\n",
                 number-of-bytes-written

                 If you replace *file* with !, take the rest of the line to be a shell
                 command (see sh(1)) whose standard input is the addressed lines.
                 Such a shell command is not remembered as the current path
                 name. This usage of the write command with ! is considered as a
                 last w command that wrote the entire buffer.

(1,$) W *file*   Write the addressed lines into *file* as the write command above
                 but append the addressed lines to the end of *file* if it exists. If
                 file does not exist, create it as described above for the w
                 command.

X   Determine whether text read for the e and r commands is
                 encrypted. A null key turns off encryption. Subsequent e, r, and w
                 commands use this key to encrypt or decrypt the text. An explicitly
                 empty key turns off encryption. Also, see the -x option of ed.

($) =   Write the number of the addressed line to standard output in the
                 following format: "%d\n" *line-number*

                 The current line number is unchanged.

`!shell` *command*

> Send the remainder of the line after the ! to the UNIX system shell
> (see sh(1)) to be interpreted as a command. Within the text of that
> command, replace the unescaped character % with the
> remembered file name; if you use a ! as the first character of the
> shell command, replace it with the text of the previous shell
> command. Thus, !! repeats the last shell command. If any
> replacements of % or ! are performed, write the modified line to the
> standard output before command is executed. The ! command
> writes !\n to standard output on completion, unless you specify
> the -s option. The current line number is unchanged. Note that a
> ! command cannot be subject to a g or v command. You cannot use
> the ! command and the ! escape from the e, r, and w commands if
> you invoke ed from a restricted shell (see sh(1)).

`(.+1)newline`

> Write the addressed line. A newline alone, equivalent to .+1p, is
> useful for stepping forward through the buffer. Set the current line
> number to the address of the written line.

If you send an interrupt signal (ASCII DEL or BREAK), ed writes a ?\n and
returns to its command level. The ed command takes the standard action for all
signals with the following exceptions:

SIGINT
> Interrupt current activity, write the string ?\n to standard output,
> and return to command mode.

SIGHUP
> If the buffer is not empty and has changed since the last write,
> write a copy of the buffer in a file. First, use the file named ed.hup
> in the current directory; if that fails, use the file named ed.hup in
> the directory named by the HOME environment variable. In any
> case, the ed command exits without returning to command mode.

Options

-C
> Simulate a C encryption command. The C command is like the X
> command, except that all text read in is assumed to have been
> encrypted.

-p *string*   Specify a prompt string. By default, there is no prompt string.

-s | -
> Suppress the writing of character counts by e, r, and w commands,
> of diagnostics from e and q commands, and of the ! prompt after a
> !shell command. Although the - option is still supported, it has
> been replaced in the documentation by the -s option that follows
> the Command Syntax Standard (see intro(1)).

-x   Simulate an X encryption command and prompt for a key. The X
             command makes an educated guess to determine whether text
             read in is encrypted or not. The temporary buffer file is encrypted
             also, using a transformed version of the key typed in for the -x
             option.

Operands

file   Simulate an e command on the named *file* before accepting
             commands from the standard input.

Examples

The following examples show some of the basic ed editing commands. First we
create a new file named edfile and use the a (append) command to append
text to it. If the file already contained text, the new input would be appended to
the end of the file. The dot (.) on a separate line at the end exits input mode.

```
castle% ed edfile
?edfile
a
Kookaburra sits in the old gum tree
Merry merry king of the bush is he
Laugh, kookaburra, laugh
Gay your life must be.

Kookaburra sits in the old gum tree
Eating all the gumdrops he can see
Laugh, kookaburra, laugh
Leave some there for me.
.
```

To save the file, we use the w (write) command. The text is written to the
buffer, and the number of characters is displayed. Then we use the q (quit)
command to quit ed.

```
w
240
q
castle%
```

Now let's open the file again by typing **ed** and the file name. The contents of
the file are written into the ed buffer, and the number of characters in the file
is displayed.

```
castle% ed edfile
240
```

To display the last line of the file, we use the p (print) command.

```
p
Leave some there for me.
```

To display the first line of the file, we use 1p.

1p
```
Kookaburra sits in the old gum tree
```

To display the first five lines of the file, we use 1,5p.

1,5p
```
Kookaburra sits in the old gum tree
Merry merry king of the bush is he
Laugh, kookaburra, laugh
Gay your life must be.
```

To display everything in the buffer, we use 1,$p.

1,$p
```
Kookaburra sits in the old gum tree
Merry merry king of the bush is he
Laugh, kookaburra, laugh
Gay your life must be.

Kookaburra sits in the old gum tree
Eating all the gumdrops he can see
Laugh, kookaburra, laugh
Leave some there for me.
```

Because ed is a line-oriented text editor, it helps a great deal to know what line you want to edit. The n (number) command is like the p (print) command except that it displays a line number at the beginning of each line. The n command uses the same syntax as the p command. In the following example, we print the contents of the buffer with line numbers.

1,$n
```
1       Kookaburra sits in the old gum tree
2       Merry merry king of the bush is he
3       Laugh, kookaburra, laugh
4       Gay your life must be.
5
6       Kookaburra sits in the old gum tree
7       Eating all the gumdrops he can see
8       Laugh, kookaburra, laugh
9       Leave some there for me.
```

To delete a line of text, use the d (delete) command. In the following example, we delete the fifth line that contains just a newline character and then use the n command again to display the contents of the buffer. As you can see, the blank line has been deleted.

5d
1,$n
```
1       Kookaburra sits in the old gum tree
2       Merry merry king of the bush is he
3       Laugh, kookaburra, laugh
4       Gay your life must be.
```

```
5        Kookaburra sits in the old gum tree
6        Eating all the gumdrops he can see
7        Laugh, kookaburra, laugh
8        Leave some there for me.
```

Now we decide to quit the file, but we've forgotten to write the changes in the buffer. ed displays a ? prompt to remind us that we haven't saved the changes. We then write the changes and quit again.

```
q
?
w
239
q
castle%
```

Usage

See largefile(5) for the description of the behavior of ed and red when encountering files greater than or equal to 2 Gbytes (2**31 bytes).

Environment Variables

See environ(5) for descriptions of the following environment variables that affect the execution of ed: HOME, LC_CTYPE, LC_COLLATE, LC_MESSAGES, and NLSPATH.

Exit Status

0	Successful completion without any file or command errors.
>0	An error occurred.

Files

$TMPDIR	If this environment variable is not null, use its value in place of /var/tmp as the directory name for the temporary work file.
/var/tmp	If /var/tmp exists, use it as the directory name for the temporary work file.
/tmp	If the environment variable TMPDIR does not exist or is null and if /var/tmp does not exist, then use /tmp as the directory name for the temporary work file.
ed.hup	Save work here if the terminal is hung up.

Attributes

See attributes(5) for descriptions of the following attributes:

/usr/bin/ed, /usr/bin/red

Attribute Type	Attribute Value
Availability	SUNWcsu
CSI	Enabled

/usr/xpg4/bin/ed

Attribute Type	Attribute Value
Availability	SUNWxcu4
CSI	Enabled

See Also

bfs(1), edit(1), grep(1), ksh(1), lex(1), sh(1), stty(1), umask(1), vi(1),
fspec(4), attributes(5), environ(5), largefile(5), regex(5), xpg4(5)

Diagnostics

?	Command errors.
?*file*	An inaccessible file. (Use the help and Help commands for detailed explanations.)

If changes have been made in the buffer since the last w command that wrote the entire buffer, ed warns you if you use the e or q commands, which would destroy the buffer. It writes ? and enables you to continue editing. Issuing a second e or q command at this point executes the command. You can inhibit this feature by using the -s command-line option.

edit — Text Editor (Variant of ex for Casual Users)

Synopsis

```
/usr/bin/edit [- | -s] [-l] [-L] [-R] [-r [filename]] [-t tag] [-v] [-V]
    [-x] [-wn] [-C] [+command | -c command] filename...
/usr/xpg4/bin/edit [- | -s] [-l] [-L] [-R] { -r [filename]]
    [-t tag] [-v] [-V] [-x] [-wn] [-C] [+command | -c command]
    filename...
```

Description

The `edit` command is a variant of the text editor `ex` and is recommended for new or casual users who want to use a command-oriented editor. It operates precisely as `ex` with the following options automatically set:

`novice`	On
`report`	On
`showmode`	On
`magic`	Off

The following brief introduction should help you get started with `edit`. If you are using a CRT terminal, you may want to learn about the display editor `vi`.

The `edit` command operates on a copy of the file it is editing; the original file remains unchanged until you issue a `w` (write) command. The copy of the text being edited resides in a temporary file called a buffer. The `edit` command also has 26 additional buffers, named `a` through `z`, that you can use as temporary storage areas for copying and moving text between files.

The `edit` command numbers the lines in the buffer, with the first line as number 1. If you execute the command `1`, then `edit` types the first line of the buffer. If you then execute the command `d`, edit deletes the first line, line 2 becomes line 1, and `edit` prints the current line (the new line 1) so you can see where you are. In general, the current line is always the last line affected by a command. The current line has the symbolic name dot (`.`).

See `ex`(1) for a complete list of `edit` commands and syntax.

Starting the Editor

To create a new file, you begin at a shell prompt by typing:

```
castle% edit filename
```

The editor displays the file name, tells you it is a new file, and displays the colon (`:`) prompt, as shown in the following example.

```
castle% edit editfile
"editfile" [New File]
:
```

To edit an existing file, you also type `edit filename` and press Return. The editor makes a copy of the file, stores it the buffer, and tells you how many lines and characters are in the file, as shown in the following example.

```
castle% edit editfile2
"editfile2" 9 lines, 263 characters
:
```

To edit the file, you type an `edit` command and press Return. The `edit` command prompt is the colon (`:`), which you should see after starting the editor. If you are editing an existing file, then you have some lines in `edit`'s buffer.

When you start editing, edit makes the last line of the file the current line. Most commands to edit use the current line if you do not tell them which line to use. Thus, if you type print (which can be abbreviated p) and press Return (as you should after all edit commands), edit prints the current line. If you delete (d) the current line, edit prints the new current line, which is usually the next line in the file. If you delete the last line, then the new last line becomes the current one.

Appending Text

If you start with an empty file or want to add some new lines, use the append (a) command. After you execute this command (pressing a Return after the word append), edit reads lines from your terminal until you type a line consisting of just a dot (.); edit places these lines after the current line. The last line you type then becomes the current line. The insert (i) command is like append but places the lines you type before, instead of after, the current line.

Changing Text

You can make a change to some text within the current line by using the substitute (s) command: s/old/new/ where old is the string of characters you want to replace and new is the string of characters you want to replace old with.

The filename (f) command tells you how many lines there are in the buffer you are editing and displays [Modified] if you have changed the buffer.

By using the d and a commands and giving line numbers to see lines in the file, you can make any changes you want. You should learn at least a few more things, however, if you use edit more than a few times.

The change (c) command changes the current line to a sequence of lines you supply (as in append, you type lines up to a line consisting of only a dot (.). You can tell change to change more than one line by giving the line numbers of the lines you want to change, for example, 3,5c.

Saving Edits and Quitting the Editor

After modifying a file, you can save the contents of the file by executing a write (w) command. You can leave the editor by issuing a quit (q) command. If you run edit on a file but do not change the file, you do not need to (but it does no harm) write the file back. If you try to quit from edit after modifying the buffer without writing it out, you receive the message No write since last change (:quit! overrides), and edit waits for another command. If you do not want to write the buffer out, issue the quit command followed by an exclamation point (q!). The buffer is then irretrievably discarded, and the shell returns.

The undo (u) command reverses the effect of the last command you executed that changed the buffer. Thus, if you execute a substitute command that does not do what you want, type u and the old contents of the line are restored. You can also undo an undo command. edit warns you when a command affects more than one line of the buffer. Note that you cannot undo commands such as `write` and `quit`.

Displaying Lines in the Buffer

`edit` provides a number of different commands that enable you to display what's in the buffer.

- Find the current line number by typing `.=`
- Use the `print` command to display a set of line numbers: `1,23p` prints the first 23 lines of the file, `1,$p` prints the complete file, and `.,$p` prints the current line plus the rest of the lines in the file.
- Use the `number` (`nu`) command to display the contents of the buffer with line numbers. You can find the number of the current line (`nu`), a range of lines (for example, `5,10nu` displays numbered lines 5 through 10), or all of the lines in the file (`1,$pnu`).
- To look at the next line in the buffer, press Return.
- To look at a number of lines, enter Control-D (while holding down the Control key, press the d key) instead of Return. This key sequence shows you a half-screen of lines on a CRT or 12 lines on a hardcopy terminal. You can look at nearby text by executing the `z` command. The current line is displayed in the middle of the text displayed, and the last line displayed becomes the current line; you can get back to the line where you were before you executed the `z` command by typing `''`. The `z` command has other options: `z-` prints a screen of text (or 24 lines) ending where you are; `z+` prints the next screenful. If you want less than a screenful of lines, type `z.11` to display five lines before and five lines after the current line. (Typing `z.n`, when n is an odd number, displays a total of n lines, centered about the current line; when n is an even number, it displays $n-1$ lines, so that the lines displayed are centered around the current line.) You can give counts after other commands; for example, with the command `d5` you can delete 5 lines starting with the current line.

You can also do arithmetic with line references. Thus, the line `$-5` is the fifth before the last and `.+20` is 20 lines after the current line.

Note — `edit` also has a `vi` mode that enables you to view the contents of the file as you edit it. For more information on using the `vi` mode, see `ex(1)`.

Finding Text

To find things in the file, you can use line numbers. You can also search backward and forward in the file for strings by giving commands of the form `/text/` to search forward for text or `?text?` to search backward for text. If a search reaches the end of the file without finding text, it wraps around and continues to search back to the line where you are. A useful feature here is a search of the form /^text/ which searches for text at the beginning of a line. Similarly, /text$/ searches for text at the end of a line. You can omit the trailing / or ? in these commands.

Copying or Moving Text

You can copy or move text within the same file by using the copy (c) or move (m) commands. You specify the line or range of lines you want to move, followed by the command and then the number of the line after which you want the text to be placed. For example, the command 5,10c 20 makes a copy of lines 5 through 10 and inserts it after line 20 in the buffer. The symbolic-name dot (.) syntax, which represents the current line, is most useful in a range of lines. To move to the last line in the file, you can refer to it by its symbolic name $. Thus, the command $d deletes the last line in the file, no matter what the current line is, and the command 10,20m $ moves lines 10 through 20 to the end of the file.

Using the Internal Buffers

The edit command has 26 internal buffers, named a through z, that you can use as temporary clipboards for copying or moving text from one file to another. Before you begin the copy or move, find the first and last line numbers you want to copy or move. For example, to move lines 10 through 20, type 10,20d a and press Return. The lines are deleted from the file and put into a buffer named a. To put the contents of buffer a after the current line, type put a and press Return. If you want to move or copy these lines to another file, first copy the lines by using the yank (y) command, then type **e *filename*** and press Return, where *filename* is the name of the other file you want to edit, for example, e chapter2.

Note — The contents of the a through z buffers are not preserved if you exit edit. When you use the e or q commands, edit does not warn you when these buffers contain text.

The /usr/xpg4/bin/edit command is identical to /usr/bin/edit.

Options

You can turn the following options on or off by using the set command in ex(1).

- | -s	Suppress all interactive user feedback. This option is useful when processing editor scripts.
-C	Simulate the C command of ex, which assumes that all text read in has been encrypted.
+*command* | -c *command*	Begin editing by executing the specified editor command (usually a search or positioning command).
-l	Set up for editing LISP programs.

-L	List the name of all files saved as the result of an editor or system crash.
-R	Set the read-only flag to prevent accidental overwriting of the file.
-r *filename*	Recover the version of *filename* that was in the buffer when a system crash occurred.
-t *tag*	Edit the file containing *tag* and position the editor at its definition.
-v	Start up in display editing state using vi. You can achieve the same effect by simply typing the vi command.
-V	Verbose. When ex commands are read by means of standard input, the input is echoed to standard error. This option is useful for processing ex commands within shell scripts.
-x	Simulate the X encryption command of ex and prompt for a key. This key encrypts and decrypts text, using the algorithm of the crypt command. The X command makes an educated guess to determine whether text read in is encrypted or not. The temporary buffer file is encrypted also, using a transformed version of the key typed in for the -x option. Note that the encryption options are provided with the Security Administration Utilities package, which is available only in the United States.
-w*n*	Set the default window size to *n*. This option is useful when you are using the editor over a slow-speed line.

The *filename* argument indicates one or more files to be edited.

Attributes

See attributes(5) for descriptions of the following attributes:

/usr/bin/edit

Attribute Type	Attribute Value
Availability	SUNWcsu
CSI	Enabled

/usr/xpg4/bin/edit

Attribute Type	Attribute Value
Availability	SUNWxcu4
CSI	Enabled

See Also

ed(1), ex(1), vi(1), attributes(5), XPG4(5)

egrep — Search a File for a Pattern, Using Full Regular Expressions

Synopsis
```
/usr/bin/egrep [-bchilnsv] [-e pattern-list] [-f file]
    [strings] [file...]
/usr/xpg4/bin/egrep [-bchilnsvx] [-e pattern-list]
    [-f file] [strings] [file...]
```

Description
The egrep (expression grep) command searches files for a pattern of characters and prints all lines that contain that pattern. egrep uses full regular expressions (expressions that have string values that use the full set of alphanumeric and special characters) to match the patterns. It uses a fast deterministic algorithm that sometimes needs exponential space.

If you specify no files, egrep assumes standard input. Normally, each line found is copied to the standard output. The file name is printed before each line found if there is more than one input file.

/usr/bin/egrep
The /usr/bin/egrep command accepts full regular expressions as described on the regexp(5) manual page, except for \ (and \ ), and with the addition of the following expressions:

- A full regular expression followed by + that matches one or more occurrences of the full regular expression.

- A full regular expression followed by ? that matches 0 or 1 occurrence of the full regular expression.

- Full regular expressions separated by | or by a newline that match strings that are matched by any of the expressions.

- A full regular expression that may be enclosed in parentheses () for grouping.

Be careful when using the characters $, *, [, ^, |, (,), and \ in full regular expression because they are also meaningful to the shell. It is safest to enclose the entire full regular expression in single quotes ' ... '.

The order of precedence of operators is [], then *?+, then concatenation, then | and newline.

/usr/xpg4/bin/egrep
/usr/xpg4/bin/egrep is a POSIX-compliant version of the /usr/bin/egrep command. See standards(5).

The /usr/xpg4/bin/egrep command uses the regular expressions described in the Extended Regular Expressions section of the regex(5) manual page.

Notes

Ideally, there should be only one `grep` command, but there is not a single algorithm that spans a wide enough range of space-time trade-offs.

Lines are limited only by the size of the available virtual memory.

The `/usr/xpg4/bin/egrep` command is identical to `/usr/xpg4/bin/grep -E` (see `grep(1)`). Portable applications should use `/usr/xpg4/bin/grep -E`.

Options

The options listed below are supported for both `/usr/bin/egrep` and `/usr/xpg4/bin/egrep` except for the `-x` option, which is available only for the `/usr/xpg4/bin/egrep` command.

`-b`	Precede each line by the block number on which it was found. This option can be useful in locating block numbers by context (first block is 0).
`-c`	Print only a count of the lines that contain the pattern.
`-e` *pattern-list*	Search for a *pattern-list* (full regular expression that begins with a -).
`-f` *file*	Take the list of full regular expressions from *file*.
`-h`	Suppress printing of file names when searching multiple files.
`-i`	Ignore upper-/lowercase distinction during comparisons.
`-l`	Print the names of files with matching lines once, separated by newlines. Do not repeat the names of files when the pattern is found more than once.
`-n`	Precede each line by its line number in the file (first line is 1).
`-s`	Work silently, that is, display nothing except error messages. This option is useful for checking the error status.
`-v`	Print all lines except those that contain the pattern.
`-x`	Consider only input lines that use all characters in the line to match an entire fixed string or regular expression to be matching lines. This option is supported for `/usr/xpg4/bin/egrep` only.

Operands

file	A path name of a file to be searched for the patterns. If you specify no file operands, use the standard input.
pattern	For `/usr/bin/egrep`, Specify a pattern to be used during the search for input. For `usr/xpg4/bin/egrep`, specify one or more patterns to be used during the search for input. This operand is treated as if it were specified as `-e` *pattern-list*.

Examples

Suppose you want to find lines in one of your files that contain the words Michigan, Ohio, or Indiana. A single grep command cannot perform searches for more than one pattern. You can use egrep to search for more than one pattern in a file or group of files with a similar extension extension.

egrep provides the following capabilities:

- The capability to search for several patterns at a time in an "either-or" condition.

- The capability to use a file containing patterns as the basis for its search.

- An extended set of regular expression metacharacters.

egrep is slower than grep but it can do more complex searches.

Note — When using the egrep command, \ (—backslash followed by open parenthesis—or \)—backslash followed by close parenthesis—match parentheses as literal text. Open parenthesis and closed parenthesis are special characters that group parts of the pattern. The reverse is true with the grep command.

The following example searches all the files in the current directory with a .doc extension, for lines containing either Michigan or Ohio.

```
castle% egrep "Michigan|Ohio" *.doc
```

The following example forces egrep to look for lines that begin with Michigan or Ohio. The -i option looks for both upper and lower case.

```
castle% egrep -i "^Michigan|^Ohio" *.doc
```

You can include search patterns in a file and specify the file name as an argument to the egrep command. Using a file is convenient when developing complex patterns that you do not want to type at the command line.

In the following example, a file named pattern.file contains the line

```
(Michigan|Ohio)
```

The patterns do not require quotes but do require parenthesis. The following example uses -f pattern.file as an egrep argument.

```
castle% egrep -f pattern.file *.doc
```

The following example searches all files with a .doc extension for lines that contain a string of one or more digits or the string ABC.

```
castle% egrep  "( [0-9]+  )|ABC)" *.doc
file1.doc: ABCDEFGHI
file5.doc: The following are numbers 1234567
file7.doc: 1 2 3 4 5 6
castle%
```

The following example searches `file1.doc` for lines that contain either the strings `bill`, `tom`, or any number that is enclosed in `()`:

```
castle% egrep "\((bill)|(tom)|(0-9)\)" file1.doc
(1)
(5)
(bill)
(tom)
castle%
```

The search does not match the following strings.

```
(123)
(bill123)
```

Usage

See `largefile`(5) for the description of the behavior of `egrep` when encountering files greater than or equal to 2 Gbytes (2**31 bytes).

Environment Variables

See `environ`(5) for descriptions of the following environment variables that affect the execution of `egrep`: LC_COLLATE, LC_CTYPE, LC_MESSAGES, and NLSPATH.

Exit Status

0	If any matches are found.
1	If no matches are found.
2	For syntax errors or inaccessible files (even if matches were found).

Attributes

See `attributes`(5) for descriptions of the following attributes:

/usr/bin/egrep

Attribute Type	Attribute Value
Availability	SUNWcsu
CSI	Enabled

/usr/xpg4/bin/egrep

Attribute Type	Attribute Value
Availability	SUNWxcu4
CSI	Enabled

See Also

```
fgrep(1), grep(1), sed(1), sh(1), attributes(5), environ(5),
largefile(5), regex(5), regexp(5), XPG4(5)
```

---

eject — Eject Media such as CD-ROM and Diskette from Drive

Synopsis

```
/usr/bin/eject [-dfnpq] [device | nickname]
```

Description

Use the eject command for those removable media devices that do not have a manual eject button, or for those that do but are managed by Volume Management (see vold(1M)). You can specify the device by its name or by a nickname; if Volume Management is running and no device is specified, eject uses the default device.

> **Note —** Only devices that support eject under program control respond to this command. eject responds differently, depending on whether or not Volume Management is running.

---

eject can also display its default device and a list of nicknames.

With Volume Management

When you use eject on media that can be ejected only manually, it does everything except remove the media, including unmounting the file system if it is mounted. In this case, eject displays a message that the media can now be manually ejected. If a window system is running, the message is displayed as a pop-up window, unless you use the -p option. If no window system is running or you use the -p option, a message is displayed both to standard error and to the system console that the media can now be physically removed.

Volume Management has the concept of a default device, which eject uses if you specify no path name or nickname. Use the -d option to check what default device is used.

Without Volume Management

When Volume Management is not running and you specify a path name, eject sends the eject command to that path name. If you supply a nickname instead of a path name, eject recognizes the nicknames shown below. To display this list, you can type **eject -n** and press Return.

Nickname	Path
fd	/dev/rdiskette
fd0	/dev/rdiskette
fd1	/dev/rdiskette1
diskette	/dev/rdiskette
diskette0	/dev/rdiskette0
diskette1	/dev/rdiskette1
rdiskette	/dev/rdiskette
rdiskette0	/dev/rdiskette0
rdiskette1	/dev/rdiskette1
floppy	/dev/rdiskette
floppy0	/dev/rdiskette0
floppy1	/dev/rdiskette1

Do not physically eject media from a device that contains mounted file systems. eject automatically searches for any mounted file systems that reside on the device and tries to unmount them before ejecting the media (see mount(1M)). If the umount operation fails, eject prints a warning message and exits. You can use the -f option to specify an eject even if the device contains mounted partitions; this option works only if Volume Management is not running.

If you have inserted a diskette, you must use volcheck(1) before ejecting the media, to inform Volume Management of the diskette's presence.

Bugs

There should be a way to change the default on a per-user basis.

If Volume Management is not running, it is possible to eject a volume that is currently mounted (see mount(1M)). For example, if you have a CD-ROM drive at /dev/dsk/c0t3d0s2 mounted on /mnt, the following command (without Volume Management running) ejects the CD-ROM because both slices s0 and s2 reference the whole CD-ROM drive.

```
castle% eject /dev/dsk/c0t3d0s0
```

Options

-d	Display the name of the default device to be ejected.
-f	Force the device to eject even if it is busy, if Volume Management is not running.
-n	Display the nickname to device name translation table.

-p	Do not try to call the `eject_popup` program.
-q	Query to see if the media are present.

Operands

device	Specify which device to eject, by the name in the `/dev` directory.
nickname	Specify which device to eject, by its nickname as known to this command.

Example

The following example uses the `-d` option to find out the default eject device. In the first example, no media is in either the diskette or CD-ROM drive. In the second example, a diskette is in the diskette drive, and the `volcheck` command is used to let the system know that it is there. In the third example, a CD is in the CD-ROM drive and nothing is in the diskette drive.

```
castle% eject -d
Default device is: nothing inserted
castle% volcheck
castle% eject -d
Default device is: /vol/dev/rdiskette0/unnamed_floppy
castle% eject
castle% eject -d
Default device is: /vol/dev/rdsk/c0t6d0/jumpingjavascript
castle% eject
```

The following example ejects a CD from its drive, while Volume Management is running (assuming only one CD-ROM drive).

```
castle% eject cdrom0
castle%
```

The following example ejects a diskette whether or not Volume Management is running.

```
castle% eject floppy0
castle%
```

The following example ejects a CD-ROM drive with path name `/dev/dsk/c0t3d0s2`, without Volume Management running.

```
# eject /dev/dsk/c0t3d0s2
#
```

Note — You must be superuser to mount, unmount, and eject a CD-ROM without Volume Management running.

Exit Status

0	The operation was successful or, with the -q option, the media is in the drive.
1	The operation was unsuccessful or, with the -q option, the media is not in the drive.
2	You specified invalid options.
3	An `ioctl()` request failed.
4	Manually ejectable media is now okay to remove.

Files

`/dev/diskette0`

Default diskette file.

`/dev/sr0`   Default CD-ROM file (deprecated).

`/dev/dsk/c0t6d0s2`

Default CD-ROM file.

`/usr/lib/vold/eject_popup`

Pop-up used for manually ejected media.

Attributes

See `attributes`(5) for descriptions of the following attributes:

Attribute Type	**Attribute Value**
Availability	SUNWcsu

See Also

```
volcancel(1), volcheck(1), volmissing(1), mount(1M), rmmount(1M),
vold(1M), ioctl(2), rmmount.conf(4), vold.conf(4), attributes(5),
volfs(7FS)
```

Diagnostics

A short help message is printed if you specify an unknown option. A diagnostic is printed if the device name cannot be opened or does not support `eject`.

`Device Busy` An attempt was made to eject a device that has a mounted file system. A warning message is printed when doing a forced eject of a mounted device.

elfdump — Dump Selected Parts of an Object File

Synopsis

```
/usr/ccs/bin/elfdump [-cdeihnprsvG][-w file][-N name] filename ..
```

Description

Use the `elfdump` command to symbolically dump selected parts of the specified object file(s). The options enable you to display specific portions of the file.

The `elfdump` command is similar in function to the `dump(1)` command, that offers an older and less user-friendly interface than `elfdump`, although `dump(1)` may be more appropriate for certain uses, such as in shell scripts.

For a complete description of the displayed information, refer to the *Linker and Libraries Guide*.

Options

`-c`	Dump section header information.
`-d`	Dump the contents of the `.dynamic` section.
`-e`	Dump the ELF header.
`-i`	Dump the contents of the `.interp` section.
`-G`	Dump the contents of the `.got` section.
`-h`	Dump the contents of the `.hash` section.
`-n`	Dump the contents of the `.note` section.
`-N name`	Qualify an option with a specific name. For example, in a file that contains more than one symbol table, you can display the `.dynsym` table using: `% elfdump -s -N .dynsym filename`
`-p`	Dump the program headers.
`-r`	Dump the contents of the relocation sections (that is, `.rel[a]`).
`-s`	Dump the contents of the symbol table sections (that is, `.dynsym` and/or `.symtab`).
`-v`	Dump the contents of the version sections (that is, `.SUNW_version`). If you also use the `-s` option, then the `st_other` entry reported for symbols from the `.dynsym` section are their version index.
`-w file`	Write the contents of a specified section to the named file. This option is useful for extracting an individual sections data for additional processing.

Operands

filename   The name of the specified object file.

Examples

The following example shows the first few lines of the output from the elfdump
command for the zipinfo command.

```
castle% /usr/ccs/bin/elfdump -c /bin/zipinfo

Section Header[1]:  sh_name: .interp
      sh_addr:       0x100d4        sh_flags:    [ SHF_ALLOC ]
      sh_size:       0x11           sh_type:     [ SHT_PROGBITS ]
      sh_offset:     0xd4           sh_entsize:  0
      sh_link:       0              sh_info:     0
      sh_addralign: 0x1

Section Header[2]:  sh_name: .hash
      sh_addr:       0x100e8        sh_flags:    [ SHF_ALLOC ]
      sh_size:       0x64c          sh_type:     [ SHT_HASH ]
      sh_offset:     0xe8           sh_entsize:  0x4
      sh_link:       3              sh_info:     0
      sh_addralign: 0x4

Section Header[3]:  sh_name: .dynsym
      sh_addr:       0x10734        sh_flags:    [ SHF_ALLOC ]
      sh_size:       0xbe0          sh_type:     [ SHT_DYNSYM ]
      sh_offset:     0x734          sh_entsize:  0x10
      sh_link:       4              sh_info:     28
      sh_addralign: 0x4
...
```

Files

liblddbg.so

Linker debugging library.

Attributes

See attributes(5) for descriptions of the following attributes:

Attribute Type	Attribute Value
Availability	SUNWbtool

See Also

dump(1), nm(1), pvs(1), attributes(5)
Linker and Libraries Guide

enable, disable — Enable/Disable LP Printers

Synopsis

```
/usr/bin/enable printer ...
/usr/bin/disable [-c | -W] [-r [reason]] printer...
```

Description

The `enable` command activates printers, enabling them to print requests submitted by the `lp` command. You must run the `enable` command on the printer server.

The `disable` command deactivates printers, disabling them from printing requests submitted by the `lp` command. By default, any requests that are currently printing on *printer* are reprinted in their entirety either on *printer* or another member of the same class of printers. You must run the `disable` command on the print server.

Use `lpstat -p` to check the status of printers.

`enable` and `disable` affect queueing only on the print server's spooling system. Executing these commands from a client system has no effect on the server.

Options

-c	Cancel any requests that are currently printing on printer. You cannot use this option with the -W option. If the printer is remote, the -c option is silently ignored.
-r [reason]	Assign a reason for the disabling of the printer(s). This reason applies to all printers specified. This reason is reported by lpstat -p. Enclose *reason* in quotes if it contains blanks. The default reasons are unknown reason for the existing printer, and new printer for a printer that has been added to the system but not yet enabled.
-W	Wait until the request currently being printed is finished before disabling *printer*. You cannot use this option with the -c option. If the printer is remote, the -W option is silently ignored.

Operands

printer	The name of the printer to be enabled or disabled. Specify *printer* using atomic name. See `printers.conf`(4) for information regarding the naming conventions for atomic names.

Exit Status

0	Successful completion.
non-zero	An error occurred.

Files

/var/spool/lp/*

LP print queue.

Attributes

See attributes(5) for descriptions of the following attributes:

Attribute Type	Attribute Value
Availability	SUNWpcu
CSI	Enabled

See Also

lp(1), lpstat(1), printers.conf(4), attributes(5)

---

env — Set Environment for Command Invocation

Synopsis

```
/usr/bin/env [-i | -] [name=value] ... [command [arg ...]]
/usr/xpg4/bin/env [-i | -] [name=value] ...[command [arg ...]]
```

Description

Using the env command with no arguments displays the current environment variable settings. The env command with options obtains the current environment, modifies it according to its arguments, then invokes the command named by the *command* operand with the modified environment.

Optional arguments are passed to *command*. If you specify no *command* operand, the resulting environment is written to the standard output, with one *name=value* pair per line.

/usr/bin/env

If env executes commands with arguments, it uses the default shell /usr/bin/sh (see sh(1)).

/usr/xpg4/bin/env

`/usr/xpg4/bin/env` is a POSIX-compliant version of the `/usr/bin/env` command. See `standards`(5).

If `env` executes commands with arguments, it uses `/usr/xpg4/bin/sh`, which is equivalent to `/usr/bin/ksh` (see `ksh`(1)).

Options

    `-i | -`   Ignore the environment that would otherwise be inherited from the current shell. Restrict the environment for *command* to that specified by the arguments.

Operands

    `name=value` Arguments of the form *name=value* modify the execution environment and are placed into the inherited environment before command is invoked.

    `command`   The name of the command to be invoked. If *command* names any of the special shell built-in commands, the results are undefined.

    `arg`   A string to pass as an argument for the invoked command.

Examples

The following example uses the `env` command without any arguments to display the current values for the environment variables. The list has been truncated to save space.

```
castle% env
MANPATH=/usr/openwin/share/man:/usr/openwin/man:/usr/share/man:/usr/dt/
    share/man:/usr/dt/man:/usr/man:/opt/SUNWrtvc/man:/opt/hpnp/man
DTDATABASESEARCHPATH=/export/home/winsor/.dt/types,/etc/dt/appconfig/ty
    pes/%L,/etc/dt/appconfig/types/C,/usr/dt/appconfig/types/%L,/usr/dt/a
    ppconfig/types/C
DTXSERVERLOCATION=local
LANG=C
HELPPATH=/usr/openwin/lib/locale:/usr/openwin/lib/help
DTSOURCEPROFILE=true
PATH=/usr/openwin/bin:/usr/dt/bin:/bin:/usr/bin:/usr/sbin:/usr/ucb:/etc
    :/usr/proc/bin:/opt/hpnp/bin:/usr/local/games:.
...
castle%
```

The following example pipes the output of the `env` command through `grep` and searches for the value for the `MANPATH` environment variable.

```
castle% env | grep MANPATH
MANPATH=/usr/openwin/share/man:/usr/openwin/man:/usr/share/man:/usr/dt/
    share/man:/usr/dt/man:/usr/man:/opt/SUNWrtvc/man:/opt/hpnp/man
castle%
```

The following command invokes the command named `mygrep` with a new PATH value as the only entry in its environment. In this case, PATH is used to locate `mygrep`, which then must reside in `/mybin`.

```
castle% env -i PATH=/mybin mygrep xyz myfile
```

Environment Variables

See `environ`(5) for descriptions of the following environment variables that affect the execution of `env`: LC_CTYPE, LC_MESSAGES, and NLSPATH.

Exit Status

If *command* is invoked, the exit status of `env` is the exit status of *command*; otherwise, the `env` command exits with one of the following values:

0	Successful completion.
1-125	An error occurred.
126	*command* was found but could not be invoked.
127	*command* could not be found.

Attributes

See `attributes`(5) for descriptions of the following attributes:

/usr/bin/env

Attribute Type	Attribute Value
Availability	SUNWcsu
CSI	Enabled

/usr/xpg4/bin/env

Attribute Type	Attribute Value
Availability	SUNWxcu4
CSI	Enabled

See Also

ksh(1), sh(1), exec(2), profile(4), attributes(5), environ(5), XPG4(5)

eqn, neqn, checkeq — Typeset Mathematics Test

Synopsis

```
/usr/bin/eqn [-dxy] [-fn] [-pn] [-sn] [file] ...
/usr/bin/neqn [file] ...
/usr/bin/checkeq [file] ...
```

Description

eqn and neqn are language processors to assist in describing equations. eqn is a preprocessor for troff(1) and is intended for devices that can print troff's output. neqn is a preprocessor for nroff(1) and is intended for use with terminals. Usage is almost always:

```
castle% eqn file ... | troff
castle% neqn file ... | nroff
```

If you specify no files, eqn and neqn read from the standard input. A line beginning with .EQ marks the start of an equation; the end of an equation is marked by a line beginning with .EN. Neither of these lines is altered, so they may be defined in macro packages to get centering, numbering, and so on. It is also possible to set two characters as delimiters; subsequent text between delimiters is also treated as eqn input.

checkeq reports missing or unbalanced delimiters and .EQ/.EN pairs.

Options

-dxy	Set equation delimiters to characters x and y with the command-line argument. The more common way to do this is with delim xy between .EQ and .EN. The left and right delimiters can be identical. Delimiters are turned off by delim off in the text. All text that is neither between delimiters nor between .EQ and .EN is passed through untouched.
-fn	Change font to n globally in the document. The font can also be changed globally in the body of the document by the gfont n directive, where n is the font specification.
-pn	Reduce subscripts and superscripts by n point sizes from the previous size. In the absence of the -p option, subscripts and superscripts are reduced by three point sizes from the previous size.
-sn	Change point size to n globally in the document. The point size can also be changed globally in the body of the document by the gsize n directive, where n is the point size.

Operands

file   The nroff or troff file processed by eqn or neqn.

Eqn Language

The nroff version of this description depicts the output of neqn to the terminal screen exactly as neqn is able to display it. Use neqn to view an accurate depiction of the printed output on the screen.

Tokens within eqn are separated by braces, double quotes, tildes, circumflexes, space, Tab, or newline characters. Braces {} are used for grouping; generally, anywhere a single character like x could appear, you can use a complicated construction enclosed in braces instead. Tilde (~) represents a full space in the output, circumflex (^), half as much.

Make subscripts and superscripts with the keywords sub and sup.

```
x sub i makes xi
2
a sub i sup 2 produces ai
 e sup {x sup 2 + y sup 2} gives ex2+y2
```

Make fractions with over.

```
a?_
a over b yields b
```

Make square roots with sqrt.

```
1
1 over sqrt {ax sup 2 +bx+c} results in  _____
\|ax2+bx+c
```

Use the keywords from and to to introduce lower and upper limits on arbitrary things.

```
lim from {n-> inf } sum from 0 to n x sub i
```

makes

```
n
lim ~?>?_xi
n->oo0
```

Note — The SIGMA symbol cannot be displayed in nroff.

Make left and right brackets and braces of the right height with left and right.

```
left [x sup 2 + y sup 2 over alpha right] ~=~1
```

produces

```
|
|  y?_2?_|  = 1.
|x2+<?a  |
|
```

The `right` clause is optional. Legal characters after `left` and `right` are braces, brackets, bars, `c` and `f` for ceiling and floor, and `" "` for nothing at all (useful for a right-side-only bracket).

Make vertical piles of things with `pile`, `lpile`, `cpile`, and `rpile`.

```
pile {a above b above c}
```

produces

```
a
b
c
```

There can be an arbitrary number of elements in a pile. `lpile` left-justifies, `pile` and `cpile` center, with different vertical spacing, and `rpile` right-justifies.

Make matrices with `matrix`.

```
matrix { lcol { x sub i above y sub 2 } ccol { 1 above 2 } }
```

produces

```
xi
y2
1
2
```

In addition, you can use `rcol` for a right-justified column.

Make diacritical marks with `dot`, `dotdot`, `hat`, `tilde`, `bar`, `vec`, `dyad`, and `under`.

```
x dot = f(t) bar
```

is

```
.  ____
x=f(t)
```

```
y dotdot bar ~=~ n under
```

is

```
 .?_.?_
 y = n?_
```

```
x vec ~=~ y dyad
```

is

$$\overline{\overline{x}} = \overline{\overline{y}}$$

Sizes and Fonts
Change sizes and font with `size` *n* or `size +-`*n*, `roman`, `italic`, `bold`, and `font` *n*. Change size and fonts globally in a document by `gsize` *n* and `gfont` *n* or by the command-line arguments `-s`*n* and `-f`*n*.

Successive Display Arguments
You can line up successive display arguments by placing `mark` before the desired lineup point in the first equation; place `lineup` at the place that is to line up vertically in subsequent equations.

Shorthands
Define shorthands or redefine existing keywords with `define`. The following statement defines a new token called *thing* that is replaced by *replacement* whenever it appears thereafter. The `%` can be any character that does not occur in *replacement*.

`define` *thing* `%` *replacement* `%`

Keywords and Shorthands
Recognized keywords are `sum` (SIGMA is not reproducible in `nroff`), `int` (integral sign is not reproducible in `nroff`), `inf` (infinity sign is not reproducible in `nroff`), and shorthands like `>=` (greater than or equal to is not reproducible in `nroff`) `->` (`->`), and `!=` (not equal to is not reproducible in `nroff`).

Greek letters
Greek letters are spelled out in the desired case, as in alpha or GAMMA.

Mathematical Words
Mathematical words like `sin`, `cos`, and `log` are made Roman automatically.
    You can use `troff`(1) four-character escapes like `\ (bu` (*o*) anywhere. Strings enclosed in double quotes `"..."` are passed through untouched to permit keywords to be entered as text. You can use them to communicate with `troff` when all else fails.

Attributes
See `attributes`(5) for descriptions of the following attributes:

Attribute Type	Attribute Value
Availability	SUNWdoc

See Also

```
nroff(1), tbl(1), troff(1), attributes(5), ms(5)
```

Bugs

To bold characters such as digits and parentheses, you must quote them, as in
`'bold "12.3"'`.

eval — Shell Built-in Functions to Execute Other Commands

Synopsis

sh and ksh
```
eval [argument...]
```

ksh
```
* eval [arg ...]
```

Description

See exec(1).

ex — Display-Based Text Editor

Synopsis

```
/usr/bin/ex [- | -s][-l][-L][-R][-r [file]][-t tag][-v][-V]
    [-x][-wn][-C][+command | -c command] file...
/usr/xpg4/bin/ex [- | -s][-l] [-L][-R][-r [file]][-t tag][-v][-V]
    [-x][-wn][-C][+command | -c command] file...
```

Description

The ex command is the root of a family of editors: ex, edit, and vi. ex is a
superset of ed(1), with the most notable extension being a display-editing
facility. Display-based editing is the focus of vi.

If you have a CRT terminal, you may want to use a display based editor; in
this case, see vi(1), which is a command that focuses on the display-editing
portion of ex.

If you have used ed, you will find that, in addition to having all of the ed
commands available, ex has a number of additional features useful on CRT
terminals. Intelligent terminals and high-speed terminals are very pleasant to
use with vi. Generally, the ex editor uses far more of the capabilities of
terminals than does ed. The ex editor uses the terminal capability database

(see terminfo(4)) and the type of the terminal you are using from the environment variable TERM to determine how to drive your terminal efficiently. The editor makes use of features such as "insert and delete character and line" in its visual command (the vi ccommand).

The ex command contains a number of features for easily viewing the text of the file. The z command gives easy access to windows of text. Entering Control-D scrolls a half-window of text and is more useful for quickly stepping through a file than just pressing Return. Of course, the screen-oriented visual mode gives constant access to editing context.

The ex command provides help when you make mistakes. The undo (u) command enables you to reverse any single change that goes astray. ex gives you a lot of feedback, normally printing changed lines, and indicates when more than a few lines are affected by a command so that it is easy to detect when a command has affected more lines than it should have.

The editor also normally prevents overwriting existing files, unless you edited them, so that you do not accidentally overwrite a file other than the one you are editing. If the system (or editor) crashes or you accidentally hang up the telephone, you can use the editor recover command (or -r file option) to retrieve your work. This facility gets you back to within a few lines of where you left off.

The ex command has several features for dealing with more than one file at a time. You can give it a list of files on the command line and use the next (n) command to deal with each in turn. You can also give the next command a list of file names, or a pattern as used by the shell, to specify a new set of files to be dealt with. In general, you can form file names in the editor with full shell metasyntax. The metacharacter % is also available in forming file names and is replaced by the name of the current file.

The editor has a group of buffers whose names are the ASCII lowercase letters (a-z). You can place text in these named buffers, where it is available to be inserted elsewhere in the file. The contents of these buffers remain available when you begin editing a new file using the edit (e) command.

Note — The editor does not warn you when you exit if you put text in named buffers and have not used them.

The & command repeats the last substitute command. In addition, ex provides a confirmed substitute command. You give a range of substitutions to be done, and the editor interactively asks whether each substitution is desired.

You can specify whether searches and substitutions are case insensitive. ex also allows regular expressions that match words to be constructed. This pattern matching is convenient, for example, in searching for the word edit if your document also contains the word editor.

ex has a set of options that you can tailor to your liking. One option that is very useful is the autoindent option, which enables the editor to supply leading white space to align text automatically. You can then use ^D as a backtab and space or Tab to move forward to align new code easily.

Miscellaneous useful features include an intelligent `join` (`j`) command that automatically supplies white space between joined lines, commands < and > that shift groups of lines, and the ability to filter portions of the buffer through commands such as `sort`.

Note — Null characters are discarded in input files and cannot appear in resultant files.

Options

`-` | `-s`	Suppress all interactive user feedback. This option is useful when processing editor scripts. Note that file input/output errors do not print a name if you use the command-line `-s` option.
`+command` | `-c command`	
	Begin editing by executing the specified editor command (usually a search or positioning command).
`-C`	Simulate the `C` command. The `C` command is like the `X` command, except that all text read in is assumed to have been encrypted.
`-l`	Set up for editing LISP programs.
`-L`	List the name of all files saved as the result of an editor or system crash.
`-R`	Set the read-only flag to prevent accidental overwriting of the file.
`-r file`	Edit `file` after an editor or system crash. (Recover the version of file that was in the buffer when the crash occurred.) Note that the message `file too large to recover with -r option` that you see when you load a file indicates that you can successfully edit and save the file. However, if the editing session is lost, you cannot recover the file with the `-r` option.
`-t tag`	Edit the file containing the `tag,` and position the editor at its definition.
`-v`	Start up in display-editing state using `vi`. You can achieve the same effect by simply typing the `vi` command.
`-V`	When `ex` commands are read by means of standard input, echo the input to standard error. This verbose option can be useful for processing `ex` commands within shell scripts.
`-wn`	Set the default window size to n. This option is useful when using the editor over a slow-speed line.

-x   Simulate the X command and prompt for an encryption key. This key encrypts and decrypts text using the algorithm of the crypt command. The X command makes an educated guess to determine whether text read in is encrypted or not. The temporary buffer file is encrypted also, using a transformed version of the key typed in for the -x option.

Note — Although the following options continue to be supported, they have been replaced in the documentation by options that follow the Command Syntax Standard (see intro(1)). The - option has been replaced by -s; a -r option that is not followed with an option-argument has been replaced by -L, and +command has been replaced by -c command.

/usr/xpg4/bin/ex

If you specify both the -t tag and the -c command options, the -t tag is processed first. That is, the file containing tag is selected by -t and then the command is executed.

Note — The standard Solaris version of ex will be replaced by the POSIX.2-conforming version (see standards(5)) in the future. Scripts that use the ex family of addressing and features should use the /usr/xpg4/bin version of these commands.

Operands

file   A path name of a file to be edited.

Usage

The states for the ex command are listed below.

State	Description
Command	Normal and initial state. Input prompted for by a colon (:). Your line-kill character cancels a partial command.
Insert	Entered by a, i, or c. You can enter arbitrary text. Insert state normally is terminated by a line having only . on it, or, abnormally, with an interrupt.
Visual	Entered by typing vi; terminated by typing Q or ^\ (Control-\).

The commands, abbreviations, and command arguments for the ex command are listed below. For /usr/xpg4/bin/ex, if you specify both a count and a range for a command that uses them, the number of lines affected

is taken from the *count* value instead of the *range*. The starting line for the
command is taken to be the first line addressed by the *range*.

Command	Abbreviation	Arguments
Abbreviate	ab	ab[brev] *word* rhs
Append	a	[*line*] a[ppend][!]
Arguments	ar	ar[gs]
Change	c	[*range*] c[hange][!] [*count*]
Change Directory	chd	chd[ir][!] [*directory*]; cd[!] [*directory*]
Copy	co	[*range*] co[py] *line* [*flags*]; [*range*] t *line* [*flags*]
Delete	d	[*range*] d[elete] [*buffer*] [*count*] [*flags*]
Edit	e	e[dit][!] [+*line*][*file*]; ex[!] [+*line*] [*file*]
File	f	f[ile] [*file*]
Global	g	[*range*] g[lobal] /*pattern*/ [*commands*]; [*range*] v /*pattern*/ [commands]
Insert	i	[*line*] i[nsert][!]
Join	j	[*range*] j[oin][!] [*count*] [*flags*]
List	l	[*range*] l[ist] [*count*] [*flags*]
Map	map	map[!] [x rhs]
Mark	ma	[*line*] ma[rk] x; [*line*] k x
Move	m	[*range*] m[ove] *line*
Next	n	n[ext][!] [*file* ...]
Number	nu	[*range*] nu[mber] [*count*] [*flags*]; [*range*] # [*count*] [*flags*]
Open	o	[*line*] o[pen] /*pattern*/ [*flags*]
Preserve	pre	pre[serve]
Print	p	[*range*] p[rint] [*count*] [*flags*]
Put	pu	[*line*] pu[t] [*buffer*]
Quit	q	q[uit][!]
Read	r	[*line*] r[ead][!] [*file*]
Recover	rec	rec[over] *file*

Command	Abbreviation	Arguments
Rewind	rew	rew[ind][!] Set se[t] [*option*[=[*value*]]...] [nooption...] [*option*?...] [all]
Shell	sh	sh[ell]
Source	so	so[urce] *file*
Substitute	s	[*range*] s[ubstitute] [/*pattern*/*repl*/[*options*] [*count*] [*flags*]]
Suspend	su	su[spend][!]; st[op][!]
Tag	ta	ta[g][!] *tagstring*
Unabbreviate	una	una[bbrev] *word*
Undo	u	u[ndo]
Unmap	unm	unm[ap][!] x
Visual	vi	[*line*] vi[sual] [*type*] [*count*] [*flags*]
Write	w	[*range*} w[rite][!] [>>] [*file*]; [*range*} w[rite] [!] [*file*]; [*range*} wq[!] [>>] [*file*]
Write and Exit	x	[*range*] x[it][!] [*file*]
Yank	ya	[*range*] ya[nk] [*buffer*] [*count*]
Adjust Window		[*line*] z [*type*] [*count*] [*flags*]
Escape		! *command* [*range*]! *command*
Shift Left		[*range*] < [*count*] [*flags*]
Shift Right		[*range*] > [*count*] [*flags*]
Resubstitute		[*range*] & [*options*] [*count*] [*flags*]; [*range*] s[ubstitute] [*options*] [*count*][*flags*]; [*range*] ~ [*options*] [*count*] [*flags*]
Scroll		EOF
Write Line Number		[*line*] = [*flags*]
Execute		@ *buffer*; * *buffer*

The ex commands are listed below.

Command	Description
C	Forced encryption.

Command	Description
X	Heuristic encryption.
&	Resubstitute.
CR	Print next.
>	Right shift.
<	Left shift.
^D	Scroll.
z	Window.
!	Shell escape.

> **Note —** The z command prints the number of logical instead of physical lines. More than one screen of output may result if long lines are present.

The ex command addresses are listed below.

Address	Description
n	Line n.
.	Current.
$	Last.
+	Next.
−	Previous.
+n	n forward.
/pat	Next with pat.
?pat	Previous with pat.
x-n	n before x.
x,y	x through y.
'x	Marked with x.
"	Previous context.
%	1,$.

The ex initialization options are listed below.

Option	Description
EXINIT	Place set commands in the EXINIT environment variable.
$HOME/.exrc	
	Editor initialization file.
./.exrc	Editor initialization file.

Option	Description
set *x*	Enable option *x*.
set no*x*	Disable option *x*.
set *x=val*	Give value *val* to option *x*.
set	Show changed options.
set al	Show all options.
set *x?*	Show value of option *x*.

The most useful `ex` options and their abbreviations are listed below.

Option	Abbrev.	Description
autoindent	ai	Supply indent.
autowrite	aw	Write before changing files.
directory		Path name of directory for temporary work files.
exrc	ex	Enable vi/ex to read the .exrc in the current directory. This option is set in the EXINIT shell variable or in the .exrc file in the $HOME directory.
ignorecase	ic	Ignore case of letters in scanning. Note that there is no easy way to do a single scan ignoring case.
list		Print ^I for Tab, $ at end.
magic		Treat . [* as special in patterns.
modelines		Execute first five lines and last five lines as vi/ex commands if they are of the form ex:*command*: or vi:*command*:.
number	nu	Number lines.
paragraphs	para	Macro names that start paragraphs.
redraw		Simulate smart terminal.
report		Inform you if the number of lines modified by the last command is greater than the value of the report variable.
scroll		Command-mode lines.
sections	sect	Macro names that start sections.
shiftwidth	sw	For < >, and input ^D.
showmatch	sm	To) and } as typed.
showmode	smd	Show insert mode in vi.
slowopen	slow	Stop updates during insert.
term		Specifies to vi the type of terminal being used (the default is the value of the environment variable TERM).

Option	Abbrev.	Description
window		Visual mode lines.
wrapmargin	wm	Automatic line splitting.
wrapscan	ws	Search around end (or beginning) of buffer.

The ex scanning pattern formations are listed below.

Pattern	Description
^	Beginning of line.
$	End of line.
.	Any character.
\<	Beginning of word.
\>	End of word.
[str]	Any character in str.
[^str]	Any character not in str.
[x-v]	Any character between x and y.
*	Any number of preceding characters.

Environment Variables

See environ(5) for descriptions of the following environment variables that affect the execution of ex: HOME, PATH, SHELL, TERM, LC_COLLATE, LC_CTYPE, LC_MESSAGES, and NLSPATH.

COLUMNS	Override the system-selected horizontal screen size.
EXINIT	Determine a list of ex commands that are executed on editor startup, before reading the first file. The list can contain multiple commands separated by the pipe (|) character.
LINES	Override the system-selected vertical screen size, used as the number of lines in a screenful and the vertical screen size in visual mode.

The editing environment defaults to certain configuration options. When you initiate an editing session, ex tries to read the EXINIT environment variable. If it exists, the editor uses the values defined in EXINIT; otherwise, the values set in $HOME/.exrc are used. If $HOME/.exrc does not exist, the default values are used.

To use a copy of .exrc located in the current directory other than $HOME, set the exrc option in EXINIT or $HOME/.exrc. Options set in EXINIT can be turned off in a local .exrc only if exrc is set in EXINIT or $HOME/.exrc.

Exit Status

0	Successful completion.
>0	An error occurred.

Files

/var/tmp/Ex*nnnnn*

          Editor temporary file.

/var/tmp/Rx*nnnnn*

          Named buffer temporary file.

/usr/lib/expreserve

          Preserve command.

/usr/lib/exrecover

          Recover command.

/usr/lib/exstrings

          Error messages.

/usr/share/lib/terminfo/*

          Describes capabilities of terminals.

/var/preserve/login

          Preservation directory (where login is the user's login).

$HOME/.exrc

          Editor startup file.

./.exrc   Editor startup file.

Attributes

See attributes(5) for descriptions of the following attributes:

/usr/bin/ex

Attribute Type	Attribute Value
Availability	SUNWcsu
CSI	Enabled

/usr/xpg4/bin/ex

Attribute Type	Attribute Value
Availability	SUNWxcu4
CSI	Enabled

See Also

ed(1), edit(1), grep(1), sed(1), sort(1), vi(1), curses(3X), term(4),
terminfo(4), attributes(5), environ(5), standards(5)
Solaris Advanced User's Guide

Author

The vi and ex commands are based on software developed by The University
of California, Berkeley California, Computer Science Division, Department of
Electrical Engineering and Computer Science.

exec, eval, source — Shell Built-in Functions to Execute Other Commands

Synopsis

sh

exec [*argument...*]
eval [*argument...*]

csh

exec *command*
eval *argument...*
source [-h] *name*

ksh

* exec [*arg ...*]
* eval [*arg ...*]

Description

Bourne Shell

The exec *command* specified by the arguments is executed in place of this shell
without creating a new process. Input/output arguments may appear and, if
you give no other arguments, they modify the shell input/output.

The arguments to the eval built-in are read as input to the shell and the
resulting command(s) executed.

C Shell

exec executes *command* in place of the current shell, which terminates.

eval reads its arguments as input to the shell and executes the resulting
command(s). This command is usually used to execute commands generated as
the result of command or variable substitution.

source reads commands from *name*. You can nest source commands, but if they are nested too deeply, the shell may run out of file descriptors. An error in a sourced file at any level terminates all nested source commands.

-h   Put commands from the file name on the history list without executing them.

Korn Shell

With the exec built-in, if you specify *arg*, the command specified by the arguments is executed in place of this shell without creating a new process. You can specify input/output arguments that affect the current process. If you specify no arguments, the effect of this command is to modify file descriptors as prescribed by the input/output redirection list. In this case, any file descriptor numbers greater than 2 that are opened with this mechanism are closed when another program is invoked.

The arguments to eval are read as input to the shell, and the resulting command(s) executed.

ksh(1) commands that are preceded by one or two asterisks (*) are treated specially in the following ways:

- Variable assignment lists preceding the command remain in effect when the command completes.
- I/O redirections are processed after variable assignments.
- Errors cause a script that contains them to abort.
- Words, following a command preceded by ** and that are in the format of a variable assignment, are expanded with the same rules as a variable assignment. Tilde substitution is performed after the equal sign, and word-splitting and file-name generation are not performed.

Attributes

See attributes(5) for descriptions of the following attributes:

Attribute Type	Attribute Value
Availability	SUNWcsu

See Also

csh(1), ksh(1), sh(1), attributes(5)

exit, return, goto — Shell Built-in Functions to Enable the Shell
to Advance Beyond Its Sequence of Steps

Synopsis

sh
```
exit [n]
return [n]
```

csh
```
exit [(expr)]
goto label
```

ksh
```
* exit [n]
* return [n]
```

Description

Bourne Shell

exit exits the calling shell or shell script with the exit status specified by n. If you omit n, the exit status is that of the last command executed (an end-of-file exits the shell).

return exits a function with the return value specified by n. If you omit n, the return status is that of the last command executed.

C Shell

exit exits the calling shell or shell script, either with the value of the status variable or with the value specified by the expression *expr*.

The goto built-in uses a specified label as a search string among commands. The shell rewinds its input as much as possible and searches for a line of the form *label*: possibly preceded by space or Tab characters. Execution continues after the indicated line. It is an error to jump to a label that occurs between a while or for built-in command and its corresponding end.

Korn Shell

exit exits the calling shell or shell script with the exit status specified by n. The value is the least significant 8 bits of the specified status. If you omit n, the exit status is that of the last command executed. When exit occurs when a trap is being executed, the last command refers to the command that executed before the trap was invoked. An end-of-file also exits the shell except for a shell that has the ignoreeof option turned on.

return returns a shell function or . script to the invoking script with the return status specified by n. The value is the least significant 8 bits of the specified status. If you omit n, the return status is that of the last command executed. If you invoke `return` while not in a function or a . script, then it is the same as an `exit`.

For the `exit` and `return` commands, ksh(1) commands that are preceded by one or two asterisks (*) are treated specially in the following ways:

1. Variable assignment lists preceding the command remain in effect when the command completes.
2. I/O redirections are processed after variable assignments.
3. Errors cause a script that contains them to abort.
4. Words, following a command preceded by ** and that are in the format of a variable assignment, are expanded with the same rules as a variable assignment. Tilde substitution is performed after the equal sign (=), and word-splitting and file-name generation are not performed.

Attributes

See `attributes`(5) for descriptions of the following attributes:

Attribute Type	Attribute Value
Availability	SUNWcsu

See Also

`break(1)`, `csh(1)`, `ksh(1)`, `sh(1)`, `attributes(5)`

---

expand, unexpand — Expand Tab Characters to Space Characters, and Vice Versa

Synopsis

```
/usr/bin/expand [-t tablist] [file...]
/usr/bin/expand [-tabstop] [-tab1,tab2,...,tabn] [file...]
/usr/bin/unexpand [-a] [-t tablist] [file...]
```

Description

expand copies files (or the standard input) to the standard output, with Tab characters expanded to space characters. Backspace characters are preserved in the output and decrement the column count for Tab calculations. expand is useful for preprocessing character files (before sorting, looking at specific columns, and so forth) that contain Tab characters.

unexpand copies files (or the standard input) to the standard output, putting Tab characters back into the data. By default, only leading space and

Tab characters are converted to strings of tabs. You can override the default behavior with the -a option.

Options

The options for the expand command are listed below.

-t *tablist* Specify the Tab stops. The argument *tablist* must consist of a single, positive decimal integer or multiple, positive, decimal integers separated by blank characters or commas, in ascending order. If you specify a single number, Tabs are set *tablist* column positions apart instead of the default 8. If you specify multiple numbers, the Tabs are set at those specific column positions.

Each Tab-stop position N must be an integer value greater than 0, and the list must be in strictly ascending order. From the start of a line of output, tabbing to position N outputs the next character in the (N+1)-th column position on that line.

If expand processes a Tab character at a position beyond the last of those specified in a multiple Tab-stop list, the Tab character is replaced by a single space character in the output.

-*tabstop*   Set Tab characters *tabstop* space characters apart, where *tabstop* is a single integer, instead of the default 8.

-*tab1,tab2,...,tabn*

Set Tab characters at the columns specified by -*tab1, tab2,...,
tabn*.

The options for the unexpand command are listed below.

-a   Insert Tab characters when replacing a run of two or more space characters would produce a smaller output file.

-t *tablist* Specify the Tab stops. The *tablist* must be a single argument consisting of a single, positive, decimal integer or multiple, positive, decimal integers separated by blank characters or commas, in ascending order. If you specify a single number, set Tabs *tablist* column positions apart instead of the default 8. If you specify multiple numbers, the tabs are set at those specific column positions.

Each Tab-stop position N must be an integer value greater than 0, and the list must be in strictly ascending order. From the start of a line of output, tabbing to position N outputs the next character in the (N+1)-th column position on that line. When you do not specify the -t option, the default is the equivalent of specifying -t 8 (except for the interaction with -a).

No space-to-Tab character conversions occur for characters at positions beyond the last of those specified in a multiple Tab-stop list.

When you specify -t, the presence or absence of the -a option is ignored; conversion is not limited to the processing of leading blank characters.

Operands.

file   The path name of a text file to be used as input.

Environment Variables

See environ(5) for descriptions of the following environment variables that affect the execution of expand and unexpand: LC_CTYPE, LC_MESSAGES, and NLSPATH.

Exit Status

0   Successful completion.

>0   An error occurred.

Attributes

See attributes(5) for descriptions of the following attributes:

Attribute Type	Attribute Value
Availability	SUNWesu
CSI	Enabled

See Also

tabs(1), attributes(5), environ(5)

export — Shell Built-in Environment Variable Function

Synopsis

sh
export [name ...]

ksh
export [name[=value]] ...

Description

See set(1).

exportfs — Translate exportfs Options to share/unshare Commands

Synopsis

```
/usr/sbin/exportfs [-aiuv] [-o options] [pathname]
```

Description

exportfs translates SunOS 4.x exportfs options to the corresponding share/unshare options and invokes share/unshare with the translated options.

With no options or arguments, exportfs invokes share to print out the list of all currently shared NFS file systems.

Note — exportfs is the BSD/Compatibility Package command of share(1M) and unshare(1M). Use share(1M)/ unshare(1M) whenever possible.

Options

-a	Invoke shareall(1M), or if -u is specified, invoke unshareall(1M).
-i	Ignore options in /etc/dfs/dfstab.
-u	Invoke unshare(1M) on path name.
-v	Verbose.
-o options	Specify a comma-separated list of optional characteristics for the file systems being exported. exportfs translates options to share-equivalent options. (See share(1M) for information about individual options.)

Attributes

See attributes(5) for descriptions of the following attributes:

Attribute Type	Attribute Value
Availability	SUNWcsu

See Also

share(1M), shareall(1M), unshare(1M), unshareall(1M), attributes(5)

expr — Evaluate Arguments as an Expression

Synopsis
```
/usr/bin/expr argument...
/usr/xpg4/bin/expr argument...
/usr/ucb/expr argument...
```

Description

The `expr` command evaluates the expression and writes the result to standard output. Each token of the expression is a separate argument, so you must separate terms of the expression by blanks. Quote strings containing blanks or other special characters. You can precede integer-valued arguments by a unary minus sign. Escape characters special to the shell. The length of the expression is limited to LINE_MAX (2048 characters).

Note — The character 0 is written to indicate a zero value and nothing is written to indicate a null string.

Operands

The operators and keywords are listed below. The list is in order of increasing precedence, with equal precedence operators grouped within { } symbols. All of the operators are left-associative.

expr \| *expr*

> Return the first *expr* if it is neither null nor 0; otherwise, return the second *expr*.

expr \& *expr*

> Return the first *expr* if neither *expr* is null or 0; otherwise, return 0.

expr { =, \>, \>=, \<, \<=, != } *expr*

> Return the result of an integer comparison if both arguments are integers; otherwise, return the result of a string comparison, using the locale-specific coalition sequence. The result of each comparison is 1 if the specified relationship is `true`, 0 if the relationship is `false`.

expr { +, - } *expr*

> Add or subtract integer-valued arguments.

expr { *, /, % } *expr*

> Multiply, divide, or remainder the integer-valued arguments.

> `expr : expr` Compare the first argument with the second argument, which must be an internationalized basic regular expression (BRE); see `regex`(5). Normally, the `/usr/bin/expr` colon (`:`) matching operator returns the number of bytes matched, and the `/usr/xpg4/bin/expr` matching operator returns the number of characters matched (0 on failure). If the second argument contains at least one BRE subexpression `[\(...\)]`, the matching operator returns the string corresponding to `\1`.

> `integer` An argument consisting only of an (optional) unary minus followed by digits.

> `string` A string argument that cannot be identified as an integer argument or as one of the expression operator symbols.

Compatibility Operators (x86 only)

The following operators are included for compatibility with INTERACTIVE UNIX System only and are not intended to be used by non-INTERACTIVE UNIX System scripts:

`index string character-list`

> Report the first position in which any one of the bytes in `character-list` matches a byte in string.

`length string`

> Return the length (that is, the number of bytes) of `string`.

`substr string integer-1 integer-2`

> Extract the substring of `string` starting at position `integer-1` and of length `integer-2` bytes. If `integer-1` has a value greater than the number of bytes in `string`, `expr` returns a null string. If you try to extract more bytes than there are in `string`, `expr` returns all the remaining bytes from `string`. Results are unspecified if either `integer-1` or `integer-2` is a negative value.

Notes

After argument processing by the shell, `expr` cannot tell the difference between an operator and an operand except by the value. If `$a` is an `=`, the command:

```
$ expr $a = '='
```

looks like:

```
$ expr = = =
```

as the arguments are passed to `expr` (and they are all taken as the = operator). The following works:

```
$ expr X$a = X=
```

Regular Expressions

Unlike some previous versions, expr uses Internationalized Basic Regular Expressions for all system-provided locales. Internationalized Regular Expressions are explained on the regex(5) manual page.

Examples

You can use expr to perform basic integer math, which is useful for simple mathematical processing and for controlling loops.

The following example performs a simple calculation.

```
castle% expr 1 + 9
10
castle%
```

You can use expr to evaluate various string comparisons, as shown in the following example.

```
a=bill
b=tom

 if expr $a = $b
then
  echo "They are the same."
else
  echo "They are different."
fi
```

The script returns:

```
They are different.
```

You can use expr to evaluate alphabetic or arithmetic variables, as shown in the following example.

```
a=bill
expr $a : '[a-zA-Z]*'
or
n=100
expr $n : '[-+]*[0-9.]*'

if [ 'expr $n : '[-+]*[0-9.]*'' -eq 'expr $n : '.*'' ]
 then
    echo "It's numeric."
 else
    echo "It's not numeric."
fi
```

The system returns:

```
It's numeric.
```

The following example adds 1 to the shell variable a.

```
a=0
a=`expr $a + 1`
```

The following example emulates basename(1). It returns the last segment of the path name $a. For $a equal to either /usr/abc/file or just file, the example returns file. (Watch out for / alone as an argument: expr takes it as the division operator.)

```
a='/etc/dfs/dfstab'
expr $a : '.*/\(.*\)' \| $a
```

The expression returns dfstab.

The following example is a better version of the previous example. The addition of the // characters eliminates any ambiguity about the division operator and simplifies the whole expression.

```
a='/etc/dfs/dfstab'
expr //$a : '.*/\(.*\)'
```

/usr/bin/expr

The following example returns the number of bytes in $VAR.

```
VAR=bill
expr "$VAR" : '.*'
```

The expression returns 4.

/usr/xpg4/bin/expr

The following example returns the number of characters in $VAR.

```
VAR=bill
expr "$VAR" : '.*'
```

Environment Variables

See environ(5) for descriptions of the following environment variables that affect the execution of expr: LC_COLLATE, LC_CTYPE, LC_MESSAGES, and NLSPATH.

Exit Status

As a side effect of expression evaluation, expr returns the following exit values:

0	The expression is neither null nor 0.
1	The expression is either null or 0.
2	Invalid expression.
>2	An error occurred.

Attributes
See `attributes`(5) for descriptions of the following attributes:

Attribute Type	Attribute Value
Availability	SUNWcsu
CSI	Enabled

See Also
`basename(1)`, `ed(1)`, `sh(1)`, `Intro(3)`, `attributes(5)`, `environ(5)`, `regex(5)`, `XPG4(5)`

Diagnostics
`syntax error` Operator and operand errors.

`non-numeric argument`
>   Arithmetic is attempted on such a string.

exstr — Extract Strings from Source Files

Synopsis
```
/usr/bin/exstr filename...
/usr/bin/exstr -e filename...
/usr/bin/exstr -r [-d] filename...
```

Description
Use the `exstr` command to extract strings from C-language source files and replace them by calls to the message retrieval function (see `gettxt`(3C)). This command extracts all character strings surrounded by double quotes, not just strings used as arguments to the `printf` command or the `printf` routine. In the first form, `exstr` finds all strings in the source files and writes them on the standard output. Each string is preceded by the source file name and a colon.

Use the following steps to extract strings from a source file:

1. Use `exstr -e` to extract a list of strings and save it in a file.
2. Examine the list and determine which strings can be translated and subsequently retrieved by the message retrieval function.
3. Modify the file by deleting lines that can't be translated and, for lines that can be translated, by adding the message file names and the message numbers as the fourth (`msgfile`) and fifth (`msgnum`) entries on a line. The message files named must have been created by `mkmsgs`(1) and exist in

/usr/lib/locale/locale/LC_MESSAGES. (The directory locale corresponds to the language in which the text strings are written; see setlocale(3C)). Use message numbers that correspond to the sequence numbers of strings in the message files.

4. Use this modified file as input to exstr -r to produce a new version of the original C-language source file in which the strings have been replaced by calls to the message retrieval function gettxt(). The msgfile and msgnum fields are used to construct the first argument to gettxt(). The second argument to gettxt() is printed if the message retrieval fails at runtime. This argument is the null string, unless you use the -d option.

The exstr command cannot replace strings in all instances. For example, a static initialized character string cannot be replaced by a function call. A second example is that a string could be in a form of an escape sequence that could not be translated. To not break existing code, you must examine the files created by invoking exstr -e and delete lines containing strings not replaceable by function calls. In some cases, the code may require modifications so that strings can be extracted and replaced by calls to the message retrieval function.

Options

-e Extract a list of strings from the named C-language source files, with positional information. This list is produced on standard output in the following format:

file:*line*:*position*:*msgfile*:*msgnum*:*string*

file	The name of a C-language source file.
line	Line number in the file.
position	Character position in the line.
msgfile	Null.
msgnum	Null.
string	The extracted text string.

Normally, you redirect this output into a file. Then, you edit this file to add the values you want to use for *msgfile* and *msgnum*:

msgfile	The file that contains the text strings that replace *string*. A file with this name must be created and installed in the appropriate place by the mkmsgs(1) command.
msgnum	The sequence number of the string in *msgfile*.

The next step is to use exstr -r to replace strings in file.

-r Replace strings in a C-language source file with function calls to the message retrieval function gettxt().

-d   Use together with the -r option. If the message retrieval fails
                            when gettxt() is invoked at runtime, then the extracted string is
                            printed. You use the capability provided by exstr on an
                            application program that needs to run in an international
                            environment and have messages print in more than one language.
                            exstr replaces text strings with function calls that point at
                            strings in a message database. The database used depends on the
                            runtime value of the LC_MESSAGES environment variable (see
                            environ(5)).

Examples

The following examples show uses of exstr.

Assume that the file example.c contains two strings.

```
main()
{
 printf("This is an example\n");
 printf("Hello world!\n");
}
```

The following example invokes the exstr command with the argument
example.c to extract strings from the named file and print them on the
standard output.

```
castle% exstr example.c
example.c:This is an example\n
example.c:Hello world!\n
castle%
```

Next, use the -e option to extract the strings and redirect the output to a file
named example.stringout.

```
castle% exstr -e example.c > example.stringout
castle% more example.stringout
example.c:3:22:::This is an example\n
example.c:4:22:::Hello world!\n
castle%
```

You must edit example.stringout to add the values you want to use for
the msgfile and msgnum fields before these strings can be replaced by calls to
the retrieval function. The following example uses UX as the name of the
message file and the numbers 1 and 2 as the sequence number of the strings in
the file to produce a file that looks like the following.

```
castle% more example.stringout
example.c:3:22:UX:1:This is an example\n
example.c:4:22:UX:2:Hello world!\n
castle%
```

Now, invoke the exstr command with the -r option to replace the strings in
the source file by the calls to the message retrieval function gettxt().

```
castle% exstr -r example.c < example.stringout > intlexample.c
castle% more intlexample.c
extern char *gettxt();
        main()
        {
                printf(gettxt("UX:1", ""));
                printf(gettxt("UX:2", ""));
        }
castle%
```

Using exstr with the -rd option displays the extracted strings as a second argument to gettxt().

```
castle% exstr -rd example.c < example.stringout > intlexample.c
castle% more intlexample.c
extern char *gettxt();
        main()
        {
                printf(gettxt("UX:1", "This is an example\n"));
                printf(gettxt("UX:2", "Hello world!\n"));
        }
castle%
```

Files

/usr/lib/locale/locale/LC_MESSAGES/*

Files created by mkmsgs(1).

Attributes

See attributes(5) for descriptions of the following attributes:

Attribute Type	Attribute Value
Availability	SUNWtoo

See Also

gettxt(1),mkmsgs(1),printf(1),srchtxt(1),gettxt(3C),setlocale(3C),,
printf(3S), attributes(5), environ(5)

Diagnostics

The error messages produced by exstr are self-explanatory. They indicate errors in the command line or format errors encountered within the input file.

F

---

factor — Obtain the Prime Factors of a Number

Synopsis

```
/usr/bin/factor [integer]
```

Description

`factor` writes to standard input all prime factors for any positive integer of fewer than 15 digits. The prime factors are written the proper number of times.

If you type `factor` without an argument, it waits for you to type an integer and press Return. After you enter the integer, `factor` factors it, writes its prime factors the proper number of times, and then waits for another integer. `factor` exits if you enter a 0 or any nonnumeric character.

If you invoke `factor` with an argument (`integer`), it writes the integer, factors it, writes all the prime factors as described above, and then exits. If the argument is 0 or nonnumeric, `factor` writes a 0 and then exits.

The maximum time to factor an integer is proportional to $sqrt(n)$, where n is the integer that you enter. `factor` takes this time when n is prime or the square of a prime.

Operands

`integer`   Any positive integer less than 15 digits.

Examples

The following example enters a number of 15 digits, and factor displays the Ouch! error message. It then factors a number of 14 digits. Type **q** and press Return to quit factor.

```
castle% factor
123456789012345
Ouch!
12345678901234
        2
        7
        73
        12079920647

q
castle%
```

Exit Status

0	Successful completion.
1	An error occurred.

Diagnostics

factor prints the error message Ouch! for input out of range or for garbage input.

Attributes

See attributes(5) for descriptions of the following attributes:

Attribute Type	Attribute Value
Availability	SUNWesu

See Also

attributes(5)

false — Provide Truth Values

Synopsis

/usr/bin/false

Description

See true(1).

fastboot, fasthalt — Reboot/Halt the System Without Checking the Disks

Synopsis

```
/usr/ucb/fastboot [boot-options]
/usr/ucb/fasthalt [halt-options]
```

Description

fastboot and fasthalt are shell scripts that invoke reboot and halt with the proper arguments.

Note — These commands are provided for BSD compatibility only.

Attributes

See attributes(5) for descriptions of the following attributes:

Attribute Type	Attribute Value
Availability	SUNWscpu

See Also

fsck(1M), halt(1M), init(1M), reboot(1M), init.d(4), attributes(5)

fc — Process Command History List

Synopsis

```
/usr/bin/fc [first[last]]
/usr/bin/fc -l [-nr][first[last]]
/usr/bin/fc -s [old=new][first]
```

ksh
```
fc -e - [old=new][command]
fc [-e ename][-nlr][first [last]]
```

Description

See history(1).

fdformat — Format Diskette or PCMCIA Memory Card

Synopsis

```
/usr/bin/fdformat [-dDeEfHlLmMUqvx] [-b label] [-B filename] [-t dos]
[-t nec] [devname]
```

Description

Use the fdformat command to format both diskettes and PCMCIA memory cards. You must format all new, blank diskettes or PCMCIA memory cards before you can use them. fdformat formats and verifies the media and indicates whether it encountered any bad sectors. All existing data on the diskette or PCMCIA memory card, if any, is destroyed by formatting. If you specify no device name, fdformat uses the diskette as a default.

By default, fdformat uses the configured capacity of the drive to format the diskette. A 3.5-inch, high-density drive uses diskettes with a formatted capacity of 1.44 megabytes. A 5.25-inch, high-density drive uses diskettes with a formatted capacity of 1.2 megabytes. In either case, you need not specify a density option to fdformat. You must, however, specify a density option when using a diskette with a lower capacity than the drive's default. Use the -H option to format high-density diskettes (1.44-megabyte capacity) in an extra-high-density (ED) drive. Use the -D option, the -l option, or the -L option to format double-density (or low-density) diskettes (720-kilobyte capacity) in an HD or ED drive. To format medium-density diskettes (1.2-megabyte capacity), use the -M option with -t nec (this is the same as using the -m option with -t nec).

Extended density uses double-sided, extended-density (or extra-high-density) (DS/ED) diskettes. Medium and high densities use the same media: double-sided, high-density (DS/HD) diskettes. Double (low) density uses double-sided, double-density (DS/DD) diskettes.

Note — Substituting diskettes of one density for diskettes of either a higher or lower density generally does not work. Data integrity cannot be assured whenever a diskette is formatted to a capacity not matching its density.

You can use the fdformat command to format a PCMCIA memory card with densities from 512-kilobytes to 64-megaytes.

fdformat writes new identification and data fields for each sector on all tracks unless you specify the -x option. For diskettes, if you specify the -v option, each sector is verified.

After formatting and verifying, fdformat writes an operating-system label on block 0. Use the -t dos option (same as the -d option) to put an MS-DOS file system on the diskette or PCMCIA memory card after the format is done. Use the -t nec option with the -M option (same as the -m option) to put an

NEC-DOS file system on a diskette. Otherwise, `fdformat` writes a SunOS label in block 0.

> **Note** — A diskette or PCMCIA memory card containing a ufs file system created on a SPARC-based system (by using `fdformat` and `newfs`(1M)) is not identical to a diskette or PCMCIA memory card containing a ufs file system created on an x86-based system. Do not interchange ufs diskettes or memory cards between these platforms; use `cpio`(1) or `tar`(1) to transfer files on diskettes or memory cards between them.
>
> A diskette or PCMCIA memory card formatted with the `-t dos` option (or `-d`) for MS-DOS does not have the necessary system files and is therefore not bootable. Trying to boot from it on a PC displays following message:
>
> ```
> Non-System disk or disk error
> Replace and strike any key when ready
> ```

Bugs

Currently, bad sector mapping is not supported on diskettes or PCMCIA memory cards. Therefore, a diskette or memory card is unusable if `fdformat` finds an error (bad sector).

Options

`-D`	Format a 720-kilobyte (3.5-inch) or 360-kilobyte (5.25-inch) double-density diskette (same as the `-l` or `-L` options). This option is the default for double-density type drives. Use it only if the drive is a high- or extended-density type.
`-e`	Eject the diskette when done. (This feature is not available on all systems.)
`-E`	Format a 2.88-megabyte (3.5-inch) extended-density diskette. This option is the default for extended-density type drives.
`-f`	Do not ask for confirmation before starting format.
`-H`	Format a 1.44-megabyte (3.5-inch) or 1.2-megabyte (5.25-inch) high-density diskette. This option is the default for high-density type drives; use it only if the drive is the extended-density type.
`-M`	Write a 1.2-megabyte (3.5-inch) medium-density format on a high-density diskette (use only with the `-t nec` option). This option is the same as using `-m`. (This feature is not available on all systems.)
`-U`	Unmount any file systems and then format.
`-q`	Do not print status messages.

-v	Verify each block of the diskette after the format.
-x	Skip the format, and write only a SunOS label or an MS-DOS file system.
-b *label*	Label the media with volume label. A SunOS volume label is restricted to 8 characters. A DOS volume label is restricted to 11 uppercase characters.
-B *filename*	

Install special boot loader in *filename* on an MS-DOS diskette. This option is meaningful only when you also specify the -d option (or -t dos).

-t dos	Install an MS-DOS file system and boot sector formatting. This is equivalent to the DOS format command or the -d option.
-t nec	Install an NEC-DOS file system and boot sector on the disk after formatting. Use this option only with the -M option. (This feature is not available on all systems.)
devname	Replace *devname* with rdiskette0 (systems without Volume Management) or floppy0 (systems with Volume Management) to use the first drive or rdiskette1 (systems without Volume Management) or floppy1 (systems with Volume Management) to use the second drive. If you omit *devname*, use the first drive, if one exists.

For PCMCIA memory cards, replace *devname* with the device name for the PCMCIA memory card that resides in /dev/rdsk/c*N*t*N*d*N*s*N* or /dev/dsk/c*N*t*N*d*N*s*N*.

If you omit *devname*, use the default diskette drive, if one exists. *N* represents a decimal number and can be specified as follows:

c*N*	Controller *N*.
t*N*	Technology type *N*.

0x1	ROM.
0x2	OTPROM.
0x3	EPROM.
0x4	EEPROM.
0x5	FLASH.
0x6	SRAM.
0x7	DRAM.

d*N*	Technology region in type *N*.
s*N*	Slice *N*.

The following options are provided for compatibility with previous versions of fdformat; their use is discouraged.

-d   Format an MS-DOS diskette or PCMCIA memory card (same as
                  -t). This option is equivalent to the MS-DOS FORMAT command.

-l   Format a 720-kilobyte (3.5-inch) or 360-kilobyte (5.25-inch)
                  double-density diskette (same as -D or -L). This option is the
                  default for double-density type drives; use it only if the drive is the
                  high- or extended-density type.

-L   Format a 720-kilobyte (3.5-inch) or 360-kilobyte (5.25-inch)
                  double-density diskette (same as -l or -D). This option is the
                  default for double-density type drives; use it only if the drive is the
                  high- or extended-density type.

-m   Write a 1.2-megabyte (3.5-inch) medium-density format on a
                  high-density diskette (use only with the -t nec option). This
                  option is the same as using -M. (This feature is not available on all
                  systems.)

Files

/vol/dev/diskette0

                  Directory providing block device access for the media in diskette
                  drive 0.

/vol/dev/rdiskette0

                  Directory providing character device access for the media in
                  diskette drive 0.

/vol/dev/aliases/floppy0

                  Symbolic link to the character device for the media in diskette
                  drive 0.

/dev/rdiskette

                  Directory providing character device access for the media in the
                  primary diskette drive, usually drive 0.

/vol/dev/dsk/cNtNdNsN

                  Directory providing block device access for the PCMCIA memory
                  card.

/vol/dev/rdsk/cNtNdNsN

                  Directory providing character device access for the PCMCIA
                  memory card.

/vol/dev/aliases/pcmemS

                  Symbolic link to the character device for the PCMCIA memory
                  card in socket S, where S represents a PCMCIA socket number.

/dev/rdsk/c*Nt*N*d*s*N*

> Directory providing character device access for the PCMCIA memory card.

/dev/dsk/c*Nt*N*d*s*N*

> Directory providing block device access for the PCMCIA memory card.

Note — See the *devname* section above for a description of the values for *N*.

Examples

In the following example, the diskette has been mounted with the volcheck command. fdformat displays an error message telling you to use the -U option to unmount the diskette before formatting it.

```
castle% volcheck
castle% fdformat
fdformat: /vol/dev/rdiskette0/unnamed_floppy is mounted (use -U flag)
castle%
```

In the following example, using the fdformat -U command, fdformat detects a formatting error, as indicated by the e, and exits.

```
castle% fdformat -U
Formatting 1.44 MB in /vol/dev/rdiskette0/unnamed_floppy
Press return to start formatting floppy.
.................................................e
fdformat: can't read format data, I/O error
castle% eject
```

The following example uses fdformat with no arguments (on a new diskette) to successfully create a SunOS file system on the diskette.

```
castle% fdformat
Formatting 1.44 MB in /vol/dev/rdiskette0/untitled
Press return to start formatting floppy.
.............................................................
.........
castle%
```

The following example uses the -d option to successfully create a DOS file system on a diskette.

```
castle% fdformat -d
Formatting 1.44 MB in /vol/dev/rdiskette0/untitled
Press return to start formatting floppy.
.............................................................
.........
castle%
```

Attributes

See `attributes`(5) for descriptions of the following attributes:

Attribute Type	Attribute Value
Availability	SUNWcsu

See Also

cpio(1), eject(1), tar(1), volcancel(1), volcheck(1), volmissing(1), *New!*
volmount(1), mount(1M), newfs(1M), rmmount(1M), vold(1M),
rmmount.conf(4), vold.conf(4), attributes(5), pcfs(7FS), volfs(7FS)

x86 Only
fd(7D)

fg — Control Process Execution

Synopsis

sh, ksh
fg [%*job-id* ...]

csh
fg [%*job-id*]

Description

See jobs(1).

fgrep — Search a File for a Fixed-Character String

Synopsis

```
/usr/bin/fgrep [-bchilnsvx][-e pattern-list]
   [-f pattern-file][pattern][file ...]
/usr/xpg4/bin/fgrep [-bchilnsvx][-e pattern-list]
   [-f pattern-file][pattern][file ...]
```

Description

The fgrep (fast grep) command searches files for a character string and prints
all lines that contain that string. fgrep is different from grep(1) and egrep(1)

because it searches for a string, instead of searching for a pattern that matches an expression. fgrep uses a fast and compact algorithm.

fgrep interprets the characters $, *, [, ^, |, (,), and \ literally; that is, fgrep does not recognize full regular expressions as does egrep. Because these characters have special meaning to the shell, it is safest to enclose the entire string in single quotes '...'.

If you specify no files, fgrep uses the standard input. Normally, each line found is copied to the standard output. The file name is printed before each line found if there is more than one input file.

Note — Ideally there should be only one grep command; however, no single algorithm spans a wide enough range of space-time trade-offs.

Lines are limited only by the size of the available virtual memory.

The /usr/xpg4/bin/fgrep command is identical to /usr/xpg4/bin/grep -F (see grep(1)). Portable applications should use /usr/xpg4/bin/grep -F.

Options

-b   Precede each line by the block number on which it was found. This option can be useful in locating block numbers by context (first block is 0).

-c   Print a count only of the lines that contain the pattern.

-e *pattern-list*

                Search for a string in *pattern-list* (useful when the string begins with a -).

-f *pattern-file*

                Take the list of patterns from *pattern-file*.

-h   Suppress printing of files when searching multiple files.

-i   Ignore upper-/lowercase distinction during comparisons.

-l   Print the names of files with matching lines once, separated by newlines. Do not repeat the names of files when the pattern is found more than once.

-n   Precede each line by its line number in the file (first line is 1).

-s   Work silently, that is, display nothing except error messages. This option is useful for checking the error status.

-v   Print all lines except those that contain the pattern.

-x   Print only lines matched entirely.

Operands

`file`	A path name of a file to be searched for the patterns. If you specify no file operands, use the standard input.
`pattern`	For `/usr/bin/fgrep`, specify a pattern to be used during the search for input. For `/usr/xpg4/bin/fgrep`, specify one or more patterns to be used during the search for input. This operand is treated as if it were specified as `-e pattern-list`.

Examples

Because you do not need to quote special characters, the `fgrep` command is useful for searching for patterns that have literal backslashes, asterisks, and the like. You can also search for more than one target string. With the `fgrep` command, you put each target on a separate line.

Suppose you have a file named `foo` that has lots of special characters.

```
$ cat foo
@ # $ &
^
\
* ( )
$
```

The following example uses the `fgrep` command to search the file `foo`.

```
$ fgrep "$
> *" foo
@ # $
* ( )
$
```

Usage

See `largefile`(5) for the description of the behavior of `fgrep` when encountering files greater than or equal to 2 Gbytes (2**31 bytes).

Environment Variables

See `environ`(5) for descriptions of the following environment variables that affect the execution of `fgrep`: LC_COLLATE, LC_CTYPE, LC_MESSAGES, and NLSPATH.

Exit Status

0	Matches are found.
1	No matches are found.
2	Syntax errors or inaccessible files (even if matches are found).

Attributes

See attributes(5) for descriptions of the following attributes:

/usr/bin/fgrep

Attribute Type	Attribute Value
Availability	SUNWcsu

/usr/xpg4/bin/fgrep

Attribute Type	Attribute Value
Availability	SUNWxcu4
CSI	Enabled

See Also

ed(1), egrep(1), grep(1), sed(1), sh(1), attributes(5), environ(5), largefile(5), XPG4(5)

---

file — Determine File Type

Synopsis

```
/usr/bin/file [-h] [-m mfile] [-f ffile]  file
/usr/bin/file [-h] [-m mfile]  -f ffile
/usr/bin/file -c [-m mfile]
```

Description

The file command performs a series of tests on each file supplied by *file* and, optionally, on each file listed in *ffile* in an attempt to classify it. If the file is not a regular file, its file type is identified. The file types directory, FIFO, block special, and character special are identified as such. If the file is a regular file and the file is 0-length, it is identified as an empty file.

If *file* is a text file, file examines the first 512 bytes and tries to determine its programming language. If *file* is an executable a.out, file prints the version stamp, provided it is greater than 0. If *file* is a symbolic link, by default the link is followed and file tests the file to which the symbolic link refers.

A magic number is a numeric or string constant that indicates the file type. By default, file tries to use the localized magic file /usr/lib/locale/locale/LC_MESSAGES/magic, if it exists, to identify files that have a magic number. If a localized magic file does not exist, file uses /etc/magic. See magic(4) for an explanation of the format of /etc/magic.

If `file` does not exist, cannot be read, or its file status could not be determined, it is not considered an error that affects the exit status. The output indicates that the file was processed, but that its type could not be determined.

Options

`-c`	Check the `magic` file for format errors. For reasons of efficiency, this validation is normally not carried out.
`-h`	Do not follow symbolic links.
`-f` `ffile`	Examine the files listed in `ffile`.
`-m` `mfile`	Use `mfile` as an alternate magic file, instead of `/etc/magic`.

Operands

`ffile`	A file containing a list of the names of files to be examined.
`file`	A path name of a file to be tested.
`mfile`	An alternate magic file.

Usage

See `largefile`(5) for the description of the behavior of `file` when encountering files greater than or equal to 2 Gbytes (2**31 bytes).

Examples

The following example displays the file types for all of the files in a directory.

```
castle% file *
Art:            directory
Design.book:    empty file
Mail:           directory
Menu.start:     empty file
bibliography:   ascii text
checknr.1:      [nt]roff, tbl, or eqn input text
dosfile:        ascii text
example.c:      c program text
example.stringout:      ascii text
kerberos:       English text
local.cshrc:    assembler program text
local.profile:  ascii text
castle%
```

The following example determines if a file is a binary executable file.

```
castle% file "$1" | grep -Fq executable && printf "%s is executable.\n"
    "$1"
```

Environment Variables

See `environ`(5) for descriptions of the following environment variables that affect the execution of `file`: LC_CTYPE, LC_MESSAGES, and NLSPATH.

Exit Status

0	Successful completion.
>0	An error occurred.

Files

`/etc/magic`   Magic number file.

Attributes

See `attributes`(5) for descriptions of the following attributes:

Attribute Type	Attribute Value
Availability	SUNWcsu
CSI	Enabled

See Also

`ls(1)`, `filehdr(4)`, `magic(4)`, `attributes(5)`, `environ(5)`, `largefile(5)`

Diagnostics

When you specify the `-h` option and `file` is a symbolic link, `file` prints the error message:

```
symbolic link to file
```

filesync — Synchronize Ordinary, Directory, or Special Files

Synopsis

New!

```
/usr/bin/filesync [-aehmnqvy][-o src | dst][-f src | dst] |old | new]
    [-r directory ...]
/usr/bin/filesync [-aehmnqvy] -s source-dir -d dest-dir filename ...
```

Description

`filesync` synchronizes files between multiple computer systems, typically a server and a portable computer. `filesync` synchronizes ordinary, directory, or special files. Although intended for use on nomadic systems, `filesync` is useful for backup and file replication on more permanently connected systems.

If files are synchronized between systems, the corresponding files on each of the systems are identical. Changing a file on one or both of the systems can unsynchronize the files. To make the files identical again, the differences between the files must be reconciled.

There are two forms of the `filesync` command. You invoke the first form of `filesync` without file arguments. This form of `filesync` reconciles differences between the files and systems specified in the `$HOME/.packingrules` file. `$HOME/.packingrules` is a packing rules list for `filesync` and `cachefspack` and contains a list of files to be kept synchronized. See `packingrules(4)` and `cachefspack(1M)`.

The second form of `filesync` copies specific files from a directory on the source system to a directory on the destination system. In addition, this form of `filesync` adds the file or files specified as arguments (`filename`) to `$HOME/.packingrules`. See `-s` and `-d` for information about specifying directories on source and destination systems.

Multiple `filesync` commands are cumulative (that is, the specified files are added to the already existing packing rules file list).

Reconciling and Synchronizing Files

`filesync` synchronizes files between computer systems by performing the following tasks:

1. `filesync` examines the directories and files specified in the packing rules file on both systems and determines whether or not they are identical. Any file that differs requires reconciliation.

2. `filesync` also maintains a baseline summary in the `$HOME/.filesync-base` file for all of the files that are being monitored. This file lists the names, types, and sizes of all files as of the last reconciliation.

3. Based on the information contained in the baseline file and the specified options, `filesync` determines which of the various copies is the correct one and makes the corresponding changes to the other system. Once this has been done, the two copies are again identical (synchronized).

4. If a source file has changed and the destination file has not, the changes on the source system are propagated to the destination system. If a destination file has changed and the corresponding source file has not, the changes on the destination file are propagated to the source system. If both systems have changed (and the files are not still identical) a warning message is printed, asking you to resolve the conflict manually.

Resolving Conflicts

When files on both sides have changed, `filesync` tries to determine which version should be chosen. If `filesync` cannot automatically determine which version should be selected, it prints out a warning message and leaves the two incompatible versions of the file unreconciled.

In these cases, you must either resolve the differences manually or tell `filesync` how to choose which file should win. Use the `-o` and `-f` options to tell `filesync` how to resolve conflicts.

Alternatively, for each conflicting file, you can examine the two versions, determine which one should be kept, and manually bring the two versions into agreement (by copying, deleting, or changing the ownership or protection to be correct). You can then rerun `filesync` to see whether any other conflicts remain.

Packing Rules File
The packing rules file `$HOME/.packingrules` contains a list of files to be kept synchronized. The syntax of this file is described in `packingrules(4)`.

If you invoke `filesync` with *filename* arguments, the `$HOME/.packingrules` file is automatically created. By using `filesync` options, you can augment the packing rules in `$HOME/.packingrules`.

Many users choose to create the packing rules file manually and edit it by hand. You can edit `$HOME/.packingrules` (using any editor) to permanently change the `$HOME/.packingrules` file or to gain access to more powerful options that are not available from the command line (such as `IGNORE` commands). By editing the `$HOME/.packingrules` file, you can easily enter complex wild-card expressions.

Baseline Files
`$HOME/.filesync-base` is the `filesync` baseline summary file. `filesync` uses the information in `$HOME/.filesync-base` to identify the differences between files during reconciliation and synchronization. You do not create or edit the baseline file. It is created automatically by `filesync` and records the last-known state of agreement between all of the files being maintained.

Custom Synchronization
Over time, the set of files you want to keep synchronized can change. It is common, for instance, to want to keep files pertaining to only a few active projects on your notebook. If you continue to synchronize files associated with every project you have ever worked on, your notebook's disk would fill up with old files. In addition, each `filesync` command would waste a lot of time updating files you no longer care about.

If you simply delete the files from your notebook, `filesync` wants to perform the corresponding deletes on the server, which is not what you want. Instead, you can tell `filesync` to stop synchronizing some of the files, in one of the following two ways:

- Edit `$HOME/.packingrules` and delete the rules for the files that you want to delete from your notebook.
- Delete `$HOME/.packingrules`. Then, use the `filesync` command to specify the files that you want synchronized.

Either way works, and you can choose the one that seems easiest to you. For minor changes, it is probably easier to edit `$HOME/.packingrules`. For major changes, it is probably easier to start from scratch.

Once `filesync` is no longer synchronizing a set of files, you can delete them from your notebook without affecting the files on the server.

Nomadic Machines

When using `filesync` to keep files synchronized between nomadic machines and a server, store the packing rules and baseline files on the nomadic machines, not the server. If, when you are logged into your notebook, the HOME environment variable does not normally point to a directory on your notebook, you can use the FILESYNC environment variable to specify an alternate location for the packing rules and baseline files.

Each nomadic machine should carry its own packing rules and baseline file. Incorrect file synchronization can result if a server carries a baseline file and multiple nomadic machines attempt to reconcile against the server's baseline file. In this case, a nomadic machine could be using a baseline file that does not accurately describe the state of its files, which might result in incorrect reconciliations.

To safeguard against the dangers associated with a single baseline file being shared by more than two machines, `filesync` adds a default rule to each new packing rules file. This default rule prevents the packing rules and baseline files from being copied.

Options

`-a`	Force the checking of Access Control Lists (ACLs) and try to make them agree for all new and changed files. If it is not possible to set the ACL for a particular file, `filesync` stops ACL synchronization for that file.
	Some file systems do not support ACLs. It is not possible to synchronize ACLs between file systems that support ACLs and those that do not; trying to do so results in numerous error messages.
`-d dest-dir`	
	Specify the directory on the destination system into which `filename` is to be copied. Use with the `-s source-dir` option and the `filename` operand. See `-s`.
`-e`	Flag all differences. It may not be possible to resolve all conflicts involving modes and ownership (unless `filesync` is being run with root privileges). If you cannot change the ownership or protections on a file, `filesync` normally ignores conflicts in ownership and protection. If you specify the `-e` (everything must agree) flag, `filesync` flags these differences.
`-f src | dst \ old | new`	*New!*
	Specify how to resolve conflicting changes. If a file has been changed on both systems and you specify the `-f` option, retain the changes made on the favored system and discard the changes made on the unfavored system.

Specify -f `src` to favor the source-system file. Specify -f `dst` to favor the destination-system file. Specify -f `old` to favor the older version of the file. Specify -f `new` to favor the newer version of the file.

You can combine the -f and -o options if they both specify the same preference (`src` or `dst`). If -f and -o conflict, ignore the -f option.

-h   Halt on error. Normally, if `filesync` encounters a read or write error while copying files, it notes the error and the program continues trying to reconcile other files. If you specify the -h option, `filesync` immediately halts when one of these errors occurs and does not process any more files.

-m   Ensure that both copies of the file have the same modification time. Set the modification time for newly copied files to the time of reconciliation by default. Order file changes by increasing modification times so that the propagated files have the same relative modification time ordering as the original changes. There is usually some time skew between any two systems, and transferring modification times from one system to another can occasionally produce strange results.

At times, using `filesync` to update some (but not all) files in a directory confuses the `make` program. If, for example, `filesync` is keeping .c files synchronized but ignoring .o files, a changed .c file may show up with a modification time before a .o file that was built from a previous version of the .c file.

-n   Display the change and reconciliation information on standard output, but do not make the changes.

Specifying both the -n and -o options analyzes the prevailing system and reports the changes that have been made on that system. Using -n and -o in combination is useful if your machine is disconnected (and you cannot access the server) but you want to know what changes have been made on the local machine.

-o src | dst

Force a one-way reconciliation, favoring either the source system (`src`) or destination system (`dst`). `filesync` aborts if it cannot access a source or destination directory.

Specify -o `src` to propagate changes from the source system to the destination system only. Ignore changes made on the destination system. `filesync` aborts if it cannot access a source or destination directory.

Specify -o `dst` to propagate changes only from the destination system to the source system. Ignore changes made on the source system.

Specifying both the -n and -o options analyzes the prevailing system and report the changes that have been made on that system. Using -n and -o in combination is useful if your machine is disconnected (and you cannot access the server) but you want to know what changes have been made on the local machine.

You can combine the -f and -o options if they both specify the same preference (src or dst). If -f and -o conflict, ignore the -f option.

-q   Suppress the standard filesync messages that describe each reconciliation action as it is performed.

The standard filesync message describes each reconciliation action in the form of a UNIX shell command (for example, mv, ln, cp, rm, chmod, chown, chgrp, setfacl, and so forth).

-r *directory*

Limit the reconciliation to *directory*. Specify multiple directories with multiple -r specifications.

-s *source-dir*

Specify the directory on the source system from which the *filename* to be copied is located. Use with the -d *dest-dir* option and the *filename* operand.

-v   Display additional information about each file comparison as it is made on the standard output.

-y   Bypass safety check prompts. Nomadic machines occasionally move between domains, and many of the files on which filesync operates are expected to be accessed by NFS. It is possible that you could ask filesync to reconcile local changes against the wrong file system or server, resulting in a large number of inappropriate copies and deletions. To prevent such a mishap, filesync performs a few safety checks before reconciliation. If large numbers of files are likely to be deleted or if high-level directories have changed their I-node numbers, filesync prompts for a confirmation before reconciliation. If you know that this is likely and do not want to be prompted, use the -y (yes) option.

Operands

filename   The name of the ordinary file, directory, symbolic link, or special file in the specified source directory (*source-dir*) to be synchronized. Specify multiple files by separating each *filename* by spaces. Use the *filename* operand with the -s and -d options.

If *filename* is an ordinary file, replicate that ordinary file (with the same *filename*) in the specified destination directory (*dest-dir*).

If *filename* is a directory, replicate that directory and all of the files and subdirectories under it (recursively) in the specified destination directory (*dest-dir*).

If *filename* is a symbolic link, replicate a copy of that symbolic link in the specified destination directory (*dest-dir*).

If *filename* is a special file, replicate a special file with the same major or minor device numbers in the specified destination directory (*dest-dir*). Only superusers can use filesync to create special files.

Files created in the destination directory (*dest-dir*) have the same owner, group, and other permissions as the files in the source directory.

If *filename* contains escaped shell wild-card characters, store the wild-card characters in $HOME/.packingrules and evaluate them each time you run filesync.

For example, the following command makes sure that the two specified files, currently in $RHOME, are replicated in $HOME.

```
castle% filesync -s $RHOME -d $HOME a.c b.c
```

The following example ensures that all of the *.c files in $RHOME are replicated in $HOME, even if those files are not created until later.

```
castle% filesync -s $RHOME -d $HOME '*.c'
```

If any of the destination files already exist, filesync ensures that they are identical and issues warnings if they are not.

Once files have been copied, the distinction between the source and destination is a relatively arbitrary one (except for its use in the -o and -f switches).

Environment Variables

FILESYNC   Specify the default location of the filesync packing rules and baseline files. The default value for this variable is $HOME. The suffixes .packingrules and .filesync-base are appended to form the names of the packing rules and baseline files.

LC_MESSAGES

Determine how diagnostic and informative messages are presented. In the C locale, the messages are presented in the default form found in the program itself (in most cases, U.S. English).

Exit Status

Normally, if all files are already up-to-date or if all files are successfully reconciled, filesync exits with a status of 0. However, if you specify the -n option or any errors occurred, the exit status is the logical OR of the following:

0	No conflicts, all files up to date.
1	Some resolvable conflicts.
2	Some conflicts requiring manual resolution.
4	Some specified files did not exist.

8	Insufficient permission for some files.
16	Errors accessing packing rules or baseline file.
32	Invalid arguments.
64	Unable to access either or both of the specified source or destination directories.
128	Miscellaneous other failures.

Files

`$HOME/.packingrules`

>   List of files to be kept synchronized.

`$HOME/.filesync-base`

>   Baseline summary file.

Attributes

See `attributes`(5) for descriptions of the following attributes:

Attribute Type	Attribute Value
Availability	SUNWesu

See Also

`cachefspack`(1M), `packingrules`(4), `attributes`(5)

find — Find Files

Synopsis

`/usr/bin/find` *path... expression*

Description

You can use the `find` command to search through any part of the file system, looking for files with a particular name. `find` recursively descends the directory hierarchy for each path, seeking files that match *expression*.

   `find` descends to arbitrary depths in a file hierarchy and does not fail because of path-length limitations (unless a path operand specified by the application exceeds PATH_MAX requirements).

Operands

path   A path name of a starting point in the directory hierarchy.

expression   Interpret the first argument that starts with a -, or is a ! or a (,
              and all subsequent arguments as an expression made up of the
              following primaries and operators. In the descriptions, wherever
              you use *n* as a primary argument, interpret it as a decimal integer
              optionally preceded by a plus (+) or minus (-) sign, as follows:

   +*n*   More than *n*.

   n   Exactly *n*.

   -*n*   Less than *n*.

Expressions

-atime *n*   true if the file was accessed *n* days ago. The access time of
              directories in path is changed by find itself.

-cpio *device*

              Always true; write the current file on device in cpio format
              (5120-byte records).

-ctime *n*   true if the file's status was changed *n* days ago.

-depth   Always true; descend the directory hierarchy so that all entries in
              a directory are acted on before the directory itself. This option can
              be useful when find is used with cpio(1) to transfer files that are
              contained in directories without write permission.

-exec *command*

              true if the executed command returns a 0 value as exit status. You
              must punctuate the end of *command* with an escaped semicolon. A
              command argument { } is replaced by the current path name.

-follow   Always true; follow symbolic links. When following symbolic links,
              find keeps track of the directories visited so that it can detect
              infinite loops. For example, such a loop would occur if a symbolic
              link pointed to an ancestor. Do not use this expression with the
              -type l expression.

-fstype *type*

              true if the file system to which the file belongs is of type *type*.

-group *gname*

              true if the file belongs to the group *gname*. If *gname* is numeric and
              does not appear in the /etc/group file, it is taken as a group ID.

-inum *n*   true if the file has inode number *n*.

-links *n*   true if the file has *n* links.

-local	true if the file-system type is not a remote file-system type as defined in the /etc/dfs/fstypes file. Use nfs as the default remote file-system type if the /etc/dfs/fstypes file is not present.
-ls	Always true; print current path name together with its associated statistics:

- Inode number.
- Size in kilobytes (1024 bytes).
- Protection mode.
- Number of hard links.
- User.
- Group.
- Size in bytes.
- Modification time.

If the file is a special file, the size field contains the major and minor device numbers.

If the file is a symbolic link, the path name of the linked-to file is printed preceded by ->. The format is identical to that of ls -gilds (see ls(1)). Formatting is done internally, without executing the ls program.

-mount	Always true; restrict the search to the file system containing the directory specified. Do not list mount points to other file systems.
-mtime *n*	true if the file's data was modified *n* days ago.
-name *pattern*	

true if *pattern* matches the current file name. You can use normal shell file-name generation characters (see sh(1)). Use a backslash (\) as an escape character within the pattern. Escape or quote the pattern when you invoke find from the shell.

-ncpio *device*

Always true; write the current file on device in cpio -c format (5120-byte records).

-newer *file*

true if the current file has been modified more recently than the argument *file*.

-nogroup	true if the file belongs to a group not in the /etc/group file.
-nouser	true if the file belongs to a user not in the /etc/passwd file.

-ok *command*

> Like -exec except print the generated command line with a
> question mark first, and execute it only if the user responds by
> typing **y**.

-perm [-]*mode*

> The *mode* argument represents file-mode bits. It is identical in
> format to the *symbolic-mode* operand described in chmod(1) and is
> interpreted in the following way. To start, assume a template with
> all file mode bits cleared. For an operator symbol of

> +   Set the appropriate mode bits in the template.

> -   Clear the appropriate bits.

> =   Set the appropriate mode bits without regard to the contents
>   of the process file-mode creation mask.

> You cannot use the - symbol as the first character of *mode*; this
> restriction avoids ambiguity with the optional leading dash.
> Because the initial mode is all bits off, no symbolic modes need to
> use - as the first character.

> If you omit the dash, the primary evaluates as true when the file
> permission bits exactly match the value of the resulting template.

> Otherwise, if mode is prefixed by a dash, the primary evaluates as
> true if at least all the bits in the resulting template are set in the
> file permission bits.

-perm [-]*onum*

> true if the file permission flags exactly match the octal number
> *onum* (see chmod(1)). If *onum* is prefixed by a dash (-), compare only
> the bits that are set in *onum* with the file permission flags and
> evaluate the expression true if they match.

-print   Always true; print the current path name.

-prune   Always true. Do not examine any directories or files in the
> directory structure below the pattern just matched.

-size *onum*[c]

> true if the file is *onum* blocks long (512 bytes per block). If you
> follow *onum* with a c, the size is in bytes.

-type *c*   true if the type of the file is c, where c is b (block special file), c
> (character special file), d (directory), l (symbolic link), p (fifo:
> named pipe), s (socket), or f (plain file).

-user *uname*

> true if the file belongs to the user *uname*. If *uname* is numeric and
> does not appear as a login name in the /etc/passwd file, take it as
> a user ID.

-xdev   Same as the -mount primary.

> **Note —** When using `find` to determine files modified within a range of time, specify the `-atime`, `-ctime`, or `-mtime` option before the `-print` option; otherwise, `find` gives all files.

The following options are obsolete and will not be supported in future releases:

`-cpio` *device*

> Always `true`; write the current file on *device* in cpio format (5120-byte records).

`-ncpio` *device*

> Always `true`; write the current file on *device* in cpio `-c` format (5120-byte records).

Complex Expressions

You can combine the primaries by using the operators listed below, in order of decreasing precedence:

(*expression*)

> `true` if the parenthesized expression is `true` (parentheses are special to the shell and must be escaped).

`!` *expression*

> The negation of a primary (`!` is the unary `not` operator).

expression `[-a]` *expression*

> Concatenation of primaries (the `and` operation is implied by the juxtaposition of two primaries).

expression `-o` expression

> Alternation of primaries (`-o` is the `or` operator).

> **Note —** When you use `find` in conjunction with cpio, if you use the `-L` option with cpio, then you must use the `-follow` expression with `find`, and vice versa. Otherwise, you get undesirable results.

If no expression is present, `-print` is used as the expression. Otherwise, if the given expression does not contain any of the primaries `-exec`, `-ok`, or `-print`, the given expression is effectively replaced by:

(*given-expression*) `-print`

The `-user`, `-group`, and `-newer` primaries each evaluate their respective arguments only once.

Usage

See `largefile`(5) for the description of the behavior of `find` when encountering files greater than or equal to 2 Gbytes (2**31 bytes).

Examples

The following commands are equivalent. Both write out the entire directory hierarchy from the current directory.

```
castle% find .
castle% find . -print
```

The following example searches from the root directory (/) and lists all core files on the system.

```
castle# find / -name core -print
/export/home/winsor/core
/files/winsor/bookgames/src/xblackjack/core
/core
castle#
```

The following example searches the current directory and silently removes all core files.

```
castle% pwd
/export/home/winsor
castle% ls core
core
castle% find . -name core -exec rm {} \;
castle% ls core
core: No such file or directory
castle%
```

If you want to see a list of the files that are removed, add the -print option to the command line as shown in the following example.

```
castle% find . -name core -exec rm {} \; -print
```

The following example recursively prints all file names whose permission mode exactly matches read, write, and execute access for user, and read and execute access for group and other.

```
castle% find . -perm u+rwx,g=rx,o=rx
./.dt
./.dt/sessions
./.dt/sessions/current
./.dt/sessions/current.old
./.dt/types
./.dt/types/fp_dynamic
./.dt/tmp
./.dt/sessionlogs
./.dt/icons
./.dt/appmanager
./.dt/help
./.dt/help/winsor-castle-0
./.dt/Trash
./.dt/palettes
./.dt/.Printers/seachild1_Print
./.dtprofile
```

```
castle% find . -perm -o+w
.
./local.cshrc
./.dt/sessions/current/dt.session
./.dt/sessions/current/dt.settings
./.dt/sessions/current/dt.resources
./.dt/sessions/current.old/dt.session
...
castle%
```

The following example removes all files in your home directory named a.out or *.o* that have not been accessed for a week.

```
castle% find $HOME \( -name a.out -o -name '*.o*' \) -atime +7 -exec rm {} \;
```

The following example recursively prints all file names in the current directory and below but skips SCCS directories.

```
castle% find . -name SCCS -prune -o -print
```

The following example recursively prints all file names in the current directory and below, skipping the contents of SCCS directories but printing out the SCCS directory name.

```
castle% find . -print -name SCCS -prune
```

The following command is basically equivalent to the -nt extension to test(1).

```
castle$ if [-n "$(find file1 -prune -newer file2)"]; then printf %s
    "file1 is newer than file2"
```

The following command recursively prints all file names whose permission mode exactly matches read, write, and execute access for user, and read and execute access for group and other.

```
castle% find . -perm u=rwx,g=rx,o=rx
```

You could also specify the above command in the following way.

```
castle% find . -perm a=rwx,g-w,o-w
```

The following command recursively prints all file names whose permissions include, but are not limited to, write access for other.

```
castle% find . -perm -o+w
```

The descriptions of -atime, -ctime, and -mtime use the terminology n 24-hour periods. The midnight boundary between days does not affect the 24-hour calculation. -atime looks for files that have been accessed, which means files that have been read or changed or directories that have been listed or changed into. -mtime looks for files that have been modified, which means files that have been altered in some way such as being edited, moved, renamed, or revised. `-ctime` looks for files that have had a change in file status such as a change of owner or a change of group.

The following example looks for a file that has been accessed no more than one day ago.

```
castle% find . -atime -1 -print
```

Suppose your disk has filled up recently and you want to find large files that are less than three days old. With the following example, you search your home directory for files that are 200c or larger. The c specifies the size in bytes. Without the c, you would be specifying blocks of 512 kilobytes.

```
castle% find $HOME -size 200c -mtime -3 -user winsor -print
```

The `-mtime -3` option looks for files modified less than three days ago. To look for files modified more than three days ago, use `-mtime +3`. To look for files modified exactly three days ago, use `-mtime 3`.

The following example looks for files older than three days but less than six days.

```
castle% find $HOME -size 200c -mtime +3 -mtime -6 -user winsor -print
```

The following example looks for files owned by `winsor` not accessed for three or more days and not modified within 14 days.

```
castle% find $HOME \( -atime +3 -o -mtime +14 \) -user winsor -print
```

The following example looks for core files older than sven days and then prompts you to verify that it is OK to remove them.

```
castle% find / -name core -mtime +7 -ok -exec {} \;
```

Environment Variables

See environ(5) for descriptions of the following environment variables that affect the execution of find: LC_COLLATE, LC_CTYPE, LC_MESSAGES, and NLSPATH.

Exit Status

0	All path operands were traversed successfully.
>0	An error occurred.

Files

/etc/passwd Password file.

/etc/group Group file.

/etc/dfs/fstypes

File that registers distributed file system packages.

Attributes

See attributes(5) for descriptions of the following attributes:

Attribute Type	Attribute Value
Availability	SUNWcsu
CSI	Enabled

See Also

chmod(1), cpio(1), ls(1), sh(1), test(1), stat(2), umask(2),
attributes(5), environ(5), largefile(5)

finger — Display Information About Local and Remote Users

Synopsis

```
/usr/bin/finger [-bfhilmpqsw][username...]
/usr/bin/finger [-l][username@hostname1[@hostname2...@hostnamen] ...
/usr/bin/finger [-l][@hostname1[@hostname2...@hostnamen] ...]
```

Description

By default, the finger command displays, in a multicolumn format, the
following information about each logged-in user:

- User name.
- User's full name.
- Terminal name (prepended with an asterisk (*) if write permission is
  denied).
- Idle time.
- Login time.
- Host name if logged in remotely.

The following example shows the output from the finger command with no
arguments.

```
castle% finger
Login       Name            TTY       Idle    When      Where
winsor          ???         console           Thu 15:38 :0
castle%
```

Idle time is displayed in minutes if it is a single integer, in hours and
minutes if a colon (:) is present, or in days and hours if a d is present.

When you specify one or more *username* arguments, more detailed
information is shown for each user name specified, whether the user is logged

in or not. *username* must be that of a local user and can be a first or last name or an account name. Information is presented in multiline format as follows:

- The user name and the user's full name.
- The user's home directory and login shell.
- Time the user logged in if currently logged in, or the time the user last logged in, and the terminal or host from which the user logged in.
- Last time the user received mail and the last time the user read mail.
- The first line of the $HOME/.project file, if it exists.
- The contents of the $HOME/.plan file, if it exists.

New!

Note — When the comment (GECOS) field in /etc/passwd includes a comma, finger does not display the information following the comma.

The following example shows the output from the finger command with three user names specified. None of these users were logged in at the time the command was invoked.

```
castle% finger ray des rob
Login name: ray
Directory: /export/home/ray                Shell: /bin/csh
Last login Tue Nov 25, 1997 on pts/6 from castle
Unread mail since Thu Nov 13 08:37:58 1997
No Plan.

Login name: des
Directory: /export/home/des                Shell: /bin/csh
Last login Thu Oct  9, 1997 on console from :0
No unread mail
No Plan.

Login name: rob
Directory: /export/home/rob                Shell: /bin/csh
Never logged in.
No unread mail
No Plan.
castle%
```

If you specify the arguments *username@hostname1*[*@hostname2...* *@hostnamen*] or *@hostname1*[*@hostname2...@hostnamen*], the request is sent first to *hostnamen* and forwarded through each *hostnamen-1* to *hostname1*. The program uses the finger user information protocol (see RFC 1288) to query that remote host for information about the named user (if you specify a *username*) or about each logged-in user. The information displayed is server dependent As required by RFC 1288, finger passes only printable, 7-bit ASCII data. A system administrator can modify this behavior by using the PASS option in /etc/default/finger. Specifying PASS=low enables all characters less than decimal 32 ASCII. Specifying PASS=high enables all

characters greater than decimal 126 ASCII. `PASS=low,high` or
`PASS=high,low` enables both characters less than 32 and greater than 126 to
pass through.

Note — The *username@hostname* form supports only the -1 option
because the `finger` user information protocol limits the options
that can be used with the remote form of this command. The
following example shows the kind of information that `finger`
displays when you specify a *username@hostname* argument.

```
castle% finger winsor@castle
[castle]
Login       Name              TTY          Idle    When     Where
winsor      ???           console      Thu 15:38  :0
winsor      ???           pts/3       2 Thu 15:39  :0.0
winsor      ???           pts/4       9 Thu 15:39  :0.0
winsor      ???           pts/5      25 Thu 15:42  :0.0
castle%
```

Options

-b	Suppress printing the user's home directory and shell in a long format printout.
-f	Suppress printing the header that is normally printed in a short format printout.
-h	Suppress printing of the .project file in a long format printout.
-i	Force idle output format, which is similar to short format except print only the login name, terminal, login time, and idle time.
-l	Force long output format.
-m	Match arguments only on user name (not first or last name).
-p	Suppress printing of the .plan file in a long format printout.
-q	Force quick output format, which is similar to short format except print only the login name, terminal, and login time.
-s	Force short output format.
-w	Suppress printing the full name in a short format printout.

Files

$HOME/.plan User's plan.

$HOME/.project

         User's projects.

/etc/default/finger

         `finger` options file.

/etc/passwd Password file.

var/adm/lastlog

> Time of last login.

/var/adm/utmp

> Accounting.

Attributes

See attributes(5) for descriptions of the following attributes:

Attribute Type	Attribute Value
Availability	SUNWcsu

See Also

passwd(1), who(1), whois(1), attributes(5)

Zimmerman, D., *The Finger User Information Protocol*, RFC 1288, Center for Discrete Mathematics and Theoretical Computer Science (DIMACS), Rutgers University, December 1991.

fmt — Simple Text Formatter

Synopsis

/usr/bin/fmt [-cs][-w *width* | -*width*][*inputfile* ...]

Description

fmt is a simple text formatter that fills and joins lines to produce output lines of (up to) the number of characters specified in the -w *width* option. The default width is 72. fmt concatenates the *inputfiles* listed as arguments. If you specify no input files, fmt formats text from the standard input.

Blank lines are preserved in the output, as is the spacing between words. For compatibility with nroff (1), fmt does not fill or split lines beginning with a dot (.). It does not fill or split a set of contiguous nonblank lines that is recognized as a mail header, the first line of which must begin with From.

Indentation is preserved in the output, and input lines with differing indentation are not joined unless you use the -c option.

You can also use fmt as an in-line text filter for vi(1). The following vi command reformats the text between the cursor location and the end of the paragraph.

!}fmt

Options

-c
      Preserve the indentation of the first two lines within a paragraph and align the left margin of each subsequent line with that of the second line. This crown width mode is useful for tagged paragraphs.

-s
      Do not join short lines to form longer ones. This split-lines-only option prevents sample lines of code, and other such formatted text, from being unduly combined.

-w *width* | -*width*
      Fill output lines to up to *width* columns. Note that the -width option is acceptable for BSD compatibility, but it may go away in future releases.

Operands

inputfile Input file.

Examples

The following example combines three files and displays the output on standard output. The original files are unaffected.

```
castle% fmt -72 kookaburra-1 kookaburra-2 kookaburra-3
Kookaburra sits in the old gum tree Merry merry king of the bush is he
Laugh, kookaburra, laugh Gay your life must be.

Kookaburra sits in the old gum tree Eating all the gumdrops he can see
Laugh, kookaburra, laugh Leave some there for me. Kookaburra sits in
the old gum tree Merry merry king of the bush is he Laugh, kookaburra,
laugh Glad your life must be.

Kookaburra sits in the old gum tree Eating all the gumdrops he can see
Laugh, kookaburra, laugh Leave some there for me. Kookaburra sits in
the old gum tree Merry merry king of the bush is he Laugh, kookaburra,
laugh Gay your life must be.

Kookaburra sits in the old gum tree Eating all the gumdrops he can see
Laugh, kookaburra, laugh Leave some there for me. Kookaburra sits in
the old gum tree Merry merry king of the bush is he Laugh, kookaburra,
laugh Glad your life must be.

Kookaburra sits in the old gum tree Eating all the gumdrops he can see
Laugh, kookaburra, laugh Leave some there for me.
castle%
```

Environment Variables

See environ(5) for a description of the LC_CTYPE environment variable that affects the execution of fmt.

Attributes
See attributes(5) for descriptions of the following attributes:

Attribute Type	Attribute Value
Availability	SUNWcsu

See Also
nroff(1), vi(1), attributes(5), environ(5)

---

fmtmsg — Display a Message on Standard Error or System Console

Synopsis
/usr/bin/fmtmsg [-c class][-u subclass][-l label][-s severity]
    [-t tag][-a action] text

Description
Based on the message classification component, fmtmsg either writes a formatted message to standard error or writes a formatted message to the console.

A formatted message consists of up to five standard components (see environment variable MSGVERB.) The classification and subclass components are not displayed as part of the standard message, but they define the source of the message and direct the display of the formatted message.

Options
-c hard | soft | firm

> Describes the source of the message as hardware, software, or firmware.

-u subclass

> A list of keywords (separated by commas) that further defines the message and directs the display of the message. Valid keywords are:
>
> | | |
> | --- | --- |
> | appl | The condition originated in an application. Do not use this keyword in combination with either util or opsys. |
> | util | The condition originated in a command. Do not use this keyword in combination with either appl or opsys. |
> | opsys | The message originated in the kernel. Do not use this keyword in combination with either appl or util. |

	recov	The application recovers from the condition. Do not use this keyword in combination with `nrecov`.
	nrecov	The application does not recover from the condition. Do not use this keyword in combination with `recov`.
	print	Print the message to the standard error stream `stderr`. You can use `print`, `console`, or both.
	console	Write the message to the system console. You can use `print`, `console`, or both.
-l *label*		Identify the source of the message.
-s *severity*		

Indicate the seriousness of the error. The keywords and definitions of the standard levels of severity are:

	halt	The application has encountered a severe fault and is halting.
	error	The application has detected a fault.
	warn	The application has detected a condition that is out of the ordinary and might be a problem.
	info	The application is providing information about a condition that is not in error.

-t *tag*	Specify the string containing an identifier for the message.
-a *action*	Specify a text string describing the first step in the error recovery process. You must write this string so that the entire *action* argument is interpreted as a single argument. `fmtmsg` precedes each action string with the `TO FIX:` prefix.
text	Specify a quoted text string describing the condition. You must write this string so that the entire *text* argument is interpreted as a single argument.

Examples

The following example of `fmtmsg` produces a complete message in the standard message format and displays it to standard error.

```
castle% fmtmsg -c soft -u recov,print,appl -l UX:cat   -s error
  -t UX:cat:001 -a "Refer to manual" "Invalid syntax"
UX:cat: ERROR: Invalid syntax
        TO FIX: Refer to manual   UX:cat:001
castle%
```

If you set the `MSGVERB` environment variable as follows in the C shell

```
castle% setenv MSGVERB severity:text:action
```

the previous example produces

```
ERROR: invalid syntax
TO FIX: refer to manual
```

If you set the environment variable SEV_LEVEL as follows in the C shell

```
castle% setenv SEV_LEVEL=note,5,NOTE
```

the following command displays the NOTE: tag on standard error.

```
castle% fmtmsg -c soft -u print -l UX:cat -s note -a "refer to manual"
    "Invalid syntax"
UX:cat: INFO: Invalid syntax
      TO FIX: refer to manual
castle%
```

Note — If you do not set the SEV_LEVEL environment variable, fmtmsg displays a syntax error message because note is not one of the default arguments for the -s option.

Environment Variables

The environment variables MSGVERB and SEV_LEVEL control the behavior of fmtmsg. MSGVERB is set by the administrator in /etc/profile for the system. You can override the value of MSGVERB set by the system by resetting MSGVERB in your own .profile files or by changing the value in the current shell session. You can use the SEV_LEVEL environment variable in shell scripts.

MSGVERB tells fmtmsg what message components to select when writing messages to standard error. The value of MSGVERB is a colon-separated list of optional keywords. You can set MSGVERB as follows for the Bourne and Korn shell.

```
$ MSGVERB=[keyword[:keyword[:...]]]
$ export MSGVERB
```

You can set MSGVERB as follows for the C shell.

```
castle% setenv MSGVERB [keyword[:keyword[:...]]]
```

Valid keywords are label, severity, text, action, and tag. If MSGVERB contains a keyword for a component and the component's value is not the component's null value, fmtmsg includes that component in the message when writing the message to stderr. If MSGVERB does not include a keyword for a message component, that component is not included in the display of the message. You can specify the keywords in any order. If MSGVERB is not defined, if its value is the null string, if its value is not of the correct format, or if it contains keywords other than the valid ones listed above, fmtmsg selects all components.

MSGVERB affects only the selection of message components for display on stderr. All message components are included in console messages.

SEV_LEVEL defines severity levels and associates print strings with them for use by fmtmsg. You cannot modify the standard severity levels shown below. You can define, redefine, and remove additional severity levels.

0   (No severity is used).

1	HALT.
2	ERROR.
3	WARNING.
4	INFO.

You set SEV_LEVEL as follows for the Bourne and Korn shell

```
$ SEV_LEVEL=[description[:description[:...]]]; export SEV_LEVEL
```

and as follows for the C shell.

```
castle% setenv SEV_LEVEL [description[:description[:...]]]
```

description is a comma-separated list containing three fields.

description=severity-keyword,level,printstring

severity-keyword
> A character string used as the keyword with the -s severity option to fmtmsg.

level   A character string that evaluates to a positive integer (other than 0, 1, 2, 3, or 4, which are reserved for the standard severity levels). If you use the keyword *severity-keyword*, *level* is the severity value passed on to fmtmsg(3C).

printstring The character string used by fmtmsg in the standard message format whenever the severity value level is used.

If SEV_LEVEL is not defined or if its value is null, no severity levels other than the defaults are available. If a description in the colon-separated list is not a comma-separated list containing three fields or if the second field of a comma-separated list does not evaluate to a positive integer, that description in the colon-separated list is ignored.

Exit Status

0	All the requested functions were executed successfully.
1	The command contains a syntax error, an invalid option, or an invalid argument to an option.
2	The function executed with partial success; however, the message was not displayed on standard error.
4	The function executed with partial success; however, the message was not displayed on the system console.
32	No requested functions were executed successfully.

Attributes

See attributes(5) for descriptions of the following attributes:

Attribute Type	Attribute Value
Availability	SUNWcsu

See Also

addseverity(3C), fmtmsg(3C), attributes(5)

---

fnattr — Update and Examine Attributes Associated with an FNS Named Object

Synopsis

```
/usr/bin/fnattr [-AL] composite-name [[-O | -U] identifier] ...
/usr/bin/fnattr [-L] composite-name [{ -a [-s][-O | -U] identifier
   [value ...] } | { -d [[-O | -U] identifier [value ...]] } |{ -m [-O |
   -U] identifier old-value new-value }] ...
```

Description

Use the fnattr command to update and examine attributes associated with a Federated Naming Service (FNS) named object. This command has four uses:

- Add an attribute or value.
- Delete an attribute or value.
- Modify an attribute's value.
- List the contents of an attribute.

Note — You cannot update built-in attributes, such as onc_unix_passwd for users, by using the fnattr command. Their contents are affected by updates to the underlying naming service, such as NIS+ or NIS.

Options

You can combine the options for adding, modifying, and deleting attributes and their values in the same command line. The modifications are executed in the order that you specify them.

Any unsuccessful modification aborts all subsequent modifications specified in the command line; any modifications already carried out remain. The unsuccessful modifications are displayed as output of `fnattr`.

-a	Add an attribute or add a value to an attribute associated with object named by *composite-name*. *identifier* is the identifier of the attribute to manipulate; its format is `FN_ID_STRING` unless you use the -O or -U option. *value* ... represents the attribute values to add. The attribute syntax used for storing value is `fn_attr_syntax_ascii`.
-A	Consult the authoritative source to get attribute information.
-d	Delete attributes associated with object named by *composite-name*. If you do not specify *identifier*, delete all attributes associated with the named object. If you specify *identifier* without accompanying values (*value...*), remove the entire attribute identified by *identifier*. If you specify individual attribute values (*value...*), then remove only these from the attribute. Removal of the last value of an attribute entails removal of the attribute as well. The format of identifier is `FN_ID_STRING` unless you use the -O or -U option.
-L	If the composite name is bound to an X/Open Federated Naming (XFN) link, manipulate the attributes associated with the object pointed to by the link. If you do not specify -L, manipulate the attributes associated with the XFN link.
-m	Modify the values of the attribute identified by *identifier* associated with the object named by *composite-name*. *old-value* is replaced by *new-value* in the specified attribute. Leave other attributes and values associated with *composite-name* unaffected. The format of identifier is `FN_ID_STRING` unless you use the -O or -U option.
-O	The format of *identifier* is `FN_ID_ISO_OID_STRING`, an ASN.1, dot-separated, integer list string.
-s	Add in supersede mode. If an attribute with the same identifier as *identifier* already exists, remove all its values, and replace with *value*. If you omit this option, the resulting values for the specified attribute is a union of the existing values and *value*.
-U	The format of identifier is `FN_ID_DCE_UUID`, a DCE UUID in string form.

Operands

composite-name

An FNS named object.

identifier The identifier of the attribute to manipulate.

Examples

Adding
Use the -a option for adding attributes and values. The following command replaces the value of the shoesize attribute of user/jane with the value 7.5.

```
castle% fnattr user/jane -as shoesize 7.5
```

The following command adds the value Chameleon to the projects attribute of user/jane.

```
castle% fnattr user/jsmith -a projects Chameleon
```

Deleting
Use the -d option for deleting attributes and values. The following command deletes the attribute shoesize associated with user/jane.

```
castle% fnattr user/jane -d shoesize
```

The following command deletes the attribute value old_project from the projects attribute associated with user/jane.

```
castle% fnattr user/jane -d projects old_project
```

The following command deletes all the attributes associated with user/jane.

```
castle% fnattr user/jane -d
```

Modifying
Use the -m option to modify an attribute value. The following command replaces the value Chameleon with Dungeon in the projects attribute associated with user/jsmith.

```
castle% fnattr user/jsmith -m projects Chameleon Dungeon
```

The following command is an example of unsuccessful modification attempts. The user executing this command does not have permission to update user/jane's attributes but is allowed to add new attributes. Executing the command adds the attribute hatsize but does not delete shoesize or modify dresssize because -d shoesize fails and the command stops.

```
castle% fnattr user/jane -a hatsize medium -d shoesize -m dresssize 5 6
```

Listing
Use the fnattr command with no options to list attributes and their values. The following command lists all the attributes associated with user/jane.

```
castle% fnattr user/jane
```

The following command lists the values of the projects attribute of user/jane.

```
castle% fnattr user/jane projects
```

   The following command lists the values of the `project` and `shoesize` attributes of `user/jane`.

```
castle% fnattr user/jane project shoesize
```

Exit Status

0	Operation was successful.
1	Operation failed.

Attributes

See `attributes(5)` for descriptions of the following attributes:

Attribute Type	Attribute Value
Availability	SUNWfns

See Also

`fnlookup(1)`, `attributes(5)`, `fns(5)`

fnbind — Bind a Reference to an FNS Name

Synopsis

```
/usr/bin/fnbind [-s] [-v] [-L] name new-name
/usr/bin/fnbind -r [-s] [-v] new-name [-O | -U]
   ref-type { [-O | -U] addr-type [-c | -x] addr-contents } ...
```

Description

   `fnbind` binds the Federated Naming Service (FNS) reference named by *name* to the name *new-name*. The second synopsis of `fnbind` (using the `-r` option) enables the binding of *new-name* to the reference constructed, using arguments supplied in the command line.

Options

-c	Store *addr-contents* in the given form; do not use XDR encoding.
-L	Create an X/Open Federated Naming (XFN) link by using *name* and bind it to *new-name*.
-O	Specify the identifier format as FN_ID_ISO_OID_STRING, an ASN.1 dot-separated integer list string.

-r	Create a reference using *ref-type* as the reference's type, and one or more pairs of *addr-type* and *addr-contents* as the reference's list of addresses, and bind this reference to *new-name*. Unless you use the -O or -U options, use FN_ID_STRING as the identifier format for *ref-type* and *addr-type*. Unless you use the -c or -x options, store *addr-contents* as an XDR-encoded string.
-s	Bind to *new-name* even if it is already bound. If you omit this option, fnbind fails if *new-name* is already bound.
-U	Specify the identifier format as FN_ID_DCE_UUID, a DCE UUID in string form.
-v	Display the reference being bound to *new-name*.
-x	Specify *addr-contents* as a hexidecimal string. Convert it to its hexidecimal representation and store it; do not use XDR encoding.

Examples

The following command binds the name thisorgunit/service/pr to the reference named by thisorgunit/service/printer. Any reference bound to thisorgunit/service/pr is overwritten.

```
castle% fnbind -s thisorgunit/service/printer thisorgunit/service/pr
```

The following example binds the name thisorgunit/service/pr to the XFN link constructed using the name thisorgunit/service/printer.

```
castle% fnbind -L thisorgunit/service/printer thisorgunit/service/pr
```

The following command binds the name thisorgunit/service/calendar to the reference with reference type SUNW_cal, address type SUNW_cal_deskset_onc, and address contents of staff@exodus.

```
castle% fnbind -r thisorgunit/service/calendar SUNW_cal
    SUNW_cal_deskset_onc staff@exodus
```

Attributes

See attributes(5) for descriptions of the following attributes:

Attribute Type	Attribute Value
Availability	SUNWfns

See Also

fnlookup(1), fnrename(1), fnunbind(1), FN_identifier_t(3N), xdr(3N), xfn_links(3N), attributes(5), fns(5)

fnlist — Display the Names and References Bound in an FNS Context

Synopsis

```
/usr/bin/fnlist [-Alv] [composite-name]
```

Description

fnlist displays the Federated Naming Service (FNS) names and references bound in the context of *composite-name*.

If you do not specify *composite-name*, the default initial context is displayed, as shown in the following example.

```
castle% fnlist
_myorgunit
. . .
_orgunit
_x500
_thisens
myens
thisens
org
orgunit
_dns
myorgunit
thisorgunit
_thisorgunit
_myens
castle%
```

Options

-A	Consult the authoritative source for information.
-l	Display the references as well as the names bound in the context of *composite-name*. Without this option, display only the names.
-v	Display the reference in detail. For onc_fn* references, this option is useful for deriving the name of the NIS+ table that stores the reference for every name that is bound in the context of *composite-name*.

Operands

composite-name

A Federated Naming Service named object. Composite names, like UNIX file names, depend on the subcontexts created.

Examples of commands with valid *composite-name* operands are:

```
castle% fnlist thisorgunit
castle% fnlist thisorgunit/service
castle% fnlist thisorgunit/service/printer
```

When FNS is deployed, the composite name is specific to the deployed site.

Examples

In the following example, the command with no operand provides the listing with reference and address types for the initial context.

```
castle% fnlist -l
name: _myorgunit
Reference type: onc_fn_nsid
Address type: onc_fn_files
   context type: namespace id

name: ...
Reference type: fn_global
Address type: initial

name: _orgunit
Reference type: onc_fn_organization
Address type: onc_fn_files
   context type: organization

name: _x500
Reference type: fn_global
Address type: x500
   Warning: empty X.500 reference address
   length: 0
   data:

name: _thisens
Reference type: onc_fn_enterprise
Address type: onc_fn_files
   context type: enterprise root

...
castle%
```

In the following examples, where you specify a user context (that is, *composite-name* = user/), FNS must first be deployed by using fncreate(1M), using one of the naming services NIS, NIS+, or files. If FNS is not deployed, there are no user contexts and the commands fails with the Name not found error message.

The following command shows the names bound in the context of user/.

```
castle% fnlist user/
```

The following command displays the names and references bound in the context of user/.

```
castle% fnlist -l user/
```

Exit Status

0   Operation was successful.

1   Operation failed.

Attributes

See `attributes`(5) for descriptions of the following attributes:

Attribute Type	Attribute Value
Availability	SUNWfns

See Also

```
fnbind(1), fnlookup(1), fnunbind(1), fncreate(1M), fndestroy(1M),
attributes(5), fns(5), fns_references(5)
```

---

fnlookup — DIsplay the Reference Bound to an FNS Name

Synopsis

```
/usr/bin/fnlookup [-ALv] composite-name
```

Description

`fnlookup` displays the Federated Naming Service (FNS) binding of
composite-name.

Options

-A   Consult the authoritative source for information.

-L   If the composite name is bound to an X/Open Federated Naming
                      (XFN) link, display the reference that the link is bound to. Without
                      the -L option, display the XFN link.

-v   Display the binding in detail. For `onc_fn_*` references, this option
                      is useful for deriving the name of the NIS+ table that stores the
                      reference for *composite-name* and a string representation of the
                      reference, if applicable.

Operands

composite-name

                      An FNS named object.

Examples

The following example shows the calendar reference to which the name
`/usr/jsmith/service/calendar` is bound.

```
castle% fnlookup user/jsmith/service/calendar
```

The following example shows the service context reference to which
`/usr/jsmith` is bound.

```
castle% fnlookup user/jsmith/service
```

If the service reference is bound to an XFN link, then the following command
displays the reference to which this link is bound.

```
castle% fnlookup -L user/jsmith/service
```

Exit Status

0   Operation was successful.

1   Operation failed.

Attributes

See `attributes`(5) for descriptions of the following attributes:

Attribute Type	Attribute Value
Availability	SUNWfns

See Also

`fnbind(1)`, `fnlist(1)`, `fnunbind(1)`, `fncreate(1M)`, `fndestroy(1M)`,
`xfn_links(3N)`, `attributes(5)`, `fns(5)`, `fns_references(5)`

fnrename — Rename the Binding of an FNS Name

Synopsis

`/usr/bin/fnrename[-s][-v]context-nameold-atomic-namenew-atomic-name`

Description

`fnrename` renames the Federated Naming Service (FNS) binding of
`old-atomic-name` to `new-atomic-name` in the context of `context-name`.
Both `old-atomic-name` and `new-atomic-name` must be atomic names, to be
resolved in the context named by `context-name`.

Options

-s   Overwrite any reference already bound to *new-atomic-name*. If
            you omit this option, fnrename fails if *new-atomic-name* is
            already bound.

-v   Display the binding being renamed.

Examples

The following example binds calendar to the reference bound to clendar in
the context named by /usr/jsmith/service and unbinds clendar.

castle% **fnrename user/jsmith/service/ clendar calendar**

Attributes

See attributes(5) for descriptions of the following attributes:

Attribute Type	Attribute Value
Availability	SUNWfns

See Also

fnbind(1), fnlist(1), fnunbind(1), fncreate(1M), fndestroy(1M),
xfn_links(3N), attributes(5), fns(5), fns_references(5)

fnsearch — Search for FNS Objects with Specified Attributes

Synopsis

/usr/bin/fnsearch [-AlLv][-n *max*][-s *scope*] *composite-name*
    [-a *ident*]... [-O | -U] *filter-expr* [*filter-arg*]...

Description

The fnsearch command displays the names and, optionally, the attributes
and references of Federated Naming Service (FNS) objects bound at or below
composite-name whose attributes satisfy a given filter expression. Specify
the filter expression in terms of logical expressions involving the identifiers and
values of the attributes and references of objects examined during the search.
    For general information about FNS, see fns(5).

Options

-a *ident*   Display the given attribute of each object that satisfies the filter expression. If you do not use the -a option, display all attributes. An empty *ident* (" " from the shell) indicates that no attributes are to be displayed. You can give multiple -a options. The syntax of *ident* is described fully under ""Displaying Selected Attributes" on page 392.

-A   Consult the authoritative source(s) for information.

-l   Display the reference of each object that satisfies the filter expression.

-L   Follow X/Open Federated Naming (XFN) links during the search.

-n *max*   Restrict the maximum number of objects displayed to the given number (a positive integer). There is no limit by default.

-s *scope*   Set the scope of the search. *scope* is one of:

      * object   Search only the object *composite-name*.

      * context   Search objects bound directly to *composite-name*.

      * subtree   Search objects bound to *composite-name* or any of its subcontexts.

      * constrained_subtree

                  Like subtree, but restrict the search to a set of subcontexts in a manner defined by the implementation context.

      You can abbreviate *scope* to any unambiguous prefix, such as o or cont.

      If you do not specify the -s *scope* option, the default behavior is -s *context*.

-v   Display in detail the reference of each object that satisfies the filter expression. This option takes precedence over -l.

Operands

composite-name

      An FNS named object.

Usage

Simple Filter Expressions

The simplest form of filter expression is one that tests for the existence of an attribute. You form this expression simply by giving the attribute's name. For example, the following command searches for objects having an attribute named for_sale.

```
% fnsearch composite-name for_sale
```

Another simple filter expression is one that tests the value of a particular attribute. The following command finds objects with ages less than 17.

```
% fnsearch composite-name "age < 17"
```

String values are indicated by enclosing the string in single quotes. For example, the following command finds all red objects.

```
% fnsearch composite-name "color == 'red'"
```

Note that the double quotes (") in this example are not part of the filter expression. Instead, they prevent the shell from interpreting the white space and single quotes that are part of the expression.

Logical Operators

You can compose simple filter expressions by using the logical operators and, or, and not, as shown in the following example.

```
% fnsearch composite-name "age >= 35 and us_citizen"
```

You can use parentheses to group expressions, as shown in the following example.

```
% fnsearch composite-name "not (make == 'olds' and \ year == 1973)"
```

The precedence of operators is as follows, in order of increasing precedence:

- or
- and
- not
- Relational operators

The logical operators and and or are left-associative.

Relational Operators

You can use the following relational operators to compare an attribute to a supplied value:

==	true if at least one value of the attribute is equal to the supplied value.
!=	true if none of the attribute's values are equal to the supplied value.
<	true if at least one value of the attribute is less than the supplied value.
<=	true if at least one value of the attribute is less than or equal to the supplied value.

>	true if at least one value of the attribute is greater than the supplied value.
>=	true if at least one value of the attribute is greater than or equal to the supplied value.
~=	true if at least one value of the attribute matches the supplied value according to some context-specific approximate matching criterion. This criterion must subsume strict equality.

Comparisons and ordering are specific to the syntax or rules of the attribute being tested.

Displaying Selected Attributes

By default, the fnsearch command displays the names and all of the attributes of each object matching the search criteria. You can restrict the list of attributes by using the -a command-line option. In the following example, only the color and shape attributes of small objects are displayed.

```
% fnsearch composite-name -a color -a shape "size == 'small'"
```

The format of an attribute identifier is taken to be *FN_ID_STRING* (an ASCII string) by default. To name an attribute identifier that is an OSI OID or a DCE UUID, prefix the attribute name by -O or -U.

-O	The identifier format is *FN_ID_ISO_OID_STRING*, an ASN.1, dot-separated, integer list string.
-U	The identifier format is *FN_ID_DCE_UUID*, a DCE UUID in string form.

The following examples show the -O and -U attributes.

```
% fnsearch composite-name -a -O 2.5.4.0 "shoe_size < 9"
% fnsearch composite-name -a -U 0006a446-5e97-105f-9828-8190285baa77
  "bowling_avg > 200"
```

Filter Arguments

You can replace some parts of a filter expression with a substitution token which is a percent sign (%) followed by a single character. The value of this portion of the expression is then given in a filter argument that follows the filter expression, in much the same way as is done in printf(1). The available substitution tokens are:

%a	Attribute
%s	String
%i	Identifier
%v	Attribute value

Note — The only syntax currently supported for %v is fn_attr_syntax_ascii.

For example, you could write the following command

```
% fnsearch composite-name "color == 'red'"
```

as

```
% fnsearch composite-name "%a == 'red'" color
```

or as

```
% fnsearch composite-name "%a == %s" color red
```

Substitution tokens are helpful for writing shell scripts when the values of the filter arguments will be generated at runtime.

By default, the format of the identifier of an attribute, such as the color attribute above, is taken to be *FN_ID_STRING* (an ASCII string). Substitution tokens enable the use of OSI OIDs and DCE UUIDs instead. Prefix the filter argument by -O or -U, with the same meaning as in the -a command-line option:

-O   The identifier format is *FN_ID_ISO_OID_STRING*, an ASN.1, dot-separated, integer list string.

-U   The identifier format is *FN_ID_DCE_UUID*, a DCE UUID in string form.

For example:

```
% fnsearch composite-name "%a -O 2.5.4.0
```

and

```
% fnsearch composite-name "%a" =='red'" -U
    0006a446-5e97-105f-9828-8190285baa77
```

Wild-carded Strings

A wild-carded string consists of a sequence of alternating wild-card specifiers and strings. The wild-card specifier is denoted by the asterisk (*) and means 0 or more occurrences of any character.

Use wild-carded strings to specify substring matches. The following are some examples of wild-carded strings and their meanings.

*   Any string.

'tom'   The string tom.

'harv'*   Any string starting with harv.

*'ing'   Any string ending with ing.

'a'*'b'   Any string starting with a and ending with b.

'jo'*'ph'*'ne'*'er'

                Any string starting with jo and containing the substring ph, and containing the substring ne in the portion of the string following ph, and ending with er.

`%s*`	Any string starting with the string supplied as a filter argument.
`'bix'*%s`	Any string starting with `bix` and ending with the string supplied as a filter argument.

Extended Operations

Extended operators are predicates (functions that return `true` or `false`) that you can freely mix with other operators in a filter expression. You specify an extended operation by giving the operation name as a quoted string, followed by an argument in parentheses. The following three extended operations are currently defined:

`'name'(WildcardedString)`

> `true` if the name of the object matches the supplied wild-carded string.

`'reftype'(Identifier)`

> `true` if the reference type of the object is equal to the supplied identifier.

`'addrtype'(Identifier)`

> `true` if any of the address types in the reference of the object are equal to the supplied identifier.

The following example shows a search for objects whose names start with `bill` and having IQ attributes over `80`.

```
% fnsearch composite-name "'name'('bill'*) and IQ > 80"
```

Grammar of Filter Expressions

The complete grammar of filter expressions is given below. It is based on the grammar defined by the X/Open Federated Naming (XFN) specification (see `FN_search_filter_t(3N)`).

String literals in this grammar are enclosed in double quotes; the quotes are not themselves part of the expression. Use braces for grouping; brackets, for optional elements. An unquoted asterisk (*) signifies 0 or more occurrences of the preceding element; a plus sign (+) signifies 1 or more occurrences.

```
FilterExpr ::=[Expr]

Expr ::=Expr "or" Expr
       | Expr "and" Expr
       | "not" Expr
       | "(" Expr ")"
       | Attribute [RelOp Value]
       | Ext

RelOp ::="==" | "!=" | "<" | "<=" | ">" | ">=" | "~="

Attribute ::=Char*
       | "%a"
```

```
Value ::=Integer
        | WildcardedString
        | "%v"

WildcardedString ::=
        "*"
        | String
        | {String "*"}+ [String]
| {"*" String}+ ["*"]
```

(that is, an alternating sequence of *String* and `"*"`)

```
String ::="'" Char* "'"
        | "%s"

Ext ::="'name'(" WildcardedString ")"
        | "'reftype'(" Identifier ")"
        | "'addrtype'(" Identifier ")"

Identifier ::= "'" Char* "'"
        | "%i"

Char ::=an element of the Portable Character Set (ASCII)
        | a character in the repertoire of a string representation
```

Note — If the filter expression is empty, it evaluates to `true` (all objects satisfy it).

If the identifier in any subexpression of the filter expression does not exist as an attribute of an object, then the innermost logical expression containing that identifier evaluates to `false`.

Exit Status

0	Operation was successful.
1	Operation failed.

Attributes

See `attributes`(5) for descriptions of the following attributes:

Attribute Type	Attribute Value
Availability	SUNWfns

See Also

```
printf(1), FN_search_control_t(3N), FN_search_filter_t(3N),
fn_attr_ext_search(3N), fn_attr_search(3N), attributes(5), fns(5)
```

fnunbind — Unbind the Reference from an FNS Name

Synopsis

```
/usr/bin/fnunbind composite-name
```

Description

fnunbind unbinds the Federated Naming Service (FNS) reference of
`composite-name`.

For example, the following command unbinds the reference to which the
name `user/jsmith/fs/` was bound.

```
castle% fnunbind user/jsmith/fs/
```

> **Note** — An fnunbind on a name of a context fails because such a
> context cannot be unbound unless it is first destroyed with the
> fndestroy command.

Attributes

See attributes(5) for descriptions of the following attributes:

Attribute Type	Attribute Value
Availability	SUNWfns

See Also

fnbind(1), fnlist(1), fnlookup(1), fnrename(1), fncreate(1M),
fndestroy(1M), attributes(5), fns(5)

fold — Filter for Folding Lines

Synopsis

```
/usr/bin/fold [-bs] [-w width | -width] [file ...]
```

Description

The fold command is a filter that folds lines from its input files, breaking the
lines to have a maximum of `width` column positions (or bytes, if you specify the
-b option). Lines are broken by inserting a newline character so that each
output line (referred to later in this section as a segment) is the maximum

width possible that does not exceed the specified number of column positions (or bytes). A line is not broken in the middle of a character. The behavior is undefined if *width* is less than the number of columns any single character in the input would occupy.

If the Return, backspace, or Tab characters are encountered in the input and you do not specify the -b option, the characters are treated specially, as described below.

Backspace	Decrement the current count of line width by 1, although the count never becomes negative. Do not insert a newline character immediately before or after any backspace character.
Return	Set the current count of line width to 0. Do not insert a newline character immediately before or after any Return character.
Tab	Advance the column position pointer to the next Tab stop for each Tab character encountered. Tab stops are at each column position n so that n modulo 8 equals 1.

Note — You can use fold and cut(1) to create text files out of files with arbitrary line lengths. Use fold when you need to keep the contents of long lines contiguous. Use cut when you need the number of lines (or records) to remain constant.

fold is frequently used to send text files to line printers that truncate, instead of fold, lines wider than the printer is able to print (usually 80 or 132 column positions).

fold may not work correctly if underlining is present.

Options

-b	Count width in bytes instead of column positions.
-s	If a segment of a line contains a blank character within the first width column positions (or bytes), break the line after the last such blank character meeting the width constraints. If no blank character meets the requirements, the - s option has no effect for that output segment of the input line.

-w *width*| -*width*

Specify the maximum line length, in column positions (or bytes if you specify -b). If *width* is not a positive decimal number, return an error. The default value is 80.

Operands

file	A path name of a text file to be folded. If you specify no *file* operands, use the standard input.

Examples

The following example folds lines for the file kookaburra at 10 characters.

```
castle% fold -w 10 kookaburra
Kookaburra
 sits in t
he old gum
 tree
Merry merr
y king of
the bush i
s he
Laugh, koo
kaburra, l
augh
Gay your l
ife must b
e.

Kookaburra
 sits in t
he old gum
 tree
Eating all
 the gumdr
ops he can
 see
Laugh, koo
kaburra, l
augh
Leave some
 there for
 me.
castle%
```

The following example folds lines for the file kookaburra at 72 characters. Because the file contains no lines longer than 72 characters, the output looks exactly like the original file.

```
castle% fold -w 72 kookaburra
Kookaburra sits in the old gum tree
Merry merry king of the bush is he
Laugh, kookaburra, laugh
Gay your life must be.

Kookaburra sits in the old gum tree
Eating all the gumdrops he can see
Laugh, kookaburra, laugh
Leave some there for me.

castle%
```

The following example submits a file of possibly long lines to the line printer (under the assumption that you know the line width of the printer to be assigned by lp(1)).

```
castle% fold -w 132 bigfile | lp
```

Environment Variables

See environ(5) for descriptions of the following environment variables that affect the execution of fold: LC_CTYPE, LC_MESSAGES, and NLSPATH.

Exit Status

0	All input files were processed successfully.
>0	An error occurred.

Attributes

See attributes(5) for descriptions of the following attributes:

Attribute Type	Attribute Value
Availability	SUNWcsu
CSI	Enabled

See Also

cut(1), pr(1), attributes(5), environ(5)

---

for, foreach, repeat — Shell Built-in Repeat Functions

Synopsis

sh
```
for word [in wordlist...] ; do actions ; done
```

csh
```
foreach word (wordlist)
 ...
end

repeat count command
```

ksh
```
for word [in wordlist ...] ; do actions ; done
```

Description

You can use loops in shell scripts to control the flow of execution in a script. A loop is an iterative mechanism that repeats a sequence of instructions until a predetermined condition is met. The for/foreach loop executes a list of commands one time for each value of a loop variable.

Bourne Shell

Each time a for command is executed, *word* is set to the next item taken from the in *wordlist*. If you omit in *wordlist* ..., then the for command executes the do *actions* once for each positional parameter that is set. Execution ends when there are no more words in the list.

C Shell

The variable *word* is successively set to each member of *wordlist*. The sequence of commands between this command and the matching end is executed for each new value of *word*. Both foreach and end must appear alone on separate lines.

repeat executes command repeatedly *count* times. *count* must be a number. *command* is restricted to a one-line statement.

Korn Shell

Each time a for command is executed, *word* is set to the next item taken from the in *wordlist*. If you omit in *wordlist* ..., then the for command executes the do *actions* once for each positional parameter that is set. Execution ends when there are no more words in the list.

Note — Both the Bourne shell, sh, and the Korn shell, ksh, can use the semicolon and the Return interchangeably in their syntax of the if, for, and while built-in commands.

Loop Interrupts

All three shells have built-in continue and break commands that you can use to break out of a for/foreach loop. continue terminates the execution of the current iteration of a for or foreach loop. The break command terminates execution of a for or foreach command.

Examples

In the examples using for/foreach, the code counts the number of lines for each file in the current directory whose name ends with a .c extension.

Bourne and Korn Shell

The following Bourne and Korn shell example counts the number of lines for each file in the current directory whose name ends with a .c extension.

```
for file in *.c ; do wc -l $file ; done
```

C Shell

The following C shell example counts the number of lines for each file in the current directory whose name ends with a `.c` extension. Notice how the syntax differs from the Bourne and Korn shell example that performs the same loop.

```
foreach file ( *.c )
wc -l $file
end
```

The `repeat` command reexecutes the single subsequent command for *count* number of times. The following example prints `I will not chew gum in class.` 500 times.

```
@ repetition = 500
repeat $repetition echo "I will not chew gum in class."
```

Attributes

See `attributes`(5) for descriptions of the following attributes:

Attribute Type	Attribute Value
Availability	SUNWcsu

See Also

`break(1), csh(1), ksh(1), sh(1), attributes(5)`

---

from — Display the Sender and Date of Newly Arrived Mail Messages

Synopsis

```
/usr/ucb/from [-s sender] [username]
```

Description

`from` prints out the mail header lines in your mailbox file to show who your mail is from. If you specify *username*, then *username*'s mailbox is examined instead of your own.

Options

`-s sender`   Display headers only for mail sent by *sender*.

Examples

The following example displays the header lines for the current user.

```
castle% from
From <IMAP4.psuedo.sims> Fri Aug 28 12:30:14 1998
From winsor Fri Aug 28 12:15:01 1998
From winsor Fri Aug 28 12:30:01 1998
From winsor Fri Aug 28 12:30:02 1998
From winsor Fri Aug 28 12:55:01 1998
From winsor Fri Aug 28 12:56:53 1998
From winsor Fri Aug 28 13:04:41 1998
From winsor Fri Aug 28 13:04:53 1998
From winsor Fri Aug 28 13:05:37 1998
From winsor Fri Aug 28 13:06:24 1998
From lp Tue Sep 29 13:11:29 1998
From lp Thu Oct  1 10:38:46 1998
castle%
```

In the following example, someone tries to use the `from` command to display the header lines for a different user.

```
castle% from ray
Can't open /var/mail/ray
castle%
```

In the following example, superuser examines the header lines for user ray.

```
castle% su
Password:
# /usr/ucb/from ray
From winsor@castle Wed Nov 12 16:37:58 1997
#
```

Usage

See `largefile`(5) for the description of the behavior of `from` when encountering files greater than or equal to 2 Gbytes (2**31 bytes).

Files

```
/var/spool/mail/*
```

Attributes

See `attributes`(5) for descriptions of the following attributes:

Attribute Type	Attribute Value
Availability	SUNWfac

See Also

`biff`(1B), `mail`(1B), `attributes`(5), `largefile`(5)

ftp — File Transfer Program

Synopsis
```
/usr/bin/ftp [-dgintv][hostname]
```

Description
The ftp command is the user interface to the Internet standard File Transfer Protocol (FTP). Use ftp to transfer files to and from a remote network site.

You can specify the client host with which ftp is to communicate on the command line. If you do so, ftp immediately tries to establish a connection to an FTP server on that host; otherwise, ftp enters its command interpreter and awaits instructions. When ftp is awaiting commands, it displays the prompt ftp>.

Use the following steps to transfer files from your local system to a remote system with the ftp command.

Note — You may need to have an account on each system and an entry in the /.rhosts file to use the file transfer program. Some systems allow read-only ftp access to anybody who logs in as anonymous and types a login name at the password prompt.

If you have an NIS or an NIS+ account, you can use your login name and network password to access a remote system, using ftp.

1. Type **ftp** and press Return. The ftp> prompt is displayed.

2. Type **open *remote-system-name*** and press Return. System connection messages are displayed, and you are asked for a user name.

3. Type the user name for your account on the remote system and press Return. If a password is required, you are asked to enter it.

4. Type the password (if required) for your account on the remote system and press Return. A system login message and the ftp> prompt are displayed.

5. Type **bin** to set binary format or type **asc** to set ASCII format and press Return. The file type is set. (The default is ASCII.)

6. Type **put *local-filename destination-filename*** and press Return. File transfer messages and the ftp> prompt are displayed.

7. Type **quit** and press Return. A goodbye message and the command prompt are displayed.

The following example establishes an ftp connection from the system oak to the system elm, specifies ASCII format, puts the file quest from oak into the /tmp/quest directory on elm, and quits the session.

```
oak% ftp
ftp> open elm
Connected to elm
220 elm FTP server (UNIX(r) System V Release 4.0) ready.

Name (elm:ignatz): ignatz
331 Password required for ignatz.
Password:
230 User ignatz logged in.
ftp> asc
ftp> put quest /tmp/quest
200 PORT command successful.

150 ASCII data connection for /tmp/quest (129.144.52.119,1333).

226 Transfer complete.
ftp> quit
221 Goodbye.
oak%
```

You can use the send command as an alternative to the put command. You can copy multiple files by using the mput command. There is no msend command.

Follow these steps to transfer files from a remote system to your local system, using ftp.

1. Type **ftp** and press Return. The ftp> prompt is displayed.

2. Type **open *remote-system-name*** and press Return. System connection messages are displayed, and you are asked for a user name.

3. Type the user name for your account on the remote system and press Return. If a password is required, you are asked to enter it.

4. Type the password (if required) for your account on the remote system and press Return. A system login message and the ftp> prompt are displayed.

5. Type **bin** to set binary format or type **asc** to set ASCII format and press Return. The file type is set.

6. Type **get *remote-filename destination-filename*** and press Return. File transfer messages and the ftp> prompt are displayed.

7. Type **quit** and press Return. A goodbye message and the command prompt are displayed.

The following example establishes an ftp connection from the system oak to the system elm, specifies ASCII format, gets the file quest from elm, puts it into the /tmp/quest directory on oak, and quits the session.

```
oak% ftp
ftp> open elm
Connected to elm
220 elm FTP server (UNIX(r)System V Release 4.0) ready.
```

```
Name (elm:ignatz): ignatz
331 Password required for ignatz.
Password:
230 User ignatz logged in.

ftp> asc
ftp> get quest /tmp/quest
200 PORT command successful.
150 ASCII data connection for /tmp/quest (129.144.52.119,1333).
226 Transfer complete.

ftp> quit
221 Goodbye.
oak%
```

Note — Correct execution of many commands depends on proper behavior by the remote server.

An error in the treatment of Returns in the 4.2 BSD code that handles transfers with a representation type of network ASCII has been corrected. This correction may result in incorrect transfers of binary files to and from 4.2 BSD servers using a representation type of network ASCII. Avoid this problem by using the `image` type.

Options

You can specify the following options for the `ftp` command either at the command line or to the `ftp` command interpreter.

-d	Enable debugging.
-g	Disable *filename* globbing.
-i	Turn off interactive prompting during multiple file transfers.
-n	Do not attempt auto-login on initial connection. If auto-login is not disabled, `ftp` checks the `.netrc` file in the user's home directory for an entry describing an account on the remote machine. If no entry exists, `ftp` prompts for the login name of the account on the remote machine (the default is the login name on the local machine), and, if necessary, prompts for a password and an account with which to log in.
-t	Enable packet tracing (unimplemented).
-v	Show all responses from the remote server, as well as report on data transfer statistics. This option is turned on by default if `ftp` is running interactively with its input coming from the user's terminal.

You can specify the following `ftp` commands to the `ftp` command interpreter.

! [*command*]   Run *command* as a shell command on the local machine. If no command is given, invoke an interactive shell.

$ *macro-name* [*args*]

Execute the macro *macro-name* that was defined with the `macdef` command. Arguments are passed unglobbed to the macro.

account [*passwd*]

Supply a supplemental password required by a remote system for access to resources once a login has been successfully completed. If no argument is included, the user is prompted for an account password in a nonechoing input mode.

append *local-file* [*remote-file*]

Append a local file to a file on the remote machine. If you do not specify *remote-file*, use the local file name, subject to alteration by any `ntrans` or `nmap` settings. File transfer uses the current settings for representation type, file structure, and transfer mode.

ascii   Set the representation type to network ASCII (the default).

bell   Sound a bell after each file transfer command is completed.

binary   Set the representation type to `image`.

bye   Terminate the FTP session with the remote server and exit `ftp`. An end-of-file also terminate the session and exits.

case   Toggle remote computer file-name case mapping during `mget` commands. When `case` is on (default is off), write remote computer file names with all letters in upper case in the local directory with the letters mapped to lower case.

cd *remote-directory*

Change the working directory on the remote machine to *remote-directory*.

cdup   Change the remote-machine working directory to the parent of the current, remote-machine working directory.

close   Terminate the FTP session with the remote server, and return to the command interpreter. Erase any defined macros.

cr   Toggle Return-stripping during network ASCII type file retrieval. Records are denoted by a Return/linefeed sequence during network ASCII type file transfer. When `cr` is on (the default), Return characters are stripped from this sequence to conform with the UNIX system single-linefeed record delimiter. Records on non-UNIX-system remote hosts can contain single linefeed characters; when a network ASCII type transfer is made, these linefeed characters can be distinguished from a record delimiter only when `cr` is off.

delete *remote-file*

> Delete the file *remote-file* on the remote machine.

debug   Toggle debugging mode. When debugging is on, ftp prints each
                command sent to the remote machine, preceded by the string -->.

dir [*remote-directory*] [*local-file*]

> Print a listing of the directory contents in the directory,
> *remote-directory*, and, optionally, place the output in
> *local-file*. If you specify no directory, use the current working
> directory on the remote machine. If you specify no local file or
> local-file is -, send output to the terminal.

disconnect A synonym for close.

form [*format-name*]

> Set the carriage control format subtype of the representation type
> to *format-name*. The only valid *format-name* is nonprint, which
> corresponds to the default "non-print" subtype.

get *remote-file* [*local-file*]

> Retrieve the *remote-file* and store it on the local machine. If you
> do not specify the local file name, give it the same name it has on
> the remote machine, subject to alteration by the current case,
> ntrans, and nmap settings. Use the current settings for
> representation type, file structure, and transfer mode while
> transferring the file.

glob   Toggle *filename expansion*, or globbing, for mdelete, mget, and
                mput. If globbing is turned off, take file names literally.

> Do globbing for mput as in sh(1). For mdelete and mget, expand
> each remote file name separately on the remote machine, and do
> not merge the lists.

> Expansion of a directory name is likely to be radically different
> from expansion of the name of an ordinary file: the exact result
> depends on the remote operating system and FTP server and can
> be previewed by executing mls *remote-files* -.

> mget and mput are not meant to transfer entire directory subtrees
> of files. You can transfer entire directory subtrees by transferring a
> tar(1) archive of the subtree (using a representation type of image
> as set by the binary command).

hash   Toggle hash sign (#) printing for each data block transferred. The
                size of a data block is 8192 bytes.

help [*command*]

> Print an informative message about the meaning of *command*. If
> you specify no argument, ftp prints a list of the known commands.

`lcd [directory]`

>   Change the working directory on the local machine. If you specify no directory, use the user's home directory.

`ls [remote-directory | -al][local-file]`

>   Print an abbreviated listing of the contents of a directory on the remote machine. If you specify no `remote-directory`, use the current working directory.

>   The `-a` option lists all entries, including those that begin with a dot (`.`), that are normally not listed. The `-l` option lists files in long format, giving mode, number of links, owner, group, size in bytes, and time of last modification for each file. If the file is a special file, the size field instead contains the major and minor device numbers instead of a size. If the file is a symbolic link, the file name is printed, followed by `->` and the path name of the referenced file.

>   If you specify no local file or if `local-file` is `-`, send the output to the terminal.

`macdef macro-name`

>   Define a macro. Store subsequent lines as the macro `macro-name`; a null line (consecutive newline characters in a file or Return characters from the terminal) terminates macro input mode. There is a limit of 16 macros and 4,096 total characters in all defined macros. Macros remain defined until you execute a `close` command.

>   The macro processor interprets $ and \ as special characters. A $ followed by a number (or numbers) is replaced by the corresponding argument on the macro invocation command line. A $ followed by an i signals the macro processor to loop the executing macro. On the first pass, $i is replaced by the first argument on the macro invocation command line; on the second pass, it is replaced by the second argument, and so on. A \ followed by any character is replaced by that character. Use the \ to prevent special treatment of the $.

`mdelete remote-files`

>   Delete the `remote-files` on the remote machine.

`mdir remote-files local-file`

>   Like `dir`, except you can specify multiple remote files. If interactive prompting is on, prompt to verify that the last argument is indeed the target local file for receiving `mdir` output.

`mget remote-files`

>   Expand the `remote-files` on the remote machine and do a `get` for each file name thus produced. See `glob` for details on the file-name expansion. Process resulting file names according to `case`, `ntrans`,

and nmap settings. Transfer files into the local working directory, which you can change with lcd *directory*; you can create new local directories with ! mkdir *directory*.

mkdir *directory-name*

Make a directory on the remote machine.

mls *remote-files local-file*

Like ls(1), except you can specify multiple remote files. If interactive prompting is on, ftp prompts you to verify that the last argument is indeed the target local file for receiving mls output.

mode [*mode-name*]

Set the transfer mode to *mode-name*. The only valid *mode-name* is stream, which corresponds to the default stream mode. This implementation supports only stream and requires that it be specified.

mput *local-files*

Expand wild-cards in the list of local files given as arguments and do a put for each file in the resulting list. See glob for details of file-name expansion. Process resulting file names according to ntrans and nmap settings.

nmap [*inpattern outpattern*]

Set or unset the file-name mapping mechanism. If you specify no arguments, unset the file-name mapping mechanism. If you specify arguments, map remote file names during mput and put commands issued without a specified remote target file name.

The nmap command is useful when connecting to a non-UNIX system remote host with different file-naming conventions or practices. The mapping follows the pattern set by *inpattern* and *outpattern*. *inpattern* is a template for incoming file names (that may have already been processed according to the ntrans and case settings). Variable templating is accomplished by including the sequences $1, $2, ..., $9 in *inpattern*. Use \ to prevent this special treatment of the $ character. All other characters are treated literally and are used to determine the nmap *inpattern* variable values.

For example, given *inpattern* $1.$2 and the remote file name, mydata.data, $1 would have the value mydata and $2 would have the value data.

The *outpattern* determines the resulting mapped file name. The sequences $1, $2, ..., $9 are replaced by any value resulting from the *inpattern* template. The sequence $0 is replaced by the original file name. Additionally, the sequence [*seq1,seq2*] is replaced by *seq1* if *seq1* is not a null string; otherwise, it is replaced by *seq2*.

For example, the command `nmap $1.$2.$3 [$1,$2].[$2,file]`
yields the output file name `myfile.data` for input file names
`myfile.data` and `myfile.data.old`; `myfile.file` for the input
file name `myfile`; and `myfile.myfile` for the input file name
`.myfile`. You can include space characters in *outpattern*, as in
the example `nmap $1 | sed "s/ *$//" > $1`. Use the \ character
to prevent special treatment of the $, [,], and , characters.

`ntrans [`*inchars* `[`*outchars*`]]`

Set or unset the file-name character translation mechanism. If you
specify no arguments, unset the file-name character translation
mechanism. If you specify arguments, translate characters in
remote file names during `mput` and `put` commands issued without
a specified remote target file name, and translate characters in
local file names during `mget` and `get` commands issued without a
specified local target file name.

The `ntrans` command is useful when connecting to a non-UNIX
system remote host with different file-naming conventions or
practices. Characters in a file name matching a character in
inchars are replaced with the corresponding character in
outchars. If the character's position in *inchars* is longer than the
length of *outchars*, delete the character from the file name.

You can translate only 16 characters when using the `ntrans`
command under `ftp`. Use `case` if you need to convert the entire
alphabet.

`open host [`*port*`]`

Establish a connection to the specified host FTP server. You can
supply an optional port number, in which case, `ftp` contacts an
FTP server at that port. If the auto-login option is on (default
setting), `ftp` also tries to automatically log the user in to the FTP
server.

`prompt`   Toggle interactive prompting. Interactive prompting occurs during
multiple file transfers to enable you to selectively retrieve or store
files. By default, prompting is turned on. If you turn prompting off,
any `mget` command transfers all files, and any `mdelete` command
deletes all files.

`proxy` *ftp-command*

Execute an FTP command on a secondary control connection. The
`proxy` command enables simultaneous connection to two remote
FTP servers for transferring files between the two servers. The
first `proxy` command should be an `open`, to establish the secondary
control connection. Enter the command `proxy ?` to see other FTP
commands executable on the secondary connection.

The following commands behave differently when prefaced by `proxy`: `open` does not define new macros during the auto-login process, `close` does not erase existing macro definitions, `get` and `mget` transfer files from the host on the primary control connection to the host on the secondary control connection, and `put`, `mputd`, and `append` transfer files from the host on the secondary control connection to the host on the primary control connection.

Third-party file transfers depend on support of the `PASV` command by the server on the secondary control connection.

put *local-file* [*remote-file*]

Store a local file on the remote machine. If you do not specify *remote-file*, use the local file name after processing according to any `ntrans` or `nmap` settings in naming the remote file. File transfer uses the current settings for representation type, file structure, and transfer mode.

pwd   Print the name of the current working directory on the remote machine.

quit   A synonym for `bye`.

quote *arg1 arg2 ...*

Send the arguments specified, verbatim, to the remote FTP server. A single FTP reply code is expected in return. (The `remotehelp` command displays a list of valid arguments.) Use `quote` only if you are an experienced user familiar with the FTP protocol.

recv *remote-file* [*local-file*]

A synonym for `get`.

remotehelp [*command-name*]

Request help from the remote FTP server. If *command-name* is specified, it is supplied to the server as well.

rename *from to*

Rename the file named *from* on the remote machine to have the name *to*.

reset   Clear reply queue. This command resynchronizes command/reply sequencing with the remote FTP server. You may need to resynchronize following a violation of the FTP protocol by the remote server.

rmdir *directory-name*

Delete a directory on the remote machine.

runique   Toggle storing of files on the local system with unique file names. If
                 a file already exists with a name equal to the target local file name
                 for a get or mget command, append a .1 to the name. If the
                 resulting name matches another existing file, append a .2 to the
                 original name. If this process continues up to .99, print an error
                 message, and abort the transfer. The generated unique file name is
                 reported. runique does not affect local files generated from a shell
                 command. The default value is off.

send *local-file* [*remote-file*]

                 A synonym for put.

sendport   Toggle the use of PORT commands. By default, ftp tries to use a
                 PORT command when establishing a connection for each data
                 transfer. The use of PORT commands can prevent delays when
                 performing multiple file transfers. If the PORT command fails, ftp
                 uses the default data port. When you disable the use of PORT
                 commands, no attempt is made to use PORT commands for each
                 data transfer. This option is useful when connected to certain FTP
                 implementations that ignore PORT commands but incorrectly
                 indicate they have been accepted.

status   Show the current status of ftp.

struct [*struct-name*]

                 Set the file structure to *struct-name*. The only valid *struct-name*
                 is file, which corresponds to the default file structure. The
                 implementation supports only file and requires that it be
                 specified.

sunique   Toggle storing of files on remote machine under unique file names.
                 The remote FTP server must support the STOU command for
                 successful completion. The remote server reports the unique name.
                 Default value is off.

tenex   Set the representation type to that needed to talk to TENEX
                 machines.

trace   Toggle packet tracing (unimplemented).

type [*type-name*]

                 Set the representation type to *type-name*. The valid *type-name*s
                 are ascii for network ASCII, binary or image for image, and
                 tenex for local byte size with a byte size of 8 (used to talk to
                 TENEX machines). If you do not specify a type, ftp prints the
                 current type. The default type is network ASCII.

user *user-name* [*password*] [*account*]

                 Identify yourself to the remote FTP server. If you do not specify the
                 password and the server requires it, ftp prompts you for it (after
                 disabling local echo). If you do not specify an account field and the
                 FTP server requires it, you are prompted for it. If you specify an
                 account field, relay an account command to the remote server

after the login sequence is completed if the remote server did not require it for logging in. Unless `ftp` is invoked with auto-login disabled, this process is done automatically on initial connection to the FTP server.

verbose   Toggle verbose mode. In verbose mode, all responses from the FTP server are displayed. In addition, if verbose mode is on, then when a file transfer completes, statistics regarding the efficiency of the transfer are reported. By default, verbose mode is on if `ftp`'s commands are coming from a terminal, and off otherwise.

? [*command*] A synonym for `help`.

You can quote command arguments that have embedded spaces with quote (`"`) marks.

If you do not specify any command argument that is not indicated as being optional, `ftp` prompts for that argument.

Aborting File Transfer

To abort a file transfer, use the terminal interrupt key. Sending transfers are immediately halted. Receiving transfers are halted by sending an FTP protocol `ABOR` command to the remote server and discarding any further data received. The speed at which this is accomplished depends on the remote server's support for `ABOR` processing. If the remote server does not support the `ABOR` command, an `ftp>` prompt is not displayed until the remote server has completed sending the requested file.

The terminal interrupt key sequence is ignored when `ftp` has completed any local processing and is awaiting a reply from the remote server. A long delay in this mode may result from the `ABOR` processing described above, or from unexpected behavior by the remote server, including violations of the `ftp` protocol. If the delay results from unexpected remote server behavior, you must kill the local `ftp` program by hand.

File-Naming Conventions

Local files specified as arguments to `ftp` commands are processed according to the following rules.

1. If you specify the file name `-`, use the standard input (for reading) or standard output (for writing).

2. If the first character of the file name is `|`, interpret the remainder of the argument as a shell command. `ftp` then forks a shell, using `popen(3S)` with the argument supplied, and reads (writes) from the standard output (standard input) of that shell. If the shell command includes space characters, you must quote the argument; for example `"| ls -lt"`. A particularly useful example of this mechanism is: `"dir | more"`.

3. Failing the above checks, if you enable globbing, then expand local file names according to the rules used in the sh(1); see the `glob` command. If the `ftp` command expects a single local file (for example, `put`), use only the first `filename` generated by the globbing operation.

4. For `mget` and `get` commands with unspecified local file names, the local `filename` is the remote `filename`, which you can alter by using a `case`, `ntrans`, or `nmap` setting. You can then alter the resulting `filename` if `runique` is on.

5. For `mput` and `put` commands with unspecified remote file names, the remote `filename` is the local `filename`, which you can alter by using an `ntrans` or `nmap` setting. The resulting `filename` can then be altered by the remote server if `sunique` is on.

File Transfer Parameters

The following parameters from the FTP specification can affect file transfers.

Representation type

> `ASCII`, `EBCDIC`, `image`, or `local byte size` with a specified byte size (for PDP-10s and PDP-20s mostly). The `network ASCII` and `EBCDIC` types have a further subtype that specifies whether vertical format control such as newline characters and formfeeds is to be passed through (nonprint), provided in TELNET format (TELNET format controls), or provided in ASA (FORTRAN) (carriage control (ASA)) format. `ftp` supports the `network ASCII` (subtype nonprint only) and `image` types, plus `local byte size` with a byte size of 8 for communicating with TENEX machines.

File structure

> `file` (no record structure), `record`, or `page`. `ftp` supports only the default value, which is `file`.

Transfer mode

> `stream`, `block`, or `compressed`. `ftp` supports only the default value, which is `stream`.

Usage

See `largefile(5)` for the description of the behavior of `ftp` when encountering files greater than or equal to 2 Gbytes (2**31 bytes).

Files

~/.netrc

Attributes

See attributes(5) for descriptions of the following attributes:

Attribute Type	Attribute Value
Availability	SUNWcsu
CSI	Enabled

See Also

ls(1), rcp(1), sh(1), tar(1), ftpd(1M), popen(3S), netrc(4),
attributes(5), largefile(5)

---

function — Shell Built-in Command to Define a Shell Function

Synopsis

ksh

```
function identifier { list ;}
identifier() { list ;}
```

Description

Korn Shell

function defines a function that is referenced by *identifier*. The body of
the function is the list of commands between the curly braces ({ }).

Alternatively, you can define a function by omitting the function keyword
and appending the identifier with a set of enclosed parentheses.

Examples

The following example creates a function called status() that returns the
name of your current working directory and then lists it.

```
$ status() { cd $*; pwd;ls; }
$
$ functions
function status
{
cd $*; pwd;ls; }
$
$ status /home
/home
TT_DB           bill            lost+found
$
```

The following example creates a function called `scp()` for safe copy. It prevents you from overwriting an existing file. When you issue the same command twice, the second command is not executed and the `scp()` function displays an error message.

```
$ scp()
> {
> if test ! -s "$2"
> then cp "$1" "$2"
> else echo "scp: cannot copy $1: $2 exists"
> fi
> }
$ scp junk junk1
$ scp junk junk1
scp: cannot copy junk: junk1 exists
$
```

Attributes

See `attributes`(5) for descriptions of the following attributes:

Attribute Type	Attribute Value
Availability	SUNWcsu

See Also

`ksh`(1), `attributes`(5)

G

gcore — Get Core Images of Running Processes

Synopsis

```
/usr/bin/gcore [-o filename] process-id ...
```

Description

gcore creates a core image of each specified process in the current working directory. By default, the name of the core image file for the process is core.*process-id*.

Options

-o *filename*

Substitute *filename* in place of core as the first part of the name of the core image files.

Operands

process-id Process ID.

Examples

The following example creates a core image of process ID 450.

```
castle% gcore 450
gcore: core.450 dumped
castle% ls -l core*
-rw-rw-rw-   1 winsor     staff          66216 Jan 16 14:16 core.450
castle% file core.450
core.450:        ELF 32-bit MSB core file SPARC Version 1, from 'cat'
castle%
```

The following example tries to create a core image for process ID 461, which doesn't exist. Notice that gcore creates an output file named core.o, but it is an empty file.

```
castle% gcore 461
castle% ls -l core*
-rw-rw-rw-   1 winsor     staff              0 Jan 14 15:50 core.o
castle%
```

Exit Status

0	On success.
non-zero	On failure, such as nonexistent process ID.

Files

core.*process-id*

Core images.

Attributes

See attributes(5) for descriptions of the following attributes:

Attribute Type	Attribute Value
Availability	SUNWtoo (32-bit) SUNWtoox (64-bit)

New!

See Also

kill(1), core(4), proc(4), attributes(5)

gencat — Generate a Formatted Message Catalog

Synopsis

```
/usr/bin/gencat catfile msgfile...
```

Description

Use the gencat command to merge the message text source file(s) *msgfile* into a formatted message database *catfile*. If the database *catfile* does not already exist, it is created. If *catfile* does exist, its messages are included in the new *catfile*. If set and message numbers collide, the new message text defined in *msgfile* replaces the old message text currently contained in *catfile*. The message text source file (or set of files) you input to gencat can contain either set and message numbers or simply message numbers, in which case the set NL_SETD (see nl_types(5)) is assumed.

Message Text Source File Format

The format of a message text source file is described below.

Note — The fields of a message text source line are separated by a single ASCII space or Tab character. Any other ASCII spaces or Tabs are considered as part of the subsequent field.

`$set n comment`

> Specify a set identifier, where *n* specifies the set identifier of the following messages until the next $set, $delset, or end-of-file. *n* must be a number in the range (1-{NL_SETMAX}). Set identifiers within a single source file need not be contiguous. Treat any string following the set identifier as a comment. If you specify no $set directive in a message text source file, locate all messages in the default message set NL_SETD.

`$delset n comment`

> Delete message set *n* from an existing message catalog. Treat any string following the set number as a comment. (Note: if *n* is not a valid set, it is ignored.)

`$ comment`

> Treat a line beginning with a dollar symbol $ followed by an ASCII space or Tab character as a comment.

`m message-text`

> The *m* denotes the message identifier, a number in the range (1-{NL_MSGMAX}). Store *message-text* in the message catalog with the set identifier specified by the last $set directive and with message identifier *m*. If *message-text* is empty and an ASCII space or Tab field separator is present, store an empty

string in the message catalog. If a message source line has a message number but neither a field separator nor message text, delete the existing message with that number (if any) from the catalog. Message identifiers need not be contiguous. The length of `message-text` must be in the range `(0-{NL_TEXTMAX})`.

`$quote c`   Specify an optional quote character `c` that can be used to surround `message-text` so that trailing spaces or null (empty) messages are visible in a message source line. By default or if you specify an empty `$quote` directive, no quoting of `message-text` is recognized.

Empty lines in a message text source file are ignored.

Text strings can contain the special characters and escape sequences defined below.

Description	Symbol	Sequence
Newline	NL(LF)	\n
Horizontal tab	HT	\t
Vertical tab	VT	\v
Backspace	BS	\b
Return	CR	\r
Formfeed	FF	\f
Backslash	\	\\
Bit pattern	*ddd*	*ddd*

The escape sequence *ddd* consists of backslash followed by 1, 2, or 3 octal digits, which are taken to specify the value of the desired character. If the character following a backslash is not one of those specified, the backslash is ignored.

You can also use a backslash followed by an ASCII newline character to continue a string on the following line. Thus, the following two lines describe a single message string:

```
1 This line continues \
to the next line
```

is equivalent to:

```
1 This line continues to the next line
```

Operands

catfile	A path name of the formatted message catalogue. If you specify -, use the standard output.
msgfile	A path name of a message text source file. If you specify - for an instance of *msgfile*, use the standard input.

Environment Variables

See environ(5) for descriptions of the following environment variables that affect the execution of gencat: LC_CTYPE, LC_MESSAGES, and NLSPATH.

Exit Status

0	Successful completion.
>0	An error occurred.

Attributes

See attributes(5) for descriptions of the following attributes:

Attribute Type	Attribute Value
Availability	SUNWloc
CSI	Enabled

See Also

mkmsgs(1), catgets(3C), catopen(3C), gettxt(3C), attributes(5), environ(5), nl_types(5)

---

genmsg — Generate a Message Source File by Extracting Messages from Source Files

Synopsis

```
/usr/bin/genmsg [-abdfrntx][-c message-tag] [-g project-file]
    [-l project-file][-m prefix][-M suffix]
    [-o message-file][-p preprocessor][-s set-tags] file ...
```

Description

genmsg extracts message strings with calls to catgets(3C) from source files and writes them in a format suitable for input to gencat(1).

Invocation

genmsg reads one or more input files and, by default, generates a message source file whose name is composed of the first input file name with a `.msg` suffix. If you specify the -o option, genmsg uses the option argument for its output file.

Command	Output File
genmsg prog.c	prog.c.msg
gensmg main.c util.c tool.c	main.c.msg
genmsg -o prog.msg mail.c util.c	prog.msg

    genmsg also enables you to invoke a preprocessor to solve the dependencies of macros and to define statements for the catgets(3C) calls.

Message Autonumbering

genmsg replaces message numbers with the calculated numbers based on the project file if the message numbers are -1. It generates copies of the input files with the new message numbers and a copy of the project file with the new maximum message numbers.

    A project file is a database that stores a list of set numbers with their maximum message numbers. Each line in a project file is composed of a set number and its maximum message number:

Set_number Maximum_message_number

    In a project file, a line beginning with a number sign (#) or an ASCII space is considered as a comment and ignored.

    genmsg also has the reverse operation to replace all message numbers with -1.

Comment Extraction

genmsg enables you to comment about messages and set numbers to inform the translator how to translate the messages. It extracts the comment, which is surrounded with the comment indicators and has the specified tag inside the comment, from the input file and writes it with a dollar ($) prefix in the output file. genmsg supports the C and C++ comment indicators, /*, */, and //.

Testing

genmsg generates two kinds of messages for testing:

- Prefixed messages enable you to check that your program is retrieving the messages from the message catalog.

- Long messages enable you to check the appearance of your window program's initial size and position.

Notes

genmsg does not handle pointers or variables in the catgets(3C) call. For example:

```
const int set_num = 1;
extern int msg_num(const char *);
const char *msg = "Hello";

catgets(catd, set_num, msg_num(msg), msg);
```

When the message autonumbering is turned on with a preprocessor, if there are multiple -1's in the catgets(3C) line, genmsg replaces all of the -1's in the line with a calculated number. For example, given the input:

```
#define MSG(id, msg) catgets(catd, 1, (id), (msg))

if (ret == -1) printf("%s0, MSG(-1, "Failed"));
```

the command

```
genmsg -l proj -p "cc -E"
```

produces

```
#define MSG(id, msg) catgets(catd, 1, (id), (msg))

if (ret == 1) printf("%s0, MSG(1, "Failed"));
```

The workaround is to split the output into two lines as follows:

```
if (ret == -1)
  printf("%s0, MSG(-1, "Failed"));
```

Options

-a	Append the output into the message file *message-file* that is specified by the -o option. If two different messages that have the same set and message number are found, keep the message in the specified message file and discard the other message in the input file.
-b	Place the extracted comment after the corresponding message in the output file. This option changes the placement behavior of the -s or -c option.
-c *message-tag*	Extract message comments having *message-tag* inside them from the input files and write them with a $ prefix as a comment in the output file.
-d	Include an original text of a message as a comment to be preserved along with its translations. With this option, the translator can see the original messages even after they are replaced with their translations.

-f   Overwrite the input files and the project file when used with the
                -l or -r option. With the -r option, overwrite only the input files.

-g *project-file*

                Generate *project-file* that has a list of set numbers and their
                maximum message numbers in the input files.

-l *project-file*

                Replace message numbers with the calculated numbers based on
                project-file if the message numbers are -1 in the input files,
                then generate copies of the input files with the new message
                numbers and a copy of *project-file* with the new maximum
                message numbers. If *project-file* is not found, use the
                maximum message number in the input file as a base number and
                generate *project-file*.

-m *prefix*   Fill in the message with *prefix*. This option is useful for testing.

-M *suffix*   Fill in the message with *suffix*. This option is useful for testing.

-n   Add comment lines to the output file indicating the file name and
                line number in the input files where each extracted string is
                encountered.

-o *message-file*

                Write the output to *message-file*.

-p *processor*

                Invoke preprocessor to preprocess macros and define statements
                for the catgets(3C) calls. genmsg first invokes the option
                argument as a preprocesser and then starts the normal process
                against the output from the preprocessor. genmsg initiates this
                process for all the input files.

-r   Replace message numbers with -1. This operation is the reverse of
                the -l option.

-s *set-tag*   Extract set number comments having *set-tag* inside them from
                the input files and write them with a $ prefix as a comment in the
                output file. If you specify multiple comments for one set number,
                extract the first one and discard the rest of them.

-t   Generate a message that is three times as long as the original
                message. This option is useful for testing.

-x   Suppress warning messages about message, set number range
                checks, and conflicts.

Operands

file   An input source file.

Examples

Suppose that you have the following source and project files.

```
castle% cat test.c
printf(catgets(catfd, 1, -1, "line too long0));
printf(catgets(catfd, 2, -1, "invalid code0));
castle% cat proj
1    10
2    20
```

The command

```
castle% genmsg -l proj test.c
```

assigns the calculated message numbers based on proj and generates the following files.

```
test.c.msg    message file
proj.new      updated project file
test.c.new    new source file
castle% cat test.c.msg
$quote "

$set    1
11      "line too long0

$set    2
21      "invalid code0
castle% cat proj.new
1    11
2    21
castle% cat test.c.new
printf(catgets(catfd, 1, 11, "line too long0));
printf(catgets(catfd, 2, 21, "invalid code0));
```

For a test.c file containing the following information

```
castle% cat test.c
/* SET: tar messages */
/* MSG: don't translate "tar". */
catgets(catfd, 1, 1, "tar: tape write error");
// MSG: don't translate "tar" and "-I".
catgets(catfd, 1, 2, "tar: missing argument for -I flag");
```

the following command extracts the comments and writes them in the test.c.msg output file.

```
castle% genmsg -s SET -c MSG test.c
castle% cat test.c.msg
$ /* SET: tar messages */
$set    1
$ /* MSG: don't translate "tar". */
1       "tar: tape write error"
$ // MSG: don't translate "tar" and "-I".
2       "tar: missing argument for -I flag"
```

The following command generates messages for testing.

```
castle% genmsg -m PRE: -M :FIX test.c
castle% cat test.c.msg
1       "PRE:OK:FIX"
2       "PRE:Cancel:FIX"
```

With the following input,

```
castle% cat example.c
#include <nl_types.h>

#define MSG1    "message1"
#define MSG2    "message2"
#define MSG3    "message3"

#define MSG(n)  catgets(catd, 1, n, MSG ## n)

void
main(int argc, char **argv)
{
        nl_catd catd = catopen(argv[0], NL_CAT_LOCALE);

        (void) printf("%s0, MSG(1));
        (void) printf("%s0, MSG(2));
        (void) printf("%s0, MSG(3));

        (void) catclose(catd);
}
```

the following command parses the MSG macros and writes the extracted messages in example.msg.

```
castle%  genmsg -p "cc -E" -o example.msg example.c
```

Suppose that you have the following header, source, and project files:

```
castle% ../inc/msg.h
#define WARN_SET                1
#define ERR_SET                 2

#define WARN_MSG(id, msg) catgets(catd, WARN_SET, (id), (msg))

#define ERR_MSG(id, msg)  catgets(catd, ERR_SET, (id), (msg))
castle% example.c
#include "msg.h"
printf("%s0, WARN_MSG(-1, "Warning error"));
printf("%s0, ERR_MSG(-1, "Fatal error"));
example % proj
1       10
2       10
```

Then, the following command assigns each of the -1 message numbers a
calculated number based on proj and overwrites the results to example.c
and proj. This command also writes the extracted messages in example.msg.

```
castle% genmsg -f -p "cc -E -I../inc" -l proj -o example.msg example.c
```

Environment Variables

See environ(5) for descriptions of the following environment variables that
affect the execution of genmsg: LC_MESSAGES and NLSPATH.

Exit Status

0	Successful completion.
>0	An error occurred.

Attributes

See attributes(5) for descriptions of the following attributes:

Attribute Type	Attribute Value
Availability	SUNWloc

See Also

gencat(1), catgets(3C), catopen(3C), attributes(5), environ(5)

get, sccs-get — Retrieve a Version of an SCCS File

Synopsis

```
/usr/ccs/bin/get [-begkmnpst] [-l[p]] [-asequence]
    [-c date-time | -cdate-time] [-Gg-file]
    [-i sid-list | -isid-list] [-r[sid]]
    [-x sid-list| -xsid-list] s.filename ...
/usr/xpg4/bin/get [-begkmnpst] [-l[p]] [-asequence]
    [-c date-time | -cdate-time] [-Gg-file]
    [-i sid-list | -isid-list] [-r sid | -rsid]
    [-x sid-list | -xsid-list] s.filename ...
```

Description

See sccs-get(1).

getconf — Get Configuration Values

Synopsis

```
/usr/bin/getconf [-v specification] system-var
/usr/bin/getconf [-v specification] path-var pathname
/usr/bin/getconf -a
```

Description

In the first synopsis form, the getconf command writes the value of the variable specified by *system-var* to the standard output. If you specify the -v option, it writes the value in accordance with *specification*.

In the second synopsis form, getconf writes the value of the variable specified by *path-var* for the path specified by *pathname* to the standard output. If you specify the -v option, it writes the value in accordance with *specification*.

In the third synopsis form, the getconf command writes the names of the current system configuration variables to the standard output.

The value of each configuration variable is determined as if it were obtained by calling the function from which it is defined. The value reflects conditions in the current operating environment.

Options

-a   Write the names of the current system configuration variables to the standard output.

-v *specification*

Give the specification that governs the selection of values for configuration variables.

Operands

path-var   A name of a configuration variable whose value is available from the pathconf(2) function. All of the following values are supported:
```
LINK_MAX
NAME_MAX
POSIX_CHOWN_RESTRICTED
MAX_CANON
PATH_MAX
POSIX_NO_TRUNC
MAX_INPUT
PIPE_BUF POSIX_VDISABLE
```

pathname   A path name for which the variable specified by *path-var* is to be determined.

system-var A name of a configuration variable whose value is available from
confstr(3C) or sysconf(3C). All of the values in the following
table are supported.

ARG_MAX	POSIX2_C_BIND
BC_BASE_MAX	POSIX2_C_DEV
BC_DIM_MAX	POSIX2_C_VERSION
BC_SCALE_MAX	POSIX2_CHAR_TERM
BC_STRING_MAX	POSIX2_COLL_WEIGHTS_MAX
CHAR_BIT	POSIX2_EXPR_NEST_MAX
CHAR_MAX	POSIX2_FORT_DEV
CHAR_MIN	POSIX2_FORT_RUN
CHARCLASS_NAME_MAX	POSIX2_LINE_MAX
CHILD_MAX	POSIX2_LOCALEDEF
CLK_TCK	POSIX2_RE_DUP_MAX
COLL_WEIGHTS_MAX	POSIX2_SW_DEV
CS_PATH	POSIX2_UPE
EXPR_NEST_MAX	POSIX2_VERSION
INT_MAX	RE_DUP_MAX
INT_MIN	SCHAR_MAX
LFS64_CFLAGS	SCHAR_MIN
LFS64_LDFLAGS	SHRT_MAX
LFS64_LIBS	SHRT_MIN
LFS64_LINTFLAGS	SSIZE_MAX
LFS_CFLAGS	STREAM_MAX
LFS_LDFLAGS	TMP_MAX
LFS_LIBS	TZNAME_MAX
LFS_LINTFLAGS	UCHAR_MAX
LINE_MAX	UINT_MAX
LONG_BIT	ULONG_MAX
LONG_MAX	USHRT_MAX
LONG_MIN	WORD_BIT
MB_LEN_MAX	XBS5_ILP32_OFF32
NGROUPS_MAX	XBS5_ILP32_OFF32_CFLAGS
NL_ARGMAX	XBS5_ILP32_OFF32_LDFLAGS
NL_LANGMAX	XBS5_ILP32_OFF32_LIBS
NL_MSGMAX	XBS5_ILP32_OFF32_LINTFLAGS

New!

NL_NMAX	XBS5_ILP32_OFFBIG
NL_SETMAX	XBS5_ILP32_OFFBIG_CFLAGS
NL_TEXTMAX	XBS5_ILP32_OFFBIG_LDFLAGS
NZERO	XBS5_ILP32_OFFBIG_LIBS
OPEN_MAX	XBS5_ILP32_OFFBIG_LINTFLAGS
_POSIX_ARG_MAX	XBS5_LP64_OFF64
_POSIX_CHILD_MAX	XBS5_LP64_OFF64_CFLAGS
_POSIX_JOB_CONTROL	XBS5_LP64_OFF64_LDFLAGS
_POSIX_LINK_MAX	XBS5_LP64_OFF64_LIBS
_POSIX_MAX_CANON	XBS5_LP64_OFF64_LINTFLAGS
_POSIX_MAX_INPUT	XBS5_LPBIG_OFFBIG
_POSIX_NAME_MAX	XBS5_LPBIG_OFFBIG_CFLAGS
_POSIX_NGROUPS_MAX	XBS5_LPBIG_OFFBIG_LDFLAGS
_POSIX_OPEN_MAX	XBS5_LPBIG_OFFBIG_LIBS
_POSIX_PATH_MAX	XBS5_LPBIG_OFFBIG_LINTFLAGS
_POSIX_PIPE_BUF	_XOPEN_CRYPT
_POSIX_SAVED_IDS	_XOPEN_ENH_I18N
_POSIX_SSIZE_MAX	_XOPEN_LEGACY
_POSIX_STREAM_MAX	_XOPEN_SHM
_POSIX_TZNAME_MAX	_XOPEN_VERSION
_POSIX_VERSION	_XOPEN_XCU_VERSION
POSIX2_BC_BASE_MAX	_XOPEN_XPG2
POSIX2_BC_DIM_MAX	_XOPEN_XPG3
POSIX2_BC_SCALE_MAX	_XOPEN_XPG4
POSIX2_BC_STRING_MAX	

New!

The symbol PATH also is recognized, yielding the same value as the confstr() name value CS_PATH.

Usage

See largefile(5) for the description of the behavior of getconf when encountering files greater than or equal to 2 Gbytes (2**31 bytes).

Examples

The following example shows the first few lines of the output generated by the getconf -a command.

```
castle% getconf -a
AIO_LISTIO_MAX:                  256
AIO_MAX:                         undefined
```

```
AIO_PRIO_DELTA_MAX:                     0
ARG_MAX:                                1048320
ATEXIT_MAX:                             32
BC_BASE_MAX:                            99
BC_DIM_MAX:                             2048
BC_SCALE_MAX:                           99
BC_STRING_MAX:                          1000
CHARCLASS_NAME_MAX:                     14
CHAR_BIT:                               8
CHAR_MAX:                               127
CHAR_MIN:                               -128
...
castle%
```

The following example returns the value of NGROUPS_MAX.

```
castle% getconf NGROUPS_MAX
16
castle%
```

The following example returns the value of NAME_MAX for a specific directory.

```
castle% getconf NAME_MAX /usr
255
castle%
```

The following example shows how to deal more carefully with results that might be unspecified.

```
if value=$(getconf PATH_MAX /usr); then
  if ["$value" = "undefined"]; then
    echo PATH_MAX in /usr is infinite.
  else
    echo PATH_MAX in /usr is $value.
  fi
else
  echo Error in getconf.
fi
```

> **Note** — sysconf(_SC_POSIX_C_BIND); and
> system("getconf POSIX2_C_BIND"); in a C program could give
> different answers. The sysconf call supplies a value that
> corresponds to the conditions when the program was either
> compiled or executed, depending on the implementation; the system
> call to getconf always supplies a value corresponding to conditions
> when the program is executed.

Environment Variables

See environ(5) for descriptions of the following environment variables that affect the execution of getconf: LC_CTYPE, LC_MESSAGES, and NLSPATH.

Exit Status

0   The specified variable is valid and information about its current
             state was written successfully.

>0   An error occurred.

Attributes

See `attributes`(5) for descriptions of the following attributes:

Attribute Type	Attribute Value
Availability	SUNWcsu

See Also

`pathconf(2)`, `confstr(3C)`, `sysconf(3C)`, `attributes(5)`, `environ(5)`,
`largefile(5)`

getfacl — Display Discretionary File Information

Synopsis

`/usr/bin/getfacl [-ad]` *file* `...`

Description

Access Control Lists (ACLs) are extensions to standard UNIX file permissions.
The ACL information is stored and associated with each file individually. You
can determine if a file has an ACL with the `getfacl` command. For each
argument that is a regular file, special file, or named pipe, `getfacl` displays
the owner, the group, and the ACL. For each directory argument, `getfacl`
displays the owner, the group, and the ACL and/or the default ACL. Only
directories contain default ACLs.

   You can execute `getfacl` on a file system that does not support ACLs. It
reports the ACL based on the base permission bits.

   If you specify no options, `getfacl` displays the file name, the owner, the
group, and both the ACL and the default ACL if it exists.

Options

-a   Display the file name, the owner, the group, and the ACL of the
             file.

-d   Display the file name, the owner, the group, and the default ACL of
             the file if it exists.

Operands

      `file`   The path name of a regular file, special file, or named pipe.

Output

The format for ACL output is as follows.

```
# file: filename
# owner: uid
# group: gid
user::perm
user:uid:perm
group::perm
group:gid:perm
mask:perm
other:perm
default:user::perm
default:user:uid:perm
default:group::perm
default:group:gid:perm
default:mask:perm
default:other:perm
```

When you specify multiple files on the command line, a blank line separates the ACLs for each file.

The ACL entries are displayed in the order in which they are evaluated when an access check is performed. The default ACL entries that may exist on a directory have no effect on access checks.

The first three lines display the file name, the file owner, and the file-owning group. Note that when you specify only the -d option and the file has no default ACL, only these three lines are displayed.

The `user` entry without a user ID indicates the permissions that are granted to the owner of the file. One or more additional user entries indicate the permissions that are granted to the specified users.

The `group` entry without a group ID indicates the permissions that are granted to the owning group of the file. One or more additional group entries indicate the permissions that are granted to the specified groups.

The `mask` entry indicates the file group mask permissions. These are the maximum permissions allowed to any user entries, except the file owner, and to any group entries, including the owning group. These permissions restrict the permissions specified in other entries.

The `other` entry indicates the permissions that are granted to others.

The default entries may exist only for directories and indicate the default entries that are added to a file created within the directory.

The `uid` is a login name or a user ID if there is no entry for the `uid` in the system password file, `/etc/passwd`. The `gid` is a group name or a group ID if there is no entry for the `gid` in the system group file, `/etc/group`. The `perm` is a three-character string composed of the letters representing the separate discretionary access rights: `r` (read), `w` (write), `x` (execute/search), or the placeholder character –. The perm is displayed in the following order: rwx. If permission is not granted by an ACL entry, the placeholder character is used.

The file-owner permission bits represent the access of the owning user ACL entry. The file-group class permission bits represent the most access that any additional user entries, additional group entries, or the owning group entry may grant. The file other-class permission bits represent the access that the other ACL entry has. If a user invokes the chmod(1) command and changes the file group class permission bits, the access granted by additional ACL entries may be restricted.

To indicate that the file group-class permission bits restrict an ACL entry, getfacl displays an additional Tab character, pound sign (#), and the actual permissions granted, following the entry.

Note — The output from getfacl is in the correct format for input to the setfacl command. If the output from getfacl is redirected to a file, the file can be used as input to setfacl. In this way, you can easily assign one file's ACL to another file.

Examples

Given file foo, with an ACL six entries long, the command

```
castle% getfacl foo
```

prints

```
# file: foo
# owner: shea
# group: staff
user::rwx
user:spy:---
user:mookie:r--
group::r--
mask::rw-
other::---
```

Continuing with the above example, after using the **chmod 700 foo** command:

```
castle% getfacl foo
```

prints

```
# file: foo
# owner: shea
# group: staff
user::rwx
user:spy:---
user:mookie:r--      #effective:---
group::r--           #effective:---
mask::---
other::---
```

Given directory doo, with an ACL containing default entries, the command

castle% **getfacl -d doo**

prints

```
# file: doo
# owner: shea
# group: staff
default:user::rwx
default:user:spy:---
default:user:mookie:r--
default:group::r--
default:mask::---
default:other::---
```

Files

/etc/passwd System password file.

/etc/group Group file.

Attributes

See attributes(5) for descriptions of the following attributes:

Attribute Type	Attribute Value
Availability	SUNWcsu

See Also

chmod(1), ls(1), setfacl(1), acl(2), aclsort(3), group(4), passwd(4), attributes(5)

getopt — Parse Command Options

Synopsis

```
set -- `getopt optstring $*`
```

Description

The /usr/bin/getopt command is superseded by the getopts command.

> **Note** — getopt is not supported in the next major release. This release provides a getoptcvt conversion tool. For more information about getopts and getoptcvt, see getopts(1)

Use `getopt` to break up options in command lines for easy parsing by shell procedures and to check for legal options; you use `getopts` in shell script loops to ensure standard syntax for command-line options. *optstring* is a string of recognized option letters; see `getopt(3C)`. If you follow a letter with a colon, the option is expected to have an argument that may or may not be separated from it by white space. Use the special option `--` to delimit the end of the options. If you use it explicitly, `getopt` recognizes it; otherwise, `getopt` generates it; in either case, `getopt` puts it at the end of the options. The positional parameters (`$1 $2 ...`) of the shell are reset so that each option is preceded by a `-` and is in its own positional parameter; each option argument is also parsed into its own positional parameter.

Reset `optind` to 1 when rescanning the options.

`getopt` does not support the part of Rule 8 of the command syntax standard (see `intro(1)`) that permits groups of option-arguments following an option to be separated by white space and quoted. For example,

```
cmd - a - b - o "xxx z yy" filename
```

is not handled correctly. To correct this deficiency, use the `getopts` command in place of `getopt`.

Examples

The following code fragment shows how you might process the arguments for a command that can take the options a or b, as well as the option o, which requires an argument.

```
set -- `getopt abo: $*`
if [$? != 0]
then
   echo $USAGE
   exit 2
fi
for i in $*
do
   case $i in
   -a | -b)   FLAG=$i; shift;;
   -o)        OARG=$2; shift 2;;
   --)        shift; break;;
   esac
done
```

This code accepts any of the following as equivalent.

```
cmd - aoarg filename1 filename2
cmd - a - o arg filename1 filename2
cmd - oarg - a filename1 filename2
cmd - a - oarg - - filename1 filename2
```

> **Note** — If an option that takes an option-argument is followed by a value that is the same as one of the options listed in *optstring*,
>
> ```
> cmd - o - a filename
> ```
>
> getopt always treats - a as an option-argument to - o; it never recognizes - a as an option. For this case, the for loop in the example shifts past the *filename* argument.

Attributes

See attributes(5) for descriptions of the following attributes:

Attribute Type	Attribute Value
Availability	SUNWcsu
CSI	Enabled

See Also

intro(1), sh(1), shell_builtins(1), getopt(3C), attributes(5)

Diagnostics

getopt prints an error message on the standard error when it encounters an option letter not included in *optstring*.

getoptcvt — Convert to getopts to Parse Command Options

Synopsis

```
/usr/lib/getoptcvt [-b] filename
/usr/lib/getoptcvt
```

Description

Use /usr/lib/getoptcvt to convert getopt output to use getopts instead. getoptcvt reads the shell script in *filename*, converts it to use getopts instead of getopt, and writes the results on the standard output.

getopts is a built-in Bourne shell command that parses positional parameters and checks for valid options. See sh(1). getopts supports all applicable rules of the command syntax standard (see Rules 3-10, intro(1)). You should use getopts instead of the getopt command. The syntax for the shell's built-in getopts command is

```
getopts optstring name [argument...]
```

optstring must contain the option letters recognized by the command using
getopts; if a letter is followed by a colon, the option is expected to have an
argument, or group of arguments, that must be separated from it by white
space.

Each time you invoke it, getopts puts the next option in the shell variable
name and the index of the next argument to be processed in the shell variable
OPTIND. Whenever you invoke the shell or a shell script, OPTIND is initialized
to 1.

When an option requires an option-argument, getopts puts it in the shell
variable OPTARG.

If getops encounters an illegal option, ? is placed in *name*.

When the end of options is encountered, getopts exits with a non-zero exit
status. You can use the special option -- to delimit the end of the options.

By default, getopts parses the positional parameters. If you specify extra
arguments (*argument* ...) on the getopts command line, getopts parses
them instead.

So that all new commands adhere to the command syntax standard
described in intro(1), they should use getopts or getopt to parse positional
parameters and should check for options that are valid for that command.

Although relaxations of the following command syntax rule (see intro(1))
are permitted under the current implementation, you should not use them
because they may not be supported in future releases of the system.

Options

-b   Make the converted script portable to earlier releases of the UNIX
            system. /usr/lib/getoptcvt modifies the shell script in
            filename so that when the resulting shell script is executed, it
            determines at runtime whether to invoke getopts or getopt.

Examples

The following fragment of a shell program shows how you might process the
arguments for a command that can take the options a or b, as well as the option
o, which requires an option-argument.

```
while getopts abo: c
  do
    case $c in
    a | b)    FLAG=$c;;
    o)        OARG=$OPTARG;;
    \?)       echo $USAGE
              exit 2;;
    esac
  done
  shift `expr $OPTIND - 1`
```

This code accepts any of the following as equivalent.

```
cmd - a - b - o "xxx z yy" filename
cmd - a - b - o "xxx z yy" -- filename
cmd - ab - o xxx,z,yy filename
cmd - ab - o "xxx z yy" filename
cmd - o xxx,z,yy - b - a filename
```

Note that a and b are options, and the option o requires an option-argument. The following example violates Rule 5: options with option-arguments must not be grouped with other options.

```
castle% cmd - aboxxx filename
```

The following example violates Rule 6: there must be white space after an option that takes an option-argument.

```
castle% cmd - ab oxxx filename
```

Changing the value of the shell variable OPTIND or parsing different sets of arguments can lead to unexpected results.

Attributes

See attributes(5) for descriptions of the following attributes:

Attribute Type	Attribute Value
Availability	SUNWcsu
CSI	Enabled

See Also

intro(1), sh(1), shell_builtins(1), getopt(3C), attributes(5)

Diagnostics

getopts prints an error message on the standard error when it encounters an option letter not included in optstring.

getopts — Parse Utility Options

Synopsis

```
/usr/bin/getopts optstring name [arg...]
```

sh
```
getopts optstring name [argument ...]
```

ksh
```
getopts optstring name [arg ...]
```

Description

/usr/bin/getopts

You can use the `getopts` command to process command-line arguments and check for legal options. You use the `getops` command in shell script loops to ensure standard syntax for command-line options.

Each time it is invoked, the `getopts` command puts the value of the next option in the shell variable specified by the *name* operand and the index of the next argument to be processed in the shell variable `OPTIND`. Whenever the shell is invoked, `OPTIND` is initialized to 1.

When the option requires an option-argument, the `getopts` command puts it in the shell variable `OPTARG`. If no option is found or if the option that was found does not have an option-argument, `OPTARG` is unset.

If an option character not contained in the *optstring* operand is found where an option character is expected, the shell variable specified by *name* is set to the question-mark (?) character. In this case, if the first character in *optstring* is a colon (:), the shell variable `OPTARG` is set to the option character found but no output is written to standard error; otherwise, the shell variable `OPTARG` is unset and a diagnostic message is written to standard error. This condition is considered to be an error detected in the way arguments were presented to the invoking application but is not an error in `getopts` processing.

If an option-argument is missing, `getopts` handles it in the following ways:

- If the first character of *optstring* is a colon, the shell variable specified by *name* is set to the colon character and the shell variable `OPTARG` is set to the option character found.

- Otherwise, the shell variable specified by *name* is set to the question-mark character, the shell variable `OPTARG` is unset and a diagnostic message is written to standard error. This condition is considered to be an error detected in the way arguments were presented to the invoking application but is not an error in `getopts` processing; a diagnostic message is written as stated, but the exit status is 0.

When the end-of-options is encountered, the `getopts` command exits with a return value greater than 0; the shell variable `OPTIND` is set to the index of the first nonoption argument, where the first `--` argument is considered to be an option-argument if no other nonoption arguments appear before it, or the value `$# + 1` if there are no nonoption arguments; the *name* variable is set to the question-mark character. Any of the following identify the end of options:

- The special option `--`.
- Finding an argument that does not begin with a `-`.
- Encountering an error.

The shell variables `OPTIND` and `OPTARG` are local to the caller of `getopts` and are not exported by default.

The shell variable specified by the *name* operand, OPTIND, or OPTARG affects the current shell execution environment.

If the application sets OPTIND to the value 1, a new set of parameters can be used: either the current positional parameters or new *arg* values. Any other attempt to invoke getopts multiple times in a single-shell execution environment with parameters (positional parameters or *arg* operands) that are not the same in all invocations, or with an OPTIND value modified to be a value other than 1, produces unspecified results.

Bourne Shell

getopts is a built-in Bourne shell command that parses positional parameters and checks for valid options. See sh(1). It supports all applicable rules of the command syntax standard (see Rules 3-10, intro(1)). You should use it instead of the getopt command.

optstring must contain the option letters recognized by the command using getopts; if a letter is followed by a colon, the option is expected to have an argument, or group of arguments, which must be separated from it by white space.

Each time getopts is invoked, it puts the next option in the shell variable *name* and the index of the next argument to be processed in the shell variable OPTIND. Whenever the shell or a shell script is invoked, OPTIND is initialized to 1. When an option requires an option-argument, getopts puts it in the shell variable OPTARG.

If an illegal option is encountered, ? is placed in *name*.

When the end of options is encountered, getopts exits with a non-zero exit status. You can use the special option -- to delimit the end of the options.

By default, getopts parses the positional parameters. If extra arguments (*argument* ...) are given on the getopts command line, getopts parses them instead.

/usr/lib/getoptcvt reads the shell script in *filename*, converts it to use getopts instead of getopt, and writes the results on the standard output.

So that all new commands adhere to the command syntax standard described in intro(1), they should use getopts or getopt to parse positional parameters and to check for options that are valid for that command.

Korn Shell

The Korn shell built-in getopts command checks *arg* for legal options. If you omit *arg*, the positional parameters are used. An option argument begins with a + or a -. An option not beginning with + or - or the argument -- ends the options. *optstring* contains the letters that getopts recognizes. If a letter is followed by a colon, that option is expected to have an argument. You can separate the options from the argument by blanks.

getopts puts the next option letter it finds inside variable *name* each time it is invoked with a + prepended when *arg* begins with a +. The index of the next *arg* is stored in OPTIND. The option argument, if any, is stored in OPTARG.

A leading : in *optstring* stores the letter of an invalid option in OPTARG, and sets *name* to ? for an unknown option and to : when a required option is missing. Otherwise, getopts prints an error message. The exit status is non-zero when there are no more options.

The following fragment of a shell program shows how you might process the arguments for a command that can take the options a or b, as well as the option o, which requires an option-argument.

```
while getopts abo: c
  do
    case $c in
    a | b)         FLAG=$c;;
    o)        OARG=$OPTARG;;
    \?)     echo $USAGE               exit 2;;
    esac
  done
shift `expr $OPTIND - 1`
```

This code accepts any of the following as equivalent.

```
cmd -a -b -o "xxx z yy" filename
cmd -a -b -o "xxx z yy" -- filename
cmd -ab -o xxx,z,yy filename
cmd -ab -o "xxx z yy" v
cmd -o xxx,z,yy -b -a filename
```

getopts prints an error message on the standard error when it encounters an option letter not included in *optstring*.

Although relaxations of the following command syntax rule (see intro(1)) are permitted under the current implementation, you should not use them because they may not be supported in future releases of the system. a and b are options, and the option o requires an option-argument. The following example violates Rule 5: options with option-arguments must not be grouped with other options.

```
castle% cmd -aboxxx filename
```

The following example violates Rule 6: there must be white space after an option that takes an option-argument.

```
castle% cmd -ab -oxxx filename
```

Changing the value of the shell variable OPTIND or parsing different sets of arguments may lead to unexpected results.

Operands

optstring   A string containing the option characters recognized by the command invoking getopts. If a character is followed by a colon, the option is expected to have an argument, which should be supplied as a separate argument. Applications should specify an option character and its option-argument as separate arguments, but getopts interprets the characters following an option

character requiring arguments as an argument whether or not
this specification is done. An explicit null option-argument need
not be recognized if it is not supplied as a separate argument when
getopts is invoked; see getopt(3C). An application must not use
the characters ? and : as option characters. The use of other
option characters that are not alphanumeric produces unspecified
results. If the option-argument is not supplied as a separate
argument from the option character, the value in OPTARG is
stripped of the option character and the -. The first character in
optstring determines how getopts behaves if an option
character is not known or if an option-argument is missing.

name   The name of a shell variable that is set by the getopts command
to the option character that was found.

The getopts command by default parses positional parameters passed to
the invoking shell procedure. If you specify *args*, they are parsed instead of the
positional parameters.

Usage

Because getopts affects the current shell execution environment, it is
generally provided as a shell regular built-in. If it is called in a subshell or
separate command-execution environment, such as one of the following,

```
(getopts abc value "$@")
nohup getopts ...
find . -exec getopts ... \;
```

it does not affect the shell variables in the caller's environment.

Note — Shell functions share OPTIND with the calling shell even
though the positional parameters are changed. Functions that use
getopts to parse their arguments usually want to save the value of
OPTIND on entry and restore it before returning. However, there are
cases when a function wants to change OPTIND for the calling shell.

Examples

The following example script parses and displays its arguments.

```
aflag=
bflag=
while getopts ab: name
do
  case $name in
  a)      aflag=1;;
  b)      bflag=1
          bval="$OPTARG";;
  ?)      printf "Usage: %s: [-a] [-b value]  args\n"
$0
      exit 2;;
```

```
    esac
done
if [! -z "$aflag"]; then
  printf "Option -a specified\n"
fi
if [! -z "$bflag"]; then
  printf 'Option -b "%s" specified\n' "$bval"
fi
shift $(($OPTIND - 1))
printf "Remaining arguments are: %s\n" "$*"
```

Environment Variables

See environ(5) for descriptions of the following environment variables that affect the execution of getopts: LC_CTYPE, LC_MESSAGES, and NLSPATH.

OPTIND   This variable is used by getopts as the index of the next argument to be processed.

Exit Status

0   An option, specified or unspecified by *optstring*, was found.

>0   The end of options was encountered or an error occurred.

Attributes

See attributes(5) for descriptions of the following attributes:

Attribute Type	Attribute Value
Availability	SUNWcsu

See Also

getopt(1), getoptcvt(1), intro(1), ksh(1), sh(1), getopt(3C), attributes(5), environ(5)

Diagnostics

Whenever an error is detected and the first character in the *optstring* operand is not a colon (:), a diagnostic message is written to standard error with the following information in an unspecified format:

- The invoking program name is identified in the message. The invoking program name is the value of the shell special parameter 0 at the time the getopts command is invoked. A name equivalent to basename "$0" can be used.

- If an option is found that was not specified in *optstring*, this error is identified and the invalid option character is identified in the message.

- If an option requiring an option-argument is found but an option-argument is not found, this error is identified and the invalid option character is identified in the message.

gettext — Retrieve Text String from Message Database

Synopsis

```
/usr/bin/gettext [textdomain] msgid
```

Description

gettext retrieves a translated text string corresponding to string *msgid* from a message object generated with msgfmt(1). The message object name is derived from the optional argument *textdomain* if present; otherwise, from the TEXTDOMAIN environment. If you specify no domain or if a corresponding string cannot be found, gettext prints *msgid*.

Ordinarily gettext looks for its message object in /usr/lib/locale/*lang*/LC_MESSAGES where *lang* is the locale name. If present, the TEXTDOMAINDIR environment variable replaces the path name component up to *lang*.

This command interprets C escape sequences such as \t for Tab. Use \\ to print a backslash. To produce a message on a line of its own, either put a \n at the end of *msgid* or use this command in conjunction with printf(1).

Note — This command is the shell equivalent of the library routine gettext(3C).

Environment Variables

LANG   Specify locale name.

LC_MESSAGES Specify messaging locale and, if present, override LANG for messages.

TEXTDOMAIN   Specify the text domain name, which is identical to the message object file name without the .mo suffix.

TEXTDOMAINDIR

               Specify the path name to the message database, and if present, use instead of /usr/lib/locale.

Attributes

See attributes(5) for descriptions of the following attributes:

Attribute Type	Attribute Value
Availability	SUNWcsu

See Also

msgfmt(1), printf(1), gettext(3C), setlocale(3C), attributes(5)

gigiplot — Graphics Filters for Various Plotters

Synopsis

/usr/ucb/plot [-Tterminal]

Description

See plot(1).

glob — Shell Built-in Function to Expand a Word List

Synopsis

glob wordlist

Description

For csh, glob performs file-name expansion and history substitutions on wordlist. This command is much the same as the echo(1) command, but glob does not recognize \ escapes. Words are delimited by null characters in the output.

Attributes

See attributes(5) for descriptions of the following attributes:

Attribute Type	Attribute Value
Availability	SUNWcsu

See Also

    csh(1), echo(1), attributes(5)

---

goto — Shell Built-in Functions

Synopsis

csh

    goto *label*

Description

See exit(1).

---

gprof — Display Call-graph Profile Data

Synopsis

    /usr/ccs/bin/gprof [-abcCDlsz] [-e *function-name*] [-E *function-name*]
        [-f *function-name*] [-F *function-name*] [*image-file*
        [*profile-file* ...]] [-n *number-of-functions*]

Description

gprof produces an execution profile of a program. The effect of called routines is incorporated in the profile of each caller. The profile data is taken from the call-graph profile file that is created by programs compiled with the -xpg option of cc(1), or by the -pg option with other compilers, or by setting the LD_PROFILE environment variable for shared objects. See ld.so.1(1). These compiler options also link in versions of the library routines that are compiled for profiling. The symbol table in the executable image file *image-file*(a.out by default) is read and correlated with the call-graph profile file *profile-file*(gmon.out by default).

The gprof command works in the following way.

1. Execution times for each routine are propagated along the edges of the call graph.

2. Cycles are discovered, and calls into a cycle are made to share the time of the cycle. The first listing shows the functions sorted according to the time they represent, including the time of their call-graph descendants. Below each function entry is shown its (direct) call-graph children and how their times are propagated to this function. A similar display above the function shows how this function's time and the time of its descendants are

propagated to its (direct) call-graph parents.

3. Cycles are also shown, with an entry for the cycle as a whole and a listing of the members of the cycle and their contributions to the time and call counts of the cycle.

4. A flat profile is given, similar to that provided by prof(1). This listing gives the total execution times and call counts for each of the functions in the program, sorted by decreasing time.

5. Finally, an index is given that shows the correspondence between function names and call-graph profile index numbers.

You can split a single function into subfunctions for profiling by means of the MARK macro. See prof(5).

> **Note** — Beware of quantization errors. The granularity of the sampling is shown but remains statistical at best. It is assumed that the time for each execution of a function can be expressed by the total time for the function divided by the number of times the function is called. Thus, the time propagated along the call-graph arcs to parents of that function is directly proportional to the number of times that arc is traversed.

The profiled program must call exit(2) or return normally for the profiling information to be saved in the gmon.out file.

64-bit Profiling
You can use 64-bit profiling freely with dynamically linked executables, and profiling information is collected for the shared objects if the objects are compiled for profiling. Apply care to interpret the profile output because it is possible for symbols from different shared objects to have the same name. If name duplication occurs in the profile output, you can use the module ID prefix before the symbol name in the symbol index listing to identify the appropriate module for the symbol.

> **Note** — Take care not to mix 32-bit profile files with 64-bit profile files when using the -s or -D option to sum multiple profile files.

32-bit Profiling
You can use 32-bit profiling with dynamically linked executables; however, you must be careful. In 32-bit profiling, you cannot use gprof to profile shared objects. Only the main portion of the image is sampled when you execute a profiled, dynamically linked program. This means that all time spent outside of the main object (time spent in a shared object) is not included in the profile summary. Thus, the total time reported for the program may be less than the total time used by the program.

Because the time spent in a shared object cannot be accounted for, you should minimize the use of shared objects whenever a program is profiled with gprof. You can link the program to the profiled version of a library (or to the standard archive version if no profiling version is available), instead of to the shared object, to get profile information on the functions of a library. Versions of profiled libraries may be supplied with the system in the /usr/lib/libp directory. Refer to compiler driver documentation on profiling.

Consider an extreme case. A profiled program dynamically linked with the shared C library spends 100 units of time in some libc routine, say, malloc(). Suppose malloc() is called only from routine B and B consumes only 1 unit of time. Suppose further that routine A consumes 10 units of time, more than any other routine in the main (profiled) portion of the image. In this case, gprof concludes that most of the time is being spent in A and almost no time is being spent in B. From this result, it is almost impossible to tell that the greatest improvement can be made by looking at routine B and not routine A. The value of the profiler in this case is severely degraded; the solution is to use archives as much as possible for profiling.

Notes

If the executable image has been stripped and has no symbol table (.symtab), then gprof reads the dynamic symbol table (.dyntab), if present. If the dynamic symbol table is used, then only the information for the global symbols is available, and the behavior is identical to that with the -a option.

LD_LIBRARY_PATH must not contain /usr/lib as a component when compiling a program for profiling. if LD_LIBRARY_PATH contains /usr/lib, the program links incorrectly with the profiling versions of the system libraries in /usr/lib/libp.

The times reported in successive, identical runs may show variances because of varying cache-hit ratios that result from sharing the cache with other processes. Even if a program seems to be the only one using the machine, hidden background or asynchronous processes may blur the data. In rare cases, the clock ticks initiating recording of the program counter may change because of loops in a program, grossly distorting measurements. Call counts are always recorded precisely, however.

Only programs that call exit or return from main are guaranteed to produce a profile file, unless a final call to monitor is explicitly coded.

Profiling can be used with dynamically linked executables, but care must be applied. Currently, shared objects cannot be profiled with gprof. Thus, when a profiled, dynamically linked program is executed, only the main portion of the image is sampled. This means that all time spent outside the main object, that is, time spent in a shared object, is not included in the profile summary; the total time reported for the program may be less than the total time used by the program.

Functions such as mcount(), _mcount(), moncontrol(), _moncontrol(), monitor(), and _monitor() may appear in the gprof report. These functions are part of the profiling implementation and thus account for some amount of the runtime overhead. Because these functions are not present in an unprofiled application, you can ignore time accumulated and call counts for these functions when evaluating the performance of an application.

Bugs

Parents that are not themselves profiled have the time of their profiled children propagated to them, but they appear to be spontaneously invoked in the call-graph listing and do not have their time propagated further. Similarly, signal catchers, even though profiled, appear to be spontaneous (although for more obscure reasons). Any profiled children of signal catchers should have their times propagated properly unless the signal catcher was invoked during the execution of the profiling routine, in which case all is lost.

Options

-a   Suppress printing statically declared functions. If you specify this option, all relevant information about the static function (for instance, time samples, calls to other functions, calls from other functions) belongs to the function loaded just before the static function in the a.out file.

-b   Suppress descriptions of each field in the profile.

-C   Demangle C++ symbol names before printing them.

-c   Discover the static call graph of the program by a heuristic that examines the text space of the object file. Indicate static-only parents or children with call counts of 0.

-D   Produce a profile file gmon.sum that represents the difference of the profile information in all specified profile files. You can give this summary profile file to subsequent executions of gprof (also with -D) to summarize profile data across several runs of an a.out file. See also the -s option.

               As an example, suppose function A calls function B *n* times in profile file gmon.sum, and *m* times in profile file gmon.out. With -D, create a new gmon.sum file showing the number of calls from A to B as *n-m*.

-E *function-name*

               Suppress printing the graph profile entry for routine *function-name* and its descendants (as -e, below) and also exclude the time spent in *function-name* and its descendants from the total and percentage time computations. You can specify more than one -E option. For example, the default is

               `-E mcount -E mcleanup'

-e *function-name*

               Suppress printing the graph profile entry for routine *function-name* and all its descendants (unless they have other ancestors that are not suppressed). You can specify more than one

-e option. You can specify only one *function-name* with each -e
option.

-F *function-name*

Print the graph profile entry only for routine *function-name* and
its descendants (as -f, below) and also use only the times of the
printed routines in total time and percentage computations. You
can specify more than one -F option. You can specify only one
function-name with each -F option. The -F option overrides the
-E option.

-f *function-name*

Print the graph profile entry only for routine *function-name* and
its descendants. You can give more than one -f option. You can
specify only one *function-name* for each -f option.

-l   Suppress the reporting of graph profile entries for all local
symbols. This option is the equivalent of placing all of the local
symbols for the specified executable image on the -E exclusion list.

-n *number-of-functions*

Limit the size of flat and graph profile listings to the top
number-of-functions offending functions.

-s   Produce a profile file *gmon.sum* that represents the sum of the
profile information in all of the specified profile files. You can give
this summary profile file to subsequent executions of gprof (also
with -s) to accumulate profile data across several runs of an a.out
file. See also the -D option.

-z   Display routines that have 0 usage (as indicated by call counts and
accumulated time). This option is useful in conjunction with the -c
option for discovering which routines are never called.

Environment Variables

PROFDIR   Put profiling output within the specified directory, in a file named
pid.programname. pid is the process ID, and *programname* is the
name of the program being profiled, as determined by removing
any path prefix from the argv[0] with which the program was
called. If the variable contains a null value, no profiling output is
produced. Otherwise, profiling output is placed in the file
gmon.out.

LD_LIBRARY_PATH must not contain /usr/lib as a component when a
program is compiled for profiling. If LD_LIBRARY_PATH contains /usr/lib,
the program is not linked correctly with the profiling versions of the system
libraries in /usr/lib/libp.

Files

`a.out`	Executable file containing *namelist*.
`gmon.out`	Dynamic call graph and profile.
`gmon.sum`	Summarized dynamic call graph and profile.
`$PROFDIR/pid.programname`	

Attributes

See `attributes`(5) for descriptions of the following attributes:

Attribute Type	Attribute Value
Availability	SUNWbtool

See Also

`cc(1)`, `ld.so.1(1)`, `prof(1)`, `exit(2)`, `pcsample(2)`, `profil(2)`, `malloc(3C)`, `monitor(3C)`, `malloc(3X)`, `attributes(5)`, `prof(5)`

Graham, S.L., Kessler, P.B., McKusick, M.K., "gprof: A Call Graph Execution Profiler," *Proceedings of the SIGPLAN '82 Symposium on Compiler Construction*, SIGPLAN Notices, Vol.17, No. 6, pp. 120-126, June 1982.
Linker and Libraries Guide

---

graph — Draw a Graph

Synopsis

```
/usr/bin/graph [-a spacing [start]] [-b] [-c string]
   [-g gridstyle] [-l label] [-m connectmode] [-s]
   [-x [l] lower [upper [spacing]]]
   [-y [l] lower [upper [spacing]]] [-h fraction]
   [-w fraction] [-r fraction] [-u fraction] [-t] ...
```

Description

If you type `graph` with no options, an se prompt is displayed. You can type a pair of numbers, separated by a comma or by white space, that are used as abscissas and ordinates of a graph. Successive points are connected by straight lines. The standard output from `graph` contains plotting instructions suitable for input to `plot`(1B) or to the command `lpr -g` (see `lpr`(1B)).

If the coordinates of a point are followed by a nonnumeric string, that string is printed as a label beginning on the point. You can surround labels with quotes `"..."`, in which case they may be empty or contain blanks and numbers; labels never contain newline characters.

graph   **453**

A legend indicating grid range is produced with a grid unless you specify the
-s option.

Bugs

graph stores all points internally and drops those for which there is no room.
Segments that run out of bounds are dropped, not windowed.
Logarithmic axes cannot be reversed.

Options

Represent each option as a separate argument. If a specified lower limit
exceeds the upper limit, the axis is reversed.

-a *spacing*[*start*]

Supply abscissas automatically (they are missing from the input);
spacing is the spacing (default 1). *start* is the starting point for
automatic abscissas (default 0 or lower limit given by -x).

-b   Break (disconnect) the graph after each label in the input.

-c *string*   Use *string* as the default label for each point.

-g *grid-*   Use *gridstyle* as the grid style. Possible values are 0, no grid, 1,
style   frame with ticks, 2, full grid (default).

-l *label*   Use *label* as the label.

-m *connectmode*

Use *connectmode* as the style or mode of connecting lines. Possible
values are 0, disconnected, 1, connected (default). Some devices
give distinguishable line styles for other small integers.

-s   Save screen. Do not erase before plotting.

-x [l] *lower* [*upper* [*spacing*]]

If you use l, make the x axis logarithmic. *lower* and *upper* specify
lower and upper x limits. If you use *spacing*, space the grid on the
x axis. Normally, these quantities are determined automatically.

-y [l] *lower* [*upper* [*spacing*]]

If you use l, make the y axis logarithmic. *lower* and *upper* specify
lower and upper x limits. If you use *spacing*, space the grid on the
x axis. Normally, these quantities are determined automatically.

-h *fraction* Use *fraction* of space for height.

-w *fraction* Use *fraction* of space for width.

-r *fraction* Use *fraction* of space to move right before plotting.

-u *fraction* Use *fraction* of space to move up before plotting.

-t   Transpose horizontal and vertical axes. Option -x now applies to
the vertical axis.

Examples

The following example uses the plot and graph capabilities. The file named data contains the following data points.

```
castle% cat data
1       1.0
2       4.0
3       5.0
4       6.5       "Optional Label"
7       10.3
8       11.4
9       9.5
10      8.9
11      7.0
12      10.5
13      5.0
14      2.8
castle%
```

The following example displays the data in a shell tool using the graph command.

```
castle% graph < data + plot -Tcrt
castle% ****************************************************************************
        *                         *                        *                     *
        *                         *                        *                     *
        *                         *                        *                     *
        *                         *              *         *                     *
        *                         *           * *          *                     *
        *                         *        **    **        *            *        *
        ******************************************************************************
        *                         *       **         **    *          * *        *
        *                         *      **           ** *      *    *            *
        *                  **     *    * *            **      *     *             *
        *                 * **    *  **               **        *   *             *
        *                  **     * **                *  ** *      *              *
        *                ***      **                  *   * *         *           *
        *               **  *                         *     *         *          *
        *                        *Optional Label       *              *          *
        *                    *        *                *                 *        *
        *                  **         *                *                  *       *
        *                 *           *                *                   *      *
        ******************************************************************************
        *              **            *                *                      *    *
        *             **             *                *                       *   *
        *           *                *                *                      *    *
        *          *                 *                *                     *     *
        *          *                 *                *                    *      *
        *          *                 *                *                           *
        *         *                  *                *                           *
        *         *                  *                *                           *
        *                            *                *                           *
        *                            *                *                           *
        ******************************************************************************
        0 -x- 15  0 -y- 15
```

graph clears the screen and displays the graph positioning the prompt at the the top of the screen. Any subsequent commands you type are displayed on top of the graph. Use the clear command to clear the screen after you display the plot.

Attributes

See attributes(5) for descriptions of the following attributes:

Attribute Type	Attribute Value
Availability	SUNWesu

See Also

spline(1), lpr(1B), plot(1B), plot(3), attributes(5)

grep — Search a File for a Pattern

Synopsis

```
/usr/bin/grep [-bchilnsvw] limited-regular-expression [filename... ]
/usr/xpg4/bin/grep [-E | -F] [-c | -l | -q] [-bhinsvwx]
  -e pattern-list [-f pattern-file] ... [file... ]
/usr/xpg4/bin/grep [-E | -F] [-c | -l | -q] [-bhinsvwx]
  [-e pattern-list -f pattern-file [file... ]
/usr/xpg4/bin/grep [-E | -F] [-c | -l | -q]
  [-bhinsvwx] pattern [file... ]
```

Description

The grep command searches files for a pattern in one or more files and prints all lines that contain that pattern. grep (which stands for global regular expression and print) uses a compact, nondeterministic algorithm.

Note — Be careful using the characters $, *, [, ^, |, (,), and \ in the *pattern-list* because they are also meaningful to the shell. It is safest to enclose the entire *pattern-list* in single quotes '...'.

If you specify no files, grep assumes standard input. Normally, each line found is copied to standard output. The file name is printed before each line found if there is more than one input file.

/usr/bin/grep

The /usr/bin/grep command uses limited regular expressions like those described on the regexp(5) manual page to match the patterns.

Lines are limited only by the size of the available virtual memory. For a line with embedded nulls, grep matches only up to the first null; if it matches, grep prints the entire line.

/usr/xpg4/bin/grep

/usr/xpg4/bin/grep is a POSIX-compliant version of the /usr/bin/grep command. See standards(5).

The options -E and -F affect the way /usr/xpg4/bin/grep interprets *pattern-list*. If you specify -E, /usr/xpg4/bin/grep interprets *pattern-list* as a full regular expression. If you specify -F, grep interprets *pattern-list* as a fixed string. If you specify neither, grep interprets *pattern-list* as a basic regular expression, as described on the regex(5) manual page.

The results are unspecified if input files contain lines longer than LINE_MAX bytes or contain binary data. LINE_MAX is defined in /usr/include/limits.a.

Options

The following options are supported for both /usr/bin/grep and /usr/xpg4/bin/grep.

-b	Precede each line by the block number on which it was found. This option can be useful in locating block numbers by context (first block is 0).
-c	Print a count only of the lines that contain the pattern.
-h	Prevent the name of the file containing the matching line from being appended to that line. Used when searching multiple files.
-i	Ignore upper-/lowercase distinction during comparisons.
-l	Print the names of files only with matching lines, separated by newline characters. Do not repeat the names of files when the pattern is found more than once.
-n	Precede each line by its line number in the file (first line is 1).
-s	Suppress error messages about nonexistent or unreadable files.
-v	Print all lines except those that contain the pattern.
-w	Search for the expression as a word as if surrounded by \< and \>.

The following options are supported only for /usr/xpg4/bin/grep.

-e *pattern-list*

Specify one or more patterns to be used during the search for input. Separate patterns in *pattern-list* by a newline character. You can specify a null pattern with two adjacent newline characters in *pattern-list*. Unless you specify the -E or -F option, treat each pattern as a basic regular expression. grep accepts multiple -e and -f options. All of the specified patterns are used when matching lines, but the order of evaluation is not specified.

-E Match, using full regular expressions. Treat each pattern specified as a full regular expression. If any entire full regular expression pattern matches an input line, the line is matched. A null full regular expression matches every line.

Interpret each pattern as a full regular expression as described on the regex(5) manual page, except for \(and \), and including:

- A full regular expression followed by + that matches one or more occurrences of the full regular expression.

- A full regular expression followed by ? that matches 0 or 1 occurrence of the full regular expression.

- Full regular expressions, separated by | or by a newline, that match strings that are matched by any of the expressions.

- A full regular expression that may be enclosed in parentheses () for grouping.

The order of precedence of operators is [], then *?+, then concatenation, then | and newline.

-f *pattern-file*

Read one or more patterns from the file named by the path name *pattern-file*. Terminate patterns in *pattern-file* with a newline character. You can specify a null pattern by an empty line in *pattern-file*. Unless you also specify the -E or -F option, treat each pattern as a basic regular expression.

-F Match, using fixed strings. Treat each pattern specified as a string instead of a regular expression. If an input line contains any of the patterns as a contiguous sequence of bytes, match the line. A null string matches every line. See fgrep(1) for more information.

-q Do not write anything to the standard output, regardless of matching lines. Exit with 0 status if an input line is selected.

-x Consider only input lines that use all characters in the line to match an entire fixed string or regular expression to be matching lines.

Operands

file A path name of a file to be searched for the patterns. If no file operands are specified, use the standard input.

/usr/bin/grep *pattern*

Specify a pattern to be used during the search for input.

`/usr/xpg4/bin/grep` *pattern*

> Specify one or more patterns to be used during the search for input. This operand is treated as if it were specified as `-e` *pattern-list*.

Usage

The `-e` *pattern-list* option has the same effect as the *pattern-list* operand but is useful when *pattern-list* begins with the hyphen delimiter. It is also useful when it is more convenient to provide multiple patterns as separate arguments.

`grep` accepts multiple `-e` and `-f` options and uses all of the patterns it is given to match input text lines.

> **Note** — The order of evaluation is not specified. If an implementation finds a null string as a pattern, it is allowed to use that pattern first, matching every line, and effectively ignore any other patterns.

The `-q` option provides a means of easily determining whether or not a pattern (or string) exists in a group of files. When searching several files, it provides a performance improvement (because `grep` can quit as soon as it finds the first match) and requires less care by the user in choosing the set of files to supply as arguments (because `grep` exits 0 if it finds a match even if `grep` detected an access or read error on earlier file operands).

Large File Behavior

See `largefile`(5) for the description of the behavior of `grep` when encountering files greater than or equal to 2 Gbytes (2**31 bytes).

Examples

The following example finds all uses of the word `Posix` (in any case) in the `standards.5` manual page and displays the line with a line number preceding it. To save space, not all of the lines are shown in this example.

```
castle% /usr/bin/grep -i -n posix standards.5
7:standards, posix, POSIX, posix.1, POSIX.1, posix.2, POSIX.2, xnet,
  XNET, xnet4, XNET4, xpg, XPG, xpg3, XPG3, xpg4, XPG4, xpg4v2, XPG4v2
  \- standards and specifications supported by Solaris
33:.IX "standards and specifications supported by Solaris" "POSIX.2" ""
  "\(em \fLPOSIX.2\fP"
34:.IX "POSIX.2" "" "\fLPOSIX.2\fP \(em standards and specifications
  supported by Solaris"
35:.IX "standards and specifications supported by Solaris" "posix.2" ""
  "\(em \fLposix.2\fP"
...
castle%
```

You can combine the grep command with other commands to find specific information. In the following example, the output of the env command is piped to grep to search for environment variables that contain the word HOME. As you can see, the search results also include longer words that contain the HOME string.

```
castle% env | grep HOME
OPENWINHOME=/usr/openwin
HOME=/export/home/winsor
castle%
```

You can use either of the following commands to find all empty lines in the standard input.

```
castle% /usr/bin/grep ^$
castle% /usr/bin/grep -v .
```

Both of the following commands print all lines containing strings abc or def or both.

```
castle% /usr/xpg4/bin/grep -E 'abc def'
castle% /usr/xpg4/bin/grep -F 'abc def'
```

Both of the following commands print all lines matching exactly abc or def.

```
castle% /usr/xpg4/bin/grep -E '^abc$ ^def$'
castle% /usr/xpg4/bin/grep -F -x 'abc def'
```

You can use the grep command to search through several files to find a particular string. The following example uses the grep command to search all of the files in a directory for the string kookaburra.

```
castle% grep kookaburra *
kookaburra:Laugh, kookaburra, laugh
kookaburra:Laugh, kookaburra, laugh
kookaburra-1:Laugh, kookaburra, laugh
kookaburra-1:Laugh, kookaburra, laugh
kookaburra-2:Laugh, kookaburra, laugh
kookaburra-2:Laugh, kookaburra, laugh
kookaburra-3:Laugh, kookaburra, laugh
kookaburra-3:Laugh, kookaburra, laugh
kookaburra-3:Laugh, kookaburra, laugh
kookaburra-3:Laugh, kookaburra, laugh
castle%
```

As you can see from the output, grep displays the name of the file at the beginning of each line that it prints. Four files in this directory contain the word kookaburra. Also note that because we did not specify the -i option to ignore case, lines containing the word Kookaburra are not displayed.

Environment Variables

See environ(5) for descriptions of the following environment variables that affect the execution of grep: LC_COLLATE, LC_CTYPE, LC_MESSAGES, and NLSPATH.

Exit Status

0	One or more matches were found.
1	No matches were found.
2	Syntax errors or inaccessible files (even if matches were found).

Attributes

See attributes(5) for descriptions of the following attributes:

/usr/bin/grep

Attribute Type	Attribute Value
Availability	SUNWfac

/usr/xpg4/bin/grep

Attribute Type	Attribute Value
Availability	SUNWfac

See Also

New!

egrep(1), fgrep(1), sed(1), sh(1), attributes(5), environ(5), largefile(5), regex(5), regexp(5), XPG4(5)

groups — Print Group Membership of User

Synopsis

/usr/bin/groups [user...]

Description

The groups command prints on standard output the groups to which you or the optionally specified *user* belong. Each user belongs to a group specified in /etc/passwd and possibly to other groups as specified in /etc/group. Note that /etc/passwd specifies the numerical ID (gid) of the group. The groups command converts gid to the group name in the output.

Examples

The following example shows the groups for users `winsor`, `ray`, and `des`.

```
castle% groups winsor ray des
winsor : staff other sysadmin
ray : staff other sysadmin
des : staff sysadmin
castle%
```

Files

`/etc/passwd` Password file.

`/etc/group` Group file.

Attributes

See `attributes`(5) for descriptions of the following attributes:

Attribute Type	Attribute Value
Availability	SUNWcsu

See Also

`group(4)`, `passwd(4)`, `attributes(5)`

grpck — Password/Group File Checkers

Synopsis

`/usr/sbin/grpck` [*filename*]

Description

See `pwck`(1).

H

hash, rehash, unhash, hashstat — Evaluate the Internal Hash
Table of the Contents of Directories

Synopsis

```
/usr/bin/hash [name]
/usr/bin/hash [- r]
```

sh
```
hash [- r] [name ...]
```

csh
```
rehash
unhash
hashstat
```

ksh
```
hash [name ...]
```

Description

Hashing is a method of indexing information by using an algorithm that
generates an index of values indicating the ordered position of each item. For
example, when the C shell starts, it finds all of the commands in directories
specified by the path environment variable and builds an internal hash table
of full path names. Then, when you execute a command, the C shell uses the

hash table instead of searching directly for the path. This hashing technique is designed to improve performance. However, if you change your path or add a command to one of the directories, the C shell does not find the command unless you force it to rebuild its hash table with the `rehash` command.

/usr/bin/hash

The `/usr/bin/hash` command affects the way the current shell environment remembers the locations of commands found. Depending on the arguments specified, it adds command locations to its list of remembered locations or it purges the contents of the list. When you specify no arguments, it reports on the contents of the list, as shown in the following example.

```
$ hash
hits    cost    command
2       3       /bin/touch
1       3       /bin/ps
0       3       /bin/grep
3       3       /bin/ls
0       3       /bin/env
$
$ hash
hits    cost    command
$
```

The `hits` column of output shows the number of times a command has been invoked by the shell process. The `cost` column of output is a measure of the work required to locate a command in the search path. If a command is found in a relative directory in the search path, after changing to that directory, the stored location of that command is recalculated. Commands for which this is done are indicated by an asterisk (*) adjacent to the `hits` information. `cost` is incremented when the recalculation is done.

hash does not report on shell built-in commands.

Bourne Shell

For each command *name*, the shell determines and remembers the location in the search path. When you use the `-r` option to the `hash` built-in, the shell forgets all remembered locations. If you specify no arguments, `hash` provides information about remembered commands.

C Shell

rehash recomputes the internal hash table of the contents of directories listed in the `path` environmental variable to account for new commands added.

unhash disables the internal hash table.

hashstat prints a statistics line indicating how effective the internal hash table has been at locating commands (and avoiding `execs`), as shown in the following example.

```
castle% hashstat
6 hits, 1 misses, 85%
castle%
```

An `exec` is attempted for each component of the path where the `hash` function indicates a possible hit and in each component that does not begin with a `/`.

Korn Shell

For each command *name*, the shell determines and remembers the location in the search path. If you specify no arguments, `hash` provides information about remembered commands.

Operands

command The name of a command to be searched for and added to the list of remembered locations.

Output

When you specify no arguments, the standard output of `hash` is used. Its format is unspecified but includes the path name of each command in the list of remembered locations for the current shell environment. This list consists of those commands named in previous `hash` invocations that have been invoked, and the list may contain those invoked and found through the normal command search process.

Environment Variables

See `environ(5)` for descriptions of the following environment variables that affect the execution of `hash`: `LC_CTYPE`, `LC_MESSAGES`, and `NLSPATH`.

PATH Determine the location of command.

Exit Status

0 Successful completion.

\>0 An error occurred.

Attributes

See `attributes(5)` for descriptions of the following attributes:

Attribute Type	Attribute Value
Availability	SUNWcsu

See Also

`csh(1)`, `ksh(1)`, `sh(1)`, `attributes(5)`, `environ(5)`

hashcheck, hashmake — Report Spelling Errors

Synopsis
```
/usr/lib/spell/hashmake
/usr/lib/spell/hashcheck spelling-list
```

Description
See spell(1).

hashstat — Evaluate the Internal Hash Table of the Contents of Directories

Synopsis

csh
```
hashstat
```

Description
See hash(1).

head — Display First Few Lines of Files

Synopsis
```
/usr/bin/head [-number | -n number] [filename...]
```

Description
The head command copies the first *number* of lines of each `filename` to the standard output. If you specify no file name, head copies lines from the standard input. The default value of *number* is 10 lines.

When you specify more than one `filename`, the start of each file displays the file name between two arrows, as shown below.
```
==> filename <==
```

The following example shows a common way to display a set of short files, identifying each one by name.

```
castle% head -9999 kookaburra1 kookaburra2
==> kookaburra1 <==
Kookaburra sits in the old gum tree
Merry merry king of the bush is he
Laugh, kookaburra, laugh, kookaburra
Gay your life must be.

Kookaburra sits in the old gum tree
Eating all the gumdrops he can see
Stop, kookaburra, stop, kookaburra
Leave some there for me.

==> kookaburra2 <==
Kookaburra sits in the old gum tree
Merry merry king of the bush is he
Laugh, kookaburra, laugh, kookaburra
Glad your life must be.

Kookaburra sits in the old gum tree
Eating all the gumdrops he can see
Stop, kookaburra, stop, kookaburra
Leave some there for me.
castle%
```

Options

-n *number*   Copy the first *number* lines of each input file to standard output. Specify the *number* option argument as a positive decimal integer.

-*number*   Specify the *number* of lines as a positive decimal integer with the same effect as the -n *number* option.

If you specify no options, head uses a default of -n 10.

Operands

file   A path name of an input file. If you specify no file operands, use the standard input.

Usage

See largefile(5) for the description of the behavior of head when encountering files greater than or equal to 2 Gbytes (2**31 bytes).

Examples

The following example writes the first 10 lines of all files (except those with a leading period) in the directory.

```
example% head *
```

Environment Variables

See environ(5) for descriptions of the following environment variables that affect the execution of head: LC_CTYPE, LC_MESSAGES, and NLSPATH.

Exit Status

0	Successful completion.
>0	An error occurred.

Attributes

See attributes(5) for descriptions of the following attributes:

Attribute Type	Attribute Value
Availability	SUNWcsu
CSI	Enabled

See Also

cat(1), more(1), pg(1), tail(1), attributes(5), environ(5), largefile(5)

help, sccs-help — Ask for Help Regarding SCCS Error or Warning Messages

Synopsis

/usr/ccs/bin/help [*argument*] ...

Description

See sccs-help(1).

history, fc — Process Command History List

Synopsis

sh

```
/usr/bin/fc [first[last]]
/usr/bin/fc -l [-nr] [first[last]]
/usr/bin/fc -s [old=new] [first]
```

csh

```
history [-hr] [n]
```

ksh

```
fc -e - [old=new] [command]
fc [-e editor] [-nlr] [first [last]]
```

Description

Command history creates a numbered list of the most recent commands that you have used. You can display these commands and reuse them as originally issued. You can also change a command by editing it. The syntax and arguments for history commands differ for each shell.

/usr/bin/fc

The fc command lists or edits and reexecutes commands previously entered to an interactive sh.

The command history list references commands by number. The first number in the list is chosen arbitrarily. The relationship of a number to its command does not change except when you log in and no other process is accessing the list, at which time the system may reset the numbering to start the oldest retained command at another number (usually 1). When the number reaches the value in HISTSIZE or 128 (whichever is greater), the shell may wrap the numbers, starting the next command with a lower number (usually 1). However, despite this optional wrapping of numbers, fc maintains the time-ordering sequence of the commands. For example, if four commands in sequence are given the numbers 32766, 32767, 1 (wrapped), and 2 as they are executed, command 32767 is considered the command previous to 1, even though its number is higher.

When you edit commands and you did not specify the -l option, the resulting lines are entered at the end of the history list and then reexecuted by sh. The fc editing command is not entered into the history list. If the editor returns a non-zero exit status, this status suppresses the entry into the history list and the command reexecution. Any command-line variable assignments or redirection operators used with fc affect both the fc command itself as well as the command that results. For example, the following command reinvokes the previous command, suppressing standard error for both fc and the previous command.

```
$ fc -s -- -1 2>/dev/null
$
```

C Shell

Use the history command to display the history list; if you specify the number *n*, display only the *n* most recent events.

-r   Reverse the order of printout to be most recent first instead of oldest first.

-h   Display the history list without leading numbers. Use this option to produce files suitable for sourcing with the -h option to the csh built-in source(1) command.

If you use any of the options together with *n*, specify the options first.

History Substitution

History substitution enables you to use words from previous command lines in the command line you are typing. This substitution simplifies spelling corrections and the repetition of complicated commands or arguments. Command lines are saved in the history list, the size of which is controlled by the history variable. You can set the history shell variable to specify the maximum number of command lines that are saved in the history file; for example, the following command enables the history list to keep track of the most recent 200 command lines.

castle% **set history = 200**

If the history variable is not set, the C shell saves only the most recent command.

Begin a history substitution with a ! (although you can change this character with the histchars variable). The ! can occur anywhere on the command line; history substitutions do not nest. You can escape the ! with a backslash (\) to suppress its special meaning.

Input lines containing history substitutions are echoed on the terminal after being expanded but before any other substitutions take place or the command is executed.

Event Designators

An event designator is a reference to a command-line entry in the history list.

!   Start a history substitution, except when followed by a space character, Tab, newline, =, or (.

!!   Refer to the previous command. By itself, this substitution repeats the previous command.

!*n*   Refer to command line *n*.

!-*n*   Refer to the current command line minus *n*.

!*str*   Refer to the most recent command starting with *str*.

!?*str*?   Refer to the most recent command containing *str*.

!?*str*? *additional*

> Refer to the most recent command containing *str*, and append *additional* to that referenced command.

!{*command*} *additional*

> Refer to the most recent command beginning with *command*, and append *additional* to that referenced command.

^*previous-word*^*replacement*^

> Repeat the previous command line, replacing the string *previous-word* with the string *replacement*. This syntax is equivalent to the history substitution:
>
> !:s/*previous-word*/*replacement*/
>
> To reexecute a specific previous command *and* make such a substitution, say, reexecuting command #6:
>
> !:6s/*previous-word*/*replacement*/

Word Designators

A colon (:) separates the event specification from the word designator. You can omit the colon if the word designator begins with a ^, $, *, -, or %. If the word is to be selected from the previous command, you can omit the second ! character from the event specification. For instance, !!:1 and !:1 both refer to the first word of the previous command, while !!$ and !$ both refer to the last word in the previous command. Word designators include:

#	The entire command line typed so far.
0	The first input word (command).
n	The *n*-th argument.
^	The first argument, that is, 1.
$	The last argument.
%	The word matched by the most recent ?*s* search.
x-y	A range of words; -*y* abbreviates 0-*y*.
*	All the arguments, or a null value if there is just one word in the event.
*x**	Abbreviates *x*-$.
x-	Like *x** but omitting word $.

Modifiers

After the optional word designator, you can add a sequence of one or more of the following modifiers, each preceded by a colon (:).

h	Remove a trailing path-name component, leaving the head.
r	Remove a trailing suffix of the form .*xxx*, leaving the basename.
e	Remove all but the suffix, leaving the extension.

`s/oldchars/replacements/`

> Substitute replacements for *oldchars*. *oldchars* is a string that may contain embedded blank spaces, whereas *previous-word* in the event designator `^oldchars^replacements^` may not.

t   Remove all leading path-name components, leaving the tail.

&   Repeat the previous substitution.

g   Apply the change to the first occurrence of a match in each word by prefixing the above modifiers (for example, `g&`).

p   Print the new command, but do not execute it.

q   Quote the substituted words, escaping further substitutions.

x   Like q, but break into words at each space character, Tab, or newline.

Unless preceded by a g, the modification is applied only to the first string that matches *oldchars*; an error results if no string matches.

The left-hand side of substitutions are character strings, not regular expressions. You can use any character as the delimiter in place of /. A backslash escapes the delimiter character. The character & in the right-hand side is replaced by the text from the left-hand side. You can escape the & with a backslash. A null *oldchars* uses the previous string either from *oldchars* or from a contextual scan string *s* from `!?s`. You can omit the rightmost delimiter if a newline immediately follows replacements; similarly, you can omit the rightmost ? in a context scan.

Without an event specification, a history reference refers either to the previous command or to a previous history reference on the command line (if any).

Korn Shell

When you use the form `fc -e - [old=new] [command]`, the *command* is reexecuted after the substitution *old=new* is performed. If you specify no command argument, the most recent command typed at this terminal is executed.

When you use the form `fc [-e editor][-nlr][first [last]]`, a range of commands from *first* to *last* is selected from the last HISTSIZE commands that were typed at the terminal. You can specify the arguments *first* and *last* as a number or as a string. A string is used to locate the most recent command starting with the given string. A negative number is used as an offset to the current command number. If you use the -l flag, the commands are listed on standard output. Otherwise, the editor program `-e editor` is invoked on a file containing these keyboard commands. If you do not specify *editor*, then the value of the variable FCEDIT (default /bin/ed) is used as the editor. When editing is complete, the edited command(s) is executed. If you do not specify *last*, then the value is set to *first*. If you do not specify *first*, the default is the previous command for editing and -16 for listing. The -r option reverses the order of the commands, and the -n option suppresses command numbers when listing. (See ksh(1) for more information about command-line editing.)

HISTFILE	If this variable is set when the shell is invoked, then the value is the path name of the file that is used to store the command history.
HISTSIZE	If this variable is set when the shell is invoked, then the number of previously entered commands that are accessible by this shell is greater than or equal to this number. The default is 128.

Command Reentry

The text of the last HISTSIZE (default 128) commands entered from a terminal device is saved in a history file. The file $HOME/.sh_history is used if the HISTFILE variable is not set or if the file it names is not writable. A shell can access the commands of all interactive shells that use the same named HISTFILE. The special command fc is used to list or edit a portion of this file. The portion of the file to be edited or listed can be selected by number or by giving the first character or characters of the command. You can specify a single command or a range of commands. If you do not specify an editor program as an argument to fc, then the value of the variable FCEDIT is used. If FCEDIT is not defined, then /bin/ed is used. The edited command(s) is printed and reexecuted on leaving the editor. The editor name – is used to skip the editing phase and to reexecute the command. In this case, you can use a substitution parameter of the form *old=new* to modify the command before execution. For example, if r is aliased to fc -e -, then typing **r bad=good c** reexecutes the most recent command that starts with the letter c, replacing the first occurrence of the string bad with the string good.

Using the fc built-in command within a compound command removes the whole command from the history file.

Options

-e *editor*	Use the editor named by *editor* to edit the commands. The *editor* string is a command name, subject to searching the PATH variable. The value in the FCEDIT variable is used as a default when you do not specify -e. If FCEDIT is null or unset, ed is used as the editor.
-h	Display the history list without leading numbers. Use this option to produce files suitable for sourcing with the -h option to the csh built-in source(1) command.
-l	List the commands instead of invoking an editor on them. Write the commands in the sequence indicated by the *first* and *last* operands, as affected by -r, with each command preceded by the command number.
-n	Suppress command numbers when listing with -l.
-r	Reverse the order of the commands listed (with -l) or edited.
-s	Reexecute the command without invoking an editor.

Operands

first last   Choose the commands to list or edit. The number of previous commands that can be accessed is determined by the value of the HISTSIZE variable. The value of *first* or *last* or both is one of the following:

      [+]number   A positive number representing a command number; you can display command numbers with the -1 option.

      -number   A negative decimal number representing the command that was executed *number* of commands previously. For example, -1 is the previous command.

      string   A string indicating the most recently entered command that begins with that string. If you do not also specify the *old=new* operand with -s, the string form of the *first* operand cannot contain an embedded equal sign.

old=new   Replace the first occurrence of string *old* in the commands to be reexecuted by the string *new*.

When you use the synopsis form with -s:

- If you omit *first*, use the previous command. For the synopsis, forms without -s.

- If you omit *last*, *last* defaults to the previous command when -1 is specified; otherwise, it defaults to *first*.

- If you omit both *first* and *last*, list the previous 16 commands or edit the previous single command (based on the -1 option).

- If you specify both *first* and *last*, edit or list all of the commands from *first* to *last*. When editing multiple commands, the editor presents all of the commands at one time, each command starting on a new line. If *first* represents a newer command than *last*, the commands are listed or edited in reverse sequence, equivalent to using -r. For example, the following commands on the first line are equivalent to the corresponding commands on the second:

```
fc -r 10   20
fc
30 40
fc 20 10
fc  -r
40 30
```

When you use a range of commands, you can specify *first* or *last* values that are not in the history list; fc substitutes the value representing the oldest or newest command in the list, as appropriate. For example, if the

history list has only 10 commands, numbered 1 to 10, the following
command lists and edits all 10 commands.

```
fc -l
fc 1 99
```

Output

When you use the -l option to list commands, the format of each command in
the list is as follows:

line-number command

If you specify both the -l and -n options, the format of each command is:

`"\t%s\n",` *command*

If the command consists of more than one line, the lines after the first are
displayed as:

`"\t%s\n",` *continued-command*

Examples

C Shell

The following C shell examples show various ways to use the history event
designators.

```
castle% history
     1  cd /etc
     2  vi passwd
     3  date
     4  cd
     5  du .
     6  ls -t
     7  history
castle% !da
date
Mon Jan 18 17:53:28 WST 1999
castle% !!
date
Mon Jan 18 17:53:34 WST 1999
castle% !5
du .
262    ./SCCS
336    .
castle% !ls ma*
ls -t malloc.c
malloc.o
malloc.c
```

Korn Shell

The following example shows the various ways to use the `fc` event designators.

```
$ fc -l
1    cd /etc
2    vi passwd
3    date
4    cd
5    du .
6    ls -t
7    fc -l
$ fc -e - d
du .
262    ./SCCS
336    .
$ fc -e - da
date
Mon Jan 18 17:59:52 WST 1999
$ !!
ksh: !!: not found
$ alias \!='fc -e -'
$ !
alias ='fc -e -'
$ !5
ksh: !5: not found
du .
262    ./SCCS
336    .


$ ! ls ma*
malloc.o
malloc.c
$
```

Environment Variables

See `environ(5)` for descriptions of the following environment variables that affect the execution of `fc`: `LC_CTYPE`, `LC_MESSAGES`, and `NLSPATH`.

FCEDIT   When expanded by the shell, this variable determines the default value for the e *editor* argument. If FCEDIT is null or unset, use ed as the editor.

HISTFILE   Determine a path name naming a command history file. If the HISTFILE variable is not set, the shell may try to access or create a file `.sh_history` in the user's home directory. If the shell cannot obtain both read and write access to, or create, the history file, it uses an unspecified mechanism that enables the history to operate properly. (References to history file in this section are understood to mean this unspecified mechanism in such cases.) `fc` may choose to access this variable only when initializing the history file. This initialization occurs when `fc` or `sh` first tries to retrieve entries from, or add entries to, the file as the result of commands issued by the user, the file named by the ENV variable, or a system startup file such as /etc/profile. (The initialization process for the history file can depend on the system startup files in that they can contain commands that effectively preempt the user's settings of HISTFILE and HISTSIZE. For example, function definition commands are recorded in the history file, unless you set the set -o nolog option. If the system administrator includes function definitions in some system startup file called before the ENV file, the history file is initialized before the user gets a chance to influence its characteristics.) The variable HISTFILE is accessed initially when the shell is invoked. Any changes to HISTFILE do not take effect until another shell is invoked.

HISTSIZE   Determine a decimal number representing the limit to the number of previous commands that are accessible. If this variable is unset, an unspecified default greater than or equal to 128 is used. The variable HISTSIZE is accessed initially when the shell is invoked. Any changes to HISTSIZE do not take effect until another shell is invoked.

Exit Status

0   Successful completion of the listing.

>0   An error occurred.

Otherwise, the exit status is that of the commands executed by fc.

Attributes

See attributes(5) for descriptions of the following attributes:

Attribute Type	Attribute Value
Availability	SUNWcsu

See Also

csh(1), ed(1), ksh(1), set(1), sh(1), source(1), set(1F), attributes(5), environ(5)

hostid — Print the Numeric Identifier of the Current Host

Synopsis

/usr/bin/hostid

Description

Use the `hostid` command to print the identifier of the current host in hexadecimal.

Example

The following example displays the host ID for the system `castle`.

```
castle% hostid
727014d0
castle%
```

Attributes

See `attributes`(5) for descriptions of the following attributes:

Attribute Type	Attribute Value
Availability	SUNWcsu

See Also

`sysinfo(2)`, `gethostid(3C)`, `attributes(5)`

hostname — Set or Print Name of Current Host System

Synopsis

`/usr/bin/hostname [name-of-host]`

Description

Use the `hostname` command to print the name of the current host, as given before the login prompt. The superuser can set the host name by giving an argument.

Example

The following example uses `hostname` with no arguments to display the host name.

```
$ hostname
castle
$
```

Attributes

See attributes(5) for descriptions of the following attributes:

Attribute Type	Attribute Value
Availability	SUNWcsu

See Also

uname(1), attributes(5)

hp7221plot, hpplot — Graphics Filters for Various Plotters

Synopsis

/usr/ucb/plot [-T*terminal*]

Description

See plot(1).

I

iAPX286, i286, i386, i486, i860 — Get Processor Type Truth Value

Synopsis
```
/usr/bin/iAPX286
/usr/bin/i386
/usr/bin/i486
/usr/bin/i860
```

Description
See machid(**1**).

iconv — Code Set Conversion Utility

Synopsis
```
/usr/bin/iconv -f fromcode -t tocode [file...]
```

481

Description

The `iconv` command converts the characters or sequences of characters in *file* from one code set to another and writes the results to standard output. Should no conversion exist for a particular character, then it is converted to the underscore (_) in the target code set.

The list of supported conversions and the locations of the associated conversion tables are provided in the `iconv(5)` manual page.

The `iconv` command can use conversion modules (`/usr/lib/iconv/*.so`) or conversion tables (`/usr/lib/iconv/*.t`). If both a conversion module and a conversion table exist for a particular code set conversion, `iconv` uses the conversion module.

Refer to the `/usr/share/man/man5/iconv_locale.5` manual page in the Asian localized releases for information on supported code sets. For example, the following command displays the manual page describing the code set conversions that are supported for the Japanese locale.

```
% man -s 5 iconv_ja
```

> **Note —** The `iconv_locale.5` manual page may not exist in every localized release. Also, the `iconv_locale.5` manual page does not exist in the U. S. (nonlocalized) release.

Options

-f *fromcode* Identify the input code set.

-t *tocode*   Identify the output code set.

Operands

file   A path name of the input file to be translated. If you omit *file*, use the standard input.

Examples

The following example converts the contents of file `mail1` from code set `8859` to `646fr` and stores the results in the file `mail.local`.

```
castle% iconv -f 8859 -t 646fr mail1 > mail.local
castle%
```

Environment Variables

See `environ(5)` for descriptions of the following environment variables that affect the execution of `iconv`: LC_CTYPE, LC_MESSAGES, and NLSPATH.

Exit Status

0	Successful completion.
1	An error has occurred.

Files

/usr/lib/iconv/*.so

Conversion modules.

/usr/lib/iconv/*.t

Conversion tables.

/usr/lib/iconv/iconv_data

List of conversions supported by conversion tables.

Attributes

See attributes(5) for descriptions of the following attributes:

Attribute Type	Attribute Value
Availability	SUNWcsu

See Also

iconv(3), attributes(5), environ(5), iconv(5), iconv_unicode(5)

if, test — Evaluate Conditions

Synopsis

```
/usr/bin/test [condition]

[ condition ]
```

sh

```
if condition; then action; fi
if condition; then action; else action2; fi
if condition; then action; elif condition2; then
  action2;
  ... ; fi
if condition; then action; elif condition2; then action2;
    ... ; else action3; fi
test condition
[ condition ]
```

csh
```
if (condition) then
   action
else if (condition2) then
   action2
else
   action3
endif

if (condition) action
```

ksh
```
if condition; then action; fi
if condition; then action; else action2; fi
if condition; then action; elif condition2; then action2;
   ... ; fi
if condition; then action; elif condition2; then action2;
   ... ; else action3; fi
test condition
[ condition ]
```

Description

When writing scripts, you frequently want to test for conditions. The simplest test is to determine whether a condition is `true` or `false`. If the expression is `true`, execute any subsequent commands; if not, continue with the script.

/usr/bin/test

The `test` command evaluates the `condition` and indicates the result of the evaluation by its exit status. An exit status of 0 indicates that the condition evaluated as `true`, and an exit status of 1 indicates that the condition evaluated as `false`.

The second form of the command uses square brackets (`[]`) instead of the `test` command; the square brackets must be separate arguments and `condition` is optional.

Bourne Shell

The condition following `if` is executed, and if it returns a 0 exit status, the `action` following the first `then` is executed. Otherwise, the `condition2` following `elif` is executed, and if its value is 0, the `action2` following the next `then` is executed. Failing the `if` and `elif` conditions, the `else` `action3` is executed. If no `else` `action` or `then` `action` is executed, the `if` command returns a 0 exit status. Any number of `elif` ... `then` ... branching pairs are allowed, but only one `else`.

`test` evaluates the `condition` condition and, if its value is `true`, sets exit status to 0; otherwise, it sets a non-zero (`false`) exit status; `test` also sets a non-zero exit status if there are no arguments. When permissions are tested, the effective user ID of the process is used.

All operators, flags, and brackets (brackets used as shown in the second Synopsis line) must be separate arguments to the `test` command; normally these items are separated by spaces.

> **Note** — Both the Bourne shell and the Korn shell can use the semicolon and the Return interchangeably in their syntax of the if, for, and while built-in commands.

Primitives

You can use the following primitives to construct *condition*:

-r *filename*

> true if *filename* exists and is readable.

-w *filename*

> true if *filename* exists and is writable.

-x *filename*

> true if *filename* exists and is executable.

-f *filename*

> true if *filename* exists and is a regular file. Alternatively, if /usr/bin/sh users specify /usr/ucb before /usr/bin in their PATH environment variable, then test returns true if *filename* exists and is not a directory. This behavior is also the default for /usr/bin/csh users. The not-a-directory alternative to the -f option is a transition aid for BSD applications and may not be supported in future releases.

-d *filename*

> true if *filename* exists and is a directory.

-h *filename*

> true if *filename* exists and is a symbolic link. With all other primitives (except -L *filename*), follow the symbolic links by default.

-c *filename*

> true if *filename* exists and is a character special file.

-b *filename*

> true if *filename* exists and is a block special file.

-p *filename*

> true if *filename* exists and is a named pipe (fifo).

-u *filename*

> true if *filename* exists and its set-user-ID bit is set.

-g *filename*

> true if *filename* exists and its set-group-ID bit is set.

-k *filename*

> true if *filename* exists and its sticky bit is set.

-s *filename*
> true if *filename* exists and has a size greater than 0.

-t [*fildes*] true if the open file whose file descriptor number is *fildes* (1 by default) is associated with a terminal device.

-z *s1*   true if the length of string *s1* is zero.

-n *s1*   true if the length of the string *s1* is non-zero.

s1 = *s2*   true if strings *s1* and *s2* are identical.

s1 != *s2*   true if strings *s1* and *s2* are not identical.

s1   true if *s1* is not the null string.

n1 -eq *n2*   true if the integers *n1* and *n2* are algebraically equal.

n1 -ne *n2*   true if the integers *n1* and *n2* are not algebraically equal.

n1 -ge *n2*   true if the *integer n1* is algebraically greater than or equal to the integer *n2*.

n1 -gt *n2*   true if the integer *n1* is algebraically greater than the integer *n2*.

n1 -le *n2*   true if the integer *n1* is algebraically less than or equal to the integer *n2*.

n1 -lt *n2*   true if the integer *n1* is algebraically less than the integer *n2*.

-L *filename*
> true if *filename* exists and is a symbolic link. With all other primitives (except -h *filename*), follow the symbolic links by default. The -L option is a migration aid for users of other shells that have similar options. It may not be supported in future releases.

Operators
You can combine these primaries with the following operators:

!   Unary negation operator.

-a   Binary and operator.

-o   Binary or operator (-a has higher precedence than -o).

(*condition*)   Parentheses for grouping. Notice also that parentheses are meaningful to the shell and, therefore, must be quoted.

If you test a file you own (the -r -w or -x tests) but the permission tested does not have the owner bit set, a non-zero (false) exit status is returned even though the file may have the group or other bit set for that permission. The correct exit status is set if you are superuser.

Note — If more than one argument follows the -r through -n operators, only the first argument is examined; the others are ignored, unless -a or -o is the second argument.

The = and != operators have a higher precedence than the -r through -n operators, and = and != always expect arguments; therefore, you cannot use = and != with the -r through -n operators.

C Shell

With the multiline form of if, if *condition* is true, the *action* up to the first else or then is executed. Otherwise, if else if *condition2* is true, the *action2* between the else if and the following else or then is executed. Otherwise, the *action3* between the else and the endif is executed.

The if must appear alone on its input line or after an else. Only one endif is needed, but it is required. The words else and endif must be the first nonwhite characters on a line. Any number of else if ... then ... branching pairs are allowed, but only one else.

With the one-line form of if, there are no else, then, or endif keywords: if the specified condition evaluates to true, the single *action* with arguments is executed. Variable substitution on *action* happens early, at the same time it does for the rest of the if command. *action* must be a simple command, not a pipeline, a command list, or a parenthesized command list.

> **Note** — I/O redirection occurs even if *condition* is false, when *action* is not executed (this is a bug).

Korn Shell

The *condition* following if is executed and, if it returns an exit status of 0, the *action* following the first then is executed. Otherwise, the *condition2* following elif is executed, and if its value is 0, the *action2* following the next then is executed. Failing that, the else *action3* is executed. If no else *action* or then *action* is executed, then the if command returns an exit status of 0. Any number of elif ... then ... branching pairs are allowed, but only one else.

For a description of the test built-in, see the ksh(1) sections Conditional Expressions and Arithmetic Evaluation and the (sh) Bourne shell's test built-in.

[*condition*] evaluates file attributes, string comparisons, and compound and or or conditions.

Operands

Present all operators and elements of primaries as separate arguments to the test command. You can use the following primaries to construct *condition*:

-a *file*	true if *file* exists.
-b *file*	true if *file* exists and is a block special *file*.
-c *file*	true if *file* exists and is a character special file.
-d *file*	true if *file* exists and is a directory.

`-e file`	true if `file` exists.
`-f file`	true if `file` exists and is a regular file.
`-g file`	true if `file` exists and its set-group-ID flag is set.
`-k file`	true if `file` exists and its sticky bit is set.
`-n string`	true if the length of string is non-zero.
`-o option`	true if option named `option` is on.
`-p file`	true if `file` is a named pipe (FIFO).
`-r file`	true if `file` exists and is readable.
`-s file`	true if `file` exists and has a size greater than 0.

`-t file-descriptor`

> true if the `file` whose file descriptor number is `file-descriptor` is open and is associated with a terminal.

`-u file`	true if `file` exists and its set-user-ID flag is set.
`-w file`	true if `file` exists and is writable. true indicates only that the write flag is on. The file is not writable on a read-only file system even if this test indicates true.
`-x file`	true if `file` exists and is executable. true indicates only that the execute flag is on. If `file` is a directory, true indicates that `file` can be searched.
`-z string`	true if the length of string `string` is 0.
`-L file`	true if `file` exists and is a symbolic link.
`-O file`	true if `file` exists and is owned by the effective user ID of this process.
`-G file`	true if `file` exists and its group matches the effective group ID of this process.
`-S file`	true if `file` exists and is a socket.

`file1 -nt file2`

> true if `file1` exists and is newer than `file2`.

`file1 -ot file2`

> true if `file1` exists and is older than `file2`.

`file1 -ef file2`

> true if `file1` and `file2` exist and refer to the same file.

`string`	true if the string `string` is not the null string.

`string = pattern`

> true if `string` matches `pattern`.

`string != pattern`

> true if `string` does not match `pattern`.

string1 = *string2*

true if the strings *string1* and *string2* are identical.

string1 ! = *string2*

true if the strings *string1* and *string2* are not identical.

string1 < *string2*

true if *string1* comes before *string2*, based on ASCII value of their characters.

string1 > *string2*

true if *string1* comes after *string2*, based on ASCII value of their characters.

n1 -eq *n2*   true if the integers *n1* and *n2* are algebraically equal.

n1 -ne *n2*   true if the integers *n1* and *n2* are not algebraically equal.

n1 -ge *n2*   true if the integer *n1* is algebraically greater than or equal to the integer *n2*.

n1 -gt *n2*   true if the integer *n1* is algebraically greater than the integer *n2*.

n1 -le *n2*   true if the integer *n1* is algebraically less than or equal to the integer *n2*.

n1 -lt *n2*   true if the integer *n1* is algebraically less than the integer *n2*.

You can combine these primaries with the following operator:

! condition

true if condition is false.

The primaries with two elements of the following form are known as unary primaries.

-primary-operator primary-operand

The primaries with three elements in either of the following two forms are known as binary primaries.

primary-operand -primary-operator primary-operand
primary-operand primary-operator primary-operand

The algorithm for determining the precedence of the operators and the return value that is generated is based on the number of arguments presented to test. (However, when you use the [. . .] form, the right-bracket final argument is not counted in this algorithm.)

In the following list, $1, $2, $3 and $4 represent the arguments presented to test.

0 *arguments*

Exit false(1).

1 *argument*

> Exit true (0) if $1 is not null; otherwise, exit false.

2 *arguments*

- If $1 is !, exit true if $2 is null, false if $2 is not null.
- If $1 is a unary primary, exit true if the unary test is true, false if the unary test is false.
- Otherwise, produce unspecified results.

3 *arguments*

- If $2 is a binary primary, perform the binary test of $1 and $3.
- If $1 is !, negate the two-argument test of $2 and $3.
- Otherwise, produce unspecified results.

4 *arguments*

- If $1 is !, negate the three-argument test of $2, $3, and $4.
- Otherwise, the results are unspecified.

Usage

Be careful when you write scripts that deal with user-supplied input that could be confused with primaries and operators. Unless you, the application writer, know all the cases that produce input to the script, write invocations like

```
test "$1" -a "$2"
```

as follows to avoid problems if a user supplied values such as $1 set to ! and $2 set to the null string.

```
test "$1" && test "$2"
```

In cases where maximal portability is of concern, replace

```
test expr1 -a expr2
```

with

```
test expr1 && test expr2
```

and replace

```
test expr1 -o expr2
```

with

```
test expr1 || test expr2
```

> **Note** — In `test`, `-a` has higher precedence than `-o`, and `&&` and `||` have equal precedence in the shell.

You can use parentheses or braces in the shell command language for grouping.

You must escape parentheses when using `sh`; for example,

```
test \( expr1 -a expr2 \) -o expr3
```

This command is not always portable outside XSI-conformant systems. Instead, you can use the following form.

```
( test expr1 && test expr2 ) || test expr3
```

The following two commands could not be used reliably on some historical systems.

```
test "$1"
test ! "$1"
```

Unexpected results occur if such a string condition is used and `$1` is expanded to `!` or a known unary primary. Better constructs are

```
test -n "$1"
test -z "$1"
```

Historical systems have also been unreliable given the common construct

```
test "$response" = "expected string"
```

One of the following is a more reliable form.

```
test "X$response" = "Xexpected string"
test "expected string" = "$response"
```

Note that the second form assumes that `"expected string"` could not be confused with any unary primary. If `"expected string"` starts with `-`, `(`, `!` or even `=`, use the first form instead. Using the preceding rules without the marked extensions, any of the three comparison forms is reliable, given any input. Note, however, that the strings are quoted in all cases.

Because the string-comparison binary primaries, `=` and `!=`, have a higher precedence than any unary primary in the `>4` argument case, unexpected results can occur if arguments are not properly prepared. For example, in the following construct, if `$1` evaluates to a possible directory name of `-`, the first three arguments are considered a string comparison, and a syntax error is displayed when the second `-d` is encountered.

```
test -d $1 -o -d $2
```

One of the following forms prevents this problem; the second is preferred.

```
test \( -d "$1" \) -o \( -d "$2" \)
test -d "$1" || test -d "$2"
```

Also in the >4 argument case, syntax errors occur if $1 evaluates to (or !.

```
test "$1" = "bat" -a "$2" = "ball"
```

One of the following forms prevents this error; the third is preferred.

```
test "X$1" = "Xbat" -a "X$2" = "Xball"
test "$1" = "bat" && test "$2" = "ball"
test "X$1" = "Xbat" && test "X$2" = "Xball"
```

See `largefile`(5) for the description of the behavior of `test` when encountering files greater than or equal to 2 Gbytes (2**31 bytes).

Examples

In the `if` command examples, three conditions are tested, and if all three evaluate as `true` or successful, then their validities are written to the screen.

The three tests are:

- If a variable set to 1 is greater than 0.
- If a variable set to 2 is equal to 2.
- If the word `root` is included in the text file /etc/passwd.

/usr/bin/test

The following example performs a `mkdir` if a directory does not exist.

```
test ! -d tempdir && mkdir tempdir
```

The following example waits for a file to become nonreadable.

```
while test -r thefile
do
  sleep 30
done
echo '"thefile" is no longer readable'
```

The following example performs a command if the argument is one of three strings (two variations).

```
if [ "$1" = "pear" ] || [ "$1" = "grape" ] || [ "$1" = "apple" ]
then
    command
fi
case "$1" in
  pear|grape|apple) command ; ;
esac
```

For the two forms of the `test` built-in command, see the Bourne shell `if` example.

Bourne Shell

```
ZERO=0 ONE=1 TWO=2 ROOT=root
if  [ $ONE -gt $ZERO ]
[ $TWO -eq 2 ]
grep $ROOT  /etc/passwd >&1 > /dev/null      # discard output
```

```
then
  echo "$ONE is greater than 0, $TWO equals 2, and $ROOT
    is a user-name in the password file"
else
  echo "At least one of the three test conditions is false"
fi
```

The following examples use the `test` built-in command.

```
test `grep $ROOT /etc/passwd >&1 /dev/null`   # discard output
echo $?                                        # test for success
[ `grep nosuchname /etc/passwd >&1 /dev/null` ]
echo $?                                        # test for failure
```

C shell

```
@ ZERO = 0; @ ONE = 1; @ TWO = 2;  set ROOT = root
grep $ROOT  /etc/passwd >&1 /dev/null  # discard output
# $status must be tested for immediately following grep
if ( "$status" == "0" && $ONE > $ZERO && $TWO == 2 ) then
  echo "$ONE is greater than 0, $TWO equals 2, and $ROOT
    is a user-name in the password file"
endif
```

Korn Shell

```
ZERO=0 ONE=1 TWO=$((ONE+ONE)) ROOT=root
if  ((ONE > ZERO))                       # arithmetical comparison
[[ $TWO = 2 ]]                           # string comparison
[ `grep $ROOT  /etc/passwd >&1 /dev/null` ] # discard output
then
   echo "$ONE is greater than 0, $TWO equals 2, and $ROOT
 is a user-name in the password file"
else
   echo "At least one of the three test conditions is false"
fi
```

The Korn shell also accepts the syntax of both the `if` command and the `test` command of the Bourne shell.

When using the brackets (`[]`) within `if` commands, you must separate both inside ends of the brackets from the inside characters with a space.

Environment Variables

See environ(5) for descriptions of the following environment variables that affect the execution of `test`: LC_CTYPE, LC_MESSAGES, and NLSPATH.

Exit Status

0	Condition evaluated to `true`.
1	Condition evaluated to `false` or condition was missing.
>1	An error occurred.

Attributes

See attributes(5) for descriptions of the following attributes:

Attribute Type	Attribute Value
Availability	SUNWcsu

See Also

csh(1), ksh(1), sh(1), test(1B), attributes(5), environ(5), largefile(5)

---

implot — Graphics Filters for Various Plotters

Synopsis

/usr/ucb/plot [-T*terminal*]

Description

See plot(1).

---

indxbib — Create an Inverted Index to a Bibliographic Database

Synopsis

/usr/bin/indxbib *database-file*...

Description

A bibliographic reference is a set of lines constituting fields of bibliographic information. Each field starts on a line beginning with a %, followed by a key letter, then a blank, and finally the contents of the field that may continue until the next line starting with %. A database contains bibliographic references (or other kinds of information) separated by blank lines.

indxbib makes an inverted index to the named *database-file* (that must reside within the current directory), typically for use by lookbib(1) and refer(1). As output, indxbib creates an entry file (with a .ia suffix), a posting file (.ib), and a tag file (.ic), in the working directory.

indxbib is a shell script that calls two programs: /usr/lib/refer/mkey and /usr/lib/refer/inv.mkey, truncates words to 6 characters, and maps upper case to lower case. It also discards words shorter than 3 characters, words among the 100 most common English words, and numbers (dates) < 1000 or > 2099. You can change these parameters.

Bugs

All dates should probably be indexed because many disciplines refer to literature written in the 1800s or earlier.

indxbib does not recognize path names.

Examples

The following example runs the indxbib command on a bibliographic database named bibliography and shows the contents of the output files.

```
castle% indxbib bibliography
castle% more bibliography.*
::::::::::::::::
bibliography.ia
::::::::::::::::
(((((((((((((((((((((((((((((,<<<<<<<<<<<<<<<<<<<<<<<<<<<<<<@PPPPPPPPPP
   PPPPPPPPPPTddddddddddd
::::::::::::::::
bibliography.ib
::::::::::::::::
ÿÿÿÿ(>ÿÿÿÿ(>ÿÿÿÿ(>ÿÿÿÿ(>ÿÿÿÿ(>ÿÿÿÿ(>ÿÿÿÿ(>ÿÿÿÿ(>ÿÿÿÿ(>ÿÿÿÿ(>ÿÿÿÿ(>ÿÿÿÿ(
   >ÿÿÿÿ(>ÿÿÿÿ
::::::::::::::::
bibliography.ic
::::::::::::::::
bibliography:0,721
bibliography:721,720
bibliography:1441,720
bibliography:2161,720
castle%
```

Files

/usr/lib/refer/mkey

Use to map the bibliographic database.

/usr/lib/refer/inv

Use to invert the bibliographic database.

x.ia   Entry file.

x.ib   Posting file.

x.ic   Tag file.

x.ig   Reference file.

Attributes

See attributes(5) for descriptions of the following attributes:

Attribute Type	Attribute Value
Availability	SUNWdoc

See Also

addbib(1), lookbib(1), refer(1), roffbib(1), sortbib(1), attributes(5)

install — Install Commands

Synopsis

```
/usr/sbin/install -c dira [-m mode] [-u user] [-g group] [-o] [-s] file
/usr/sbin/install -f dirb [-m mode] [-u user] [-g group] [-o] [-s] file
/usr/sbin/install -n dirc [-m mode] [-u user] [-g group] [-o] [-s] file
/usr/sbin/install -d|-i [-m mode] [-u user] [-g group] [-o] [-s] dirx...
/usr/sbin/install [-m mode] [-u user] [-g group] [-o] [-s] file [dirx...]
```

Description

The install command is most commonly used in makefiles (see makc(1S)) to install a file in a specific location or to create directories within a file system. Each file is installed by being copied into the appropriate directory.

install uses no special privileges to copy files from one place to another. The implications of this are:

- You must have permission to read the files to be installed.

- You must have permission to copy into the destination directory.

- You must have permission to change the modes on the final copy of the file if you want to use the -m option.

- You must be superuser if you want to specify the ownership of the installed file with the -u or -g options. If you are not the superuser, the installed file is owned by you, regardless of who owns the original.

install prints messages telling you exactly what files it is replacing or creating and where they are going.

If you specify no options or directories (dirx ...), install searches a set of default directories (/bin, /usr/bin, /etc, /lib, and /usr/lib, in that order) for a file with the same name as file. When it finds the first occurrence, install issues a message saying that it is overwriting that file with file and proceeds to do so. If the file is not found, the program states this and exits.

If you specify one or more directories (*dirx* . . .) after file, those directories are searched before the default directories.

Options

-c *dira*	Install *file* in the directory specified by *dira* if *file* does not yet exist. If it is found, issue a message saying that the file already exists, and exit without overwriting it.
-f *dirb*	Force *file* to be installed in given directory, even if the file already exists. If the file being installed does not already exist, set the mode to 755 and the owner to bin. If the file already exists, the mode and owner are those of the already existing file.
-n *dirc*	If *file* is not found in any of the searched directories, put it in the directory specified in *dirc*. Set the mode of the new file to 755 and the owner to bin.
-d	Create a directory. Missing parent directories are created as required as in mkdir -p. If the directory already exists, set the owner, group, and mode to the values given on the command line.
-i	Ignore default directory list, searching only through the given directories (*dirx*. . .).
-m *mode*	Set the mode of the new file to *mode*. Set to 0755 by default.
-u *user*	Set the owner of the new file to *user*. Only available to the superuser. Set to bin by default.
-g *group*	Set the group ID of the new file to *group*. Only available to the superuser. Set to bin by default.
-o	If *file* is found, save the found file by copying it to OLDFILE in the directory in which it was found. This option is useful for installing a frequently used file such as /bin/sh or /lib/saf/ttymon, where you cannot remove the existing file.
-s	Suppress printing of messages other than error messages.

Usage

See largefile(5) for the description of the behavior of install when encountering files greater than or equal to 2 Gbytes (2**31 bytes).

Attributes

See attributes(5) for descriptions of the following attributes:

Attribute Type	Attribute Value
Availability	SUNWcsu

See Also

```
chgrp(1), chmod(1), chown(1), cp(1), mkdir(1), chown(1M), make(1S),
attributes(5), largefile(5)
```

Intro, intro — Introduction to Commands and Application Programs

Synopsis

This section describes, in alphabetical order, commands available with this operating system.

Pages of special interest are categorized as follows:

1B	Commands found only in the SunOS/BSD Compatibility Package. Refer to the *Source Compatibility Guide* for more information.
1C	Commands for communicating with other systems.
1F	Commands associated with Form and Menu Language Interpreter (FMLI).
1S	Commands specific to the SunOS system.

Note — This book does not include the FMLI commands.

Other Sections

The following other sections of the manual pages provide more information.

Section 1M	System maintenance commands.
Section 4	Information on file formats.
Section 5	Descriptions of publicly available files and miscellaneous information pages.
Section 6	Computer demonstrations.

For tutorial information about these commands and procedures, see:
Solaris Advanced User's Guide
Programming Utilities Guide

Manual Page Command Syntax

Unless otherwise noted, commands described in the Synopsis section of a manual page accept options and other arguments according to the following syntax and should be interpreted as explained below.

name [*-option*...] [*cmdarg*...]

where

[ ]	Surround an *option* or *cmdarg* is not required.
...	Indicate multiple occurrences of the *option* or *cmdarg*.
name	Specify the name of an executable file.
{ }	Indicate interdependent options and/or arguments, so that everything enclosed is treated as a unit.
option	Always preceded by a dash (-) *noargletter*... or *argletter* *optarg*[,...].
noargletter	A single letter represents an option without an option-argument. Note that you can group more than one *noargletter* option after one dash (-) (Rule 5, below).
argletter	A single letter represents an option that requires an option-argument.
optarg	An option-argument (character string) that satisfys a preceding *argletter*. Note that groups of *optargs* following an *argletter* must be separated by commas or separated by a Tab or space character and quoted (Rule 8, below).
cmdarg	Specify a path name (or other command argument) not beginning with a dash (-) or - by itself, indicating the standard input.

Command Syntax Standard: Rules

These command syntax rules are not followed by all current commands, but all new commands obey them. All shell procedures should use getopts(1) to parse positional parameters and to check for legal options. getopts supports Rules 3-10 below. The enforcement of the other rules must be done by the command itself.

1. Command names (*name* above) must be between two and nine characters long.
2. Command names must include only lowercase letters and digits.
3. Option names (*option* above) must be one character long.
4. All options must be preceded by a dash (-).
5. Options with no arguments may be grouped after a single dash (-).
6. The first option-argument (*optarg* above) following an option must be preceded by a Tab or space character.
7. Option-arguments cannot be optional.

8. Groups of option-arguments following an option must either be
    separated by commas or separated by Tab or space character and quoted
    (-o xxx,z,yy or -o "xxx z yy").
9. All options must precede operands (*cmdarg* above) on the command line.
10. You can use a double dash (--) to indicate the end of the options.
11. The order of the options relative to one another should not matter.
12. The relative order of the operands (*cmdarg* above) may affect their
    significance in ways determined by the command.
13. Use a dash preceded and followed by a space character (-) only to
    mean standard input.

Attributes

See attributes(5) for a discussion of the attributes listed in this section.

See Also

getopts(1), wait(1), exit(2), wait(3B), getopt(3C), attributes(5)

Diagnostics

On termination, each command returns two bytes of status, one supplied by the
system and giving the cause for termination, and (in the case of "normal"
termination) one supplied by the program [see wait(3B) and exit(2)]. The
former byte is 0 for normal termination; the latter is customarily 0 for
successful execution and non-zero to indicate troubles such as erroneous
parameters, or bad or inaccessible data. It is called variously "exit code," "exit
status," or "return code," and is described only where special conventions are
involved. In this book, the Exit Status section for each command describes the
values returned on command termination.

Warnings

Some commands produce unexpected results when processing files containing
null characters. These commands often treat text input lines as strings and
therefore become confused on encountering a null character (the string
terminator) within a line.

List of Commands

An asterisk (*) next to a command name indicates that the command is new or
revised in the Solaris 7 release. A dagger next to a command name indicates
that the command is not included in this book.

Intro(1)*	Introduction to commands and application programs,
Mail(1)	See mailx(1),
NIS+(1)*	See nis+(1).
acctcom(1)	Search and print process accounting files.

adb(1)*	General-purpose debugger.
addbib(1)	Create or extend a bibliographic database.
admin(1)	See sccs-admin(1).
aedplot(1B)	See plot(1B).
alias(1)	Create or remove a pseudonym or shorthand for a command or series of commands.
answerbook2(1)*	Online documentation system.
appletviewer(1)*	View Java applets.
apropos(1)	Locate commands by keyword lookup.
ar(1)	Maintain portable archive or library.
arch(1)	Display the architecture of the current host.
as(1)*	Assembler.
asa(1)	Convert FORTRAN carriage control output to printable form.
at(1)	Execute commands at a later time.
atoplot(1B)	See plot(1B).
atq(1)	Display the jobs queued to run at specified times.
atrm(1)	Remove jobs spooled by at or batch.
audioconvert(1)	Convert audio file formats.
audioplay(1)	Play audio files.
audiorecord(1)	Record an audio file.
awk(1)	Pattern scanning and processing language.
banner(1)	Make posters.
basename(1)	Deliver portions of path names.
basename(1B)	Display portions of path names.
batch(1)	See at(1).
bc(1)	Arbitrary precision arithmetic language.
bdiff(1)	Big diff.
bfs(1)	Big file scanner.
bg(1)	See jobs(1).
bgplot(1B)	See plot(1B).
biff(1B)	Give notice of incoming mail messages.
break(1)	Shell built-in functions to escape from or advance within a controlling while, for, foreach, or until loop.
cal(1)	Display a calendar.
calendar(1)	Reminder service.

cancel(1)	Cancel print request.
case(1)	Shell built-in functions to choose from among a list of actions.
cat(1)	Concatenate and display files.
cc(1B)	C compiler.
cd(1)	Change working directory.
cdc(1)	See sccs-cdc(1).
chdir(1)	See cd(1).
checkeq(1)	See eqn(1).
checknr(1)	Check nroff and troff input files; report possible errors.
chgrp(1)	Change file group ownership.
chkey(1) *	Change user's secure RPC key pair.
chmod(1)	Change the permissions mode of a file.
chown(1) *	Change file ownership.
chown(1B)	Change owner.
ckdate(1) †	Prompt for and validate a date.
ckgid(1) †	Prompt for and validate a group ID.
ckint(1) †	Display a prompt; verify and return an integer value.
ckitem(1) †	Build a menu; prompt for and return a menu item.
ckkeywd(1) †	Prompt for and validate a keyword.
ckpath(1) †	Display a prompt; verify and return a path name.
ckrange(1) †	Prompt for and validate an integer.
ckstr(1) †	Display a prompt; verify and return a string answer.
cksum(1) †	Write file checksums and sizes.
cktime(1) †	Display a prompt; verify and return a time of day.
ckuid(1) †	Prompt for and validate a user ID.
ckyorn(1) †	Prompt for and validate yes/no.
clear(1)	Clear the terminal screen.
cmp(1)	Compare two files.
cocheck(1F) †	See coproc(1F).
cocreate(1F) †	See coproc(1F).
codestroy(1F) †	See coproc(1F).
col(1)	Reverse linefeeds filter.
comb(1)	See sccs-comb(1).
comm(1)	Select or reject lines common to two files.
command(1)	Execute a simple command.

compress(1)	Compress, uncompress files or display expanded files.
continue(1)	See break(1).
coproc(1F) †	Communicate with a process.
coreceive(1F) †	See coproc(1F).
cosend(1F) †	See coproc(1F).
cp(1)	Copy files.
cpio(1)	Copy file archives in and out.
cpp(1) *	The C-language preprocessor.
crontab(1)	Edit/display user crontab file.
crtplot(1B)	See plot(1B).
crypt(1)	Encode or decode a file.
csh(1)	Shell command interpreter with a C-like syntax.
csplit(1)	Split files based on context.
ct(1C)	Spawn login to a remote terminal.
ctags(1)	Create a tags file for use with ex and vi.
cu(1C)	Call another UNIX system.
cut(1)	Cut out selected fields of each line of a file.
date(1)	Write the date and time.
dc(1)	Desk calculator.
delta(1)	See sccs-delta(1).
deroff(1)	Remove nroff/troff, tbl, and eqn constructs.
df(1B)	Display status of disk space on file systems.
dhcpinfo(1)	Display value of parameters received through DHCP.
diff(1)	Display line-by-line differences between pairs of text files.
diff3(1)	Three-way differential file comparison.
diffmk(1)	Mark differences between versions of a troff input file.
dircmp(1)	Directory comparison.
dirname(1)	See basename(1).
dirs(1)	See cd(1).
dis(1) *	Object code disassembler.
disable(1)	See enable(1).
dispgid(1)	Display a list of all valid group names.
dispuid(1)	Display a list of all valid user names.
dos2unix(1)	Convert text file from DOS format to ISO format.
download(1)	Host-resident PostScript font downloader.
dpost(1)	troff postprocessor for PostScript printers.

du(1B)	Display the number of disk blocks used per directory or file.
dumbplot(1B)	See plot(1B).
dump(1)	Dump selected parts of an object file.
dumpcs(1)	Show codeset table for the current locale.
dumpkeys(1)	See loadkeys(1).
echo(1)	Echo arguments.
echo(1B)	Echo arguments to standard output.
echo(1F) †	Put string on virtual output.
ed(1)	Text editor.
edit(1)	Text editor (variant of ex for casual users).
egrep(1)	Search a file for a pattern, using full regular expressions.
eject(1)	Eject media such as CD-ROM and floppy from drive.
elfdump(1) *	Dump selected parts of an object file.
enable(1)	Enable/disable LP printers.
env(1)	Set environment for command invocation.
eqn(1)	Typeset mathematics test.
errange(1) †	See ckrange(1).
errdate(1) †	See ckdate(1).
errgid(1) †	See ckgid(1).
errint(1) †	See ckint(1).
erritem(1) †	See ckitem(1).
error(1) †	Insert compiler error messages at right source lines.
errpath(1) †	See ckpath(1).
errstr(1) †	See ckstr(1).
errtime(1) †	See cktime(1).
erruid(1) †	See ckuid(1).
erryorn(1) †	See ckyorn(1).
eval(1)	See exec(1).
ex(1)	Text editor.
exec(1)	Shell built-in functions to execute other commands.
exit(1)	Shell built-in functions to enable the execution of the shell to advance beyond its sequence of steps.
expand(1)	Expand Tab characters to space characters, and vice versa.
export(1)	See set(1).
exportfs(1B)	Translate exportfs options to share/unshare commands.
expr(1)	Evaluate arguments as an expression.

expr(1B)	Evaluate arguments as a logical, arithmetic, or string expression.
exstr(1)	Extract strings from source files.
face(1)†	Executable for the Framed Access Command Environment Interface.
factor(1)	Obtain the prime factors of a number.
false(1)	See true(1).
fastboot(1B)	Reboot/halt the system without checking the disks.
fasthalt(1B)	See fastboot(1B).
fc(1)	See history(1).
fdformat(1)*	Format floppy diskette or PCMCIA memory card.
fg(1)	See jobs(1).
fgrep(1)	Search a file for a fixed character string.
file(1)	Determine file type.
file(1B)	Determine the type of a file by examining its contents.
filesync(1)*	Synchronize ordinary, directory, or special files.
find(1)*	Find files.
finger(1)	Display information about local and remote users.
fmlcut(1F)†	Cut out selected fields of each line of a file.
fmlexpr(1F)†	Evaluate arguments as an expression.
fmlgrep(1F)†	Search a file for a pattern.
fmli(1)†	Invoke the Form and Menu Language Interpreter.
fmt(1)	Simple text formatters.
fmtmsg(1)	Display a message on stderr or system console.
fnattr(1)	Update and examine attributes associated with a Federated Naming Service (FNS) named object.
fnbind(1)	Bind a reference to an FNS name.
fnlist(1)	Display the names and references bound in an FNS context.
fnlookup(1)	Display the reference bound to an FNS name.
fnrename(1)	Rename the binding of an FNS name.
fnsearch(1)	Search for FNS objects with specified attributes.
fnunbind(1)	Unbind the reference from an FNS name.
fold(1)	Filter for folding lines.
for(1)	Shell built-in functions to repeatedly execute action(s) for a selected number of times.
foreach(1)	See for(1).

`from(1B)`	Display the sender and date of newly arrived mail messages.
`ftp(1)`	File transfer program.
`function(1)`	Shell built-in command to define a function that is usable within this shell.
`gcore(1)` *	Get core images of running processes.
`gencat(1)`	Generate a formatted message catalog.
`genmsg(1)`	Generate a message source file by extracting messages from source files.
`get(1)` *	See `sccs-get`(1).
`getconf(1)` *	Get configuration values.
`getfacl(1)`	Display discretionary file information.
`getfrm(1F)` †	Return the current frame ID number.
`getitems(1F)` †	Return a list of currently marked menu items.
`getopt(1)`	Parse command options.
`getoptcvt(1)`	Convert to `getopts` to parse command options.
`getopts(1)`	Parse command options.
`gettext(1)`	Retrieve text string from message database.
`gettxt(1)`	Retrieve a text string from a message database.
`gigiplot(1B)`	See `plot`(1B).
`glob(1)`	Shell built-in function to expand a word list.
`goto(1)`	See `exit`(1).
`gprof(1)` *	Display call-graph profile data.
`graph(1)`	Draw a graph.
`grep(1)`	Search a file for a pattern.
`groups(1)`	Print group membership of user.
`groups(1B)`	Display a user's group memberships.
`grpck(1B)`	Check group database entries.
`hash(1)`	Evaluate the internal hash table of the contents of directories.
`hashcheck(1)`	See `spell`(1).
`hashmake(1)`	See `spell`(1).
`hashstat(1)`	See `hash`(1).
`head(1)`	Display first few lines of files.
`help(1)` *	See `sccs-help`(1).
`helpdate(1)` †	See `ckdate`(1).
`helpgid(1)` †	See `ckgid`(1).

`helpint(1)`†	See `ckint`(1).
`helpitem(1)`†	See `ckitem`(1).
`helppath(1)`†	See `ckpath`(1).
`helprange(1)`†	See `ckrange`(1).
`helpstr(1)`†	See `ckstr`(1).
`helptime(1)`†	See `cktime`(1).
`helpuid(1)`†	See `ckuid`(1).
`helpyorn(1)`†	See `ckyorn`(1).
`history(1)`	Process command history list.
`hostid(1)`	Print the numeric identifier of the current host.
`hostname(1)`	Set or print name of current host system.
`hp7221plot(1B)`	See `plot`(1B).
`hpplot(1B)`	See `plot`(1B).
`i286(1)`	See `machid`(1).
`i386(1)`	See `machid`(1).
`i486(1)`	See `machid`(1).
`i860(1)`	See `machid`(1).
`iAPX286(1)`	See `machid`(1).
`iconv(1)`	Convert code set.
`if(1)`	Evaluate condition(s) or make execution of actions dependent on the evaluation of condition(s).
`implot(1B)`	See `plot`(1B).
`indicator(1F)`†	Display application-specific alarms and/or the "working" indicator.
`indxbib(1)`	Create an inverted index to a bibliographic database.
`install(1B)`	Install files.
`ipcrm(1)`	Remove a message queue, semaphore set, or shared memory ID.
`ipcs(1)`*	Report interprocess communication facilities status.
`isainfo(1)`*	Describe instruction set architecture.
`isalist(1)`	Display the native instruction sets executable on this platform.
`jobs(1)`	Control process execution.
`join(1)`	Relational database operator.
`jsh(1)`	See `sh`(1).

kbd(1)	Manipulate the state of keyboard or display the type of keyboard or change the default keyboard abort sequence effect.
kdestroy(1)	Destroy Kerberos tickets.
kerberos(1)	Introduction to the Kerberos system.
keylogin(1)*	Decrypt and store secret key with keyserv.
keylogout(1)	Delete stored secret key with keyserv.
kill(1)	Terminate or signal processes.
kinit(1)	Kerberos login command.
klist(1)	List currently held Kerberos tickets.
ksh(1)*	Korn shell, a standard/restricted command and programming language.
ksrvtgt(1)	Fetch and store Kerberos ticket-granting ticket, using a service key.
last(1)	Display login and logout information about users and terminals.
lastcomm(1)	Display the last commands executed, in reverse order.
ld(1)*	Link editor for object files.
ld(1B)	Link editor, dynamic link editor.
ldapadd(1)*	See ldapmodify(1).
ldapdelete(1)*	Delete entry tool for ldap.
ldapmodify(1)*	Addition and modification tool for ldap.
ldapmodrdn(1)*	Modify entry RDN tool for ldap.
ldapsearch(1)*	Search tool for ldap.
ldd(1)	List dynamic dependencies of executable files or shared objects.
ld.so.1(1)*	Runtime linker for dynamic objects.
let(1)	Shell built-in function to evaluate one or more arithmetic expressions.
lex(1)	Generate programs for lexical tasks.
limit(1)*	Set or get limitations on the system resources available to the current shell and its descendants.
line(1)	Read one line.
lint(1B)	Verify C programs.
listusers(1)	List user login information.
ln(1)	Make hard or symbolic links to files.
ln(1B)	Make hard or symbolic links to files.

loadfont(1)	Display or change font information in the RAM of the video card on an x86 system in text mode.
loadkeys(1)	Load and dump keyboard translation tables.
locale(1)	Get locale-specific information.
localedef(1)*	Define locale environment.
logger(1)	Add entries to the system log.
logger(1B)	Add entries to the system log.
login(1)*	Sign on to the system.
logname(1)	Return user's login name.
logout(1)	Shell built-in function to exit from a login session.
longline(1F)†	See readfile(1F).
look(1)	Find words in the system dictionary or lines in a sorted list.
lookbib(1)	Find references in a bibliographic database.
lorder(1)	Find ordering relation for an object or library archive.
lp(1)*	Submit print request.
lpc(1B)	Line printer control program.
lpq(1B)	Display the content of a print queue.
lpr(1B)	Submit print requests.
lprm(1B)	Remove print requests from the print queue.
lpstat(1)	Print information about the status of the print service.
lptest(1B)	Generate line printer ripple pattern.
ls(1)	List contents of a directory.
ls(1B)	List contents of a directory.
m4(1)	Macro processor.
mach(1)	Display the processor type of the current host.
machid(1)	Get processor type truth value.
mail(1)	Read mail or send mail to users.
mail(1B)	See mailx(1).
mailcompat(1)	Provide SunOS compatibility for Solaris mailbox format.
mailq(1)*	Print the mail queue.
mailstats(1)*	Print statistics collected by sendmail.
mailx(1)	Interactive message processing system.
make(1S)	Maintain, update, and regenerate related programs and files.
makekey(1)	Generate encryption key.
man(1)	Find and display reference manual pages.

mconnect(1)	Connect to SMTP mail server socket.
mcs(1)	Manipulate the comment section of an object file.
mesg(1)	Permit or deny messages.
message(1F) †	Put arguments on the Form and Menu Language Interpreter message line.
mkdir(1)	Make directories.
mkmsgs(1)	Create message files for use by gettxt.
mkstr(1B)	Create an error message file by massaging C source files.
more(1)	Browse or page through a text file.
msgfmt(1)	Create a message object from a message file.
mt(1)	Control magnetic tapes.
mv(1)*	Move files.
nawk(1)	Pattern scanning and processing language.
neqn(1)	See eqn(1).
newaliases(1)*	Rebuild the database for the mail aliases file.
newform(1)	Change the format of a text file.
newgrp(1)	Log in to a new group.
news(1)	Print news items.
nice(1)	Invoke a command with an altered scheduling priority.
nis+(1)*	A new version of the network information name service.
nis(1)	See nis+(1).
niscat(1)	Display NIS+ tables and objects.
nischgrp(1)	Change the group owner of an NIS+ object.
nischmod(1)	Change access rights on an NIS+ object.
nischown(1)	Change the owner of an NIS+ object.
nischttl(1)	Change the time-to-live value of an NIS+ object.
nisdefaults(1)	Display NIS+ default values.
niserror(1)	Display NIS+ error messages.
nisgrep(1)*	See nismatch(1).
nisgrpadm(1)*	NIS+ group administration command.
nisln(1)	Symbolically link NIS+ objects.
nisls(1)	List the contents of an NIS+ directory.
nismatch(1)*	Command for searching NIS+ tables.
nismkdir(1)	Create NIS+ directories.
nispasswd(1)*	Change NIS+ password information.
nisrm(1)	Remove NIS+ objects from the namespace.

`nisrmdir(1)`	Remove NIS+ directories.
`nistbladm(1)`	Administer NIS+ tables.
`nistest(1)*`	Return the state of the NIS+ namespace, using a conditional expression.
`nl(1)`	Filter line numbers.
`nm(1)`	Print name list of an object file.
`nohup(1)`	Run a command immune to hangups.
`notify(1)`	See `jobs(1)`.
`nroff(1)*`	Format documents for display or line printer.
`od(1)`	Octal dump.
`on(1)`	Execute a command on a remote system, but with the local environment.
`onintr(1)`	See `trap(1)`.
`optisa(1)`	Determine which variant instruction set is optimal to use.
`pack(1)`	Compress and expand files.
`page(1)`	See `more(1)`.
`pagesize(1)`	Display the size of a page of memory.
`passwd(1)`	Change login password and password attributes.
`paste(1)`	Merge corresponding or subsequent lines of files.
`patch(1)`	Apply changes to files.
`pathchk(1)`	Check path names.
`pathconv(1F)†`	Search Form and Menu Language Interpreter criteria for file name.
`pax(1)`	Portable archive interchange.
`pcat(1)`	See `pack(1)`.
`pcmapkeys(1)`	Set keyboard extended map and scancode translation for the PC console in text mode.
`pcred(1)*`	See `proc(1)`.
`pdp11(1)`	See `machid(1)`.
`pfiles(1)*`	See `proc(1)`.
`pflags(1)*`	See `proc(1)`.
`pg(1)`	Files perusal filter for CRTs.
`pgrep(1)*`	Find or signal processes by name and other attributes.
`pkginfo(1)`	Display software package information.
`pkgmk(1)`	Produce an installable package.
`pkgparam(1)`	Display package parameter values.
`pkgproto(1)`	Generate prototype file entries for input to `pkgmk` command.

pkgtrans(1)	Translate package format.
pkill(1)*	See pgrep(1)
pldd(1)*	See proc(1).
plimit(1)	Get or set the resource limits of running processes.
plot(1B)	Graphics filters for various plotters.
plottoa(1B)	See plot(1B).
pmap(1)*	See proc(1).
popd(1)	See cd(1).
postdaisy(1)	PostScript translator for Diablo 630 daisy-wheel files.
postdmd(1)	PostScript translator for DMD bitmap files.
postio(1)	Serial interface for PostScript printers.
postmd(1)	Matrix display program for PostScript printers.
postplot(1)	PostScript translator for plot(4) graphics files.
postprint(1)	PostScript translator for text files.
postreverse(1)	Reverse the page order in a PostScript file.
posttek(1)	PostScript translator for Tektronix 4014 files.
pr(1)	Print files.
prex(1)*	Control tracing in a process or the kernel.
print(1)	Shell built-in function to output characters to the screen or window.
printenv(1B)	Display environment variables currently set.
printf(1)	Write formatted output.
priocntl(1)	Display or set scheduling parameters of specified process(es).
proc(1)*	proc tools.
prof(1)*	Display profile data.
prs(1)*	See sccs-prs(1).
prt(1)	See sccs-prt(1).
prun(1)*	See proc(1).
ps(1)*	Report process status.
ps(1B)	Display the status of current processes.
psig(1)*	See proc(1).
pstack(1)*	See proc(1).
pstop(1)*	See proc(1).
ptime(1)*	See proc(1).
ptree(1)*	See proc(1).

pushd(1)	See cd(1).
pvs(1)	Display the internal version information of dynamic objects.
pwait(1)*	See proc(1).
pwd(1)	Return working directory name.
pwdx(1)*	See proc(1).
ranlib(1)	Convert archives to random libraries.
rcp(1)	Remote file copy.
rdist(1)	Remote file distribution program.
read(1)	Read a line from standard input.
readfile(1F)†	Read file; get longest line.
readonly(1)	Shell built-in function to protect the value of the given variable from reassignment.
red(1)	See ed(1).
refer(1)	Expand and insert references from a bibliographic database.
regcmp(1)	Regular expression compile.
regex(1F)†	Match patterns against a string.
rehash(1)	See hash(1).
reinit(1F)†	Run an initialization file.
remote_shell(1)	See rsh(1).
remsh(1)	See rsh(1).
renice(1)	Alter priority of running processes.
repeat(1)	See for(1).
reset(1B)	See tset(1B).
reset(1F)†	Reset the current form field to its default values.
return(1)	See exit(1).
rksh(1)*	See ksh(1).
rlogin(1)	Remote login.
rm(1)	Remove directory entries.
rmail(1)	See mail(1).
rmdel(1)	See sccs-rmdel(1).
rmdir(1)	See rm(1).
roffbib(1)	Format and print a bibliographic database.
rpcgen(1)	An RPC protocol compiler.
rsh(1)	Remote shell.

`run(1F)`†	Run an executable.
`rup(1)`	Show host status of remote machines (RPC version).
`rup(1C)`	Show host status of remote machines (RPC version).
`ruptime(1)`	Show host status of local machines.
`rusage(1B)`	Print resource usage for a command.
`rusers(1)`	Report who is logged in on remote machines.
`rwho(1)`	Report who is logged in on local machines.
`sact(1)`	See `sccs-sact(1)`.
`sag(1)`*	Graph system activity.
`sar(1)`	System activity reporter.
`sccs(1)`*	Front end for the Source Code Control System (SCCS).
`sccs-admin(1)`	Create and administer SCCS history files.
`sccs-cdc(1)`	Change the delta commentary of an SCCS delta.
`sccs-comb(1)`	Combine SCCS deltas.
`sccs-delta(1)`	Make a delta to an SCCS file.
`sccsdiff(1)`	See `sccs-sccsdiff(1)`.
`sccs-get(1)`*	Retrieve a version of an SCCS file.
`sccs-help(1)`*	Ask for help regarding SCCS error or warning messages.
`sccs-prs(1)`*	Display selected portions of an SCCS history.
`sccs-prt(1)`	Display delta table information from an SCCS file.
`sccs-rmdel(1)`	Remove a delta from an SCCS file.
`sccs-sact(1)`*	Show editing activity status of an SCCS file.
`sccs-sccsdiff(1)`	Compare two versions of an SCCS file.
`sccs-unget(1)`	Undo a previous get of an SCCS file.
`sccs-val(1)`	Validate an SCCS file.
`script(1)`	Make record of a terminal session.
`sdiff(1)`	Print differences between two files side-by-side.
`sed(1)`*	Stream editor.
`sed(1B)`	Stream editor.
`select(1)`	See `case(1)`.
`set(1)`	Shell built-in functions to determine the characteristics for environmental variables of the current shell and its descendants.
`set(1F)`†	Set and unset local or global environment variables.
`setcolor(1F)`†	Redefine or create a color.
`setenv(1)`	See `set(1)`.

setfacl(1)*	Modify the Access Control List (ACL) for a file or files.
settime(1)*	See touch(1).
sh(1)	Standard and job control shell and command interpreter.
shell(1F)†	Run a command, using shell.
shell_builtins(1)	Shell command interpreter built-in functions.
shift(1)	Shell built-in function to traverse either a shell's argument list or a list of field-separated words.
shutdown(1B)	Close down the system at a given time.
size(1)	Print section sizes in bytes of object files.
sleep(1)	Suspend execution for an interval.
smart2cfg(1)	Compaq Smart-2 EISA/PCI and Smart-2SL PCI Array Controller ioctl command.
soelim(1)	Resolve and eliminate .so requests from nroff or troff input.
solregis(1)	Solaris user registration.
sort(1)	Sort, merge, or sequence-check text files.
sortbib(1)	Sort a bibliographic database.
sotruss(1)	Trace shared library procedure calls.
source(1)	See exec(1).
sparc(1)	See machid(1).
spell(1)	Report spelling errors.
spellin(1)	See spell(1).
spline(1)	Interpolate smooth curve.
split(1)	Split a file into pieces.
srchtxt(1)	Display contents of, or search for a text string in, message databases.
stop(1)	See jobs(1).
strchg(1)	Change or query stream configuration.
strconf(1)	See strchg(1).
strings(1)	Find printable strings in an object or binary file.
strip(1)	Strip symbol table, debugging, and line number information from an object file.
stty(1)	Set the options for a terminal.
stty(1B)	Set the options for a terminal.
sum(1)	Print checksum and block count for a file.
sum(1B)	Calculate a checksum for a file.
sun(1)	See machid(1).

suspend(1)	Shell built-in function to halt the current shell.
switch(1)	See case(1).
symorder(1)	Rearrange a list of symbols.
sysV-make(1) *	Maintain, update, and regenerate groups of programs.
t300(1)	See tplot(1).
t300(1B)	See plot(1B).
t300s(1)	See tplot(1).
t300s(1B)	See plot(1B).
t4013(1B)	See plot(1B).
t4014(1)	See tplot(1).
t450(1)	See tplot(1).
t450(1B)	See plot(1B).
tabs(1)	Set Tabs on a terminal.
tail(1)	Deliver the last part of a file.
talk(1)	Talk to another user.
tar(1) *	Create tape archives and add or extract files.
tbl(1)	Format tables for nroff or troff.
tcopy(1)	Copy a magnetic tape.
tee(1)	Replicate the standard output.
tek(1)	See tplot(1).
tek(1B)	See plot(1B).
telnet(1) *	User interface to a remote system, using the TELNET protocol.
test(1)	See if(1).
test(1B)	Condition evaluation command.
test(1F) †	Condition evaluation command.
tftp(1)	Trivial file transfer program.
time(1)	Time a simple command.
times(1)	Shell built-in function to report time usages of the current shell.
timex(1)	Time a command; report process data and system activity.
tip(1)	Connect to remote system.
tnfdump(1)	Convert binary Trace Normal Form file to ASCII.
tnfxtract(1)	Extract kernel probes output into a trace file.
touch(1) *	Change file access and modification times.
touch(1B)	Change file access and modification times.

tplot(1)	Graphics filters for various plotters.
tput(1)	Initialize a terminal or query terminfo database.
tr(1)	Translate characters.
tr(1B)	Translate characters.
trap(1)	Shell built-in functions to respond to hardware signals.
troff(1)*	Typeset or format documents.
true(1)	Provide truth values.
truss(1)*	Trace system calls and signals.
tset(1B)	Establish or restore terminal characteristics.
tsort(1)	Topological sort.
tty(1)	Return user's terminal name.
type(1)	Write a description of command type.
typeset(1)	Shell built-in functions to set/get attributes and values for shell variables and functions.
u370(1)	See machid(1).
u3b(1)	See machid(1).
u3b15(1)	See machid(1).
u3b2(1)	See machid(1).
u3b5(1)	See machid(1).
ucblinks(1B)	Add /dev entries to give SunOS 4.x-compatible names to SunOS 5.x devices.
ul(1)	Underline text.
ulimit(1)*	See limit(1).
umask(1)	Get or set the file-mode creation mask.
unalias(1)	See alias(1).
uname(1)	Print name of current system.
uncompress(1)	See compress(1).
unexpand(1)	See expand(1).
unget(1)	See sccs-unget(1).
unhash(1)	See hash(1).
unifdef(1)	Resolve and remove ifdef'ed lines from C program source.
uniq(1)	Report or filter out repeated lines in a file.
units(1)	Convert quantities expressed in standard scales to other scales.
unix2dos(1)	Convert text file from ISO format to DOS format.
unlimit(1)*	See limit(1).

unpack(1)	See pack(**1**).
unset(1)	See set(**1**).
unset(1F) †	See set(**1F**).
unsetenv(1)	See set(**1**).
until(1)	See while(**1**).
uptime(1)	Show how long the system has been up.
users(1B)	Display a compact list of users logged in.
uucp(1C)	UNIX-to-UNIX system copy.
uudecode(1C)	See uuencode(**1C**).
uuencode(1C)	Encode a binary file, or decode its encoded representation.
uuglist(1C)	Print the list of service grades that are available on this UNIX system.
uulog(1C)	See uucp(**1C**).
uuname(1C)	See uucp(**1C**).
uupick(1C)	See uuto(**1C**).
uustat(1C)	UUCP status inquiry and job control.
uuto(1C)	Public UNIX-to-UNIX system file copy.
uux(1C)	UNIX-to-UNIX system command execution.
vacation(1)	Reply to mail automatically.
val(1)	See sccs-val(**1**).
valdate(1)	See ckdate(**1**).
valgid(1)	See ckgid(**1**).
valint(1)	See ckint(**1**).
valpath(1)	See ckpath(**1**).
valrange(1)	See ckrange(**1**).
valstr(1)	See ckstr(**1**).
valtime(1)	See cktime(**1**).
valuid(1)	See ckuid(**1**).
valyorn(1)	See ckyorn(**1**).
vax(1)	See machid(**1**).
vc(1)	Version control.
vedit(1) *	See vi(**1**).
ver(1)	See tplot(**1**).
vgrind(1) *	Format program listings.
vi(1) *	Screen-oriented (visual) display editor based on ex.
view(1) *	See vi(**1**).

vipw(1B)	Edit the password file.
volcancel(1)	Cancel user's request for removable media that is not currently in drive.
volcheck(1)	Check for media in a drive, and, by default, check all floppy media.
volmissing(1)	Notify user that volume requested is not in the CD-ROM or diskette drive.
volrmmount(1)	Call rmmount to mount or unmount media.
vplot(1B)	See plot(1B).
vsig(1F)†	Synchronize a coprocess with the controlling Form and Menu Language Interpreter application.
w(1)	Display information about currently logged-in users.
wait(1)*	Await process completion.
wc(1)	Display a count of lines, words, and characters in a file.
what(1)	Extract SCCS version information from a file.
whatis(1)	Display a one-line summary about a keyword.
whence(1)	See typeset(1).
whereis(1B)	Locate the binary, source, and manual page files for a command.
which(1)	Locate a command; display its path name or alias.
while(1)	Shell built-in functions to repetitively execute a set of actions while/until conditions are evaluated true.
who(1)	Report who is on the system.
whoami(1B)	Display the effective current user name.
whocalls(1)	Report on the calls to a specific procedure.
whois(1)	Internet user name directory service.
write(1)	Write to another user.
xargs(1)	Construct argument lists and invoke command.
xgettext(1)	Extract gettext call strings from C programs.
xstr(1)	Extract strings from C programs to implement shared strings.
yacc(1)	Yet another compiler-compiler.
ypcat(1)	Print values in an NIS database.
ypmatch(1)	Print the value of one or more keys from an NIS map.
yppasswd(1)	Change your network password in the NIS database.
ypwhich(1)	Return name of NIS server or map master.
zcat(1)	See compress(1).

ipcrm — Remove a Message Queue, Semaphor Set, or Shared Memory ID

Synopsis
```
/usr/bin/ipcrm [-m shmid] [-q msqid] [-s semid] [-M shmkey] [-Q msgkey]
    [-S semkey]
```

Description
ipcrm removes one or more messages, semaphores, or shared memory identifiers.

If you specify either the -C or -N flag, the real and effective UID/GID is set to the real UID/GID of the user invoking ipcs.

Note — Things can change while ipcs is running; the information it gives is guaranteed to be accurate only when it was retrieved.

Options

-m shmid Remove the shared memory identifier shmid from the system. Destroy the shared memory segment and data structure associated with it after the last detach.

-q msqid Remove the message queue identifier msqid from the system and destroy the message queue and data structure associated with it.

-s semid Remove the semaphore identifier semid from the system and destroy the set of semaphores and data structure associated with it.

-M shmkey Remove the shared memory identifier, created with key shmkey, from the system. Destroy the shared memory segment and data structure associated with it after the last detach.

-Q msgkey Remove the message queue identifier, created with key msgkey, from the system and destroy the message queue and data structure associated with it.

-S semkey Remove the semaphore identifier, created with key semkey, from the system and destroy the set of semaphores and data structure associated with it.

The details of the removals are described in msgctl(2), shmctl(2), and semctl(2). Use the ipcs command to find the identifiers and keys.

Attributes

See attributes(5) for descriptions of the following attributes:

Attribute Type	Attribute Value
Availability	SUNWipc

See Also

ipcs(1), msgctl(2), msgget(2), msgrcv(2), msgsnd(2), semctl(2), semget(2), semop(2), shmctl(2), shmget(2), shmop(2), attributes(5)

---

ipcs — Report Interprocess Communication Facilities Status

Synopsis

/usr/bin/ipcs [-aAbcimopqst] [-C corefile] [-N namelist]   *New!*

Description

The ipcs command prints information about active interprocess communication facilities. The information that is displayed is controlled by the options you supply. Without options, information is printed in short format for message queues, shared memory, and semaphores that are currently active in the system, as shown in the following example.

```
castle% ipcs
IPC status from <running system> as of Tue Jan 19 17:16:05 1999
Message Queue facility not in system.
T         ID      KEY         MODE         OWNER     GROUP
Shared Memory:
m         0    0x50018325  --rw-r--r--    root      root
Semaphores:
castle%
```

Note — If you specify either the -C or -N option, the real and effective UID/GID is set to the real UID/GID of the user invoking ipcs.

Things can change while ipcs is running; the information it gives is guaranteed to be accurate only when it was retrieved.

Options

-a	Use all XCU5 print options. (A shorthand notation for -b, -c, -o, -p, and -t.)

New!　-A　　　Use all print options. (A shorthand notation for -b, -c, -o, -p, and -t.)

-b　　　Print information on biggest allowable size: maximum number of bytes in messages on queue for message queues, size of segments for shared memory, and number of semaphores in each set for semaphores.

-c　　　Print creator's login name and group name.

-C *corefile*

Use the file *corefile* in place of /dev/mem and /dev/kmem. Use a core dump obtained from savecore(1M) in place of

/dev/mem and /dev/kmem. Without the -C option (default), use the running system image.

New!　-i　　　Print number of ISM attaches to shared memory segments.

-m　　　Print information about active shared memory segments.

-N *namelist*

Use the file *namelist* in place of /dev/ksyms.

-o　　　Print information on outstanding usage: number of messages on queue, total number of bytes in messages on queue for message queues, and number of processes attached to shared memory segments.

-p　　　Print process number information: process ID of last process to send a message, process ID of last process to receive a message on message queues, process ID of creating process, and process ID of last process to attach or detach on shared memory segments.

-q　　　Print information about active message queues.

-s　　　Print information about active semaphores.

If you specify -m, -q, or -s, print information about only those indicated. If you specify none of these options, print information about all three, subject to the following options: -a, -A, -b, -c, -C, -o, -i, -p, and -t.

-t　　　Print time information: time of the last control operation that changed the access permissions for all facilities, time of last msgsnd(2) and last msgrcv(2) on message queues, time of last shmat(2) and last shmdt(2) on shared memory (see shmop(2)), time of last semop(2) on semaphores.

The column headings and the meaning of the columns in an ipcs listing are shown below; the letters in parentheses indicate the options that display the corresponding heading; (all) means that the heading is always shown.

Note — These options determine only what information is provided for each facility; they do not determine what facilities are listed.

T   (all) Type of the facility:

q   Message queue.

m   Shared memory segment.

s   Semaphore.

ID   (all) The identifier for the facility entry.

KEY   (all) The key used as an argument to msgget(2), semget(2), or shmget(2) to create the facility entry. (Note: The key of a shared memory segment is changed to IPC_PRIVATE when the segment has been removed until all processes attached to the segment detach it.)

MODE   (all) The facility access modes and flags: The mode consists of 11 characters that are interpreted as follows. The first two characters are any two of the following:

R   A process is waiting on a msgrcv(2).

S   A process is waiting on a msgsnd(2).

D   Remove the associated shared memory segment. It is removed when the last process attached to the segment detaches it. (Note: If the shared memory segment identifier is removed by an IPC_RMID call to shmctl(2) before the process has detached from the segment with shmdt(2), the segment is no longer visible to ipcs and it does not appear in the ipcs output.)

C   Clear the associated shared memory segment when the first attach is executed.

–   The corresponding special flag is not set.

The next nine characters are interpreted as three sets of three bits each. The first set refers to the owner's permissions; the next, to permissions of others in the user group of the facility entry; and the last, to all others. Within each set, the first character indicates permission to read, the second character indicates permission to write or alter the facility entry, and the last character is currently unused.

The permissions are indicated as follows:

r   Read permission is granted.

w   Write permission is granted.

a   Alter permission is granted.

–   The indicated permission is not granted.

OWNER   (all) The login name of the owner of the facility entry.

GROUP	(all) The group name of the group of the owner of the facility entry.
CREATOR	(a, A, c) The login name of the creator of the facility entry.
CGROUP	(a, A, c) The group name of the group of the creator of the facility entry.
CBYTES	(a, A, o) The number of bytes in messages currently outstanding on the associated message queue.
QNUM	(a, A, o) The number of messages currently outstanding on the associated message queue.
QBYTES	(a, A, b) The maximum number of bytes allowed in messages outstanding on the associated message queue.
LSPID	(a, p) The process ID of the last process to send a message to the associated queue.
LRPID	(a, A, p) The process ID of the last process to receive a message from the associated queue.
STIME	(a, A, t) The time the last message was sent to the associated queue.
RTIME	(a, A, t) The time the last message was received from the associated queue.
CTIME	(a, A, t) The time when the associated entry was created or changed.
ISMATTCH	(a, i) The number of ISM attaches to the associated shared memory segments.
NATTCH	(a, A, o) The number of processes attached to the associated shared memory segment.
SEGSZ	(a, A, b) The size of the associated shared memory segment.
CPID	(a, A, p) The process ID of the creator of the shared memory entry.
LPID	(a, A, p) The process ID of the last process to attach or detach the shared memory segment.
ATIME	(a, A, t) The time the last attach to the associated shared memory segment was completed.
DTIME	(a, A, t) The time the last detach on the associated shared memory segment was completed.
NSEMS	(a, A, b) The number of semaphores in the set associated with the semaphore entry.
OTIME	(a, A, t) The time the last semaphore operation on the set associated with the semaphore entry was completed.

New! (marginal note beside ISMATTCH)

Environment Variables

See environ(5) for descriptions of the following enviornment variables that affect the execution of ipcs: LANG, LC_ALL, LC_CTYPE, LC_MESSAGES, and NLSPATH.

TZ   Determine the time zone for the time strings written by ipcs.

Files

/etc/group Group names.

/etc/passwd User names.

/dev/mem   Memory.

/dev/ksyms System namelist.

Attributes

See attributes(5) for descriptions of the following attributes:

Attribute Type	Attribute Value	
Availability	SUNWcsu (32-bit)	*New!*
	SUNWipcx (64-bit)	

See Also

savecore(1M), msgget(2), msgrcv(2), msgsnd(2), semget(2), semop(2), shmctl(2), shmget(2), shmop(2), attributes(5), environ(5)

isainfo — Describe Instruction Set Architectures

New!

Synopsis

/usr/bin/isainfo [-vknb]

Description

Use the isainfo command to identify various attributes of the instruction set architectures supported on the currently running system. Among the questions it can answer are whether 64-bit applications are supported, or whether the running kernel uses 32-bit or 64-bit device drivers.

When invoked with no options, isainfo prints the name(s) of the native instruction sets for applications supported by the current version of the operating system. These names are a subset of the list returned by isalist(1). The subset corresponds to the basic applications environments supported by the currently running system.

Options

-b   Print the number of bits in the address space of the native instruction set.

-k   Print the name of the instruction set(s) used by the operating system kernel components such as device drivers and STREAMS modules.

-n   Print the name of the native instruction set used by portable applications supported by the current version of the operating system.

-v   Print more detailed information about the other options.

Examples

The following are examples of invoking the isainfo command on different operating systems.

On a 32-bit x86 platform,

```
% isainfo -v
32-bit i386 applications
% isainfo -k
i386
%
```

On a system running the 32-bit operating system on a 64-bit SPARC processor,

```
% isainfo -n
sparc
% isainfo -v
32-bit sparc applications
% isainfo -kv
32-bit sparc kernel modules
%
```

On a system running the 64-bit operating system on a 64-bit SPARC processor,

```
% isainfo
sparcv9 sparc
% isainfo -n
sparcv9
% isainfo -v
64-bit sparcv9 applications
32-bit sparc applications
% isainfo -vk
64-bit sparcv9 kernel modules
%
```

Exit Status

Non-zero options are either not specified correctly, or the command is unable to recognize attributes of the system on which it is running. An error message is printed to standard error.

Attributes

See attributes(5) for descriptions of the following attributes:

Attribute Type	Attribute Value
Availability	SUNWcsu

See Also

isalist(1),uname(1),psrinfo(1M),sysinfo(2),attributes(5),isalist(5)

---

isalist — Display the Native Instruction Sets for This Platform

Synopsis

/usr/bin/isalist

Description

isalist prints the names of the native instruction sets executable on this platform on the standard output, as returned by the SI_ISALIST command of sysinfo(2).

The names are space-separated and are ordered in the sense of best performance. That is, earlier-named instruction sets may contain more instructions than later-named instruction sets; a program that is compiled for an earlier-named instruction set most likely runs faster on this machine than does the same program compiled for a later-named instruction set.

Programs compiled for instruction sets that do not appear in the list most likely experience performance degradation or do not run at all on this machine.

The instruction set names known to the system are listed in isalist(5). These names may or may not match predefined names or compiler options in the C-language compilation system,

Example

The following example runs isalist on a SPARCstation 10.

```
castle% isalist
sparcv8 sparcv8-fsmuld sparcv7 sparc
castle%
```

Attributes

See attributes(5) for descriptions of the following attributes:

Attribute Type	Attribute Value
Availability	SUNWcsu

See Also

New!

optisa(1), uname(1), sysinfo(2), attributes(5), isalist(5)

J

jar — Java Archive Tool

Synopsis

```
/usr/java/bin/jar[-c][-f][-M][-m][-o][-t][-v][-xfile][manifest-file]
    destination input-file [input-files]
```

Description

The jar (Java Archive) tool is a stand-alone, command-line Java application that you use for general-purpose archiving and to create a digital signature and the associated scripts in a JAR file, which always has a .jar suffix.

The JAR file type is a registered Internet MIME type that is based on the standard cross-platform ZIP and ZLIB compression format. The JAR file acts as a digital envelope for a compressed collection of files. The format is a set of conventions for associating digital signatures, installer scripts, and other information with files in a package.

jar was designed mainly to facilitate the packaging of Java applets or applications into a single archive. When you combine the components of an applet or application (.class files, images, and sounds) into a single archive, a Java agent (such as a browser) can download them in a single HTTP transaction instead of requiring a new connection for each piece. Download time dramatically improves. The jar tool also compresses files and so further improves download time. In addition, it enables the applet author to sign

529

individual entries in a file with a digital signature so that their origin can be authenticated.

Note — The syntax for the `jar` tool is almost identical to the syntax for the `tar(1)` command.

The three types of files for the `jar` tool are:

- Manifest file (optional).
- Destination `jar` file.
- Files to be archived.

The following example of typical usage puts all of the `.class` files in the current directory into a file named `myjarfile`.

```
castle% jar cf myjarfile *.class
```

The `jar` tool automatically generates a manifest file, which is always the first entry in the `jar` file. By default, it is named `META-INF/MANIFEST.INF`. The manifest file stores any metainformation about the archive. For details about how metainformation is stored in the manifest file, refer to:

```
http://sun.com/products/jdk/1.1/docs/guide/jar/manifest.html
```

To use a preexisting manifest file to create a new `jar` archive, specify the old manifest file with the `-m` option, as shown in the following example.

```
castle% jar cmf myManifestFile myJarFile *.class
```

When you add files to a `jar` archive, the file and its MD5 and SHA hashes are stored. The hashes are entered to the manifest file. It is easy to view and process the contents of the manifest file because it uses RFC822 ASCII format.

Options

`-c`	Create a new or empty archive on the standard output.
`-f`	The second argument specifies a `jar` file to process. When creating an archive, this refers to the name of the `jar` file to be created (instead of on standard output). For `table` or `xtract`, the second argument identifies the `jar` file to be listed or extracted.
`-M`	Include manifest information from specified preexisting manifest file. For example, `jar cmf myManifestFile myJarFile *.class`.
`-m`	Do not create a manifest file for the entries.
`-o`	Store only, without using ZIP compression.
`-t`	List the table of contents from standard output.
`-v`	Generate verbose output on standard error.

-x *file* Extract all files or just the named files from standard input. If you omit *file*, extract all files; otherwise, extract only the specified file or files.

If any of the files is a directory, then process that directory recursively.

Examples

The following example adds all of the files in a particular directory to an archive named `bundle.jar`.

```
castle% ls
0.au        3.au        6.au        9.au           at_work.gif
1.au        4.au        7.au        Animator.class monkey.jpg
e.au        5.au        8.au        Wave.class     spacemusic.au
castle% jar cvf bundle.jar *
adding: 0.au
adding: 1.au
adding: 2.au
adding: 3.au
adding: 4.au
adding: 5.au
adding: 6.au
adding: 7.au
adding: 8.au
adding: 9.au
adding: Animator.class
adding: Wave.class
adding: at_work.gif
adding: monkey.jpg
adding: spacemusic.au
castle%
```

If subdirectories for images, audio files, and classes already exist in an HTML directory, use `jar` to archive each directory to a single `jar` file, as shown in the following example.

```
castle% ls
audio classes images
castle% jar cvf bundle.jar audio classes images
adding: audio/1.au
adding: audio/2.au
adding: audio/3.au
adding: audio/spacemusic.au
adding: classes/Animator.class
adding: classes/Wave.class
adding: images/monkey.jpg
adding: images/at_work.gif
castle% ls -l
total 142
drwxr-xr-x    2 brown      green          512 Aug  1 22:33 audio
-rw-r--r--    1 brown      green        68677 Aug  1 22:36 bundle.jar
drwxr-xr-x    2 brown      green          512 Aug  1 22:26 classes
```

```
drwxr-xr-x   2 brown     green        512 Aug  1 22:25 images
castle%
```

The following example displays the entry names in the `jar` file, using the `jar` tool and the `-t` option.

```
castle% ls
audio bundle.jar classes images
castle% jar tf bundle.jar
META-INF/MANIFEST.MF
audio/1.au
audio/2.au
audio/3.au
audio/spacemusic.au
classes/Animator.class
classes/Wave.class
images/monkey.jpg
images/at_work.gif
castle%
```

The following example uses the `-v` option to display more information about the files in the archive, such as their size and last modified date.

```
castle% jar tvf bundle.jar
145 Thu Aug 01 22:27:00 PDT 1996 META-INF/MANIFEST.MF
946 Thu Aug 01 22:24:22 PDT 1996 audio/1.au
1039 Thu Aug 01 22:24:22 PDT 1996 audio/2.au
993 Thu Aug 01 22:24:22 PDT 1996 audio/3.au
48072 Thu Aug 01 22:24:23 PDT 1996 audio/spacemusic.au
16711 Thu Aug 01 22:25:50 PDT 1996 classes/Animator.class
3368 Thu Aug 01 22:26:02 PDT 1996 classes/Wave.class
12809 Thu Aug 01 22:24:48 PDT 1996 images/monkey.jpg
527 Thu Aug 01 22:25:20 PDT 1996 images/at_work.gif
castle%
```

Attributes

See `attributes`(5) for descriptions of the following attributes:

Attribute Type	Attribute Value
Availability	SUNWjvrt

See Also

`javakey`(1)

JAR Guide

http://java.sun.com/products/jdk/1.1/docs/guide/jar/
  jarGuide.html

Manifest Format

http://sun.com/products/jdk/1.1/docs/guide/jar/manifest.html

For information on related topics, use the search link at
`http://java.sun.com/`

javac — Java Compiler

Synopsis
```
/usr/java/bin/javac [-classpath path] [-d directory] [-depend]
    [-deprecation] [-encodingencoding-name] [-g] [-Jjavaoption] [-nowarn]
    [-O] [-verbose] filename.java ...
/usr/java/bin/javac_g [-classpath path] [-d directory] [-depend]
    [-deprecation] [-encodingencoding-name] [-g] [-Jjavaoption] [-nowarn]
    [-O] [-verbose] filename.java ...
```

Description
The `javac` command compiles Java source code into Java bytecodes that can
then be interpreted by the `java(1)` interpreter.

Java source code must be contained in files with file names that end in the
`.java` extension. If the class is public or is referenced from another source file,
the file name must be constructed from the class name, as `classname.java`.

For every class defined in each source file compiled by `javac`, the compiler
stores the resulting bytecodes in a class file with a name of the form
`classname.class`. Unless you specify the `-d` option, the compiler puts each
class file in the same directory as the corresponding source file.

When the compiler must refer to your own classes, you must specify their
location with either the `-classpath` option or CLASSPATH environment
variable. The class path is a sequence of directories (or files) that `javac`
searches for classes not already defined in any of the files specified directly as
command arguments. The compiler looks in the class path for both a source file
and a class file, recompiling the source (and regenerating the class file) if it is
newer.

Set the property `javac.pipe.output` to `true` to send output messages to
`System.out`. Set `javac.pipe.output` to `false` (that is, do not set it) to send
output messages to `System.err`.

`javac_g` is a nonoptimized version of `javac` suitable for use with debuggers
like `jdb(1)` for debugging `javac` itself. Using `javac_g` is not equivalent to
using the command `javac -g`.

Options

-classpath *path*

> Specify a colon-separated list of directories as the path used to
> look up classes needed to run `javac` or to find records by other
> classes you are compiling. Override the default or the `CLASSPATH`
> environment variable if it is set. It is often useful for the directory
> containing the source files to be on the class path. Always include
> the system classes at the end of the path. For example:
>
> `% javac -classpath`
> `.:/home/avh/classes:/usr/local/java/classes ...`

-d *directory*

> Specify the root directory of the class file hierarchy. In other
> words, specify a destination directory for your compiled classes.
> For example,
> `% javac -d /home/avh/classes MyProgram.java`
> saves the compiled class files for the classes in the
> MyProgram.java source file in the directory
> /home/avh/classes/demos/awt.Ifyourclassesaredefinedinthe
> package demos/awt, the class files are placed in the directory
> /home/avh/classes/demos/awt.

-depend

> Make the compiler consider recompiling class files that are
> referenced from other class files. Without this option, only
> recompile missing or out-of-date class files that are referred to
> from source code.

-deprecation

> Generate a warning for every use or override of a deprecated
> member or class. A member or class is deprecated if its
> documentation comment contains the @deprecated tag. The
> compiler displays a warning at the end of compilation regardless
> of whether you use -deprecation; this option notes the location of
> each individual use or override.
>
> Deprecated members or classes are deliberately not mentioned if
> the source file containing the deprecation is being recompiled.
> This can happen because the file is on the command line or
> because you use -depend and the source file was out of date.

-encoding *encoding-name*

> Specify the source file encoding name, such as EUCJIS/SJIS.
> Otherwise, use the platform default converter.

-g

> Enable generation of debugging tables. Debugging tables contain
> information about line numbers and local variables information
> used by Java debugging tools. By default, only line numbers are
> generated, unless you turn on optimization (-O).

-J*javaoption*

> Pass the *javaoption* string through as a single argument to the java(1) interpreter that runs the compiler. The argument should not contain spaces. Begin multiple argument words with the prefix -J, which is stripped. This option is useful for adjusting the compiler's execution environment or memory usage.

-nowarn   Turn off warnings. The compiler does not print any warnings.

-O

> Direct the compiler to try to generate faster code by inlining static, final, and private methods. This option can slow down compilation, make larger class files, and/or make it difficult to debug. -O implicitly turns on -depend and turns off -g.
>
> This option informs the compiler that all generated class files are guaranteed to be delivered and upgraded as a unit, enabling optimizations that may otherwise break binary compatibility. Use this option with discretion.

-verbose   Print compiler and linker messages about what source files are being compiled and what class files are being loaded.

Note — The -d and -classpath options have independent effects. The compiler reads only from the class path and writes only to the destination directory. It is often useful for the destination directory to be on the class path. If you do not specify the -d option, the source files should be stored in a directory hierarchy that reflects the package structure so that the resulting class files can be easily located.

The Java Language Specification section 13.4.21 describes situations in which it is legal to use a Java compiler to inline methods. The compiler optimizes code only for source that is available during the compilation, so the only .java files discoverable by the compiler should be for classes intended to be delivered or upgraded as a unit. In particular, ensure that no sources for other classes are accessible on CLASSPATH, keeping in mind that the present working directory (.) is appended to CLASSPATH.

To ensure that a product is able to run on JDK 1.1 as well as future binary-compatible Java virtual machines, ensure that any sources for JDK 1.1 classes are never available along CLASSPATH while using -O.

Example

When the source files are located in /home/ws/src/java/awt/*.java, the following example compiles the two specified classes.

```
castle% cd /home/ws/src/java/awt/
castle% javac Button.java Canvas.java
```

Environment Variables

CLASSPATH   Provide the system with a path to user-defined classes. Separate directories with colons, for example,
`.:/home/avh/classes:/usr/local/java/classes`.

Attributes

See `attributes(5)` for descriptions of the following attributes:

Attribute Type	Attribute Value
Availability	SUNWjvdev

See Also

`java(1), javadoc(1), javah(1), javap(1), jdb(1), attributes(5)`

---

javadoc — Java API Documentation Generator

Synopsis

```
/usr/java/bin/javadoc [-author][-classpath path][-d directory]
    [-d][-docencoding name][-encoding name][-J flag][-nodeprecated]
    [-noindex][-notree][-package][-private][-protected][-public]
    [-sourcepath path]  [-verbose][-version][package | source.java]*
```

Description

The `javadoc` command parses the declarations and documentation comments in a set of Java source files and produces a set of HTML pages describing, by default, the public and protected classes, interfaces, constructors, methods, and fields. As an argument to `javadoc`, you pass either a series of Java package names or source files.

`javadoc` generates one `.html` file for each `.java` file and each package it encounters. In addition, it produces a class hierarchy (`tree.html`) and an index of those members (`AllNames.html`).

When `javadoc` parses the class and member declarations, it picks up their signatures for inclusion. You can add further documentation by including documentation comments in the source code.

Commenting the Source Code

You can include documentation comments in the source code. A documentation comment consists of the characters between the `/**` that begins the comment and the `*/` that ends it. The text is divided into one or more lines, each beginning with an asterisk (`*`). When `javadoc` parses a documentation comment, it discards leading * characters on each line. For lines other than the first, it also discards blanks and Tabs preceding the initial * characters. These comments can include HTML tags. Here is an example of a documentation comment.

```
/**
 * This is a <b>doc</b> comment.
 */
```

Make the first sentence of each documentation comment a summary sentence containing a concise but complete description of the declared entity. This sentence ends at the first period that is followed by a blank, Tab, or line terminator or at the first tag (as defined below). javadoc copies this first sentence to the member summary at the top of the .html file.

Documentation comments are recognized only when placed immediately before class, interface, constructor, method, or field declarations.

When you embed HTML tags within a documentation comment, do not use heading tags such as <h1> and <h2> because javadoc creates an entire structured document and these structural tags interfere with the formatting of the generated document.

For the specification on documentation comments, see Chapter 18, "Documentation Comments," in *The Java Language Specification*, by James Gosling, Bill Joy, and Guy Steele.

Tagged Paragraphs

javadoc parses special tags that are recognized when they are embedded within a Java documentation comment. These documentation tags enable you to autogenerate a complete, well-formatted API from your source code. The tags start with an at sign (@).

Tags must start at the beginning of a line. Keep tags with the same name together within a documentation comment. For example, put all @author tags together so that javadoc can tell where the list ends.

The tags fall into three categories:

- Class and interface tags.
- Field tags.
- Constructor and method tags.

Each of the tag categories is described in the following sections.

Class and Interface Documentation Tags

@author *name-text*

> Create an Author entry. The text has no special internal structure. A documentation comment can contain multiple @author tags.

`@deprecated` *deprecated-text*

> Add a deprecated comment indicating that this API should no longer be used (even though it may continue to work). The convention is to describe the API that serves as a replacement. For example:
>
> `@deprecated Replaced by setBounds(int, int, int,`
>
> If the member is obsolete and there is no replacement, the argument to `@deprecated` should be `No replacement`.

`@since` *since-text*

> Add a `Since` entry. The text has no special internal structure. This tag means that this change or feature has existed since the release number of the software specified by the *since-text* (such as the JDK).

`@see` *classname*

> Add a hyperlinked `See Also` entry to the class. Some examples are:
>
> `@see java.lang.String@see String`
> `@see String#equals`
> `@see java.lang.Object#wait(int)`
> `@see Character#MAX_RADIX`
> `@see <a href="spec.html">Java Spec</a>`
>
> You use the # character to separate the name of a class from the name of one of its fields, methods, or constructors. You can select one of several overloaded methods or constructors by including a parenthesized list of argument types after the method or constructor name. White space in `@see` *classname* is significant. If there is more than one argument, use a single blank character between the arguments. For example:
>
> `@seejava.io.File#File(java.io.Filejava.lang.String)`
>
> A documentation comment can contain more than one `@see` tag.

`@version` *version-text*

> Add a `Version` entry. The text has no special internal structure. A documentation comment *can* contain only one `@version` tag. *version* normally refers to the version of the software (such as the JDK) that contains this feature.

The following example shows a class comment.

```
/**
 * A class representing a window on the screen.
 * For example:
 * <pre>
 *    Window win = new Window(parent);
 *    win.show();
 * </pre>
 *
```

```
 * @author   Sami Shaio
 * @version 1.5, 04/20/98
 * @see      java.awt.BaseWindow
 * @see      java.awt.Button
 */
class Window extends BaseWindow {
  ...
}
```

Field Documentation Tags

A field comment can contain only @see, @since, and @deprecated tags (as
described above).

The following example shows a field comment.

```
/**
 * The X-coordinate of the window.
 *
 * @see window#1
 */
int x = 1263732;
```

Constructor and Method Documentation Tags

Constructor and method documentation tags can contain @see tags as well as
tags from the following list.

@param *parameter-name description*

> Add a parameter to the Parameters section. You can continue the
> description on the next line.

@return *description*

> Add a Returns section that contains the description of the return
> value.

@exception *fully-qualified-class-name description*

> Add a Throws section that contains the name of the exception that
> can be thrown by the method. The exception is linked to its class
> documentation.

@see *classname*

> Add a hyperlinked See Also entry to the method. This tag is
> described above.

@since *deprecated-text*

> See the description above.

@since *since-text*

> See the description above.

The following example shows a method documentation comment.

```
/**
 * Returns the character at the specified index. An index
 * ranges from <code>0</code> to <code>length() - 1</code>.
```

```
*
* @param      index the index of the desired character.
* @return     the desired character.
* @exception StringIndexOutOfRangeException
*                 if the index is not in the range <code>0</code>
*                 to <code>length()-1</code>.
* @see        java.lang.Character#charValue()
*/
public char charAt(int index) {
  ...
}
```

Options

-author   Include @author tags, which are omitted by default.

-classpath *path*

> In general, you should not use -classpath because it is normally not needed; use sourcepath instead to specify .java files. Specify the directories from which javadoc is to load the .class files used to execute the javadoc tool. If you do not specify -sourcepath, this option also specifies the path javadoc uses to look up the .java files to document. Override the default or the CLASSPATH environment variable if it is set. The path can contain multiple, colon-separated paths. Set the path the same way you do for the CLASSPATH environment variable. The following example sets two paths: current directory (.) and /home/opus/myclasses.

```
javadoc -classpath .:/home/opus/myclasses
myPackage.MyClass
```

> You do not need to use the -classpath option if you call the javadoc wrapper script directly. Normally, if you specify classpath, it must precede sourcepath. However, the order of these two options does not matter if you are using the wrapper script.

> The value of classpath defaults to the current directory plus the classes location, as described in the CLASSPATH environment variable.

-d *directory*

> Specify the destination directory where javadoc stores the generated HTML files. The directory can be absolute or relative to the current working directory. For example, the following command generates the documentation for the java.lang package (using CLASSPATH to find it) and stores the results in the directory specified by the -d option.

```
castle% javadoc -d /home/opus/public_html/doc
java.lang -docencoding name
```

`-docencoding` *name*

> Specify the output HTML file-encoding name.

`-encoding` *name*

> Specify the source file encoding name, such as `EUCJIS`/`SJIS`. If you do not specify this option, use the platform default converter.

`-J` *flag*   Pass *flag* directly to the runtime system. For example, if you need to ensure that the system sets aside 32 megabytes of memory to hold the generated documentation, use `-J`, as follows:

> `castle% `**`javadoc -J-mx32m -J-ms32m ...`**

`-nodeprecated`

> Exclude paragraphs with the `@deprecated` tag.

> Please note that the `-doctype` option is no longer available. Only HTML documentation can be produced.

`-noindex`   Omit the default package index.

`-notree`   Omit the default class and interface hierarchy.

`-package`   Show only package, protected, and public classes and members.

`-private`   Show all classes and members.

`-protected` Show only protected and public classes and members. This is the default.

`-public`   Show only public classes and members.

`-sourcepath` *path*

> Specify the search path for source files. Do not affect the loading of class files. The path you specify depends on whether you specify packages or classes as `javadoc` command arguments.

> When generating documentation for packages, you specify the source path as the directory in the source tree that contains the topmost parent package of those you are documenting. The default for the source path is the current `-classpath` directory. For example, suppose you want to document a package called `java.lang` whose source files are located at:

> `/myapp/src/share/java/lang/*.java`

> Because `java`(1) is the topmost parent package, specify as the source path the directory that contains `java`.

> `castle% `**`javadoc -sourcepath /myapp/src/share`**

> When generating documentation for discrete classes, specify the source path as the directory in the source tree that contains the classes you are documenting. Note that this is different from the source path you used when documenting packages. For example, suppose you want to document a class named `java.lang.java.lang.String` whose source file is located at `/myapp/src/share/java/lang/String.java`

Specify the directory containing the class `String.java` as the source path.

```
castle%javadoc-sourcepath/myapp/src/share/java/lang
```

You can omit the `-sourcepath` option if you first switch to the directory you would have specified.

`-verbose`   Print additional messages specifying the number of milliseconds taken to parse each source file. Without the verbose option, display messages for loading the source files, generating the documentation (one message per source file), and sorting.

`-version`   Include `@version` tags (omitted by default).

Examples

Each package name has a corresponding directory name. In the following examples, the source files are located at `/home/ws/src/java/awt/*java`. The destination directory is `/home/ws/html`.

One or More Packages

For package documentation, the source files (`*.java`) for that package must be located in a directory having the same name as the package. If a package name is made up of several identifiers (separated by dots), each identifier represents a different directory. Thus, all `java.awt` classes must reside in a directory named `java/awt/`.

First, change to the parent directory of the topmost package (or supply the `sourcepath` option with that directory). Then, run `javadoc`, supplying one or more fully specified package names. For example, the following command documents the source files in the `java.awt` package located at `/home/ws/src/java/awt/*.java` and its subpackage `java.awt.event`.

```
castle% cd /home/ws/src/
castle% javadoc -d /home/ws/html java.awt java.awt.event
```

This command generates HTML-formatted documentation for the public classes in packages `java.awt` and `java.awt.event` and puts them in the specified destination directory (`/home/ws/html`).

One or More Classes

To document one or more classes, change to the directory containing the class (or supply the `sourcepath` option with that directory). Then, run `javadoc`, supplying one or more class names, as shown below.

```
castle% cd /home/ws/src/java/awt
castle% javadoc -d /home/ws/html Button.java Canvas.java
```

This command generates HTML-formatted documentation for the two classes and puts them in the specified destination directory (`/home/ws/html`).

Environment Variables

CLASSPATH   Provide the system with a path to user-defined classes. Separate
directories with colons; for example,
`.:/home/avh/classes:/usr/local/java/classes`

Files

AllNames.html

An index of members.

tree.html   A hierarchy of classes.

Attributes

See attributes(5) for descriptions of the following attributes:

Attribute Type	Attribute Value
Availability	SUNWjvdev

See Also

java(1), javac(1), javadoc(1), javap(1), jdb(1), jre(1), attributes(5)

The Java Language Specification
http://java.sun.com/docs/books/jls/index.html

For information on related topics, use the search link
http://java.sun.com/

javah — C Header and Stub File Generator

Synopsis

```
/usr/java/bin/javah [-classpath path][-d directory][-help] [-jni]
    [-o outputfile][-stubs][-td directory] [-trace][-v][-version]
    classname. . .
/usr/java/bin/javah_g [-classpath path][-d directory][-help][-jni]
    [-o outputfile] [-stubs][-td directory] [-trace][-v][-version]
    classname. . .
```

Description

The javah command generates the C header and source files that are needed
to implement native methods. The generated header and source files are used
by C programs to reference instance variables of an object from native source

code. The .h file contains a structure definition whose layout parallels that of the corresponding class. The fields in the structure correspond to instance variables in the class.

The name of the header file and the structure declared within it are derived from the name of the class. If the class passed to javah is inside a package, the package name is prepended to both the header file name and the structure name. Underscores (_) are used as name delimiters.

By default, javah creates a header file for each class listed on the command line and puts the files in the current directory. Use the -stubs option to create source files. Use the -o option to concatenate the results for all listed classes into a single file.

The new native method interface, Java Native Interface (JNI), does not require header information or stub files. You can still use the javah command with the -jni option to generate native method function prototypes needed for JNI-style native methods. The result is placed in the .h file.

The javah_g version is a nonoptimized version of javah suitable for use with debuggers like jdb.

Options

-classpath *path*

> Specify the path javah uses to look up classes. Override the default of the CLASSPATH environment variable if it is set. Directories are separated by colons. Thus, the general format for path is:
>
> .:*your-path*
>
> For example:
>
> .:/home/avh/classes:/usr/local/java/classes

-d *directory*

> Set the directory where javah saves the header files or the stub files.

-help   Print help message.

-jni   Create an output file containing JNI-style native method function prototypes.

-o *outputfile*

> Concatenate the resulting header or source files for all the classes listed on the command line into *outputfile*.

-stubs   Generate C declarations from the Java object file.

-td *directory*

> Override the default directory where javah stores temporary files. The default is /tmp.

-trace   Add tracing information to the stubs file.

-v   Print a message to standard output concerning the status of the
               generated files.

-version   Print build version.

Environment Variables

CLASSPATH   Provide the system with a path to user-defined classes. Separate
               directories with colons; for example,
               .:/home/avh/classes:/usr/local/java/classes

Attributes

See attributes(5) for descriptions of the following attributes:

Attribute Type	Attribute Value
Availability	SUNWjvdev

See Also

java(1), javac(1), javadoc(1), javap(1), jdb(1), attributes(5)

javald — Create Java Application Wrappers

Synopsis

/usr/java/bin/javald [-C path] [-H dir] [-j option-list] [-o outfile] [-R
  path] classname

Description

The javald command creates a convenient wrapper that captures the
necessary environment needed to run a Java application specified by
classname. This wrapper sets the necessary environment variables needed by
java(1) before it executes the class specified by classname.

If you specify the -o option, the resulting executable wrapper is outfile. If
you do not specify the -o option, the default used is the name of the class.

If you specify the -H option, the wrapper sets JAVA_HOME to the path
specified by the option. If you do not specify the -H option, the wrapper tries to
use the JAVA_HOME environment if set; otherwise, it assumes a default
JAVA_HOME of /usr/java.

Paths specified as arguments to the -C and -R options of the javald
command are treated differently.

The path arguments, which may include shell variables, are subject to
deferred evaluation. They are evaluated when the wrapper is executed.

Relative path names are treated as path names relative to the directory where the wrapper is installed, not the current working directory.

This behavior is designed to support applications that consist of several classes in a directory hierarchy instead of a single executable. Using relative path names enables you to more easily move this directory hierarchy (thus the application) to different file systems.

The default CLASSPATH created by the wrapper if no -C options are used is equivalent to specifying -C.

The default interpreter executed by the wrapper is $JAVA_HOME/bin/java.

Options

-C *path*	Add *path*, to the runtime CLASSPATH to specify where java(1) searches for Java classes.
	You can repeat the -C option.
	castle% **javald -C /usr/class -C /optjava...**
-H *dir*	Set JAVA_HOME to *dir*.
-j *option-list*	
	Specify the list of options to be passed to the invocation of java(1). If you specify multiple options, you must quote them to ensure that they are passed into the resulting wrapper.
-o *outfile*	Put the wrapper in *outfile*.
R *path*	Add *path* to the runtime LD_LIBRARY_PATH to specify where java(1) searches for native methods.

Examples

In the following example, a wrapper app1 is created in /opt/acme/bin.

castle% **javald -o /opt/acme/bin/app1 -C /opt/acme/classes acmeApp**

It contains the following environment variables.

```
JAVA_HOME=${JAVA_HOME:-/usr/java}
CLASSPATH=/opt/acme/classes
```

When you run app1, java(1) tries to invoke the main() method of the acmeApp class. The java(1) interpreter searches for acmeApp in /opt/acme/classes, then in the default system class directory, ${JAVA_HOME}/lib/classes.zip.

The following command creates a script called myapp.

castle% **javald -o myapp -j '-noverify -ms8m' myapp**

It contains the following invocation of the java(1) interpreter.

```
exec {JAVA_HOME}/bin/java -noverify -ms8m myapp
```

Environment Variables

JAVA_HOME   Specify the java (1) runtime.

Files

/usr/java/lib/classes.zip

> Archive of Java runtime classes. Note that you do not need to unzip the archive.

Attributes

See attributes(5) for descriptions of the following attributes:

Attribute Type	Attribute Value
Availability	SUNWjvrt

See Also

java(1)
> The Java Tutorial at
http://java.sun.com:80/docs/books/tutorial/index.html
> For information on related topics, use the search link at
http://java.sun.com/

javap — Java Class File Disassembler

Synopsis

/usr/java/bin/javap [-b] [-c] [-classpath path] [-h] [-Jflag] [-l] [-package]
[-private] [-protected] [-public] [-s] [-verbose] [-verify] [-version]
class...

Description

Use the javap command to disassemble a Java class file. The options determine the output. If you specify no options, javap displays the public fields and methods of the classes passed to it. The javap command displays its output to standard output. For example, compile the following class declaration:

```
import java.awt.*;
import java.applet.*;

public class DocFooter extends Applet {
String date;
String email;

public void init() {
    resize(500,100);

date = getParameter("LAST_UPDATED");
    email = getParameter("EMAIL");
}

    public void paint(Graphics g) {
    g.drawString(date + " by ",100, 15);
    g.drawString(email,290,15);
}
}
```

The output from `javap DocFooter` yields:

```
Compiled from DocFooter.java
public class DocFooter extends java.applet.Applet {
    java.lang.String date;
    java.lang.String email;
    public void init();
    public void paint(java.awt.Graphics);
    public DocFooter();
}
```

Options

-b   Ensure backward compatibility with `javap` in JDK 1.1.

-c   Print disassembled code, that is, the instructions that make up the Java bytecodes, for each of the methods in the class.

-classpath *path*

           Specify the path `javap` uses to look up classes. Override the default or the CLASSPATH environment variable if it is set. Separate directories with colons. Thus, the general format for path is:

           `.:your-path`

           For example:

           `.:/home/avh/classes:/usr/local/java/classes`

-h   Generate code that can be put in a C header file.

-J *flag*   Pass *flag* directly to runtime system.

-l   Display line and local variable tables.

-package	Show only package, protected, and public classes and members (the default).
-private	Show all classes and members.
-protected	Show only protected and public classes and members.
-public	Show only public classes and members.
-s	Display internal type signatures.
-verbose	Print stack size, number of locals, and arguments for methods.
-verify	Run the verifier.
-version	Print the javap version string.

Environment Variables

CLASSPATH	Provide the system with a path to user-defined classes. Separate directories with colons. For example, .:/home/avh/classes:/usr/local/java/classes

Attributes

See attributes(5) for descriptions of the following attributes:

Attribute Type	Attribute Value
Availability	SUNWjvdev

See Also

java(1), javac(1), javadoc(1), javah(1), jdb(1), attributes(5)

---

jdb — Java Debugger

Synopsis

/usr/java/bin/jdb [-host *hostname*] [-password *password*] [*classname*]

Description

The Java debugger, jdb, is a dbx-like command-line debugger for Java classes. It uses the Java debugger API to provide inspection and debugging of a local or remote Java interpreter.

Starting a jdb Session

Like dbx, jdb can be used for debugging in two ways. The most frequently used way is to use jdb to start java(1) with the class to be debugged. You do this by substituting the command jdb for java(1) in the command line. For example, to start appletviewer(1) under jdb, use one of the following commands.

```
castle% jdb sun.applet.AppletViewer
castle% jdb -classpath INSTALL_DIR/classes sun.applet.AppletViewer
```

When started this way, jdb invokes a second Java interpreter with any specified parameters, loads the specified class, and stops the interpreter before executing the first instruction of that class.

The second way to use jdb is by attaching it to a running Java interpreter session. For security reasons, you can debug Java interpreters only if you start them with the -debug option. When you start with the -debug option, the Java interpreter displays a password for the Java debugger to use.

To attach jdb to a running Java interpreter (once the session password is known), invoke it as follows.

```
castle% jdb -host hostname -password password
```

Basic jdb Commands

The following list describes the basic jdb commands. The Java debugger supports other commands that you can list with the help command.

Note — To browse local (stack) variables, you must compile the class with the -g option.

---

dump	Dump an object's instance variables. Specify objects by their object ID (a hexadecimal integer). Specify classes either by their object ID or by name. If a class is already loaded, you can use a substring, such as Thread for java.lang.Thread. If a class isn't loaded, you must specify its full name, and the class is loaded as a side effect. This command is needed to set breakpoints in referenced classes before an applet runs.
	The dump command supports Java expressions such as dump 0x12345678.myCache[3].foo. Method invocation is not currently supported.
help, or ?	Display the list of recognized commands with a brief description (the most important jdb command).
print	Browse Java objects. Call the toString() method of the object so it is formatted differently depending on its class.
	You specify classes either by their object ID or by name. If a class is already loaded, you can use a substring, such as Thread for java.lang.Thread.
	The print subcommand supports Java expressions, such as print MyClass.clsVar. Method invocation is not currently supported.

`threads`	List the current threads, organized by thread group. Threads are referenced by their object ID, or if they are in the current thread group, with the form t@*index*, such as t@3.
`where`	With no arguments, dump the stack of the current thread (which is set with the `thread` command). With the `all` subcommand, dump the stack of all threads in the current thread group. With the `threadid` subcommand, dump the stack of the specified thread. The `threadid` subcommand takes the form of t@*index*, such as t@3. If a requested thread is suspended (either because it's at a breakpoint or with the `suspend` command), you can browse local (stack) and instance variables with the `print` and `dump` commands. Use the `up` and `down` commands to choose which stack frame is current.

Breakpoint Commands

Set breakpoints in `jdb` in classes as follows:

`clear at class:line`

> Remove breakpoints, using a syntax similar to `stop`.

`cont`	Continue execution.
`step`	Execute single step lines.

`stop at class:line`

> Specify the source file line number or the name of the method (the breakpoint is then set at the first instruction of that method). For example, `stop at MyClass:45`

Exception Commands

When an exception occurs for which there is no `catch` statement anywhere up a Java program's stack, the Java runtime normally dumps an exception trace and exits. When running under `jdb`, however, that exception is treated as a nonrecoverable breakpoint and `jdb` stops at the offending instruction. If that class was compiled with the `-g` option, you can print instance and local variables to determine the cause of the exception.

`catch`	Break for specific exception. You can catch specific exceptions with the `catch` command; for example,
	`catch FileNotFoundException`
	or
	`catch mypackage.BigTroubleException`
	
	The Java debugging facility keeps a list of these exceptions and, when one is thrown, treats it as if a breakpoint is set on the instruction that caused the exception.

`ignore`	Remove exception classes from this list. Note that only the debugger ignores specific exceptions. The Java interpreter does not.

Options

When jdb is used in place of the Java interpreter on the command line, jdb accepts the same options as the java(1) command.

When jdb is used to attach to a running Java interpreter session, jdb accepts the following options.

-host *hostname*

> Set the name of the host machine on which the interpreter session is to attach when running.

-password *password*

> Log in to the active interpreter session. This is the password printed by the Java interpreter when invoked with the -debug option.

Environment Variables

CLASSPATH Provide the system a path to user-defined classes. Separate directories with colons; for example,

.:/home/avh/classes:/usr/local/java/classes

Attributes

See attributes(5) for descriptions of the following attributes:

Attribute Type	Attribute Value
Availability	SUNWjvdev

See Also

java(1), javac(1), javadoc(1), javah(1), javap(1), http://java.sun.com/

jobs, fg, bg, stop, notify — Control Process Execution

Synopsis

jsh
```
jobs [-p | -l] [%job-id ...]
jobs -x command [arguments]
fg [%job-id ...]
bg [%job-id ...]
stop %job-id ...
stop pid ...
```

csh
```
jobs[-l]
fg [%job-id]
bg [%job-id] ...
notify [%job-id] ...
stop %job-id ...
stop pid ...
```

ksh
```
jobs [-lnp] [%job-id ...]
fg [%job-id ...]
bg [%job-id ...]
stop %job-id ...
stop pid ...
```

Description

Job control enables you to move currently executing commands into the foreground or background and to stop, suspend, or restart them as needed. There is always one job in the foreground, which is the job that accepts your keyboard input. The foreground job may be a shell or another command such as an editor that accepts keyboard input.

When you execute a command line or start a job in the foreground, input to the terminal window is blocked and you cannot enter additional commands until that job completes. You can use the job control commands to push that job into the background to regain control of your terminal window. Similarly, you can bring a background job back to the foreground so that you can control it or enter data from the terminal window. Job control enables you to perform these actions within the current layer or window.

Each command or pipeline that you enter at a terminal window is assigned a positive numeric *job-id*. The shell keeps track of current and previous jobs. The current job is the most recent job to be started or restarted. The previous job is the first noncurrent job.

All jobs exist in one of the following states.

- A *foreground* job has read and write access to the controlling terminal.

- A *background* job is denied read access and has conditional write access to the *controlling* terminal (see stty(1)).

- A stopped job is a job that has been placed in a suspended state, usually as a result of a SIGTSTP signal (see signal(5)).

The Korn and C shells and the jsh job control shell of the Bourne shell all support job control.

Output

For all of the shells, if you specify no options, the output is a series of lines of the following form.
```
[%d] %c %s %s\n, job-number, current, state, command
```

The fields are described below.

job-number   A number used to identify the process group to the wait, fg, bg, and kill commands. With these commands, you can identify the job by prefixing the job number with %.

current   The + character identifies the job that would be used as a default for the fg or bg commands; you can also specify this job with *job-id* %+ or %% . The - character identifies the job that would become the default if the current default job were to exit; you can also specify this job with *job-id* %-. For other jobs, this field is a space character. You can identify one job with + and one job with -. If there is any suspended job, then the current job is a suspended job. If there are at least two suspended jobs, then the previous job is also a suspended job.

state   One of the following strings (in the POSIX locale):

Running   The job has not been suspended by a signal and has not exited.

Done   The job completed and returned exit status 0.

Done(*code*)   The job completed normally and it exited with the specified non-zero exit status, *code*, expressed as a decimal number.

Stopped
Stopped (SIGTSTP)

    The job was suspended by the SIGTSTP signal.

Stopped (SIGSTOP)

    The job was suspended by the SIGSTOP signal.

Stopped (SIGTTIN)

    The job was suspended by the SIGTTIN signal.

Stopped (SIGTTOU)

    The job was suspended by the SIGTTOU signal.

The implementation may substitute the string Suspended in place of Stopped. If the job was terminated by a signal, the format of state is unspecified, but it is visibly distinct from all of the other state formats shown here and indicates the name or description of the signal that terminated the job.

command   The associated command that was given to the shell.

If you specify the -l option, a field containing the process group ID is inserted before the state field. Also, more processes in a process group may be output on separate lines, using only the process ID and command fields.

For jsh and ksh, if you specify the -p option, the output consists of one line for each process ID.

The following jsh example lists two jobs.

```
$ jobs
[1]  - Running                         spider
[2]  + Done(0)                         find . -name core -print
$
```

Bourne Job Control Shell

jsh is the Bourne job control shell. jsh provides all of the functionality of sh in addition to the built-in job control commands. Typically, you use jsh only as an interactive shell; noninteractive shells typically do not benefit from the added functionality of job control.

The jsh built-in jobs commands reports all jobs that are stopped or executing in the background. If you omit %*job-id*, the jobs command reports all jobs that are stopped or running in the background. The following options modify or enhance the output of jobs.

-l	Report the process group ID and working directory of the jobs.
-p	Report only the process group ID of the jobs.
-x	Replace any *job-id* found in command or arguments with the corresponding process group ID and then execute *command*, passing it arguments.

The acceptable syntax for a job identifier is of the form:

%*job-id*

You can specify *job-id* in any of the following formats:

% or +	The current job.
-	The previous job.
?*string*	The job for which the command line uniquely contains *string*.
n	Job number *n*, where *n* is a job number
pref	A unique prefix of the command name (for example, if the command ls -l *name* were running in the background, it could be referred to as %ls); *pref* cannot contain blanks unless you quote it.

The fg (foreground) command resumes the execution of a stopped job in the foreground and moves an executing background job into the foreground. If you omit %*job-id*, the current job is assumed.

The bg (background) command resumes the execution of a stopped job in the background. If you omit %*job-id*, the current job is assumed.

The stop command stops the execution of a background job(s) by using its *job-id*, or of any process by using its *pid*; see ps(1).

C Shell

The C shell built-in jobs command without an argument lists the active jobs under job control.

The following option modifies/enhances the output of jobs.

-1   List process IDs, in addition to the normal information.

The shell associates a numbered *job-id* with each command sequence to keep track of those commands that are running in the background or have been stopped with TSTP signals (typically Control-Z). When you start a command or command sequence (semicolon-separated list) in the background by using the & metacharacter at the end of the command line, the shell displays a line with the job number in brackets and a list of associated process numbers:

[1] 567

Note — To see the current list of jobs, use the jobs built-in command. The job most recently stopped (or put into the background if none are stopped) is referred to as the current job and is indicated with a plus sign (+). The previous job is indicated with a dash (-); when the current job is terminated or moved to the foreground, this job takes its place (becomes the new current job).

To manipulate jobs, use the bg, fg, kill, stop, and % built-in commands. A reference to a job begins with a percent sign (%). By itself, the percent sign refers to the current job.

% %+ %%   The current job.

%-   The previous job.

%*j*   Refer to job *j* as in: kill -9 %*j*. *j* can be a job number or a string that uniquely specifies the command line that started it; for example, fg %vi might bring a stopped vi job to the foreground.

%?*string*   Specify the command-line job that uniquely contains *string*.

A job running in the background stops when it tries to read from the terminal. Background jobs can normally produce output, but you can suppress this feature with the stty tostop command.

The following list describes the additional C shell built-in job control commands.

fg   Bring the current or specified *job-id* into the foreground.

bg   Run the current or specified jobs in the background.

stop   Stop the execution of a background job(s) by using its *job-id*, or of any process by using its *pid*; see ps(1).

notify   Notify you asynchronously when the status of the current job or specified jobs changes.

Korn Shell

The Korn shell built-in jobs command displays the status of the jobs that were started in the current shell environment. When jobs reports the termination status of a job, the shell removes its process ID from the list of those known in the current shell execution environment.

The following options modify or enhance the output of jobs.

-1   (The letter ell.) Provide more information about each job listed. This information includes the job number, current job, process group ID, state, and the command that formed the job.

-n   Display only jobs that have stopped or exited since you were last notified.

-p   Display only the process IDs for the process group leaders of the selected jobs.

By default, jobs displays the status of all the stopped jobs, running background jobs, and any job whose status has changed and has not been reported by the shell.

If the monitor option of the set command is turned on, an interactive shell associates a job with each pipeline. It keeps a table of current jobs, printed by the jobs command, and assigns them small integer numbers. When a job is started asynchronously with &, the shell prints a line that looks like [1] 567, indicating that the job that was started asynchronously was job number 1 and has one (top-level) process, whose process ID is 567.

If you are running a job and want to do something else, you can use the ^Z (Control-Z) key combination to send a STOP signal to the current job. The shell normally indicates that the job has been stopped and displays another prompt. You can then manipulate the state of this job, putting it in the background with the bg command, or you can run some other commands and then eventually bring the job back into the foreground with the fg command. A ^Z takes effect immediately and is like an interrupt in that pending output and unread input are discarded.

You can refer to jobs in the shell by their process ID or by any of the following.

%*number*   The job with the given number.

%*string*   Any job whose command line begins with *string*. This syntax works only in the interactive mode when the history file is active.

%?*string*   Any job whose command line contains *string*. This syntax works only in the interactive mode when the history file is active.

%%   Current job.

%+   Equivalent to %%.

%-   Previous job.

The shell learns immediately whenever a process changes state. It normally informs you whenever a job becomes blocked so that no further progress is possible, but only just before it displays a prompt. The warning is done in this way so that it does not otherwise disturb your work. When the monitor mode is on, each background job that completes triggers any trap set for CHLD. When you try to leave the shell while jobs are running or stopped, you are warned

You have stopped (running) jobs. You can use the jobs command to see what the stopped jobs are. If you do this or immediately try to exit again, the shell does not warn you a second time, and the stopped jobs are terminated.

The following list describes the additional Korn shell job control commands.

fg
Move a background job from the current environment into the foreground. Using fg to place a job in the foreground removes its process ID from the list of those known in the current shell execution environment. The fg command is available only on systems that support job control. If you do not specify a *job-id*, the current job is brought into the foreground.

bg
Resume suspended jobs from the current environment by running them as background jobs. If the job specified by *job-id* is already a running background job, bg has no effect and exits successfully. Using bg to place a job into the background makes its process ID known in the current shell execution environment as if it had been started as an asynchronous list. The bg command is available only on systems that support job control. If you do not specify *job-id*, the current job is placed in the background.

stop
Stop the execution of a background job(s) by using its *job-id*, or of any process by using its *pid*; see ps(1).

Environment Variables

See environ(5) for descriptions of the following environment variables that affect the execution of jobs, fg, and bg: LC_CTYPE, LC_MESSAGES, and NLSPATH.

Exit Status

0
Successful completion.

>0
An error occurred.

Attributes

See attributes(5) for descriptions of the following attributes:

Attribute Type	Attribute Value
Availability	SUNWcsu

See Also

csh(1), kill(1), ksh(1), ps(1), sh(1), shell_builtins(1), stop(1), stty(1), wait(1), attributes(5), environ(5), signal(5)

join — Relational Database Operator

Synopsis

```
/usr/bin/join [-a filenumber | -v filenumber] [-1 fieldnumber]
   [-2 fieldnumber] [-o list] [-e string][-t char] file1 file2
/usr/bin/join [-a filenumber] [-j fieldnumber][-j1 fieldnumber]
   [-j2 fieldnumber][-o list] [-e string] [-t char] file1 file2
```

Description

The `join` command forms a join of the two relations specified by the lines of *file1* and *file2* and displays the result on standard output.

The output has one line for each pair of lines in *file1* and *file2* that have identical join fields. The output line normally consists of the common field, then the rest of the line from *file1*, then the rest of the line from *file2*. You can change this format with the `-o` option. Use the `-a` option to add unmatched lines to the output. Use the `-v` option to output only unmatched lines.

The default input field separators are blank, Tab, or newline. Multiple separators count as one field separator, and leading separators are ignored. The default output field separator is a blank.

If the input files are not in the appropriate collating sequence, the results are unspecified.

Note — With default field separation, the collating sequence is that of `sort -b`; with `-t`, the sequence is that of a plain `sort`.

The conventions of the `join`, `sort`, `comm`, `uniq`, and `awk` commands are wildly incongruous.

Options

Some of the options below use the argument *filenumber*. This argument should be a 1 or a 2 referring to either *file1* or *file2*, respectively.

`-a` *filenumber*

In addition to the normal output, produce a line for each unpairable line in file *filenumber*, where *filenumber* is 1 or 2. If you specify both `-a 1` and `-a 2`, output all unpairable lines.

`-e` *string*   Replace empty output fields with *string*.

`-j` *fieldnumber*

Equivalent to `-1` *fieldnumber* `-2` *fieldnumber*.

`-j1` *fieldnumber*

Equivalent to `-1` *fieldnumber*.

-j2 *fieldnumber*

>   Equivalent to -2 *fieldnumber*. Fields are numbered starting
>   with 1.

-o *list*   Include the fields specified in *list* in each output line Fields
>   selected by *list* that do not appear in the input are treated as
>   empty output fields. (See the -e option.) Each element has either
>   the form *filenumber.fieldnumber* or 0, which represents the join
>   field. Do not print the common field unless specifically requested.

-t *char*   Use character *char* as a separator. Every appearance of *char* in a
>   line is significant. Use the character *char* as the field separator for
>   both input and output. When you specify this option, the collating
>   term should be the same as sort without the -b option.

-v *filenumber*

>   Instead of the default output, produce a line only for each
>   unpairable line in *filenumber*, where *filenumber* is 1 or 2. If you
>   specify both -v 1 and -v 2, output all unpairable lines.

-1 *fieldnumber*

>   Join on the *fieldnumber*-th field of *file1*. Fields are decimal
>   integers starting with 1.

-2 *fieldnumber*

>   Join on the *fieldnumber*-th field of *file2*. Fields are decimal
>   integers starting with 1.

Operands

file1   A path name of a file to be joined. If either of the *file1* or *file2*
file2   operands is -, use the standard input in its place.

   file1 and *file2* must be sorted in increasing collating sequence as
determined by LC_COLLATE on the fields on which they are to be joined,
normally, the first in each line (see sort(1)).

Usage

See largefile(5) for the description of the behavior of join when
encountering files greater than or equal to 2 Gbytes (2**31 bytes).

Examples

The following command line joins the password file and the group file,
matching on the numeric group ID and outputing the login name, the group
name, and the login directory. It is assumed that the files have been sorted in
ASCII collating sequence on the group ID fields.

```
castle% join -j1 4 -j2 3 -o 1.1 2.1 1.6 -t: /etc/passwd /etc/group
root:other:/
daemon:other:/
```

```
bin:bin:/usr/bin
sys:sys:/
adm:adm:/var/adm
lp:lp:/usr/spool/lp
nuucp:nuucp:/var/spool/uucppublic
```

The `-o 0` field essentially selects the union of the join fields. For example, given file `phone`:

```
!Name         Phone Number
Don           +1 123-456-7890
Hal           +1 234-567-8901
Yasushi       +2 345-678-9012
```

and file `fax`:

```
!Name         Fax Number
Don           +1 123-456-7899
Keith         +1 456-789-0122
Yasushi       +2 345-678-9011
```

(where the large expanses of white space are meant to each represent a single Tab character), the command

example% **join -t "<tab>" a 1 -a 2 -e '(unknown)' o 0,1.2,2.2 phone ax**

produces

```
!Name         Phone Number           Fax Number
Don           +1 123-456-7890        +1 123-456-7899
Hal           +1 234-567-8901        (unknown)
Keith         (unknown)              +1 456-789-0122
Yasushi       +2 345-678-9012        +2 345-678-9011
```

Environment Variables

See `environ(5)` for descriptions of the following environment variables that affect the execution of `join`: LC_CTYPE, LC_MESSAGES, LC_COLLATE, and NLSPATH.

Exit Status

0	All input files were output successfully.
>0	An error occurred.

Attributes

See `attributes`(5) for descriptions of the following attributes:

Attribute Type	Attribute Value
Availability	SUNWcsu
CSI	Enabled

See Also

`awk(1)`, `comm(1)`, `sort(1)`, `uniq(1)`, `attributes(5)`, `environ(5)`, `largefile(5)`

---

jre — Java Runtime Interpreter

Synopsis

```
/usr/java/bin/jre [-classpath path(s)][-cp path(s)]
   [-DpropertyName=newValue][-help] [-msx][-mxx][-noasyncgc]
   [-noclassgc][-nojit][-noverify][-ossx][-ssx][-v | -verbose]
   [-verbosegc][-verify][-verifyremote] classname args
```

Description

The `jre` command executes Java class files. The `classname` argument is the name of the class to be executed. Any arguments to be passed to the class must be placed after the `classname` on the command line.

Options

`-classpath path(s)`

> Specify the path or paths that `jre` uses to look up classes. Override the default or the CLASSPATH environment variable if it is set. If you specify more than one path, separate the paths with colons. Each path should end with the directory containing the class files to be executed. However, if a file to be executed is a `zip` or `jar`(1) file, the path to that file must end with the file name. Following is an example of an argument for `-classpath` that specifies three paths consisting of the current directory and two additional paths.
>
> `.:/home/xyz/classes:/usr/local/java/classes/MyClasses.jar`

-cp *path*(s) Prepend the specified path or paths to the base classpath or path given by the CLASSPATH environment variable. If you specify more than one path, separate them with colons. Each path should end with the directory containing the class file(s) to be executed. However, if a file to be executed is a zip or jar file, the path to that file must end with the file name. Following is an example of an argument for -cp that specifies three paths consisting of the current directory and two additional paths.

```
.:/home/xyz/classes:/usr/local/java/classes/MyClasses.
jar
```

-D*propertyName=newValue*

Define a property value. *propertyName* is the name of the property whose value you want to change, and *newValue* is the value to change it to. For example, the following command line sets the value of the property awt.button.color to green.

```
castle% jre -Dawt.button.color=green ...
```

jre accepts any number of -D options on the command line.

-help Print a usage message.

-ms*x* Set the startup size of the memory allocation pool (the garbage collection heap) to *x*. The default is 16 megabytes of memory. The *x* value must be greater than or equal to 1,000 bytes.

By default, measure *x* in bytes. You can specify *x* in either kilobytes or megabytes by appending k for kilobytes or m for megabytes.

-mx*x* Set the maximum size of the memory allocation pool (the garbage collection heap) to *x*. The default is 1 megabyte of memory. The *x* value must be greater than 1,000 bytes.

By default, measure *x* in bytes. You can specify *x* in either kilobytes or megabytes by appending k for kilobytes or m for megabytes.

-noasyncgc Turn off asynchronous garbage collection. When activated, no garbage collection takes place unless it is explicitly called or the program runs out of memory. Normally, garbage collection runs as an asynchronous thread in parallel with other threads.

-noclassgc Turn off garbage collection of Java classes. By default, the Java interpreter reclaims space for unused Java classes during garbage collection.

-nojit Ignore any JIT compiler and invoke the default Java interpreter.

-noverify Turn verification off.

-oss*x*   Set the maximum stack size that can be used by Java code in a thread to *x*. Each Java thread has two stacks: one for Java code and one for C code. Every thread that is spawned during the execution of the program passed to jre has *x* as its Java stack size. The default units for *x* are bytes. The value of *x* must be greater than or equal to 1,000 bytes.

You can modify the meaning of *x* by appending either the letter k for kilobytes or the letter m for megabytes. The default stack size is 400 kilobytes (-oss400k).

-ss*x*   Set the maximum stack size that can be used by C code in a thread to *x*. Each Java thread has two stacks: one for Java code and one for C code. Every thread that is spawned during the execution of the program passed to jre has *x* as its C stack size. The default units for *x* are bytes. The value of *x* must be greater than or equal to 1,000 bytes.

You can modify the meaning of *x* by appending either the letter k for kilobytes or the letter m for megabytes. The default stack size is 128 kilobytes (-ss128k).

-v | -verbose

Print a message to standard output each time a class file is loaded.

-verbosegc   Print garbage collector messages whenever garbage collection frees memory.

-verify   Perform byte code verification on the class file. Note, however, that jre -verify does not perform a full verification in all situations. Any code path that is not actually executed by the interpreter is not verified and therefore cannot be relied upon to certify class files unless all code paths in the class file are actually run.

-verifyremote

Run the verifier on all code that is loaded into the system with a class loader. This option is the default for the interpreter.

Environment Variables

CLASSPATH   Specify the path to the class file or files that you want to execute. Specify CLASSPATH as a colon-separated list of directories that contain the class files to be executed. For example:
.:/home/xyz/classes

If the file to be executed is a zip file or a jar file, end the path with the file name. For example:
.:/usr/local/java/classes/MyClasses.jar

Attributes

See attributes(5) for descriptions of the following attributes:

Attribute Type	Attribute Value
Availability	SUNWjvrt

See Also

jar(1), attributes(5)

jsh — Standard and Job Control Shell and Command Interpreter

Synopsis

/usr/bin/jsh [-acefhiknprstuvx] [*argument*...]

Description

See jobs(1) and sh(1).

K

---

kbd — Keyboard Command

Synopsis
```
/usr/bin/kbd [-r] [-t] [-c on | off] [-a enable | disable]
  [-d keyboard device]
/usr/bin/kbd -i [-d keyboard device]
```

Description
Use the kbd command to manipulate the state of the keyboard, display the keyboard type, or change the default keyboard abort sequence effect. The default keyboard device being set is /dev/kbd.

The -i option reads and processes default values for the keyclick and keyboard abort settings from the keyboard default file, /etc/default/kbd, shown below.

```
castle% more /etc/default/kbd
#pragma ident   "@(#)kbd.dfl    1.2     96/06/07 SMI"
#
# Copyright 1996, Sun Microsystems, Inc.
# All Rights Reserved.
#
# /etc/default/kbd
#
# kbd default settings processed via kbd(1).
#
```

```
# KEYBOARD_ABORT affects the default behavior of the keyboard abort
# sequence, see kbd(1) for details.  The default value is "enable".
# The optional value is "disable".  Any other value is ignored.
#
# KEYCLICK affects the default keyclick behavior. Possible values are
# 'on' and 'off'.  Any other value is ignored. The default behavior is
# to leave the current keyclick setting unchanged.
#
# Uncomment the following lines to change the default values.
#
#KEYBOARD_ABORT=enable
#KEYCLICK=off
castle%
```

Only keyboards that support a clicker respond to the -c option. You can change the keyclick setting for a session with the -c option from the command line.

To turn clicking on by default, edit the /etc/default/kbd file, remove the comment (#) from the beginning of the KEYCLICK variable line, and change the default value to on, as shown below.

KEYCLICK=on

Then, run the command kbd -i to change the current setting. Valid settings for the KEYCLICK variable are the values on and off. Other values are ignored. If the variable is not specified in the default file, the setting is unchanged.

On most systems, the default effect of the keyboard abort sequence is to suspend the operating system and enter the debugger or the monitor. The abort sequence on most systems is L1-A or STOP-A on the keyboard and BREAK on the serial console input device.

> **Note —** Some systems have key switches with a secure position. On these systems, the key switch in the secure position overrides any software default set with the kbd command.
>
> There is no way to determine the state of the keyboard click setting when set from a command line.

Only superuser can use the -a option to change the keyboard abort sequence. Superuser can change the keyboard abort sequence from the command line.

To permanently change the software default effect of the keyboard abort sequence, as superuser, edit the /etc/default/kbd file, remove the comment (#) from the beginning of the KEYBOARD_ABORT line, and change the default value to disable, as shown below.

KEYBOARD_ABORT=disable

Then, run the command kbd -i to change the current setting. Valid settings for the KEYBOARD_ABORT variable are the values enable and disable. Other values are ignored. If the variable is not specified in the default file, the setting is unchanged.

Options

`-a enable/disable state`

Enable or disable the keyboard abort sequence effect. By default, a keyboard abort sequence (typically, Stop-A or L1-A on the keyboard and BREAK on the serial console device) suspends the operating system on most systems. This option can be used only by the superuser.

`enable`   Enable the default effect of the keyboard abort sequence, which is to suspend the operating system and enter the debugger or the monitor.

`disable`   Disable the default effect and ignore keyboard abort sequences.

`-c on/off state`

Turn the clicking of the keyboard on or off.

`on`   Enable clicking.

`off`   Disable clicking.

`-d keyboard device`

Specify the keyboard device being set. The default is `/dev/kbd`.

`-i`   Set keyboard defaults from the keyboard default file. This option is mutually exclusive with all other options except for the `-d` keyboard device option. This option instructs the keyboard command to read and process keyclick and keyboard abort default values from the `/etc/default/kbd` file. This option can be used only by the superuser.

`-r`   Reset the keyboard as if power-up.

`-t`   Return the type of the keyboard being used.

Examples

The following example displays the keyboard type.

```
castle% kbd -t
Type 4 Sun keyboard
castle%
```

The following example sets keyboard defaults as specified in the keyboard default file.

```
castle% kbd -i
castle%
```

The following example turns clicking on from the command line.

```
castle% kbd -c on
castle%
```

Files

/dev/kbd   Keyboard device file.

/etc/default/kbd

Keyboard default file containing software defaults for keyboard configurations.

/etc/rcS   Shell script containing commands to put the system in single-user mode.

Attributes

See attributes(5) for descriptions of the following attributes:

Attribute Type	Attribute Value
Architecture	SPARC
Availability	SUNWcsu

See Also

loadkeys(1), kadb(1M), keytables(4), attributes(5), kb(7M)

---

kdestroy — Destroy Kerberos Tickets

Synopsis

/usr/bin/kdestroy [-fnq]

Description

Kerberos is an authentication system that uses Data Encryption Standard (DES) to authenticate a user logging in to the system. Authentication is based on the capability of the sending system to use a common key to encrypt a ticket containing the current time that the receiving system can decrypt and check against its current time.

You destroy Kerberos tickets by using the kdestroy command. You should destroy Kerberos tickets when the session is over so that an unauthorized user cannot gain access to them.

kdestroy destroys the user's active Kerberos authorization tickets by writing zeros to the file that contains them. If the ticket file does not exist, kdestroy displays a message to that effect. After overwriting the file, kdestroy removes the file from the system. The command displays a message indicating the success or failure of the operation. If kdestroy is unable to destroy the ticket file, it warns you by making your terminal beep.

In addition to removing the ticket file, kdestroy also invalidates all Kerberos credentials for this user being held in the kernel for use with NFS requests. You can put the kdestroy command in your .logout file so that your tickets are destroyed automatically when you log out.

> **Note** — When you put kdestroy in your .logout file, NFS operations done on your behalf fail after you log out.

Bugs

Only the tickets in the user's current ticket file are destroyed. Separate ticket files are used to hold root instance and password changing tickets. These files should probably be destroyed too, or all of a user's tickets should be kept in a single ticket file.

Options

-f	Do not display the status message.
-n	Do not invalidate NFS credentials in the kernel. The credentials continue to be valid until their normal expiration time, although new ones cannot be obtained until you run kinit(1) again for this user.
-q	Do not make your terminal beep if kdestroy fails to destroy the tickets.

Examples

The following example shows how to destroy Kerberos tickets. After the tickets are destroyed, if the user tries to change to or list a Kerberos-protected directory, the ticket server denies access.

```
castle% kdestroy
Tickets destroyed
castle% ls /mntkrb
Can't get Kerberos key: No ticket file (tf_util)
NSF getattr failed for server castle: RPC: Authentication error
cannot access directory /mntkrb.
castle%
```

Files

The file specified by the KRBTKFILE environment variable if set; otherwise, /tmp/tktuid.

Attributes

See `attributes`(5) for descriptions of the following attributes:

Attribute Type	Attribute Value
Availability	SUNWcsu

See Also

`kerberos(1)`, `kinit(1)`, `klist(1)`, `attributes(5)`

Authors

Steve Miller, MIT Project Athena/Digital Equipment Corporation; Clifford
Neuman, MIT Project Athena; Bill Sommerfeld, MIT Project Athena

kerberos — Introduction to the Kerberos Security System

Description

The Kerberos system authenticates individual users in a network
environment. After authenticating yourself to Kerberos, you can use the
`kerberos` authentication option of network services such as NFS. In addition,
in some environments you can use network commands such as `rlogin(1)`,
`rcp(1)`, and `rsh(1)` without having to present passwords to remote hosts and
without needing entries in `.rhosts` files. See your system administrator for
more information about Kerberos support at your site.

Before you can use Kerberos, you must be registered as a user in the
Kerberos database. You can use the `kinit(1)` command to find out your status.
This command tries to log you in to the Kerberos system. `kinit` prompts you
for a user name and password. Enter your user name and password. If the
command lets you log in without giving you a message, you have already been
registered.

If you enter your user name and `kinit` responds with the following
message, you have not been registered as a Kerberos user. See your system
administrator.

```
Principal unknown (kerberos)
```

A Kerberos name contains three parts.

- The principal name, usually a user's or service's name.

- The instance, usually null for a user. Some users, such as root or admin, may have privileged instances. In the case of a service, the instance is the name of the system on which it runs; that is, there can be an NFS service running on the system ABC that is different from the NFS service running on the system XYZ.
- The realm. The realm corresponds to the Kerberos service providing authentication for the principal. For example, at MIT there is a Kerberos running at the Laboratory for Computer Science and one running at Project Athena.

When writing a Kerberos name, the principal name is separated from the instance (if not null) by a period, and the realm (if not the local realm) follows, preceded by an @ sign. The following are examples of valid Kerberos names.

```
billb
jis.admin
srz@lcs.mit.edu
treese.root@athena.mit.edu
```

When you authenticate yourself with Kerberos, typically with the kinit command, Kerberos gives you an initial Kerberos ticket, that is, an encrypted protocol message that provides authentication. Kerberos uses this ticket for network commands such as NFS, rlogin, and rcp. The ticket transactions are done transparently, so you do not have to worry about their management.

Note — Tickets expire. Privileged tickets, such as root instance tickets, expire in a few minutes, whereas tickets that carry more ordinary privileges may be good for several hours or a day, depending on the installation's policy. If your login session extends beyond the time limit, you have to use the kinit command to reauthenticate yourself to Kerberos to get new tickets.

If you use the kinit command to get your tickets, you can use the kdestroy(1) command to destroy your tickets before you end your login session. For more information about the kinit and kdestroy commands, see the kinit(1) and kdestroy(1) manual pages.

Currently, Kerberos supports NFS and other RPC network services using the AUTH_KERB authentication type. In some environments, the following network services are also supported: rlogin, rsh, and rcp. Other services, such as the pop mail system, are being worked on but are not yet available.

Bugs

Kerberos does not do authentication forwarding. In other words, if you use rlogin to log in to a remote host, you cannot use Kerberos services from that host until you authenticate yourself explicitly on that host. Although you may need to authenticate yourself on the remote host, be aware that when you do so, rlogin sends your password across the network in clear text.

See Also
kdestroy(1), kinit(1), klist(1), kerbd(1M), kerberos(3N), krb.conf(4)

Authors
Steve Miller, MIT Project Athena/Digital Equipment Corporation, and Clifford Neuman, MIT Project Athena.

The following people helped out on various aspects of the system:

Jeff Schiller designed and wrote the administration server and its user interface, kadmin. He also wrote the dbm version of the database management system.

Mark Colan developed the Kerberos versions of rlogin, rsh, and rcp, as well as contributing work on the servers.

John Ostlund developed the Kerberos versions of passwd and userreg.

Stan Zanarotti pioneered Kerberos in a foreign realm (LCS) and made many contributions based on that experience.

Many people contributed code and/or useful ideas. These include, Jim Aspnes, Bob Baldwin, John Barba, Richard Basch, Jim Bloom, Bill Bryant, Rob French, Dan Geer, David Jedlinsky, John Kohl, John Kubiatowicz, Bob McKie, Brian Murphy, Ken Raeburn, Chris Reed, Jon Rochlis, Mike Shanzer, Bill Sommerfeld, Jennifer Steiner, Win Treese, and Ted Ts'o.

Restrictions
COPYRIGHT 1985,1986 Massachusetts Institute of Technology.

keylogin — Decrypt and Store Secret Key with keyserv

Synopsis
/usr/bin/keylogin [-r]

Description
The keylogin command is part of the set of Secure RPC commands. Before you can use keylogin, a system administrator must use the newkey(1M), nisaddcred(1M), or nisclient(1M) commands to generate a public and secret key. Each user has a unique public key and secret key. The key can be found in the /etc/publickey file (see publickey(4)) or the NIS map publickey.byname or the NIS+ table cred.org_dir in the user's home domain. The sources and their lookup order are specified in the /etc/nsswitch.conf file (see nsswitch.conf(4)).

The keylogin command prompts for a password and uses it to decrypt the user's secret key. Once decrypted, the secret key is stored by the local key server process, keyserv(1M). This stored key is used when issuing requests to any secure RPC services, such as NFS or NIS+. You can delete the key stored by keyserv with the keylogout(1) command.

keylogin fails if it cannot get the caller's key or if the password is incorrect. For a new user or host, a new key can be added with newkey(1M), nisaddcred(1M), or nisclient(1M).

When multiple authentication mechanisms are configured for a system, each of the configured mechanism's secret keys is decrypted and stored by keyserv(1M). See nisauthconf(1M) for information on configuring multiple authentication mechanisms.

Options

-r   Update the /etc/.rootkey file. This file holds the unencrypted secret key of the superuser. Only the superuser can use this option. Processes running as superuser can issue authenticated requests without requiring that the administrator explicitly run keylogin as superuser at system startup time (see keyserv(1M)). The administrator should use the -r option when the host's entry in the publickey database has changed and the /etc/.rootkey file has become out of date with the actual key pair stored in the publickey database. The permissions on the /etc/.rootkey file are read and write by the superuser but by no other user on the system.

If multiple authentication mechanisms are configured for the system, the /etc/.rootkey file stores each of the secret keys.

Files

/etc/.rootkey

Superuser's secret key.

Attributes

See attributes(5) for descriptions of the following attributes:

Attribute Type	Attribute Value
Availability	SUNWcsu

See Also

chkey(1), keylogout(1), login(1), keyserv(1M), newkey(1M), nisaddcred(1M), nisauthconf(1M), nisclient(1M), nsswitch.conf(4), publickey(4), attributes(5)

keylogout — Delete Stored Secret Key with keyserv

Synopsis
```
/usr/bin/keylogout [-f]
```

Description
The keylogout command is part of the set of Secure RPC commands. keylogout deletes the key stored by the key server process keyserv(1M). Further access to the key is revoked; however, current session keys may remain valid until they expire or are refreshed.

When you delete the keys stored by keyserv, any background jobs or scheduled at(1) jobs that need secure RPC services fail. Because only one copy of the key is kept on a system, it is a bad idea to place a call to this command in your .logout file because it affects other sessions on the same machine.

Options
-f   Force keylogout to delete the secret key for superuser. By default, keylogout by superuser is disallowed because it would break all RPC services, such as NFS, that are started by superuser.

Attributes
See attributes(5) for descriptions of the following attributes:

Attribute Type	Attribute Value
Availability	SUNWcsu

See Also
at(1), chkey(1), login(1), keylogin(1), keyserv(1M), newkey(1M), publickey(4), attributes(5)

kill — Terminate or Signal Processes

Synopsis

```
/usr/bin/kill -s signal pid...
/usr/bin/kill -l [exit-status]
/usr/bin/kill [-signal] pid...
```

sh, csh, and ksh

```
kill [-sig] [pid] [%job-id]...
kill -l
```

Description

At times, you may need to eliminate a process entirely because you want to stop a large job before it completes or you detect a process that is hung or not working properly. To delete a process, use the `kill` command. The `kill` command sends a signal to the process or processes specified by each *pid* operand. Use the `ps(1)` command to find the process ID for the process you want to kill.

When you kill a process, you are actually telling the system to send the process a signal. There are 36 numbered signals and 4 unnumbered ones. Refer to the `signal(5)` manual page for the complete list.

You can specify a signal either by its number or by its logical signal name as listed in the `signal(5)` manual page, with the `SIG` part removed. The following example specifies signal 15 by number and then by name.

```
castle% kill -15 456
castle% kill -TERM 457
```

When you specify no signal, the `kill` command sends signal 15 (`SIGTERM`) by default. Signal 15 terminates the process if it can and is the preferred method for killing a process. Sometimes processes do not die when you use the `kill` command. The three most common cases are:

- The process is waiting for a device, such as a tape drive, to complete an operation before exiting.

- The process is waiting for resources that are unavailable because of NFS problems. For such processes, use signal 3 (`SIGQUIT`).

- The process is a zombie, as shown by the message `defunct` in the `ps` report. A zombie process is one that has had all its resources freed but has not received an acknowledgment from a parent process, receipt of which would ordinarily remove its entry from the process table. The next time a system is booted, zombie processes are cleared. Zombies do not affect system performance, and you do not need to remove them.

When a process does not die with a signal 15, use signal 9 (`SIGKILL`) to force the process to die.

```
castle% kill -9 458
castle% kill -KILL 459
```

Built-in Shell kill Commands

The Bourne job control shell jsh, the Korn shell, and the C shell have built-in versions of kill that provide the functionality of the kill command for processes identified with a *job-id*.

The csh kill built-in sends the TERM (terminate) signal, by default, or the signal specified, to the specified process ID, the job indicated, or the current job. Specify signals either by number or by name. There is no default. Typing kill does not send a signal to the current job. If the signal being sent is TERM (terminate) or HUP (hangup), then the job or process is sent a CONT (continue) signal as well.

The Korn shell kill sends either the TERM (terminate) signal or the specified signal to the specified jobs or processes. Specify signals either by number or by names (as given in signal(5) but stripped of the prefix SIG). If the signal being sent is TERM (terminate) or HUP (hangup), then the job or process is sent a CONT (continue) signal if it is stopped. The *job-id* argument can be the process ID of a process that is not a member of one of the active jobs.

Options

-l   (The letter ell.) Write all values of *signal* supported by the implementation for jsh, ksh, and csh. For /usr/bin/kill, write all values of *signal* if you do not specify the *exit-status* operand. If you specify an *exit-status* operand and it has a value of the ? shell special parameter and wait corresponding to a process that was terminated by a signal, write the *signal* corresponding to the signal that terminated the process. If you give an *exit-status* operand and it is the unsigned decimal integer value of a signal number, write the *signal* corresponding to that signal. Otherwise, the results are unspecified.

-s *signal*   Send the specified signal to the process or job ID, using either the signal number or the symbolic name as defined in the signal(5) manual page. Values of *signal* are case independent, without the SIG prefix. In addition, the symbolic name 0 is recognized, representing the signal value 0. Typical values used with the kill command are -15 (TERM)—the default—and 9 (KILL).

Operands

pid   One of the following:

- A decimal integer specifying a process or process group to be signaled. The process or processes selected by positive, negative, and 0 values of the *pid* operand are as described for the kill command. If you specify process number 0, then all processes in the process group are signaled. If the first *pid* operand is negative, precede it with -- to keep it from being interpreted as an option.

- A job control job ID that identifies a background process group to be signaled. The job control job ID notation is applicable only for invocations of kill in the current shell execution environment.

exit-status

         A decimal integer specifying a signal number or the exit status of a process terminated by a signal.

Note — The job control job ID type of *pid* is available only on systems supporting the job control option.

Usage

You can find process ID numbers by using ps(1).

The job control job ID notation is not required to work as expected when kill is operating in its own command execution environment. For example, in both of the following examples, kill operates in a different environment and does not share the shell's understanding of job numbers.

```
nohup kill %1 &
system( "kill %1" );
```

Output

When you do not specify the -l option, the standard output is not used. When you specify the -l option, the symbolic name of each signal is written in the following format:

```
%s%c, signal, separator
```

where the *signal* is in upper case, without the SIG prefix, and the *separator* is either a newline or a space. For the last signal written, *separator* is a newline.

When you specify both the -l option and *exit-status* operand for /usr/bin/kill, the symbolic name of the corresponding signal is written in the following format.

```
%s\n, signal
```

Examples

The following example uses the -l option to list the available signals for /usr/bin/kill.

```
castle% /usr/bin/kill -l
EXIT HUP INT QUIT ILL TRAP ABRT EMT FPE KILL BUS SEGV SYS PIPE ALRM TERM
    USR1 USR2 CLD PWR WINCH URG POLL STOP TSTP CONT TTIN TTOU VTALRM PROF
    XCPU XFSZ WAITING LWP FREEZE THAW CANCEL LOST RTMIN RTMIN+1 RTMIN+2
    RTMIN+3 RTMAX-3 RTMAX-2 RTMAX-1 RTMAX
castle%
```

If the sending process has permission to send the signal, any of the following commands sends the SIGKILL signal to an existing process whose process ID is 100 and to all existing processes whose process group ID is 165.

```
# kill -9 100 -165
# kill -s kill 100 -165
# kill -s KILL 100 -165
```

To avoid an ambiguity of an initial negative number argument specifying either a signal number or a process group, the signal number is always specified. Therefore, to send the default signal to a process group (for example, 123), an application should use a command similar to one of the following:

```
# kill -TERM -123
# kill -- -123
```

The following example uses the ps command to find the process ID for the game spider and then uses the kill command to kill it by process ID.

```
castle% ps -ef | grep spider
  winsor   544   419  0 15:45:42 pts/3     0:00 grep spider
  winsor   542   419  1 15:45:35 pts/3     0:00 spider.exe
castle% kill 542
[1]    Exit 1                spider
castle%
```

The following example uses the jobs command to find the job number for the game spider and then uses the kill command to kill it by job ID.

```
castle% jobs
[2]  + Running              spider
castle% kill %2
castle%
[2]    Exit 1                spider
castle%
```

Environment Variables

See environ(5) for descriptions of the following environment variables that affect the execution of kill: LC_CTYPE, LC_MESSAGES, and NLSPATH.

Exit Status

0	At least one matching process was found for each `pid` operand, and the specified signal was successfully processed for at least one matching process.
>0	An error occurred.

Attributes

See `attributes`(5) for descriptions of the following attributes:

Attribute Type	Attribute Value
Availability	SUNWcsu

See Also

csh(1), jobs(1), ksh(1), ps(1), sh(1), shell_builtins(1), wait(1),
kill(2), signal(3C), attributes(5), environ(5), signal(5)

---

kinit — Kerberos Login Command

Synopsis

/usr/bin/kinit [-ilrv] [*username*]

Description

The `kinit` command is used to log in to the Kerberos authentication and authorization system. Note that only registered Kerberos users can use the Kerberos system. For information about registering as a Kerberos user, see the kerberos(1) manual page.

When you use `kinit` without options, the command prompts for your user name and Kerberos password and tries to authenticate your login with the local Kerberos server. You can specify the user name on the command line if you want.

If Kerberos authenticates the login attempt, `kinit` retrieves your initial ticket (that is, the ticket-granting ticket) and puts it in the ticket file specified by your KRBTKFILE environment variable. If this variable is undefined, your ticket is stored in the file /tmp/tkt*uid*, where *uid* specifies your user identification number. Tickets expire after a specified lifetime, after which you must run `kinit` again to refresh the tickets. The default ticket lifetime is 8 hours.

Use the kdestroy(1) command to destroy any active tickets before you end your login session.

Options

-i   Prompt for a Kerberos instance.

-l   Prompt for a ticket lifetime in minutes. Because of protocol restrictions in Kerberos Version 4, this value must be between 5 and 1275 minutes; values less than 5 are set to 5; values greater than 1275 are set to 1275; values between the limits are rounded down to a multiple of 5 (for example, a value of 7 is set to 5, 9 is set to 5, 10 remains unchanged).

-r   Prompt for a Kerberos realm. This option lets you authenticate yourself with a remote Kerberos server. Note that the -r option has not been fully implemented

-v   Print a status message indicating the success or failure of your login attempt.

Examples

The following example uses the kinit command to connect to the client system seachild.

```
# kinit root.seachild
Password:
#
```

Attributes

See attributes(5) for descriptions of the following attributes:

Attribute Type	Attribute Value
Availability	SUNWcsu

See Also

kdestroy(1), kerberos(1), klist(1), attributes(5)

Authors

Steve Miller, MIT Project Athena/Digital Equipment Corporation; Clifford Neuman, MIT Project Athena

klist — List Currently Held Kerberos Tickets

Synopsis

```
/usr/bin/klist [-st] [-file name] [-srvtab]
```

Description

Use the `klist` command to list Kerberos tickets. `klist` prints the name of the ticket file, the identity of the principal that the tickets are for (as listed in the ticket file), and the principal names of all Kerberos tickets currently held by the user, along with the issuance and expiration time for each authenticator. Principal names are listed in the form *name.instance@realm*, with the dot (.) omitted if the instance is null and the at sign (@) omitted if the realm is null.

The value of the `KRBTKFILE` environment variable is used as the name of the ticket file. If this environment variable is not set, then the file `/tmp/tktuid` is used, where *uid* is the current user ID of the user.

Bugs

When a file is read as a service key file, very little sanity or error checking is performed.

Options

`-s`	Do not print the issuance and expiration times, the name of the ticket file, or the identity of the principal.
`-t`	Check for the existence of a nonexpired ticket-granting-ticket in the ticket file. If one is present, exit with status 0, else exit with status 1. When you specify this option, generate no output.
`-file name`	Use file *name* as the ticket file. The default file is `/etc/srvtab`.
`-srvtab`	Treat the file as a service key file, and print the names of the keys contained therein. If you do not specify a file with a `-file` option, the default is `/etc/srvtab`.

Examples

The following example lists a Kerberos ticket for user `ray`.

```
castle% klist
Ticket file: /tmp/tkt8765
Principal: ray@Castle.Abc.COM
  Issued             Expires            Principal
 Oct 10 15:15:56 Oct 10:16:15:56 krbtgt.Castle.Abc.COM@Castle.Abc.com
castle%
```

Files

/etc/krb.conf

> The name of the local realm.

/tmp/tktuid

> The default ticket file.

/etc/srvtab The default service key file.

Attributes

See attributes(5) for descriptions of the following attributes:

Attribute Type	Attribute Value
Availability	SUNWcsu

See Also

kdestroy(1), kerberos(1), kinit(1), ksrvtgt(1), attributes(5)

---

ksh, rksh — Korn Shell, a Standard/Restricted Command and Programming Language

Synopsis

New!

```
/usr/bin/ksh [± abCefhikmnoprstuvx] [± o option]... [arg...]
/usr/bin/ksh -c [± abCefhikmnoprstuvx] [± o option]...
   command-string [command-name [arg...]]
/usr/xpg4/bin/sh [± abCefhikmnoprstuvx] [± o option]... [arg...]
/usr/xpg4/bin/sh -c [± abCefhikmnoprstuvx] [± o option]...
   command-string [command-name [arg...]]
/usr/bin/ksh [± abCefhikmnoprstuvx] [± o option]... [arg...]
/usr/bin/ksh -c [± abCefhikmnoprstuvx] [± o option]...
   command-string [command-name [arg...]]
```

Description

The Korn shell, written by David Korn of AT&T Bell Laboratories, was designed to be compatible with the Bourne shell and to offer interactive features comparable to the C shell. The Korn shell includes convenient programming features such as built-in integer arithmetic, arrays, and string-manipulation facilities. The Korn shell runs faster than the C shell and runs virtually all scripts that are written for the Bourne shell.

The Korn shell command is /usr/bin/ksh or /usr/xpg4/bin/ksh. These two commands are identical.

/usr/bin/rksh is a restricted version of the command interpreter ksh; it is used to set up login names and execution environments whose capabilities are more controlled than those of the standard shell.

The default prompt for the Korn shell is a dollar sign ($). The root prompt is a pound sign (#).

The Korn shell discussion uses the following definitions.

- A *metacharacter* is one of the following characters: ; & ( ) | < > newline space Tab.

- A *blank* is a Tab or a space.

- An *identifier* is a sequence of letters, digits, or underscores starting with a letter or underscore. Identifiers are used as names for functions and variables.

- A *word* is a sequence of characters separated by one or more nonquoted metacharacters.

- A *command* is a sequence of characters in the syntax of the shell language. The shell reads each command and carries out the desired action either directly or by invoking separate commands.

- A *special command* is a command that is carried out by the shell without creating a separate process. Except for documented side effects, most special commands can be implemented as separate commands.

Initialization

If the shell is invoked by exec(2) and the first character of argument 0 ($0) is -, then the shell is assumed to be a login shell and it reads commands in the following sequence:

1. Execute commands in /etc/profile.
2. Execute commands from either .profile in the current directory or $HOME/.profile if either file exists.
3. Read commands from the file named by performing parameter substitution on the value of the environment variable ENV if the file exists. If the -s option is not present and *arg* is -, then perform a path search on the first *arg* to determine the name of the script to execute. The script *arg* must have read permission, and any setuid and setgid settings are ignored. If the script is not found in the path, process *arg* as if it named a built-in command or function. Commands are then read as described.

The following options are interpreted by the shell when it is invoked.

-c   Read commands from the *command-string* operand. Set the value
      of the special parameter 0 from the value of the *command-name*
      operand and the positional parameters ($1, $2, and so on) in
      sequence from the remaining *arg* operands. Read no commands
      from the standard input.

-i   If you specify -i or if the shell input and output are attached to a
      terminal (as told by ioctl(2)), this shell is interactive. In this
      case, ignore TERM (so that kill 0 does not kill an interactive shell)
      and catch and ignore INTR (so that wait is interruptible). In all
      cases, ignore QUIT.

-r   Specify a restricted shell.

-s   If you specify the -s option or if no arguments remain, read
      commands from the standard input. Write shell output, except for
      the output of the special sommands, to file descriptor 2.

Restricted Korn Shell

Use the restricted Korn shell, rksh, to set up login names and execution
environments with more controlled capabilities than those of the standard
shell. The actions of rksh are identical to those of ksh, except that the
following actions are not enabled:

- Changing directory (see cd(1)).
- Setting the value of SHELL, ENV, or PATH.
- Specifying path or command names containing /.
- Redirecting output (>, >|, <>, and >>).
- Changing group (see newgrp(1)).

The restrictions above are enforced after the .profile and ENV files are
interpreted. When a command to be executed is found to be a shell procedure,
rksh invokes ksh to execute it. Thus, you can provide shell procedures that
have access to the full power of the standard shell while imposing a limited
menu of commands; this scheme assumes that the user does not have write and
execute permissions in the same directory.

The net effect of these rules is that the writer of the .profile has complete
control over user actions, by performing guaranteed setup actions and leaving
the user in an appropriate directory (probably not the login directory).

The system administrator often sets up a directory of commands (that is,
/usr/rbin) that can be safely invoked by rksh.

Interactive Operation

After startup processing is complete, an interactive Korn shell begins reading
commands from the terminal. The default prompts are a dollar sign ($) for
normal use or a pound sign (#) for superuser.

The following list describes some of the key features of using ksh as an interactive shell.

- *Command-line editing.* ksh provides an emacs-like and a vi-like interface that you can use to edit the current line. You can use the same interface to make changes to previous commands, which ksh keeps in a history file.

- *Command history mechanism.* ksh uses a history file to store the commands that you enter. You can access the history file with emacs or vi editor directives or by using the built-in fc command. The history file is maintained across login sessions and can be shared by several simultaneous instances of ksh.

- *Aliasing.* You can customize command name and option combinations by defining shorthand names, called aliases, for frequently used commands.

- *Job control.* ksh can display a completion message at the prompt after a background job terminates. You can stop jobs and move them to and from background processing.

- *Tilde expansion.* You can symbolically refer to the home directory of any user and the last directory that you were in. You do not need to know the name of the directory or type it in.

When you use the Korn shell interactively, it prompts with the parameter expanded value of PS1 before reading a command. If at any time you type a newline and the shell needs further input to complete a command, then the secondary prompt (that is, the value of PS2) is displayed.

Programming Language Operation

The Korn shell programming language provides the following benefits.

- *I/O mechanism.* You can simultaneously open and read more than one file. You can specify the number of columns printed for each item of information.

- *Arithmetic evaluation.* ksh can perform integer arithmetic in any base from 2 through 36 by using constants and ksh variables.

- *Substring operators.* ksh can generate substrings derived from the values of shell variables.

- *Array variables and attributes.* You can convert strings to lower case or upper case. You can use one-dimensional arrays of strings or numbers.

- *Function facility.* You can define local variables within functions to enable you to write recursive procedures. You can specify code to be executed whenever the function terminates.

- *Coprocessing facility.* You can run one or more programs in the background and send queries to and receive responses from it. This capability enables you to use shell scripts as a front end to another application such as a database management system.

Warning — The use of `setuid` shell scripts is strongly discouraged because of potential security risks.

Commands

A simple command is a sequence of blank-separated words that can be preceded by a variable assignment list. The first word specifies the name of the command to be executed. Except as specified below, the remaining words are passed as arguments to the invoked command. The command name is passed as argument 0 (see `exec`(2)). The value of a simple command is its exit status if it terminates normally or (octal) 200+ status if it terminates abnormally (see `signal`(3C) for a list of status values).

A pipeline is a sequence of one or more commands separated by |. The standard output of each command but the last is connected by a `pipe`(2) to the standard input of the next command. Each command is run as a separate process; the shell waits for the last command to terminate. The exit status of a pipeline is the exit status of the last command.

A list is a sequence of one or more pipelines separated by `;`, `&`, `&&`, or ||, and optionally terminated by `;`, `&`, or |`&`. Of these five symbols, `;`, `&`, and |`&` have equal precedence, which is lower than that of `&&` and ||. The symbols `&&` and || also have equal precedence. A semicolon (`;`) sequentially executes the preceding pipeline; an ampersand (`&`) asynchronously executes the preceding pipeline (that is, the shell does not wait for that pipeline to finish). The symbol |`&` asynchronously executes the preceding command or pipeline with a two-way pipe established to the parent shell.

The standard input and output of the spawned command can be written to and read from by the parent shell with the `-p` option of the special commands `read` and `print` described in "Special Commands" on page 623. The symbol `&&` (||) executes the list following it only if the preceding pipeline returns 0 (or a non-zero) value. You can use an arbitrary number of newlines in a list, instead of a semicolon, to delimit a command.

A command is either a simple command or one of the following. Unless otherwise stated, the value returned by a command is that of the last simple command executed in the command.

`for` *identifier* [in *word*...] `;` `do` *list* `;` `done`

        Each time a `for` command is executed, set *identifier* to the next word taken from the `in` *word* list. If you omit `in` *word*. . ., execute the `do` *list* once for each positional parameter that is set. Execution ends when there are no more words in the list.

```
select identifier [in word...] ; do list ; done
```

> Print to standard error (file descriptor 2) the set of words, each
> preceded by a number. If you omit in word..., use the positional
> parameters instead (see Parameter Substitution). Print the PS3
> prompt, and read a line from the standard input. If this line
> consists of the number of one of the listed words, then set the value
> of the variable identifier to the word corresponding to this number.
> If this line is empty, print the selection list again. Otherwise, set
> the value of the variable identifier to null. Save the contents of
> the line read from standard input in the shell variable REPLY.
> Execute the list for each selection until a break or EOF is
> encountered. If the REPLY variable is set to null by the execution
> of list, then print the selection list before displaying the PS3
> prompt for the next selection.

```
case word in [pattern [| pattern] ) list ;;]... esac
```

> A case command executes the list associated with the first
> pattern that matches word. The form of the patterns is the same as
> that used for file-name generation.

```
if list ; then list ; [elif list ; then list;...][else list ;] fi
```

> Execute the list following if and, if it returns an exit status of 0,
> execute the list following the first then. Otherwise, execute the
> list following elif, and, if its value is 0, execute the list
>
> following the next then. Failing that, execute the else list. If no
> else list or then list is executed, then return 0 exit status.

```
while list ; do list ; done
until list ; do list ; done
```

> Repeatedly execute the while list, and, if the exit status of the
> last command in the list is 0, execute the do list; otherwise,
> terminate the loop. If no commands in the do list are executed,
> then return 0 exit status; you can use until in place of while to
> negate the loop termination test.

(list)   Execute list in a separate environment. Note that if two adjacent
> open parentheses are needed for nesting, you must insert a space
> to avoid arithmetic evaluation.

{list}   Execute list. Note that unlike the metacharacters (and), { and
> } are reserved words and must occur at the beginning of a line or
> after a semicolon to be recognized.

```
[[expression]]
```

> Evaluate expression and return 0 exit status when expression
> is true. See "Conditional Expressions" on page 619 for a
> description of expression.

```
function identifier { list ;} identifier() { list ;}
```
> Define a function that is referenced by *identifier*. The body of
> the function is the list of commands between { and }. (See
> Functions.)

```
time pipeline
```
> Execute the pipeline and print the elapsed time as well as the user
> and system time to standard error.

The following reserved words are recognized only as the first word of a
command and when not quoted.

```
! if then else elif fi case esac for while until do done { } function
    select time [[]]
```

Inline Editing Option

Normally, you simply type each command line from a terminal device followed
by a newline (Return or linefeed). However, if the emacs, gmacs, or vi option is
active, you can edit the command line. To be in one of these edit modes, you
must set the corresponding option. An editing option is automatically selected
each time the VISUAL or EDITOR variable is assigned a value ending with one
of the editing option names.

The editing features require that your terminal accept Return as Return
without linefeed and that a space must overwrite the current character on the
screen. The editing modes implement the concept that you are looking through
a window at the current line. The window width is the value of COLUMNS if it is
defined; otherwise, it is 80 characters. If the window width is too small to
display the prompt and leaves at least 8 columns for input, the prompt is
truncated from the left. If the line is longer than the window width minus two,
a mark is displayed at the end of the window. As the cursor moves and reaches
the window boundaries, the window is centered about the cursor. The mark is
a > if the line extends on the right side of the window, < if the line extends on
the left, and * if the line extends on both sides of the window. The search
commands in each edit mode provide access to the history file. Only strings are
matched, not patterns, although a leading ^ in the string restricts the match to
begin at the first character in the line.

emacs Editing Mode

You enter emacs editing mode by enabling either the emacs or gmacs option.
The only difference between these two modes is the way they handle ^T. To edit,
move the cursor to the point needing correction and then insert or delete
characters or words as needed. All the editing commands are control characters
or escape sequences. The notation for control characters is a caret (^) followed
by the control character.

For example, ^F is the notation for Control-F. You enter this key sequence by
holding down the Control key and typing f. Do not press the Shift key. (The
notation ^? indicates the Delete key.)

The notation for escape sequences is M- followed by a character. For example, enter M-f (pronounced Meta f) by pressing Escape (ASCII 033) followed by f. (M-F would be the notation for Escape followed by Shift (capital) F.)

All edit commands operate from any place on the line (not just at the beginning).

Note — Do not press either the Return or the linefeed key after edit commands except when noted.

^F	Move cursor forward (right) one character.
M-f	Move cursor forward one word. (The emacs editor considers a word to be a string of characters consisting of only letters, digits, and underscores.)
^B	Move cursor backward (left) one character.
M-b	Move cursor backward one word.
^A	Move cursor to start of line.
^E	Move cursor to end of line.
^]*char*	Move cursor forward to character *char* on current line.
M-^]*char*	Move cursor backward to character *char* on current line.
^X^X	Interchange the cursor and mark.
erase	Delete previous character. The user-defined erase character, usually ^H or #, is defined by the stty(1) command.
^D	Delete current character.
M-d	Delete current word.
M-^H	(Meta-backspace) Delete previous word.
M-h	Delete previous word.
M-^?	(Meta-Delete) Delete previous word (if your interrupt character is ^? (Delete, the default), then this command does not work).
^T	Transpose current character with next character in emacs mode. Transpose two previous characters in gmacs mode.
^C	Capitalize current character.
M-c	Capitalize current word.
M-l	Change the current word to lower case.
^K	Delete from the cursor to the end of the line. If preceded by a numerical parameter whose value is less than the current cursor position, then delete from given position up to the cursor. If preceded by a numerical parameter whose value is greater than the current cursor position, then delete from cursor up to given cursor position.
^W	Kill from the cursor to the mark.
M-p	Push the region from the cursor to the mark on the stack.

kill　　　　　　　Kill the entire current line. If you enter two kill characters in
　　　　　　　　　succession, all kill characters from then on insert a linefeed
　　　　　　　　　(useful when using paper terminals). The user-defined kill
　　　　　　　　　character, usually ^G or @, is defined by the stty(1) command.

^Y　　　　　　　　Restore last item removed from line. (Yank item back to the line.)

^L　　　　　　　　Linefeed and print current line.

^@　　　　　　　　(null character) Set mark.

M-space　　　　　(Meta-space) Set mark.

J　　　　　　　　(Newline) Execute the current line.

M　　　　　　　　(Return) Execute the current line.

eof　　　　　　　Process end-of-file character, normally ^D, as an End-of-File only if
　　　　　　　　　the current line is null.

^P　　　　　　　　Fetch previous command. Each time you enter ^P, access the
　　　　　　　　　previous command back in time. Move back one line when not on
　　　　　　　　　the first line of a multiline command.

M-<　　　　　　　Fetch the least recent (oldest) history line.

M->　　　　　　　Fetch the most recent (youngest) history line.

^N　　　　　　　　Fetch next command line. Each time you enter ^N, access the next
　　　　　　　　　command line forward in time.

^R*string*　　　Reverse search history for a previous command line containing
　　　　　　　　　string. If you give a parameter of 0, search forward. Terminate
　　　　　　　　　string with a Return or newline. If you precede *string* with a ^,
　　　　　　　　　the matched line must begin with *string*. If you omit *string*,
　　　　　　　　　then access the next command line containing the most recent
　　　　　　　　　string. In this case, a parameter of 0 reverses the direction of the
　　　　　　　　　search.

^O　　　　　　　　Execute the current line and operate on the next line relative to
　　　　　　　　　the current line from the history file.

M-*digits*　　　Define numeric parameter for Escape. The digits are taken as a
　　　　　　　　　parameter to the next command. The commands that accept a
　　　　　　　　　parameter are ^F, ^B, erase, ^C, ^D, ^K, ^R, ^P, ^N, ^], M-., M-^],
　　　　　　　　　M-_, M-b, M-c, M-d, M-f, M-h, M-l, and M-^H.

M-*letter*　　　Search your alias list for an alias with the name _*letter* and, if
　　　　　　　　　an alias of this name is defined, insert its value on the input
　　　　　　　　　queue. The letter must not be one of the above metafunctions.

M-[*letter*　　Search your alias list for an alias with the name __*letter* and, if
　　　　　　　　　an alias of this name is defined, insert its value on the input
　　　　　　　　　queue. You can use this option to program functions keys on many
　　　　　　　　　terminals.

M-.　　　　　　　Insert the last word of the previous command on the line. If
　　　　　　　　　preceded by a numeric parameter, the value of this parameter
　　　　　　　　　determines what word to insert instead of the last word.

M-_	Same as M- .
M-*	Append an asterisk to the end of the word and try a file-name expansion.
M-Escape	Complete file name by replacing the current word with the longest common prefix of all file names matching the current word with an asterisk appended. If the match is unique, append a / if the file is a directory and a space if the file is not a directory.
M-=	List files matching current word pattern if an asterisk is appended.
^U	Multiply parameter of next command by 4.
\	Escape next character. You can enter editing characters and erase, kill, and interrupt (normally ^?) characters in a command line or in a search string if you precede them with a \. The \ removes the next character's editing features (if any).
^V	Display version of the shell.
M-#	Insert a # at the beginning of the line and execute it. This command also inserts a comment in the history file.

vi Editing Mode

vi has an input and a control mode. Initially, when you enter a command, you are in input mode. To edit, press Escape (033) to enter control mode, move the cursor to the point that needs correction, and then insert or delete characters or words as needed. Most control commands accept an optional repeat count to the command.

In vi mode on most systems, canonical processing is initially enabled and the command is echoed again if the speed is 1200 baud or greater and it contains any control characters or if less than one second has elapsed since the prompt was printed. The Escape character terminates canonical processing for the remainder of the command and you can then modify the command line. This scheme has the advantages of canonical processing with the type-ahead echoing of raw mode.

If the option viraw is also set, the terminal always has canonical processing disabled. This mode is implicit for systems that do not support two alternate end-of-line delimiters and may be helpful for certain terminals.

vi Input Edit Commands

By default the editor is in input mode.

erase	Delete previous character. The user-defined erase character, usually ^H or #, is defined by the stty(1) command.
^W	Delete the previous blank-separated word.
^D	Terminate the shell.

^V	Escape the next character. You can enter editing characters and the erase or kill characters in a command line or in a search string if preceded by a ^V. The ^V removes the next character's editing features (if any).
\	Escape the next erase or kill character.

vi Motion Edit Commands

The following commands move the cursor.

[*count*]l	Move cursor forward (right) one character.
[*count*]w	Move cursor forward one alphanumeric word.
[*count*]W	Move cursor to the beginning of the next word that follows a blank.
[*count*]e	Move cursor to end of word.
[*count*]E	Move cursor to end of the current blank delimited word.
[*count*]h	Move cursor backward (left) one character.
[*count*]b	Move cursor backward one word.
[*count*]B	Move cursor to preceding blank-separated word.
[*count*]|	Move cursor to column *count*.
[*count*]f*c*	Find the next character *c* in the current line.
[*count*]F*c*	Find the previous character *c* in the current line.
[*count*]t*c*	Equivalent to f followed by h.
[*count*]T*c*	Equivalent to F followed by l.
[*count*];	Repeat *count* times, the last, single-character find command, f, F, t, or T.
[*count*],	Reverse the last single-character find command *count* times.
0	Move cursor to start of line.
^	Move cursor to first nonblank character in line.
$	Move cursor to end of line.
%	Move to balancing (,), {, }, [, or]. If the cursor is not on one of the above characters, first search the remainder of the line for the first occurrence of one of the above characters.

vi Search Edit Commands

Use these commands to access your command history.

[*count*]k	Fetch previous command. Each time you enter k, access the previous command back in time.
[*count*]-	Equivalent to k.
[*count*]j	Fetch next command. Each time you enter j, access the next command forward in time.

`[count]+`	Equivalent to j.
`[count]G`	Fetch the command number *count*. The default is the least recent history command.
`/string`	Search backward through history for a previous command containing *string*. Terminate *string* with a Return or newline. If you precede *string* with a ^, the matched line must begin with *string*. If *string* is null, use the previous string.
`?string`	Same as / except search forward.
n	Search for next match of the last pattern to / or ? commands.
N	Search for next match of the last pattern to / or ?, but in reverse direction. Search history for the *string* entered by the previous / command.

vi Text Modification Edit Commands

Use these commands to modify the line.

a	Enter input mode and enter text after the current character.
A	Append text to the end of the line. Equivalent to $a.
`[count]cmotion c[count]motion`	
	Delete current character through the character that *motion* would move the cursor to, and enter input mode. If *motion* is c, delete the entire line and enter input mode.
C	Delete the current character through the end of line and enter input mode. Equivalent to c$.
`[count]s`	Delete *count* characters and enter input mode.
S	Delete entire line and enter input mode. Equivalent to cc.
`[count]dmotion d[count]motion`	
	Delete current character through the character that *motion* would move to. If *motion* is d, delete the entire line.
D	Delete the current character through the end of line. Equivalent to d$.
i	Enter input mode and insert text before the current character.
I	Insert text before the beginning of the line. Equivalent to 0i.
`[count]P`	Put the previous text modification before the cursor.
`[count]p`	Put the previous text modification after the cursor.
R	Enter input mode and replace, in overlay fashion, characters on the screen with characters you type.
`[count]rc`	Replace the *count* character(s) starting at the current cursor position with *c*, and advance the cursor.
`[count]x`	Delete current character.

[*count*]X	Delete preceding character.
[*count*].	Repeat the previous text modification command.
[*count*]~	Invert the case of the *count* character(s) starting at the current cursor position, and advance the cursor.
[*count*]_	Append the *count* word of the previous command and enter input mode. If you omit *count*, use the last word.
*	Append an asterisk (*) to the current word and try file-name generation. If no match is found, ring the bell. Otherwise, replace the word with the matching pattern and enter input mode.
\	Perform file-name completion by replacing the current word with the longest common prefix of all file names matching the current word with an asterisk appended. If the match is unique, append a / if the file is a directory and a space if the file is not a directory.

vi Other Edit Commands

Miscellaneous commands.

[*count*]y*motion* y[*count*]*motion*

         Yank current *character* through *character* that *motion* would move the cursor to and put them into the delete buffer. Leave the text and cursor unchanged.

Y	Yank from current position to end of line. Equivalent to y$.
u	Undo the last text-modifying command.
U	Undo all the text-modifying commands performed on the line.
[*count*]v	Return the command fc -e ${VISUAL:-${EDITOR:-vi}} *count* in the input buffer. If you omit *count*, then use the current line.
^L	Linefeed and print current line. Has effect only in control mode.
J	(Newline) Execute the current line, regardless of mode.
M	(Return) Execute the current line, regardless of mode.
#	If the first character of the command is a #, then delete this # and each # that follows a newline. Otherwise, send the line after inserting a # in front of each line in the command. Useful for inserting the current line in the history as a comment and removing comments from previous comment commands in the history file.
=	List the file names that match the current word if an asterisk is appended to it.
@*letter*	Search your alias list for an alias by the name _*letter* and if an alias of this name is defined, insert its value on the input queue for processing.

Command History

Commands you enter from a terminal device are saved in a history file. The HISTSIZE environment variable determines the number of commands that are saved. The default is 128. If the HISTFILE variable is not set or if the file it names is not writable, ksh uses the file $HOME/.sh_history to store the history list. A shell can access the commands of all interactive shells that use the same named HISTFILE. Use the special command fc to list or edit a portion of this file. You can specify the portion of the file to be edited or listed by the number assigned in the history list or by specifying the first character or characters of the command. You can specify a single command or a range of commands. If you do not specify an editor program as an argument to fc, then the value of the variable FCEDIT is used. If FCEDIT is not defined, then /bin/ed is used as the editor. The edited commands are printed and reexecuted on leaving the editor. Use the editor name - to skip the editing phase and to reexecute the command. In this case. you can use a substitution parameter of the form *old=new* to modify the command before execution. For example, if r is aliased to fc -e -, then typing r bad=good c reexecutes the most recent command that starts with the letter c, replacing the first occurrence of the string bad with the string good. For more details, see history(1).

> **Note** — Using the fc built-in command within a compound command removes the whole command from the history file.

Aliasing

If you have defined an alias for a word, the first word of each command is replaced by the text of the alias. An alias name consists of any number of characters excluding metacharacters, quoting characters, file-expansion characters, parameter and command substitution characters, and =. The replacement string can contain any valid shell script including the metacharacters listed above. The first word of each command in the replaced text, other than any that are in the process of being replaced, is tested for aliases. If the last character of the alias value is a blank, then the word following the alias is also checked for alias substitution. You can use aliases to redefine special built-in commands, but you cannot use them to redefine the reserved words.

Create, list, and export aliases with the alias command. Remove them with the unalias command. Exported aliases remain in effect for scripts invoked by name but must be reinitialized for separate invocations of the shell. To prevent infinite loops in recursive aliasing, if the shell is not currently processing an alias of the same name, the word is replaced by the value of the alias; otherwise, it is not replaced.

Aliasing is performed when scripts are read, not while they are executed. Therefore, for an alias to take effect, the alias definition command has to be executed before the command that references the alias is read. Aliases are frequently used as a shorthand for full path names. An option to the aliasing facility enables the value of the alias to be automatically set to the full path name of the corresponding command. These aliases are called *tracked aliases*. The value of a tracked alias is defined the first time the corresponding command is looked up and becomes undefined each time the PATH variable is reset. These aliases remain tracked so that the next subsequent reference redefines the value. Several tracked aliases are compiled into the shell. The –h option of the set command makes each referenced command name into a tracked alias. The following exported aliases are compiled into (and built into) the shell, but you can unset or redefine them.

```
autoload='typeset -fu'
false='let 0'
functions='typeset -f'
hash='alias -t'
history='fc -l'
integer='typeset -i'
nohup='nohup '
r='fc -e -'
true=':'
type='whence -v'
```

The following example shows a problem involving trailing blank characters and reserved words. If you type the commands

```
$ alias foo="/bin/ls "
$ alias while="/"
```

then the effect of executing the following commands is a never-ending sequence of Hello, World strings.

```
$ while true
> do
> echo "Hello, World"
> done
```

If, however, you type the following command, the result is an ls listing of /.

```
$ foo while
```

Because the alias substitution for foo ends in a space character, the next word is checked for alias substitution. The next word, while, has also been aliased, so it is substituted as well. Because it is not in the proper position as a command word, it is not recognized as a reserved word.

If you type

```
$ foo; while
```

while retains its normal reserved-word properties.

Note — If a command that is a tracked alias is executed, and then a command with the same name is installed in a directory in the search path before the directory where the original command was found, the shell continues to execute the original command. Use the -t option of the alias command to correct this situation.

Tilde Substitution

After alias substitution is performed, each word is checked to see if it begins with an unquoted tilde (~). If it does, then the word up to a / is checked to see if it matches a user name. If a match is found, the ~ and the matched login name are replaced with the login directory of the matched user. This action is called a *tilde substitution*. If no match is found, the original text is left unchanged. A ~ by itself, or in front of a /, is replaced by $HOME. A ~ followed by a + or - is replaced by $PWD and $OLDPWD, respectively. In addition, tilde substitution is attempted when the value of a variable assignment begins with a ~.

Job Control

Job control enables you to move currently executing commands into the foreground or background and to stop, suspend, or restart them as needed. There is always one job in the foreground, which is the job that accepts your keyboard input. The foreground job may be a shell or another command such as an editor that accepts keyboard input.

When you execute a command line or start a job in the foreground, input to the terminal window is blocked and you cannot enter additional commands until that job completes. You can use the job control commands to push that job into the background to regain control of your terminal window. Similarly, you can bring a background job back to the foreground so that you can control it or enter data from the terminal window. Job control enables you to perform these actions within the current layer or window.

When the monitor option of the set command is turned on, an interactive shell associates a job with each pipeline. Each command or pipeline that you enter at a terminal window is then assigned a positive numeric *job-id*. The shell keeps track of current and previous jobs. The current job is the most recent job to be started or restarted. The previous job is the first noncurrent job.

When a job is started asynchronously with &, the shell prints a line that looks like [1] 567, indicating that the job that was started asynchronously was job number 1 and has one (top-level) process whose process ID is 567.

All jobs exist in one of the following states.

- A *foreground* job has read and write access to the controlling terminal.
- A *background* job is denied read access and has conditional write access to the *controlling* terminal (see stty(1)).

- A *stopped* job has been placed in a suspended state, usually as a result of a SIGTSTP signal (see signal(5)).

If you specify no options, the output is a series of lines of the following form.

```
[%d] %c %s %s\n, job-number, current, state, command
```

The following example lists two jobs.

```
$ jobs
[1] - Running                           spider
[2] + Done(0)                           find . -name core -print
$
```

The fields are described below.

job-number A number used to identify the process group to the wait, fg, bg, and kill commands. Using these commands, you can identify the job by prefixing the job number with %.

current The character + identifies the job that would be used as a default for the fg or bg commands; this job can also be specified using the *job-id* %+ or %% . The character - identifies the job that would become the default if the current default job were to exit; this job can also be specified with the *job-id* %-. For other jobs, this field is a space character. One job can be identified with +, and one job can be identified with -. If there is any suspended job, then the current job is a suspended job. If there are at least two suspended jobs, then the previous job is also a suspended job.

state One of the following strings (in the POSIX locale):

Running   The job has not been suspended by a signal and has not exited.

Done   The job completed and returned exit status 0.

Done(*code*)   The job completed normally and exited with the specified non-zero exit status, *code*, expressed as a decimal number.

Stopped
Stopped (SIGTSTP)

                   The job was suspended by the SIGTSTP signal.

Stopped (SIGSTOP)

                   The job was suspended by the SIGSTOP signal.

Stopped (SIGTTIN)

                   The job was suspended by the SIGTTIN signal.

Stopped (SIGTTOU)

                   The job was suspended by the SIGTTOU signal.

The implementation may substitute the string Suspended in place of Stopped. If the job was terminated by a signal, the format of state is unspecified, but it is visibly distinct from all of the other state formats shown here and indicates the name or description of the signal that terminated the job.

command　　The associated command that was given to the shell.

If you specify the -l option, a field containing the process group ID is inserted before the state field. Also, more processes in a process group may be output on separate lines, using only the process ID and command fields.

If you specify the -p option, the output consists of one line for each process ID.

The built-in jobs command displays the status of the jobs that were started in the current shell environment. When jobs reports the termination status of a job, the shell removes its process ID from the list of those known in the current shell execution environment.

The following options modify or enhance the output of jobs.

-l　　　　(The letter ell.) Provide more information about each job listed. This information includes the job number, current job, process group ID, state and the command that formed the job.

-n　　　　Display only jobs that have stopped or exited since last notified.

-p　　　　Display only the process IDs for the process group leaders of the selected jobs.

By default, jobs displays the status of all the stopped jobs, running background jobs, and all jobs whose status has changed and have not been reported by the shell.

If you are running a job and want to do something else, you can use the ^Z (Control-Z) key combination to send a STOP signal to the current job. The shell normally indicates that the job has been stopped and displays another prompt. You can then manipulate the state of this job, putting it in the background with the bg command, or run some other commands and then eventually bring the job back into the foreground with the fg command. A ^Z takes effect immediately and is like an interrupt in that pending output and unread input are discarded.

You can refer to jobs in the shell by their process ID or by any of the following.

%*number*　　The job with the given number.

%*string*　　Any job whose command line begins with *string*. This syntax works only in the interactive mode when the history file is active.

%?*string*　　Any job whose command line contains *string*. This syntax works only in the interactive mode when the history file is active.

%%　　　　Current job.

%+   Equivalent to %%.

%-   Previous job.

The following list describes the additional Korn shell job control commands.

fg   Move a background job from the current environment into the
            foreground. Using fg to place a job in the foreground removes its
            process ID from the list of those known in the current shell
            execution environment. The fg command is available only on
            systems that support job control. If you do not specify a *job-id*,
            the current job is brought into the foreground.

bg   Resume suspended jobs from the current environment by running
            them as background jobs. If the job specified by *job-id* is already
            a running background job, bg has no effect and exits successfully.
            Using bg to place a job into the background makes its process ID
            known in the current shell execution environment as if it had been
            started as an asynchronous list. The bg command is available only
            on systems that support job control. If you do not specify *job-id*,
            the current job is placed in the background.

stop   Stop the execution of a background job(s) by using its *job-id*, or of
            any process by using its *pid*; see ps(1).

The shell learns immediately whenever a process changes state. It normally
informs you whenever a job becomes blocked so that no further progress is
possible, but only just before it displays a prompt. The warning is done in this
way so that it does not otherwise disturb your work. When the monitor mode
is on, each background job that completes triggers any trap set for CHLD.

When you try to leave the shell while jobs are running or stopped, you are
warned that You have stopped(running) jobs. You can use the jobs
command to see what they are. If you do this or immediately try to exit again,
the shell does not warn you a second time, and the stopped jobs are terminated.
If you have nohup'ed jobs running when you attempt to log out, you are warned
with the message

You have jobs running.

You then need to log out a second time to actually log out; however, your
background jobs continue to run.

Signals
The INT and QUIT signals for an invoked command are ignored if the command
is followed by & and the monitor option is not active. Otherwise, signals have
the values inherited by the shell from its parent (but see also the trap special
command.

Tilde Expansion
A tilde-prefix consists of an unquoted tilde character (~) at the beginning of a
word, followed by all of the characters preceding the first unquoted slash in the

word, or all the characters in the word if there is no slash. In an assignment, you can use multiple tilde-prefixes: at the beginning of the word (that is, following the equal sign of the assignment), following any unquoted colon, or both. A tilde-prefix in an assignment is terminated by the first unquoted colon or slash. If none of the characters in the tilde-prefix are quoted, the characters in the tilde-prefix following the tilde are treated as a possible login name from the user database.

A portable login name cannot contain characters outside the set given in the description of the LOGNAME environment variable. If the login name is null (that is, the tilde-prefix contains only the tilde), the tilde-prefix is replaced by the value of the variable HOME. If HOME is unset, the results are unspecified. Otherwise, the tilde-prefix is replaced by a path name of the home directory associated with the login name obtained with the getpwnam function. If the system does not recognize the login name, the results are undefined.

Tilde expansion generally occurs only at the beginning of words, but an exception based on historical practice has been included:

```
PATH=/posix/bin:~dgk/bin
```

is eligible for tilde expansion because the tilde follows a colon and none of the relevant characters are quoted. Consideration was given to prohibiting this behavior because any of the following are reasonable substitutes.

```
PATH=$(printf %s ~karels/bin : ~bostic/bin)
for Dir in ~maart/bin ~srb/bin...
do
 PATH=${PATH:+$PATH:}$Dir
done
```

With the first command, explicit colons are used for each directory. In all cases, the shell performs tilde expansion on each directory because all are separate words to the shell.

Note — Expressions in operands such as:

```
make -k mumble LIBDIR=~chet/lib
```

do not qualify as shell variable assignments, and tilde expansion is not performed (unless the command does so itself, which make does not). The special sequence $~ has been designated for future implementations to evaluate as a means of forcing tilde expansion in any word.

Because of the requirement that the word not be quoted, the following are not equivalent; only the last does tilde expansion.

```
\~hlj/  ~h\lj/  ~"hlj"/  ~hlj\/  ~hlj/
```

The results of specifying tilde with an unknown login name are undefined because the Korn shell ~+ and ~- constructs make use of this condition. In general it is an error to give an incorrect login name with tilde. The results of having HOME unset are unspecified because some historical shells treat this as an error.

Command Substitution

The standard output from a command enclosed in parentheses preceded by a dollar sign $(*command*) or a pair of grave accents (` `) can be used as part or all of a word; trailing newlines are removed. In the second (archaic) form, the string between the quotes is processed for special quoting characters before the command is executed. (See "Quoting (Escaping) Characters" on page 618.) The command substitution $(cat *file*) can be replaced by the equivalent but faster (<file). Command substitution of most special commands that do not perform input/output redirection are carried out without creating a separate process. Command substitution enables the output of a command to be substituted in place of the command name itself. Command substitution occurs when the command is enclosed as follows:

$(*command*)

or (backquoted version):

` *command* `

The shell expands the command substitution by executing *command* in a subshell environment and replacing the command substitution (the text of *command* plus the enclosing $( ) or backquotes) with the standard output of the command, removing sequences of one or more newline characters at the end of the substitution. Embedded newline characters before the end of the output are not removed; however, they can be treated as field delimiters and eliminated during field splitting, depending on the value of IFS and quoting that is in effect.

Within the backquoted style of command substitution, backslash retains its literal meaning, except when followed by $ ` \ (dollar sign, backquote, backslash). The search for the matching backquote is satisfied by the first backquote found without a preceding backslash; during this search, if a nonescaped backquote is encountered within a shell comment, a here-document, an embedded command substitution of the $(*command*) form, or a quoted string, undefined results occur. A single- or double-quoted string that begins, but does not end, within the ` . . . ` sequence produces undefined results.

With the $(*command*) form, all characters following the opening parenthesis to the matching closing parenthesis constitute the command. Any valid shell script can be used for command; however,

- A script consisting solely of redirections produces unspecified results.

- See the restriction on single subshells described below.

The result of command substitution is that field splitting and path-name expansion are processed for further tilde expansion, parameter expansion, command substitution, or arithmetic expansion. If a command substitution occurs inside double quotes, it is not performed on the results of the substitution.

Command substitution can be nested. To specify nesting within the backquoted version, precede the inner backquotes with backslashes; for example:

`` `\`command\`` ``

The `$( )` form of command substitution solves a problem of inconsistent behavior when backquotes are used. For example:

Command	Output
`echo '\$x'`	`\$x`
`` echo `echo '\$x'` ``	`$x`
`echo $(echo '\$x')`	`\$x`

Additionally, the backquoted syntax has historical restrictions on the contents of the embedded command. Whereas the new `$( )` form can process any kind of valid embedded script, the backquoted form cannot handle some valid scripts that include backquotes. For example, these otherwise valid embedded scripts do not work in the left column, but do work on the right:

```
echo `                        echo $(
cat <<eeof                     cat <<eeof
a here-doc with `              a here-doc with )
eof                            eof
`                              )


echo `                        echo $(
echo abc # a comment with `    echo abc # a comment with )
`                              )


echo `                        echo $(
echo '`'                       echo ')'
`                              )
```

Because of these inconsistent behaviors, the backquoted variety of command substitution is not recommended for new applications that nest command substitutions or attempt to embed complex scripts.

If the command substitution consists of a single subshell, such as:

```
$( (command) )
```

a portable application must separate the $(and (into two tokens (that is, separate them with white space). This space is required to avoid any ambiguities with arithmetic expansion.

Input/Output
Before a command is executed, you can redirect its input and output by using a special notation interpreted by the shell. The following syntax can be used anywhere in a simple command or can precede or follow a command without being passed on to the invoked command. Command and parameter substitution occur before *word*, or *digit* is used except as noted below. File-name generation occurs only if the pattern matches a single file, and blank interpretation is not performed.

`<word`	Use file *word* as standard input (file descriptor 0).
`>word`	Use file *word* as standard output (file descriptor 1). If the file does not exist, then create it. If the file exists and the `noclobber` option is on, an error occurs; otherwise, truncate it to 0 length.
`>|word`	Same as >, except override the `noclobber` option.
`>>word`	Use file *word* as standard output. If the file exists, then seek to the EOF and append output to it; otherwise, create the file.
`<>word`	Open file *word* for reading and writing as standard input.
`<< [-]word`	Read the shell input up to a line that is the same as *word* or to an end-of-file. Perform no parameter substitution, command substitution, or file-name generation on *word*. The resulting document, called a *here-document*, becomes the standard input. If any character of *word* is quoted, then put no interpretation on the characters of the document; otherwise, parameter and command substitution occur, \newline is ignored, and \ must be used to quote the characters \, $, `, and the first character of *word*. If you append - to <<, then strip all leading tabs from *word* and from the document.
`<&digit`	Duplicate the standard input from file descriptor *digit* (see dup(2)). Similarly for the standard output using `>&digit`.
`<&-`	Close the standard input. Similarly for the standard output using `>&-`.
`<&p`	Move the input from the coprocess to standard input.
`>&p`	Move the output to the coprocess to standard output.

If one of the above is preceded by a digit, then the file descriptor number referred to is that specified by the digit (instead of the default 0 or 1). For example, . . . `2>&1` means file descriptor 2 is to be opened for writing as a duplicate of file descriptor 1.

The specified order of redirections is significant. The shell evaluates each redirection in terms of the (file descriptor, file) association at the time of evaluation. For example, ... `1>fname 2>&1` first associates file descriptor 1 with file `fname`. It then associates file descriptor 2 with the file associated with file descriptor 1 (that is, `fname`). If the order of redirections is reversed, file descriptor 2 is associated with the terminal (assuming file descriptor 1 had been) and then file descriptor 1 is associated with file `fname`. If a command is followed by `&` and job control is not active, then the default standard input for the command is the empty file `/dev/null`. Otherwise, the environment for the execution of a command contains the file descriptors of the invoking shell as modified by input/output specifications.

Execution

Each time a command is executed, the above substitutions are carried out in the following sequence.

- If the command name matches one of the special commands, it is executed within the current shell process.

- The command name is checked to see if it matches one of the user-defined functions. If it does, the positional parameters are saved and then reset to the arguments of the function call. When the function completes or issues a return, the positional parameter list is restored and any trap set on `EXIT` within the function is executed. The value of a function is the value of the last command executed. A function is also executed in the current shell process.

- If a command name is not a special command or a user-defined function, a process is created and an attempt is made to execute the command with `exec(2)`. The shell variable `PATH` defines the search path for the directory containing the command. Alternative directory names are separated by a colon (`:`). The default path is `/bin:/usr/bin:.` (specifying `/bin`, `/usr/bin`, and the current directory, in that order). The current directory can be specified by two or more adjacent colons or by a colon at the beginning or end of the path list. If the command name contains a `/`, then the search path is not used. Otherwise, each directory in the path is searched for an executable file. If the file has execute permission but is not a directory or an `a.out` file, it is assumed to be a file containing shell commands. A subshell is spawned to read it. All nonexported aliases, functions, and variables are removed in this case. A parenthesized command is executed in a subshell without removing nonexported quantities.

Arithmetic Expansion

An arithmetic expression enclosed in double parentheses preceded by a dollar sign `$((arithmetic-expression))` is replaced by the value of the arithmetic expression within the double parentheses. Arithmetic expansion provides a mechanism for evaluating an arithmetic expression and substituting its value. The format for arithmetic expansion is as follows:

```
$((expression))
```

The expression is treated as if it were in double quotes, except that a double-quote inside the expression is not treated specially. The shell expands all tokens in the expression for parameter expansion, command substitution, and quote removal.

Next, the shell treats it as an arithmetic expression and substitutes the value of the expression. The arithmetic expression is processed according to the rules of the ISO C with the following exceptions:

- Only integer arithmetic is required.

- The sizeof() operator and the prefix and postfix ++ and -- operators are not required.

- Selection, iteration, and jump statements are not supported. As an extension, the shell may recognize arithmetic expressions beyond those listed. If the expression is invalid, the expansion fails and the shell writes a message to standard error indicating the failure.

The following simple example uses arithmetic expansion.

```
# repeat a command 100 times
x=100
while [$x -gt 0]
do
command
x=$(($x-1))
done
```

Process Substitution

Note — Process substitution is available in SunOS and only on versions of the UNIX operating system that support the /dev/fd directory for naming open files.

Each command argument of the form `<(list)` or `>(list)` runs process *list* asynchronously connected to some file in /dev/fd. The name of this file becomes the argument to the command. If you use the form with >, then writing to this file provides input for *list*. If you use <, then the file passed as an argument contains the output of the list process. For example,

```
paste <(cut -f1 file1) <(cut -f3 file2) |
tee >( process1) >( process2)
```

cuts fields 1 and 3 from the files *file1* and *file2* respectively, pastes the results together, and sends it to the processes *process1* and *process2*, as well as putting it onto the standard output.

Note — The file passed as an argument to the command is a UNIX
pipe(2) so programs that expect to execute lseek(2) on the file do
not work.

Parameter Substitution

A parameter is an identifier of one or more digits or any of the characters *, @,
#, ?, -, $, and !. A variable (a parameter denoted by an identifier) has a value
and zero or more attributes. You can assign values and attributes to variables
by using the typeset special command. The attributes supported by the shell
are described with the typeset special command. Exported variables pass
values and attributes to the environment.

The shell supports a one-dimensional array facility. An element of an array
variable is referenced by a subscript. A subscript is denoted by a [, followed by
an arithmetic expression followed by a]. To assign values to an array, use

```
set -A name value....
```

The value of all subscripts must be in the range of 0 through 1023. Arrays
need not be declared. Any reference to a variable with a valid subscript is legal,
and an array is created if necessary. Referencing an array without a subscript
is equivalent to referencing the element 0. If you use an array identifier with
subscript * or @, then the value for each of the elements is substituted
(separated by a field separator character).

You can assign the value of a variable in the following way:

```
name=value [name=value]...
```

If the integer attribute, -i, is set for *name*, the value is subject to arithmetic
evaluation as described below. Positional parameters, parameters denoted by a
number, may be assigned values with the set special command. Parameter $0
is set from argument 0 when the shell is invoked. If parameter is one or more
digits, then it is a positional parameter. You must enclose a positional
parameter of more than one digit in braces.

Parameter Expansion

The format for parameter expansion is as follows:

```
${expression}
```

where expression consists of all characters until the matching }. Any } escaped
by a backslash or within a quoted string, and characters in embedded
arithmetic expansions, command substitutions, and variable expansions are
not examined in determining the matching }.

The simplest form for parameter expansion is:

```
${parameter}
```

The value, if any, of *parameter* is substituted.

You can enclose the parameter name or symbol in braces, which are optional except for positional parameters with more than one digit or when parameter is followed by a character that could be interpreted as part of the name. The matching closing brace is determined by counting brace levels, skipping over enclosed quoted strings and command substitutions.

If you do not enclose the parameter name or symbol in braces, the expansion uses the longest valid name whether the symbol represented by that name exists. When the shell is scanning its input to determine the boundaries of a name, it is not bound by its knowledge of what names are already defined. For example, if F is a defined shell variable, the following command does not echo the value of $F followed by red.

```
echo $Fred
```

Instead, it selects the longest possible valid name, Fred, which might be unset.

If a parameter expansion occurs inside double-quotes:

- Path name expansion is not performed on the results of the expansion.
- Field splitting is not performed on the results of the expansion, with the exception of @.

In addition, a parameter expansion can be modified by one of the following formats. In each case that a value of *word* is needed (based on the state of parameter, as described below), *word* is subjected to tilde expansion, parameter expansion, command substitution, and arithmetic expansion. If *word* is not needed, it is not expanded.

The } character that delimits the following parameter expansion modifications is determined as described previously in this section. (For example, ${foo-bar}xyz} results in the expansion of foo followed by the string xyz} if foo is set; otherwise, the expanded string is barxyz}.)

${*parameter*:-*word*}

> Use default values. If *parameter* is unset or null, substitute the expansion of *word*; otherwise, substitute the value of *parameter*.

${*parameter*:=*word*}

> Assign default values. If parameter is unset or null, assign the expansion of *word* to *parameter*. In all cases, substitute the final value of *parameter*. You can assign only variables in this way, not positional parameters or special parameters.

${*parameter*:?[*word*]}

> Indicate error if null or unset. If *parameter* is unset or null, write to standard error the expansion of *word* (or a message indicating it is unset if you omit *word*) and exit with a non-zero exit status. Otherwise, substitute the value of *parameter*. An interactive shell need not exit.

${parameter:+[word]}

> Use alternative value. If *parameter* is unset or null, substitute
> null; otherwise, substitute the expansion of *word*.

In the above parameter expansions, use of the colon in the format results in
a test for a parameter that is unset or null; omitting the colon results in a test
for a parameter that is only unset. The following table summarizes the effect of
the colon:

Format	Parameter set and not null	Parameter set but null	Parameter unset
${parameter:-word}	Substitute *parameter*	Substitute *word*	Substitute *word*
${parameter-word}	Substitute *parameter*	Substitute null	Substitute *word*
${parameter:=word}	Substitute *parameter*	Assign *word*	Assign *word*
${parameter=word}	Substitute *parameter*	Substitute *parameter*	Assign null
${parameter:?word}	Substitute *parameter*	Error; exit	Error; exit
${parameter?word}	Substitute *parameter*	Substitute null	Error; exit
${parameter:+word}	Substitute *word*	Substitute null	Substitute null
${parameter+word}	Substitute *word*	Substitute *word*	Substitute null

All cases shown with Substitute replace the expression with the value
shown. All cases shown with Assign assign *parameter* that value, which also
replaces the expression.

${#parameter}

> String length. Specify the length, in characters, of the value of
> *parameter*. If *parameter* is * or @, then substitute all the positional
> parameters, starting with $1 separated by a field separator
> character.

The following four varieties of parameter expansion provide for substring
processing. In each case, pattern matching notation (see patmat), instead of
regular expression notation, is used to evaluate the patterns. If parameter is *

or @, then all the positional parameters, starting with $1, are substituted (separated by a field separator character). Enclosing the full parameter expansion string in double quotes does not cause the following four varieties of pattern characters to be quoted, whereas quoting characters within the braces does have this effect.

${*parameter%word*}

> Remove smallest suffix pattern. Expand *word* to produce a pattern. The parameter expansion then results in *parameter*, with the smallest portion of the suffix matched by the pattern deleted.

${*parameter%%word*}

> Remove largest suffix pattern. Expand *word* to produce a pattern. The parameter expansion then results in *parameter*, with the largest portion of the suffix matched by the pattern deleted.

${*parameter#word*}

> Remove smallest prefix pattern. Expand *word* to produce a pattern. The parameter expansion then results in *parameter*, with the smallest portion of the prefix matched by the pattern deleted.

${*parameter##word*}

> Remove largest prefix pattern. Expand *word* to produce a pattern. The parameter expansion then results in *parameter*, with the largest portion of the prefix matched by the pattern deleted.

Pattern Expansion Examples

The following examples illustrate each of the pattern expansion forms.

In the first example, ls is executed only if x is null or unset. (The $(ls) command substitution notation is explained in "Command Substitution" on page 604.)

${*parameter:-word*}

```
${x:-$(ls)}
```

${*parameter:=word*}

```
unset X
echo ${X:=abc}
abc
```

${*parameter:?word*}

```
unset posix
echo ${posix:?}
sh: posix: parameter null or not set
```

${*parameter:+word*}

```
set a b c
echo ${3:+posix}
```

```
        posix
```

${#*parameter*}

```
        HOME=/usr/posix
        echo ${#HOME}
        10
```

${*parameter*%v}

```
        x=file.c
        echo ${x%.c}.o
        file.o
```

${*parameter*%%*word*}

```
        x=posix/src/std
        echo ${x%%/*}
        posix
```

${*parameter*#*word*}

```
        x=$HOME/src/cmd
        echo ${x#$HOME}
        /src/cmd
```

${*parameter*##*word*}

```
        x=/one/two/three
        echo ${x##*/}
        three
```

Parameters Set by Shell

The shell automatically sets the following parameters.

#	The number of positional parameters in decimal.
-	Options supplied to the shell on invocation or by the set command.
?	The decimal value returned by the last executed command.
$	The process number of this shell.
_	Initially, the value of _ is an absolute path name of the shell or script being executed as passed in the environment. Subsequently, it is assigned the last argument of the previous command. This parameter is not set for commands that are asynchronous. This parameter is also used to hold the name of the matching MAIL file when checking for mail.
!	The process number of the last background command invoked.
ERRNO	The value of errno as set by the most recently failed system call. This value is system dependent and is intended for debugging purposes.
LINENO	The line number of the current line within the script or function being executed.
OLDPWD	The previous working directory set by the cd command.

OPTARG	The value of the last option argument processed by the getopts special command.
OPTIND	The index of the last option argument processed by the getopts special command.
PPID	The process number of the parent of the shell.
PWD	The present working directory set by the cd command.
RANDOM	Each time this variable is referenced, generate a random integer, uniformly distributed between 0 and 32767. You can initialize the sequence of random numbers by assigning a numeric value to RANDOM.
REPLY	This variable is set by the select statement and by the read special command when you supply no arguments.
SECONDS	Each time this variable is referenced, return the number of seconds since shell invocation. If this variable is assigned a value, then the value returned on reference is the value that was assigned plus the number of seconds since the assignment.

Variables Used by Shell

The shell gives default values to PATH, PS1, PS2, PS3, PS4, MAILCHECK, FCEDIT, TMOUT, and IFS, while HOME, SHELL ENV, and MAIL are not set at all by the shell (although HOME is set by login(1)). On some systems MAIL and SHELL are also set by login. The shell uses the following variables.

CDPATH	Specify the search path for the cd command.
COLUMNS	If this variable is set, use the value to define the width of the edit window for the shell edit modes and for printing select lists.
EDITOR	If the value of this variable ends in emacs, gmacs, or vi and the VISUAL variable is not set, then turn on the corresponding option (see the set special command).
ENV	When the shell is invoked, subject this variable to parameter expansion by the shell and use the resulting value as a path name of a file containing shell commands to execute in the current environment. The file need not be executable. If the expanded value of ENV is not an absolute path name, the results are unspecified. ENV is ignored if the user's real and effective user IDs or real and effective group IDs are different. You can use this variable to set aliases and other items local to the invocation of a shell. The file referred to by ENV differs from $HOME/.profile so that .profile is typically executed at session startup, whereas the ENV file is executed at the beginning of each shell invocation. The ENV value is interpreted in a manner similar to a dot script, in that the commands are executed in the current environment and the file needs to be readable but not executable. However, unlike dot scripts, no PATH searching is performed as a guard against Trojan horse security breaches.

FCEDIT	Specify the default editor for the fc command.
FPATH	Specify the search path for function definitions. By default, search the FPATH directories after the PATH variable. If an executable file is found, then read and execute it in the current environment. FPATH is searched before PATH when a function with the -u attribute is referenced. The autoload preset alias creates a function with the -u attribute.
IFS	Specify the internal field separators, normally space, Tab, and newline, used to separate command words that result from command or parameter substitution and for separating words with the read special command. The first character of the IFS variable is used to separate arguments for the $* substitution.
HISTFILE	If this variable is set when the shell is invoked, use the value as the file to store the command history.
HISTSIZE	If this variable is set when the shell is invoked, specify the number of commands to store in the history file. The default is 128.
HOME	Specify the default argument (home directory) for the cd command.
LC_ALL	A default value for the LC_* variables.
LC_COLLATE	Determine the behavior of range expressions, equivalence classes, and multibyte character-collating elements within pattern matching.
LC_CTYPE	Determine how the shell handles characters. When LC_CTYPE is set to a valid value, the shell can display and handle text and file names containing valid characters for that locale. If LC_CTYPE (see environ(5)) is not set in the environment, the operational behavior of the shell is determined by the value of the LANG environment variable. If LC_ALL is set, its contents override both the LANG and the other LC_* variables.
LC_MESSAGES	Determine the language for messages.
LANG	Provide a default value for the internationalization variables that are unset or null. If any of the internationalization variables contains an invalid setting, the command behaves as if none of the variables are defined.
LINENO	Set by the shell to a decimal number representing the current sequential line number (numbered starting with 1) within a script or function before it executes each command. If the user unsets or resets LINENO, the variable may lose its special meaning for the life of the shell. If the shell is not currently executing a script or function, the value of LINENO is unspecified.
LINES	If this variable is set, use the value to determine the column length for printing select lists. Select lists print vertically until about two-thirds of LINES' lines are filled.

MAIL If this variable is set to the name of a mail file and the MAILPATH variable is not set, then inform the user of arrival of mail in the specified file.

MAILCHECK Specify how often (in seconds) the shell checks for changes in the modification time of any of the files specified by the MAILPATH or MAIL variables. The default value is 600 seconds. When the time has elapsed, the shell checks before issuing the next prompt.

MAILPATH A colon-separated list of file names. If this variable is set, then inform the user of any modifications to the specified files that have occurred within the last MAILCHECK seconds. Each file name can be followed by a ? and a message that is printed. The message undergoes parameter substitution with the variable $_ defined as the name of the file that has changed. The default message is: you have mail in $_.

NLSPATH Determine the location of message catalogs for the processing of LC_MESSAGES.

PATH Specify the search path for commands. The user cannot change PATH if executing under rksh (except in .profile).

PPID Set by the shell to the decimal process ID of the process that invoked the shell. In a subshell, PPID is set to the same value as that of the parent of the current shell. For example, echo $PPID and (echo $PPID) would produce the same value.

PS1 Expand the value of this variable for parameter substitution to define the primary prompt string, by default, $. Replace the character ! in the primary prompt string by the command number. Two successive occurrences of ! produce a single ! when the prompt string is printed.

PS2 Specify the secondary prompt string, by default, >.

PS3 Specify the selection prompt string used within a select loop, by default, #?.

PS4 Expand the value of this variable for parameter substitution and precede each line of an execution trace. If omitted, the execution trace prompt is +.

SHELL Store the path name of the shell in the environment. At invocation, if the basename of this variable is rsh, rksh, or krsh, then the shell becomes restricted.

TMOUT If set to a value greater than 0, terminate if a command is not entered within the prescribed number of seconds after the PS1 prompt is issued. (Note that the shell can be compiled with a maximum bound for this value which cannot be exceeded.)

VISUAL If the value of this variable ends in emacs, gmacs, or vi, then turn on the corresponding option.

Blank Interpretation

After parameter and command substitution, the results of substitutions are scanned for the field separator characters (those found in IFS) and split into distinct arguments when such characters are found. Explicit null arguments (" ") or (' ') are retained. Implicit null arguments (those resulting from parameters that have no values) are removed.

File-Name Generation

Following substitution, each command word is scanned for the characters *, ?, and [, unless you specify the -f option. If one of these characters appears, the word is regarded as a pattern. The word is replaced with lexicographically sorted file names that match the pattern. If no file name that matches the pattern is found, the word is left unchanged. When a pattern is used for file-name generation, the character dot (.) at the start of a file name or immediately following a /, as well as the character / itself, must be matched explicitly. A file name beginning with a dot is not matched with a pattern with the dot inside parentheses; that is, ls .@(r*) would locate a file named .restore, but ls @(.r*) would not.

In other instances of pattern matching, the / and . are not treated specially.

*	Match any string, including the null string.
?	Match any single character.
[...]	Match any one of the enclosed characters. A pair of characters separated by - matches any character lexically between the pair, inclusive. If the first character following the opening square bracket ([ ) is an exclamation mark (!), then any character not enclosed is matched. You can include a dash (-) in the character set by putting it as the first or last character.

A *pattern-list* is a list of one or more patterns separated from each other with a |. You can form composite patterns with one or more of the following.

?(*pattern-list*)

   Optionally match any one of the given patterns.

*(*pattern-list*)

   Match zero or more occurrences of the given patterns.

+(*pattern-list*)

   Match one or more occurrences of the given patterns.

@(*pattern-list*)

   Match exactly one of the given patterns.

!(*pattern-list*)

   Match anything except one of the given patterns.

Quoting (Escaping) Characters

Each of the metacharacters has a special meaning to the shell. To remove the normal meaning, you can quote it. (Note that in other contexts, the term escape is used to describe this action.) You can quote a single character (that is, make it stand for itself) by preceding it with a backslash. The pair \newline is removed.

To quote a string of characters, you can enclose them in quotes.

- All characters enclosed between a pair of single quote marks (' ') are quoted. A single quote cannot appear within single quotes.

- Inside double-quote marks (""), parameter and command substitution occur, and \ quotes the characters \, `, ", and $. The meaning of $* and $@ is identical when not quoted or when used as a parameter assignment value or as a file name. However, when used as a command argument, $* is equivalent to $1d$2d..., where d is the first character of the IFS variable, whereas $@ is equivalent to $1 $2....

- Inside grave quote marks (` `), \ quotes the characters \, `, and $. If the grave quotes occur within double quotes, then \ also quotes the character ".

You can remove the special meaning of reserved words or aliases by quoting any character of the reserved word. The recognition of function names or special command names cannot be altered by quoting them.

Arithmetic Evaluation

The let special command provides the capability of performing integer arithmetic. Evaluations are performed using long arithmetic. Constants are of the form [base#] n, where base is a decimal number between 2 and 36 representing the arithmetic base and n is a number in that base. If you omit base, then base 10 is used. An arithmetic expression uses the same syntax, precedence, and associativity of expression as the C language. All the integral operators, other than ++, --, ?:, and , are supported. You can reference variables by name within an arithmetic expression without using the parameter substitution syntax. When you reference a variable, its value is evaluated as an arithmetic expression.

You can specify an internal integer representation of a variable with the -i option of the typeset special command. Arithmetic evaluation is performed on the value of each assignment to a variable with the -i attribute. If you do not specify an arithmetic base, the first assignment to the variable determines the arithmetic base. This base is used when parameter substitution occurs.

Because many of the arithmetic operators require quoting, an alternative form of the let command is provided. For any command that begins with a ((, all the characters until a matching)) are treated as a quoted expression. More precisely, ((...)) is equivalent to let "...".

Conditional Expressions

Use conditional expressions with the [[compound command to test attributes of files and to compare strings.

Word splitting and file-name generation are not performed on the words between [[and]]. Each expression can be constructed from one or more of the following unary or binary expressions.

-a *file*	true if *file* exists.
-b *file*	true if *file* exists and is a block special file.
-c *file*	true if *file* exists and is a character special file.
-d *file*	true if *file* exists and is a directory.
-e *file*	true if *file* exists.
-f *file*	true if *file* exists and is an ordinary file.
-g *file*	true if *file* exists and has its setgid bit set.
-k *file*	true if *file* exists and has its sticky bit set.
-n *string*	true if length of *string* is non-zero.
-o *option*	true if option named *option* is on.
-p *file*	true if *file* exists and is a fifo special file or a pipe.
-r *file*	true if *file* exists and is readable by current process.
-s *file*	true if *file* exists and has size greater than 0.
-t *fildes*	true if file descriptor number *fildes* is open and associated with a terminal device.
-u *file*	true if *file* exists and has its setuid bit set.
-w *file*	true if *file* exists and is writable by current process.
-x *file*	true if *file* exists and is executable by current process. If *file* exists and is a directory, then the current process has permission to search in the directory.
-z *string*	true if length of *string* is 0.
-L *file*	true if *file* exists and is a symbolic link.
-O *file*	true if *file* exists and is owned by the effective user ID of this process.
-G *file*	true if *file* exists and its group matches the effective group ID of this process.
-S *file*	true if *file* exists and is a socket.
file1 -nt *file2*	true if *file1* exists and is newer than *file2*.
file1 -ot *file2*	true if *file1* exists and is older than *file2*.

file1 -ef *file2*

> true if *file1* and *file2* exist and refer to the same file.

string   true if the string *string* is not the null string.

string = *pattern*

> true if *string* matches *pattern*.

string != *pattern*

> true if *string* does not match *pattern*.

string1 = *string2*

> true if the strings *string1* and *string2* are identical.

string1 ! = *string2*

> true if the strings *string1* and *string2* are not identical.

string1 < *string2*

> true if *string1* comes before *string2* based on strings interpreted as appropriate to the locale setting for category LC_COLLATE.

string1 > *string2*

> true if *string1* comes after *string2* based on strings interpreted as appropriate to the locale setting for category LC_COLLATE.

exp1 -eq *exp2*

> true if *exp1* is equal to *exp2*.

exp1 -ne *exp2*

> true if *exp1* is not equal to *exp2*.

exp1 -lt *exp2*

> true if *exp1* is less than *exp2*.

exp1 -gt *exp2*

> true if *exp1* is greater than *exp2*.

exp1 -le *exp2*

> true if *exp1* is less than or equal to *exp2*.

exp1 -ge *exp2*

> true if *exp1* is greater than or equal to *exp2*.

In each of the above expressions, if *file* is of the form /dev/fd/*n*, where *n* is an integer, then the test is applied to the open file whose descriptor number is *n*.

You can construct a compound expression from these primitives by using any of the following, listed in decreasing order of precedence.

(*expression*)

> true if *expression* is true. Use to group expressions.

! *expression*

> true if *expression* is false.

expression1 && *expression2*

> true if *expression1* and *expression2* are both true.

expression1 || *expression2*

> true if either *expression1* or *expression2* is true.

Environment Variables

The environment (see environ(5)) is a list of name-value pairs that is passed to an executed program in the same way as a normal argument list. The names must be identifiers, and the values are character strings. The shell interacts with the environment in several ways. On invocation, the shell scans the environment and creates a variable for each name found, giving it the corresponding value and marking it export. Executed commands inherit the environment. If the user modifies the values of these variables or creates new ones by using the export or typeset -x commands, they become part of the environment. The environment seen by any executed command is thus composed of any name-value pairs originally inherited by the shell, whose values may be modified by the current shell, plus any additions that must be noted in export or typeset -x commands.

You can augment the environment for any simple command or function by prefixing it with one or more variable assignments. A variable assignment argument is a word of the form *identifier*=*value*. Thus:

TERM=450 *cmd args*

and

(export TERM; TERM=450; *cmd args*)

are equivalent (as far as the above execution of *cmd* is concerned except for special commands listed in "Special Commands" on page 623 that are preceded with an asterisk).

If the -k option is set, all variable assignment arguments are placed in the environment, even if they occur after the command name. The following example first prints a=b c and then c:

```
$ echo a=b c
a=b c
$ set -k
```

```
$ echo a=b c
c
$
```

Note — Because this feature is intended for use with scripts written for early versions of the shell, its use in new scripts is strongly discouraged. The feature is likely to disappear someday.

Functions

Use the `function` reserved word to define shell functions. Shell functions are read in and stored internally. Alias names are resolved when the function is read. Functions are executed like commands with the arguments passed as positional parameters.

Functions execute in the same process as the caller and share all files and present working directory with the caller. Traps caught by the caller are reset to their default action inside the function. A trap condition that is not caught or ignored by the function terminates the function and passes the condition on to the caller. A trap on `EXIT` set inside a function is executed after the function completes in the environment of the caller. Ordinarily, variables are shared between the calling program and the function. However, the `typeset` special command used within a function defines local variables whose scope includes the current function and all functions it calls.

Use the `return` special command to return from function calls. Errors within functions return control to the caller.

`typeset +f` lists the names of all functions. `typeset -f` lists all function names as well as the text of all functions. `typeset -f` *function-names* lists the text of the named functions only. You can undefine functions with the `-f` option of the `unset` special command.

Ordinarily, functions are unset when the shell executes a shell script. The `-xf` option of the `typeset` command enables you to export a function to scripts that are executed without a separate invocation of the shell. Specify functions that need to be defined across separate invocations of the shell in the ENV file with the `-xf` option of `typeset`.

Function Definition Command

A function is a user-defined name that is used as a simple command to call a compound command with new positional parameters. A function is defined with a function definition command. The format of a function definition command is as follows:

fname() compound-command[io-redirect...]

The function is named *fname*; it must be a name. An implementation may allow other characters in a function name as an extension. The implementation maintains separate name spaces for functions and variables. The `()` in the function definition command consists of two operators. Therefore, intermixing blank characters with the *fname*, (, and) is allowed, but unnecessary. The argument *compound-command* represents a compound command.

When you declare a function, none of the expansions in `wordexp` are performed on the text in *compound-command* or *io-redirect*; all expansions are performed as normal each time you call the function. Similarly, the optional *io-redirect* redirections and any variable assignments within *compound-command* are performed during the execution of the function itself, not the function definition.

When a function is executed, it has the syntax-error and variable-assignment properties described for the special built-in commands.

The *compound-command* is executed whenever the function name is specified as the name of a simple command The operands to the command temporarily become the positional parameters during the execution of the *compound-command*; the special parameter # is also changed to reflect the number of operands. The special parameter 0 is unchanged. When the function completes, the values of the positional parameters and the special parameter # are restored to the values they had before the function was executed. If the special built-in return is executed in the *compound-command*, the function completes and execution resumes with the next command after the function call.

The following example shows how you can use a function definition wherever a simple command is allowed.

```
# If variable i is equal to "yes",
# define function foo to be ls -l
#
["$i" = yes] && foo() {
  ls -l
}
```

The exit status of a function definition is 0 if the function was declared successfully; otherwise, it is greater than 0. The exit status of a function invocation is the exit status of the last command executed by the function.

Special Commands

The following simple commands are executed in the shell process. Input/output redirection is permitted. Unless otherwise indicated, the output is written on file descriptor 1 and the exit status, when there is no syntax error, is 0.

Commands that are preceded by one or two asterisks (*) are treated specially in the following ways.

- Variable assignment lists preceding the command remain in effect when the command completes.

- I/O redirections are processed after variable assignments.

- Errors abort a script that contains them.

- Words following a command preceded by ** that are in the format of a variable assignment are expanded with the same rules as a variable assignment. This means that tilde substitution is performed after the equal sign and word-splitting and file-name generation are not performed.

* : [*arg...*]

> Expand only parameters.

* . *file* [*arg...*]

> Read the complete file, then execute the commands. Execute the commands in the current shell environment. Use the search path specified by PATH to find the directory containing *file*. If you specify any arguments *arg*, they become the positional parameters. Otherwise, the positional parameters are unchanged. The exit status is the exit status of the last command executed.

** alias [-tx] [*name*[=*value*]]...

> With no arguments, print the list of aliases in the form *name*=*value* on standard output. An alias is defined for each *name* whose *value* is given. A trailing space in value checks the next word for alias substitution. Use the -t option to set and list tracked aliases. The value of a tracked alias is the full path name corresponding to the given name. The value becomes undefined when the value of PATH is reset, but the aliases remained tracked. Without the -t option, for each name in the argument list for which no value is given, print the name and value of the alias. Use the -x option to set or print exported aliases. An exported alias is defined for scripts invoked by name. The exit status is non-zero if you specify a *name* but no *value* and if no alias has been defined for the *name*.

bg [%*job*...]

> Available only on systems that support job control. Puts each specified job into the background. If you specify no *job*, put the current job in the background. See "Job Control" on page 599 for a description of the format of *job*.

* break [*n*] Exit from the enclosed for, while, until, or select loop, if any. If you specify *n*, then break *n* levels.

* continue [*n*]

> Resume the next iteration of the enclosed for, while, until, or select loop. If you specify *n*, then resume at the *n*-th enclosed loop.

cd [*arg*]   In the first form, change the current directory to *arg*. If *arg* is -,
cd *old new*   change the directory to the previous directory. The shell variable
               HOME is the default *arg*. The variable PWD is set to the current
               directory. The shell variable CDPATH defines the search path for the
               directory containing *arg*. Alternative directory names are
               separated by a colon (:). The default path is null (specifying the
               current directory). Note that the current directory is specified by a
               null path name, which can appear immediately after the equal sign
               or between the colon delimiters anywhere else in the path list. If
               arg begins with a /, do not use the search path. Otherwise, search
               each directory in the path for *arg*. The second form substitutes the
               string *new* for the string *old* in the current directory name, PWD,
               and tries to change to this new directory. The cd command may not
               be executed by rksh.

command [-p] [*command-name*] [*argument*...]
command [-v -V] *command-name*

               The command command treats the arguments as a simple
               command, suppressing the shell function lookup. The -p option
               performs the command search, using a default value for PATH that
               is guaranteed to find all of the standard commands. The -v option
               writes a string to standard output that indicates the path name or
               command used by the shell, in the current shell execution
               environment, to invoke *command-name*. The -V option writes a
               string to standard output that indicates how the name given in the
               command-name operand is interpreted in the current shell
               execution environment.

echo [*arg*...]   *New!*

               See echo(1) for usage and description.

* eval [*arg*...]

               Read the arguments as input to the shell and execute the resulting
               command(s).

* exec [*arg*...]

               If you specify *arg*, execute the command specified by the
               arguments in place of this shell without creating a new process.
               Input/output arguments can appear and affect the current process.
               If you specify no arguments, modify file descriptors as prescribed
               by the input/output redirection list. In this case, any file descriptor
               numbers greater than 2 that are opened with this mechanism are
               closed when another program is invoked.

* exit [*n*]   Exit the calling shell or shell script with the exit status specified by *n*. The value is the least significant 8 bits of the specified status. If you omit *n*, then the exit status is that of the last command executed. When exit occurs when executing a trap, the last command refers to the command that executed before the trap was invoked. An EOF exits the shell except for a shell that has the ignoreeof option turned on.

** export [*name*[=*value*]]...

Mark the given names for automatic export to the environment of subsequently executed commands.

fc [-e *ename*] [-nlr] [*first* [*last*]]
fc -e - [*old=new*] [*command*]

In the first form, choose a range of commands from *first* to *last* from the last HISTSIZE commands that were typed at the terminal. You can specify the arguments *first* and *last* as a number or as a string. Use a string to locate the most recent command starting with the given string. Use a negative number as an offset to the current command number. If you use the -l option, list the command on standard output. Otherwise, invoke the editor program *ename* on a file containing these keyboard commands. If you do not supply *ename*, use the value of the variable FCEDIT (default /bin/ed) as the editor. When editing is complete, execute the edited command(s). If you do not specify *last*, then the command is set to *first*. If you do not specify *first*, the default is the previous command for editing and -16 for listing. The -r option reverses the order of the commands, and the -n option suppresses command numbers when listing. In the second form, the command is reexecuted after it performs the substitution *old=new*. If you specify no command argument, execute the most recent command typed at this terminal.

fg [%*job*...]

On systems that support job control only, bring each job specified to the foreground. Otherwise, bring the current job into the foreground. See "Job Control" on page 599 for a description of the format of *job*.

getopts *optstring name* [*arg*...]

Check *arg* for legal options. If you omit *arg*, use the positional parameters. Begin an option argument with a + or a -. An option not beginning with + or - or the argument -- ends the options. *optstring* contains the letters that getopts recognizes. If you follow a letter by a :, that option is expected to have an argument. You can separate the options from the argument by blanks. getopts places the next option letter it finds inside variable *name* each time it is invoked with a + prepended when *arg* begins with a +. The index of the next *arg* is stored in OPTIND. The option argument, if any, is stored in OPTARG. A leading : in *optstring* stores the letter of an invalid option in OPTARG and sets name to ? for an unknown option and to : when a required option is missing. Otherwise, getopts prints an error message. The exit status is non-zero when there are no more options. See getoptcvt(1) for usage and description.

hash [*name...*]

For each *name*, determine the location in the search path of the command specified by *name* and remember it. The -r option forgets all remembered locations. If you give no arguments, present information about remembered commands. In the hash output, Hits is the number of times a command has been invoked by the shell process. Cost is a measure of the work required to locate a command in the search path. If a command is found in a relative directory in the search path, after changing to that directory, recalculate the stored location of that command. Recalculated commands are indicated by an asterisk (*) adjacent to the Hits information. Cost is incremented when the recalculation is done.

jobs [-lnp] [%*job...*]

List information about each given job; or, if you omit *job*, list all active jobs. The -l option lists process IDs in addition to the normal information. The -n option displays only jobs that have stopped or exited since last notified. The -p option lists only the process group. See "Job Control" on page 599 and jobs(1) for a description of the format of *job*.

kill [-*sig*] %*job...*
kill [-*sig*] *pid...*
kill -l

Send either the TERM (terminate) signal or the specified signal to the specified jobs or processes. You can specify signals either by number or by name (as given in signal(5) stripped of the prefix SIG, with the exception that SIGCHD is named CHLD). If you send TERM (terminate) or HUP (hangup), then the job or process is sent a CONT (continue) signal if it is stopped. The argument *job* can be the process ID of a process that is not a member of one of the active jobs. See "Job Control" on page 599 for a description of the format of *job*. The third form, kill -l, lists the signal names.

let *arg...*   Each *arg* is a separate arithmetic expression to be evaluated. The exit status is 0 if the value of the last expression is non-zero, and 1 otherwise.

login *argument...*

Equivalent to exec login *argument....* See login(1) for usage and description.

* newgrp [*arg*...]

> Equivalent to exec /bin/newgrp *arg*....

print [-Rnprsu[n]] [*arg*...]

> The shell output mechanism. With no options or with option - or --, print the arguments on standard output as described by echo(1). The exit status is 0, unless the output file is not open for writing.

-n
> Suppress newline from being added to the output.

-R | -r
> Ignore the escape conventions of echo. The -R option prints all subsequent arguments and options other than -n.

-p
> Write the arguments to the pipe of the process spawned with |& instead of standard output.

-s
> Write the arguments to the history file instead of standard output.

-u [*n*]
> Specify a one-digit file descriptor unit number *n* on which the output is placed. The default is 1.

pwd
> Equivalent to print -r - $PWD.

Read
> Read one line.

read [-prsu[n]] [*name*?*prompt*] [*name*...]

> Break up the shell input into fields, using the characters in IFS as separators. Use the escape character (\) to remove any special meaning for the next character and for line continuation. In raw mode, -r, the \ character is not treated specially. Assign the first field to the first *name*, the second field to the second *name*, and so on, with leftover fields assigned to the last *name*. The -p option takes the input line from the input pipe of a process spawned by the shell using |&.

> If you specify the -s option, save the input as a command in the history file. Use the -u option to specify a one-digit file descriptor unit *n* to read from. The file descriptor can be opened with the exec special command. The default value of *n* is 0. If you omit *name*, then use REPLY as the default name. The exit status is 0 unless the input file is not open for reading or an end-of-file is encountered. An end-of-file with the -p option cleans up for this process so that another can be spawned. If the first argument contains a ?, use the remainder of this word as a prompt on standard error when the shell is interactive. The exit status is 0 unless an end-of-file is encountered.

** readonly [*name*[=*value*]]...

> Mark the given names read-only. You cannot change these names by subsequent assignment.

```
* return [n]
```

Return the invoking script for a shell function or . script with the
return status specified by *n*. The value is the least significant 8 bits
of the specified status. If you omit *n*, then the return status is that
of the last command executed. If you invoke `return` while not in a
function or a . script, then it is the same as an exit.

```
set [± abCefhkmnopstuvx] [± o option]... [± A name] [arg...]
```

New!

The options for this command have meaning as follows.

-A	Unset the variable name and assign array values sequentially from the list *arg*. If you use +A, do not first unset the variable name.
-a	Automatically export all subsequent variables that are defined.
-b	Notify the user asynchronously of background job completions. The following message is written to standard error:

`"[%d]%c %s%s\n"`, *job-number*, *current*, *status*, *job-name*

where the fields are as follows:

current	The + character identifies the job that would be used as a default for the fg or bg commands. You can also specify this job with the *job-id* %+ or %%. The - character identifies the job that would become the default if the current default job were to exit. You can also specify this job with the *job-id* %-. For other jobs, this field is a space character. At most one job can be identified with +, and at most one job can be identified with -. If there is any suspended job, then the current job is a suspended job. If there are at least two suspended jobs, then the previous job is also a suspended job.
job-name	Unspecified. When the shell notifies the user that a job has been completed, it may remove the job's process ID from the list of those known in the current shell execution environment. Asynchronous notification is not enabled by default.
job-number	A number used to identify the process group to the wait, fg, bg, and kill commands. Using these commands, you can identify the job by prefixing the job number with %.
status	Unspecified.
-C	Prevent existing files from being overwritten by the shell's > redirection operator; the >| redirection operator overrides this `noclobber` option for an individual file.

`-e`	If a command has a non-zero exit status, execute the ERR trap, if set, and exit. This mode is disabled while profiles are read.
`-f`	Disable file-name generation.
`-h`	Make each command a tracked alias when first encountered.
`-k`	Put all variable assignment arguments in the environment for a command, not just those that precede the command name.
`-m`	Run background jobs in a separate process group and print a line on completion. Report the exit status of background jobs in a completion message. On systems with job control, this option is turned on automatically for interactive shells.
`-n`	Read commands and check them for syntax errors, but do not execute them. Ignored for interactive shells.
`-o`	The argument for this option can be one of the following names:

`allexport`	Same as `-a`.
`errexit`	Same as `-e`.
`bgnice`	Run all background jobs at a lower priority. This mode is the default.
`emacs`	Put you in an `emacs`-style inline editor for command entry.
`gmacs`	Put you in a `gmacs`-style inline editor for command entry.
`ignoreeof`	Do not exit on end-of-file. You must use the `exit` command.
`keyword`	Same as `-k`.
`markdirs`	Append a trailing / to all directory names resulting from file-name generation.
`monitor`	Same as `-m`.
`noclobber`	Prevent redirection > from truncating existing files. Require >| to truncate a file when turned on. Equivalent to `-C`.
`noexec`	Same as `-n`.
`noglob`	Same as `-f`.
`nolog`	Do not save function definitions in history file.
`notify`	Equivalent to `-b`.

	`nounset`	Same as -u.
	`privileged`	Same as -p.
	`verbose`	Same as -v.
	`trackall`	Same as -h.
	`vi`	Put you in insert mode of a `vi`-style inline editor until you press escape character 033 to enter control mode. A Return sends the line.
	`viraw`	Process each character as it is typed in `vi` mode.
	`xtrace`	Same as -x.

If you supply no option name, then print the current option settings.

-p   Disable processing of the `$HOME/.profile` file and use the file `/etc/suid_profile` instead of the ENV file. This mode is on whenever the effective UID is not equal to the real UID, or when the effective GID is not equal to the real GID. Turning this option off sets the effective UID and GID to the real UID and GID.

-s   Sort the positional parameters lexicographically.

-t   Exit after reading and executing one command.

-u   Treat unset parameters as an error when substituting.

-v   Print shell input lines as they are read.

-x   Print commands and their arguments as they are executed.

–   Turn off -x and -v options and stop examining arguments for options.

––   Do not change any of the options; useful in setting $1 to a value beginning with -. If no arguments follow this option, unset the positional parameters. Using + instead of - turns these options off. You can also use these options on invocation of the shell. The current set of options can be found in `$-`. Unless you specify -A, assign the remaining arguments as positional parameters, in order, to $1 $2 . . . . If you specify no arguments, print the names and values of all variables on the standard output.

* `shift [n]` Rename the positional parameters from $n+1 $n+1 . . . as $1 . . ., default n is 1. The parameter n can be any arithmetic expression that evaluates to a nonnegative number less than or equal to $#.

```
stop %job-id...
stop pid...
```

Stop the execution of a background job(s) by using its `job-id`, or of any process by using its `pid` (see `ps(1)`).

suspend   Stop the execution of the current shell (but not if it is the login shell).

test *expression*

Evaluate conditional expressions. See "Conditional Expressions" on page 619 and `test(1)` for usage and description.

* times   Print the accumulated user and system times for the shell and for processes run from the shell.

* trap [*arg sig*...] *arg*

Read and execute the command when the shell receives signal(s) `sig`. Scan `arg` once when the trap is set and once when the trap is taken. You can specify `sig` as a signal number or signal name. Execute `trap` commands in order of signal number. Any attempt to set a trap on a signal number that was ignored on entry to the current shell is ineffective. If `arg` is -, reset each `sig` to the default value. If `arg` is null (`' '`), ignore each specified `sig` if it arises. Otherwise, read and execute `arg` when one of the corresponding `sig`s arises.

The action of the trap overrides a previous action (either default action or one explicitly set). The value of `$?` after the trap action completes is the value it had before the trap was invoked. `sig` can be EXIT, 0 (equivalent to EXIT) or a signal specified using a symbolic name, without the SIG prefix, for example, HUP, INT, QUIT, TERM. If `sig` is 0 or EXIT and the trap statement is executed inside the body of a function, execute the command `arg` after the function completes. If `sig` is 0 or EXIT for a trap set outside any function, execute the command `arg` on exit from the shell. If `sig` is ERR. execute `arg` whenever a command has a non-zero exit status. If `sig` is DEBUG, execute `arg` after each command. The environment in which the shell executes a trap on EXIT is identical to the environment immediately after the last command executed before the trap on EXIT was taken. Each time the trap is invoked, process `arg` in a manner equivalent to `eval "$arg"`.

You cannot trap or reset signals that were ignored on entry to a noninteractive shell, although no error need be reported when attempting to do so. An interactive shell may reset or catch signals ignored on entry. Traps remain in place for a given shell until explicitly changed with another `trap` command. When a subshell is entered, traps are set to the default `args`. This does not imply that you cannot use the `trap` command within the subshell to set new traps. The `trap` command with no arguments writes to standard output a list of commands associated with each `sig`. The format is:

```
trap -- %s %s... arg, sig...
```

The shell formats the output, including the proper use of quoting, so that it is suitable for reinput to the shell as commands that achieve the same trapping results. For example:

```
save_traps=$(trap)
...
eval "$save_traps"
```

If the trap name or number is invalid, return a non-zero exit status; otherwise, return 0. For both interactive and noninteractive shells, invalid signal names or numbers are not considered a syntax error and do not abort the shell. Traps are not processed while a job is waiting for a foreground process. Thus, a trap on CHLD won't be executed until the foreground job terminates.

type *name*...

For each *name*, indicate how it would be interpreted if used as a command name.

** typeset [± HLRZfilrtux[n]] [*name*[=*value*]]...

Set attributes and values for shell variables and functions. When you invoke typeset inside a function, create a new instance of the variable *name*. Restore the variables *value* and *type* when the function completes. You can specify the following attributes.

-H	Provide UNIX to host-name file mapping on non-UNIX machines.
-L	Left-justify and remove leading blanks from *value*. If *n* is non-zero, it defines the width of the field; otherwise, determine it by the width of the value of first assignment. When the variable is assigned, it is filled on the right with blanks or truncated, if necessary, to fit into the field. Leading 0s are removed if the -Z option is also set. The -R option is turned off.
-R	Right-justify and fill with leading blanks. If *n* is non-zero, it defines the width of the field; otherwise, determine it by the width of the value of first assignment. The field is left-filled with blanks or truncated from the end if the variable is reassigned. The -L option is turned off.
-Z	Right-justify and fill with leading 0s if the first non-blank character is a digit and you have not used the -L option. If *n* is non-zero, it defines the width of the field; otherwise, determine it by the width of the value of first assignment.
-f	The names refer to function names instead of variable names. No assignments can be made, and the only other valid options are -t, -u, and -x.

-i	Parameter is an integer. This makes arithmetic faster. If *n* is non-zero, it defines the output arithmetic base; otherwise, the first assignment determines the output base.
-l	Convert all uppercase characters to lower case. The -u uppercase option is turned off.
-r	Mark the given names read-only. You cannot change these names by subsequent assignment.
-t	Tag the variables. Tags are user definable and have no special meaning to the shell.
-u	Convert all lowercase characters to uppercase characters. The -l lowercase option is turned off.
-x	Mark the given names for automatic export to the environment of subsequently executed commands.

You cannot specify the -l attribute along with -R,-L, -Z, or -f.

Using + instead of - turns these options off. If you specify no *name* arguments but specify options, print a list of names (and optionally the values) of the variables that have these options set. (Using + instead of - keeps the values from being printed.) If you specify no names or if options are given, print the names and attributes of all variables.

ulimit [-HSacdfnstv] [*limit*]

Set or display a resource limit. The available resources limits are listed below. Many systems do not contain one or more of these limits. When you specify a limit for a specific resource, it is set. The value of *limit* can be a number in the unit specified below with each resource, or the value unlimited. The H and S options specify whether the hard limit or the soft limit for the given resource is set. Once a hard limit is set, you cannot increase it. You can increase a soft limit up to the value of the hard limit. If you specify neither the H nor S option, the limit applies to both. Print the current resource limit when you omit *limit*. In this case, print the soft limit unless you specified H. When you specify more than one resource, print the limit name and unit before the value.

-a	List all of the current resource limits.
-c	The number of 512-byte blocks on the size of core dumps.
-d	The number of Kbytes on the size of the data area.
-f	The number of 512-byte blocks on files written by child processes (files of any size may be read).
-n	The number of file descriptors plus 1.
-s	The number of Kbytes on the size of the stack area.
-t	The number of seconds to be used by each process.

-v   The number of Kbytes for virtual memory. If you specify
            no option, assume -f.

umask [-S] [*mask*]

Set the user file-creation mask to *mask* (see umask(2)). *mask* can be
either an octal number or a symbolic value as described in
chmod(1). If you specify a symbolic value, the new umask value is
the complement of the result of applying *mask* to the complement of
the previous umask value. If you omit *mask*, print the current value
of the mask. The -S option produces symbolic output.

unalias *name*...

Remove the aliases given by the list of names from the alias list.

unset [-f] *name*...

Unassign the variables given by the list of names, that is, erase
their values and attributes. You cannot unset read-only variables.
If you specify the -f, option, the names refer to function names.
Unsetting ERRNO, LINENO, MAILCHECK, OPTARG, OPTIND, RANDOM,
SECONDS, TMOUT, and _ removes their special meaning even if they
are subsequently assigned.

* wait [*job*]

Wait for the specified job and report its termination status. If you
do not specify *job*, wait for all currently active child processes. The
exit status from this command is that of the process waited for. See
"Job Control" on page 599 for a description of the format of *job*.

whence [-pv] *name*...

For each *name*, indicate how it would be interpreted if used as a
command name. The -v option produces a more verbose report. The
-p option does a path search for *name* even if *name* is an alias, a
function, or a reserved word.

Errors

Errors detected by the shell, such as syntax errors, return a non-zero exit
status. Otherwise, the shell returns the exit status of the last command
executed (see also the exit command). If the shell is being used
noninteractively, then execution of the shell file is abandoned. Runtime errors
detected by the shell are reported by printing the command or function name
and the error condition. If the line number at which the error occurred is
greater than 1, then the line number is also printed in square brackets ([ ])
after the command or function name. For a noninteractive shell, an error

condition encountered by a special built-in or other type of command writes a diagnostic message to standard error and exits as shown in the following table.

Error	Special Built-in	Other Utilities
Shell language syntax error	Exit	Exit
Utility syntax error (option or operand error)	Exit	Do not exit
Redirection error	Exit	Do not exit
Variable assignment error	Exit	Do not exit
Expansion error	Exit	Exit
Command not found	N/A	May exit
Dot script not found	Exit	N/A

An expansion error is one that occurs when the shell expansions are carried out (for example, ${x!y}, because ! is not a valid operator); an implementation may treat these as syntax errors if it is able to detect them during tokenization instead of during expansion.

If any of the errors shown as (may) exit occur in a subshell, the subshell (may) exit with a non-zero status, but the script containing the subshell does not exit because of the error.

In all of the cases shown in the table, an interactive shell writes a diagnostic message to standard error without exiting.

Notes

Some very old shell scripts contain a ^ as a synonym for the pipe character |.

The built-in command . *file* reads the whole file before executing any commands. Therefore, alias and unalias commands in the file do not apply to any functions defined within the file.

When the shell executes a shell script that tries to execute a nonexistent command interpreter, the shell returns an erroneous diagnostic message that the shell script file does not exist.

Usage

See largefile(5) for the description of the behavior of ksh and rksh when encountering files greater than or equal to 2 Gbytes (2**31 bytes).

Exit Status

Each command has an exit status that can influence the behavior of other shell commands. The exit status of commands that are not treated as commands is documented in this section. The exit status of the standard commands is documented in their respective sections.

If a command is not found, the exit status is 127. If the command name is found, but the command is not executable, the exit status is 126. Applications that invoke commands without using the shell should use these exit status values to report similar errors.

If a command fails during word expansion or redirection, its exit status is greater than 0.

When reporting the exit status with the special parameter ?, the shell reports the full 8 bits of exit status available. The exit status of a command that terminated because it received a signal is reported as greater than 128.

Files

```
/etc/profile
/etc/suid_profile
$HOME/.profile
/tmp/sh*
/dev/null
```

Attributes

See attributes(5) for descriptions of the following attributes:

/usr/bin/ksh, /usr/bin/rksh

Attribute Type	Attribute Value
Availability	SUNWcsu
CSI	Enabled

/usr/xpg4/bin/ksh

Attribute Type	Attribute Value
Availability	SUNWxcu4
CSI	Enabled

See Also

cat(1), cd(1), chmod(1), cut(1), echo(1), env(1), getoptcvt(1), jobs(1), login(1), newgrp(1), paste(1), ps(1), shell_builtins(1), stty(1), test(1), vi(1), dup(2), exec(2), fork(2), ioctl(2), lseek(2), pipe(2), ulimit(2), umask(2), wait(2), rand(3C), signal(3C), a.out(4), profile(4), attributes(5), environ(5), largefile(5), signal(5), xpg4(5)

Morris I. Bolsky and David G. Korn, *The Korn Shell Command and Programming Language*, Prentice Hall, 1989.

ksrvtgt — Fetch and Store Kerberos Ticket-Granting Ticket, Using a Service Key

Synopsis

    /usr/bin/ksrvtgt name instance [[realm] srvtab]

Description

The `ksrvtgt` command is part of the set of Secure RPC commands. `ksrvtgt` performs the following actions:

- Retrieves a Kerberos ticket-granting ticket with a lifetime of five minutes for the principal `name.instance@realm` (or `name.instance@localrealm` if you do not supply `realm` on the command line).
- Decrypts the response, using the service key found in the file `srvtab` (or in `/etc/srvtab` if you do not specify `srvtab` on the command line).
- Stores the ticket in the standard ticket cache.

Note — This command is intended primarily for use in shell scripts and other batch-type facilities.

Diagnostics

Generic `kerberos` failure (`kfailure`) can indicate a whole range of problems, the most common of which is the inability to read the service key file.

Files

    /etc/krb.conf

> To get the name of the local realm.

    /tmp/tktuid

> The default ticket file.

    /etc/srvtab

> The default service key file.

Attributes

See `attributes`(5) for descriptions of the following attributes:

Attribute Type	Attribute Value
Availability	SUNWcsu

See Also

kdestroy(1), kerberos(1), kinit(1), klist(1), attributes(5)

L

last — Display Login and Logout Information

Synopsis

```
/usr/bin/last [-n number | -number] [-f filename] [name | tty]...
```

Description

Use the `last` command to display login and logout information about users and terminals. The `last` command looks in the `/var/adm/wtmpx` file, which records all logins and logouts. You can use the arguments to specify names of users or terminals of interest. If you specify multiple arguments, the information applicable to the arguments is printed. For example, `last root console` lists all of root's sessions, as well as all sessions on the console terminal. `last` displays the sessions of the specified users and terminals, most recent first, indicating the times at which the session began, the duration of the session, and the terminal on which the session took place. `last` also indicates whether the session is continuing or was cut short by a reboot.

The pseudo-user `reboot` logs in when the system reboots. Thus, the following example shows the mean time between reboots.

```
castle% last reboot
reboot    system boot                    Thu Mar  4 11:10
reboot    system boot                    Thu Mar  4 07:35
reboot    system boot                    Wed Mar  3 18:40
```

641

```
wtmp begins Wed Mar   3 18:40
castle%
```

last with no arguments displays a record of all logins and logouts, in reverse order, as shown in the following example.

```
castle% last
winsor    console      :0        Thu Mar  4 11:13    still logged in
reboot    system boot            Thu Mar  4 11:10
winsor    console      :0        Thu Mar  4 07:38 - 08:46  (01:07)
reboot    system boot            Thu Mar  4 07:35
root      console      :0        Wed Mar  3 19:55 - 19:55  (00:00)
winsor    console      :0        Wed Mar  3 19:52 - 19:54  (00:02)
winsor    console      :0        Wed Mar  3 19:51 - 19:52  (00:00)
root      console      :0        Wed Mar  3 18:44 - 19:51  (01:06)
root      console                Wed Mar  3 18:43 - 18:43  (00:00)
reboot    system boot            Wed Mar  3 18:40

wtmp begins Wed Mar   3 18:40
castle%
```

If last is interrupted, it indicates how far the search has progressed in /var/adm/wtmpx. If interrupted with a quit signal (generated by a Control-\), last indicates how far the search has progressed and then continues the search.

Options

-n *number*|-*number*

> Limit the number of entries displayed to that specified by *number*. These options are identical; the -*number* option is provided as a transition tool only and will be removed in future releases.

-f *filename*

> Use *filename* as the name of the accounting file instead of /var/adm/wtmpx.

Environment Variables

Date and time format is based on locale specified by the LC_ALL, LC_TIME, or LANG environments, in that order of priority.

Files

/var/adm/wtmpx

> Accounting file.

Attributes

See attributes(5) for descriptions of the following attributes:

Attribute Type	Attribute Value
Availability	SUNWesu

See Also

utmp(4), attributes(5)

---

lastcomm — Display the Last Commands Executed, in Reverse Order

Synopsis

/usr/bin/lastcomm [*command-name*]...[*user-name*]...[*terminal-name*]...

Description

The lastcomm command shows information about previously executed accounting commands that are stored in the /var/adm/pacct file. lastcomm with no arguments displays information about all the commands recorded during the current accounting file's lifetime. If you specify arguments, lastcomm displays only accounting entries with a matching *command-name*, *user-name*, or *terminal-name*.

If *terminal-name* is - -, there was no controlling TTY for the process. The process was probably executed during boot time. If *terminal-name* is ??, the controlling TTY could not be decoded into a printable name.

For each process entry, lastcomm displays the following information:

- The command name under which the process was called.
- One or more flags indicating special information about the process. The flags have the following meanings:

  F   The process performed a fork but not an exec.

  S   The process ran as a setuid program.

- The name of the user who ran the process.
- The terminal where the user was logged in at the time (if applicable).
- The amount of CPU time used by the process (in seconds).
- The date and time the process exited.

Examples

The following command lists all the executions of commands named a.out by user root while using the terminal term/01.

```
castle% lastcomm a.out root term/01
```

The following command lists all of the commands executed by user root.

```
example% lastcomm root
```

Files

/var/adm/pacct

Accounting file.

Attributes

See attributes(5) for descriptions of the following attributes:

Attribute Type	Attribute Value
Availability	SUNWesu

See Also

last(1), sigvec(3B), acct(4), core(4), attributes(5)

ld — Link Editor for Object Files

Synopsis

```
/usr/ccs/bin/ld [-a|-r][-b][-G][-i][-m][-s][-t][-V]
   [-B dynamic | static][-B group][-B local][-B eliminate]
   [-B reduce][-B symbolic][-d y|n][-D token][-e epsym]
   [-F name | -f name][-h name][-I name][-L path][-l x][-M mapfile]
   [-N string][-o outfile][-Q y | n][-R path][-u symname][-Y P,dirlist]
   [-z allextract | defaultextract | weakextract][-z ccombreloc][-
   z defs | nodefs][-z ignore | record][-z lazyload | nolazyload]
   [-z initfirst][-zloadfltr][-zmuldefs][-znodelete][-znodlopen][-z
   nopartial][-z noversion][-z now][-z origin][-z redlocsym]
   [-z text | textwarn | textoff] filename...
```

New!

Description

The ld command is the link editor for object files. It is often automatically invoked by compiler commands such as cc.

The ld command combines relocatable object files, performs relocation, and resolves external symbols. ld operates in two modes, static or dynamic, as governed by the -d option. Specify -dn for static mode and -dy for dynamic mode.

In -dn static mode, relocatable object files specified as arguments are combined to produce an executable object file. If you specify the -r option, relocatable object files are combined to produce one relocatable object file.

In -dy dynamic mode (the default), relocatable object files you specify as arguments are combined to produce an executable object file that is linked at execution with any shared object files you specify as arguments. If you specify the -G option, relocatable object files are combined to produce a shared object. In all cases, the output of ld is left in a.out by default.

If any argument is a library, ld searches exactly once at the point it encounters the library in the argument list. The library can be either a relocatable archive or a shared object. For an archive library, ld loads only those routines that define an unresolved external reference. ld searches the archive library symbol table sequentially with as many passes as are needed to resolve external references that can be satisfied by library members. See ar(4). Thus, the order of members in the library is functionally unimportant unless multiple library members exist that define the same external symbol.

A shared object consists of an indivisible, whole unit that has been generated by a previous link edit of one or more input files. When the link editor processes a shared object, the entire contents of the shared object become a logical part of the resulting output file image. The shared object is not physically copied during the link edit as its actual inclusion is deferred until process execution. This logical inclusion means that all symbol entries defined in the shared object are made available to the link editing process.

No specific option tells ld to link 64-bit objects; the class of the first object that gets processed by ld determines whether it is to perform a 32-bit or a 64-bit link edit.

New!

Options

-a   In static mode only, produce an executable object file. Display errors for undefined references (the default for static mode). You cannot use -a with the -r option.

-b   In dynamic mode only, when creating an executable, do not do special processing for relocations that reference symbols in shared objects. Without the -b option, create special position-independent relocations for references to functions defined in shared objects and arrange for data objects defined in shared objects to be copied into the memory image of the executable by the runtime linker. With the -b option, the output code may be more efficient but it is less sharable.

-B dynamic | static

Options governing library inclusion. -B dynamic is valid in dynamic mode only. You can specify these options any number of times on the command line as toggles: if you use the -B static option, no shared objects are accepted until `-B dynamic` is seen. See also the `-l` option.

`-B eliminate`

Do not assign any global symbols to a version definition to be eliminated from the symbol table. This option achieves the same symbol elimination as the `auto-elimination` directive available as part of a mapfile version definition.

`-B group`   Establish a shared object and its dependencies as a group. Objects within the group are bound to other members of the group at runtime. The runtime processing of an object containing this option mimics what happens if the object is added to a process by `dlopen(3X)` with the `RTLD_GROUP` mode. As the group must be self-contained, use of the `-B group` option also asserts the `-z defs` option.

`-B local`   Reduce any global symbols not assigned to a version definition to `local`. You can supply version definitions from a mapfile and indicate the global symbols that should remain visible in the generated object. This option achieves the same symbol reduction as the `auto-reduction` directive available as part of a mapfile version definition and can be useful when combining versioned and nonversioned relocatable objects.

`-B reduce`   When generating a relocatable object, reduce the symbolic information defined by any version definitions. You can supply version definitions from a mapfile to indicate the global symbols that should remain visible in the generated object. When a relocatable object is generated, by default version definitions are recorded only in the output image. The actual reduction of symbolic information is carried out when the object itself is used in the construction of a dynamic executable or shared object. This option is applied automatically when a dynamic executable or shared object is created.

`-B symbolic`

In dynamic mode only. When building a shared object, bind references to global symbols to their definitions, if available, within the object. Normally, references to global symbols within shared objects are not bound until runtime even if definitions are available, so that definitions of the same symbol in an executable or other shared object can override the object's own definition. `ld` issues warnings for undefined symbols unless `-z defs` overrides.

`-dy | n`   When you specify `-dy` (the default), use dynamic linking; when you specify `-dn`, use static linking. See also `-B dynamic|static`.

`-D token, token, ...`

Print debugging information to the standard error as specified by each token. The special token `help` shows the full list of available tokens.

-e *epsym*	Set the entry point address for the output file to be that of the symbol *epsym*.
-f *name*	Useful only when building a shared object. Specify that the symbol table of the shared object is used as an auxiliary filter on the symbol table of the shared object specified by *name*. You can use multiple instances of this option. You cannot combine this option with the -F option.
-F *name*	Useful only when building a shared object. Specify that the symbol table of the shared object is used as a filter on the symbol table of the shared object specified by *name*. You can use multiple instances of this option. You cannot combine this option with the -f option.
-G	In dynamic mode only, produce a shared object. Allow undefined symbols.
-h *name*	In dynamic mode only, when building a shared object, record *name* in the object's dynamic section. *name* is recorded in executables that are linked with this object instead of the object's UNIX system file name. Accordingly, *name* is used by the runtime linker as the name of the shared object to search for at runtime.
-i	Ignore LD_LIBRARY_PATH setting. This option is useful when an LD_LIBRARY_PATH setting is in effect to influence the runtime library search, which would interfere with performing link editing.
-I *name*	When building an executable, use *name* as the path name of the interpreter to be written into the program header. The default in static mode is no interpreter; in dynamic mode, the default is the name of the runtime linker, ld.so.1(1). You can override either case by -I *name*. exec(2) loads this interpreter when it loads a.out and passes control to the interpreter instead of directly to a.out.
-l *x*	Search a library libx.so or libx.a, the conventional names for shared object and archive libraries, in that order. In dynamic mode, unless you use the -B static option, search each directory specified in the library search path for a libx.so or libx.a file. Stop the directory search at the first directory containing either. Choose the file ending in .so if -l *x* expands to two files with names of the form libx.so and libx.a. If no libx.so is found, accept libx.a. In static mode or when the -B static option is in effect, choose only the file ending in .a. ld searches a library when it encounters its name, so the placement of -l is significant.
-L *path*	Add *path* to the library search directories. Search for libraries first in any directories specified by the -L options and then in the standard directories. This option is useful only if it precedes the -l options to which it applies. You can use the environment variable LD_LIBRARY_PATH to supplement the library search path.
-m	Produce a memory map or listing of the input/output sections, together with any nonfatal, multiply defined symbols, on the standard output.

-M *mapfile*	Read *mapfile* as a text file of directives to ld. You can specify this option multiple times. If *mapfile* is a directory, then process all regular files within the directory, as defined by stat(2). See *Linker and Libraries Guide* for description of mapfiles.
-N *string*	Add a DT_NEEDED entry to the .dynamic section of the object being built. The value of the DT_NEEDED string is the string specified on the command line. This option is position dependent, and the DT_NEEDED .dynamic entry is relative to the other dynamic dependencies discovered on the link edit line.
-o *outfile*	Produce an output object file named *outfile*. The name of the default object file is a.out.
-Q y|n	For -Qy, add an ident string to the .comment section of the output file to identify the version of the link editor used to create the file. When there are multiple linking steps, such as when using ld -r, multiple ld idents result. This option is identical to the default action of the cc command. For -Qn, suppress version identification.
-r	Combine relocatable object files to produce one relocatable object file. Do not complain about unresolved references. You cannot use this option in dynamic mode or with -a.
-R *path*	Specify a colon-separated list of directories used as library search directories by the runtime linker. If present and not null, *path* is recorded in the output object file and passed to the runtime linker. Multiple instances of this option are concatenated, with each path separated by a colon.
-s	Strip symbolic information from the output file. Remove any debugging information, that is, .debug, .line, and .stab sections, and their associated relocation entries. Except for relocatable files or shared objects, also remove the symbol table and string table sections from the output object file.
-t	Turn off the warning about multiply defined symbols that are not the same size.
-u *symname*	Enter *symname* as an undefined symbol in the symbol table. This option is useful for loading entirely from an archive library because initially the symbol table is empty and an unresolved reference is needed to force the loading of the first routine. The placement of this option on the command line is significant; put it before the library that defines the symbol.
-V	Display a message giving information about the version of ld being used.
-Y P,*dirlist*	
	Change the default directories used for finding libraries. *dirlist* is a colon-separated path list.

`-z allextract | defaultextract | weakextract`

> Alter the extraction criteria of objects from any archives that follow. By default, extract archive members to satisfy undefined references and to promote tentative definitions with data definitions. Weak symbol references do not trigger extraction. For `-z allextract`, extract all archive members from the archive. For `-z weakextract`, weak references trigger archive extraction. `-z defaultextract` provides a way of returning to the default following use of the former extract options.

`-z combreloc`

> Combine multiple relocation sections. This option reduces overhead when objects are loaded into memory.

`-z defs`   Force a fatal error if any undefined symbols remain at the end of the link. This option is the default when an executable is built. It is also useful when building a shared object to ensure that the object is self-contained, that is, that all its symbolic references are resolved internally.

`-z ignore | record`

> Ignore or record dynamic dependencies that are not referenced as part of the link edit. `-z record` is the default.

`-z initfirst`

> Mark the object so that its runtime initialization occurs before the runtime initialization of any other objects brought into the process at the same time. In addition, the object runtime finalization occurs after the runtime finalization of any other objects removed from the process at the same time. This option is meaningful only when building a shared object.

`-z lazyload | nolazyload`

> Enable or disable the marking of dynamic dependencies to be lazily loaded. Dynamic dependencies that are marked `lazyload` are not loaded at initial process startup but instead are delayed until the first binding to the object is made.

`-z loadfltr`

> Mark the object to require that when building a filter, filtered objects are processed immediately at runtime. Normally, filter processing is delayed until a symbol reference is bound to the filter. The runtime processing of an object that contains this flag mimics that which occurs if the `LD_LOADFLTR` environment variable is in effect. See `ld.so.1`(1).

`-z muldefs`   Enable multiple symbol definitions. By default, multiple symbol definitions that occur between relocatable objects result in a fatal error. This option suppresses the error condition and enables the first symbol definition to be taken.

-z nodefs   Enable undefined symbols. This option is the default when a shared object is built. When used with executables, the behavior of references to such undefined symbols is unspecified.

-z nodelete

    Mark the object as nondeletable at runtime. The runtime processing of an object that contains this flag mimics that which occurs if the object is added to a process by dlopen(3X) with the RTLD_NODELETE mode.

-z nodlopen

    Mark the object as not available to dlopen(3X), either as the object specified by the dlopen() or as any form of dependency required by the object specified by dlopen(). This option is meaningful only when building a shared object.

New!   -z nopartial

    Expand the partially initialized symbols when the output file is generated if any exist in the input relocatable object files.

-z noversion

    Do not record any versioning sections. Any version sections or associated .dynamic section entries are not generated in the output image.

-z now   Mark the object to override the runtime linker's default mode and require nonlazy runtime binding. This option is similar to adding the object to the process by using dlopen(3X) with the RTLD_NOW mode or by setting the LD_BIND_NOW environment variable. See ld.so.1(1).

New!   -z origin   Mark the object as requiring immediate $ORIGIN processing at runtime.

-z redlocsym

    Eliminate all local symbols except for the SECT symbols from the symbol table SHT_SYMTAB. Update all relocations that refer to local symbols to now refer to the corresponding SECT symbol.

-z text   In dynamic mode only, force a fatal error if any relocations against nonwritable, allocatable sections remain.

New!   -z textoff In dynamic mode only, allow relocations against all allocatable sections including nonwritable ones. This option is the default when building a shared object.

New!   -z textwarn

    In dynamic mode only, list a warning if any relocations against nonwritable, allocatable sections remain. This option is the default when building an executable.

Options No Longer Supported

The following SunOS 4.x.y options do not have any replacement in this release: -B nosymbolic (this option is now the default if you do not use -B symbolic), -d, -dc, and -dp, (these options are now the default; see -b above to override the default), -M, -S, -t, -x, -X, and -ysym.

The following SunOS 4.x.y options are not supported: -align datum, -A name, -D hex, -p, -T[text] hex, -T data hex. Much of the functionality of these options can be achieved with the -M mapfile option.

Obsolete Options

The SunOS 4.x.y options -n, -N, and -z are obsolete in this release.

Environment Variables

LD_LIBRARY_PATH

> A list of directories to search for libraries specified with the -l option. Separate multiple directories with a colon. In the most general case, the variable contains two directory lists separated by a semicolon:
>
> dirlist1;dirlist2
>
> If ld is called with any number of occurrences of -L, as in:
>
> ld... -Lpath1... -Lpathn...
>
> then the search path ordering is:
>
> dirlist1 path1... pathn dirlist2 LIBPATH
>
> When the list of directories does not contain a semicolon, it is interpreted as dirlist2.
>
> The LD_LIBRARY_PATH environment variable also affects the runtime linkers searching for dynamic dependencies.

LD_LIBRARY_PATH_64

New!

> Similar to the LD_LIBRARY_PATH environment variable. Override LD_LIBRARY_PATH when searching for 64-bit dependencies.

LD_OPTIONS A default set of options to ld. LD_OPTIONS is interpreted by ld just as though its value had been placed on the command line, immediately following the name used to invoke ld, as in:

> ld $LD_OPTIONS... other-arguments...

LD_RUN_PATH An alternative mechanism for specifying a run path to the link editor (see -R option). If both LD_RUN_PATH and the -R option are specified, -R supersedes.

Note — Environment-variable names beginning with the characters LD_ are reserved for possible future enhancements to ld and ld.so.1(1).

Files

`libx.so`	Libraries.
`libx.a`	Libraries.
`a.out`	Output file.
`LIBPATH`	Usually `/usr/ccs/lib:/usr/lib`.

New! `/usr/lib/ld/map.default`

Mapfile showing default layout of 32-bit programs.

New! `/usr/lib/ld/sparcv9/map.default`

Mapfile showing default layout of 64-bit SPARC V9 programs.

New! `/usr/lib/ld/sparcv9.map.above4G`

Mapfile showing suggested layout above 4 Gbytes of 64-bit SPARC V9 programs.

New! `/usr/lib/ld/sparcv9/map.below4G`

Mapfile showing suggested layout below 4 Gbytes of 64-bit SPARC V9 programs.

Attributes

See `attributes(5)` for descriptions of the following attributes:

Attribute Type	Attribute Value
Availability	SUNWtoo

See Also

`as(1)`, `gprof(1)`, `ld.so.1(1)`, `pvs(1)`, `exec(2)`, `stat(2)`, `elf(3E)`, `dlopen(3X)`, `a.out(4)`, `ar(4)`, `attributes(5)`

New! **ldapadd** — ldap Entry Addition and Modification Tools

Synopsis

```
/opt/SUNWconn/ldap/bin/ldapadd [-b][-c][-n][-v][-F]
   [-d debuglevel][-D binddn][-w passwd][-h ldaphost][-p ldapport]
   [-f file][-l nb-ldap-connections]
```

Description

See `ldapmodify(1)`.

ldapdelete — ldap Delete Entry Tool   *New!*

Synopsis

```
/usr/bin/ldapdelete [-n][-v][-c][-d debuglevel][-f file][-D binddn]
    [-w passwd][-h ldaphost][-M authentication][-p ldapport][dn...]
```

Description

ldapdelete opens a connection to an LDAP server and binds and deletes one or more entries. If you specify one or more *dn* arguments, entries with those distinguished names are deleted. If you specify no *dn* arguments, a list of distinguished names (DNs) is read from *file*, if you specify the -f option, or from standard input.

Options

-c   Continuous operation mode. Report errors but continue with deletions. The default is to exit after reporting an error.

-d *debuglevel*

Set the LDAP debugging level. Useful levels of debugging for ldapmodify and ldapadd are:

1   Trace.

2   Packets.

4   Arguments.

32   Filters.

128   Access control.

To request more than one category of debugging information, add the masks. For example, to request trace and filter information, specify a debug level of 33.

-D *binddn*   Use the distinguished name *binddn* to bind to the directory.

-f *file*   Read the entry deletion information from *file* instead of from standard input.

-h *ldaphost* Specify an alternate host on which the slapd server is running.

-M *authentication*

Specify the authentication mechanism used to bind to the directory. This option can have the value CRAM-MD5. The bind DN and bind password are mandatory with this option.

-n   Show what would be done, but don't actually delete entries. Useful in conjunction with -v and -d for debugging.

-p *ldapport*

> Specify an alternate TCP port where the slapd server is listening.

-v   Use verbose mode and write diagnostics to standard output.

-w *passwd*   Use *passwd* as the password for authentication to the directory.

Operands

dn   Specify one or several distinguished names of entries to delete.

Examples

The following example deletes the entry named with commonName "Delete Me" directly below the XYZ Corporation organizational entry.

```
castle% ldapdelete "cn=Delete Me, o=XYZ, c=US" -D "cn=Administrator,
    o=XYZ, c=US" -w password
```

Exit Status

0   No errors occurred.

non-zero   Errors result and a diagnostic message is written to standard error.

Attributes

See attributes(5) for descriptions of the following attributes:

Attribute Type	Attribute Value
Availability	SUNWllldap (32-bit)
	SUNWldapx (64-bit)
Stability Level	Evolving

See Also

ldapadd(1), ldapmodify(1), ldapmodrdn(1), ldapsearch(1)

ldapmodify, ldapadd — ldap Entry Addition and Modification Tools

New!

Synopsis

```
/usr/bin/ldapmodify [-a][-b][-c][-r][-n][-v][-F][-d debuglevel]
    [-D binddn][-w passwd][-h ldaphost][-M authentication][-p ldapport]
    [-f file][-l nb-ldap-connections]
/opt/SUNWconn/ldap/bin/ldapadd [-b][-c][-n][-v][-F][-d debuglevel]
    [-D binddn][-w passwd][-h ldaphost][-p ldapport][-f file]
    [-l nb-ldap-connections]
```

Description

ldapmodify opens a connection to an LDAP server and binds, modifies, or adds entries. The entry information is read from standard input or from *file*, specified with the -f option. ldapadd is implemented as a hard link to ldapmodify. When invoked as ldapadd, the -a (add new entry) option is turned on automatically.

Both ldapadd and ldapmodify reject duplicate attribute-name/value pairs for the same entry.

Options

-a   Add new entries. The default for ldapmodify is to modify existing entries. If invoked as ldapadd, this option is always set.

-b   Assume that any value that starts with a / is the path name of a file containing the actual attribute value. This option is useful for attribute values in binary format.

-c   Continuous operation mode. Report errors and continue with modifications. The default is to exit after reporting an error.

-d *debuglevel*

Set the LDAP debugging level. Useful levels of debugging for ldapmodify and ldapadd are:

1   Trace.

2   Packets.

4   Arguments.

32   Filters.

128   Access control.

To request more than one category of debugging information, add the masks. For example, to request trace and filter information, specify a debug level of 33.

-D *binddn*	Use the distinguished name *binddn* to bind to the directory.
-f *file*	Read the entry modification information from *file* instead of from standard input.
-F	Force application of all changes regardless of the content of input lines that begin replica:. By default, replica: lines are compared against the LDAP server host and port in use to decide whether to apply a replog record.
-h *ldaphost*	Specify an alternate host on which the slapd server is running.
-l *nb-ldap-connections*	
	Specify the number of LDAP connections ldappadd or ldapmodify open to process the modifications in the directory. The default is one connection.
-M *authentication*	
	Specify the authentication mechanism used to bind to the directory. This option can have the value CRAM-MD5. Bind DN and bind password are mandatory with this option.
-n	Preview modifications but make no changes to entries. Useful in conjunction with -v and -d for debugging.
-p *ldapport*	
	Specify an alternate TCP port where the slapd server is listening.
	Specify the number of LDAP connections that ldapadd or ldapmodify opens to process the modifications in the directory. The default is one connection.
-r	Replace existing value with the specified value (the default for ldapmodify). When you call ldapadd or if you specify the -a option, the -r option is ignored.
-v	Use verbose mode, and write diagnostics to standard output.
-w *passwd*	Use *passwd* as the password for authentication to the directory.

Examples

The format of the content of file (or standard input if you specify no -f option) is shown in the following examples.

The file /tmp/entrymods contains the following modification instructions:

```
dn: cn=Modify Me, o=XYZ, c=US
changetype: modify
replace: mail
mail: modme@atlanta.xyz.com
-
add: title
title: System Manager
-
add: jpegPhoto
```

```
jpegPhoto: /tmp/modme.jpeg
-
delete: description
-
```

The following command modifies the Modify Me entry as described below.

castle% **ldapmodify -b -r -f /tmp/entrymods**

1. Replace the current value of the mail attribute with the value modme@atlanta.xyz.com.
2. Add a title attribute with the value System Manager.
3. Add a jpegPhoto attribute using the contents of the file /tmp/modme.jpeg as the attribute value.
4. Remove the description attribute.

In the following example, the file /tmp/newentry contains the information for creating a new entry:

```
dn: cn=Ann Jones, o=XYZ, c=US
objectClass: person
cn: Ann Jones
cn: Annie Jones
sn: Jones
title: Director of Research and Development
mail: ajones@londonrd.xyz.us.com
uid: ajones
```

The following command uses the information in the newentry file to add a new entry for Ann Jones.

castle% **ldapadd -f /tmp/newentry**

In the following example, the file /tmp/badentry contains the information about an entry to be deleted.

```
dn: cn=Ann Jones, o=XYZ, c=US
changetype: delete
```

The following command removes Ann Jones' entry.

castle% **ldapmodify -f /tmp/badentry**

Exit Status

0	No errors.
non-zero	Errors occur and a diagnostic message is written to standard error.

Attributes

See attributes(5) for descriptions of the following attributes:

Attribute Type	Attribute Value
Availability	SUNW11dap (32-bit)
	SUNW1dapx (64-bit)
Stability Level	Evolving

See Also

ldapadd(1), ldapdelete(1), ldapmodrdn(1), ldapsearch(1)

New! **ldapmodrdn** — ldap Modify Entry RDN Tool

Synopsis

```
/usr/bin/ldapmodrdn [-r][-n][-v][-c][-d debuglevel][-D binddn]
    [-w passwd][-h ldaphost][-M authentication][-p ldapport][-f file]
    [dn rdn]
```

Description

ldapmodrdn opens a connection to an LDAP server and binds and modifies the relative distinguished name (RDN) of entries. The entry information is read from standard input, from *file* with the -f option, or from the command-line pair *dn* and *rdn*.

Options

-c   Continuous operation mode. Report errors and continue with modifications. The default is to exit after reporting an error.

-d *debuglevel*

Set the LDAP debugging level. Useful values of debug level for ldapmodrdn are:

1	Trace.
2	Packets.
4	Arguments.
32	Filters.
128	Access control.

To request more than one category of debugging information, add the masks. For example, to request trace and filter information, specify a debug level of 33.

-D *binddn*   Use the distinguished name *binddn* to bind to the directory.

-f *file*   Read the entry modification information from *file* instead of from standard input or the command line.

-h *ldaphost* Specify an alternate host on which the slapd server is running.

-M *authentication*

Specify the authentication mechanism used to bind to the directory. This option can have the value CRAM-MD5. The bind DN and bind password are mandatory with this option.

-n   Show what would be done, but don't actually change entries. Useful in conjunction with -v for debugging.

-p *ldapport*

Specify an alternate TCP port where the slapd server is listening.

-r   Remove old RDN values from the entry. By default, keep the old values.

-v   Use verbose mode and write diagnostics to standard output.

-w *passwd* Use *passwd* as the password for authentication to the directory.

Input Format

If you specify the command-line arguments *dn* and *rdn*, *rdn* replaces the relative distinguished name (RDN) of the entry specified by the distinguished name (DN), *dn*.

Otherwise, the contents of *file* (or standard input if you do not specify the -f option) must consist of one or more pairs of lines:

```
Distinguished Name (DN)
Relative Distinguished Name (RDN)
```

Use one or more blank lines to separate each DN/RDN pair.

Examples

In the following example, the file /tmp/entrymods contains the following lines:

```
cn=Modify Me, o=XYZ, c=US
cn=The New Me
```

The following command changes the RDN of the Modify Me entry from Modify Me to The New Me and removes the old cn, Modify Me.

```
example% ldapmodify -r -f /tmp/entrymods
```

Exit Status

0   No errors occurred.

non-zero   Errors result and a diagnostic message is written to standard error.

Attributes

See attributes(5) for descriptions of the following attributes:

Attribute Type	Attribute Value
Availability	SUNW11dap (32-bit)
	SUNW1dapx (64-bit)
Stability Level	Evolving

See Also

ldapadd(1), ldapdelete(1), ldapmodify(1), ldapsearch(1)

New! **ldapsearch** — ldap Search Tool

Synopsis

```
/usr/bin/ldapsearch [-n][-u][-v][-t][-A][-B][-L][-R][-d debuglevel]
    [-F sep][-S attr][-f file][-D binddn][-w passwd][-h ldaphost]
    [-M authentication][-p ldapport][-b searchbase][-s scope][-a deref]
    [-l time limit][-z size limit] filter [attrs....]
```

Description

ldapsearch opens a connection to an LDAP server and binds and performs a search using the *filter* filter.

If ldapsearch finds one or more entries, the attributes specified by *attrs* are retrieved and the entries and values are printed to standard output. If no *attrs* are listed, all attributes are returned.

Options

-a *deref*   Specify how aliases dereferencing is done. The possible values for *deref* are never, always, search, or find to specify that aliases are never dereferenced, always dereferenced, dereferenced when searching, or dereferenced only when finding the base object for the search. The default is to never dereference aliases.

-A   Retrieve attributes only (no values). This option is useful when you just want to see whether an attribute is present in an entry and are not interested in the specific value.

-b *searchbase*

Use *searchbase* as the starting point for the search instead of the default.

-B   Do not suppress display of non-ASCII values. This option is useful
            when dealing with values that appear in alternate character sets
            such as ISO-8859.1. This option is automatically set by the -L
            option.

-d *debuglevel*

            Set the LDAP debugging level. Useful levels of debugging for
            ldapsearch are:

            1   Trace.

            2   Packets.

            4   Arguments.

            32   Filters.

            128   Access control.

            To request more than one category of debugging information, add
            the masks. For example, to request trace and filter information,
            specify a debug level of 33.

-D *binddn*   Use the distinguished name *binddn* to bind to the directory.

-f *file*   Read a series of lines from *file*, performing one LDAP search for
            each line. In this case, treat the filter given on the command line
            as a pattern where the first occurrence of %s is replaced with a line
            from *file*. If *file* is a single - character, then read the lines from
            standard input.

-F *sep*   Use *sep* as the field separator between attribute names and
            values. The default separator is =. If you specify the -L option, this
            option is ignored.

-h *ldaphost* Specify an alternate host on which the slapd server is running.

-l *timelimit*

            Wait at most *timelimit* seconds for a search to complete.

-L   Display search results in a modified format. Turn on the -B option,
            and ignore the -F option.

-M *authentication*

            Specify the authentication mechanism used to bind to the
            directory. This option can have the value CRAM-MD5. The bind DN
            and bind password are mandatory with this option.

-n   Show what would be done, but don't actually perform the search.
            Useful in conjunction with -v and -d for debugging.

-p *ldapport* Specify an alternate TCP port where the slapd server is listening.

-R   Do not automatically follow referrals returned while searching.

-s *scope*   Specify the scope of the search. The possible values of *scope* are
            base, one, or sub to specify a base object, one-level, or subtree
            search. The default is sub.

`-S attribute`

> Based on `attribute`, sort the entries returned. If `attribute` is a zero-length string (" "), sort the entries by the components of their Distinguished Name. Note that `ldapsearch` normally prints entries as it receives them. Retrieve, then sort, then print all entries. The default is not to sort entries returned.

`-t`
> Write retrieved values to a set of temporary files. This option is useful for dealing with non-ASCII values such as `jpegPhoto` or `audio`.

`-u`
> Include the user-friendly form of the Distinguished Name (DN) in the output.

`-v`
> Run in verbose mode and write diagnostics to standard output.

`-w passwd`   Use `passwd` as the password for authentication to the directory.

`-z sizelimit`
> Retrieve at most `sizelimit` entries for a search to complete.

Output Format

If one or more entries are found, each entry is written to standard output in the form:

```
Distinguished Name (DN)
User Friendly Name (if you specify the -u option)
attributename=value
attributename=value
attributename=value
...
```

Multiple entries are separated with a single blank line. If you use the `-F` option to specify a different separator character, this character is used instead of the = character. If you use the `-t` option, the name of a temporary file is returned in place of the actual value. If you use the `-A` option, only the `attributename` is returned and not the attribute value.

Examples

The following command performs a subtree search (using the default search base) for entries with a `commonName` of `mark smith`. The `commonName` and `telephoneNumber` values are retrieved and printed to the standard output.

```
castle% ldapsearch "cn=mark smith' cn telephoneNumber
cn=Mark D Smith, ou=Sales, ou=Atlanta, ou=People, o=XYZ, c=US
cn=Mark Smith
cn=Mark David Smith
cn=Mark D Smith 1
cn=Mark D Smith
telephoneNumber=+1 123 456-7890
cn=Mark C Smith, ou=Distribution, ou=Atlanta, ou=People, o=XYZ, c=US
cn=Mark Smith
```

```
cn=Mark C Smith 1
cn=Mark C Smith
telephoneNumber=+1 123 456-9999
castle%
```

The following command performs a substring search, using the default search base for entries with user ID of `mcs`. The user-friendly form of the entry's DN is output after the line that contains the DN itself, and the `jpegPhoto` and `audio` values are retrieved and written to temporary files. The output might look like this if one entry with one value for each of the requested attributes is found.

```
castle% ldapsearch -u -t "uid=mcs" jpegPhoto audio
cn=Mark C Smith, ou=Distribution, ou=Atlanta, ou=People, o=XYZ, c=US
Mark C Smith, Distribution, Atlanta, People, XYZ, US
audio=/tmp/ldapsearch-audio-a19924
jpegPhoto=/tmp/ldapsearch-jpegPhoto-a19924
castle%
```

The following command performs a one-level search at the `c=US` level for all organizations whose `organizationName` begins with `XY`. Search results are displayed in the `LDIF` format. The `organizationName` and `description` attribute values are retrieved and printed to standard output, resulting in output similar to this.

```
castle% ldapsearch -L -s one -b "c=US" "o=XY*" o description
dn: o=XYZ, c=US
o: XYZ
description: XYZ Corporation
dn: o="XY Trading Company", c=US
o: XY Trading Company
description: Import and export specialists

dn: o=XYInternational, c=US
o: XYInternational
o: XYI
o: XY International
castle%
```

Exit Status

0	No errors occurred.
non-zero	Errors result and a diagnostic message is written to standard error.

Attributes

See attributes(5) for descriptions of the following attributes:

Attribute Type	Attribute Value
Availability	SUNW11dap (32-bit)
	SUNW1dapx (64-bit)
Stability Level	Evolving

See Also

ldapadd(1), ldapdelete(1), ldapmodify(1), ldapmodrdn(1)

ldd — List Dynamic Dependencies of Executable Files or Shared Objects

Synopsis

/usr/bin/ldd [-d | -r] [-f] [-i] [-l] [-s] [-v] *filename*...

Description

The ldd (list dynamic dependencies) command lists the dynamic dependencies of executable files or shared objects. If *filename* is an executable file, ldd lists the path names of all shared objects that would be loaded when *filename* is loaded.

If *filename* is a shared object, ldd lists the path names of all shared objects that would be loaded when *filename* is loaded. ldd expects shared objects to have execute permission and if they don't, ldd issues a warning before trying to process the file.

ldd processes its input one file at a time. For each input file ldd performs one of the following:

- Lists the object dependencies if they exist.
- Succeeds quietly if dependencies do not exit.
- Prints an error message if processing fails.

Note — ldd does not list shared objects explicitly attached using dlopen(3X).

Using the -d or -r option with shared objects can give misleading results. ldd does a worst-case analysis of the shared object. However, in practice, some or all of the symbols reported as unresolved can be resolved by the executable file referencing the shared object.

ldd uses the same algorithm as the runtime linker to locate shared objects.

Options

ldd can also check the compatibility of *filename* with the shared objects it uses. With each of the following options, ldd prints warnings for any unresolved symbol references that would occur if *filename* were executed.

-d	Check references to data objects. You cannot use -d with -r.
-r	Check references to both data objects and functions. You cannot use -r with -d.
-f	Force a check for an executable file that is not secure. When ldd is invoked by a superuser, by default, it does not process any executable that it finds not secure. An executable is considered not secure if the interpreter it specifies does not reside in /usr/lib or /etc/lib or if the interpreter cannot be determined.
-i	Display the order of execution of initialization sections.
-l	Force the immediate processing of any filters so that all filtered objects and their dependencies are listed.
-s	Display the search path used to locate shared object dependencies.
-v	Display all dependency relationships incurred when processing *filename*. This option also displays any dependency version requirements. See pvs(1).

Superuser should use the -f option only if the executable to be examined is known to be trustworthy, as use of -f on an untrustworthy executable by superuser can compromise system security. If you do not know whether the executable to be examined is trustworthy, temporarily become a regular user and invoke ldd as that regular user. You can safely examine untrustworthy objects with dump(1) and with adb(1) as long as you do not use the :r subcommand. In addition, a non-superuser can use either the :r subcommand of adb or truss(1) to examine an untrustworthy executable without too much risk of compromise. To minimize risk when using ldd, adb :r, or truss on an untrustworthy executable, use the user ID nobody.

Examples

The following example uses the -s option to display the search path used to locate shared object dependencies. Because the file is not an executable, a warning message is also displayed.

```
castle% ldd -s /usr/lib/adb/adbsub.o
warning: ldd: /usr/lib/adb/adbsub.o: is not executable
    search path=/usr/lib  (default)
```

```
    trying path=/usr/lib/libld.so.2
    search path=/usr/lib   (default)
    trying path=/usr/lib/libc.so.1

   find library=libdl.so.1; required by /usr/lib/libc.so.1
    search path=/usr/lib   (default)
    trying path=/usr/lib/libdl.so.1

  find library=/usr/platform/SUNW,SPARCstation-10/lib/libc_psr.so.1;
   required by /usr/lib/libc.so.1
      search path=/usr/lib   (default)
      trying path=/usr/lib/libelf.so.1
castle%
```

Files

```
/usr/lib/lddstub
```
> Fake executable loaded to check the dependencies of shared objects.

Attributes

See `attributes`(5) for descriptions of the following attributes:

Attribute Type	Attribute Value
Availability	SUNWtoo

See Also

`adb`(1), `dump`(1), `ld`(1), `ld.so.1`(1), `pvs`(1), `truss`(1), `dlopen`(3X), `attributes`(5)
> *Linker and Libraries Guide*

Diagnostics

`ldd` prints the record of shared object path names to standard output. The optional list of symbol resolution problems is printed to standard error. If *filename* is not an executable file or a shared object or if it cannot be opened for reading, a non-zero exit status is returned.

ld.so.1 — Runtime Linker for Dynamic Objects

Synopsis

```
/usr/lib/ld.so.1
/etc/lib/ld.so.1
```

Description

Dynamic applications consist of one or more dynamic objects, typically a dynamic executable and its shared object dependencies. As part of the initialization and execution of a dynamic application, an interpreter is called to complete the binding of the application to its shared object dependencies. In Solaris, this interpreter is referred to as the runtime linker.

During the link editing of a dynamic executable, a special .interp section is created along with an associated program header. This section contains a path name specifying the program's interpreter. You can specify the path name to the interpreter when the executable is being constructed with the -I option to ld(1), the link editor. The default name supplied by the link editor is that of the runtime linker, /usr/lib/ld.so.1.

During the process of executing a dynamic executable, the kernel maps the file and locates the required interpreter. See exec(2) and mmap(2). The kernel maps this interpreter and transfers control to it, passing sufficient information to enable the interpreter to continue binding the application and then to run it.

In addition to initializing an application, the runtime linker provides services that enable the application to extend its address space by mapping additional shared objects and binding to symbols within them.

The runtime linker performs the following functions:

- Analyzes the application's dynamic information section (.dynamic) and determines which shared object dependencies are required.

- Locates and maps in these dependencies, then analyzes their dynamic information sections to determine if any additional shared object dependencies are required.

- Once all shared object dependencies are located and mapped, performs any necessary relocations to bind these shared objects in preparation for process execution.

- Calls any initialization functions provided by the shared object dependencies. By default, these functions are called in the reverse order of the topologically sorted dependencies. Should cyclic dependencies exist, the initialization functions are called, using the sorted order with the cycle removed. ldd(1) can be used to display the initialization order of shared object dependencies. See also LD_BREADTH.

- Passes control to the application.

- During the application's execution, the runtime linker can be called on to perform any delayed function binding.

- Calls any finalization functions on deletion of shared objects from the process. By default, these functions are called in the order of the topologically sorted dependencies.

- The application can also call on the runtime linker's services to acquire additional shared objects by dlopen(3X) and bind to symbols within these objects with dlsym(3X).

You can find further details on each of the above topics in the *Linker and Libraries Guide*.

The runtime linker uses a prescribed search path for locating the dynamic dependencies of an object. The default search paths are the run path recorded in the object, followed by /usr/lib. You specify the run path when the dynamic object is constructed with the -R option to ld(1). You can use LD_LIBRARY_PATH to indicate directories to be searched before the default directories.

Note — The user compatibility library /usr/lib/0@0.so.1 provides a mechanism that establishes a value of 0 at location 0. Some applications exist that erroneously assume a null character pointer should be treated the same as a pointer to a null string. Such applications produce a segmentation violation when they access a null character pointer. If this library is added to such an application at runtime, using LD_PRELOAD, it provides an environment that is sympathetic to this errant behavior. However, the user compatibility library is intended neither to enable the generation of such applications nor to endorse this particular programming practice.

Environment Variables

LD_AUDIT   Specify a colon-separated list of objects that are loaded by the runtime linker. As each object is loaded, it is examined for Link-Auditing interfaces. The routines that are present are called as specified in the Link-Auditing interface described in the *Linker and Libraries Guide*.

LD_BIND_NOW   Override the runtime linker's default mode of performing lazy binding by setting the environment variable LD_BIND_NOW to any non-null value. With this setting, the runtime linker performs both data reference and function reference relocations during process initialization before transferring control to the application. Also see the -z now option of ld(1).

LD_BREADTH   Call any initialization functions in reverse breadth-first order. Call any finalization functions in breadth-first order.

LD_DEBUG   Specify a comma-separated list of tokens so that the runtime linker can print debugging information to the standard error. The help special token indicates the full list of tokens available. You can also supply the environment variable LD_DEBUG_OUTPUT to specify a file to which the debugging information is sent. The file name is suffixed with the process ID of the application generating the debugging information.

LD_LIBRARY_PATH

> Enhance the search path that the runtime linker uses to find dynamic dependencies. LD_LIBRARY_PATH specifies a colon-separated list of directories that are to be searched before the default directories. Also note that LD_LIBRARY_PATH adds additional semantics to ld(1).

LD_LIBRARY_PATH-64

New!

> Override LD_LIBRARY_PATH for 64-bit dependencies. Similar to the LD_LIBRARY_PATH environment variable.

LD_LOADFLTR Set to any non-null value to process filters immediately when they are loaded. Filters are a form of shared object. They enable an alternative shared object to be selected at runtime and provide the implementation for any symbols defined within the filter. See the -f and -F options of ld(1). By default, defer the alternative shared object processing until symbol resolution occurs against the filter. Also see the -z loadfltr option of ld(1).

LD_NOAUXFLTR

> Set to any non-null value to disable alternative shared lookup. Auxiliary filters are a form of shared object. They enable an alternative shared object to be selected at runtime and provide the implementation for any symbols defined within the filter. See the -f option of ld(1).

LD_NOVERSION

> Set to any non-null value to disable the runtime linker version checking. By default the runtime linker verifies version dependencies for the primary executable and all of its dependencies.

LD_ORIGIN Trigger the immediate processing of $ORIGIN by setting the environment variable LD_ORIGIN to any non-null value. This variable can be useful for applications that invoke chdir(2) before locating dependencies that use the $ORIGIN string token.

New!

LD_PRELOAD Provide a white-space-separated list of shared objects that are to be interpreted by the runtime linker. The specified shared objects are linked after the program is executed but before any other shared objects that the program references.

LD_PROFILE Define a shared object that is profiled by the runtime linker. When profiling is enabled, create and map a profiling buffer file. The name of the buffer file is the name of the shared object being profiled with a .profile extension. By default, this buffer is placed in /var/tmp. You can also use the environment variable LD_PROFILE_OUTPUT to indicate an alternative directory in which to place the profiling buffer. This buffer contains profil(2) and call count information similar to the gmon.out information generated by programs that have been linked with the -xpg option of cc(1). Any applications that use the named shared object and that run while this environment variable is set accumulate data in the profile buffer. You can use gprof(1) to examine the profile buffer information. Note that this profiling technique is an alternative to any that may be provided by the compilation system. The shared object being profiled does not have to be instrumented in any way, and LD_PROFILE should not be combined with a profile-instrumented application.

Note — Environment-variable names beginning with the characters LD_ are reserved for possible future enhancements to ld and ld.so.1(1).

Security

To prevent malicious dependency substitution or symbol interposition, some restrictions may apply to the evaluation of the dependencies of secure processes.

The runtime linker categorizes a process as secure if the user is not a superuser and either the real user and effective user identifiers are not equal or the real group and effective group identifiers are not equal. See getuid(2), geteuid(2), getgid(2), and getegid(2).

New!

If an LD_LIBRARY_PATH environment variable is in effect for a secure process, only the trusted directories specified by this variable are used to augment the runtime linker's search rules. Presently, the only trusted directory known to the runtime linker is /usr/lib, or /usr/lib/sparcv9 for 64-bit SPARC V9 objects.

In a secure process, any run-path specifications provided by the application or any of its dependencies are used, provided they are full path names; that is, the path name starts with a /.

You can load additional objects with a secure process by using the LD_PRELOAD environment variable, provided the objects are specified as simple file names with no / in the name. These objects are located subject to the search path restrictions previously described.

Files

/usr/lib/ld.so.1

> Default runtime linker.

/etc/lib/ld.so.1

> Alternate runtime linker.

/usr/lib/libc.so.

> Alternate interpreter for SVID ABI compatibility.

/usr/lib/ld.so

> AOUT(BCP) runtime linker.

/usr/lib/0@0.so.1

> Null character pointer compatibility library.

/usr/lib/sparcv9/ld.so.1

> Default runtime linker for the SPARC V9 architecture.

/usr/lib/sparcv9/0@0so.1

> Null character pointer compatibility library for the SPARC V9 architecture.

Attributes

See attributes(5) for descriptions of the following attributes:

Attribute Type	Attribute Value
Availability	SUNWcsu

See Also

gprof(1), ld(1), ldd(1), exec(2), getegid(2), geteuid(2), getuid(2), mmap(2), profil(2), dladdr(3X), dlclose(3X), dldump(3X), dlerror(3X), dlopen(3X), dlsym(3X), attributes(5)
> *Linker and Libraries Guide*

let — Shell Built-in Function to Evaluate One or More Arithmetic Expressions

Synopsis

ksh
```
let "arg"...
```

Description

ksh

Use the let command to perform integer arithmetic as specified by one or more arguments. Each *arg* can contain numbers, operators, constants, and shell variables that define a separate arithmetic expression to be evaluated. Use double quotes with any arguments that contain spaces or other special characters. You can also use double parentheses ((...)) instead of double quotes for arguments that contain white space.

The exit status is 0 if the value of the last expression is non-zero, and 1 otherwise.

Examples

The following example sets the variable X to the sum of 1 + 1.

```
$ let "X=1 + 1"
$ print $X
2
$
```

Attributes

See attributes(5) for descriptions of the following attributes:

Attribute Type	Attribute Value
Availability	SUNWcsu

See Also

ksh(1), set(1), typeset(1), attributes(5)

lex — Generate Programs for Lexical Tasks

Synopsis

/usr/ccs/bin/lex [-cntv][-e | -w][-V -Q [y | n]][*file*]...

Description

The lex command generates C programs to be used in lexical processing of character input that can also be used as an interface to yacc. The C programs are generated from lex source code and conform to the ISO C standard. Usually, the lex command writes the program it generates to the file lex.yy.c; the state of this file is unspecified if lex exits with a non-zero exit status.

Options

-c	Indicate C-language action (default option).
-e	Generate a program that can handle EUC characters (cannot be used with the -w option). yytext[] is of type unsigned char[].
-n	Suppress the summary of statistics usually written with the -v option. If no table sizes are specified in the lex source code and you do not specify the -v option, then -n is implied.
-t	Write the resulting program to standard output instead of lex.yy.c.

-v   Write a summary of lex statistics to the standard error. If table
              sizes are specified in the lex source code and you do not specify the
              -n option, the -v option may be enabled.

-w   Generate a program that can handle EUC characters (cannot be
              used with the -e option). Unlike the -e option, yytext[] is of type
              wchar_t[].

-V   Print version information on standard error.

-Q[y|n]   Print version information to output file lex.yy.c by using -Qy.
              The -Qn option does not print out version information and is the
              default.

Operands

file   A path name of an input file. If you specify more than one such file,
              concatenate all files to produce a single lex program. If you specify
              no file operands or if a file operand is -, use the standard input.

Output

Standard Output

If you specify the -t option, the text file of C source code output of lex is
written to standard output.

Standard Error

If you specify the -t option, informational, error, and warning messages
concerning the contents of lex source code input are written to the standard
error.
   If you do not specify the -t option:

- Informational error and warning messages concerning the contents of
  lex source code input are written to either the standard output or
  standard error.

- If you specify the -v option and do not specify the -n option, lex statistics
  are also written to standard error. These statistics may also be generated
  if table sizes are specified with a % operator as long as you do not specify
  the -n option.

Output Files

A text file containing C source code is written to lex.yy.c or to the standard
output if you use the -t option.

Extended Description

Each input file contains lex source code, which is a table of regular expressions
with corresponding actions in the form of C-program fragments.

When `lex.yy.c` is compiled and linked with the `lex` library (using the `-1 1` operand with `c89` or `cc`), the resulting program reads character input from the standard input and partitions it into strings that match the given expressions.

When an expression is matched, the following actions occur:

- The input string that was matched is left in `yytext` as a null-terminated string; `yytext` is either an external character array or a pointer to a character string. You can explicitly select the type with the `%array` or `%pointer` declarations. The default is `%array`.
- The external `int yyleng` is set to the length of the matching string.
- The expression's corresponding program fragment, or action, is executed.

During pattern matching, `lex` searches the set of patterns for the single longest possible match. The rule given first is chosen from the rules that match the same number of characters.

The general format of `lex` source is:

New!

```
Definitions %%
Rules %%
User Subroutines
```

The first `%%` is required to mark the beginning of the rules (regular expressions and actions); the second `%%` is required only if user subroutines follow.

Any line in the `Definitions` section beginning with a blank character is assumed to be a C-program fragment and is copied to the external definition area of the `lex.yy.c` file. Similarly, anything in the `Definitions` section included between delimiter lines containing only `%{` and `%}` is also copied unchanged to the external definition area of the `lex.yy.c` file.

Any such input (beginning with a blank character or within `%{` and `%}` delimiter lines) appearing at the beginning of the `Rules` section before any rules are specified is written to `lex.yy.c` after the declarations of variables for the `yylex` function and before the first line of code in `yylex`. Thus, user variables local to `yylex` can be declared here as well as application code to execute on entry to `yylex`.

The action taken by `lex` is undefined when `lex` encounters any input beginning with a blank character or within `%{` and `%}` delimiter lines appearing in the `Rules` section but coming after one or more rules. The presence of such input may result in an erroneous definition of the `yylex` function.

Definitions in lex

Definitions in `lex` appear before the first `%%` delimiter. Any line in this section not contained between `%{` and `%}` lines and not beginning with a blank character is assumed to define a `lex` substitution string. The format of these lines is:

```
name substitute
```

If a *name* does not meet the requirements for identifiers in the ISO C standard, the result is undefined. The string substitute replaces the string { *name* } when it is used in a rule. The *name* string is recognized in this context only when the braces are provided and when it does not appear within a bracket expression or within double quotes.

In the Definitions section, any line beginning with a % (percent sign) character and followed by an alphanumeric word beginning with either s or S defines a set of start conditions. Any line beginning with a % followed by a word beginning with either x or X defines a set of exclusive start conditions. When the generated scanner is in a %s state, patterns with no state specified are also active; in a %x state, such patterns are not active. The rest of the line after the first word is considered to be one or more blank-character-separated names of start conditions. Start condition names are constructed in the same way as definition names. Start conditions can be used to restrict the matching of regular expressions to one or more states.

Implementations accept either of the following two mutually exclusive declarations in the Definitions section.

%array   Declare the type of yytext to be a null-terminated character array.

%pointer   Declare the type of yytext to be a pointer to a null-terminated character string.

Note — When using the %pointer option, you cannot use the yyless function to alter yytext.

%array is the default. If you specify %array (or do not specify either %array or %pointer), the correct way to make an external reference to yytext is with a declaration of the following form.

```
extern char yytext[]
```

If you specify %pointer, the correct way to make an external reference to yytext is with a declaration of the following form.

```
extern char *yytext;
```

lex accepts declarations in the Definitions section for setting certain internal table sizes. The declarations are shown in the following table.

Declaration	Description	Default
%p n	Number of positions	2500
%n n	Number of states	500
%a n	Number of transitions	2000
%e n	Number of parse tree nodes	1000

Declaration	Description	Default
%k n	Number of packed character classes	10000
%o n	Size of the output array	3000

Programs generated by lex need either the -e or -w option to handle input that contains EUC characters from supplementary codesets. If you specify neither of these options, yytext is of the type char[], and the generated program can handle only ASCII characters.

When you use the -e option, yytext is of the type unsigned char[] and yyleng gives the total number of bytes in the matched string. With this option, the macros input(), unput(c), and output(c) should do a byte-based I/O in the same way as with the regular ASCII lex. Two more variables are available with the -e option, yywtext and yywleng, which behave the same as would yytext and yyleng under the -w option.

When you use the -w option, yytext is of the type wchar_t[] and yyleng gives the total number of characters in the matched string. If you supply your own input(), unput(c), or output(c) macros with this option, they must return or accept EUC characters in the form of wide character (wchar_t). This enables a different interface between your program and the lex internals to expedite some programs.

Rules in lex

The Rules source files are a table in which the left column contains regular expressions and the right column contains actions (C-program fragments) to be executed when the expressions are recognized.

```
ERE action
ERE action
...
```

The extended regular expression (ERE) portion of a row is separated from action by one or more blank characters. A regular expression containing blank characters is recognized under one of the following conditions:

- The entire expression appears within double quotes.
- The blank characters appear within double quotes.
- Each blank character is preceded by a backslash character.

User Subroutines in lex

Anything in the user subroutines section is copied to lex.yy.c following yylex.

Regular Expressions in lex

The lex command supports the set of Extended Regular Expressions (EREs) described in regex(5) with the following additions and exceptions to the syntax.

. . . Any string enclosed in double quotes represents the characters within the double quotes as themselves, except that backslash escapes (which appear in the following table) are recognized. Any backslash-escape sequence is terminated by the closing quote. For example, `"\01""1"` represents a single string: the octal value 1 followed by the character 1.

<state>r <state1, state2,...>r

Match the regular expression *r* only when the program is in one of the start conditions indicated by *state*, *state1*, and so forth. (As an exception to the typographical conventions of the rest of this document, in this case *<state>* does not represent a metavariable, but the literal angle-bracket characters surrounding a symbol.) The start condition is recognized as such only at the beginning of a regular expression.

r/x Match the regular expression *r* only if it is followed by an occurrence of regular expression *x*. The token returned in yytext matches only *r*. If the trailing portion of *r* matches the beginning of *x*, the result is unspecified. The *r* expression cannot include further trailing context nor the $ (match-end-of-line) operator; *x* cannot include the ^ (match-beginning-of-line) operator, nor trailing context, nor the $ operator. That is, only one occurrence of trailing context is allowed in a lex regular expression, and you can use the ^ operator only at the beginning of such an expression.

{name} When *name* is one of the substitution symbols from the Definitions section, replace the string, including the enclosing braces, with the substitute value. Treat the substitute value in the extended regular expression as if it were enclosed in parentheses. No substitution occurs if *{name}* occurs within a bracket expression or within double quotes.

Within an ERE, a backslash character (\\, \a, \b, \f, \n, \r, \t, \v) is considered to begin an escape sequence. In addition, the escape sequences in the following table are recognized.

You cannot use a literal newline character within an ERE; you cannot use the \n escape sequence to represent a newline character. A newline character cannot be matched by a period operator.

Escape Sequences in lex

Sequence	Description	Meaning
\digits	A backslash character followed by the longest sequence of one, two, or three octal-digit characters (01234567). If all of the digits are 0, (that is, representation of the null character), the behavior is undefined.	The character whose encoding is represented by the one-, two-, or three-digit octal integer. Multibyte characters require multiple concatenated escape sequences of this type, including the leading \ for each byte.
\xdigits	A backslash character followed by the longest sequence of hexadecimal-digit characters (01234567 abcdefABCDEF). If all of the digits are 0, (that is, representation of the null character), the behavior is undefined.	The character whose encoding is represented by the hexadecimal integer.
\c	A backslash character followed by any character not described in this table (\\, \a, \b, \f, \n, \r, \t, \v).	The character c, unchanged.

ERE Precedence in lex
The order of precedence given to extended regular expressions for lex is as shown in the following table, from high to low.

Note — The escaped characters entry is not meant to imply that these are operators. They are included in the table to show their relationships to the true operators. The start condition, trailing context, and anchoring notations have been omitted from the table because of the placement restrictions described in this section; they can only appear at the beginning or ending of an ERE.

[= =][: :][. .]	Collation-related bracket symbols.
\<special character>	Escaped characters.
[]	Bracket expression.
"..."\grouping ( )	Quoting.

{*name*}	Definition.
* + ?	Single-character RE duplication concatenation.
{*m*, *n*}	Interval expression.
|	Alternation.

The ERE anchoring operators (^ and $) do not appear in the table. With `lex` regular expressions, use of these operators is restricted. You can use the ^ operator only at the beginning of an entire regular expression and the $ operator only at the end. The operators apply to the entire regular expression. Thus, for example, the pattern (^abc) | (def$) is undefined. Instead, you can write it as two separate rules, one with the regular expression ^abc and one with def$, that share a common action via the special | action. If you write the pattern ^abc|def$, it would match either of abc or def on a line by itself.

Unlike the general ERE rules, embedded anchoring is not allowed by most historical `lex` implementations. An example of embedded anchoring is for patterns such as (^) foo ($) to match foo when it exists as a complete word. You can achieve this functionality with existing `lex` features, as shown below.

```
^foo/[\n] |
" foo"/[\n]   /* found foo as a separate word */
```

Note also that $ is a form of trailing context (it is equivalent to / \n) and as such you cannot use it with regular expressions containing another instance of the operator.

You can use the additional regular expressions trailing-context operator / as an ordinary character if presented within double-quotes, " / "; preceded by a backslash, \ /; or within a bracket expression, [/]. The start-condition < and > operators are special only in a start condition at the beginning of a regular expression; elsewhere in the regular expression they are treated as ordinary characters.

The following examples clarify the differences between `lex` regular expressions and regular expressions appearing elsewhere in this document. For regular expressions of the form *r*/*x*, the string matching *r* is always returned; confusion may arise when the beginning of *x* matches the trailing portion of *r*. For example, given the regular expression a*b/cc and the input aaabcc, yytext would contain the string aaab on this match. But, given the regular expression x*/xy and the input xxxy, the token xxx, not xx, is returned by some implementations because xxx matches x*.

In the rule ab*/bc, the b* at the end of *r* extends *r*'s match into the beginning of the trailing context, so the result is unspecified. If this rule were ab/bc, however, the rule matches the text ab when it is followed by the text bc. In this latter case, the matching of *r* cannot extend into the beginning of *x*, so the result is specified.

Actions in lex

The action to be taken when an ERE is matched can be a C-program fragment or the special actions described below. The program fragment can contain one or more C statements and can also include special actions. The empty C statement ; is a valid action; any string in the lex.yy.c input that matches the pattern portion of such a rule is effectively ignored or skipped. However, the absence of an action is not valid, and the action lex takes in such a condition is undefined.

The specification for an action, including C statements and special actions, can extend across several lines if you enclose them in braces.

```
ERE <one or more blanks> { program statement program statement }
```

The default action is to copy the string to the output when a string in the input to a lex.yy.c program is not matched by any expression. Because the default behavior of a program generated by lex is to read the input and copy it to the output, a minimal lex source program that has just %% generates a C program that simply copies the input to the output unchanged.

Four special actions are available: | ECHO; REJECT; BEGIN.

| | The action for the next rule is the action for this rule. Unlike the other three actions, you cannot enclose | in braces or terminate it with a semicolon. You must specify it alone with no other actions. |

ECHO;   Write the contents of the string yytext on the output.

REJECT;   Usually only a single expression is matched by a given string in the input. REJECT means continue to the next expression that matches the current input and execute whatever rule was the second choice after the current rule for the same input. Thus, you can match and execute multiple rules for one input string or overlapping input strings. For example, given the regular expressions xyz and xy and the input xyz, usually only the regular expression xyz would match. The next attempted match would start after z. If the last action in the xyz rule is REJECT, both this rule and the xy rule would be executed. The REJECT action can be implemented so that flow of control does not continue after it, as if it were equivalent to a goto to another part of yylex. Using REJECT can result in somewhat larger and slower scanners.

BEGIN   The action

```
BEGIN newstate;
```

switches the state (start condition) to *newstate*. If you have not previously declared the string *newstate* as a start condition in the Definitions, the results are unspecified. The initial state is indicated by the digit 0 or the token INITIAL.

The functions or macros described below are accessible to user code included in the lex input. It is unspecified whether they appear in the C code output of lex or are accessible only through the -l l operand to c89 or cc (the lex library).

int yylex(void)

> Perform lexical analysis on the input; this is the primary function generated by the lex command. The function returns 0 when the end of input is reached; otherwise it returns non-zero values (tokens) determined by the actions that are selected.

int yymore(void)

> When called, indicate that when the next input string is recognized, append it to the current value of yytext instead of replacing it; adjust the value in yyleng accordingly.

int yyless(int *n*)

> Retain *n* initial characters in yytext, null terminated, and treat the remaining characters as if they had not been read; adjust the value in yyleng accordingly.

int input(void)

> Return the next character from the input or 0 on end-of-file. Obtain input from the stream pointer yyin, although possibly via an intermediate buffer. Thus, once scanning has begun, the effect of altering the value of yyin is undefined. Remove the character read from the input stream of the scanner without any processing by the scanner.

int unput(int *c*)

> Return the character *c* to the input; yytext and yyleng are undefined until the next expression is matched. The result of using unput for more characters than have been input is unspecified.

The following functions appear only in the lex library, accessible through the -l l operand. They can, therefore, be redefined by a portable application.

int yywrap(void)

> Called by yylex at end-of-file; the default yywrap always returns 1. If the application requires yylex to continue processing with another source of input, then the application can include a function yywrap, which associates another file with the external variable FILE *yyin and returns a value of 0.

int main(int argc, char *argv[])

> Call yylex to perform lexical analysis, then exit. The user code can contain main to perform application-specific operations, calling yylex as applicable.

The reason for breaking these functions into two lists is that only those functions in libl.a can be reliably redefined by a portable application.

Except for input, unput, and main, all external and static names generated by lex begin with the prefix yy or YY.

Usage

Portable applications are warned that in the `Rules` section, an ERE without an action is not acceptable but need not be detected as erroneous by `lex`. This may result in compilation or runtime errors.

The purpose of `input` is to take characters off the input stream and discard them as far as the lexical analysis is concerned. A common use is to discard the body of a comment once the beginning of a comment is recognized.

The `lex` command is not fully internationalized in its treatment of regular expressions in the `lex` source code or generated lexical analyzer. It would seem desirable to have the lexical analyzer interpret the regular expressions given in the `lex` source according to the environment specified when the lexical analyzer is executed, but this is not possible with the current `lex` technology. Furthermore, the very nature of the lexical analyzers produced by `lex` must be closely tied to the lexical requirements of the input language being described, which frequently are locale specific anyway. (For example, writing an analyzer that is used for French text is not automatically useful for processing other languages.)

Note — If routines such as `yyback()`, `yywrap()`, and `yylock()` in `.l` (ell) files are to be `extern C` functions, the command line to compile a C++ program must define the `__EXTERN_C__` macro, for example:

```
castle% CC -D__EXTERN_C__ ... file
```

Examples

The following example of a `lex` program implements a rudimentary scanner for a Pascal-like syntax.

```
%{
/* need this for the call to atof() below */
#include <math.h>
/* need this for printf(), fopen() and stdin below */
#include <stdio.h>
%}
DIGIT [0-9]
ID [a-z][a-z0-9]*
%%
{DIGIT}+ {
    printf("An integer: %s (%d)\n", yytext,
    atoi(yytext));
    }
{DIGIT}+"."{DIGIT}*   {
    printf("A float: %s (%g)\n", yytext,
    atof(yytext));
    }
if|then|begin|end|procedure|function   {
    printf("A keyword: %s\n", yytext);
    }
```

```
{ID} printf("An identifier: %s\n", yytext);
"+"|"-"|"*"|"/"    printf("An operator: %s\n", yytext);
"{"[^}\n]*"}"  /* eat up one-line comments */
[\t\n]+ /* eat up white space */
    printf("Unrecognized character: %s\n", yytext);
%%
int main(int argc, char *argv[])
{
    ++argv, --argc;  /* skip over program name */
    if (argc > 0)
    yyin = fopen(argv[0], "r");
    else
    yyin = stdin;
    yylex();
}
```

Environment Variables

See environ(5) for descriptions of the following environment variables that affect the execution of lex: LC_COLLATE, LC_CTYPE, LC_MESSAGES, and NLSPATH.

Exit Status

0	Successful completion.
>0	An error occurred.

Attributes

See attributes(5) for descriptions of the following attributes:

Attribute Type	Attribute Value
Availability	SUNWbtool

See Also

yacc(1), attributes(5), environ(5), regex(5)

limit, ulimit, unlimit — Set or Get Limitations on Available System Resources

Synopsis

```
/usr/bin/ulimit [-f][blocks]
```

sh
```
ulimit [-[HS][a | cdfnstv]]
ulimit [-[HS]] c | d | f | n | s | t | v]] limit
```

csh
```
limit [-h][resource [limit]]
unlimit [-h][resource]
```

ksh
```
ulimit [-HSacdfnstv][limit]
```

Description

/usr/bin/ulimit

The ulimit command sets or reports the file-size writing limit imposed on files written by the shell and its child processes (files of any size can be read). Only a process with appropriate privileges can increase the limit.

Bourne Shell

The Bourne shell built-in function, ulimit, prints or sets hard or soft resource limits. These limits are described in getrlimit(2).

If you specify limit, ulimit prints the specified limits. You can print any number of limits at one time. The -a option prints all limits, as shown in the following example.

```
$ ulimit -a
time(seconds) unlimited
file(blocks) unlimited
data(kbytes) unlimited
stack(kbytes) 8192
coredump(blocks) unlimited
nofiles(descriptors) 64
memory(kbytes) unlimited
$
```

If limit is present, ulimit sets the specified limit to limit. The string unlimited requests the largest valid limit. You can set limits for only one resource at a time. Any user can set a soft limit to any value below the hard limit. Any user can lower a hard limit. Only superuser can raise a hard limit; see su(1M).

The -H option specifies a hard limit. The -S option specifies a soft limit. If you specify neither option, ulimit sets both limits and prints the soft limit.

The following options specify the resource whose limits are to be printed or set. If you specify no option, the file size limit is printed or set.

-c	Maximum corefile size (in 512-byte blocks).
-d	Maximum size of data segment or heap (in kilobytes).
-f	Maximum file size (in 512-byte blocks).
-n	Maximum file descriptor plus 1.
-s	Maximum size of stack segment (in kilobytes).
-t	Maximum CPU time (in seconds).
-v	Maximum size of virtual memory (in kilobytes).

C Shell

The C shell `limit` built-in function limits the consumption by the current process or any process it spawns, each not to exceed *limit* on the specified resource. If you omit *limit*, current limit is displayed. If you omit *resource*, all limits are displayed. (Run the `sysdef`(1M) command to obtain the maximum possible limits for your system. The values reported are in hexadecimal, but you can translate them into decimal numbers with the `bc`(1) command).

-h	Use hard limits instead of the current limits. Hard limits impose a ceiling on the values of the current limits. Only superuser can raise the hard limits.

resource is one of the following:

cputime	Maximum CPU seconds per process.
filesize	Largest single file allowed; limited to the size of the file system (see `df`(1M)).
datasize	The maximum size of a process's heap in bytes.
stacksize	Maximum stack size for the process (see `swap`(1M)).
coredumpsize	
	Maximum size of a core dump (file). This value is limited to the size of the file system.
descriptors	Maximum number of file descriptors. (Run `sysdef()`.)
memorysize	Maximum size of virtual memory.

limit is a number, with an optional scaling factor, as follows:

*n*h	Hours (for `cputime`).
*n*k	*n* kilobytes (the default for all but `cputime`).
*n*m	*n* megabytes or minutes (for `cputime`).
mm:*ss*	Minutes and seconds (for `cputime`).

unlimit removes a limitation on resource. If you specify no resource, all resource limitations are removed. See the description of the limit command for the list of resource names.

-h	Remove corresponding hard limits. Only superuser can use this option.

Korn Shell

The Korn shell built-in function, ulimit, sets or displays a resource limit. The available resources limits are listed below. Many systems do not contain one or more of these limits. The limit for a specified resource is set when you specify limit. The value of limit can be a number in the unit specified below with each resource, or the value unlimited. The -H and -S flags specify whether to set the hard limit or the soft limit for the given resource. Once you set a hard limit, you cannot increase it. You can increase a soft limit up to the value of the hard limit. If you specify neither the -H nor -S option, the limit applies to both. When you omit limit, the current resource limit is printed.

In this case, the soft limit is printed unless you specify -H. When you specify more than one resource, the limit name and unit are printed before the value.

-a	List all of the current resource limits.
-c	The number of 512-byte blocks on the size of core dumps.
-d	The number of kilobytes on the size of the data area.
-f	The number of 512-byte blocks on files written by child processes (files of any size can be read).
-n	The number of file descriptors plus 1.
-s	The number of kilobytes on the size of the stack area.
-t	The number of seconds (CPU time) to be used by each process.
-v	The number of kilobytes for virtual memory.

If you specify no option, -f is assumed.

Options

-f	Set (or report, if no blocks operand is present), the file size limit in blocks. The -f option is also the default case.

Operands

blocks	The number of 512-byte blocks to use as the new file size limit.

Examples

/usr/bin/ulimit
The following example limits the stack size to 512 kilobytes.

```
castle% ulimit -s 512
castle% ulimit -a
```

```
time(seconds) unlimited
file(blocks) 100
data(kbytes) 523256
stack(kbytes) 512
coredump(blocks) 200
nofiles(descriptors) 64
memory(kbytes) unlimited
castle%
```

Bourne and Korn Shells

The following example limits the number of file descriptors to 12.

```
$ ulimit -n 12
$ ulimit -a
time(seconds) unlimited
file(blocks) 41943
data(kbytes) 523256
stack(kbytes) 8192
coredump(blocks) 200
nofiles(descriptors) 12
vmemory(kbytes) unlimited
$
```

C Shell

The following example limits the size of a core dump file size to 0 kilobytes.

```
castle% limit coredumpsize 0
castle% limit
cputime          unlimited
filesize         unlimited
datasize         unlimited
stacksize        8192 kbytes
coredumpsize     0 kbytes
descriptors      64
memorysize       unlimited
castle%
```

The following example removes the above limitation for the corefile size.

```
castle% unlimit coredumpsize
castle% limit
cputime          unlimited
filesize         unlimited
datasize         unlimited
stacksize        8192 kbytes
coredumpsize     unlimited
descriptors      64
memorysize       unlimited
castle%
```

Environment Variables

See environ(5) for descriptions of the following environment variables that affect the execution of ulimit: LC_CTYPE, LC_MESSAGES, and NLSPATH.

Exit Status

0   Successful completion.

>0   A request for a higher limit was rejected or an error occurred.

Attributes

See `attributes`(5) for descriptions of the following attributes:

Attribute Type	Attribute Value
Availability	SUNWcsu

See Also

bc(1), csh(1), ksh(1), sh(1), df(1M), su(1M), swap(1M), sysdef(1M),
getrlimit(2), attributes(5), environ(5)

line — Read One Line

Synopsis

/usr/bin/line

Description

The `line` command copies one line (up to and including a newline) from the
standard input and writes it on the standard output. It returns an exit status
of 1 on end-of-file and always prints at least a newline. It is often used within
shell files to read from the user's terminal.

Examples

When you invoke the `line` command, it enters a newline and waits for you to
type a line. When you press Return, the line is echoed to standard output, as
shown in the following example.

```
castle% line
This is a line
This is a line
castle%
```

Exit Status

0   Successful completion.

>0   End-of-file on input.

Attributes

See `attributes`(5) for descriptions of the following attributes:

Attribute Type	Attribute Value
Availability	SUNWcsu

See Also

sh(1), read(2), attributes(5)

---

lint — C Program Verifier

Synopsis

/usr/ucb/lint [*options*]

Description

Use the `lint` command to detect portability problems, bugs, and other potential errors in C programs. /usr/ucb/lint is the interface to the BSD Compatibility Package C program verifier. It is a script that looks for the link /usr/ccs/bin/ucblint to the C program verifier. /usr/ccs/bin/ucblint is available only with the SPROcc package, whose default location is /opt/SUNWspro. /usr/ucb/lint is identical to /usr/ccs/bin/ucblint, except that BSD headers are used and BSD libraries are linked before base libraries. The /opt/SUNWspro/man/man1/lint.1 manual page is available only with the SPROcc package.

Options

/usr/ucb/lint accepts the same options as /usr/ccs/bin/ucblint, with the following exceptions.

-I*dir*   Search *dir* for included files whose names do not begin with a slash (/) before searching the usual directories. Search the directories for multiple -I options in the order specified. The preprocessor first searches for #include files in the directory containing a source file, and then in directories named with -I options (if any), then /usr/ucbinclude, and finally, /usr/include.

-L*dir*   Add *dir* to the list of directories searched for libraries by /usr/ccs/bin/ucblint. This option is passed to /usr/ccs/bin/ld. Directories specified with this option are searched before /usr/ucblib and /usr/lib.

-Y P, *dir*   Change the default directory used for finding libraries.

Exit Status

0   Successful completion.

>0   An error occurred.

Files

`/usr/lint/bin/ld`

Link editor.

`/usr/lib/libc`

C library.

`/usr/ucbinclude`

BSD compatibility directory for header files.

`/usr/ucblib` BSD compatibility directory for libraries.

`/usr/ucblib/libucb`

BSD compatibility C library.

`/usr/lib/libsocket`

Library containing socket routines.

`/usr/lib/libnsl`

Library containing network functions.

`/usr/lib/libelf`

Library containing routines to process ELF object files.

`/usr/lib/libaio`

Library containing asynchronous I/O routines.

Attributes

See `attributes`(5) for descriptions of the following attributes:

Attribute Type	Attribute Value
Availability	SUNWscpu

See Also

`ld(1), a.out(4), attributes(5)`

listusers — List User Login Information

Synopsis

```
/usr/bin/listusers [-g groups][-l logins]
```

Description

Executed without any options, the listusers command lists all user logins sorted by login. The output shows the login ID and the account field value from the system's password database as specified by /etc/nsswitch.conf, as shown in the following example.

```
castle% listusers
des
noaccess        No Access User
nobody          Nobody
nobody4         SunOS 4.x Nobody
ray
rob
winsor
castle%
```

A user login is one that has a UID of 100 or greater.

You can combine the -l and -g options. User logins are listed only once, even if they belong to more than one of the selected groups.

Options

-g *groups* List all user logins belonging to *groups*, sorted by login. You can specify multiple groups as a comma-separated list.

-l *logins* List the user login or logins specified by *logins*, sorted by login. You can specify multiple logins as a comma-separated list.

Attributes

See attributes(5) for descriptions of the following attributes:

Attribute Type	Attribute Value
Availability	SUNWcsu

See Also

```
nsswitch.conf(4), attributes(5)
```

ln — Make Hard or Symbolic Links to Files

Synopsis
```
/usr/bin/ln [-fns] source-file [target]
/usr/bin/ln [-fns] source-file... target
/usr/xpg4/bin/ln [-fs] source-file [target]
/usr/xpg/bin/ln [-fs] source-file... target
```

Description
At times it is useful to have one file accessible from several directories. Linking a file can reduce the amount of disk space used and make it easier to maintain consistency in files used by several people. Use the ln (link) command to create links between directory entries in a single file system to make a single file accessible at two ore more locations in the directory hierarchy.

Symbolic links (-s) can link files across file systems. A symbolic link has a name and a location in the directory tree but has no contents. It simply points to another file or directory.

Use the ln command to create both hard links and symbolic links. A hard link is a pointer to a file and is indistinguishable from the original directory entry. Any changes to a file are effective independently of the name used to reference the file. Hard links cannot span file systems and cannot refer to directories.

By default, ln creates hard links. source-file is linked to target. If target is a directory, another file named source-file is created in target and linked to the original source-file.

In the first synopsis form, the ln command creates a new directory entry (link) for the file specified by source-file, at the destination path specified by target. If you do not specify target, the link is made in the current directory. This first synopsis form is assumed when the final operand does not name an existing directory; if you specify more than two operands and the final operand is not an existing directory, an error results.

In the second synopsis form, the ln command creates a new directory entry for each file specified by a source-file operand at a destination path in the existing directory named by target.

/usr/bin/ln
If target is a file, its contents are overwritten. If /usr/bin/ln determines that the mode of target forbids writing, it prints the mode (see chmod(1)), asks for a response, and reads the standard input for one line. If the response is affirmative, the link occurs if permissible; otherwise, the command exits.

/usr/xpg4/bin/ln
If target is a file and you do not specify the -f option, /usr/xpg4/bin/ln writes a diagnostic message to standard error, does nothing more with the current source-file, and goes on to any remaining source-files. A

symbolic link is an indirect pointer to a file; its directory entry contains the name of the file to which it is linked. Symbolic links can span file systems and can refer to directories.

File permissions for *target* can differ from those displayed with a -l listing of the ls(1) command. To display the permissions of *target*, use ls -lL. See stat(2) for more information.

Notes

A symbolic link to a directory behaves differently than you might expect in certain cases. While an ls(1) on such a link displays the files in the pointed-to directory, an ls -l displays information about the link itself, as shown in the following example.

```
castle% ln -s dir link
castle% ls link
file1 file2 file3 file4
castle% ls -l link
lrwxrwxrwx  1 user              7 Jan 11 23:27 link -> dir
castle%
```

When you use cd(1) to change to a directory through a symbolic link, you wind up in the pointed-to location within the file system. This means that the parent of the new working directory is not the parent of the symbolic link but, rather, the parent of the pointed-to directory. For instance, in the following case, the final working directory is /usr and not /home/user/linktest.

```
castle% pwd
/home/user/linktest
castle% ln -s /usr/tmp symlink
castle% cd symlink
castle% cd ..
castle% pwd
/usr
castle%
```

C shell users can avoid any resulting navigation problems by using the pushd and popd built-in commands instead of cd.

Options

The following options are supported for both /usr/bin/ln and /usr/xpg4/bin/ln.

    -f   Link files without questioning even if the mode of *target* forbids writing (the default if the standard input is not a terminal).

    -s   Create a symbolic link.

If you use the -s option with two arguments, *target* can be an existing directory or a nonexistent file. If *target* already exists and is not a directory, an error is returned. *source-file* can be any path name and need not exist. If it exists, it can be a file or directory and can reside on a different file system from *target*. If *target* is an existing directory, a file is created in directory *target* whose name is *source-file* or the last component of *source-file*. This file is a symbolic link that references *source-file*. If *target* does not exist, a file with name *target* is created and is a symbolic link that references *source-file*.

If you use the -s option with more than two arguments, *target* must be an existing directory or an error is returned. For each *source-file*, a link is created in *target* whose name is the last component of *source-file*; each new *source-file* is a symbolic link to the original *source-file*. The files and *target* can reside on different file systems.

/usr/bin/ln

-n   If the link is an existing file, do not overwrite the contents of the file. The -f option overrides this option. This behavior is the default for /usr/xpg4/bin/ln and is silently ignored.

Operands

source-file

A path name of a file to be linked. This file can be either a regular or special file. If you specify the -s option, *source-file* can also be a directory.

target   The path name of the new directory entry to be created or of an existing directory in which the new directory entries are to be created.

Usage

See largefile(5) for the description of the behavior of ln when encountering files greater than or equal to 2 Gbytes (2**31 bytes).

Environment Variables

See environ(5) for descriptions of the following environment variables that affect the execution of ln: LC_CTYPE, LC_MESSAGES, and NLSPATH.

Exit Status

0   All the specified files were linked successfully.

>0   An error occurred.

Attributes

See attributes(5) for descriptions of the following attributes:

/usr/bin/ln

Attribute Type	Attribute Value
Availability	SUNWcsu
CSI	Enabled

/usr/xpg4/bin/ln

Attribute Type	Attribute Value
Availability	SUNWxcu4
CSI	Enabled

See Also

chmod(1), ls(1), stat(2), attributes(5), environ(5), largefile(5), XPG4(5)

loadfont — Display or Change X86 Video Card Font Information

Synopsis

/bin/loadfont [-f *BDF-file* | -c *codeset*] [-m *mode*] [-d]

Description

The loadfont command enables you to load and activate a different font into the RAM of the video card used by the console of Solaris for the x86 operating system in text mode. You can also use loadfont to display information about the fonts currently in use. In addition, you can use the -m option to change the size of the characters on the screen and the number of lines per screen. loadfont always reads from standard output; this feature enables a system administrator to use it from a remote terminal.

When used without arguments, loadfont displays the different ways the command can be used, as shown in the synopsis.

> **Note** — The default fonts on the system are those of the ISO 8859-1 codeset. The optional IBM DOS 437 codeset is supported only at internationalization level 1. That is, if you choose to download fonts of the optional IBM DOS 437 codeset, nonstandard U.S. date, time, currency, numbers, unit, and collation are not

supported. There is no support for non-English message and text presentation and no multibyte character support. Therefore, non-Windows users should use only IBM DOS 437 codeset in the default C locale.

Options

-f *BDF-file*

>Read the contents of *BDF-file* and subsequently load the font specified in the file into the RAM of the video card. The file must be in the Binary Distribution Format version 2.1 as developed by Adobe Systems, Inc. (See loadfont(4).)

-c *codeset* Specify the name of a *codeset* available for the current font size. This font is loaded into the RAM of the video card and activated. Use ? to find out the valid codesets available. This option is a shorthand form of -f.

-m *mode* Change the mode of the console as specified to display a different font size and/or different number of lines and columns on the screen. Use ? to find out the valid modes available.

-d Read the font information from the video RAM and write it to standard output in a format compatible with the Binary Distribution Format version 2.1 as developed by Adobe Systems, Inc. (See loadfont(4).)

Fonts

A font is the representation of characters by images. The need to use different fonts can be imposed by:

- The codeset used to represent the characters internally.
- The resolution used to display the characters.

Each font contains exactly 256 images. All supported fonts are fixed size (constant width and constant height), that is, each character takes the same amount of space on the screen. When the monitor is not being used in graphics mode, the loadfont command enables you to modify the font used by the video card so that different images are displayed on the screen of the console for the various characters. The same video card can support different text modes. Video cards typically differ by the number of pixels they use to represent a single character. On any given video card, the same number of pixels is used for each character. For the standard VGA video cards, 8 by 16 (8 horizontally and 16 vertically) resolution is supported.

When you invoke loadfont to modify the existing font, it tries to do so for the font size currently in use. Use the -m option to switch to another font size.

loadfont and pcmapkeys

There is an almost one-to-one relationship between the use of the `loadfont`
command and the `pcmapkeys` command. Whereas `loadfont` lists or modifies
the images that correspond with the various characters, the `pcmapkeys`
command determines how characters are generated from the keyboard and
which code (a single bytecode) is used to represent the character internally. The
default representation is the ISO 8859-1 codeset.

When you use a different codeset, both a different `pcmapkeys` input file and
a different font set are required. If the default font does not satisfy your needs
(because a different font size or a customized font is required, such as a Greek
font), you need a `loadfont` description file to be used with the `-f` option. A
sample file that describes the IBM extended ASCII font for an 8 by 16
resolution is supplied (`/usr/share/lib/fonts/437.bdf`). A second sample
file, `/usr/share/lib/fonts/646g.bdf`, contains a font file for German
ASCII. See `pcmapkeys`(1) and `loadfont`(4) for additional details.

Warnings

When you try to switch to a mode that the video card does not support, you get
a blank screen. There is nothing wrong with the system; as superuser, simply
type in the command to set the default mode back, for example:

```
loadfont -m V80x25
```

Files

`/usr/share/lib/fonts/8859-1.bdf`

> The Binary Distribution Format (BDF) file for the default fonts.

`/usr/share/lib/fonts/437.bdf`

> Sample Binary Distribution Format (BDF) file for IBM 437 font on
> a VGA.

`/usr/share/lib/fonts/646g.bdf`

> Sample BDF file for German ASCII.

Attributes

See `attributes`(5) for descriptions of the following attributes:

Attribute Type	Attribute Value
Architecture	X86, PowerPC Edition
Availability	SUNWcsu

See Also

`pcmapkeys`(1), `loadfont`(4), `attributes`(5)

loadkeys, dumpkeys — Load and Dump Keyboard Translation Tables

Synopsis

```
/usr/bin/loadkeys [filename]
/usr/bin/dumpkeys
```

Description

loadkeys reads the file specified by *filename* and modifies the keyboard streams module's translation tables. If you specify no file and the keyboard is a Type-4 keyboard, a default file for the layout indicated by the DIP switches on the keyboard is used. The file is in the format specified by keytables(4).

By default, loadkeys loads the file

```
/usr/share/lib/keytables/type_tt/layout_dd
```

where *tt* is the value returned by the KIOCTYPE ioctl and *dd* is the value returned by the KIOCLAYOUT ioctl (see kb(7M)). On self-identifying keyboards, the value returned by the KIOCLAYOUT ioctl is set from the DIP switches. These files specify only the entries that change between the different Type-4 keyboard layouts.

dumpkeys writes to the standard output the current contents of the keyboard streams module's translation tables in the format specified by keytables(4).

Examples

The following example shows the first few lines output by the dumpkeys command for a Type-4 keyboard.

```
castle% dumpkeys
key 0     all hole
key 1     all buckybits+systembit up buckybits+systembit
key 2     all hole
key 3     all lf(2)
key 4     all hole
key 5     all tf(1)
key 6     all tf(2)
key 7     all tf(10)
key 8     all tf(3)
key 9     all tf(11)
key 10    all tf(4)
key 11    all tf(12)
key 12    all tf(5)
...
```

Files

/usr/share/lib/keytables/layout_dd
>
> Default keytable files.

Attributes

See attributes(5) for descriptions of the following attributes:

Attribute Type	Attribute Value
Architecture	SPARC, x86
Availability	SUNWcsu

See Also

kbd(1), keytables(4), attributes(5), kb(7M)

---

locale — Get Locale-Specific Information

Synopsis

```
/usr/bin/locale [-a | -m]
/usr/bin/locale [-ck] name...
```

Description

The locale command writes information to the standard output about the current locale environment or all public locales. For the purposes of this command, a public locale is one provided by the implementation that is accessible to the application.

When you use the locale command without any arguments, it summarizes the current locale environment for each locale category as determined by the settings of the environment variables. If the LANG environment variable is set with the following format

```
LANG=locale_x LC_COLLATE=locale_y
```

locale displays the results in the following format.

```
LANG=locale_x
LC_CTYPE=locale_x
LC_NUMERIC=locale_x
LC_TIME=locale_x
LC_COLLATE=locale_y
LC_MONETARY=locale_x
LC_MESSAGES=locale_x
LC_ALL=
```

When you specify operands, `locale` writes values that have been assigned to the keywords in the locale categories, as follows:

- Specifying a keyword name selects the named keyword and the category containing that keyword.
- Specifying a category name selects the named category and all keywords in that category.

Note — If you specify `LC_CTYPE` or keywords in the category `LC_CTYPE`, only the values in the range `0x00-0x7f` are displayed.

If you specify `LC_COLLATE` or keywords in the category `LC_COLLATE`, no actual values are written.

Options

`-a`	Write information about all available public locales. The available locales include `POSIX`, representing the POSIX locale.
`-c`	Write the names of selected locale categories. The `-c` option increases readability when you specify more than one category (for example, with more than one keyword name or a category name). It is valid both with and without the `-k` option.
`-k`	Write the names and values of selected keywords. The implementation can omit values for some keywords.
`-m`	Write names of available `charmaps`; see `localedef`(1).

Operands

name	Specify the name of a locale category (such as `LC_NUMERIC`), the name of a keyword in a locale category (such as `decimal_point`), or the reserved name `charmap`. The named category or keyword is used for output. If a single name represents both a locale category name and a keyword name in the current locale, the results are unspecified; otherwise, you can specify both category and keyword names as *name* operands, in any sequence.

Examples

The following example shows the output of the locale command with no arguments for an Australian locale.

```
castle% locale
LANG=en_AU
LC_CTYPE=en_AU
LC_NUMERIC=en_AU
LC_TIME=en_AU
LC_COLLATE=en_AU
LC_MONETARY=en_AU
LC_MESSAGES=C
```

```
LC_ALL=
castle%
```

If LC_ALL is set to POSIX, the following example shows the first few lines of
the values for the LC_ALL environment variable.

```
castle% setenv LC_ALL=POSIX
castle% locale -ck LC_ALL
LC_CTYPE
lower="a";"b";"c";"d";"e";"f";"g";"h";"i";"j";"k";"l";"m";"n";"o";"p";"
  q";"r";"s";"t";"u";"v";"w";"x";"y";"z"
upper="A";"B";"C";"D";"E";"F";"G";"H";"I";"J";"K";"L";"M";"N";"O";"P";"
  Q";"R";"S";"T";"U";"V";"W";"X";"Y";"Z"
alpha="A";"B";"C";"D";"E";"F";"G";"H";"I";"J";"K";"L";"M";"N";"O";"P";"
  Q";"R";"S";"T";"U";"V";"W";"X";"Y";"Z";"a";"b";"c";"d";"e";"f";"g";"h
  ";"i";"j";"k";"l";"m";"n";"o";"p";"q";"r";"s";"t";"u";"v";"w";"x";"y"
  ;"z"
digit="0";"1";"2";"3";"4";"5";"6";"7";"8";"9"
space="\x09";"\x0a";"\x0b";"\x0c";"\x0d";" "
...
```

The following example displays the values for the LC_NUMERIC category.

```
castle% locale -ck LC_NUMERIC
LC_NUMERIC
decimal_point="."
thousands_sep=""
grouping=-1
castle%
```

You can check for the value of specific elements within an environment
variable by specifying the keyword as arguments to the locale command. The
following example displays the decimal_point value of the LC_NUMERIC
category.

```
castle% locale -ck decimal_point
LC_NUMERIC
decimal_point="."
castle%
```

The following example uses the locale command to determine whether a
user-supplied response is affirmative.

```
if printf "%s\n" "$response" | /usr/xpg4/bin/grep -Eq "$(locale yesexpr)"
then
 affirmative processing goes here
else
  non-affirmative processing goes here
fi
```

Environment Variables

See environ(5) for the descriptions of LANG, LC_ALL, LC_CTYPE,
LC_MESSAGES, and NLSPATH.

The LANG, LC_*, and NLSPATH environment variables must specify the current locale environment to be written; they are used if you do not specify the -a option.

Exit Status

| 0 | All the requested information was found and output successfully. |
| >0 | An error occurred. |

Attributes

See attributes(5) for descriptions of the following attributes:

Attribute Type	Attribute Value
Availability	SUNWloc
CSI	Enabled

See Also

localedef(1), attributes(5), charmap(5), environ(5), locale(5)

localedef — Define Locale Environment

Synopsis

New!

```
localedef [-c][-C compiler-options [-f charmap]
    [-i sourcefile][-L linker-options][-m model][-W cc, arg]
    [-x extensions-file] localename
```

Description

The localedef command converts source definitions for locale categories into a format usable by the functions and commands whose operational behavior is determined by the setting of the locale environment variable (see environ(5)).

The command reads source definitions for one or more locale categories belonging to the same locale from the file named in the -i option (if specified) or from standard input.

Each category source definition is identified by the corresponding environment variable name and terminated by an END category-name statement. The following categories are supported.

LC_CTYPE   Define character classification and case conversion.

LC_COLLATE Define collation rules.

LC_MONETARY

> Define the format and symbols used in the formatting of monetary information.

LC_NUMERIC Define the decimal delimiter, grouping, and grouping symbol for nonmonetary numeric editing.

LC_TIME Define the format and content of date and time information.

LC_MESSAGES

> Define the format and values of affirmative and negative responses.

Options

-c Create permanent output even if warning messages have been issued.

-C *compiler-options*

> Pass the *compiler-options* to the C compiler (cc). If you specify more than one option, you must enclose all of them in quotes (" ").

-f *charmap* Specify the path name of a file containing a mapping of character symbols and collating element symbols to actual character encodings. You must specify this option if you use symbolic names (other than collating symbols defined in a collating-symbol keyword). If you do not use the -f option, use the default character mapping.

-i *sourcefile*

> Specify the path name of a file containing the source definitions. If you do not use this option, read source definitions from standard input.

-L *linker-options*

> Pass the *linker-options* to the C compiler (cc) that follows the C source file name. If you specify more than one option, you must enclose all of them in quotes (" ").

-m *model* Specify whether localedef generates a 64-bit or a 32-bit locale object. To generate a 32-bit object, specify model as ilp32. To generate a 64-bit locale object, specify lp64. The default is -m ilp32.

New!

-W cc,*arg* Pass *arg* options to the C compiler. Separate each argument from the preceding with just a comma. (You can make a comma part of an argument by immediately preceding it with a backslash character to escape it. The backslash is removed from the resulting argument.)

New!

-x *extensions-file*

>Specify the name of an extension file where various `localedef` options are listed. See `locale`(5).

If you specify the `-c` option and warnings occur, permanent output is created. The following conditions issue warning messages:

- If you use a symbolic name not found in the `charmap` file for the descriptions of the `LC_CTYPE` or `LC_COLLATE` categories (for other categories, this is an error condition).

- If optional keywords not supported by the implementation are present in the source.

Operands

localename   Identify the locale. If the name contains one or more slash characters, interpret *localename* as a path name where the created locale definitions are stored. This capability can be restricted to users with appropriate privileges. (You can process one category by specifying just one *localename*, although you can process several categories in one execution.)

Output

`localedef` creates a temporary C source file that represents the locale's data. `localedef` then calls the C compiler to compile this C source file into a shared object. This object is named `localename.so.1`. `localedef` also creates a text file named `localename` that is for information only.

If you do not specify the `-m` option, `localedef` generates a shared object for the 32-bit environment. It also generates a shared object for the 32-bit environment if you specify the `-m ilp32` option. If you specify the `-m lp64` option, `localedef` generates a shared object for the 64-bit environment.

You must move the share object for the 32-bit environment to:

`/usr/lib/locale/`*localename*`/`*localename*`.so.`*version_number*

You must move the shared object for the 64-bit environment to:

`/usr/lib/locale/`*localename*`/sparcv9/`*localename*`.so.`*version_number*

The `localename` text file is not needed.

Environment Variables

See `environ`(5) for definitions of the following environment variables that affect the execution of `localedef`: `LC_CTYPE`, `LC_MESSAGES`, and `NLSPATH`.

Exit Status

0	No errors occurred and the locales were successfully created.
1	Warnings occurred and the locales were successfully created.
2	The locale specification exceeded implementation limits or the coded character set or sets used were not supported by the implementation, and no locale was created.
3	The capability to create new locales is not supported by the implementation.
>3	Warnings or errors occurred and no output was created.

If an error is detected, no permanent output is created.

Files

/usr/lib/localedef/generic_eucbc.*x*

Describes what a generic EUC locale uses in the system (the default).

/usr/lib/localedef/single_byte.*x*

Describes a generic single-byte file used in the system.

/usr/lib/locale/*localename*/*localename*.so.*version_number*   *New!*

The shared object for the 32-bit environment.

/usr/lib/locale/*localename*/sparcv9/*localename*.so.*version_number*   *New!*

The shared object for the 64-bit environment on SPARC.

Attributes

See attributes(5) for descriptions of the following attributes:

Attribute Type	Attribute Value
Availability	SUNWcsu

See Also

locale(1), nl_langinfo(3C), strftime(3C), attributes(5), charmap(5), environ(5), extensions(5), locale(5)

logger — Add Entries to the System Log

Synopsis

/usr/bin/logger [-i] [-f *file*] [-p *priority*] [-t *tag*] [*message*]...

Description

The logger command provides a method for adding one-line entries to the system log file from the command line. You can specify one or more message arguments on the command line, in which case each is logged immediately. If you specify no command-line arguments, either the file indicated with -f or the standard input is added to the log. Otherwise, you can specify a file with a set of lines to be logged. If you specify no options, logger reads and logs messages on a line-by-line basis from the standard input.

Options

-f *file*   Use the contents of file as the message to log.

-i   Log the process ID of the logger process with each line.

-p *priority*

                Enter the message with the specified priority. The message
                priority can be specified numerically or as a *facility.level* pair.
                For example, -p local3.info assigns the message priority to the
                information level in the local3 facility. The default priority is
                user.notice.

-t *tag*   Mark each line added to the log with the specified tag.

Operands

message   One of the string arguments whose contents are concatenated in
                the order specified, separated by single-space characters.

Examples

The following example logs the message System rebooted to the default priority level notice to be treated by syslogd in the same way as other messages to the facility user.

```
castle% logger System rebooted
castle%
```

The following example reads from the file /dev/idmc and logs each line in that file as a message with the tag HOSTIDM at priority level notice to be treated by syslogd in the same way as other messages to the facility local0.

```
castle% logger -p local0.notice -t HOSTIDM -f /dev/idmc
```

Environment Variables

See environ(5) for descriptions of the following environment variables that affect the execution of logger: LC_CTYPE, LC_MESSAGES, and NLSPATH.

Exit Status

0	Successful completion.
>0	An error occurred.

Attributes

See attributes(5) for descriptions of the following attributes:

Attribute Type	Attribute Value
Availability	SUNWcsu

See Also

mailx(1), write(1), syslogd(1M), syslog(3), attributes(5), environ(5)

login — Sign On to the System

Synopsis

```
/usr/bin/login [-p] [-d device] [-h hostname [terminal]] | -r hostname]
    [name [environ...]]
```

Description

Use the login command at the beginning of each terminal session to identify yourself to the system. login is invoked by the system when a connection is first established and after the previous user has terminated the login shell by issuing the exit command.

If you invoke login as a command, it must replace the initial command interpreter. To invoke login in this way, from the initial shell, type:

exec login

The C shell and Korn shell have their own built-in login commands. See ksh(1) and csh(1) for descriptions of login built-ins and usage.

login asks for your user name if it is not supplied as an argument and for your password if appropriate. Where possible, echoing is turned off while you type your password so that it does not appear on the written record of the session.

If you make any mistake in the login procedure, the following message is displayed and a new login prompt is displayed.

`Login incorrect`

If you make five incorrect login attempts, all five may be logged in `/var/adm/loginlog`, if it exists. The TTY line is dropped.

If password aging is turned on and the password has aged (see `passwd`(1) for more information), you are forced to changed the password. In this case, the `/etc/nsswitch.conf` file is consulted to determine password repositories (see `nsswitch.conf`(4)). The password update configurations supported are limited to the following five cases.

- `passwd: files`
- `passwd: files nis`
- `passwd: files nisplus`
- `passwd: compat (==> files nis)`
- `passwd: compat (==> files nisplus) passwd_compat: nisplus`

Failure to comply with these configurations prevents you from logging in to the system because `passwd`(1) fails. If you do not complete the login successfully within a certain period of time, it is likely that you will be silently disconnected.

After a successful login, accounting files are updated. Device owner, group, and permissions are set according to the contents of the `/etc/logindevperm` file, and the time you last logged in is printed (see `logindevperm`(4)).

The user ID, group ID, supplementary group list, and working directory are initialized, and the command interpreter specified in your password file is started.

The basic environment is initialized to:

```
HOME=your-login-directory
LOGNAME=your-login-name
PATH=/usr/bin:
SHELL=last-field-of-passwd-entry
MAIL=/var/mail/your-login-name
TZ=timezone-specification
```

For Bourne shell and Korn shell logins, the shell executes `/etc/profile` and `$HOME/.profile` if it exists. For C shell logins, the shell executes `/etc/.login`, `$HOME/.cshrc`, and `$HOME/.login`. The default `/etc/profile` and `/etc/.login` files check quotas (see `quota`(1M)), print `/etc/motd`, and check for mail. None of the messages are printed if the file `$HOME/.hushlogin` exists. The name of the command interpreter is set to - (dash), followed by the last component of the interpreter's path name, for example, `-sh`.

If the login-shell field in the password file (see passwd(4)) is empty, then the default command interpreter, /usr/bin/sh, is used. If this field is * (asterisk), then the named directory becomes the root directory. At that point, login is reexecuted at the new level, which must have its own root structure.

You can expand or modify the environment (except for PATH and SHELL) by supplying additional arguments to login, either at execution time or when login requests your login name. The arguments can take either the form *xxx* or *xxx=yyy*. Arguments without an equal sign (=) are put into the environment as:

L*n*=*xxx*

where *n* is a number starting at 0 which is incremented each time a new variable name is required. Variables containing an = (equal sign) are put into the environment without modification. If these variables already appear in the environment, then they replace the older values.

You cannot change the PATH and SHELL environment variables to prevent people who are logged in to restricted shell environments from spawning secondary shells that are not restricted. login understands simple single-character quoting conventions. Typing a backslash (\) in front of a character quotes it and allows you to include characters such as spaces and tabs.

Alternatively, you can pass the current environment by supplying the -p option to login. This option indicates that login should pass all currently defined environment variables, if possible, to the new environment. This option does not bypass any environment variable restrictions mentioned above. Environment variables specified on the login line take precedence if a variable is passed by both methods.

To enable remote logins by root, edit the /etc/default/login file and insert a pound sign (#) before the CONSOLE=/dev/console entry.

Security

login uses pam(3) for authentication, account management, session management, and password management. The PAM configuration policy, listed through /etc/pam.conf, specifies the modules to be used for login. Below is a partial pam.conf file with entries for the login command and using the UNIX authentication, account management, session management, and password management module.

```
login auth      required  /usr/lib/security/pam_unix.so.1
login account   required  /usr/lib/security/pam_unix.so.1
login session   required  /usr/lib/security/pam_unix.so.1
login password  required  /usr/lib/security/pam_unix.so.1
```

If the login service has no entries, then the entries for the other service are used. If multiple authentication modules are listed, then the user may be prompted for multiple passwords.

When `login` is invoked through `rlogind` or `telnetd`, the service name used by PAM is `rlogin` or `telnet`.

Warnings

Users with a UID greater than 76695844 are not subject to password aging and the system does not record their last login time.

If you use the `CONSOLE` setting to disable root logins, you should arrange that remote command execution by root is also disabled. See `rsh(1)`, `rcmd(3N)`, and `hosts.equiv(4)` for further details.

Options

`-d device`	Specify the path name of the TTY port `login` is to operate on. The device option can improve login performance because `login` does not need to call `ttyname(3C)`. The `-d` option is available only to users whose UID and effective UID are `root`. Any other attempt to use `-d` exits quietly.

`-h hostname [terminal]`

Pass information about the remote host and terminal type from `in.telnetd(1M)`.

`-p`	Pass environment variables to the login shell.
`-r hostname`	Pass information about the remote host from `in.rlogind(1M)`.

Exit Status

0	Successful operation.
non-zero	Error.

Files

`$HOME/.cshrc`

Initial commands for each `csh`.

`$HOME/.hushlogin`

Suppress login messages.

`$HOME/.login`

User's login commands for `csh`.

`$HOME/.profile`

User's login commands for `sh` and `ksh`.

`$HOME/.rhosts`

Private list of trusted hostname/username combinations.

`/etc/.login`

Systemwide `csh` login commands.

/etc/logindevperm

> Login-based device permissions.

/etc/motd   Message-of-the-day.

/etc/nologin

> Message displayed to users attempting to log in during system shutdown.

/etc/passwd   Password file.

/etc/profile

> Systemwide sh and ksh login commands.

/etc/shadow   List of users' encrypted passwords.

/usr/bin/sh

> User's default command interpreter.

/var/adm/lastlog

> Time of last login.

/var/adm/loginlog

> Record of failed login attempts.

/var/adm/utmp

> Accounting.

/var/adm/wtmp

> Accounting.

/var/mail/*your-name*

> Mailbox for user *your-name*.

/etc/default/login

> Default value that can be set for the flags in /etc/default/login. For example, TIMEZONE=EST5EDT

The following list describes the variables that can be set in /etc/default/login.

TIMEZONE	Set the TZ environment variable of the shell (see environ(5)).
HZ	Set the HZ environment variable of the shell.
ULIMIT	Set the file size limit for the login. Units are disk blocks. Default is 0 (no limit).
CONSOLE	If set, root can log in on that device only. This setting does not prevent execution of remote commands with rsh(1). Comment out this line to enable login by root.
PASSREQ	Determine if login requires a password.
ALTSHELL	Determine if login should set the SHELL environment variable.

PATH	Set the initial shell PATH variable.
SUPATH	Set the initial shell PATH variable for root.
TIMEOUT	Set the number of seconds (between 0 and 900) to wait before abandoning a login session.
UMASK	Set the initial shell file-creation mode mask. See umask(1).
SYSLOG	Determine whether the syslog(3) LOG_AUTH facility should be used to log all root logins at level LOG_NOTICE and multiple failed login attempts at LOG_CRIT.
SLEEPTIME	If present, set the number of seconds to wait before login failure is printed to the screen and another login attempt is allowed. Default is 4 seconds. Minimum is 0 seconds. Maximum is 5 seconds.
RETRIES	Set the number of retries for logging in (see pam(3)). The default is 5.

Attributes

See attributes(5) for descriptions of the following attributes:

Attribute Type	Attribute Value
Availability	SUNWcsu

See Also

csh(1), exit(1), ksh(1), mail(1), mailx(1), newgrp(1), passwd(1), rlogin(1), rsh(1), sh(1), shell_builtins(1), telnet(1), umask(1), admintool(1M), in.rlogind(1M), in.telnetd(1M), logins(1M), quota(1M), su(1M), syslogd(1M), useradd(1M), userdel(1M), pam(3), syslog(3), ttyname(3C), rcmd(3N), hosts.equiv(4), logindevperm(4), loginlog(4), nologin(4), nsswitch.conf(4), pam.conf(4), passwd(4), profile(4), shadow(4), utmp(4), wtmp(4), attributes(5), environ(5), pam_unix(5), termio(7I)

Diagnostics

Login incorrect

The user name or the password cannot be matched.

Not on system console

Root login denied. Check the CONSOLE setting in /etc/default/login.

No directory! Logging in with home=/

The user's home directory named in the passwd(4) database cannot be found or has the wrong permissions. Contact your system administrator.

No shell   Cannot execute the shell named in the passwd(4) database.
              Contact your system administrator.

NO LOGINS: System going down in *N* minutes

              The system is in the process of being shut down and logins have
              been disabled.

logname — Return User's Login Name

Synopsis

/usr/bin/logname

Description

The logname command writes your login name to standard output as shown in
the following example.

```
castle% logname
winsor
castle%
```

The login name is the string returned by the getlogin(3C) function. Under
the conditions where getlogin() would fail, logname writes a diagnostic
message to standard error and exits with a non-zero exit status.

Environment Variables

See environ(5) for descriptions of the following environment variables that
affect the execution of logname: LC_CTYPE, LC_MESSAGES, and NLSPATH.

Exit Status

0   Successful completion.

>0   An error occurred.

Files

/etc/profile

              Environment for user at login time.

/var/adm/utmp

              User and accounting information.

Attributes

See attributes(5) for descriptions of the following attributes:

Attribute Type	Attribute Value
Availability	SUNWesu

See Also

env(1), login(1), getlogin(3C), utmp(4), attributes(5), environ(5)

---

logout — Shell Built-in Function to Exit from a Login Session

Synopsis

csh
logout

Description

The logout command terminates a login C shell. If the shell is not a login shell, the message Not login shell is displayed.

Attributes

See attributes(5) for descriptions of the following attributes:

Attribute Type	Attribute Value
Availability	SUNWcsu

See Also

csh(1), login(1), attributes(5)

---

look — Find Words in the System Dictionary or Lines in Sorted List

Synopsis

/usr/bin/look [-d][-f][-tc] *string* [*filename*]

Description

The look command consults a sorted *filename* and prints all lines that begin with *string*. If you specify no file name, look uses /usr/share/lib/dict/words with collating sequence -df.

look limits the length of a search to 256 characters.

Options

-d	Dictionary order. Use only letters, digits, Tabs, and space characters in comparisons.
-f	Fold case. Do not distinguish uppercase letters from lowercase letters in comparisons.
-t*c*	Set termination character. Ignore all characters to the right of *c* in *string*.

Examples

The following example uses the default dictionary to list all lines that begin with the string sun.

```
castle% look sun
sun
sunbeam
sunbonnet
sunburn
sunburnt
Sunday
sunder
sundew
sundial
sundown
sundry
sunfish
sunflower
sung
sunglasses
sunk
sunken
sunlight
sunlit
sunny
Sunnyvale
sunrise
sunscreen
sunset
sunshade
sunshine
sunshiny
sunspot
suntan
suntanned
suntanning
```

```
SUNY
castle%
```

Files

/usr/share/lib/dict/words
Spelling list.

Attributes

See attributes(5) for descriptions of the following attributes:

Attribute Type	Attribute Value
Availability	SUNWesu

See Also

grep(1), sort(1), attributes(5)

lookbib — Find References in a Bibliographic Database

Synopsis

/usr/bin/lookbib *database*

Description

A bibliographic reference is a set of lines, constituting fields of bibliographic information. Each field starts on a line beginning with a percent sign (%), followed by a key letter, then a blank, and finally the contents of the field, which may continue until the next line starting with %.

lookbib uses an inverted index made by indxbib to find sets of bibliographic references. It reads keywords typed after the > prompt on the terminal and retrieves records containing all these keywords. If nothing matches, nothing is returned except another > prompt.

You can search multiple databases as long as they have a common index made by indxbib(1). In that case, only the first argument given to indxbib is specified to lookbib.

If lookbib does not find the index files (the .i[abc] files), it looks for a reference file with the same name as the argument without the suffixes. It creates a file with an .ig suffix, suitable for use with fgrep (see grep(1)). lookbib then uses this fgrep file to find references. This method is simpler to use, but the .ig file is slower to use than the .i[abc] files and does not allow the use of multiple reference files.

Bugs

All dates should probably be indexed because many disciplines refer to literature written in the 1800s or earlier.

Examples

The following example accesses the bibliographic file named `bibliography`, displays instructions, and searches for references to the keyword `dreams`.

```
castle% lookbib bibliography
Instructions? y

Type keywords (such as author and date) after the > prompt.
References with those keywords are printed if they exist;
        if nothing matches you are given another prompt.
To quit lookbib, press CTRL-d after the > prompt.

> dreams
%A Janice Winsor
%T Opening the Dream Door
%P 153
%I Merrill-West Publishing
%C Carmel, California
%D 1998
%K dreams, psychic development
%X Not just another dream interpretation book! Opening the Dream Door
is a practical guide to psychic development. Written in a
friendly, personal style, Opening the Dream Door does not
attempt to interpret dream symbology. It is the author's belief
that each person has their own personal myths and symbols that
cannot be deciphered in a collective fashion. By using her own
dreams as an example, Janice Winsor makes practical suggestions
for expanding the subconscious life and connecting to other realms.
Processes for remembering and accessing dreams are taught in an
easy to understand style.
~
~
~
"bibliography" 27 lines, 946 characters
> ^D
castle%
```

To exit `lookbib`, press Control-D at the > prompt.

Files

`x.ia`	
`x.ib`	
`x.ic`	Index files.
`x.ig`	Reference file.

Attributes

See attributes(5) for descriptions of the following attributes:

Attribute Type	Attribute Value
Availability	SUNWdoc

See Also

addbib(1), grep(1), indxbib(1), refer(1), roffbib(1), sort bib(1), attributes(5)

---

lorder — Find Ordering Relation for an Object or Library Archive

Synopsis

/usr/ccs/bin/lorder *filename*...

Description

Use the lorder command to search a list of object file names and display a list of related pairs. The input is one or more object or library archive file names (see ar(1)). The standard output is a list of pairs of object file or archive member names; the first file of the pair refers to external identifiers defined in the second.

lorder accepts as input any object or archive file regardless of its suffix, provided there is more than one input file. If there is a single input file, its suffix must be .o.

You can process the output by tsort(1) to find an ordering of a library suitable for one-pass access by ld.

Note — The link editor ld is capable of multiple passes over an archive in the portable archive format (see ar(4)) and does not require that you use lorder when building an archive. The usage of the lorder command may, however, allow for a more efficient access of the archive during the link edit process.

The following example builds a new library from existing .o files.

```
castle% ar -cr library `lorder *.o | tsort`
```

Files

TMPDIR/*symref

> Temporary files.

TMPDIR/*symdef

> Temporary files.

TMPDIR   Usually /var/tmp but you can redefine by setting the
            environment variable TMPDIR (see tempnam() in tmpnam(3S)). The
            length of the file name for TMPDIR is limited to whatever sed
            allows.

Attributes

See attributes(5) for descriptions of the following attributes:

Attribute Type	Attribute Value
Availability	SUNWbtool

See Also

ar(1), ld(1), tsort(1), tmpnam(3S), ar(4), attributes(5)

lp — Submit Print Request

Synopsis

```
/usr/bin/lp [-c][-m][-p][-s][-w][-d destination][-f form-name]
    [-H special-handling][-n number][-o option][-P page-list]
    [-q priority-level][-S character-set|print-wheel][-t title]
    [-T content-type [-r]][-y mode-list][file...]
/usr/bin/lp -i request-ID... [-c][-m][-p][-s][-w][-d destination]
    [-f form-name][-H special-handling][-n number][-o option]
    [-P page-list] [-q priority-level][-S character-set|print-wheel]
    [-t title][-T content-type [-r]][-y mode-list]
```

Description

lp submits print requests to a destination. The lp command has two formats.

- The first form of lp prints files (*file*) and associated information
  (collectively called a print request). If you do not specify *file*, lp assumes
  the standard input. Use a dash (-) with *file* to specify the standard
  input. Files are printed in the order you specify them on the command
  line.

New!

- The second form of lp changes print request options. You can use this form of lp only in a Solaris 2.6 operating environment or compatible versions of the LP print server. The print request identified by *request-ID* is changed according to the printing options specified. The printing options available are the same as those with the first form of the lp. If the request has finished printing when the lp command is executed, the change is rejected. If the request is in the process of printing, it is stopped and restarted from the beginning (unless you specify the -P option).

The print client commands locate destination information in a specific order. See printers(4) and printers.conf(4) for details.

Options

Printers that have a 4.x- or BSD-based print server are not configured to handle BSD protocol extensions. lp handles print requests sent to such printers in the following ways.

- Print requests with more than 52 file names are truncated to 52 files. lp displays a warning message.
- The -f, -H, -o, -P, -p, -q, -S, -T, and -y options may require a protocol extension to pass to a print server. If lp cannot handle the print request, it displays the following warning message.

```
LP administrators enable protocol extensions by setting a
printer's bsdaddr entry in /etc/printers.conf. Changing the
bsdaddr entry in /etc/printers.conf to:
```

destination:bsdaddr=*server*,*destination*,Solaris

```
generates a set of BSD print protocol extensions that can be pro-
cessed by a Solaris print server. lp supports only Solaris proto-
col extensions at this time.
```

-c   Copy *file* before printing. Unless you specify -c, you should not remove any file before the print request has completely printed. Changes made to *file* after the print request is made but before it is printed are reflected in the printed output. *file* is linked (as opposed to copied).

-d *destination*

                Print *file* on a specific *destination*. *destination* can be either a printer of a class of printers, (see lpadmin(1M)). Specify destination using atomic, POSIX-style (*server:destination*) or Federated Naming Service (FNS) (*.../service/printer/...*) names. See printers.conf(4) for information regarding the naming conventions for atomic and FNS names, and standards(5) for information regarding POSIX.

-f *form-name*

> Print file on *form-name*. The LP print service ensures that the form is mounted on the printer. The print request is rejected if the printer does not support *form-name*, if *form-name* is not defined for the system, or if the user is not allowed to use *form-name* (see lpforms(1M)).

-H *special-handling*

> Print the print request according to the value of *special-handling*. The following *special-handling* values are acceptable:

> | | |
> |---|---|
> | hold | Do not print the print request until notified. If printing has already begun, stop it. Other print requests go ahead of a request that has been put on hold (held print request) until the print request is resumed. |
> | resume | Resume a held print request. If the print request had begun to print when held, it is the next print request printed unless it is superseded by an immediate print request. |
> | immediate | Print the print request next. If more than one print request is assigned, print the most recent print request next. If a print request is currently printing on the desired printer, you must issue a hold request to enable the immediate request to print. The immediate request is available only to LP administrators. |

-m

> Send mail after file has printed (see mail(1)). By default, send no mail on normal completion of a print request.

-n *number*

> Print a specific number of copies of file. Specify number as a digit. The default for *number* is 1.

-o *option*

> Specify printer-dependent options. Specify several options by specifying -o *option* multiple times (-o *option* -o *option* -o *option*). You can also specify printer-dependent options by using the -o key letter once followed by a list of options enclosed in double quotes (o "*option option option*"). The following options are valid.

> | | |
> |---|---|
> | nobanner | Do not print a banner page with the request. This option can be disallowed by the LP administrator. |
> | nofilebreak | Print multiple files without inserting a formfeed between them. |

> length=*number*i | *number*c | *number*

> > Print the print request with pages of a specific length. Specify length in inches, centimeters, or

number of lines. Use *number* to specify the number of inches, centimeters, or lines. Indicate inches or centimeters by appending to *number* the letter i for inches, c for centimeters. Indicate the number of lines by specifying *number* alone. length=66 indicates a page length of 66 lines. length=11i indicates a page length of 11 inches. length=27.94c indicates a page length of 27.94 centimeters. You cannot use this option with the -f option.

width=*numberi* | *numberc* | *number*

Print the print request with pages of a specific width. Specify width in inches, centimeters, or number of columns. Use *number* to specify the number of inches, centimeters, or lines. Indicate inches or centimeters by appending to *number* the letter i for inches, c for centimeters. Indicate the number of lines by specifying *number* alone. width=65 indicates a page width of 65 columns. width=6.5i indicates a page width of 6.5 inches. width=10c indicates a page width of 10 centimeters. You cannot use this option with the -f option.

lpi=*number*   Print the print request with the line pitch set to *number* lines in an inch. Use *number* to specify the number of lines in an inch. You cannot use this option with the -f option.

cpi=*number*|pica|elite|compressed

Print the print request with the character pitch set to *number* characters in an inch. Use *number* to specify the number of characters in an inch. Use pica to set character pitch to pica (10 characters per inch), or elite to set character pitch to elite (12 characters per inch). Use compressed to set character pitch to as many characters as the printer can handle. There is no standard number of characters per inch for all printers; see the terminfo database (see terminfo(4)) for the default character pitch for your printer. You cannot use this option with the -f option.

stty=*stty-option-list*

Print the request, using a list of options valid for the stty command (see stty(1)). Enclose the list in single quotes (′ ′) if it contains blanks.

-P *page-list*

> Print the pages specified in *page-list* in ascending order. Specify *page-list* as a range of numbers, single-page number, or a combination of both. You can use -P only if there is a filter available to handle it; otherwise, the print request is rejected.

-p

> Enable notification on completion of the print request. Delivery of the notification is dependent on additional software.

-q *priority-level*

> Assign the print request a priority in the print queue. Specify *priority-level* as an integer between from 0 and 39. Use 0 to indicate the highest priority; 39 to indicate the lowest priority. If you specify no priority, the default priority for a print service is assigned by the LP administrator. The LP administrator can also assign a default priority to individual users.

-s

> Suppress the display of messages sent from lp.

-S *character-set*|*print-wheel*

> Print the request using the *character-set* or *print-wheel*. If a form was requested and requires a character set or print wheel other than the one specified with the -S option, reject the request. Printers using mountable print wheels or font cartridges use the print wheel or font cartridge mounted at the time of the print request unless you specify the -S option.

> Printers using print wheels: If *print-wheel* is not one listed by the LP administrator as acceptable for the printer, the request is rejected unless the print wheel is already mounted on the printer.

> Printers using selectable or programmable character sets. If you do not specify the -S option, lp uses the standard character set. If *character-set* is not defined in the terminfo database for the printer (see terminfo(4)) or is not an alias defined by the LP administrator, the request is rejected.

-t *title*

> Print a title on the banner page of the output. Enclose *title* in quotes if it contains blanks. If you do not specify *title*, print the name of the file on the banner page.

-T *content-type* [-r]

> Print the request on a printer that can support the specified *content-type*. If no printer accepts this type directly, use a filter to convert the content into an acceptable type. If you specify the -r option, use no filter. If you specify -r and no printer accepts the *content-type* directly, reject the request. If the *content-type* is not acceptable to any printer, either directly or with a filter, the request is rejected.

-w

> Write a message on the user's terminal after the files have been printed. If the user is not logged in, then send mail instead.

```
-y mode-list
```
> Print the request according to the printing modes listed in
> *mode-list*. The allowed values for *mode-list* are locally defined.
> You can use this option only if there is a filter available to handle
> it; otherwise, the print request is rejected.

Operands

```
file
```
> The name of the file to be printed. Specify *file* as a path name or
> as a dash (–) to indicate the standard input. If you do not specify
> *file*, use the standard input.

Usage

See largefile(5) for the description of the behavior of lp when encountering
files greater than or equal to 2 Gbytes (2**31 bytes).

Exit Status

0	Successful completion.
non-zero	An error occurred.

Files

```
/var/spool/lp/*
```
> LP print queue.

```
$HOME/.printers
```
> User-configurable printer database.

```
/etc/printers.conf
```
> System printer configuration database.

```
printers.conf.byname
```
> NIS version of /etc/printers.conf.

```
fns.ctx_dir.domain
```
> NIS+ version of /etc/printers.conf.

Attributes

See attributes(5) for descriptions of the following attributes:

Attribute Type	**Attribute Value**
Availability	SUNWpcu
CSI	Enabled

Note — CSI capability assumes that printer names are composed of ASCII characters.

See Also

cancel(1), enable(1), lpstat(1), mail(1), postprint(1), pr(1), stty(1), *New!*
lpq(1B), lpr(1B), lprm(1B), accept(1M), lpadmin(1M), lpfilter(1M),
lpforms(1M), lpsched(1M), lpshut(1M), lpsystem(1M), lpusers(1M),
printers(4), printers.conf(4), terminfo(4), attributes(5), environ(5),
largefile(5), standards(5)

lpc — Line Printer Control Program

Synopsis

/usr/ucb/lpc [command [parameter...]]

Description

Use the lpc (line printer control) command to control the operation of printers. lpc performs the following functions.

- Starts or stops a printer.
- Disables or enables a printer's spooling queue.
- Rearranges the order of jobs in a print queue.
- Displays the status of a printer print queue and printer daemon

You can run lpc from the command line or interactively. Specifying lpc with the optional *command* and *parameter* arguments interprets the first argument as an lpc command and all other arguments as parameters to that command. Specifying lpc without arguments runs it interactively, prompting for lpc commands with lpc>. If you redirect the standard input, lpc can read commands from a file.

Usage

You can type lpc commands in their entirety or abbreviate them to an unambiguous substring. Some lpc commands are available to all users; others are available only to superusers.

All users can execute the following lpc commands.

? [command...] | help [command...]

> Display a short description of *command*. *command* is an lpc command. If *command* is not specified, display a list of lpc commands.

exit | quit Exit from lpc.

restart [all | *printer*...]

> Try to start a new printer daemon. restart is useful when a print daemon dies unexpectedly and leaves jobs in the print queue. all performs this command on all locally attached printers.
>
> *printer* performs this command on specific printers. Specify *printer* as an atomic name. See printers.conf(4) for information regarding naming conventions for atomic names.

status [all | *printer*...]

> Display the status of print daemons and print queues. all performs this command on all locally attached printers. *printer* performs this command on specific printers. Specify *printer* as an atomic name. See printers.conf(4) for information regarding naming conventions for atomic names.

Only superuser can execute the following lpc commands.

abort [all | *printer*...]

> Terminate an active spooling daemon. Disable printing (by preventing new daemons from being started by lpr(1B)) for *printer*. all performs this command on all locally attached printers. *printer* performs this command on specific printers. Specify *printer* as an atomic name. See printers.conf(4) for information regarding naming conventions for atomic names.

clean [all | *printer*...]

> Remove files created in the print spool directory by the print daemon from *printer*'s print queue. all performs this command on all locally attached printers. *printer* performs this command on specific printers. Specify *printer* as an atomic name. See printers.conf(4) for information regarding naming conventions for atomic names.

disable [all | *printer*...]

> Turn off the print queue for *printer*. Prevent new printer jobs from being entered into the print queue for *printer* by lpr(1B). all performs this command on all locally attached printers.
>
> *printer* performs this command on specific printers. Specify *printer* as an atomic name. See printers.conf(4) for information regarding naming conventions for atomic names.

down [all | *printer*...] [*message*]

> Turn off the queue for *printer* and disable printing on *printer*. Insert *message* in the printer status file. You do not need to quote *message*; treat multiple arguments to *message* in the same way as arguments to echo(1). Use down to take a printer down and inform users. all performs this command on all locally attached printers. *printer* performs this command on specific printers. Specify

printer as an atomic name. See `printers.conf`(4) for information regarding naming conventions for atomic names.

enable [all | *printer*...]

Enable `lpr`(1B) to add new jobs to the spool queue. `all` performs this command on all locally attached printers. *printer* performs this command on specific printers. Specify *printer* as an atomic name. See `printers.conf`(4) for information regarding naming conventions for atomic names.

start [all | *printer*...]

Enable printing. Start a spooling daemon for the printer. `all` performs this command on all locally attached printers. *printer* performs this command on specific printers. Specify *printer* as an atomic name. See `printers.conf`(4) for information regarding naming conventions for atomic names.

stop [all | *printer*...]

Stop a spooling daemon after the current job is complete. Disable printing at that time. `all` performs this command on all locally attached printers. *printer* performs this command on specific printers. Specify *printer* as an atomic name. See `printers.conf`(4) for information regarding naming conventions for atomic names.

topq printer [*request-ID*...] [*user*...]

Move *request-ID* or print jobs belonging to *user* on *printer* to the beginning of the print queue. Specify *user* as a user's login name. Specify *printer* as an atomic name. See `printers.conf`(4) for information regarding naming conventions for atomic names.

up [all | *printer*...]

Turn the queue on for *printer* and enable printing. Delete the message in the printer status file (inserted by `down`). Use `up` to undo the effects of `down`. `all` performs this command on all locally attached printers. *printer* performs this command on specific printers. Specify *printer* as an atomic name. See `printers.conf`(4) for information regarding naming conventions for atomic names.

Exit Status

0   Successful completion.

non-zero   An error occurred.

Files

/var/spool/lp/*

LP print queue.

/var/spool/lp/system/pstatus

Printer status information file.

Attributes

See attributes(5) for descriptions of the following attributes:

Attribute Type	Attribute Value
Availability	SUNWscplp

See Also

echo(1), lpstat(1), lpq(1B), lpr(1B), lprm(1B), lpsched(1M),
attributes(5)

Diagnostics

Ambiguous command

> The lpc command or abbreviation matches more than one command.

?Invalid command

> The lpc command or abbreviation is not recognized.

?Privileged command

> The lpc command or abbreviation can be executed only by superuser.

lpc: printer: unknown printer to the print service

> That printer does not exist in the LP database. Check that printer was correctly specified. Use lpstat -p or the status command (see lpstat(1)) to check the status of printers.

lpc: error on opening queue to spooler

> The connection to lpsched failed. Usually means that the printer server has died or is hung. Use /usr/lib/lp/lpsched to check if the printer spooler daemon is running.

lpc: Can't send message to LP print service
lpc: Can't receive message from LP print service

> The LP print service stopped. Contact the LP administrator.

lpc: Received unexpected message from LP print service

> A problem with the software. Contact the LP administrator.

lpq — Display the Contents of a Print Queue

Synopsis

```
/usr/ucb/lpq [-P destination][-1][+ [interval]][request-ID][user]
```

Description

The lpq command displays the information about the contents of a print
queue. A print queue comprises print requests that are waiting in the process
of being printed.

lpq displays the following information to the standard output.

- The user name of the person associated with a print request.
- The position of a print request in the print queue.
- The name of file or files comprising a print request.
- The job number of a print request.
- The size of the file requested by a print request. File size is reported in
  bytes.

Normally, only as much information as fits on one line is displayed. If the
name of the input file associated with a print request is not available, the input
file field indicates the standard input.

The print client commands locate destination information in a specific order.
See printer.conf(4) and printers(4) for details.

Options

-P destination

        Display information about printer or class of printers (see
        lpadmin(1M)). Specify destination using atomic, POSIX-style
        (server:destination) or Federated Naming Service (FNS)
        (.../service/printer/...) names. See printers.conf(4) for
        information regarding the naming conventions for atomic and FNS
        names, and standards(5) for information regarding POSIX.

-1   Display information in long format. Long format includes the name
        of the host from which a print request originated.

+ [interval]

        Display information at specific time intervals. Stop displaying
        information when the print queue is empty. Clear the screen before
        displaying the print queue. Specify interval as the number of
        seconds between displays. If interval is not specified, execute only
        once.

Operands

request-ID   The job number associated with a print request.

user   The name of the user about whose jobs lpq reports information.
              Specify user as a valid user name.

Exit Status

0   Successful completion.

non-zero   An error occurred.

Files

/var/spool/print/[cd]f*

              Spooling directory and request files for jobs awaiting transfer.

Attributes

See attributes(5) for descriptions of the following attributes:

Attribute Type	Attribute Value
Availability	SUNWscplo

See Also

lp(1), lpstat(1), lpc(1B), lpr(1B), lprm(1B), lpadmin(1M), printers(4),
printers.conf(4), attributes(5), standards(5)

lpr — Submit BSD Print Requests

Synopsis

/usr/ucb/lpr [-P destination] [-# number] [-C class] [-J job]
[-T title] [-i [number]] [-1|-2|-3|-4 font] [-w number]
[-m] [-h] [-s] [-filter-option] [file...]

Description

The lpr command submits print requests to a destination. lpr prints files
(file) and associated information, collectively called a print request. If you do
not specify file, lpr assumes the standard input.

The print client commands locate destination information in a specific order.
See printers(4) and printers.conf(4) for details.

Print requests with more than 52 files specified are truncated to 52 files. `lpr` displays a warning message.

Options

-P *destination*

Print file on a specific printer or class of printers (see lpadmin(1M)). Specify *destination* using atomic, POSIX-style (*server:destination*) or Federated Naming Service (FNS) (*.../service/printer/...*) names. See printers.conf(4) for information regarding the naming conventions for atomic and FNS names, and standards(5) for information regarding POSIX.

-# *number*
Print a specific number of copies. Specify *number* as a positive integer. The default for number is 1.

-C *class*
Print *class* as the job classification on the banner page of the output. Enclose *class* in double quotes if it contains blanks. If you do not specify *class*, print the name of the system (as returned by host name) as the job classification. See hostname(1).

-J *job*
Print *job* as the job name on the banner page of the output. Enclose *job* in double quotes if it contains blanks. If you do not specify *job*, print *file* (or in the case of multiple files, the first file specified on the command line) as the job name on the banner page of the output.

-T *title*
Print a title on the banner page of the output. Enclose *title* in double quotes if it contains blanks. If you do not specify *title*, print file name on the banner page.

-i [*number*]
Indent the output a specific number of space characters. Use *number* to indicate the number of space characters to be indented. Specify *number* as a positive integer. Eight space characters is the default.

-1|-2|-3|-4 *font*

Mount the specified font in the font position 1, 2, 3, or 4. Specify *font* as a valid font name.

-w *number*
Print *file* with pages of a specific width. *number* indicates the number of columns.

-m
Send mail after *file* has printed (see mail(1)). By default, send no mail on normal completion of a print request.

-h
Suppress printing of the banner page of the output.

-s
Use full path names (as opposed to symbolic links) to *file* instead of trying to copy them. File should not be modified or removed until it has completed printing. -s prevents only copies of local files from being made on the local system. -s works only with specified files. If the lpr command is at the end of a pipeline, *file* is copied to the spool.

- *filter-options*

> Notifies the print spooler that *file* is not a standard text file. Enable the spooling daemon to use the appropriate filters to print *file*. *filter-options* offer a standard user interface. All options may not be available for, or applicable to, all printers. Specify *filter-options* as a single character. If you do not specify *filter-options* and the printer can interpret PostScript(Reg.), inserting % ! as the first two characters of *file* interprets the file as PostScript. The following *filter-options* are supported.

p	Use pr to format the files.
l	Print control characters and suppress page breaks.
t	File contains troff (cat phototypesetter) binary data.
n	File contains ditroff data from device-independent troff.
d	File contains tex data from in DVI format from Stanford.
g	File contains standard plot data produced by plot(1B) routines.
v	File contains a raster image. *printer* must support an appropriate imaging model such as PostScript to print the image.
c	File contains data produced by cifplot.
f	Interpret the first character of each line as a standard FORTRAN carriage control character.

Operands

file	The name of the file to be printed. Specify *file* as a path name. If you do not specify *file*, use the standard input.

Usage

See largefile(5) for the description of the behavior of lpr when encountering files greater than or equal to 2 Gbytes (2**31 bytes).

Exit Status

0	Successful completion.
non-zero	An error occurred.

Files

`/var/spool/print/.seq`

> File containing the sequence numbers for job ID assignment.

`/var/spool/print/[cd]f*`

> Spooling directories and files.

Attributes

See `attributes`(5) for descriptions of the following attributes:

Attribute Type	Attribute Value
Availability	SUNWscplo
CSI	Enabled

Note — `lpr` is CSI enabled except for the printer name.

See Also

`hostname(1)`, `lp(1)`, `lpstat(1)`, `mail(1)`, `pr(1)`, `troff(1)`, `lpc(1B)`, `lpq(1B)`,`lprm(1B)`,`plot(1B)`,`lpadmin(1M)`,`printers(4)`,`printers.conf(4)`, `attributes(5)`, `largefile(5)`, `standards(5)`

Diagnostics

`lpr:` *destination* `|: unknown destination`

> *destination* was not found in the LP configuration database. Usually this error results from a typing mistake; however, it may indicate that the destination does not exist on the system. Use `lpstat -p` to display information about the status of the print service.

lprm — Remove Print Requests from the Print Queue

Synopsis

`/usr/ucb/lprm [-P destination][-][request-ID...][user...]`

Description

Use the `lprm` command to remove print requests (`request-ID`) from the print queue.

Without arguments, lprm deletes the current print request. lprm reports the name of the file associated with print requests that it removes. lprm is silent if there are no applicable print requests to remove.

You can only remove print requests associated with your own user name. If a superuser executes lprm and specifies the *user* operand, lprm removes all print requests belonging to the specified user.

The print client commands locate destination information in a specific order. See printers(4) and printers.conf(4) for details.

Note — You can only remove print requests associated with your own user name. By default, you can only remove print requests on the host from which the print request was submitted. If a superuser has set user-equivalence=true in /etc/printers.conf on the print server, you can remove print requests associated with your user name on any host. Superusers can remove print requests on the host from which the print request was submitted. Superusers can also remove print requests from the print server.

Options

-P *destination*

Specify the name of the printer or class of printers (see lpadmin(1M)) from which to remove print requests. Specify *destination* using atomic, POSIX-style (*server:destination*) or Federated Naming Service (FNS) (*.../service/printer/...*) names. See printers.conf(4) for information regarding the naming conventions for atomic and FNS names, and standards(5) for information regarding POSIX.

-

Remove all print requests owned by the user. If a superuser specifies this option, remove all requests in the print queue. Job ownership is determined by the user's login name and host name on the system from which lpr was executed.

Operands

user

Remove print requests associated with a specific user. Specify *user* as a valid user name. Only superuser can use this option.

request-ID

Remove a specific print request. Specify *request-ID* as the job number associated with a print request and reported by lpq. See lpq(1B).

Examples

The following example removes *request-ID* 385 from destination killtree.

```
castle% lprm -P killtree 385
```

Exit Status

    0   Successful completion.

    non-zero   An error occurred.

Files

    `/var/spool/print/[cd]f*`

        Spooling directories and files.

Attributes

See `attributes`(5) for descriptions of the following attributes:

Attribute Type	Attribute Value
Availability	SUNWscplp
CSI	Enabled

See Also

`lp(1)`, `lpstat(1)`, `lpc(1B)`, `lpq(1B)`, `lpr(1B)`, `lpadmin(1M)`, `printers(4)`, `printers.conf(4)`, `attributes(5)`, `standards(5)`

lpstat — Display Information About the Status of the Print Service

Synopsis

```
/usr/bin/lpstat [-d] [-r] [-R] [-s] [-t] [-a [list]] [-c [list]] [-f [list]
     [-l]] [-o [list]] [-p [list] [-D] [-l]] [-S [list] [-l]]
     [-u [login-ID-list]] [-v [list]]
```

Description

`lpstat` displays information about the current status of the LP print service to standard output.

If you specify no options, `lpstat` prints the status of all your print requests made by `lp` (see `lp(1)`). Any arguments that are not options are assumed to be *request-ID*s as returned by `lp`. The `lpstat` command prints the status of such requests. You can specify options in any order and can repeat and intermix them with other arguments. You can follow some key letters with an optional list that can be in one of two forms: a list of items separated from one another by a comma, or a list of items separated from one another by spaces enclosed in quotes. For example:

```
castle% lpstat -u "user1 user2 user3"
```

Specifying `all` after any key letter that takes *list* as an argument prints all information relevant to the key letter. For example, the following command prints the status of all output requests.

```
castle% lpstat -o all
```

Omitting a list following such key letters prints all information relevant to the key letter. For example, the following command prints the status of all output requests.

```
castle% lpstat -o
```

The print client commands locate printer information in a specific order. See `printers.conf(4)` and `printers(4)` for details.

Options

`-d`	Print the default destination for output requests.
`-o [list]`	Print the status of output requests. *list* is a list of intermixed printer names, class names, and *request-ID*s. You can omit the key letter `-o`. Specify printer and class names using atomic, POSIX-style (*server*:*destination*) or Federated Naming Service (FNS) (`.../service/printer/...`) names. See `printers.conf(4)` for information regarding the naming conventions for atomic and FNS names, and `standards(5)` for information regarding POSIX.
`-r`	Print the status of the LP request scheduler.
`-R`	Print a number showing the position of each request in the print queue.
`-s`	Print a status summary, including the status of the LP scheduler, the default destination, a list of printers and their associated devices, a list of the systems sharing print services, a list of all forms currently mounted, and a list of all recognized character sets and print wheels.
`-t`	Print all status information. This includes all the information obtained with the `-s` option, plus the acceptance and idle/busy status of all printers.
`-u [login-ID-list]`	Print the status of output requests for users. The *login-ID-list* argument can include any or all of the following constructs:

login-ID	A user on any system.
system-name!*login-ID*	A user on system *system-name*.
system-name!all	All users on system *system-name*.
all!*login-ID*	A user on all systems.

-v [*list*]   Print the names of printers and the path names of the devices associated with them or remote system names for network printers. *list* is a list of printer names.

The following options return accurate results only if they are issued from a Solaris 2.x LP print server.

-a [*list*]   Report whether print destinations are accepting requests. *list* is a list of intermixed printer names and class names.

-c [*list*]   Print name of all classes and their members. *list* is a list of class names.

-f [*list*] [-l]

Print a verification that the forms in *list* are recognized by the LP print service. *list* is a list of forms; the default is all. The -l option lists the form descriptions.

-p [*list*] [-D] [-l]

Print the status of printers. *list* is a list of printer names. If you specify the -D option, print a brief description for each printer in *list*. If you specify the -l option and the printer is on the local system, return a full description of each printer's configuration, including the form mounted, the acceptable content and printer types, a printer description, and the interface used.

-S [*list*] [-l]

Print a verification that the character sets or the print wheels specified in *list* are recognized by the LP print service. Items in *list* can be character sets or print wheels; the default for the list is all. If you specify the -l option, append to each line a list of printers that can handle the print wheel or character set. The list also shows whether the print wheel or character set is mounted or specifies the built-in character set into which it maps.

-d   Print the default destination for output requests.

-o [*list*]   Print the status of output requests. *list* is a list of intermixed printer names, class names, and request IDs. You can omit the key letter -o.

-r   Print the status of the LP request scheduler.

-R   Print a number showing the position of each request in the print queue.

-s   Print a status summary, including the status of the LP scheduler, the default destination, a list of printers and their associated devices, a list of the systems sharing print services, a list of all forms currently mounted, and a list of all recognized character sets and print wheels.

-t   Print all status information, including all the information
                       obtained with the -s option, plus the acceptance and idle/busy
                       status of all printers.

-u [*login-ID-list*]

                       Print the status of output requests for users. The *login-ID-list*
                       argument can include any or all of the following constructs:

                       login-ID   A user on any system.

                       system-name!*login-I*   A user on system
                                                           system-name.

                       system-name!all   All users on system
                                                           system-name.

                       all!*login-ID*   A user on all systems.

                       all   All users on all systems.

-v [*list*]   Print the names of printers and the path names of the devices
                       associated with them or remote system names for network
                       printers. *list* is a list of printer names.

Exit Status

0   Successful completion.

non-zero   An error occurred.

Files

/var/spool/print/*

                       LP print queue.

$HOME/.printers

                       User-configurable printer database.

/etc/printers.conf

                       System configuration database.

Attributes

See attributes(5) for descriptions of the following attributes:

Attribute Type	Attribute Value
Availability	SUNWpcu

See Also

cancel(1), lp(1), lpq(1B), lpr(1B), lprm(1B), printers(4),
printers.conf(4), attributes(5), standards(5)

lptest — Generate Line Printer Ripple Pattern

Synopsis

```
/usr/ucb/lptest [length [count]]
```

Description

lptest writes the traditional ripple test pattern to the standard output. In 96 lines, the ripple test pattern prints all 96 printable ASCII characters in each position. The ripple test pattern was originally created to test printers. It is also useful for testing terminals, driving terminal ports, debugging, and performing tasks that require a quick supply of random data.

Note — This command is obsolete.

Options

length	Specify the length of the output line in characters. The default is 79 characters.
count	Specify the number of output lines. The default is 200 lines. If you specify count, you must also specify length.

Exit Status

0	Successful completion.
non-zero	An error occurred.

Attributes

See attributes(5) for descriptions of the following attributes:

Attribute Type	Attribute Value
Availability	SUNWscplp

See Also

attributes(5)

ls — List Contents of Directory

Synopsis

```
/usr/bin/ls [-aAbcCdfFgilLmnopqrRstux1] [file...]
/usr/xpg4/bin/ls [-aAbcCdfFgilLmnopqrRstux1] [file...]
/usr/ucb/ls [-aAcCdfFgilLqrRstu1] file...
```

Description

Use the `ls` command to list the contents of a directory and display permissions, links, ownership, group, size (in bytes), modification date and time, and file name for files.

For each file that is a directory, `ls` lists the contents of the directory; for each file that is an ordinary file, `ls` repeats its name and any other information requested. The output is sorted alphabetically by default. When you specify no arguments, `ls` lists the contents of the current directory. When you specify several arguments, the arguments are first sorted appropriately, with file arguments before directories and their contents.

`ls` has three major listing formats.

- The default format for output directed to a terminal is multicolumn with entries sorted down the columns.
- The `-1` option displays single-column output.
- The `-m` option displays stream output format. Files are listed all on the same line separated by a comma and a space.

To determine output formats for the `-C`, `-x`, and `-m` options, `ls` uses an environment variable, COLUMNS, to determine the number of character positions available on one output line. If this variable is not set, the terminfo(4) database is used to determine the number of columns, based on the environment variable TERM. If this information cannot be obtained, 80 columns are assumed.

The mode printed with the `-1` option consists of ten characters. The first character is one of the following.

d	The entry is a directory.
D	The entry is a door.
l	The entry is a symbolic link.
b	The entry is a block special file.
c	The entry is a character special file.
p	The entry is a FIFO (or named pipe) special file.
s	The entry is an AF_UNIX address family socket.
-	The entry is an ordinary file.

The next nine characters are interpreted as three sets of three bits each. The first set refers to the owner's permissions; the next, to permissions of others in the user-group of the file; and the last, to all others. Within each set, the three characters indicate permission to read, to write, and to execute the file as a program. For a directory, execute permission is interpreted as permission to search the directory for a specified file.

For user and group permissions, the third position can be occupied by x (execute), – (deny access), or s (set user ID). The s permission designation refers to the state of the set-ID bit, whether it be the user's or the group's. For example, the ability to assume the same ID as the user during execution is used during login where you begin the process as root but then assume the identity of your user login.

For group permissions, l can occupy the third position. l refers to mandatory file and record locking. This permission describes a file's ability to allow other files to lock its reading or writing permissions during access.

For others permissions, the third position can be occupied by t or T. These refer to the state of the sticky bit and execution permissions.

The permissions are indicated as follows.

r	The file is readable.
w	The file is writable.
x	The file is executable.
–	The indicated permission is not granted.
s	The setuser-ID or setgroup-ID bit is on, and the corresponding user or group execution bit is also on.
S	Undefined bit-state (the setuser-ID bit is on, and the user execution bit is off).
t	The 1000 (octal) bit, or sticky bit, is on (see chmod(1)), and execution is on.
T	The 1000 bit is on, and execution is off (undefined bit state).
l	Mandatory locking occurs during access (the setgroup-ID bit is on, and the group execution bit is off) (/usr/bin/ls).
L	Mandatory locking occurs during access (the setgroup-ID bit is on and the group execution bit is off) (/usr/xpg4/bin/ls).

ls -l (the long list) prints its output as follows for the POSIX locale:

```
-rwxrwxrwx+  1 winsor   staff    10876  May 16 9:42 part2
```

Reading from right to left, the current directory holds one file, named part2. The last time that file's contents were modified was 9:42 A.M. on May 16. The file contains 10,876 characters or bytes. The owner of the file, or the user, belongs to the group staff, and the login name is winsor. The number, in this case, 1, indicates the number of links to file part2 (see cp(1)). The plus sign indicates that there is an access control list (ACL) associated with the file.

Finally, the dash and letters tell you that user, group, and others have permissions to read, write, and execute `part2`.

Note — Unprintable characters in file names may confuse the columnar output options.

The total block count is incorrect if there are hard links among the files.

Options

`-a`	List all entries, including those that begin with a dot (`.`), which are normally not listed.
`-A`	List all entries, including those that begin with a dot (`.`) with the exception of the working directory (`.`) and the parent directory (`..`).
`-b`	Force printing of nonprintable characters to be in the octal `\ddd` notation.
`-c`	Use time of last modification of the inode (file created, mode changed, and so forth) for sorting (`-t`) or printing (`-l` or `-n`).
`-C`	Display multicolumn output and sort entries down the columns. This format is the default.
`-d`	If an argument is a directory, list only its name (not its contents); often used with `-l` to get the status of a directory.
`-f`	Force each argument to be interpreted as a directory, and list the name found in each slot. This option turns off `-l`, `-t`, `-s`, and `-r`, and turns on `-a`; the order is the order in which entries appear in the directory.
`-F`	Mark directories with a trailing slash (`/`), doors with a trailing greater-than sign (`>`), executable files with a trailing asterisk (`*`), FIFOs with a trailing vertical bar (`|`), symbolic links with a trailing at-sign (`@`), and `AF_UNIX` address family sockets with a trailing equal sign (`=`).
`-g`	The same as `-l`, except do not print the owner.
`-i`	For each file, print the inode number in the first column of the report.
`-l`	List in long format, giving mode, ACL indication, number of links, owner, group, size in bytes, and time of last modification for each file. If the file is a special file, the size field contains the major and minor device numbers. If the time of last modification is greater than six months ago, it is shown in the format *month date year* for the POSIX locale. When the LC_TIME locale category is not set to the POSIX locale, a different format of the time field may be used. Files modified within six months show *month date time*. If

the file is a symbolic link, the file name is printed followed by ->
and the path name of the referenced file.

-L	If an argument is a symbolic link, list the file or directory the link references instead of the link itself.
-m	Stream output format; list files across the page, separated by commas and spaces.
-n	The same as -l, except print the owner UID and group GID numbers instead of the associated character strings.
-o	The same as -l, except do not print the group.
-p	Put a slash (/) after each file name if the file is a directory.
-q	Force printing of nonprintable characters in file names as the character question mark (?).
-r	Reverse the order of sort to get reverse alphabetic or oldest first as appropriate.
-R	Recursively list subdirectories.
-s	Give size in blocks, including indirect blocks, for each entry.
-t	Sort by timestamp (latest first) instead of by name. The default is the last modification time. (See -u and -c.)
-u	Use time of last access instead of last modification for sorting (with the -t option) or printing (with the -l option).
-x	Display multicolumn output and sort entries across instead of down the page.
-1	Print one entry per line of output.

Specifying more than one of the options in the following mutually exclusive pairs is not considered an error: -C and -1 (one), -c and -u. The last option specified in each pair determines the output format.

/usr/bin/ls
Specifying more than one of the options in the following mutually exclusive pairs is not considered an error: -C and -1 (ell), -m and -1 (ell), -x and -1 (ell). The -1 option overrides the other option specified in each pair.

/usr/xpg4/bin/ls
Specifying more than one of the options in the following mutually exclusive pairs is not considered an error: -C and -1 (ell), -m and -1 (ell), -x and -1 (ell). The last option specified in each pair determines the output format.

Operands

file	A path name of a file to be listed. If the specified file is not found, display a diagnostic message on standard error.

Usage

See `largefile`(5) for the description of the behavior of `ls` when encountering files greater than or equal to 2 Gbytes (2**31 bytes).

Examples

The following example of file permissions describes a file that is readable, writable, and executable by the user and readable by the group and others.

```
-rwxr--r--
```

The following example describes a file that is readable, writable, and executable by the user, readable and executable by the group and others, and enables its user ID to be assumed, during execution, by the user presently executing it.

```
-rwsr-xr-x
```

The following example describes a file that is readable and writable only by the user and the group and that can be locked during access.

```
-rw-rwl---
```

The following command displays the names of all files in the current directory, including those that begin with a dot (.), which normally are not displayed.

```
castle% ls -a
```

The following example provides information on all files, including those that begin with a dot (the -a option), the i-number—the memory address of the inode associated with the file—printed in the left-hand column (the -i option); the size (in blocks) of the files, printed in the column to the right of the i-numbers (the -s option); finally, the report is displayed in the numeric version of the long list (the -n option), printing the UID (instead of user name) and GID (instead of group name) numbers associated with the files.

```
castle% ls -aisn
total 10272
   297874     2 drwxr-xr-x    6 1001     10       512 Mar  9 13:50 .
   296220     2 drwxr-xr-x    6 0        1        512 Mar  3 18:49 ..
   297877     2 -rw-r--r--    1 1001     10       411 Mar  3 19:05 .cshrc
   407708     2 drwxr-xr-x   14 1001     10       512 Mar  9 13:15 .dt
   297878    10 -rwxr-xr-x    1 1001     10      5111 Mar  3 19:52 .dtprofile
    41663     2 drwxr-xr-x    2 1001     10       512 Mar  4 07:42 .hotjava
    81587     2 drwxrwxrwx    2 1001     10       512 Mar  4 11:22 .jetadmin
   297875     2 -rw-r--r--    1 1001     10       581 Mar  3 18:48 .login
   297884     2 -rw-------    1 1001     10        36 Mar  6 16:52 .sh_history
    36679     2 drwx------    2 1001     10       512 Mar  9 13:15 .solregis
   297890     2 -rw-------    1 1001     10       100 Mar  9 13:15 .Xauthority
   297880     8 -rw-r--r--    1 1001     10      3985 Mar  4 11:26 .Xdefaults
   297885     0 -rw-r--r--    1 1001     10         0 Mar  8 12:55 a.out
   297888     2 -rw-r--r--    1 1001     10       783 Mar  8 18:08 bibliography
   297881   240 -rw-------    1 1001     10    111560 Mar  5 10:33 core
```

```
      297879    4 -rw-------   1 1001     10      1068 Mar  8 18:11 examples
      297887    2 -rw-r--r--   1 1001     10       265 Mar  8 18:00 kookaburra-1
      297876 9984 -rw-r--r--   1 1001     10   5097472 Mar  3 19:03 SOLd515.pkg
castle%
```

When the sizes of the files in a directory are listed, a total count of blocks, including indirect blocks, is printed.

Environment Variables

See environ(5) for descriptions of the following environment variables that affect the execution of ls: LC_COLLATE, LC_CTYPE, LC_TIME, LC_MESSAGES, NLSPATH, and TZ.

COLUMNS   Determine the preferred column position width for writing multiple text-column output. If this variable contains a string representing a decimal integer, the ls command calculates how many path-name text columns to write (see -C) based on the width provided. If COLUMNS is not set or is invalid, use 80. The column width chosen to write the names of files in any given directory is constant. File names are not truncated to fit into the multiple text column output.

Exit Status

0   All information was written successfully.

>0   An error occurred.

Files

/etc/group   Group IDs for ls -l and ls -g.

/etc/passwd User IDs for ls -l and ls -o.

/usr/share/lib/terminfo/?/*

               Terminal information database.

Attributes

See attributes(5) for descriptions of the following attributes:

/usr/bin/ls

Attribute Type	Attribute Value
Availability	SUNWcsu
CSI	Enabled

/usr/xpg4/bin/ls

Attribute Type	Attribute Value
Availability	SUNWcsu

See Also

chmod(1), cp(1), setfacl(1), terminfo(4), attributes(5), environ(5), largefile(5), XPG4(5)

M

m4 — Macro Processor

Synopsis
```
/usr/ccs/bin/m4 [-e] [-s] [-Bint] [-Hint] [-Sint] [-Tint] [-Dname [=val]]
   ... [-U name] ... [file...]
/usr/xpg4/bin/m4 [-e] [-s] [-Bint] [-Hint] [-Sint] [-Tint] [-Dname [=val]]
   ... [-U name] ... [file...]
```

Description
The m4 command is a macro processor front end for C, assembler, and other languages. Each of the argument files is processed in order; if there are no files or if a file is -, the standard input is read. The processed text is written to the standard output.

Macro Syntax
Macro calls have the form:

```
name(arg1,arg2,..., argn)
```

The (must immediately follow the name of the macro. If the name of a defined macro is not followed by a (, it is considered to be a call of that macro with no arguments. Potential macro names consist of alphanumeric characters and underscore (_), where the first character is not a digit.

Leading unquoted blanks, Tabs, and newlines are ignored while arguments are collected. Left and right single quotes are used to quote strings. The value of a quoted string is the string stripped of the quotes.

Macro Processing

When a macro name is recognized, its arguments are collected by searching for a matching right parenthesis. If fewer arguments are supplied than are in the macro definition, the trailing arguments are taken to be `null`. Macro evaluation proceeds normally during the collection of the arguments, and any commas or right parentheses that happen to turn up within the value of a nested call are as effective as those in the original input text. After argument collection, the value of the macro is pushed back onto the input stream and rescanned.

Options

`-e`	Operate interactively. Ignore interrupts and buffer the output.
`-s`	Enable line sync output for the C preprocessor (`#line...`)
`-B` *int*	Change the size of the push-back and argument-collection buffers from the default of 4,096.
`-H` *int*	Change the size of the symbol table hash array from the default of 199. The size should be prime.
`-S` *int*	Change the size of the call stack from the default of 100 slots. Macros take three slots, and nonmacro arguments take one.
`-T` *int*	Change the size of the token buffer from the default of 512 bytes.

To be effective, put the above options before any file names and before any `-D` or `-U` options.

`-D` *name[=val]*	
	Define *name* to *val* or to `null` in *val*'s absence.
`-U` *name*	Undefine *name*.

Operands

file	A path name of a text file to be processed. If you specify no file or if it is `-`, read the standard input.

Usage

The `m4` command makes the following built-in macros available. You can redefine these macros, but if you do so, you lose their original meaning. Macro values are `null` unless otherwise stated.

`changequote`

> Change quote symbols to the first and second arguments. The symbols can be up to five characters long. `changequote` without arguments restores the original values (that is, ` ' `).

changecom   Change left and right comment markers from the default # and newline. With no arguments, the comment mechanism is effectively disabled. With one argument, the left marker becomes the argument and the right marker becomes newline. With two arguments, both markers are affected. Comment markers can be up to five characters long.

decr   Return the value of the argument decremented by 1.

define   The second argument is installed as the value of the macro whose name is the first argument. Replace each occurrence of $n in the replacement text, where n is a digit, with the n-th argument. Argument 0 is the name of the macro. Replace missing arguments with the null string. Replace $# with the number of arguments. Replace $* with a list of all the arguments separated by commas. $@ is like $* but quotes each argument with the current quotes.

defn   Return the quoted definition of the argument(s). This macro is useful for renaming macros, especially built-ins.

divert   Change the current output stream to the (*digit-string*) argument. m4 maintains 10 output streams, numbered 0-9. The final output is the concatenation of the streams in numerical order; initially, stream 0 is the current stream. Output diverted to a stream other than 0 through 9 is discarded.

divnum   Return the value of the current output stream.

dnl   Read and discard characters up to and including the next newline.

dumpdef   Print current names and definitions for the named items or for all if you specify no arguments.

errprint   Print the argument on the diagnostic output file.

/usr/ccs/bin/m4

eval   Evaluate the argument as an arithmetic expression using 32-bit signed-integer arithmetic. The following operators are supported: parentheses, unary –, unary +, !, ~, *, /, %, +, –, relationals, bitwise &, |, &&, and ||. You can specify octal and hex numbers as in C. The second argument specifies the radix for the result; the default is 10. You can use the third argument to specify the minimum number of digits in the result.

/usr/xpg4/bin/m4

eval   Evaluate the argument as an arithmetic expression using 32-bit signed-integer arithmetic. The following operators are supported: parentheses, unary –, unary +, !, ~, *, /, %, +, –, <<, >>, relationals, bitwise &, |, &&, and ||. Precedence and associativity are as in C. You can also specify octal and hex numbers as in C. The second argument specifies the radix for the result; the default is 10. You can use the third argument to specify the minimum number of digits in the result.

ifdef	If the first argument is defined, use the value of the second argument; otherwise, use the third. If there is no third argument, the value is `null`. The word `unix` is predefined.
ifelse	This macro has three or more arguments. If the first argument is the same string as the second, then use the value of the third argument. If not and if there are more than four arguments, repeat the process with arguments 4, 5, 6, and 7. Otherwise, the value is either the fourth string or, if it is not present, `null`.
include	Return the contents of the file named in the argument.
incr	Return the value of the argument incremented by 1. The value of the argument is calculated by interpreting an initial digit-string as a decimal number.
index	Return the position in the first argument where the second argument begins (0 origin), or `-1` if there is no second argument.
len	Return the number of characters in the argument.
m4exit	Exit from `m4`. Argument 1, if specified, is the exit code; the default is `0`.
m4wrap	Push back argument 1 at final EOF; for example, `m4wrap('cleanup()')`.
maketemp	Fill in a string of `X` characters in the argument with the current process ID.
popdef	Remove current definition of the argument(s), exposing the previous one, if any.
pushdef	Like `define`, but save any previous definition.
shift	Return all but the first argument. Quote and push back the other arguments with commas in between. The quoting nullifies the effect of the extra scan that is subsequently performed.
sincludd	Identical to `include`, except say nothing if the file is inaccessible.
substr	Return a substring of the first argument. The second argument is a 0-origin number selecting the first character; the third argument indicates the length of the substring. A missing third argument is taken to be large enough to extend to the end of the first string.
syscmd	Execute the command given in the first argument. Return no value.
sysval	Return the return code from the last call to `syscmd`.
translit	Transliterate the characters in the first argument from the set given by the second argument to the set given by the third. Permit no abbreviations.
traceon	Turn on tracing for all macros (including built-ins) with no arguments. Otherwise, turn on tracing for named macros.

traceoff   Globally turn off `trace` and for any macros specified. Macros specifically traced by `traceon` can be untraced only by specific calls to `traceoff`.

undefine   Remove the definition of the macro named in the argument.

undivert   Immediately output the text from diversions named as arguments, or all diversions if you specify no argument. Text can be undiverted into another diversion. Undiverting discards the diverted text.

Examples

An example of a single m4 input file capable of generating two output files follows. The file `file1.m4` could contain lines such as the following.

```
if(VER, 1, do_something)
if(VER, 2, do_something)
```

The makefile for the program could include the following lines.

```
file1.1.c :        file1.m4
                   m4 -D VER=1 file1.m4 > file1.1.c...
file1.2.c :        file1.m4
                   m4 -D VER=2 file1.m4 > file1.2.c
                   . . .
```

You can use the -U option to undefine VER. If `file1.m4` contains the following statements,

```
if(VER, 1, do_something)
if(VER, 2, do_something)
ifndef(VER, do_something)
```

then the makefile would contain

```
file1.0.c :        file1.m4
                   m4 -U VER file1.m4 > file1.0.c
                   . . .
file1.1.c :        file1.m4
                   m4 -D VER=1 file1.m4 > file1.1.c
                   . . .
file1.2.c :        file1.m4
                   m4 -D VER=2 file1.m4 > file1.2.c
                   . . .
```

Environment Variables

See `environ(5)` for descriptions of the following environment variables that affect the execution of m4: LC_CTYPE, LC_MESSAGES, and NLSPATH.

Exit Status

0	Successful completion.
>0	An error occurred.

If you use the m4 exit macro, the exit value can be specified by the input file.

Attributes

See attributes(5) for descriptions of the following attributes:

/usr/ccs/bin/m4

Attribute Type	Attribute Value
Availability	SUNWcsu

/usr/xpg4/bin/m4

Attribute Type	Attribute Value
Availability	SUNWcsu

See Also

as(1), attributes(5), environ(5), xpg4(5)

mach — Display the Processor Type of the Current Host

Synopsis

/usr/bin/mach

Description

The mach command displays the processor type of the current host.

> **Note —** mach and uname -p return equivalent values. Independent software vendors and others who need to ascertain processor type are encouraged to use uname with the -p option instead of the mach command. The mach command is provided for compatibility with previous releases, but generally its use is discouraged.

Attributes

See `attributes`(5) for descriptions of the following attributes:

Attribute Type	Attribute Value
Availability	SUNWcsu

See Also

`arch(1)`, `uname(1)`, `attributes(5)`

---

machid — Get Processor Type Truth Value

Synopsis

```
/usr/bin/sun
/usr/bin/iAPX286
/usr/bin/i386
/usr/bin/pdp11
/usr/bin/sparc
/usr/bin/u3b
/usr/bin/u3b2
/usr/bin/u3b5
/usr/bin/u3b15
/usr/bin/vax
/usr/bin/u370
```

Description

> **Note** — The `machid` family of commands is obsolete. Use `uname -p` and `uname -m` instead.

The following commands return a `true` value (exit code of 0) if you are using an instruction set that the command name indicates.

sun	true if you are on a Sun system.
iAPX286	true if you are on a computer using an iAPX286 processor.
i386	true if you are on a computer using an iAPX386 processor.
pdp11	true if you are on a PDP-11/45 or PDP-11/70.
sparc	true if you are on a computer using a SPARC family processor.
u3b	true if you are on a 3B20 computer.
u3b2	true if you are on a 3B2 computer.
u3b5	true if you are on a 3B5 computer.

u3b15	true if you are on a 3B15 computer.
vax	true if you are on a VAX-11/750 or VAX11/780.
u370	true if you are on an IBM (Reg.) System/370 computer.

The commands that do not apply return a `false` (non-zero) value. These commands are often used within `make` files (see `make(1S)`) and shell scripts (see `sh(1)`) to increase portability.

Attributes

See `attributes(5)` for descriptions of the following attributes:

Attribute Type	Attribute Value
Availability	SUNWcsu

See Also

`sh(1)`, `test(1)`, `true(1)`, `uname(1)`, `make(1S)`, `attributes(5)`

---

mail, rmail — Read Mail or Send Mail to Users

Synopsis

Sending Mail
```
/usr/bin/mail [-tw] [-m message-type] recipient...
/usr/bin/rmail [-tw] [-m message-type] recipient...
```

Reading Mail
```
/usr/bin/mail [-ehpPqr] [-f file]
```

Debugging
```
/usr/bin/mail [-x debug-level] [other-mail-options] recipient...
```

Description

A *recipient* is usually a user name recognized by `login(1)`. When you specify recipients, `mail` assumes a message is being sent. It reads from the standard input up to an end-of-file (Control-D) or, if reading from a terminal device, until it reads a line consisting of just a period. When either of those indicators is received, `mail` adds the letter to the mail file for each recipient.

A letter is composed of some header lines followed by a blank line followed by the message content. The header lines section of the letter consists of one or more UNIX postmarks:

From *sender date-and-time* [remote from *remote-system-name*]

followed by one or more standardized message header lines of the form:

keyword-name: [*printable text*]

where *keyword-name* consists of any printable, non-white-space characters
other than colon (:). A `Content-Length:` header line indicating the number
of bytes in the message content is always present unless the letter consists of
only header lines with no message content. A `Content-Type:` header line that
describes the type of the message content (such as text, binary, or multipart) is
also present unless the letter consists of only header lines with no message
content. Header lines can be continued on the following line if that line starts
with white space.

Options

Sending Mail

-m *message-type*

        Add a `Message-Type:` line to the message header with the value of
        message-type.

-t   Add a `To:` line to the message header for each of the intended
        recipients.

-w   Send a letter to a remote recipient without waiting for the
        completion of the remote transfer program.

    If a letter is found to be undeliverable, it is returned to the sender with
diagnostics that indicate the location and nature of the failure. If mail is
interrupted during input, the message is saved in the file dead.letter to
enable editing and resending. dead.letter is always appended to, thus
preserving any previous contents. The initial attempt to append to (or create)
dead.letter is in the current directory. If this attempt fails, dead.letter is
appended to (or created in) the user's login directory. If the second attempt also
fails, no dead.letter processing is done.

    rmail permits only the sending of mail; uucp(1C) uses rmail as a security
precaution. Any application programs that generate mail messages should be
sure to invoke rmail instead of mail for message transport and/or delivery.

    If the local system has the Basic Networking Utilities installed, you can send
mail to a recipient on a remote system. There are numerous ways to address
mail to recipients on remote systems, depending on the transport mechanisms
available to the local system. The two most prevalent addressing schemes are
domain style and UUCP style. Consult your local system administrator for
details on which addressing conventions are available on the local system.

Domain-Style Addressing

For domain-style addressing, you specify remote recipients by appending an @ and domain (and possibly subdomain) information to the recipient name (such as *user*@sf.att.com).

UUCP-Style Addressing

For UUCP-style addressing, you specify remote recipients by prefixing the recipient name with the remote system name and an exclamation point, such as sysa!user. If csh(1) is the default shell, use sysa\!user. You can use a series of system names separated by exclamation points to direct a letter through an extended network (such as sysa!sysb!sysc!*user* or sysa\!sysb\!sysc\!*user*).

Reading Mail

-e	Do not print mail. Return an exit status of 0 if the user has mail; otherwise, return an exit status of 1.
-h	Initially display a window of headers instead of the latest message. The display is followed by the ? prompt.
-p	Print all messages without prompting for disposition.
-P	Print all messages with all header lines displayed instead of the default selective header line display.
-q	Terminate mail after interrupts. Normally, an interrupt terminates only the message being printed.
-r	Print messages in first-in, first-out order.
-f *file*	Use *file* (such as mbox) instead of the default mail file.

mail, unless otherwise influenced by command-line arguments, prints mail messages in last-in, first-out order. The default mode for printing messages is to display only those header lines of immediate interest. These include, but are not limited to, the UNIX From and >From postmarks, From:, Date:, Subject:, and Content-Length: header lines, and any recipient header lines such as To:, Cc:, Bcc:, and so forth. After the header lines have been displayed, mail displays the contents (body) of the message only if it contains no unprintable characters. Otherwise, mail issues a warning statement about the message having binary content and does not display the content. (You can override this feature with the p command.)

For each message, you are prompted with a ? and a line is read from the standard input. The following commands are available to determine the disposition of the message.

#	Print the number of the current message.
-	Print previous message.
newline | + | n	
	Print the next message.

`! command`	Escape to the shell to execute `command`.
`a`	Print message that arrived during the mail session.
`d ǀ dp`	Delete the current message and print the next message.
`d n`	Delete message number `n`. Do not go on to next message.
`dq`	Delete message and quit `mail`.
`h`	Display a window of headers around current message.
`h n`	Display a window of headers around message number `n`.
`h a`	Display headers of all messages in your mail file.
`h d`	Display headers of messages scheduled for deletion.
`m [persons]`	Mail (and delete) the current message to the named persons.
`n`	Print message number `n`.
`p`	Print current message, again overriding any indications of binary (that is, unprintable) content.
`P`	Override default brief mode and print current message, again displaying all header lines.
`q ǀ Control-D`	Put undeleted mail back in the mail file and quit `mail`.
`r [users]`	Reply to the sender and other users, then delete the message.
`s [files]`	Save message in the named files (mbox is default) and delete the message.
`u [n]`	Undelete message number `n` (default is last read).
`w [files]`	Save message content without any header lines in the named `files` (mbox is default) and delete the message.
`x`	Put all mail back in the mail file unchanged and exit `mail`.
`y [files]`	Same as the -w option.
`?`	Print a command summary.

When you log in, `mail` informs you if you have any mail. It also notifies you if new mail arrives while you are using `mail`.

You can manipulate the permissions of the mail file with chmod(1) in two ways to alter the function of `mail`. The permissions of the file for others can be read-write (`0666`), read-only (`0664`), or neither read nor write (`0660`) to permit different levels of privacy. If you change others permissions to anything besides the default (mode `0660`), the file is preserved even when empty to perpetuate the desired permissions. (The administrator can override this file preservation with the `DEL_EMPTY_MAILFILE` option of `mailcnfg`.)

The group ID of the mail file must be `mail` to enable new messages to be delivered, and the mail file must be writable by group `mail`.

Debugging

The following command-line argument provides mail debugging information.

    -x debug-level

> Create a trace file containing debugging information.

The -x option creates a file named /tmp/MLDBGprocess_id that contains debugging information relating to how mail processed the current message. The absolute value of *debug-level* controls the verboseness of the debug information. 0 implies no debugging. If *debug-level* is greater than 0, the debug file is retained only if mail encountered some problem while processing the message. If *debug-level* is less than 0 the debug file is always retained. The *debug-level* specified with -x overrides any specification of DEBUG in /etc/mail/mailcnfg. The information provided by the -x option is esoteric and is probably useful only to system administrators.

Delivery Notification

mail provides several forms of notification, including one of the following lines in the message header:

    Transport-Options: [/options]
    Default-Options: [/options]
    >To: recipient [/options]

where the /*options* can be one or more of the following.

/delivery	Inform the sender that the message was successfully delivered to the recipient's mailbox.
/nodelivery	Do not inform the sender of successful deliveries.
/ignore	Do not inform the sender of failed deliveries.
/return	Inform the sender if mail delivery fails. Return the failed message to the sender.
/report	Same as /return except that the original message is not returned.

The default is /nodelivery/return. If you use contradictory options, the first is recognized and any later, conflicting, terms are ignored.

Notes

The interpretation and resulting action taken because of the header lines described in the Delivery Notification section occur only if this version of mail is installed on the system where the delivery (or failure) happens. Earlier versions of mail may not support any types of delivery notification.

Conditions sometimes result in a failure to remove a lock file.

After an interrupt, the next message may not be printed; you can force printing by typing p.

Operands

recipient   A user login name.

Usage

See largefile(5) for the description of the behavior of mail and rmail when encountering files greater than or equal to 2 Gbytes (2**31 bytes).

Environment Variables

See environ(5) for descriptions of the following environment variables that affect the execution of mail: LC_CTYPE, LC_MESSAGES, and NLSPATH.

TZ   Determine the time zone used with date and time strings.

Exit Status

0   Successful completion when the user had mail.

1   The user had no mail or an initialization error occurred.

>1   An error occurred after initialization.

Files

dead.letter Unmailable text.

/etc/passwd Used to identify sender and locate recipients.

$HOME/mbox Saved mail.

$MAIL   Variable containing path name of mail file.

/tmp/ma*   Temporary file.

/tmp/MLDBG* Debug trace file.

/var/mail/*.lock

                Lock for mail directory.

/var/mail/:saved

                Directory for holding temp files to prevent loss of data in the event of a system crash.

/var/mail/user

                Incoming mail for user; that is, the mail file.

Attributes

See attributes(5) for descriptions of the following attributes:

Attribute Type	Attribute Value
Availability	SUNWcsu

See Also
chmod(1), csh(1), login(1), mailx(1), vacation(1), write(1), uucp(1C), uuencode(1C), attributes(5), environ(5), largefile(5)
Solaris Advanced User's Guide

---

mailcompat — Provide Compatibility for Solaris Mailbox

Format
/usr/bin/mailcompat

Description
The mailcompat command provides 4.x compatibility for the Solaris mailbox format. You typically run mailcompat to be able to read mail on a workstation running 4.x when your mail server is running Solaris.

Enabling mailcompat creates an entry in an existing .forward file in your home directory. If the .forward file does not exist, mailcompat creates it. Disabling mailcompat removes the entry from the .forward file and, if this was the only entry, removes the entire file.

To execute mailcompat, log in to the Solaris mail server and enter mailcompat on the command line. Answer the queries provided by the program.

Usage
See largefile(5) for the description of the behavior of mailcompat when encountering files greater than or equal to 2 Gbytes (2**31 bytes).

Examples
The following example enables the mailcompat feature and displays the contents of the .forward file.

```
castle% mailcompat
This program can be used to store your mail in a format
that you can read with SunOS 4.X based mail readers
To enable the mailcompat feature a ".forward" file is created.
Would you like to enable the mailcompat feature? y
Mailcompat feature ENABLED. Run mailcompat with no arguments to remove it
castle% more .forward
"|/usr/bin/mailcompat winsor"
castle%
```

The following example disables the mailcompat feature for user winsor.

```
castle% mailcompat
This program can be used to store your mail in a format
that you can read with SunOS 4.X based mail readers
```

```
You have a .forward file in your home directory  containing:
    "|/usr/bin/mailcompat winsor"
Would you like to remove it and disable the mailcompat feature? y
Back to normal reception of mail.
castle%
```

Files

~/.forward List of recipients for forwarding messages.

Attributes

See attributes(5) for descriptions of the following attributes:

Attribute Type	Attribute Value
Availability	SUNWcsu

See Also

mailx(1), attributes(5), largefile(5)

mailq — Print the Mail Queue

New!

Synopsis

/usr/bin/mailq [-q Xstring] [-v]

Description

mailq displays a summary of the mail messages queued for future delivery.

The first line displayed for each mail message shows the internal identifier used on this host for the message, the size of the message in bytes, the date and time the message was accepted into the queue, and the envelope sender of the message. The second line of the display shows the error message that retained this message in the queue. This line is not displayed if the message is being processed for the first time.

The mailq command is identical to sendmail -bp.

Options

-q *Xstring*   Run the queue once, limiting the jobs to those matching *Xstring*. The *Xstring* argument consists of a key letter (*X*) followed by *string*. The key letter *X* can be an I, R, or S. Use I to limit based on queue identifier. Use R to limit based on recipient. Use S to limit based on sender. Accept a particular queued job when one of the corresponding addresses contains the specified string.

-v   Print verbose information. This option adds the priority of the message and a single character indicator (+ or blank) indicating whether a warning message has been sent on the first line of the message. Additionally, extra lines may be intermixed with the recipients indicating the "controlling user"; this information shows who owns any programs that are executed on behalf of this message and the name of the alias this command is expanded from, if any.

Exit Status

0   Successful completion.

>0   An error occurred.

Attributes

See attributes(5) for descriptions of the following attributes:

Attribute Type	Attribute Value
Availability	SUNWsndmu

See Also

sendmail(1M), attributes(5)

mailstats — Print Statistics Collected by sendmail

Synopsis

/usr/bin/mailstats [-c *configfile*] [-f *statisticsfile*] *file*

Description

The mailstats command prints out the statistics collected by the sendmail(1M) program on mailer usage. These statistics are collected if the file indicated by the S configuration option of sendmail (defined in /etc/mail/sendmail.cf) exists. The default statistics file is

/etc/mail/sendmail.st. The mailstats command first prints the time that the statistics file was created and the last time it was modified. It then prints a table with one row for each mailer specified in the configuration file. The first column is the mailer number, followed by the total number of messages sent from this mailer. The next two columns refer to the number of messages received by sendmail, and the last two columns refer to messages sent by sendmail. The number of messages and their total size (in 1024-byte units) is shown. No numbers are printed if no messages were sent (or received) for any mailer.

You might want to add an entry to /var/spool/cron/crontabs/root to reinitialize the statistics file once a night. Copy /dev/null into the statistics file or otherwise truncate it to reset the counters.

> **Note** — The mailstats command should read the configuration file instead of having a hard-wired table mapping mailer numbers to names.

Options

-c *configfile*

Specify a sendmail configuration file.

-f *statisticsfile*

Specify a sendmail statistics file.

Examples

The following example shows the output for a new sendmail.st file with a local mailer and one message.

```
castle% mailstats
Statistics from Sun Mar 14 12:16:39 1999
 M   msgsfr  bytes_from   msgsto   bytes_to  msgsrej msgsdis  Mailer
 3        1          1K        0         0K        0       0  local
=============================================================
 T        1          1K        0         0K        0       0
castle%
```

Usage

See largefile(5) for the description of the behavior of mailstats when encountering files greater than or equal to 2 Gbytes (2**31 bytes).

Files

/dev/null   Zero-lined file.

/var/spool/cron/crontabs/root

Default scheduler file used by the cron(1M) daemon.

```
/etc/mail/sendmail.st
```
Default `sendmail` statistics file.

```
/etc/mail/sendmail.cf
```
Default `sendmail` configuration file.

Attributes

See `attributes`(5) for descriptions of the following attributes:

Attribute Type	Attribute Value
Availability	SUNWsndmu

New!

See Also

`cron`(1M), `sendmail`(1M), `attributes`(5), `largefile`(5)

Diagnostics

```
mailstats: file size changed
```
The statistics file is zero-length and has not yet been filled with data.

mailx, mail, Mail — Interactive Message Processing System

Synopsis
```
mailx [-BdeHiInNUvV~][-f [file|+folder]][-T file][-u user]
mailx [-BdFintUv~][-b bcc][-c cc][-h number][-r address][-s subject]
   recipient...
/usr/ucb/mail...
/usr/ucb/Mail...
```

Description

The mail commands listed above provide a comfortable, flexible environment for sending and receiving mail messages electronically.

When mail is being read, the mail commands facilitate saving, deleting, and responding to messages. When mail is being sent, the mail commands enable editing, reviewing, and other modification of the message as you enter it.

Incoming mail for each user is stored in a standard file, called the `mailbox`. When the mail commands are called to read messages, the `mailbox` is the default place to find them. As messages are read, they are marked to be moved to a secondary file for storage, unless specific action is taken, so that the messages need not be seen again. This secondary file is called the mbox and is normally located in the user's HOME directory. You can save messages in other secondary files with names you specify. Messages remain in a secondary file until forcibly removed.

You can access a secondary file by using the -f option. You can then read or otherwise process messages in the secondary file, using the same commands you use for the primary mailbox. When you access a secondary file with the -f option, that file is considered the current mailbox.

Options

On the command line, options start with a dash (-). Any other arguments are taken to be destinations (recipients). If you specify no recipients, mailx tries to read messages from the mailbox.

-B	Do not buffer standard input or standard output.
-b *bcc*	Set the blind carbon copy list to *bcc*. Enclose *bcc* in quotes if it contains more than one name.
-c *cc*	Set the carbon copy list to *cc*. Enclose *cc* in quotes if it contains more than one name.
-d	Turn on debugging output. (Neither particularly interesting nor recommended.)
-e	Test for the presence of mail. mailx prints nothing and exits with a successful return code if there is mail to read.
-F	Record the message in a file named after the first recipient. Override the record variable, if set.
-f [*file*]	Read messages from *file* instead of mailbox. If you specify no file, use the mbox.
-f [+*folder*]	Use the file *folder* in the folder directory (same as the folder command). The name of this directory is listed in the folder variable.
-H	Print header summary only.
-h *number*	The number of network hops made so far. This option is provided for network software to avoid infinite delivery loops. This option and its argument are passed to the delivery program.
-I	Include the newsgroup and article ID header lines when printing mail messages. This option requires that you also specify the -f option.
-i	Ignore interrupts.
-N	Do not print initial header summary.
-n	Do not initialize from the system default mailx.rc or Mail.rc file.

-r *address*	Use *address* as the return address when invoking the delivery program. Disable all tilde commands. This option and its argument are passed to the delivery program.
-s *subject*	Set the Subject header field to *subject*. You must enclose *subject* in quotes if it contains embedded white space.
-T *file*	Record message ID and article ID header lines in *file* after the message is read. This option also sets the -I option.
-t	Scan the input for To:, Cc:, and Bcc: fields. Ignore any recipients on the command line.
-U	Convert UUCP-style addresses to Internet standards. Override the conv environment variable.
-u *user*	Read *user*'s mailbox. This option is effective only if *user*'s mailbox is not read protected.
-V	Print the mailx version number and exit.
-v	Pass the -v flag to sendmail(1M).
-~	Interpret tilde escapes in the input even if not reading from a TTY.

Operands

recipient	Addressee of message.

Usage

Starting Mail

At startup time, mailx executes the system startup file
/etc/mail/mailx.rc. If invoked as mail or Mail, the system startup file
/etc/mail/Mail.rc is used instead.

The system startup file sets up initial display options and alias lists and
assigns values to some internal variables. These variables are flags and valued
parameters that are set and cleared with the set and unset commands. See
"Internal Variables" on page 779. If mailx is started with the -n option, the
mail commands do not execute the system startup file.

Regular commands are legal inside startup files except for the following
commands: !, Copy, edit, followup, Followup, hold, mail, preserve,
reply, Reply, shell, and visual. When the startup file contains an error, the
remaining lines are ignored.

After executing the system startup file, the mail commands execute the
optional personal startup file $HOME/.mailrc, which you can use to override
the values of the internal variables as set by the system startup file.

Many system administrators include the following commands in the system
startup files (to be compatible with past Solaris behavior), but these commands
do not meet standards requirements for mailx.

```
set appenddeadletter
unset replyall
unset pipeignore
```

To get standard behavior for `mailx`, either use the `-n` option or include the following commands in a personal startup file.

```
unset appenddeadletter
set replyall
set pipeignore
```

When mail is being read, the mail commands are in command mode. A header summary of the first several messages is displayed, followed by a prompt indicating that mail commands can accept regular commands (see "Commands" on page 769). When mail is being sent, the mail commands are in input mode. If you specify no subject on the command line and the `asksub` variable is set, you are prompted for the subject.

As you type the message, the mail commands read the message and store it in a temporary file. You can enter commands by beginning a line with the tilde (~) escape character followed by a single command letter and optional arguments. See "Tilde Escapes" on page 777 for a summary of these commands.

Reading Mail

> **Note** — To read mail on a workstation running Solaris 1.x when your mail server is running Solaris 2.x, first execute the `mailcompat(1)` program.

Each message is assigned a sequential number. The current message is marked by a right angle bracket (>) in the header summary. Many commands take an optional list of messages (`message-list`) to operate on. In most cases, the current message is set to the highest-numbered message in the list after the command is finished executing.

The default for `message-list` is the current message. A `message-list` is a list of message identifiers separated by spaces, which may include the following.

n	Message number *n*.
.	The current message.
^	The first undeleted message.
$	The last message.
*	All messages.
+	The next undeleted message.
−	The previous undeleted message.
n−m	An inclusive range of message numbers.
user	All messages from *user*.

/string	All messages with *string* in the Subject line (case ignored).
:*c*	All messages of type *c*, where *c* is one of the following.

d	Deleted messages.
n	New messages.
o	Old messages.
r	Read messages.
u	Unread messages.

Note — The context of the command determines whether the type of message specification makes sense.

Other arguments are usually arbitrary strings whose usage depends on the command involved. File names, where expected, are expanded according to the normal shell conventions (see sh(1)). Special characters are recognized by certain commands and are documented with the commands listed in "Commands."

Sending Mail
Recipients listed on the command line can be of three types:

- Login names.
- Shell commands.
- Alias groups.

Login names can be any network address, including mixed network addressing. If mail is found to be undeliverable, an attempt is made to return it to the sender's mailbox. If the recipient name begins with a pipe symbol (|) the rest of the name is taken to be a shell command to pipe the message through. This provides an automatic interface with any program that reads the standard input, such as lp(1), for recording outgoing mail on paper. Alias groups are set by the alias command or in a system startup file (for example, $HOME/.mailrc). Aliases are lists of recipients of any type.

Note — Full Internet addressing is not fully supported by mailx. The new standards need some time to settle down.

Replies do not always generate correct return addresses. Try resending the errant reply with onehop set.

Forwarding Mail
To forward a specific message, include it in a message to the desired recipients with the ~f or ~m tilde escapes. See "Tilde Escapes" on page 777. To forward mail automatically, add a comma-separated list of addresses for additional recipients to the .forward file in your home directory. This format is different

from the format of the `alias` command, which takes a space-separated list instead.

> **Note** — Forwarding addresses must be valid or the messages bounce. For example, you cannot reroute your mail to a new host by forwarding it to your new address if it is not yet listed in the NIS `aliases` domain.

Commands

Regular commands are of the form

```
[command] [message-list] [arguments]
```

In input mode, commands are recognized by the escape character, tilde (~), and lines not treated as commands are taken as input for the message.

If you specify no command in command mode, next is assumed.

The following is a complete list of `mailx` commands.

`!shell-command`

> Escape to the shell. Note that where `shell-command` is valid, arguments are not always allowed. Experimentation is recommended.

`# comment`   Null command (comment). Useful in `mailrc` files.

`=`   Print the current message number.

`?`   Print a summary of commands.

`alias alias name...`
`group alias name...`

> Declare an alias for the given `names`. Substitute names when you use `alias` as a recipient. This command is useful in the `mailrc` file. With no arguments, display the list of defined aliases.

`alternates name...`

> Declare a list of alternate names for your login. When responding to a message, remove these names from the list of recipients for the response. With no arguments, print the current list of alternate names. See also `allnet` in "Internal Variables" on page 779.

`cd [directory]` `chdir [directory]`

> Change directory. If you specify no `directory`, use $HOME.

`copy [file]`
`copy [message-list] file`

> Copy messages to the file without marking the messages as saved. Otherwise, equivalent to the `save` command.

Copy [*message-list*]

> Save the specified messages in a file whose name is derived from the author of the message to be saved without marking the messages as saved. Otherwise, equivalent to the Save command.

delete [*message-list*]

> Delete messages from the mailbox. If autoprint is set, print the next message after the last one (see "Internal Variables" on page 779).

discard [*header-field...*]
ignore [*header-field...*]

> Suppress printing of the specified header fields when displaying messages on the screen. Examples of header fields to ignore are Status and Received. Include the fields when the message is saved unless the alwaysignore variable is set. The More, Page, Print, and Type commands override this command. If you specify no header, print the current list of header fields being ignored. See also the undiscard and unignore commands.

dp [*message-list*]
dt [*message-list*]

> Delete the specified messages from the mailbox and print the next message after the last one deleted. Roughly equivalent to a delete command followed by a print command.

echo string...

> Echo the given strings. (Like echo(1).)

edit [*message-list*]

> Edit the given messages. Put each message in a temporary file and invoke the program named by the EDITOR variable to edit it. Default editor is ed(1).

exit   Exit from mailx, without changing the mailbox. Save no messages
xit   in the mbox (see also quit).

field [*message-list*] *header-file*

> Display the value of the header field in the specified message.

file [*file*]
folder [*file*]

> Quit from the current file of messages and read in the specified file. The following special characters are recognized when used as file names.

> % is the current mailbox.

> %*user* is the mailbox for *user*.

> # is the previous mail file.

             `&` is the current `mbox`.

             `+file` is the named file in the folder directory (listed in the `folder` variable).

             With no arguments, print the name of the current mail file and the number of messages and characters it contains.

`folders`   Print the names of the files in the directory set by the `folder` variable (see "Internal Variables" on page 779).

`Followup` [*message*]

             Respond to a message, recording the response in a file whose name is derived from the author of the message. Override the `record` variable if set. If the `replyall` variable is set, reverse the actions of `Followup` and `followup`. See also the `followup`, `Save`, and `Copy` commands, `outfolder` in "Internal Variables" on page 779, and "Starting Mail" on page 766.

`followup` [*message-list*]

             Respond to the first message in the *message-list*, sending the message to the author of each message in the *message-list*. Take the subject line from the first message and record the response in a file whose name is derived from the author of the first message. If the `replyall` variable is set, reverse the actions of `followup` and `Followup`. See also the `Followup`, `Save`, and `Copy` commands, `outfolder` in "Internal Variables" on page 779, and "Starting Mail" on page 766.

`from` [*message-list*]

             Print the header summary for the specified messages. If you specify no messages, print the header summary for the current message.

`group` *alias name*...
`alias` *alias name*...

             Declare an alias for the given names. The names are substituted when *alias* is used as a recipient. Useful in the `mailrc` file.

`headers` [*message*]

             Print the page of headers that include the message specified. The screen variable sets the number of headers per page (see "Internal Variables" on page 779). See also the `z` command.

`help`   Print a summary of commands.

`hold` [*message-list*]
`preserve` [*message-list*]

             Hold the specified messages in the mailbox.

```
if s | r | t
mail-commands
else
mail-commands
endif
```

Conditional execution, where s executes following `mail-commands`
up to an `else` or `endif` if the program is in send mode. `r` executes
the `mail-commands` only in receive mode. `t` executes the
`mail-commands` only if `mailx` is being run from a terminal. Useful
in the `mailrc` file.

```
ignore [header-field...]
discard [header-field...]
```

Suppress printing of the specified header fields when displaying
messages on the screen. Examples of header fields to ignore are
`Status` and `Cc`. Include all fields when the message is saved. The
`More`, `Page`, `Print`, and `Type` commands override this command. If
you specify no header, print the current list of header fields being
ignored. See also the `undiscard` and `unignore` commands.

`inc`   Incorporate messages that arrive while you are reading the system
mailbox. Add the new messages to the message list in the current
mail session. This command does not commit changes made during
the session and does not renumber prior messages.

`list`   Print all commands available. No explanation is given.

`load [message] file`

Replace the specified message by the message in the named file.
`file` should contain a single mail message including mail headers
(as saved by the `save` command).

`mail recipient...`

Mail a message to the specified recipients.

`Mail recipient...`

Mail a message to the specified recipients and record it in a file
whose name is derived from the author of the message. Override the
`record` variable if set. See also the `Save` and `Copy` commands and
`outfolder` in "Internal Variables" on page 779.

`mbox [message-list]`

Arrange for the given messages to end up in the standard `mbox` save
file when `mailx` terminates normally. See `MBOX` in "Environment
Variables" on page 783 for a description of this file. See also the
`exit` and `quit` commands.

```
more [message-list]
page [message-list]
```
> Print the specified messages. If crt is set, page through the
> messages that are longer than the number of lines specified by the
> crt variable, using the command specified by the PAGER variable.
> The default command is pg(1), or if the bsdcompat variable is set,
> the default is more(1). See "Environment Variables" on page 783.
> Same as the print and type commands.

```
More [message-list]
Page [message-list]
```
> Print the specified messages on the screen, including all header
> fields. Override suppression of fields by the ignore command. Same
> as the Print and Type commands.

```
new [message-list]
New [message-list]
unread [message-list]
Unread [message-list]
```
> Take a message list and mark each message as not having been
> read.

```
next [message]
```
> Go to the next message matching message. If you do not supply
> message, find the next message that was not deleted or saved. If you
> specify a message-list, the first valid message in the list is the
> only one used. This command is useful for jumping to the next
> message from a specific user because, otherwise, the name would be
> taken as a command in the absence of a real command. See the
> discussion of message-list above for a description of possible
> message specifications.

```
pipe [message-list][shell-command]
| [message-list][shell-command]
```
> Pipe the message through the given shell-command. Treat the
> message as if it were read. If you specify no arguments, pipe the
> current message through the command specified by the value of the
> cmd variable. If the page variable is set, insert a formfeed character
> after each message (see "Internal Variables" on page 779).

```
preserve [message-list]
hold [message-list]
```
> Preserve the specified messages in the mailbox.

```
print [message-list]
type [message-list]
```
> Print the specified messages. If crt is set, page through the
> messages that are longer than the number of lines specified by the
> crt variable, using the command specified by the PAGER variable.
> The default command is pg(1), or if the bsdcompat variable is set,

the default is more(1). See "Environment Variables" on page 783. Same as the more and page commands.

Print [*message-list*]
Type [*message-list*]

Print the specified messages on the screen, including all header fields. Override suppression of fields by the ignore command. Same as the More and Page commands.

put [*file*]
put [*message-list*] file

Save the specified message in the given file. Use the same conventions as the print command for which header fields are ignored.

Put [*file*]
Put [*message-list*] file

Save the specified message in the given file. Override suppression of fields by the ignore command.

quit

Exit from mailx, storing messages that were read in mbox and unread messages in the mailbox. Delete messages that have been explicitly saved in a file unless the keepsave variable is set.

reply [*message-list*]
respond [*message-list*]
replysender [*message-list*]

Send a response to the author of each message in the *message-list*. Take the subject line from the first message. If record is set to a file, add a copy of the reply to that file. If the replyall variable is set, reverse the actions of Reply/Respond and reply/respond. The replysender command is not affected by the replyall variable but sends each reply only to the sender of each message. See "Starting Mail" on page 766.

Reply [*message*]
Respond [*message*]
replyall [*message*]

Reply to the specified message, including all other recipients of that message. If the variable record is set to a file, add a copy of the reply to that file. If the replyall variable is set, reverse the actions of Reply/Respond and reply/respond. The replyall command is not affected by the replyall variable but always sends the reply to all recipients of the message. See "Starting Mail" on page 766.

retain

Add the list of header fields named to the retained list. Show only the header fields in the retain list on your terminal when you print a message. Suppress all other header fields. Override any list of ignored fields specified by the ignore command. You can use the

Type and Print commands to print a message in its entirety. If you execute retain with no arguments, it lists the current set of retained fields.

Save [*message-list*]

Save the specified messages in a file whose name is derived from the author of the first message. The name of the file is taken to be the author's name with all network addressing stripped off. See also the Copy, followup, and Followup commands, and outfolder in "Internal Variables" on page 779.

save [*file*]
save [*message-list*] file

Save the specified messages in the given file. Create the file if it does not exist. The file defaults to mbox. Delete the message from the mailbox when mailx terminates unless keepsave is set (see also "Internal Variables" on page 779 and the exit and quit commands).

set
set *variable*
set *variable=string*
set *variable=number*

Define a variable. To assign a value to variable, separate the variable name from the value by an equal sign (=). Do not follow the equal sign with a space. You can give a null, string, or numeric value. To embed space characters within a value, enclose the value in quotes.

With no arguments, set displays all defined variables and any values they might have. See "Internal Variables" on page 779 for a description of all predefined mail variables.

shell   Invoke an interactive shell. See also SHELL in "Environment Variables" on page 783.

size [*message-list*]

Print the size in characters of the specified messages.

source *file*   Read commands from the given file and return to command mode.

top [*message-list*]

Print the top few lines of the specified messages. If the toplines variable is set, take it as the number of lines to print (see "Internal Variables" on page 779). The default is 5.

touch [*message-list*]

Touch the specified messages. If any message in *message-list* is not specifically saved in a file, on normal termination, put it in the mbox or in the file specified in the MBOX environment variable. See exit and quit.

```
Type [message-list]
Print [message-list]
```

> Print the specified messages on the screen, including all header fields. Override suppression of fields by the `ignore` command.

```
type [message-list]
print [message-list]
```

> Print the specified messages. If `crt` is set, use the command specified by the `PAGER` variable to page through the messages that are longer than the number of lines specified by the `crt` variable. The default command is `pg`(1).

```
unalias [alias]...
ungroup [alias]...
```

> Remove the definitions of the specified aliases.

```
undelete [message-list]
```

> Restore the specified deleted messages. Restore only messages deleted in the current mail session. If `autoprint` is set, print the last message of those restored (see "Internal Variables" on page 779).

```
undiscard [header-field...]
unignore [header-field...]
```

> Remove the specified header fields from the list being ignored. If you specify no header fields, remove all header fields from the list being ignored.

```
unread [message-list]
Unread [message-list]
```

> Same as the `new` command.

```
unretain [header-field...]
```

> Remove the specified header fields from the list being retained. If you specify no header fields, remove all header fields from the list being retained.

```
unset variable...
```

> Erase the specified variables. If the variable was imported from the environment (that is, an environment variable or exported shell variable), you cannot unset it from within `mailx`.

```
version
```
> Print the current version and release date of the `mailx` command.

```
visual [message-list]
```

> Edit the given messages with a screen editor. Put each message in a temporary file and invoke the program named by the `VISUAL` variable to edit it (see "Environment Variables" on page 783). Note that the default visual editor is `vi`.

```
write [message-list] file
```
> Write the given messages on the specified file, minus the header and trailing blank line. Otherwise, equivalent to the save command.

```
xit
exit
```
> Exit from mailx, without changing the mailbox. Save no messages in the mbox (see also quit).

```
z[+|-]
```
> Scroll the header display forward or backward by one full screen. The number of headers displayed is set by the screen variable (see "Internal Variables" on page 779).

Tilde Escapes

You can use the following tilde escape commands when composing mail to send. You can enter them only from input mode by beginning a line with the tilde escape character (~). See escape in "Internal Variables" on page 779 for information on how to change this special character. You can enter the escape character as text by typing it twice.

```
~!shell-command
```
> Escape to the shell. If present, run *shell-command*.

```
~.
```
> Simulate end-of-file (terminate message input).

```
~:mail-command
~_mail-command
```
> Perform the command-level request. Valid only when sending a message while reading mail.

```
~?
```
> Print a summary of tilde escapes.

```
~A
```
> Insert the autograph string Sign into the message (see "Internal Variables" on page 779).

```
~a
```
> Insert the autograph string sign into the message (see "Internal Variables" on page 779).

```
~b name...
```
> Add the names to the blind carbon copy (Bcc) list. This escape is like the carbon copy (Cc) list, except that the names in the Bcc list are not shown in the header of the mail message.

```
~c name...
```
> Add the names to the carbon copy (Cc) list.

```
~d
```
> Read in the dead-letter file. See DEAD in "Environment Variables" on page 783 for a description of this file.

```
~e
```
> Invoke the editor on the partial message. See also EDITOR in "Environment Variables" on page 783.

```
~f [message-list]
```
> Forward the specified message or the current message being read. Valid only when sending a message while reading mail. The messages are inserted into the message without alteration (as opposed to ~m escape).

~F [*message-list*]

> Forward the specified message or the current message being read, including all header fields. Override the suppression of fields by the ignore command.

~h

> Prompt for Subject line and To, Cc, and Bcc lists. If the field is displayed with an initial value, you can edit it as if you had just typed it.

~i *variable*

> Insert the value of the named *variable* into the text of the message. For example, ~A is equivalent to ~i Sign. Environment variables set and exported in the shell are also accessible with ~i.

~m [*message-list*]

> Insert the listed messages or the current message being read into the letter. Valid only when sending a message while reading mail. Shift the text of the message to the right and insert the string contained in the indentprefix variable as the leftmost characters of each line. If indentprefix is not set, insert a Tab character into each line.

~M [*message-list*]

> Insert the listed messages or the current message being read, including the header fields, into the letter. Valid only when sending a message while reading mail. Shift the text of the message to the right and insert the string contained in the indentprefix variable as the leftmost characters of each line. If indentprefix is not set, insert a Tab character into each line. Override the suppression of fields by the ignore command.

~p

> Print the message being entered.

~q

> Quit from input mode by simulating an interrupt. If the body of the message is not null, save the partial message in deadletter. See DEAD in "Environment Variables" on page 783 for a description of this file.

~R

> Mark message for return receipt.

~r *file* ~< *file* ~< ! *shell-command*

> Read in the specified file. If the argument begins with an exclamation point (!), take the rest of the string as an arbitrary shell command and execute it with the standard output inserted into the message.

~s *string...*

> Set the subject line to string.

~t *name...*   Add the given names to the To list.

~v   Invoke a preferred screen editor on the partial message. The
            default visual editor is vi(1). See also VISUAL in "Environment
            Variables" on page 783.

~w *file*   Write the message, without the header, into the specified file.

~x   Exit as with ~q, except do not save the message in deadletter.

~| *shell-command*

            Pipe the body of the message through the given *shell-command*. If
            the *shell-command* returns a successful exit status, replace the
            message with the output of the command.

Internal Variables

The following variables are internal variables. You can import them from the
execution environment or set them by using the set command at any time. You
can use the unset command to erase variables.

> **Note** — You cannot unset internal variables that are imported from
> the execution environment.

allnet   Treat all network names whose last component (login name) match
            as identical. The *message-list* message specifications behave
            similarly. Disabled by default. See also the alternates command
            and the metoo variable.

alwaysignore

            Ignore header fields with ignore everywhere, not just during print
            or type. Affects the save, Save, copy, Copy, top, pipe, and write
            commands and the ~m and ~f tilde escapes. Enabled by default.

append   On termination, append messages to the end of the mbox file instead
            of prepending them. Although disabled by default, append is set in
            the system startup file (which you can suppress with the -n
            command-line option).

appenddeadletter

            Append to the deadletter file instead of overwriting it. Although
            disabled by default, appenddeadletter is frequently set in the
            system startup file. See "Starting Mail" on page 766.

askbcc   Prompt for the Bcc list after you enter the Subject if it is not
            specified on the command line with the -b option. Disabled by
            default.

askcc   Prompt for the Cc list after you enter the Subject if it is not specified
            on the command line with the -c option. Disabled by default.

asksub   Prompt for Subject if it is not specified on the command line with the
            -s option. Enabled by default.

autoinc
Automatically incorporate new messages into the current session as they arrive. This variable has an effect similar to issuing the inc command every time the command prompt is displayed. Disabled by default, but autoinc is set in the default system startup file for mailx; it is not set for /usr/ucb/mail or /usr/ucb/Mail.

autoprint
Enable automatic printing of messages after delete and undelete commands. Disabled by default.

bang
Enable the special casing of exclamation points (!) in shell escape command lines as in vi(1). Disabled by default.

bsdcompat
Set automatically if mailx is invoked as mail or Mail. Use /etc/mail/Mail.rc as the system startup file. Change the default pager to more(1).

cmd=*shell-command*

Set the default command for the pipe command. No default value.

conv=*conversion*

Convert uucp addresses to the specified address style, which can be either of the following values:

internet: Require a mail delivery program conforming to the RFC822 standard for electronic mail addressing.

optimize: Remove loops in uucp(1C) address paths (typically generated by the reply command). Perform no rerouting; mail has no knowledge of UUCP routes or connections.

Conversion is disabled by default. See also sendmail(1M) and the -U command-line option.

crt[=*number*]

Pipe messages having more than *number* lines through the command specified by the value of the PAGER variable (pg(1) or more(1) by default). If you do not specify *number*, use the current window size. Disabled by default.

debug
Enable verbose diagnostics for debugging. Do not deliver messages. Disabled by default.

dot
Take a period on a line by itself, or EOF during input from a terminal, as end-of-file. Disabled by default, but dot is set in the system startup file (which you can suppress with the -n command line option).

escape=*c*
Substitute *c* for the ~ escape character. Takes effect with next message sent.

flipr
Reverse the effect of the followup/Followup and reply/Reply command pairs. If both flipr and replyall are set, the effect is as if neither was set.

`folder=directory`

> The directory for saving standard mail files. Expand user-specified file names beginning with a plus (+) by preceding the file name with this directory name to obtain the real file name. If `directory` does not start with a slash (/), prepend `$HOME` to it. There is no default for the `folder` variable. See also `outfolder`.

`header`   Enable printing of the header summary when entering `mailx`. Enabled by default.

`hold`   Preserve all messages that are read in the mailbox instead of putting them in the standard `mbox` save file. Disabled by default.

`ignore`   Ignore interrupts while entering messages. Handy for noisy dial-up lines. Disabled by default.

`ignoreeof` Ignore end-of-file during message input. Input must be terminated by a period (.) on a line by itself or by the ~ . command. See also `dot` above. Disabled by default.

`indentprefix=string`

> Use `string` to mark indented lines from messages included with ~m. The default is a Tab character.

`iprompt=string`

> Display the specified prompt string before each line on input when sending a message.

`keep`   When the mailbox is empty, truncate it to 0 length instead of removing it. Disabled by default.

`keepsave`   Keep messages that have been saved in other files in the mailbox instead of deleting them. Disabled by default.

`makeremote` When replying to all recipients of a message, if an address does not include a machine name, assume it to be relative to the sender of the message. Normally not needed when dealing with hosts that support RFC822.

`metoo`   If your login appears as a recipient, do not delete it from the list. Disabled by default.

`mustbang`   Force all mail addresses to be in bang format.

`onehop`   Disable alteration of the recipients' addresses, improving efficiency in a network where all machines can send directly to all other machines (that is, those that are one hop away). When responding to a message that was originally sent to several recipients, the other recipient addresses are normally forced to be relative to the originating author's machine for the response. Disabled by default.

`outfolder` Locate the files used to record outgoing messages in the directory specified by the `folder` variable unless the path name is absolute. Disabled by default. See `folder` and the `Save`, `Copy`, `followup`, and `Followup` commands.

page   Used with the `pipe` command to insert a formfeed after each message
                sent through the pipe. Disabled by default.

pipeignore   Omit ignored header when outputting to the `pipe` command.
                Although disabled by default, `pipeignore` is frequently set in the
                system startup file. See "Starting Mail" on page 766.

postmark   Include your real name in the `From` line of messages you send. By
                default this value is derived from the comment field in your
                `passwd`(4) file entry.

prompt=*string*

                Set the command mode prompt to *string*. Default is `?` unless the
                `bsdcompat` variable is set; then, the default is `&`.

quiet   Refrain from printing the opening message and version when
                entering `mailx`. Disabled by default.

record=*file*   Record all outgoing mail in *file*. Disabled by default. See also
                `outfolder`. Note that `mailx` does not lock your record file. So, if you
                use a record file and send two or more messages simultaneously, lines
                from the messages may be interleaved in the record file.

replyall   Reverse the effect of the `reply` and `Reply` and `followup` and
                `Followup` commands. Although set by default, `replyall` is
                frequently unset in the system startup file. See `flipr` and "Starting
                Mail" on page 766.

save   Enable saving of messages in `deadletter` on interrupt or delivery
                error. See DEAD in "Environment Variables" on page 783 for a
                description of this file. Enabled by default.

screen=*number*

                Set the number of lines in a full screen of headers for the headers
                command. *number* must be a positive number. The default is set
                according to baud rate or window size. With a baud rate less than
                1200, *number* defaults to 5; if baud rate is exactly 1200, it defaults to
                10. If you are in a window, *number* defaults to the default window size
                minus 4. Otherwise, the default is 20.

sendmail=*shell-command*

                Alternate command for delivering messages. Note that, in addition to
                the expected list of recipients, `mail` also passes the `-i` and `-m` options
                to the command. Because these options are not appropriate to other
                commands, you may have to use a shell script that strips them from
                the arguments list before invoking the desired command. Default is
                `/usr/bin/rmail`.

sendwait   Wait for background mailer to finish before returning. Disabled by
                default.

showname   Show the sender's real name (if known) in the message header
                instead of the mail address. Disabled by default, but `showname` is set
                in the `/etc/mail/mailx.rc` system startup file for `mailx`.

showto   When displaying the header summary and the message is from you, print the recipient's name instead of the author's name.

sign=*string* Insert the variable into the text of a message when the ~a (autograph) command is used. No default (see also ~i in "Tilde Escapes" on page 777).

Sign=*string* Insert the variable into the text of a message when the ~A command is used. No default (see also ~i in "Tilde Escapes" on page 777).

toplines=*number*

      Set the number of lines of header to print with the top command. Default is 5.

verbose   Invoke sendmail(1M) with the –v flag.

translate   Use the translate program to translate mail addresses. The program receives mail addresses as arguments. It produces, on the standard output, lines containing the following data, in this order:

- The postmark for the sender (see the postmark variable).

- Translated mail addresses, one per line, corresponding to the program's arguments. Each translated address replaces the corresponding address in the mail message being sent.

- A line containing only y or n. If the line contains y, you are asked to confirm that the message should be sent.

      The translate program is invoked for each mail message to be sent. If the program exits with a non-zero exit status or fails to produce enough output, the message is not sent.

Usage

See largefile(5) for the description of the behavior of mailx when encountering files greater than or equal to 2 Gbytes (2**31 bytes).

Environment Variables

See environ(5) for descriptions of the following environment variables that affect the execution of mailx: HOME, LANG, LC_CTYPE, LC_TIME, LC_MESSAGES, NLSPATH, and TERM.

DEAD   The name of the file used to save partial letters in case of untimely interrupt. Default is $HOME/dead.letter.

EDITOR   The command to run when the edit or ~e command is used. Default is ed(1).

LISTER   The command (and options) to use when listing the contents of the folder directory. The default is ls(1).

MAIL   The name of the initial mailbox file to read (in lieu of the standard system mailbox).The default is /var/mail/*username*.

MAILRC   The name of the startup file. Default is $HOME/.mailrc.

MAILX_HEAD Include the specified string at the beginning of the body of each message that is sent.

MAILX_TAIL Include the specified string at the end of the body of each message that is sent.

MBOX The name of the file in which to save messages that have been read. The exit command overrides this function, as does saving the message explicitly in another file. Default is $HOME/mbox.

PAGER The command to use as a filter for paginating output. You can also use this variable to specify the options to be used. Default is pg(1), or if the bsdcompat variable is set, the default is more(1). See "Internal Variables" on page 779.

SHELL The name of a preferred command interpreter. Default is sh(1).

VISUAL The name of a preferred screen editor. Default is vi(1).

Exit Status

When you specify the -e option, the following exit values are returned:

0 Mail was found.

>0 Mail was not found or an error occurred.

Otherwise, the following exit values are returned:

0 Successful completion. Note that this status implies that all messages were sent, but it gives no assurances that any of them were actually delivered.

>0 An error occurred.

Files

$HOME/.mailrc
  Personal startup file.

$HOME/mbox Secondary storage file.

$HOME/.Maillock
  Lock file to prevent multiple writers of system mailbox.

/etc/mail/mailx.rc
  Optional system startup file for mailx only.

/etc/mail/Mail.rc
  BSD compatibility systemwide startup file for /usr/ucb/mail and /usr/ucb/Mail.

/tmp/R[emqsx]*
  Temporary files.

```
/usr/share/lib/mailx/mailx.help*
```
         Help message files.

`/var/mail/*` Post office directory.

Attributes

See `attributes(5)` for descriptions of the following attributes:

Attribute Type	Attribute Value
Availability	SUNWcsu

See Also

```
echo(1), ed(1), ex(1), fmt(1), lp(1), ls(1), mail(1), mailcompat(1),
more(1), newaliases(1), pg(1), sh(1), vacation(1), vi(1), biff(1B),
uucp(1C),sendmail(1M),aliases(4),passwd(4),attributes(5),environ(5),
largefile(5), standards(5)
```

.

make — Maintain, Update, and Regenerate Related Programs and Files

Synopsis

```
/usr/ccs/bin/make [-d][-dd][-D][-DD][-e][-i][-k][-n][-p][-P][-q]
    [-r][-s][-S][-t][-V][-f makefile]...[-K statefile]...
    [target][macro=value]
/usr/xpg4/bin/make [-d][-dd][-D][-DD][-e][-i][-k][-n][-p][-P][-q]
    [-r][-s][-S][-t][-V][-f makefile]...[target][macro=value]
```

Description

Use the `make` command to reduce the compilation time for large projects. You use a `makefile` to specify a list of dependencies between source files and the target application. The `make` command uses `makefile` to determine the minimum recompilation needed to rebuild the application. `make` uses file-system modification dates to determine which files are newer than their dependents. Then, `make` rebuilds the modules and reconstructs the application.

The `make` command executes a list of shell commands associated with each `target`, typically to create or update a file of the same name. `makefile` contains entries that describe how to bring a `target` up-to-date with its dependencies. Because each dependency is a `target`, it can have dependencies of its own. Targets, dependencies, and subdependencies constitute a tree structure that `make` traces when deciding whether or not to rebuild a `target`.

The make command recursively checks each *target* against its dependencies, beginning with the first target entry in *makefile* if you supply no *target* argument on the command line. If, after processing all of its dependencies, a target file is either missing or older than any of its dependencies, make rebuilds it. Optionally, with this version of make, you can treat a *target* as out-of-date when the commands used to generate it have changed since the last time the target was built.

To build a given target, make executes the list of commands, called a rule. You can list this rule explicitly in the target's *makefile* entry, or it can be supplied implicitly by make.

If you specify no *target* on the command line, make uses the first target defined in *makefile*.

If a target has no *makefile* entry or if its entry has no rule, make tries to derive a rule by each of the following methods, in turn, until a suitable rule is found. Each method is described under "Reading Makefiles and the Environment" on page 788.

1. Pattern matching rules.

2. Implicit rules read in from a user-supplied *makefile*.

3. Standard implicit rules (also known as suffix rules), typically read in from the file /usr/share/lib/make/make.rules.

4. SCCS retrieval. make retrieves the most recent version from the SCCS history file (if any). See the description of the .SCCS_GET: special-function target for details.

5. The rule from the .DEFAULT: target entry, if there is such an entry in the *makefile*.

6. If the target has no *makefile* entry for a target, if no rule can be derived for building it, and if no file by that name is present, make issues an error message and halts.

Options

-d	Display the reasons why make chooses to rebuild a target. Display any and all dependencies that are newer. In addition, display options read in from the MAKEFLAGS environment variable.
-dd	Display the dependency check and processing in vast detail.
-D	Display the text of the makefiles read in.
-DD	Display the text of the makefiles, make.rulesfile, the state file, and all hidden dependency reports.
-e	Specify that environment variables override assignments within makefiles.

-f *makefile*

> Use the description file *makefile*. A - as the *makefile* argument denotes the standard input. The contents of *makefile*, when it is present, override the standard set of implicit rules and predefined macros. When you specify more than one -f *makefile* argument pair, use the concatenation of those files in order of appearance.
>
> When you specify no *makefile*, /usr/ccs/bin/make tries the following in sequence, except when in POSIX mode (see the "Special-Function Targets" on page 792).
>
> - If there is a file named *makefile* in the working directory, use that file. If an SCCS history file (SCCS/s.makefile) is newer, try to retrieve and use the most recent version.
>
> - In the absence of the above file(s), if a file named Makefile is present in the working directory, try to use it. If an SCCS history file (SCCS/s.Makefile) is newer, try to retrieve and use the most recent version.
>
> When you specify no *makefile*, /usr/ccs/bin/make in POSIX mode and /usr/xpg4/bin/make try the following files in sequence:
>
> - ./makefile, ./Makefiles
>
> - .makefile, SCCS/s.makefile
>
> - s.Makefile, SCCS/s.Makefile

-i

> Ignore error codes returned by commands. Equivalent to the special-function target .IGNORE:.

-k

> When a non-zero error status is returned by a rule or when make cannot find a rule, abandon work on the current target but continue with other dependency branches that do not depend on it.

-K *statefile*

> Use the state file *statefile*. A dash (-) as the *statefile* argument denotes the standard input. The contents of *statefile*, when present, override the standard set of implicit rules and predefined macros. When you specify more than one -K *statefile* argument pair, use the concatenation of those files, in order of appearance. (See also .KEEP_STATE and .KEEP_STATE_FILE in "Special-Function Targets" on page 792).

-n

> Print commands but do not execute them. Print lines beginning with an @. However, if a command line contains a reference to the $(MAKE) macro, always execute that line (see the discussion of MAKEFLAGS in "Reading Makefiles and the Environment" on page 788). When in POSIX mode, execute lines beginning with a plus (+).

-p

> Print the complete set of macro definitions and target descriptions.

-P

> Merely report dependencies instead of building them.

`-q`	Return a 0 or non-zero status code depending on whether the target file is up-to-date. When in POSIX mode, execute lines beginning with a plus (+).
`-r`	Do not read the default makefile `/usr/share/lib/make/make.rules`.
`-s`	Do not print command lines before executing them. Equivalent to the special function target `.SILENT:`.
`-S`	Undo the effect of the `-k` option. Stop processing when a command returns a non-zero exit status.
`-t`	Touch the target files (bringing them up-to-date) instead of performing their rules. This option can be dangerous when files are maintained by more than one person. When the `.KEEP_STATE:` target appears in the *makefile*, update the state file just as if the rules had been performed. When in POSIX mode, execute lines beginning with a plus (+).
`-V`	Put make into SysV mode. Refer to `sysVmake(1)` for details.

Operands

target   Target names.

macro=value

Macro definition. This definition overrides any regular definition for the specified macro within the *makefile* itself or in the environment. However, you can still override this definition with conditional macro assignments.

Usage

Refer to make in *Programming Utilities Guide* for tutorial information.

Reading Makefiles and the Environment

When make first starts, it reads the MAKEFLAGS environment variable to obtain any of the following options specified present in its value: -d, -D, -e, -i, -k, -n, -p, -q, -r, -s, -S, or -t. Because of the implementation of POSIX.2 (see POSIX.2(5), the MAKEFLAGS values contain a leading - character. The make command then reads the command line for additional options, which also take effect.

Next, make reads in a default makefile that typically contains predefined macro definitions, target entries for implicit rules, and additional rules such as the rule for retrieving SCCS files. If present, make uses the file make.rules in the current directory; otherwise it reads the file /usr/share/lib/make/make.rules, which contains the standard definitions and rules. Use the following directive in your local make.rules file to include them.

```
include /usr/share/lib/make/make.rules
```

Next, make imports variables from the environment (unless you specify the -e option), and treats them as defined macros. Because make uses the most recent definition it encounters, a macro definition in the makefile normally overrides an environment variable of the same name. When you specify -e, however, environment variables are read in after all makefiles have been read. In that case, the environment variables take precedence over definitions in the makefile.

Next, make reads any makefiles you specify with -f or one of makefile or Makefile, as described above, and then the state file in the local directory if it exists. If the makefile contains a .KEEP_STATE_FILE: target, then make reads the state file that follows the target. Refer to special target .KEEP_STATE_FILE: for details.

Next, (after reading the environment if you specify -e), make reads in any macro definitions supplied as command-line arguments. These macro definitions override macro definitions both in the makefile and the environment, but only for the make command itself.

make exports environment variables, using the most recently defined value. Macro definitions supplied on the command line are not normally exported unless the macro is also an environment variable.

make does not export macros defined in the makefile. If an environment variable is set and you define a macro with the same name on the command line, make exports its value as defined on the command line. Unless you specify -e, macro definitions within the makefile take precedence over those imported from the environment.

The macros MAKEFLAGS, MAKE, SHELL, HOST_ARCH, HOST_MACH, and TARGET_MACH are special cases. See "Special-Purpose Macros" on page 795 for details.

Makefile Target Entries

A target entry has the following format:

target... [:|::] [*dependency*]... [; *command*]... [*command*]

The first line contains the name of a target or a space-separated list of target names terminated with a colon or double colon. A list of targets is equivalent to having a separate entry of the same form for each target. The colon(s) can be followed by a dependency or a dependency list. make checks this list before building the target. You can terminate the dependency list with a semicolon (;), which in turn can be followed by a single Bourne shell command. Subsequent lines in the target entry begin with a Tab and contain Bourne shell commands. These commands constitute the rule for building the target.

You can continue shell commands across input lines by escaping the newline with a backslash (\). The continuing line must also start with a Tab.

To rebuild a target, make expands macros, strips off initial Tab characters, and either executes the command directly (if it contains no shell metacharacters) or passes each command line to a Bourne shell for execution.

The first line that does not begin with a Tab or # begins another target or macro definition.

Special Characters

This section lists global special characters and targets and dependencies.

Global

Start a comment. The comment ends at the next newline. If the # follows the Tab in a command line, pass that line to the shell (which also treats # as the start of a comment).

include *filename*

           If the word include appears as the first seven letters of a line and is followed by a space or Tab, take the string that follows as a file name to interpolate at that line. You can nest include files to a depth of no more than about 16. If *filename* is a macro reference, expand it.

Targets and Dependencies

:   Target list terminator. Add words following the colon to the dependency list for the target or targets. If you name a target in more than one colon-terminated target entry, add the dependencies for all its entries to form that target's complete dependency list.

::   Target terminator for alternate dependencies. When used in place of a :, the double colon enables a target to check and update from alternate dependency lists. When the target is out-of-date with dependencies listed in the first alternate, build it according to the rule for that entry. When out-of-date with dependencies in another alternate, build it according to the rule in that other entry. Implicit rules do not apply to double-colon targets; you must supply a rule for each entry. If you specify no dependencies, the rule is always performed.

target [+ *target*...] :

           Use the rule in the target entry to build all the indicated targets as a group. It is normally performed only once per make run but is checked for command dependencies every time a target in the group is encountered in the dependency scan.

%   Match any string of zero or more characters in a target name or dependency, in the target portion of a conditional macro definition or within a pattern-replacement macro reference. (Like the * shell wild-card.) Note that a target, dependency name, or pattern-replacement macro reference can have only one %.

./pathname Ignore the leading . / characters from targets with names given as path names relative to dot (the working directory).

Macros

=	Macro definition. The word to the left of this character is the macro name; words to the right constitute its value. Strip leading and trailing white space characters from the value. A word break following the = is implied.
$	Macro reference. Interpret the following character or the parenthesized or bracketed string as a macro reference. Expand the reference (including the $) by replacing it with the macro's value.
( ) { }	Macro-reference name delimiters. Take a parenthesized or bracketed word appended to a $ as the name of the macro being referred to. Without the delimiters, make recognizes only the first character as the macro name.
$$	A reference to the dollar sign macro, the value of which is the character $. Used to pass variable expressions beginning with $ to the shell, to refer to environment variables that are expanded by the shell, or to delay processing of dynamic macros within the dependency list of a target until that target is actually processed.
\$	Escaped dollar sign character. Interpreted as a literal dollar sign within a rule.
+=	When used in place of =, append a string to a macro definition (must be surrounded by white space, unlike =).
:=	Conditional macro assignment. When preceded by a list of targets with explicit target entries, the macro definition that follows takes effect when processing only those targets and their dependencies.
:sh =	Define the value of a macro to be the output of a command (see "Command Substitutions" on page 810).
:sh	In a macro reference, execute the command stored in the macro and replace the reference with the output of that command (see "Command Substitutions" on page 810).

Rules

+	Always execute the commands preceded by a plus (+), even when you specify -n.
–	Ignore any non-zero error code returned by a command line for which the first non-Tab character is a dash (–). This character is not passed to the shell as part of the command line. make normally terminates when a command returns non-zero status unless you specify the -i or -k options or the .IGNORE: special-function target.
@	If the first non-Tab character is an @, do not print the command line before executing it. This character is not passed to the shell.

? Escape command-dependency checking. Do not subject command lines starting with this character to command-dependency checking.

! Force command dependency checking. Apply command dependency checking to command lines for which it would otherwise be suppressed. This checking is normally suppressed for lines that contain references to the ? dynamic macro (for example, $?).

When any combinations of +, -, @, ?, or ! are the first characters after the Tab, all that are present apply. None are passed to the shell.

Special-Function Targets

When incorporated in a makefile, the following target names perform special functions.

.DEFAULT: If it has an entry in the makefile, use the rule for this target to process a target when there is no other entry for it, no rule for building it, and no SCCS history file from which to retrieve a current version. make ignores any dependencies for this target.

.DONE: If defined in the makefile, process this target and its dependencies after all other targets are built. This target is also performed when make halts with an error unless the .FAILED: target is defined.

.FAILED: Perform this target along with its dependencies instead of .DONE: when defined in the makefile and halt with an error.

.GET_POSIX: Retrieve the current version of an SCCS file from its history file in the current working directory. Use this rule when running in POSIX mode.

.IGNORE: Ignore errors. When this target appears in the makefile, ignore non-zero error codes returned from commands. When used in POSIX mode, .IGNORE: can be followed only by target names, for which the errors are ignored.

.INIT: If defined in the makefile, build this target and its dependencies before processing any other targets.

.KEEP_STATE:

This target has no effect if used in POSIX mode. If this target is in effect, update the .make.state state file in the current directory. Also activate command dependencies and hidden dependency checks. If either the .KEEP_STATE: target is in the makefile or the environment variable KEEP_STATE is set ("setenv KEEP_STATE"), rebuild everything to collect dependency information even if all the targets were up-to-date because of previous make runs. See also "Environment Variables" on page 811.

.KEEP_STATE_FILE:

> This target has no effect if used in POSIX mode. This target implies .KEEP_STATE:. If the target is followed by a file name, use it as the state file. If the target is followed by a directory name, look for a .make.state file in that directory. If the target is not followed by any name, look for a .make.state file in the current working directory.

.MAKE_VERSION:

> A target-entry of the form
>
> .MAKE_VERSION: VERSION-*number*
>
> enables version checking. If the version of make differs from the version indicated, make issues a warning message.

.NO_PARALLEL:

> Reserved for future use.

.PARALLEL: Reserved for future use.

.POSIX: Enable POSIX mode.

.PRECIOUS: Specify a list of files not to delete. Do not remove any of the files listed as dependencies for this target when interrupted. make normally removes the current target when it receives an interrupt. When used in POSIX mode, if the target is not followed by a list of files, assume all the files are precious.

.SCCS_GET: Contain the rule for retrieving the current version of an SCCS file from its history file. To suppress automatic retrieval, add an entry for this target with an empty rule to your makefile.

.SCCS_GET_POSIX:

> Contain the rule for retrieving the current version of an SCCS file from its history file. make uses this rule when it is running in POSIX mode.

.SILENT: Run silently. Do not echo commands before executing them. When used in POSIX mode, it could be followed by target names, and only those are executed silently.

.SUFFIXES: Specify the suffixes list for selecting implicit rules.

.WAIT: Reserved for future use.

Clearing Special Targets

In this version of make, you can clear the definition of the following special targets by supplying entries for them with no dependencies and no rule. .DEFAULT:, .SCCS_GET:, and .SUFFIXES:.

Command Dependencies

When the .KEEP_STATE: target is in effect, make checks the command for building a target against the state file. If the command has changed since the last make run, make rebuilds the target.

Hidden Dependencies

When the .KEEP_STATE: target is in effect, make reads reports from cpp(1) and other compilation processors for any "hidden" files, such as #include files. If the target is out-of-date with any of these files, make rebuilds it.

Macros

Entries of the following form define macros.

```
macro=value
```

macro is the name of the macro and *value*, which consists of all characters up to a comment character or unescaped newline, is the value. make strips both leading and trailing white space in accepting the value.

Subsequent references to the macro, of the forms $(name) or ${name} are replaced by *value*. You can omit the parentheses or brackets in a reference to a macro with a single-character name.

Macro references can contain references to other macros, in which case nested references are expanded first.

Suffix Replacement Macro References

Substitutions within macros can be made as follows,

```
$(name:string1=string2)
```

where *string1* is either a suffix or a word to be replaced in the macro definition, and *string2* is the replacement suffix or word. Words in a macro value are separated by space, Tab, and escaped newline characters.

Pattern Replacement Macro References

Pattern-matching replacements can also be applied to macros, with a reference of the following form,

```
$(name: op%os= np%ns)
```

where *op* is the existing (old) prefix and *os* is the existing (old) suffix, *np* and *ns* are the new prefix and new suffix, and the pattern matched by % (a string of zero or more characters) is carried forward from the value being replaced. For example, the following statements set the value of DEBUG to tmp/fabricate-g.

```
PROGRAM=fabricate
DEBUG= $(PROGRAM:%=tmp/%-g)
```

> **Note** — You cannot use pattern replacement macro references in the dependency list of a pattern-matching rule; the % characters are not evaluated independently. Also, any number of % metacharacters can appear after the equal sign.

Appending to a Macro

You can append words to macro values as shown below.

macro += word...

Special-Purpose Macros

When the MAKEFLAGS variable is present in the environment, make takes options from it in combination with options entered on the command line. make retains this combined value as the MAKEFLAGS macro and exports it automatically to each command or shell it invokes.

Flags passed by way of MAKEFLAGS are only displayed when you use the -d or -dd options.

The MAKE macro is another special case. It has the value make by default and temporarily overrides the -n option for any line in which it is referred to. The following syntax enables you to write nested invocations of make to run recursively with the -n flag in effect for all commands but make.

$(MAKE)...

You can use make -n to test an entire hierarchy of makefiles.

For compatibility with the 4.2 BSD make, the MFLAGS macro is set from the MAKEFLAGS variable by prepending a -. MFLAGS is not automatically exported.

The SHELL macro, when set to a single-word value such as /usr/bin/csh, indicates the name of an alternate shell to use. The default is /bin/sh. Note that make executes commands that contain no shell metacharacters. Built-in commands, such as dirs in the C shell, are not recognized unless the command line includes a metacharacter (for instance, a semicolon). This macro is neither imported from, nor exported to, the environment, regardless of -e. To be sure it is set properly, you must define this macro within every makefile that requires it.

The following macros are provided for use with cross-compilation.

HOST_ARCH   The machine architecture of the host system. By default, the output of the arch(1) command prepended with -. In normal circumstances, you should never alter this value.

HOST_MACH   The machine architecture of the host system. By default, the output of the mach(1), prepended with -. In normal circumstances, you should never alter this value.

TARGET_ARCH
            The machine architecture of the target system. By default, the output of mach, prepended with -.

Dynamic Macros

Several dynamically maintained macros are useful as abbreviations within rules. They are shown here as references. If you define them, make simply overrides the definition.

`$*`	The basename of the current target, derived as if selected for use with an implicit rule.
`$<`	The name of a dependency file, derived as if selected for use with an implicit rule.
`$@`	The name of the current target. This macro is the only one whose value is strictly determined when used in a dependency list (in which case, it takes the form `$$@`).
`$?`	The list of dependencies that are newer than the target. Command dependency checking is automatically suppressed for lines that contain this macro just as if you had prefixed the command with a `?`. See the description of `?`. You can force this check with the `!` command-line prefix.
`$%`	The name of the library member being processed. (See "Library Maintenance" on page 809.)

To refer to the `$@` dynamic macro within a dependency list, precede the reference with an additional `$` character (as in, `$$@`). Because make assigns `$<` and `$*` as it would for implicit rules (according to the suffixes list and the directory contents), they may be unreliable when used within explicit target entries.

You can modify these macros to apply either to the file-name part (`F`) or the directory part (`D`) of the strings they stand for, by adding an uppercase `F` or `D` and enclosing the resulting name in parentheses or braces. Thus, `$(@D)` refers to the directory part of the string `$@`; if there is no directory part, `.` is assigned. `$(@F)` refers to the file-name part.

Conditional Macro Definitions

A macro definition of the following form indicates that when processing any of the targets listed and their dependencies, *macro* is to be set to the value supplied.

```
target-list := macro = value
```

> **Note** — If a conditional macro is referred to in a dependency list, the `$` must be delayed (use `$$` instead). Also, *target-list* can contain a `%` pattern, in which case the macro is conditionally defined for all targets encountered that match the pattern. You can use a pattern replacement reference within the value.

You can temporarily append to a macro's value with a conditional definition of the following form.

```
target-list := macro += value
```

Predefined Macros

make supplies the macros shown in the following table for compilers and their options, host architectures, and other commands. Unless these macros are read in as environment variables, their values are not exported by make. If you run make with any of these macros set in the environment, it is a good idea to add commentary to the makefile to indicate what value each is expected to take. If you use the -r option, make does not read the default makefile (./make.rules or /usr/share/lib/make/make.rules) in which these macro definitions are supplied.

The following table lists the predefined macros and shows their default values.

Table of Predefined Macros

Use	Macro	Default Value
Library archives	AR ARFLAGS	ar rv
Assembler commands	AS ASFLAGS COMPILE.s COMPILE.S	as $(AS) $(ASFLAGS) $(CC) $(ASFLAGS) $(CPPFLAGS) -c
C compiler commands	CC CFLAGS CPPFLAGS COMPILE.c LINK.c	cc $(CC) $(CFLAGS) $(CPPFLAGS) -c $(CC) $(CFLAGS) $(CPPFLAGS) $(LDFLAGS)
C++ compiler commands	CCC CCFLAGS CPPFLAGS COMPILE.cc LINK.cc COMPILE.C LINK.C	CC CFLAGS $(CCC) $(CCFLAGS) $(CPPFLAGS) -c $(CCC) $(CCFLAGS) $(CPPFLAGS) $(LDFLAGS) $(CCC) $(CCFLAGS) $(CPPFLAGS) -c $(CCC) $(CCFLAGS) $(CPPFLAGS) $(LDFLAGS)
FORTRAN 77 compiler commands	FC FFLAGS COMPILE.f LINK.f COMPILE.F LINK.F	f77 $(FC) $(FFLAGS) -c $(FC) $(FFLAGS) $(LDFLAGS) $(FC) $(FFLAGS) $(CPPFLAGS) -c $(FC) $(FFLAGS) $(CPPFLAGS) $(LDFLAGS)

Use	Macro	Default Value
FORTRAN 90 compiler commands	FC F90FLAGS COMPILE.f90 LINK.f90 COMPILE.ftn LINK.ftn	f90 $(F90C) $(F90FLAGS) -c $(F90C) $(F90C) $(F90FLAGS) $(CPPFLAGS) -c $(F90C) $(F90FLAGS) $(CPPFLAGS) $(LDFLAGS)
lex command	LEX LFLAGS LEX.1	lex $(LEX) $(LFLAGS) -t
Link editor command	LD LDFLAGS	ld
lint command	LINT LINTFLAGS LINT.c	lint $(LINT) $(LINTFLAGS) $(CPPFLAGS)
Modula 2 commands	M2C M2FLAGS MODFLAGS DEFFLAGS COMPILE.def COMPILE.mod	m2c $(M2C) $(M2FLAGS) $(DEFFLAGS) $(M2C) $(M2FLAGS) $(MODFLAGS)
Pascal compiler commands	PC PFLAGS COMPILE.p LINK.p	pc $(PC) $(PFLAGS) $(CPPFLAGS) -c $(PC) $(PFLAGS) $(CPPFLAGS) $(LDFLAGS)
Ratfor compilation commands	RFLAGS COMPILE.r LINK.r	 $(FC) $(FFLAGS) $(RFLAGS) -c $(FC) $(FFLAGS) $(RFLAGS) $(LDFLAGS)
rm command	RM	rm -f
sccs command	SCCSFLAGS SCCSGETFLAGS	 -s
yacc command	YACC YFLAGS YACC.y	yacc $(YACC) $(YFLAGS)

Use	Macro	Default Value
Suffixes list	SUFFIXES	.o .c .c~ .cc .cc~ .y .y~ .l .l~ .s .s~ .sh .sh~ .S .S~ .ln .h .h~ ..f .f~ .F .F~ .mod .mod~ .sym .def .def~ .p .p~ .r .r~ .cps .cps~ .C .C~ .Y .Y~ .L .L .f90 .f90~ .ftn .ftn~

Implicit Rules

When a target has no entry in the makefile, make tries to determine its class (if any) and apply the rule for that class. An implicit rule describes how to build any target of a given class from an associated dependency file. The class of a target determines, either by a pattern or by a suffix, the corresponding dependency file (with the same basename) from which such a target might be built. In addition to a predefined set of implicit rules, make enables you to define your own rules, either by pattern or by suffix.

Pattern-Matching Rules

A target entry of the following form is a pattern-matching rule in which *tp* is a target prefix, *ts* is a target suffix, *dp* is a dependency prefix, and *ds* is a dependency suffix (any of which can be null).

```
tp%ts: dp%ds    rule
```

The % stands for a basename of zero or more characters that is matched in the target and is used to construct the name of a dependency. When make encounters a match in its search for an implicit rule, it uses the rule in that target entry to build the target from the dependency file. Pattern-matching implicit rules typically make use of the $@ and $< dynamic macros as placeholders for the target and dependency names. Other, regular dependencies can occur in the dependency list; however, none of the regular dependencies can contain %. An entry of the following form is a valid pattern-matching rule.

```
tp%ts: [dependency...] dp%ds [dependency...] rule
```

Suffix Rules

When no pattern-matching rule applies, make checks the target name to see if it ends with a suffix in the known suffixes list. If so, make checks for any suffix rules, as well as a dependency file with same root and another recognized suffix, from which to build it.

The target entry for a suffix rule takes the following form:

```
DsTs: rule
```

where *Ds* is the suffix of the dependency file, *Ts* is the suffix of the target, and *rule* is the rule for building a target in the class. Both *Ds* and *Ts* must appear in the suffixes list. (A suffix need not begin with a . to be recognized.)

A suffix rule with only one suffix describes how to build a target having a null (or no) suffix from a dependency file with the indicated suffix. For instance, you could use the .c rule to build an executable program named *file* from a C source file named *file*.c. If a target with a null suffix has an explicit dependency, make omits the search for a suffix rule.

The following table lists the standard implicit (suffix) rules.

Use	**Implicit Rule Name**	**Command Line**
Assembly files	.s.o	$(COMPILE.s) -o $@ $<
	.s.a	$(COMPILE.s) -o $% $<
		$(AR) $(ARFLAGS) $@ $%
		$(RM) $%
	.s~.o	$(-s1GET) $(-s1GFLAGS) -p $< > $*.s
		$(-s1COMPILE.s) -o $@ $*.s
	.S.o	$(COMPILE.S) -o $@ $<
	.S.a	$(COMPILE.S) -o $% $<
		$(AR) $(ARFLAGS) $@ $%
		$(RM) $%
	.S~.o	$(GET) $(GFLAGS) -p $< > $*.S
		$(COMPILE.S) -o $@ $*.S
	.S~.a	$(GET) $(GFLAGS) -p $< > $*.S
		$(COMPILE.S) -o $% $*.S
		$(AR) $(ARFLAGS) $@ $%
		$(RM) $%
C files	.c	$(LINK.c) -o $@ $< $(LDLIBS)
	.c.ln	$(LINT.c) $(OUTPUT_OPTION) -i $<
	.c.o	$(COMPILE.c) $(OUTPUT_OPTION) $<
	.c.a	$(COMPILE.c) -o $% $<
		$(AR) $(ARFLAGS) $@ $%
		$(RM) $%

Use	Implicit Rule Name	Command Line
	`..c~`	`$(GET) $(GFLAGS) -p $< > $*.c`
		`$(CC) $(CFLAGS) $(LDFLAGS) -o $@ $*.c`
	`..c~.o`	`$(GET) $(GFLAGS) -p $< > $*.c`
		`$(CC) $(CFLAGS) -c $*.c`
	`..c~.ln`	`$(GET) $(GFLAGS) -p $< > $*.c`
		`$(LINT.c) $(OUTPUT_OPTION) -c $*.c`
	`..c~.a`	`$(GET) $(GFLAGS) -p $< > $*.c`
		`$(COMPILE.c) -o $% $*.c`
		`$(AR) $(ARFLAGS) $@ $%`
		`$(RM) $%`
C++ files	`.cc`	`$(LINK.cc) -o $@ $< $(LDLIBS)`
	`.cc.o`	`$(COMPILE.cc) $(OUTPUT_OPTION) $<`
	`.cc.a`	`$(COMPILE.cc) -o $% $<`
		`$(AR) $(ARFLAGS) $@ $%`
		`$(RM) $%`
	`.cc~`	`$(GET) $(GFLAGS) -p $< > $*.cc`
		`$(LINK.cc) -o $@ $*.cc $(LDLIBS)`
	`.cc.o`	`$(COMPILE.cc) $(OUTPUT_OPTION) $<`
	`.cc~.o`	`$(GET) $(GFLAGS) -p $< > $*.cc`
		`$(COMPILE.cc) $(OUTPUT_OPTION) $*.cc`
	`.cc.a`	`$(COMPILE.cc) -o $% $<`
		`$(AR) $(ARFLAGS) $@ $%`
		`$(RM) $%`
	`.cc~.a`	`$(GET) $(GFLAGS) -p $< > $*.cc`
		`$(COMPILE.cc) -o $% $*.cc`
		`$(AR) $(ARFLAGS) $@ $%`

Use	Implicit Rule Name	Command Line
		`$(RM) $%`
	.C	`$(LINK.C) -o $@ $< $(LDLIBS)`
	.C~	`$(GET) $(GFLAGS) -p $< > $*.C`
		`$(LINK.C) -o $@ $*.C $(LDLIBS)`
	.C.o	`$(COMPILE.C) $(OUTPUT_OPTION) $<`
	.C~.o	`$(GET) $(GFLAGS) -p $< > $*.C`
		`$(COMPILE.C) $(OUTPUT_OPTION) $*.C`
	.C.a	`$(COMPILE.C) -o $% $<`
		`$(AR) $(ARFLAGS) $@ $%`
		`$(RM) $%`
	.C~.a	`$(GET) $(GFLAGS) -p $< > $*.C`
		`$(COMPILE.C) -o $% $*.C`
		`$(AR) $(ARFLAGS) $@ $%`
		`$(RM) $%`
FORTRAN 77 files	.f	`$(LINK.f) -o $@ $< $(LDLIBS)`
	.f.o	`$(COMPILE.f) $(OUTPUT_OPTION) $<`
	.f.a	`$(COMPILE.f) -o $% $<`
		`$(AR) $(ARFLAGS) $@ $%`
		`$(RM) $%`
	.f	`$(LINK.f) -o $@ $< $(LDLIBS)`
	.f~	`$(GET) $(GFLAGS) -p $< > $*.f`
		`$(FC) $(FFLAGS) $(LDFLAGS) -o $@ $*.f`
	.f~.o	`$(GET) $(GFLAGS) -p $< > $*.f`
		`$(FC) $(FFLAGS) -c $*.f`
	.f~.a	`$(GET) $(GFLAGS) -p $< > $*.f`
		`$(COMPILE.f) -o $% $*.f`

Use	Implicit Rule Name	Command Line
		`$(AR) $(ARFLAGS) $@ $%`
		`$(RM) $%`
	.F	`$(LINK.F) -o $@ $< $(LDLIBS)`
	.F.o	`$(COMPILE.F) $(OUTPUT_OPTION) $<`
	.F.a	`$(COMPILE.F) -o $% $<`
		`$(AR) $(ARFLAGS) $@ $%`
		`$(RM) $%`
	.F~	`$(GET) $(GFLAGS) -p $< > $*.F`
		`$(FC) $(FFLAGS) $(LDFLAGS) -o $@ $*.F`
	.F~.o	`$(GET) $(GFLAGS) -p $< > $*.F`
		`$(FC) $(FFLAGS) -c $*.F`
	.F~.a	`$(GET) $(GFLAGS) -p $< > $*.F`
		`$(COMPILE.F) -o $% $*.F`
		`$(AR) $(ARFLAGS) $@ $%`
		`$(RM) $%`
FORTRAN 90 files	.f90	`$(LINK.f90) -o $@ $< $(LDLIBS)`
	.f90~	`$(GET) $(GFLAGS) -p $< > $*.f90`
		`$(LINK.f90) -o $@ $*.f90 $(LDLIBS)`
	.f90.o	`$(COMPILE.f90) $(OUTPUT_OPTION) $<`
	.f90~.o	`$(GET) $(GFLAGS) -p $< > $*.f90`
		`$(COMPILE.f90) $(OUTPUT_OPTION) $*.f90`
	.f90.a	`$(COMPILE.f90) -o $% $<`
		`$(AR) $(ARFLAGS) $@ $%`
		`$(RM) $%`
	.f90~.a	`$(GET) $(GFLAGS) -p $< > $*.f90`
		`$(COMPILE.f90) -o $% $*.f90`

Use	**Implicit Rule Name**	**Command Line**
		`$(AR) $(ARFLAGS) $@ $%`
		`$(RM) $%`
	`.ftn`	`$(LINK.ftn) -o $@ $< $(LDLIBS)`
	`.ftn~`	`$(GET) $(GFLAGS) -p $< > $*.ftn`
		`$(LINK.ftn) -o $@ $*.ftn $(LDLIBS)`
	`.ftn.o`	`$(COMPILE.ftn)$(OUTPUT_OPTION)$<`
	`.ftn~.o`	`$(GET) $(GFLAGS) -p $< > $*.ftn`
		`$(COMPILE.ftn) $(OUTPUT_OPTION) $*.ftn`
	`.ftn.a`	`$(COMPILE.ftn) -o $% $<`
		`$(AR) $(ARFLAGS) $@ $%`
		`$(RM) $%`
	`.ftn~.a`	`$(GET) $(GFLAGS) -p $< > $*.ftn`
		`$(COMPILE.ftn) -o $% $*.ftn`
		`$(AR) $(ARFLAGS) $@ $%`
		`$(RM) $%`
lex files	`.l`	`$(RM) $*.c`
		`$(LEX.l) $< > $*.c`
		`$(LINK.c) -o $@ $*.c $(LDLIBS)`
		`$(RM) $*.c`
	`.l.c`	`$(RM) $@`
		`$(LEX.l) $< > $@`
	`.l.ln`	`$(RM) $*.c`
		`$(LEX.l) $< > $*.c`
		`$(LINT.c) -o $@ -i $*.c`
		`$(RM) $*.c`
	`.l.o`	`$(RM) $*.c`
		`$(LEX.l) $< > $*.c`

Use	Implicit Rule Name	Command Line
		`$(COMPILE.c) -o $@ $*.c`
		`$(RM) $*.c`
	.l~	`$(GET) $(GFLAGS) -p $< > $*.l`
		`$(LEX) $(LFLAGS) $*.l`
		`$(CC) $(CFLAGS) -c lex.yy.c`
		`rm -f lex.yy.c`
		`mv lex.yy.c $@`
	.l~.c	`$(GET) $(GFLAGS) -p $< > $*.l`
		`$(LEX) $(LFLAGS) $*.l`
		`mv lex.yy.c $@`
	.l~.ln	`$(GET) $(GFLAGS) -p $< > $*.l`
		`$(RM) $*.c`
		`$(LEX.l) $*.l > $*.c`
		`$(LINT.c) -o $@ -i $*.c`
		`$(RM) $*.c`
	.l~.o	`$(GET) $(GFLAGS) -p $< > $*.l`
		`$(LEX) $(LFLAGS) $*.l`
		`$(CC) $(CFLAGS) -c lex.yy.c`
		`rm -f lex.yy.c`
		`mv lex.yy.c $@`
Modula 2 files	.mod	`$(COMPILE.mod) -o $@ -e $@ $<`
	.mod.o	`$(COMPILE.mod) -o $@ $<`
	.def.sym	`$(COMPILE.def) -o $@ $<`
	.def~.sym	`$(GET) $(GFLAGS) -p $< > $*.def`
		`$(COMPILE.def) -o $@ $*.def`
	.mod~	`$(GET) $(GFLAGS) -p $< > $*.mod`
		`$(COMPILE.mod) -o $@ -e $@ $*.mod`

Use	Implicit Rule Name	Command Line
	`.mod~.o`	`$(GET) $(GFLAGS) -p $< > $*.mod`
		`$(COMPILE.mod) -o $@ $*.mod`
	`.mod~.a`	`$(GET) $(GFLAGS) -p $< > $*.mod`
		`$(COMPILE.mod) -o $% $*.mod`
		`$(AR) $(ARFLAGS) $@ $%`
		`$(RM) $%`
NeWS files	`.cps.h`	`cps $*.cps`
	`.cps~.h`	`$(GET) $(GFLAGS) -p $< > $*.cps`
		`$(CPS) $(CPSFLAGS) $*.cps`
Pascal files	`.p`	`$(LINK.p) -o $@ $< $(LDLIBS)`
	`.p.o`	`$(COMPILE.p) $(OUTPUT_OPTION) $<`
	`.p~`	`$(GET) $(GFLAGS) -p $< > $*.p`
		`$(LINK.p) -o $@ $*.p $(LDLIBS)`
	`.p~.o`	`$(GET) $(GFLAGS) -p $< > $*.p`
		`$(COMPILE.p)$(OUTPUT_OPTION)$*.p`
	`.p~.a`	`$(GET) $(GFLAGS) -p $< > $*.p`
		`$(COMPILE.p) -o $% $*.p`
		`$(AR) $(ARFLAGS) $@ $%`
		`$(RM) $%`
Ratfor files	`.r`	`$(LINK.r) -o $@ $< $(LDLIBS)`
	`.r.o`	`$(COMPILE.r) $(OUTPUT_OPTION) $<`
	`.r.a`	`$(COMPILE.r) -o $% $<`
		`$(AR) $(ARFLAGS) $@ $%`
		`$(RM) $%`
	`.r~`	`$(GET) $(GFLAGS) -p $< > $*.r`
		`$(LINK.r) -o $@ $*.r $(LDLIBS)`

Use	Implicit Rule Name	Command Line
	`.r~.o`	`$(GET) $(GFLAGS) -p $< > $*.r`
		`$(COMPILE.r)$(OUTPUT_OPTION)$*.r`
	`.r~.a`	`$(GET) $(GFLAGS) -p $< > $*.r`
		`$(COMPILE.r) -o $% $*.r`
		`$(AR) $(ARFLAGS) $@ $%`
		`$(RM) $%`
SCCS files	`.SCCS_GET`	`sccs $(SCCSFLAGS) get $(SCCSGET-FLAGS) $@ -G$@`
	`.SCCS_GET_POSIX`	`sccs $(SCCSFLAGS) get $(SCCSGET-FLAGS) $@`
	`.GET_POSIX`	`$(GET) $(GFLAGS) s.$@`
Shell scripts	`.sh`	`cat $< >$@`
	`chmod +x $@`	
	`.sh~`	`$(GET) $(GFLAGS) -p $< > $*.sh`
		`cp $*.sh $@`
		`chmod a+x $@`

yacc files	`.y`	`$(YACC.y) $<`
		`$(LINK.c) -o $@ y.tab.c $(LDLIBS)`
		`$(RM) y.tab.c`

	`.y.c`	`$(YACC.y) $<`
		`mv y.tab.c $@`
	`.y.ln`	`$(YACC.y) $<`
		`$(LINT.c) -o $@ -i y.tab.c`
		`$(RM) y.tab.c`
	`.y.o`	`$(YACC.y) $<`
		`$(COMPILE.c) -o $@ y.tab.c`
		`$(RM) y.tab.c`
	`.y~`	`$(GET) $(GFLAGS) -p $< > $*.y`
		`$(YACC) $(YFLAGS) $*.y`

Use	Implicit Rule Name	Command Line
		`$(COMPILE.c) -o $@ y.tab.c`
		`$(RM) y.tab.c`
	`.y~.c`	`$(GET) $(GFLAGS) -p $< > $*.y`
		`$(YACC) $(YFLAGS) $*.y`
		`mv y.tab.c $@`
	`.y~.ln`	`$(GET) $(GFLAGS) -p $< > $*.y`
		`$(YACC.y) $*.y`
		`$(LINT.c) -o $@ -i y.tab.c`
		`$(RM) y.tab.c`
	`.y~.o`	`$(GET) $(GFLAGS) -p $< > $*.y`
		`$(YACC) $(YFLAGS) $*.y`
		`$(CC) $(CFLAGS) -c y.tab.c`
		`rm -f y.tab.c`
		`mv y.tab.o $@`

make reads in the standard set of implicit rules from the file
`/usr/share/lib/make/make.rules` unless `-r` is in effect or there is a
`make.rules` file in the local directory that does not include that file.

The Suffixes List

The suffixes list is given as the list of dependencies for the `.SUFFIXES:`
special-function target. The default list is contained in the `SUFFIXES` macro
(See "Table of Predefined Macros" on page 797 for the standard list of suffixes).
You can define additional `.SUFFIXES:` targets; a `.SUFFIXES:` target with no
dependencies clears the list of suffixes. Order is significant within the list;
make selects a rule that corresponds to the target's suffix and the first
dependency-file suffix found in the list. To put suffixes at the head of the list,
clear the list and replace it with the new suffixes followed by the default list, as
shown below.

```
.SUFFIXES:
.SUFFIXES: suffixes $(SUFFIXES)
```

A tilde (~) indicates that if a dependency file with the indicated suffix (minus
the ~) is under SCCS, its most recent version should be retrieved, if necessary,
before the target is processed.

Library Maintenance

A target name of the following form refers to a member, or a space-separated list of members, in an ar(1) library.

```
lib(member...)
```

You must give the dependency of the library member on the corresponding file as an explicit entry in the makefile. This entry can be handled with a pattern matching rule of the following form:

```
lib(%.s): %.s
```

where `.s` is the suffix of the member; this suffix is typically `.o` for object libraries.

A target name of the following form refers to the member of a randomized object library that defines the entry point named *symbol*.

```
lib((symbol))
```

Command Execution

Command lines are executed one at a time, each by its own process or shell. Shell commands, notably `cd`, are ineffectual across an unescaped newline in the makefile. A line is printed (after macro expansion) just before being executed. This printing is suppressed if the line starts with a `@`, if there is a `.SILENT:` entry in the makefile, or if you run `make` with the `-s` option. Although the `-n` option specifies printing without execution, lines containing the macro `$(MAKE)` are executed regardless, and lines containing the `@` special character are printed. The `-t` (touch) option updates the modification date of a file without executing any rules. This behavior can be dangerous when sources are maintained by more than one person.

`make` invokes the shell with the `-e` (exit-on-errors) argument. Thus, with semicolon-separated command sequences, execution of the later commands depends on the success of the former. This behavior can be overridden by starting the command line with a `-` or by writing a shell script that returns a non-zero status only as appropriate.

Bourne Shell Constructs

To use the Bourne shell `if` control structure for branching, use a command line of the following form.

```
if expression ; \
    then command ; \
        ... ; \
    else command ; \
        ... ; \
    fi
```

Although composed of several input lines, the escaped newline characters ensure that `make` treats them all as one (shell) command line.

To use the Bourne shell `for` control structure for loops, use a command line of the following form.

```
for var in list ; \
  do command; \
    ... ; \
  done
```

To refer to a shell variable, use a double dollar sign ($$). This syntax prevents expansion of the dollar sign by `make`.

Command Substitutions

To incorporate the standard output of a shell command in a macro, use a definition of the following form.

```
MACRO:sh =command
```

The *command* is executed only once, standard error output is discarded, and newline characters are replaced with spaces. If the command has a non-zero exit status, `make` halts with an error.

To capture the output of a shell command in a macro reference, use a reference of the following form:

```
$(MACRO:sh)
```

where *MACRO* is the name of a macro containing a valid Bourne shell command line. In this case, the command is executed whenever the reference is evaluated. As with shell command substitutions, the reference is replaced with the standard output of the command. If the command has a non-zero exit status, `make` halts with an error.

In contrast to commands in rules, the command is not subject to macro substitution; therefore, you do not need to replace a dollar sign ($) with a double dollar sign ($$).

Signals

`INT`, `SIGTERM`, and `QUIT` signals received from the keyboard halt `make` and remove the target file being processed unless that target is in the dependency list for `.PRECIOUS:.`

Examples

The following makefile says that `pgm` depends on two files, `a.o` and `b.o`, and that they in turn depend on their corresponding source files (`a.c` and `b.c`) along with a common file `incl.h`.

```
pgm: a.o b.o
      $(LINK.c) -o $@ a.o b.o
a.o: incl.h a.c
      cc -c a.c
b.o: incl.h b.c
      cc -c b.c
```

The following makefile uses implicit rules to express the same dependencies:

```
pgm: a.o b.o
     cc a.o b.o -o pgm
a.o b.o: incl.h
```

Environment Variables

See `environ(5)` for descriptions of the following environment variables that affect the execution of `make`: `LC_CTYPE`, `LC_MESSAGES`, and `NLSPATH`.

KEEP_STATE Produce the same effect as the `.KEEP_STATE:` special-function target. Enable command dependencies, hidden dependencies, and writing of the state file.

USE_SVR4_MAKE

    Invoke the generic System V version of `make` (`/usr/ccs/lib/svr4.make`). See `sysV-make(1)`.

MAKEFLAGS Specify a character string representing a series of option characters to be used as the default options. The implementation accepts both of the following formats (but need not accept them when intermixed):

- The characters are option letters without the leading dashes or blank-character separation used on a command line.

- The characters are formatted in a manner similar to a portion of the `make` command line: options are preceded by dashes and are blank-character separated. The *macro=name* macro definition operands can also be included. The difference between the contents of `MAKEFLAGS` and the command line is that the contents of the variable are not subject to the word expansions (see `wordexp(3C)`) associated with parsing the command-line values.

When you use the command-line options `-f` or `-p`, they take effect regardless of whether they also appear in `MAKEFLAGS`. If they otherwise appear in `MAKEFLAGS`, the result is undefined.

The `MAKEFLAGS` variable is accessed from the environment before the makefile is read. At that time, all of the options (except `-f` and `-p`) and command-line macros not already included in `MAKEFLAGS` are added to the `MAKEFLAGS` macro. The `MAKEFLAGS` macro is passed into the environment as an environment variable for all child processes. If the `MAKEFLAGS` macro is subsequently set by the makefile, it replaces the `MAKEFLAGS` variable currently found in the environment.

Exit Status

When you specify the -q option, the make command exits with one of the following values.

0   Successful completion.

1   The target was not up-to-date.

>1   An error occurred.

When you do not specify the -q option, the make command exits with one of the following values.

0   Successful completion.

>0   An error occurred.

Files

makefile
Makefile Current version(s) of make description file.

s.makefile SCCS history files for the above makefile(s) in the current
s.Makefile directory.

SCCS/s.makefile

      SCCS history files for the above makefile(s).

make.rules Default file for user-defined targets, macros, and implicit rules.

/usr/share/lib/make/make.rules

      Makefile for standard implicit rules and macros (not read if
      make.rules is read).

.make.state State file in the local directory.

Attributes

See attributes(5) for descriptions of the following attributes:

/usr/ccs/bin/make

Attribute Type	Attribute Value
Availability	SUNWsprot

/usr/xpg4/bin/make

Attribute Type	Attribute Value
Availability	SUNWxcu4t

See Also

ar(1), cd(1), lex(1), sh(1), sccs-get(1), sysV-make(1) yacc(1),
passwd(4), attributes(5), POSIX.2(5)
 Solaris Advanced User's Guide and *Programming Utilities Guide*

Diagnostics

Don't know how to make target *target*

> There is no makefile entry for *target*, and none of make's implicit
> rules apply (there is no dependency file with a suffix in the suffixes
> list, or the target's suffix is not in the list).

*** *target* removed

> make was interrupted while building *target*. Instead of leaving a
> partially completed version that is newer than its dependencies,
> make removes the file named *target*.

*** *target* not removed

> make was interrupted while building *target*, and *target* was not
> present in the directory.

*** *target* could not be removed, *reason*

> make was interrupted while building *target*, which was not
> removed for the indicated *reason*.

Read of include file *file* failed

> The makefile indicated in an include directive was not found or
> was inaccessible.

Loop detected when expanding macro value *macro*

> A reference to the macro being defined was found in the definition.

Could not write state file *file*

> You used the .KEEP_STATE: target, but you do not have write
> permission on the state file.

*** Error code *n*

> The previous shell command returned a non-zero error code.

*** *signal message*

> The previous shell command was aborted because of a signal. If
> - core dumped appears after the message, a core file was created.

Conditional macro conflict encountered

> Displayed only when -d is in effect, this message indicates that
> two or more parallel targets currently being processed depend on
> a target that is built differently for each by virtue of conditional
> macros. Because the target cannot simultaneously satisfy both
> dependency relationships, it is conflicted.

Bugs

Some commands return non-zero status inappropriately; to overcome this difficulty, prefix the offending command line in the rule with a -.

File names with the characters =, :, or @ do not work.

You cannot build `file.o` from `lib(file.o)`.

Options supplied by MAKEFLAGS should be reported for nested make commands. Use the -d option to find out what options the nested command picks up from MAKEFLAGS.

This version of make is incompatible with previous versions in the following ways.

- The -d option output is much briefer in this version. -dd now produces the equivalent voluminous output.

- make tries to derive values for the dynamic macros $*, $<, and $? while processing explicit targets. It uses the same method as for implicit rules; in some cases, this can lead either to unexpected values or to an empty value being assigned. (Actually, this was true for earlier versions as well, even though the documentation stated otherwise.)

- make no longer searches for SCCS history (s.) files.

- Suffix replacement in macro references is now applied after the macro is expanded.

There is no guarantee that makefiles created for this version of make work with earlier versions.

If there is no make.rules file in the current directory and the file /usr/share/lib/make/make.rules is missing, make stops before processing any targets. To force make to run anyway, create an empty make.rules file in the current directory.

Once a dependency is made, make assumes the dependency file is present for the remainder of the run. If a rule subsequently removes that file and future targets depend on its existence, unexpected errors may result.

When hidden dependency checking is in effect, the $? macro's value includes the names of hidden dependencies. This can lead to improper file-name arguments to commands when $? is used in a rule.

Pattern replacement macro references cannot be used in the dependency list of a pattern-matching rule.

Unlike previous versions, this version of make strips a leading ./ from the value of the $@ dynamic macro.

With automatic SCCS retrieval, this version of make does not support tilde suffix rules.

The only dynamic macro whose value is strictly determined when used in a dependency list is $@ (takes the form $$@).

make invokes the shell with the -e argument, which cannot be inferred from the syntax of the rule alone.

makekey — Generate Encryption Key

Synopsis

```
/usr/lib/makekey
```

Description

makekey improves the usefulness of encryption schemes depending on a key by increasing the amount of time required to search the key space. It reads 10 bytes from its standard input and writes 13 bytes on its standard output. The output depends on the input in a way intended to be difficult to compute (that is, to require a substantial fraction of a second).

The first eight input bytes (the input key) can be arbitrary ASCII characters. The last two (the salt) are best chosen from the set of digits, upper- and lowercase letters, and . and /. The salt characters are repeated as the first two characters of the output. The remaining eleven output characters are chosen from the same set as the salt and constitute the output key.

The transformation performed is essentially the following: The salt is used to select one of 4,096 cryptographic machines all based on the National Bureau of Standards data encryption standard (DES) algorithm but modified in 4,096 different ways. Using the input key as key, a constant string is fed into the machine and recirculated a number of times. The 64 bits that come out are distributed into the 66 useful key bits in the result.

makekey is intended for programs that perform encryption (for instance, ed(1) and crypt(1)). Usually, makekey's input and output are pipes.

See Also

```
crypt(1), ed(1)
```

man — Find and Display Reference Manual Pages

Synopsis

```
/usr/bin/man[-][-adFlrt][-Mpath][-Tmacro-package][-ssection]name...
/usr/bin/man [-M path] -k keyword...
/usr/bin/man [-M path] -f file...
```

New!

Description

Use the man command to display information from the online reference manuals. man displays complete manual pages that you specify by name or one-line summaries that you specify either with keyword (-k) or with the name of an associated file (-f). If no manual page is located, man prints an error message.

Source Format

Reference manual pages are marked up with either nroff(1) or sgml(5) (Standard Generalized Markup Language) tags. The man command recognizes the type of markup and processes the file accordingly. The various source files are kept in separate directories depending on the type of markup.

Location of Manual Pages

The online reference manual page directories are conventionally located in /usr/share/man. The nroff sources are located in the /usr/share/man/man* directories. The SGML sources are located in the /usr/share/man/sman* directories. Each directory corresponds to a section of the manual. Because these directories are optionally installed, they may not reside on your host; you may have to mount /usr/share/man from a host on which they do reside.

If there are preformatted, up-to-date versions in the corresponding cat* or fmt* directories, man displays or prints those versions. If the preformatted version of interest is out-of-date or missing, man reformats it before displaying it and stores the preformatted version if cat* or fmt* is writable. The windex database is not updated. See catman(1M). If directories for the preformatted versions are not provided, man reformats a page whenever it is requested; it uses a temporary file to store the formatted text during display.

If the standard output is not a terminal or if you specify the - option, man pipes its output through cat(1); otherwise, man pipes its output through more(1) to handle paging and underlining on the screen.

Options

-	Pipe output through cat(1) instead of more(1).
-a	Show all manual pages in the order found matching *name* within the MANPATH search path.
-d	Display what a section-specifier evaluates to, method used for searching, and paths searched by man.
-f *file*...	Locate manual pages related to any of the given files. Strip the leading path-name components from each file and print one-line summaries containing the resulting basename or names. This option uses the windex database.
-F	Force man to search all directories specified by MANPATH or the man.cf file instead of using the windex lookup database. This option is useful if the database is not up-to-date. If the windex database does not exist, this option is assumed.

`-k keyword...`

Print one-line summaries from the `windex` database (table of contents) that contain any of the given keywords. The `windex` database is created with `catman`(1M).

`-l`   List all manual pages found matching *name* within the search path.

`-M path`   Specify an alternate search path for manual pages. *path* is a colon-separated list of directories that contain manual page directory subtrees. For example, if path is `/usr/share/man:/usr/local/man`, man searches for *name* in the standard location and then in `/usr/local/man`. When used with the `-k` or `-f` options, the `-M` option must be first. Each directory in the path is assumed to contain subdirectories of the form `man*`, one for each section. This option overrides the `MANPATH` environment variable.

`-r`   Reformat the manual page, but do not display it. This option replaces the `man - -t` *name* combination.

`-s section...`

Specify sections of the manual for man to search. The directories searched for *name* are limited to those specified by *section*. *section* can be a digit (perhaps followed by one or more letters), a word (for example: `local`, `new`, `old`, `public`), or a letter. To specify multiple sections, separate each section with a comma. This option overrides the `MANPATH` environment variable and the `man.cf` file.

`-t`   Process with `troff` and send specified manual pages to a suitable raster output device (see `troff`(1). If you use both the `-` and `-t` flags, man updates the troffed versions of each named *name* (if needed) but does not display the names.

`-T macro-package`

Format manual pages, using *macro-package* instead of the standard `-man` macros defined in `/usr/share/lib/tmac`.

Note — The `-f` and `-k` options use the `windex` database, which is created by `catman`(1M).

Operands

name   A keyword or the name of a standard command.

Usage

Manual Page Sections
Entries in the reference manuals are organized into sections. A section name consists of a major section name, typically a single digit, optionally followed by a subsection name, typically one or more letters. For example, the command

lpr(1B) is in Section (1), User Commands, and belongs to the BSD Compatibility Package subsection. An unadorned major section name acts as an abbreviation for the section of the same name along with all of its subsections. Each section contains descriptions appropriate to a particular reference category, with subsections refining these distinctions. See the intro manual pages for an explanation of the classification used in this release.

Search Path

Before searching for a given name, man constructs a list of candidate directories and sections. man searches for *name* in the directories specified by the MANPATH environment variable. If this variable is not set, /usr/share/man is searched by default.

Within the manual page directories, man confines its search to the sections specified, in the following order:

- Sections specified on the command line with the -s option.
- Sections embedded in the MANPATH environment variable.
- Sections specified in the man.cf file for each directory specified in the MANPATH environment variable

If none of the above exist, man searches each directory in the manual page path and displays the first matching manual page found.

The man.cf file has the following format:

MANSECTS=*section*[,*section*]...

Lines beginning with # and blank lines are considered comments and are ignored. Each directory specified in MANPATH can contain a manual page configuration file specifying the default search order for that directory.

Formatting Manual Pages

New!

Manual pages are marked up in nroff(1) or sgml(5). nroff manual pages are processed by nroff(1) or troff(1) with the -man macro package. Please refer to man(5) for information on macro usage. SGML-tagged manual pages are processed by an SGML parser and are passed to the formatter.

Preprocessing nroff Manual Pages

When formatting an nroff manual page, man examines the first line to determine whether it requires special processing. If the first line is a string of the following form,

'\" *X*

where *X* is separated from the " by a single space and consists of any combination of characters in the following list, then man pipes its input to troff(1) or nroff(1) through the corresponding preprocessors.

e   eqn(1), or neqn for nroff.

r   refer(1).

t	tbl(1).
v	vgrind(1).

If eqn or neqn is invoked, man automatically reads the file /usr/pub/eqnchar (see eqnchar(5)). If nroff(1) is invoked, col(1) is automatically used.

Referring to Other nroff Manual Pages

If the first line of the nroff manual page is a reference to another manual page entry fitting the following pattern, man processes the indicated file in place of the current one.

```
.so man*/ sourcefile
```

You must express the reference as a path name relative to the root of the manual page directory subtree.

When the second or any subsequent line starts with .so, man ignores it; troff(1) or nroff(1) processes the request in the usual manner.

Processing SGML Manual Pages

New!

Manual pages are identified as being marked up in SGML by the presence of the string <!DOCTYPE. If the file also contain the string SHADOW_PAGE, the file refers to another manual page for the content. The reference is made with a file entity reference to the manual page that contains the text. This mechanism is similar to the .so mechanism used in the nroff-formatted manual pages.

Bugs

The manual is supposed to be reproducible either on a phototypesetter or on an ASCII terminal. However, on a terminal some information (indicated by font changes, for instance) is lost.

Some dumb terminals cannot process the vertical motions produced by the e (see eqn(1)) preprocessing flag. To prevent garbled output on these terminals, when you use e also use t to invoke col(1) implicitly. This workaround has the disadvantage of eliminating superscripts and subscripts even on those terminals that can display them. Use Control-Q to clear a terminal that gets confused by eqn(1) output.

Environment Variables

See environ(5) for descriptions of the following environment variables that affect the execution of man: LC_CTYPE, LC_MESSAGES, and NLSPATH.

MANPATH	A colon-separated list of directories; each directory can be followed by a comma-separated list of sections. If set, its value overrides /usr/share/man as the default directory search path and the man.cf file as the default section search path. The -M and -s options, in turn, override these values.

PAGER	A program to use for interactively delivering man's output to the screen. If not set, more -s is used. See more(1).
TCAT	The name of the program to use to display troffed manual pages.
TROFF	The name of the formatter to use when you specify the -t option. If not set, troff(1) is used.

Exit Status

0	Successful completion.
>0	An error occurred.

Files

/usr/share/man

    Root of the standard manual page directory subtree.

/usr/share/man/man?/*

    Unformatted nroff manual entries.

New! /usr/share/man/sman?/*

    Unformatted SGML manual entries.

/usr/share/man/cat?/*

    Nroffed manual entries.

/usr/share/man/fmt?/*

    Troffed manual entries.

/usr/share/man/windex

    Table of contents and keyword database.

/usr/share/lib/tmac/an

    Standard -man macro package.

New! /usr/share/lib/sgml/locale/C/dtd/*

    SGML document type definition files.

New! /usr/share/lib/sgml/locale/C/solbook/*

    SGML style sheet and entity definitions directories.

/usr/share/lib/pub/eqnchar

    Standard definitions for eqn and neqn.

man.cf   Default search order by section.

Attributes

See attributes(5) for descriptions of the following attributes:

Attribute Type	Attribute Value
Availability	SUNWdoc
CSI	Enabled

Note — The man command is CSI capable. However, some commands invoked by the man command, namely, troff, eqn, neqn, refer, tbl, and vgrind, are not verified to be CSI capable. Because of this, the man command with the -t option may not handle non-EUC data. Also, if the man command is used to display manual pages that require special processing through eqn, neqn, refer, tbl, or vgrind, man may not be CSI capable.

See Also

apropos(1), cat(1), col(1), eqn(1), more(1), nroff(1), refer(1), tbl(1), *New!*
troff(1), vgrind(1), whatis(1), catman(1M), attributes(5), environ(5),
eqnchar(5), man(5), sgml(5)

mconnect — Connect to SMTP Mail Server Socket

Synopsis

/usr/bin/mconnect [-p port] [-r] [hostname]

Description

mconnect opens a connection to the mail server on a given host so that the mail server can be tested independently of all other mail software. If no host is given, the connection is made to the local host. Servers expect to speak the Simple Mail Transfer Protocol (SMTP) on this connection. Exit by typing the quit command. Typing EOF sends an end-of-file to the server. An interrupt closes the connection immediately and exits.

Options

-p port   Specify the port number instead of the default SMTP port (number 25) as the next argument.

-r   Disable the default line buffering and input handling to operate in raw mode. This option produces an effect similar to telnet to port number 25.

Files

/etc/mail/sendmail.hf

Help file for SMTP commands.

Attributes

See attributes(5) for descriptions of the following attributes:

Attribute Type	Attribute Value
Availability	SUNWcsu

See Also

sendmail(1M), attributes(5)

Postel, Jonathan B., *Simple Mail Transfer Protocol*, RFC 821, Information Sciences Institute, University of Southern California, August 1982.

mcs — Manipulate the Comment Section of an Object File

Synopsis

/usr/ccs/bin/mcs { -c | -d | -p | -V | -a *string* | -n *name* }... *file*...

Description

Use the mcs command to manipulate a section in an ELF object file. The default section is .comment. mcs is used to add to, delete, print, and compress the contents of a section in an ELF object file and print only the contents of a section in a Common Object File Format (COFF) object file. COFF is an object file format that preceded ELF on some computer architectures. mcs cannot add, delete or compress the contents of a section that is contained within a segment.

If the input file is an archive (see ar(4)), the archive is treated as a set of individual files. For example, if you specify the -a option, the string is appended to the comment section of each ELF object file in the archive; if the archive member is not an ELF object file, then it is left unchanged.

> **Note —** When mcs deletes a section with the -d option, it tries to bind together sections of type SHT_REL and target sections pointed to by the sh_info section header field. If one is to be deleted, mcs tries to delete the other of the pair.

Options

You must specify one or more of the options described below. Each specified option is applied, in order, to each file.

-a *string*   Append *string* to the comment section of the ELF object files. If *string* contains embedded blanks, enclose it in quotation marks.

-c   Compress the contents of the comment section of the ELF object files. Remove all duplicate entries. The ordering of the remaining entries is not disturbed.

-d   Delete the contents of the comment section from the ELF object files. Also remove the section header for the comment section.

-n *name*   Specify the name of the comment section to access if other than .comment. By default, mcs deals with the section named .comment. You can use this option to specify another section. You can specify multiple -n options to specify multiple section comments.

-p   Print the contents of the comment section on the standard output. Tag each section printed with the name of the file from which it was extracted, using the format file[*member_name*]: for archive files and file: for other files.

-V   Print on standard error the version number of mcs.

Examples

The following example prints the comments section from elf.file.

```
castle% mcs -p elf.file
```

The following example appends string xyz to the comment section of elf.file.

```
castle% mcs -a xyz elf.file
```

Files

/tmp/mcs*   Temporary files.

Attributes

See attributes(5) for descriptions of the following attributes:

Attribute Type	Attribute Value
Availability	SUNWbtool

See Also

ar(1), as(1), ld(1), elf(3E), tmpnam(3S), a.out(4), ar(4), attributes(5)

mesg — Permit or Deny Messages

Synopsis
```
/usr/bin/mesg [-n | -y | n | y]
```

Description
The `mesg` command controls whether other users can send messages to a terminal device by using `write(1)`, `talk(1)`, or other commands. The terminal device affected is determined by searching for the first terminal in the sequence of devices associated with standard input, standard output, and standard error. With no arguments, `mesg` reports the current state without changing it. Processes with appropriate privileges may be able to send messages to the terminal independently of the current state.

Options

`-n` | `n`	Deny permission to other users to send message to the terminal. See `write(1)`.
`-y` | `y`	Grant permission to other users to send messages to the terminal.

Examples
The following example uses the `mesg` command with no arguments to display the current state, and first turns off, then turns on, the ability to receive messages from another terminal.
```
castle% mesg
is y
castle% mesg -n
castle% mesg
is n
castle% mesg -y
castle% mesg
is y
castle%
```

Environment Variables
See `environ(5)` for descriptions of the following environment variables that affect the execution of `mesg`: LC_CTYPE, LC_MESSAGES, and NLSPATH.

Exit Status

0	Messages are receivable.
1	Messages are not receivable.
2	Error.

Files

/dev/tty*   Terminal devices.

/dev/pts*   Terminal devices.

Attributes

See attributes(5) for descriptions of the following attributes:

Attribute Type	Attribute Value
Availability	SUNWcsu

See Also

talk(1), write(1), attributes(5), environ(5)

---

mkdir — Make Directories

Synopsis

/usr/bin/mkdir [-m *mode*][-p] *dir*...

Description

Use the mkdir command to create new directories. If you specify a complete path name, the new directory is created at the bottom of the specified path. If you specify a directory name, the new directory is created as a subdirectory of the current directory. You must have write permission for the parent directory. When a new directory is created, standard entries in a directory (for instance, the files . for the directory itself and .. for its parent) are made automatically.

By default, new directories are created with mode 777 permissions. These permissions are altered by the file-mode creation mask (see umask(1)).

The owner ID and group ID of the new directories are set to the effective user-ID and group-ID of the process. mkdir calls the mkdir(2) system call.

setgid and mkdir

To change the setgid bit on a newly created directory, you must use chmod g+s or chmod g-s.

The setgid bit setting is inherited from the parent directory.

Options

-m *mode*   Specify the mode to be used for new directories. Choices for modes can be found in chmod(1).

-p   Create *dir* by first creating all the nonexisting parent directories. The mode given to intermediate directories is the difference between 777 and the bits set in the file-mode creation mask. The difference must be at least 300 (write and execute permission for the user).

Operands

dir   A path name of a directory to be created.

Usage

See largefile(5) for the description of the behavior of mkdir when encountering files greater than or equal to 2 Gbytes (2**31 bytes).

Examples

The following example creates the subdirectory structure ltr/jw/jan.

```
castle% mkdir -p ltr/jw/jan
castle% ls -lsa
total 6
    2 drwxr-xr-x   3 winsor    staff        512 Mar 15 15:30 .
    2 drwxr-xr-x  10 winsor    staff        512 Mar 15 15:30 ..
    2 drwxr-xr-x   3 winsor    staff        512 Mar 15 15:30 ltr
castle% cd ltr
castle% ls -lsa
total 6
    2 drwxr-xr-x   3 winsor    staff        512 Mar 15 15:30 .
    2 drwxr-xr-x   3 winsor    staff        512 Mar 15 15:30 ..
    2 drwxr-xr-x   3 winsor    staff        512 Mar 15 15:30 jw
castle% cd jw
castle% ls -lsa
total 6
    2 drwxr-xr-x   3 winsor    staff        512 Mar 15 15:30 .
    2 drwxr-xr-x   3 winsor    staff        512 Mar 15 15:30 ..
    2 drwxr-xr-x   2 winsor    staff        512 Mar 15 15:30 jan
castle% cd jan
castle% ls -lsa
total 4
    2 drwxr-xr-x   2 winsor    staff        512 Mar 15 15:30 .
    2 drwxr-xr-x   3 winsor    staff        512 Mar 15 15:30 ..
castle%
```

Environment Variables

See environ(5) for descriptions of the following environment variables that affect the execution of mkdir: LC_CTYPE, LC_MESSAGES, and NLSPATH.

Exit Status

0	All the specified directories were created successfully, or the -p option was specified and all the specified directories now exist.
>0	An error occurred.

Attributes

See `attributes`(5) for descriptions of the following attributes:

Attribute Type	Attribute Value
Availability	SUNWcsu
CSI	Enabled

See Also

`rm(1)`, `sh(1)`, `umask(1)`, `intro(2)`, `mkdir(2)`, `attributes(5)`, `environ(5)`, `largefile(5)`

---

mkmsgs — Create Message Files for Use by gettxt

Synopsis

```
/usr/bin/mkmsgs [-o][-i locale] input-strings msgfile
```

Description

Use the `mkmsgs` command to create a file of text strings that can be accessed by the text retrieval tools (see `gettxt`(1), `srchtxt`(1), `exstr`(1), and `gettxt`(3C)). `mkmsgs` takes as input a file of text strings for a particular geographic locale (see `setlocale`(3C)) and creates a file of text strings in a format that can be retrieved by both `gettxt`(1) and `gettxt`(3C). By using the `-i` option, you can install the created file under the `/usr/lib/locale/`*locale*`/LC_MESSAGES` directory (*locale* corresponds to the language in which the text strings are written).

input-strings is the name of the file that contains the original text strings. *msgfile* is the name of the output file where `mkmsgs` writes the strings in a format that is readable by `gettxt`(1) and `gettxt`(3C). The name of *msgfile* can be up to 14 characters in length but cannot contain either \0 (null) or the ASCII code for slash (/) or colon (:).

The input file contains a set of text strings for the particular geographic locale. Separate text strings with a newline character. Represent nongraphic characters as alphabetic escape sequences. Messages are transformed and copied sequentially from *input-strings* to *msgfile*. To generate an empty message in *msgfile*, leave an empty line at the correct place in *input-strings*.

You can change strings by editing the *input-strings* file. Add new strings only at the end of the file; then, create a new *msgfile* file and install it in the correct place. If you do not follow this procedure, the retrieval function retrieves the wrong string and software compatibility will be broken.

Options

-o   Overwrite *msgfile* if it exists.

-i *locale*   Install *msgfile* in the /usr/lib/locale/locale/LC_MESSAGES directory. Create directories under /usr/lib/locale if they do not exist. Only someone who is superuser or a member of group bin can create or overwrite files in this directory.

Examples

The following example shows an input message source file C.str.

```
File %s:\t cannot be opened\n
%s: Bad directory\n
.
.
.
write error\n
.
.
```

The following command uses the input strings from C.str to create text strings in the appropriate format in the file UX in the current directory.

castle% **mkmsgs C.str UX**

The following command uses the input strings from FR.str to create text strings in the appropriate format in the file UX in the directory /usr/lib/locale/fr/LC_MESSAGES.

castle% **mkmsgs -i fr FR.str UX**

You would be able to access these text strings if you had set the environment variable LC_MESSAGES=fr and then invoked one of the gettxt(1), srchtxt(1), or exstr(1) text retrieval tools.

Files

/usr/lib/locale/locale/LC_MESSAGES/*

Message files created by mkmsgs.

Attributes

See `attributes`(5) for descriptions of the following attributes:

Attribute Type	Attribute Value
Availability	SUNWloc

See Also

`exstr`(1),`gettxt`(1),`srchtxt`(1),`gettxt`(3C),`setlocale`(3C),`attributes`(5)

mkstr — Create an Error Message File by Massaging C Source Files

Synopsis

`/usr/ucb/mkstr [-]` *messagefile prefix filename...*

Description

`mkstr` creates files of error messages. You can use `mkstr` to make smaller programs from those that have a large numbers of error diagnostics. You reduce system overhead in running such programs because the error messages do not have to be constantly swapped in and out.

`mkstr` processes each of the specified file names, placing a massaged version of the input file in a file with a name consisting of the specified prefix and the original source file name. A typical example of using `mkstr` is.

```
mkstr pistrings processed *.c
```

This command puts all the error messages from the C source files in the current directory in the file `pistrings` and puts processed copies of the source for these files into files whose names are prefixed with `processed`.

To process the error messages in the source to the message file, `mkstr` keys on the string `error("` in the input stream. Each time it occurs, the C string starting at the `"` is placed in the message file, followed by a null character and a newline character. The null character terminates the message so it can be easily used when retrieved. The newline character makes it possible to sensibly use `cat` on the error message file to see its contents. The massaged copy of the input file then contains an `lseek` pointer into the file that can be used to retrieve the message.

```
char efilname[] = "/usr/lib/pi_strings";
     int efil = -1;
error(a1, a2, a3, a4)
     {
```

```
     char
            buf[256];
            if (efil < 0) {
efil = open(efilname, 0);
      if (efil < 0) {
oops:
      perror (efilname);
      exit (1);
            }
      }
      if (lseek(efil, (long) a1, 0) || read(efil, buf, 256) <= 0)
            goto oops;
      printf(buf, a2, a3, a4);
}
```

Notes

/usr/bin/more
Skipping backward is slow on large files.

usr/xpg4/bin/more
This command does not behave correctly if the terminal is not set up properly.

Options

- Put error messages at the end of the specified message file for recompiling part of a large mkstred program.

Attributes

See attributes(5) for descriptions of the following attributes:

Attribute Type	Attribute Value
Availability	SUNWscpu

See Also

xstr(1), attributes(5)

more, page — Browse or Page Through a Text File

Synopsis

```
/usr/bin/more [-cdflrsuw] [-lines] [+linenumber] [+/pattern] [file...]
/usr/bin/page [-cdflrsuw] [-lines] [+linenumber] [+/pattern] [file...]
/usr/xpg4/bin/more [-cdeisu] [-nnumber] [-pcommand] [-ttagstring] [file...]
/usr/xpg4/bin/more [-cdeisu] [-nnumber] [+command] [-ttagstring] [file...]
```

Description

The `more` command is a filter that displays the contents of a text file on the terminal, one screen at a time. It normally pauses after each screen. `/usr/bin/more` prints `--More--` and `/usr/xpg4/bin/more` prints *file* at the bottom of the screen. If `more` is reading from a file instead of a pipe, the percentage of characters displayed so far is also shown.

Press Return to scroll one more line. Press the space bar to display another screen. Other commands are listed below.

The `page` command clears the screen before displaying the next screen of text; it provides only a one-line overlap between screens.

The `more` command sets the terminal to NOECHO mode so that the output can be continuous. Commands that you type do not normally show up on your terminal except for the / and ! commands.

The `/usr/bin/more` command exits after displaying the last specified file; `/usr/xpg4/bin/more` prompts for a command at the last line of the last specified file.

If the standard output is not a terminal, `more` acts just like `cat(1)`, except that a header is printed before each file in a series.

Options

The following options are supported for both `/usr/bin/more` and `/usr/xpg4/bin/more`.

`-c`	Clear before displaying. Redraw the screen instead of scrolling for faster displays. Ignore this option if the terminal does not have the ability to clear to the end of a line.
`-d`	Display error messages instead of ringing the terminal bell if you use an unrecognized command. This option is helpful for inexperienced users.
`-s`	Replace multiple blank lines with a single blank line. This squeezing is helpful when viewing `nroff(1)` output.

/usr/bin/more

`-f`	Do not fold long lines. This option is useful when lines contain nonprinting characters or escape sequences, such as those generated when `nroff(1)` output is piped through `ul(1)`.
`-l`	Do not treat formfeed characters (Control-L) as page breaks. If you do not use `-l`, `more` pauses to accept commands after any line containing a ^L character (Control-L). Also, if a file begins with a formfeed, clear the screen before printing the file.
`-r`	Display control characters such as ^C, where C stands for any control character. Normally, `more` ignores control characters that it does not interpret in some way.

-u   Suppress generation of underlining escape sequences. Normally,
                more handles underlining, such as that produced by nroff(1), in a
                manner appropriate to the terminal. If the terminal can perform
                underlining or has a standout mode, supply appropriate escape
                sequences as called for in the text file.

-w   Prompt and wait for any key to be pressed before exiting.
                Normally, more exits when it comes to the end of its input.

-*lines*   Display the indicated number of lines in each screen instead of the
                default (the number of lines in the terminal screen less two).

+*linenumber*   Start at *linenumber*.

+/*pattern*   Start two lines above the line containing the regular expression
                pattern. Note that, unlike editors, this construct should not end
                with a slash (/). If it does, then take the trailing slash as a
                character in the search pattern.

/usr/xpg4/bin/more

-e   Exit immediately after writing the last line of the last file in the
                argument list.

-i   Perform pattern matching in searches without regard to case.

-n *number*   Specify the number of lines per screen. The *number* argument is a
                positive decimal integer. The -n option overrides any values
                obtained from the environment.

-p *command*   For each file examined, initially execute the more command in the
+*command*   *command* argument. If *command* is a positioning command such as a
                line number or a regular expression search, set the current
                position to represent the final results of the command without
                writing any intermediate lines of the file. For example, the two
                commands:

                more -p 1000j file

                more -p 1000G file

                are equivalent and start the display with the current position at
                line 1000, bypassing the lines that j would write and scroll off the
                screen if it had been issued during the file examination. If the
                positioning command is unsuccessful, the first line in the file is the
                current position.

-t*tagstring*   Write the screen of the file containing the tag named by the
                tagstring argument. See the ctags(1) command.

-u   Treat a backspace character as a printable control character,
                displayed as a ^H (Control-H), suppressing backspacing and the
                special handling that produces underlined or standout-mode text
                on some terminal types. Also, do not ignore a Return character at
                the end of a line.

If you specify both the -t *tagstring* and -p *command* (or the obsolescent +*command*) options, the -t *tagstring* is processed first.

Usage

Environment
more uses the terminfo(4) entry for the terminal to determine its display characteristics.

more looks in the environment variable MORE for any preset options. For instance, to page through files using the -c mode by default, set the value of this variable to -c. (Normally, the command sequence to set up this environment variable is put in the .login or .profile file).

Commands
The commands take effect immediately. It is not necessary to press Return unless the command requires a file, command, tagstring, or pattern. Up to the time you type the command character itself, you can type the line-kill character to cancel the numerical argument. In addition, you can type the erase character to redisplay the --More--(*xx*%) or *file* message.

In the following commands, *i* is a numerical argument (1 by default).

*i*space	Display another screen, or *i* more lines if *i* is specified.
*i*Return	Display another line, or *i* more lines, if specified.
*i*b | *i*^B	(Control-B) Skip back *i* screens and then print a screen.
*i*d | *i*^D	(Control-D) Scroll forward half a screen or *i* more lines. If *i* is specified, the count becomes the default for subsequent d and u commands.
*i*f	Skip *i* screens and then print a screen.
h	Give a description of all the more commands.
^L	(Control-L) Refresh.
*i*n	Search for the *i*-th occurrence of the last pattern entered.
q | Q	Exit from more.
*i*s	Skip *i* lines and then print a screen.
v	Drop into the vi editor at the current line of the current file.
*i*z	Same as space except that *i*, if present, becomes the new default number of lines per screen.
=	Display the current line number.

i/pattern	Search forward for the *i*-th occurrence of the regular expression *pattern*. Display the screen, starting two lines before the line that contains the *i*-th match for the regular expression pattern or the end of a pipe, whichever comes first. If more is displaying a file and there is no match, its position in the file remains unchanged. You can edit regular expressions by using the erase and kill characters. Erasing back past the first column cancels the search command.
!command	Invoke a shell to execute *command*. Replace the characters % and !, when used within command, with the current file name and the previous shell command. If there is no current file name, do not expand %. Prepend a backslash to these characters to escape expansion.
:f	Display the current file name and line number.
i:n	Skip to the *i*-th next file name given in the command line or to the last file name in the list if *i* is out of range.
i:p	Skip to the *i*-th previous file name given in the command line or to the first file name if *i* is out of range. If used while more is positioned within a file, go to the beginning of the file. If more is reading from a pipe, ring the terminal bell.
:q | :Q	Exit from more (same as q or Q).

/usr/bin/more
The following commands are available only in /usr/bin/more.

'	Single quote. Go to the point from which the last search started. If no search has been performed in the current file, go to the beginning of the file.
.	Repeat the previous command.
^\	Halt a partial display of text. Stop sending output and display the usual --More- prompt. Some output is lost as a result.

/usr/xpg4/bin/more
The following commands are available only in /usr/xpg4/bin/more.

i^F	(Control-F) Skip *i* full screens and print a screen. (Same as *i*f.)
^G	(Control-G) Display the current line number (same as =).
*i*g	Go to line number *i* with the default of the first line in the file.
*i*G	Go to line number *i* with the default of the last line in the file.
*i*j	Display another line or *i* more lines if specified. (Same as *i*Return.)
*i*k	Scroll backward one or *i* lines if specified.
m*letter*	Mark the current position with the name letter.
N	Reverse direction of search.

r	Refresh the screen.
R	Refresh the screen, discarding any buffered input.
*i*u *i*^U	(Control-U) Scroll backward half a screen of *i* lines if specified. If you specify *i*, the count becomes the new default for subsequent d and u commands.
ZZ	Exit from more (same as q).
:e *file*	Examine (display) a new file. If you specify no file, redisplay the current file.
:t *tagstring*	

Go to the tag named by the *tagstring* argument and scroll/rewrite the screen with the tagged line in the current position. See the ctags command.

'*letter*	Return to the position that was previously marked with the name *letter*.
''	Return to the position from which the last move of more than a screen was made. Default to the beginning of the file.
i?[!]*pattern*	

Search backward in the file for the *i*-th line containing the *pattern*. The ! specifies to search backward for the *i*-th line that does not contain the pattern.

i/!*pattern*	Search forward in the file for the *i*-th line that does not contain the *pattern*.
![*command*]	Invoke a shell or the specified command.

Usage

See largefile(5) for the description of the behavior of more and page when encountering files greater than or equal to 2 Gbytes (2**31 bytes).

Environment Variables

See environ(5) for descriptions of the following environment variables that affect the execution of more: LC_COLLATE

For /usr/xpg4/bin/more only: LC_CTYPE, LC_MESSAGES, NLSPATH, and TERM.

/usr/xpg4/bin/more

The following environment variables also affect the execution of /usr/xpg4/bin/more.

COLUMNS	Override the system-selected horizontal screen size.
EDITOR	Used by the v command to select an editor.
LINES	Override the system-selected vertical screen size. The -n option has precedence over LINES in determining the number of lines in a screen.

MORE   A string specifying options. As in a command line, separate the
              options with blank characters and start each option specification
              with a –. Process any command-line options after those specified
              in MORE as though the command line were:

              more $MORE *options operands*

Exit Status

0   Successful completion.

>0   An error occurred.

Files

/usr/lib/more.help

              Help file for /usr/bin/more and /usr/bin/page.

Attributes

See attributes(5) for descriptions of the following attributes:

/usr/bin/more /usr/bin/page

Attribute Type	Attribute Value
Availability	SUNWcsu
CSI	Not enabled

/usr/xpg4/bin/more

Attribute Type	Attribute Value
Availability	SUNWxcu4
CSI	Enabled

See Also

cat(1), csh(1), ctags(1), man(1), nroff(1), script(1), sh(1), ul(1),
environ(4), terminfo(4), attributes(5), environ(5), largefile(5)

/usr/bin/more /usr/bin/page

regcomp(3C)

/usr/xpg4/bin/more

regex(5), xpg4(5)

msgfmt — Create a Message Object from a Message File

Synopsis

```
/usr/bin/msgfmt [-v] [-o output-file] filename.po...
```

Description

msgfmt creates message object files from portable object files (*filename*.po), without changing the portable object files.

The .po file contains messages displayed to users by system commands or by application programs. You can edit .po files and rewrite the messages in them in any language supported by the system.

You can use the xgettext(1) command to create .po files from scripts or programs.

msgfmt interprets data as characters according to the current setting of the LC_CTYPE locale category.

Note — Neither msgfmt nor any gettext() routine imposes a limit on the total length of a message. However, each line in the *.po file is limited to MAX_INPUT (512) bytes.

Installing message catalogs under the C locale is pointless because they are ignored for the sake of efficiency.

Portable Object Files

Formats for all .po files are the same. Each .po file contains one or more lines, with each line containing either a comment or a statement. Comments start the line with a hash mark (#) and end with the newline character. All comments are ignored. The format of a statement is:

directive value

Each *directive* starts at the beginning of the line and is separated from *value* by white space such as one or more spaces or Tab characters. *value* consists of one or more quoted strings separated by white space. Use any of the following types of directives:

```
domain domainname
msgid message_identifier
msgstr message_string
```

The behavior of the domain directive is affected by the options used. See "Options" on page 838 for the behavior when you specify the -o option. If you do not specify the -o option, the behavior of the domain directive is as follows.

- Put all *msgids* from the beginning of each .po file to the first domain directive into a default message object file, messages.mo.

- When msgfmt encounters a domain *domainname* directive in the .po
  file, put all following *msgids* until the next domain directive into the
  message object file domainname.mo.
- Define duplicate *msgids* in the scope of each domain. That is, a *msgid* is
  considered a duplicate only if the identical *msgid* exists in the same
  domain.
- Ignore all duplicate *msgids*.
- The msgid directive specifies the value of a message identifier associated
  with the directive that follows it. The *message_identifier* string
  identifies a target string to be used at retrieval time. Each statement
  containing a *msgid* directive must be followed by a statement containing
  a msgstr directive.
- The msgstr directive specifies the target string associated with the
  message_identifier string declared in the immediately preceding
  msgid directive.
- Message strings can contain the escape sequences \n for newline, \t for
  Tab, \v for vertical Tab, \b for backspace, \r for Return, \f for formfeed,
  \\ for backslash, \" for double quote, \ *ddd* for octal bit pattern, and \x*DD*
  for hexadecimal bit pattern.

Options

-v   List duplicate message identifiers. Message strings are not
               redefined.

-o *output-file*

               Specify output file name as *output-file*. Ignore all domain
               directives and duplicate *msgids* in the .po file.

Examples

In the following example, module1.po and module2.po are portable message
objects files.

```
castle% cat module1.po
# default domain "messages.mo"
msgid "msg 1"
msgstr "msg 1 translation"
#
domain "help_domain"
msgid "help 2"
msgstr "help 2 translation"
#
domain "error_domain"
msgid "error 3"
msgstr "error 3 translation"
castle% cat module2.po
# default domain "messages.mo"
```

```
msgid "mesg 4"
msgstr "mesg 4 translation"
#
domain "error_domain"
msgid "error 5"
msgstr "error 5 translation"
#
domain "window_domain"
msgid "window 6"
msgstr "window 6 translation"
castle%
```

The following command produces the output files, messages.mo, help_domain.mo, and error_domain.mo.

```
castle% msgfmt module1.po
```

The following command produces the output files, messages.mo, help_domain.mo, error_domain.mo, and window_domain.mo.

```
castle% msgfmt module1.po module2.po
```

The following example produces the output file hello.mo.

```
castle% msgfmt -o hello.mo module1.po module2.po
```

Install message object files in /usr/lib/locale/*locale*/LC_MESSAGES/*domain*.mo, where *locale* is the message locale as set by setlocale(3C), and *domain* is text domain as set by textdomain(). Optionally, you can change the /usr/lib/locale portion by calling bindtextdomain(). See gettext(3C).

Environment Variables

See environ(5) for descriptions of the following environmental variables that affect the execution of msgfmt: LC_CTYPE, LC_MESSAGES, and NLSPATH.

Attributes

See attributes(5) for descriptions of the following attributes:

Attribute Type	Attribute Value
Availability	SUNWloc

See Also

xgettext(1), gettext(3C), setlocale(3C), attributes(5), environ(5)

mt — Magnetic Tape Control

Synopsis
```
/usr/bin/mt [-f tapename] command... [count]
```

Description
mt sends commands to a magnetic tape drive. If you do not specify
-f tapename, the environment variable TAPE is used. If TAPE does not exist,
mt uses the device /dev/rmt/0n.

Bugs
Not all devices support all options. Some options are hardware dependent.
Refer to the corresponding device manual page.

mt is architecture sensitive. Heterogeneous operation (that is, Sun-3 to
Sun-4 or the reverse) is not supported.

Options
-f tapename   Specify the raw tape device.

Operands

count	The number of times that the requested operation is to be performed. By default, mt performs command once; you can specify multiple operations of command with count.
command	Available commands that can be sent to a magnetic tape drive. You need specify only as many characters as are required to uniquely identify a command.

eof, weof	Write count EOF marks at the current position on the tape.
fsf	Forward space over count EOF marks. Position the tape on the first block of the file.
fsr	Forward space count records.
bsf	Backspace over count EOF marks. Position the tape on the beginning-of-tape side of the EOF mark.
bsr	Backspace count records.
nbsf	Backspace count files. Position the tape on the first block of the file. Equivalent to count+1 bsf followed by one fsf.
asf	Absolute space to count file number. This is equivalent to a rewind followed by an fsf.

If *count* is specified with any of the following commands, ignore the count and perform the command only once.

eom   Space to the end of recorded material on the tape. Useful for appending files onto previously written tapes.

rewind   Rewind the tape.

offline, rewoffl   Rewind the tape and, if appropriate, take the drive unit off-line by unloading the tape. The drive unit cycles through all four tapes.

status   Print status information about the tape unit.

retension   Rewind the cartridge tape completely, then wind it forward to the end of the reel and back to beginning-of-tape to smooth out tape tension.

reserve   Allow the tape drive to remain reserved after closing the device. The drive must then be explicitly released.

release   Reestablish the default behavior of releasing at close.

forcereserve

     Break the reservation of the tape drive held by another host and then reserve the tape drive. This command can be executed only with superuser privileges.

erase   Erase the entire tape. Erasing a tape may take a long time, depending on the device and/or tape. Refer to the device-specific manual for time details.

Exit Status

0   All operations were successful.

1   Command was unrecognized or mt was unable to open the specified tape drive.

2   An operation failed.

Files

/dev/rmt/*   Magnetic tape interface.

Attributes

See `attributes`(5) for descriptions of the following attributes:

Attribute Type	Attribute Value
Availability	SUNWcsu

See Also

`tar`(1), `tcopy`(1), `ar`(4), `attributes`(5), `environ`(5), `mtio`(7I), `st`(7D)

---

mv — Move Files

Synopsis

```
/usr/bin/mv [-fi] source target-file
/usr/bin/mv [-fi] source... target-dir
/usr/xpg4/bin/mv [-fi] source target-file
/usr/xpg4/bin/mv [-fi] source... target-dir
```

Description

Use the `mv` command to move files from one place to another or to change the name of a file.

In the first synopsis form, the `mv` command moves the file named by the `source` operand to the destination specified by `target-file`. `source` and `target-file` cannot have the same name. If `target-file` does not exist, `mv` creates a file named `target-file`. If `target-file` exists, its contents are overwritten. This first synopsis form is assumed when the final operand does not name an existing directory.

In the second synopsis form, `mv` moves each file named by a `source` operand to a destination file in the existing directory named by the `target-dir` operand. The destination path for each source is the concatenation of the target directory, a single slash character (`/`), and the last path-name component of the source. This second form is assumed when the final operand names an existing directory.

If `mv` determines that the mode of `target-file` forbids writing, it prints the mode (see `chmod`(2)), asks for a response, and reads the standard input for one line. If the response is affirmative, the move occurs if permissible; otherwise, the command exits.

Note that the mode displayed may not fully represent the access permission if the target is associated with an access control list (ACL). When the parent directory of source is writable and has the sticky bit set, one or more of the following conditions must be true:

- The user must own the file.
- The user must own the directory.
- The file must be writable by the user.
- The user must be a privileged user.

If *source* is a file and *target-file* is a link to another file with links, the other links remain and *target-file* becomes a new file.

If *source* and *target-file* or *target-dir* are on different file systems, *New!* mv copies the source and deletes the original; any hard links to other files are lost. mv tries to duplicate the source file characteristics to the target, that is, the owner and group ID, permission modes, modification and access times, and ACLs if applicable. For symbolic links, mv preserves only the owner and group of the link itself.

If unable to preserve owner and group ID, mv clears the setuid and setgid *New!* bits in the target. mv prints a diagnostic message to standard error if unable to clear these bits, though the exit code is not affected. Only /usr/xpg4/bin/mv prints a diagnostic message to standard error for all other failed attempts to duplicate file characteristics; the exit code is not affected.

To preserve the source file characteristics, you must have the appropriate *New!* file access permissions, including being superuser or having the same owner ID as the destination file.

Note — You can use -- to explicitly mark the end of any command-line options, enabling mv to recognize file-name arguments that begin with a -. As an aid to BSD migration, mv accepts - as a synonym for --. This migration aid may disappear in a future release. If a -- and a - both appear on the same command line, the second is interpreted as a file name.

Options

-f   Move the file(s) without prompting even if it is writing over an existing target. Note that this is the default if the standard input is not a terminal.

-i   Prompt for confirmation whenever the move would overwrite an existing target. An affirmative answer means that the move should proceed. Any other answer prevents mv from overwriting the target.

usr/bin/mv

Specifying both the -f and the -i options is not considered an error. The -f option overrides the -i option.

/usr/xpg4/bin/mv

Specifying both the -f and the -i options is not considered an error. The last option specified determines the behavior of mv.

Operands

source A path name of a file or directory to be moved.

target-file

A new path name for the file or directory being moved.

target-dir A path name of an existing directory into which to move the input files.

Usage

See largefile(5) for the description of the behavior of mv when encountering files greater than or equal to 2 Gbytes (2**31 bytes).

Environment Variables

See environ(5) for descriptions of the following environment variables that affect the execution of mv: LC_CTYPE, LC_MESSAGES, and NLSPATH.

Exit Status

0   All input files were moved successfully.

>0   An error occurred.

Attributes

See attributes(5) for descriptions of the following attributes:

Attribute Type	Attribute Value
Availability	SUNWcsu
CSI	Enabled

/usr/xpg4/bin/mv

Attribute Type	Attribute Value
Availability	SUNWxcu4
CSI	Enabled

See Also

cp(1), cpio(1), ln(1), rm(1), setfacl(1), chmod(2), attributes(5), environ(5), largefile(5), XPG4(5)

N

native2ascii — Native-to-ASCII Converter

Synopsis

```
/usr/java/bin/native2ascii [-encoding encoding-name] [-reverse]
   [inputfile [outputfile]]
```

Description

The javac(1) compiler and other Java tools can process only files that contain Latin-1 or Unicode-encoded (\udddd notation) characters. The native2ascii command converts files that contain other character encoding into files containing Latin-1 or Unicode-encoded characters.

If you omit *outputfile*, standard output is used for output. If you also omit *inputfile*, standard input is used for input.

Options

-encoding *encoding-name*

>   Specify the encoding name that is used by the conversion procedure. The default encoding is taken from system property file.encoding. This encoding-name string must be one that can be passed as the argument of class CharacterEncoding.

Converter Class	Description
8859_1	ISO 8859-1.
8859_2	ISO 8859-2.
8859_3	ISO 8859-3.
8859_4	ISO 8859-4.
8859_5	ISO 8859-5.
8859_6	ISO 8859-6.
8859_7	ISO 8859-7.
8859_8	ISO 8859-8.
8859_9	ISO 8859-9.
Big5	Big5, Traditional Chinese.
CNS11643	CNS 11643, Traditional Chinese.
Cp037	USA, Canada (Bilingual, French), Netherlands, Portugal, Brazil, Australia.
Cp1006	IBM AIX Pakistan (Urdu).
Cp1025	IBM Multilingual Cyrillic: Bulgaria, Bosnia, Herzegovina, Macedonia(FYR).
Cp1026	IBM Latin-5, Turkey.
Cp1046	IBM Open Edition US EBCDIC.
Cp1097	IBM Iran (Farsi)/Persian.
Cp1098	IBM Iran (Farsi)/Persian (PC).
Cp1112	IBM Latvia, Lithuania.
Cp1122	IBM Estonia.
Cp1123	IBM Ukraine.
Cp1124	IBM AIX Ukraine.
Cp1125	IBM Ukraine (PC).
Cp1250	Windows Eastern European.
Cp1251	Windows Cyrillic.
Cp1252	Windows Latin-1.
Cp1253	Windows Greek.
Cp1254	Windows Turkish.
Cp1255	Windows Hebrew.
Cp1256	Windows Arabic.
Cp1257	Windows Baltic.
Cp1258	Windows Vietnamese.

Converter Class	Description
Cp1381	IBM OS/2, DOS People's Republic of China (PRC).
Cp1383	IBM AIX People's Republic of China (PRC).
Cp273	IBM Austria, Germany.
Cp277	IBM Denmark, Norway.
Cp278	IBM Finland, Sweden.
Cp280	IBM Italy.
Cp284	IBM Catalan/Spain, Spanish Latin America.
Cp285	IBM United Kingdom, Ireland.
Cp297	IBM France.
Cp33722	IBM-EUCJP - Japanese (superset of 5050).
Cp420	IBM Arabic.
Cp424	IBM Hebrew.
Cp437	MS-DOS United States, Australia, New Zealand, South Africa.
Cp500	EBCDIC 500V1.
Cp737	PC Greek.
Cp775	PC Baltic.
Cp838	IBM Thailand extended SBCS.
Cp850	MS-DOS Latin-1.
Cp852	MS-DOS Latin-2.
Cp855	IBM Cyrillic.
Cp857	IBM Turkish.
Cp860	MS-DOS Portuguese.
Cp861	MS-DOS Icelandic.
Cp862	PC Hebrew.
Cp863	MS-DOS Canadian French.
Cp864	PC Arabic.
Cp865	MS-DOS Nordic.
Cp866	MS-DOS Russian.
Cp868	MS-DOS Pakistan.
Cp869	IBM Modern Greek.
Cp870	IBM Multilingual Latin-2.
Cp871	IBM Iceland.

Converter Class	Description
Cp874	IBM Thai.
Cp875	IBM Greek.
Cp918	IBM Pakistan (Urdu).
Cp921	IBM Latvia, Lithuania (AIX, DOS).
Cp922	IBM Estonia (AIX, DOS).
Cp930	Japanese Katakana-Kanji mixed with 4370 UDC, superset of 5026.
Cp933	Korean mixed with 1880 UDC, superset of 5029.
Cp935	Simplified Chinese Host mixed with 1880 UDC, superset of 5031.
Cp937	Traditional Chinese Host mixed with 6204 UDC, superset of 5033.
Cp939	Japanese Latin Kanji mixed with 4370 UDC, superset of 5035.
Cp942	Japanese (OS/2), superset of 932.
Cp948	OS/2 Chinese (Taiwan), superset of 938.
Cp949	PC Korean.
Cp950	PC Chinese (Hong Kong, Taiwan).
Cp964	AIX Chinese (Taiwan).
Cp970	AIX Korean.
EUCJIS	JIS, EUC encoding, Japanese.
GB2312	GB2312, EUC encoding, Simplified Chinese.
GBK	GBK, Simplified Chinese.
ISO2022CN	ISO 2022 CN, Chinese.
ISO2022CN_CNS	CNS 11643 in ISO-2022-CN form, T. Chinese.
ISO2022CN_GB	GB 2312 in ISO-2022-CN form, S. Chinese.
ISO2022KR	ISO 2022 KR, Korean.
JIS	JIS, Japanese.
JIS0208	JIS 0208, Japanese.
KOI8_R	KOI8-R, Russian.
KSC5601	KS C 5601, Korean.
MS874	Windows Thai.
MacArabic	Macintosh Arabic.

Converter Class	Description
MacCentralEurope	Macintosh Latin-2.
MacCroatian	Macintosh Croatian.
MacCyrillic	Macintosh Cyrillic.
MacDingbat	Macintosh Dingbat.
MacGreek	Macintosh Greek.
MacHebrew	Macintosh Hebrew.
MacIceland	Macintosh Iceland.
MacRoman	Macintosh Roman.
MacRomania	Macintosh Romania.
MacSymbol	Macintosh Symbol.
MacThai	Macintosh Thai.
MacTurkish	Macintosh Turkish.
MacUkraine	Macintosh Ukraine.
SJIS	Shift-JIS, Japanese.
UTF8	UTF-8.

-reverse   Perform the reverse operation: convert a file with Latin-1 or Unicode-encoded characters to one with native-encoded characters.

Attributes
See attributes(5) for descriptions of the following attributes:

Attribute Type	Attribute Value
Availability	SUNWjvdev

See Also
attributes(5)

nawk — New Pattern Scanning and Processing Language

Synopsis
```
/usr/bin/nawk [-F ERE][-v assignment]
  'program' | -f progfile argument...]
/usr/xpg4/bin/awk [-F ERE][-v assignment 'program' |
  -f progfile [argument...]
```

Description

The awk command is a complete programming language that is very useful for computation and pattern matching. The name awk is an acronym composed of the last initials of the three developers of the language: Aho, Weinberger, and Kernighan. The nawk (new awk) command is a greatly enhanced and optimized version of awk.

The /usr/bin/nawk and /usr/xpg4/bin/awk commands execute programs written in the nawk programming language, which is specialized for manipulating textual data. A nawk program is a sequence of patterns and corresponding actions. You must enclose the string specifying *program* in single quotes (') to protect it from interpretation by the shell. You can specify the sequence of pattern-action statements in the command line as *program* or in one or more files that you specify with the -f *progfile* option. When input that matches a pattern is read, the action associated with the pattern is performed.

Input is interpreted as a sequence of records. By default, a record is a line, but you can change this default by using the RS built-in variable. Each record of input is matched to each pattern in the program. For each pattern matched, the associated action is executed.

The nawk command interprets each input record as a sequence of fields where, by default, a field is a string of nonblank characters. You can change this default white-space field delimiter (blanks and/or tabs) by using the FS built-in variable or the -F *ERE* option. The nawk command denotes the first field in a record as $1, the second $2, and so forth. The symbol $0 refers to the entire record; setting any other field reevaluates $0. Assigning to $0 resets the values of all fields and the NF built-in variable.

Notes

nawk is a new version of awk that provides capabilities unavailable in previous versions. This version becomes the default version of awk in the next major release.

Input white space is not preserved on output if fields are involved.

There are no explicit conversions between numbers and strings. To force an expression to be treated as a number, add 0 to it; to force it to be treated as a string, concatenate the null string (" ") to it.

Options

-F *ERE*   Define the input field separator to be the extended regular expression *ERE*, before any input is read (can be a character).

-f *progfile*

    Specify the path name of the file *progfile* containing a nawk program. If you specify multiple instances of this option, process the concatenation of the files in the order specified in *progfile*. Alternatively, you can specify the nawk program in the command line as a single argument.

```
-v assignment
```

The `assignment` argument must be in the same form as an `assignment` operand. The assignment is of the form `var=value`, where `var` is the name of one of the variables described below. The specified assignment occurs before the nawk program is executed including the actions associated with BEGIN patterns (if any). You can specify this option multiple times.

Operands

`program` If you specify no -f option, the first operand to nawk is the text of the nawk program. The application supplies the `program` operand as a single argument to nawk. If the text does not end in a newline character, nawk interprets the text as if it did.

`argument` You can intermix either of the following two types of arguments.

`file` A path name of a file that contains the input to be read, which is matched against the set of patterns in the program. If you specify no file operands or if a file operand is -, use the standard input.

`assignment` An operand that begins with an underscore or alphabetic character from the portable character set, followed by a sequence of underscores, digits, and alphabetics from the portable character set, followed by the = character specifies a variable assignment instead of a path name. The characters before the = represent the name of a nawk variable; if that name is a nawk reserved word, the behavior is undefined. The characters following the equal sign are interpreted as if they appeared in the nawk program preceded and followed by a double-quote (") character, as a STRING token. When the last character is an unescaped backslash, it is interpreted as a literal backslash instead of as the first character of the sequence " \ ". The variable is assigned the value of that STRING token. If the value is considered a numeric string, the variable is assigned its numeric value. Each such variable assignment is performed just before the processing of the following file (if any). Thus, an assignment before the first file argument is executed after the BEGIN actions (if any), while an assignment after the last file argument is executed before the END actions (if any). If there are no file arguments, execute assignments before processing the standard input.

Input Files

Input files to the nawk program can come from any of the following sources:

- Any file operands or their equivalents, achieved by modifying the nawk variables ARGV and ARGC.

- Standard input in the absence of any file operands.

- Text file arguments to the getline function. Whether the variable RS is set to a value other than a newline character, for these files, implementations support records terminated with the specified separator up to {LINE_MAX} bytes and can support longer records.

- Text file arguments to the -f *progfile* option containing a nawk program.

- The standard input when you specify no file operands or if a file operand is -.

Extended Description

A nawk program is composed of pairs of the form:

pattern { action }

You can omit either the *pattern* or the *action*, including the enclosing brace characters. Separate pattern-action statements by a semicolon or by a newline.

A missing pattern matches any record of input, and a missing action is equivalent to an action that writes the matched record of input to standard output.

Execution of the nawk program is done as follows.

1. The actions associated with all BEGIN patterns are executed in the order they occur in the program.

2. Each file operand (or standard input if no files were specified) is processed by reading data from the file until a record separator is seen (a newline character by default).

3. The current record is split into fields, using the current value of FS, evaluating each pattern in the program in the order of occurrence and executing the action associated with each pattern that matches the current record.

4. The action for a matching pattern is executed before evaluating subsequent patterns.

5. The actions associated with all END patterns are executed in the order they occur in the program.

Expressions in nawk

Expressions describe computations used in patterns and actions. The following table lists valid expression operations from highest to lowest precedence. In expression evaluation where the grammar is formally ambiguous, higher precedence operators are evaluated before lower precedence operators. In the table, *expr*, *expr1*, *expr2*, and *expr3* represent any expression, while *lvalue* represents any entity that can be assigned to (that is, on the left side of an assignment operator).

Syntax	Name	Type of Result	Associativity
(*expr*)	Grouping	Type of *expr*	N/A
$*expr*	Field reference	String	N/A
++ *lvalue*	Pre-increment	Numeric	N/A
-- *lvalue*	Pre-decrement	Numeric	N/A
lvalue ++	Post-increment	Numeric	N/A
lvalue --	Post-decrement	Numeric	N/A
expr ^ *expr*	Exponentiation	Numeric	Right
! *expr*	Logical NOT	Numeric	N/A
+ *expr*	Unary plus	Numeric	N/A
- *expr*	Unary minus	Numeric	N/A
expr * *expr*	Multiplication	Numeric	Left
expr / *expr*	Division	Numeric	Left
expr % *expr*	Modulus	Numeric	Left
expr + *expr*	Addition	Numeric	Left
expr - *expr*	Subtraction	Numeric	Left
expr *expr*	String concatenation	String	Left
expr < *expr*	Less than	Numeric	None
expr <= *expr*	Less than or equal to	Numeric	None
expr != *expr*	Not equal to	Numeric	None
expr == *expr*	Equal to	Numeric	None
expr > *expr*	Greater than	Numeric	None
expr >= *expr*	Greater than or equal to	Numeric	None

Syntax	Name	Type of Result	Associativity
expr ~ *expr*	ERE match	Numeric	None
expr !~ *expr*	ERE nonmatch	Numeric	None
expr in array (*index*) in array	Array membership Multidimension array membership	Numeric Numeric	Left Left
expr && *expr*	Logical AND	Numeric	Left
expr || *expr*	Logical OR	Numeric	Left
expr1 ? *expr2* : *expr3*	Conditional *expr*ession	Type of selected *expr2* or *expr3*	Right
lvalue ^= *expr*	Exponentiation assignment	Numeric	Right
lvalue %= *expr*	Modulus assignment	Numeric	Right
lvalue *= *expr*	Multiplication assignment	Numeric	Right
lvalue /= *expr*	Division assignment	Numeric	Right
lvalue += *expr*	Addition assignment	Numeric	Right
lvalue -= *expr*	Subtraction assignment	Numeric	Right
lvalue = *expr*	Assignment	Type of *expr*	Right

Each expression has a string value, a numeric value, or both. Except as stated for specific contexts, the value of an expression is implicitly converted to the type needed for the context in which it is used. A string value is converted to a numeric value by the equivalent of the following calls.

```
setlocale(LC_NUMERIC, ""); numeric_value = atof(string_value);
```

A numeric value that is exactly equal to the value of an integer is converted to a string by the equivalent of a call to the sprintf function, with the string %d as the fmt argument and the numeric value being converted as the first and only *expr* argument. Any other numeric value is converted to a string by the equivalent of a call to the sprintf function, with the value of the variable CONVFMT as the fmt argument and the numeric value being converted as the first and only *expr* argument.

A string value is considered to be a numeric string in the following cases.

- Any leading and trailing blank characters are ignored.
- If the first unignored character is a + or -, it is ignored.
- If the remaining unignored characters would be lexically recognized as a NUMBER token, the string is considered a numeric string.
- If a - character is ignored in the above steps, the numeric value of the numeric string is the negation of the numeric value of the recognized NUMBER token. Otherwise the numeric value of the numeric string is the numeric value of the recognized NUMBER token. Whether a string is a numeric string is relevant only in contexts where that term is used in this section.
- When an expression is used in a Boolean context, if it has a numeric value, a value of 0 is treated as `false` and any other value is treated as `true`. Otherwise, a string value of the null string is treated as `false`, and any other value is treated as `true`. A Boolean context is one of the following:
  - The first subexpression of a conditional expression.
  - An expression operated on by logical NOT, logical AND, or logical OR.
  - The second expression of a `for` statement.
  - The expression of an `if` statement.
  - The expression of the `while` clause in either a `while` or `do...while` statement.
  - An expression used as a pattern (as in Overall Program Structure).

The `nawk` language supplies arrays that are used for storing numbers or strings. Arrays need not be declared. They are initially empty and their sizes change dynamically. The subscripts or element identifiers are strings, providing a type of associative array capability. You can use an array name followed by a subscript within square brackets as an *lvalue* and as an expression, as described in the grammar. Unsubscripted array names are used only in the following contexts.

- A parameter in a function definition or function call.
- The NAME token following any use of the keyword `in`.

A valid array index consists of one or more comma-separated expressions, similar to the way that multidimensional arrays are indexed in some programming languages. Because `nawk` arrays are really one dimensional, `nawk` converts such a comma-separated list to a single string by concatenating the string values of the separate expressions, each separated from the other by the value of the SUBSEP variable. Thus, the following two index operations are equivalent.

```
var[expr1, expr2,... exprn]
var[expr1 SUBSEP expr2 SUBSEP... SUBSEP exprn]
```

You must enclose in parentheses a multidimensioned index used with the in operator. The in operator, which tests for the existence of a particular array element, does not create the element if it does not exist. Any other reference to a nonexistent array element automatically creates it.

Variables and Special Variables

You can use variables in a nawk program by referencing them. With the exception of function parameters, variables are not explicitly declared. Uninitialized scalar variables and array elements have both a numeric value of 0 and a string value of the empty string.

Field variables are designated by a $ followed by a number or numerical expression. The effect of the field number expression evaluating to anything other than a nonnegative integer is unspecified. You do not need to convert uninitialized variables or string values to numeric values in this context. Create new field variables by assigning a value to them. References to nonexistent fields (that is, fields after $NF) produce the null string. However, assigning to a nonexistent field (for example, $(NF+2) = 5) increases the value of NF, creates any intervening fields with the null string as their values and recomputes the value of $0 with the fields separated by the value of OFS. Each field variable has a string value when created. When the decimal-point character from the current locale is changed to a period character, the string is considered a *numeric string*; the field variable also has the numeric value of the *numeric string*.

nawk sets the following special variables.

ARGC   The number of elements in the ARGV array.

ARGV   An array of command-line arguments excluding options and the program argument, numbered from 0 to ARGC-1.

You can modify or add to the arguments in ARGV. You can alter ARGC. As each input file ends, nawk treats the next non-null element of ARGV, up to the current value of ARGC-1, inclusive, as the name of the next input file. Setting an element of ARGV to null means that it is not treated as an input file. The name – indicates the standard input. If an argument matches the format of an assignment operand, this argument is treated as an assignment instead of a file argument.

/usr/xpg4/bin/awk

CONVFMT   The printf format for converting numbers to strings (except for output statements, where OFMT is used); %.6g by default.

ENVIRON   The variable ENVIRON is an array representing the value of the environment. The indices of the array are strings consisting of the names of the environment variables, and the value of each array element is a string consisting of the value of that variable. If the value of an environment variable is considered a numeric string, the array element also has its numeric value.

In all cases where nawk behavior is affected by environment variables (including the environment of any commands that nawk executes via the system function or via pipeline redirections with the print statement, the printf statement, or the getline function), the environment used is the environment at the time nawk began executing.

FILENAME	A path name of the current input file. Inside a BEGIN action, the value is undefined. Inside an END action, the value is the name of the last input file processed.
FNR	The ordinal number of the current record in the current file. Inside a BEGIN action, the value is 0. Inside an END action, the value is the number of the last record processed in the last file processed.
FS	Input field separator regular expression; by default, a space character.
NF	The number of fields in the current record. Inside a BEGIN action, the use of NF is undefined unless a getline function without a var argument is executed previously. Inside an END action, NF retains the value it had for the last record read unless a subsequent, redirected getline function without a var argument is performed before entering the END action.
NR	The ordinal number of the current record from the start of input. Inside a BEGIN action, the value is 0. Inside an END action, the value is the number of the last record processed.
OFMT	The printf format for converting numbers to strings in output statements; by default, "%.6g". The result of the conversion is unspecified if the value of OFMT is not a floating-point format specification.
OFS	The print statement output field separator; by default, a space character.
ORS	The print output record separator; by default, a newline character.
LENGTH	The length of the string matched by the match function.
RS	The first character of the string value of RS is the input record separator; by default, a newline character. If RS contains more than one character, the results are unspecified. If RS is null, records are separated by sequences of one or more blank lines: leading or trailing blank lines do not produce empty records at the beginning or end of input, and the field separator is always newline, no matter what the value of FS.
RSTART	The starting position of the string matched by the match function, numbering from 1. This value is always equivalent to the return value of the match function.
SUBSEP	The subscript separator string for multidimensional arrays; the default value is 1.

Regular Expressions

The nawk command uses the extended regular expression notation (see regex(5)) except that it allows the use of C-language conventions to escape special characters within the EREs, namely, \\, \a, \b, \f, \n, \r, \t, \v, and those specified in the following table. These escape sequences are recognized both inside and outside bracket expressions.

Note — You do not need to separate records with newline characters, and string constants can contain newline characters, so even the \n sequence is valid in nawk EREs. Using a slash character within the regular expression requires escaping as shown in the table below.

Escape Sequence	Description	Meaning
\"	Backslash quotation mark.	Quotation mark character.
\/	Backslash slash.	Slash character.
ddd	A backslash character followed by the longest sequence of one-, two-, or three-digit octal characters (01234567). If all of the digits are 0 (null character), the behavior is undefined.	The character encoded by the one-, two-, or three-digit octal integer. Multibyte characters require multiple concatenated escape sequences, including the leading \ for each byte.
\c	A backslash character followed by any character not described in this table or the special characters \\, \a, \b, \f, \n, \r, \t, \v.	Undefined.

A regular expression can be matched against a specific field or string by one of the two regular expression matching operators, ~ and !~. These operators interpret their right-hand operand as a regular expression and their left-hand operand as a string. If the regular expression matches the string, the ~ expression evaluates to the value 1, and the !~ expression evaluates to the value 0. If the regular expression does not match the string, the ~ expression evaluates to the value 0, and the !~ expression evaluates to the value 1. If the right-hand operand is any expression other than the lexical token ERE, the string value of the expression is interpreted as an extended regular expression, including the escape conventions described above. Note that these same escape conventions also are applied in determining the value of a string literal (the lexical token STRING) and are applied a second time when a string literal is used in this context.

When an ERE token appears as an expression in any context other than as the right-hand side of the ~ or ! ~ operator or as one of the built-in function arguments described below, the value of the resulting expression is the equivalent of $0 ~ /ere/.

The *ere* argument to the gsub, match, and sub functions and the *fs* argument to the split function (see "String Functions" on page 863) are interpreted as extended regular expressions. These ERE tokens or arbitrary expressions are interpreted in the same manner as the right-hand side of the ~ or ! ~ operator.

An extended regular expression can be used to separate fields by using the -F *ERE* option or by assigning a string containing the expression to the built-in variable FS. The default value of the FS variable is a single-space character.

FS behaves in the following way.

1. If FS is a single character,
   - Skip leading and trailing blank characters; fields are delimited by sets of one or more blank characters.
   - Otherwise, if FS is any other character *c*, fields are delimited by each single occurrence of *c*.

2. Otherwise, the string value of FS is considered to be an extended regular expression. Each occurrence of a sequence matching the extended regular expression delimits fields.

Except in the gsub, match, split, and sub built-in functions, regular expression matching is based on input records; that is, record separator characters (the first character of the value of the variable RS, a newline character by default) cannot be embedded in the expression, and no expression matches the record separator character. If the record separator is not a newline character, newline characters embedded in the expression can be matched. In those four built-in functions, regular expression matching is based on text strings. So, any character (including the newline character and the record separator) can be embedded in the pattern, and an appropriate pattern matches any character. However, in all nawk regular expression matching, the use of one or more null characters in the pattern, input record, or text string produces undefined results.

Patterns

A pattern is any valid expression, a range specified by two expressions separated by comma, or one of the two special patterns, BEGIN or END.

Special Patterns

The nawk command recognizes two special patterns, BEGIN and END. Each BEGIN pattern is matched once and its associated action executed before the first record of input is read (except possibly by use of the getline function in a prior BEGIN action) and before command-line assignment is done. Each END pattern is matched once, and its associated action is executed after the last record of input has been read. These two patterns have associated actions.

BEGIN and END do not combine with other patterns. Multiple BEGIN and END patterns are allowed. The actions associated with the BEGIN patterns are executed in the order specified in the program, as are the END actions. An END pattern can precede a BEGIN pattern in a program.

If a nawk program consists of only actions with the pattern BEGIN and the BEGIN action contains no getline function, nawk exits without reading its input when the last statement in the last BEGIN action is executed. If a nawk program consists of only actions with the pattern END or only actions with the patterns BEGIN and END, the input is read before the statements in the END actions are executed.

Expression Patterns

An expression pattern is evaluated as if it were an expression in a Boolean context. If the result is true, the pattern is considered to match, and the associated action (if any) is executed. If the result is false, the action is not executed.

Pattern Ranges

A pattern range consists of two expressions separated by a comma. In this case, the action is performed for all records between a match of the first expression and the following match of the second expression, inclusive. At this point, the pattern range can be repeated, starting at input records subsequent to the end of the matched range.

Actions

An action is a sequence of statements. A statement can be one of the following.

```
if ( expression ) statement [else statement]
while ( expression ) statement
do statement while ( expression )
for ( expression ; expression ; expression ) statement
for ( var in array ) statement
delete array[subscript]        #delete an array element
break
continue
{ [statement]... }
expression              # commonly, variable = expression
print [expression-list] [>expression]
printf format [, expression-list] [>expression]
next                    # skip remaining patterns on this input line
exit [expr]             # skip the rest of the input; exit status is expr
return [expr]
```

You can replace any single statement with a statement list enclosed in braces. Terminate statements with newline characters or semicolons. Statements are executed sequentially in the order that they appear.

The next statement abandons all further processing of the current input record. The behavior is undefined if a next statement appears or is invoked in a BEGIN or END action.

The `exit` statement invokes all END actions in the order that they occur in the program source and then terminates the program without reading further input. An `exit` statement inside an END action terminates the program without further execution of END actions. If an expression is specified in an `exit` statement, its numeric value is the exit status of nawk unless subsequent errors are encountered or a subsequent `exit` statement with an expression is executed.

Output Statements

Both `print` and `printf` statements write to standard output by default. The output is written to the location specified by output redirection if one is supplied, as follows.

```
>  expression
>> expression
|  expression
```

In all cases, the expression is evaluated to produce a string that is used as a full path name to write into (for > or >>) or as a command to be executed (for |). Using the first two forms, if the file of that name is not currently open, it is opened. If necessary it is created. With the first form, the file is truncated. The output then is appended to the file. As long as the file remains open, subsequent calls in which *expression* evaluates to the same string value simply append output to the file. The file remains open until the `close` function is called with an expression that evaluates to the same string value.

The third form writes output onto a stream piped to the input of a command. The stream is created if no stream is currently open, with the value of *expression* as its command name. The stream created is equivalent to one created by a call to the popen(3S) function, with the value of *expression* as the command argument and a value of w as the mode argument. As long as the stream remains open, subsequent calls, in which *expression* evaluates to the same string value, write output to the existing stream. The stream remains open until the `close` function is called with an expression that evaluates to the same string value. At that time, the stream is closed as if by a call to the pclose function.

These output statements take a comma-separated list of expressions referred to in the grammar by the nonterminal symbols expr_list, print_expr_list, or print_expr_list_opt. This list is referred to here as the expression list, and each member is referred to as an expression argument.

The `print` statement writes the value of each expression argument onto the indicated output stream separated by the current output field separator (see variable OFS) and terminated by the output record separator (see variable ORS). All expression arguments are taken as strings, converted if necessary; with the exception that the `printf` format in OFMT is used instead of the value in CONVFMT. An empty expression list stands for the whole input record ($0).

The `printf` statement produces output based on a notation similar to the File Format Notation used to describe file formats in this document. Output is produced as specified, with the first expression argument as the string format and subsequent expression arguments as the strings arg1 to argn, inclusive, with the following exceptions.

- The format is an actual character string instead of a graphical representation. Therefore, it cannot contain empty character positions. The space character in the format string, in any context other than a flag of a conversion specification, is treated as an ordinary character

- If the character set contains a / \ character and that character appears in the format string, it is treated as an ordinary character that is copied to the output.

- The escape sequences beginning with a backslash character are treated as sequences of ordinary characters that are copied to the output. Note that these same sequences are interpreted lexically by nawk when they appear in literal strings, but they are not treated specially by the printf statement.

- A field width or precision can be specified as the * character instead of a digit string. In this case, the next argument from the expression list is fetched, and its numeric value is taken as the field width or precision.

- The implementation does not precede or follow output from the d or u conversion specifications with blank characters not specified by the format string.

- The implementation does not precede output from the o conversion specification with leading 0s not specified by the format string.

- For the c conversion specification: if the argument has a numeric value, the character whose encoding is that value is output. If the value is 0 or is not the encoding of any character in the character set, the behavior is undefined. If the argument does not have a numeric value, the first character of the string value is output; if the string does not contain any characters, the behavior is undefined.

- For each conversion specification that consumes an argument, the next expression argument is evaluated. With the exception of the c conversion, the value is converted to the appropriate type for the conversion specification.

- If there are insufficient expression arguments to satisfy all the conversion specifications in the format string, the behavior is undefined.

- If any character sequence in the format string begins with a % character but does not form a valid conversion specification, the behavior is unspecified. Both print and printf can output at least {LINE_MAX} bytes.

Functions
The nawk language has a variety of built-in functions: arithmetic, string, input/output, and general.

Arithmetic Functions

The arithmetic functions, except for `int`, are based on the ISO C standard. The behavior is undefined in cases where the ISO C standard specifies that an error be returned or that the behavior is undefined. Although the grammar permits built-in functions to appear with no arguments or parentheses, unless the argument or parentheses are indicated as optional in the following list (by displaying them within the `[]` brackets), such use is undefined.

`atan2(y,x)`	Return arctangent of y/x.
`cos(x)`	Return cosine of x, where x is in radians.
`sin(x)`	Return sine of x, where x is in radians.
`exp(x)`	Return the exponential function of x.
`log(x)`	Return the natural logarithm of x.
`sqrt(x)`	Return the square root of x.
`int(x)`	Truncate its argument to an integer. Truncate toward 0 when $x > 0$.
`rand()`	Return a random number n, such that $0 < n < 1$.
`srand([expr])`	

Set the seed value for `rand` to *expr* or use the time of day if *expr* is omitted. Return the previous seed value.

String Functions

The string functions in the following list are supported. Although the grammar permits built-in functions to appear with no arguments or parentheses, unless the argument or parentheses are indicated as optional in the following list (by displaying them within the `[]` brackets), such use is undefined.

`gsub(ere,repl[,in])`

Behave like `sub` (see below), except replace all occurrences of the regular expression (like the `ed` command global substitute) in `$0` or in the *in* argument, when specified.

`index(s,t)`

Return the position, in characters, numbering from 1, in string *s* where string *t* first occurs, or 0 if it does not occur at all.

`length[([s])]`

Return the length, in characters, of its argument taken as a string, or of the whole record, `$0`, if there is no argument.

`match(s,ere)`

Return the position, in characters, numbering from 1, in string *s* where the extended regular expression *ere* occurs, or 0 if it does not occur at all. Set RSTART to the starting position (which is the same as the returned value), 0 if no match is found; set RLENGTH to the length of the matched string, -1 if no match is found.

split(*s*,*a*[,*fs*])

> Split the string *s* into array elements *a*[1], *a*[2],..., *a*[n], and return *n*. Do the separation with the extended regular expression *fs* or with the field separator FS if you do not specify *fs*. Each array element has a string value when created. When any occurrence of the decimal-point character from the current locale is changed to a period character, a string assigned to any array element is considered a numeric string; the array element also has the numeric value of the numeric string. The effect of a null string as the value of *fs* is unspecified.

sprintf(fmt, *expr*, *expr*,...)

> Format the expressions according to the printf format given by fmt and return the resulting string.

sub(*ere*, *repl*[,*in*])

> Substitute the string *repl* in place of the first instance of the extended regular expression *ere* in string *in*, and return the number of substitutions. Replace an ampersand (&) in the string *repl* with the string from *in* that matches the regular expression. For each occurrence of backslash (\) encountered when scanning the string *repl* from beginning to end, take the next character literally and lose its special meaning (for example, interpret \& as a literal ampersand character). Except for & and \, it is unspecified what the special meaning of any such character is. If you specify *in* and it is not an *lvalue*, the behavior is undefined. If you omit *in*, substitute in the current record ($0).

substr(*s*, *m*[,*n*])

> Return at most the *n*-character substring of *s* that begins at position *m*, numbering from 1. If *n* is missing, limit the length of the substring by the length of the string *s*.

tolower(*s*) Return a string based on the string *s*. In the returned string, replace each character in *s* that is an uppercase letter specified to have a tolower mapping by the LC_CTYPE category of the current locale with the lowercase letter specified by the mapping. Other characters in *s* are unchanged in the returned string.

toupper(*s*) Return a string based on the string *s*. In the returned string, replace each character in *s* that is a lowercase letter specified to have a toupper mapping by the LC_CTYPE category with the uppercase letter specified by the mapping. Other characters in *s* are unchanged in the returned string.

All of the preceding functions that take *ERE* as a parameter expect a pattern or a string-valued expression that is a regular expression as defined below.

Input/Output and General Functions
The input/output and general functions are listed below.

close(*expression*)

> Close the file or pipe opened by a print or printf statement or a call to getline with the same string-valued expression. If the close was successful, return 0; otherwise, return non-zero.

expression | getline [*var*]

> Read a record of input from a stream piped from the output of a command. If no stream is currently open, create the stream with the value of *expression* as its command name. The stream created is equivalent to one created by a call to the popen function with the value of expression as the command argument and a value of r as the mode argument. As long as the stream remains open, subsequent calls in which expression evaluates to the same string value read subsequent records from the file. The stream remains open until the close function is called with an expression that evaluates to the same string value. At that time, the stream is closed as if by a call to the pclose function. If *var* is missing, $0 and NF are set; otherwise, *var* is set.

> The getline operator can form ambiguous constructs when there are operators that are not in parentheses (including concatenate) to the left of the | (to the beginning of the expression containing getline). In the context of the $ operator, | behaves as if it had a lower precedence than $. The result of evaluating other operators is unspecified, and all such uses of portable applications must be put in parentheses properly.

getline

> Set $0 to the next input record from the current input file. This form of getline sets the NF, NR, and FNR variables.

getline *var*

> Set variable *var* to the next input record from the current input file. This form of getline sets the FNR and NR variables.

getline [*var*] < *expression*

> Read the next record of input from a named file. The expression is evaluated to produce a string that is used as a full path name. If the file of that name is not currently open, open it. As long as the stream remains open, subsequent calls in which *expression* evaluates to the same string value read subsequent records from the file. The file remains open until the close function is called with an expression that evaluates to the same string value. If *var* is missing, $0 and NF are set; otherwise, *var* is set.

> The getline operator can form ambiguous constructs when there are binary operators that are not in parentheses (including concatenate) to the right of the < (up to the end of the expression containing the getline). The result of evaluating such a construct is unspecified, and all such uses of portable applications must be put in parentheses properly.

```
system(expression)
```
> Execute the command given by *expression* in a manner equivalent to the system(3S) function and return the exit status of the command.

All forms of getline return 1 for successful input, 0 for end-of-file, and -1 for an error.

Where strings are used as the name of a file or pipeline, the strings must be textually identical. The terminology "same string value" implies that "equivalent strings," even those that differ only by space characters, represent different files.

User-Defined Functions

The nawk language also provides user-defined functions. You can define such functions with the following syntax.

```
function name(args,...) { statements }
```

You can refer to a function anywhere in a nawk program; in particular, you can use it before it is defined. The scope of a function is global.

Function arguments can be either scalars or arrays; the behavior is undefined if an array name is passed as an argument that the function uses as a scalar or if a scalar expression is passed as an argument that the function uses as an array. Function arguments are passed by value if scalar, and by reference if array name. Argument names are local to the function; all other variable names are global. The same name is not used both as an argument name and as the name of a function or a special nawk variable. The same name must not be used both as a variable name with global scope and as the name of a function. The same name must not be used within the same scope both as a scalar variable and as an array.

The number of parameters in the function definition need not match the number of parameters in the function call. Excess formal parameters can be used as local variables. If fewer arguments are supplied in a function call than are in the function definition, the extra parameters that are used in the function body as scalars are initialized with a string value of the null string and a numeric value of 0 and the extra parameters that are used in the function body as arrays are initialized as empty arrays. If more arguments are supplied in a function call than are in the function definition, the behavior is undefined.

When invoking a function, put no white space between the function name and the opening parenthesis. You can nest function calls and make recursive calls on functions. On return from any nested or recursive function call, the values of all of the calling function's parameters are unchanged except for array parameters passed by reference. You can use the return statement to return a value. If a return statement appears outside a function definition, the behavior is undefined.

In the function definition, newline characters are optional before the opening brace and after the closing brace. Function definitions can appear anywhere in the program where a pattern-action pair is allowed.

Usage

Do not confuse the `index`, `length`, `match`, and `substr` functions with similar functions in the ISO C standard; the `nawk` versions deal with characters, whereas the ISO C standard deals with bytes.

Because the concatenation operation is represented by adjacent expressions instead of an explicit operator, you often need to use parentheses to enforce the proper evaluation precedence.

See `largefile`(5) for the description of the behavior of `nawk` when encountering files greater than or equal to 2 Gbytes (2**31 bytes).

Examples

The `nawk` program specified in the command line is most easily specified within single quotes (for example, `'program'`) for applications using `sh`, because `nawk` programs commonly contain characters that are special to the shell, including double quotes. In the cases where a `nawk` program contains single-quote characters, it is usually easiest to specify most of the program as strings within single quotes concatenated by the shell with quoted single-quote characters. The following example prints all lines from the standard input containing a single quote character prefixed with `quote:`.

```
awk '/'\''/ { print "quote:", $0 }'
```

The rest of the examples show simple `nawk` programs.

The following example writes to the standard output all input lines for which field 3 is greater than 5.

```
$3 > 5
```

The following example writes every tenth line.

```
(NR % 10) == 0
```

The following example writes any line with a substring matching the regular expression.

```
/(G|D)(2[0-9][[:alpha:]]*)/
```

The following example prints any line with a substring containing a G or D, followed by a sequence of digits and characters. It uses character classes `digit` and `alpha` to match language-independent digit and alphabetic characters.

```
/(G|D)([[:digit:][:alpha:]]*)/
```

The following example writes any line in which the second field matches the regular expression and the fourth field does not.

```
$2 ~ /xyz/ && $4 !~ /xyz/
```

The following example writes any line in which the second field contains a backslash.

```
$2 ~ /\\/
```

The following example writes any line in which the second field contains a backslash. Note that backslash escapes are interpreted twice, once in lexical processing of the string and once in processing the regular expression.

```
$2 ~ "\\\\"
```

The following example writes the penultimate and the last field in each line with fields separated by colons.

```
{OFS=":";print $(NF-1), $NF}
```

The following example writes the line number and number of fields in each line. The three strings representing the line number, the colon, and the number of fields are concatenated and that string is written to standard output.

```
{print NR ":" NF}
```

The following example writes lines longer than 72 characters.

```
{length($0) > 72}
```

The following example writes the first two fields in opposite order separated by the OFS.

```
{ print $2, $1 }
```

The following example writes the first two fields in opposite order with input fields separated by comma, or space and Tab characters, or both.

```
BEGIN { FS = ",[\t]*|[\t]+" }
  { print $2, $1 }\
```

The following example adds up the first column and prints the sum and average.

```
{s += $1 }
END {print "sum is ", s, " average is", s/NR}
```

The following example writes the fields in reverse order, one per line (many lines out for each line in).

```
{ for (i = NF; i > 0; --i) print $i }
```

The following example writes all lines between occurrences of the strings start and stop.

```
/start/, /stop/
```

The following example writes all lines whose first field is different from the previous one.

```
$1 != prev { print; prev = $1 }
```

The following example simulates the echo command.

```
BEGIN {
 for (i = 1; i < ARGC; ++i)
 printf "%s%s", ARGV[i], i==ARGC-
 1?"\n":""
}
```

The following example writes the path prefixes contained in the PATH environment variable, one per line.

```
BEGIN {
 n = split (ENVIRON["PATH"], path, ":")
 for (i = 1; i <= n; ++i)
 print path[i]
```

In the following example, if a file named input contains page headers of the following form

```
Page#
```

and a file named program contains the following lines

```
/Page/{ $2 = n++; }
 { print }
```

then the following command prints the file input, filling in page numbers starting at 5.

```
nawk -f program n=5 input
```

Environment Variables

See environ(5) for descriptions of the following environment variables that affect execution of nawk: LC_COLLATE, LC_CTYPE, LC_MESSAGES, LC_NUMERIC, and NLSPATH.

Exit Status

0	All input files were processed successfully.
>0	An error occurred.

You can alter the exit status within the program by using an exit expression.

Attributes

See attributes(5) for descriptions of the following attributes:

/usr/bin/nawk

Attribute Type	Attribute Value
Availability	SUNWcsu

/usr/xpg4/bin/awk

Attribute Type	Attribute Value
Availability	SUNWxcu4

See Also

awk(1), ed(1), egrep(1), grep(1), lex(1), sed(1), popen(3S), printf(3S), system(3S), attributes(5), environ(5), largefile(5), regex(5), xpg4(5)

Aho, A. V., B. W. Kernighan, and P. J. Weinberger, *The AWK Programming Language*, Addison-Wesley, 1988.

Diagnostics

If any file operand is specified and the named file cannot be accessed, nawk writes a diagnostic message to standard error and terminates without any further action.

If the program specified by either the *program* operand or a *progfile* operand is not a valid nawk program, the behavior is undefined.

---

neqn — Typeset Mathematics Test

Synopsis

/usr/bin/neqn [*file*]...

Description

See eqn(1).

newaliases — Rebuild the Database for the Mail Aliases File

Synopsis
```
/usr/bin/newaliases
```

Description
The `newaliases` command rebuilds the random access database for the mail aliases file `/etc/mail/aliases`. It is run automatically by `sendmail`(1M) (in the default configuration) whenever `/etc/mail/aliases` is newer than `/etc/mail/aliases.pag`.

    `newaliases` accepts all the flags that `sendmail`(1M) accepts. However, most of these flags have no effect, except for the `-C` option and three of the processing options that can be set from a configuration file with the `-o` option.

`-C /path/to/alt/config/file`

        Use alternate configuration file.

`-oAfile`   Specify possible alias `file`(s).

`-oLn`   Set the default log level to n. Default is 9.

`-on`   Validate the RHS of aliases when rebuilding the `aliases`(4) database.

    `newaliases` automatically runs in verbose mode (`-v` option).

Examples
To run `newaliases` on an alias file different from the `/etc/mail/aliases` default in `sendmail`(1M):

```
castle% newaliases -oA/path/to/alternate/alias/file
```

Exit Status
`newaliases` returns an exit status describing what it did. The codes are defined in `/usr/include/sysexits.h`.

New!

`EX_OK`   Successful completion on all addresses.

`EX-NOUSER`   User name not recognized.

`EX_UNAVAILABLE`

        Necessary resources were not available. This exit status is a catchall.

`EX_SYNTAX`   Syntax error in address.

`EX_SOFTWARE`

        Internal software error including bad arguments.

EX-OSERR   Temporary operating system error such as cannot fork.

EX-NOHOST   Host name not recognized.

EX_TEMPFAIL

Message could not be sent immediately but was queued.

Files

/etc/aliases

Symbolic link to /etc/mail/aliases.

/etc/mail/aliases.pag

/etc/mail/aliases.dir

ndbm files maintained by newaliases.

Attributes

See attributes(5) for descriptions of the following attributes:

Attribute Type	Attribute Value
Availability	SUNWnisu

See Also

newform(1), sendmail(1M), aliases(4), attributes(5)

---

newform — Change the Format of a Text File

Synopsis

/usr/bin/newform [-s] [-itabspec] [-otabspec] [-bn] [-en] [-pn] [-an] [-f]
 [-cchar] [-ln] [filename...]

Description

Use the newform command to reformat files according to the specified options.
newform reads lines from the named file names, or the standard input if you
specify no input file, and reproduces the lines on the standard output. Lines are
reformatted in accordance with the specified command-line options.

Except for -s, you can specify options in any order, repeat them, and
intermingle them with optional file names. Command-line options are
processed in the order specified. This means that option sequences such as
-e15 -l60 yield results different from -l60 -e15. Options are applied to all
file names on the command line.

Notes

newform normally keeps track only of physical characters; however, for the -i
and -o options, newform keeps track of backspaces to be able to line up Tabs in
the appropriate logical columns.

newform does not prompt you if a *tabspec* is to be read from the standard
input (by use of -i-- or -o--).

If you use the -f option and the last -o option specified was -o--, and it was
preceded by either a -o-- or a -i--, the Tab specification format line is
incorrect.

Options

-a*n*	Same as -p*n*, except append characters to the end of a line.
-b*n*	Truncate *n* characters from the beginning of the line when the line length is greater than the effective line length (see -l*n*). Default is to truncate the number of characters necessary to obtain the effective line length. The default value is used when you specify -b with no *n*. You can use this option to delete the sequence numbers from a COBOL program as follows: newform -l1 -b7 *filename*
-c*char*	Change the prefix/append character to *char*. Default character for *char* is a space.
-e*n*	Same as -b*n*, except truncate characters from the end of the line.
-f	Write the Tab specification format line on the standard output before any other lines are output. The Tab specification format line that is printed corresponds to the format specified in the last -o option. If you specify no -o option, the line that is printed contains the default specification of -8.
-i*tabspec*	Expand Tabs to spaces according to the Tab specifications given. *tabspec* recognizes all Tab specification forms described in tabs(1). In addition, *tabspec* can be --, in which case, newform assumes that the Tab specification is to be found in the first line read from the standard input (see fspec(4)). If you specify no *tabspec*, *tabspec* defaults to -8. A *tabspec* of -0 expects no Tabs; if any are found, they are treated as -1.
-l*n*	Set the effective line length to *n* characters. If you do not specify *n*, -l defaults to 72. The default line length without the -l option is 80 characters. Note that Tabs and backspaces are considered to be one character (use -i to expand Tabs to spaces). You must use -l1 to set the effective line length shorter than any existing line in the file so that the -b option is activated.
-o*tabspec*	Replace spaces with Tabs according to the Tab specifications given. The Tab specifications are the same as for -i *tabspec*. If you specify no *tabspec*, *tabspec* defaults to -8. A *tabspec* of -0 means that no spaces are converted to Tabs on output.

-p*n*   Prefix *n* characters (see -c*char*) to the beginning of a line when the line length is less than the effective line length. Default is to prefix the number of characters necessary to obtain the effective line length.

-s   Shear off leading characters on each line up to the first Tab and put up to eight of the sheared characters at the end of the line. If more than eight characters (not counting the first Tab) are sheared, replace the eighth character with a * and discard any characters to the right of it. Always discard the first Tab.

   Save the characters sheared off internally until all other options specified are applied to that line. Then, add the characters at the end of the processed line.

   For example, you have a file with leading digits, one or more Tabs, and text on each line. You want to convert that file to a file beginning with the text, all Tabs after the first expanded to spaces, padded with spaces out to column 72 (or truncated to column 72), and the leading digits placed starting at column 73. The command is: newform -s -i -1 -a -e *filename*
If you use this option on a file without a Tab on each line, newform displays an error message and exits.

New! Operands

  filename Input file.

Examples

The following example first uses the cat command to display a file with leading numbers and Tabs. Then it uses the newform -s command to strip the numbers and Tabs from the beginning of each line and append the numbers to the end of the line. The first Tab is always discarded.

```
castle% cat kookaburra-1
1.      Kookaburra sits in the old gum tree
2.      Merry merry king of the bush is he.
3.      Laugh, kookaburra, laugh, kookaburra
4.      Gay your life must be.
5.
6.      Kookaburra sits in the old gum tree
7.      Eating all the gumdrops he can see.
8.      Stop, kookaburra, stop, kookaburra
9.      Leave some there for me.
castle% newform -s kookaburra-1
Kookaburra sits in the old gum tree1.
Merry merry king of the bush is he.2.
Laugh, kookaburra, laugh, kookaburra3.
Gay your life must be.4.
5.
Kookaburra sits in the old gum tree6.
Eating all the gumdrops he can see.7.
```

```
Stop, kookaburra, stop, kookaburra8.
Leave some there for me.9.
castle%
```

Exit Status

New!

0	Successful operation.
1	Operation failed.

Attributes

See attributes(5) for descriptions of the following attributes:

Attribute Type	Attribute Value
Availability	SUNWesu

See Also

csplit(1), tabs(1), fspec(4), attributes(5)

Diagnostics

All diagnostics are fatal.

usage:...

> newform was called with a bad option.

"not -s format"

> There was no Tab on one line.

"can't open file"

> Self-explanatory.

"internal line too long"

> A line exceeds 512 characters after being expanded in the internal work buffer.

"tabspec in error"

> A Tab specification is incorrectly formatted, or specified Tab stops are not ascending.

"tabspec indirection illegal"

> A *tabspec* read from a file (or standard input) may not contain a *tabspec* referencing another file (or standard input).

newgrp — Log In to a New Group

Synopsis

    /usr/bin/newgrp [- | -l][group]

sh

    newgrp [argument]

ksh

    *
    newgrp [argument...]

Description

Use the newgrp command to log in to a new group by changing your real and effective group ID. You remain logged in and the current directory is unchanged. The execution of newgrp always replaces the current shell with a new shell even if the command terminates with an error (unknown group).

Any variable that is not exported is reset to null or its default value. Exported variables retain their values. System variables (such as PS1, PS2, PATH, MAIL, and HOME) are reset to default values unless they have been exported by the system or the user. For example, when you have a primary prompt string (PS1) other than $ (default) and have not exported PS1, your PS1 is set to the default prompt string $, even if newgrp terminates with an error.

> **Note** — The shell command export (see sh(1) and set(1)) is the method to export variables so that they retain their assigned value when invoking new shells.

With no operands and options, newgrp changes your group IDs (real and effective) back to the group specified in your password file entry. This way you can exit the effect of an earlier newgrp command.

A password is demanded if the group has a password and you are not listed in /etc/group as being a member of that group.

> **Note** — The only way to create a password for a group is to use passwd(1), then cut and paste the encrypted password from /etc/shadow to /etc/group. Group passwords are antiquated and not often used.

Bourne Shell

Equivalent to exec newgrp argument where argument represents the options or operand of the newgrp command.

Korn Shell

Equivalent to exec /bin/newgrp argument where argument represents the options or operand of the newgrp command.

For the `newgroup` command, `ksh(1)` commands that are preceded by one or two asterisks (`*`) are treated specially in the following ways.

- Variable assignment lists preceding the command remain in effect when the command completes.
- I/O redirections are processed after variable assignments.
- Errors cause a script that contains them to abort.
- Words following a command preceded by `**` and that are in the format of a variable assignment are expanded with the same rules as a variable assignment. This means that tilde substitution is performed after the `=` sign, and word splitting and file-name generation are not performed.

Options

`-l | -`   Change the environment to what would be expected if the user actually logged in again as a member of the new group.

Operands

group   A group name from the group database or a nonnegative numeric group ID. Specify the group ID used to set the real and effective group IDs. If group is a nonnegative numeric string and exists in the group database as a group name (see `getgrnam(3C)`), use the numeric group ID associated with that group name as the group ID.

argument   `sh` and `ksh` only. Options and/or operand of the `newgrp` command.

Environment Variables

See `environ(5)` for descriptions of the following environment variables that affect the execution of `newgrp`: `LC_CTYPE`, `LC_MESSAGES`, and `NLSPATH`.

Exit Status

If `newgrp` succeeds in creating a new shell execution environment, whether or not the group identification was changed successfully, the exit status is the exit status of the shell. Otherwise, the following exit value is returned.

`>0`   An error occurred.

Files

`/etc/group` System group file.

`/etc/passwd` System password file.

Attributes

See attributes(5) for descriptions of the following attributes:

Attribute Type	Attribute Value
Availability	SUNWcsu

See Also

login(1), ksh(1), set(1), sh(1), intro(2), getgrnam(3C), group(4), passwd(4), attributes(5), environ(5)

---

news — Print News Items

Synopsis

/usr/bin/news [-a][-n][-s][*items*]

Description

The news command consults the /var/news directory for information about current events. Use news to keep informed of current events. By convention, these events are described by files in the directory /var/news.

When invoked without arguments, news prints the contents of all current files in /var/news, most recent first, with each preceded by an appropriate header. news stores the currency time as the modification date of a file named .news_time in the user's home directory (the identity of this directory is determined by the environment variable $HOME); only files more recent than this currency time are considered current.

Options

-a	Print all items, regardless of currency. In this case, the stored time is not changed.
-n	Report the names of the current items without printing their contents and without changing the stored time.
-s	Report how many current items exist, without printing their names or contents and without changing the stored time. It is useful to include such an invocation of news in your .profile file or in the system's /etc/profile.

All other arguments are assumed to be specific news items that are to be printed.

If you press the Delete key during the printing of a news item, printing stops and the next item is started. Another delete within one second of the first terminates the program.

Examples

The following example displays one news item.

```
castle% news

stocknews (root) Thu Mar 18 14:46:34 1999
    Today the U.S. Stock Market broke the 10,000 barrier.

castle%
```

When all news items have been read, typing news simply returns the prompt, as shown in the following example.

```
castle% news
castle%
```

You can display all news items by using the -a option, as shown in the following example.

```
castle% news -a

stocknews (root) Thu Mar 18 14:46:34 1999
    Today the U.S. Stock Market broke the 10,000 barrier.

castle%
```

You can display individual news items by name by typing the name of the article as an argument to news, as shown in the following example.

```
castle% news stocknews

stocknews (root) Thu Mar 18 14:46:34 1999
    Today the U.S. Stock Market broke the 10,000 barrier.

castle%
```

nice — Invoke a Command with an Altered Scheduling Priority

Synopsis

```
/usr/bin/nice [-increment | -n increment] command [argument...]
/usr/xpg4/bin/nice [-increment | -n increment]
  command [argument...]
```

csh Built-in

```
nice [-increment | +increment] [command]
```

Description

Use the nice command to raise or lower the priority of a command or a process. When you use the nice command without an argument, the default is to increase the nice number by ten units, thus lowering the priority of the process.

The priocntl(1) command is a more general interface to scheduler functions.

The invoking process (generally, the user's shell) must be in a scheduling class that supports nice.

If you use the C shell (see csh(1)), you must specify the full path of the nice command; otherwise, the csh built-in version of nice is invoked. See C Shell Built-in below.

/usr/bin/nice

If nice executes commands with arguments, it uses the default shell /usr/bin/sh (see sh(1)).

/usr/xpg4/bin/nice

If nice executes commands with arguments, it uses /usr/xpg4/bin/sh, which is equivalent to /usr/bin/ksh (see ksh(1)).

C Shell Built-in

nice is also a csh built-in command with behavior different from the command versions. See csh(1) for a description.

Options

```
-increment | -n increment
```

> increment must be in the range 1-19; if not specified, assume an increment of 10. An increment greater than 19 is equivalent to 19.

The superuser can run commands with priority higher than normal by using a negative increment such as --10. A negative increment assigned by an unprivileged user is ignored.

Operands

command	The name of a command that is to be invoked. If command names any of the special built-in commands (see shell_builtins(1)), the results are undefined.
argument	Any string to be supplied as an argument when invoking command.

Examples

The following example lowers the priority of a command by four units (the default).

```
castle% /usr/bin/nice command
```

The following example lowers the priority of a command by increasing the `nice` number by 10 units.

```
castle% /usr/bin/nice +1- command
```

Note — The plus sign is optional for positive numbers. The minus sign is required for negative numbers.

The following example raises the priority of a command by lowering the `nice` number by 10 units. The first minus sign is the option sign and the second minus sign indicates a negative number.

```
# /usr/bin/nice - -10 command
```

Environment Variables

See `environ`(5) for descriptions of the following environment variables that affect the execution of `nice`: LC_CTYPE, LC_MESSAGES, PATH, and NLSPATH.

Exit Status

If *command* is invoked, the exit status of `nice` is the exit status of *command*; otherwise, `nice` exits with one of the following values.

1-125	An error occurred.
126	*command* was found but could not be invoked.
127	*command* could not be found.

Attributes

See `attributes`(5) for descriptions of the following attributes:

/usr/bin/nice

Attribute Type	Attribute Value
Availability	SUNWcsu
CSI	Enabled

/usr/xpg4/bin/nice

Attribute Type	Attribute Value
Availability	SUNWxcu4
CSI	Enabled

See Also

```
csh(1),ksh(1),nohup(1),priocntl(1),sh(1),shell_builtins(1),nice(2),
attributes(5), environ(5), XPG4(5)
```

nis+, NIS+, nis — New Version of the Network Information Name Service

Description

NIS+ is a new version of the network information name service. This version differs in several significant ways from version 2, which is referred to as NIS or YP in earlier releases. Specific areas of enhancement include the ability to scale to larger networks, security, and the administration of the service.

The manual pages for NIS+ are divided into three basic categories. Section 1 manual pages describe the user commands that are most often executed from a shell script or directly from the command line. Section 1M manual pages describe commands that can be used by the network administrator to administer the service itself. Section 3N manual pages describe the NIS+ programming API.

All commands and functions that use NIS version 2 are prefixed by the letters yp as in ypmatch(1), ypcat(1), yp_match(3N), and yp_first(3N). Commands and functions that use the new replacement software NIS+ are prefixed by the letters nis as in nismatch(1), nischown(1), nis_list(3N), and nis_add_entry(3N). See "List of Commands" on page 893 for a complete list of NIS+ commands.

This manual page introduces the NIS+ terminology. It also describes the NIS+ namespace, authentication, and authorization policies.

NIS+ Namespace

The naming model of NIS+ is based on a tree structure. Each node in the tree corresponds to an NIS+ object. NIS+ has six types of objects:

- Directory
- Table
- Group
- Link
- Entry
- Private

NIS+ Directory Object

Each NIS+ namespace has at least one NIS+ directory object. An NIS+ directory is like a UNIX file-system directory that contains other NIS+ objects, including NIS+ directories. The NIS+ directory that forms the root of the NIS+ namespace is called the root directory. NIS+ has two special directories.

- `org_dir` consists of all the systemwide administration tables such as `passwd`, `hosts`, and `mail_aliases`.
- `groups_dir` holds NIS+ group objects that are used for access control.

The collection of `org_dir`, `groups_dir`, and their parent directory is referred to as an NIS+ domain. You can arrange NIS+ directories in a treelike structure so that the NIS+ namespace can match the organizational or administrative hierarchy.

NIS+ Table Object

NIS+ tables (not files) contained within NIS+ directories store the actual information about some particular type. For example, the `hosts` system table stores information about the IP address of the hosts in that domain. NIS+ tables are multicolumn, and you can search the tables through any of the searchable columns. Each table object defines the schema for its table. The NIS+ tables consist of NIS+ entry objects. For each entry in the NIS+ table, there is an NIS+ entry object. NIS+ entry objects conform to the schema defined by the NIS+ table object.

NIS+ Group Object

NIS+ group objects are used for access control at group granularity. NIS+ group objects, contained within the `groups_dir` directory of a domain, contain a list of all the NIS+ principals within a certain NIS+ group. An NIS+ principal is a user or a machine making NIS+ requests.

NIS+ Link Object

NIS+ link objects are like UNIX symbolic file-system links. They are typically used for shortcuts in the NIS+ namespace.

Refer to `nis_objects`(3N) for more information about the NIS+ objects.

NIS+ Names

The NIS+ service defines two forms of names.

- Simple names identify NIS+ objects contained within the NIS+ namespace.
- Indexed names identify NIS+ entries contained within NIS+ tables.

Furthermore, entries within NIS+ tables are returned to the caller as NIS+ objects of type entry. NIS+ objects are implemented as a union structure that is described in the file `rpcsvc/nis_object.x`. The differences between the various types and the meanings of the components of these objects are described in `nis_objects`(3N).

Simple Names

Simple names consist of a series of labels that are separated by the dot (.) character. Each label is composed of printable characters from the ISO Latin-1 set. Each label can be of any non-zero length provided that the fully qualified name is fewer than NIS_MAXNAMELEN octets including the separating dots. (See rpcsvc/nis.h for the actual value of NIS_MAXNAMELEN in the current release.) Labels that contain special characters (see "Grammar" on page 885) must be quoted. The NIS+ namespace is organized as a singly rooted tree. Simple names identify nodes within this tree. These names are constructed so that the leftmost label in a name identifies the leaf node and all of the labels to the right of the leaf identify the parent node of the object. The parent node is referred to as the leaf's directory. The leaf directory is a naming directory and should not be confused with a file-system directory.

For example, the name example.simple.name. is a simple name with three labels, where example is the leaf node in this name. The directory of this leaf is simple.name. which by itself is a simple name, the leaf of which is simple, and its directory is simply name.

The function nis_leaf_of(3N) returns the first label of a simple name. The function nis_domain_of(3N) returns the name of the directory that contains the leaf. Iterative use of these two functions can break a simple name into each of its label components.

The name dot (.) is reserved to name the global root of the namespace. For systems that are connected to the Internet, this global root is served by a Domain Name Service. When an NIS+ server is serving a root directory whose name is not dot (.), this directory is referred to as a local root.

NIS+ names are said to be fully qualified when the name includes all of the labels identifying all of the directories, up to the global root. Names without the trailing dot are called partially qualified.

Indexed Names

Indexed names are compound names that are composed of a search criterion and a simple name. The search criterion component is used to select entries from a table; the simple name component is used to identify the NIS+ table that is to be searched. The search criterion is a series of column names and their desired values enclosed in bracket characters ([]). This criterion takes the following form.

```
[column_name=value, column_name=value,...]
```

A search criterion is combined with a simple name to form an indexed name by concatenating the two parts, separated by a comma as follows.

```
[search-criterion],table.directory.
```

When multiple column name/value pairs are present in the search criterion, only those entries in the table that have the appropriate value in all columns specified are returned. When no column name/value pairs are specified in the search criterion, [], all entries in the table are returned.

Grammar

The following text represents a context-free grammar that defines the set of legal NIS+ names. The terminals in this grammar are the characters dot (.), open bracket ([), close bracket (]), comma (,), equal (=), and white space. Use the vertical bar (|) character to separate alternate productions. Read this syntax as "this production OR this production."

name	::=	. | *simple-name* | *indexed-name*
simple name	::=	*string.* | *string.simple-name*
indexed name	::=	*search-criterion,simple-name*
search criterion	::=	[*attribute-list*]
attribute list	::=	*attribute* | *attribute,attribute-list*
attribute	::=	*string = string*
string	::=	ISO Latin-1 character set except the character slash (/). The initial character cannot be a terminal character or the characters at (@), plus (+), or dash (–).

Terminals that appear in strings must be quoted with double quote ("). You can quote the " character by quoting it with itself (""").

Name Expansion

The NIS+ service accepts only fully qualified names. However, because such names can be unwieldy, the NIS+ commands in section 1 use a set of standard expansion rules that try to fully qualify a partially qualified name. This expansion is actually done by the NIS+ library function nis_getnames(3N), which generates a list of names by using the default NIS+ directory search path or the NIS_PATH environment variable. The default NIS+ directory search path includes all the names in its path. nis_getnames() is invoked by the functions nis_lookup(3N) and nis_list(3N) when the EXPAND_NAME flag is used.

The NIS_PATH environment variable contains an ordered list of simple names. The names are separated by the colon (:) character. If any name in the list contains colons, the colon should be quoted as described in the Grammar section. When the list is exhausted, the resolution function returns the error NIS_NOTFOUND. This error message may mask the fact that the name existed but a server for it was unreachable. If the name presented to the list or lookup interface is fully qualified, the EXPAND_NAME flag is ignored. In the list of names from the NIS_PATH environment variable, the dollar sign ($) character is treated specially. Simple names that end with the label $ have this character replaced by the default directory (see nis_local_directory(3N)). Using $ as a name in this list results in this name being replaced by the list of directories between the default directory and the global root that contain at least two labels.

Below is an example of this expansion. With a default directory of some.long.domain.name. and the NIS_PATH variable set to `fred.bar.:org_dir.$:$`, the path is initially broken up into the following list.

```
1 fred.bar.
2 org_dir.$
3 $
```

The dollar sign in the second component is replaced with the default directory. The dollar sign in the third component is replaced with the names of the directories between the default directory and the global root that have at least two labels in them. The effective path values become:

```
1  fred.bar.
2a org_dir.some.long.domain.name.
3a some.long.domain.name.
3b long.domain.name.
3c domain.name.
```

Each of these simple names is appended to the partially qualified name that was passed to the `nis_lookup`(3N) or `nis_list`(3N) interface. Each is tried in turn until NIS_SUCCESS is returned or the list is exhausted.

If the NIS_PATH variable is not set, the path $ is used.

The library function `nis_getnames`(3N) can be called from user programs to generate the list of names that would be attempted. The program `nisdefaults`(1) with the -s option can also be used to show the fully expanded path.

Concatenation Path

Normally, all the entries for a certain type of information are stored within the table itself. However, at times it is desirable for the table to point to other tables where entries can be found. For example, you may want to store all the IP addresses in the `host` table for their own domain and want to still be able to resolve hosts in some other domain without explicitly specifying the new domain name. NIS+ provides a mechanism for concatenating different but related tables with an NIS+ concatenation path. With a concatenation path, you can create a sort of flat namespace from a hierarchical structure. You can also create a table with no entries and just point the hosts or any other table to its parent domain. Note that with such a setup, you are moving the administrative burden of managing the tables to the parent domain. The concatenation path slows down the request response time because more tables and more servers are searched. It also decreases the availability of tables if all the servers are incapacitated for a particular directory in the table path.

The NIS+ concatenation path is also referred to as the *table path*. This path is set up at table creation time with `nistbladm`(1). You can specify more than one table to be concatenated, and the tables are searched in the given order. Note that the NIS+ client libraries, by default, do not follow the concatenation path set in site-specific tables. Refer to `nis_list`(3N) for more details.

Namespaces

The NIS+ service defines two additional disjoint namespaces for its own use. These namespaces are:

- The NIS+ principal namespace.
- The NIS+ group namespace.

The names associated with the group and principal namespaces are syntactically identical to simple names. However, the information they represent cannot be obtained by directly presenting these names to the NIS+ interfaces. Instead, special interfaces are defined to map these names into NIS+ names so that they can then be resolved.

Principal Names

NIS+ principal names are used to uniquely identify users and machines that are making NIS+ requests. These names have the following form.

principal.domain

Here, domain is the fully qualified name of an NIS+ directory where the named principal's credentials can be found. See "Directories and Domains" on page 889 for more information on domains. Note that this name, *principal*, is not a leaf in the NIS+ namespace.

Credentials are used to map the identity of a host or user from one context, such as a process UID, into the NIS+ context. They are stored as records in an NIS+ table named `cred`, which always appears in the `org_dir` subdirectory of the directory named in the principal name.

This mapping can be expressed as a replacement function with the following syntax.

principal.domain ->[cname=*principal.domain*],cred.org_dir.*domain*

This replacement name is an NIS+ name that can be presented to the `nis_list`(3N) interface for resolution. NIS+ principal names are administered with the `nisaddcred`(1M) command.

The `cred` table contains five columns named cname, auth_name, auth_type, public_data, and private_data. This table contains one record for each identity mapping for an NIS+ principal. The current service supports three types of mappings.

LOCAL   Map from the UID of a given process to the NIS+ principal name associated with that UID. If no mapping exists, return the name nobody. When the effective UID of the process is 0 (for example, the superuser), return the NIS+ name associated with the host. Note that UIDs are sensitive to the context of the machine on which the process is executing.

DES   Map to and from a Secure RPC netname into an NIS+ principal name. See `secure_rpc(3N)` for more information on netnames. Note that because netnames contain the notion of a domain, they span NIS+ directories.

DH*nnn-m*   Map netnames and NIS+ principal names for extended Diffie-Hellman keys, for example, `DH640-0`, `DH1024-0`. See `nisauthconf(1M)` for further information.

The NIS+ client library function `nis_local_principal(3N)` uses the `cred.org_dir` table to map the UNIX notion of an identity, a process UID, into an NIS+ principal name. Shell programs can use the program `nisdefaults(1)` with the `-p` option to return this information.

Mapping from UIDs to an NIS+ principal name is accomplished by constructing a query of the following form.

```
[auth_type=LOCAL, auth_name=uid],cred.org_dir.defaultdomain.
```

This query returns a record containing the NIS+ principal name associated with this UID, in the machine's default domain.

The NIS+ service uses the Data Encryption Standard (DES) mapping to map the names associated with Secure RPC requests into NIS+ principal names. RPC requests that use Secure RPC include the netname of the client making the request in the RPC header. This netname has the following form.

```
unix.UID@domain
```

The service constructs a query by using this name of the following form where the *domain* part is extracted from the netname instead of using the default domain.

```
[auth_type=DES, auth_name=netname],cred.org_dir.domain.
```

This query is used to look up the mapping of this netname into an NIS+ principal name in the domain where it was created.

This mechanism of mapping UID and netnames into an NIS+ principal name guarantees that a client of the NIS+ service has only one principal name. This principal name is used as the basis for authorization described below. All objects in the NIS+ namespace and all entries in NIS+ tables must have an owner specified for them. This owner field always contains an NIS+ principal name.

Group Names

Like NIS+ principal names, NIS+ group names take the following form.

```
group_name.domain
```

All objects in the NIS+ namespace and all entries in NIS+ tables can optionally have a group owner specified for them. This group owner field, when filled in, always contains the fully qualified NIS+ group name.

The NIS+ client library defines several interfaces (nis_groups(3N)) for dealing with NIS+ groups. These interfaces internally map NIS+ group names into an NIS+ simple name that identifies the NIS+ group object associated with that group name. This mapping can be shown as follows.

```
group.domain -> group.groups_dir.domain
```

This mapping eliminates collisions between NIS+ group names and NIS+ directory names. For example, without this mapping, a directory with the name engineering.foo.com. would make it impossible to have a group named engineering.foo.com because of the restriction that within the NIS+ namespace, a name unambiguously identifies a single object. With this mapping, the NIS+ group name engineering.foo.com. maps to the NIS+ object name engineering.groups_dir.foo.com.

The contents of a group object are a list of NIS+ principal names and the names of other NIS+ groups. See nis_groups(3N) for a more complete description of their use.

NIS+ Security

NIS+ defines a security model to control access to information managed by the service. The service defines access rights that are selectively granted to individual clients or groups of clients. Principal names and group names define clients and groups of clients that may be granted or denied access to NIS+ information. These principals and groups are associated with NIS+ domains as defined below.

The security model also uses the notion of a class of principals, called nobody, that contains all clients whether or not they have authenticated themselves to the service. The class world includes any client who has been authenticated.

Directories and Domains

Some directories within the NIS+ namespace are referred to as NIS+ domains. Domains are those NIS+ directories that contain the subdirectories groups_dir and org_dir. Further, the subdirectory org_dir should contain the table named cred. NIS+ group names and NIS+ principal names always include the NIS+ domain name after their first label.

Authentication

The NIS+ name service uses Secure RPC for the integrity of the NIS+ service. Secure RPC requires that users of the service and their machines must have a Secure RPC key pair associated with them. This key is initially generated with either the nisaddcred(1M) or nisclient(1M) commands and modified with the chkey(1) or nispasswd(1) commands.

The use of Secure RPC enables private information that is not available to untrusted machines or users on the network to be stored in the name service.

In addition to the Secure RPC key, users need a mapping of their UID into an NIS+ principal name. This mapping is created by the system administrator, using the `nisclient`(1M) or `nisaddcred`(1M) commands.

Users that are using machines in several NIS+ domains must ensure that they have a local credential entry in each of those domains. This credential should be created with the NIS+ principal name of the user in their "home" domain. For the purposes of NIS+ and Secure RPC, the home domain is defined to be the one where the user's Secure RPC key pair is located.

New!

Although extended Diffie-Hellman keys use an alternative to Secure RPC, administration is done through the same commands. See `nisauthconf`(1M).

Authorization

The NIS+ service defines four access rights that can be granted or denied to clients of the service. These rights are:

- Read
- Modify
- Create
- Destroy

These access rights are specified in the object structure at creation time and can be modified later with the `nischmod`(1) command. In general, the rights granted for an object apply only to that object. However, for purposes of authorization, rights granted to clients reading directory and table objects are granted to those clients for all of the objects "contained" by the parent object. This notion of containment is abstract. The objects do not actually contain other objects within them. Note that group objects do contain the list of principals within their definition.

Access rights are interpreted as follows.

read	Grant read access to an object. For directory and table objects, having read access on the parent object conveys read access to all of the objects that are direct children of a directory or to entries within a table.
modify	Grant modification access to an existing object. Read access is not required for modification. However, in many applications, one needs to read an object before modifying it. Such modify operations fail unless read access is also granted.
create	Grant a client permission to create new objects where one had not previously existed. `create` is used only in conjunction with directory and table objects. Having create access for a table enables a client to add additional entries to the table. Having create access for a directory enables a client to add new objects to an NIS+ directory.

destroy   Grant a client permission to destroy or remove an existing object
               or entry. When a client tries to destroy an entry or object by
               removing it, the service first checks to see if the table or directory
               containing that object grants the client destroy access. If it does,
               the operation proceeds; if the containing object does not grant this
               right, then the object itself is checked to see if it grants this right
               to the client. If the object grants the right, then the operation
               proceeds; otherwise, the request is rejected.

Each of these rights can be granted to any one of four different categories.

owner   Grant a right to the owner of an object. The owner is the NIS+
               principal identified in the owner field. The owner can be changed
               with the nischown(1) command. Note that if the owner does not
               have modification access rights to the object he cannot change any
               access rights to the object unless he has modification access rights
               to its parent object.

group owner   Grant a right to the group owner of an object. This grants the right
               to any principal that is identified as a member of the group
               associated with the object. The group owner can be changed with
               the nischgrp(1) command. The object owner need not be a
               member of this group.

world   Grant a right to everyone in the world. This grants the right to all
               clients who have authenticated themselves with the service.

nobody   Grant a right to the nobody principal. This has the effect of
               granting the right to any client that makes a request of the
               service, regardless of whether the client is authenticated.

Note that for bootstrapping reasons, directory objects that are NIS+
domains, the org_dir subdirectory, and the cred table within that
subdirectory must grant read access to the nobody principal. This permission
makes navigation of the namespace possible when a client is in the process of
locating its credentials. Granting this access does not enable the contents of
other tables within org_dir to be read (such as the entries in the password
table) unless the table itself gives "real" access rights to the nobody principal.

Directory Authorization

Additional capabilities grant access rights to clients for directories. These
rights are contained within the object access rights (OAR) structure of the
directory. This structure enables the NIS+ service to grant rights that are not
granted by the directory object for objects contained by the directory of a
specific type.

An example of this capability is a directory object that does not grant create
access to all clients but does grant create access in the OAR structure for
objects of type group to clients who are members of the NIS+ group associated
with the directory. In this example the only objects that could be created as
children of the directory would have to be of the type group.

Another example is a directory object that grants create access only to the owner of the directory and then additionally grants create access through the OAR structure for objects of type `table`, `link`, group, and `private` to any member of the directory's group. The group thus gains nearly complete create access to the group with the exception of creating subdirectories. The creation of new NIS+ domains are restricted because creating a domain requires creating both a `groups_dir` and `org_dir` subdirectory.

Note — There is currently no command-line interface to set or change the OAR of the directory object.

Table Authorization

As with directories, additional capabilities are provided for granting access to entries within tables. Rights granted to a client by the access rights field in a table object apply to the table object and all of the entry objects "contained" by that table. If an access right is not granted by the table object, it can be granted by an entry within the table. This authorization holds for all rights except `create`.

For example, a table cannot grant read access to a client performing an `nis_list(3N)` operation on the table. However, the access rights field of entries within that table can grant read access to the client. Note that access rights in an entry are granted to the owner and group owner of the entry and not the owner or group of the table. When the list operation is performed, all entries to which the client has read access are returned. Those entries that do not grant read access are not returned. If none of the entries that match the search criterion grant read access to the client making the request, no entries are returned and the result status contains the `NIS_NOTFOUND` error code.

Access rights that are granted by the rights field in an entry are granted for the entire entry. However, in the table object, an additional set of access rights is maintained for each column in the table. These rights apply to the equivalent column in the entry. The rights are used to grant access when neither the table nor the entry itself grants access. The access rights in a column specification apply to the owner and group owner of the entry instead of the owner and group owner of the table object.

When a `read` operation is performed, if read access is not granted by the table and is not granted by the entry but is granted by the access rights in a column, that entry is returned with the correct values in all columns that are readable and the string `*NP*` (No Permission) in columns where read access is not granted.

As an example, consider a client who has performed a list operation on a table that does not grant read access to that client. Each entry object that satisfied the search criterion specified by the client is examined to see if it grants read access to the client. If it does, it is included in the returned result. If it does not, then each column is checked to see if it grants read access to the client. If any columns grant read access to the client, data in those columns is returned. Columns that do not grant read access have their contents replaced by the string `*NP*`. If none of the columns grant read access, then the entry is not returned.

List of Commands

The following list shows all commands and programming functions related to NIS+.

NIS+ User Commands

`nisaddent(1M)`

Add `/etc` files and NIS maps into their corresponding NIS+ tables.

`niscat(1)`   Display NIS+ tables and objects.

`nischgrp(1)` Change the group owner of an NIS+ object.

`nischmod(1)` Change access rights on an NIS+ object.

`nischown(1)` Change the owner of an NIS+ object.

`nischttl(1)` Change the time-to-live value of an NIS+ object.

`nisdefaults(1)`

Display NIS+ default values.

`niserror(1)` Display NIS+ error messages.

`nisgrep(1)`   Search NIS+ tables.

`nisgrpadm(1)`

Administer NIS+ groups.

`nisln(1)`   Symbolically link NIS+ objects.

`nisls(1)`   List the contents of an NIS+ directory.

`nismatch(1)` Search NIS+ tables.

`nismkdir(1)` Create NIS+ directories.

`nispasswd(1)`

Change NIS+ password information.

`nisrm(1)`   Remove NIS+ objects from the namespace.

`nisrmdir(1)` Remove NIS+ directories.

`nisshowcache(1M)`

Print the contents of the shared cache file.

`nistbladm(1)`

Administer NIS+ tables.

`nistest(1)`   Return the state of the NIS+ namespace, using a conditional expression.

NIS+ Administrative Commands

aliasadm(1M)

> Manipulate the NIS+ aliases map.

nis_cachemgr(1M)

> Cache location information about NIS+ servers.

nisaddcred(1M)

> Create NIS+ credentials.

nisaddent(1M)

> Create NIS+ tables from corresponding /etc files or NIS maps.

nisauthconf(1M)

> Configure extended Diffie-Hellman keys.

nisclient(1M)

> Initialize NIS+ credentials for NIS+ principals.

nisd(1M)   NIS+ service daemon.

nisd_resolv(1M)

> NIS+ service daemon.

nisinit(1M) Initialize NIS+ clients and servers.

nislog(1M)   Display the contents of the NIS+ transaction log.

nisping(1M) Send ping to NIS+ servers.

nispopulate(1M)

> Populate the NIS+ tables in an NIS+ domain.

nisserver(1M)

> Set up NIS+ servers.

nissetup(1M)

> Initialize an NIS+ domain.

nisshowcache(1M)

> Print the contents of the shared cache file.

nisstat(1M) Report NIS+ server statistics.

nisupdkeys(1M)

> Update the public keys in an NIS+ directory object.

rpc.nisd(1M)

> NIS+ service daemon.

rpc.nisd_resolv(1M)

> NIS+ service daemon.

```
sysidnis(1M)
```
New!

System configuration.

NIS+ Programming API

```
__nis_map_group(3N)
```

NIS+ group manipulation functions.

```
db_add_entry(3N)
```

NIS+ database access functions.

```
db_checkpoint(3N)
```

NIS+ database access functions.

```
db_create_table(3N)
```

NIS+ database access functions.

```
db_destroy_table(3N)
```

NIS+ database access functions.

```
db_first_entry(3N)
```

NIS+ database access functions.

```
db_free_result(3N)
```

NIS+ database access functions.

```
db_initialize(3N)
```

NIS+ database access functions.

```
db_list_entries(3N)
```

NIS+ database access functions.

```
db_next_entry(3N)
```

NIS+ database access functions.

```
db_remove_entry(3N)
```

NIS+ database access functions.

```
db_reset_next_entry(3N)
```

NIS+ database access functions.

```
db_standby(3N)
```

NIS+ database access functions.

```
db_table_exists(3N)
```

NIS+ database access functions.

```
db_unload_table(3N)
```

NIS+ database access functions.

```
nis_add(3N)
```
NIS+ namespace functions.

`nis_add_entry`(3N)

> NIS+ table functions.

`nis_addmember`(3N)

> NIS+ group-manipulation functions.

`nis_checkpoint`(3N)

> Miscellaneous NIS+ log administration functions.

`nis_clone_object`(3N)

> NIS+ subroutines.

`nis_creategroup`(3N)

> NIS+ group-manipulation functions.

`nis_db`(3N)   NIS+ database access functions.

`nis_destroy_object`(3N)

> NIS+ subroutines.

`nis_destroygroup`(3N)

> NIS+ group manipulation functions.

`nis_dir_cmp`(3N)

> NIS+ subroutines.

`nis_domain_of`(3N)

> NIS+ subroutines.

`nis_error`(3N)

> Display NIS+ error messages.

`nis_first_entry`(3N)

> NIS+ table functions.

`nis_freenames`(3N)

> NIS+ subroutines.

`nis_freeresult`(3N)

> NIS+ namespace functions.

`nis_freeservlist`(3N)

> Miscellaneous NIS+ functions.

`nis_freetags`(3N)

> Miscellaneous NIS+ functions.

`nis_getnames`(3N)

> NIS+ subroutines.

`nis_getservlist`(3N)

> Miscellaneous NIS+ functions.

```
nis_groups(3N)
```
NIS+ group manipulation functions.
```
nis_ismember(3N)
```
NIS+ group manipulation functions.
```
nis_leaf_of(3N)
```
NIS+ subroutines.
```
nis_lerror(3N)
```
Display some NIS+ error messages.
```
nis_list(3N)
```
NIS+ table functions.
```
nis_local_directory(3N)
```
NIS+ local names.
```
nis_local_group(3N)
```
NIS+ local names.
```
nis_local_host(3N)
```
NIS+ local names.
```
nis_local_names(3N)
```
NIS+ local names.
```
nis_local_principal(3N)
```
NIS+ local names.
```
nis_lookup(3N)
```
NIS+ namespace functions.
```
nis_map_group(3N)
```
NIS+ group manipulation functions.
```
nis_mkdir(3N)
```
Miscellaneous NIS+ functions.
```
nis_modify(3N)
```
NIS+ namespace functions.
```
nis_modify_entry(3N)
```
NIS+ table functions.
```
nis_name_of(3N)
```
NIS+ subroutines.
```
nis_names(3N)
```
NIS+ namespace functions.
```
nis_next_entry(3N)
```
NIS+ table functions.

nis_objects(3N)

> NIS+ object formats.

nis_perror(3N)

> Display NIS+ error messages.

nis_ping(3N)

> Miscellaneous NIS+ log administration functions.

nis_print_group_entry(3N)

> NIS+ group-manipulation functions.

nis_print_object(3N)

> NIS+ subroutines.

nis_remove(3N)

> NIS+ namespace functions.

nis_remove_entry(3N)

> NIS+ table functions.

nis_removemember(3N)

> NIS+ group-manipulation functions.

nis_rmdir(3N)

> Miscellaneous NIS+ functions.

nis_server(3N)

> Miscellaneous NIS+ functions.

nis_servstate(3N)

> Miscellaneous NIS+ functions.

nis_sperrno(3N)

> Display NIS+ error messages.

nis_sperror(3N)

> Display NIS+ error messages.

nis_sperror_r(3N)

> Display NIS+ error messages.

nis_stats(3N)

> Miscellaneous NIS+ functions.

nis_subr(3N)

> NIS+ subroutines.

nis_tables(3N)

> NIS+ table functions.

nis_verifygroup(3N)

> NIS+ group-manipulation functions.

NIS+ Files and Directories

`nisfiles(4)` NIS+ database files and directory structure.

Files

`rpcsvc/nis_object.x`

>Protocol description of an NIS+ object.

`rpcsvc/nis.x`

>Defines the NIS+ protocol, using the RPC language as described in the *ONC+ Developer's Guide.*

`rpcsvc/nis.h`

>Should be included by all clients of the NIS+ service.

See Also

`nischown(1), nisdefaults(1), nismatch(1), nispasswd(1), admintool(1M), newkey(1M), nisaddcred(1M), nisclient(1M), nispopulate(1M), nisserver(1M), nis_add_entry(3N), nis_domain_of(3N), nis_getnames(3N), nis_groups(3N), nis_leaf_of(3N), nis_list(3N), nis_local_directory(3N), nis_lookup(3N), nis_objects(3N)`

ONC+ Developer's Guide

>Describes the application programming interfaces for networks including NIS+.

Solaris Naming Setup and Configuration Guide

>Describes how to plan for and configure an NIS+ namespace.

Solaris Naming Administration Guide

>Describes how to administer a running NIS+ namespace and modify its security.

NIS+ Transition Guide

>Describes how to make the transition from NIS to NIS+.

Solaris Advanced User's Guide

>Describes the `admintool(1M)` window interface for modifying the data in NIS+ tables.

niscat — Display NIS+ Tables and Objects

Synopsis

```
/usr/bin/niscat [-AhLMv][-s sep] tablename...
/usr/bin/niscat [-ALMP] -o name...
```

Description

Use the niscat command to display information in NIS+ tables and objects. In the first synopsis, niscat displays the contents of the NIS+ tables named by *tablename*. In the second synopsis, niscat displays the internal representation of the NIS+ objects named by *name*.

Note — Columns without values in a table are displayed by two adjacent separator characters.

Options

-A	Display the data within the table and all of the data in tables in the initial table's concatenation path.
-h	Display the header line before displaying the table. The header consists of the hash (#) character followed by the name of each column. The column names are separated by the table separator character.
-L	If *tablename* or *name* names an object of type LINK, follow the link and display the object or table named by the link.
-M	Master server only. Send the request to the master server of the named data. This option guarantees that the most up-to-date information is seen, at the possible expense of increasing the load on the master server and increasing the possibility of the NIS+ server being unavailable or busy for updates.
-o *name*	Display the internal representation of the named NIS+ object(s). If *name* is an indexed name (see nismatch(1)), then display each of the matching entry objects. Use this option to display access rights and other attributes of individual columns.
-P	Follow the concatenation path of a table if the initial search is unsuccessful. This option is useful only when using an indexed name for *name* and the -o option.
-s *sep*	Specify the character used to separate the table columns. If you specify no character, use the default separator (a space) for the table.
-v	Display columns containing binary data on the standard output. Without this option, display binary data as the string *BINARY*.

Examples

The following example displays the contents of the hosts table.

```
castle% niscat -h hosts.org_dir
# cname name addr comment
client1 client1 129.144.201.100 Joe Smith
crunchy crunchy 129.144.201.44 Jane Smith
```

```
crunchy softy 129.144.201.44
castle%
```

The string *NP* is returned in those fields where the user has insufficient access rights.

The following example displays `passwd.org_dir` on the standard output.

```
castle% niscat passwd.org_dir
```

The following example displays the contents of table `frodo` and the contents of all tables in its concatenation path.

```
castle% niscat -A frodo
```

The following example displays the entries in the table `groups.org_dir` as NIS+ objects. Note that the brackets are protected from the shell by single quotes.

```
castle% niscat -o '[]groups.org_dir'
```

The following example displays the table object of the `passwd.org_dir` table.

```
castle% niscat -o passwd.org_dir
```

The previous example displays the `passwd` table object and not the `passwd` table. The table object includes information such as the number of columns, column type, searchable or not searchable, separator, access rights, and other defaults.

The following example displays the directory object for `org_dir`, which includes information such as the access rights and replica information.

```
castle% niscat -o org_dir
```

Environment Variables

NIS_PATH   If this variable is set and the NIS+ name is not fully qualified, search each directory specified until the object is found (see `nisdefaults(1)`).

Exit Status

0   Successful completion.

1   An error occurred.

Attributes

See attributes(5) for descriptions of the following attributes:

Attribute Type	Attribute Value
Availability	SUNWnisu

See Also

nis+(1), nisdefaults(1), nismatch(1), nistbladm(1), nis_objects(3N), nis_tables(3N), attributes(5)

---

nischgrp — Change the Group Owner of an NIS+ Object

Synopsis

/usr/bin/nischgrp [-AfLP] group name...

Description

Use the nischgrp command to change the group owner of the NIS+ objects or entries specified by *name* to the specified NIS+ *group*. Specify entries, using indexed names (see nismatch(1)). If *group* is not a fully qualified NIS+ group name, it is resolved using the directory search path (see nisdefaults(1)).

The only restriction on changing an object's group owner is that you must have modify permissions for the object.

This command fails if the master NIS+ server is not running.

Note — The NIS+ server checks the validity of the group name before making the change.

Options

-A	Modify all entries in all tables in the concatenation path that match the search criteria specified in *name*. This option implies the -P option.
-f	Force the operation and fail silently if it does not succeed.
-L	Follow links and change the group owner of the linked object or entries instead of the group owner of the link itself.
-P	Follow the concatenation path within a named table. This option makes sense only when either name is an indexed name or when you also specify the -L option and the named object is a link pointing to entries.

Examples

The following examples show how to change the group owner of an object to a group in a different domain and how to change the group owner in the local domain.

```
castle% nischgrp newgroup.remote.domain. object
castle% nischgrp my-buds object
```

The following example shows how to change the group owner for a password entry. admins is an NIS+ group in the same domain.

```
castle% nischgrp admins '[uid=99],passwd.org_dir'
```

The following two examples change the group owner of the object or entries pointed to by a link, and the group owner of all entries in the hobbies table.

```
castle% nischgrp -L my-buds linkname
castle% nischgrp my-buds '[],hobbies'
```

Environment Variables

NIS_PATH   If this variable is set and the NIS+ name is not fully qualified, search each specified directory until the object is found (see nisdefaults(1)).

Exit Status

0   Success.

1   Failure.

Attributes

See attributes(5) for descriptions of the following attributes:

Attribute Type	Attribute Value
Availability	SUNWnisu

See Also

nis+(1), nischmod(1), nischown(1), nisdefaults(1), nisgrpadm(1), nis_objects(3N), attributes(5)

nischmod — Change Access Rights on an NIS+ Object

Synopsis

```
/usr/bin/nischmod [-AfLP] mode name...
```

Description

Use the nischmod command to change the access rights (mode) of the NIS+ objects or entries specified by *name* to *mode*. Specify entries, using indexed names (see nismatch(1)). Only principals with modify access to an object can change its mode.

 mode has the following form.

```
rights [, rights]...
```

rights has the form:

```
[who] op permission [op permission]...
```

 who is a combination of the following identities.

n	Nobody's permissions.
o	Owner's permissions.
g	Group's permissions.
w	World's permissions.
a	All or owg.

 If you omit *who*, the default is a.
 op is one of the following operators.

+	To grant the permission.
-	To revoke the permission.
=	To set the permissions explicitly.

 permission is any combination of the following permissions.

r	Read.
m	Modify.
c	Create.
d	Destroy.

> **Note** — Unlike the system chmod(1) command, the nischmod command does not accept an octal notation.

Options

-A	Modify all entries in all tables in the concatenation path that match the search criteria specified in *name*. This option implies the -P option.
-f	Force the operation and fail silently if it does not succeed.
-L	Follow links and change the permission of the linked object or entries instead of the permission of the link itself.
-P	Follow the concatenation path within a named table. This option is applicable only when either *name* is an indexed name or you specify the -L option and the named object is a link pointing to an entry.

Examples

The following example gives everyone read access to an object (that is, access for owner, group, and all).

```
castle% nischmod a+r object
```

The following example denies create and modify privileges to group and unauthenticated clients (nobody).

```
castle% nischmod gn-cm object
```

The following example sets a complex set of permissions for an object.

```
castle% nischmod o=rmcd,g=rm,w=rc,n=r object
```

The following example sets the permissions of an entry in the password table so that the group owner can modify them.

```
castle% nischmod g+m '[uid=55],passwd.org_dir'
```

The following example changes the permissions of a linked object.

```
castle% nischmod -L w+mr linkname
```

Environment Variables

NIS_PATH	If this variable is set and the NIS+ name is not fully qualified, search each specified directory until the object is found (see nisdefaults(1)).

Exit Status

0	Success.
1	Failure.

Attributes

See attributes(5) for descriptions of the following attributes:

Attribute Type	Attribute Value
Availability	SUNWnisu

See Also

chmod(1), nis+(1), nischgrp(1), nischown(1), nisdefaults(1), nis_objects(3N), attributes(5)

---

nischown — Change the Owner of an NIS+ Object

Synopsis

/usr/bin/nischown [-AfLP] owner name...

Description

Use the nischown command to change the owner of the NIS+ objects or entries specified by name to owner. Specify entries, using indexed names (see nismatch(1)). If owner is not a fully qualified NIS+ principal name (see nisaddcred(1M)), the default domain (see nisdefaults(1)) is appended to it.

The only restriction on changing an object's owner is that you must have modify permissions for the object.

> **Note** — If you are the current owner of an object and you change ownership, you may not be able to regain ownership unless you have modify access to the new object.

The NIS+ server checks the validity of the name before making the modification. The nischown command fails if the master NIS+ server is not running.

Options

-A	Modify all entries in all tables in the concatenation path that match the search criteria specified in name. This option implies the -P option.
-f	Force the operation and fail silently if it does not succeed.
-L	Follow links and change the owner of the linked object or entries instead of the owner of the link itself.

`-P`	Follow the concatenation path within a named table. This option is meaningful only when either *name* is an indexed name or you also specify the `-L` option and the named object is a link pointing to entries.

Examples

The following two examples show how to change the owner of an object to a principal in a different domain and how to change it to a principal in the local domain.

```
castle% nischown bob.remote.domain. object
castle% nischown skippy object
```

The following example shows how to change the owner of an entry in the `passwd` table.

```
castle% nischown bob.remote.domain. '[uid=99],passwd.org_dir'
```

The following example shows how to change the object or entries pointed to by a link.

```
castle% nischown -L skippy linkname
```

Environment Variables

`NIS_PATH`	If this variable is set and the NIS+ name is not fully qualified, search each specified directory until the object is found (see `nisdefaults(1)`).

Exit Status

`0`	Success.
`1`	Failure.

Attributes

See `attributes`(5) for descriptions of the following attributes:

Attribute Type	Attribute Value
Availability	SUNWnisu

See Also

```
nis+(1), nischgrp(1), nischmod(1), nischttl(1), nisdefaults(1),
nisaddcred(1M), nis_objects(3N), attributes(5)
```

nischttl — Change the Time-to-Live Value of an NIS+ Object

Synopsis

```
nischttl [-AfLP] time name...
```

Description

Use the nischttl command to change the time-to-live value (ttl) of the NIS+ objects or entries specified by *name* to *time*. Specify entries using indexed names (see nismatch(1)).

The time-to-live value is used by object caches to set the expiration time of objects within their cache. When an object is read into the cache, this value is added to the current time in seconds, yielding the time when the cached object would expire. The object can be returned from the cache while the current time is earlier than the calculated expiration time. When the expiration time has been reached, the object is flushed from the cache.

You can specify the time-to-live time in seconds or in days, hours, minutes, seconds format. The latter format uses a suffix letter of d, h, m, or s to identify the units of time.

The command fails if the master NIS+ server is not running.

Note — Setting a high ttl value enables objects to persist in caches for a longer period and can improve performance. However, when an object changes, in the worst case, the number of seconds in this attribute must pass before that change is visible to all clients. Setting a ttl value of 0 does not cache the object at all.

A high ttl value is a week, a low value is less than a minute. Password entries should have ttl values of about 12 hours (easily allowing one password change per day), entries in the RPC table can have ttl values of several weeks (this information is effectively unchanging). Only directory and group objects are cached in this implementation.

Options

-A	Modify all tables in the concatenation path that match the search criterion specified in *name*. This option implies the -P option.
-f	Force the operation and fail silently if it does not succeed.
-L	Follow links and change the time-to-live of the linked object or entries instead of the time-to-live of the link itself.

-P   Follow the concatenation path within a named table. This option
               makes sense only when either *name* is an indexed name or you also
               specify the -L option and the named object is a link pointing to
               entries.

Examples

The following example changes the ttl of an object, using the seconds format
and the days, hours, minutes, seconds format. The ttl of the second object is set
to 1 day and 12 hours.

```
castle% nischttl 184000 object
castle% nischttl 1d12h object
```

The following example changes the ttl for a password entry.

```
castle% nischttl 1h30m '[uid=99],passwd.org_dir'
```

The next two examples change the ttl of the object or entries pointed to by a
link and the ttl of all entries in the hobbies table.

```
castle% nischttl -L 12h linkname
castle% nischttl 3600 '[],hobbies
```

Environment Variables

NIS_PATH   If this variable is set and the NIS+ name is not fully qualified,
               search each specified directory until the object is found (see
               nisdefaults(1)).

Exit Status

0   Success.

1   Failure.

Attributes

See attributes(5) for descriptions of the following attributes:

Attribute Type	Attribute Value
Availability	SUNWnisu

See Also

```
nis+(1), nischgrp(1), nischmod(1), nischown(1), nisdefaults(1),
nis_objects(3N), attributes(5)
```

nisdefaults — Display NIS+ Default Values

Synopsis

```
/usr/bin/nisdefaults [-adghprstv]
```

Description

Use the `nisdefaults` command to print the default values that are returned by calls to the NIS+ local name functions (see `nis_local_names(3N)`). When you specify no options, all defaults are printed in a verbose format. With options, information for that option only is displayed in a terse form suitable for shell scripts.

Options

`-a`	Print all defaults in a terse format.
`-d`	Print the default domain name.
`-g`	Print the default group name.
`-h`	Print the default host name.
`-p`	Print the default principal name.
`-r`	Print the default access rights with which new objects are created.
`-s`	Print the default directory search path.
`-t`	Print the default time-to-live value.
`-v`	Print the defaults in a verbose format. This option prepends an identifying string to the output.

Examples

The following example prints the NIS+ defaults for a root process on machine `castle` in the `foo.bar.` domain.

```
castle% nisdefaults
Principal Name : castle.foo.bar
Domain Name : foo.bar
Host Name : castle.foo.bar
Group Name :
Access Rights : ----rmcdr---r---
Time to live : 12:00:00
Search Path : foo.bar.
```

The following example sets a variable in a shell script to the default domain.

```
DOMAIN=`nisdefaults -d`
```

The following example prints out the default time-to-live in a verbose format.

```
castle% nisdefaults -tv
Time to live : 12:00:00
```

The following example prints out the time-to-live in the terse format.

```
castle% nisdefaults -t
43200
```

Environment Variables

Several environment variables affect the defaults associated with a process.

NIS_DEFAULTS

> Specify a defaults string that overrides the NIS+ standard defaults. The defaults string is a series of tokens separated by colons. These tokens represent the default values to be used for the generic object properties. All of the legal tokens are described below.

> ttl=*time*   Set the default time-to-live for objects that are created. Specify the *time* value in the format defined by the nischttl(1) command. The default value is 12 hours.

> owner=*ownername*
> > Specify that the NIS+ principal *ownername* should own created objects. The default for this value is the principal who is executing the command.

> group=*groupname*
> > Specify that the group *groupname* should be the group owner for created objects. The default is null.

> access=*rights*
> > Specify the set of access rights that are to be granted for created objects. Specify the *rights* value in the format defined by the nischmod(1) command. The default value is ----rmcdr---r---.

NIS_GROUP   The name of the local NIS+ group. If the name is not fully qualified, append the default domain to it.

NIS_PATH   Override the default NIS+ directory search path. Specify an ordered list of directories separated by colons. The dollar sign character ($) is treated specially. Append the default domain to directory names that end in $. Replace a $ by itself with the list of directories between the default domain and the global root that are at least two levels deep. The default NIS+ directory search path is $.

Refer to the Name Expansion subsection in `nis+(1)` for more details.

Attributes

See `attributes(5)` for descriptions of the following attributes:

Attribute Type	Attribute Value
Availability	SUNWnisu

See Also

`nis+(1)`, `nis_local_names(3N)`, `attributes(5)`

---

niserror — Display NIS+ Error Messages

Synopsis

```
/usr/bin/niserror error-num
```

Description

Use the `niserror` command to print the NIS+ error associated with status value *error-num* on the standard output. This command is used in shell scripts to translate returned NIS+ error numbers into text messages.

Examples

The following example prints the error associated with the error number 20.

```
castle% niserror 20
Not Found, no such name
castle%
```

The following example prints the error associated with the error number 21.

```
castle% niserror 21
Name/entry isn't unique
castle%
```

Attributes

See `attributes(5)` for descriptions of the following attributes:

Attribute Type	Attribute Value
Availability	SUNWnisu

See Also
nis+(1), nis_error(3N), attributes(5)

---

nisgrep — Search NIS+ Tables

Synopsis
```
/usr/bin/nisgrep [-AchiMov] [-s sep] keypat tablename
/usr/bin/nisgrep [-AchiMov] [-s sep] colname=keypat... tablename
```

New!

Description
See nismatch(1).

---

nisgrpadm — NIS+ Group Administration Command

Synopsis
```
/usr/bin/nisgrpadm -a| -r| -t] [-s] group principal...
/usr/bin/nisgrpadm -d| -l [-M] [-s] group
/usr/bin/nisgrpadm -c [-D defaults] [-M] [-s] group
```

New!

Description
Use the nisgrpadm command to administer NIS+ groups and the membership lists for groups. nisgrpadm can create, destroy, or list NIS+ groups and can be used to administer a group's membership list. It can add or delete principals to the group or test principals for membership in the group.

The names of NIS+ groups are syntactically similar to names of NIS+ objects, but they occupy a separate namespace. A group named a.b.c.d. is represented by an NIS+ group object named a.groups_dir.b.c.d.; the functions described here all expect the name of the group, not the name of the corresponding group object.

There are three types of group members.

- An explicit member is just an NIS+ principal name, for example, wickedwitch.west.oz..

- An implicit ("domain") member, written *.west.oz., means that all principals in the given domain belong to this member. No other forms of wild-carding are allowed: wickedwitch.*.oz. is invalid, as is wickedwitch.west.*.. Note that principals in subdomains of the given domain are not included.

- A recursive ("group") member, written @cowards.oz., refers to another group; all principals that belong to that group are considered to belong here.

You can make any member negative by prefixing it with a minus sign (–). A group can thus contain explicit, implicit, recursive, negative explicit, negative implicit, and negative recursive members.

A principal is considered to belong to a group if it belongs to at least one nonnegative group member of the group and belongs to no negative group members.

Note — Principal names must be fully qualified, whereas groups can be abbreviated on all operations except create.

Options

-a	Add the list of NIS+ principals specified to group. The principal name should be fully qualified.
-c	Create group in the NIS+ namespace. The NIS+ group name should be fully qualified.
-d	Destroy (remove) group from the namespace.

New!   -D defaults

Specify a different set of defaults to be used when creating objects. The defaults string is a series of colon-separated tokens that represent the default values to be used for the generic object properties. All of the legal tokens are described below.

ttl=time   Set the default time-to-live for objects created with this command. You specify the time value in the format as defined by the nischttl(1) command. The default value is 12 hours.

owner=ownername

Specify that the NIS+ principal ownername owns the created object. Normally, this value is the same as the principal who is executing the command.

group=groupname

Specify that the group groupname is the group owner for the created object. The default value is null.

access=rights

Specify the set of access rights that are to be granted for the given object. You specify the rights value in the format defined by the nischmod(1) command. The default value is ----rmcdr---r---.

-l	List the membership list of the specified group. (see -M.)
-M	Master server only. Send the lookup to the master server of the named data. This option guarantees that the most up-to-date information is seen, at the possible expense that the master server may be busy. Note that the -M option is applicable only with the -l option.
-r	Remove the list of principals specified from group. The principal name should be fully qualified.
-s	Work silently. Return results, using the exit status of the command. This status can be translated into a text string by the niserror(1) command.
-t	Display whether the principals specified are members in group.

Examples

Administering Groups
The following example creates a group in the foo.com. domain.

```
castle% nisgrpadm -c my_buds.foo.com.
```

The following example removes the group from the current domain.

```
castle% nisgrpadm -d freds_group
```

Administering Members
The following example shows how you would add two principals, bob and betty, to the group my_buds.foo.com..

```
castle% nisgrpadm -a my_buds.foo.com. bob.bar.com. betty.foo.com.
```

The following example removes betty from freds_group.

```
castle% nisgrpadm -r freds_group betty.foo.com.
```

Environment Variables

NIS_DEFAULTS	
	Specify a default string that overrides the NIS+ standard defaults.
NIS_PATH	If this variable is set and the NIS+ name is not fully qualified, search each specified directory until the object is found (see nisdefaults(1)).

New!

Attributes

See attributes(5) for descriptions of the following attributes:

Attribute Type	Attribute Value
Availability	SUNWnisu

See Also

nis+(1), nischgrp(1), nischmod(1), nischttl(1), nisdefaults(1),
niserror(1), nis_groups(3N), attributes(5)

Diagnostics

NIS_SUCCESS

On success, return an exit status of 0.

NIS_PERMISSION

This error is returned when you do not have the needed access
right to change the group.

NIS_NOTFOUND

This error is returned when the group does not exist.

NIS_TRYAGAIN

This error is returned when the server for the group's domain is
currently checkpointing or otherwise in a read-only state. Retry
the command at a later date.

NIS_MODERROR

This error is returned when the group was modified by someone
else during the execution of the command. Reissue the command
and optionally recheck the group membership list.

nisln — Symbolically Link NIS+ Objects

Synopsis

/usr/bin/nisln [-L] [-D *defaults*] *name linkname*

Description

Use the nisln command to link an NIS+ object named *name* to an NIS+
linkname. If *name* is an indexed name (see nismatch(1)), the link points to
entries within an NIS+ table. Clients who want to look up information in the
name service can use the FOLLOW_LINKS flag to force the client library to

follow links to the name they point to. Further, all of the NIS+ administration commands accept the -L option indicating they should follow links (see nis_names(3N) for a description of the FOLLOW_LINKS flag).

> **Note** — When creating the link, nisln verifies that the linked object exists. Once the link is created, you can delete or replace the linked object without affecting the link. At that time the link becomes invalid and attempts to follow it return NIS_LINKNAMEERROR to the client. When the path attribute in tables specifies a link instead of another table, the link is followed if the flag FOLLOW_LINKS was present in the call to nis_list() (see nis_tables(3N)) and ignored if the flag is not present. If the flag is present and the link is no longer valid, a warning is sent to the system logger and the link is ignored.

Options

-D *defaults*

Specify a different set of defaults to be used for the creation of the link object. The defaults string is a series of tokens separated by colons. These tokens represent the default values to be used for the generic object properties. All of the legal tokens are described below.

ttl=*time*   Set the default time-to-live for objects created with this command. You specify the *time* value in the format as defined by the nischttl(1) command. The default value is 12 hours.

owner=*ownername*

Specify that the NIS+ principal *ownername* owns the created object. Normally, this value is the same as the principal who is executing the command.

group=*groupname*

Specify that the group *groupname* is the group owner for the created object. The default value is null.

access=*rights*

Specify the set of access rights that are to be granted for the given object. You specify the *rights* value in the format defined by the nischmod(1) command. The default value is ----rmcdr---r---.

-L   If *name* is itself a link, follow it to the linked object that it points to. The new link points to that linked object instead of to *name*.

Examples

The following example creates a link in the domain `foo.com.` named `hosts` that points to the `hosts.bar.com.` object.

```
castle% nisln hosts.bar.com. hosts.foo.com.
```

The following example makes a link `example.sun.com.` that points to an entry in the `hosts` table in `eng.sun.com..`

```
castle% nisln '[name=example],hosts.eng.sun.com.' example.sun.com.
```

Environment Variables

NIS_PATH   If this variable is set and the NIS+ name is not fully qualified, search each specified directory until the object is found (see `nisdefaults(1)`).

Exit Status

0   Success.

1   Failure.

Attributes

See `attributes(5)` for descriptions of the following attributes:

Attribute Type	Attribute Value
Availability	SUNWnisu

See Also

`nisdefaults(1)`, `nismatch(1)`, `nisrm(1)`, `nistbladm(1)`, `nis_names(3N)`, `nis_tables(3N)`, `attributes(5)`

nisls — List the Contents of an NIS+ Directory

Synopsis

```
/usr/bin/nisls [-dglLmMR][name...]
```

Description

Use the `nisls` command to list the contents of NIS+ directories or objects. For each *name* that is an NIS+ directory, `nisls` lists the contents of the directory. For each *name* that is an NIS+ object other than a directory, `nisls` simply echoes *name*. If you specify no *name*, the first directory in the search path (see nisdefaults(1)) is listed.

Options

-d	Treat NIS+ directories like other NIS+ objects instead of listing their contents.
-g	Display group owner instead of owner when listing in long format.
-l	List in long format, displaying additional information about the objects such as their type, creation time, owner, and access rights. List the access rights in the following order in long mode: nobody, owner, group owner, and world.
-L	Follow links. If *name* actually points to a link, follow it to the linked object.
-m	Display modification time instead of creation time when listing in long format.
-M	Master only. Return information from the master server of the named object. This option guarantees that the most up-to-date information is seen, at the possible expense that the master server may be busy.
-R	List directories recursively. This option reiterates the list for each subdirectory found in the process of listing each name.

Environment Variables

NIS_PATH	If this variable is set and the NIS+ name is not fully qualified, search each specified directory until the object is found (see nisdefaults(1)).

Exit Status

0	Success.
1	Failure.

Attributes

See attributes(5) for descriptions of the following attributes:

Attribute Type	Attribute Value
Availability	SUNWnisu

See Also

nisdefaults(1), nisgrpadm(1), nismatch(1), nistbladm(1), nis_objects(3N), attributes(5)

nismatch, nisgrep — Search NIS+ Tables

Synopsis

```
/usr/bin/nismatch [-AchMoPv][-s sep]  key tablename
/usr/bin/nismatch [-AchMoPv][-s sep]  colname=key... tablename
/usr/bin/nismatch [-AchMoPv][-s sep]  indexedname
/usr/bin/nisgrep [-AchiMov][-s sep]  keypat tablename
/usr/bin/nisgrep [-AchiMov][-s sep]  colname=keypat... tablename
```

New!

Description

Use the nismatch and nisgrep commands to search NIS+ tables. The nisgrep command differs from the nismatch command in its ability to accept regular expressions *keypat* for the search criteria instead of simple text matches.

Because nisgrep uses a callback function, it is not constrained to searching only those columns that are specifically made searchable at the time of table creation. It is slower but more flexible than nismatch.

With nismatch, the server does the searching; with nisgrep, the server returns all the readable entries and then the client does the pattern matching.

With both commands, the parameter *tablename* is the NIS+ name of the table to be searched. If you specify only one key or key pattern without the column name, then the first column is searched. You can search specific named columns by using the *colname=key* syntax. When you search multiple columns, only entries that match in all columns are returned. This result is the equivalent of a logical join operation.

nismatch accepts an additional form of search criteria, *indexedname*, which is an NIS+ indexed name of the form:

```
[colname=value,...],tablename
```

Options

-A	Return all data within the table and all of the data in tables in the initial table's concatenation path.
-c	Print only a count of the number of entries that matched the search criteria.
-h	Display a header line before the matching entries that contains the names of the table's columns.
-i	Ignore upper/lowercase distinction during comparisons.
-M	Master server only. Send the lookup to the master server of the named data. This option guarantees that the most up-to-date information is seen, at the possible expense that the master server may be busy.

New!

`-o`	Display the internal representation of the matching NIS+ object(s).
`-P`	Follow concatenation path. Specify that the lookup should follow the concatenation path of a table if the initial search is unsuccessful.
`-s sep`	Specify the character used to separate the table columns. If you specify no character, use the default separator (a space) for the table.
`-v`	Do not suppress the output of binary data when displaying matching entries. Without this option, display binary data as the string *BINARY*.

Examples

The following example searches a table named `passwd` in the `org_dir` subdirectory of the `zotz.com.` domain. It returns the entry that has the user name of `skippy`. In the following example, all the work is done on the server.

```
castle% nismatch name=skippy passwd.org_dir.zotz.com.
```

The following example is similar to the one above except that it uses `nisgrep` to find all users in the table named `passwd` that are using either `ksh`(1) or `csh`(1).

```
castle% nisgrep 'shell=[ck]sh' passwd.org_dir.zotz.com.
```

Environment Variables

`NIS_PATH`	If this variable is set and the NIS+ name is not fully qualified, search each specified directory until the object is found (see `nisdefaults`(1)).

Exit Status

0	Successfully matched some entries.
1	Successfully searched the table and no matches were found.
2	An error condition occured. An error message is also printed.

Attributes

See `attributes`(5) for descriptions of the following attributes:

Attribute Type	**Attribute Value**
Availability	SUNWnisu

See Also

niscat(1), nisdefaults(1), nisls(1), nistbladm(1), nis_objects(3N), attributes(5)

Diagnostics

No memory   An attempt to allocate memory for the search failed.

tablename is not a table

>The object with the name *tablename* was not a table object.

Can't compile regular expression

>The regular expression in *keypat* was malformed.

column not found: *colname*

>The column named *colname* does not exist in the table named *tablename*.

nismkdir — Create NIS+ Directories

Synopsis

/usr/bin/nismkdir [-D *defaults*] [-m *hostname*] [-s *hostname*] *dirname*

Description

Use the nismkdir command to create new NIS+ subdirectories within an existing domain. You can also use it to create replicated directories. Without options, this command creates a subdirectory with the same master and the replicas as its parent directory.

It is advisable to use nisserver(1M) to create an NIS+ domain that consists of the specified directory along with the org_dir and groups_dir subdirectories.

The two primary aspects that are controlled when making a directory are its access rights and its degree of replication.

dirname is the fully qualified NIS+ name of the directory that has to be created.

Note — A host that serves an NIS+ directory must be an NIS+ client in a directory above the one it is serving. The exceptions to this rule are the root NIS+ servers, which are both clients and servers of the same NIS+ directory.

When the host's default domain is different from the default domain on the client where the command is executed, the host name supplied as an argument to the -s or -m options must be fully qualified.

Options

-D *defaults*   Specify a different set of defaults to be used when creating new directories. The defaults string is a series of tokens separated by colons. These tokens represent the default values to be used for the generic object properties. All of the legal tokens are described below.

> ttl=*time*   Set the default time-to-live for objects that are created by this command. Specify the *time* value in the format defined by the nischttl(1) command. The default value is 12 hours.
>
> owner=*ownername*
>
> > Specify that the NIS+ principal *ownername* should own the created object. The default for this value is the principal who is executing the command.
>
> group=*groupname*
>
> > Specify that the group *groupname* should be the group owner for the object that is created. The default value is null.
>
> access=*rights*
>
> > Specify the set of access rights that are to be granted for the given object. Specify the *rights* value in the format defined by the nischmod(1) command. The default value is ----rmcdr---r---.

-m *hostname*   If the directory named by *dirname* does not exist, then create a new directory that is not replicated with host *hostname* as its master server. If the directory name by *dirname* does exist, then the host named by *hostname* is made its master server.

-s *hostname*   Specify that the host *hostname* is a replica for an existing directory named *dirname*.

Examples

The following example creates a new directory bar under the foo.com. domain that shares the same master and replicas as the foo.com. directory.

```
castle% nismkdir bar.foo.com.
```

The following example creates a new directory bar.foo.com. that is not replicated under the foo.com. domain.

```
castle% nismkdir -m myhost.foo.com. bar.foo.com.
```

The following example adds a replica server of the bar.foo.com. directory.
castle% **nismkdir -s replica.foo.com. bar.foo.com.**

Environment Variables

NIS_DEFAULTS

Specify a defaults string that overrides the NIS+ standard
defaults. If you use the -D option, then those values override both
the NIS_DEFAULTS variable and the standard defaults.

If this variable is set and the NIS+ directory name is not fully qualified,
search each specified directory until the directory is found (see
nisdefaults(1)).

Exit Status

0   Success.

1   Failure.

Attributes

See attributes(5) for descriptions of the following attributes:

Attribute Type	Attribute Value
Availability	SUNWnisu

See Also

nis+(1), nischmod(1), nisdefaults(1), nisls(1), nisrmdir(1),
nisserver(1M), attributes(5)

nispasswd — Change NIS+ Password Information

Synopsis

```
/usr/bin/nispasswd [-ghs][-D domainname][username]
/usr/bin/nispasswd -a
/usr/bin/nispasswd -D domainname [-d [username]]
/usr/bin/nispasswd [-l][-f][-n min][-x max][-w warn][-D domainname]
    username
```

Description

> **Note** — The use of nispasswd is discouraged, as it is now only a
> link to the passwd(1) command, which you should use instead.
> Using passwd(1) with the -r nisplus option achieves the same
> result and is consistent across all the different name services
> available.
>
> The login program, file access display programs (for example,
> ls -l), and network programs that require user passwords (such
> as rlogin(1) and ftp(1)) use the standard getpwnam(3C) and
> getspnam(3C) interfaces to get password information. These
> programs get the NIS+ password information that is modified by
> nispasswd only if the passwd: entry in the /etc/nsswitch.conf
> file includes nisplus. See nsswitch.conf(4) for more details.

Use the nispasswd command to change a password, comment (finger) field (-g
option), home directory (-h option), or login shell (-s option) associated with
the *username* (invoker by default) in the NIS+ passwd table.

Additionally, you can use the command to view or modify aging information
associated with the user specified if the invoker has the right NIS+ privileges.

nispasswd uses secure RPC to communicate with the NIS+ server and,
therefore, never sends unencrypted passwords over the communication
medium.

nispasswd does not read or modify the local password information stored in
the /etc/passwd and /etc/shadow files.

When used to change a password, nispasswd prompts nonprivileged users
for their old password. It then prompts for the new password twice to forestall
typing mistakes. When you enter the old password, nispasswd checks to see if
it has "aged" sufficiently. If aging is insufficient, nispasswd terminates; see
getspnam(3C).

The old password is used to decrypt the user-name's secret key. If the
password does not decrypt the secret key, nispasswd prompts for the old
secure-RPC password. It uses this password to decrypt the secret key. If this
fails, it gives the user one more chance. The old password is also used to ensure
that the new password differs from the old by at least three characters.
Assuming aging is sufficient, a check is made to ensure that the new password
meets construction requirements, described below. When you enter the new
password a second time, the two copies of the new password are compared. If
the two copies are not identical, the cycle of prompting for the new password is
repeated twice. The new password is used to reencrypt the user's secret key.
Hence, it also becomes the user's secure-RPC password, and the secure-RPC is
no longer a different password from the user's password.

Construct passwords to meet the following requirements.

- Each password must have at least six characters. Only the first eight
  characters are significant.

- Each password must contain at least two alphabetic characters and at least one numeric or special character. In this case, "alphabetic" refers to all upper- or lowercase letters.
- Each password must differ from the login user name and any reverse or circular shift of that login username. For comparison purposes, an uppercase letter and its corresponding lowercase letter are equivalent.
- New passwords must differ from the old by at least three characters. For comparison purposes, an uppercase letter and its corresponding lowercase letter are equivalent.

Network administrators who own the NIS+ password table can change any password attributes if they establish their credentials (see keylogin(1)) before invoking nispasswd. nispasswd does not prompt these privileged users for the old password, and they are not forced to comply with password aging and password construction requirements.

Any user can use the -d option to display password attributes for his or her own login name. The format of the display is:

```
username status mm/dd/yy min max warn
```

or, if password aging information is not present,

```
username status
```

where

username	The login ID of the user.
status	The password status of username: PS means the password exists or is locked, LK means locked, and NP means no password.
mm/dd/yy	The date password was last changed for username. (Note that all password aging dates are determined from Greenwich Mean Time (Universal Time) and, therefore, may differ by as much as a day in other time zones.)
min	The minimum number of days required between password changes for username.
max	The maximum number of days the password is valid for username.
warn	The number of days, relative to max, before the password expires that the username is warned.

Options

-a	Show the password attributes for all entries. This option shows only the entries in the NIS+ passwd table in the local domain that the invoker is authorized to read.

-d [*username*]

　　　　　　　Display password attributes for the caller or the user specified if
　　　　　　　the invoker has the right privileges.

-D *domainname*

　　　　　　　Consult the passwd.org_dir table in *domainname*. If you do not
　　　　　　　specify this option, use the default *domainname* returned by
　　　　　　　nis_local_directory(). This *domainname* is the same as that
　　　　　　　returned by domainname(1M).

-f　　　　　　Force the user to change password at the next login by expiring
　　　　　　　the password for *username*.

-g　　　　　　Change the comment (finger) information.

-h　　　　　　Change the home directory.

-l　　　　　　Lock the password entry for *username*. Subsequently, login(1)
　　　　　　　disallows logins with this NIS+ password entry.

-n *min*　　　Set minimum field for *username*. The *min* field contains the
　　　　　　　minimum number of days between password changes for
　　　　　　　username. If *min* is greater than *max*, the user cannot change the
　　　　　　　password. Always use this option with the -x option, unless *max* is
　　　　　　　set to -1 (aging turned off). In that case, *min* need not be set.

-s　　　　　　Change the login shell. By default, only the NIS+ administrator
　　　　　　　can change the login shell. Users are prompted for the new login
　　　　　　　shell.

-w *warn*　　Set *warn* field for *username*. The *warn* field contains the number of
　　　　　　　days before the password expires that the user is warned when
　　　　　　　logging in.

-x *max*　　　Set maximum field for *username*. The *max* field contains the
　　　　　　　number of days that the password is valid for *username*. The aging
　　　　　　　for *username* is turned off immediately if *max* is set to -1. If it is set
　　　　　　　to 0, then the user is forced to change the password at the next
　　　　　　　login session and aging is turned off.

Exit Status

0　　　　　　Success.

1　　　　　　Permission denied.

2　　　　　　Invalid combination of options.

3　　　　　　Unexpected failure. NIS+ passwd table unchanged.

4　　　　　　NIS+ passwd table missing.

5　　　　　　NIS+ was busy. Try again later.

6　　　　　　Invalid argument to option.

7　　　　　　Aging was disabled.

Attributes

See attributes(5) for descriptions of the following attributes:

Attribute Type	Attribute Value
Availability	SUNWnisu

See Also

keylogin(1), login(1), nis+(1), nistbladm(1), passwd(1), rlogin(1), domainname(1M), getspnam(3C), getpwnam(3C), nis_local_directory(3N), nsswitch.conf(4), passwd(4), shadow(4), attributes(5)

nisrm — Remove NIS+ Objects from the Namespace

Synopsis

/usr/bin/nisrm [-if] *name*...

Description

Use the nisrm command to remove NIS+ objects named *name* from the NIS+ namespace.

This command fails if the NIS+ master server is not running.

Note — This command does not remove directories (see nisrmdir(1)), nor does it remove tables that are not empty (see nistbladm(1)).

Options

-f Attempt a forced removal and, if it fails for permission reasons, try an nischmod(1) operation and retry the removal. If the command fails, it fails silently.

-i Like the system rm(1) command, interactively ask for confirmation before removing an object. If the name specified by *name* is not a fully qualified name, force this option on. This option prevents the removal of unexpected objects.

Examples

The following example removes the objects foo, bar, and baz from the namespace.

castle% **nisrm foo bar baz**

Environment Variables

NIS_PATH   If this variable is set and the NIS+ name is not fully qualified, search each specified directory until the object is found (see nisdefaults(1)).

Exit Status

0   Success.

1   Failure.

Attributes

See attributes(5) for descriptions of the following attributes:

Attribute Type	Attribute Value
Availability	SUNWnisu

See Also

nis+(1), nischmod(1), nisdefaults(1), nisrmdir(1), nistbladm(1), rm(1), attributes(5)

nisrmdir — Remove NIS+ Directories

Synopsis

/usr/bin/nisrmdir [-if][-s *hostname*] *dirname*

Description

Use the nisrmdir command to delete existing NIS+ subdirectories. You can remove a directory outright or simply remove replicas from serving a directory.

This command modifies the object that describes the directory *dirname* and then notifies each replica to remove the directory named *dirname*. If the notification of any of the affected replicas fails, the directory object is returned to its original state unless you specify the -f option.

This command fails if the NIS+ master server is not running.

Options

-f   Force the command to succeed even though it may not be able
          to contact the affected replicas. Use this option when a replica
          is known to be down and is not able to respond to the removal
          notification. When the replica is finally rebooted, it reads the
          updated directory object, notes that it is no longer a replica for
          that directory, and stops responding to lookups on that
          directory. You can manually clean up the files that held the now
          removed directory by removing the appropriate files in the
          /var/nis directory (see nisfiles(4) for more information).

-i   Like the system rm(1) command, interactively ask for
          confirmation before removing a directory. If the name specified
          by *dirname* is not a fully qualified name, force this option on.
          This option prevents the removal of unexpected directories.

-s *hostname*

          Remove the host *hostname* as a replica for the directory named
          dirname. If this option is not present, remove all replicas and
          the master server for a directory and remove the directory from
          the namespace.

Examples

The following example removes a directory bar under the foo.com. domain.

castle% **nisrmdir bar.foo.com.**

The following example removes a replica that is serving the bar.foo.com.
directory.

castle% **nisrmdir -s replica.foo.com. bar.foo.com.**

The following example forces the removal of the bar.foo.com. directory
from the namespace.

castle% nisrmdir **-f bar.foo.com.**

Environment Variables

NIS_PATH   If this variable is set and the NIS+ name is not fully qualified,
             search each specified directory until the object is found (see
             nisdefaults(1)).

Exit Status

0   Success.

1   Failure.

Attributes
See attributes(5) for descriptions of the following attributes:

Attribute Type	Attribute Value
Availability	SUNWnisu

See Also
nis+(1), nisdefaults(1), nisrm(1), nisfiles(4), attributes(5)

---

nistbladm — Administer NIS+ Tables

Synopsis
```
/usr/bin/nistbladm -a|-A [-D defaults] colname=value... tablename
/usr/bin/nistbladm -a|-A [-D defaults] indexedname
/usr/bin/nistbladm -c [-D defaults][-p path][-s sep] type
   colname=[flags][,access]... tablename
/usr/bin/nistbladm -d tablename
/usr/bin/nistbladm -e|-E colname=value... indexedname
/usr/bin/nistbladm -m colname=value... indexedname
/usr/bin/nistbladm -r|-R [colname=value...] tablename
/usr/bin/nistbladm -r|-R indexedname
/usr/bin/nistbladm -u [-p path][-s sep][-t type][colname=access...]
   tablename
```

Description
Use the nistbladm command to administer NIS+ tables. It performs five
primary operations:

- Creating tables.
- Deleting tables.
- Adding entries to tables.
- Modifying entries within tables.
- Removing entries from tables.

Although NIS+ does not place restrictions on the size of tables or entries, the
size of data has an impact on the performance and the disk space requirements
of the NIS+ server. NIS+ is not designed to store huge pieces of data such as
files.

NIS+ design is optimized to support 10,000 objects with a total size of 10
megabytes. If the requirements exceed the above, it is suggested that you
create the domain hierarchy or store pointers to the data in the tables instead
of storing the data itself.

When creating tables, you must specify a table type, *type*, and a list of column definitions.

type is a string that is stored in the table and later used by the service to verify that entries being added to it are of the correct type. Column definitions use the following syntax.

colname=[*flags*][,*access*]

flags is a combination of:

S   Searches can be done on the column's values (see nismatch(1)).

I   Searches ignore case (makes sense only in combination with S).

C   Encrypt column values.

B   Binary data (does not make sense in combination with S). If not set, the column's values are expected to be null-terminated ASCII strings.

X   XDR encode data (makes sense only in combination with B).

access is specified in the format as defined by the nischmod(1) command.

When manipulating entries, this command takes two forms of entry name. The first uses a series of space-separated *colname=value* pairs that specify column values in the entry. The second is an NIS+ indexed name, *indexedname*, of the following form.

[*colname=value*, . . .],*tablename*

Options

-a | A   Add entries to an NIS+ table. The difference between the lowercase a and the uppercase A is in the treatment of preexisting entries. The entry's contents are specified by the *column=value* pairs on the command line. Note that you must specify values for all columns when adding entries to a table.

             Normally, NIS+ reports an error if you try to add an entry to a table that would overwrite an entry that already exists. This feature prevents multiple parties from adding duplicate entries and having one of them get overwritten. The uppercase A specifies that the entry is to be added even if it already exists. This option is analogous to a modify operation on the entry.

-c   Create a table named *tablename* in the namespace. The table that is created must have at least one column, and at least one column must be searchable.

-d *tablename*

             Destroy the table named *tablename*. The table that is being destroyed must be empty. First delete the table's contents with the -R option.

-D *defaults*

> When creating objects, specify a different set of defaults to be used during this operation. The *defaults* string is a series of tokens separated by colons. These tokens represent the default values to be used for the generic object properties. All of the legal tokens are described below.
>
> ttl=*time*
>
>> Set the default time-to-live for objects that are created by this command. Specify the *time* value in the format defined by the nischttl(1) command. The default value is 12 hours.
>
> owner=*ownername*
>
>> Specify that the NIS+ principal *ownername* should own the created object. Normally, this value is the same as the principal who is executing the command.
>
> group=*groupname*
>
>> Specify that the group *groupname* should be the group owner for the object that is created. The default value is null.
>
> access=*rights*
>
>> Specify the set of access rights that are to be granted for the given object. Specify the *rights* value in the format defined by the nischmod(1) command. The default value is ----rmcdr---r---.

-e|E

> Edit the entry in the table that is specified by *indexedname*. *indexedname* must uniquely identify a single entry. It is possible to edit the value in a column that would change the indexed name of an entry.
>
> The change (*colname=value*) can affect other entries in the table if the change results in an entry whose indexed name is different from *indexedname* and matches that of another existing entry. In this case, the -e option fails and an error is reported. The -E option forces the replacement of the existing entry by the new entry (effectively removing two old entries and adding a new one).

-m

> A synonym for -E. This option has been superseded by the -E option.

-p *path*

> When creating or updating a table, specify the table's search path. When you invoke an nis_list() function, you can specify the flag FOLLOW_PATH to tell the client library to continue searching tables in the table's path if the search criteria used do not yield any entries. The path consists of an ordered list of table names, separated by colons. The names in the path must be fully qualified.

When creating or updating a table, specify the table's separator character. The separator character is used by `niscat(1)` when displaying tables on the standard output. Its purpose is to separate column data when the table is in ASCII form. The default value is a space.

-r|R   Remove entries from a table. Specify the entry by either a series of `column=value` pairs on the command line or an indexed name that is specified as `entryname`. The difference between the interpretation of the lowercase `r` and the uppercase `R` is in the treatment of nonunique entry specifications. Normally, the NIS+ server disallows an attempt to remove an entry when the search criterion specified for that entry resolves to more than one entry in the table. However, you sometimes want to be able to remove more than one entry, for example, when you are trying to remove all of the entries from a table. In this case, using the uppercase `R` forces the NIS+ server to remove all entries matching the passed search criterion. If that criterion is null and no column values are specified, then all entries in the table are removed.

-t type   When updating a table, specify the table's `type` string.

-u   Update attributes of a table. This option enables the concatenation path (-p), separation character specified with the (-s), column access rights, and table type string (-t) of a table to be changed. Neither the number of columns nor the columns that are searchable can be changed.

Examples

The following example creates a table named `hobbies` in the directory `foo.com.` of the type `hobby_tbl` with two searchable columns, `name` and `hobby`.

```
castle% nistbladm -c hobby_tbl name=S,a+r,o+m hobby=S,a+r
    hobbies.foo.com.
```

The column `name` has read access for all (that is, owner, group, and world) and modify access for only the owner. The column `hobby` is readable by all but not modifiable by anyone.

In the following example, if the access rights had not been specified, the table's access rights would have come from either the standard defaults or the `NIS_DEFAULTS` variable.

The following examples add entries to this table.

```
castle% nistbladm -a name=bob hobby=skiing hobbies.foo.com.
castle% nistbladm -a name=sue hobby=skiing hobbies.foo.com.
castle% nistbladm -a name=ted hobby=swimming hobbies.foo.com.
```

The following example adds to the concatenation path.

```
castle% nistbladm -u -p hobbies.bar.com.:hobbies.baz.com. hobbies
```

The following example deletes the skiers from the list.

```
castle% nistbladm -R hobby=skiing hobbies.foo.com.
```

Note — The previous example uses the -R option. Using the -r option would fail because there are two entries with the value of skiing.

To create a table with a column that is named with no flags set, you supply only the name and the equal (=) sign as follows.

```
castle% nistbladm -c notes_tbl name=S,a+r,o+m note= notes.foo.com.
```

The following example created a table, named notes.foo.com., of type notes_tbl, with two columns name and note. The note column is not searchable.

When entering data for columns in the form of a value string, protect the characters equal (=), comma (,), left bracket ([), right bracket (]), and space ( ) with single or double quotes. These characters are parsed by NIS+ within an indexed name. Protect these characters by enclosing the entire value in double quote (") characters as follows.

```
castle% nistbladm -a fullname="Joe User" nickname=Joe nicknames
```

If there is any doubt about how the string is parsed, it is best to enclose it in quotes.

Environment Variables

NIS_DEFAULTS

    This variable contains a defaults string that overrides the NIS+ standard defaults. If you use the –D option, those values then override both the NIS_DEFAULTS variable and the standard defaults.

NIS_PATH   If this variable is set and the NIS+ table name is not fully qualified, search each specified directory until the table is found (see nisdefaults(1)).

Exit Status

0   Success.

1   Failure

Attributes

See attributes(5) for descriptions of the following attributes:

Attribute Type	Attribute Value
Availability	SUNWnisu

See Also

nis+(1), niscat(1), nischmod(1), nischown(1), nisdefaults(1), nismatch(1), nissetup(1M), attributes(5)

Warnings

To modify one of the entries, say, for example, from bob to robert, the following command is incorrect.

```
castle% nistbladm -m name=robert [name=bob],hobbies
```

[name=bob],hobbies is an indexed name and the characters [(open bracket) and] (close bracket) are interpreted by the shell. When typing entry names in the form of NIS+ indexed names, you must protect the name by using single quotes, as shown below.

```
castle% nistbladm -m name=robert '[name=bob],hobbies'
```

It is possible to specify a set of defaults so that you cannot read or modify the table object later.

nistest — Return the State of the NIS+ Namespace, Using Conditional Expression

Synopsis

```
/usr/bin/nistest [-ALMP][-a rights | -t type] object
/usr/bin/nistest [-ALMP][-a rights] indexedname
/usr/bin/nistest -c dir1 op dir2
```

New!

Description

Use the nistest command as a way for shell scripts and other programs to test for the existence, type, and access rights of objects and entries. Entries are named using indexed names (see nismatch(1)). With the -c option, you can compare directory names to test where they lie in relation to each other in the namespace.

New!

Options

-a *rights*   Verify that the current process has the desired or required access rights on the named object or entries. The access rights are specified in the same way as the nischmod(1) command.

-A   Return all data within the table and all of the data in tables in the initial table's concatenation path. This option is valid only when using indexed names or following links.

-c   Test whether two directory names have a certain relationship to each other; for example, higher than (ht) or lower than (lt). You can display the complete list of values for *op* by using the -c option with no arguments. The complete list of *op* values is shown below.

<	Lower than.
lt	Lower than.
<=	Lower than or equal.
le	Lower than or equal.
=	Equal.
eq	Equal.
>	Higher than.
ht	Higher than.
gt	Higher than.
>=	Higher than or equal.
he	Higher than or equal.
ge	Higher than or equal.
!=	Not equal.
ne	Not equal.
ns	Not sequential.

-L   If the object named by object or the *tablename* component of *indexedname* names a LINK type object, follow the link.

-M   Master server only. Send the lookup to the master server of the named data. This option guarantees that the most up-to-date information is seen, at the possible expense that the master server may be busy.

-P   Follow the concatenation path of a table if the initial search is unsuccessful. This option is valid only when using indexed names or following links.

-t *type*   Test the type of object. The value of *type* can be one of the following:

D	Return true if the object is a directory object.
G	Return true if the object is a group object.
L	Return true if the object is a link object.

P	Return `true` if the object is a private object.
T	Return `true` if the object is a table object.

Examples

When testing for access rights, `nistest` returns success (`0`) if the specified rights are granted to the current user. Thus, the following test for access rights tests that all authenticated NIS+ clients have read and modify access to the `skippy.domain` object.

```
castle% nistest -a w=mr skippy.domain
```

You can test for access on a particular entry in a table by using the indexed name syntax. The following example tests to see if an entry in the password table can be modified.

```
castle% nistest -a o=m '[uid=99],passwd.org_dir'
```

New!

The following example tests if a directory lies higher in the namespace than another directory by using the `-c` option with an *op* of `ht` (higher than). The test returns `true`.

```
castle% nistest -c dom.com. ht lower.dom.com.
```

Environment Variables

`NIS_PATH`   If this variable is set and the NIS+ name is not fully qualified, search each specified directory until the object is found (see `nisdefaults(1)`).

Exit Status

0	Success.
1	Failure because the object was not present, not of specified type, and/or no such access.
2	Failure because of illegal usage.

Attributes

See `attributes(5)` for descriptions of the following attributes:

Attribute Type	Attribute Value
Availability	SUNWnisu

See Also

`nis+(1)`, `nischmod(1)`, `nisdefaults(1)`, `nismatch(1)`, `attributes(5)`

nl — Line Numbering Filter

Synopsis

```
/usr/bin/nl [-p] [-b[type]] [-d[delim]] [-f[type]] [-h[type]] [-i[incr]]
    [-l[num]] [-n[format]] [-s[sep]] [-w[width]] [-v[startnum]] [file]
/usr/xpg4/bin/nl [-p] [-b type] [-d delim] [-f type] [-h type] [-i incr]
    [-l num] [-n format] [-s sep] [-w width] [-v startnum] [file]
```

Description

Use the nl command to number the lines of a file. The nl command divides
pages into logical segments and restarts the line numbering at the top of each
new page. A logical page consists of a header, a body, and a footer section.
Empty sections are valid.

The nl command reads lines from the named file, or the standard input if no
file is named, and reproduces the lines on the standard output. Lines are
numbered on the left in accordance with the specified command options.

Different line numbering options are independently available for header,
body, and footer. For example, -bt (the default) numbers nonblank lines in the
body section and does not number any lines in the header and footer sections.

The start of logical page sections is signaled by input lines containing
nothing but the following delimiter character(s).

Line contents	Start of
\:\:\:	Header.
\:\:	Body.
\:	Footer.

Unless optioned otherwise, nl assumes the text being read is in a single
logical page body.

Notes

Internationalized Regular Expressions are used in the POSIX and C locales. In
other locales, Internationalized Regular Expressions are used if the following
two conditions are met:

- /usr/lib/locale/*locale*/LC_COLLATE/CollTable is present, and
- /usr/lib/locale/*locale*/LC_COLLATE/coll.so is not present;

otherwise, Simple Regular Expressions are used. Internationalized Regular
Expressions are explained on regex(5). Simple Regular Expressions are
explained on regexp(5).

Options

You can specify options in any order and intermingle them with an optional file name. You can name only one file. The specified default is used when the option is not entered on the command line. /usr/xpg4/bin/nl options require option arguments. A space character can separate options from option arguments. /usr/bin/nl options can have arguments. If you do not specify arguments for /usr/bin/nl, the default options are used.

-b*type*   Specify which logical page body lines are to be numbered. Recognized types and their meanings are:

      a   Number all lines.

      t   Number all nonempty lines.

      n   No line numbering.

      p*exp*   Number only lines that contain the regular expression specified in *exp*. Default type for logical page body is t (text lines numbered).

-f*type*   Same as -b*type* except for footer. Default type for logical page footer is n (no lines numbered).

-d*delim*   Change the two delimiter characters specifying the start of a logical page section from the default characters (\:) to two user-specified characters. If you enter only one character, the second character remains the default character (:). Do not include a space between the -d and the delimiter characters. To enter a backslash, use two backslashes.

-h*type*   Same as -b*type* except for header. Default type for logical page header is n (no lines numbered).

-i*incr*   Specify the increment value used to number logical page lines. Default *incr* is 1.

-l*num*   Specify the number of blank lines to be considered as one. For example, -l2 results in only the second adjacent blank being numbered (if the appropriate -ha, -ba, or -fa option is set). Default *num* is 1.

-n*format*   Specify the line numbering format. Recognized values are:

      ln   Left-justified, leading zeros suppressed.

      rn   Right-justified, leading zeros suppressed.

      rz   Right-justified, leading zeros kept. Default format is rn (right-justified).

-p   Do not restart numbering at logical page delimiters.

-s*sep*   Specify the character(s) used in separating the line number and the corresponding text line. Default *sep* is a Tab.

-v*startnum*   Specify the initial value used to number logical page lines. Default *startnum* is 1.

`-wwidth`	Specify the number of characters to be used for the line number. Default width is 6.

Operands

`file`	A path name of a text file to be line numbered.

Examples

The following example uses the default options to add line numbers to the file `kookaburra-1`.

```
castle% nl kookaburra-1
     1  Kookaburra sits in the old gum tree
     2  Merry merry king of the bush is he.
     3  Laugh, kookaburra, laugh, kookaburra
     4  Gay your life must be.
     5
     6  Kookaburra sits in the old gum tree
     7  Eating all the gumdrops he can see.
     8  Stop, kookaburra, stop, kookaburra
     9  Leave some there for me.
castle%
```

The following command numbers the first line of the page body 10, the second line of the page body, 20, the third 30, and so forth. The logical page delimiters are ++.

```
castle% nl -v10 -i10 -d++ kookaburra-2
    10  Kookaburra sits in the old gum tree
    20  Merry merry king of the bush is he.
    30  Laugh, kookaburra, laugh, kookaburra
    40  Gay your life must be.
    50
    60  Kookaburra sits in the old gum tree
    70  Eating all the gumdrops he can see.
    80  Stop, kookaburra, stop, kookaburra
    90  Leave some there for me.

castle%
```

Environment Variables

See `environ`(5) for descriptions of the following environment variables that affect the execution of `nl`: LC_COLLATE, LC_CTYPE, LC_MESSAGES, and NLSPATH.

Exit Status

`0`	Successful completion.
`>0`	An error occurred.

Files

/usr/lib/locale/locale/LC_COLLATE/CollTable

Collation table generated by localedef.

/usr/lib/locale/locale/LC_COLLATE/coll.so

Shared object containing string transformation library routines.

Attributes

See attributes(5) for descriptions of the following attributes:

/usr/bin/nl

Attribute Type	Attribute Value
Availability	SUNWesu

/usr/xpg4/bin/nl

Attribute Type	Attribute Value
Availability	SUNWxcu4

See Also

pr(1), attributes(5), environ(5), regex(5), regexp(5)

nm — Print Name List of an Object File

Synopsis

/usr/ccs/bin/nm [-ACDhlnPprRsTuVv] [-efox] [-g | -u] [-t format] file...
/usr/xpg4/bin/nm [-ACDhlnPprRsTuVv] [-efox] [-g | -u] [-t format] file...

Description

The nm command displays the symbol table of each ELF object file that is specified by file.

If no symbolic information is available for a valid input file, the nm command reports that fact but does not consider it an error condition.

Options

You can specify options in any order, either singly or in combination, and can put them anywhere on the command line. When you specify conflicting options (such as -v and -n; and -o and -x) the first is taken and the second ignored with a warning message. (See -R for exception.)

-A	Write the full path name or library name of an object on each line.
-C	Demangle C++ symbol names before printing them.
-D	Display the SHT_DYNSYM symbol table used by ld.so.1 that is present even in stripped dynamic executables. By default, the SHT_SYMTab symbol table is displayed.
-g	Write only external (global) symbol information.
-h	Do not display the output heading data.
-l	Distinguish between WEAK and GLOBAL symbols by appending an asterisk (*) to the key letter for WEAK symbols.
-n	Sort external symbols by name before they are printed.
-o	Print the value and size of a symbol in octal instead of decimal. (equivalent to -t o).
-p	Produce easy-to-parse, terse output. Precede each symbol name by its value (blanks if undefined) and one of the letters:

A	Absolute symbol.
B	bss (uninitialized data space) symbol.
D	Data object symbol.
F	File symbol.
N	Symbol has no type.
S	Section symbol.
T	Text symbol.
U	Undefined.

If the symbol's binding attribute is:

LOCAL	The key letter is lower case.
WEAK	The key letter is upper case; if you specify the -l modifier, the uppercase key letter is followed by *.
GLOBAL	The key letter is upper case.

-P	Write information in a portable output format, as specified in "Standard Output" on page 944.
-r	Prepend the name of the object file or archive to each output line.
-R	Print the archive name (if present), followed by the object file and symbol name. If you also specify the -r option, ignore this option.
-s	Print section name instead of section index.
-t *format*	Write each numeric value in the specified format. The format is dependent on the single character used as the format option-argument.

d	Write the offset in decimal (default).
o	Write the offset in octal.
x	Write the offset in hexadecimal.

The following options are obsolete because of changes to the object file format and will be deleted in a future release.

-e	Print only external and static symbols. The symbol table now contains only static and external symbols. Automatic symbols no longer appear in the symbol table. They do appear in the debugging information produced by cc -g, which you can examine by using dump(1).
-f	Produce full output. Redundant symbols (such as .text and .data) that existed previously no longer exist. Producing full output is identical to the default output.
-T	By default, nm prints the entire name of the symbols listed. Because symbol names have been moved to the last column, the problem of overflow is removed; truncating the symbol name is no longer necessary.

/usr/ccs/bin/nm

-u	Print undefined symbols only.

/usr/xpg4/bin/nm

-u	Print long listing for each undefined symbol.
-v	Sort external symbols by value before they are printed.
-V	Print the version of the nm command executing on the standard error output.
-x	Print the value and size of a symbol in hexadecimal instead of decimal (equivalent to -t x).

Operands

file	A path name of an object file, executable file, or object-file library.

Output

Standard Output

For each symbol, the following information is printed:

Index	The index of the symbol. (The index appears in brackets.)
Value	The value of the symbol is one of the following.

- A section offset for defined symbols in a relocatable file.
- Alignment constraints for symbols whose section index is SHN_COMMON.

- A virtual address in executable and dynamic library files.

Size   The size in bytes of the associated object.

Type   A symbol is of one of the following types.

    NOTYPE   No type was specified.

    OBJECT   A data object such as an array or variable.

    FUNC   A function or other executable code.

    SECTION   A section symbol.

    FILE   Name of the source file.

Bind   The symbol's binding attributes.

    LOCAL   Limit scope to the object file containing their definition.

    GLOBAL   Visible to all object files being combined.

    WEAK   Specify that global symbols have a lower precedence than GLOBAL.

Other   Reserved for future use, currently contains 0.

Shndx   Except for three special values, this is the section header table index in relation to which the symbol is defined. The following special values exist.

    ABS   The symbol's value does not change through relocation.

    COMMON   An unallocated block and the value provide alignment constraints.

    UNDEF   An undefined symbol.

Name   The name of the symbol.

Object Name The name of the object or library if you specify -A.

If you specify the -P option, the previous information is displayed, using the following portable format. The three versions differ depending on whether you specify -t d, -t o or -t x.

```
%s%s %s %d %d\n, library/object-name, name, type, value, size
%s%s %s %o %o\n, library/object-name, name, type, value, size
%s%s %s %x %x\n, library/object-name, name, type, value, size
```

where *library/object-name* is formatted as follows.

- If you specify -A, *library/object-name* is an empty string.

- If you specify -A and the corresponding file operand does not name a library: %s: , *file*

- If you specify -A and the corresponding file operand names a library. In this case, *object-file* names the object file in the library containing the symbol being described: %s[%s]: , *file, object-file*

If you do not specify -A, if you specify more than one file operand, or if you specify only one file operand and it names a library, nm writes a line identifying the object containing the following symbols before the lines containing those symbols, in one of the following forms.

- If the corresponding file operand does not name a library: %s:\n, *file*
- If the corresponding file operand names a library; in this case, *object-file* is the name of the file in the library containing the following symbols: %s[%s]:\n, *file*, *object-file*

If you specify -P but not -t, the format is as if you had specified -t x.

Examples

The following example shows the first few lines of output from the zipinfo command.

```
castle% /usr/ccs/bin/nm /bin/zipinfo
[Index]     Value      Size    Type   Bind   Other  Shndx    Name
```

[Index]	Value	Size	Type	Bind	Other	Shndx	Name
[20]	216572	0	SECT	LOCL	0	19	
[2]	65748	0	SECT	LOCL	0	1	
[3]	65768	0	SECT	LOCL	0	2	
[4]	67380	0	SECT	LOCL	0	3	
[5]	70420	0	SECT	LOCL	0	4	
[6]	73532	0	SECT	LOCL	0	5	
[7]	73564	0	SECT	LOCL	0	6	
[8]	73588	0	SECT	LOCL	0	7	
[9]	73624	0	SECT	LOCL	0	8	
[10]	74296	0	SECT	LOCL	0	9	
[11]	148616	0	SECT	LOCL	0	10	
[12]	148672	0	SECT	LOCL	0	11	
[13]	148728	0	SECT	LOCL	0	12	
[14]	148732	0	SECT	LOCL	0	13	
[15]	148924	0	SECT	LOCL	0	14	
[16]	215644	0	SECT	LOCL	0	15	
[17]	215648	0	SECT	LOCL	0	16	
[18]	216372	0	SECT	LOCL	0	17	
[19]	216540	0	SECT	LOCL	0	18	
[21]	232300	0	SECT	LOCL	0	20	
[39]	0	0	NOTY	LOCL	0	UNDEF	
[22]	233152	0	SECT	LOCL	0	21	
[23]	0	0	SECT	LOCL	0	22	
[24]	0	0	SECT	LOCL	0	23	
[25]	0	0	SECT	LOCL	0	24	
[26]	0	0	SECT	LOCL	0	25	
[27]	0	0	SECT	LOCL	0	26	
[28]	0	0	SECT	LOCL	0	27	
[38]	0	0	NOTY	LOCL	0	UNDEF	
[566]	215996	0	FUNC	GLOB	0	UNDEF	.div
[473]	216008	0	FUNC	GLOB	0	UNDEF	.rem
[565]	216188	0	FUNC	GLOB	0	UNDEF	.udiv
[471]	216116	0	FUNC	GLOB	0	UNDEF	.urem
[484]	216608	4	OBJT	GLOB	0	19	___Argv

```
[522]     |     216604|     4|OBJT  |GLOB  |0     |19       |__cg89_used
[523]     |     216604|     4|OBJT  |GLOB  |0     |19       |__cg92_used
. . .
```

Environment Variables

See environ(5) for descriptions of the following environment variables that affect the execution of nm: LC_COLLATE, LC_CTYPE, LC_MESSAGES, and NLSPATH.

Exit Status

0	Successful completion.
>0	An error occurred.

Attributes

See attributes(5) for descriptions of the following attributes:

/usr/ccs/bin/nm

Attribute Type	Attribute Value
Availability	SUNWbtool

/usr/xpg4/bin/nm

Attribute Type	Attribute Value
Availability	SUNWxcu4

See Also

ar(1),as(1),dump(1),ld(1),ld.so.1(1),a.out(4),ar(4),attributes(5), environ(5), XPG4(5)

nohup — Run a Command Immune to Hangups

Synopsis

```
/usr/bin/nohup command [argument...]
/usr/xpg4/bin/nohup command [argument...]
```

Description

Use the nohup command to run background jobs that keep running even if you log out. The nohup command invokes the named command with the arguments supplied. When the command is invoked, nohup arranges for the SIGHUP signal to be ignored by the process.

When a shell exits, the system sends its children SIGHUP signals which, by default, kill them. You can, however, use the nohup command when you know that *command* takes a long time to run and you want to be able to log out of the terminal without interrupting the command. When you precede a command invocation with the nohup command (or if the process programmatically has chosen to ignore SIGHUP), all stopped, running, and background jobs ignore SIGHUP and continue running.

nohup automatically sends command output, including standard error, to the nohup.out file.

/usr/bin/nohup

Processes run by /usr/bin/nohup are immune to SIGHUP (hangup) and SIGQUIT (quit) signals.

/usr/xpg4/bin/nohup

Processes run by /usr/xpg4/bin/nohup are immune to SIGHUP.

The nohup command does not arrange to make processes immune to a SIGTERM (terminate) signal, so they receive it unless you arrange for the processes to be immune to SIGTERM or unless the shell makes them immune to SIGTERM.

If nohup.out is not writable in the current directory, output is redirected to $HOME/nohup.out. If a file is created, the file has read and write permission (600, see chmod(1)). If the standard error is a terminal, output is redirected to the standard output; otherwise, it is not redirected. The priority of the process run by nohup is not altered.

Warnings

If you are running the Korn shell (ksh(1)) as your login shell and have nohup'ed jobs running when you attempt to log out, you are warned with the message

```
You have jobs running.
```

You then need to log out a second time to actually log out; however, your background jobs continue to run.

Notes

The C shell (csh(1)) has a built-in nohup command that provides immunity from SIGHUP but does not redirect output to nohup.out. Commands executed with & are automatically immune to HUP signals while in the background.

nohup does not recognize command sequences. In the case of the following command, the nohup command applies only to *command1*.

```
$ nohup command1; command2
```

The following command is syntactically incorrect.

```
$ nohup (command1; command2)
```

Operands

command   The name of a command that is to be invoked. If the *command* operand names any of the special `shell_builtins(1)` commands, the results are undefined.

argument   Any string to be supplied as an argument when invoking the command operand.

Examples

It is frequently desirable to apply `nohup` to pipelines or lists of commands. You can do this only by placing pipelines and command lists in a single file, called a shell script. If you run the script with the following command, then `nohup` applies to everything in the file.

```
$ nohup sh file
```

If the shell script file is to be executed often, you can eliminate the need to type `sh` by giving *file* execute permission.

When you add an ampersand, the contents of *file* are run in the background with interrupts also ignored (see `sh(1)`).

```
$ nohup file &
```

Environment Variables

See `environ(5)` for descriptions of the following environment variables that affect the execution of `nohup`: LC_CTYPE, LC_MESSAGES, PATH, and NLSPATH.

HOME   Determine the path name of the user's home directory. If the output file `nohup.out` cannot be created in the current directory, the `nohup` command uses the directory named by HOME to create the file.

Exit Status

126   Command was found but could not be invoked.

127   An error occurred in `nohup`, or command could not be found.

Otherwise, the exit values of `nohup` are those of the *command* operand.

Files

nohup.out   The output file of the nohup execution if standard output is a terminal and if the current directory is writable.

$HOME/nohup.out

The output file of the nohup execution if standard output is a terminal and if the current directory is not writable.

Attributes

See attributes(5) for descriptions of the following attributes:

/usr/bin/nohup

Attribute Type	Attribute Value
Availability	SUNWcsu
CSI	Enabled

/usr/xpg4/bin/nohup

Attribute Type	Attribute Value
Availability	SUNWxcu4
CSI	Enabled

See Also

batch(1), chmod(1), csh(1), ksh(1), nice(1), sh(1), shell_builtins(1), signal(3C), attributes(5), environ(5), xpg4(5)

notify — Control Process Execution

Synopsis

csh
notify [%*job-id*]...

Description

See jobs(1).

nroff — Format Documents for Display or Line Printer

Synopsis

```
/usr/bin/nroff [-ehiq] [-mname] [-nN] [-opagelist] [-raN] [-sN] [-Tname]
```

Description

nroff formats text in the named files for typewriter-like devices. See also troff(1).

If you specify no *file* argument, nroff reads the standard input. An argument consisting of a dash (-) is taken to be a file name corresponding to the standard input.

Notes

Previous documentation incorrectly described the numeric register yr as being the "Last two digits of current year". yr is in actuality the number of years since 1900. To correctly obtain the last two digits of the current year through the year 2099, you can include the following definition of string register yy in a document to display a two-digit year. Note that you can substitute any other available one- or two-character register name for yy.

```
.\" definition of new string register yy--last two digits of year
.\" use yr (# of years since 1900) if it is < 100
.ie \n(yr<100 .ds yy \n(yr
.el \{          .\" else, subtract 100 from yr, store in ny
.nr ny \n(yr-100
.ie \n(ny>9 \{    .\" use ny if it is two digits
.ds yy \n(ny
.\" remove temporary number register ny
.rr ny \}
.el \{.ds yy 0
.\" if ny is one digit, append it to 0
.as yy \n(ny
.rr ny \} \}
```

Options

You can specify options in any order as long as they appear before the files.

-e	Produce equally spaced words in adjusted lines, using full terminal resolution.
-h	Use output Tab characters during horizontal spacing to speed output and reduce output character count. Tab settings are assumed to be every eight nominal character widths.
-i	Read the standard input after the input files are exhausted.
-mname	Prepend the macro file /usr/share/lib/tmac/tmac.*name* to the input files.

-n*N*	Number the first generated page *N*.
-o*pagelist*	Print pages whose page numbers appear only in the comma-separated list of numbers and ranges. A range *N-M* means pages *N* through *M*; an initial *-N* means from the beginning to page *N*; and a final *N-* means from *N* to the end.
-q	Invoke the simultaneous input-output mode of the rd(9F) request.
-ra*N*	Set register a (one-character) to *N*.
-s*N*	Stop every *N* pages (default N=1) to allow paper loading or changing. Resume on receipt of a newline.
-T*name*	Prepare output for a device of the specified name. Known names are:

37	Teletype Corporation Model 37 terminal (the default).
lp | tn300	GE Any line printer or terminal without half-line capability.
300	DASI-300.
300-12	DASI-300–12-pitch.
300S	DASI-300S.
300S-12	DASI-300S.
382	DASI-382 (fancy DTC 382).
450	DASI-450 (Diablo Hyterm).
450-12	DASI-450 (Diablo Hyterm)–12pitch.
832	AJ 832.

Examples

The following example formats user.guide, using the -me macro package and stopping every four pages.

```
castle% nroff -s4 -me users.guide
```

Environment Variables

See environ(5) for descriptions of the following environment variables that affect the execution of nroff: LC_CTYPE, LC_MESSAGES, and NLSPATH.

Files

/usr/tmp/trtmp*

    Temporary file.

/usr/share/lib/tmac/tmac.*

    Standard macro files.

```
/usr/share/lib/nterm/*
```
        Terminal driving tables for `nroff`.

```
/usr/share/lib/nterm/README
```
        Index to terminal description files.

Note — `/usr/tmp` is currently a symbolic link to `/var/tmp`.   *New!*

Attributes

See `attributes`(5) for descriptions of the following attributes:

Attribute Type	Attribute Value
Availability	SUNWdoc
CSI	Enabled

See Also

checknr(1), col(1), eqn(1), man(1), tbl(1), troff(1), attributes(5),
environ(5), me(5), ms(5), term(5), rd(9F)

O

od — Octal Dump

Synopsis

```
/usr/bin/od [-bcCDdFfOoSsvXx][-][file][offset_string]
/usr/bin/od [-bcCDdFfOoSsvXx][-A address-base][-j skip][-N count]
    [-t type-string] ... [-][file]
/usr/xpg4/bin/od [-bcCDdFfOoSsvXx][-][file][offset-string]
/usr/xpg4/bin/od [-bcCDdFfOoSsvXx][-A address-base] [-j skip]
    [-N count][-t type-string [-][file]
```

Description

The od command sequentially copies each input file to standard output and transforms the input data according to the output types specified with the -t or -bcCDdFfOoSsvXx options. If you specify no output type, the default output is as if you specified -t o2. You can specify multiple types by using multiple -bcCDdFfOoSstvXx options. Output lines are written for each type specified in the order in which the types are specified. If you specify no file, the standard input is used. The [offset-string] operand is mutually exclusive from the -A, -j, -N, and -t options. For the purposes of this description, the following terms are used:

word   A 16-bit unit, independent of the word size of the system.

long word   A 32-bit unit.

double long word

> A 64-bit unit.

Options

-A *address-base*

> Specify the input offset base. The *address-base* argument must be a character. The characters d, o, or x specify that the offset base is written in decimal, octal, or hexadecimal. The character n specifies that the offset is not written. Unless you specify -A, the output line is preceded by the input offset, cumulative across input files, of the next byte to be written. In addition, the offset of the byte following the last byte written is displayed after all the input data has been processed. Without the -A *address-base* option and the [*offset-string*] operand, the input offset base is displayed in octal.

-b

> Interpret bytes in octal. This option is equivalent to -t o1.

/usr/bin/od

-c

> Display single-byte characters. Certain nongraphic characters appear as C-language escapes:

> | | |
> |---|---|
> | \0 | Null. |
> | \b | Backspace. |
> | \f | Formfeed. |
> | \n | Newline. |
> | \r | Return. |
> | \t | Tab. |

> Others appear as 3-digit octal numbers. For example:

```
echo "hello world" | od -c
0000000 h e l l o   w o r l d \n
0000014
```

/usr/xpg4/bin/od

-c

> Interpret bytes as single- or multibyte characters according to the current setting of the LC_CTYPE locale category. Write printable multibyte characters in the area corresponding to the first byte of the character; write the two-character sequence * * in the area corresponding to each remaining byte in the character as an indication that the character is continued. Nongraphic characters appear the same as they would with the -C option.

-C   Interpret bytes as single- or multibyte characters according to the current setting of the LC_CTYPE locale category. Write printable multibyte characters in the area corresponding to the first byte of the character; write the two-character sequence * * in the area corresponding to each remaining byte in the character as an indication that the character is continued. Certain nongraphic characters appear as C escapes:

\0	Null.
\b	Backspace.
\f	Formfeed.
\n	Newline.
\r	Return.
\t	Tab.

Other nonprintable characters appear as one 3-digit octal number for each byte in the character.

-d   Interpret words in unsigned decimal. This option is equivalent to -t u2.

-D   Interpret long words in unsigned decimal. This option is equivalent to -t u4.

-f   Interpret long words in floating point. This option is equivalent to -t f4.

-F   Interpret double-long words in extended precision. This option is equivalent to -t f8.

-j *skip*   Jump over *skip* bytes from the beginning of the input. The od command reads or seeks past the first *skip* bytes in the concatenated input files. If the combined input is not at least *skip* bytes long, write a diagnostic message to standard error and exit with a non-zero exit status.

By default, the *skip* argument is interpreted as a decimal number. With a leading 0x or 0X, the offset is interpreted as a hexadecimal number; otherwise, with a leading 0, the offset is interpreted as an octal number. Appending the character b, k, or m to offset interprets it as a multiple of 512, 1,024 or 1,048,576 bytes. If the *skip* number is hexadecimal, consider any appended b to be the final hexadecimal digit. Display the address starting at 0000000, and do not imply its base by the base of the *skip* argument.

-N *count*   Format no more than *count* bytes of input. By default, *count* is interpreted as a decimal number. With a leading 0x or 0X, *count* is interpreted as a hexadecimal number; otherwise, with a leading 0, it is interpreted as an octal number. If *count* bytes of input (after successfully skipping if -j *skip* is specified) are not available, it is not considered an error; the od command formats the input that is available. The base of the address displayed is not implied by the base of the *count* argument.

-o   Interpret words in octal. This option is equivalent to -t o2.

-O   Interpret long words in unsigned octal. This option is equivalent to -t o4.

-s   Interpret words in signed decimal. This option is equivalent to -t d2.

-S   Interpret long words in signed decimal. This option is equivalent to -t d4.

-t *type-string*

Specify one or more output types. The *type-string* argument must be a string specifying the types to be used when writing the input data. The string must consist of the type specification characters.

a   Interpret bytes as named characters. Use only the least significant seven bits of each byte for this type specification. Bytes with the values listed in the following table are written using the corresponding names of those characters.

Value	Name	Value	Name	Value	Name	Value	Name
\000	nul	\001	soh	\002	stx	\003	etx
\004	eot	\005	enq	\006	ack	\007	bel
\010	bs	\011	ht	\012	lf	\013	vt
\014	ff	\015	cr	\016	so	\017	si
\020	dle	\021	dc1	\022	dc2	\023	dc3
\024	dc4	\025	nak	\026	syn	\027	etb
\030	can	\031	em	\032	sub	\033	esc
\034	fs	\035	gs	\036	rs	\037	us
\040	sp	\177	del				

c   Interpret bytes as single- or multibyte characters specified by the current setting of the LC_CTYPE locale category. Write printable multibyte characters in the area corresponding to the first byte of the character; write the two-character sequence ** in the area corresponding to each remaining byte in the character, as an indication that the character is continued. Certain nongraphic characters appear as C escapes: \0, \a, \b, \f, \n, \r, \t, \v. Other nonprintable characters appear as one 3-digit octal number for each byte in the character.

You can follow the type specification characters d, f, o, u, and x with an optional, unsigned decimal integer that specifies the number of bytes to be transformed by each instance of the output type.

f   Can be followed by an optional F, D, or L, applying the conversion to an item of type float, double, or long double.

d, o, u, and x

Signed decimal, octal, unsigned decimal, and hexadecimal. Can be followed by an optional C, S, I, or L, applying the conversion to an item of type char, short, int, or long.

You can concatenate multiple types within the same *type-string* and specify multiple -t options. Write output lines for each type specified in the order in which the type specification characters are specified.

-v   Show all input data (verbose). Without the -v option, replace all groups of output lines that would be identical to the immediately preceding output line (except for byte offsets) with an asterisk (*).

-x   Interpret words in hex. This option is equivalent to -t x2.

-X   Interpret long words in hex. This option is equivalent to -t x4.

Operands

The following operand is supported for both /usr/bin/od and /usr/xpg4/bin/od.

-        Use the standard input in addition to any files specified. When you do not specify this operand, use the standard input only if no file operands are specified.

/usr/bin/od

The following operands are supported for /usr/bin/od only.

file   A path name of a file to be read. If you specify no *file* operands, use the standard input. If there are no more than two operands, none of the -A, -j, -N, or -t options are specified and any of the following are true, then the corresponding operand is assumed to be an offset operand instead of a file operand.

- The first character of the last operand is a plus sign (+).
- The first character of the second operand is numeric.
- The first character of the second operand is x, and the second character of the second operand is a lowercase hexadecimal character or digit.
- The second operand is named x.

- The second operand is named `..`

Without the `-N count` option, the display continues until an end-of-file is reached.

```
[+][0] offset [.][b|B]
[+][0][offset][.]
[+][0x|x][offset]
[+][0x|x] offset[B]
```

The *offset-string* operand specifies the byte offset in the file where dumping is to commence. The *offset* is interpreted in octal bytes by default. If *offset* begins with 0, interpret it in octal. If offset begins with x or 0x, interpret it in hexadecimal and consider any appended b to be the final hexadecimal digit. If . is appended, interpret the offset in decimal. If b or B is appended, interpret the offset in units of 512 bytes. If you omit the *file* argument, the offset argument must be preceded by a plus sign (+). Display the address starting at the given offset. The radix of the address is the same as the radix of the offset if specified; otherwise, it is octal. Decimal overrides octal, and it is an error to specify both hexadecimal and decimal conversions in the same *offset* operand.

/usr/xpg4/bin/od

The following operands are supported for `/usr/xpg4/bin/od` only.

file   Same as `/usr/bin/od`, except only one of the first two conditions must be true.

```
[+][0] offset [.][b|B]
+ [offset][.]
[+][0x][offset]
[+][0x] offset[B]
+x [offset]
+xoffset [B
```

Description of *offset-string* is the same as for `/usr/bin/od`.

Environment Variables

See environ(5) for descriptions of the following environment variables that affect the execution of od: LC_CTYPE, LC_MESSAGES, LC_NUMERIC, and NLSPATH.

Exit Status

0   Successful completion.

>0   An error occurred.

Attributes

See attributes(5) for descriptions of the following attributes:

/usr/bin/od

Attribute Type	Attribute Value
Availability	SUNWtoo
CSI	Enabled

/usr/xpg4/bin/od

Attribute Type	Attribute Value
Availability	SUNWxcu4
CSI	Enabled

See Also

sed(1), attributes(5), environ(5), XPG4(5)

on — Execute a Command on a Remote System, Using the Local Environment

Synopsis

/usr/bin/on [-i][-d][-n] *host command* [*argument*] ...

Description

Use the on command to execute commands on another system in an environment similar to that invoking the program. All environment variables are passed through, and the current working directory is preserved. To preserve the working directory, the working file system must either be already mounted on the host or be exported to it. Relative path names work only if they are within the current file system; absolute path names may cause problems.

The standard input is connected to the standard input of the remote command, and the standard output and the standard error from the remote command are sent to the corresponding files for the on command.

Bugs

When the working directory is remote-mounted over NFS, a Control-Z hangs the window.

Root cannot use on.

Options

-i	Use remote echoing and special character processing. This option is needed for programs that expect to be talking to a terminal. All terminal modes and window size changes are propagated.
-d	Print debugging messages as work is being done.
-n	Get end-of-file when on reads from the standard input instead of passing the standard input from the standard input of the on program. For example, you need to use the -n option when running commands in the background with job control.

Attributes

See attributes(5) for descriptions of the following attributes:

Attribute Type	**Attribute Value**
Availability	SUNWcsu

See Also

chkey(1), rlogin(1), rsh(1), telnet(1), attributes(5)

Diagnostics

unknown host

> Host name not found.

cannot connect to server

> Host down or not running the server.

can't find Problem finding the working directory.

can't locate mount point

> Problem finding current file system.

RPC: Authentication error

> The server requires DES authentication and you do not have a secret key registered with keyserv. Perhaps you logged in without a password. Try to use keylogin. If that fails, try to set your public key with chkey.

Other diagnostic messages may be passed back from the server.

onintr — Shell Built-in Functions to Respond to (Hardware) Signals

Synopsis

csh
```
onintr [-| label]
```

Description

See trap(1).

optisa — Determine Which Variant Instruction Set Is Optimal

Synopsis
```
/usr/bin/optisa instruction-set...
```

Description

optisa prints the instruction set out of the ones specified in the command that performs best on this machine. Best is defined by the order in which instruction set names are returned by isalist(1). Possible values for *instruction-set* are given in isalist(5).

> **Note** — optisa is preferable to uname -p or uname -m in determining which of several binary versions of a given program should be used on the given machine.

Examples

The following example displays the isalist instruction set and then uses the optisa command to find the command that performs best on a SPARCstation 10.

```
castle% isalist
sparcv8 sparcv8-fsmuld sparcv7 sparc
castle% optisa sparcv8 sparcv8-fsmuld sparcv7 sparc
sparcv8
castle%
```

Attributes

See attributes(5) for descriptions of the following attributes:

Attribute Type	Attribute Value
Availability	SUNWcsu

New! Exit Status

0	One of the *instruction-set* values you specified is printed.
1	No output; that is, this system cannot use any *instruction-set* that you specified with the optisa command.

New! See Also

isalist(1), uname(1), attributes(5), isalist(5)

Diagnostics

Exit status is 0 if one of the *instruction-set* values you specified is printed by this command. Exit status is 1 if there is no output; that is, this machine cannot use any *instruction-set* that you specified with the optisa command.

P

---

pack, pcat, unpack — Compress and Expand Files

Synopsis

```
/usr/bin/pack [-f][-] file...
/usr/bin/pcat file...
/usr/bin/unpack file...
```

Description

pack

The pack command stores the specified files in a compressed form. Wherever possible (and useful), each specified input file is replaced by a packed file named *file*.z with the same access modes, access and modified dates, and owner as those of *file*. When the pack is successful, the original file is removed.

The size of the input file and the character frequency distribution determine the amount of compression. Because a decoding tree forms the first part of each .z file, it is usually not worthwhile to pack files smaller than three blocks. You may find it worthwhile, however, to pack small files such as printer plots or pictures in which the character frequency distribution is very skewed.

Text files are typically reduced to 60–75 percent of their original size. Load modules, which use a larger character set and have a more uniform distribution of characters, show little compression. The packed versions are usually about 90 percent of the original size.

pack returns a value that is the number of files that it failed to compress. No packing is done under the following conditions.

- The file is already packed.
- The file name has more than 14 bytes.
- The file has links.
- The file is a directory.
- The file cannot be opened.
- The file is empty.
- No disk storage blocks are saved by packing.
- A file named *file*.z already exists.
- The .z file cannot be created.
- An I/O error occurs during processing.

The file name must contain no more than 14 bytes to allow space to append the .z extension. You cannot compress directories.

pcat

Use the pcat command on packed files in the same way that you use the cat(1) command on ordinary files. You cannot use pcat as a filter. The specified files are unpacked and written to the standard output.

pcat returns the number of files it was unable to unpack. Unpacking can fail in the following conditions.

- The file cannot be opened.
- The file is not output from the pack command.

unpack

The unpack command expands files created by pack. For each file specified in the command, a search is made for a file called *file*.z (or just *file*, if *file* ends in .z). If this file appears to be a packed file, it is replaced by its expanded version. The new file has the .z suffix stripped from its name and has the same access modes, access and modification dates, and owner as those of the packed file.

unpack returns a value that is the number of files it was unable to unpack. Unpacking can fail under the following conditions.

- The file cannot be opened.
- The file is not output from the pack command.
- A file with the unpacked name already exists.
- The unpacked file cannot be created.
- The file name (excluding the .z extension) has more than 14 bytes.

Options

-f   Force packing of file. This option is useful for packing entire directories even if some of the files do not save disk storage blocks. You can restore packed files to their original form with either the unpack or pcat commands.

-                    pack uses Huffman (minimum redundancy) codes on a byte-by-byte basis. With the – argument, set an internal flag that prints to standard output the number of times each byte is used, the relative frequency, and the code for the bytes. Additional use of – in place of *file* sets and resets the internal flag.

Operands

file   A path name of a file to be packed, packed with pcat, or unpacked. *file* can either include or omit the .z suffix.

Examples

In the following example, the passwd file is too small to save any disk storage blocks by packing. The termcap file is big enough to compress, and it is compressed 29.8 percent.

```
castle% pack passwd
pack: passwd: no saving - file unchanged
castle% pack termcap
pack: termcap: 29.8% Compression
castle%
```

In the following example, the pcat command displays the contents of the compressed termcap.z file and pipes the output through the more command. To save space, only the first line of the output is shown here.

```
castle% pcat termcap.z | more
#ident "@(#)termcap 1.13 93/03/27 SMI" /* SunOS 4,1,3 termcap */
. . .
```

The following example unpacks the termcap.z file.

```
castle% unpack termcap.z
unpack: termcap: unpacked
castle%
```

Environment Variables

See environ(5) for descriptions of the following environment variables that affect the execution of pack, pcat, and unpack: LC_CTYPE, LC_MESSAGES, and NLSPATH.

Exit Status

0   Successful completion.

>0   The number of files the command failed to pack or unpack.

Attributes

See attributes(5) for descriptions of the following attributes:

Attribute Type	Attribute Value
Availability	SUNWcsu
CSI	Enabled

See Also

cat(1), compress(1), zcat(1), attributes(5), environ(5), largefile(5)

---

page — Browse or Page through a Text File

Synopsis

/usr/bin/page [-cdflrsuw] [-lines] [+linenumber] [+/pattern] [file...]

Description

See more(1).

---

pagesize — Display the Size of a Page of Memory

Synopsis

/usr/bin/pagesize

Description

Use the pagesize command to print the size of a page of memory, in bytes, as returned by getpagesize(3C). This program is useful in constructing portable shell scripts.

Example

```
castle% /usr/bin/pagesize
4096
castle%
```

Attributes

See `attributes`(5) for descriptions of the following attributes:

Attribute Type	Attribute Value
Availability	SUNWcsu

See Also

`getpagesize(3C)`, `attributes(5)`

passwd — Change Login Password and Password Attributes

Synopsis

```
/usr/bin/passwd [-r files | -r nis| -r nisplus][name]
/usr/bin/passwd [-r files][-egh][name]
/usr/bin/passwd [-r files] -s [-a]
/usr/bin/passwd [-r files] -s [name]
/usr/bin/passwd [-r files][-d | -l][-f][-n min][-w warn][-x max] name
/usr/bin/passwd -r nis [-egh][name]
/usr/bin/passwd -r nisplus [-egh][-D domainname][name]
/usr/bin/passwd -r nisplus -s [-a]
/usr/bin/passwd -r nisplus [-D domainname] -s [name]
/usr/bin/passwd -r nisplus [-l][-f][-n min][-w warn][-x max]
    [-D domainname] name
```

Description

Note — The `passwd` command replaces the `nispasswd` and `yppasswd` commands and should be used in their place.

Use the `passwd` command to change the password or list password attributes associated with the user's login name. Additionally, superuser can use `passwd` to install or change passwords and attributes associated with any login name.

When used to change a password, `passwd` prompts for the old password if any. It then prompts again for the new password. When you type the old password, `passwd` checks to see if it has aged sufficiently. If aging is insufficient, `passwd` terminates. See `pwconv`(1M), `nistbladm`(1), and `shadow`(4) for additional information.

When NIS or NIS+ is in effect on a system, passwd changes the NIS or NIS+ database. The NIS or NIS+ password can be different from the password on the local machine. If NIS or NIS+ is running, use passwd -r to change password information on the local machine.

The pwconv command creates and updates /etc/shadow with information from /etc/passwd. pwconv relies on a special value of x in the password field of the /etc/passwd file. The value of x indicates that the password for the user is already in /etc/shadow and should not be modified.

If aging is sufficient, a check is made to ensure that the new password meets construction requirements. When you type the new password a second time, the two copies of the new password are compared. If the two copies are not identical, the cycle of prompting for the new password is repeated for, at most, two more times.

Passwords must be constructed to meet the following requirements.

- Each password must have at least PASSLENGTH characters, where PASSLENGTH is defined in /etc/default/passwd and is set to 6. Only the first eight characters are significant.

- Each password must contain at least two alphabetic characters and at least one numeric or special character. In this case, alphabetic refers to all upper- or lowercase letters.

- Each password must differ from the user's login name and any reverse or circular shift of that login name. For comparison purposes, an uppercase letter and its corresponding lowercase letter are equivalent.

- New passwords must differ from the old by at least three characters. For comparison purposes, an uppercase letter and its corresponding lowercase letter are equivalent.

If all requirements are met, by default, the passwd command consults /etc/nsswitch.conf to determine which repositories to update. It searches the passwd and passwd_compat entries. The sources (repositories) associated with these entries are updated. However, the password update configurations supported are limited to the following five cases. Failure to comply with the configurations prevents users from logging in to the system.

- passwd: files
- passwd: files nis
- passwd: files nisplus
- passwd: compat (==> files nis)
- passwd: compat (==> files nisplus)
- passwd_compat: nisplus

Network administrators who own the NIS+ password table can change any password attributes.

In the case of files, superuser (anyone with real and effective UID equal to 0, see id(1M) and su(1M)) can change any password. passwd does not prompt superuser for the old password. Superuser is not forced to comply with password aging or password construction requirements.

Superuser can create a null password by pressing Return in response to the prompt for a new password. (This procedure differs from `passwd -d` because the `password` prompt is still displayed.) If NIS is in effect, superuser on the root master can change any password without being prompted for the old NIS password and is not forced to comply with password construction requirements.

Users can use the `-s` option to show password attributes for their own login name provided they use the `-r nisplus` argument. Otherwise, the `-s` argument is restricted to the superuser.

The format of the display is:

```
name status mm/dd/yy min max warn
```

or, if password aging information is not present,

```
name status
```

name	*name* is the login ID of the user. *status* is the password status of *name*: PS means having a password or locked, LK means locked, and NP means no password.
mm/dd/yy	The date the password was last changed for *name*. Note that all password aging dates are determined from Greenwich Mean Time (Universal Time) and, therefore, can differ by as much as a day in other time zones.
min	The minimum number of days required between password changes for name. MINWEEKS is found in /etc/default/passwd and is set to null.
max	The maximum number of days the password is valid for *name*. MAXWEEKS is found in /etc/default/passwd and is set to null.
warn	The number of days relative to *max* before the password expires and *name* is warned.

Security

`passwd` uses `pam(3)` for password management. The PAM configuration policy, listed in `/etc/pam.conf`, specifies the password modules to be used for `passwd`. Here is the `passwd` entry from a `pam.conf` file and using the UNIX password module.

```
passwd    password required    /usr/lib/security/pam_unix.so.1
```

If there are no entries for the `passwd` service, then the entries for the `other` service, shown below, are used.

```
# Password management
#
other    password required        /usr/lib/security/pam_unix.so.1
```

If multiple password modules are listed, then the user may be prompted for multiple passwords.

Options

-a
: Show password attributes for all entries. Use only with the -s option; you must not specify *name*. For the nisplus repository, this option shows only the entries in the NIS+ password table in the local domain that the invoker is authorized to read. For the files repository, this option is restricted to superuser.

-D *domainname*
: Consult the passwd.org_dir table in *domainname*. If you do not specify this option, the default *domainname* returned by nis_local_directory(3N) is used. This domain name is the same as that returned by domainname(1M).

-e
: Change the login shell. For the files repository, this option works only for superuser. Normal users can change the nis or nisplus repositories.

-g
: Change the comment (finger) information. For the files repository, this option works only for superuser. Normal users can change the nis or nisplus repositories.

-h
: Change the home directory.

-r
: Specify the repository to which an operation is applied. The supported repositories are files, nis, and nisplus.

-s *name*
: Show password attributes for the login *name*. For the nisplus repository, this option works for everyone. However, for the files repository, this option works only for superuser. It does not work at all for the nis repository, which does not support password aging.

Superuser Options

Only superuser can use the following options.

-d
: Delete password for *name*. The login name is not prompted for password. It is only applicable to the files repository.

-f
: Force the user to change password at the next login by expiring the password for *name*.

-l
: Lock password entry for *name*.

-n *min*
: Set minimum field for *name*. The *min* field contains the minimum number of days between password changes for *name*. If *min* is greater than *max*, the user cannot change the password. Always use this option with the -x option, unless *max* is set to -1 (aging turned off). In that case, *min* need not be set.

-w *warn*
: Set *warn* field for *name*. The *warn* field contains the number of days before the password expires and the user is warned. This option is not valid if password aging is disabled.

-x *max*	Set maximum field for *name*. The *max* field contains the number of days that the password is valid for *name*. The aging for *name* is turned off immediately if *max* is set to -1. If it is set to 0, then the user is forced to change the password at the next login session and aging is turned off.

Operands

name	User login name.

Environment Variables

If any of the LC_* variables (LC_CTYPE, LC_MESSAGES, LC_TIME, LC_COLLATE, LC_NUMERIC, and LC_MONETARY) (see environ(5)) are not set in the environment, the operational behavior of passwd for each corresponding locale category is determined by the value of the LANG environment variable. If LC_ALL is set, its contents are used to override both the LANG and the other LC_* variables. If none of the above variables are set in the environment, the C (U.S. style) locale determines how passwd behaves.

LC_CTYPE	Determine how passwd handles characters. When LC_CTYPE is set to a valid value, passwd can display and handle text and file names containing valid characters for that locale. passwd can display and handle Extended Unix Code (EUC) characters where any individual character can be 1, 2, or 3 bytes. passwd can also handle EUC characters of 1, 2, or more column widths. In the C locale, only characters from ISO 8859-1 are valid.

LC_MESSAGES

Determine how diagnostic and informative messages are presented. This presentation includes the language and style of the messages and the correct form of affirmative and negative responses. In the C locale, the messages are presented in the default form found in the program itself (in most cases, U.S. English).

Exit Status

0	Success.
1	Permission denied.
2	Invalid combination of options.
3	Unexpected failure. Password file unchanged.
4	Unexpected failure. Password file(s) missing.
5	Password file(s) busy. Try again later.
6	Invalid argument to option.
7	Aging option was disabled.

Files

/etc/oshadow
/etc/passwd

Password files.

/etc/shadow

Shadow password file.

/etc/default/passwd

Default values can be set for the following flags in
/etc/default/passwd. For example, MAXWEEKS=26.

MAXWEEKS	Maximum time period that password is valid.
MINWEEKS	Minimum time period before the password can be changed.
PASSLENGTH	Minimum length of password, in characters.
WARNWEEKS	Time period until warning of date of password's pending expiration.

Attributes

See attributes(5) for descriptions of the following attributes:

Attribute Type	Attribute Value
Availability	SUNWcsu
CIS	Enabled

See Also

finger(1), login(1), nispasswd(1), nistbladm(1), yppasswd(1),
domainname(1M), eeprom(1M), id(1M), passmgmt(1M), pwconv(1M), su(1M),
useradd(1M), userdel(1M), usermod(1M), pam(3), crypt(3C), getpwnam(3C),
getspnam(3C), nis_local_directory(3N), loginlog(4), nsswitch.conf(4),
pam.conf(4), passwd(4), shadow(4), attributes(5), environ(5), pam_unix(5)

paste — Merge Corresponding or Subsequent Lines of Files

Synopsis

/usr/bin/paste [-s][-d *list*] *file*...

Description

Use the `paste` command to join files together line by line, writing the output to standard output. You can use `paste` to create new tables by pasting together fields or columns from between 1 and 12 files. Each line of each input file is considered to be one field for the output line. By default, `paste` adds a Tab character as the delimiter between the contributions of each file. `paste` takes one or more file names as arguments, reads a line from each file, and combines the lines into a single line. If some of the files have fewer lines than others, `paste` simply puts in the delimiters and leaves the field empty. You can specify a dash (-) as one or more of the file names to read standard input.

Options

-d *list*   Unless you use a backslash character (\) in *list*, specify each character in *list* as a delimiter character. If you use a backslash character, specify it and one or more characters following it as a delimiter character, as described below. These elements specify one or more delimiters to use instead of the default Tab character that replaces the newline character of each of the input lines. The elements in *list* are used circularly; that is, when the list is exhausted, the first element from the list is reused.

When you specify the -s option:

- Do not modify the last newline character in a file.
- Reset the delimiter to the first element of *list* after each *file* operand is processed.

When you do not specify the -s option:

- Do not modify the newline characters in the file specified by the last *file*.
- Reset the delimiter to the first element of *list* each time a line is processed from each file.

If a backslash character appears in *list*, use it and the character following it to represent the following delimiter characters.

\n   Newline character.

\t   Tab character.

\\\\   Backslash character.

\0   Empty string (not a null character). If \0 is immediately followed by the character x, the character X, or any character defined by the LC_CTYPE digit keyword, the results are unspecified.

If any other characters follow the backslash, the results are unspecified.

-s   Concatenate all of the lines of each separate input file in command-line order. Replace the newline character of every line except the last line in each input file with the Tab character, unless otherwise specified by the -d option.

Operands

file   A path name of an input file. If you specify - for one or more of the files, use the standard input; read the standard input one line at a time, circularly, for each instance of -. Implementations support pasting of at least 12 file operands.

Usage

See largefile(5) for the description of the behavior of paste when encountering files greater than or equal to 2 Gbytes (2**31 bytes).

Examples

The following example uses the paste command to list the files in a directory in one column, using a space character as the delimiter.

```
castle% ls | paste -d" " -
085X01.DOC
085X02.DOC
085X03~1.DOC
085X042.DOC
085X08R.DOC
085X09E.RTF
085XDOCS.ZIP
085XFILE.ZIP
085XINTR.ZIP
a.out
bibliography
bibliography.ig
C.str
DeadLetters
examples
file1
kookaburra-1
ltr
Mail
new
castle%
```

The following example lists the contents of a directory in four columns, using the default Tab delimiter.

```
castle% ls | paste - - - -
085X01.DOC      085X02.DOC      085X03~1.DOC    085X042.DOC
085X08R.DOC     085X09E.RTF     085XDOCS.ZIP    085XFILE.ZIP
085XINTR.ZIP    a.out   bibliography    bibliography.ig
C.str   DeadLetters     examples        file1
```

```
kookaburra-1     ltr      Mail     new
castle%
```

The following example combines pairs of lines from one file into single lines. The lines in the file `kookaburra-1` are numbered to make it easier for you to see the results.

```
castle% paste -s -d"\t\n" kookaburra-1
   1  Kookaburra sits in the old gum tree          2  Merry merry king
of the bush is he.
   3  Laugh, kookaburra, laugh, kookaburra         4  Gay your life
must be.
     5         6   Kookaburra sits in the old gum tree
   7  Eating all the gumdrops he can see.          8  Stop,
kookaburra, stop, kookaburra
   9  Leave some there for me.              10
  11  Kookaburra sits in the old gum tree         12  Merry merry king
of the bush is he.
  13  Laugh, kookaburra, laugh, kookaburra        14  Gay your life
must be.
          15   Kookaburra sits in the old gum tree
  16  Eating all the gumdrops he can see.         17  Stop,
kookaburra, stop, kookaburra
  18  Leave some there for me.
castle%
```

Environment Variables

See `environ`(5) for descriptions of the following environment variables that affect the execution of `paste`: LC_CTYPE and LC_MESSAGES.

Exit Status

0	Successful completion.
>0	An error occurred.

Attributes

See `attributes`(5) for descriptions of the following attributes:

Attribute Type	Attribute Value
Availability	SUNWesu
CSI	Enabled

See Also

cut(1), grep(1), pr(1), attributes(5), environ(5), largefile(5)

Diagnostics

"line too long"

Output lines are restricted to 511 characters.

"too many files"

Except with the -s option, you can specify no more than 12 input files.

"no delimiters"

The -d option was specified with an empty list.

"cannot open file"

The specified file cannot be opened.

patch — Apply Changes to Files

Synopsis

/usr/bin/patch [-blNR][-c | -e | -n][-d dir][-D define]
  [-i patchfile][-o outfile][-p num][-r rejectfile][file]

Description

Use the patch command to edit text files created by diff(1). patch reads a source (patch) file containing any of the three forms of difference (diff) listings produced by the diff(1) command (normal, context, or in the style of ed(1)) and applies those differences to a file. By default, patch reads from the standard input.

patch tries to determine the type of the diff listing unless overruled by a -c, -e, or -n option.

If the patch file contains more than one patch, patch tries to apply each patch as if it came from a separate patch file. (In this case, the name of the patch file must be determinable for each diff listing.)

Options

-b

Before applying the differences, save a copy of the original contents of each modified file in a file of the same name with the suffix .orig appended to it. If the file already exists, overwrite it; if multiple patches are applied to the same file, write the .orig file only for the first patch. When you also specify the -o outfile option, do not create file.orig; if outfile already exists, create outfile.orig.

-c

Interpret the patch file as a context difference (the output of the command diff when you specify the -c or -C option).

-d *dir*   Change the current directory to *dir* before processing.

-D *define*   Mark changes with the C preprocessor construct.

> #ifdef *define*
>
> . . .
>
> #endif
>
> Use *define* as the differentiating symbol.

-e   Interpret the patch file as an ed script instead of a diff script.

-i *patchfile*

> Read the patch information from the file named by the path name *patchfile* instead of from the standard input.

-l   Match any sequence of blank characters in the difference script with any sequence of blank characters in the input file. Match other characters exactly.

-n   Interpret the script as a normal difference.

-N   Ignore patches where the differences have already been applied to the file; by default, reject already applied patches.

-o *outfile* Instead of modifying the files (specified by the *file* operand or the difference listings) directly, write a copy of the file referenced by each patch to *outfile* with the appropriate differences applied. Apply multiple patches for a single file to the intermediate versions of the file created by any previous patches, and write multiple, concatenated versions of the file to *outfile*.

-p *num*   For all path names in the patch file that indicate the names of files to be patched, delete *num* path-name components from the beginning of each path name. If the path name in the patch file is absolute, consider any leading slashes as the first component (that is, -p 1 removes the leading slashes). Specifying -p 0 uses the full path name. If you do not specify -p, use only the basename (the final path-name component).

-R   Reverse the sense of the patch script; that is, assume that the difference script was created from the new version to the old version. You cannot use the -R option with ed scripts; patch tries to reverse each portion of the script before applying it. Save rejected differences in swapped format. If you do not specify this option and until a portion of the patch file is successfully applied, patch tries to apply each portion in its reversed sense as well as in its normal sense. If the attempt is successful, prompt the user to determine if the -R option should be set.

-r *rejectfile*

> Override the default reject file name. In the default case, the reject file has the same name as the output file, with the suffix .rej appended to it.

Operands

file   A path name of a file to patch.

Usage

The -R option does not work with ed scripts because there is too little information to reconstruct the reverse operation.

The -p option makes it possible to customize a patchfile to local user directory structures without manually editing the patchfile. For example, if the file name in the patch file was

/curds/whey/src/blurfl/blurfl.c

then setting -p 0 results in the entire path name unmodified. Setting -p 1 returns the following path.

curds/whey/src/blurfl/blurfl.c

Without the leading slash, -p 4 returns the following path.

blurfl/blurfl.c

Not specifying -p at all returns the following path.

blurfl.c.

When using -b in some file-system implementations, the saving of a .orig file can produce unwanted results. With 12-, 13- or 14-character file names on file systems supporting 14-character maximum file names, the .orig file overwrites the new file.

Environment Variables

See environ(5) for descriptions of the following environment variables that affect the execution of patch: LC_CTYPE, LC_MESSAGES, LC_TIME, and NLSPATH.

Output Files

The output of patching the save files (.orig suffixes) and the reject files (.rej suffixes) is text files.

Extended Description

A patchfile can contain patching instructions for more than one file. When you specify the -b option, for each patched file, the original is saved in a file of the same name with the suffix .orig appended to it.

For each patched file, a reject file can also be created as noted in "Patch Application" on page 981. In the absence of a -r option, the name of this file is formed by appending the suffix .rej to the original file name.

Patch-file Format

The patch file must contain zero or more lines of header information followed by one or more patches. Each patch must contain zero or more lines of file-name identification in the format produced by `diff -c` and one or more sets of `diff` output, which are customarily called hunks.

`patch` recognizes the following expression in the header information.

`Index: `*`pathname`*`   The file to be patched is named `*`pathname`*`.`

If all lines (including headers) within a patch begin with the same leading sequence of blank characters, `patch` removes this sequence before proceeding. Within each patch, if the type of difference is `context`, `patch` recognizes the following expressions.

`*** `*`filename timestamp`*` The patches arose from `*`filename`*`.`
`--- `*`filename timestamp`*` The patches should be applied to `*`filename`*`.`

Each hunk within a patch must be the `diff` output to change a line range within the original file. The line numbers for successive hunks within a patch must occur in ascending order.

File-name Determination

If you specify no *`file`* operand, `patch` performs the following steps to obtain a path name.

1. If the patch contains the strings `***` and `---`, `patch` strips components from the beginning of each path name (depending on the presence or value of the `-p` option), then it tests for the existence of both files in the current directory (or directory specified with the `-d` option).

2. If both files exist, `patch` assumes that no path name can be obtained from this step. If the header information contains a line with the string `Index:`, `patch` strips components from the beginning of the path name (depending on `-p`), then tests for the existence of this file in the current directory (or directory specified with the `-d` option).

3. If an SCCS directory exists in the current directory, `patch` tries to perform a `get -e SCCS/s.`*`filename`* command to retrieve an editable version of the file.

4. If no path name can be obtained by applying the previous steps or if the path names obtained do not exist, `patch` writes a prompt to standard output and requests a file name interactively from standard input.

Patch Application

If you specify the `-c`, `-e`, or `-n` options, `patch` interprets information within each hunk as a context difference, an `ed` difference, or a normal difference. In the absence of any of these options, `patch` determines the type of difference on the basis of the format of information within the hunk.

For each hunk, `patch` begins to search for the place to apply the patch at the line number at the beginning of the hunk plus or minus any offset used in applying the previous hunk. If lines matching the hunk context are not found, patch scans both forward and backward at least 1,000 bytes for a set of lines that match the hunk context.

If no such place is found and it is a context difference, then patch does another scan, ignoring the first and last line of context. If that fails, the first two and last two lines of context are ignored and another scan is made. Implementations can search more extensively for installation locations.

If no location can be found, patch appends the hunk to the reject file. The rejected hunk is written in context-difference format regardless of the format of the patch file. If the input was a normal or ed style difference, the reject file can contain differences with zero lines of context. The line numbers on the hunks in the reject file can be different from the line numbers in the patch file because they reflect the approximate locations for the failed hunks in the new file instead of the old one.

If the type of patch is an ed diff, the implementation can accomplish the patching by invoking the ed command.

Examples

diff(1) compares two text files and creates a third text file containing the differences. This output file created by diff contains lines that look like ed(1) commands. You can use the output to make file1 look like file2 by running the diff command.

The following example shows the contents of file1 and file2.

```
# cat file1
bill
tom
pete
joe
mike
# cat file2
patti
bill
tom
pete
joe
mike
glenda
#
```

Then, running diff redirects the output to file3, as shown below.

```
# diff file1 file2 > file3
```

The file3 output from diff is shown below.

```
# cat file3
0a1
> patti
5a7
```

```
> glenda
#
```

Now you can use the `patch` command on `file3` to make it look like `file1`.

```
# patch -i file3 file1
  Looks like a normal diff.
done
#
```

The following example shows the contents of `file1`.

```
# cat file1
patti
bill
tom
pete
joe
mike
glenda
#
```

Exit Status

0	Successful completion.
1	One or more lines were written to a reject file.
>1	An error occurred.

Attributes

See `attributes`(5) for descriptions of the following attributes:

Attribute Type	Attribute Value
Availability	SUNWcsu

See Also

ed(1), diff(1), attributes(5), environ(5)

pathchk — Check Path Names

Synopsis

```
/usr/bin/pathchk [-p] path...
```

Description

The `pathchk` command checks that one or more path names are valid (that is, they could be used to access or create a file without causing syntax errors) and that they are portable (that is, no file-name truncation results). More extensive portability checks are provided by the -p option.

By default, `pathchk` checks each component of each *path* operand based on the underlying file system. A diagnostic is written for each *path* operand that:

- Is longer than PATH_MAX bytes.
- Contains any component longer than NAME_MAX bytes in its containing directory.
- Contains any component in a directory that is not searchable.
- Contains any character in any component that is not valid in its containing directory.

The format of the diagnostic message is not specified but indicates the error detected and the corresponding path operand.

It is not considered an error if one or more components of a *path* operand do not exist as long as a file that matches the path name specified by the missing components could be created and that such a file does not violate any of the checks specified above.

Options

-p   Instead of performing checks based on the underlying file system, write a diagnostic for each path operand that:

- Is longer than _POSIX_PATH_MAX bytes.
- Contains any component longer than _POSIX_NAME_MAX bytes.
- Contains any character in any component that is not in the portable file-name character set.

Operands

path   A path to be checked.

Usage

See largefile(5) for the description of the behavior of pathchk when encountering files greater than or equal to 2 Gbytes (2**31 bytes).

Examples

The following example verifies that all paths in an imported data interchange archive are legitimate and unambiguous on the current system.

```
pax -f archive | sed -e '/ == .*/s///' | xargs pathchk
   if [$? -eq 0]
      then
         pax -r -f archive
```

```
    else
       echo Investigate problems before importing files.
    exit 1
 fi
```

The following example verifies that all files in the current directory hierarchy could be moved to any system conforming to the X/Open specification that also supports the pax(1) command.

```
find . -print | xargs pathchk -p
  if [$? -eq 0]
    then
       pax -w -f archive .
    else
       echo Portable archive cannot be created.
       exit 1
  fi
```

The following example verifies that a user-supplied path specifies a readable file and that the application can create a file extending the given path without truncation and without overwriting any existing file.

```
case $- in
  *C*)     reset="";;
  *)       reset="set +C"
     set -C;;
esac
test -r "$path" && pathchk "$path.out" &&
  rm "$path.out" > "$path.out"
if [$? -ne 0]; then
  printf "%s: %s not found or %s.out fails \
  creation checks.\n" $0 "$path" "$path"
     $reset    # reset the noclobber option in case a trap
               # on EXIT depends on it
     exit 1
fi
$reset
PROCESSING < "$path" > "$path.out"
```

The following assumptions are made in the previous example.

- PROCESSING represents the code that is used by the application to use $path once it is verified that $path.out works as intended.
- The state of the noclobber option is unknown when this code is invoked and should be set on exit to the state it was in when this code was invoked. (The reset variable is used in this example to restore the initial state.)
- Note the usage of rm "$path.out" > "$path.out".
  - The pathchk command has already verified, at this point, that $path.out is not truncated.
  - With the noclobber option set, the shell verifies that $path.out does not already exist before invoking rm.

- If the shell succeeded in creating $path.out, rm removes it so that the application can create the file again in the PROCESSING step.
- If the PROCESSING step expects the file to exist already when it is invoked, replace rm "$path.out" > "$path.out" with > "$path.out", which verifies that the file did not already exist but leaves $path.out in place for use by PROCESSING.

Environment Variables

See environ(5) for descriptions of the following environment variables that affect the execution of pathchk: LC_CTYPE, LC_MESSAGES, and NLSPATH.

Exit Status

0	All path operands passed all of the checks.
>0	An error occurred.

Attributes

See attributes(5) for descriptions of the following attributes:

Attribute Type	Attribute Value
Availability	SUNWcsu

See Also

pax(1), test(1), attributes(5), environ(5), largefile(5)

pax — Portable Archive Interchange

Synopsis

```
/usr/bin/pax [-cdnv][-f archive][-s replstr]...[pattern...]
/usr/bin/pax -r [-cdiknuv][-f archive][-o options]...[-p string]...
   [-s replstr]... [pattern...]
/usr/bin/pax -w [-dituvX][-b blocksize][-a][-f archive][-o options]...
   [-s replstr]... [-x format][v...]
/usr/bin/pax -r -w [-diklntuvX][-p string]...[-s replstr]... [file...]
   directory
```

Description

The pax (portable archive exchange) command provides better portability for POSIX-compliant systems than do the tar or cpio commands. Use the pax command to copy files, special files, file systems that require multiple tape volumes, or files that you want to copy to and from POSIX-compliant systems. Disadvantages of the pax command are that it is not aware of file-system boundaries and that the full path-name length cannot exceed 255 characters.

pax reads, writes, and writes lists of the members of archive files and copies directory hierarchies. A variety of archive formats are supported; see the -x format option.

Modes of Operations

The action to be taken depends on the presence of the -r (read) and -w (write) options. The four combinations of -r and -w are referred to as the four modes of operation: list, read, write, and copy modes, which correspond to the four forms shown in the Synopsis.

list
: When you specify neither -r nor -w, write to the standard output the names of the members of the archive file read from the standard input with path names matching the specified patterns. If a named file is of type *directory*, write the file hierarchy rooted at that file as well.

read
: When you specify -r but not -w, extract the members of the archive file read from the standard input with path names matching the specified patterns. If an extracted file is of type *directory*, extract the file hierarchy rooted at that file as well. Create the extracted files relative to the current file hierarchy. The ownership, access and modification times, and file mode of the restored files are discussed under the -p option.

write
: When you specify -w but not -r, write the contents of the file operands to the standard output in an archive format. If you specify no file operands, read a list of files to copy, one per line, from the standard input. A file of type *directory* includes all of the files in the file hierarchy rooted at the file.

copy
: When you specify both -r and -w, copy the *file* operands to the destination *directory*.

    If you specify no *file* operands, read a list of files to copy, one per line, from the standard input. A file of type *directory* includes all of the files in the file hierarchy rooted at the file.

    The effect of the copy is as if the copied files were written to an archive file and then subsequently extracted, except that there may be hard links between the original and the copied files. If the destination *directory* is a subdirectory of one of the files to be copied, the results are unspecified. It is an error if *directory* does not exist, is not writable by the user, or is not a directory.

    In read or copy modes, if intermediate directories are needed to extract an archive member, pax performs actions equivalent to the mkdir(2) function, called with the following arguments.

    • Use the intermediate directory as the *path* argument.

- Use the octal value of 777 or rwx (read, write, and execute permissions) as the mode argument (see chmod(1)).

If any specified *pattern* or *file* operands are not matched by at least one file or archive member, pax writes a diagnostic message to standard error for each one that did not match and exits with a non-zero exit status.

The supported archive formats are automatically detected on input. The default output archive format is tar(1).

If the selected archive format supports the specification of linked files, it is an error if these files cannot be linked when the archive is extracted. Any of the various names in the archive that represent a file can be used to select the file for extraction.

Options

-r   Read an archive file from standard input.

-w   Write files to the standard output in the specified archive format.

-a   Append files to the end of the archive. This option does not work for some archive devices, such as 1/4-inch streaming tapes and 8mm tapes.

-b *blocksize*

                Block the output at a positive, decimal-integer number of bytes per write to the archive file. Devices and archive formats can impose restrictions on blocking. Blocking is automatically determined on input. Portable applications must not specify a blocksize value larger than 32,256. Default blocking when creating archives depends on the archive format. (See the -x option.)

-c   Match all file or archive members except those specified by the *pattern* or *file* operands.

-d   Copy files of type *directory* or archive members of type *directory* being extracted to match only the file or archive member itself and not the file hierarchy rooted at the file.

-f *archive*   Specify the path name of the input or output archive overriding the default standard input (in list or read modes) or the standard output (write mode).

-i   Interactively rename files or archive members. For each archive member matching a *pattern* operand or file matching a *file* operand, write a prompt to the file /dev/tty. The prompt contains the name of the file or archive member. Then, read a line from /dev/tty. If the line is blank, skip the file or archive member. If the line consists of a single period, process the file or archive member with no modification to its name. Otherwise, replace its name with the contents of the line. Exit immediately with a non-zero exit status if an end-of-file is encountered when reading a response or if /dev/tty cannot be opened for reading and writing.

-k Prevent the overwriting of existing files.

-l Link files. In copy mode, make hard links between the *source* and *destination* file hierarchies whenever possible.

-n Use the first archive member that matches each *pattern* operand. Match no more than one archive member for each *pattern* (although members of type directory still match the file hierarchy rooted at that file).

-o *options* Reserved for special format-specific options.

-p *string* Specify one or more file characteristic options (privileges). The string argument must be a string specifying file characteristics to be retained or discarded on extraction. The string consists of the specification characters a, e, m, o, and p. You can concatenate multiple characteristics within the same string and specify multiple -p options. The meaning of the specification characters is as follows.

a Do not preserve file access times.

e Preserve the user ID, group ID, file-mode bits, access time, and modification time.

m Do not preserve file modification times.

o Preserve the user ID and group ID.

p Preserve the file-mode bits. Other, implementation-dependent file-mode attributes can be preserved.

In the preceding list, p indicates that an attribute stored in the archive is given to the extracted file, subject to the permissions of the invoking process; otherwise, the attribute is determined as part of the normal file creation action.

If you specify neither the e nor the o character or the user ID and group ID are not preserved for any reason, pax does not set the setuid and setgid bits of the file mode.

If the preservation of any of these items fails for any reason, pax writes a diagnostic message to standard error. Failure to preserve these items affects the final exit status but does not delete the extracted file.

If file-characteristic letters in any of the *string* arguments are duplicated or conflict with each other, the ones given last take precedence. For example, if you specify -p eme, file modification times are preserved.

-s *replstr*   Modify file or archive member names named by *pattern* or *file* operands according to the substitution expression *replstr*, which is based on the ed(1) s (substitution) command, using the regular expression syntax on the regex(5) manual page. The concepts of address and line are meaningless in the context of the pax command and must not be supplied. The format is:

-s / *old*/*new*/ [gp]

where, as in ed, *old* is a basic regular expression and *new* can contain an ampersand (&) or a *n* backreference, where *n* is a digit. The *old* string also is permitted to contain newline characters.

You can use any non-null character as a delimiter (/ shown here). You can specify multiple -s expressions; the expressions are applied in the order specified, terminating with the first successful substitution. The optional trailing g is as defined in the ed command. The optional trailing p writes successful substitutions to standard error. File or archive member names that substitute to the empty string are ignored when archives are read and written.

-t   Reset the access times of the archived files to the same values they had before being read by pax.

-u   Ignore files that are older (having a less-recent file modification time) than a preexisting file or archive member with the same name.

read mode   Extract an archive member with the same name as a file in the file system if the archive member is newer than the file.

write mode Supersede an archive file member with the same name as a file in the file system if the file is newer than the archive member.

copy mode   Replace the file in the destination hierarchy by the file in the source hierarchy or by a link to the file in the source hierarchy if the file in the source hierarchy is newer.

-v   In list mode, produce a verbose table of contents. Otherwise, write archive member path names to standard error.

-x *format* Specify the output archive format. The pax command recognizes the following formats.

cpio   The extended cpio interchange format; see the IEEE 1003.1(1990) specifications. The default blocksize for this format for character special archive files is 5,120. Implementations support all blocksize values less than or equal to 32,256 that are multiples of 512.

This archive format allows files with UIDs and GIDs up to 262,143 to be stored in the archive. Files with UIDs and GIDs greater than this value are archived with the UID and GID of 60001.

ustar   The extended `tar` interchange format; see the IEEE 1003.1(1990) specifications. The default blocksize for this format for character special archive files is 10,240. Implementations support all blocksize values less than or equal to 32,256 that are multiples of 512.

Any attempt to append to an archive file in a format different from the existing archive format exits immediately with a non-zero exit status.

This archive format allows files with UIDs and GIDs up to 2,097,151 to be stored in the archive. Files with UIDs and GIDs greater than this value are archived with the UID and GID of 60001.

-X   When traversing the file hierarchy specified by a path name, pax does not descend into directories that have a different device ID (st_dev, see stat(2)).

The options that operate on the names of files or archive members (-c, -i, -n, -s, -u, and -v) interact as follows.

- In read mode, the archive members are selected on the basis of user-specified pattern operands as modified by the -c, -n, and -u options. Then, any -s and -i options modify, in that order, the names of the selected files. The -v option writes names resulting from these modifications.

- In write mode, the files are selected on the basis of user-specified path names as modified by the -n and -u options. Then, any -s and -i options, in that order, modify the names of these selected files. The -v option writes names resulting from these modifications.

- If you specify both the -u and -n options, pax does not consider a file selected unless it is newer than the file to which it is compared.

Operands

directory   The destination directory path name for copy mode.

file   A path name of a file to be copied or archived.

pattern   A pattern matching one or more path names of archive members. A pattern must conform to the pattern-matching notation found on the fnmatch(5) manual page. The default, if no pattern is specified, is to select all members in the archive.

Output

Standard Output

In write mode, if you do not specify -f, the standard output is the archive formatted according to cpio or ustar. (See -x *format*.)

In list mode, the table of contents of the selected archive members is written to standard output, using the following format.

```
"%s\n" pathname
```

If you specify the -v option in list mode, the table of contents of the selected archive members is written to standard output, using the following formats for path names.

For path names representing hard links to previous members of the archive:

```
"%s/\==/\%s\n" ls -l listing, linkname
```

For all other path names:

```
pathname "%s\n" ls -l listing
```

where ls -l *listing* is the format specified by the ls command with the -l option. When path names are written in this format, it is unspecified what is written for fields for which the underlying archive format does not have the correct information, although the correct number of blank-separated fields are written.

In list mode, standard output is not buffered more than a line at a time.

Standard Error

If you specify -v in read, write, or copy modes, pax writes the path names it processes to the standard error output, using the following format.

```
"%s\n" pathname
```

These path names are written as soon as processing is begun on the file or archive member and are flushed to standard error. The trailing newline character, which is not buffered, is written when the file has been read or written.

If you specify the -s option and the replacement string has a trailing p, substitutions are written to standard error in the following format.

```
"%s/\>>/\%s\n" original-pathname, new-pathname
```

In all operating modes of pax, optional messages of unspecified format concerning the input archive format and volume number, the number of files, blocks, volumes, and media parts, as well as other diagnostic messages can be written to standard error.

In all formats for both standard output and standard error, it is unspecified how nonprintable characters in path names or link names are written.

Errors

If pax cannot create a file or a link when reading an archive; cannot find a file when writing an archive; or cannot preserve the user ID, group ID, or file mode when you specify the -p option, processing continues, a diagnostic message is written to standard error, and a non-zero exit status is returned. When pax cannot create a link to a file, pax does not, by default, create a second copy of the file.

If the extraction of a file from an archive is prematurely terminated by a signal or error, pax may have only partially extracted the file or (if you did not specify the -n option) may have extracted a file of the same name as that specified but that is not the file you wanted. Additionally, the file modes of extracted directories may have additional bits from the read, write, execute mask set, as well as incorrect modification and access times.

Usage

The -p (privileges) option was invented to reconcile differences between historical tar(1) and cpio(1) implementations. In particular, the two commands use -m in diametrically opposed ways. The -p option also provides a consistent means of extending the ways in which future file attributes can be addressed, such as for enhanced security systems or high-performance files. Although it may seem complex, the following two modes are most commonly used.

-p e   Preserve everything. Superuser can use this option to preserve all aspects of the files as they are recorded in the archive. The e flag is the sum of o, p, and other implementation-dependent attributes.

-p p   Preserve the file-mode bits. Users with regular privileges can use this option to preserve aspects of the file other than the ownership. The file times are preserved by default, but two other flags are offered to disable these and to use the time of extraction.

See largefile(5) for the description of the behavior of pax when encountering files greater than or equal to 2 Gbytes (2**31 bytes).

Examples

The following example copies the contents of the current directory to tape drive 1, medium density (assuming historical System V device naming procedures. The historical BSD device name would be /dev/rmt9).

```
castle% pax -w -f /dev/rmt/1m .
castle%
```

The following example copies the olddir directory hierarchy to newdir.

```
castle% mkdir newdir
castle% pax -rw olddir newdir
castle%
```

The following example reads the archive a.pax with all files rooted in /usr in the archive extracted relative to the current directory.

```
castle% pax -r -s ',^//*usr//*,,' -f a.pax
castle%
```

Environment Variables

See environ(5) for descriptions of the following environment variables that affect the execution of pax: LC_CTYPE, LC_MESSAGES, LC_TIME, and NLSPATH.

LC_COLLATE Determine the locale for the behavior of ranges, equivalence classes, and multicharacter collating elements used in the pattern-matching expressions for the *pattern* operand, the basic regular expression for the -s option, and the extended regular expression defined for the yesexpr locale keyword in the LC_MESSAGES category.

Exit Status

0   All files were processed successfully.

>0   An error occurred.

Attributes

See attributes(5) for descriptions of the following attributes:

Attribute Type	Attribute Value
Availability	SUNWcsu

See Also

chmod(1), cpio(1), ed(1), tar(1), mkdir(2), stat(2), attributes(5), environ(5), fnmatch(5), largefile(5), regex(5)

pcat — Compress and Expand Files

Synopsis

```
/usr/bin/pcat file...
```

Description

See pack(1).

pcmapkeys — Set Keyboard Extended Map and Scan Code Translation for the PC Console in Text Mode

Synopsis

```
/bin/pcmapkeys [-f mapfile | -n | -g | -d | -e]
```

Description

The pcmapkeys command enables you, in text mode, to activate character mapping on input and output and keyboard extended mapping on the PC console. The keyboard extended mapping consists of the support for the deadkey and compose key sequences.

Consistent Keyboard-Display Mapping

The original UNIX operating system was written to support the ASCII codeset. ASCII is one of many standards used to represent characters internally as certain numbers. ASCII typically supports 128 different characters, each represented by a single byte, of which the 8th bit is not used. Many UNIX system applications, including the shell, took advantage of this representation. Starting with UNIX System V Release 3.1, most of these applications have been modified to properly support characters represented as a byte with the 8th bit also set. With the 8th bit set, 256 characters can be supported at the same time. However, a consistent coding convention needs to be applied. In the IBM PC world, an 8-bit coding, referred to as IBM extended ASCII, has been used for several years; MS-DOS users are familiar with that codeset. In heterogeneous UNIX system environments, a different codeset, called ISO 8859, has been promoted. In both codesets, characters found in the ASCII codeset are represented in the same way. The other 128 characters are encoded differently, however, and some characters found in one codeset are missing in the other. The Solaris for x86 system supports any 8-bit, one-byte codeset, which includes the IBM extended ASCII and ISO 8859 codesets.

To be able to use characters from the French, German, Finnish, and other alphabets, systems available on the market generate 7-bit codes but display the above-mentioned characters on the screen instead of the ones found on a U.S. console. The keyboard has an equal number of keys but uses different characters on the key caps. Other keyboards can support 256 different characters at a time but use their own proprietary codesets.

For example, if you are using the Solaris for x86 system with a console and a French keyboard and you do not use pcmapkeys to map the French keyboard tables, then if you edit a file and use the French character é in text, the actual code generated is ASCII 123, which is the code normally used for the left curly brace. If you look at the edited file on the console, the letter actually appears to be a curly brace. Using pcmapkeys to map in the French keyboard enables consistent input and output mappings.

Note — The default keyboard mappings on the system are those of the ISO 8859-1 codeset. The optional IBM DOS 437 codeset is supported only at internationalization level 1. That is, if you choose to download keyboard mappings of the optional IBM DOS 437 codeset, nonstandard U.S. date, time, currency, numbers, unit, and collation are not supported. Non-English message and text presentation and multibyte characters are also not supported. Therefore, non-Windows users should only use the IBM DOS 437 codeset in the default C locale.

Input Mapping

On input, any byte can be mapped to any byte. Using the example above, you could map 123 to 130, the code used for é in the IBM extended ASCII codeset.

Output Mapping

On output, any byte can be mapped to either a byte or a string. In the above example, 130 would be mapped back to 123 to properly display the character on the screen. If the connected device is a printer that does not support the é character, it could be mapped to the string e backspace.

Deadkeys

On typewriters, keys can be found that do not move when you press them. Control (^) and the grave accent (`) are such characters. When ` is followed by an e, the letter è is generated. This is called a deadkey or a nonspacing character. The Solaris for x86 system supports the use of deadkeys. Typically, the ^ character, the ` character, and the umlaut (¨) character are used as deadkeys.

Compose Sequences

Characters can also be generated by a compose sequence. A dedicated compose character followed by two other keystrokes generates a single character. As an example, COMPOSE followed by the plus and the minus sign could generate the plus/minus sign (±). Compose sequences can also be used as an alternative for deadkeys, for example, COMPOSE ^ e instead of ^ e.

Numeric Compose Sequences

By pressing the compose key followed by three digits, you can generate compose sequence characters such as graphics characters that are not present on the keyboard and cannot be intuitively composed by some key sequence.

Toggle Key

You can define an optional toggle key to temporarily disable the current mapping from within an application. The toggle key can be useful when, for example, a German programmer wants easy access to the curly braces and the brackets. Use of the toggle key is analogous to use of the -d and -e command line options.

Scancode Mapping

The keyboards of the console and some other peripherals such as SunRiver workstations behave differently than those of regular terminals. They generate what are called scancodes. They also have a number of keys, such as the Alt key, that are not found on regular terminals. Scancodes generated by PC keyboards typically represent the location of the key on the keyboard. The keyboard driver has to properly translate these scancodes. The different national variants of a PC keyboard not only have non-English characters printed on some of the keycaps but the order of some of the keys is different as well. Without changing the scancode translation, a French user would type A and see Q on his screen. Several status keys can influence the translated code as well. The keyboard driver, and thus the pcmapkeys program, makes a distinction between two sets of key combinations that can be translated.

Function Keys

Up to 60 key combinations are recognized as function keys. The first 12 are the 12 function keys of a 101-key PC keyboard (the first 10 on an 84-key keyboard).

If you do not know whether you have an 84- or 101-key keyboard, you can determine which type you have in the following way.

- If your keyboard has arrow keys that are separate from the ones on the numeric keypad, then you have a 101-key keyboard.

- If the arrow keys on your keyboard are located on the numeric keypad only, then you have an 84-key keyboard.

F13 to F24 are the same keys used in combination with Shift, F25 to F36 when used with Control, and F37 to F48 when used with Control and Shift together. F49 to F60 are the keys on the numeric keypad, in the following order.

```
7
8
9
-
4
5
6
+
1
2
3
INS
```

Each of these function keys can be given a string as a value. The total length of all strings should not exceed 512 characters.

Regular Keys

Scancodes generated by all keys on the PC keyboard can be translated in a different way as well. For each key, you can specify a different translation for each of the following four cases.

- The key is pressed.
- The key and the Shift key are pressed simultaneously.
- The key and the Alt key are pressed simultaneously.
- The key, the Shift, and the Alt keys are pressed simultaneously.

For each of these cases, the scancode can be translated into one of the following.

- A single byte.
- A single byte preceded by Escape N.
- A single byte preceded by Escape O.
- A single byte preceded by Escape [.

Internally, special bits are set to indicate that an escape sequence needs to be generated. Other bits are used to indicate whether the translated code should be influenced by some special keys.

Num Lock	If the Num Lock bit is set, swap the regular and Shift values as well as the Alt and Shift Alt values whenever the Num Lock LED is on. By default, only the keys on the numeric keypad have this bit set. That is why these keys generate 7, 8, 9, and so on when the Num Lock LED is on, which is the same value that would be produced if Shift were used with these keys.
Caps Lock	Has the same effect as the Num Lock key. By default, this bit is set for all letters and not set for punctuation marks.
Control	When a key is translated into a single byte (no escape sequence) and this bit is set, generate the corresponding control character when the Control key is pressed simultaneously with another key. This setting is equally valid for the Shift, Alt, and Shift Alt combination. When this bit is not used, the Control key combination does not generate anything.

Mapfile

This section describes the layout of the *mapfile* that is read by the pcmapkeys program.

A mapfile is a text file that consists of several sections. You can use the pound sign (#) to include comments. Everything following the # until the end of the line is ignored by the pcmapkeys program. Inside a line, you can also use C-style comments (/* */). Indicate the beginning of each section by a keyword. Spaces and Tabs are silently ignored and can be used at all times to improve readability. The section that defines the compose character is required; all other sections are optional. The sections must appear in the following predefined order.

```
input:
toggle:
dead:
compose:
output:
scancodes:
```

You can describe characters in several different ways. ASCII characters can be described by putting the character between single quotes. For example:

```
'a'  '{'
```

You can list control characters between single quotes by using a circumflex sign before the character that needs to be quoted. For example:

```
'^x'
```

When you use a backslash (\), the subsequent sequence is interpreted as a decimal, octal (leading 0), or hexadecimal (leading x or X) representation of the character, although the use of single quotes is not mandatory. For example:

```
'\x88'
```

is the same as:

```
0x88
```

The 0 is needed when the sequence is not quoted, and

```
'\007'
```

is the same as

```
007
```

When strings are needed, use a list of character representations. Quoted strings will be supported in the future.

The following paragraphs describe what goes in each section of the *mapfile*.

Input Section

The input section describes which input characters should be mapped into a single byte. A very small sample input section could be:

```
input:
'A'  'B'       # map A into B on input
'#'  0x9c      # map sharp sign into pound sign
```

Toggle Section

The toggle section is a one-line section that defines which key is to toggle between mapping and no mapping. For example:

```
toggle:
'^y'              # ctrl y is the toggle key
```

Deadkey Section

The deadkey section defines which keys should be treated as deadkeys. For each character, use the `dead:` keyword followed by the specification of the character. The subsequent lines describe what key should be generated for each key following the deadkey. A deadkey followed by a key not described in this part of the mapfile does not generate any key, and a beep tone is produced on the terminal. For example:

```
dead:   '^'     # circumflex is a deadkey
' '     '^'     # circumflex followed by space generates circumflex
'e'     0x88    # circumflex followed by e generates e circumflex
dead:   '"'     # double quote used as a deadkey
' '     '"'     # double quote space generates double quote
'a'     0x84    # double quote a generates an umlaut
```

Compose Section

The first line of the compose section defines the compose character. That line must always be present in a mapfile. Subsequent lines consist of three character representations indicating that the third character needs to be generated on input when the compose character is followed by the first two. Group the compose sequences with the same first character. For example:

```
compose: '^x'
'"'   'e'   0x89   # e with umlaut is generated when typing ^x " e
'"'   'a'   0x84   # a with umlaut
'e'   '"'   0x89   # e with umlaut is generated when typing ^x e "
'a'   '"'   0x84   # a with umlaut
```

The following incorrect example gives the wrong result. Instead, you should group all lines starting with the same character specification.

```
compose: '^x'
'"'   'e'   0x89   # e with umlaut is generated when typing ^x " e
'e'   '"'   0x89   # e with umlaut is generated when typing ^x e "
'"'   'a'   0x84   # a with umlaut
'a'   '"'   0x84   # a with umlaut
```

Output Section

The output section describes the mapping on output, either single byte to single byte, or single byte to string. A string is a series of character specifications. For example:

```
output:
0x82 '{'              # map e with accent to { to display e with accent
'^u' '(''K''I''L''L'')' # print (KILL) when kill character is used
```

Scancodes Section

The scancodes section has an effect only when your terminal is a scancode device. No error message is produced if this section is in your mapfile when not needed because the pcmapkeys program determines whether the terminal is a scancode device. The lines in this section can have two different formats. One format describes what the values of the function keys must be. The other format describes the translation of scancodes into a byte or an escape sequence. No specific order is required.

Function Keys
The following line is an example of how to define a string for a function key.

```
F13   'd''a''t''e''0     # Shift F1 is the date command
```

The numbering convention of the function keys is described in a previous section. Currently, the use of quoted strings such as `"date\n"` is not supported.

Scancodes
Specifying how to translate a scancode is a more complex task. A line has the following general format.

```
scancode normal shift alt shiftalt flags
```

scancode should list the hexadecimal representation of a scancode generated by a key (unquoted). How keys correspond with scancodes can be found in keyboard(7D).

normal, *shift*, *alt*, and *shiftalt* are character representations in one of the formats described throughout this document, optionally followed by one of the following special keywords.

	C	The key is influenced by the Control key.
	N	Esc N should precede the specified character.
	O	Esc O should precede the specified character.
	[	Esc [should precede the specified character.

The *normal* field defines how the scancode is translated when no other key is pressed, the *shift* field defines the translation when the Shift key is used simultaneously, the *alt* field specifies what to do when the Alt key is pressed together with this key, and the *shiftalt* field contains the information on what to generate when both the Shift and Alt keys are pressed.

You must fill in the first five fields. When no translation is requested (that is, the current active translation does not need to be changed) you can use a dash (-). The sixth, *flags*, field is optional. *flags* can contain the special keyword CAPS or NUM or both, to indicate whether or not the Caps Lock key or Num Lock key status has any effect. The following sample line describes the default translation for the Q key.

```
0x10 'q'|C   'Q'|C   'q'|N   'Q'|N   CAPS
```

If the *normal* or *shift* field is filled in for a scancode that represents a function key, a self-explanatory message is produced and that translation information is ignored.

The following example shows a scancodes section in more detail.

```
scancodes:
# the w key
0x11 'w'|C    'W'|C    'w'|N    'W'|N    CAPS
# left square bracket and curly brace key
# control shift [does not generate anything (no C flag)
0x1a '['|C    '{'       '['|N    '{'|N
# 9 on numeric keypad
0x49 'V'|[ '9'       '9'|N    '9'|N    NUM
F13 'd''a''t''e''0 # SHIFT F1
```

For complete examples of mapfiles, look in the /usr/share/lib/keyboards directory.

Options

-d and -e	Temporarily disable the compose key and deadkey sequences if the keyboard extended mapping is installed.
-e	Enable extended keyboard mapping.
-f *mapfile*	Install the contents of the file *mapfile* and set the corresponding mapping as supported by the console driver.
-g	Display the current mappings and keyboard extended mapping (if one is installed) in hex values (see /usr/include/sys/emap.h). This option is used mainly for debugging.
-n	Disable and dismantle the current keyboard extended mapping. Use the -f option to reinstall the keyboard extended mapping.

Files

/usr/share/lib/keyboards/8859/*

Sample mapfiles to be used in conjunction with ISO-8859-1 fonts (see loadfont(1)).

/usr/share/lib/keyboards/437/*

Sample mapfiles to be used in conjunction with IBM 437 fonts (see loadfont(1)).

Attributes

See attributes(5) for descriptions of the following attributes:

Attribute Type	Attribute Value
Architecture	SUNWx86
Availability	SUNWcsu

See Also

```
loadfont(1), attributes(5)
```

pcred — Proc Tools

Synopsis

```
/usr/proc/bin/pcred pid...
```

Description

See proc(1).

pdp11 — Get Processor Type Truth Value

Synopsis

```
/usr/bin/pdp11
```

Description

See machid(1).

pfiles, pflags — Proc Tools

Synopsis

```
/usr/proc/bin/pfiles pid...
/usr/proc/bin/pflags pid...
```

Description

See proc(1).

pg — Files Perusal Filter

Synopsis

```
/usr/bin/pg [-number][-p string][-cefnrs][+linenumber][+/pattern/]
    [filename...]
```

Description

The pg command is a filter that enables you to examine files one screen at a time. If you press Return, another page is displayed; other possibilities are listed below.

This command is different from previous paginators in that it enables you to back up and review something that has already moved off the screen. The method for backing up is explained below.

To determine terminal attributes, pg scans the terminfo(4) database for the terminal type specified by the environment variable TERM. If TERM is not defined, the terminal type dumb is assumed.

Notes

While waiting for terminal input, pg responds to BREAK, Control-C, and Control-\ by terminating execution. Between prompts, however, these signals interrupt the current task and display the prompt. Use these key combinations with caution when input is being read from a pipe because an interrupt is likely to terminate the other commands in the pipeline.

If terminal Tabs are not set every eight positions, undesirable results may occur.

When pg is used as a filter with another command that changes the terminal I/O options, terminal settings may not be restored correctly.

Options

-number	Specify the size (in lines) of the window that pg is to use instead of the default. (On a terminal containing 24 lines, the default window size is 23).
+linenumber	
	Start up at linenumber.
+/pattern/	Start up at the first line containing the regular expression pattern.
-c	Home the cursor and clear the screen before displaying each page. This option is ignored if clear_screen is not defined for this terminal type in the terminfo(4) database.
-e	Do not pause at the end of each file.

-f Inhibit split lines. Without this option, pg splits lines longer than the screen width but some sequences of characters in the text being displayed (for instance, escape sequences for underlining) generate undesirable results.

-n Normally, commands must be terminated by a newline character. This option automatically ends the command as soon as a command letter is entered.

-p *string* Use *string* as the prompt. If the prompt string contains a %d, the first occurrence of %d in the prompt is replaced by the current page number when the prompt is issued. The default prompt string is a colon (:).

-r Disallow the shell escape. Print an error message but do not exit.

-s Print all messages and prompts in the standard output mode (usually inverse video).

Operands

filename A path name of a text file to be displayed. If no file name is given or if it is -, read the standard input.

Usage

Commands
When pg pauses, you can respond with three types of commands:

- Those enabling further perusal.
- Those that search.
- Those that modify the perusal environment.

Commands that enable further perusal normally take a preceding address, which is an optionally signed number indicating the point from which further text should be displayed. This address is interpreted in either pages or lines, depending on the command. A signed address specifies a point relative to the current page or line, and an unsigned address specifies an address relative to the beginning of the file. Each command has a default address that is used if none is provided.

The perusal commands and their defaults are as follows.

(+1)newline | blank

Display one page. The address is specified in pages.

(+1) l With a relative address, scroll the screen forward or backward the number of lines specified. With an absolute address, print a screen beginning at the specified line.

(+1) d Scroll half a screen forward or backward.
^D

`if`	Skip i screens of text.
`iz`	Same as newline except that i, if present, becomes the new default number of lines per screen.

The following perusal commands take no address.

`. |^L`	Redisplay the current page of text.
`$`	Display the last screen in the file. Use with caution when the input is a pipe.

The following commands are available for searching for text patterns in the text. The regular expressions are described on the `regex(5)` manual page. They must always be terminated by a newline even if you specify the `-n` option.

`i/pattern/`	Search forward for the i-th (default $i=1$) occurrence of `pattern`. Begin searching immediately after the current page and continue to the end of the current file without wraparound.
`i^pattern^` `i?pattern?`	Search backward for the i-th (default $i=1$) occurrence of `pattern`. Begin searching immediately before the current page and continue to the beginning of the current file without wraparound. The ^ notation is useful for Adds 100 terminals that do not properly handle the ?.

Note — You can omit the final /, ^, or ? from the searching commands.

After searching, pg normally displays the line found at the top of the screen. You can modify this behavior by appending m or b to the search command to leave the line found in the middle or at the bottom of the window from now on. Use the t suffix to restore the original situation.

You can modify the perusal environment with the following commands.

`in`	Begin perusing the i-th next file in the command line. The i is an unsigned number; default is 1.
`ip`	Begin perusing the i-th previous file in the command line. i is an unsigned number; default is 1.
`iw`	Display another window of text. If i is present, set the window size to i.
`s filename`	Save the input in the named file. Save only the current file being perused. The white space between the s and `filename` is optional. You must always terminate this command with a newline, even if you specify the `-n` option.
`h`	Help by displaying an abbreviated summary of available commands.
`q or Q`	Quit.

!*command*   Pass *command* to the shell specified in the SHELL environment
                variable. If this shell is not available, use the default shell. You
                must always terminate this command with a newline, even if you
                specify the -n option.

You can use the quit key (normally Control-\) or the interrupt (BREAK) key
at any time to stop sending output and display the prompt. You can then enter
one of the above commands in the normal manner. Unfortunately, some output
is lost when this is done because any characters waiting in the terminal's
output queue are flushed when the quit signal occurs.

If the standard output is not a terminal, then pg acts just like cat(1), except
that a header is printed before each file (if there is more than one).

Large File Behavior
See largefile(5) for the description of the behavior of pg when encountering
files greater than or equal to 2 Gbytes (2**31 bytes).

Examples
The following example uses pg to read the system news.

```
castle% news | pg -p "(Page %d):"
```

Environment Variables
See environ(5) for descriptions of the following environment variables that
affect the execution of pg: LC_CTYPE, LC_MESSAGES, and NLSPATH.

The following environment variables also affect the execution of pg.

COLUMNS   Determine the horizontal screen size. If unset or null, use the
             value of TERM, the window size, baud rate, or some combination of
             these, to indicate the terminal type for the screen size calculation.

LINES   Determine the number of lines to be displayed on the screen. If
             unset or null, use the value of TERM, the window size, baud rate, or
             some combination of these, to indicate the terminal type for the
             screen size calculation.

SHELL   Determine the name of the command interpreter executed for a
             !*command*.

TERM   Determine terminal attributes. Optionally, try to search a
             system-dependent database, keyed on the value of the TERM
             environment variable. If no information is available, assume a
             terminal incapable of cursor-addressable movement.

Exit Status

0   Successful completion.

>0   An error occurred.

Files

`/tmp/pg*`   Temporary file when input is from a pipe.

`/usr/share/lib/terminfo/?/*`

         Terminal information database.

Attributes

See `attributes(5)` for descriptions of the following attributes:

Attribute Type	Attribute Value
Availability	SUNWcsu
CSI	Enabled

See Also

`cat(1)`, `grep(1)`, `more(1)`, `terminfo(4)`, `attributes(5)`, `environ(5)`, `largefile(5)`, `regex(5)`

New! pgrep, pkill — Find or Signal Processes

Synopsis

```
/usr/bin/pgrep [-flnvx] [-d delim] [-P ppidlist] [-g pgrplist] [-s sidlist]
     [-u euidlist] [-U uidlist] [-G gidlist] [-t termlist] [pattern]
/usr/bin/pkill [-signal] [-fnvx] [-P ppidlist] [-g pgrplist] [-s sidlist]
     [-u euidlist] [-U uidlist] [-G gidlist] [-t termlist] [pattern]
```

Description

The `pgrep` command examines the active processes on the system and reports the process IDs of the processes whose attributes match the criteria specified on the command line. Each process ID is printed as a decimal value and is separated from the next ID by a delimiter string, which is a newline by default. For each attribute option, you can specify a comma-separated set of possible values on the command line. For example, the following command matches processes whose real group ID is other OR daemon.

```
castle% pgrep -G other,daemon
120
castle%
```

If you specify multiple criteria options, `pgrep` matches processes whose attributes match the logical AND of the criteria options. For example, the following command matches processes whose attributes are (real group ID is other OR daemon) AND (real user ID is root OR daemon).

```
castle% pgrep -G other,daemon -U root,daemon
120
castle%
```

pkill functions identically to pgrep except that each matching process is signaled as if by kill(1) instead of displaying its process ID. You can specify a signal name or number as the first command-line option to pkill.

Both commands match the ERE pattern argument against either the pr_fname or pr_psargs fields of the /proc/*nnnnn*/psinfo files. The lengths of these strings are limited according to definitions in sys/procfs.h. Patterns that can match strings longer than the current limits may fail to match the intended set of processes.

If the pattern argument contains ERE metacharacters that are also shell metacharacters, you may need to enclose the pattern with appropriate shell quotes.

Defunct processes are never matched by either pgrep or pkill.

The current pgrep or pkill process never considers itself a potential match.

Options

-d *delim*   Specify the output delimiter to be printed between each matching process ID. If you specify no -d option, the default is a newline character. The -d option is valid only when specified as an option to pgrep.

-f   Match the regular expression pattern against the full process argument string (obtained from the pr_psargs field of the /proc/*nnnnn*/psinfo file). If you specify no -f option, match the expression only against the name of the executable file (obtained from the pr_fname field of the /proc/*nnnnn*/psinfo file).

-g *pgrplist* Match only processes whose process group ID is in the given list. If you include group 0 in the list, interpret it as the process group ID of the pgrep or pkill process.

-G *gidlist* Match only processes whose real group ID is in the given list. You can specify each group ID as either a group name or a numerical group ID.

-l   Print the process name along with the process ID of each matching process. The process name is obtained from the pr_psargs or pr_fname field, depending on whether you specified the -f option. The -l option is valid only when specified as an option to pgrep.

-n   Match only the newest (most recently created) process that meets all other specified matching criteria.

-P *ppidlist*

              Match only processes whose parent process ID is in the given list.

-s *sidlist*   Match only processes whose process session ID is in the given list. If you include ID 0 in the list, interpret it as the session ID of the pgrep or pkill process.

-t *termlist*   Match only processes that are associated with a terminal in the given list. Each terminal is specified as the suffix following /dev/ of the terminal's device path name in /dev, for example, term/a or pts/0.

-u *euidlist*   Match only processes whose effective user ID is in the given list. You can specify each user ID either as a login name or as a numerical user ID.

-U *uidlist*   Match only processes whose real user ID is in the given list. You can specify each user ID either as a login name or as a numerical user ID.

-v   Reverse the sense of the matching. Match all processes except those that meet the specified matching criteria.

-x   Consider only processes to be matching whose argument string or executable file name exactly matches the specified pattern. The pattern match is considered to be exact when all characters in the process argument string or executable file name match the pattern.

-*signal*   Specify the signal to send to each matched process. If no signal is specified, send SIGTERM by default. The value of *signal* can be one of the symbolic names defined in signal(5) without the SIG prefix, or the corresponding signal number as a decimal value. The -*signal* option is valid only when specified as the first option to pkill.

Operands

pattern   Specify an Extended Regular Expression (ERE) pattern to match against either the executable file name or full process argument string. See regex(5) for a complete description of the ERE syntax.

Examples

The following example obtains the process ID of sendmail.

```
castle% pgrep -x -u root sendmail
336
castle%
```

The following example terminates the most recently created xterm.

```
castle% pkill -n xterm
castle%
```

Exit Status

0	One or more processes were matched.
1	No processes were matched.
2	Invalid command line options were specified.
3	A fatal error occurred.

Files

/proc/*nnnnn*/psinfo

Process information files.

Attributes

See attributes(5) for descriptions of the following attributes:

Attribute Type	Attribute Value
Availability	SUNWcsu

See Also

kill(1), proc(1), ps(1), truss(1), kill(2), proc(4), attributes(5), regex(5), signal(5)

pkginfo — Display Software Package Information

Synopsis

```
/usr/bin/pkginfo [-q | -x | -l][-p | -i][-r][-a arch][-v version]
   [-c category ...][pkginst...]
/usr/bin/pkginfo [-d device][-R root-path][-q | -x | -l][-a arch]
   [-v version] [-c category...][pkginst...]
```

Description

Use the pkginfo command to check which packages are installed on a system (with the first synopsis). By default, pkginfo displays information about currently installed packages. You can also use the pkginfo command to display packages that are on mounted distribution media or that reside in a particular directory (with the second synopsis).

Without options, pkginfo lists the primary category, package instance, and the names of all completely installed and partially installed packages. It displays one line for each package selected.

Options

Note — The -p and -i options are meaningless if used in conjunction with the -d option. The options -q, -x, and -l are mutually exclusive.

-a *arch*	Specify the architecture of the package as *arch*.
-c *category*	Display packages that match *category*. Categories are defined with the CATEGORY parameter in the pkginfo(4) file. If you supply more than one *category*, the package needs to match only one category in the list. The match is not case specific.
-d *device*	Define a device, *device*, on which the software resides. *device* can be an absolute directory path name or the identifiers for tape, diskette, removable disk, and so forth. You can use the special token spool to indicate the default installation spool directory (/var/spool/pkg).
-i	Display information only for fully installed packages.
-l	Specify long format, which includes all available information about the designated package(s).
-p	Display information only for partially installed packages.
-q	Do not list any information. Use from a program to check whether or not a package has been installed.
-r	List the installation base for relocatable packages.
-R *root-path*	Define the full path name of a directory to use as the *root-path*. All files, including package system information files, are relocated to a directory tree starting in the specified *root-path*.
-v *version*	Specify the version of the package as *version*. You define the version with the VERSION parameter in the pkginfo(4) file. You can request all compatible versions by preceding the version name with a tilde (~). Replace multiple white spaces with a single white space during version comparison.
-x	Designate an extracted listing of package information. The listing contains the package abbreviation, package name, package architecture (if available), and package version (if available).

Operands

pkginst	Specify a package designation by its instance. An instance can be the package abbreviation or a specific instance (for example, inst.1 or inst.2). You can request all instances of a package with inst.*.

The asterisk character (*) is a special character to some shells and may need to be escaped. In the C shell, * must be surrounded by single quotes (') or preceded by a backslash (\).

Examples

The following example shows the first few packages from a system.

```
castle% pkginfo
application HPNP             JetAdmin for Unix
ALE         SUNW5xmft       Chinese/Taiwan BIG5 X Windows Platform
   minimum required Fonts Package
system      SUNWab2m        Solaris Documentation Server Lookup
system      SUNWaccr        System Accounting, (Root)
system      SUNWaccu        System Accounting, (Usr)
system      SUNWadmap       System administration applications
system      SUNWadmc        System administration core libraries
system      SUNWadmfw       System & Network Administration Framework
system      SUNWadmr        System & Network Administration Root
system      SUNWapppr       PPP/IP Asynchronous PPP daemon configuration
   files
system      SUNWapppu       PPP/IP Asynchronous PPP daemon and PPP login
   service
system      SUNWarc         Archive Libraries
...
```

Exit Status

0	Successful completion.
>0	An error occurred.

Files

/var/spool/pkg

Default installation spool directory.

Attributes

See attributes(5) for descriptions of the following attributes:

Attribute Type	Attribute Value
Availability	SUNWcsu

See Also

pkgtrans(1), pkgadd(1M), pkgask(1M), pkgchk(1M), pkgrm(1M), pkginfo(4), attributes(5)

Application Packaging Developer's Guide

pkgmk — Produce an Installable Package

Synopsis

/usr/bin/pkgmk [-o] [-a arch] [-b base-src-dir] [-d device] [-f prototype]
   [-l limit] [-p pstamp] [-r root-path] [-v version]
   [variable=value ...] [pkginst]

Description

Use the pkgmk command to produce an installable package to be used as input to the pkgadd(1M) command. The package contents are in directory structure format.

The command uses the package prototype(4) file as input and creates a pkgmap(4) file. The contents for each entry in the prototype file are copied to the appropriate output location. Information concerning the contents (checksum, file size, modification date) is computed and stored in the pkgmap file along with attribute information specified in the prototype file.

You can provide architecture information on the command line with the -a option or in the prototype(4) file. If you supply no architecture information, pkgmk uses the output of uname -m.

You can provide version information on the command line with the -v option or in the pkginfo(4) file. If you supply no version information, a default based on the current date is provided.

Command-line definitions for both architecture and version override the prototype(4) definitions.

Options

-a arch
Override the architecture information provided in the pkginfo(4) file with arch.

-b base-src-dir
Prepend the indicated base-src-dir to locate relocatable objects on the source machine.

-d device
Create the package on device. device can be an absolute directory path name or the identifiers for a diskette or removable disk (for example, /dev/diskette). The default device is the installation spool directory (/var/spool/pkg).

-f prototype
Use the file prototype as input to the command. The default prototype file name is Prototype or prototype.

-l limit
Specify the maximum size in 512-byte blocks of the output device as limit. By default, if the output file is a directory or a mountable device, pkgmk uses the df(1M) command to

dynamically calculate the amount of available space on the output device. This option is useful in conjunction with pkgtrans(1) to create a package with a datastream format.

-o   Overwrite the same instance of the package if it already exists.

-p *pstamp*   Override the production stamp definition in the pkginfo(4) file with *pstamp*.

-r *root-path*

Ignore destination paths in the prototype(4) file. Instead, use the indicated *root-path* with the source path name appended to locate objects on the source machine.

-v *version*   Override the version information provided in the pkginfo(4) file with *version*.

variable=value

Place the indicated variable in the packaging environment. (See prototype(4) for definitions of variable specifications.)

Operands

pkginst   A package designation by its instance. An instance can be the package abbreviation or a specific instance (for example, inst.1 or inst.2). You can request all instances of a package with inst.*.

     The asterisk character (*) is a special character to some shells and may need to be escaped. In the C shell, you must surround * with single quotes (') or precede it with a backslash (\).

Exit Status

0   Successful completion.

>0   An error occurred.

Attributes

See attributes(5) for descriptions of the following attributes:

Attribute Type	Attribute Value
Availability	SUNWcsu

See Also

pkgparam(1), pkgproto(1), pkgtrans(1), uname(1), df(1M), pkgadd(1M), pkginfo(4), pkgmap(4), prototype(4), attributes(5)

Application Packaging Developer's Guide

pkgparam — Display Package Parameter Values

Synopsis
```
/usr/bin/pkgparam [-v][-d device][-R root-path] pkginst [param...]
/usr/bin/pkgparam -f filename [-v][param...]
```

Description
Use the pkgparam command to display the value associated with the parameter or parameters requested on the command line. The values are located in either the pkginfo(4) file for *pkginst* or from the specific file named with the -f option.

One parameter value is shown per line. Only the value of a parameter is given unless you use the -v option. With the -v option, the output of the command is in the following format.

```
parameter1='value1'
parameter2='value2'
parameter3='value3'
```

The following example shows the output of the -v option for the SUNWdthj package.

```
castle% pkgparam -v SUNWdthj
CLASSES='base docs runtime'
BASEDIR='/usr'
TZ='Australia/West'
PATH='/sbin:/usr/sbin:/usr/bin:/usr/sadm/install/bin'
OAMBASE='/usr/sadm/sysadm'
ARCH='sparc'
PKG='SUNWdthj'
NAME='HotJava Browser for Solaris'
VERSION='1.0.1,REV=1998.02.13'
PRODNAME='HotJava'
PRODVERS='1.0.1'
SUNW_PKGTYPE='usr'
MAXINST='1000'
CATEGORY='system'
DESC='HotJava Browser for Solaris'
VENDOR='Sun Microsystems, Inc.'
HOTLINE='Please contact your local service provider'
EMAIL=''
HOTJAVA='dt/appconfig/hotjava'
PSTAMP='pavoni980213183227'
PKGINST='SUNWdthj'
PKGSAV='/var/sadm/pkg/SUNWdthj/save'
INSTDATE='Feb 15 1999 09:33'
castle%
```

If you specify no parameters on the command line, values for all parameters associated with the package are shown.

Options

-d device
: Specify the device on which a *pkginst* is stored. *device* can be a directory path name or the identifiers for tape, diskette, or removable disk (for example, /var/tmp, /dev/diskette, and /dev/dsk/c1d0s0). You can use the special token spool to represent the default installation spool directory (/var/spool/pkg).

-f filename
: Read *filename* for parameter values. *filename* should be in the same format as a pkginfo(4) file. For example, you might create such a file during package development and use it for testing.

-R root-path
: Define the full path name of a subdirectory to use as the *root-path*. Relocate all files, including package system information files, to a directory tree starting in the specified *root-path*.

-v
: Display the name of *param* and its value.

Operands

pkginst
: Define a specific package instance for which to display parameter values.

param
: Define a specific parameter whose value should be displayed.

Examples

The following example lists the information for the SUNWdthj package.

```
castle% pkgparam SUNWdthj
base docs runtime
/usr
Australia/West
/sbin:/usr/sbin:/usr/bin:/usr/sadm/install/bin
/usr/sadm/sysadm
sparc
SUNWdthj
HotJava Browser for Solaris
1.0.1,REV=1998.02.13
HotJava
1.0.1
usr
1000
system
HotJava Browser for Solaris
Sun Microsystems, Inc.
```

```
Please contact your local service provider

dt/appconfig/hotjava
pavoni980213183227
SUNWdthj
/var/sadm/pkg/SUNWdthj/save
Mar 03 1999 17:51
castle%
```

Exit Status

0	Successful completion.
>0	An error occurred.

If parameter information is not available for the indicated package, the command exits with a non-zero status.

Attributes

See `attributes`(5) for descriptions of the following attributes:

Attribute Type	Attribute Value
Availability	SUNWcsu

See Also

`pkgmk(1)`, `pkgproto(1)`, `pkgtrans(1)`, `pkginfo(4)`, `attributes(5)`
Application Packaging Developer's Guide

---

pkgproto — Generate Prototype File Entries for Input to pkgmk Command

Synopsis

```
/usr/bin/pkgproto [-i][-c class][path1]
/usr/bin/pkgproto [-i][-c class][path1=path2...]
```

Description

The `pkgproto` command scans the indicated paths and generates `prototype`(4) file entries that can be used as input to the `pkgmk`(1) command.

If you specify no paths on the command line, standard input is assumed to be a list of paths. If the path name listed on the command line is a directory, the contents of the directory are searched. However, if input is read from the standard input, a directory specified as a path name is not searched.

By default, pkgproto creates symbolic link entries for any symbolic link encountered (ftype=s). When you use the -i option, pkgproto creates a file entry for symbolic links (ftype=f). You would have to edit the prototype(4) file to assign such file types as v (volatile), e (editable), or x (exclusive directory). pkgproto detects linked files. If multiple files are linked together, the first path encountered is considered the source of the link.

By default, pkgproto prints prototype entries to the standard output. However, you should save the output in a file (named Prototype or prototype) to be used as input to the pkgmk(1) command.

Options

-i   Ignore symbolic links and record the paths as ftype=f (a file) or
               ftype=s (a symbolic link).

-c *class*   Map the class of all paths to *class*.

Operands

path1   Path name where objects are located.

path2   Path name that should be substituted on output for *path1*.

Examples

The following examples show uses of pkgproto and a partial listing of the output produced.

```
castle% pkgproto /bin=bin /usr/bin=usrbin /etc=etc
f none bin/sed=/bin/sed 0775 bin bin
f none bin/sh=/bin/sh 0755 bin daemon
f none bin/sort=/bin/sort 0755 bin bin
f none usrbin/sdb=/usr/bin/sdb 0775 bin bin
f none usrbin/shl=/usr/bin/shl 4755 bin bin
d none etc/master.d 0755 root daemon
f none etc/master.d/kernel=/etc/master.d/kernel 0644 root daemon
f none etc/rc=/etc/rc 0744 root daemon

castle% find / -type d -print | pkgproto
d none / 755 root root
d none /bin 755 bin bin
d none /usr 755 root root
d none /usr/bin 775 bin bin
d none /etc 755 root root
d none /tmp 777 root root
castle%
```

Exit Status

0   Successful completion.

>0   An error occurred.

Attributes

See `attributes`(5) for descriptions of the following attributes:

Attribute Type	Attribute Value
Availability	SUNWcsu

See Also

`pkgmk(1)`, `pkgparam(1)`, `pkgtrans(1)`, `prototype(4)`, `attributes(5)`
Application Packaging Developer's Guide

pkgtrans — Translate Package Format

Synopsis

`/usr/bin/pkgtrans [-inos]` *device1 device2* `[`*pkginst...*`]`

Description

The `pkgtrans` command translates an installable package from one format to another. It performs the following translations.

- A file-system format to a datastream.
- A datastream to a file-system format.
- One file-system format to another file-system format.

Device specifications can be either the special node name (for example, `/dev/diskette`) or a device alias (for example, `diskette1`). The device `spool` indicates the default spool directory. Source and destination devices cannot be the same.

By default, `pkgtrans` does not translate any instance of a package if any instance of that package already exists on the destination device. Using the `-n` option creates a new instance if an instance of this package already exists. Using the `-o` option overwrites an instance of this package if it already exists. Neither of these options is useful if the destination device is a datastream.

Options

`-i`	Copy only the `pkginfo`(4) and `pkgmap`(4) files.
`-n`	Create a new instance of the package on the destination device if any instance of this package already exists, up to the number specified by the `MAXINST` variable in the `pkginfo`(4) file.
`-o`	Overwrite the same instance on the destination device if it already exists.

-s   Write the package to *device2* as a datastream instead of as a file
                       system. The default behavior is to write a file-system format on
                       devices that support both formats.

Operands

device1   The source device. The package or packages on this device are
                       translated and placed on *device2*.

device2   The destination device. Translated packages are placed on this
                       device.

pkginst   Specify which package instance or instances on *device1* should be
                       translated. You can use the token all to indicate all packages. You
                       can use *pkginst*.* to indicate all instances of a package. If no
                       packages are defined, a prompt shows all packages on the device
                       and asks which to translate.

The asterisk character (*) is a special character to some shells and may need
to be escaped. In the C shell, you must surround * with single quotes (') or
precede it with a backslash (\).

Examples

The following example translates all packages on the diskette drive
/dev/diskette and places the translations on /tmp.

```
castle% pkgtrans /dev/diskette /tmp all
```

The following example translates packages pkg1 and pkg2 on /tmp and
puts their translations (that is, a datastream) on the 9track1 output device.

```
castle% pkgtrans /tmp 9track1 pkg1 pkg2
```

The following example translates pkg1 and pkg2 on /tmp and puts them on
the diskette in a datastream format.

```
castle% pkgtrans -s /tmp /dev/diskette pkg1 pkg2
```

Environment Variables

The MAXINST variable is set in the pkginfo(4) file and declares the maximum
number of package instances.

Exit Status

0   Successful completion.

>0   An error occurred.

Attributes

See attributes(5) for descriptions of the following attributes:

Attribute Type	Attribute Value
Availability	SUNWcsu

See Also

pkginfo(1),pkgmk(1),pkgparam(1),pkgproto(1),installf(1M),pkgadd(1M),
pkgask(1M),pkgrm(1M),removef(1M),pkginfo(4),pkgmap(4),attributes(5)
Application Packaging Developer's Guide

New! **pkill** — Find or Signal Processes

Synopsis

```
/usr/bin/pkill [-signal] [-fnvx] [-P ppidlist] [-g pgrplist] [-s sidlist]
    [-u euidlist] [-U uidlist] [-G gidlist] [-t termlist] [pattern]
```

Description

See pgrep(1).

---

pldd — Proc Tools

Synopsis

```
/usr/proc/bin/pldd pid...
```

Description

See proc(1).

New! **plimit** — Get or Set the Resource Limits of Running Processes

Synopsis

```
/usr/bin/plimit [-km] pid...
/usr/bin/plimit -cdfnstv soft,hard... pid...
```

Description

With no arguments, plimit reports the resource limits of the processes identified by *pid*. When you specify one or more of the cdfnstv options, plimit sets the *soft* (current) limit and/or the *hard* (maximum) limit of the indicated resource(s) in the processes identified by *pid*.

Only the owner of a process or the superuser is permitted either to get or to set the resource limits of a process. Only the superuser can increase the *hard* limit.

Options

-k	Show file sizes in kilobytes (1,024 bytes) instead of in 512-byte blocks.
-m	Show file and memory sizes in megabytes (1,024*1,024 bytes).

The following options change specified resource limits. They each accept an argument of the form:

soft,hard

where *soft* specifies the soft (current) limit and *hard* specifies the hard (maximum) limit. If you do not specify a hard limit, you can omit the comma. If the soft limit is an empty string, only the hard limit is set. Each limit is either the literal string unlimited or a number with an optional scaling factor, as follows:

*n*k	*n* kilobytes.
*n*m	*n* megabytes (minutes for CPU time).
*n*h	*n* hours (for CPU time only).
mm:ss	Minutes and seconds (for CPU time only).

The soft limit cannot exceed the hard limit.

-c *soft,hard*

Set corefile size limits (default unit is 512-byte blocks).

-d *soft,hard*

Set data segment (heap) size limits (default unit is kilobytes).

-f *soft,hard*

Set file size limits (default unit is 512-byte blocks).

-n *soft,hard*

Set file descriptor limits (no default unit).

-s *soft,hard*

Set stack segment size limits (default unit is kilobytes).

-t *soft,hard*

Set CPU time limits (default unit is seconds).

-v *soft,hard*

> Set virtual memory size limits (default unit is kilobytes).

Operands

pid   Process ID list.

Examples

The following example shows the current settings for the Volume Management daemon, vold.

```
# plimit 213
213:    /usr/sbin/vold
   resource              current           maximum
   time(seconds)         unlimited         unlimited
   file(blocks)          unlimited         unlimited
   data(kbytes)          unlimited         unlimited
   stack(kbytes)         8192              2097148
   coredump(blocks)      unlimited         unlimited
   nofiles(descriptors)  1024              1024
   vmemory(kbytes)       unlimited         unlimited
#
```

Exit Status

0   Success.

non-zero   Failure such as no such process, permission denied, or invalid option.

Files

/proc/pid/* Process information and control files.

Attributes

See attributes(5) for descriptions of the following attributes:

Attribute Type	Attribute Value
Availability	SUNWesu

See Also

proc(1), ulimit(1), getrlimit(2), setrlimit(2), proc(4), attributes(5)

plot, aedplot, atoplot, bgplot, crtplot, dumbplot, gigiplot —
Graphics Filters for Various Plotters

Synopsis
`/usr/ucb/plot [-T`*terminal*`]`

Description
The `plot` command reads plotting instructions (see `plot`(4B)) from the standard input and produces plotting instructions suitable for a particular terminal on the standard output.

If you do not specify a terminal, the environment variable TERM is used. The default terminal is `tek`.

Environment Variables
Except for `ver`, you can use the following terminal types with `lpr -g` (see `lpr`) to produce plotted output.

`2648	2648a	h8	hp2648	hp2648a`	
	Hewlett-Packard® 2648 graphics terminal.
`hp7221	hp7	h7`	
	Hewlett-Packard 7221 plotter.
`300`	DASI 300 or GSI terminal (Diablo mechanism).
`300s	300S`	
	DASI 300s terminal (Diablo mechanism).
`450`	DASI Hyterm 450 terminal (Diablo mechanism).
`4013`	Tektronix 4013 storage scope.
`4014	tek`	Tektronix 4014 and 4015 storage scope with Enhanced Graphics Module. (Use 4013 for Tektronix 4014 or 4015 without the Enhanced Graphics Module).
`aed`	AED 512 color graphics terminal.
`bgplot	bitgraph`	
	BBN bitgraph graphics terminal.
`crt`	Any CRT terminal capable of running `vi`(1).
`dumb	un	unknown`	
	Dumb terminals without cursor addressing or line printers.
`gigi	vt125`	
	DEC® vt125 terminal.
`implot`	Imagen® plotter.

var   Benson Varian printer-plotter

ver   Versatec D1200A printer-plotter. The output is scan-converted and suitable input to `lpr -v`.

Files

```
/usr/ucb/aedplot
/usr/ucb/atoplot
/usr/ucb/bgplot
/usr/ucb/crtplot
/usr/ucb/dumbplot
/usr/ucb/gigiplot
/usr/ucb/hp7221plot
/usr/ucb/hpplot
/usr/ucb/implot
/usr/ucb/plot
/usr/ucb/plottoa
/usr/ucb/t300
/usr/ucb/t300s
/usr/ucb/t4013
/usr/ucb/t450
/usr/ucb/tek
/usr/ucb/vplot
```

Attributes

See `attributes`(5) for descriptions of the following attributes:

Attribute Type	Attribute Value
Availability	SUNWscpu

See Also

`graph(1)`, `tplot(1)`, `vi(1)`, `lpr(1B)`, `plot(4B)`, `attributes(5)`

pmap — Proc Tools

Synopsis
```
/usr/proc/bin/pmap [-r] pid...
```

Description
See proc(1).

popd — Change Working Directory

Synopsis
```
/usr/bin/cd [directory]
```

sh
```
popd [+n]
```

Description
See cd(1).

postdaisy — PostScript Translator for Diablo 630 Daisy-Wheel Files

Synopsis
```
/usr/lib/lp/postdaisy [-c num] [-f num] [-h num] [-m num] [-n num]
    [-o list] [-p mode] [-r num] [-s num] [-v num] [-x num] [-y num] [file...]
/usr/lib/lp/postscript/postdaisy
```

Description
The postdaisy filter translates Diablo 630 daisy-wheel files into PostScript and writes the results to the standard output. If you specify no files or if - is one of the input files, the standard input is read.

Options

-c num   Print num copies of each page. By default, only one copy is printed.

-f *name*	Print files, using font *name*. You can use any PostScript font, although the best results are obtained only with constant-width fonts. The default font is `Courier`.
-h *num*	Set the initial horizontal motion index to *num*. Determine the character advance and the default point size unless you use the -s option. The default is 12.
-m *num*	Magnify each logical page by the factor *num*. Scale pages uniformly about the origin, which is located near the upper-left corner of each page. The default magnification is 1.0.
-n *num*	Print *num* logical pages on each piece of paper, where *num* can be any positive integer. By default, *num* is set to 1.
-o *list*	Print pages whose numbers are given in the comma-separated list. The *list* contains single numbers *N* and ranges *N1* - *N2*. A missing *N1* means the lowest-numbered page, a missing *N2* means the highest. The page range is an expression of logical pages instead of physical sheets of paper. For example, if you are printing two logical pages to a sheet and you specified a range of 4, then two sheets of paper containing four page layouts would print. If you specified a page range of 3-4 when requesting two logical pages to a sheet, then only page 3 and page 4 layouts would print, and they would appear on one physical sheet of paper.
-p *mode*	Print files in either p (portrait) or 1 (landscape) mode. Only the first character of *mode* is significant. The default mode is portrait.
-r *num*	Choose Return and linefeed behavior. If *num* is 1, a linefeed generates a Return. If *num* is 2, a Return generates a linefeed. Setting *num* to 3 enables both modes.
-s *num*	Use point size *num* instead of the default value set by the initial horizontal motion index.
-v *num*	Set the initial vertical motion index to *num*. The default is 8.
-x *num*	Translate the origin *num* inches along the positive x axis. The default coordinate system has the origin fixed near the upper-left corner of the page, with positive x to the right and positive y down the page. Positive *num* moves everything right. The default offset is 0.25 inches.
-y *num*	Translate the origin *num* inches along the positive y axis. Positive *num* moves text up the page. The default offset is -0.25 inches.

Exit Status

0	Successful completion.
non-zero	An error occurred.

Files

/usr/lib/lp/postscript/forms.ps

/usr/lib/lp/postscript/ps.requests

Attributes

See attributes(5) for descriptions of the following attributes:

Attribute Type	Attribute Value
Availability	SUNWpsf

See Also

download(1), dpost(1), postdmd(1), postio(1), postmd(1), postprint(1),
postreverse(1), posttek(1), attributes(5)

---

postdmd — PostScript Translator for DMD Bitmap Files

Synopsis

/usr/lib/lp/postdmd [-b num][-c num][-f][-m num][-n num][-o list]
  [-p mode][-x num][-y num][file...]
/usr/lib/lp/postscript/postdmd

Description

The postdmd command translates DMD bitmap files produced by dmdps or
files written in the Ninth Edition bitfile(9.5) format into PostScript and
writes the results to the standard output. If no files are specified or if - is one
of the input files, the standard input is read.

Options

-b num	Pack the bitmap in the output file, using num byte patterns. A value of 0 turns off all packing of the output file. By default, num is 6.
-c num	Print num copies of each page. By default, only one copy is printed.
-f	Flip the sense of the bits in files before printing the bitmaps.
-m num	Magnify each logical page by the factor num. Scale pages uniformly about the origin which, by default, is located at the center of each page. The default magnification is 1.0.
-n num	Print num logical pages on each piece of paper where num can be any positive integer. By default, num is set to 1.

`-o list`	Print pages whose numbers are given in the comma-separated list. The `list` contains single numbers `N` and ranges `N1-N2`. A missing `N1` means the lowest-numbered page, a missing `N2` means the highest. The page range is an expression of logical pages instead of physical sheets of paper. For example, if you are printing two logical pages to a sheet and you specified a range of 4, then two sheets of paper containing four page layouts would print. If you specified a page range of 3-4 when requesting two logical pages to a sheet, then only page 3 and page 4 layouts would print and they would appear on one physical sheet of paper.
`-p mode`	Print files in either p (portrait) or 1 (landscape) mode. Only the first character of `mode` is significant. The default mode is portrait.
`-x num`	Translate the origin `num` inches along the positive x axis. The default coordinate system has the origin fixed at the center of the page, with positive x to the right and positive y up the page. Positive `num` moves everything right. The default offset is 0 inches.
`-y num`	Translate the origin `num` inches along the positive y axis. Positive `num` moves everything up the page. The default offset is 0.

Only one bitmap is printed on each logical page, and each of the input files must contain complete descriptions of at least one bitmap. Decreasing the pattern size with the -b option may help throughput on printers with fast processors (such as PS-810s), while increasing the pattern size often is the right move on older models (such as PS-800s).

Exit Status

0	Successful completion.
non-zero	An error occurred.

Files

/usr/lib/lp/postscript/forms.ps

/usr/lib/lp/postscript/ps.requests

Attributes

See attributes(5) for descriptions of the following attributes:

Attribute Type	Attribute Value
Availability	SUNWpsf

See Also

download(1), dpost(1), postdaisy(1), postio(1), postmd(1), postprint(1), postreverse(1), posttek(1), attributes(5)

postio — Serial Interface for PostScript Printers

Synopsis

```
/usr/lib/lp/postio -l line [-D][-i][-q][-t][-S][-b speed][-B num]
    [-L file][-P string][-R num][file...]
/usr/lib/lp/postscript/postio
```

Description

The postio command sends files to the PostScript printer attached to *line*. If you specify no files, the standard input is sent.

Notes

The input files are handled as a single PostScript job. Sending several different jobs, each with its own internal end-of-job mark (^D) is not guaranteed to work properly. postio can quit before all the jobs have completed and could be restarted before the last one finishes.

All the capabilities described below may not be available on every machine or even across the different versions of the UNIX system that are currently supported by the program.

There may be no default line, so using the -l option is strongly recommended. If you omit the -l option, postio may try to connect to the printer using the standard output. If Datakit is involved, the -b option may be ineffective and attempts by postio to impose flow control over data in both directions may not work. The -q option can help if the printer is connected to RADIAN. The -S option is not generally recommended and should be used only if all other attempts to establish a reliable connection fail.

Options

The following group of options should be sufficient for most applications.

-b *speed*	Transmit data over line at baud rate *speed*. Recognized baud rates are 1200, 2400, 4800, 9600, and 19200. The default speed is 9600 baud.
-B *num*	Set the internal buffer size for reading and writing files to *num* bytes. By default, *num* is 2048 bytes.
-D	Enable debug mode. Guarantee that everything read on line is added to the log file (standard error by default).
-l *line*	Connect to the printer attached to *line*. In most cases, there is no default and postio must be able to read and write *line*. If the line does not begin with a /, it may be treated as a Datakit destination.

-L *file*   Put data received on line in *file*. The default log file is standard error. Printer or status messages that don't show a change in state are not normally written to *file* but can be forced with the -D option.

-P *string*   Send *string* to the printer before any of the input files. The default string is simple PostScript code that disables timeouts.

-R *num*   Run postio as a single process if *num* is 1 or as separate read and write processes if *num* is 2. By default, postio runs as a single process.

-q   Prevent status queries while files are being sent to the printer. When status queries are disabled, append a dummy message to the log file before each block is transmitted.

The next two options are for users who expect to run postio on their own. Neither is suitable for use in spooler interface programs.

-i   Run the program in interactive mode. First, send any files, followed by the standard input. Force separate read and write processes and override many other options. To exit interactive mode, use your interrupt or quit character. To get a friendly interactive connection with the printer, type executive on a line by itself.

-t   Write data received on *line* and not recognized as printer or status information to the standard output. Force separate read and write processes. Convenient if you have a PostScript program that is returning useful data to the host.

The following option is not generally recommended and should be used only if all else fails to provide a reliable connection.

-S   Slow the transmission of data to the printer. Severely limit throughput, run as a single process, disable the -q option, limit the internal buffer size to 1,024 bytes. This option can use an excessive amount of CPU time and does nothing in interactive mode.

The best performance is usually obtained by using a large internal buffer (the -B option) and by running the program as separate read and write processes (the -R 2 option). Inability to fork the additional process continues as a single read/write process. When one process is used, only data sent to the printer is flow controlled.

The options are not all mutually exclusive. The -i option always wins, selecting its own settings for whatever is needed to run interactive mode independently of anything else found on the command line. Interactive mode runs as separate read and write processes, and few of the other options accomplish anything in the presence of the -i option. The -t option needs a reliable two-way connection to the printer and therefore tries to force separate read and write processes. The -S option relies on the status query mechanism, so -q is disabled and the program runs as a single process.

In most cases, postio starts by making a connection to *line* and then tries to force the printer into the IDLE state by sending an appropriate sequence of ^T (status query), ^C (interrupt), and ^D (end-of-job) characters. When the printer goes IDLE, files are transmitted along with an occasional ^T (unless you used the -q option). After all the files are sent, the program waits until it is likely that the job is complete. Printer-generated error messages received at any time except while establishing the initial connection (or when running interactive mode) exit postio with a non-zero status. In addition to being added to the log file, printer error messages are also echoed to standard error.

Examples

The following example runs as a single process at 9600 baud and sends file1 and file2 to the printer attached to /dev/tty01.

```
castle% postio -l /dev/tty01 file1 file2
```

The following example is the same as the previous one except that two processes are used, the internal buffer is set to 4,096 bytes, and data returned by the printer gets put in file log.

```
castle% postio -R 2 -B 4096 -l/dev/tty01 -L log file1 file2
```

The following example establishes an interactive connection with the printer at Datakit destination my/printer.

```
castle% postio -i -l my/printer
```

The following example sends file program to the printer connected to /dev/tty22, recovers any data in file results, and puts log messages in file log.

```
castle% postio -t -l /dev/tty22 -L log program >results
```

Exit Status

0	Successful completion.
non-zero	An error occurred.

Attributes

See attributes(5) for descriptions of the following attributes:

Attribute Type	Attribute Value
Availability	SUNWpsf

See Also

download(1),dpost(1),postdaisy(1),postdmd(1),postmd(1),postprint(1), postreverse(1), posttek(1), attributes(5)

postmd — Matrix Display Program for PostScript Printers

Synopsis

```
/usr/lib/lp/postmd [-b num] [-c num] [-d dimen] [-g list] [-i list]
   [-m num] [-n num] [-o list] [-p mode] [-w window] [-x num] [-y num]
   [file...]
/usr/lib/lp/postscript/postmd
```

Description

The postmd filter reads a series of floating-point numbers from files, translates them into a PostScript grayscale image, and writes the results to the standard output. In a typical application the numbers might be the elements of a large matrix written in row major order, while the printed image could help locate patterns in the matrix. If you specify no files or if - is one of the input files, the standard input is read.

Notes

The largest matrix that can be adequately displayed is a function of the interval and grayscale lists, the printer resolution, and the paper size. A 600 by 600 matrix is an optimistic upper bound for a two-element interval list (that is, five regions) using 8.5 by 11 inch paper on a 300 dpi printer.

Using white (that is, 255) in a grayscale list is not recommended. It does not show in the legend and bar graph that postmd displays below each image.

Options

-b *num*	Pack the bitmap in the output file, using *num* byte patterns. A value of 0 turns off all packing of the output file. By default, *num* is 6.
-c *num*	Print *num* copies of each page. By default, only one copy is printed.
-d *dimen*	Set the default matrix dimensions for all input files to *dimen*. You can give the *dimen* string as rows or rows times columns. If you omit the columns value, set it to rows. By default, postmd assumes each matrix is square and sets the number of rows and columns to the square root of the number of elements in each input file.
-g *list*	Use *list*, a comma- or space-separated string of integers each lying between 0 and 255 inclusive, to assign PostScript grayscales to the regions of the real line chosen by the -i option. 255 corresponds to white, and 0, to black. The postmd filter assigns a default grayscale that omits white (that is, 255) and gets darker as the regions move from left to right along the real line.

-i *list*   Use *list*, a comma-, space- or slash- (/) separated string of *N*
            floating-point numbers, to partition the real line into 2*N*+1 regions.
            Specify the list in increasing numerical order. The partitions are
            used to map floating-point numbers read from the input files into
            grayscale integers that are either assigned automatically by
            postmd or that are arbitrarily chosen by using the -g option. The
            default interval list is -1,0,1, which partitions the real line into
            seven regions.

-m *num*   Magnify each logical page by the factor *num*. Scale pages uniformly
            about the origin which, by default, is located at the center of each
            page. The default magnification is 1.0.

-n *num*   Print *num* logical pages on each piece of paper, where *num* can be
            any positive integer. By default, *num* is set to 1.

-o *list*   Print pages whose numbers are given in the comma-separated
            list. The *list* contains single numbers *N* and ranges *N1*–*N2*. A
            missing *N1* means the lowest-numbered page, a missing *N2* means
            the highest. The page range is an expression of logical pages
            instead of physical sheets of paper. For example, if you are
            printing two logical pages to a sheet and you specified a range of 4,
            then two sheets of paper containing four page layouts would print.
            If you specified a page range of 3–4 when requesting two logical
            pages to a sheet, then only page 3 and page 4 layouts would print
            and they would appear on one physical sheet of paper.

-p *mode*   Print files in either p (portrait) or l (landscape) mode. Only the
            first character of *mode* is significant. The default mode is portrait.

-w *window* Use *window*, a comma- or space-separated list of four positive
            integers, to choose the upper-left and lower-right corners of a
            submatrix from each of the input files. Row and column indices
            start at 1 in the upper-left corner and the numbers in the input
            files are assumed to be written in row major order. By default, the
            entire matrix is displayed.

-x *num*   Translate the origin *num* inches along the positive x axis. The
            default coordinate system has the origin fixed at the center of the
            page with positive x to the right and positive y up the page.
            Positive *num* moves everything right. The default offset is 0 inches.

-y *num*   Translate the origin *num* inches along the positive y axis. Positive
            num moves everything up the page. The default offset is 0.

   One matrix only is displayed on each logical page, and each of the input files
must contain complete descriptions of exactly one matrix. Matrix elements are
floating-point numbers arranged in row major order in each input file. White
space, including newlines, is not used to determine matrix dimensions. By
default, postmd assumes each matrix is square and sets the number of rows
and columns to the square root of the number of elements in the input file.
Supplying default dimensions on the command line with the -d option

overrides this default behavior, and in that case, the dimensions apply to all input files.

You can supply an optional header with each input file that is used to set the matrix dimensions, the partition of the real line, the grayscale map, and a window into the matrix. The header consists of keyword/value pairs, each on a separate line. It begins on the first line of each input file and ends with the first unrecognized string, which should be the first matrix element. Values set in the header take precedence but apply only to the current input file. Recognized header keywords are `dimension`, `interval`, `grayscale`, and `window`. The syntax of the value string that follows each keyword parallels what is accepted by the `-d`, `-i`, `-g`, and `-w` options.

Examples

Suppose `file` initially contains the 1,000 numbers in a 20 x 50 matrix. Then, you can produce exactly the same output by completing three steps. First, issue the following command.

```
castle% postmd -d20x50 -i"-100 100" -g0,128,254,128,0 file
```

Next, prepend the following header to `file`.

```
dimension 20x50
interval -100.0 .100e+3
grayscale 0 128 254 128 0
```

Then, issue the following command.

```
castle% postmd file
```

The interval list partitions the real line into five regions, and the grayscale list maps numbers less than -100 or greater than 100 into 0 (that is, black), numbers equal to -100 or 100 into 128 (that is, 50 percent black), and numbers between -100 and 100 into 254 (that is, almost white).

Files

/usr/lib/lp/postscript/forms.ps

/usr/lib/lp/postscript/ps.requests

Exit Status

0	Successful completion.
non-zero	An error occurred.

Attributes

See attributes(5) for descriptions of the following attributes:

Attribute Type	Attribute Value
Availability	SUNWpsf

See Also

dpost(1), postdaisy(1), postdmd(1), postio(1), postprint(1), postreverse(1), posttek(1), attributes(5)

---

postplot — PostScript Translator for plot(4) Graphics Files

Synopsis

```
/usr/lib/lp/postplot [-c num][-f name][-m num][-n num][-o list]
   [-p mode][-w num] [-x num][-y num][filename...]
/usr/lib/lp/postscript/postplot
```

Description

The postplot filter translates plot(1B) graphics file names into PostScript and writes the results to the standard output. If you specify no file names or if – is one of the input file names, the standard input is read.

Note — The default line width is too small for write-white print engines such as the one used by the PS-2400.

Options

-c num	Print num copies of each page. By default, only one copy is printed.
-f name	Print text, using font name. You can use any PostScript font, although the best results are obtained only with constant-width fonts. The default font is Courier.
-m num	Magnify each logical page by the factor num. Scale pages uniformly about the origin which, by default, is located at the center of each page. The default magnification is 1.0.
-n num	Print num logical pages on each piece of paper where num can be any positive integer. By default, num is set to 1.
-o list	Print pages whose numbers are given in the comma-separated list. The list contains single numbers N and ranges N1-N2. A missing N1 means the lowest-numbered page, a missing N2 means the highest.

-p *mode*   Print file names in either p (portrait) or 1 (landscape) mode. Only the first character of *mode* is significant. The default mode is landscape.

-w *num*   Set the line width used for graphics to *num* points, where a point is approximately 1/72 of an inch. By default, *num* is set to 0 points, which forces lines to be one pixel wide.

-x *num*   Translate the origin *num* inches along the positive x axis.The default coordinate system has the origin fixed at the center of the page with positive x to the right and positive y up the page. Positive *num* moves everything right.The default offset is 0.0 inches.

-y *num*   Translate the origin *num* inches along the positive y axis. Positive *num* moves everything up the page. The default offset is 0.0.

Files

```
/usr/lib/lp/postscript/forms.ps
/usr/lib/lp/postscript/postplot.ps
/usr/lib/lp/postscript/ps.requests
```

Attributes

See attributes(5) for descriptions of the following attributes:

Attribute Type	Attribute Value
Availability	SUNWlps

See Also

```
download(1), dpost(1), postdaisy(1), postdmd(1), postio(1), postmd(1),
postprint(1), postreverse(1), plot(1B), attributes(5)
```

Diagnostics

An exit status of 0 is returned if file names were successfully processed.

postprint — PostScript Translator for Text Files

Synopsis

```
/usr/lib/lp/postprint [-c num][-f name][-l num][-m num][-n num]
   [-o list][-p mode][-r num][-s num][-t num][-x num][-y num][file...]
/usr/lib/lp/postscript/postprint
```

Description

The postprint filter translates text files into PostScript and writes the results to the standard output. If you specify no files or if – is one of the input files, the standard input is read.

Options

-c *num*	Print *num* copies of each page. By default, print only one copy.
-f *name*	Print files, using font *name*. You can use any PostScript font, although the best results are obtained only with constant-width fonts. The default font is Courier.
-l *num*	Set the length of a page to *num* lines. By default, *num* is 66. Setting *num* to 0 is allowed, and postprint guesses a value, based on the point size.
-m *num*	Magnify each logical page by the factor *num*. Scale pages uniformly about the origin, which is located near the upper-left corner of each page. The default magnification is 1.0.
-n *num*	Print *num* logical pages on each piece of paper where *num* can be any positive integer. By default, *num* is set to 1.
-o *list*	Print pages whose numbers are given in the comma-separated *list*. The *list* contains single numbers *N* and ranges *N1*–*N2*. A missing *N1* means the lowest-numbered page, a missing *N2* means the highest. The page range is an expression of logical pages instead of physical sheets of paper. For example, if you are printing two logical pages to a sheet and you specified a range of 4, then two sheets of paper containing four page layouts would print. If you specified a page range of 3–4 when requesting two logical pages to a sheet, then only page 3 and page 4 layouts would print and they would appear on one physical sheet of paper.
-p *mode*	Print files in either p (portrait) or l (landscape) mode. Only the first character of *mode* is significant. The default mode is portrait.
-r *num*	Choose Return behavior. Ignore Returns if *num* is 0, go to column 1 if *num* is 1, and generate a newline if *num* is 2. The default *num* is 0.
-s *num*	Print files, using point size *num*. When printing in landscape mode, scale *num* by a factor that depends on the imaging area of the device. The default size for portrait mode is 10. Note that increasing point size increases virtual image size, so you either need to load larger paper or use the -l0 option to scale the number of lines per page.
-t *num*	Assume Tabs are set every *num* columns, starting with the first column. By default, Tabs are set every 8 columns.

-x *num*	Translate the origin *num* inches along the positive x axis. The default coordinate system has the origin fixed near the upper-left corner of the page, with positive x to the right and positive y down the page. Positive *num* moves everything to the right. The default offset is 0.25 inches.
-y *num*	Translate the origin *num* inches along the positive y axis. Positive *num* moves text up the page. The default offset is -0.25 inches.

A new logical page is started after 66 lines have been printed on the current page or whenever an ASCII formfeed character is read. You can change the number of lines per page with the -l option. Unprintable ASCII characters are ignored, and lines that are too long are silently truncated by the printer.

Examples

The following example prints file1 and file2 in landscape mode.

```
castle% postprint -pland file1 file2
```

The following example prints three logical pages on each physical page in portrait mode.

```
castle% postprint -n3 file
```

Exit Status

0	Successful completion.
non-zero	An error occurred.

Files

/usr/lib/lp/postscript/forms.ps

/usr/lib/lp/postscript/ps.requests

Attributes

See attributes(5) for descriptions of the following attributes:

Attribute Type	Attribute Value
Availability	SUNWpsf

See Also

download(1), dpost(1), postdaisy(1), postdmd(1), postio(1), postmd(1), postreverse(1), posttek(1), attributes(5)

postreverse — Reverse the Page Order in a PostScript File

Synopsis

```
/usr/lib/lp/postreverse [-o list][-r][file]
/usr/lib/lp/postscript/postreverse
```

Description

The postreverse filter reverses the page order in files that conform to Adobe's Version 1.0 or Version 2.0 file structuring conventions and writes the results to the standard output. Only one input file is allowed, and, if you specify no file, the standard input is read.

The postreverse filter can handle a limited class of files that violate page independence, provided all global definitions are bracketed by %%BeginGlobal and %%EndGlobal comments. In addition, files that mark the end of each page with %%EndPage: label ordinal comments also reverse properly, provided the prologue and trailer sections can be located. If postreverse fails to find an %%EndProlog or %%EndSetup comment, the entire file is copied, unmodified, to the standard output.

Because global definitions are extracted from individual pages and put in the prologue, the output file can be minimally conforming even if the input file was not.

> **Note** — No attempt has been made to deal with redefinitions of global variables or procedures. If standard input is used, the input file is read three times before being reversed.

Options

-o *list*   Print pages whose numbers are given in the comma-separated list. The *list* contains single numbers *N* and ranges *N1-N2*. A missing *N1* means the lowest-numbered page, a missing *N2* means the highest. The page range is an expression of logical pages instead of physical sheets of paper. For example, if you are printing two logical pages to a sheet and you specified a range of 4, then two sheets of paper containing four page layouts would print. If you specified a page range of 3-4 when requesting two logical pages to a sheet, then only page 3 and page 4 layouts would print and they would appear on one physical sheet of paper.

-r   Do not reverse the pages in *file*.

Examples

The following example reverses pages 1 to 100 from file.

```
castle% postreverse -o1-100 file
```

The following example prints four logical pages on each physical page and reverses all the pages.

```
example% postprint -n4 file | postreverse
```

The following example produces a minimally conforming file from output generated by dpost without reversing the pages.

```
example% dpost file | postreverse -r
```

Exit Status

0	Successful completion.
non-zero	An error occurred.

Attributes

See attributes(5) for descriptions of the following attributes:

Attribute Type	Attribute Value
Availability	SUNWpsf

See Also

download(1), dpost(1), postdaisy(1), postdmd(1), postio(1), postmd(1), postprint(1), posttek(1), attributes(5)

---

posttek — PostScript Translator for Tektronix 4014 Files

Synopsis

```
/usr/lib/lp/posttek [-c num][-f name][-m num][-n num][-o list]
   [-p mode][-w num][-x num][-y num][file...]
/usr/lib/lp/postscript/posttek
```

Description

The posttek filter translates Tektronix 4014 graphics files into PostScript and writes the results to the standard output. If you specify no files or if - is one of the input files, the standard input is read.

> **Note —** The default line width is too small for write-white print engines such as the one used by the PS-2400.

Options

-c *num*	Print *num* copies of each page. By default, only one copy is printed.
-f *name*	Print text, using font *name*. You can use any PostScript font, although the best results are obtained only with constant-width fonts. The default font is `Courier`.
-m *num*	Magnify each logical page by the factor *num*. Scale pages uniformly about the origin which is located near the upper-left corner of each page. The default magnification is `1.0`.
-n *num*	Print *num* logical pages on each piece of paper where *num* can be any positive integer. By default, *num* is set to `1`.
-o *list*	Print pages whose numbers are given in the comma-separated list. The `list` contains single numbers *N* and ranges *N1-N2*. A missing *N1* means the lowest-numbered page, a missing *N2* means the highest. The page range is an expression of logical pages instead of physical sheets of paper. For example, if you are printing two logical pages to a sheet and you specified a range of 4, then two sheets of paper containing four page layouts would print. If you specified a page range of 3-4 when requesting two logical pages to a sheet, then only page 3 and page 4 layouts would print and they would appear on one physical sheet of paper.
-p *mode*	Print files in either p (portrait) or 1 (landscape) mode. Only the first character of *mode* is significant. The default mode is portrait.
-w *num*	Set the line width used for graphics to *num* points, where a point is approximately 1/72 of an inch. By default, *num* is set to 0 points, which forces lines to be 1 pixel wide.
-x *num*	Translate the origin *num* inches along the positive x axis. The default coordinate system has the origin fixed at the center of the page, with positive x to the right and positive y up the page. Positive *num* moves everything right. The default offset is `0.0` inches.
-y *num*	Translate the origin *num* inches along the positive y axis. Positive *num* moves everything up the page. The default offset is `0.0`.

Exit Status

0	Successful completion.
non-zero	An error occurred.

Files

```
/usr/lib/lp/postscript/forms.ps
/usr/lib/lp/postscript/ps.requests
```

Attributes

See attributes(5) for descriptions of the following attributes:

Attribute Type	Attribute Value
Availability	SUNWpsf

See Also

download(1), dpost(1), postdaisy(1), postdmd(1), postio(1), postmd(1), postprint(1), postreverse(1), attributes(5)

pr — Print Files

Synopsis

```
/usr/bin/pr[+page] [-column] [-adFmrt] [-e[char] [gap]] [-header] [-i[char]
    [gap]] [-l lines] [-n[char] [width]] [-o offset] [-s[char]] [-w width]
    [-fp] [file...]
/usr/xpg4/bin/pr [+page] [-column | -c column] [-adFmrt] [-e[char] [gap]]
    [-h header] [-i[char] [gap]] [-l lines] [-n[char] [width]] [-o offset]
    [-s[char]] [-w width] [-fp] [file...]
```

Description

The pr command is a printing and pagination filter. If you specify multiple input files, each is read, formatted, and written to standard output. By default, the input is separated into 66-line pages, each with:

- A 5-line header that includes the page number, date, time, and the path name of the file.
- A 5-line trailer consisting of blank lines.

If standard output is associated with a terminal, diagnostic messages are deferred until the pr command has completed processing.

When you specify options for multicolumn output, output text columns are of equal width; input lines that do not fit into a text column are truncated. By default, text columns are separated with at least one blank character.

Options

In the following option descriptions, column, lines, offset, page, and width are positive decimal integers; gap is a nonnegative decimal integer. Some of the arguments are optional, and some of the arguments cannot be specified as arguments separate from the preceding option letter. In particular, the -s option requires that you keep the option letter with its argument, and the options -e, -i, and -n require that both arguments, if present, be kept with the option letter.

The following options are supported for both /usr/bin/pr and /usr/xpg4/bin/pr.

+*page*	Begin output at page number *page* of the formatted input.
-*column*	Produce multicolumn output that is arranged in *column* columns (default is 1) and is written down each column in the order in which the text is received from the input file. Do not use this option with -m. The -e and -i options are assumed for multiple text-column output. Whether text columns are produced with identical vertical lengths is unspecified, but a text column never exceeds the length of the page (see the -l option). When used with -t, use the minimum number of lines to write the output.
-a	Modify the effect of the -*column* option so that the columns are filled across the page in a round-robin order (for example, when *column* is 2, the first input line heads column 1, the second heads column 2, the third is the second line in column 1, and so forth).
-d	Produce output that is double-spaced; append an extra newline character following every newline character found in the input.
-e[*char*][*gap*]	
	Expand each input Tab character to the next greater column position specified by the formula $n * gap+1$, where n is an integer >0. If *gap* is omitted or it is 0, it defaults to 8. Expand all Tab characters in the input into the appropriate number of space characters. If any nondigit character, *char*, is specified, use it as the input Tab character.
-f	Use a formfeed character for new pages instead of the default behavior that uses a sequence of newline characters. Pause before beginning the first page if the standard output is associated with a terminal.
-h *header*	Use the string *header* to replace the contents of the file operand in the page header.
-l *lines*	Override the 66-line default and reset the page length to *lines*. If *lines* is not greater than the sum of both the header and trailer depths (in lines), suppress both the header and trailer, as if the -t option were in effect.
-m	Merge files. Format standard output to write one line from each file specified by *file*, side by side, into text columns of equal fixed widths in terms of the number of column positions. Implementations support merging of at least nine files.

-n[*char*][*width*]

> Provide *width*-digit line numbering (default for *width* is 5). The number occupies the first *width* column positions of each text column of default output or each line of -m output. If you specify *char* (any nondigit character), append to the line number to separate it from whatever follows (default for *char* is a Tab character).

-o *offset* Precede each line of output by *offset* spaces. If you do not specify the -o option, the default offset is 0. The space taken is in addition to the output line width (see -w option).

-p Pause before beginning each page if the standard output is directed to a terminal (write an ALERT character to standard error and wait for a Return character to be read on /dev/tty).

-r Write no diagnostic reports on failure to open files.

-s[*char*] Separate text columns by the single character *char* instead of by the appropriate number of space characters (default for *char* is the Tab character).

-t Write neither the 5-line identifying header nor the 5-line trailer usually supplied for each page. Quit writing after the last line of each file without spacing to the end of the page.

-w *width* Set the width of the line to *width* column positions for multiple text-column output only. If you do not specify the -w option and specify the -s option, the default width is 72. If you do not specify the -w option and specify the -s option, the default width is 512. For single column output, input lines are not truncated.

/usr/bin/pr
The following options are supported for /usr/bin/pr only.

-F Fold the lines of the input file. When used in multicolumn mode (with the -a or -m options), fold lines to fit the current column's width; otherwise, fold them to fit the current line width (80 columns).

-i[*char*][*gap*]

> In output, replace space characters with Tab characters wherever one or more adjacent space characters reach column positions *gap*+1, 2**gap+1, 3**gap+1, and so forth. If *gap* is 0 or is omitted, set default Tabs at every eighth column position. If you specify any nondigit character, *char*, use it as the output Tab character.

/usr/xpg4/bin/pr
The following options are supported for /usr/xpg4/bin/pr only.

-F Use a formfeed character for new pages instead of the default behavior that uses a sequence of newline characters.

`-i[char][gap]`

> In output, replace multiple space characters with Tab characters wherever two or more adjacent space characters reach column positions $gap+1$, $2*gap+1$, $3*gap+1$, and so forth. If gap is 0 or is omitted, set default Tabs at every eighth column position. If any nondigit character, $char$, is specified, use it as the output Tab character.

Operands

`file`   A path name of a file to be written. If you specify no file operands or if a file operand is -, use the standard input.

Examples

The following example prints a numbered list of all files in the current directory.

```
$ ls -a | pr -n -h "Files in $(pwd)."
```

```
Mar 26 16:29 1999  Files in $(pwd). Page 1


    1    .
    2    ..
    3    .cshrc
    4    .dt
    5    .dtprofile
    6    .hotjava
    7    .jetadmin
    8    .login
    9    .news_time
   10    .sh_history
   11    .solregis
   12    .Xauthority
   13    .Xdefaults
   14    bibliography
   15    DeadLetters
   16    examples
   17    file1
   18    kookaburra-1
   19    ltr
   20    Mail
  ...  (extra linefeeds removed)
$
```

The following example prints `kookaburra-1` and `bibliography` as a double-spaced, three-column listing headed by "file list".

```
$ pr -3d -h "file list" kookaburra-1 bibliography
```

```
Mar 25 16:52 1999   file list Page 1


    1  Kookaburra sits     8  Stop, kookaburr     14  Gay your life m

    2  Merry merry kin     9  Leave some ther

    3  Laugh, kookabur    10                      15  Kookaburra sits

    4  Gay your life m    11  Kookaburra sits     16  Eating all the

    5                     12  Merry merry kin     17  Stop, kookaburr

    6  Kookaburra sits    13  Laugh, kookabur     18  Leave some ther

    7  Eating all the

... (extra linefeeds removed)

Mar 18 08:35 1999   file list Page 1


%A Janice Winsor          friendly, personal styl ~

%T Opening the Dream Do attempt to interpret dr ~

%P 153                    that each person has th %A Janice Winsor

%I Merrill-West Publish cannot be deciphered in %T Opening the Dream Do

%C Carmel, California   dreams as an example, J %P 153

%D 1998                  for expanding the subco %I Merrill-West Publish

%K dreams, psychic deve Processes for rememberi %C Carmel, California

%X Not just another dre easy to understand styl %D 1998

is a practical guide to                         %K dreams, psychic deve
...
```

The following example writes file1 on file2, expanding Tabs to columns 10, 19, 28, and so on.

```
$ pr -e9 -t <file1 >file2
```

Environment Variables

See environ(5) for descriptions of the following environment variables that affect the execution of pr: LC_CTYPE, LC_MESSAGES, LC_TIME, TZ, and NLSPATH.

Exit Status

0	Successful completion.
>0	An error occurred.

Attributes

See `attributes`(5) for descriptions of the following attributes:

/usr/bin/pr

Attribute Type	Attribute Value
Availability	SUNWcsu
CSI	Enabled

/usr/xpg4/bin/pr

Attribute Type	Attribute Value
Availability	SUNWxcu4
CSI	Enabled

See Also

`expand(1)`, `lp(1)`, `attributes(5)`, `environ(5)`, `XPG4(5)`

prex — Control Tracing in a Process or the Kernel

Synopsis

```
/usr/bin/prex [-o trace-file-name] [-l libraries] [-s kbytes-size] cmd
    [cmd-args...]
/usr/bin/prex [-o trace-file-name] [-l libraries] [-s kbytes-size] -p pid
/usr/bin/prex -k [-s kbytes-size]
```

Description

The `prex` command is the part of the Solaris tracing architecture that controls probes in a process or the kernel. See `tracing`(3X) for an overview of this tracing architecture and for example source code.

`prex` is the application used for external control of probes. It locates all the probes in a target executable or the kernel and provides an interface for you to manipulate them. `prex` enables you to turn on a probe for tracing, debugging, or both. Tracing generates a TNF trace file that you can convert to ASCII with `tnfdump`(1) and use for performance analysis. Debugging generates a line to standard error whenever the probe is hit at runtime.

Note — prex does not work on static executables. It works only on dynamic executables.

Invoking prex

You can invoke prex in three ways.

- Use prex to start the target application *cmd*. In this case, the target application need not be built with a dependency on libtnfprobe. See TNF_PROBE(3X). prex sets the environment variable LD_PRELOAD to load libtnfprobe into the target process. See ld(1). prex then uses the environment variable PATH to find the target application.

- Attach prex to a running application. In this case, the running target application should have libtnfprobe already linked in. Alternatively, you can manually set LD_PRELOAD to include libtnfprobe.so.1 before invoking the target.

- Use prex with the -k option to set it to kernel mode. You can then use prex to control probes in the Solaris kernel. In kernel mode, additional commands are defined and some commands that are valid in other modes are invalid.

Control File Format and Command Language

In a future release of prex, the command language may be moved to a syntax that is supported by an existing scripting language like ksh(1). In the meantime, the interface to prex is uncommitted.

- Specify commands in ASCII.
- Terminate each command with the newline character.
- Continue a command onto the next line by ending the previous line with the backslash (\) character.
- Separate tokens in a command by white space (one or more spaces or Tabs).
- Use the # character to indicate that the rest of the line is a comment.

Control File Search Path

You can communicate with prex in two different ways:

- By specifications in a control file. During startup, prex searches for a file named .prexrc in the directories specified below. prex does not stop at the first file it finds. You can use the control file to override any defaults. The search order is: $HOME/ ./.

- By typing commands at the prex prompt.

The command language for both methods is the same and is specified in "Usage" on page 1052. The commands that return output do not make sense in a control file. The output goes to standard output.

When prex is used on a target process, the target is in one of two states: running or stopped. You can detect the state by the presence or absence of the prex> prompt. If the prompt is absent, it means that the target process is running. Typing Control-C stops the target process and returns the prompt. There is no guarantee that Control-C returns to a prex prompt immediately. For example, if the target process is stopped on a job control stop (SIGSTOP), then Control-C in prex waits until the target has been continued (SIGCONT). See "Signals to Target Program" on page 1056 for more information on signals and the target process.

Notes

Currently, the only probe function that is available is the &debug function. When this function is executed, it prints the arguments sent in to the probe as well as the value associated with the sunw%debug attribute in the detail field (if any) to standard error.

For example, for the following probe point,

```
TNF_PROBE_2(input_values, "testapp main",
"sunw%debug 'have read input values successfully'",
tnf_long, int_input, x,
tnf_string, string_input, input);
```

if x was 100 and input was the string "success", then the output of the debug probe function would be

```
probe input_values; sunw%debug "have read input values successfully";
int_input=100; string_input="success";
```

Some non-SPARC hardware lacks a true high-resolution timer so that gethrtime() returns the same value multiple times in succession. As a result, some tools can have problems interpreting the trace file. You can improve this situation by interposing a version of gethrtime(), shown below, that artificially increments these successive values by one nanosecond.

```
hrtime_t
gethrtime()
{
    static mutex_t lock;
    static hrtime_t (*real_gethrtime)(void) = null;
    static hrtime_t last_time = 0;

    hrtime_t this_time;
    if (real_gethrtime == null) {
        real_gethrtime =
            (hrtime_t (*)(void)) dlsym(RTLD_NEXT, "gethrtime");
    }
    this_time = real_gethrtime();

    mutex_lock(&lock);
    if (this_time <= last_time)
        this_time = ++last_time;
```

```
      else
            last_time = this_time;
      mutex_unlock(&lock);
      return (this_time);
}
```

Of course, this workaround does not increase the resolution of the timer, so timestamps for individual events are still relatively inaccurate. However, this technique does maintain ordering so that if event A causes event B, B never seems to happen before or at the same time as A.

dbx is available with the Sun Workshop Products.

Options

-k
Control probes in the Solaris kernel. Kernel mode defines additional commands and invalidates commands valid in other modes. See "Kernel Mode" on page 1056.

-l *libraries*
Link *libraries*, a space-separated string of library names enclosed in double quotes, into the target application, using LD_PRELOAD (see ld(1)). You cannot use this option when attaching to a running process. Specify library names, following the LD_PRELOAD rules on how libraries should be specified and where they are found.

-o *trace-file-name*
Use *trace-file-name* to trace output. *trace-file-name* is assumed to be relative to the current working directory of prex (that is, the directory that you were in when you started prex).

If prex attaches to a process that is already tracing, do not use the new *trace-file-name* (if provided). If you specify no *trace-file-name*, the default is /$TMPDIR/trace-*pid*, where *pid* is the process ID of the target program. If TMPDIR is not set, use /tmp.

-s *kbytes-size*
Set the maximum size of the output trace file in kilobytes. The default size of the trace *kbytes-size* is 4096 or 4 megabytes for normal usage and 384 or 384 kilobytes in kernel mode. You can think of the trace file as a least-recently used circular buffer. Once the file has been filled, newer events overwrite the older ones.

Usage

Grammar
Specify probes as a list of space-separated selectors. Selectors are of the form:

attribute=value

(see TNF_PROBE(3X)). The *attribute=* is optional. If you do not specify it, the defaults is keys=.

The *attribute* or *value* (generically called spec) can be any of the following.

IDENT   Any sequence of letters, digits, _, \, ., % not beginning with a digit. IDENT implies an exact match.

QUOTED_STR   Usually used to escape reserved words (any commands in the command language). QUOTED_STR implies an exact match and must be enclosed in single quotes (' ').

REGEXP   An ed(1) regular expression pattern match. Enclose REGEXP in slashes (/ /). You can include a / in a REGEXP by escaping it with a backslash \.

The following grammar explains the syntax.

```
selector_list ::=   |                       /* empty */
                    selector_list selector
selector ::=        spec=spec |             /* white space around = opt */
                    spec
spec ::=            IDENT |
                    QUOTED_STR |
                    REGEXP
```

The terminals in the above grammar are shown below.

```
IDENT =             [a-zA-Z_\.%]{[a-zA-Z0-9_\.%]}+
QUOTED_STR =        '[^\n']*'         /* any string in single quotes */
REGEXP =            /[^\n/]*/         /* a regexp has to be in / / */
```

The following list shows the remaining grammar that is needed to understand the syntax of the command language (defined in next subsection).

```
filename ::=        QUOTED_STR        /* QUOTED_STR defined above */
spec_list ::=       /* empty */ |
                    spec_list spec    /* spec defined above */
fcn_handle ::=      &IDENT            /* IDENT defined above */
set_name ::=        $IDENT            /* IDENT defined above */
```

Command Language

Set Creation and Set Listing

```
create $set_name selector_list
list    sets                        # list the defined sets
```

You can use create to define a set that contains probes that match the *selector_list*. The set $all is predefined as /.*/. It matches all the probes.

Function Listing

```
list      fcns                    # list the available fcn_handle
```

You can list the different functions that can be connected to probe points. Currently, only the &debug function is available.

Commands to Connect and Disconnect Probe Functions

```
connect &fcn_handle $set_name
connect &fcn_handle selector_list
clear $set_name
clear selector_list
```

Use the connect command to connect probe functions (which must be prefixed by &) to probes. The probes are specified either as a single set (with a $) or by explicitly listing the probe selectors in the command. The probe function has to be one that is listed by the list fcns command. This command does not enable the probes.

Use the clear command to disconnect all connected probe functions from the specified probes.

Commands to Toggle the Tracing Mode

```
trace $set_name
trace selector_list
untrace $set_name
untrace selector_list
```

Use the trace and untrace commands to toggle the tracing action of a probe point (that is, whether or not a probe emits a trace record if it is hit). This command does not enable the probes specified. Probes have tracing on by default. The most efficient way to turn off tracing is by using the disable command. untrace is useful if you want debug output but do no tracing. If so, set the state of the probe to enabled, untraced, and the debug function to connected.

Commands to Enable and Disable Probes

```
enable $set_name
enable selector_list
disable $set_name
disable selector_list
list history    # lists probe control command history
```

Use the enable and disable commands to control whether the probes perform the action for which they have been set up. To trace a probe, the probe has to be both enabled and traced (using the trace command). Probes are disabled by default. Use the list history command to list the probe control commands issued: connect, clear, trace, untrace, enable, and disable. These commands are executed whenever a new shared object is brought in to the target program by dlopen(3X). See "dlopen'ed Libraries" on page 1055 for more information.

List History

The `list` history command displays a list of the probe control commands previously issued in the tracing session, for example, `connect`, `clear`, `trace`, `disable`. Commands in the history list are executed whenever a new shared object is brought into the target program by `dlopen(3X)`.

Commands to List Probes or List Values

```
list spec_list probes $set_name        # e.g., list probes $all
list spec_list probes selector_list    # e.g., list name probes
                                       # file=test.c
list values spec_list                  # e.g., list values keys
```

The first two commands list the selected attributes and values of the specified probes. You can use them to check the state of a probe. The third command lists the various values associated with the selected attributes.

Help Command

```
help topic
```

Invoke the `help` command with no arguments to view a list of the available help topics. If a topic argument is specified, help is printed for that topic.

Source a File

```
source filename
```

You can use the `source` command to source a file of `prex` commands. `source` can be nested (that is, a file can source another file).

Process Control

```
continue        # resume the target process
quit kill       # quit prex, kill target
quit resume     # quit prex, continue target
quit suspend    # quit prex, leave target suspended
quit            # quit prex, continue or kill target
```

The default `quit` continues the target process if `prex` is attached to it. Instead, if `prex` had started the target program, `quit` kills the target process.

dlopen'ed Libraries

Probes in shared objects that are brought in by `dlopen(3X)` are automatically set up according to the command history of `prex`. When a shared object is removed by a `dlclose(3X)`, `prex` again needs to refresh its understanding of the probes in the target program. This requirement implies that there is more work to do for `dlopen(3X)` and `dlclose(3X)`, so they take slightly longer. If you are not interested in this feature and do not want to interfere with `dlopen(3X)` and `dlclose(3X)`, detach `prex` from the target to inhibit this feature.

Signals to Target Program

prex does not interfere with signals that are delivered directly to the target program. However, prex receives all signals normally generated from the terminal, for example, Control-C (SIGINT), and Control-Z (SIGSTOP), and does not forward them to the target program. To signal the target program, use the kill(1) command from a shell.

Interactions with Other Applications

Process managing applications like dbx, truss(1), and prex cannot operate on the same target program simultaneously. prex is not able to attach to a target that is being controlled by another application. You can trace and debug a program serially by the following method: first, attach prex to target (or start target through prex), set up the probes by using the command language, and then type quit suspend. You can then attach dbx to the suspended process and debug it. You can also suspend the target by sending it a SIGSTOP signal, and then by typing quit resume to prex. In this case, you should also send a SIGCONT signal after invoking dbx on the stopped process, or else dbx hangs.

Failure of Event Writing Operations

There are a few failure points, such as system call failures, that are possible when writing events to a trace file. These failures result in a failure code being set in the target process. The target process continues normally, but no trace records are written. Whenever you type Control-C to prex to get to a prex prompt, prex checks the failure code in the target and informs you if there was a tracing failure.

Target Executing a fork or exec

If the target program does a fork(2), any probes that the child encounters log events to the same trace file. Events are annotated with a process ID, so it is possible to determine which process a particular event came from. In multithreaded programs, a race condition results with a thread doing a fork while the other threads are still running. For the trace file not to be corrupted, either use fork1(2) or make sure that all other threads are quiescent when doing a fork(2),

If the target program itself (not any children it may fork) does an exec(2), prex detaches from the target and exits. You can reconnect prex with prex -p *pid*.

A vfork(2) is generally followed quickly by an exec(2) in the child and, in the interim, the child borrows the parent's process while the parent waits for the exec(2). Any events logged by the child from the parent process appear to have been logged by the parent.

Kernel Mode

Invoking prex with the -k flag runs prex in kernel mode. In kernel mode, prex controls probes in the Solaris kernel. See tnf_kernel_probes(4) for a list of available probes in the Solaris kernel. A few prex commands are unavailable in kernel mode; many other commands are valid only in kernel mode.

The -l, -o, and -p options are not valid in kernel mode (that is, you cannot combine them with the -k option).

The rest of this section describes the differences in the prex command language when prex runs in kernel mode.

prex Does Not Stop the Kernel

When prex attaches to a running user program, it stops the user program. Obviously, it cannot do so when attaching to the kernel. Instead, prex provides a tracing master switch: no probes have any effect unless the tracing master switch is on. This switch enables you to iteratively select probes to enable, then to enable them all at once by turning on the master switch.

Use the following command to inspect and set the value of the master switch.

```
ktrace [on | off]
```

Without an argument, prex reports the current state of the master switch.

Because prex does not stop or kill the kernel, the quit resume and quit kill commands are not valid in kernel mode.

No Functions Can Be Attached to Probes in the Kernel

The debug function is not available in kernel mode.

Trace Output is Written to an In-Core Buffer

In kernel mode, a trace output file is not generated directly to enable probes to be placed in time-critical code. Instead, trace output is written to an in-core buffer and copied out by a separate program, tnfxtract(1).

The in-core buffer is not automatically created. The following prex command controls buffer allocation and deallocation.

```
buffer [alloc [size] | dealloc]
```

Without an argument, the buffer command reports the size of the currently allocated buffer if any. With an argument of alloc [size], prex allocates a buffer of the given size in bytes, with an optional suffix of k or m specifying a multiplier of 1,024 or 1,048,576. If you specify no size, the size specified on the command line with the -s option is used as a default. If you do not use the -s option, the default is 384 kilobytes.

With an argument of dealloc, prex deallocates the trace buffer in the kernel.

prex rejects attempts to turn on the tracing master switch when no buffer is allocated and to deallocate the buffer when the tracing master switch is on. prex refuses to allocate a buffer when one is already allocated; use buffer dealloc first.

prex does not allocate a buffer larger than one-half of physical memory.

prex Supports Per-Process Probe Enabling in the Kernel

In kernel mode you can choose a set of processes for which probes are enabled. No trace output is written when other processes traverse these probe points.

This mode is called "process filter mode." By default, process filter mode is off, and all processes generate trace records when they hit an enabled probe.

Some kernel events such as interrupts cannot be associated with a particular user process. By convention, these events are considered to be generated by process ID 0.

prex provides commands to turn process filter mode on and off, to get the current status of the process filter mode switch, to add and delete processes (by process ID) from the process filter set, and to list the current process filter set.

The process filter set is maintained even when process filter mode is off but has no effect unless process filter mode is on.

When a process in the process filter set exits, its process ID is automatically deleted from the process filter set.

The following command controls the process filter switch and process filter set membership.

```
pfilter [on | off | add pidlist | delete pidlist]
```

With no arguments, pfilter prints the current process filter set and the state of the process filter mode switch. on or off sets the state of the process filter mode switch.

```
add pidlist
delete pidlist
```

add or delete processes from the process filter set. pidlist is a comma-separated list of one or more process IDs.

Examples

See tracing(3X) for complete examples showing, among other things, the use of prex for simple probe control.

When either the process or kernel is started, all probes are disabled.

```
# Set creation and set listing
create $out name=/out/    # $out = probes with "out" in
                          #    value of "name" attribute
create $foo /page/ name=biodone   # $foo = union of
       # probes with "page" in value of keys attribute
       # probes with "biodone" as value of "name" attribute
list sets                 # list the defined sets
list fcns                 # list the defined probe fcns

# Commands to trace and connect probe functions

trace foobar='on'         # exact match on foobar attribute
trace $all                # trace all probes (predefined set $all)
connect &debug $foo       # connect debug func to probes in $foo

# Commands to enable and disable probes

enable  $all              # enable all probes
enable /vm/ name=alloc    # enable the specified probes
```

```
disable $foo              # disable probes in set $foo
list history              # list probe control commands issued

# Process control

continue                  # resumes the target process
^C                        # stop target; give control to prex
quit resume               # exit prex, leave process running

# Kernel mode

buffer alloc 2m           # allocate a 2-megabyte buffer
enable $all               # enable all probes
trace $all                # trace all probes
ktrace on                 # turn tracing on
ktrace off                # turn tracing off
pfilter on                # turn process filter mode on
pfilter add 1379          # add pid 1379 to process filter
ktrace on                 # turn tracing on
                          # (only pid 1379 will be traced)
```

Files

.prexrc   Local prex initialization file.

~/.prexrc   User's prex initialization file.

/proc/*nnnnn* Process files.

Attributes

See attributes(5) for descriptions of the following attributes:

Attribute Type	Attribute Value
Availability	SUNWtnfs (32-bit)
	SUNWtnfcs (64-bit)

See Also

ed(1), kill(1), ksh(1), ld(1), tnfdump(1), tnfxtract(1), truss(1),
exec(2), fork(2), fork1(2), vfork(2), dlclose(3X), dlopen(3X),
gethrtime(3C), libtnfctl(3X), TNF_DECLARE_RECORD(3X), TNF_PROBE(3X),
tnf_process_disable(3X), tracing(3X), tnf_kernel_probes(4),
attributes(5)

Bugs

prex should issue a notification when a process ID has been automatically
deleted from the filter set.

A known bug in prex can result in the following message:

```
Tracing shut down in target program due to an internal
error - Please restart prex and target
```

When you run `prex` as root, the target process is not root and you put the tracefile in a directory where it cannot be removed and recreated (such as a directory like /tmp with the sticky bit on), then the target process is not able to open the tracefile when it needs to, thus disabling tracing.

Changing any of the circumstances listed above should fix the problem. Either don't run `prex` as root, run the target process as root, or specify the tracefile in a directory other than /tmp.

print — Shell Built-in Function to Output Characters to the Screen or Window

Synopsis

ksh
```
print [-Rnprsu[n]] [arg...]
```

Description

Korn Shell

The `print` built-in function is the mechanism used by the Korn shell to display *arg*. With no options or with - or --, the arguments are printed on standard output as described by echo(1). The exit status is 0, unless the output file is not open for writing.

Options

-n	Suppress newline from being added to the output.
-R | -r	Ignore the escape conventions of echo. The -R option prints all subsequent arguments and options other than -n.
-p	Write the arguments onto the pipe of the process spawned with |& instead of to standard output.
-s	Write the arguments into the history file instead of to standard output.
-u [n]	Use the *n* argument to specify a one-digit file descriptor unit number on which the output is placed. The default is 1.

Attributes

See attributes(5) for descriptions of the following attributes:

Attribute Type	Attribute Value
Availability	SUNWcsu

See Also

echo(1), ksh(1), attributes(5)

---

printenv — Display Current Environment Variable

Synopsis

/usr/ucb/printenv [*variable*]

Description

Use the printenv command to print the values of the variables in the environment. If a variable is specified, only its value is printed.

Examples

The following example displays the value for the EDITOR environment variable.

```
castle% printenv EDITOR
/usr/dt/bin/dtpad
castle%
```

Attributes

See attributes(5) for descriptions of the following attributes:

Attribute Type	Attribute Value
Availability	SUNWscpu

See Also

csh(1), echo(1), sh(1), stty(1), tset(1B), attributes(5), environ(5)

Diagnostics

If a variable is specified and it is not defined in the environment, printenv returns an exit status of 1.

---

printf — Write Formatted Output

Synopsis

/usr/bin/printf *format* [*argument*...]

Description

The `printf` command writes formatted operands to the standard output. The *argument* operands are formatted under control of the *format* operand.

Operands

format   A string describing the format used to write the remaining operands. Use the *format* operand as the format string described on the `formats`(5) manual page, with the following exceptions.

- In any context other than a flag of a conversion specification, treat a space character in the format string as an ordinary character that is copied to the output.

- Treat a delta character in the format string as a delta character, not as a space character.

- In addition to the escape sequences described on the `formats`(5) manual page (\\, \a, \b, \f, \n, \r, \t, \v), write *ddd*, where *ddd* is a one-, two- or three-digit octal number, as a byte with the numeric value specified by the octal number.

- Do not precede or follow output from the d or u conversion specifications with blank characters not specified by the *format* operand.

- Do not precede output from the o conversion specification with 0s not specified by the *format* operand.

- An additional conversion character, b, is supported as follows. Take the argument to be a string that can contain backslash-escape sequences. The following backslash-escape sequences are supported.

  - Convert the escape sequences listed on the `formats`(5) manual page (\\, \a, \b, \f, \n, \r, \t, \v) to the characters they represent.

  - Convert \0*ddd*, where *ddd* is a zero-, one-, two-, or three-digit octal number to a byte with the numeric value specified by the octal number.

  - Write \c and ignore any remaining characters in the string operand containing it, any remaining string operands, and any additional characters in the format operand.

The interpretation of a backslash followed by any other sequence of characters is unspecified.

Write bytes from the converted string until reaching the end of the string or the number of bytes indicated by the precision specification. If the precision is omitted, take it to be infinite, so write all bytes up to the end of the converted string. For each specification that consumes an argument, evaluate the next argument operand and convert it to the appropriate type for the conversion, as specified below. Reuse the format operand as often as needed to satisfy the argument operands. Evaluate any extra c or s conversion specifications as if a null string argument were supplied; evaluate other extra conversion specifications as if a 0 argument were supplied. If the format operand contains no conversion specifications and argument operands are present, the results are unspecified. If a character sequence in the format operand begins with a % character but does not form a valid conversion specification, the behavior is unspecified.

argument   Specify the strings to be written to standard output under the control of *format*. Treat the argument operands as strings if the corresponding conversion character is b, c, or s; otherwise, evaluate it as a C constant, as described by the ISO C standard, with the following extensions:

- Allow a leading + or – sign.

- If the leading character is a single or double quote, the value is the numeric value in the underlying codeset of the character following the single or double quote.

If an *argument* operand cannot be completely converted into an internal value appropriate to the corresponding conversion specification, write a diagnostic message to standard error, do not exit with a 0 exit status, continue processing any remaining operands, and write to standard output the value accumulated at the time the error was detected.

Usage

Note that the printf command, like the printf(3S) function on which it is based, makes no special provision for dealing with multibyte characters when using the %c conversion specification or when a precision is specified in a %b or %s conversion specification. Application programmers should be extremely cautious about using either of these features when there are multibyte characters in the character set.

You cannot specify field widths and precisions as *.

For compatibility with previous versions of SunOS 5.x, the $ format specifier is supported for formats containing only %s specifiers.

The %b conversion specification is not part of the ISO C standard; it has been added here as a portable way to process backslash escapes expanded in string operands as provided by the echo command. See also the echo(1) manual page for ways to use printf as a replacement for all of the traditional versions of the echo command.

If an argument cannot be parsed correctly for the corresponding conversion specification, the printf command reports an error. Thus, overflow and extraneous characters at the end of an argument being used for a numeric conversion are reported as errors.

It is not considered an error if an *argument* operand is not completely used for a c or s conversion or if a string operand's first or second character is used to get the numeric value of a character.

Examples

The following example alerts the user and then prints and reads a series of prompts.

```
printf "\aPlease fill in the following: \nName: "
read name
printf "Phone number: "
read phone
```

The following example read a list of right and wrong answers from a file, calculates the percentages correctly, and prints them out. The numbers are right-justified and separated by a single Tab character. The percentage is written to one decimal place of accuracy.

```
while read right wrong ; do
  percent=$(echo "scale=1;($right*100)/($right+$wrong)" | bc)
  printf "%2d right\t%2d wrong\t(%s%%)\n" \
     $right $wrong $percent
done < database_file
```

The command

```
printf "%5d%4d\n" 1 21 321 4321 54321
```

produces

```
   1  21
3214321
54321   0
```

Note that the format operand is used three times to print all of the given strings and that a 0 was supplied by printf to satisfy the last %4d conversion specification.

The printf command tells the user when conversion errors are detected while producing numeric output; thus, the following results would be expected on an implementation with 32-bit twos-complement integers when %d is specified as the format operand.

Standard Argument	Output	Diagnostic Output
5a	5	printf: 5a not completely converted
9999999999	2147483647	printf: 9999999999: Results too large
-9999999999	-2147483648	printf: -9999999999: Results too large

Standard Argument	Output	Diagnostic Output
ABC	0	printf: ABC expected numeric value

Note that the value shown on standard output is what would be expected as the return value from the function strtol(3C). A similar correspondence exists between %u and strtoul(3C), and %e, %f, %g and strtod(3C).

In a locale using the ISO/IEC 646:1991 standard as the underlying codeset, the command

```
printf "%d\n" 3 +3 -3 \'3 \"+3 "'-3"
```

produces:

3	Numeric value of constant 3.
3	Numeric value of constant 3.
-3	Numeric value of constant -3.
51	Numeric value of the character 3 in the ISO/IEC 646:1991 standard codeset.
43	Numeric value of the character + in the ISO/IEC 646:1991 standard codeset.
45	Numeric value of the character - in the SO/IEC 646:1991 standard codeset.

Note — In a locale with multibyte characters, the value of a character is intended to be the value of the equivalent of the wchar_t representation of the character.

If an *argument* operand cannot be completely converted into an internal value appropriate to the corresponding conversion specification, a diagnostic message is written to standard error and the command returns a 0 exit status, continues processing any remaining operands, and writes the value accumulated at the time the error was detected to standard output.

Environment Variables

See environ(5) for descriptions of the following environment variables that affect the execution of printf: LC_COLLATE, LC_CTYPE, LC_MESSAGES, LC_TIME, TZ, and NLSPATH.

Exit Status

0	Successful completion.
>0	An error occurred.

Attributes

See attributes(5) for descriptions of the following attributes:

Attribute Type	Attribute Value
Availability	SUNWloc
CSI	Enabled

See Also

awk(1), bc(1), echo(1), strtod(3C), strtol(3C), strtoul(3C), printf(3S), attributes(5), environ(5), formats(5)

priocntl — Display or Set Scheduling Parameters of Specified Process(es)

Synopsis

```
/usr/bin/priocntl -l
/usr/bin/priocntl -d [-i idtype][idlist]
/usr/bin/priocntl -s [-c class][class-specific options]
   [-i idtype][idlist]
/usr/bin/priocntl -e [-c class][class-specific options] command
   [argument(s)]
```

Description

Use the priocntl (priority control) command to assign processes to a priority class and to manage process priorities within a class. You can also use priocntl to display the current configuration information for the system process scheduler or to execute a command with specified scheduling parameters.

Processes fall into distinct classes with a separate scheduling policy applied to each class. The process classes currently supported are:

- Real-time.
- Timesharing.
- Interactive.

The characteristics of these classes and the class-specific options they accept are described below. With appropriate permissions, the priocntl command can change the class and other scheduling parameters associated with a running process.

The class-specific parameters to be set are specified by the class-specific options, as explained under the appropriate heading below. If you omit the -c class option, idtype and idlist must specify a set of processes that are all in the same class; otherwise, an error results. If you specify no class-specific options, the class-specific parameters of the process are set to the default values for the class specified by -c *class* (or to the default parameter values for the process's current class if you also omit the -c *class* option).

For the scheduling parameters of a process to be changed with priocntl, the real or effective user ID or group ID) of the user invoking priocntl must match the real or effective user ID or group ID of the receiving process; otherwise, the effective user ID must be superuser. These are the minimum permission requirements enforced for all classes. An individual class can impose additional permissions requirements when setting processes to that class or when setting class-specific scheduling parameters.

When *idtype* and *idlist* specify a set of processes, priocntl acts on the processes in the set in an implementation-specific order. If priocntl encounters an error for one or more of the target processes, it may or may not continue through the set of processes, depending on the nature of the error.

If the error is related to permissions, priocntl prints an error message and then continues through the process set, resetting the parameters for all target processes for which the user has appropriate permissions. If priocntl encounters an error other than permissions, it does not continue through the process set but prints an error message and exits immediately.

Real-Time Class

The real-time class provides a fixed-priority, preemptive scheduling policy for those processes requiring fast and deterministic response and absolute user/application control of scheduling priorities. If the real-time class is configured in the system, it should have exclusive control of the highest range of scheduling priorities on the system. This control ensures that a runnable real-time process is given CPU service before any process belonging to any other class.

The real-time class has a range of real-time priority (*rtpri*) values that can be assigned to processes within the class. Real-time priorities range from 0 to *x*, where the value of *x* is configurable and can be displayed for a specific installation that has already configured a real-time scheduler, with the following command.

```
castle% priocntl -l
CONFIGURED CLASSES
==================

SYS (System Class)

TS (Time Sharing)
        Configured TS User Priority Range: -60 through 60

IA (Interactive)
        Configured IA User Priority Range: -60 through 60
castle%
```

The real-time scheduling policy is a fixed-priority policy. The scheduling priority of a real-time process never changes except as the result of an explicit request by the user/application to change the `rtpri` value of the process.

For processes in the real-time class, the `rtpri` value is, for all practical purposes, equivalent to the scheduling priority of the process. The `rtpri` value completely determines the scheduling priority of a real-time process relative to other processes within its class. Numerically higher `rtpri` values represent higher priorities. Because the real-time class controls the highest range of scheduling priorities in the system, it is guaranteed that the runnable real-time process with the highest `rtpri` value is always selected to run before any other process in the system.

In addition to controlling priority, `priocntl` can control the length of the time quantum allotted to processes in the real-time class. The time quantum value specifies the maximum amount of time a process can run, assuming that it does not complete or enter a resource or event wait state (sleep). Note that if another process becomes runnable at a higher priority, the currently running process can be preempted before receiving its full time quantum.

The following command displays the real-time priority and time quantum (in millisecond resolution) for each real-time process in the set specified by `idtype` and `idlist`.

```
priocntl -d [-i idtype] [idlist]
```

You can use any combination of the -p and -t options with `priocntl -s` or `priocntl -e` for the real-time class. If you omit an option and the process is currently real-time, the associated parameter is unaffected. If you omit an option when changing the class of a process to real-time from some other class, the associated parameter is set to a default value. The default value for `rtpri` is 0, and the default for the time quantum is dependent on the value of `rtpri` and on the system configuration; see `rt_dptbl(4)`.

When using the -t `tqntm` option, you can optionally specify a resolution using the -r `res` option. (If you specify no resolution, millisecond resolution is assumed.) If you specify `res`, it must be a positive integer between 1 and 1,000,000,000 inclusive and the resolution used is the reciprocal of `res` in seconds. For example, specifying -t 10 -r 100 sets the resolution to hundredths of a second and the resulting time-quantum length to one-tenth of a second (10/100). Although you can specify very fine (nanosecond) resolution, the time-quantum length is rounded up by the system to the next integral multiple of the system clock's resolution. Requests for time quanta of 0 or quanta greater than the (typically very large) implementation-specific maximum quantum result in an error.

To change the class of a process to real-time (from any other class), you must have superuser privileges. To change the `rtpri` value or time quantum of a real-time process, you must either be superuser or must currently be in the real-time class (shell running as a real-time process) with a real or effective user ID matching the real or effective user ID of the target process.

The real-time priority and time quantum are inherited across the fork(2) and exec(2) system calls.

Timesharing Class

The timesharing scheduling policy provides for a fair and effective allocation of the CPU resource among processes with varying CPU consumption characteristics. The objectives of the timesharing policy are to provide good response time to interactive processes and good throughput to CPU-bound jobs while providing a degree of user or application control over scheduling.

The timesharing class has a range of timesharing user priority (*tsupri*) values that can be assigned to processes within the class. User priorities range from $-x$ to $+x$, where the value of x is configurable. You can display the range for a specific installation with the priocntl -l command.

The user priority provides some degree of user or application control over the scheduling of processes in the timesharing class. Raising or lowering the *tsupri* value of a process in the timesharing class raises or lowers the scheduling priority of the process. However, it is not guaranteed that a timesharing process with a higher *tsupri* value runs before one with a lower *tsupri* value, because the *tsupri* value is just one factor used to determine the scheduling priority of a timesharing process. The system can dynamically adjust the internal scheduling priority of a timesharing process based on other factors such as recent CPU usage.

In addition to the systemwide limits on user priority (displayed with priocntl -l), a per process user priority limit (*tsuprilim*) specifies the maximum *tsupri* value that can be set for a given process.

The priocntl -d [-i *idtype*] [*idlist*] command displays the user priority and user priority limit for each timesharing process in the set specified by *idtype* and *idlist*.

Any timesharing process can lower its own *tsuprilim* (or that of another process with the same user ID). Only a timesharing process with superuser privilege can raise a *tsuprilim*. When changing the class of a process to timesharing from some other class, superuser privilege is required to set the initial *tsuprilim* to a value greater than 0.

Any timesharing process can set its own *tsupri* (or that of another process with the same user ID) to any value less than or equal to the process's *tsuprilim*. Attempts to set the *tsupri* above the *tsuprilim* (and/or set the *tsuprilim* below the *tsupri*) set the *tsupri* equal to the *tsuprilim*.

You can use any combination of the -m and -p options with priocntl -s or priocntl -e for the timesharing class. If you omit an option and the process is currently timesharing, the associated parameter is normally unaffected. The exception is when you omit the -p option and use -m to set a *tsuprilim* below the current *tsupri*. In this case, the *tsupri* is set equal to the *tsuprilim* that is being set. If you omit an option when changing the class of a process to timesharing from some other class, the associated parameter is set to a default value. The default value for *tsuprilim* is 0, and the default for *tsupri* is to be set equal to the *tsuprilim* value that is being set.

The timesharing user priority and user priority limit are inherited across the fork(2) and exec(2) system calls.

Interactive Class

The interactive scheduling policy provides for a fair and effective allocation of the CPU resource among processes with varying CPU consumption characteristics while providing good responsiveness for user interaction. The objectives of the interactive policy are to provide good response time to interactive processes and good throughput to CPU-bound jobs. You can change the priorities of processes in the interactive class in the same way as those in the timesharing class, although the modified priorities continue to be adjusted to provide good responsiveness for user interaction.

In the default configuration, a runnable real-time process runs before any other process. Therefore, inappropriate use of real-time processes can have a dramatic negative impact on system performance.

If an *idlist* is present, it must appear last on the command line and the elements of the list must be separated by white space. If no *idlist* is present an *idtype* argument of pid, ppid, pgid, sid, class, uid, or gid specifies the process ID, parent process ID, process group ID, session ID, class, user ID, or group ID of the priocntl command itself.

The following command displays the class and class-specific scheduling parameters of the process(es) specified by *idtype* and *idlist*.

```
priocntl -d [-i idtype] [idlist]
```

The following example uses the -d option with no arguments.

```
castle% priocntl -d
INTERACTIVE CLASS PROCESSES:
    PID    IAUPRILIM    IAUPRI    IAMODE
    422        0           0         1
castle%
```

The following command sets the class and class-specific parameters of the specified processes to the values given on the command line.

```
# priocntl -s [-c class] [class-specific options] [-i idtype] [idlist]
```

The -c class option specifies the class to be set. (The valid class arguments are RT for real-time, TS for timesharing, or IA for interactive.)

sys Scheduling Class

A special sys scheduling class exists to schedule the execution of certain special system processes (such as the swapper process). It is not possible to change the class of any process in the sys class. In addition, priocntl disregards any processes in the sys class that are included in the set of processes specified by *idtype* and *idlist*.

For example, if *idtype* were uid, an *idlist* consisting of a 0 would specify all processes with a UID of 0 except processes in the sys class and (if changing the parameters with the -s option) the init process.

The init process (process ID 1) is a special case. For the priocntl command to change the class or other scheduling parameters of the init process, *idtype* must be pid and *idlist* must consist of only a 1. The init process can be assigned to any class configured on the system, but the timesharing class is almost always the appropriate choice. (Other choices can be highly undesirable; see the *System Administration Guide* for more information.)

The following command executes the specified command with the class and scheduling parameters specified on the command line (*argument* is the arguments to the command).

```
priocntl -e [-c class][class-specific options] command [argument...]
```

If you omit the -c *class* option, the command is run in the user's current class.

Options

-c *class*	Specify the *class* to be set. (The valid class arguments are RT for real-time, TS for timesharing, or IA for interactive.) If the specified class is not already configured, configure it automatically.
-d	Display the scheduling parameters associated with a set of processes.
-e	Execute a specified command with the class and scheduling parameters associated with a set of processes.
-i *idtype*	Specify (together with the *idlist* arguments if any) one or more processes to which the priocntl command is to apply. The interpretation of *idlist* depends on the value of *idtype*. The valid *idtype* arguments and corresponding interpretations of *idlist* are as follows.

	-i pid	A list of process IDs. The priocntl command applies to the specified processes.
	-i ppid	A list of parent process IDs. The priocntl command applies to all processes whose parent process ID is in the list.
	-i pgid	A list of process group IDs. The priocntl command applies to all processes in the specified process groups.
	-i sid	A list of session IDs. The priocntl command applies to all processes in the specified sessions.

`-i class`	A single class name (RT for real-time, TS for timesharing, or IA for interactive). The `priocntl` command applies to all processes in the specified class.
`-i uid`	A list of user IDs. The `priocntl` command applies to all processes with an effective user ID equal to an ID from the list.
`-i gid`	A list of group IDs. The `priocntl` command applies to all processes with an effective group ID equal to an ID from the list.
`-i all`	All existing processes. No `idlist` should be specified (if one is, ignore it). The permission restrictions described below still apply.

If you omit the `-i` `idtype` option when using the `-d` or `-s` options, assume the default `idtype` of `pid`.

`-l`	Display a list of the classes currently configured in the system along with class-specific information about each class.
`-s`	Set the scheduling parameters associated with a set of processes.

The valid class-specific options for setting real-time parameters are:

`-p rtpri`	Set the real-time priority of the specified process(es) to `rtpri`.
`-t tqntm [-r res]`	
	Set the time quantum of the specified process(es) to `tqntm`. You can optionally specify a resolution as explained below.

The valid class-specific options for setting timesharing parameters are:

`-m tsuprilim`	
	Set the user priority limit of the specified process(es) to `tsuprilim`.
`-p tsupri`	Set the user priority of the specified process(es) to `tsupri`.

The valid class-specific options for setting interactive parameters are:

New!

`-m iauprilim`	
	Set the user priority limit of the specified process(es) to `iauprilim`.

New!

`-p iaupri`	
	Set the user priority of the specified process(es) to `iaupri`.

Examples

The following real-time class example sets the class of any non-real-time processes selected by `idtype` and `idlist` to real-time and sets their real-time priority to the default value of 0.

```
castle% priocntl -s -c RT -t 1 -r 10 -i idtype idlist
```

The real-time priorities of any processes currently in the real-time class are unaffected. The time quanta of all of the specified processes are set to 1/10 second.

The following example executes *command* in the real-time class with a real-time priority of 15 and a time quantum of 20 milliseconds.

```
castle% priocntl -e -c RT -p 15 -t 20 command
```

The following timesharing class example sets the class of any non-timesharing processes selected by *idtype* and *idlist* to timesharing and sets both their user priority limit and user priority to 0. Processes already in the timesharing class are unaffected.

```
castle% priocntl -s -c TS -i idtype idlist
```

The following example executes *command* with the *arguments* arguments in the timesharing class with a user priority limit of 0 and a user priority of -15.

```
castle% priocntl -e -c TS -m 0 -p -15 command [arguments]
```

Exit Status

New!

The following exit values are returned for the -d, -l, and -s options.

0	Successful operation.
1	Error condition.

The following exit values are returned for the -e option.

Exit status of executed command.

0	Successful operation.
1	Command could not be executed at the specified priority.

Attributes

See attributes(5) for descriptions of the following attributes:

Attribute Type	Attribute Value
Availability	SUNWcsu
CSI	Enabled

See Also

nice(1),ps(1),exec(2),fork(2),priocntl(2),rt_dptbl(4),attributes(5)
System Administration Guide, Volume I

New!

Diagnostics

`Process(es) not found`

> None of the specified processes exist.

`Specified processes from different classes`

> The -s option is being used to set parameters, the -c *class* option is not present, and processes from more than one class are specified.

`Invalid option or argument`

> An unrecognized or invalid option or option argument is used.

---

proc, pflags, pcred, pmap, pldd, psig, pstack, pfiles, pwdx, pstop, prun, pwait, ptree, ptime — Proc Tools

Synopsis

New!
```
/usr/proc/bin/pflags [-r] pid...
/usr/proc/bin/pcred pid...
```
New!
```
/usr/proc/bin/pmap [-rxlF] pid...
```
New!
```
/usr/proc/bin/pldd [-F] pid...
/usr/proc/bin/psig pid...
```
New!
```
/usr/proc/bin/pstack [-F] pid...
```
New!
```
/usr/proc/bin/pfiles [-F] pid...
/usr/proc/bin/pwdx [-F] pid...
/usr/proc/bin/pstop pid...
/usr/proc/bin/prun pid...
/usr/proc/bin/pwait [-v] pid...
/usr/proc/bin/ptree [-a][[pid|user]...]
/usr/proc/bin/ptime command [arg...]
```

Description

The `proc` tools are commands that exercise features of /proc (see proc(4)). Most of them take a list of process IDs (*pid*); those that do also accept /proc/*nnn* as a process ID, so you can use the shell expansion /proc/* to specify all processes in the system.

pflags	Print the /proc tracing flags, the pending and held signals, and other /proc status information for each lightweight process (lwp) in each process.
pcred	Print the credentials (effective, real, and saved UIDs and GIDs) of each process.
pmap	Print the address space map of each process.

pldd	List the dynamic libraries linked into each process, including shared objects explicitly attached by means of dlopen(3X). See also ldd(1).
psig	List the signal actions of each process. See signal(5).
pstack	Print a hex+symbolic stack trace for each lwp in each process.
pfiles	Report fstat(2) and fcntl(2) information for all open files in each process.
pwdx	Print the current working directory of each process.
pstop	Stop each process (PR_REQUESTED stop).
prun	Set each process running (inverse of pstop).
pwait	Wait for all of the specified processes to terminate.
ptree	Print the process trees containing the specified *pid*s or *user*s, with child processes indented from their respective parent processes. Take an argument of all digits to be a process ID; otherwise, assume it is a user login name. Default is all processes.
ptime	Time a command, such as the time(1) command, but using microstate accounting for reproducible precision.

The pfiles, pldd, pmap, pstack, and pwdx commands stop their target *New!*
processes while inspecting them and reporting the results. While a process is
stopped, it can do nothing. For example, if you are inspecting the X server with
one of these proc tools running in a window under the X server's control, the
whole window system can become deadlocked because the proc tool would try
to print its results to a window that cannot be refreshed. To clear the deadlock
in this case, log in from another system by using rlogin(1) and kill the
offending proc tool.

Exercise caution when using the -F option. Imposing two controlling *New!*
processes on one victim process can lead to chaos. Safety is assured only if the
primary controlling process, typically a debugger, has stopped the victim
process and the primary controlling process is doing nothing at the moment of
applying the specific proc tool.

Options

-a	(ptree only) Include children of process 0.	*New!*
-F	Force a grab of the target process even if another process has control.	*New!*
-l	(pmap only) Print unresolved dynamic linker map names.	
-r	(pflags only) If the process is stopped, display its machine registers.	*New!*
-r	(pmap only) Print the process's reserved addresses.	
-v	(pwait only) Report each termination to standard output.	
-x	(pmap only) Print resident/shared/private mapping details.	*New!*

Exit Status

0   Success.

non-zero An error has occurred.

Files

/proc/* Process files.

/usr/proc/lib/*

     proc tools supporting files.

Attributes

See attributes(5) for descriptions of the following attributes:

Attribute Type	Attribute Value
Availability	SUNWesu (32-bit) SUNWesxu (64-bit)

See Also

ldd(1), ps(1), pwd(1), rlogin(1), time(1), truss(1), wait(1), fcntl(2), fstat(2), dlopen(3X), proc(4), attributes(5), signal(5)

---

prof — Display Profile Data

Synopsis

/usr/ccs/bin/prof [-ChsVz] [-a | c | n | t] [-o | x] [-g | l]
 [-m *mdata*] [*prog*]

Description

The prof command interprets a profile file produced by the monitor function. The symbol table in the object file prog (a.out by default) is read and correlated with a profile file (mon.out by default). For each external text symbol, the percentage of time spent executing between the address of that symbol and the address of the next is printed, together with the number of times that function was called and the average number of milliseconds per call.

Notes

The times reported in successive identical runs can vary because of varying cache-hit ratios that result from sharing the cache with other processes. Even if a program seems to be the only one using the system, hidden background or asynchronous processes can blur the data. In rare cases, the clock ticks initiating recording of the program counter may cycle with loops in a program, grossly distorting measurements. Call counts are always recorded precisely, however.

Only programs that call `exit` or `return` from `main` are guaranteed to produce a profile file unless a final call to `monitor` is explicitly coded.

The times for static functions are attributed to the preceding external text symbol if you do not use the `-g` option. However, the call counts for the preceding function are still correct; that is, the static function call counts are not added to the call counts of the external function.

If you specify more than one of the options `-t`, `-c`, `-a`, and `-n`, the last option specified is used and you are warned.

`LD_LIBRARY_PATH` must not contain `/usr/lib` as a component when compiling a program for profiling. If `LD_LIBRARY_PATH` does contain `/usr/lib`, the program is not linked correctly with the profiling versions of the system libraries in `/usr/lib/libp`. See `gprof(1)`.

Functions such as `mcount()`, `_mcount()`, `moncontrol()`, `_moncontrol()`, `monitor()`, and `_monitor()` can appear in the `prof` report. These functions are part of the profiling implementation and, thus, account for some amount of the runtime overhead. Because these functions are not present in an unprofiled application, time accumulated and call counts for these functions can be ignored when the performance of an application is evaluated.

64-bit Profiling

You can use 64-bit profiling freely with dynamically linked executables, and profiling information is collected for the share objects if the objects are compiled for profiling. Apply care in interpreting the profile output because it is possible for symbols from different shared objects to have the same name. If you see duplicate names in the profile output, it is better to use the `-s` (summary) option to prefix a module ID before each symbol that is duplicated. You can then map the symbols to the appropriate modules by looking at the module's information in the summary.

If you use the `-a` option with a dynamically linked executable, sorting is done on a per-shared-object basis. Because there is a high likelihood of symbols from different shared objects having the same value, this sorting results in an output that is more understandable. If you use the `-s` option, a blank line separates the symbols from different shared objects.

32-bit Profiling

You can use 32-bit profiling with dynamically linked executables, but you must be careful. In 32-bit profiling, you cannot use `prof` to profile shared objects. Thus, when you execute a profiled, dynamically linked program, only the `main` portion of the image is sampled. All time spent outside of the `main` object—time spent in a shared object—is not included in the profile summary. Consequently, the total time reported for the program can be less than the total time used by the program.

Because the time spent in a shared object cannot be accounted for, minimize the use of shared objects whenever you use `prof` to profile a program. You can link the program to the profiled version of a library (or to the standard archive version if no profiling version is available) instead of the shared object to get profile information on the functions of a library. Versions of profiled libraries can be supplied with the system in the `/usr/lib/libp` directory. Refer to compiler driver documentation on profiling.

Consider an extreme case. A profiled program dynamically linked with the shared C library spends 100 units of time in some `libc` routine, say, `malloc()`. Suppose `malloc()` is called only from routine B and B consumes only 1 unit of time. Suppose further that routine A consumes 10 units of time, more than any other routine in the `main` (profiled) portion of the image. In this case, `prof` concludes that most of the time is being spent in A and almost no time is being spent in B. From this, it is almost impossible to tell that the greatest improvement can be made by looking at routine B and not routine A. The value of the profiler in this case is severely degraded; the solution is to use archives as much as possible for profiling.

Options

The mutually exclusive options -a, -c, -n, and -t determine the type of sorting of the output lines.

-a	Sort by increasing symbol address.
-c	Sort by decreasing number of calls.
-n	Sort lexically by symbol name.
-t	Sort by decreasing percentage of total time (default).

The mutually exclusive options -o and -x specify the printing of the address of each symbol monitored.

-o	Print each symbol address (in octal) along with the symbol name.
-x	Print each symbol address (in hexadecimal) along with the symbol name.

The mutually exclusive options -g and -l control the type of symbols to be reported. Use the -l option with care; it applies the time spent in a static function to the preceding (in memory) global function instead of giving the static function a separate entry in the report. If all static functions are properly located, this feature can be very useful. If not, the resulting report can be misleading.

Assume that A and B are global functions and only A calls static function S. If S is located immediately after A in the source code (that is, if S is properly located), then, with the -l option, the amount of time spent in A can easily be determined, including the time spent in S. If, however, both A and B call S, then, if you use the -l option, the report is misleading; the time spent during

B's call to S is attributed to A, making it seem as if more time had been spent in A than really had been. In this case, function S cannot be properly located.

-g	List the time spent in static (nonglobal) functions separately. The -g option function is the opposite of the -l function.
-l	Suppress printing statically declared functions. Allocate time spent executing in a static function to the closest global function loaded before the static function in the executable. This option is the default. It is the opposite of the -g function and should be used with care.

The following options can be used in any combination.

-C	Demangle C++ symbol names before printing them.
-h	Suppress the heading normally printed on the report. This option is useful if the report is to be processed further.
-m *mdata*	Use file *mdata* instead of mon.out as the input profile file.
-s	Print a summary of several of the monitoring parameters and statistics on the standard error output.
-V	Print prof version information on the standard error output.
-z	Include all symbols in the profile range, even if associated with 0 number of calls and 0 time.

A program creates a profile file if it has been link edited with the -p option of cc(1B). This option to the cc(1B) command arranges for calls to monitor at the beginning and end of execution. The call to monitor at the end of execution writes a profile file. The number of calls to a function is tallied if you use the -p option when compiling the file containing the function.

A single function can be split into subfunctions for profiling by means of the MARK macro. See prof(5).

Environment Variables

PROFDIR	Specify the name of the file created by a profiled program. If PROFDIR is not set, produce mon.out in the directory current when the program terminates. If PROFDIR=*string*, *string/pid.progname* is produced, where *progname* consists of argv[0] with any path prefix removed and *pid* is the process ID of the program. If PROFDIR is set but null, produce no profiling output.

Files

mon.out	Default profile file.
a.out	Default name list (object) file.

Attributes

See `attributes(5)` for descriptions of the following attributes:

Attribute Type	Attribute Value
Availability	SUNWbtool

See Also

New!

`gprof(1)`, `cc(1B)`, `exit(2)`, `profil(2)`, `psample(2)`, `malloc(3C)`, `monitor(3C)`, `malloc(3X)`, `attributes(5)`, `prof(5)`
Programming Utilities Guide

---

prs, sccs-prs — Display Selected Portions of an SSCS History

Synopsis

`/usr/ccs/bin/prs[-ael] [-cdate-time] [-ddataspec] [-rsid]s.filename...`

Description

See `sccs-prs(1)`.

---

prt, sccs-prt — Display Delta Table Information from an SCCS File

Synopsis

`/usr/ccs/bin/prt [-abdefistu] [-cdate-time] [-rdate-time] [-ysid] s.filename...`

Description

See `sccs-prt(1)`.

---

prun — Proc Tools

Synopsis

`/usr/proc/bin/prun pid...`

Description

See `proc(1)`.

ps — Report Process Status

Synopsis

```
/usr/bin/ps [-aAcdefjlLPy][-g grplist][-n namelist [[-o format]...]
    [-p proclist][-s sidlist][-t term][-u uidlist][-U uidlist]
    [-G gidlist]
```

Description

Use the ps command to determine process status and get detailed information about an individual process, such as:

- PID (process ID).
- UID (user ID).
- Priority.
- Control terminal.
- Memory use.
- CPU time.
- Current status.

The ps command takes a snapshot of system activity at the time you type the command. Some data printed for defunct processes is irrelevant. If you are monitoring system activity by time, be aware that the results are already slightly out-of-date by the time you read them.

When you type the ps command without options, ps prints information about processes associated with the controlling terminal. The output contains only the PID, terminal identifier, cumulative execution time, and the command name. The other information that you can access by using the ps command is controlled with the options.

If you use no options to select processes, ps reports all processes associated with the controlling terminal. If there is no controlling terminal, only the headers are printed.

Options

The most frequently used options for the ps command are listed below.

-a	List information about all processes most frequently requested: all those except process group leaders and processes not associated with a terminal.
-e	Report information about all processes now running.
-f	Show the owner of the process, by name instead of by UID, in the first column. This option turns off -1, -t, -s, and -r and turns on -a.
-1	Generate a long report that includes all fields except STIME.

Additional options for the ps command are listed below. Some options accept lists as arguments. You can separate items in a list either by using commas or by enclosing the entire argument in quotes and separating the items with commas or spaces. Many of the options are used to select processes to list. If you specify any processes, the default list is ignored and the ps command chooses the processes represented by the inclusive OR of all the selection-criteria options. Note that the *proclist* and *grplist* options require numeric values.

-A	List information for all processes. Identical to -e.
-c	Print information in a format that reflects scheduler properties as described in priocntl(1). The -c option affects the output of the -f and -l options.
-d	List information about all processes except session leaders.
-g *grplist*	List only process data whose group leader's ID number(s) appears in *grplist*. (A group leader is a process whose process ID number is identical to its process group ID number.)
-G *gidlist*	List information for processes whose real group ID numbers are given in *gidlist*. The *gidlist* must be a single argument in the form of a blank or comma-separated list.
-j	Print session ID and process group ID.
-L	Print information about each lightweight process (lwp) in each selected process.
-n *namelist*	Specify the name of an alternative system *namelist* file in place of the default. This option is accepted for compatibility but is ignored.
-o *format*	Print information according to the format specification given in *format*. This option is described fully in "Creating Custom Reports" on page 1086. You can specify multiple -o options; interpret the format specification as the space-character-separated concatenation of all the *format* arguments.
-p *proclist*	List only process data whose process ID numbers are given in *proclist*.
-P	Print the number of the processor to which the process or lwp is bound, if any, under an additional column header, PSR.
-s *sidlist*	List information on all session leaders whose IDs appear in *sidlist*.
-t *term*	List only process data associated with *term*. You specify terminal identifiers as a device file name, and an identifier. For example, term/a or pts/0.
-u *uidlist*	List only process data whose effective user ID number or login name is given in *uidlist*. Print the numerical user ID unless you specify the -f option to print the login name.

-U *uidlist*   List information for processes whose real user ID numbers or login names are given in *uidlist*. Specify *uidlist* as a single argument in the form of a blank- or comma-separated list.

-y   Under a long listing (-1), omit the obsolete F and ADDR columns and include an RSS column to report the resident set size of the process. Report both RSS and SZ in units of kilobytes instead of pages.

Note — ps -if or ps -o *stime* may report an earlier time when a gutty was last respawned on the tty line instead of the actual start of a TTY login session.

Command Report Formats

The ps -e command displays a report that looks like the following.

```
castle% ps -e
   PID TTY        TIME CMD
     0 ?          0:01 sched
     1 ?          0:00 init
     2 ?          0:00 pageout
     3 ?          0:20 fsflush
   242 ?          0:01 vold
   186 ?          0:00 nscd
   302 ?          0:00 sac
   113 ?          0:00 rpcbind
   103 ?          0:00 in.route
   140 ?          0:00 inetd
   115 ?          0:00 keyserv
   162 ?          0:00 automoun
   145 ?          0:00 statd
   147 ?          0:00 lockd
   305 ?          0:00 listen
   166 ?          0:01 syslogd
   180 ?          0:00 cron
   196 ?          0:00 lpsched
   217 ?          0:00 sendmail
   205 ?          0:02 lp
   307 ?          0:14 Xsun
   214 ?          0:00 powerd
... (More information not shown here)
```

The columns are described below.

PID   Process identification number.

TTY   The terminal from which the process (or its parent) started. If the process has no controlling terminal, this column contains a question mark (?). Processes with question marks usually are system processes.

TIME   The cumulative amount of CPU time used by the process.

COMD   The name of the command that generated the process. Note that, for the ps -e command, only the first eight characters of the file name are displayed.

   When you type ps -el and press Return, you get a listing that looks like the following example.

```
castle% ps -el
  F S   UID   PID  PPID  C PRI NI     ADDR    SZ    WCHAN TTY    TIME CMD
 19 T     0     0     0  0   0 SY f0274e38     0            ?    0:01 sched
  8 S     0     1     0  0  41 20 f5b2d888     4 f5b2da80 ?    0:00 init
 19 S     0     2     0  0   0 SY f5b2d1c8     0 f02886a4 ?     :00 pageout
 19 S     0     3     0  1   0 SY f5b2cb08     0 f028aeb4 ?    0:21 fsflush
  8 S     0   242     1  0  59 20 f5b2b6c8   515 f5d387de ?      01 vold
  8 S     0   186     1  0  46 20 f5b2c448   480 f5b2c640 ?     :00 nscd
  8 S     0   302     1  0  41 20 f5b2bd88   350 f5a81c78 ?    0:00 sac
  8 S     0   113     1  0  41 20 f5b2b008   445 f5d38f36 ?    0:00 rpcbind
  8 S     0   103     1  0  41 20 f5d2d890   340 f5d38f86 ?    0:00 in.route
  8 S     0   140     1  0  54 20 f5d2d1d0   446 f5d38e6e ?    0:00 inetd
  8 S     0   115     1  0  57 20 f5d2cb10   461 f5d38ebe ?    0:00 keyserv
  8 S     0   162     1  0  41 20 f5d2c450   560    3e39c ?    0:00 automoun
  8 S     0   145     1  0  47 20 f5d2bd90   501 f5d38e96 ?    0:00 statd
  8 S     0   147     1  0  65 20 f5d2b6d0   409 f5d38df6 ?    0:00 lockd
  8 S     0   305   302  0  41 20 f5d2b010   352 f597e0ce ?    0:00 listen
  8 S     0   166     1  0  46 20 f5e18898   702 f5d38c66 ?    0:01 syslogd
  8 S     0   180     1  0  51 20 f5e181d8   358 f5a81eb8 ?    0:00 cron
  8 S     0   196     1  0  67 20 f5e17b18   652 f5d38a5e ?    0:00 lpsched
  8 S     0   217     1  0  41 20 f5e17458   448 f5d38a0e ?    0:00 sendmail
  8 S     0   205     1  0  41 20 f5e16d98   462 f5e16f90 ?    0:02 lp
  8 S  1001   307   293  2  41 20 f5e166d8   343 f5d38586 ?    0:17 Xsun
  8 S     0   214     1  0  58 20 f5e16018   215 f5e16210 ?    0:00 powerd
  8 S     0   227     1  0  41 20 f5e808a0   214 f5d38a36 ?    0:00 utmpd
  8 S     0   232     1  0  40 20 f5e801e0   483 f5d3896e ?    0:00 hpnpd
  8 S     1   250     1  0  66 20 f5e7fb20  1429 f5e7fb90 ?    0:00 dwhttpd
  8 S     0   310     1  0  40 20 f5e7f460   471 f5d38496 ?    0:00 fbconsol
  8 S     1   251   250  0  41 20 f5e7eda0  1551 f5d38806 ?    0:01 dwhttpd
```
(*More information not shown here*)

   The fields in a ps -el long listing report are described below.

F   Hexadecimal flags which, added together, indicate the process's current state. These flags are available for historical purposes only.

S   The current state of the process, as shown by one of the following letters:

       O   Currently running on the processor.

       S   Sleeping; waiting for an I/O event to complete.

       R   Ready to run.

       I   Idle; process is being created.

       Z   Zombie. The process has terminated and the parent is not waiting, but the dead process is still in the process table.

       T   Stopped because parent is tracing the process.

X	Waiting for more memory.
UID	The user ID of the owner of the process.
PID	The process ID number.
PPID	The parent process ID number.
C	The CPU use (that is, an estimate of the percentage of CPU time used by the process).
CLS	Scheduling class. Printed only when you use the -c option.
PRI	The scheduling priority. Higher numbers mean lower priority.
NI	The nice number, which contributes to the scheduling priority of the process. Making a process nicer means lowering its priority so it does not use as much CPU time.
ADDR	The memory address of the process.
SZ	The amount of virtual memory required by the process. This number indicates how much demand the process puts on system memory.
WCHAN	The address of an event for which the process is sleeping. If this column is blank, the process is running.
TTY	The terminal from which the process (or its parent) started or a question mark to indicate there is no controlling terminal (which usually indicates a system process).
TIME	The total amount of CPU time used by the process since it began.
COMD	The command that generated the process.

The fields in a ps -f report are listed below.

UID	The user ID of the owner of the process.
PID	The process ID number.
PPID	The parent process ID number.
C	The CPU use (that is, an estimate of the percentage of CPU time used by the process).
STIME	The starting time of the process in hours, minutes, and seconds. A process that began more than 24 hours before the ps command is executed is shown in months and days.
TTY	The terminal from which the process (or its parent) started or a question mark to indicate there is no controlling terminal (which usually indicates a system process).
TIME	The total amount of CPU time used by the process since it began.
CMD	The command that generated the process.

When you specify the -j option, the following two additional columns are printed.

PGID	The process ID of the process group leader.

SID   The process ID of the session leader.

When you specify the -L option, the following two additional columns are printed.

LWP   The lwp ID of the lightweight process being reported.

NLWP   The number of lwps in the process if you also specify the -f option.

When you use the -L option, one line is printed for each lwp in the process and the STIME and TIME fields show the values for the lwp, not for the process. A traditional single-threaded process contains only one lwp.

A process that has exited and has a parent but has not yet been waited for by the parent is marked <defunct>.

Creating Custom Reports

You can use the -o option to create your own custom reports that display only columns of information that are of interest to you. You specify the format by providing a list of the columns you want to view as a single argument. The names must be either a comma-separated list or a quoted list separated by spaces or by commas, as shown in the following examples.

```
castle% ps -o "user pcpu nice args"
    USER %CPU NI COMMAND
  winsor  0.0 20 /bin/csh
castle% ps -o user,pcpu,nice,args
    USER %CPU NI COMMAND
  winsor  0.0 20 /bin/csh
castle%
```

Each variable has a default header. You can overwrite the default header by appending an equal sign and the new text of the header as part of the argument to the -o option.

The report writes the fields in the order specified on the command line and arranges the output in columns. The width of the fields is chosen by the system to be at least as wide as the header text. If the header text is null (as specified by -o user=), the field is at least as wide as the default header text. If all header text fields are null, no header line is displayed.

The -o option has both a set of POSIX and Solaris format names. You can use names from either name set and combine them in the same argument. The following example shows the output for the Solaris environment.

```
castle% ps -o user,pid,ppid=MOM -o args
   USER  PID  MOM COMMAND
  winsor  413  401 /bin/csh
castle%
```

The following table shows an alphabetical list of the names recognized in the POSIX locale along with the default header.

Name	Default Header	Description
args	COMMAND	The command with all its arguments as a string. Applications cannot depend on being able to modify their argument list and having that modification be reflected in the output of the ps command. The Solaris implementation limits the string to 80 bytes; the string is the version of the argument list as it was passed to the command when it started.
comm	COMMAND	The name of the command being executed (argv[0] value) as a string.
etime	ELAPSED	The elapsed time since the process was started, in the form [[dd-]hh:]mm.ss where dd is the number of days, hh is the number of hours, mm is the number of minutes, and ss is the number of seconds.
group	GROUP	The effective group ID of the process displayed as text if it can be obtained and if the field width permits. Otherwise, the decimal GID value is displayed.
nice	NI	The decimal value of the system scheduling priority of the process. See nice(1).
pcpu	%CPU	The ratio of CPU time used recently to CPU time available in the same period expressed as a percentage. The meaning of "recently" in this context is not specified. The CPU time available is determined in an unspecified manner.
pgid	PGID	The decimal value of the process group ID.
pid	PID	The decimal value of the process ID.
ppid	PPID	The decimal value of the parent process ID.
rgroup	RGROUP	The real group ID of the process displayed as text if it can be obtained and the field width permits. Otherwise, the decimal value is displayed.
ruser	RUSER	The real user ID of the process displayed as text if it can be obtained and the field width permits. Otherwise, the decimal value is displayed.
time	TIME	The cumulative CPU time of the process, in the form [dd-]hh:mm:ss.
TTY	TT	The name of the controlling terminal of the process (if any) in the same format used by the who(1) command.

Name	Default Header	Description
user	USER	The effective user ID of the process displayed as text if it can be obtained and the field width permits. Otherwise, the decimal value is displayed.
vsz	VSZ	The total size of the process in virtual memory, in kilobytes.

The following table shows an alphabetical list of the names recognized by the Solaris implementation along with the default header.

Name	Default Header	Description
addr	ADDR	The memory address of the process.
c	C	Processor use for scheduling (obsolete).
class	CLS	The scheduling class of the process.
f	F	Flags (hexadecimal and additive) associated with the process.
fname	COMMAND	The first eight bytes of the basename of the process's executable file.
gid	GID	The effective group ID number of the process as a decimal integer.
lwp	LWP	The decimal value of the lwp ID. This option prints one line for each lightweight process.
nlwp	NLWP	The number of lwps in the process.
opri	PRI	The obsolete priority of the process. Lower numbers mean higher priority.
osz	SZ	The total size of the process in virtual memory, in pages.
pmem	%MEM	The ratio of the resident set size of the process to the physical memory on the machine, expressed as a percentage.
pri	PRI	The priority of the process. Higher numbers mean higher priority.
psr	PSR	The number of the processor to which the process or lwp is bound.
rgid	RGID	The real group ID number of the process as a decimal integer.
rss	RSS	The resident set size of the process in kilobytes.
ruid	RUID	The real user ID number of the process as a decimal integer.
s	S	The state of the process.
sid	SID	The process ID of the session leader.

Name	Default Header	Description
stime	STIME	The starting time or date of the process, printed with no blanks.
uid	UID	The effective user ID number of the process as a decimal integer.
wchan	WCHAN	The address of an event for which the process is sleeping. If the process is running, - is displayed.

Using the ps Report

When you need to check on which processes or daemons are running, use the ps -e option. If you need more detailed information about a process, use the ps -el options. With experience, you will learn how the report should look and how to judge what is out of the ordinary.

Use the following guidelines to spot potential problems.

- Look for many identical jobs owned by the same user. This condition can result from someone running a script that starts a lot of background jobs without waiting for any of the jobs to terminate. Talk to the user to find out if that is the case. If necessary, use the kill command to terminate some of the processes. See kill(1) for more information on killing a process.

- Look at the TIME field for processes that have accumulated a large amount of CPU time. Such processes might be in an endless loop.

- Look at the C field to find unimportant processes that consume a large percentage of CPU time. If you do not think a process warrants so much attention, use the priocntl command to lower its priority. See the priocntl(1) manual page for more information.

- Look at the SZ field for processes that consume too large a percentage of memory. If a process is a memory hog, kill the process. If many processes are using lots of memory, the system may need more memory.

- Watch for a runaway process that progressively uses more and more CPU time. You can check this condition by using the -f option to see the start time (STIME) of the process and by watching the TIME field for the accumulation of CPU time.

Environment Variables

See environ(5) for descriptions of the following environment variables that affect the execution of ps: LC_CTYPE, LC_MESSAGES, LC_TIME, and NLSPATH. COLUMNS can override the system-selected horizontal screen size used to determine the number of text columns to display.

Exit Status

0	Successful completion.
>0	An error occurred.

Files

/dev/pts/* Terminal (TTY) names searcher files.

/dev/term/*

Terminal (TTY) names searcher files.

/etc/passwd

UID information supplier.

/proc*   Process control files.

/tmp/ps_data

Internal data structure.

Attributes

See attributes(5) for descriptions of the following attributes:

Attribute Type	Attribute Value
Availability	SUNWcsu
CSI	Enabled

Note — ps is CSI enabled except for login names (user names).

See Also

kill(1), nice(1), pagesize(1), priocntl(1), who(1), getty(1M), proc(4), ttysrch(4), attributes(5), environ(5)

psig, pstack, pstop, ptime, ptree — Proc Tools

Synopsis

```
/usr/proc/bin/psig pid...
/usr/proc/bin/pstack pid...
/usr/proc/bin/pstop pid...
/usr/proc/bin/ptree [[pid|user]...]
/usr/proc/bin/ptime command [arg...]
```

Description

See proc(1).

pushd — Change Working Directory

Synopsis

csh
```
pushd [+n | dir]
```

Description

See cd(1).

pvs — Display the Internal Information of Dynamic Objects

Synopsis

```
/usr/bin/pvs [-dlnorsv][-N name] file...
```

Description

Use the pvs command to display any internal version information contained in an executable and linking format (ELF) object file. Commonly, ELF files are dynamic executables, shared objects, and possibly relocatable objects. This version information can fall into one of two categories.

- Version definitions describe the interfaces made available by an ELF file. Each version definition is associated with a set of global symbols provided by the file. Version definitions can be assigned to a file during its creation by the link editor, using the -M option and the associated mapfile directives (see the *Linker and Libraries Guide* for more details).

- Version dependencies describe the binding requirements of dynamic objects on the version definitions of any shared object dependencies. When a dynamic object is built with a shared object, the link editor records information within the dynamic object, indicating that the shared object is a dependency. This dependency must be satisfied at runtime. If the shared object also contains version definitions, then those version definitions that satisfy the global symbol requirements of the dynamic object are also recorded in the dynamic object being created. At process initialization, the runtime linker uses any version dependencies as a means of validating the interface requirements of the dynamic objects used to construct the process.

Options

If you specify neither the -d nor -r option, both are enabled.

-d	Print version definition information.
-l	When used with the -s option, print any symbols that have been reduced from global to local binding because of versioning. By convention, these symbol entries are located in the .symtab section and fall between the FILE symbol representing the output file and the FILE symbol representing the first input file used to generate the output file.
	These reduced symbol entries are assigned the fabricated version definition _REDUCED_. No reduced symbols are printed if the file has been stripped (see strip(1)) or if the symbol entry convention cannot be determined.
-n	Normalize version definition information. By default, display all version definitions within the object. However, version definitions can inherit other version definitions and, under normalization, only the head of each inheritance list is displayed.
-o	Create one-line version definition output. By default, file, version definitions, and any symbol output are indented to ease human inspection. This option prefixes each output line with the file and version definition name and may be more useful for analysis with automated tools.
-r	Print version dependency (requirements) information.
-s	Print the symbols associated with each version definition. Accompany any data symbols with the size, in bytes, of the data item.
-v	Show any weak version definitions and any version definition inheritance. When used with the -N and -d options, also show the inheritance of the base version definition. When used with the -s option, also show the version symbol definition.
N name	Print only the information for the given version definition name and any of its inherited version definitions (when used with the -d option) or for the given dependency file name (when used with the -r option).

Operands

file	The ELF file about which internal version information is displayed.

Examples

The following example displays the version definitions of libelf.so.1.

```
castle% pvs -d /usr/lib/libelf.so.1
        libelf.so.1;
```

```
        SUNW_1.2;
        SUNW_1.1;
        SUNW_0.7;
        SUNWprivate_1.1;
castle%
```

The following example uses the -n and -o options to produce a normalized, one-line display suitable for creating a mapfile version-control directive.

```
castle% pvs -don /usr/lib/libelf.so.1
/usr/lib/libelf.so.1 -  SUNW_1.2; /usr/lib/libelf.so.1 -
   SUNWprivate_1.1;
castle%
```

The following example displays the version requirements of ldd and pvs.

```
castle% pvs -r /usr/bin/ldd /usr/bin/pvs
/usr/bin/ldd:
        libelf.so.1 (SUNW_1.2);
        libc.so.1 (SUNW_1.1);
/usr/bin/pvs:
        libelf.so.1 (SUNW_1.2);
        libc.so.1 (SUNW_1.1);
castle%
```

Exit Status

If the requested version information is not found, a non-zero value is returned; otherwise, a 0 value is returned.

Version information is not found when any of the following is true:

- You specify the -d option, and no version definitions are found.
- You specify the -r option, and no version requirements are found.
- You specify neither the -d nor -r option, and no version definitions or version requirements are found.

Attributes

See attributes(5) for descriptions of the following attributes:

Attribute Type	Attribute Value
Availability	SUNWtoo

See Also

ld(1), ldd(1), strip(1), elf(3E), attributes(5)
Linker and Libraries Guide

---

pwait — Proc Tools

Synopsis
```
/usr/proc/bin/pwait [-v] pid...
```

Description
See proc(1).

---

pwd — Return Working Directory Name

Synopsis
```
/usr/bin/pwd
```

Description
Use the pwd (print working directory) command to display the absolute path name of the current working directory to standard output.

Both the Bourne shell, sh(1), and the Korn shell, ksh(1), also have a built-in pwd command.

> **Note** — If you move the current directory or one above it, pwd may not give the correct response. Use the cd(1) command with a full path name to correct this situation.

Example
The following example displays the current directory, changes to another directory, and displays the new current directory.
```
castle% pwd
/export/home/winsor
castle% cd /etc
castle% pwd
/etc
castle%
```

Environment Variables
See environ(5) for descriptions of the following environment variables that affect the execution of pwd: LC_MESSAGES and NLSPATH.

Exit Status

0	Successful completion.
>0	An error occurred.

If an error is detected, output is not written to standard output, a diagnostic message is written to standard error, and the exit status is not 0.

Attributes

See attributes(5) for descriptions of the following attributes:

Attribute Type	Attribute Value
Availability	SUNWcsu
CSI	Enabled

See Also

cd(1), ksh(1), sh(1), shell_builtins(1), attributes(5), environ(5)

Diagnostics

Cannot open... and Read error in... indicate possible file-system trouble. Consult a UNIX system administrator if you see one of these error messages.

pwxd — Proc Tools

Synopsis

/usr/proc/bin/pwdx *pid*...

Description

See proc(1).

R

---

ranlib — Convert Archives to Random Libraries

Synopsis
```
/usr/ccs/bin/ranlib archive
```

Description

> **Note** — The `ranlib` command was used in SunOS 4.x to add a
> table of contents to archive libraries. It converted each archive to a
> form that could be linked more rapidly. This command is no longer
> needed because the `ar(1)` command automatically provides all the
> functionality of `ranlib`.

This command is provided as a convenience for software developers who
need to maintain makefiles that are portable across a variety of operating
systems.

Exit Status
`ranlib` has exit status 0.

Attributes

See `attributes`(5) for descriptions of the following attributes:

Attribute Type	**Attribute Value**
Availability	SUNWbtool

See Also

`ar(1)`, `ar(4)`, `attributes(5)`

rcp — Remote File Copy

Synopsis

```
/usr/bin/rcp [-p] filename1 filename2
/usr/bin/rcp [-pr] filename... directory
```

Description

Use the `rcp` command to copy files between systems. Each file name or directory argument is either a local file name (containing no colon (`:`) or backslash (`\`) characters) or a remote file name of the following form.

`hostname:path`

If a file name is not a full path name, it is interpreted relative to your home directory on `hostname`. You can quote a path on a remote host by using `\`, `"`, or `'`, so that the metacharacters are interpreted remotely.

`rcp` does not prompt for passwords; your current local user name must exist on `hostname` and allow remote command execution by `rsh(1)`.

`rcp` handles third-party copies where neither source nor target files are on the current system. Host names can also take the following form with `username` as the user name on the remote host instead of your current local user name.

`username@hostname:filename`

`rcp` also supports Internet domain addressing of the remote host, so that the following form specifies the `username`, the `hostname`, and the `domain` in which that host resides.

`username@host.domain:filename`

File names that are not full path names are interpreted relative to the home directory of the user named `username` on the remote host.

Notes

rcp is designed to copy between different hosts; trying to remotely copy a file onto itself, as with the following command, results in a severely corrupted file.

```
rcp tmp/file myhost:/tmp/file
```

rcp may not fail correctly when the target of a copy is a file instead of a directory.

rcp can become confused by output generated by commands in a $HOME/.profile on the remote host.

rcp requires that the source host have permission to execute commands on the remote host when doing third-party copies.

rcp does not properly handle symbolic links. Use tar (see tar(1)) or cpio (see cpio(1)) piped to rsh to obtain remote copies of directories containing symbolic links or named pipes.

If you forget to quote metacharacters intended for the remote host, you get an incomprehensible error message.

rcp fails if you copy access control lists (ACLs) to a file system that does not support them.

Options

-p	Try to give each copy the same modification times, access times, modes, and access control lists (ACLs) as the original file if applicable.
-r	Copy each subtree rooted at *filename*; the destination must be a directory.

Usage

See largefile(5) for the description of the behavior of rcp when encountering files greater than or equal to 2 Gbytes (2**31 bytes).

Files

$HOME/.profile

Attributes

See attributes(5) for descriptions of the following attributes:

Attribute Type	Attribute Value
Availability	SUNWcsu
CSI	Enabled

Note — rcp is CSI enabled except for the handling of *username*,
hostname, and *domain*.

See Also

cpio(1), ftp(1), rlogin(1), rsh(1), setacl(1), tar(1), hosts.equiv(4),
attributes(5), largefile(5)

---

rdist — Remote File Distribution Program

Synopsis

/usr/bin/rdist[-b] [-D] [-h] [-i] [-n] [-q] [-R] [-v] [-w] [-y] [-d *macro=value*]
    [-f *distfile*] [-m *host*]...
/usr/bin/rdist[-b] [-D] [-h] [-i] [-n] [-q] [-R] [-v] [-w] [-y] -c*pathname*...
    [*login*@] *hostname* [:*destpath*]

Description

Use the rdist (remote distribution) command to maintain copies of files on
multiple hosts. It preserves the owner, group, mode, and modification time of
the master copies and can update programs that are executing.

Note — rdist does not propagate ownership or mode changes
when the file contents have not changed.

Normally, a copy on a remote host is updated if its size or modification time
differs from the original on the local host. rdist reads the indicated *distfile*
for instructions on updating files and/or directories. If *distfile* is -, the
standard input is used. If you do not specify the -f option, rdist first looks in
its working directory for *distfile*, and then for Distfile, for instructions.
    For rdist to be used across systems, each host system must have a
/etc/host.equiv file, or the user must have an entry in the .rhosts file in
the home directory. See hosts.equiv(4) for more information.

Options

-b   Perform a binary comparison and update files if they differ instead
                of merely comparing dates and sizes.

-c *pathname*... [*login*@]*hostname*[:*destpath*]

                Update each path name on the named host. (Take relative file
                names as relative to your home directory.) If you specify the
                login@ prefix, perform the update with the user ID of *login*. If
                you specify the :*destpath*, install the remote file, using that path
                name.

-d *macro=value*

> Define *macro* to have *value*. Use this option to define or override macro definitions in the *distfile*. *value* can be the empty string, one name, or a list of names surrounded by parentheses and separated by white space.

-D

> Enable debugging.

-f *distfile*

> Use the description file *distfile*. A dash (-) as the *distfile* argument denotes the standard input.

-h

> Follow symbolic links. Copy the file that the link points to instead of the link itself.

-i

> Ignore unresolved links. rdist normally tries to maintain the link structure of files being transferred and warns you if all the links cannot be found.

-m *host*

> Limit which systems are to be updated. You can specify multiple -m arguments to limit updates to a subset of the hosts listed in the *distfile*.

-n

> Print the commands without executing them. This option is useful for debugging a *distfile*.

-q

> Do not display the files being updated on the standard output.

-R

> Remove extraneous files. If a directory is being updated, remove files on the remote host that do not correspond to those in the master (local) directory. This option is useful for maintaining truly identical copies of directories.

-v

> Verify that the files are up-to-date on all the hosts. Display any files that are out-of-date, update no files, and send no mail.

-w

> Append the whole file name to the destination directory name. Normally, only the last component of a name is used when files are renamed. This option preserves the directory structure of the files being copied instead of flattening it. For instance, renaming a list of files such as dir1/dir2 to dir3 would create files dir3/dir1 and dir3/dir2 instead of dir3 and dir3. When you use the -w option with a file name that begins with ~, append everything except the home directory to the destination name.

-y

> Do not update remote copies that are younger than the master copy, but issue a warning message instead.

Usage

White-Space Characters

Newline, Tab, and space characters are all treated as white space; a mapping continues across input lines until the start of the next mapping: either a single file name followed by a -> or the opening parenthesis of a file-name list.

Comments

Comments begin with # and end with a newline.

Macros

`rdist` has a limited macro facility. Macros are expanded only in *filename* or *hostname* lists and in the argument lists of certain primitives. Macros cannot be used to stand for primitives or their options, or the -> or : : symbols.

A macro definition is a line of the following form.

macro = value

A macro reference is a string of the following form,

$ {macro}

although (as with make(1S)) you can omit the braces if the macro name consists of just one character.

Metacharacters

The shell metacharacters [,], {, }, *, and ? are recognized and expanded (on the local host only) just as they are with csh(1). You can escape metacharacters by preceding them with a backslash.

The ~ character is also expanded in the same way as with csh; however, it is expanded separately on the local and destination hosts.

File Names

File names that do not begin with / or ~ are taken to be relative to user's home directory on each destination host; they are not relative to the current working directory. Enclose multiple file names within parentheses.

Primitives

You can use the following primitives to specify actions `rdist` is to take when updating remote copies of each file.

`install  [-b] [-h] [-i] [-R] [-v] [-w] [-y] [newname]`

> Copy out-of-date files and directories recursively. If you use no *newname* operand, give the name of the local file to the copy on the remote host. If absent from the remote host, create parent directories in the path of the file name. To help prevent disasters, do not replace a nonempty directory on a target host with a regular file or a symbolic link. However, when using the -R option, remove a nonempty directory if the corresponding file name is completely absent on the master host.

The options for `install` have the same semantics as their command-line counterparts but are limited in scope to a particular map. The login name used on the destination host is the same as the local host unless the destination name is of the format *login*@host. In that case, perform the update under the *username* login.

notify *address*...

Send mail to the indicated TCP/IP address of the form:

user@host

listing the files updated and any errors that may have occurred. If an address does not contain an @*host* suffix, use the name of the destination host to complete the address.

except *filename*...

Omit from updates the files named as arguments.

except_pat *pattern*...

Omit from updates the file names that match each regular-expression pattern (see ed(1) for more information on regular expressions). Note that you must escape \ and $ characters in the *distfile*. You can also use shell variables within a pattern; however, shell file-name expansion is not supported.

special [*filename*]... "*command-line*"

Specify a Bourne shell, sh(1), command line to execute on the remote host after each named file is updated. If you provide no *filename* argument, the command line is performed for every updated file, with the shell variable FILE set to the name of the file on the local host.

The quotation marks enable *command-line* to span input lines in the *distfile*; separate multiple shell commands by semicolons (;).

The default working directory for the shell executing each command line is the user's home directory on the remote host.

Examples

The following sample *distfile* instructs rdist to maintain identical copies of a shared library, a shared-library initialized data file, several include files, and a directory, on hosts named hermes and magus. On magus, commands are executed as superuser. rdist notifies merlin@druid whenever it discovers that a local file has changed relative to a timestamp file.

```
HOSTS = ( hermes root@magus )
FILES = ( /usr/local/lib/libcant.so.1.1
    /usrlocal/lib/libcant.sa.1.1 /usr/local/include/{*.h}
    /usr/local/bin )
```

```
(${FILES}) -> (${HOSTS})
    install -R ;
${FILES} :: /usr/local/lib/timestamp
    notify merlin@druid ;
```

Files

~/.rhosts   User's trusted hosts and users.

/etc/host.equiv

System trusted hosts and users.

/tmp/rdist*

Temporary file for update lists.

Attributes

See attributes(5) for descriptions of the following attributes:

Attribute Type	Attribute Value
Availability	SUNWcsu

See Also

csh(1), ed(1), sh(1), make(1S), stat(2), hosts.equiv(4), attributes(5)

Diagnostics

A complaint about mismatch of rdist version numbers can really stem from some problem with starting your shell, for example, you are in too many groups.

Warnings

The superuser does not have the accustomed access privileges on NFS-mounted file systems. Using rdist to copy to such a file system may fail or the copies may be owned by user nobody.

Bugs

Source files must reside on or be mounted on the local host.

There is no easy way to have a special command executed only once after all files in a directory have been updated.

Variable expansion works only for name lists; there should be a general macro facility.

rdist aborts on files that have a negative modification time (before Jan. 1, 1970).

There should be a "force" option to enable replacement of nonempty directories by regular files or symbolic links. A means of updating file modes and owners of otherwise identical files is also needed.

read — Read a Line from Standard Input

Synopsis

```
/usr/bin/read [-r] var...
```

sh
```
read name...
```

csh
```
set variable = $<
```

ksh
```
read [-prsu[n]] [name?prompt] [name...]
```

Description

/usr/bin/read

The read command reads a single line from standard input.

By default, unless you specify the -r option, backslash (\) acts as an escape character. If standard input is a terminal device and the invoking shell is interactive, read prompts for a continuation line in the following cases:

- When the shell reads an input line ending with a backslash, unless you specify the -r option.

- When a here-document is not terminated after a newline character is entered.

The line is split into fields as in the shell; the first field is assigned to the first variable *var*, the second field to the second variable *var*, and so forth. If you specify fewer *var* operands than there are fields, the leftover fields and their intervening separators are assigned to the last *var*. If you specify fewer fields than *var*s, the remaining *var*s are set to empty strings.

The setting of variables specified by the *var* operands affect the current shell execution environment. If read is called in a subshell or separate command execution environment, such as one of the following, read does not affect the shell variables in the caller's environment.

```
(read foo)
        nohup read...
        find . -exec read... \;
```

The standard input must be a text file.

Bourne Shell

One line is read from the standard input and, using the IFS internal field separator (normally space or Tab) to delimit word boundaries, the first word is assigned to the first *name*, the second word to the second *name*, and so forth, with leftover words assigned to the last *name*. Lines can be continued using

\newline. You can quote characters other than newline by preceding them with a backslash. These backslashes are removed before words are assigned to names, and no interpretation is done on the character that follows the backslash. The return code is 0 unless an end-of-file is encountered.

C Shell

The following notation loads one line of standard input as the value for a variable. (See *csh*(1)).

```
set variable = $<
```

Korn Shell

One line is read and is broken up into fields, using the characters in IFS as separators. The escape character (\) is used to remove any special meaning for the next character and for line continuation. In -r raw mode, the \ character is not treated specially. The first field is assigned to the first *name*, the second field to the second *name*, and so forth, with leftover fields assigned to the last *name*. The -p option takes the input line from the input pipe of a process spawned by the shell, using |&. If you specify the -s option, the input is saved as a command in the history file. You can use the -u option to specify a one-digit file descriptor unit *n* to read from. The file descriptor can be opened with the exec special command. The default value of *n* is 0. If you omit *name*, then REPLY is used as the default name. The exit status is 0 unless the input file is not open for reading or an end-of-file is encountered. An end-of-file with the -p option cleans up for this process so that another can be spawned. If the first argument contains a ?, the remainder of this word is used as a prompt on standard error when the shell is interactive. The exit status is 0 unless an end-of-file is encountered.

Options

-p	Read from the output of a |& process.
-r	Do not treat a backslash character in any special way. Consider each backslash to be part of the input line.
-s	Save input as command in the history file.
-u[*n*]	Read input from file descriptor *n* (default is 0).

Operands

var	The name of an existing or nonexisting shell variable.

Examples

The following example for /usr/bin/read prints a file with the first field of each line moved to the end of the line.

```
while read -r xx yy
do
  printf "%s %s\n" "$yy" "$xx"
done < input_file
```

Environment Variables

See environ(5) for descriptions of the following environment variables that affect the execution of read: LC_CTYPE, LC_MESSAGES, and NLSPATH.

IFS   Determine the internal field separators used to delimit fields.

PS2   Provide the prompt string that an interactive shell writes to standard error when a line ending with a backslash is read and you did not specify the -r option or if a here-document is not terminated after you enter a newline character.

Exit Status

0   Successful completion.

>0   End-of-file was detected or an error occurred.

Attributes

See attributes(5) for descriptions of the following attributes:

Attribute Type	Attribute Value
Availability	SUNWcsu

See Also

csh(1), ksh(1), line(1), set(1), sh(1), attributes(5), environ(5)

readonly — Shell Built-in Function to Protect the Value of the Given Variable from Reassignment

Synopsis

sh
readonly [*name*...]

ksh
```
**
readonly [*name*[=*value*]]...
```

Description

Bourne Shell
The names you specify are marked `readonly`, and the values of the names cannot be changed by subsequent assignment. If you specify no arguments, a list of all `readonly` names is printed.

Korn Shell
The given names are marked `readonly` and cannot be changed by subsequent assignment.

For the `readonly` command, `ksh(1)` commands that are preceded by one or two asterisks (`*`) are treated specially in the following ways.

- Variable assignment lists preceding the command remain in effect when the command completes.
- I/O redirections are processed after variable assignments.
- Errors abort a script that contains them.
- Words following a command preceded by `**` that are in the format of a variable assignment are expanded with the same rules as a variable assignment. This means that tilde substitution is performed after the equal sign and word splitting and file-name generation are not performed.

Attributes

See `attributes(5)` for descriptions of the following attributes:

Attribute Type	Attribute Value
Availability	SUNWcsu

See Also
`ksh(1)`, `sh(1)`, `typeset(1)`, `attributes(5)`

---

red — Text Editor

Synopsis
`/usr/bin/red [-s|-] [-p string] [-x] [-C] [file]`

Description
See ed(1).

refer — Expand and Insert References from a Bibliographic Database

Synopsis

```
/usr/bin/refer[-ben][-ar][-cstring][-kx][-lm,n][-pfilename][-skeys]
    filename...
```

Description

The `refer` command is a preprocessor for `nroff`(1) or `troff`(1) that finds and formats references. The input files (by default, the standard input) are copied to the standard output, except for lines between `.[` and `.]` command lines. Such lines are assumed to contain keywords, as for `lookbib`(1), and are replaced by information from a bibliographic data base. You can avoid the search, override fields from it, or add new fields. The reference data, from whatever source, is assigned to a set of `troff` strings. Macro packages such as `ms`(5) print the finished reference text from these strings. A flag is placed in the text at the point of reference. By default, the references are indicated by numbers.

When you use `refer` with `eqn`(1), `neqn`, or `tbl`(1), use `refer` first in the sequence, to minimize the volume of data passed through pipes.

Options

`-ar`	Reverse the first `r` author names (Jones, J. A. instead of J. A. Jones). If you omit `r`, reverse all author names.
`-b`	Do not put any flags in text (neither numbers nor labels).
`-cstring`	Capitalize (with SMALL CAPS) the fields whose key letters are in *string*.
`-e`	Accumulate references instead of leaving the references where encountered until a sequence of the following form is encountered.

```
.[
$LIST$
.]
```

Then, write out all references collected so far. Collapse references to the same source.

`-kx`	Instead of numbering references, use labels as specified in a reference data line beginning with the characters %x; By default, x is L.
`-lm,n`	Instead of numbering references, use labels from the senior author's last name and the year of publication. Use only the first m letters of the last name and the last n digits of the date. If you omit either m or n, use the entire name or date.
`-n`	Do not search the default file.

-p *filename*   Take the next argument as a file of references to be searched. Search the default file last.

-s*keys*   Sort references by fields whose key letters are in the *keys* string and permute reference numbers in the text accordingly. Using this option also uses the -e option. You can follow the key letters in *keys* with a number indicating how many such fields are used. Use a + sign to indicate a very large number. The default is AD, which sorts on the senior author and date. For example, to sort on all authors and then the date, use the option sA+T.

Files

/usr/lib/refer

Directory of programs.

/usr/lib/refer/papers

Directory of default publication lists and indexes.

Attributes

See attributes(5) for descriptions of the following attributes:

Attribute Type	Attribute Value
Availability	SUNWdoc

See Also

addbib(1), eqn(1), indxbib(1), lookbib(1), nroff(1), roffbib(1), sortbib(1), tbl(1), troff(1), attributes(5)

regcmp — Compile Regular Expressions

Synopsis

/usr/ccs/bin/regcmp [-] *filename*...

Description

The regcmp command performs a function similar to the regcmp(3C) C language library function. In most cases, the regcmp(1) command precludes the need for calling the regcmp(3C) function from C programs. Bypassing regcmp(3C) saves on both execution time and program size. The regcmp command compiles the regular expressions in *filename* and puts the output in *filename*.i.

Options

–	Put the output in *filename*.c. The format of entries in *filename* is a name (C variable), followed by one or more blanks, followed by one or more regular expressions, enclosed in double quotes. The output of regcmp is C source code. Compiled regular expressions are represented as extern char vectors. *filename*.i files can thus be #included in C programs, and *filename*.c files can be compiled and later loaded. In the C program that uses the regcmp output, regex(abc,line) applies the regular expression named abc to line. Diagnostics are self-explanatory.

Examples

In the following example, the three arguments to telno must all be entered on one line.

```
name      "([A-Za-z][A-Za-z0-9_]*)$0"
telno     "\({0,1}([2-9][01][1-9])$0\){0,1} *"
          "([2-9][0-9]{2})$1[-]{0,1}"
          "([0-9]{4})$2"
```

In the C program that uses the regcmp output, the following statement applies the regular expression named telno to line.

```
regex(telno, line, area, exch, rest)
```

Environment Variables

See environ(5) for a general description of the LC_* environment variables.

LC_CTYPE	Determine how regcmp handles characters. When LC_CTYPE is set to a valid value, regcmp can display and handle text and file names containing valid characters for that locale.
LC_MESSAGES	Determine how diagnostic and informative messages are presented, including the language and style of the messages and the correct form of affirmative and negative responses. In the C locale, the messages are presented in the default form found in the program itself (in most cases, U.S. English).

Attributes

See attributes(5) for descriptions of the following attributes:

Attribute Type	Attribute Value
Availability	SUNWtoo
CSI	Enabled

See Also

regcmp(3C), attributes(5), environ(5)

---

rehash — Evaluate the Internal Hash Table of the Contents of Directories

Synopsis

csh
rehash

Description

See hash(1).

---

remote_shell, remsh — Remote Shell

Synopsis

remsh [-n][-l *username*] *hostname command*
remsh *hostname* [-n][-l *username*] *command hostname* [-n][-l *username*]
  command

Description

See rsh(1).

---

renice — Alter Priority of Running Processes

Synopsis

/usr/bin/renice [-n *increment*][-g | -p | -u] *ID*...
/usr/bin/renice *priority* [-p] *pid*... [-g *gid*...][-p *pid*...][-u *user*...]
/usr/bin/renice *priority* -g *gid*... [-g *gid*...][-p *pid*...][-u *user*...]
/usr/bin/renice *priority* -u*user* [-g *gid*...][-p *pid*...][-u *user*...]

Description

> **Note** — The `priocntl` command subsumes the function of `renice`.

Use the `renice` command to alter the scheduling priority of one or more running processes. By default, specify the processes to be affected by their process IDs.

If the first operand is a number within the valid range of priorities (-20 to 20), `renice` treats it as a priority (as in all but the first synopsis form); otherwise, `renice` treats it as an ID (as in the first synopsis form).

Altering Process Priority

Users other than superuser can alter only the priority of processes they own and can monotonically increase only their `nice` value within the range 0 to 19. This limitation prevents you from overriding administrative fiats. Superuser can alter the priority of any process and set the priority to any value in the range -20 to 19. Useful priorities are:

- 19—Run the affected processes only when nothing else in the system wants to run.

- 0—The "base" scheduling priority.

- Any negative value—Make things go very fast.

20 is an acceptable `nice` value, but it is rounded down to 19.

Notes

If you make the priority very negative, then the process cannot be interrupted. To regain control you must make the priority greater than 0.

Users other than superuser cannot increase scheduling priorities of their own processes even if they were the ones that decreased the priorities in the first place.

Options

- The *priority* operand must precede the options and can be a multidigit option.

- The -g, -p, and -u options can each take multiple arguments.

- You can use the *pid* argument without its -p option.

-g   Interpret all operands or just the *gid* arguments as unsigned decimal integer process group IDs.

-n *increment*

          Specify how to adjust the system scheduling priority of the specified process or processes. *increment* is a positive or negative decimal integer.

Positive *increment* values schedule a lower system priority. Negative *increment* values can require appropriate privileges and schedule a higher system priority.

-p *pid*   Interpret all operands or just the *pid* arguments as unsigned decimal integer process IDs. The -p option is the default.

-u *user*   Interpret all operands or just the *user* argument as users. If a user exists with a user name equal to the operand, then use the user ID of that user in further processing. Otherwise, if the operand represents an unsigned decimal integer, use it as the numeric user ID of the user.

Operands

ID   A process ID, process group ID, or user name/user ID, depending on the option selected.

priority   The value specified is taken as the actual system scheduling priority instead of as an increment to the existing system scheduling priority. Specifying a scheduling priority higher than that of the existing process can require appropriate privileges.

Examples

The following example adjusts the system scheduling priority so that process IDs 987 and 32 have a lower scheduling priority.

```
castle% renice -n 5 -p 987 32
castle%
```

The following example adjusts the system scheduling priority so that group IDs 324 and 76 have a higher scheduling priority if the user has the appropriate privileges to raise the priority.

```
castle% renice -n -4 -g 324 76
castle%
```

The following example adjusts the system scheduling priority so that numeric user ID 1002 and user ray have a lower scheduling priority.

```
castle% renice -n 4 -u 1002 ray
castle%
```

Environment Variables

See environ(5) for descriptions of the following environment variables that affect the execution of renice: LC_CTYPE, LC_MESSAGES, and NLSPATH.

Exit Status

0   Successful completion.

>0   An error occurred.

Files

/etc/passwd
>   Map user names to user IDs.

Attributes

See attributes(5) for descriptions of the following attributes:

Attribute Type	Attribute Value
Availability	SUNWcsu

See Also

nice(1), passwd(1), priocntl(1), attributes(5), environ(5)

---

repeat — Shell Built-in Function to Repeat Actions

Synopsis

csh
repeat *count command*

Description

See for(1).

---

reset — Establish or Restore Terminal Characteristics

Synopsis

/usr/ucb/reset [-] [-ec] [-I] [-kc] [-n] [-Q] [-r] [-s] [-m [*indent*]
   [*test baudrate*]: *type*] ... [*type*]

Description

See tset(1B).

return — Shell Built-in Function to Advance Beyond a Sequence of Steps

Synopsis

sh
return [*n*]

csh
* return [*n*]

Description
See exit(1).

rksh — Korn Shell, a Standard/Restricted Command and Programming Language

Synopsis
/usr/bin/rksh [±abCefhikmnoprstuvx] [±o *option*] ... [-c *string*] [*arg...*]

Description
See ksh(1).

rlogin — Remote Login

Synopsis
/usr/bin/rlogin [-8EL] [-ec] [-l *username*] *hostname*

Description
Use rlogin to establish a remote login session from your terminal to the remote system named *hostname*.

Host names are listed in the hosts database, which can be contained in the /etc/hosts file, the Network Information Service (NIS) hosts map, the Internet domain name server, or a combination of these. Each host has one official name (the first name in the database entry) and, optionally, one or more nicknames. You can specify either official host names or nicknames as *hostname*.

> **Note** — The Network Information Service (NIS) was formerly known as Sun Yellow Pages (YP). The functionality of the two remains the same; only the name has changed.

Each remote system can have a file named /etc/hosts.equiv containing a list of trusted host names with which it shares user names. Users with the same *username* on both the local and remote system can invoke rlogin from the systems listed in the remote /etc/hosts.equiv file without supplying a password. Individual users can set up a similar private equivalence list with the file .rhosts in their home directories. Each line in this file contains two names: a *hostname* and a *username* separated by a space. An entry in a remote user's .rhosts file permits the user named *username* who is logged into *hostname* to log in to the remote system as a remote user without supplying a password. If the name of the local host is not found in the /etc/hosts.equiv file on the remote system and the local *username* and *hostname* are not found in the remote user's .rhosts file, then the remote system prompts for a password. Host names listed in /etc/hosts.equiv and .rhosts files must be the official host names listed in the hosts database; nicknames cannot be used in either of these files.

> **Note** — When a system is listed in hosts.equiv, its security must be as good as local security. One insecure system listed in hosts.equiv can compromise the security of the entire system.

For security reasons, the .rhosts file must be owned either by the remote user or by root.

The remote terminal type is the same as your local terminal type (as given in your TERM environment variable). The terminal or window size is also copied to the remote system if the server supports the option, and changes in size are reflected as well. All echoing takes place at the remote site so that (except for delays) the remote login is transparent. Flow control with Control-S and Control-Q and flushing of input and output on interrupts are handled properly.

> **Note** — This implementation can use only the TCP network service.

Options

-8	Pass 8-bit data across the net instead of 7-bit data.
-e*c*	Specify a different escape character, *c*, for the line used to disconnect from the remote host.
-E	Stop any character from being recognized as an escape character.
-l *username*	Specify a different *username* for the remote login. If you do not use this option, the remote *username* used is the same as your local *username*.

New!

-L   Run the `rlogin` session in `litout` mode.

Escape Sequences

Lines that you type that start with the tilde character are escape sequences (you can change the escape character with the `-e` option).

~.   Disconnect from the remote host. This action is not the same as a logout because the local host breaks the connection with no warning to the remote end.

~*susp*   Suspend the login session (only if you are using a shell with job control). *susp* is your suspend character, usually Control-Z; see `tty`(1).

~*dsusp*   Suspend the input half of the login, but output is still seen (only if you are using a shell with job control). `dsusp` is your "deferred suspend" character, usually Control-Y; see `tty`(1).

New! Operands

hostname   The name of the remote system on which `rlogin` establishes the remote login session.

Files

`/etc/passwd`

         Contains information about users' accounts.

`/usr/hosts/*`

         For host-name version of the command.

`/etc/hosts.equiv`

         List of trusted host names with shared user names.

`/etc/nologin`

         Message displayed to users attempting to log in during system shutdown.

`$HOME/.rhosts`

         Private list of trusted *hostname*/*username* combinations.

Attributes

See `attributes`(5) for descriptions of the following attributes:

Attribute Type	Attribute Value
Availability	SUNWcsu

See Also

rsh(1), stty(1), tty(1), in.named(1M), hosts(4), hosts.equiv(4), nologin(4), attributes(5)

Diagnostics

NO LOGINS: System going down in *N* minutes

> The system is in the process of being shut down and logins have been disabled.

---

rm, rmdir — Remove Directory Entries

Synopsis

```
/usr/bin/rm [-f][-i] file...
/usr/bin/rm -rR [-f][-i] dirname...[file...]
/usr/xpg4/bin/rm [-fiRr] file...
/usr/bin/rmdir [-ps] dirname...
```

Description

/usr/bin/rm, /usr/xpg4/bin/rm

Use the rm command to remove files. The rm command removes the entry specified by each *file* argument. If a file has no write permission and the standard input is a terminal, the full set of permissions (in octal) for the file is printed, followed by a question mark. The question mark is a prompt for confirmation. If your answer begins with y (for yes), the file is deleted; otherwise, the file remains.

If *file* is a symbolic link, the link is removed but the file or directory to which it refers is not deleted. You do not need write permission to remove a symbolic link provided you have write permissions in the directory.

If you specify multiple files and removal of any file fails for any reason, rm writes a diagnostic message to standard error, does nothing more to the current file, and goes on to any remaining files.

If the standard input is not a terminal, the command operates as if you specified the -f option.

Note — A - enables you to explicitly mark the end of any command-line options, allowing rm to recognize file arguments that begin with a -. As an aid to BSD migration, rm accepts - as a synonym for --. This migration aid may disappear in a future release. If you use - twice in the same command line, the second is interpreted as a file.

New!

/usr/bin/rmdir

Use the `rmdir` command to remove empty directories.

Directories are processed in the order specified. If you specify a directory and a subdirectory of that directory in a single invocation of `rmdir`, then you must specify the subdirectory before the parent directory so that the parent directory is empty when `rmdir` tries to remove it.

Options

The following options are supported for `/usr/bin/rm` and `/usr/xpg4/bin/rm`.

-r
: Recursively remove directories and subdirectories in the argument list. The directory is emptied of files and removed. You are normally prompted for removal of any write-protected files that the directory contains. If you specify the `-f` option, however, the write-protected files are removed without prompting. The write-protected files are also removed if the standard input is not a terminal and you do not use the `-i` option.

: Do not traverse symbolic links that are encountered with this option.

: If you try to remove a nonempty, write-protected directory, the command always fails (even if you use the `-f` option), resulting in an error message.

-R
: Same as `-r` option.

The following options are supported for `/usr/bin/rm` only.

-f
: Remove all files (whether write-protected or not) in a directory without prompting. In a write-protected directory, however, never remove files (whatever their permissions are) and display no messages. If you try to remove a write-protected directory, this option does not suppress an error message.

-i
: Prompt for confirmation before removing any files. This option overrides the `-f` option and remains in effect even if the standard input is not a terminal.

The following options are supported for `/usr/xpg4/bin/rm` only.

-f
: Do not prompt for confirmation. Do not write diagnostic messages or modify the exit status in the case of nonexistent operands. Ignore any previous occurrences of the `-i` option.

-i
: Prompt for confirmation. Ignore the `-f` option.

The following options are supported for `/usr/bin/rmdir` only.

-p
: Remove the directory *dirname* and its parent directories that become empty. Print a message on the standard error about whether the whole path is removed or part of the path remains for some reason.

-s	Suppress the message printed on the standard error when you also use the -p option.

Operands

file	A path name of a directory entry to be removed.
dirname	A path name of an empty directory to be removed.

Usage

See largefile(5) for the description of the behavior of rm and rmdir when encountering files greater than or equal to 2 Gbytes (2**31 bytes).

Examples

/usr/bin/rm /usr/xpg4/bin/rm

The following example removes the files a.out and core.

```
castle% rm a.out core
castle%
```

The following example removes the junk directory and all its contents without prompting.

```
castle% rm -rf junk
castle%
```

/usr/bin/rmdir

If directory a in the current directory is empty except that it contains a directory b, and a/b is empty except that it contains directory c, the following example removes all three directories.

```
castle% rmdir -p a/b/c
castle%
```

Environment Variables

See environ(5) for descriptions of the following environment variables that affect the execution of rm and rmdir: LC_COLLATE, LC_CTYPE, LC_MESSAGES, and NLSPATH.

Exit Status

0	If you do not specify the -f option, all the named directory entries are removed; otherwise, all the existing named directory entries are removed.
>0	An error occurred.

Attributes

See attributes(5) for descriptions of the following attributes:

/usr/bin/rm /usr/bin/rmdir

Attribute Type	Attribute Value
Availability	SUNWcsu
CSI	Enabled

/usr/xpg4/bin/rm

Attribute Type	Attribute Value
Availability	SUNWxcu4
CSI	Enabled

See Also

New!

rmdir(2), unlink(2), attributes(5), environ(5), largefiles(5), XPG4(5)

Diagnostics

All messages are generally self-explanatory.

You cannot remove the files . and .. to avoid the consequences of inadvertently doing something like the following.

```
castle% rm -r .*
```

rmail — Read Mail or Send Mail to Users

Synopsis

/usr/bin/rmail [-tw] [-m *message-type*] *recipient*...

Description

See mail(1).

rmdel — Remove a Delta from an SCCS File

Synopsis
```
/usr/ccs/bin/rmdel -rsid s.filename...
```

Description
See sccs-rmdel(1).

rmdir — Remove Directory Entries

Synopsis
```
/usr/bin/rmdir [-ps] dirname...
```

Description
See rm(1).

rmic — Java RMI Stub Compiler

Synopsis
```
/usr/java/bin/rmic [-classpath path] [-d directory] [-depend]
    [-g] [-keepgenerated] [-nowarn] [-O] [-show] [-verbose]
    package-qualified-class-names
```

Description
The rmic compiler generates stub and skeleton class files for remote objects from the names of compiled Java classes that contain remote object implementations.

A skeleton for a remote object is a server-side entity containing a method that dispatches calls to the remote object implementation.

A stub is a proxy for a remote object that is responsible for forwarding method invocations on remote objects to the server where the actual remote object implementation resides. Therefore, a client's reference to a remote object is actually a reference to a local stub.

A remote object is one that implements the interface java.rmi.Remote. The classes named in the rmic command must have compiled successfully with the javac(1) command and be fully package qualified. The following example

runs `rmic` on the class file named `HelloImpl` to create the
`HelloImpl_Skel.class` and `HelloImpl_Stub.class` files.

```
castle% rmic hello.HelloImpl
```

    The stub implements the remote interfaces only, not the local interfaces also
implemented by the remote object. Because the stub implements exactly the
same set of remote interfaces as the remote object, a client can use the Java
language's built-in operators for casting and type-checking.

Options

-classpath *path*

> Specify the path `rmic` uses to look up classes. Override the default
> or the CLASSPATH environment variable. Separate directories with
> colons. The general format for path is:
>
> `.:`*your-path*
>
> For example:
>
> `.:/usr/local/java/classes`

-d *directory*

> Specify the root directory of the class hierarchy. Use this option to
> specify a destination directory for the stub and skeleton files. For
> example, the following command puts the stub and skeleton
> classes derived from `MyClass` into the directory
> `/java/classes/foo`.
>
> `% rmic -d /java/classes/foo.MyClass`
>
> If you do not use the -d option, ignore the package hierarchy of the
> target class and put stub and skeleton files in the current
> directory.

-depend

> Recompile classes referenced by other classes. Normally, the
> compiler recompiles only missing or out-of-date classes referred to
> in source code.

-g

> Enable debugging table generation. Debugging tables contain
> information about line numbers and local variables. This
> information is used by Java debugging tools. By default, generate
> only line numbers unless you specify optimization (-O).

-keepgenerated

> Retain the generated `.java` source files for the stubs and
> skeletons. If you specify the -d option, -keepgenerated writes the
> `.java` source file to the same directory as the `.class` files.

-nowarn

> Turn off warnings. The compiler does not print warnings.

-O

> Optimize compiled code by inlining static, final, and private
> methods. Note that your classes may get larger.

-show	Show the graphical user interface for the rmic compiler. Enter one or more package-qualified class names (separated by spaces) and press either the Enter key or the Show button to create stubs and skeletons.
-verbose	Display compiler and linker messages about the classes being compiled and what class files are being loaded.

Environment Variables

CLASSPATH	Provide the system with a path to user-defined classes. Separate directories with colons. For example: `.:/usr/local/java/classes`

Attributes

See attributes(5) for descriptions of the following attributes:

Attribute Type	**Attribute Value**
Availability	SUNWjvdev

See Also

javac(1), attributes(5)

---

rmiregistry — Register Remote Java Objects

Synopsis

/usr/java/bin/rmiregistry [*port*]

Description

The Java rmiregistry command creates and starts a remote object registry on the specified port on the current host. If you omit the port number, the registry is started on port 1099. The rmiregistry command produces no output and is typically run in the background. For example:

castle% **rmiregistry &**

A remote object registry is a bootstrap naming service that is used by RMI servers on a host to bind remote objects to names. Clients can then look up remote objects and make remote method invocations.

The registry is typically used to locate the first remote object on which an application needs to invoke methods. That object, in turn, provides application-specific support for finding other objects.

The methods of the `java.rmi.registry.LocateRegistry` class are used to get a registry operating on a particular host or host and port.

The URL-based methods of the `java.rmi.Naming` class operate on a registry, and you can use them to look up a remote object, bind a simple (string) name to a remote object, rebind a new name to a remote object (overriding the old binding), unbind a remote object, and list the URLs bound in the registry.

Attributes

See `attributes`(5) for descriptions of the following attributes:

Attribute Type	Attribute Value
Availability	SUNWjvrt

See Also

attributes(5)

java.rmi.Naming

http://java.sun.com/products/jdk/1.1/docs/api/java.rmi.registry. LocateRegistry.html#_top_

java.rmi.registry.LocateRegistry

http://java.sun.com/products/jdk/1.1/docs/api/java.rmi.Naming.html#_top_

For information on related topics, use the search link
http://java.sun.com/

---

roffbib — Format and Print a Bibliographic Database

Synopsis

/usr/bin/roffbib [-e] [-h] [-m *filename*] [-np] [-o*list*] [-Q] [-ra*N*] [-s*N*]
    [-T*term*] [-V] [-x] [*filename*] . . .

Description

Use the `roffbib` command to print all records in a bibliographic database in bibliography format instead of as footnotes or endnotes. Generally, `roffbib` is used in conjunction with `sortbib`(1).

castle% **sortbib database | roffbib**

Options

roffbib accepts all options understood by nroff(1) except -i and -q.

-e	Produce equally spaced words in adjusted lines, using full terminal resolution.
-h	Use output Tabs during horizontal spacing to speed output and reduce output character count. Tab settings are assumed to be every 8 nominal character widths.
-m *filename*	Prepend the macro file /usr/share/lib/tmac/tmac.name to the input files. Leave a space between the –m and the macro *filename*. This set of macros replaces the ones defined in /usr/share/lib/tmac/tmac.bib.
-n*p*	Number the first generated page *p*.
-o*list*	Print only page numbers that appear in the comma-separated list of numbers and ranges. A range *N-M* means pages *N* through *M*; an initial -*N* means from the beginning to page *N*; a final *N*- means from page *N* to end.
-Q	Queue output for the phototypesetter. Set page offset to 1 inch.
-ra*N*	Set register a (single character) to *N*. The command-line argument -r*N*1 numbers the references starting at 1.
	Four command-line registers control formatting style of the bibliography, much like the number registers of ms(5). The flag -rV2 double-spaces the bibliography, whereas -rV1 double-spaces references and single-spaces annotation paragraphs. You can change the line length from the default 6.5 inches to 6 inches with the -rL6i argument, and you can set the page offset from the default of 0 to 1 inch by specifying -rO1i (capital O, not 0).
-s*N*	Halt before every *N* pages for paper loading or changing (default N=1). To resume, press newline or Return.
-T*term*	Specify *term* as the terminal type.
-V	Send output to the Versatec. Set page offset to 1 inch.
-x	If abstracts or comments are entered following the %X field key, roffbib formats them into paragraphs for an annotated bibliography. You can use several %X fields if you want several annotation paragraphs.

Files

/usr/share/lib/tmac/tmac.bib

> File of macros used by nroff/troff.

Attributes

See attributes(5) for descriptions of the following attributes:

Attribute Type	Attribute Value
Availability	SUNWdoc

See Also

addbib(1), indxbib(1), lookbib(1), nroff(1), refer(1), sortbib(1), troff(1), attributes(5)

Bugs

Users must rewrite macros to create customized formats.

rpcgen — RPC Protocol Compiler

Synopsis

```
/usr/bin/rpcgen infile
/usr/bin/rpcgen [-a][-A][-b][-C][-Dname [= value]][-i size]
   [-I [-K seconds]] [-L][-M][-N][-T][-Y pathname] infile
/usr/bin/rpcgen [-c | -h | -l | -m | -t | -Sc | -Ss | -Sm]
   [-o outfile][infile]
/usr/bin/rpcgen [-s nettype][-o outfile][infile]
/usr/bin/rpcgen [-n netid][-o outfile][infile]
```

Description

The rpcgen command is a tool that generates C code to implement a Remote Procedure Call (RPC) protocol. The input to rpcgen is a C-like language known as RPC Language (Remote Procedure Call Language).

rpcgen is normally used as in the first synopsis where it takes an input file and generates output files. If the infile is named proto.x, then rpcgen generates a header in proto.h, XDR routines in proto_xdr.c, server-side stubs in proto_svc.c, and client-side stubs in proto_clnt.c. With the -T option, rpcgen also generates the RPC dispatch table in proto_tbl.i.

rpcgen can also generate sample client and server files that can be customized to suit a particular application. The -Sc, -Ss, and -Sm options generate sample client, server, and makefile. The -a option generates all files, including sample files. If the infile is proto.x, then the client-side sample file is written to proto_client.c, the server-side sample file to proto_server.c, and the sample makefile to makefile.proto.

The server created can be started both by the port monitors (for example, inetd or listen) or by itself. When the server is started by a port monitor, it creates servers only for the transport for which the file descriptor 0 was passed. You must specify the name of the transport by setting up the PM_TRANSPORT environment variable. When the server generated by rpcgen is executed, it creates server handles for all the transports specified in the NETPATH environment variable or, if it is unset, it creates server handles for all the visible transports from the /etc/netconfig file.

> **Note** — The transports are chosen at runtime and not at compile time. When the server is self-started, it puts itself in background by default. You can use the special define symbol, RPC_SVC_FG, to run the server process in foreground.

The second synopsis provides special features that enable the creation of more sophisticated RPC servers. These features include support for user-provided #defines and RPC dispatch tables. The entries in the RPC dispatch table contain:

- Pointers to the service routine corresponding to that procedure.
- A pointer to the input and output arguments.
- The size of these routines.

A server can use the dispatch table to check authorization and then to execute the service routine; a client library can use the dispatch table to deal with the details of storage management and XDR data conversion.

The other three synopses are used when you want to generate a particular output file. See "Examples" on page 1132 for examples of rpcgen usage. When you execute rpcgen with the -s option, rpcgen creates servers for that particular class of transports.When you execute rpcgen with the -n option, it creates a server for the transport specified by netid. If you do not specify *infile*, rpcgen accepts the standard input.

You can use all the options mentioned in the second synopsis with the other three synopses, but the changes are made only to the specified output file.

The C preprocessor cc -E is run on the input file before it is actually interpreted by rpcgen. For each type of output file, rpcgen defines a special preprocessor symbol for use by the rpcgen programmer.

RPC_HDR   Defined when compiling into headers.

RPC_XDR   Defined when compiling into XDR routines.

RPC_SVC   Defined when compiling into server-side stubs.

RPC_CLNT   Defined when compiling into client-side stubs.

RPC_TBL   Defined when compiling into RPC dispatch tables.

Any line beginning with % is passed directly into the output file, uninterpreted by rpcgen. To specify the path name of the C preprocessor, use the -Y option.

For every data type referred to in *infile*, rpcgen assumes that a routine exists with the string xdr_ prepended to the name of the data type. If this routine does not exist in the RPC/XDR library, you must provide it. Providing an undefined data type enables customization of XDR routines.

Options

-a
: Generate all files, including sample files.

-A
: Enable the Automatic MT mode in the server main program. In this mode, the RPC library automatically creates threads to service client requests. This option generates multithread-safe stubs by implicitly turning on the -M option. You can set server multithreading modes and parameters with the rpc_control(3N) call. rpcgen-generated code does not change the default values for the Automatic MT mode.

-b
: Generate transport-specific RPC code for older versions of the operating system.

-c
: Compile into XDR routines.

-C
: Generate header and stub files that can be used with ANSI C compilers. You can also use headers generated with this option with C++ programs.

-Dname[=value]
: Define a symbol name. Equivalent to the #define directive in the source. If you specify no value, value is defined as 1. You can specify this option more than once.

-h
: Compile into C data-definitions (a header). You can use this option together with the -T option to produce a header that supports RPC dispatch tables.

-i size
: Specify the size at which to start generating inline code. This option is useful for optimization. The default size is 5.

-I
: Compile support for inetd(1M) in the server-side stubs. Such servers can be self-started or can be started by inetd. When the server is self-started, it puts itself in background by default. You can use the special define symbol RPC_SVC_FG to run the server process in foreground, or you can simply compile without the -I option. If there are no pending client requests, the inetd servers exit after 120 seconds (default). You can change the default with the -K option. All of the error messages for inetd servers are always logged with syslog(3).

: Note: This option is supported for backward compatibility only. You should always use it in conjunction with the -b option, which generates backward-compatible code. By default (that is, when you do not specify -b), rpcgen generates servers that can be invoked through port monitors.

-K *seconds*	Change the default 120-second time that services, created by rpcgen and invoked through port monitors, wait after servicing a request before exiting. To create a server that exits immediately on servicing a request, use -K 0. To create a server that never exits, use -K -1.
	When monitoring for a server, some port monitors, like listen(1M), always spawn a new process in response to a service request. If you know that a server is used with such a monitor, the server should exit immediately on completion. For such servers, use rpcgen with -K 0.
-l	Compile into client-side stubs.
-L	When the servers are started in foreground, use syslog(3) to log the server errors instead of printing them on the standard error.
-m	Compile into server-side stubs, but do not generate a main routine. This option is useful for doing callback routines and for users who need to write their own main routine to do initialization.
-M	Generate multithread-safe stubs for passing arguments and results between rpcgen-generated code and user-written code. This option is useful if you want to use threads in your code.
-N	Enable procedures to have multiple arguments. This option uses a style of parameter passing that closely resembles C. So, when passing an argument to a remote procedure, you do not have to pass a pointer to the argument but can pass the argument itself. This behavior is different from the old style of rpcgen-generated code. To maintain backward compatibility, this option is not the default.
-n *netid*	Compile into server-side stubs for the transport specified by *netid*. The netconfig database should contain an entry for *netid*. You can specify this option more than once to compile a server that serves multiple transports.
-o *outfile*	Specify the name of the output file. If none is specified, use standard output (-c, -h, -l, -m, -n, -s, -Sc, -Sm, -Ss, and -t modes only).
-s *nettype*	Compile into server-side stubs for all the transports belonging to the class *nettype*. The supported classes are netpath, visible, circuit_n, circuit_v, datagram_n, datagram_v, tcp, and udp (see rpc(3N) for the meanings associated with these classes). You can specify this option more than once. Note that the transports are chosen at runtime and not at compile time.
-Sc	Generate sample client code that uses remote procedure calls.
-Sm	Generate a sample Makefile that can be used for compiling the application.
-Ss	Generate sample server code that uses remote procedure calls.
-t	Compile into RPC dispatch table.

-T Generate the code to support RPC dispatch tables.

Use the options -c, -h, -l, -m, -s, -Sc, -Sm, -Ss, and -t exclusively to generate a particular type of file. The options -D and -T are global and can be used with the other options.

-Y *pathname*

Specify the name of the directory where rpcgen starts looking for the C preprocessor.

Operands

infile Input file.

Examples

The following example generates all these five files: prot.h, prot_clnt.c, prot_svc.c, prot_xdr.c, and prot_tbl.i.

castle% **rpcgen -T prot.x**

The following example sends the C data-definitions (header) to the standard output.

castle% **rpcgen -h prot.x**

The following example sends the test version of the -DTEST, server-side stubs for all the transport belonging to the class datagram_n to standard output.

castle% **rpcgen -s datagram_n -DTEST prot.x**

The following example creates the server-side stubs for the transport indicated by *netid* tcp.

castle% **rpcgen -n tcp -o prot_svc.c prot.x**

Exit Status

0 Successful operation.

>0 An error occurred.

Attributes

See attributes(5) for descriptions of the following attributes:

Attribute Type	Attribute Value
Availability	SUNWcsu

See Also

cc(1B), inetd(1M), listen(1M), syslog(3), rpc(3N), rpc_control(3N), rpc_svc_calls(3N), netconfig(4), attributes(5)
The rpcgen chapter in the *ONC+ Developer's Guide*.

---

rsh, remsh, remote_shell — Remote Shell

Synopsis

```
/usr/bin/rsh [-n][-l username] hostname command
/usr/bin/rsh hostname [-n][-l username] command
/usr/bin/remsh [-n][-l username] hostname command
/usr/bin/remsh hostname [-n][-l username] command
/usr/bin/hostname [-n][-l username] command
```

Description

Use the rsh (remote shell) command to connect to the specified *hostname* and execute the specified *command*. rsh copies its standard input to the remote command, the standard output of the remote command to its standard output, and the standard error of the remote command to its standard error. Interrupt, quit, and terminate signals are propagated to the remote *command*; rsh normally terminates when the remote command does.

If you omit *command*, instead of executing a single command, rsh logs you in on the remote host, using rlogin(1).

Shell metacharacters that are not quoted are interpreted on the local system, whereas quoted metacharacters are interpreted on the remote system.

Notes

You cannot run an interactive command (such as vi(1)) with rsh; use rlogin if you want to run an interactive command.

Stop signals stop the local rsh process only; this is arguably wrong, but currently hard to fix.

The current local environment is not passed to the remote shell.

Options

-l *username*

        Use *username* as the remote *username* instead of your local *username*. If you do not specify this option, the remote *username* is the same as your local *username*.

-n   Redirect the input of rsh to /dev/null. You sometimes need this
            option to avoid unfortunate interactions between rsh and the shell
            that invokes it. For example, if you are running rsh and invoke an
            rsh in the background without redirecting its input away from the
            terminal, it blocks even if no reads are posted by the remote
            command. The -n option prevents this behavior.

            The type of remote shell (sh, rsh, or other) is determined by the
            user's entry in the file /etc/passwd on the remote system.

Sometimes you need to use the -n option for reasons that are less than
obvious. For example, the following command puts your shell into a strange
state.

```
castle% rsh somehost dd if=/dev/nrmt0 bs=20b | tar xvpBf -
```

Evidently, what happens is that the tar terminates before the rsh. The rsh
then tries to write into the broken pipe and, instead of terminating neatly,
proceeds to compete with your shell for its standard input. Invoking rsh with
the -n option avoids such incidents.

This bug occurs only when rsh is at the beginning of a pipeline and is not
reading standard input. Do not use the -n option if rsh actually needs to read
standard input. For example, the following command does not produce the bug.

```
castle% tar cf - . | rsh sundial dd of=/dev/rmt0 obs=20b
```

If you use the -n in a case like this, rsh incorrectly reads from /dev/null
instead of from the pipe.

Operands

command   The command to be executed on the specified *hostname*.

hostname   The official host name or a nickname of the specified host system.

Usage

See largefile(5) for the description of the behavior of rsh and remsh when
encountering files greater than or equal to 2 Gbytes (2**31 bytes).

Host names are specified in the hosts database, which may be contained in
the /etc/hosts file, the Internet domain name database, or both. Each host
has one official name (the first name in the database entry) and, optionally, one
or more nicknames. You can specify official host names or nicknames as
hostname.

If the name of the file from which you execute rsh is anything other than
rsh, rsh takes this name as its *hostname* argument. This feature enables you
to create a symbolic link to rsh in the name of a host that, when executed,
invokes a remote shell on that host. By creating a directory and populating it
with symbolic links in the names of commonly used hosts and then including
the directory in your shell's search path, you can run rsh by typing *hostname*
to your shell.

If you invoke rsh with the basename remsh, rsh checks for the existence of the file /usr/bin/remsh. If this file exists, rsh behaves as if remsh is an alias for rsh. If /usr/bin/remsh does not exist, rsh behaves as if remsh is a host name.

Each remote system can have a file named /etc/hosts.equiv containing a list of trusted host names with which it shares user names. Users with the same user name on both the local and remote system can run rsh from the systems listed in the remote system /etc/hosts file. Individual users can set up a similar private equivalence list with the file .rhosts in their home directories. Each line in this file contains two names: a *hostname* and a *username* separated by a space. The entry permits the user named *username* who is logged into *hostname* to use rsh to access the remote system as the remote user. If the name of the local host is not found in the /etc/hosts.equiv file on the remote system and the local *username* and *hostname* are not found in the remote user's .rhosts file, then the access is denied. The host names listed in the /etc/hosts.equiv and .rhosts files must be the official host names listed in the hosts database; nicknames cannot be used in either of these files.

Note — When a system is listed in hosts.equiv, its security must be as good as local security. One insecure system listed in hosts.equiv can compromise the security of the entire system.

---

rsh does not prompt for a password if access is denied on the remote system unless you omit the *command* argument.

Examples

The following command appends the remote file lizard.file from the system called lizard to the file called castle.file on the system called castle.

```
castle% rsh lizard cat lizard.file >> castle.file
```

The following example appends the file lizard.file on the system called lizard to the file lizard.file2 which also resides on the system called lizard.

```
castle% rsh lizard cat lizard.file ">>" lizard.file2
```

Files

/etc/hosts Internet host table.

/etc/hosts.equiv

Trusted remote hosts and users.

/etc/passwd System password file.

Exit Status

0	Successful completion.
1	An error occurred.

Attributes

See attributes(5) for descriptions of the following attributes:

Attribute Type	Attribute Value
Availability	SUNWcsu
CSI	Enabled

See Also

on(1), rlogin(1), telnet(1), vi(1), in.named(1M), hosts(4), hosts.equiv(4), attributes(5), largefile(5)

rup — Show Host Status of Remote Systems (RPC Version)

Synopsis

```
/usr/bin/rup [-hlt]
/usr/bin/rup [host...]
```

Description

Use the rup command to find out how long a system has been up and to display the load average. rup gives a status similar to uptime for remote systems. It broadcasts on the local network and displays the responses it receives.

Normally, the listing is in the order that responses are received, but you can change this order by specifying one of the options listed below.

When you specify *host* arguments, instead of broadcasting, rup queries only the list of specified hosts.

A remote host responds only if it is running the rstatd daemon, which is normally started up from inetd(1M).

Options

    `-h`   Sort the display alphabetically by host name.

    `-l`   Sort the display by load average.

    `-t`   Sort the display by uptime.

Examples

The following example shows the uptime and load average for the system `castle`.

```
castle% rup castle
        castle    up          3:55,    load average: 0.06, 0.02, 0.01
castle%
```

Files

`/etc/servers`

Attributes

See `attributes`(5) for descriptions of the following attributes:

Attribute Type	Attribute Value
Availability	SUNWesu

See Also

`ruptime(1)`, `inetd(1M)`, `attributes(5)`
Solaris Advanced Installation Guide

Bugs

Broadcasting does not work through gateways.

ruptime — Show Host Status of Local Systems

Synopsis

`/usr/bin/ruptime [-alrtu]`

Description

Use the `ruptime` command to view a status line like `uptime` for each system on the local network; these statistics are formed from packets broadcast by each host on the network once a minute.

Systems for which no status report has been received for 5 minutes are shown as being down.

Normally, the listing is sorted by host name, but you can change this order by specifying one of the options listed below.

Options

`-a`	Count even those users who have been idle for an hour or more.
`-l`	Sort the display by load average.
`-r`	Reverse the sorting order.
`-t`	Sort the display by uptime.
`-u`	Sort the display by number of users.

Files

`/var/spool/rwho/whod.*`

Data files.

Attributes

See `attributes`(5) for descriptions of the following attributes:

Attribute Type	Attribute Value
Availability	SUNWcsu

See Also

`rwho(1)`, `in.rwhod(1M)`, `attributes(5)`

rusage — Print Resource Usage for a Command

Synopsis

`/usr/ucb/rusage command`

Description

The `rusage` command is similar to `time`(1). It runs the given *command*, which you must specify; that is, *command* is not optional as it is in the C shell timing facility. When the command is complete, `rusage` displays the real (wall clock), the system CPU, and the user CPU times that elapsed during execution of the command, plus other fields in the `rusage` structure, all on one long line. Times are reported in seconds and hundredths of a second.

Examples

The following example shows the format of rusage output.

```
castle% rusage wc /kookaburra-1
        9        47       264 kookaburra-1
0.07 real 0.02 user 0.03 sys 0 pf 0 pr 0 sw 0 rb 0 wb 0 vcx 0 icx 0 mx 0
   ix 0 id 0 is
castle%
```

Each of the fields identified corresponds to an element of the rusage structure, described in getrusage(3C), as follows.

```
real                   elapsed real time
user    ru_utime       user time used
sys     ru_stime       system time used
pf      ru_majflt      page faults requiring physical I/O
pr      ru_minflt      page faults not requiring physical I/O
sw      ru_nswap       swaps
rb      ru_inblock     block input operations
wb      ru_oublock     block output operations
vcx     ru_nvcsw       voluntary context switches
icx     ru_nivcsw      involuntary context switches
mx      ru_maxrss      maximum resident set size
ix      ru_ixrss       currently 0
id      ru_idrss       integral resident set size
is      ru_isrss       currently 0
```

Attributes

See attributes(5) for descriptions of the following attributes:

Attribute Type	Attribute Value
Availability	SUNWscpu

See Also

csh(1), time(1), getrusage(3C), attributes(5)

Bugs

When the command being timed is interrupted, the timing values displayed may be inaccurate.

rusers — Display Who Is Logged In on Remote Systems

Synopsis

```
/usr/bin/rusers [-ahilu] host...
```

Description

The `rusers` command produces output similar to who(1), but for remote systems. The listing is in the order that responses are received, but you can change this order by specifying one of the options listed below.

The default is to print out the names of the users logged in. When you specify the `-l` option, additional information is printed for each user.

```
userid hostname:terminal login date login time idle time login host
```

If `hostname` and `login host` are the same value, the `login host` field is not displayed. Likewise, if `hostname` is not idle, the idle time is not displayed.

A remote host responds only if it is running the `rusersd` daemon, which can be started from inetd(1M) or listen(1M).

Options

-a	Report for a system even if no users are logged on.
-h	Sort alphabetically by host name.
-i	Sort by idle time.
-l	Display a longer listing in the style of who(1).
-u	Sort by number of users.

Examples

The following example shows the output of the `rusers` command for a small network.

```
castle% rusers
Sending broadcast for rusersd protocol version 3...
castle          winsor
seachild        ray
g3              des
castle%
```

The following example shows a longer listing for the system `castle`.

```
castle% rusers -l castle
winsor          castle:console          Mar 30 08:04          (:0)
castle%
```

Attributes

See attributes(5) for descriptions of the following attributes:

Attribute Type	Attribute Value
Availability	SUNWesu

See Also

who(1), inetd(1M), listen(1M), pmadm(1M), sacadm(1M), attributes(5)

rwho — Display Who Is Logged In on Local Systems

Synopsis

/usr/bin/rwho [-a]

Description

Use the rwho command to display a list of the users logged in to all systems in your network with the login TTY port and the date and time. rwho is similar to who(1). If no report has been received from a system for 5 minutes, rwho assumes the system is down and does not report users last known to be logged in to that system.

If a user has not typed to the system for a minute or more, rwho reports this idle time. If a user has not typed to the system for an hour or more, the user is omitted from the output of rwho unless you specify the -a option.

Notes

rwho does not work through gateways.

The directory /var/spool/rwho must exist on the host from which you run rwho.

This service takes up progressively more network bandwith as the number of hosts on the local net increases. For large networks, the cost becomes prohibitive.

The rwho service daemon, in.rwhod(1M), must be enabled for this command to return useful results.

Options

-a   Report all users whether or not they have typed to the system in the past hour.

Files

`/var/spool/rwho/whod.*`

Information about other systems.

Attributes

See `attributes`(5) for descriptions of the following attributes:

Attribute Type	Attribute Value
Availability	SUNWcsu

See Also

`finger(1)`, `ruptime(1)`, `who(1)`, `in.rwhod(1M)`, `attributes(5)`

S

---

sact — Show Editing Activity Status of an SCCS File

Synopsis

```
/usr/ccs/bin/sact s.filename...
```

Description

See sccs-sact(1).

---

sag — System Activity Graph

Synopsis

```
/usr/sbin/sag [-e time] [-f file] [-i sec] [-s time] [-T term] [-x spec]
    [-y spec]
```

Description

Use the sag command to graphically display the system activity data stored in
a binary data file by a previous sar(1) run. You can plot any of the sar data
items singly or in combination, as cross-plots or versus time. You can specify
simple arithmetic combinations of data. sag invokes sar and finds the desired

data by string-matching the data column header (run `sar` to see what is available). The `sag` command requires a graphic terminal to draw the graph, and uses `tplot`(1) to produce its output. When running Solaris 2.3 and OpenWindows, perform the following steps:

1. As root, type **xterm -t** and press Return to run `xterm` as a Tektronics terminal.
2. In the `xterm` window, type **sag -T tek *options*** and press Return.

Options

The following options are passed through to `sar`.

`-e time`	Choose data up to `time`. Default is `18:00`.
`-f file`	Use `file` as the data source for `sar`. Default is the current daily data file `/usr/adm/sa/sadd`.
`-i sec`	Choose data at intervals as close as possible to `sec` seconds.
`-s time`	Choose data later than `time` in the form `hh[:mm]`. Default is `08:00`.

Other options:

`-T term`	Produce output suitable for terminal `term`. See `tplot`(1) for known terminals. Default for `term` is `$TERM`.
`-x spec`	Specify the x axis with `spec` in the form:

`name[op name]...[lo hi]`

`name` is either a string that matches a column header in the `sar` report with an optional device name in square brackets, for example, `r+w/s[dsk-1]`, or an integer value. `op` is `+ - *` or `/` surrounded by blank spaces. You can specify up to five names. Parentheses are not recognized. Contrary to custom, + and – have precedence over * and /. Evaluation is left-to-right. Thus, `A / A + B * 100` is evaluated as `(A/(A+B))*100`, and `A + B / C + D` is `(A+B)/(C+D)`. `lo` and `hi` are optional numeric scale limits. If unspecified, they are deduced from the data.

Enclose `spec` in double quotes (`" "`) if it includes white space.

A single `spec` is permitted for the x axis. If unspecified, `time` is used.

`-y spec`	Specify the y axis with `spec` in the same form as for `-x`. You can specify up to five `spec` arguments separated by a semicolon (;). The default is:

`-y "%usr 0 100; %usr + %sys 0 100; %usr + %sys + %wio 0 100"`

Examples

The following example shows today's CPU use.

```
castle$ sag
```

The following example shows activity of all disk drives over 15 minutes.

```
$ TS=`date +%H:%M`
$ sar -o /tmp/tempfile 60 15

SunOS castle 5.7 Generic sun4m     03/31/99

11:49:38    %usr    %sys    %wio    %idle
11:50:38       4      29      48      18
11:51:38       4      20      45      32
11:52:38       0       1       0      99
11:53:38       0       0       0     100
11:54:38       0       0       0     100
11:55:38       0       0       0     100
11:56:38       0       0       0      99
11:57:38       0       0       0     100
11:58:38       0       0       0     100
11:59:38       0       0       0     100
12:00:38       0       0       0     100
12:01:38       0       0       0      99
12:02:38       5      30      51      14
12:03:38       3      15      38      44
12:04:39       0       0       0      99

Average        1       7      12      80
$ TE=`date +%H:%M`
$ sag -f /tmp/tempfile -s $TS -e $TE -y "r+w/s[dsk]"
terminal type not known
$
```

Files

```
/usr/adm/sa/sadd
```

> Daily data file for day *dd*.

Attributes

See `attributes`(5) for descriptions of the following attributes:

Attribute Type	Attribute Value
Availability	SUNWaccu

See Also

```
sar(1), tplot(1), attributes(5)
```

sar — System Activity Reporter

Synopsis

```
/usr/sbin/sar [-aAbcdgkmpqruvwy] [-o filename] t [n]
/usr/sbin/sar [-aAbcdgkmpqruvwy] [-e time] [-f filename] [-i sec] [-s time]
```

Description

Use the `sar` command to view a complete profile of all system activity during an interval of time. In the first synopsis format, `sar` samples cumulative activity counters in the operating system at *n* intervals of *t* seconds, where *t* should be 5 or greater. If you specify *t* with more than one option, all headers are printed together and the output can be difficult to read. (If the sampling interval is less than 5, the activity of `sar` itself can affect the sample.) If you specify the `-o` option, `sar` saves the samples in *filename* in binary format. The default value of *n* is 1.

In the second synopsis format, you specify no sampling interval. Instead, `sar` extracts data from a previously recorded file name, either the one specified by the `-f` option or, by default, the standard, system-activity, daily data file /var/adm/sa/sa*dd* for the current day *dd*. You can bound the starting and ending times of the report with the `-e` and `-s` arguments with time specified in the form *hh*[:*mm*[:*ss*]]. The `-i` option selects records at *sec* second intervals. Otherwise, all intervals found in the data file are reported.

Options

The following options modify the subsets of information reported by `sar`.

`-a`	Report use of file access system routines `iget/s`, `namei/s`, `dirblk/s`.
`-A`	Report all data. Equivalent to `-abcdgkmpqruvwy`.
`-b`	Report buffer activity:

`bread/s, bwrit/s`

> Transfers per second of data between system buffers and disk or other block devices.

`lread/s, lwrit/s`

> Access system buffers.

`%rcache, %wcache`

> Cache hit ratios, that is, (1-bread/lread) as a percentage.

`pread/s, pwrit/s`

> Transfers by raw (physical) device mechanism.

-c   Report system calls.

      scall/s   System calls of all types.

      sread/s, swrit/s, fork/s, exec/s

             Specific system calls.

      rchar/s, wchar/s

             Characters transferred by read and write system calls. Report no incoming or outgoing exec(2) or fork(2) calls.

-d   Report activity for each block device (for example, disk or tape drive) with the exception of XDC disks and tape drives. The device specification dsk- is generally used to represent a disk drive. The device specification used to represent a tape drive is machine dependent. The activity data reported is:

      %busy, avque

             Portion of time device was busy servicing a transfer request, average number of requests outstanding during that time.

      read/s, write/s, blks/s

             Number of read/write transfers from or to device, number of bytes transferred in 512-byte units.

      avseek   Number of milliseconds per average seek.

      For more-general system statistics, use iostat(1M), sar(1M), or vmstat(1M).

-e *time*   Select data up to *time*. Default is 18:00.

-f *filename*

      Use *filename* as the data source for sar. Default is the current daily data file /usr/adm/sa/sa*dd*.

-g   Report paging activities:

      pgout/s   Page-out requests per second.

      ppgout/s   Pages paged out per second.

      pgfree/s   Pages per second placed on the free list by the page-stealing daemon.

      pgscan/s   Pages per second scanned by the page-stealing daemon.

      %ufs_ipf   The percentage of UFS inodes that were taken off the free list by iget and that had reusable pages associated with them. These pages are flushed and cannot be reclaimed by processes. Thus, this value is the percentage of igets with page flushes.

-i *sec*   Select data at intervals as close as possible to *sec* seconds.

`-k`   Report kernel memory allocation (KMA) activities.

         `sml_mem, alloc, fail`

                 Information about the memory pool reserving and allocating space for small requests: the amount of memory in bytes that KMA has for the small pool, the number of bytes allocated to satisfy requests for small amounts of memory, and the number of requests for small amounts of memory that were not satisfied (failed).

         `lg_mem, alloc, fail`

                 Information for the large memory pool (analogous to the information for the small memory pool).

         `ovsz_alloc, fail`

                 The amount of memory allocated for oversize requests and the number of oversize requests that could not be satisfied (because oversized memory is allocated dynamically, there is not a pool).

`-m`   Report message and semaphore activities.

         `msg/s, sema/s`

                 Primitives per second.

`-o` *filename*   Save samples in *filename* in binary format.

`-p`   Report paging activities.

         `atch/s`   Page faults per second that are satisfied by reclaiming a page currently in memory (attaches per second).

         `pgin/s`   Page-in requests per second.

         `ppgin/s`   Pages paged in per second.

         `pflt/s`   Page faults from protection errors per second (illegal access to page) or "copy on writes."

         `vflt/s`   Address translation page faults per second (valid page not in memory).

         `slock/s`   Faults per second from software lock requests that require physical I/O.

`-q`   Report average queue length while occupied, and report percent of time occupied.

         `runq-sz, %runocc`

                 Run queue of processes in memory and runnable.

         `swpq-sz, %swpocc`

                 No longer reported by `sar`.

`-r`   Report unused memory pages and disk blocks.

	`freemem`	Average pages available to user processes.
	`freeswap`	Disk blocks available for page swapping.
`-s time`		Select data later than *time* in the form *hh*[:*mm*]. Default is 08:00.
`-u`		Report CPU use (the default).
	`%usr, %sys, %wio, %idle`	
		Portion of time running in user mode, running in system mode, idle with some process waiting for block I/O, and otherwise idle.
`-v`		Report status of process, inode, file tables.
	`proc-sz, inod-sz, file-sz, lock-sz`	
		Entries/size for each table, evaluated once at sampling point.
	`ov`	Overflows that occur between sampling points for each table.
`-w`		Report system swapping and switching activity.
	`swpin/s, swpot/s, bswin/s, bswot/s`	
		Number of transfers and number of 512-byte units transferred for swap-ins and swap-outs (including initial loading of some programs).
	`pswch/s`	Process switches.
`-y`		Report TTY device activity.
	`rawch/s, canch/s, outch/s`	
		Input character rate, input character rate processed by canon, output character rate.
	`rcvin/s, xmtin/s, mdmin/s`	
		Receive, transmit, and modem interrupt rates.

Examples

The following example displays today's CPU activity.

```
castle% sar

SunOS castle 5.7 Generic sun4m     03/31/99

10:49:47     %usr     %sys     %wio    %idle
10:50:47        1        8       33       58
10:51:47        4       25       71        0
10:52:47        3       19       78        0
10:53:47        1        5       25       69
10:54:47        3       27       63        7
10:55:47        2        9       27       63
10:56:47        2       11       37       50
10:57:47        4       30       66        0
```

```
10:58:47        3       22      60       14
10:59:47        0        1      14       84
11:00:47        0        0       0       99
11:01:47        0        0       0      100
11:02:47        0        1       0       98
11:03:47        0        1       0       99
11:04:47        0        1       0       99

Average         2       11      32       56
castle%
```

The following example watches CPU activity evolve for 10 minutes and saves the data to a file named `temp`.

```
castle% sar -o temp 60 10

SunOS castle 5.7 Generic sun4m      03/31/99

12:30:27      %usr    %sys    %wio    %idle
12:31:27         0       1       0       99
12:32:27         0       0       0       99
12:33:27         0       0       0       99
12:34:27         0       0       0       99
12:35:27         0       0       0      100
12:36:27         0       0       0       99
12:37:27         0       1       0       99
12:38:27         0       0       0       99
12:39:27         0       0       0      100
12:40:27         0       0       0       99

Average          0       0       0       99
castle%
```

You can later review disk and tape activity from that period. The following example (truncated to save space) shows the results from the first two minutes.

```
castle% sar -d -f temp

SunOS castle 5.7 Generic sun4m      03/31/99

12:30:27   device        %busy   avque   r+w/s   blks/s  avwait  avserv

12:31:27   fd0               0     0.0       0        0     0.0     0.0
           nfs1              0     0.0       0        0     0.0     0.0
           sd0               0     0.0       0        4     0.0    90.8
           sd0,a             0     0.0       0        2     0.0    81.5
           sd0,b             0     0.0       0        0     0.0    30.6
           sd0,c             0     0.0       0        0     0.0     0.0
           sd0,d             0     0.0       0        0     0.0     0.0
           sd0,f             0     0.0       0        0     0.0    44.2
           sd0,g             0     0.0       0        2     0.0   119.8
           sd1               0     0.0       0        0     0.0    20.2
           sd1,a             0     0.0       0        0     0.0    20.2
           sd1,c             0     0.0       0        0     0.0     0.0
```

sd2	0	0.0	0	1	0.0	23.8
sd2,c	0	0.0	0	0	0.0	0.0
sd2,h	0	0.0	0	1	0.0	23.8
sd6	0	0.0	0	0	0.0	0.0

... (*More information not shown*)
```
castle%
```

Files

/var/adm/sa/sa*dd*

Daily data file, where *dd* is digits representing the day of the month.

Attributes

See attributes(5) for descriptions of the following attributes:

Attribute Type	Attribute Value
Availability	SUNWaccu

See Also

sag(1), iostat(1M), sar(1M), vmstat(1M), exec(2), fork(2), attributes(5)
System Administration Guide, Volume I

New!

sccs — Front End for the Source Code Control System (SCCS)

Synopsis

```
/usr/ccs/bin/sccs [-r][-drootprefix][-psubdir] subcommand
[option...][file...]
/usr/xpg4/bin/sccs [-r][-d rootprefix][-p subdir] subcommand
[option...][file...]
```

Description

The sccs command is a comprehensive, straightforward front end to the various command programs of the Source Code Control System (SCCS).

The complete set of SCCS tools provides document management and version control for source code as well as for text documents. When you have a large project, managing the files and changes can be a difficult task. As documents change over time, it can be difficult to track and archive the original documents and all subsequent versions along with their dates and comments.

With SCCS, you administer a single history file that contains all changes to a document. You can add changed versions, called *deltas*, to the file at any time, without destroying older versions. Then, you can retrieve any version from the master file as needed with the SCCS `get` command.

SCCS keeps version numbers for each new delta that is added to the history file. When you create a file, it is assigned version number 1.1. When you get that version from the history file, make changes, and return the new version to the history file, it is marked as version 1.2, and so on.

The name of an SCCS history file is derived by adding an `s.` prefix to the file name of a working copy. The `sccs` command normally expects these `s.` files to reside in an SCCS subdirectory. Thus, when you supply `sccs` with a file argument, it normally applies the subcommand to a file named `s.file` in the SCCS subdirectory. If `file` is a path name, `sccs` looks for the history file in the SCCS subdirectory of that file's parent directory. If `file` is a directory, however, `sccs` applies the subcommand to every `s.` file it contains. Thus, the following command applies the `get` subcommand to a history file named `SCCS/s.program.c`.

```
castle% sccs get program.c
```

By contrast, the following command applies the `get` subcommand to every `s.` file in the SCCS subdirectory.

```
castle% sccs get SCCS
```

You specify options for the `sccs` command itself before the subcommand argument. Specify options for a given subcommand after the subcommand argument. These options are specific to each subcommand and are described along with the subcommands themselves.

Running Setuid

The `sccs` command also includes the capability to run setuid to provide additional protection. However, this capability does not apply to subcommands such as `sccs-admin(1)` because it would enable anyone to change the authorizations of the history file. Commands that could change the history file are always run as the real user.

Options

`-d rootprefix`

> Define the root portion of the path name for SCCS history files. The default root portion is the current directory. `rootprefix` is prepended to the entire file argument even if `file` is an absolute path name. `-d` overrides any directory specified by the `PROJECTDIR` environment variable.

`-p subdir` Define the (sub)directory within which a history file is expected to reside. SCCS is the default.

`-r` (`/usr/xpg4/bin/sccs` only) Run `sccs` with the real user ID instead of setting it to the effective user ID.

Operands

subcommand　An SCCS command name or the name of one of the pseudo-commands.

options　An option or argument to be passed to *subcommand*.

operands　An operand to be passed to *subcommand*.

Usage

Subcommands

Many of the following sccs subcommands invoke programs that reside in /usr/ccs/bin. Many of these subcommands accept additional arguments that are documented in the manual page for the command program the subcommand invokes.

admin　Modify the flags or checksum of an SCCS history file. See sccs-admin(1) for more information about the admin command. Although you can use admin to initialize a history file, you may find that the create subcommand is simpler to use for this purpose.

cdc -*rsid* [-y[*comment*]] (/usr/ccs/bin/sccs)

cdc -*rsid* | -*rsid* [-y[*comment*]] (/usr/xpg4/bin/sccs)

　　Annotate (change) the delta commentary. See sccs-cdc(1). You can use the fix subcommand to replace the delta instead of merely annotating the existing commentary.

　　-*rsid* (/usr/ccs/bin/sccs)

　　-r *sid* | -*rsid* (/usr/xpg4/bin/sccs)

　　　　Specify the SCCS delta ID (*sid*) to which the change notation is to be added. The *sid* for a given delta is a number, in Dewey decimal format, composed of two or four fields: the release and level fields and, for branch deltas, the branch and sequence fields. For instance, the *sid* for the initial delta is normally 1.1.

　　-y[*comment*]

　　　　Specify the comment with which to annotate the delta commentary. If you omit -y, prompt for a comment. A null comment results in an empty annotation.

check [-b][-u[*username*]] (/usr/ccs/bin/sccs)

check [-b][-u [*username*] | -U] (/usr/xpg4/bin/sccs)

　　Check for files currently being edited. Like info and tell, but return an exit code instead of producing a listing of files. check returns a non-zero exit status if anything is being edited.

`-b`	Ignore branches.

`-u[`*`username`*`]` `(/usr/ccs/bin/sccs)`

`-u [`*`username`*`]| -U` `(/usr/xpg4/bin/sccs)`

> Check only files being edited by you. When you specify *username*, check only files being edited by that user. For `/usr/xpg4/bin/sccs`, the `-U` option is equivalent to `-u` *current-user*.

`clean [-b]` Remove everything in the current directory that can be retrieved from an SCCS history. Do not remove files that are being edited.

> `-b`　　　　Do not check branches to see if they are being edited. `clean -b` is dangerous when branch versions are kept in the same directory.

`comb` Generate scripts to combine deltas. See `sccs-comb`(1).

`create` Create (initialize) history files. `create` performs the following steps.

- Renames the original source file to `,program.c` in the current directory.

- Creates the history file called `s.program.c` in the SCCS subdirectory.

- Performs an `sccs get` on `program.c` to retrieve a read-only copy of the initial version.

`deledit [-s][-y[`*`comment`*`]]`

> Equivalent to an `sccs delta` and then an `sccs edit`. The `deledit` subcommand checks in a delta and checks the file back out again but leaves the current working copy of the file intact.

> `-s`　　　　Do not report delta numbers or statistics.

> `-y [`*`comment`*`]` Supply a comment for the `delta` commentary. If you omit `-y`, delta prompts for a comment. A null comment results in an empty comment field for the delta.

`delget [-s][-y[`*`comment`*`]]`

> Perform an `sccs delta` and then an `sccs get` to check in a delta and retrieve read-only copies of the resulting new version. See the `deledit` subcommand for a description of `-s` and `-y`. `sccs` performs a `delta` command on all the files specified in the argument list and then a `get` on all the files. If an error occurs during the `delta`, the `get` is not performed.

`delta [-s][-y[`*`comment`*`]]`

> Check in pending changes. Record the line-by-line changes introduced while the file was checked out. The effective user ID must be the same as the ID of the person who has the file checked

out. See sccs-delta(1). See the deledit subcommand for a
description of -s and -y.

diffs [-C][-I][-c*date-time*][-r*sid*] *diff-options*
(/usr/ccs/bin/sccs)   *New!*

diffs [-C][-I][-c*date-time* | -c *date-time*][-r*sid* | -r *sid*]   *New!*
   diff-options (/usr/xpg4/bin/sccs)

       Compare (in diff(1) format) the working copy of a file that is
checked out for editing, with a version from the SCCS history. Use
the most recent checked-in version by default. The diffs
subcommand accepts the same options as diff.

       Any -r, -c, -i, -x, and -t options are passed to the get   *New!*
subcommand. Any -l, -s, -e, -f, -h, and -b options are passed to
the diff command. A -C option is passed to diff as -c. An -I
option is passed to diff as -i.

       -c*date-time* (/usr/ccs/bin/sccs)

       -c *date-time* | -c*date-time* (/usr/xpg4/bin/sccs)

       Use the most recent version checked in before the indicated date
and time for comparison. date-time takes the form
yy[*mm*[*dd*[*hh*[*mm*[*ss*]]]]]. Omitted units default to their
maximum possible values; that is, -c7502 is equivalent to
-c750228235959.

       -r*sid* (/usr/ccs/bin/sccs)

       -r *sid* | -r*sid* (/usr/xpg4/bin/sccs)

              Use the version corresponding to the indicated
delta for comparison.

edit   Retrieve a version of the file for editing. Extract a version of the
file that is writable by you; create a p.*file* in the SCCS
subdirectory as a lock on the history file so that no one else can
check that version in or out. Retrieve ID keywords in unexpanded
form. edit accepts the same options as get. See sccs-get(1) for a
list of ID keywords and their definitions.

enter   Similar to create, but omit the final sccs get. You can use this
subcommand if you are performing an sccs edit immediately
after initializing the history file.

fix -r*sid* (/usr/ccs/bin/sccs)

fix -r *sid* | -r*sid* (/usr/xpg4/bin/sccs)

       Revise a (leaf) delta. Remove the indicated delta from the SCCS
history, but leave a working copy of the current version in the
directory. This subcommand is useful for incorporating trivial
updates for which you need no audit record or for revising the
delta commentary. You must follow fix with a -r option to specify
the *sid* of the delta to remove. The indicated delta must be the
most recent (leaf) delta in its branch. Use fix with caution

because it does not leave an audit trail of differences (although the previous commentary is retained within the history file).

```
get [-ekmps][-cdate-time][-r[sid]] (/usr/ccs/bin/sccs)
```

New!
```
get [-ekmps][-c date-time | -cdate-time][-r sid | -rsid]
(/usr/xpg4/bin/sccs)
```

Retrieve a version from the SCCS history. By default, this copy is a read-only working copy of the most recent version; ID keywords are in expanded form. See `sccs-get(1)` for a list of ID keywords and their definitions.

`-e`	Retrieve a version for editing. Same as `sccs edit`.
`-k`	Retrieve a writable copy, but do not check out the file. ID keywords are unexpanded.
`-m`	Precede each line with the `sid` of the delta in which it was added.
`-p`	Produce the retrieved version to the standard output. Direct reports that would normally go to the standard output (delta IDs and statistics) to the standard error.
`-s`	Do not report version numbers or statistics.

`-cdate-time` (/usr/ccs/bin/sccs)

`-c date-time | -cdate-time` (/usr/xpg4/bin/sccs)

Retrieve the latest version checked in before the date and time indicated by the `date-time` argument. `date-time` takes the form `yy[mm[dd [hh[mm[ss]]]]]`.

`-r[sid]`   Retrieve the version corresponding to the indicated `sid`. If you specify no `sid`, retrieve the latest `sid` for the specified file.

`-r sid | -rsid`

Retrieve the version corresponding to the indicated `sid`.

```
help message-code|sccs-command
```

`help stuck`   Supply more information about SCCS diagnostics. `help` displays a brief explanation of the error when you supply the code displayed by an SCCS diagnostic message. If you supply the name of an SCCS command, `help` prints a usage line. `help` also recognizes the keyword `stuck`. See `sccs-help(1)`.

```
info [-b][-u[username]] (/usr/ccs/bin/sccs)
info [-b][-u [username] | -U] (/usr/xpg4/bin/sccs)
```

Display a list of files being edited, including the version number checked out, the version to be checked in, the name of the user who holds the lock, and the date and time the file was checked out.

-b   Ignore branches.

-u[*username*] (/usr/ccs/bin/sccs)

-u [*username*] | -U (usr/xpg4/bin/sccs)

List only files checked out by you. When you specify *username*, list only files checked out by that user. For /usr/xpg4/bin/sccs, the -U option is equivalent to -u *current-user*.

print   Print the entire history of each named file. Equivalent to sccs prs -e followed by sccs get -p -m.

prs [-el][-c*date-time*][-r*sid*] (/usr/ccs/bin/sccs)

prs [-el][-c *date-time* | -c*date-time*][-r *sid* | -r*sid*] (/usr/xpg4/bin/sccs)

Peruse (display) the delta table or other portion of an s. file. See sccs-prs(1).

-e   Display delta table information for all deltas earlier than the one specified with -r (or all deltas if you specify none).

-l   Display information for all deltas later than, and including, that specified by -c or -r.

-c*date-time* (/usr/ccs/bin/sccs)

-c *date-time* | -c*date-time*

Specify the latest delta checked in before the indicated date and time. The *date-time* argument takes the form *yy*[*mm*[*dd* [*hh*[*mm*[*ss*]]]]].

-r*sid* (/usr/ccs/bin/sccs)

-r *sid* | -r*sid* (/usr/xpg4/bin/sccs)

Specify a given delta by *sid*.

prt [-y]   Display the delta table, but omit the MR field (see sccs-file(4) for more information on this field). See sccs-prt(1).

-y   Display the most recent delta table entry. The format is a single output line for each file argument; this format is convenient for use in a pipeline with awk(1) or sed(1).

```
rmdel -rsid (/usr/ccs/bin/sccs)
rmdel -r sid (/usr/xpg4/bin/sccs)
```

> Remove the indicated delta from the history file. That delta must be the most recent (leaf) delta in its branch. See sccs-rmdel(1).

sact   Show editing activity status of an SCCS file. See sccs-sact(1).

```
sccsdiff -rold-sid -rnew-sid diff-options
```

> Compare two versions corresponding to the indicated sids (deltas), using diff. See sccs-sccsdiff(1).

```
tell [-b][-u[username]] (/usr/ccs/bin/sccs)
tell [-b][-u [username] | -U] (/usr/xpg4/bin/sccs)
```

> Display the list of files that are currently checked out, one file per line.
>
> -b   Ignore branches.
>
> -u[username] (/usr/ccs/bin/sccs)
>
> -u [username] | -U (/usr/xpg4/bin/sccs)
>
> > List only files checked out to you. When you specify username, list only files checked out to that user. For /usr/xpg4/bin/sccs, the -U option is equivalent to -u current-user.

unedit   Undo the last edit or get -e, and return the working copy to its previous condition. unedit backs out all pending changes made since the file was checked out.

unget   Same as unedit. See sccs-unget(1).

val   Validate the history file. See sccs-val(1).

what   Display any expanded ID keyword strings contained in a binary (object) or text file. See what(1) for more information.

Examples

The following example checks out a file, edits it, and checks it back in again.

```
castle% sccs edit program.c
1.1
new delta 1.2
14 lines
castle% vi program.c
your editing session
castle% sccs delget program.c
comments? clarified cryptic diagnostic
1.2
3 inserted
2 deleted
12 unchanged
1.2
```

```
15 lines
castle%
```

The following example defines the root portion of the command path name.

```
castle% sccs -d/usr/src/include get stdio.h
/usr/ccs/bin/get    /usr/src/include/SCCS/s.stdio.h
castle%
```

The following example redefines the resident subdirectory.

```
castle% sccs -pprivate get include/stdio.h
/usr/ccs/bin/get    include/private/s.stdio.h
castle%
```

The following example initializes the history file for a source file named program.c, creates the SCCS subdirectory, and then uses sccs create to create the history file.

```
castle% mkdir SCCS
castle% sccs create program.c
program.c:
1.1
14 lines
castle%
```

After verifying the working copy, you can remove the backup file that starts with a comma, as shown in the following example.

```
castle% diff program.c ,program.c
castle% rm ,program.c
castle%
```

The following two examples retrieve a file from another directory into the current directory.

```
castle% sccs get /usr/src/sccs/cc.c
castle% sccs -p/usr/src/sccs/ get cc.c
```

The following example checks out all files under SCCS in the current directory.

```
castle% sccs edit SCCS
```

The following example checks in all files currently checked out to you.

```
castle% sccs delta `sccs tell -u`
```

Environment Variables

See environ(5) for descriptions of the following environment variables that affect the execution of sccs: LC_CTYPE, LC_MESSAGES, and NLSPATH.

PROJECTDIR

> Specify an absolute path name (beginning with a slash) for sccs to use to search for SCCS history files. If PROJECTDIR does not begin with a slash, take it as the name of a user and search the src or source subdirectory of that user's home directory for history files. If sccs finds such a directory, use it. Otherwise, use the value as a relative path name.

Exit Status

0   Successful completion.

>0   An error occurred.

Files

SCCS   SCCS subdirectory.

SCCS/d.*file*

> Temporary file of differences.

SCCS/p.*file*

> Lock (permissions) file for checked-out versions.

SCCS/q.*file*

> Temporary file.

SCCS/s.*file*

> SCCS history file.

SCCS/x.*file*

> Temporary copy of the s. file.

SCCS/z.*file*

> Temporary lock file.

/usr/ccs/bin/*

> SCCS command programs.

Attributes

See attributes(5) for descriptions of the following attributes:

/usr/ccs/bin/sccs

Attribute Type	Attribute Value
Availability	SUNWsprot

/usr/xpg4/bin/sccs

Attribute Type	Attribute Value
Availability	SUNWxcu4t

See Also

awk(1),diff(1),sccs-admin(1),sccs-cdc(1),sccs-comb(1),sccs-delta(1),
sccs-get(1), sccs-help(1), sccs-prs(1), sccs-rmdel(1), sccs-sact(1),
sccs-sccsdiff(1), sccs-unget(1), sccs-val(1), sed(1), what(1),
sccs-file(4), attributes(5), XPG4(5)
Programming Utilities Guide

---

sccs-admin, admin — Create and Administer SCCS History Files

Synopsis

/usr/ccs/bin/admin [-bhnz][-a *username* | *groupid*]... [-d *flag*...
    [-e *username* | *groupid*]... [-f *flag value*]]... [-i [*filename*]]
    [-m *mr-list*][-r *release*][-t [*description- file*]] [-y[*comment*]]
    s.*filename*...

Description

Use the SCCS admin command to create or modify the flags and other parameters of SCCS history files. File names of SCCS history files begin with the s. prefix and are referred to as s. files, or history files.

The named s. file is created if it does not already exist. Its parameters are initialized or modified according to the options you specify. Parameters not specified are given default values when the file is initialized; otherwise, they remain unchanged.

If you use a directory name in place of the s.*filename* argument, the admin command applies to all s. files in that directory. Unreadable s. files produce an error. The use of a dash (-) as the s.*filename* argument indicates that the names of files are to be read from the standard input, one s. file per line.

Options

-a *username* | *groupid*

> Add a user name or a numerical group ID to the list of users who can check deltas in or out. If the list is empty, any user is allowed to check deltas in or out.

-b   Force encoding of binary data. Files that contain ASCII `null` or other control characters or that do not end with a newline are recognized as binary data files. Store the contents of such files in the history file in encoded form. See `uuencode(1C)` for details about the encoding. This option is normally used in conjunction with `-i` to force `admin` to encode initial versions not recognized as containing binary data.

-d *flag*   Delete the indicated *flag* from the SCCS file. You can specify the `-d` option only for existing `s.` files. See `-f` for the list of recognized flags.

-e *username* | *groupid*

Erase a user name or group ID from the list of users allowed to make deltas.

-f *flag* [*value*]

Set the indicated *flag* to the (optional) value specified. The following flags are recognized.

b   Enable branch deltas. When b is set, you can create branches with the `-b` option of the SCCS `get` command (see `sccs-get(1)`).

c *ceil*   Set a ceiling on the releases that can be checked out. *ceil* is a number less than or equal to 9999. If you do not set c, the ceiling is 9999.

f *floor*   Set a floor on the releases that can be checked out. The *floor* is a number greater than 0 but less than 9999. If you do not set f, the floor is 1.

d *sid*   The default delta number (*sid*) to be used by an SCCS `get` command.

i   Treat the `No ID keywords` (`ge6`) message issued by an SCCS `get` or `delta` command as an error instead of a warning.

j   Allow concurrent updates.

la *lrelease*[, *release*...]

Lock the indicated list of releases against deltas. If you use a, lock out deltas to all releases. An SCCS `get -e` command fails when applied against a locked release.

n   Create empty releases when releases are skipped. These `null` (empty) deltas serve as anchor points for branch deltas.

q *value*   Supply a value to which the `%Q%` keyword is to expand when retrieving a read-only version with the SCCS `get` command.

m *module*   Supply a value for the module name to which the %M% keyword is to expand. If you do not specify the m flag, the value assigned is the name of the SCCS file with the leading s. removed.

t *type*   Supply a value for the module type to which the %Y% keyword is to expand.

v[*program*]   Specify a validation program for the Modification Request (MR) numbers associated with a new delta. The optional *program* specifies the name of an MR number validity-checking program. If you set this flag when creating an SCCS file, you must also use the -m option, in which case the list of MRs can be empty.

-h   Check the structure of an existing s. file (see sccs-file(4)) and compare a newly computed checksum with one stored in the first line of that file. -h inhibits writing to the file and, thus, nullifies the effect of any other options.

-i[*filename*]

Initialize the history file with text from the indicated file. This text constitutes the initial delta or set of checked-in changes. If you omit *filename*, obtain the initial text from the standard input. Omitting the -i option altogether creates an empty s. file. Using -i, you can initialize only one s. file with text. This option implies the -n option.

-m[*mr-list*]   Insert the indicated Modification Request (MR) numbers into the commentary for the initial version. When specifying more than one MR number on the command line, specify *mr-list* as a quoted, space-separated list. A warning results if you do not set the v flag or the MR validation fails.

-n   Create a new SCCS history file.

-r *release*   Specify the release for the initial delta. You can use -r only in conjunction with -i. The initial delta is inserted into release 1 if you omit this option. The level of the initial delta is always 1; initial deltas are named 1.1 by default.

-t[*description-file*]

Insert descriptive text from the file *description-file*. When you use -t in conjunction with -n or -i to initialize a new s. file, you must supply the *description-file*. When modifying the description for an existing file, a -t option without a *description-file* removes the descriptive text if any; a -t option with a *description-file* replaces the existing text.

-y[*comment*]   Insert the indicated comment in the Comments: field for the initial delta. Valid only in conjunction with -i or -n. If you omit the -y option, insert a default comment line that notes the date and time the history file was created.

-z   Recompute the file checksum and store it in the first line of the s. file. Caution: It is important to verify the contents of the history file (see sccs-val(1), and the print subcommand in sccs(1)) because using -z on a truly corrupted file can prevent detection of the error.

Exit Status

0   Successful completion.

1   An error occurred.

Files

s.*   History file.

SCCS/s.*   History file in SCCS subdirectory.

z.*   Temporary lock file.

Attributes

See attributes(5) for descriptions of the following attributes:

Attribute Type	Attribute Value
Availability	SUNWsprot

See Also

sccs(1), sccs-cdc(1), sccs-delta(1), sccs-get(1), sccs-help(1), sccs-rmdel(1), sccs-val(1), sccs-file(4), attributes(5)
Programming Utilities Guide

Diagnostics

Use the SCCS help command for explanations (see sccs-help(1)).

Warnings

The last component of all SCCS file names must have the s. prefix. New SCCS files are given permission mode 444 (see chmod(1)). All writing done by admin is to a temporary file with an x. prefix, created with mode 444 for a new SCCS file or with the same mode as an existing SCCS file. After successful execution of admin, the existing s. file is removed and replaced with the x. file. This sequence ensures that changes are made to the SCCS file only when no errors have occurred.

It is recommended that directories containing SCCS files have permission mode 755 and that the s. files themselves have mode 444. The mode for directories allows only the owner to modify the SCCS files contained in the directories, and the mode of the s. files prevents all modifications except those performed with SCCS commands.

If you need to patch an SCCS file for any reason, the owner can change the mode to 644 to allow use of a text editor. However, take extreme care when editing an SCCS file. Always process the edited file with an admin -h to check for corruption followed by an admin -z to generate a proper checksum. Another admin -h is recommended to ensure that the resulting s. file is valid.

admin also uses a temporary lock s. file, starting with the z. prefix, to prevent simultaneous updates to the s. file. See sccs-get(1) for further information about the z. file.

sccs-cdc, cdc — Change the Commentary of an SCCS Delta

Synopsis

```
/usr/ccs/bin/cdc -r sid [-m mr-list][-y [comment]] s.filename...
```

Description

Use the SCCS cdc (change delta commentary) command to annotate the delta commentary for the SCCS delta ID (*sid*) specified by the -r option in each named s. file.

If the v flag is set in the s. file, you can also use cdc to update the Modification Request (MR) list.

If you checked in the delta or if you own the file and directory and have write permission, you can use cdc to annotate the commentary.

Instead of replacing the existing commentary, cdc inserts the new comment you supply, followed by a line of the following form above the existing commentary.

```
*** CHANGED *** yy/mm/dd hh/mm/ss username
```

If a directory is named as the s.*filename* argument, the cdc command applies to all s. files in that directory. Unreadable s. files produce an error; processing continues with the next file (if any). If you specify a dash (-) as the s.*filename* argument, each line of the standard input is taken as the name of an SCCS history file to be processed and you must also use the -m and -y options.

Options

-m *mr-list*   Specify one or more MR numbers to add or delete. When specifying more than one MR on the command line, specify *mr-list* as a quoted, space-separated list. To delete an MR number, precede it with a ! character (an empty MR list has no effect). Put a list of deleted MRs in the comment section of the delta commentary. If you do not use the -m option and the standard input is a terminal, cdc prompts with MRs? for the list (before issuing the comments? prompt). -m is useful only when the v flag is set in the s. file. If that flag has a value, take it to be the name of a program to validate the MR numbers. If that validation program returns a non-zero exit status, cdc terminates and the delta commentary remains unchanged.

-r *sid*   Specify the *sid* of the delta to change.

-y[*comment*]   Use *comment* as the annotation in the delta commentary. Retain the previous comments; add the comment along with a notation that the commentary was changed. A null comment leaves the commentary unaffected. If you do not specify -y and the standard input is a terminal, cdc prompts with comments? for the text of the notation to be added. You terminate the annotation text with an unescaped newline character.

Examples

The following example produces annotated commentary for delta 1.6 in s.program.c.

```
castle% cdc -r1.6 -y"corrected commentary" s.program.c

D 1.6 88/07/05 23:21:07 username 9 0 00001/00000/00000
MRs:
COMMENTS:
corrected commentary
*** CHANGED *** 88/07/07 14:09:41 username
performance enhancements in main()
```

Files

z.*file*   Temporary lock file.

Attributes

See attributes(5) for descriptions of the following attributes:

Attribute Type	Attribute Value
Availability	SUNWsprot

See Also

sccs(1), sccs-admin(1), sccs-comb(1), sccs-delta(1), sccs-help(1), sccs-prs(1), sccs-prt(1), sccs-rmdel(1), what(1), sccs-file(4), attributes(5)

Programming Utilities Guide

Diagnostics

Use the SCCS help command for explanations (see sccs-help(1)).

---

sccs-comb, comb — Combine SCCS Deltas

Synopsis

/usr/ccs/bin/comb [-os][-c *sid-list*][-p *sid*] s.*filename* ...

Description

Use the SCCS comb command to generate a shell script (see sh(1)) that you can use to reconstruct the indicated s. files. This script is written to the standard output.

If you use a directory name in place of the s.*filename* argument, the comb command applies to all s. files in that directory. Unreadable s. files produce an error; processing continues with the next file (if any). The use of a dash (-) as the s.*filename* argument indicates that the names of files are to be read from the standard input, one s. file per line.

If you specify no options, comb preserves only the most recent (leaf) delta in a branch and the minimal number of ancestors needed to preserve the history.

Options

-c *sid-list*

Include the indicated list of deltas. Omit all other deltas. *sid-list* is a comma-separated list of SCCS delta IDs (*sid*s). To specify a range of deltas, use a a dash (-) separator instead of a comma between two *sid*s in the list.

-o

For each get -e generated, access the reconstructed file at the release of the delta to be created. Otherwise, access the reconstructed file at the most recent ancestor. Using -o can decrease the size of the reconstructed s. file. It can also alter the shape of the delta tree of the original file.

-p *sid*

Specify the *sid* of the oldest delta to be preserved.

    -s   Generate scripts to gather statistics instead of combining deltas. When run, the shell scripts report the file name, size (in blocks) after combining, original size (in blocks), and the percentage size change, computed by the formula: `100 * (original - combined) / original`. You can use this option to calculate the space that is saved before actually doing the combining.

Files

    `s.COMB`   Reconstructed SCCS file.

    `comb?????`   Temporary file.

Attributes

See `attributes`(5) for descriptions of the following attributes:

Attribute Type	Attribute Value
Availability	SUNWsprot

See Also

`sccs(1)`, `sccs-admin(1)`, `sccs-cdc(1)`, `sccs-delta(1)`, `sccs-help(1)`, `sccs-prs(1)`, `sccs-prt(1)`, `sccs-rmdel(1)`, `sccs-sccsdiff(1)`, `what(1)`, `sccs-file(4)`, `attributes(5)`
Programming Utilities Guide

Diagnostics

Use the SCCS `help` command for explanations (see `sccs-help(1)`).

Bugs

`comb` can rearrange the shape of the tree of deltas. It may not save any space; in fact, it is possible for the reconstructed file to actually be larger than the original.

sccs-delta, delta — Make a Delta to an SCCS File

Synopsis

```
/usr/ccs/bin/delta [-dnps][-g sid-list | -g sid-list]
    [-m mr-list | -m mr-list][-r sid | -r sid][-y[comment]]
    s.filename...
/usr/xpg4/bin/delta [-dnps][-g sid-list | -g sid-list]
    [-m mr-list| -m mr-list][-r sid | -r sid][-y[comment]]
    s.filename...
```

Description

Use the SCCS `delta` command to check in a record of the line-by-line differences made to a checked-out version of a file under SCCS control. These changes are taken from the writable working copy that was retrieved with the SCCS `get` command (see `sccs-get`(1)). This working copy does not have the `s.` prefix and is also referred to as a g-file.

If you specify a directory name in place of the `s.filename` argument, the `delta` command applies to all `s.` files in that directory. Unreadable `s.` files produce an error; processing continues with the next file (if any). The use of a dash (-) as the `s.filename` argument indicates that the names of files are to be read from the standard input, one `s.` file per line (requires -y, and in some cases, -m).

`delta` can issue prompts to the standard output depending on the options specified, the flags that are set in the `s.` file (see `sccs-admin`(1), and the -m and -y options.

/usr/xpg4/bin/delta

The `sid` of the delta is not echoed to standard output.

Options

-d	Use the `diff`(1) command instead of `bdiff`(1). Return exit status 2 if you do not specify the `s.filename` argument.
-g `sid-list` | -g`sid-list`	
	Specify a list of deltas to omit when the file is accessed at the SCCS version ID (`sid`) created by this delta. `sid-list` is a comma-separated list of `sids`. To specify a range of deltas, use a hyphen (-) separator, instead of a comma, between two `sids` in the list.
-m `mr-list` | -m`mr-list`	
	If the SCCS file has the v flag set (see `sccs-admin`(1)), you must supply one or more Modification Request (MR) numbers for the new delta. When you specify more than one MR number on the command line, `mr-list` takes the form of a quoted, space-separated list. If you do not use -m and the standard input is a terminal, delta prompts with MRs? for the list (before displaying the comments? prompt). If the v flag in the `s.` file has a value, take it to be the name of a program to validate the MR numbers. If that validation program returns a non-zero exit status, terminate without checking in the changes.
-n	Retain the edited g-file that is normally removed at the completion of processing.
-p	Display line-by-line differences (in `diff`(1) format) to the standard output.

`-r sid | -rsid`

> When two or more versions are checked out, specify the version to check in. This `sid` value can be either the `sid` specified on the `get` command line or the `sid` of the new version to be checked in as reported by `get`. A diagnostic results if the specified `sid` is ambiguous or if one is required but not supplied.

`-s`

> Do not display warning or confirmation messages. Do not suppress error messages (which are written to standard error).

`-y[comment]`

> Supply a comment for the delta table (version log). A `null` comment is accepted and produces an empty commentary in the log. If you do not specify `-y` and the standard input is a terminal, `delta` prompts with `comments?`. You terminate the comment with an unescaped newline.

Exit Status

0	Successful completion.
1	An error occurred, and you did not specify the `-d` option.
2	An error occurred because you specified the `-d` option but did not include the `s.filename` argument.

Files

`d.file`	Temporary file of differences.
`p.file`	Lock file for a checked-out version.
`q.file`	Temporary file.
`s.file`	SCCS history file.
`x.file`	Temporary copy of the `s.` file.
`z.file`	Temporary file.

Attributes

See `attributes`(5) for descriptions of the following attributes:

/usr/ccs/bin/delta

Attribute Type	Attribute Value
Availability	SUNWsprot

/usr/xpg4/bin/delta

Attribute Type	Attribute Value
Availability	SUNWxcu4

See Also

bdiff(1), diff(1), sccs(1), sccs-admin(1), sccs-cdc(1), sccs-get(1),
sccs-help(1),sccs-prs(1),sccs-prt(1),sccs-rmdel(1),sccs-sccsdiff(1),
sccs-unget(1), what(1), sccs-file(4), attributes(5), XPG4(5)
Programming Utilities Guide

Diagnostics

Use the SCCS help command for explanations (see sccs-help(1)).

Warnings

Lines beginning with an ASCII SOH character (binary 001) cannot be put into
the SCCS file unless you escape the SOH. This character has special meaning
to SCCS (see sccs-file(4)) and produces an error.

sccsdiff — Compare Two Versions of an SCCS File

Synopsis

```
/usr/ccs/bin/sccsdiff [-p] -r sid -r sid [diff-options]
   s.filename
```

Description

See sccs-sccsdiff(1).

sccs-get, get — Retrieve a Version of an SCCS File

Synopsis

```
/usr/ccs/bin/get [-begkmnpst][-l[p]][-a sequence]
   [-c date-time | -c date-time][-G g- file]
   [-i sid-list | -i sid-list][-r[sid]]
   [-x sid-list | -x sid-list] s.filename...
/usr/xpg4/bin/get [-begkmnpst][-l[p]][-a sequence]
   [-c date-time | -c date-time][-G g- file]
   [-i sid-list | -i sid-list][-r sid | -r sid]
   [-x sid-list | -x sid-list] s.filename ...
```

Description

Use the SCCS `get` command to retrieve a working copy from the SCCS history file, using the specified options.

For each `s.filename` argument, `get` displays the SCCS delta ID (`sid`) and number of lines retrieved.

If you use a directory name in place of the `s.filename` argument, the `get` command applies to all `s.` files in that directory. Unreadable `s.` files produce an error; processing continues with the next file (if any). The use of a dash (-) as the `s.filename` argument indicates that the names of files are to be read from the standard input, one `s.` file per line.

The retrieved file normally has the same file-name base as the `s.` file, less the prefix, and is referred to as the g-file.

For each file processed, `get` responds (to the standard output) with the `sid` being accessed and with the number of lines retrieved from the `s.` file.

Options

-a `sequence`

> Retrieve the version corresponding to the indicated delta sequence number. This option is used primarily by the SCCS `comb` command (see `sccs-comb(1)`); `-r` is an easier way for you to specify a version. `-a` supersedes `-r` when both are used.

-b

> Create a new branch. Use with the `-e` option to indicate that the new delta should have an `sid` in a new branch. Instead of incrementing the level for the version to be checked in, indicate in the `p.` file for the delta to be checked in to either initialize a new branch and sequence (if there is no existing branch at the current level) or to increment the branch component of the `sid`. If the b flag is not set in the `s.` file, ignore this option.

-c `date-time` | -c`date-time`

> Retrieve the latest version checked in before the date and time indicated by the `date-time` argument. `date-time` takes the form `yy[mm[dd[hh[mm[ss]]]]]`. Units omitted from the indicated date and time default to their maximum possible values; that is, `-c7502` is equivalent to `-c750228235959`. Any number of nonnumeric characters can separate the various 2-digit components. If white-space characters occur, you must quote the `date-time` specification.

-e

> Retrieve a version for editing. Put a lock on the `s.` file so that no one else can check in changes to the version you have checked out. If the j flag is set in the `s.` file, the lock is advisory: `get` issues a warning message. Concurrent use of `get -e` for different `sid`s is allowed; however, `get` does not check out a version of the file if a writable version is present in the directory. All SCCS file protections stored in the `s.` file, including the release ceiling, floor, and authorized user list, are honored by `get -e`.

| -g | Get the SCCS version ID, without retrieving the version itself. Use to verify the existence of a particular *sid*. |

-G *newname* Use *newname* as the name of the retrieved version.

-i *sid-list* | -i*sid-list*

> Specify a list of deltas to include in the retrieved version. The included deltas are noted in the standard output message. *sid-list* is a comma-separated list of *sid*s. To specify a range of deltas, use a a hyphen (-) separator instead of a comma between two *sid*s in the list.

| -k | Suppress expansion of ID keywords. -k is implied by -e. |

-l[p] Retrieve a summary of the delta table (version log) and write it to a listing file with the l. prefix (called l. file). When you use -lp, write the summary to the standard output.

-m Precede each retrieved line with the *sid* of the delta in which it was added to the file. The *sid* is separated from the line with a Tab.

-n Precede each line with the %M% ID keyword and a Tab. When you use both the -m and -n options, the ID keyword precedes the *sid* and the line of text.

-p Write the text of the retrieved version to the standard output. Write all messages that normally go to the standard output to the standard error instead.

-s Suppress all output normally written to the standard output. However, fatal error messages (which always go to the standard error) are unaffected.

-t Retrieve the most recently created (top) delta in a given release, for example, -r1.

/usr/ccs/bin/get

-r[*sid*] Retrieve the version corresponding to the indicated *sid* (delta).

The *sid* for a given delta is a number, in Dewey decimal format, composed of two or four fields: the release and level fields and, for branch deltas, the branch and sequence fields. For instance, if 1.2 is the *sid*, 1 is the release and 2 is the level number. If 1.2.3.4 is the *sid*, 3 is the branch and 4 is the sequence number.

You need not specify the entire *sid* to retrieve a version with get. When you omit -r altogether or when you omit both release and level, get normally retrieves the highest release and level. If the d flag is set to an *sid* in the s. file and you omit the *sid*, get retrieves the default version indicated by that flag.

When you specify a release but omit the level, get retrieves the highest level in that release. If that release does not exist, get retrieves the highest level from the next-highest existing release.

Similarly with branches, if you specify a release, level, and branch, `get` retrieves the highest sequence in that branch.

/usr/xpg4/bin/get

`-r sid | -rsid`

> Same as for `/usr/ccs/bin/get` except that `sid` is mandatory.

`-x sid-list | -xsid-list`

> Exclude the indicated deltas from the retrieved version. The excluded deltas are noted in the standard output message. `sid-list` is a comma-separated list of `sid`s. To specify a range of deltas, use a hyphen (-) separator, instead of a comma, between two `sid`s in the list.

Output

/usr/ccs/bin/get

The `/usr/ccs/bin/get` command has the following output format.

`"%s\n%d lines\n", sid, number-of-lines`

/usr/xpg4/bin/get

The `/usr/xpg4/bin/get` command has the following output format.

`"%s\n%d\n", sid, number-of-lines`

Usage

ID Keywords

In the absence of `-e` or `-k`, `get` expands the following ID keywords by replacing them with the indicated values in the text of the retrieved source.

`%A%`	Shorthand notation for an ID line with data `forwhat(1)` in the format `%Z%%Y% %M% %I%%Z%`.
`%B%`	`sid` branch component.
`%C%`	Current line number. Intended for identifying messages output by the program such as "this shouldn't have happened" errors. It is not intended to be used on every line to provide sequence numbers.
`%D%`	Current date, in the format *yy*/*mm*/*dd*.
`%E%`	Date newest applied delta was created, in the format *yy*/*mm*/*dd*.
`%F%`	SCCS `s.` file name.
`%G%`	Date newest applied delta was created, in the format *mm*/*dd*/*yy*.
`%H%`	Current date, in the format *mm*/*dd*/*yy*.
`%I%`	`sid` of the retrieved version, in the format `%R%.%L%.%B%.%S%`.
`%L%`	`sid`-level component.

`%M%`	Module name, either the value of the m flag in the s. file (see `sccs-admin`(1)) or the name of the s. file less the prefix.
`%P%`	Fully qualified s. file name.
`%Q%`	Value of the q flag in the s. file.
`%R%`	*sid* release component.
`%S%`	*sid* sequence component.
`%T%`	Current time, in the format *hh:mm:ss*.
`%U%`	Time the newest applied delta was created, in the format *hh:mm:ss*.
`%W%`	Shorthand notation for an ID line with data `forwhat`, in the format `%Z%%M%  %I%`.
`%Y%`	Module type value of the t flag in the s. file.
`%Z%`	Four-character string: `@(#)` recognized by `what`.

ID String

The table below explains how the SCCS identification string is determined for retrieving and creating deltas.

Determination of SCCS Identification String

SID(1) Specified	-b Option Used (2)	Other Conditions	SID Retrieved	SID of Delta to Be Created
`none(3)`	No	R defaults to mR	`mR.mL`	`mR.(mL+1)`
`none(3)`	Yes	R defaults to mR	`mR.mL`	`mR.mL.(mB+1).1`
`R`	No	R > mR	`mR.mL`	`R.1(4)`
`R`	No	R = mR	`mR.mL`	`mR.(mL+1)`
`R`	Yes	R > mR	`mR.mL`	`mR.mL.(mB+1).1`
`R`	Yes	R = mR	`mR.mL`	`mR.mL.(mB+1).1`
`R`	–	R < mR, and R does not exist	`hR.mL(5)`	`hR.mL.(mB+1).1`
`R`	–	Trunk succ.(6) in release > R, and R exists	`R.mL`	`R.mL.(mB+1).1`
`R.L`	No	No trunk succ.	`RL`	`R.(L+1)`
`R.L`	Yes	No trunk succ.	`RL`	`R.L.(mB+1).1`
`R.L`	–	Trunk succ. in release ≥ R	`R.L`	`R.L.(mB+1).1`

SID(1) Specified	-b Option Used (2)	Other Conditions	SID Retrieved	SID of Delta to Be Created
`R.L.B`	No	No branch succ.	`R.L.B.mS`	`R.L.B.(mS+1)`
`R.L.B`	Yes	No branch succ.	`R.L.B.mS`	`R.L.(mB+1).1`
`R.L.B.S`	No	No branch succ.	`R.L.B.S`	`R.L.B.(S+1)`
`R.L.B.S`	Yes	No branch succ.	`R.L.B.S`	`R.L.(mB+1).1`
`R.L.B.S`	–	Branch succ.	`R.L.B.S`	`R.L.(mB+1).1`

1. R, L, B, and S are the release, level, branch, and sequence components of the *sid*; m means maximum. Thus, for example, R.mL means the maximum level number within release R; R.L.(mB+1).1 means the first sequence number on the new branch (that is, maximum branch number plus 1) of level L within release R. Note that if the *sid* specified is of the form R.L, R.L.B, or R.L.B.S, each of the specified components must exist.

2. The -b option is effective only if the b flag is present in the file. An entry of a dash (-) means the -b option is not relevant.

3. This case applies if the d (default *sid*) flag is not present in the file. If the d flag is present in the file, the *sid* obtained from the d flag is interpreted as if it had been specified on the command line. Thus, one of the other cases in this table applies.

4. Force creation of the first delta in a new release.

5. hR is the highest existing release that is lower than the specified, nonexistent release R.

6. Successor.

Files

`g-file`	Version retrieved by get.
`l.file`	File containing extracted delta table information.
`p.file`	Permissions (lock) file.
`z.file`	Temporary copy of s. file.

Attributes

See attributes(5) for descriptions of the following attributes:

/usr/ccs/bin/get

Attribute Type	Attribute Value
Availability	SUNWsprot

/usr/ccs/bin/get

Attribute Type	Attribute Value
Availability	SUNWxcu4

See Also

```
sccs(1), sccs-admin(1), sccs-delta(1), sccs-help(1), sccs-prs(1),
sccs-prt(1), sccs-sact(1), sccs-unget(1), what(1), sccs-file(4),
attributes(5), XPG4(5)
```
Programming Utilities Guide

Diagnostics

Use the SCCS help command for explanations (see sccs-help(1)).

Bugs

If the effective user has write permission (either explicitly or implicitly) in the directory containing the SCCS files but the real user does not, you can name only one file when using -e.

sccs-help, help — Ask for Help Regarding SCCS Error or Warning Messages

Synopsis

```
/usr/ccs/bin/help [argument]...
```

Description

Use the SCCS help command to retrieve information to further explain errors, messages, and warnings from SCCS commands. help also provides some information about SCCS command usage. If you specify no arguments, help prompts for one.

An *argument* can be a message number (which normally appears in parentheses following each SCCS error or warning message) or an SCCS command name. help responds with an explanation of the message or a usage line for the command.

When all else fails, try /usr/ccs/bin/help stuck.

Files

`/usr/lib/help`

Directory containing files of message text.

Attributes

See `attributes`(5) for descriptions of the following attributes:

Attribute Type	Attribute Value
Availability	SUNWsprot

See Also

`sccs`(1), `sccs-admin`(1), `sccs-cdc`(1), `sccs-comb`(1), `sccs-delta`(1), `sccs-get`(1), `sccs-prs`(1), `sccs-prt`(1), `sccs-rmdel`(1), `sccs-sact`(1), `sccs-sccsdiff`(1), `sccs-unget`(1), `sccs-val`(1), `what`(1), `sccs-file`(4), `attributes`(5)

---

sccs-prs, prs — Display Selected Portions of an SCCS History

Synopsis

`/usr/ccs/bin/prs [-ael][-c date-time][-d dataspec][-r sid]`
   `s.filename...`

Description

Use the SCCS `prs` (peruse) command to display part or all of the SCCS file (see `sccs-file`(4)) in a user-supplied format.

If you use a directory name in place of the `s.filename` argument, the `prs` command applies to all `s.` files in that directory. Unreadable `s.` files produce an error; processing continues with the next file (if any). The use of a dash (-) as the `s.filename` argument indicates that the names of files are to be read from the standard input, one `s.` file per line.

Options

In the absence of options, `prs` displays the delta table (version log). In the absence of `-d` or `-l`, `prs` displays the entry for each delta indicated by the other options.

  `-a`   Include all deltas including those marked as removed (see `sccs-rmdel`(1)).

  `-e`   Request information for all deltas created earlier than, and including, the delta indicated with `-r` or `-c`.

-l   Request information for all deltas created later than, and
                  including, the delta indicated with -r or -c.

-c *date-time*

                  Display information on the latest delta checked in before the date
                  and time indicated by the *date-time* argument. *date-time* takes
                  the form *yy*[*mm*[*dd*[*hh*[*mm*[*ss*]]]]].

                  Units omitted from the indicated date and time default to their
                  maximum possible values; that is, -c7502 is equivalent to
                  -c750228235959. Any number of nonnumeric characters can
                  separate the various 2-digit components. If white space characters
                  occur, you must quote the *date-time* specification.

-d *dataspec*   Produce a report according to the indicated data specification.
                  Specify *dataspec* as a quoted text string that includes embedded
                  data keywords of the form ': key:'. The prs command expands
                  these keywords in the output it produces. To specify a Tab
                  character in the output, use \t; to specify a newline in the output,
                  use \n.

-r *sid*   Specify the SCCS delta ID (*sid*) of the delta for which you want
                  information. If you specify no *sid*, use the most recently created
                  delta.

Usage

Data Keywords

Data keywords specify which parts of an SCCS file are to be retrieved. All parts
of an SCCS file (see sccs-file(4)) have an associated data keyword. A data
keyword can appear any number of times in a data specification argument to
-d. These data keywords are listed in the following table.

In the File Section column, B = body, D = delta table, F = flags, and U = user
names. In the Format column, S = simple format and M = multiline format.

Keyword	Data Item	File Section	Value	Format
:A:	Format for the what string	N/A	:Z::Y: :M: :I::Z:	S
:B:	Branch number	D	*nnnn*	S
:BD:	Body	B	*text*	M
:BF:	Branch flag	F	yes or no	S
:CB:	Ceiling boundary	F	:R:	S

Keyword	Data Item	File Section	Value	Format
:C:	Comments for delta	D	*text*	M
:D:	Date delta created	D	:Dy:/:Dm:/:Dd:	S
:Dd:	Day delta created	D	*nn*	S
:Dg:	Deltas ignored (seq #)	D	:DS: :DS:...	S
:DI:	Seq # of deltas included	D	:Dn:/:Dx:/:Dg:	S excluded, ignored
:DL:	Delta line statistics	D	:Li:/:Ld:/:Lu:	S
:Dm:	Month delta created	D	*nn*	S
:Dn:	Deltas included (seq #)	D	:DS: :DS:...	S
:DP:	Predecessor delta seq #	D	*nnnn*	S
:Ds:	Default *sid*	F	:I:	S
:DS:	Delta seq #	D	*nnnn*	S
:Dt:	Delta information	D	:DT::I::D::T::P::DS::DP:	S
:DT:	Delta type	D	D or R	S
:Dx:	Deltas excluded (seq #)	D	:DS: ...	S
:Dy:	Year delta created	D	*nn*	S
:F:	s.*filename*	N/A text	S	
:FB:	Floor boundary	F	:R:	S
:FD:	File descriptive text	C	*text*	M
:FL:	Flag list	F	*text*	M

Keyword	Data Item	File Section	Value	Format
:GB:	Gotten body	B	*text*	M
:I:	SCCS delta ID (*sid*)	D	:R:.:L:.:B:.:S:	S
:J:	Joint edit flag	F	yes **or** no	S
:KF:	Keyword error/warning flag	F	yes **or** no	S
:L:	Level number	D	*nnnn*	S
:Ld:	Lines deleted by delta	D	*nnnnn*	S
:Li:	Lines inserted by delta	D	*nnnnn*	S
:LK:	Locked releases	F	:R:...	S
:Lu:	Lines unchanged by delta	D	*nnnnn*	S
:M:	Module name	F	*text*	S
:MF: MR	Validation flag	F	yes **or** no	S
:MP: MR	Validation program	F	*text*	S
:MR: MR	Numbers for delta	D	*text*	M
:ND:	Null delta flag	F	yes **or** no	S
:Q:	User-defined keyword	F	*text*	S
:P:	User who created delta	D	*username*	S
:PN:	s. file path name	N/A text	S	
:R:	Release number	D	*nnnn*	S

Keyword	Data Item	File Section	Value	Format
`:S:`	Sequence number	D	*nnnn*	S
`:T:`	Time delta created	D	`:Th:::Tm:::Ts:`	S
`:Th:`	Hour delta created	D	*nn*	S
`:Tm:`	Minutes delta created	D	*nn*	S
`:Ts:`	Seconds delta created	D	*nn*	S
`:UN:`	User names	U	*text*	M
`:W:`	A form of `what` string	N/A	`:Z::M:\t:I:`	S
`:Y:`	Module type flag	F	*text*	S
`:Z:`	`what` string delimiter	N/A	@(#)	S

Examples

The following command:

```
castle% /usr/ccs/bin/prs -e -d":I:\t:P:" program.c
```

produces:

```
1.6   username
1.5   username
...
```

Files

```
/tmp/pr?????
```

Temporary file.

Attributes

See attributes(5) for descriptions of the following attributes:

Attribute Type	Attribute Value
Availability	SUNWsprot

See Also

sccs(1), sccs-cdc(1), sccs-delta(1), sccs-get(1), sccs-help(1), sccs-prt(1), sccs-sact(1), sccs-sccsdiff(1), what(1), sccs-file(4), attributes(5)

Programming Utilities Guide

Diagnostics

Use the SCCS help command for explanations (see sccs-help(1)).

---

sccs-prt, prt — Display Delta Table Information from an SCCS File

Synopsis

```
/usr/ccs/bin/prt [-abdefistu][-c date-time][-r date-time][-y sid]
    s.filename...
```

Description

Use the SCCS prt (print) command to print selected portions of an SCCS file. By default, prt prints the delta table (version log).

If you use a directory name in place of the s.*filename* argument, the prt command applies to all s. files in that directory. Unreadable s. files produce an error; processing continues with the next file (if any). The use of a dash (-) as the s.*filename* argument indicates that the names of files are to be read from the standard input, one s. file per line.

Options

If you supply any option other than -y, -c, or -r, the name of each file being processed (preceded by one newline and followed by two newline characters) appears above its contents.

If you use none of the -u, -f, -t, or -b options, -d is assumed. -s and -i are mutually exclusive, as are -c and -r.

-a   Display log entries for all deltas including those marked as removed.

-b   Print the body of the s. file.

-c *date-time*

Exclude delta table entries that have the specified cutoff date and time. Print each entry as a single line preceded by the name of the SCCS file. This format (also produced by -r and -y) makes it easy to sort multiple delta tables in chronological order. When you supply both -y and -c or both -y and -r, stop printing when the first of the two conditions is met.

-d   Print delta table entries (the default).

-e   Do everything. This option implies -d, -i, -u, -f, and -t.

-f   Print the flags of each named s. file.

-i   Print the serial numbers of included, excluded, and ignored deltas.

-r *date-time*

Exclude delta table entries that are newer than the specified cutoff date and time.

-s   Print only the first line of the delta table entries; that is, only up to the statistics.

-t   Print the descriptive text contained in the s. file.

-u   Print the user names and/or numerical group IDs of users allowed to make deltas.

-y *sid*   Exclude delta table entries made before the specified *sid*. If no delta in the table has the specified *sid*, print the entire table. If you specify no *sid*, print the most recent delta.

Usage

Output Format
The following format is used to print those portions of the s. file that are specified by the various options.

- Newline.
- Type of delta (D or R).
- Space.
- SCCS delta ID (*sid*).
- Tab.
- Date and time of creation in the format *yy*/*mm*/*dd hh*/*mm*/*ss*.
- Space.
- User name of the delta's creator.
- Tab.
- Serial number of the delta.

- Space.
- Predecessor delta's serial number.
- Tab.
- Line-by-line change statistics in the format
  inserted/*deleted*/*unchanged*.
- Newline.
- List of included deltas followed by a newline (only if there were any such deltas and you used the -i option).
- List of excluded deltas followed by a newline (only if there were any such deltas and you used the -i option).
- List of ignored deltas followed by a newline (only if there were any such deltas and you used the -i option).
- List of Modification Requests (MRs) followed by a newline (only if you supplied any MR numbers).
- Lines of the delta commentary (if any) followed by a newline.

Examples

The following example produces a one-line display of the delta table entry for the most recent version.

```
castle% /usr/ccs/bin/prt -y program.c
s.program.c: D 1.6 88/07/06 21:39:39 username 5 4 00159/00080/00636...
```

Attributes

See attributes(5) for descriptions of the following attributes:

Attribute Type	Attribute Value
Availability	SUNWsprot

See Also

sccs(1), sccs-cdc(1), sccs-delta(1), sccs-get(1), sccs-help(1),
sccs-prs(1), sccs-sact(1), sccs-sccsdiff(1), what(1), sccs-file(4),
attributes(5)

Diagnostics

Use the SCCS help command for explanations (see sccs-help(1)).

sccs-rmdel, rmdel — Remove a Delta from an SCCS File

Synopsis

`/usr/ccs/bin/rmdel -r` *sid* `s.`*filename*`...`

Description

Use the SCCS `rmdel` command to remove the delta specified by the SCCS delta ID (*sid*) supplied with the `-r` option. The delta to be removed must be the most recent (leaf) delta in its branch. In addition, the *sid* must *not* be that of a version checked out for editing: it must not appear in any entry of the version lock file (`p.` file).

If you created the delta or if you own the file and directory and have write permission, you can remove it with `rmdel`.

If you use a directory name in place of the `s.`*filename* argument, the `rmdel` command applies to all `s.` files in that directory. Unreadable `s.` files produce an error; processing continues with the next file (if any). The use of a dash (-) as the `s.`*filename* argument indicates that the names of files are to be read from the standard input, one `s.` file per line.

Options

    `-r` *sid*   Remove the version corresponding to the indicated *sid* (delta).

Files

`p. file`	Permissions file.
`s. file`	History file.
`z. file`	Temporary copy of the `s.` file.

Attributes

See `attributes`(5) for descriptions of the following attributes:

Attribute Type	Attribute Value
Availability	SUNWsprot

See Also

`sccs(1)`, `sccs-admin(1)`, `sccs-cdc(1)`, `sccs-comb(1)`, `sccs-delta(1)`, `sccs-help(1)`, `sccs-prs(1)`, `sccs-prt(1)`, `sccs-sccsdiff(1)`, `sccs-unget(1)`, `what(1)`, `sccs-file(4)`, `attributes(5)`

Programming Utilities Guide

Diagnostics

Use the SCCS `help` command for explanations (see `sccs-help(1)`).

---

sccs-sact, sact — Show Editing Activity Status of an SCCS File

Synopsis

```
/usr/ccs/bin/sact s.filename...
```

Description

Use the SCCS `sact` command to list any SCCS files that are checked out for editing.

The output for each named file consists of the following five fields separated by space characters.

- `sid` of a delta that currently exists in the SCCS file to which changes are made to create the new delta.
- `sid` for the new delta to be created.
- User name of the person who has the file checked out for editing.
- Date on which the version was checked out.
- Time at which the version was checked out.

If you use a directory name in place of the `s.filename` argument, the `sact` command applies to all `s.` files in that directory. Unreadable `s.` files produce an error; processing continues with the next file (if any). The use of a dash (-) as the `s.filename` argument indicates that the names of files are to be read from the standard input, one `s.` file per line.

Attributes

See `attributes(5)` for descriptions of the following attributes:

Attribute Type	Attribute Value
Availability	SUNWsprot

See Also

```
sccs(1), sccs-delta(1), sccs-get(1), sccs-help(1), sccs-prs(1),
sccs-prt(1), what(1), sccs-file(4), attributes(5)
```
Programming Utilities Guide

Diagnostics

Use the SCCS `help` command for explanations (see `sccs-help(1)`).

Bugs

`sact` is not recognized as a subcommand of `sccs(1)`.

sccs-sccsdiff, sccsdiff — Compare Two Versions of an SCCS File

Synopsis

```
/usr/ccs/bin/sccsdiff [-p] -r sid -r sid [diff-options] s.filename
```

Description

Use the SCCS `sccsdiff` command to compare two versions of an SCCS file and display the differences between the two versions. You can specify any number of SCCS files; the options specified apply to all named `s.` files.

Options

`-p`	Pipe output for each file through `pr(1)`.
`-r sid`	Specify a version corresponding to the indicated SCCS delta ID (`sid`) for comparison. Versions are passed to `diff(1)` in the order given.
`diff-options`	
	Pass options to `diff(1)`, including `-c`, `-e`, `-f`, `-h`, `-b`, and `-D`.

Files

`/tmp/get?????`	
	Temporary files.

Attributes

See `attributes(5)` for descriptions of the following attributes:

Attribute Type	Attribute Value
Availability	SUNWsprot

See Also

```
diff(1),sccs(1),sccs-delta(1),sccs-get(1),sccs-help(1),sccs-prs(1),
sccs-prt(1), what(1), sccs-file(4), attributes(5)
```
Programming Utilities Guide

Diagnostics

`filename`: No differences

> The two versions are the same.

Use the SCCS `help` command for explanations of other messages (see `sccs-help`(1)).

sccs-unget, unget — Undo a Previous Get of an SCCS File

Synopsis

```
/usr/ccs/bin/unget [-ns][-r sid] s.filename...
```

Description

Use the SCCS `unget` command to undo the effect of a `get -e` done before the creation of the pending delta.

If you use a directory name in place of the `s.filename` argument, the `unget` command applies to all `s.` files in that directory. Unreadable `s.` files produce an error; processing continues with the next file (if any). The use of a dash (-) as the `s.filename` argument indicates that the names of files are to be read from the standard input, one `s.` file per line.

Options

`-n`	Retain the retrieved version that would otherwise be removed.
`-s`	Suppress display of the SCCS delta ID (`sid`).
`-r sid`	When multiple versions are checked out, specify which pending delta to abort. A diagnostic results if the specified `sid` is ambiguous or if it is needed but you omit it from the command line.

Attributes

See `attributes`(5) for descriptions of the following attributes:

Attribute Type	Attribute Value
Availability	SUNWsprot

See Also

sccs(1), sccs-delta(1), sccs-get(1), sccs-help(1), sccs-prs(1),
sccs-prt(1), sccs-rmdel(1), sccs-sact(1), sccs-sccsdiff(1), what(1),
sccs-file(4), attributes(5)

Diagnostics

Use the SCCS help command for explanations (see sccs-help(1)).

sccs-val, val — Validate an SCCS File

Synopsis

/usr/ccs/bin/val -
/usr/ccs/bin/val [-s][-m *name*][-r *sid*][-y *type*] s.*filename*...

Description

Use the SCCS val (validate) command to determine if the specified s. files
meet the characteristics specified by the indicated arguments. val can process
up to 50 files on a single command line.

val has a special dash (-) argument that reads the standard input until the
end-of-file condition is detected. Each line read is independently processed as if
it were a command-line argument list.

val generates diagnostic messages to the standard output for each
command line and file processed and also returns a single 8-bit code on exit as
described below.

The 8-bit code returned by val is a disjunction of the possible errors, that is,
it can be interpreted as a bit string where (moving from left to right) the bits set
are interpreted as follows.

- Bit 0 = Missing file argument.
- Bit 1 = Unknown or duplicate option.
- Bit 2 = Corrupted s. file.
- Bit 3 = Cannot open file or file not in s. file format.
- Bit 4 = The SCCS delta ID (*sid*) is invalid or ambiguous.
- Bit 5 = The *sid* does not exist.
- Bit 6 = Mismatch between %Y% and the -y argument.
- Bit 7 = Mismatch between %M% and the -m argument.

val can process two or more files on a given command line and, in turn, can
process multiple command lines (when reading the standard input). In these
cases, an aggregate code is returned that is the logical OR of the codes
generated for each command line and file processed.

Options

-s	Suppress the normal error or warning messages.
-m *name*	Compare *name* with the %M% ID keyword in the s. file.
-r *sid*	Check to see if the indicated *sid* is ambiguous, invalid, or absent from the s. file.
-y *type*	Compare *type* with the %Y% ID keyword.

Attributes

See attributes(5) for descriptions of the following attributes:

Attribute Type	Attribute Value
Availability	SUNWsprot

See Also

sccs(1), sccs-admin(1), sccs-delta(1), sccs-get(1), sccs-help(1),
what(1), sccs-file(4), attributes(5)
Programming Utilities Guide

Diagnostics

Use the SCCS help command for explanations (see sccs-help(1)).

script — Make Record of a Terminal Session

Synopsis

/usr/bin/script [-a][*filename*]

Description

Use the script command to copy to a file everything that is displayed on your terminal, including your input and the system prompts and output. The record is written to *filename*. If you specify no file name, the record is saved in the file typescript.

The script command forks and creates a subshell, using the value of $SHELL, and records the text from this session. The script ends when the forked shell exits or when you type Control-D.

Options

-a	Append the session record to *filename* instead of overwriting it.

Examples

The following example starts `script` using the default `typescript` file and
then displays the comments of the `typescript` file.

```
castle% script
Script started, file is typescript
castle% who
winsor        console      Apr  1 07:53     (:0)
winsor        pts/3        Apr  1 07:54     (:0.0)
winsor        pts/4        Apr  1 07:54     (:0.0)
winsor        pts/5        Apr  1 07:54     (:0.0)
winsor        pts/6        Apr  1 07:54     (:0.0)
castle% ps -ef | grep script
  winsor    491    408   0 16:34:25 pts/6     0:00 script
  winsor    492    491   0 16:34:25 pts/6     0:00 script
  winsor    497    493   0 16:34:36 pts/7     0:00 grep script
castle% ^D Script done, file is typescript
castle% more typescript
Script started on Thu Apr 01 16:34:25 1999
castle% who
winsor        console      Apr  1 07:53     (:0)
winsor        pts/3        Apr  1 07:54     (:0.0)
winsor        pts/4        Apr  1 07:54     (:0.0)
winsor        pts/5        Apr  1 07:54     (:0.0)
winsor        pts/6        Apr  1 07:54     (:0.0)
castle% ps -ef | grep script
  winsor    491    408   0 16:34:25 pts/6     0:00 script
  winsor    492    491   0 16:34:25 pts/6     0:00 script
  winsor    497    493   0 16:34:36 pts/7     0:00 grep script
castle% ^D
script done on Thu Apr 01 16:34:38 1999
castle%
```

Attributes

See `attributes`(5) for descriptions of the following attributes:

Attribute Type	Attribute Value
Availability	SUNWcsu
CSI	Enabled

See Also

`attributes`(5)

sdiff — Print, Side-by-Side, Differences Between Two Files

Synopsis

```
/usr/bin/sdiff [-l][-s][-o output][-w n] filename1 filename2
```

Description

The sdiff command uses the output of the diff command to produce a side-by-side listing of two files, indicating lines that are different.
Differences are shown in the following ways.

- A blank gutter is printed between the lines if they are identical.
- A < is shown in the gutter if the line appears only in *filename1*.
- A > is shown in the gutter if the line appears only in *filename2*.
- A ! is shown between the lines if they are different.

Options

-l	Print only the left side of any lines that are identical.
-s	Do not print identical lines.
-o *output*	Use the *output* argument as the name of a third file that is created as a merge of *filename1* and *filename2*. Copy identical lines of *filename1* and *filename2* to *output*. Print sets of differences as produced by diff when a set of differences share a common gutter character. After printing each set of differences, prompt with a % and wait for you to type one of the following commands.

	l	Append the left column to the output file.
	r	Append the right column to the output file.
	s	Turn on silent mode; do not print identical lines.
	v	Turn off silent mode.
	e l	Call the editor with the left column.
	e r	Call the editor with the right column.
	e b	Call the editor with the concatenation of left and right.
	e	Call the editor with a 0-length file.
	q	Exit from the program. On exit from the editor, concatenate the resulting file to the end of the *output* file.

-w *n*	Use the argument *n* as the width of the output line. The default line length is 130 characters.

Usage

See largefile(5) for the description of the behavior of sdiff when encountering files greater than or equal to 2 Gbytes (2** 31 bytes).

Examples

The following example shows output of sdiff.

```
x    |    y
a         a
b    <
c    <
d         d
     >    c
```

Environment Variables

If any of the LC_* variables (LC_CTYPE, LC_MESSAGES, LC_TIME, LC_COLLATE, LC_NUMERIC, and LC_MONETARY) (see environ(5)) are not set in the environment, the operational behavior of sdiff for each corresponding locale category is determined by the value of the LANG environment variable. If LC_ALL is set, its contents are used to override both the LANG and the other LC_* variables. If none of the above variables are set in the environment, the C locale determines how sdiff behaves.

LC_CTYPE   Determine how sdiff handles characters. When LC_CTYPE is set to a valid value, sdiff can display and handle text and file names containing valid characters for that locale.

Attributes

See attributes(5) for descriptions of the following attributes:

Attribute Type	Attribute Value
Availability	SUNWesu
CSI	Enabled

See Also

diff(1), ed(1), attributes(5), environ(5), largefile(5)

sed — Stream Editor

Synopsis

```
/usr/bin/sed [-n] script [file...]
/usr/bin/sed [-n][-e script]...[-f script-file]... [file...]
/usr/xpg4/bin/sed [-n] script [file...]
/usr/xpg4/bin/sed [-n][-e script]...[-f script-file]... [file...]
```

Description

The sed command is a noninteractive stream editor that reads one or more text files, makes editing changes according to a script of editing commands, and writes the results to standard output. sed obtains the script from either the *script* operand string or a combination of the option-arguments from the -e *script* and -f *script-file* options.

sed is a text editor. It cannot edit binary files or files containing ASCII null (\0) characters or very long lines.

Options

-e *script*   *script* is an edit command for sed. See "Usage" for more information on the format of *script*. If there is just one -e option and no -f option, you can omit the -e option.

-f *script-file*

Take the script from *script-file*, which consists of editing commands, one per line.

-n   Suppress the default output.

You can specify multiple -e and -f options. All commands are added to the script in the order specified, regardless of their origin.

Operands

file   A path name of a file whose contents are read and edited. If you specify multiple file operands, read the named files in the order specified and edit the concatenation. If you specify no file operands, use the standard input.

script   A string to be used as the script of editing commands. The application must not present a *script* that violates the restrictions of a text file, except that the final character need not be a newline character.

Usage

A script consists of editing commands, one per line, of the following form.

[*address* [, *address*]] *command* [*arguments*]

Zero or more blank characters are accepted before the first address and before *command*. Any number of semicolons are accepted before the first *address*.

In normal operation, sed cyclically copies a line of input (less its terminating newline character) into a pattern space (unless there is something left after a D command), applies in sequence all commands whose addresses select that pattern space, copies the resulting pattern space to the standard output (except with the -n option), and deletes the pattern space. Whenever the pattern space is written to standard output or a named file, sed immediately follows it with a newline character.

Some of the commands use a hold space to save all or part of the pattern space for subsequent retrieval. The pattern and hold spaces are each able to hold at least 8,192 bytes.

sed Addresses

An *address* can have the following contents.

- Empty.

- A decimal number that counts input lines cumulatively across files.

- A $ that addresses the last line of input.

- A context address that consists of a /*regularexpression*/, as described on the regexp(5) manual page.

A command line with no addresses selects every pattern space.

A command line with one address selects each pattern space that matches the address.

A command line with two addresses selects the inclusive range from the first pattern space that matches the first address through the next pattern space that matches the second address. Thereafter, the process is repeated, looking again for the first address. (If the second address is a number less than or equal to the line number selected by the first address, only the line corresponding to the first address is selected.)

Typically, addresses are separated from each other by a comma (,). They can also be separated by a semicolon (;).

sed Regular Expressions

sed supports the basic regular expressions described on the regexp(5) manual page, with the following additions.

*c*RE*c*   In a context address, the construction *c*RE*c*, where *c* is any character other than a backslash or newline character, is identical to /*RE*/. If the character designated by *c* follows a backslash, then it is considered to be that literal character and does not terminate the *RE*. For example, in the context address \xabc\xdefx, the second x stands for itself, so that the regular expression is abcxdef.

\n	The escape sequence \n matches a newline character embedded in the pattern space. You must not use a literal newline character in the regular expression of a context address or in the substitute command.

Editing commands can be applied only to nonselected pattern spaces by use of the negation command ! (described below).

sed Editing Commands

The following list of editing commands indicates the maximum number of permissible addresses for each function.

The r and w commands take an optional *rfile* (or *wfile*) parameter, separated from the command letter by one or more blank characters.

You can specify multiple commands by separating them with a semicolon (;) on the same command line.

The *text* argument consists of one or more lines, all but the last of which end with \ to hide the newline. You must precede each embedded newline character in the text with a backslash. Other backslashes in text are removed and the following character is treated literally. Backslashes in text are treated like backslashes in the replacement string of an s command and can be used to protect initial blanks and Tabs against the stripping that is done on every script line. The *rfile* or *wfile* argument must terminate the command line and must be preceded by exactly one blank. The use of the *wfile* parameter creates that file initially if it does not exist or replaces the contents of an existing file. There can be at most ten distinct *wfile* arguments.

Regular expressions match entire strings, not just individual lines, but a newline character is matched by \n in a sed *RE*; a newline character is not allowed in an *RE*. Also note that you cannot use \n to match a newline character at the end of an input line; newline characters appear in the pattern space as a result of the N editing command.

Two of the commands take a command list that is a list of sed commands separated by newline characters, as follows.

```
{ command
  command
}
```

You can precede the { with blank characters and follow it with white space. You can precede the s command with white space. You must precede the terminating } with a newline character and precede or follow it with blanks. You can precede or follow the braces with blanks. You can precede the command with blanks but cannot follow it with blanks.

The following table lists the editing commands.

Max. No. of Addresses	Command	Description
2	{ *command-list* }	Execute *command-list* only when the pattern space is selected.

Max. No. of Addresses	Command	Description
1	a\ *text*	Append by executing N command or beginning a new cycle. Place *text* on the output before reading the next input line.
2	b *label*	Branch to the : command bearing the label. If *label* is empty, branch to the end of the script. Labels are recognized as unique up to eight characters.
2	c\ *text*	Change by deleting the pattern space. Put *text* on the output. Start the next cycle.
2	d	Delete the pattern space. Start the next cycle.
2	D	Delete the initial segment of the pattern space through the first newline. Start the next cycle. (See the N command.)
2	g	Replace the contents of the pattern space with the contents of the hold space.
2	G	Append the contents of the hold space to the pattern space.
2	h	Replace the contents of the hold space with the contents of the pattern space.
2	H	Append the contents of the pattern space to the hold space.
1	i\ *text*	Insert *text* to the standard output.
2	l	/usr/bin/sed: List the pattern space to the standard output in an unambiguous form. Display nonprintable characters in octal notation, and fold long lines.
		/usr//xpg4/bin/sed: List the pattern space to the standard output in an unambiguous form. Display nonprintable characters in octal notation, and fold long lines. Write the characters (\\, \a, \b, \f, \r, \t, and \v) as the corresponding escape sequences. Write nonprintable characters not in that table as one 3-digit octal number (with a preceding backslash character) for each byte in the character (most significant byte first). If the size of a byte on the system is greater than 9 bits, the format used for nonprintable characters is implementation dependent.

Max. No. of Addresses	Command	Description
		Fold long lines, with the point of folding indicated by writing a backslash followed by a newline character; the length at which folding occurs is unspecified but should be appropriate for the output device. Mark the end of each line with a $.
2	n	Copy the pattern space to the standard output if default is not suppressed. Replace the pattern space with the next line of input.
2	N	Append the next line of input to the pattern space with an embedded newline. (The current line number changes.) If the end of input is reached, the N command verb branches to the end of the script and quits without starting a new cycle.
2	p	Print the pattern space to the standard output.
2	P	Print the initial segment of the pattern space through the first newline to the standard output.
1	q	Quit by branching to the end of the script. Do not start a new cycle.
2	r *rfile*	Read the contents of *rfile*. Put them on the output before reading the next input line.
2	t *label*	Test by branching to the : command bearing the label if any substitutions have been made since the most recent reading of an input line or execution of a t. If *label* is empty, branch to the end of the script.
2	w *wfile*	Write by appending the pattern space to *wfile*. The first occurrence of w clears *wfile*. Subsequent invocations of w append. Each time you use the sed command, *wfile* is overwritten.
2	x	Exchange the contents of the pattern and hold spaces.
2	! *command*	Apply the command (or group, if *command* is { }) only to lines not selected by the address(es).
0	: *label*	Hold a *label* for b and t commands to branch to.
1	=	Put the current line number to the standard output as a line.

Max. No. of Addresses	Command	Description
2	{ command-list }	Execute command-list only when the pattern space is selected.
0		Ignore an empty command.
0	#	If a # is the first character on a line of a script file, then treat that entire line as a comment with one exception: if a # is on the first line and the character after the # is an n, then suppress the default output. Also, ignore the rest of the line after #n. A script file must contain at least one noncomment line.

The following list describes the maximum command using strings.

2		s/regular expression/replacement/flags

Substitute the replacement string for instances of the regular expression in the pattern space. You can use any character other than backslash or newline instead of a slash to delimit the RE and the replacement. Within the RE and the replacement, you can use the RE delimiter itself as a literal character if you precede it with a backslash.

Replace an ampersand (&) appearing in the replacement with the string matching the RE. You can suppress the special meaning of & in this context by preceding it with a backslash. Replace the characters \ n, where n is a digit, with the text matched by the corresponding backreference expression. For each backslash (\) encountered in scanning replacement from beginning to end, the character that follows loses its special meaning (if any). It is unspecified what special meaning is given to any character other than &, \, or digits.

You can split a line by substituting a newline character into it. The application must escape the newline character in replacement by preceding it with a backslash. A substitution is considered to have been performed even if the replacement string is identical to the string that it replaces. For a fuller description see ed(1). flags is zero or more of the following.

n	n= 1 - 512. Substitute for just the n-th occurrence of the regular expression.
g	Globally substitute all nonoverlapping instances of the regular expression instead of just the first one. If you use both g and n, the results are unspecified.
p	Print the pattern space if a replacement was made.

| P | Print the initial segment of the pattern space through the first newline to the standard output. | *New!* |

| w *wfile* | Write by appending the pattern space to *wfile* if a replacement was made. The first occurrence of w clears *wfile*. Subsequent invocations of w append. Each time you use the sed command, *wfile* is overwritten. |

2   y/*string1*/*string2*/

Replace all occurrences of characters in *string1* with the corresponding characters in *string2*. *string1* and *string2* must have the same number of characters or, if any of the characters in *string1* appear more than once, the results are undefined. You can use any character other than backslash and newline instead of slash to delimit the strings. Within *string* and *string2*, you can use the delimiter itself as a literal character if it is preceded with a backslash. For example, y/abc/ABC/ replaces a with A, b with B, and c with C.

See largefile(5) for the description of the behavior of sed when encountering files greater than or equal to 2 Gbytes (2** 31 bytes).

Examples

The following sed script simulates the BSD cat -s command by squeezing excess blank lines from standard input.

```
sed -n '
# Write nonempty lines.
/./     {
        p
        d
        }
# Write a single empty line, then look for more empty lines.
/^$/        p
# Get next line, discard the held newline (empty line),
# and look for more empty lines.
:Empty

    /^$/            {
        N
        s/.//
        b Empty
        }
# Write the nonempty line before going back to search
# for the first in a set of empty lines.
        p
    '
```

Environment Variables

See environ(5) for descriptions of the following environment variables that affect the execution of sed: LC_COLLATE, LC_CTYPE, LC_MESSAGES, and NLSPATH.

Exit Status

| 0 | Successful completion. |
| >0 | An error occurred. |

Attributes

See attributes(5) for descriptions of the following attributes:

/usr/bin/sed

Attribute Type	Attribute Value
Availability	SUNWcsu
CSI	Not enabled

/usr/xpg4/bin/sed

Attribute Type	Attribute Value
Availability	SUNWxcu4
CSI	Enabled

See Also

awk(1), ed(1), grep(1), attributes(5), environ(5), largefile(5), regexp(5), XPG4(5)

---

select — Shell Built-in Functions to Choose from a List of Actions

Synopsis

ksh

select identifier [in word...]; do list; done

Description

See case(1).

serialver — Show Serial Version

Synopsis
```
/usr/java/bin/serialver [-show][classname]
```

Description
The `serialver` command returns the `serialVersionUID` for one or more Java classes in a form suitable for copying into an evolving class. When invoked with no arguments, it prints a usage line.

Options
`-show`	Display a simple user interface. You type the full class name and either press the Enter key or click on the Show button to display the `serialVersionUID`.

Examples
The following example shows the window that is displayed when you type **serialver -show**.

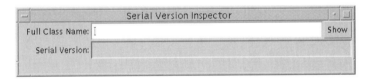

Attributes
See `attributes`(5) for descriptions of the following attributes:

Attribute Type	Attribute Value
Availability	SUNWjvdev

See Also
```
attributes(5)
```

java.io.ObjectStreamClass
```
http://www.javasoft.com/products/jdk/1.1/docs/api/java.io.
   ObjectStreamClass.html
```

Class Descriptor
```
http://www.javasoft.com/products/jdk/1.1/docs/guide/serialization/
    spec/class.doc.html
```

For information on related topics, use the search link
`http://java.sun.com/`

set, unset, setenv, unsetenv, export — Shell Environment Variable Built-in Functions

Synopsis

sh
```
set [--aefhkntuvx [argument...]]
unset [name...]
export [name...]
```

csh
```
set [var [= value]]
set var[n] = word
unset pattern
setenv [VAR [word]]
unsetenv variable
```

ksh
```
set [±aefhkmnopstuvx][±o option]... [±A name] [arg...]
unset [-f] name...
**
export [name[= value]]...
```

Description

Bourne Shell

The Bourne shell `set` command has the following options.

-a	Mark variables that are modified or created for export.
-e	Exit immediately if a command exits with a non-zero exit status.
-f	Disable file-name generation.
-h	Locate and remember function commands as you define functions (function commands are normally located when the function is executed).
-k	Put all keyword arguments in the environment for a command, not just those that precede the command name.
-n	Read commands but do not execute them.
-t	Exit after reading and executing one command.
-u	Treat unset variables as an error when substituting.
-v	Print shell input lines as they are read.
-x	Print commands and their arguments as they are executed.

--   Do not change any of the options; useful in setting $1 to -.

Using + instead of - turns these options off. You can also use these options when invoking the shell. The current set of options is found in $-. The remaining arguments are positional parameters and are assigned, in order, to $1, $2, ... If you specify no arguments, the values of all names are printed.

For each name, unset removes the corresponding variable or function value. You cannot unset the variables PATH, PS1, PS2, MAILCHECK, and IF.

With the export built-in, the given names are marked for automatic export to the environment of subsequently executed commands. If you specify no arguments, variable names that have been marked for export during the current shell's execution are listed. Function names are not exported.

C Shell

With no arguments, set displays the values of all shell variables. Multiword values are displayed as a parenthesized list. With the *var* argument alone, set assigns an empty (null) value to the variable *var*. With arguments of the form *var* = *value*, set assigns *value* to *var*, where *value* is one of the following.

word   A single *word* (or quoted string).

(*wordlist*)   A space-separated list of words enclosed in parentheses.

Values are command- and file-name-expanded before being assigned. The form set *var*[*n*] = *word* replaces the *n*-th word in a multiword value with *word*.

unset removes variables whose names match (file-name substitution) *pattern*. All variables are removed by unset *; this command has noticeably distasteful side effects.

With no arguments, setenv displays all environment variables. With the *VAR* argument, setenv sets the environment variable *VAR* to an empty (null) value. (By convention, environment variables are normally given uppercase names.) When you specify both the *VAR* and *word* arguments, setenv sets *VAR* to *word*, which must be either a single word or a quoted string. The PATH variable can take multiple word arguments, separated by colons. The most commonly used environment variables, USER, TERM, and PATH, are automatically imported to and exported from the csh variables user, term, and path. Use setenv if you need to change these variables. In addition, the shell sets the PWD environment variable from the csh variable cwd whenever the latter changes.

The environment variables LC_CTYPE, LC_MESSAGES, LC_TIME, LC_COLLATE, LC_NUMERIC, and LC_MONETARY take immediate effect when changed within the C shell. See environ(5) for descriptions of these environment variables.

unsetenv removes *variable* from the environment. As with unset, pattern matching is not performed.

Korn Shell

The options for the `set` built-in command have the following meanings.

-A   Unset the variable name, and assign values sequentially from the list *arg*. If you use +A, do not first unset the variable name.

-a   Automatically export all subsequent variables that are defined.

-e   If a command has a non-zero exit status, execute the ERR trap if set, and exit. This mode is disabled while reading profiles.

-f   Disable file-name generation.

-h   Interpret each command as a tracked alias when first encountered.

-k   Put all variable assignment arguments in the environment for a command, not just those that precede the command name.

-m   Run background jobs in a separate process group, and print a line on completion. Report the exit status of background jobs in a completion message. On systems with job control, this option is turned on automatically for interactive shells.

-n   Read commands and check them for syntax errors, but do not execute them. Ignored for interactive shells.

-o   Specify one of the following option names.

allexport	Same as -a.
errexit	Same as -e.
bgnice	Run all background jobs at a lower priority (the default).
emacs	Put you in an emacs-style line editor for command entry.
gmacs	Put you in a gmacs-style inline editor for command entry.
ignoreeof	Do not exit the shell on end-of-file. You must use the exit command.
keyword	Same as -k.
markdirs	Append a trailing slash (/) to all directory names resulting from file-name generation.
monitor	Same as -m.
noclobber	Prevent redirection > from truncating existing files. Require >| to truncate a file when turned on.
noexec	Same as -n.
noglob	Same as -f.
nolog	Do not save function definitions in history file.
nounset	Same as -u.
privileged	Same as -p.

verbose	Same as -v.
trackall	Same as -h.
vi	Put you in insert mode of a vi-style inline editor until you hit escape character 033, which puts you in control mode. A Return sends the line.
viraw	Each character is processed as it is typed in vi mode.
xtrace	Same as -x. If you supply no option name, then print the current option settings.

-p	Disable processing of the $HOME/.profile file, and use the file /etc/suid_profile instead of the ENV file. This mode is on whenever the effective UID is not equal to the real UID or when the effective GID is not equal to the real GID. Turning this option off sets the effective UID and GID to the real UID and GID.
-s	Sort the positional parameters lexicographically.
-t	Exit after reading and executing one command.
-u	Treat unset parameters as an error when substituting.
-v	Print shell input lines as they are read.
-x	Print commands and their arguments as they are executed.
-	Turn off -x and -v options, and stop examining arguments for options.
--	Do not change any of the options; useful in setting $1 to a value beginning with -. If no arguments follow this option, then unset the positional parameters.

Using + instead of - turns these options off. You can also use these options on invocation of the shell. The current set of options is found in $-. Unless you specify -A, the remaining arguments are positional parameters and are assigned, in order, to $1 $2 . . . . If you specify no arguments, then the names and values of all variables are printed to the standard output.

The variables given by the list of names are unassigned; that is, their values and attributes are erased. You cannot unset read-only variables. If you use the -f option, then the names refer to function names. Unsetting ERRNO, LINENO, MAILCHECK, OPTARG, OPTIND, RANDOM, SECONDS, TMOUT, and _ removes their special meaning even if they are subsequently assigned.

With the export built-in, the given names are marked for automatic export to the environment of subsequently executed commands.

ksh(1) commands that are preceded by one or two asterisks (*) are treated specially in the following ways.

1. Variable assignment lists preceding the command remain in effect when the command completes.

2. I/O redirections are processed after variable assignments.

3. Errors abort a script that contains them.

4. Words following a command preceded by `**` that are in the format of a variable assignment are expanded with the same rules as a variable assignment. This means that tilde substitution is performed after the equal sign and word splitting and file-name generation are not performed.

Examples

C Shell

The following example sets the PATH variable to search for files in the /bin, /usr/bin, /usr/bin, and /usr/bin directories, in that order.

```
castle% setenv PATH "/bin:/usr/bin:/usr/sbin:usr/ucb/bin"
castle%
```

Attributes

See attributes(5) for descriptions of the following attributes:

Attribute Type	Attribute Value
Availability	SUNWcsu

See Also

csh(1), ksh(1), read(1), sh(1), typeset(1), attributes(5), environ(5)

setfacl — Modify the Access Control List (ACL) for a File or Files

Synopsis

```
/usr/bin/setfacl [-r] -s acl-entries file...
/usr/bin/setfacl [-r] -md acl-entries file...
/usr/bin/setfacl [-r] -f acl-file file...
```

Description

Access Control Lists (ACLs) are extensions to standard UNIX file permissions. The ACL information is stored and associated with each file individually. Use the setfacl to set, add, modify, and delete ACL entries. For each file specified, setfacl either replaces its entire ACL, including the default ACL on a directory, or it adds, modifies, or deletes one or more ACL entries, including default entries on directories.

Setting an ACL on a file also modifies the file permission bits. The user entry modifies the file owner permission bits. If you do not specify a mask entry, the group entry modifies the file group owner permission bits. If you specify a

New!

mask entry, the group owner permission bits of the file are modified, based on the intersection (bitwise AND) of the group and mask entries. The other entry modifies the other permission bits.

If you use the chmod(1) command to change the group owner permissions on a file with ACL entries, both the group owner permissions and the ACL mask are changed to the new permissions. Be aware that the new ACL mask permissions can change the effective permissions for additional users and groups who have ACL entries on the file.

A directory can contain default ACL entries. If you create a file in a directory that contains default ACL entries, the newly created file has permissions generated according to the intersection of umask(1), the default ACL entries, and the permissions requested at creation time. If a default ACL is specified for a specific user (or users), the file has a regular ACL created; otherwise, only the mode bits are initialized according to the intersection described above. The default ACL should be thought of as the maximum discretionary access permissions that can be granted.

Syntax for acl-entries

For the -m and -s options, *acl-entries* is one or more comma-separated ACL entries.

An ACL entry consists of the following fields separated by colons.

entry-type Type of ACL entry on which to set file permissions. For example, *entry-type* can be user (the owner of a file) or mask (the ACL mask).

uid | gid User name or user identification number. Or group name or group identification number.

perms The permissions that are set on *entry-type*. You can indicate *perms* by the symbolic characters rwx or a number (the same permissions numbers used with the chmod(1) command.

The following list describes the valid ACL entries. (You can specify default entries only for directories.)

u[ser]::*perms*

File owner permissions.

g[roup]::*perms*

Group owner permissions.

o[ther]:*perms*

Permission for users other than the file owner or members of file group owner.

m[ask]:*perms*

The ACL mask specifying the maximum permissions permitted for users (other than the owner) and for groups. The mask is a quick way to change permissions on all users and groups.

u[ser]:*uid*:*perms*

> Permissions for a specific user. For *uid*, use either a user name or a numeric ID.

g[roup]:*gid*:*perms*

> Permissions for a specific group. For *gid*, use either a group name or a numeric GID.

d[efault]:u[ser]::*perms*

> Default file owner permissions.

d[efault]:g[roup]::*perms*

> Default group owner permissions.

d[efault]:o[ther]:*perms*

> Default permissions for users other than the file owner or members of the file group owner.

d[efault]:m[ask]:*perms*

> Default ACL mask.

d[efault]:u[ser]:*uid*:*perms*

> Default permissions for a specific user. For *uid*, use either a user name or a numeric ID.

d[efault]:g[roup]:*gid*:*perms*

> Default permissions for a specific group. For *gid*, use either a group name or a numeric ID.

For the -d option, *acl-entries* is one or more comma-separated ACL entries without permissions, selected from the following Options list. Note that the entries for file owner, owning group, file group class, and others cannot be deleted.

Options

New!

-s *acl-entries*

> Set the ACL for a file. Remove all old ACL entries, and replace with the newly specified ACL. You can specify the entries in any order. They are sorted by the command before being applied to the file.

Required entries:

- Exactly one user entry specified for the owner of the file.
- Exactly one group entry for the owning group of the file.
- Exactly one other entry specified.

If there are additional user and group entries:

- Exactly one mask entry specified for the file group class of the file.

- Must not be duplicate user entries with the same *uid*.
- Must not be duplicate `group` entries with the same *gid*.

If file is a directory:

- Exactly one `default:user` entry for the owner of the file.
- Exactly one `default:group` entry for the owning group of the file.
- Exactly one `default:mask` entry for the file group class of the file.
- Exactly one `default:other` entry.

You can specify additional `default:user` entries and additional `default:group` entries, but there cannot be duplicate additional `default:user` entries with the same *uid* or duplicate default group entries with the same *gid*. The entries need not be in any specific order. They are sorted by the command before being applied to the file.

-m *acl-entries*

Add one or more new ACL entries to the file, and/or modify one or more existing ACL entries on the file. If an entry already exists for a specified *uid* or *gid*, replace the current permissions with the specified permissions. If an entry does not exist for the specified *uid* or *gid*, create it.

-d *acl-entries*

Delete one or more entries from the file. You cannot delete the entries for the file owner, the owning group, and others from the ACL. Note that deleting an entry does not necessarily have the same effect as removing all permissions from the entry.

-f *acl-file*

Set the ACL for a file, using the ACL entries contained in the file named *acl-file*. The same constraints on specified entries hold as with the -s option. The entries are not required to be in any specific order in the file.

You can use the # character in an *acl-file* to indicate a comment. Starting with the #, all characters until the end of the line are ignored. Note that if the *acl-file* has been created as the output of the getfacl(1) command, any effective permissions that follow a # are ignored.

-r

Recalculate the permissions for the group class entry, that is, the `mask` entry. Ignore the permissions specified in the group class entry, and replace them with the maximum permissions needed to grant the access in any additional user, owning group, and additional group entries in the ACL. Leave the permissions in the additional user, owning group, and additional group entries unchanged.

Examples

The following example lists the permissions on file `foo`. It then adds one ACL entry to file `foo`, giving user `ray` read permission only and lists the permissions again. The + at the end of the permission listing from the `ls -l` command shows that an ACL exists for the file. Then, the example uses the `getfacl` command to list the ACL information for the file.

```
castle% ls -l foo
-rw-r--r--   1 winsor     staff           0 Apr   2 14:23 foo
castle% setfacl -m user:ray:r-- foo
castle% ls -l foo
-rw-r--r--+  1 winsor     staff           0 Apr   2 14:23 foo
castle% getfacl foo

# file: foo
# owner: winsor
# group: staff
user::rw-
user:ray:r--              #effective:r--
group::r--                #effective:r--
mask:r--
other:r--
castle%
```

The following example replaces the entire ACL for the file `foo`, adding an entry for user `ray` allowing read/write access, an entry for the file owner allowing all access, an entry for the group allowing read access only, an entry for group class allowing read/write, and an entry for others disallowing all access.

```
castle% setfacl -s user:ray:rw-,user::rwx,group::r--,mask:rw-,other:--- foo
castle% getfacl foo

# file: foo
# owner: winsor
# group: staff
user::rwx
user:ray:rw-              #effective:rw-
group::r--                #effective:r--
mask:rw-
other:---
castle%
```

Note — Following this command, the file permission bits are set to `rwxr-----`.

Even though the file-owning group has only read permission, the maximum permissions available to all additional user ACL entries and all group ACL entries are read and write because the mask entry specifies these permissions.

The following example sets the same ACL on file `bar` as the file `foo`.

```
castle% getfacl foo | setfacl -f - bar
castle% getfacl bar

# file: bar
# owner: winsor
# group: staff
user::rwx
user:ray:rw-                    #effective:rw-
group::r--                      #effective:r--
mask:rw-
other:---
castle%
```

Files

/etc/passwd

> Password file.

/etc/group Group file.

Attributes

See attributes(5) for descriptions of the following attributes:

Attribute Type	Attribute Value
Availability	SUNWcsu

See Also

chmod(1), getfacl(1), umask(1), aclcheck(3), aclsort(3), group(4), *New!*
passwd(4), attributes(5)

settime — Change File Access and Modification Times   *New!*

Synopsis

/usr/bin/settime [-f *ref-file*] *file*...

Description

See touch(1).

sh, jsh — Standard and Job Control Shell and Command Interpreter

Synopsis
```
/usr/bin/sh [-acefhiknprstuvx][argument...]
/usr/xpg4/bin/sh [± abCefhikmnoprstuvx][± o option]...
   [-c string][arg...]
/usr/bin/jsh [-acefhiknprstuvx][argument...]
```

Description
The Bourne shell, written by Steve Bourne when he was at AT&T Bell Laboratories, is the original UNIX shell. This shell is preferred for shell programming because of its programming capabilities and its universal availability. It lacks features, such as built-in arithmetic, for interactive use. The Bourne shell is the default login shell for the root account, and it serves as the default user login shell if you do not specify another shell in your passwd file. The Bourne shell is used for all system-supplied administration scripts.

The Bourne shell command is /bin/sh. The default prompt is a dollar sign ($). The root prompt is a pound sign (#).

The /usr/bin/sh command is a command programming language that executes commands read from a terminal or a file.

The /usr/xpg4/bin/sh command is identical to /usr/bin/ksh. See ksh(1).

The jsh command is an interface to the shell that provides all of the functionality of sh and also enables job control (see "Job Control" on page 1229).

Arguments to the shell are listed in "Invocation" on page 1228.

Definitions
A *blank* is a Tab or a space. A *name* is a sequence of ASCII letters, digits, or underscores, beginning with a letter or an underscore. A *parameter* is a name, a digit, or any of the characters *, @, #, ?, -, $, and !.

Usage

Commands
A *simple command* is a sequence of nonblank words separated by blanks. The first word specifies the name of the command to be executed. Except as specified below, the remaining words are passed as arguments to the invoked command. The command name is passed as argument 0 (see exec(2)). The value of a command is its exit status if it terminates normally, or (octal) 200+*status* if it terminates abnormally; see signal(5) for a list of status values.

A *pipeline* is a sequence of one or more commands separated by |. The standard output of each command but the last is connected by a pipe(2) to the standard input of the next command. Each command is run as a separate process; the shell waits for the last command to terminate. The exit status of a pipeline is the exit status of the last command in the pipeline.

A *list* is a sequence of one or more pipelines separated by ;, &, &&, or ||, and optionally terminated by ; or &. Of these four symbols, ; and & have equal precedence that is lower than that of && and ||. The symbols && and || also have equal precedence. A semicolon (;) sequentially executes the preceding pipeline (that is, the shell waits for the pipeline to finish before executing any commands following the semicolon); an ampersand (&) asynchronously executes the preceding pipeline (that is, the shell does not wait for that pipeline to finish). The symbol && (||) executes the list following it only if the preceding pipeline returns a 0 exit status. An arbitrary number of newlines can appear in a list instead of semicolons to delimit commands.

Note — Only the last process in a pipeline can be waited for.

A command is either a simple command or one of the following. Unless otherwise stated, the value returned by a command is that of the last simple command executed in the command.

for *name* [in *word*...] do *list* done

> Each time a for command is executed, set *name* to the next *word* taken from the in *word* list. If you omit in *word*..., then execute the do list once for each positional parameter that is set (see "Parameter Substitution" on page 1217). Execution ends when there are no more words in the list.

case *word* in [*pattern* [| *pattern*])*list*;;]... esac

> Execute the *list* associated with the first *pattern* that matches *word*. The form of the patterns is the same as that used for file-name generation (see "File-Name Generation" on page 1220) except that a slash, a leading dot, or a dot immediately following a slash need not be matched explicitly.

if *list* ; then *list* ; [elif *list* ; then *list* ;]

   [else *list* ;] fi

> Execute the *list* following if, and if it returns a 0 exit status, execute the *list* following the first then. Otherwise, execute the *list* following elif. If its value is 0, then execute the *list* following the next then. Failing that, execute the else *list*. If no else *list* or then *list* is executed, the if command returns a 0 exit status.

while *list* do *list* done	Repeatedly execute the while *list* and, if the exit status of the last command in the list is 0, execute the do *list*; otherwise, the loop terminates. If no commands in the do *list* are executed, then the while command returns a 0 exit status. You can use until in place of while to negate the loop termination test.
(*list*)	Execute *list* in a subshell.
{ *list*; }	Execute *list* in the current (that is, parent) shell. The { must be followed by a space.
name () { *list*; }	
	Define a function that is referenced by *name*. The body of the function is the *list* of commands between { and }. The { must be followed by a space. Execution of functions is described below (see "Execution" on page 1222). The { and } are not needed if the body of the function is a command as defined above, under Commands.

The following words are recognized only as the first word of a command and when not quoted.

```
if then else elif fi case esac for while until do done { }
```

Note — Because commands in pipelines are run as separate processes, variables set in a pipeline have no effect on the parent shell.

Comments Lines
All characters following a word beginning with # are ignored up to a newline.

Command Substitution
The shell reads commands from the string between two grave accents (` `) and the standard output from these commands can be used as all or part of a word. Trailing newlines are removed from the standard output.

No interpretation is done on the string before the string is read except to remove backslashes (\) used to escape other characters. You can use backslashes to escape a grave accent (` ) or another backslash (\). The leading backslashes are removed before the command string is read. Escaping grave accents enables nested command substitution. If the command substitution lies within a pair of double quotes (" ...` ...` ... "), a backslash used to escape a double quote (\") is removed; otherwise, it is left intact.

If you use a backslash to escape a newline character (\newline), both the backslash and the newline are removed (see "Quoting" on page 1221). In addition, backslashes used to escape dollar signs (\$) are removed. Because no parameter substitution is done on the command string before it is read, inserting a backslash to escape a dollar sign has no effect. Backslashes that precede characters other than \, `, ", newline, and $ are left intact when the command string is read.

Parameter Substitution

The $ character is used to introduce substitutable parameters. The shell has two types of parameters: positional and keyword. If parameter is a digit, it is a positional parameter. Positional parameters can be assigned values by `set`. You can assign values to keyword parameters (also known as variables) by writing:

name= *value* [*name=* *value*] ...

Pattern matching is not performed on *value*. You cannot use a function and a variable with the same name.

`${`*parameter*`}`

>Substitute the value, if any, of the parameter. The braces are required only when *parameter* is followed by a letter, digit, or underscore that is not to be interpreted as part of its name. If *parameter* is `*` or `@`, substitute all the positional parameters starting with `$1` and separated by spaces. Parameter `$0` is set from argument 0 when the shell is invoked.

`${`*parameter*`:-` *word*`}`

>If *parameter* is set and is non-null, substitute its value; otherwise substitute *word*.

`${`*parameter*`:=` *word*`}`

>If *parameter* is not set or is `null` set it to *word*; otherwise, substitute the value of the parameter. You cannot assign positional parameters in this way.

`${`*parameter*`:?` *word*`}`

>If *parameter* is set and is non-null, substitute its value; otherwise, print *word* and exit from the shell. If you omit *word*, print the message `parameter null or not set`.

`${`*parameter*`:+` *word*`}`

>If *parameter* is set and is non-null, substitute *word*; otherwise, substitute nothing. In the above, *word* is not evaluated unless it is to be used as the substituted string, so that, in the following example, pwd is executed only if d is not set or is `null`:

>`echo ${d:-`pwd`}`

>If you omit the colon (`:`) from the above expressions, the shell checks only whether parameter is set or not set.

The following parameters are automatically set by the shell.

`#`

>The number of positional parameters in decimal.

`-`

>Options supplied to the shell on invocation or by the `set` command.

?	The decimal value returned by the last synchronously executed command.
$	The process number of this shell.
!	The process number of the last background command invoked.

The following parameters are used by the shell. The parameters in this section are also referred to as environment variables.

HOME	The default argument (home directory) for the cd command, set to the user's login directory by login(1) from the password file (see passwd(4)).
PATH	The search path for commands (see "Execution" on page 1222).
CDPATH	The search path for the cd command.
MAIL	If this parameter is set to the name of a mail file and the MAILPATH parameter is not set, the shell informs you of the arrival of mail in the specified file.
MAILCHECK	Specify how often (in seconds) the shell checks for the arrival of mail in the files specified by the MAILPATH or MAIL parameters. The default value is 600 seconds (10 minutes). If set to 0, the shell checks before each prompt.
MAILPATH	A colon-separated list of file names. If this parameter is set, the shell informs the user of the arrival of mail in any of the specified files. Each file name can be followed by % and a message that is printed when the modification time changes. The default message is, you have mail.
PS1	Primary prompt string; by default, $.
PS2	Secondary prompt string; by default. >.
IFS	Internal field separators, normally space, Tab, and newline (see "Blank Interpretation" on page 1218).
SHACCT	If this parameter is set to the name of a file writable by the user, write an accounting record in the file for each shell procedure executed.
SHELL	When the shell is invoked, it scans the environment (see "Environment" on page 1221) for this name.

See environ(5) for descriptions of the following environment variables that affect the execution of sh: LC_CTYPE and LC_MESSAGES.

The shell gives default values to PATH, PS1, PS2, MAILCHECK, and IFS. HOME and MAIL are set by login(1).

Blank Interpretation
After parameter and command substitution, the results of substitution are scanned for internal field separator characters (those found in IFS) and split into distinct arguments where such characters are found. Explicit null

arguments (`" "` or `' '`) are retained. Implicit null arguments (those resulting from parameters that have no values) are removed.

Input/Output Redirection

You can redirect the input and output of a command by using a special notation interpreted by the shell. The following constructs can appear anywhere in a command or can precede or follow a command and are not passed on as arguments to the invoked command.

> **Note** — Parameter and command substitution occurs before *word* or *digit* is used.

`< word`	Use file *word* as standard input (file descriptor 0).
`> word`	Use file *word* as standard output (file descriptor 1). If the file does not exist, create it; otherwise, truncate it to 0 length.
`>> word`	Use file *word* as standard output. If the file exists, append output to it (by first seeking to the end-of-file); otherwise, create the file.
`<> word`	Open file *word* for reading and writing as standard input.
`<<[-] word`	After parameter and command substitution is done on *word*, read the shell input up to the first line that literally matches the resulting word, or to an end-of-file. If, however, – is appended to `<<`:

- Strip leading tabs from *word* before reading the shell input (but after parameter and command substitution is done on *word*).

- Strip leading Tabs from the shell input as it is read and before each line is compared with *word*.

- Read shell input up to the first line that literally matches the resulting *word*, or to an end-of-file.

If any character of *word* is quoted, do no additional processing to the shell input. If no characters of *word* are quoted:

- Do parameter and command substitution.

- Remove (escaped) \newlines.

- Use \ to quote the characters \, $, and `.

The resulting document becomes the standard input.

`<& digit`	Use the file associated with file descriptor *digit* as standard input. Similarly for the standard output, using `>& digit`.
`<&-`	Close the standard input. Similarly for the standard output, using `>&-`.

If any of the above is preceded by a digit, the file descriptor that is associated with the file is that specified by the digit (instead of the default 0 or 1). For example, the following statement associates file descriptor 2 with the file currently associated with file descriptor 1.

```
... 2>&1
```

The order in which you specify redirections is significant. The shell evaluates redirections left-to-right. For example, the following statement first associates file descriptor 1 with file xxx. It associates file descriptor 2 with the file associated with file descriptor 1 (that is, xxx).

```
... 1> xxx 2>&1
```

If the order of redirections were reversed, file descriptor 2 would be associated with the terminal (assuming file descriptor 1 had been so associated) and file descriptor 1 would be associated with file xxx.

Using the terminology introduced under "Commands" on page 1214, if a command is composed of several simple commands, redirection is evaluated for the entire command before it is evaluated for each simple command. That is, the shell evaluates redirection for the entire list, then each pipeline within the list, then each command within each pipeline, then each list within each command.

If a command is followed by &, the default standard input for the command is the empty file /dev/null. Otherwise, the environment for the execution of a command contains the file descriptors of the invoking shell as modified by input/output specifications.

File-Name Generation

Before a command is executed, each command word is scanned for the characters *, ?, and [. If one of these characters is found, the word is regarded as a *pattern*. The word is replaced with alphabetically sorted file names that match the pattern. If no file name is found that matches the pattern, the word is left unchanged. The character . at the start of a file name or immediately following a /, as well as the character / itself, must be matched explicitly.

*	Match any string, including the null string.
?	Match any single character.
[...]	Match any one of the enclosed characters. A pair of characters separated by – matches any character lexically between the pair, inclusive. If the first character following the opening [is a !, match any character not enclosed.

Note — Words used for file names in input/output redirection are not interpreted for file-name generation. For example, cat file1 > a* creates a file named a*.

All quoted characters (see below) must be matched explicitly in a file name.

Quoting

The following characters have a special meaning to the shell and terminate a word unless quoted.

```
; & ( ) | ^ < > newline space tab
```

You can quote or escape a character (that is, make it stand for itself) by preceding it with a backslash (\) or by inserting it between a pair of quote marks (' ' or " "). During processing, the shell can quote certain characters to prevent them from taking on a special meaning. Backslashes used to quote a single character are removed from the word before the command is executed. The pair \newline is removed from a word before command and parameter substitution.

All characters enclosed between a pair of single quote marks (' ') except a single quote, are quoted by the shell. Backslash has no special meaning inside a pair of single quotes. You can quote a single quote inside a pair of double-quote marks (for example, " ' ") but you cannot quote a single quote inside a pair of single quotes.

Inside a pair of double quote marks (" "), parameter and command substitution occurs and the shell quotes the results to avoid blank interpretation and file-name generation. If $* is within a pair of double quotes, the positional parameters are substituted and quoted, separated by quoted spaces ("$1 $2 ... "); however, if $@ is within a pair of double quotes, the positional parameters are substituted and quoted, separated by unquoted spaces ("$1" "$2" ...). \ quotes the characters \, `, and $. The pair \newline is removed before parameter and command substitution. If a backslash precedes characters other than \, `, $, and newline, then the backslash itself is quoted by the shell.

Prompting

When used interactively, the shell prompts with the value of PS1 before reading a command. If at any time you press newline and further input is needed to complete a command, the secondary prompt (that is, the value of PS2) is displayed.

Environment

The environment (see environ(5)) is a list of name-value pairs that is passed to an executed program in the same way as a normal argument list. The shell interacts with the environment in several ways. On invocation, the shell scans the environment and creates a parameter for each name found, giving it the corresponding value. If you modify the value of any of these parameters or create new parameters, none of these affect the environment unless you use the export command to bind the shell's parameter to the environment (see also set -a). You can remove a parameter from the environment with the unset command. The environment seen by any executed command is thus composed of any unmodified name-value pairs originally inherited by the shell, minus any pairs removed by `unset`, plus any modifications or additions, all of which must be noted in `export` commands.

You can augment the environment for any command by prefixing it with one or more assignments to parameters. Thus:

```
TERM=450 command
```

and

```
(export TERM; TERM=450; command)
```

are equivalent as far as the execution of *command* is concerned if *command* is not a special command (see "Special Commands" on page 1223). If command is a special command, then

```
TERM=450 command
```

modifies the `TERM` variable in the current shell.

If the `-k` option is set, all keyword arguments are placed in the environment, even if they occur after the command name.

The following example first prints a=b c and c.

```
$ echo a=b c
a=b c
$ set -k
$ echo a=b c
c
$
```

Note — If a command is executed and a command with the same name is installed in a directory in the search path before the directory where the original command was found, the shell continues to execute the original command. Use the `hash` command to correct this situation.

Signals

The `INTERRUPT` and `QUIT` signals for an invoked command are ignored if the command is followed by `&`; otherwise, signals have the values inherited by the shell from its parent, with the exception of signal 11 (but see also the `trap` command).

Execution

Each time a command is executed, the command substitution, parameter substitution, blank interpretation, input/output redirection, and file-name generation listed above are carried out. If the command name matches the name of a defined function, the function is executed in the shell process (note how this differs from the execution of shell script files that require a subshell for invocation). If the command name does not match the name of a defined function but matches one of the special commands listed below, it is executed in the shell process. The positional parameters $1, $2, . . . are set to the arguments of the function. If the command name matches neither a special command nor the name of a defined function, a new process is created and an attempt is made to execute the command via exec(2).

The shell parameter PATH defines the search path for the directory containing the command. Alternative directory names are separated by a colon (:). The default path is /usr/bin. The current directory is specified by a null path name that can appear immediately after the equal sign, between two colon delimiters anywhere in the path list, or at the end of the path list. If the command name contains a /, the search path is not used. Otherwise, each directory in the path is searched for an executable file. If the file has execute permission but is not an a.out file, it is assumed to be a file containing shell commands. A subshell is spawned to read it. A parenthesized command is also executed in a subshell.

The location in the search path where a command was found is remembered by the shell (to help avoid unnecessary exec commands later). If the command was found in a relative directory, its location must be redetermined whenever the current directory changes. The shell forgets all remembered locations whenever the PATH variable is changed or the hash -r command is executed (see below).

Special Commands

Input/output redirection is now permitted for these commands. File descriptor 1 is the default output location. When job control is enabled, additional special commands are added to the shell's environment (see "Job Control" on page 1229).

:	Do nothing. Return a 0 exit code.
. *filename*	Read and execute commands from *filename* and return. Use the search path specified by PATH to find the directory containing *filename*.
bg [*%jobid* ...]	When job control is enabled, add the bg command to your environment to manipulate jobs. Resume the execution of a stopped job in the background. If you omit *%jobid*, assume the current job. (See "Job Control" on page 1229 for more detail.)
break [*n*]	Exit from the enclosing for or while loop if any. If you specify *n*, break *n* levels.
cd [*argument*]	Change the current directory to *argument*. The shell parameter HOME is the default argument. The shell parameter CDPATH defines the search path for the directory containing argument. Separate alternative directory names with a colon (:). The default path is null (specifying the current directory). Note that the current directory is specified by a null path name that can appear immediately after the equal sign or between the colon delimiters

anywhere else in the path list. If *argument* begins with a /, do not use the search path. Otherwise, search each directory in the path for *argument*.

chdir [*dir*]   Change the shell's working directory to *dir*. If you specify no argument, change to your home directory. If *dir* is a relative path name not found in the current directory, check for it in those directories listed in the CDPATH variable. If *dir* is the name of a shell variable whose value starts with a /, change to the directory named by that value.

continue [*n*]

Resume the next iteration of the enclosing for or while loop. If *n* is specified, resume at the *n*-th enclosing loop.

echo [*arguments...*]

Write the words in *arguments* to the standard output separated by space characters. See echo(1) for fuller usage and description.

eval [*argument...*]

Read the argument(s) as input to the shell and execute the resulting command(s).

exec [*argument...*]

Execute the command specified by the arguments in place of this shell without creating a new process. Input/output arguments can appear, and if no other arguments are given, modify the shell input/output.

exit [*n*]   Exit the calling shell or shell script with the exit status specified by n. If you omit n, use the exit status of the last command executed (an end-of-file also exits the shell.)

export [*name...*]

Mark the given names for automatic export to the environment of subsequently executed commands. If you specify no arguments, list the variable names that have been marked for export during the current shell's execution. (Variable names exported from a parent shell are listed only if they have been exported again during the current shell's execution.) Function names are not exported.

fg [*%jobid...*]

When job control is enabled, add the fg command to your environment to manipulate jobs. Resume the execution of a stopped job in the foreground; also move an executing background job into the foreground. If you omit *%jobid*, assume the current job. (See "Job Control" on page 1229 for more detail.)

getopts   Use in shell scripts to support command syntax standards (see intro(1)); parse positional parameters and check for legal options. See getoptcvt(1) for usage and description.

```
hash [-r][name ...]
```

> For each *name*, determine the location in the search path of the
> command specified by *name* and remembered by the shell. The -r
> option forgets all remembered locations. If you specify no
> arguments, present information about remembered commands.
> Hits is the number of times a command has been invoked by the
> shell process. Cost is a measure of the work required to locate a
> command in the search path. If a command is found in a relative
> directory in the search path, then after changing to that directory,
> recalculate the stored location of that command. Commands for
> which this are done are indicated by an asterisk (*) adjacent to the
> Hits information. Cost is incremented when the recalculation is
> done.

```
jobs [-p|-l][%jobid ...]
```

```
jobs -x command [argument s]
```

> Report all jobs that are stopped or executing in the background. If
> you omit %*jobid*, report all jobs that are stopped or running in the
> background.

```
kill [-sig] %job ...
```

```
kill -1     Send either the TERM (terminate) signal or the specified signal to
```
> the specified jobs or processes. Give signals either by number or by
> names (as given in signal(5) stripped of the SIG prefix, with the
> exception that SIGCHD is named CHLD). If the signal being sent is
> TERM (terminate) or HUP (hangup), then send the job or process a
> CONT (continue) signal if stopped. The *job* argument can be the
> process ID of a process that is not a member of one of the active
> jobs. See "Job Control" on page 1229 for a description of the format
> of *job*. In the second form, kill -1, list the signal numbers and
> names. (See kill(1)).

```
login [argument...]
```

> Equivalent to exec login *argument*. . . . See login(1) for usage
> and description.

```
newgrp [argument]
```

> Equivalent to exec newgrp *argument*. See newgrp(1) for usage
> and description.

```
pwd        Print the current working directory. See pwd(1) for usage and
```
> description.

```
read name...
```

> Read one line from the standard input and, using the IFS internal
> field separator (normally space or Tab) to delimit word boundaries,
> assign the first *word* to the first *name*, the second *word* to the second
> *name*, and so forth, with leftover words assigned to the last *name*.
> You can continue lines with \newline. You can quote characters

other than newline by preceding them with a backslash. These backslashes are removed before words are assigned to names, and no interpretation is done on the character that follows the backslash. The return code is 0 unless an end-of-file is encountered.

readonly [*name*...]

Mark the given names read-only. You cannot change the values of these names by subsequent assignment. If you specify no arguments, print a list of all read-only names.

return [*n*] Exit the function with the return value specified by *n*. If you omit *n*, the return status is that of the last command executed.

set [--aefhkntuvx [*argument*...]]

-a Mark variables that are modified or created for export.

-e Exit immediately if a command exits with a non-zero exit status.

-f Disable file-name generation.

-h Locate and remember function commands as functions are defined (function commands are normally located when the function is executed).

-k Put all keyword arguments in the environment for a command, not just those that precede the command name.

-n Read commands, but do not execute them.

-t Exit after reading and executing one command.

-u Treat unset variables as an error when substituting.

-v Print shell input lines as they are read.

-x Print commands and their arguments as they are executed.

-- Do not change any of the options; useful in setting $1 to -.

Using + instead of - turns these options off. You can also use these options on invocation of the shell. The current set of options can be found in $-. The remaining arguments are positional parameters and are assigned, in order, to $1, $2, ... If you specify no arguments, print the values of all names.

shift [*n*] The positional parameters from $*n*+1 ... are renamed $1 .... If you do not specify *n*, it is assumed to be 1.

stop *pid*...

Halt execution of the process number *pid*. (see ps(1)).

suspend Stop the execution of the current shell (but not if it is the login shell).

test   Evaluate conditional expressions. See test(1) for usage and
            description.

times   Print the accumulated user and system times for processes run
            from the shell.

trap [*argument n* [*n 2...*]]

            Read and execute the command argument when the shell receives
            numeric or symbolic signal(s) (*n*). (Note that *argument* is scanned
            once when the trap is set and once when the trap is taken.) Trap
            commands are executed in order of signal number or
            corresponding symbolic names. Any attempt to set a trap on a
            signal that was ignored on entry to the current shell is ineffective.
            An attempt to trap on signal 11 (memory fault) produces an error.
            If you do not specify *argument*, reset all trap(s) *n* to their original
            values. If *argument* is the null string, the shell and the commands
            it invokes ignore this signal. If *n* is 0, execute the command
            argument on exit from the shell. The trap command with no
            arguments prints a list of commands associated with each signal
            number.

type [*name...*]

            For each *name*, indicate how it would be interpreted if used as a
            command name.

ulimit [-[HS][a | cdfnstv]]

ulimit [-[HS][c | d | f | n | s | t | v]] *limit*

            Print or set hard or soft resource limits. These limits are described
            in getrlimit(2).

            If *limit* is not present, print the specified limits. You can print any
            number of limits at one time. The -a option prints all limits.

            If *limit* is present, set the specified limit to *limit*. The string
            unlimited requests the largest valid limit. You can set limits for
            only one resource at a time. Any user can set a soft limit to any
            value below the hard limit. Any user can lower a hard limit. Only
            a superuser can raise a hard limit; see su(1M).

            The -H option specifies a hard limit. The -S option specifies a soft
            limit. If you specify neither option, ulimit sets both limits and
            prints the soft limit.

            The following options specify the resource whose limits are to be
            printed or set. If you specify no option, print or set the file size
            limit.

            -c   Maximum corefile size (in 512-byte blocks).

            -d   Maximum size of data segment or heap (in kilobytes).

            -f   Maximum file size (in 512-byte blocks).

            -n   Maximum file descriptor plus 1.

`-s`	Maximum size of stack segment (in kilobytes).
`-t`	Maximum CPU time (in seconds).
`-v`	Maximum size of virtual memory (in kilobytes).

Run the `sysdef`(1M) command to obtain the maximum possible limits for your system. The values reported are in hexadecimal, but you can use the `bc`(1) command to translate them into decimal numbers. (See `swap`(1M).)

Example of `ulimit`: to limit the size of a corefile dump to 0 megabytes, type the following:

```
ulimit -c 0
```

`umask [nnn]` Set the user file-creation mask to *nnn* (see `umask`(1)). If you omit *nnn*, print the current value of the mask.

`unset [name...]`

For each *name*, remove the corresponding variable or function value. You cannot unset the variables `PATH`, `PS1`, `PS2`, `MAILCHECK`, and `IFS`.

`wait [n]` Wait for your background process whose process ID is *n* and report its termination status. If you omit *n*, wait for all your shell's currently active background processes. The return code is 0.

Invocation
If the shell is invoked through `exec`(2) and the first character of argument 0 is `-`, commands are initially read from `/etc/profile` and from `$HOME/.profile`, if such files exist. Thereafter, commands are read as described below, which is also the case when the shell is invoked as `/usr/bin/sh`. The options below are interpreted by the shell on invocation only.

Note — Unless you specify the `-c` or `-s` option, the first argument is assumed to be the name of a file containing commands and the remaining arguments are passed as positional parameters to that command file.

`-c string`	Read commands from *string*.
`-i`	If you specified the `-i` option or if the shell input and output are attached to a terminal, this shell is interactive. In this case, ignore `TERMINATE` (so that `kill 0` does not kill an interactive shell), and catch and ignore `INTERRUPT` (so that `wait` is interruptible). In all cases, ignore `QUIT`.
`-p`	Do not set the effective user and group IDs to the real user and group IDs.
`-r`	Restrict the shell (see `rsh`(1M)).

-s   Read commands from the standard input. Any remaining
                      arguments specify the positional parameters. Write shell output
                      (except for special commands) to file descriptor 2.

The remaining options and arguments are described under the set
command above.

Job Control

When you invoke the shell as jsh, job control is enabled in addition to all of the
functionality described previously for sh. Typically, job control is enabled only
for the interactive shell. Noninteractive shells typically do not benefit from the
added functionality of job control.

With job control enabled, every command or pipeline you enter at the
terminal is called a *job*. All jobs exist in one of the following states.

- Foreground jobs have read and write access to the controlling terminal.
- Background jobs are denied read access and have conditional write access
  to the controlling terminal (see tty(1)).
- Stopped jobs have been put in a suspended state, usually as a result of a
  SIGTSTP signal (see signal(5)).

Every job that the shell starts is assigned a positive integer, called a *job
number*, that is tracked by the shell and is used as an identifier to indicate a
specific job. Additionally the shell keeps track of the current and previous jobs.
The current job is the most recent job to be started or restarted. The previous
job is the first noncurrent job.

The acceptable syntax for a job identifier has the form

%*jobid*

where you can specify *jobid* in any of the following formats.

% or +   The current job.

-             The previous job.

? <*string*> The job for which the command line uniquely contains *string*.

n   Job number *n*, where *n* is a job number.

pref   A unique prefix of the command name (for example, if the
              command ls -l was running in the background, you could refer to
              it as %ls); *pref* cannot contain blanks unless it is quoted.

When job control is enabled, the following commands are added to your
environment to manipulate jobs.

bg [%*jobid*...]

                      Resume the execution of a stopped job in the background. If you
                      omit %*jobid*, assume the current job.

`fg [%jobid...]`

> Resume the execution of a stopped job in the foreground, and also move an executing background job into the foreground. If you omit `%jobid`, assume the current job.

`jobs [-p|-l][%jobid ...]`
`jobs -x command [arguments]`

> Report jobs that are stopped or executing in the background. If you omit `%jobid`, report all jobs that are stopped or running in the background. The following options modify or enhance the output of `jobs`.

> `-l`   Report the process group ID and the working directory of the jobs.

> `-p`   Report only the process group ID of the jobs.

> `-x`   Replace any `jobid` found in `command` or `arguments` with the corresponding process group ID, and then execute `command`, passing it `arguments`.

`kill [-signal] %jobid`

> Built-in version of `kill` to provide the functionality of the `kill` command for processes identified with a `jobid`.

`stop %jobid...`

> Stop the execution of a background job(s).

`suspend`   Stop the execution of the current shell (but not if it is the login shell).

`wait [%jobid...]`

> Wait for the background process specified by `%jobid` and report its termination status. If you omit `%jobid`, `wait` behaves as described in "Special Commands" on page 1223.

Note — Because the shell implements both foreground and background jobs in the same process group, they all receive the same signals, which can lead to unexpected behavior. It is, therefore, recommended that you use other job control shells, especially in an interactive environment.

Large File Behavior

See `largefile`(5) for the description of the behavior of `sh` and `jsh` when encountering files greater than or equal to 2 Gbytes (2** 31 bytes).

Exit Status

Errors detected by the shell, such as syntax errors, return a non-zero exit status. If you are using the shell noninteractively, execution of the shell file is

abandoned. Otherwise, the shell returns the exit status of the last command
executed (see also the exit command).

jsh Only
If you invoke the shell as jsh and try to exit the shell while there are stopped
jobs, the shell issues one warning.

```
There are stopped jobs.
```

> This is the only message. If you try to exit again and there are still
> stopped jobs, the jobs are sent a SIGHUP signal from the kernel and
> the shell is exited.

Files

```
$HOME/.profile

/dev/null

/etc/profile

/tmp/sh*
```

Attributes

See attributes(5) for descriptions of the following attributes:

/usr/bin/sh /usr/bin/jsh

Attribute Type	Attribute Value
Availability	SUNWcsu
CSI	Enabled

/usr/xpg4/bin/sh

Attribute Type	Attribute Value
Availability	SUNWxcu4
CSI	Enabled

See Also

bc(1), echo(1), getoptcvt(1), intro(1), kill(1), ksh(1), login(1),
newgrp(1), ps(1), pwd(1), shell_builtins(1), stty(1), test(1), umask(1),
wait(1), rsh(1M), su(1M), swap(1M), sysdef(1M), dup(2), exec(2), fork(2),
getrlimit(2), pipe(2), ulimit(2), setlocale(3C), passwd(4), profile(4),
attributes(5), environ(5), largefile(5), signal(5), XPG4(5)

Diagnostics

If you get the error message cannot fork, too many processes, try using
the wait(1) command to clean up your background processes. If this doesn't

help, the system process table is probably full or you have too many active foreground processes. (Your login has a limited number of process IDs, and the system can track a limited number.)

When the shell executes a shell script that tries to execute a nonexistent command interpreter, the shell returns an erroneous diagnostic message that the shell script file does not exist.

Warnings

For security reasons, the use of setuid shell scripts is strongly discouraged.

---

shell_builtins — Shell Command Interpreter Built-in Functions

Description

The sh(1), csh(1), and ksh(1) shell command interpreters have special built-in functions that are interpreted by the shell as commands. Many of these built-in commands are implemented by more than one of the shells, and some are unique to a particular shell. The commands are listed in the following table.

Command	Bourne Shell	Korn Shell	C Shell
alias		X	X
bg	X	X	X
break	X	X	X
case	X	X	X
cd	X	X	X
chdir	X		X
continue	X	X	X
dirs			X
echo	X	X	X
eval	X	X	X
exec	X	X	X
exit	X	X	X
export	X	X	
fc		X	
fg	X	X	X
for	X	X	
foreach			X
function		X	
getopts	X	X	
glob			X
goto			X

Command	Bourne Shell	Korn Shell	C Shell
hash	x	x	
hashstat			x
history			x
if	x	x	x
jobs	x	x	x
kill	x	x	x
let		x	
limit			x
login	x	x	x
logout	x	x	x
nice			x
newgrp	x	x	
notify			x
onintr			x
popd			x
print		x	
pushd			x
pwd	x	x	
read	x	x	
readonly	x	x	
rehash			x
repeat			x
return	x	x	
select		x	
set	x	x	x
setenv			x
shift	x	x	x
source			x
stop	x	x	x
suspend	x	x	x
switch			x
test	x	x	
time			x
times	x	x	
trap	x	x	
type	x	x	
typeset		x	
ulimit	x	x	
umask	x	x	x

Command	Bourne Shell	Korn Shell	C Shell
unalias		x	x
unhash			x
unlimit			x
unset	x	x	x
unsetenv			x
until	x	x	
wait	x	x	x
whence		x	
while	x	x	x

Bourne Shell Special Commands

Input/output redirection is now permitted for these commands. File descriptor 1 is the default output location. When job control is enabled, additional special commands are added to the shell's environment.

In addition to these built-in reserved command words, sh also uses:

:	Do nothing. Return a 0 exit code.
. *filename*	Read and execute commands from *filename* and return. Use the search path specified by PATH to find the directory containing *filename*.

C Shell

Built-in commands are executed within the C shell. If a built-in command occurs as any component of a pipeline except the last, it is executed in a subshell. Additional to these built-in reserved command words, csh also uses:

:	Interpret this command but perform no action.

Korn Shell Special Commands

Input/output redirection is permitted. Unless otherwise indicated, the output is written on file descriptor 1, and the exit status, when there is no syntax error, is 0. Commands that are preceded by one or two asterisks (*) are treated specially in the following ways.

1. Variable assignment lists preceding the command remain in effect when the command completes.
2. I/O redirections are processed after variable assignments.
3. Errors abort a script that contains them.
4. Words following a command preceded by ** that are in the format of a variable assignment are expanded with the same rules as a variable assignment. This means that tilde substitution is performed after the equal sign and word splitting and file-name generation are not performed.

In addition to these built-in reserved command words, ksh also uses:

`*: [arg...]`

> Expand only parameters.

`*`
`. file [arg...]`

> Read the complete file, then execute the commands in the current shell environment. Use the search path specified by PATH to find the directory containing `file`. If you specify any `arg` arguments, they become the positional parameters. Otherwise, leave the positional parameters unchanged. The exit status is the exit status of the last command executed: the loop termination test.

See Also

alias(1), break(1), case(1), cd(1), chmod(1), csh(1), echo(1), exec(1), exit(1), find(1), for(1), function(1), getoptcvt(1) getopts(1), glob(1), hash(1), history(1), if(1), intro(1), jobs(1), kill(1), ksh(1), let(1), limit(1), login(1), logout(1), newgrp(1), nice(1), nohup(1), print(1), pwd(1), read(1), readonly(1), repeat(1), set(1), sh(1), shift(1), suspend(1), time(1), times(1), trap(1), typeset(1), umask(1), wait(1), while(1), test(1B), chdir(2), chmod(2), creat(2), umask(2), getopt(3C), profile(4), environ(5)

---

shift — Shell Built-in Function to Traverse Either a Shell's Argument List or a List of Field-Separated Words

Synopsis

sh
`shift [n]`

csh
`shift [variable]`

ksh
`*`
`shift [n]`

Description

The `shift` command is a shell built-in command that traverses either the argument list of the shell or a list of field-separated words.

Bourne Shell

The positional parameters from `$n+1`... are renamed `$1`.... The default `n` is 1.

C Shell

The components of `argv`, or *variable*, if supplied, are shifted to the left, discarding the first component. It is an error for the variable not to be set or to have a `null` value.

Korn Shell

The positional parameters from $n+1 $n+1... are renamed $1.... The default *n* is 1. The parameter *n* can be any arithmetic expression that evaluates to a nonnegative number less than or equal to $#.

`ksh(1)` commands that are preceded by one or two asterisks (*) are treated specially in the following ways.

- Variable assignment lists preceding the command remain in effect when the command completes.
- I/O redirections are processed after variable assignments.
- Errors abort a script that contains them.
- Words following a command preceded by ** that are in the format of a variable assignment are expanded with the same rules as a variable assignment. This means that tilde substitution is performed after the equal sign and word splitting and file-name generation are not performed.

Attributes

See `attributes(5)` for descriptions of the following attributes:

Attribute Type	Attribute Value
Availability	SUNWcsu

See Also

`csh(1)`, `ksh(1)`, `sh(1)`, `attributes(5)`

shutdown — Close Down the System at a Given Time

Synopsis

```
/usr/ucb/shutdown [-fhknr] time [warning-message...]
```

Description

Use the `/usr/ucb/shutdown` command as root when shutting down a system with multiple users. The `shutdown` command sends a warning message to all users who are logged in, waits 60 seconds (the default), and then shuts down the system to single-user state. You can choose a different default wait time and specify a different warning message.

Note — The default /usr/sbin/shutdown(1M) command has different options.

The shutdown command provides an automated procedure to notify users when the system is to be shut down. *time* specifies when shutdown brings the system down; you can specify the word now (indicating an immediate shutdown) or a future time in either the format +*number* or *hour*:*min*. The first form brings the system down in *number* minutes, and the second brings the system down at the time of day, indicated in 24-hour notation.

At intervals that get closer as the shutdown time approaches, warning messages are displayed at terminals of all logged-in users and of users who have remote mounts on that machine.

At shutdown time, a message is written to the system log daemon, syslogd(1M), containing the time of shutdown, the instigator of the shutdown, and the reason. Then, a terminate signal is sent to init; this action brings the system down to single-user mode.

Note — /usr/ucb/shutdown enables you to bring the system down between now and 23:59 only if you use the absolute time.

Options

As an alternative to the above procedure, you can specify the following options.

-f	Arrange, in the manner of fastboot(1B), that when the system is rebooted, the file systems are not checked.
-h	Execute halt(1M).
-k	Simulate shutdown of the system. Do not actually shut down the system.
-n	Prevent the normal sync(2) before stopping.
-r	Execute reboot(1M).

Examples

The following example uses the -k option to simulate the shutdown of a system.

```
# /usr/ucb/shutdown -k +1
Shutdown at 15:22 (in 1 minute) [pid 519]
#

        *** System shutdown message from winsor@castle ***

System going down in 60 seconds
```

```
          *** FINAL System shutdown message from winsor@castle ***

   System going down in 30 seconds


          *** FINAL System shutdown message from winsor@castle ***

   System going down IMMEDIATELY

   System shutdown time has arrived
   but you'll have to do it yourself

   #
```

Files

/etc/rmtab Remote mounted file-system table.

Attributes

See attributes(5) for descriptions of the following attributes:

Attribute Type	Attribute Value
Availability	SUNWscpu

See Also

login(1), fastboot(1B), halt(1M), reboot(1M), syslogd(1M), sync(2), rmtab(4), attributes(5)

size — Print Section Sizes of Object Files in Bytes

Synopsis

/usr/ccs/bin/size [-f][-F][-n][-o][-V][-x] *filename...*

Description

The size command produces segment or section size information in bytes for each loaded section in ELF object files. size prints out the size of the text, data, and bss (uninitialized data) segments (or sections) and their total.

size processes ELF object files named on the command line. If an archive file name is input to the size command, the information for each object file in the archive is displayed.

When calculating segment information, the size command prints the total file size of the nonwritable segments, the total file size of the writable segments, and the total memory size of the writable segments minus the total file size of the writable segments.

If it cannot calculate segment information, `size` calculates section information. When calculating section information, `size` prints out the total size of sections that are allocatable, nonwritable, and not `NOBITS`; the total size of the sections that are allocatable, writable, and not `NOBITS`; and the total size of the writable sections of type `NOBITS`. `NOBITS` sections do not actually take up space in the file name.

If `size` cannot calculate either segment or section information, it prints an error message and stops processing the file.

Note — Because the size of bss sections is not known until link edit time, the `size` command does not give the true total size of prelinked objects.

Options

-f	Print the size of each allocatable section, the name of the section, and the total of the section sizes. If there is no section data, print an error message and stop processing the file.
-F	Print the size of each loadable segment, the permission options of the segment, and the total of the loadable segment sizes. If there is no segment data, print an error message and stop processing the file.
-n	Print nonloadable segment or nonallocatable section sizes. If segment data exists, print the memory size of each loadable segment or file size of each nonloadable segment, the permission options, and the total size of the segments. If there is no segment data, then for each allocatable and nonallocatable section, print the memory size, the section name, and the total size of the sections. If there is no segment or section data, print an error message and stop processing.
-o	Print numbers in octal.
-V	Print the version information for the `size` command to the standard output.
-x	Print numbers in hexadecimal.

Examples

The following examples show typical size output.

```
castle% size /usr/ccs/bin/admin
44711 + 1972 + 12400 = 59083
castle% size -f /usr/ccs/bin/admin
17(.interp) + 1752(.hash) + 3600(.dynsym) + 3116(.dynstr) +
   64(.SUNW_version) + 24(.rela.ex_shared) + 60(.rela.bss) +
   912(.rela.plt) + 31460(.text) + 56(.init) + 56(.fini) +
   4(.exception_ranges) + 4(.rodata) + 3371(.rodata1) + 4(.got) +
```

```
    964(.plt) + 160(.dynamic) + 32(.ex_shared) + 188(.data) + 624(.data1)
    + 12396(.bss) = 58864
castle% size -F /usr/ccs/bin/admin
44711(r-x) + 14372(rwx) = 59243
castle%
```

Attributes

See attributes(5) for descriptions of the following attributes:

Attribute Type	Attribute Value
Availability	SUNWbtool

See Also

as(1), ld(1), cc(1B), a.out(4), ar(4), attributes(5)

---

sleep — Suspend Execution for an Interval

Synopsis

```
/usr/bin/sleep time
```

Description

The sleep command suspends execution for at least the integral number of seconds specified by the *time* operand.

If the sleep command receives a SIGALRM signal, one of the following actions is taken.

- Terminate normally with a 0 exit status.
- Effectively ignore the signal.

The sleep command takes the standard action for all other signals.

Operands

time   A nonnegative decimal integer specifying the number of seconds to suspend execution.

Examples

The following example executes a command after 105 seconds.

```
castle% (sleep 105; find . -name core -print)&
castle%
```

The following example executes a command every so often.

```
while true
 do
   command sleep 37
 done
```

Environment Variables

See environ(5) for descriptions of the following environment variables that affect the execution of sleep: LC_CTYPE, LC_MESSAGES, and NLSPATH.

Exit Status

0	The execution was successfully suspended for at least *time* seconds, or a SIGALRM signal was received.
>0	An error has occurred.

Attributes

See attributes(5) for descriptions of the following attributes:

Attribute Type	Attribute Value
Availability	SUNWcsu

See Also

wait(1), alarm(2), wait(3B), sleep(3C), attributes(5), environ(5)

smart2cfg — Compaq Smart-2 EISA/PCI and Smart-2SL PCI Array Controller ioctl Command

Synopsis

```
/bin/smart2cfg -c [controller-num]
/bin/smart2cfg -d [controller-num]
/bin/smart2cfg -h
/bin/smart2cfg -l logical-drive-num [controller-num]
/bin/smart2cfg -p physical-drive-num bus-num [controller-num]
```

Description

The smart2cfg x86 command issues controller-specific ioctls to the Compaq Smart-2 EISA/PCI and Smart-2SL PCI array controller using the smartii(7) driver.

smart2cfg provides information about the Smart-2 and Smart2SL controllers installed on the system, the logical and physical drives, and the details of the ReadWrite cache present on each controller. The command is text based and is driven by command-line arguments. smart2cfg and the smartii(7) driver communicate by using ioctls. smart2cfg also supports multiple commands.

Note — If you do not specify the controller, the first controller is taken as default.

Options

-c *controller-num*

        Print cache details of the cache on controller *controller-num*.

-d *controller-num*

        Print details of all the physical disks, all the logical drives, and the cache on controller *controller-num*.

-h   Show online help for the smart2cfg command.

-l *logical-drive-num controller-num*m

        Print logical drive details of the drive *logical-drive-num* on controller *controller-num*.

-p *physical-drive-num bus-num controller-num*

        Print physical drive details of the disk *physical-drive-num bus-num* on controller*controller-num*.

Examples

The following example shows details of the physical disk with SCSI ID 0, on bus 0, on controller 0.

smart2cfg -p 0 0 0

The following example shows logical drive details of logical drive 0 on controller 0.

smart2cfg -l 0 0

The following example shows cache details of controller 0.

smart2cfg -c 0

The following example shows information on all physical disks, logical drives, and cache on controller 0.

smart2cfg -d

The following example shows details of the disk with SCSI ID 0, on bus 0, on controller 0, and logical drive details of logical drive 0 on controller 1.

```
smart2cfg -p 0 0 0 -1 0 1
```

Files

```
/devices/eisa/smartii@instance,ioaddr:ioctlnode

/devices/pci@0,bus-num/pci1014,22@device-num/pcie11,4030@0:
  ioctlnode

/devices/pci@0,bus-num/pci1014,22@device-num/pcie11,4031@0:
  ioctlnode
```

Attributes

See `attributes`(5) for descriptions of the following attributes:

Attribute Type	Attribute Value
Architecture	x86

See Also

```
attributes(5),  smartii(7D)
```

---

soelim — Resolve and Eliminate .so Requests from nroff or troff Input

Synopsis

```
/usr/bin/soelim [filename...]
```

Description

The `soelim` command is a preprocessor that reads `nroff`/`troff` input and performs the textual inclusion implied by the `nroff`(1) directives of the form `.so somefile` when they appear at the beginning of input lines. This command is useful because programs such as `tbl`(1) do not normally do this preprocessing. With the `soelim` command, you can place individual tables in separate files to be run as a part of a large document.

An argument consisting of a dash (-) is taken to be a file name corresponding to the standard input.

Note — You can suppress inclusion by using ' in place of ., for example, ` ' so /usr/share/lib/tmac/tmac.s`

Examples

The following example shows a typical use of soelim.

```
castle% soelim exum?.n | tbl | nroff -ms | col | lpr
```

Attributes

See attributes(5) for descriptions of the following attributes:

Attribute Type	Attribute Value
Availability	SUNWdoc

See Also

more(1), nroff(1), tbl(1), attributes(5)

solregis — Solaris User Registration

Synopsis

```
/usr/dt/bin/solregis [-dc]
```

Description

The solregis command initiates the Solaris user registration procedure, which enables you to register with Sun Microsystems and receive information about Solaris. Normally, solregis is executed in conditional mode as a part of desktop login so that you are prompted at desktop startup time to register unless you have already done so.

Options

-d	Delay display of the initial screen until a window manager has asserted control of the X display.
-c	Exit without any dialog displayed if $HOME/.solregis/disable exists, DISABLE=1 is specified in /etc/default/solregis, or the user has already registered.

Exit Status

0	Successful completion.
>0	An error occurred.

Usage

The following resources can control the behavior and appearance of solregis.

Name	Class	Value Type	Default
disable	Disable	Boolean	False
localeChoices	LocaleChoices	Int	1
action0	Action	String	/usr/dt/bin/hotjava
initialURL0	URL	String	file:///usr/dt/ app-config/ solregis/EReg.html
localeChoice*n*	LocaleChoice	String	null
action*n*	Action	String	null for $n>0$
initialURL*n*	URL	String	null for $n>0$
printContext	PrintContext	String	thisorgunit

disable   If true when executed in conditional mode, exit without displaying anything.

localeChoices

Specify the number of localeChoice*n*, action*n*, and initialURL*n* sets. The first set is 0, so if localeChoices is 1, localeChoice0, action0, and initialURL0 are the only active resources. If localeChoices is 1, display none of the localeChoice*n* strings and use action0 and so forth. If localeChoices is greater than 1, make each localeChoice*n* string an element in an exclusive choice list and apply the index of the selected item controls for the action*n* and initialURL*n* resources.

localeChoice*n*

Specify the string presented to the user for this choice.

action*n*   Specify the file name of the command to be executed (normally expected to be a World Wide Web browser) when you choose Register Now, or the special string print. If you specify print, the initialURL*n* string must be a file name on the local system naming a file that is to be printed after prompting for a print destination.

initialURL*n*

> Specify the argument to be passed to action*n* for initial registration. This argument is normally the Uniform Resource Locator for the initial page to be displayed by the World Wide Web browser.

printContext

> Specify the XFN naming context to be displayed if you choose the special print action. For example, if you use the default printContext thisorgunit, display the printers in thisorgunit/service/printer.

Environment Variables

See environ(5) for descriptions of the following environment variables that affect the execution of solregis: HOME, LANG, LC_MESSAGES, and NLSPATH.

Files

/etc/default/solregis

> Default values.

/$HOME/.solregis/uprops

> User registration information.

/$HOME/.solregis/disable

> Users disabled from registration.

/usr/dt/app-defaults/C/Solregis

> Default locale resources.

/usr/dt/app-defaults/$LANG/Solregis

> Default localized resources.

/etc/dt/app-defaults/C/Solregis

> Default installation resources.

/usr/dt/app-defaults/$LANG/Solregis

> Localized installation resources.

Attributes

See attributes(5) for descriptions of the following attributes:

Attribute Type	Attribute Value
Availability	SUNWsregu

See Also

attributes(5), environ(5)

---

sort — Sort, Merge, or Sequence Check Text Files

Synopsis

```
/usr/bin/sort [-bcdfimMnru][-k keydef][-o output][-t char]          New!
    [-T directory][-y [k mem]][-z recs z][+pos1 [-pos2]][file...]
/usr/xpg4/bin/sort [-bcdfimMnru][-k keydef][-o output][-t char]     New!
    [-T directory][-y [k mem]][-z recs z][+pos1 [-pos2]][file...]
```

Description

Use the sort command to rearrange the lines in a file in alphabetic (the default) or numeric order and write the result to the standard output.

By default, the sort command uses the beginning of the line as the key field to sort on. However, you can specify any field in the file as the key field. Lines are sorted according to the collating sequence of the current locale. By default, sort uses the ASCII collating sequence, which sorts white space first, followed by most punctuation marks, followed by numbers, uppercase letters, and finally lowercase letters. When the first characters in the key field are identical, sort looks at each subsequent character up to the newline if needed to determine the correct sorting order.

For numeric sorts, numbers are not sorted in true numeric order unless you use the -n option. Instead, numerical sorted results could look like the following example.

```
1
10
11
2
20
21
3
30
```

You get this result because all of the lines starting with 1 are grouped together followed by all of the lines starting with 2, and so forth.

Note — When the last line of an input file is missing a newline character, sort appends one, prints a warning message, and continues. sort does not guarantee preservation of relative line ordering on equal keys.

Options

/usr/bin/sort

-c   Check that the single input file is ordered as specified by the
                arguments and the collating sequence of the current locale. Set
                the exit code, and produce no output unless the file is out of sort
                sequence.

/usr/xpg4/bin/sort

-c   Same as /usr/bin/sort, except produce no output under any
                circumstances.

-m   Merge only. Assume the input files are already sorted.

-u   Sort uniquely by suppressing all but one in each set of lines having
                equal keys. If used with the -c option, check that there are no lines
                with duplicate keys, in addition to checking that the input file is
                sorted.

-o *output*   Specify the name of an output file to be used instead of the
                standard output. This file can be the same as one of the input files.

-T *directory*

                Specify the name of a directory to use for temporary files.

-y k *mem*   Specify the amount of main memory used initially. Start using
                that number of kilobytes of memory unless the administrative
                minimum or maximum is exceeded, in which case use the
                corresponding extremum. Thus, -y 0 is guaranteed to start with
                minimum memory. -y with no k *mem* argument starts with
                maximum memory. If you omit this option, begin using a system
                default memory size and continue to use more space as needed.

-z *recs z*   (Obsolete). Use to prevent abnormal termination when lines
                longer than the system-dependent default buffer size are
                encountered. Because sort now automatically allocates buffers
                large enough to hold the longest line, this option has no effect.

Ordering Options

The following options override the default ordering rules. When ordering
options appear independently of any key field specifications, the requested field
ordering rules are applied globally to all sort keys. When attached to a specific
key, the specified ordering options override all global ordering options for that
key. In the obsolescent forms, if one or more of these options follow a +*pos1*
option, only the key field specified by that preceding option is affected.

-d   Sort in dictionary order. Consider only letters, digits, and blanks
                (spaces and Tabs) significant in comparisons.

-f   Fold lowercase letters into upper case.

-i   Ignore nonprintable characters.

-M   Compare as months. Fold the first three nonblank characters of
            the field to upper case and compare. For example, in English the
            sorting order is JAN < FEB < ... < DEC. Compare invalid fields lower
            than JAN. Invalid fields beginning with one of the letters of the
            month confuse sort. The -M option implies the -b option.

-n   Restrict the sort key to an initial numeric string consisting of
            optional blank characters, optional minus sign, and zero or more
            digits with an optional radix character and thousands separators
            (as defined in the current locale), which is sorted by arithmetic
            value. An empty digit string is treated as 0. Leading 0s and signs
            on 0s do not affect ordering.

-r   Reverse the sense of comparisons.

Field Separator Options

You can alter the treatment of field separators by using the following options.

-b   Ignore leading blank characters when determining the starting
            and ending positions of a restricted sort key. If you specify the -b
            option before the first sort key option, apply it to all sort key
            options. Otherwise, you can attach the -b option independently to
            each -k *field-start*, *field-end*, or +*pos1* or -*pos2* argument.

-t *char*   Use *char* as the field separator character. *char* is not considered to
            be part of a field (although you can include it in a sort key). Each
            occurrence of *char* is significant (for example, *charchar* delimits
            an empty field). If you do not specify -t, use blank characters as
            default field separators; each maximal nonempty sequence of
            blank characters that follows a nonblank character is a field
            separator.

Sort Key Options

You can specify sort keys, using the following option.

-k *keydef*   Define a restricted sort key.

The format of this definition is:

`-k field-start [type][, field-end [type]]`

where *field-start* and *field-end* define a key field restricted to a portion
of the line.

type is a modifier from the list of characters bdfiMnr. The b modifier
behaves like the -b option but applies only to the *field-start* or *field-end*
to which it is attached. Characters within a field are counted from the first
nonblank character in the field. (This rule applies separately to
first-character and *last-character*.) The other modifiers behave like
the corresponding options but apply only to the key field to which they are
attached. They have this effect if specified with *field-start*, *field-end*, or

both. If any modifier is attached to a *field-start* or to a *field-end*, no option applies to either.

When there are multiple key fields, later keys are compared only after all earlier keys compare equal. Except when you specify the -u option, lines that otherwise compare equal are ordered as if none of the options -d, -f, -i, -n, or -k were present (but with -r still in effect, if you specified it) and with all bytes in the lines significant to the comparison.

The following notation defines a key field that begins at *field-start* and ends at *field-end* inclusive, unless *field-start* falls beyond the end of the line or after *field-end*, in which case the key field is empty.

`-k field-start[type][, field-end[type]]`

A missing *field-end* means the last character of the line.

A field comprises a maximal sequence of nonseparating characters and, in the absence of option -t, any preceding field separator.

The *field-start* portion of the *keydef* option argument has the form:

`field-number[. first-character]`

Fields and characters within fields are numbered starting with 1. *field-number* and *first-character*, interpreted as positive decimal integers, specify the first character to be used as part of a sort key. If you omit . *first-character*, the default is the first character of the field.

The *field-end* portion of the *keydef* option argument has the form

`field-start[. last-character]`

The *field-number* is as described above for *field-start*. *last-character*, interpreted as a nonnegative decimal integer, specifies the last character to be used as part of the sort key. If *last-character* evaluates to 0 or you omit . *last-character*, the default is the last character of the field specified by *field-number*.

If the -b option or b *type* modifier is in effect, characters within a field are counted from the first nonblank character in the field. (This applies separately to *first-character* and *last-character*.)

The following syntax is obsolete.

`[+pos1[-pos2]]`

It provides functionality equivalent to the -k *keydef* option.

pos1 and *pos2* each have the form m.n optionally followed by one or more of the options bdfiMnr. A starting position specified by +m.n is interpreted to mean the n+1st character in the m+1st field. A missing .n means .0, indicating the first character of the m+1st field. If the b option is in effect, n is counted from the first nonblank in the m+1st field; +m.0b refers to the first nonblank character in the m+1st field.

A last position specified by -m.n is interpreted to mean the n-th character (including separators) after the last character of the m-th field. A missing .n means .0, indicating the last character of the m-th field. If the b option is in effect, n is counted from the last leading blank in the $m+1$st field; $-m.1$b refers to the first nonblank in the $m+1$st field.

The fully specified $+pos1$ $-pos2$ form with type modifiers T and U

```
+w.xT -y.zU
```

is equivalent to:

```
undefined          (z==0 & U contains b & -t is present)
-k w+1.x+1T,y.0U   (z==0 otherwise)
-k w+1.x+1T,y+1.zU (z > 0)
```

Implementations support at least nine occurrences of the sort keys (the -k option and obsolescent $+pos1$ and $-pos2$) that are significant in command-line order. If you specify no sort key, a default sort key of the entire line is used.

Operands

file   A path name of a file to be sorted, merged, or checked. If you specify no file operands or if a file operand is -, use the standard input.

Usage

See largefile(5) for the description of the behavior of sort when encountering files greater than or equal to 2 Gbytes (2** 31 bytes).

Examples

The following example uses the sort -M command to sort a file by months. Notice that of the names in the list that are not months, those that begin with the same letters as the month confuse the sort command. They are sorted alphabetically with the months and are not pushed to the top of the list.

```
castle% cat sortmonth
Janice
Maris
March
July
February
December
June
April
January
Ray
Fred
Juno
castle% sort -M sortmonth
Fred
Ray
Janice
January
February
```

```
March
Maris
April
June
Juno
July
December
castle%
```

The following example shows the contents of the file named `sortnum`, sorts it without using the -n option, then sorts it using the -n option.

```
castle% cat sortnum
2000
1998
1999
1
10
40
20
3
2

castle% sort sortnum
1
10
1998
1999
2
20
2000
3
40

castle% sort -n sortnum
1
2
3
10
20
40
1998
1999
2000
castle%
```

The following examples show both nonobsolescent and obsolescent ways of specifying sort keys as an aid to understanding the relationship between the two forms.

Either of the following commands sorts the contents of `infile` with the second field as the sort key.

```
castle% sort -k 2,2 infile
castle% sort +1 -2 infile
castle% sort -k 2,2 kookaburra-1

Eating all the gumdrops he can see.
Laugh, kookaburra, laugh, kookaburra
Stop, kookaburra, stop, kookaburra
Merry merry king of the bush is he.
Kookaburra sits in the old gum tree
Kookaburra sits in the old gum tree
Leave some there for me.
Gay your life must be
castle%
```

Either of the following commands sorts, in reverse order, the contents of infile1 and infile2, placing the output in outfile and using the second character of the second field as the sort key (assuming that the first character of the second field is the field separator).

```
castle% sort -r -o outfile -k 2.2,2.2 infile1 infile2
castle% sort -r -o outfile +1.1 -1.2 infile1 infile2

castle% sort -r -o outfile -k 2.2,2.2 kookaburra-1 kookaburra-2
castle% cat outfile
Gay your life must be
Leave some there for me.
Kookaburra sits in the old gum tree
Kookaburra sits in the old gum tree
Merry merry king of the bush is he.
Stop, kookaburra, stop, kookaburra
Laugh, kookaburra, laugh, kookaburra
Eating all the gumdrops he can see.
     8  Leave some there for me.
     7  Stop, kookaburra, stop, kookaburra
     6  Eating all the gumdrops he can see.
     5  Kookaburra sits in the old gum tree
     4  Gay your life must be
     3  Laugh, kookaburra, laugh, kookaburra
     2  Merry merry king of the bush is he.
     1  Kookaburra sits in the old gum tree


castle%
```

Either of the following commands sorts the contents of infile1 and infile2, using the second nonblank character of the second field as the sort key.

```
castle% sort -k 2.2b,2.2b infile1 infile2
castle% sort +1.1b -1.2b infile1 infile2

castle% sort -k 2.2b,2.2b kookaburra-1 kookaburra-2
```

```
      3   Laugh, kookaburra, laugh, kookaburra
      4   Gay your life must be
      6   Eating all the gumdrops he can see.
      2   Merry merry king of the bush is he.
      8   Leave some there for me.
Merry merry king of the bush is he.
Kookaburra sits in the old gum tree
Kookaburra sits in the old gum tree
Eating all the gumdrops he can see.
      1   Kookaburra sits in the old gum tree
      5   Kookaburra sits in the old gum tree
Gay your life must be
Laugh, kookaburra, laugh, kookaburra
Leave some there for me.
Stop, kookaburra, stop, kookaburra
      7   Stop, kookaburra, stop, kookaburra
castle%
```

Either of the following commands prints the passwd(4) file (user database) sorted by the numeric user ID (the third colon-separated field).

```
castle% sort -t : -k 3,3n /etc/passwd
castle% sort -t : +2 -3n /etc/passwd

castle% sort -t : -k 3,3n /etc/passwd
root:x:0:1:Super-User:/:/sbin/sh
daemon:x:1:1::/:
bin:x:2:2::/usr/bin:
sys:x:3:3::/:
adm:x:4:4:Admin:/var/adm:
uucp:x:5:5:uucp Admin:/usr/lib/uucp:
nuucp:x:9:9:uucp Admin:/var/spool/uucppublic:/usr/lib/uucp/uucico
listen:x:37:4:Network Admin:/usr/net/nls:
lp:x:71:8:Line Printer Admin:/usr/spool/lp:
winsor:x:1001:10::/export/home/winsor:/bin/csh
ray:x:1002:10::/export/home/ray:/bin/csh
des:x:1003:10::/esport/home/des:/bin/csh
rob:x:1004:10::/export/home/rob:/bin/csh
nobody:x:60001:60001:Nobody:/:
noaccess:x:60002:60002:No Access User:/:
nobody4:x:65534:65534:SunOS 4.x Nobody:/:
castle%
```

Either of the following commands prints the lines of the already sorted file infile, suppressing all but one occurrence of lines having the same third field.

```
castle% sort -um -k 3.1,3.0 infile
castle% sort -um +2.0 -3.0 infile

castle% sort -um -k 3.1,3.0 kookaburra-1
Kookaburra sits in the old gum tree
Merry merry king of the bush is he.
Laugh, kookaburra, laugh, kookaburra
Gay your life must be
```

```
Kookaburra sits in the old gum tree
Eating all the gumdrops he can see.
Stop, kookaburra, stop, kookaburra
Leave some there for me.
castle%
```

Environment Variables

See environ(5) for descriptions of the following environment variables that affect the execution of sort: LC_COLLATE, LC_MESSAGES, and NLSPATH.

LC_CTYPE   Determine the locale for the interpretation of sequences of bytes of text data as characters (for example, single- versus multibyte characters in arguments and input files) and the behavior of character classification for the –b, -d, -f, -i, and –n options.

LC_NUMERIC Determine the locale for the definition of the radix character and thousands separator for the -n option.

Exit Status

0   All input files were output successfully, or you specified – c and the input file was correctly sorted.

1   With the – c option, the file was not ordered as specified or, if you specified both the – c and –u options, two input lines were found with equal keys.

>1   An error occurred.

Files

/var/tmp/stm???

        Temporary files.

Attributes

See attributes(5) for descriptions of the following attributes:

/usr/bin/sort

Attribute Type	Attribute Value
Availability	SUNWesu
CSI	Enabled

/usr/xpg4/bin/sort

Attribute Type	Attribute Value
Availability	SUNWxcu4
CSI	Enabled

See Also

comm(1), join(1), uniq(1), passwd(4), attributes(5), environ(5),
largefile(5), XPG4(5)

Diagnostics

The sort command comments and exits with non-zero status for various
trouble conditions (for example, when input lines are too long) and for disorders
discovered under the -c option.

---

sortbib — Sort a Bibliographic Database

Synopsis

/usr/bin/sortbib [-s *KEYS*] *database*...

Description

Use the sortbib command to sort files of records containing refer(1) key
letters by keys you specify. Records can be separated by blank lines, or by . [
and .] delimiters, but the two styles cannot be mixed together. This command
reads through each database and pulls out key fields, which are sorted
separately. The sorted key fields contain the file pointer, byte offset, and length
of corresponding records. These records are delivered by disk seeks and reads,
so sortbib cannot be used in a pipeline to read standard input.

The most common key letters and their meanings are given below.

%A	Author's name.
%B	Book containing article referenced.
%C	City (place of publication).
%D	Date of publication.
%E	Editor of book containing article referenced.
%F	Footnote number or label (supplied by refer).
%G	Government order number.
%H	Header commentary, printed before reference.
%I	Issuer (publisher).
%J	Journal containing article.
%K	Keywords to use in locating reference.
%L	Label field used by -k option of refer.
%M	Bell Labs memorandum (undefined).
%N	Number within volume.
%O	Other commentary printed at end of reference.

%P	Page number(s).
%Q	Corporate or foreign author (unreversed).
%R	Report, paper, or thesis (unpublished).
%S	Series title.
%T	Title of article or book.
%V	Volume number.
%X	Abstract. Used by roffbib, not by refer.
%Y,Z	Ignored by refer.

By default, sortbib alphabetizes by the first %A and the %D fields, which contain the senior author and date.

sortbib sorts on the last word on the %A line which is assumed to be the author's last name. A word in the final position, such as jr. or ed., is ignored if the name before it ends with a comma. Authors with two-word last names or unusual constructions can be sorted correctly with the nroff convention \0 in place of a blank. A %Q field is considered to be the same as %A except that sorting begins with the first, not the last, word. sortbib sorts on the last word of the %D line, usually the year. It also ignores leading articles (like A or The) when sorting by titles in the %T or %T fields; it ignores articles of any modern European language. If a sort-significant field is absent from a record, %T puts that record before other records containing that field.

No more than 16 databases can be sorted together at one time. Records longer than 4,096 characters are truncated.

Options

-s *KEYS*   Specify new *KEYS*. For instance, -sATD sorts by author, title, and date, whereas -sA+D sorts by all authors and date. Sort keys past the fourth are not meaningful.

Attributes

See attributes(5) for descriptions of the following attributes:

Attribute Type	Attribute Value
Availability	SUNWdoc

See Also

addbib(1), indxbib(1), lookbib(1), refer(1), roffbib(1), attributes(5)

Bugs

Records with missing author fields should probably be sorted by title.

sotruss — Trace Shared Library Procedure Calls

Synopsis

```
/usr/bin/sotruss [-f][-F bindfromlist][-T bindtolist]
   [-o outputfile] executable [executable arguments...]
```

Description

The sotruss command executes the specified command and produces a trace of the library calls that it performs. Each line of the trace output reports what bindings are occurring between dynamic objects as each procedure call is executed. sotruss traces all of the procedure calls that occur between dynamic objects via the Procedure Linkage Table, so only those procedure calls that are bound via the Procedure Linkage Table are traced. See *Linker and Libraries Guide*.

Options

-f   Follow all children created by fork(), and print truss output on each child process. This option also outputs a PID on each truss output line.

-F *bindfromlist*

         Specify a colon-separated list of libraries that are to be traced. Trace only calls from these libraries. The default is to trace calls from the main executable only.

-o *outputfile*

         Direct output to the *outputfile*. If you combine this option with the -f option, then the PID of the executing program is put at the end of the file name. By default, output goes to standard error.

-T *bindtolist*

         Specify a colon-separated list of libraries that are to be traced. Trace calls only to these libraries. The default is to trace all calls.

Examples

The following simple example shows the tracing of an ls command.

```
castle% sotruss ls | more
ls                 ->         libc.so.1:*atexit(0xef7d9e8c, 0x24000, 0x0)
ls                 ->         libc.so.1:*atexit(0x13bec, 0xef7d9e8c, 0xef674498)
ls                 ->         libc.so.1:*setlocale(0x6, 0x13c2c, 0xef674490)
ls                 ->         libc.so.1:*textdomain(0x13c30, 0x13c2c, 0xef674490)
ls                 ->         libc.so.1:*time(0x0, 0xef671f98, 0xef674490)
ls                 ->         libc.so.1:*isatty(0x1, 0xef671f98, 0x0)
ls                 ->         libc.so.1:*getopt(0x1, 0xeffff46c, 0x13c40)
ls                 ->         libc.so.1:*malloc(0x100, 0x0, 0x0)
```

```
ls                    ->      libc.so.1:*malloc(0x9000, 0x0, 0x0)
ls                    ->      libc.so.1:*lstat64(0x241b8, 0xeffff310, 0x0)
ls                    ->      libc.so.1:*qsort(0x249d0, 0x1, 0x4)
ls                    ->      libc.so.1:*opendir(0x241b8, 0xef7a1750, 0xef5cea9a)
ls                    ->      libc.so.1:*readdir64(0x2dae0, 0x24480, 0xf000)
ls                    ->      libc.so.1:*readdir64(0x2dae0, 0x0, 0xf000)
ls                    ->      libc.so.1:*readdir64(0x2dae0, 0x0, 0xf000)
ls                    ->      libc.so.1:*readdir64(0x2dae0, 0xb, 0x24d18)
ls                    ->      libc.so.1:*readdir64(0x2dae0, 0xb, 0x24f58)
ls                    ->      libc.so.1:*readdir64(0x2dae0, 0x6, 0x25198)
ls                    ->      libc.so.1:*closedir(0x2dae0, 0x70, 0x25198)
ls                    ->      libc.so.1:*qsort(0x249d4, 0x3, 0x4)
ls                    ->      libc.so.1:*strcoll(0x24d18, 0x24f58, 0x8000)
ls                    ->      libc.so.1:*.mul(0x1, 0xffffffff, 0x24f58)
ls                    ->      libc.so.1:*strcoll(0x24d18, 0x25198, 0x8000)
ls                    ->      libc.so.1:*.mul(0x1, 0xfffffff3, 0x25198)
ls                    ->      libc.so.1:*strcoll(0x24d18, 0x24f58, 0x8000)
ls                    ->      libc.so.1:*.mul(0x1, 0xffffffff, 0x24f58)
ls                    ->      libc.so.1:*strcoll(0x24f58, 0x25198, 0x8000)
ls                    ->      libc.so.1:*.mul(0x1, 0xfffffff3, 0x25198)
ls                    ->      libc.so.1:*printf(0x13d24, 0x24d18, 0x241c0)
ls                    ->      libc.so.1:*printf(0x13d24, 0x24f58, 0x241c0)
ls                    ->      libc.so.1:*printf(0x13d24, 0x25198, 0x241c0)
ls                    ->      libc.so.1:*exit(0x0, 0x244f8, 0x244f4)
addusr-1.rs
addusr-2.rs
newdir
castle%
```

Attributes

See attributes(5) for descriptions of the following attributes:

Attribute Type	Attribute Value
Availability	SUNWtoo

See Also

ld.so.1(1), truss(1), whocalls(1), fork(2), attributes(5)
Linker and Libraries Guide

---

source — Shell Built-in Function to Execute Other Commands

Synopsis

csh

source [-h] *name*

Description

See exec(1).

---

sparc — Get Processor Type Truth Value

Synopsis

```
/usr/bin/sparc
```

Description

See machid(1).

---

spell, hashmake, spellin, hashcheck — Report Spelling Errors

Synopsis

```
/usr/bin/spell [-bilvx] [+ local-file] [file]...
/usr/lib/spell/hashmake
/usr/lib/spell/spellin n
/usr/lib/spell/hashcheck spelling-list
```

Description

Use the spell command to check spelling in one or more files. The spell command collects words from the named files and looks them up in a spelling list. Words that neither occur among nor are derivable (by applying certain inflections, prefixes, or suffixes) from words in the spelling list are written to the standard output.

If you specify no *file* arguments, words to check are collected from the standard input. spell ignores most troff(1), tbl(1), and eqn(1) constructs. Copies of all output words are accumulated in the history file (spellhist), and a stop list filters out misspellings (for example, their=thy-y+ier) that would otherwise pass.

By default, spell (like deroff(1)) follows chains of included files (.so and .nx troff(1) requests) unless the names of such included files begin with /usr/lib.

The standard spelling list is based on many sources and, while more haphazard than an ordinary dictionary, it is also more effective for proper names and popular technical words. Coverage of the specialized vocabularies of biology, medicine, and chemistry is light.

Three programs help maintain and check the hash lists used by spell.

hashmake   Reads a list of words from the standard input and writes the corresponding nine-digit hash code to the standard output.

spellin   Reads *n* hash codes from the standard input and writes a compressed spelling list to the standard output.

hashcheck   Reads a compressed *spelling-list* and recreates the nine-digit hash codes for all the words in it. It writes these codes to the standard output.

You can monitor misspelled words by default by setting the H_SPELL variable in /usr/bin/spell to the name of a file that has permission mode 666.

spell works only on English words defined in the U.S. ASCII codeset.

Note — Because copies of all output are accumulated in the spellhist file, spellhist can grow quite large and require purging.

Options

-b   Check British spelling. Besides preferring centre, colour, programme, speciality, travelled, and so forth, this option insists on -ise in words like standardise.

-i   Instruct deroff(1) to ignore .so and .nx commands. If deroff(1) is not present on the system, then this option is ignored.

-l   Follow the chains of all included files.

-v   Print all words not literally in the spelling list as well as plausible derivations from the words in the spelling list.

-x   Print every plausible stem, one per line, with = preceding each word.

+ *local-file*

Specify a set of words that are correct spellings (in addition to spell's own spelling list) for each job. *local-file* is the name of a user-provided file that contains a sorted list of words, one per line. Words found in *local-file* are removed from spell's output. Use sort(1) to order *local-file* in ASCII collating sequence. If this ordering is not followed, some entries in *local-file* may be ignored.

Operands

file   A path name of a text file to check for spelling errors. If you specify no files, collect words from the standard input.

Examples

The following example runs the `spell` command on the file `kookaburra-1`. Notice that both lowercase and uppercase spellings of `kookaburra` are listed in the output.

```
castle% spell kookaburra-1
Kookaburra
kookaburra
castle%
```

Environment Variables

See `environ(5)` for descriptions of the following environment variables that affect the execution of `spell`: LC_CTYPE, LC_MESSAGES, and NLSPATH.

Exit Status

0   Successful completion.

>0   An error occurred.

Files

D_SPELL=/usr/lib/spell/hlist[ab]

Hashed spelling lists, American and British.

S_SPELL=/usr/lib/spell/hstop

Hashed stop list.

H_SPELL=/var/adm/spellhist

History file.

/usr/share/lib/dict/words

Master dictionary.

Attributes

See `attributes(5)` for descriptions of the following attributes:

Attribute Type	Attribute Value
Availability	SUNWesu

See Also

`deroff(1)`, `eqn(1)`, `sort(1)`, `tbl(1)`, `troff(1)`, `attributes(5)`, `environ(5)`

Bugs

The spelling list's coverage is uneven; new installations may want to monitor the output for several months to gather local additions.

British spelling was compiled by an American.

spline — Interpolate Smooth Curve

Synopsis
```
/usr/bin/spline [-aknpx]...
```

Description
The `spline` command takes pairs of numbers from the standard input as abscissas and ordinates of a function. It produces a similar set, which is approximately equally spaced and includes the input set, to the standard output. The cubic `spline` output has two continuous derivatives, and sufficient points to look smooth when plotted, for example, by graph(1).

Options

-a	Supply abscissas automatically (they are missing from the input); specify spacing by the next argument or assume it is 1 if the next argument is not a number.
-k	Use the constant k in the boundary value computation (2nd derivative at end) = k*(2nd derivative next to end) is set by the next argument. By default, k=0.
-n	Space output points so that approximately n intervals occur between the lower and upper x limits. (By default, n = 100.)
-p	Make output periodic, that is, match derivatives at ends. First and last input values should normally agree.
-x	Next 1 (or 2) arguments are lower (and upper) x limits. Normally, these limits are calculated from the data. Automatic abscissas start at lower limit (default, 0).

Examples
The following example uses the `plot` and `graph` capabilities. The file named `data` contains the following data points.

```
castle% cat data
1       1.0
2       4.0
3       5.0
4       6.5      "Optional Label"
7       10.3
8       11.4
9       9.5
10      8.9
11      7.0
12      10.5
13      5.0
```

```
14       2.8
castle%
```

The following example displays the data in a shell tool using the `graph` command.

```
castle% graph < data + plot -Tcrt
castle% **************************************************************************
  *                    *                        *                        *
  *                    *                        *                        *
  *                    *                        *                        *
  *                    *                        *                        *
  *                    *                        *                        *
  *                    *                        *                        *
  *                    *                        *                        *
  *                    *                        *                        *
  *                    *               *        *                        *
  *                    *            *   *        *                        *
  *                    *         **    **        *          *            *
  ****************************************************************************
  *                    *          **              *          *  *         *
  *                    *       **          **   *        *   *           *
  *                    *   **              **          *     *          *
  *                    * **                **        *     *           *
  *                  **                    *  **    *      *          *
  *              ***                       *   *  *       *          *
  *          **   *                        *       *      *          *
  *        *Optional Label                 *              *          *
  *      *       *                         *              *          *
  *    **        *                         *              *          *
  *   *          *                         *              *          *
  ****************************************************************************
  *        **    *                         *                *          *
  *      **      *                         *                  *        *
  *   *         *                          *                   *       *
  *  *          *                          *                    *      *
  * *           *                          *                     *     *
  *  *          *                          *                           *
  *   *         *                          *                           *
  *             *                          *                           *
  *             *                          *                           *
  ****************************************************************************
  0 -x- 15   0 -y- 15
```

`graph` clears the screen and displays the graph positioning the prompt at the the top of the screen. Any subsequent commands you type are displayed on top of the graph. Use the `clear` command to clear the screen after you display the plot.

To create a better, smoother, plot, the following example uses the `spline` command.

```
castle% spline < data | graph | plot -Tcrt
castle% ***********************************************************************
```

```
0 -x- 15   0 -y- 15
```

Attributes

See attributes(5) for descriptions of the following attributes:

Attribute Type	Attribute Value
Availability	SUNWesu

See Also

graph(1), attributes(5)

R. W. Hamming, *Numerical Methods for Scientists and Engineers*, 2nd ed.

Diagnostics

When data is not strictly monotonic in x, spline reproduces the input without interpolating extra points.

Bugs

A limit of 1,000 input points is silently enforced.

split — Split a File into Pieces

Synopsis

```
/usr/bin/split [-linecount|-l linecount] [-a suffixlength] [file [name]]
/usr/bin/split -b n[k|m] [-a suffixlength] [file [name]]
```

Description

The split command reads *file* and writes it in *linecount*-line pieces into a set of output files. The name of the first output file is *name* with *aa* appended, and so on lexicographically, up to *zz* (a maximum of 676 files). The maximum length of *name* is two characters less than the maximum file-name length allowed by the file system. See statvfs(2). If you specify no output name, x is used as the default. Output files are named xaa, xab, and so forth.

Options

-linecount | -l *linecount*

Specify the number of lines in each piece. Default is 1000 lines.

-a *suffixlength*

Use *suffixlength* letters to form the suffix portion of the file names of the split file. If you do not specify -a, the default suffix length is 2. If the sum of the *name* operand and the *suffixlength* argument would create a file name exceeding NAME_MAX bytes, an error results; split exits with a diagnostic message and creates no files.

-b *n*   Split a file into pieces *n* bytes in size.

-b *nk*   Split a file into pieces *n**1024 bytes in size.

-b *nm*   Split a file into pieces *n**1048576 bytes in size.

Operands

file   The path name of the ordinary file to be split. If you specify no input file or *file* is -, use the standard input.

name   The prefix to be used for each of the files resulting from the split operation. If you specify no *name* argument, use x as the prefix of the output files. The combined length of the basename of the prefix and *suffixlength* cannot exceed NAME_MAX bytes.

Example

The following example splits a file into 50-line pieces.

```
castle% ls -l testfile
-rw-r--r--   1 winsor    staff          6452 Mar  3 08:58 testfile
castle% split -50 testfile
castle% ls -l x*
-rw-r--r--   1 winsor    staff          1933 Apr  5 12:16 xaa
-rw-r--r--   1 winsor    staff          1451 Apr  5 12:16 xab
-rw-r--r--   1 winsor    staff          1852 Apr  5 12:16 xac
-rw-r--r--   1 winsor    staff          1216 Apr  5 12:16 xad
castle%
```

Usage

See largefile(5) for the description of the behavior of split when encountering files greater than or equal to 2 Gbytes ($2^{**}31$ bytes).

Environment Variables

See environ(5) for descriptions of the following environment variables that affect the execution of split: LC_CTYPE, LC_MESSAGES, and NLSPATH.

Exit Status

0   Successful completion.

>0   An error occurred.

Attributes

See attributes(5) for descriptions of the following attributes:

Attribute Type	Attribute Value
Availability	SUNWesu
CSI	Enabled

See Also

csplit(1), statvfs(2), attributes(5), environ(5), largefile(5)

srchtxt — Display Contents of, or Search for, a Text String in Message Databases

Synopsis

```
/usr/bin/srchtxt [-s][-l locale][-m msgfile,...][text]
```

Description

Use the srchtxt command to display all the text strings in message databases or to search for a text string in message databases (see mkmsgs(1)). These databases are files in the directory /usr/lib/locale/*locale*/LC_MESSAGES (see setlocale(3C)), unless a file name given with the -m option contains a /. The directory *locale* is the name of the language in which the text strings are written. If you do not specify the -l option, the file accessed is determined by the value of the environment variable LC_MESSAGES. If LC_MESSAGES is not set, the files accessed are determined by the value of the environment variable LANG. If LANG is not set, the files accessed are in the directory /usr/lib/locale//C/LC_MESSAGES, which contains default strings.

If you specify no *text* argument, then all the text strings in the files accessed are displayed.

If you specify the -s option, the displayed text is prefixed by message sequence numbers. The message sequence numbers are enclosed in angle brackets: <*msgfile: msgnum*>.

msgfile	Name of the file where the displayed text occurred.
msgnum	Sequence number in *msgfile* where the displayed text occurred. This display is in the format used by gettxt(1) and gettxt(3C).

Options

-s	Suppress printing of the message sequence numbers of the messages being displayed.
-l *locale*	Access files in the directory /usr/lib/locale/*locale*/LC_MESSAGES. If you also specify -m *msgfile*, *locale* is ignored for *msgfiles* containing a /.
-m *msgfile*	Access files specified by one or more *msgfiles*. If *msgfile* contains a / character, then *msgfile* is interpreted as a path name; otherwise, it is assumed to be in the directory determined as described above. To specify more than one *msgfile*, separate the file names with commas.
text	Search for the text string specified by *text*, and display each one that matches. *text* can take the form of a regular expression; see regexp(5).

Examples

> **Note** — A bug in srchtxt results in a segmentation error.
> ```
> # srchtxt
> <ibfirmware:1>
> <ibfirmware:2>
> <ibfirmware:3>
> <ibfirmware:4>
> <ibfirmware:5>
> <ibfirmware:6>
> <ibfirmware:7>
> Segmentation Fault - core dumped
> #
> ```

The following examples show uses of srchtxt.

If message files have been installed by mkmsgs(1) in a locale named french, then you could display the entire set of text strings in the french locale (/usr/lib/locale/french/LC_MESSAGES/*) by typing:

```
castle% srchtxt -l french
```

If a set of error messages associated with the operating system has been installed in the file UX in the french locale (/usr/lib/locale/french/LC_MESSAGES/UX), then, using the value of the LANG environment variable to determine the locale to be searched, you could search that file in that locale for all error messages dealing with files.

```
castle% setenv LANG=french; export LANG
castle% srchtxt -m UX "[Ff]ichier"
```

If /usr/lib/locale/french/LC_MESSAGES/UX contained the following strings

```
Erreur E/S\n
Liste d'arguments trop longue\n
Fichier inexistant\n
Argument invalide\n
Trop de fichiers ouverts\n
Fichier trop long\n
Trop de liens\n
Argument hors du domaine\n
Identificateur supprim\n
Etreinte fatale\n
  .
  .
  .
```

then the following strings would be displayed:

```
<UX:3>Fichier inexistant\n
<UX:5>Trop de fichiers ouverts\n
<UX:6>Fichier trop long\n
```

If a set of error messages associated with the operating system has been installed in the file UX and a set of error messages associated with the INGRESS database product has been installed in the file ingress, both in the german locale, then you could search for the pattern [Dd]atei in both the files UX and ingress in the german locale with the following command.

castle% **srchtxt -l german -m UX,ingress "[Dd]atei"**

Environment Variables

See environ(5) for a description of the LC_CTYPE environment variable that affects the execution of srchtxt.

Files

/usr/lib/locale/C/LC_MESSAGES/*

    Default files created by mkmsgs(1).

/usr/lib/locale/*locale*/LC_MESSAGES/*

    Message files created by mkmsgs(1).

Attributes

See attributes(5) for descriptions of the following attributes:

Attribute Type	Attribute Value
Availability	SUNWloc

See Also

exstr(1), gettxt(1), locale(1), mkmsgs(1), gettxt(3C), setlocale(3C), attributes(5), environ(5), locale(5), regexp(5)

Diagnostics

The error messages produced by srchtxt are intended to be self-explanatory. They indicate an error in the command line or errors encountered while searching for a particular locale and/or message file.

stop — Control Process Execution

Synopsis

sh, csh, ksh
```
stop %job-id...
stop pid...
```

Description

See jobs(1).

---

strchg, strconf — Change or Query Stream Configuration

Synopsis

```
/usr/bin/strchg -h module 1[, module 2...]
/usr/bin/strchg -p [-a | -u module]
/usr/bin/strchg -f filename
/usr/bin/strconf [-m | -t module]
```

Description

Use these commands to alter or query the configuration of the stream associated with the standard input. The strchg command pushes modules on or pops modules off the stream. The strconf command queries the configuration of the stream. Only the superuser or owner of a STREAMS device can alter the configuration of that stream.

Invoked without any arguments, strconf prints a list of all the modules in the stream as well as the topmost driver. The list is printed with one name per line; the first name printed is the topmost module on the stream (if one exists), and the last item printed is the name of the driver.

If you are neither the owner of the stream nor superuser, the strchg command fails. If you do not have read permissions on the stream and are not superuser, the strconf command fails.

Note — If modules are pushed in the wrong order, you could end up with a stream that does not function as expected. For TTYs, if the line discipline module is not pushed in the correct place, you could have a terminal that does not respond to any commands.

Options

The following options apply to strchg; -h, -f, and -p are mutually exclusive.

-h module1 [, module2...]
> Push modules onto a stream. Specify as arguments the names of one or more pushable streams modules. Push these modules in order; that is, push module1 first, push module2 second, and so forth.

-p
> Pop modules off the stream. With the -p option alone, pop the topmost module from the stream.

-a module
> Pop all the modules above the topmost driver off the stream. This option requires the -p option.

-u *module*   Pop all modules above but not including *module* off the stream. This
option requires the -p option.

-f *filename*

> Specify a *filename* that contains a list of modules representing the
> desired configuration of the stream. Each module name must
> appear on a separate line; the first name represents the topmost
> module, and the last name represents the module that should be
> closest to the driver. strchg determines the current configuration
> of the stream and pops and pushes the necessary modules to end up
> with the desired configuration.

The following options apply to strconf; -m and -t are mutually exclusive.

-m *module*   Determine if the named *module* is present on a stream. If it is,
print the message yes and return 0. If not, print the message no
and return a non-zero value. The -t and -m options are mutually
exclusive.

-t *module*   Print only the topmost module (if one exists). The -t and -m
options are mutually exclusive.

Examples

The following command pushes the module ldterm on the stream associated
with the standard input.

```
castle% strchg -h ldterm
```

The following command pops the topmost module from the stream
associated with /dev/term/24. You must be the owner of this device or the
superuser.

```
castle% strchg -p < /dev/term/24
```

If the file fileconf contains the following lines

```
ttcompat
ldterm
ptem
```

then the following command configures the standard input stream so that the
module ptem is pushed over the driver, followed by ldtrm and ttcompat
closest to the stream head:

```
castle% strchg -f fileconf
```

The strconf command with no arguments lists the modules and topmost
driver on the stream; for a stream that has only the module ldterm pushed
above the zs driver, you would get the following output.

```
castle% strconf
ldterm
```

```
zs
castle%
```

The following command asks if `ldterm` is on the stream and returns an exit status of 0.

```
castle% strconf -m ldterm
yes
castle%
```

Attributes

See `attributes`(5) for descriptions of the following attributes:

Attribute Type	Attribute Value
Availability	SUNWcsu

See Also

`attributes`(5), `streamio`(7I)

Diagnostics

`strchg` returns 0 on success. It prints an error message and returns non-zero status for various error conditions, including usage error, bad module name, too many modules to push, failure of an ioctl on the stream, or failure to open `filename` from the `-f` option.

`strconf` returns 0 on success (for the `-m` or `-t` option, success means the named or topmost module is present). It returns a non-zero status if invoked with the `-m` or `-t` option and the module is not present. It prints an error message and returns non-zero status for various error conditions, including usage error or failure of an ioctl on the stream.

---

strings — Find Printable Strings in an Object or Binary File

Synopsis

`/usr/bin/strings [-a | -] [-t format | -o] [-n number | - number] [file...]`

Description

The `strings` command looks for ASCII strings in a binary file. A string is any sequence of four or more printing characters ending with a newline or a null character.

`strings` is useful for identifying random object files and many other things.

> **Note** — The algorithm for identifying strings is extremely primitive.

For backward compatibility, the -a and - options are interchangeable.

Options

-a | -   Look everywhere in the file for strings. If you omit this option, strings looks only in the initialized data space of object files.

-n *number* | -*number*

     Use *number* as the minimum string length instead of the default, which is 4.

-o   Equivalent to -t d option.

-t *format*   Write each string preceded by its byte offset from the start of the file. The format is dependent on the single character used as the *format* argument.

     d   Write the offset in decimal.

     o   Write the offset in octal.

     x   Write the offset in hexadecimal.

Operands

file   A path name of a regular file to be used as input. If you specify no *file* operand, read from the standard input.

Environment Variables

See environ(5) for descriptions of the following environment variables that affect the execution of strings: LC_CTYPE, LC_MESSAGES, and NLSPATH.

Exit Status

0   Successful completion.

>0   An error occurred.

Attributes

See attributes(5) for descriptions of the following attributes:

Attribute Type	Attribute Value
Availability	SUNWtoo
CSI	Enabled

See Also

od(1), attributes(5), environ(5)

strip — Strip Symbol Table, Debugging, and Line Number Information from an Object File

Synopsis

/usr/ccs/bin/strip [-blrVx] *file*...

Description

Use the strip command to reduce the file storage overhead incurred by an object file. The strip command removes the symbol table, debugging information, and line number information from ELF object files. Once this stripping process has been done, no symbolic debugging access is available for that file; therefore, you normally run this command only on production modules that have been debugged and tested.

If you execute strip on a common archive file (see ar(4)), then in addition to processing the members, strip removes the archive symbol table. You must restore the archive symbol table by executing the ar(1) command with the -s option before the archive can be linked with the ld(1) command. strip produces appropriate warning messages when this situation arises.

> **Note** — The symbol table section is not removed if it is contained within a segment or if the file is either a relocatable or dynamic shared object.
>
> The line number and debugging sections are not removed if they are contained within a segment or if their associated relocation section is contained within a segment.

Options

You can control the amount of information stripped from the ELF object with the following options.

-b	Same effect as the default behavior. This option is obsolete and will be removed in the next release.
-l	Strip line number information only; do not strip the symbol table or debugging information.
-r	Same effect as the default behavior. This option is obsolete and will be removed in the next release.
-V	Print to standard error the version number of strip.

-x   Do not strip the symbol table; debugging and line number
          information may be stripped.

Operands

file   A path name referring to an executable file.

Environment Variables

See environ(5) for descriptions of the following environment variables that
affect the execution of strip: LC_CTYPE, LC_MESSAGES, and NLSPATH.

Exit Status

0   Successful completion.

>0   An error occurred.

Files

/tmp/strp* Temporary files.

Attributes

See attributes(5) for descriptions of the following attributes:

Attribute Type	Attribute Value
Availability	SUNWbtool

See Also

ar(1), as(1), ld(1), elf(3E), tmpnam(3S), a.out(4), ar(4), attributes(5),
environ(5)

stty — Set the Options for a Terminal

Synopsis

```
/usr/bin/stty [-a][-g]
/usr/bin/stty [modes]
/usr/xpg4/bin/stty [-a | -g]
/usr/xpg4/bin/stty [modes]
```

Description

The stty command sets certain terminal I/O options for the device that is the current standard input; without arguments, it reports the settings of certain options.

In this section, if a character is preceded by a caret (^), then the value of that option is the corresponding control character (for example, ^h is Control-H; Control-H is the same as the backspace key.) The sequence ^ means that an option has a null value.

See termio(7I) for detailed information about the modes listed from "Control Modes through Local Modes." For detailed information about the modes listed under "Hardware Flow Control Modes" and "Clock Modes," see termiox(7I).

Operands described in the "Combination Modes" section are implemented, by options described in the earlier sections. Note that many combinations of options make no sense but no sanity checking is performed. Hardware flow control and clock modes options may not be supported by all hardware interfaces.

Options

-a   Write to standard output all of the option settings for the terminal.

-g   Report current settings in a form that can be used as an argument to another stty command. Emit termios-type output if the underlying driver supports it; otherwise, emit termio-type output.

Operands

Control Modes

parenb (-parenb)

           Enable (disable) parity generation and detection.

parext (-parext)

           Enable (disable) extended parity generation and detection for mark and space parity.

parodd (-parodd)

           Select odd (even) parity, or mark (space) parity if parext is enabled.

cs5 cs6 cs7 cs8

           Select character size (see termio(7I)).

0   Hang up line immediately.

110 300 600 1200 1800 2400 4800 9600 19200 38400 357600 76800
115200 153600 230400 307200 460800

> Set terminal baud rate to the number given if possible. (All speeds
> are not supported by all hardware interfaces.)

ispeed 0 110 300 600 1200 1800 2400 4800 9600 19200 38400 57600
76800 115200 153600 230400 307200 460800

> Set terminal input baud rate to the number given if possible. (Not
> all hardware supports split baud rates.) If the input baud rate is
> set to 0, use the value of the output baud rate to specify the input
> baud rate.

ospeed 0 110 300 600 1200 1800 2400 4800 9600 19200 38400 57600
76800 115200 153600 230400 307200 460800

> Set terminal output baud rate to the number given if possible.
> (Not all hardware supports split baud rates.) If the output baud
> rate is set to 0, hang up the line immediately.

hupcl (-hupcl)

> Hang up (do not hang up) connection on last close.

hup (-hup)   Same as hupcl (-hupcl).

cstopb (-cstopb)

> Use two (one) stop bits per character.

cread (-cread)

> Enable (disable) the receiver.

crtscts (-crtscts)

> Enable output hardware flow control. Raise the RTS (Request to
> Send) modem control line. Suspend output until the CTS (Clear to
> Send) line is raised.

crtsxoff (-crtsxoff)

> Enable (disable) input hardware flow control. Raise the RTS
> (Request to Send) modem control line to receive data. Suspend
> input when RTS is low.

clocal (-clocal)

> Assume a line without (with) modem control.

loblk (-loblk)

> Block (do not block) output from a noncurrent layer.

defeucw

> Set the widths of multibyte Extended Unix Code (EUC) characters
> in struct eucioc to default values for the current locale specified
> by LC_CTYPE; width is expressed in terms of bytes per character,
> and screen or display columns per character (see getwidth(3C)
> and ldterm(7M)).

Input Modes

ignbrk (-ignbrk)

> Ignore (do not ignore) break on input.

brkint (-brkint)

> Signal (do not signal) interrupt (INTR) on break.

ignpar (-ignpar)

> Ignore (do not ignore) parity errors.

parmrk (-parmrk)

> Mark (do not mark) parity errors (see termio(7I)).

inpck (-inpck)

> Enable (disable) input parity checking.

istrip (-istrip)

> Strip (do not strip) input characters to seven bits.

inlcr (-inlcr)

> Map (do not map) NL to CR on input.

igncr (-igncr)

> Ignore (do not ignore) CR on input.

icrnl (-icrnl)

> Map (do not map) CR to NL on input.

iuclc (-iuclc)

> Map (do not map) uppercase alphabetics to lower case on input.

ixon (-ixon)

> Enable (disable) START/STOP output control. Stop output by sending STOP control character, and start it by sending the START control character.

ixany (-ixany)

> Allow any character (only DC1) to restart output.

ixoff (-ixoff)

> Request that the system send (not send) START/STOP characters when the input queue is nearly empty/full.

imaxbel (-imaxbel)

> Echo (do not echo) BEL when the input line is too long.

Output Modes

opost (-opost)

> Postprocess output (do not postprocess output; ignore all other output modes).

olcuc (-olcuc)

    Map (do not map) lowercase alphabetics to upper case on output.

onlcr (-onlcr)

    Map (do not map) NL to CR-NL on output.

ocrnl (-ocrnl)

    Map (do not map) CR to NL on output.

onocr (-onocr)

    Do not (do) output CRs at column 0.

onlret (-onlret)

    On the terminal, NL performs (does not perform) the CR function.

ofill (-ofill)

    Use fill characters (use timing) for delays.

ofdel (-ofdel)

    Fill characters are DELs (null).

cr0 cr1 cr2 cr3

    Select style of delay for Returns (see termio(7I)).

nl0 nl1   Select style of delay for linefeeds (see termio(7I)).

tab0 tab1 tab2 tab3

    Select style of delay for horizontal Tabs (see termio(7I)).

bs0 bs1   Select style of delay for backspaces (see termio(7I)).

ff0 ff1   Select style of delay for formfeeds (see termio(7I)).

vt0 vt1   Select style of delay for vertical Tabs (see termio(7I)).

Local Modes

isig (-isig)

    Enable (disable) the checking of characters against the special control characters INTR, QUIT, SWTCH, and SUSP.

icanon (-icanon)

    Enable (disable) canonical input (ERASE and KILL processing). Does not set MIN or TIME.

xcase (-xcase)

    Canonical (unprocessed) upper/lowercase presentation.

echo (-echo)

    Echo back (do not echo back) every character typed.

echoe (-echoe)

> Echo (do not echo) ERASE character as a backspace-space-backspace string. Note that this mode erases the ERASEd character on many CRT terminals; however, it does not keep track of column position and, as a result, it can be confusing for escaped characters, Tabs, and backspaces.

echok (-echok)

> Echo (do not echo) NL after KILL character.

lfkc (-lfkc)

> The same as echok (-echok); obsolete.

echonl (-echonl)

> Echo (do not echo) NL.

noflsh (-noflsh)

> Disable (enable) flush after INTR, QUIT, or SUSP.

stwrap (-stwrap)

> Disable (enable) truncation of lines longer than 79 characters on a synchronous line.

tostop (-tostop)

> Send (do not send) SIGTTOU when background processes write to the terminal.

echoctl (-echoctl)

> Echo (do not echo) control characters as ^*char*; delete as ^?.

echoprt (-echoprt)

> Echo (do not echo) erase character as character is erased.

echoke (-echoke)

> BS-SP-BS erase (do not BS-SP-BS erase) entire line on line kill.

flusho (-flusho)

> Output is (is not) being flushed.

pendin (-pendin)

> Retype (do not retype) pending input at next read or input character.

iexten (-iexten)

> Enable (disable) special control characters not currently controlled by icanon, isig, ixon, or ixoff: VEOLZ, VSWTCH, VREPRINT, VDISCARD, VDSUSP, VWERASE, and VLNEXT.

stflush (-stflush)

> Enable (disable) flush on a synchronous line after every write(2).

```
stappl (-stappl)
```
> Use application mode (use line mode) on a synchronous line.

Hardware Flow Control Modes

```
rtsxoff (-rtsxoff)
```
> Enable (disable) RTS hardware flow control on input.

```
ctsxon (-ctsxon)
```
> Enable (disable) CTS hardware flow control on output.

```
dtrxoff (-dtrxoff)
```
> Enable (disable) DTR hardware flow control on input.

```
cdxon (-cdxon)
```
> Enable (disable) CD hardware flow control on output.

```
isxoff (-isxoff)
```
> Enable (disable) isochronous hardware flow control on input.

Clock Modes

xcibrg	Get transmit clock from internal baud rate generator.
xctset	Get the transmit clock from transmitter-signal-element timing (DCE source) lead, CCITT V.24 circuit 114, EIA-232-D pin 15.
xcrset	Get transmit clock from receiver-signal-element timing (DCE source) lead, CCITT V.24 circuit 115, EIA-232-D pin 17.
rcibrg	Get receive clock from internal baud rate generator.
rctset	Get receive clock from transmitter-signal-element timing (DCE source) lead, CCITT V.24 circuit 114, EIA-232-D pin 15.
rcrset	Get receive clock from receiver-signal-element timing (DCE source) lead, CCITT V.24 circuit 115, EIA-232-D pin 17.
tsetcoff	Transmitter-signal-element timing clock not provided.
tsetcrbrg	Output receive baud rate generator on transmitter-signal-element timing (DTE source) lead, CCITT V.24 circuit 113, EIA-232-D pin 24.
tsetctbrg	Output transmit baud rate generator on transmitter-signal-element timing (DTE source) lead, CCITT V.24 circuit 113, EIA-232-D pin 24.
tsetctset	Output transmitter-signal-element timing (DCE source) on transmitter-signal-element timing (DTE source) lead, CCITT V.24 circuit 113, EIA-232-D pin 24.
tsetcrset	Output receiver-signal-element timing (DCE source) on transmitter-signal-element timing (DTE source) lead, CCITT V.24 circuit 113, EIA-232-D pin 24.

rsetcoff	Receiver-signal-element timing clock not provided.
rsetcrbrg	Output receive baud rate generator on receiver-signal-element timing (DTE source) lead, CCITT V.24 circuit 128, no EIA-232-D pin.
rsetctbrg	Output transmit baud rate generator on receiver-signal-element timing (DTE source) lead, CCITT V.24 circuit 128, no EIA-232-D pin.
rsetctset	Output transmitter-signal-element timing (DCE source) on receiver-signal-element timing (DTE source) lead, CCITT V.24 circuit 128, no EIA-232-D pin.
rsetcrset	Output receiver-signal-element timing (DCE source) on receiver-signal-element timing (DTE source) lead, CCITT V.24 circuit 128, no EIA-232-D pin.

Control Assignments

control-character c

Set *control-character* to c where *control-character* is ctab, discard, dsusp, eof, eol, eol2, erase, intr, kill, lnext, quit, reprint, start, stop, susp, swtch, or werase (ctab is used with -stappl; see termio(7I)).

c

If *c* is a single character, set the control character to that character. In the POSIX locale, if *c* is preceded by a caret (^), indicating an escape from the shell, and is one of those listed in the ^c column of the following table, then use its value (in the Value column) as the corresponding control character (for example, ^d is a Control-D). ^? is interpreted as DEL and ^- is interpreted as undefined.

^*c*	Value	^*c*	Value	^*c*	Value
a, A	\<SOH>	l, L	\<FF>	w, W	\<ETB>
b, B	\<STX>	m, M	\<CR>	x, X	\<CAN>
c, C	\<ETX>	n, N	\<SO>	y, Y	\<EM>
d, D	\<EOT>	o, O	\<SI>	z, Z	\<SUB>
e, E	\<ENQ>	p, P	\<DLE>	[	\<ESC>
f, F	\<ACK>	q, Q	\<DC1>	\	\<FS>
g, G	\<BEL>	r, R	\<DC2>	]	\<GS>
h, H	\<BS>	s, S	\<DC3>	^	\<RS>
i, I	\<HT>	t, T	\<DC4>	_	\<US>

$^{\wedge}c$	**Value**	$^{\wedge}c$	**Value**	$^{\wedge}c$	**Value**
j, J	<LF>	u, U	<NAK>	?	<DEL>
k, K	<VT>	v, V	<SYN>		

min *number*

time *number*

> Set the value of min or time to *number*. MIN and TIME are used in noncanonical mode input processing (-icanon).

line *i*   Set line discipline to i (0<*i*<127).

Combination Modes

savedsettings

> Set the current terminal characteristics to the saved settings produced by the -g option.

evenp or parity

> Enable parenb and cs7 or disable parodd.

oddp   Enable parenb, cs7, and parodd.

spacep   Enable parenb, cs7, and parext.

markp   Enable parenb, cs7, parodd, and parext.

-parity or -evenp

> Disable parenb, and set cs8.

-oddp   Disable parenb and parodd, and set cs8.

-spacep   Disable parenb and parext, and set cs8.

-markp   Disable parenb, parodd, and parext, and set cs8.

raw (-raw or cooked)

> Enable (disable) raw input and output. Raw mode is equivalent to setting:
>
> stty cs8 -icanon min 1 time 0 -isig -xcase -inpck
> -opost

/usr/bin/stty

nl (-nl)   Unset (set) icrnl, onlcr. In addition, -nl unsets inlcr, igncr, ocrnl, and onlret.

/usr/xpg4/bin/stty

nl (-nl)   Set (unset) icrnl. In addition, -nl unsets inlcr, igncr, ocrnl, and onlret; -nl sets onlcr, and nl unsets onlcr.

lcase (-lcase)

>   Set (unset) xcase, iuclc, and olcuc.

LCASE (-LCASE)

>   Same as lcase (-lcase).

tabs (-tabs or tab3)

>   Preserve (expand to spaces) Tabs when printing.

ek   Reset ERASE and KILL characters back to normal # and @.

sane   Reset all modes to some reasonable values.

term   Set all modes suitable for the terminal type *term*, where *term* is
            one of tty33, tty37, vt05, tn300, ti700, or tek.

async   Set normal asynchronous communications, where clock settings
            are xcibrg, rcibrg, tsetcoff, and rsetcoff.

Window Size

rows *n*   Set window size to *n* rows.

columns *n*   Set window size to *n* columns.

cols *n*   Set window size to *n* columns. Note that cols is a shorthand alias
                 for columns.

ypixels *n*   Set vertical window size to *n* pixels.

xpixels *n*   Set horizontal window size to *n* pixels.

Usage

The -g option is designed to facilitate the saving and restoring of terminal
state from the shell level. For example, a program can do the following.

```
saveterm="$(stty -g)"          # save terminal state
stty (new settings)            # set new state
...                            # ...
stty $saveterm                 # restore terminal state
```

Because the -a format is so loosely specified, scripts that save and restore
terminal settings should use the -g option.

Examples

The following example shows the output from the stty command when no
options are specified.

```
castle% stty
ispeed 89376 baud; ospeed 89360 baud; -parity cstopb hupcl loblk
rows = 37; columns = 80; ypixels = 491; xpixels = 570;
quit = <undef>; erase = ^h; swtch = <undef>;
-inpck -istrip icrnl -ixany ixoff onlcr
echo echoe echok echoctl echoke iexten
castle%
```

Environment Variables

See environ(5) for descriptions of the following environment variables that affect the execution of stty: LC_CTYPE, LC_MESSAGES, and NLSPATH.

Exit Status

| 0 | Successful completion. |
| >0 | An error occurred. |

Attributes

See attributes(5) for descriptions of the following attributes:

/usr/bin/stty

Attribute Type	Attribute Value
Availability	SUNWcsu

/usr/xpg4/bin/stty

Attribute Type	Attribute Value
Availability	SUNWxcu4

See Also

tabs(1), ioctl(2), write(2), getwidth(3C), attributes(5), environ(5), ldterm(7M), termio(7I), termiox(7I)

---

sum — Print Checksum and Block Count for a File

Synopsis

```
/usr/bin/sum [-r][file...]
/usr/ucb/sum [file...]
```

Description

The sum command calculates and prints a 16-bit checksum for the named *file* and the number of 512-byte blocks in the file. It is typically used to look for bad spots or to validate a file communicated over some transmission line.

Portable applications should use cksum(1).

> **Note —** sum and /usr/ucb/sum (see sum(1B)) return different checksums.

Options

-r   Use an alternate (machine-dependent) algorithm in computing
            the checksum.

Operands

file   A path name of a file. If you specify no files, use the standard
            input.

Examples

The following example displays a checksum for the file kookaburra-1.

```
castle% sum kookaburra-1
23823 1 kookaburra-1
castle%
```

Usage

See largefile(5) for the description of the behavior of sum when encountering
files greater than or equal to 2 Gbytes (2** 31 bytes).

Environment Variables

See environ(5) for descriptions of the following environment variables that
affect the execution of sum: LC_CTYPE, LC_MESSAGES, and NLSPATH.

Exit Status

0   Successful completion.

>0   An error occurred.

Attributes

See attributes(5) for descriptions of the following attributes:

Attribute Type	Attribute Value
Availability	SUNWesu
CSI	Enabled

See Also

cksum(1), sum(1B), wc(1), attributes(5), environ(5), largefile(5)

Diagnostics

Read error is indistinguishable from end-of-file on most devices; check the
block count.

---

sun — Get Processor Type Truth Value

Synopsis
```
/usr/bin/sun
```

Description
See machid(1).

---

suspend — Shell Built-in Function to Halt the Current Shell

Synopsis
sh, csh, and ksh
```
suspend
```

Description
Bourne and Korn Shell
Stops the execution of the current shell (but not if it is the login shell).

C Shell
Stop the shell in its tracks much as if it had been sent a stop signal with ^Z.
This function is most often used to stop shells started by su.

Attributes
See attributes(5) for descriptions of the following attributes:

Attribute Type	Attribute Value
Availability	SUNWcsu

See Also
csh(1), kill(1), ksh(1), sh(1), su(1M), attributes(5)

switch — Shell Built-in Function to Choose from a List of Actions

Synopsis

csh
```
switch (expression)
case comparison1:
  actions
  breaksw
case comparison2:
  actions
  breaksw
...
default:
  endsw
```

Description
See case(1).

symorder — Rearrange a List of Symbols

Synopsis
```
/usr/ccs/bin/symorder [-s] objectfile symbolfile
```

Description
The symorder command was used in SunOS 4.x specifically to cut down on the overhead of getting symbols from vmunix. This command is no longer applicable because kernel symbol entries are dynamically obtained through /dev/ksyms.

This script is provided as a convenience for software developers who need to maintain scripts that are portable across a variety of operating systems.

Exit Status
symorder has exit status 0.

Attributes
See `attributes`(5) for descriptions of the following attributes:

Attribute Type	Attribute Value
Availability	SUNWbtool

See Also
`nlist(3E), attributes(5), ksyms(7D)`

---

sysV-make — Maintain, Update, and Regenerate Groups of Programs

Synopsis

New!

`/usr/lib/svr4.make [-f makefile][-eiknpqrst][names]`

Description

The `sysV-make` command is the vanilla System V version of `make`. If the environment variable `USE_SVR4_MAKE` is set, then the `make` command invokes this version of `make`.

`make` enables the programmer to maintain, update, and regenerate groups of computer programs. `make` executes commands in `makefile` to update one or more target `names` (`names` are typically programs). If you do not specify the `-f` option, then `makefile`, `Makefile`, and the Source Code Control System (SCCS) files `s.makefile`, and `s.Makefile` are tried in order. If `makefile` is a dash (-), the standard input is taken. You can specify more than one `-f` `makefile` argument pair.

`make` updates a target only if its dependents are newer than the target. All prerequisite files of a target are added recursively to the list of targets. Missing files are deemed to be outdated.

You can include the directives from the following list in `makefile` to extend the options provided by `make`. The directives are used in `makefile` as if they were targets.

`.DEFAULT`:	If a file must be made but there are no explicit commands or relevant built-in rules, use the commands associated with the name `.DEFAULT` if it exists.
`.IGNORE`:	Same as the `-i` option.
`.PRECIOUS`:	Do not remove dependents of the `.PRECIOUS` entry when quit or interrupt is pressed.
`.SILENT`:	Same as the `-s` option.

> **Note** — Some commands return status inappropriately; use -i or a dash (-) command-line prefix to overcome the difficulty.
>
> File names containing the characters =, :, and @ do not work. Commands that are directly executed by the shell, notably cd(1), are ineffectual across newlines in make. The syntax lib(file1.o file2.o file3.o) is illegal. You cannot build lib(file.o) from file.o.

Options

-e   Environment variables override assignments within makefiles.

-f *makefile*

Specify the name of a description file.

-i   Ignore error codes returned by invoked commands.

-k   Abandon work on the current entry if it fails, but continue on other branches that do not depend on that entry.

-n   Print commands, but do not execute them. Print command lines even if they begin with an @.

-p   Print the complete set of macro definitions and target descriptions.

-q   Question whether the target file has been updated. make returns a 0 or non-zero status code.

-r   Do not use the built-in rules.

-s   Do not print command lines before executing.

-t   Touch the target files (updating them) instead of issuing the usual commands.

Creating the makefile

The *makefile* invoked with the -f option is a carefully structured file of explicit instructions for updating and regenerating programs. It contains a sequence of entries that specify dependencies. The first line of an entry is a blank-separated, non-null list of targets, then a :, then a (possibly null) list of prerequisite files or dependencies. Text following a ; and all following lines that begin with a Tab are shell commands to be executed to update the target. The first nonempty line that does not begin with a Tab or # begins a new dependency or macro definition. You can continue shell commands across lines with a backslash-newline (\-newline) sequence. Everything printed by make (except the initial Tab) is passed directly to the shell as is. Thus, the following sequence

```
echo a\
b
```

produces

```
ab
```

exactly as the shell would. Number sign (#) and newline surround comments including contained \-newline sequences.

The following *makefile* says that pgm depends on two files, a.o and b.o, and that they, in turn, depend on their corresponding source files (a.c and b.c) and a common file incl.h.

```
pgm: a.o b.o
cc a.o b.o -o pgm
a.o: incl.h a.c
     cc -c a.c
b.o: incl.h b.c
     cc -c b.c
```

Command lines are executed one at a time, each by its own shell. You can use the SHELL environment variable to specify which shell make should use to execute commands. The default is /usr/bin/sh. The first one or two characters in a command can be @, -, @-, or -@. If @ is present, printing of the command is suppressed. If a dash (-) is present, make ignores an error. A line is printed when it is executed unless you specify the -s option, the entry .SILENT: is included in *makefile*, or the initial character sequence contains a @. The -n option specifies printing without execution; however, if the command line has the string $(MAKE) in it, the line is always executed (see the discussion of the MAKEOPTIONS macro in "make Environment" on page 1292). The -t (touch) option updates the modified date of a file without executing any commands.

Commands returning non-zero status normally terminate make. If you specify the -i option, if the entry .IGNORE: is included in *makefile*, or if the initial character sequence of the command contains a dash (-), the error is ignored. If you specify the -k option, work is abandoned on the current entry but continues on other branches that do not depend on that entry.

Interrupt and quit delete the target unless the target is a dependent of the directive .PRECIOUS:.

make Environment

The environment is read by make. All variables are assumed to be macro definitions and are processed as such. The environment variables are processed before any *makefile* and after the internal rules; thus, macro assignments in a *makefile* override environment variables. The -e option overrides the macro assignments in a *makefile*. Suffixes and their associated rules in the *makefile* override any identical suffixes in the built-in rules.

The MAKEFLAGS environment variable is processed by make as containing any legal input option (except -f and -p) defined for the command line.

Further, on invocation, make "invents" the variable if it is not in the environment, puts the current options into it, and passes it on to invocations of commands. Thus, MAKEFLAGS always contains the current input options. This feature proves very useful for "supermakes." In fact, as noted above, when you use the -n option, the command $ (MAKE) is executed anyway; hence, you can perform a make -n recursively on a whole software system to see what would have been executed. This result is possible because the -n is put in MAKEFLAGS and passed to further invocations of $ (MAKE). This usage is one way of debugging all of the makefiles for a software project without actually doing anything.

Include Files

If the string include appears as the first seven letters of a line in a *makefile* and is followed by a blank or a Tab, the rest of the line is assumed to be a file name and is read by the current invocation after any macros are substituted.

Macros

Entries of the form *string1* = *string2* are macro definitions.

    string2 is defined as all characters up to a comment character or an unescaped newline. Subsequent appearances of $ (*string1* [: *subst1*=[*subst2*]]) are replaced by *string2*. The parentheses are optional if you use a single-character macro name and there is no substitute sequence. The optional : *subst1*= *subst2* is a substitute sequence. If you specify it, all nonoverlapping occurrences of *subst1* in the named macro are replaced by *subst2*. Strings (for the purposes of this type of substitution) are delimited by blanks, Tabs, newline characters, and beginnings of lines. An example of the use of the substitute sequence is shown in "Libraries" on page 1295.

Internal Macros

Five internally maintained macros are useful for writing rules for building targets.

$*	The file name part of the current dependent with the suffix deleted. Evaluated only for inference rules.
$@	The full target name of the current target. Evaluated only for explicitly named dependencies.
$<	Evaluated only for inference rules or the .DEFAULT rule. It is the module that is outdated with respect to the target (the "manufactured" dependent file name). Thus, in the .c.o rule, the $< macro would evaluate to the .c file. An example for making optimized .o files from .c files is:

```
.c.o:
    cc -c -O $*.c
```

or

```
.c.o:
    cc -c -O $<
```

$?   Evaluated when explicit rules from the *makefile* are evaluated. It is the list of prerequisites that are outdated with respect to the target and, essentially, those modules that must be rebuilt.

$%   Evaluated only when the target is an archive library member of the form lib(file.o). In this case, $@ evaluates to lib and $% evaluates to the library member, file.o.

All macros except $? can have alternative forms. When you append an uppercase D or F to any of the four macros, the meaning is changed to "directory part" for D and "file part" for F. Thus, $(@D) refers to the directory part of the string $@. If there is no directory part, ./ is generated.

Suffixes

Certain names (for instance, those ending with .o) have inferable prerequisites such as .c, .s, and so forth. If no update commands for such a file appear in *makefile* and if an inferable prerequisite exists, that prerequisite is compiled to make the target. In this case, make has inference rules that enable it to build files from other files by examining the suffixes and determining an appropriate inference rule to use. The current default inference rules are:

```
.c      .c~     .f      .f~     .s      .s~     .sh     .sh~    .C      .C~
.c.a    .c.o    .c~.a   .c~.c   .c~.o   .f.a    .f.o    .f~.a   .f~.f   .f~.o
.h~.h   .l.c    .l.o    .l~.c   .l~.l   .l~.o   .s.a    .s.o    .s~.a   .s~.o
.s~.s   .sh~.sh .y.c    .y.o    .y~.c   .y~.o   .y~.y   .C.a    .C.o    .C~.a
.C~.C   .C~.o   .L.C    .L.o    .L~.C   .L~.L   .L~.o   .Y.C    .Y.o    .Y~.C
```

The internal rules for make are contained in the source file make.rules for the make program. These rules can be locally modified. To print out the rules compiled into the make on any machine in a form suitable for recompilation, use the following command.

```
make -pf - 2>/dev/null </dev/null
```

A tilde in the above rules refers to an SCCS file (see sccs-file(4)). Thus, the rule .c~.o would transform an SCCS C source file into an object file (.o). Because the s. of the SCCS files is a prefix, it is incompatible with the make suffix point of view. Hence, the tilde is a way of changing any file reference into an SCCS file reference.

A rule with only one suffix (for example, .c:) is the definition of how to build x from x.c. In effect, the other suffix is null. This feature is useful for building targets from only one source file, for example, shell procedures and simple C programs.

Additional suffixes are given as the dependency list for .SUFFIXES. Order is significant: the first possible name for which both a file and a rule exist is inferred as a prerequisite. The default list is:

```
.SUFFIXES: .o .c .c~.y .y~ .l .l~ .s .s~ .sh .sh~ .h .h~ .f .f~ .C .C~
    .Y .Y~ .L .L~
```

Here again, the above command for printing the internal rules displays the list of suffixes implemented on the current machine. Multiple suffix lists accumulate; .SUFFIXES: with no dependencies clears the list of suffixes.

Inference Rules

The first example can be done more briefly.

```
pgm: a.o b.o
              cc a.o b.o -o pgm
a.o b.o: incl.h
```

This abbreviation is possible because make has a set of internal rules for building files. You can add rules to this list by simply putting them in the makefile.

Certain macros are used by the default inference rules to permit the inclusion of optional matter in any resulting commands. For example, CFLAGS, LFLAGS, and YFLAGS are used for compiler options to cc(1B). Again, the previous method for examining the current rules is recommended.

The inference of prerequisites can be controlled. The rule to create a file with suffix .o from a file with suffix .c is specified as an entry with .c.o: as the target and no dependents. Shell commands associated with the target define the rule for making a .o file from a .c file. Any target that has no slashes in it and starts with a dot is identified as a rule and not a true target.

Libraries

If a target or dependency name contains parentheses, it is assumed to be an archive library. The string within parentheses refers to a member within the library. Thus, lib(file.o) and $(LIB)(file.o) both refer to an archive library that contains file.o. (This example assumes the LIB macro has been previously defined.) The expression $(LIB)(file1.o file2.o) is not legal. Rules pertaining to archive libraries have the form .XX.a, where the XX is the suffix from which the archive member is to be made. An unfortunate byproduct of the current implementation requires the XX to be different from the suffix of the archive member. Thus, you cannot have lib(file.o) depend on file.o explicitly. The most common use of the archive interface follows. Here, we assume the source files are all C type source.

```
lib: lib(file1.o) lib(file2.o) lib(file3.o)
@echo lib is now up-to-date
.c.a:
    $(CC) -c $(CFLAGS) $<
    $(AR) $(ARFLAGS) $@ $*.o
    rm -f $*.o
```

In fact, the `.c.a` rule listed above is built into `make` and is unnecessary in this example. A more interesting but more limited example of an archive library maintenance construction is the following.

```
lib: lib(file1.o) lib(file2.o) lib(file3.o)
$(CC) -c $(CFLAGS) $(?:.o=.c)
      $(AR) $(ARFLAGS) lib $?
      rm $?
      @echo lib is now up-to-date
.c.a:;
```

Here, the substitution mode of the macro expansions is used. The `$?` list is defined to be the set of object file names (inside `lib`) whose C source files are outdated. The substitution mode translates the `.o` to `.c`. (Unfortunately, you cannot as yet transform to `.c~`; however, this transformation may become possible in the future.) Also note the disabling of the `.c.a:` rule, which would have created each object file, one by one. This particular construct speeds up archive library maintenance considerably. This type of construct becomes very cumbersome if the archive library contains a mix of assembly programs and C programs.

Environment Variables

USE_SVR4_MAKE

> If this environment variable is set, then the `make` command invokes the System V version of `make`. If this variable is not set, then the default version of `make(1S)` is invoked.

You can set USE_SVR4_MAKE as follows (Bourne shell).

```
$ USE_SVR4_MAKE=""; export USE_SVR4_MAKE
```

The C shell syntax is as follows.

```
% setenv USE_SVR4_MAKE
```

Files

[Mm]akefile and s.[Mm]akefile

> Default makefiles.

/usr/bin/sh

> Default shell for make.

/usr/share/lib/make/make.rules

> Default rules for make.

Attributes

See attributes(5) for descriptions of the following attributes:

Attribute Type	Attribute Value
Availability	SUNWsprot

See Also

cd(1), sh(1), cc(1B), make(1S), printf(3S), sccs-file(4), attributes(5)

Programming Utilities Guide

T

t300, t300s, t4014, t450 — Graphics Filters for Various Plotters

Synopsis

```
/usr/bin/tplot [-Tterminal]
```

Description

See tplot(1).

---

tabs — Set Tabs on a Terminal

Synopsis

```
/usr/bin/tabs [-n | --file | [[-code] -a | -a2 | -c | -c2 | -c3 |
    -f | -p | -s | -u]][+m[n]][-T type]
/usr/bin/tabs [-T type][+m[n]] n1[,n2,...]
```

Description

Use the `tabs` command to clear any previous settings and reset the Tab stops
on your terminal according to a Tab specification. Your terminal must have
remotely settable hardware Tabs.

Different terminals are inconsistent in how they clear Tabs and set the left margin.

`tabs` clears only 20 Tabs (on terminals requiring a long sequence) but it can set up to 64.

Note — The syntax for setting tabs with the `tabs` command is slightly different from the one used with the `newform` command. For example, `tabs -8` sets tabs at every eighth position, whereas `newform -i-8` sets Tabs at every eighth position.

Options

If you use a given option more than once, `tabs` uses the last value.

-T *type* Set the Tabs and margins by specifying *type* as a name listed in `term`(5). If you do not specify the -T option, use the value of the environment variable TERM. If the value of TERM is `null` or TERM is not defined in the environment (see `environ`(5)), use `ansi+tabs` as the terminal type to provide a sequence that works for many terminals.

+m[*n*] For some terminals, move all Tabs over *n* columns by making column *n*+1 the left margin. If you specify +m without a value of *n*, the default value is `10`. For a TermiNet, the first value in the Tab list should be `1` or the margin moves even farther to the right. Specify the normal (leftmost) margin on most terminals with +m0. The margin for most terminals is reset only when you specify the +m option.

Tab Specification

The following four types of Tab specification are accepted.

- Canned.
- Repetitive (-*n*).
- Arbitrary (*n1,n2,* . . .).
- File (--*file*).

If you provide no Tab specification, the default value is -8, that is, UNIX system "standard" Tabs. The lowest column number is 1.

Note — For Tabs, column 1 always refers to the leftmost column on a terminal, even one whose column markers begin at 0, for example, the DASI 300, DASI 300s, and DASI 450.

Canned

Use one of the codes listed below to select a canned set of Tabs that you specify with the -*code* option. If you specify more than one *code*, the last code option is used. The legal codes and their meanings are shown below.

-a	1,10,16,36,72 Assembler, IBM S/370, first format.
-a2	1,10,16,40,72 Assembler, IBM S/370, second format.
-c	1,8,12,16,20,55 COBOL, normal format.
-c2	1,6,10,14,49 COBOL compact format (columns 1-6 omitted). When this code is used, the first typed character corresponds to card column 7, one space gets you to column 8, and a Tab reaches column 12. Files using this Tab setup should include a format specification as shown below (see fspec(4)).

```
<:t-c2 m6 s66 d:>
```

-c3	1,6,10,14,18,22,26,30,34,38,42,46,50,54,58,62,67 COBOL compact format (columns 1-6 omitted), with more Tabs than -c2. This format is recommended for COBOL. The appropriate format specification is shown below (see fspec(4)).

```
<:t-c3 m6 s66 d:>
```

-f	1,7,11,15,19,23 FORTRAN.
-p	1,5,9,13,17,21,25,29,33,37,41,45,49,53,57,61 PL/I.
-s	1,10,55 SNOBOL.
-u	1,12,20,44 UNIVAC 1100 Assembler.

Repetitive

-*n*	A repetitive specification requests Tabs at columns $1+n$, $1+2*n$, and so forth, where *n* is a single-digit decimal number. Of particular importance is the value 8, which represents the UNIX system standard Tab setting and is the most likely Tab setting to be found at a terminal. When you use -0, the Tab stops are cleared and no new ones are set.

Arbitrary

See "Operands."

File

--file   If you specify the name of a file, tabs reads the first line of the file, searching for a format specification (see fspec(4)). If it finds one there, set the Tab stops according to it; otherwise, set them as -8. You can use this type of specification to make sure that a Tabbed file is printed with correct Tab settings. You would use it with the pr command, as shown in the following example.

castle% **tabs -- *file*; pr *file***

The standard output performs Tab and margin setting.

Operands

n1[,n2,...]   The arbitrary format consists of Tab-stop values separated with commas or spaces. The Tab-stop values must be positive decimal integers in ascending order. Up to 40 numbers are allowed. If you precede any number (except the first one) by a plus sign, take it as an increment to be added to the previous value. Thus, the formats 1,10,20,30, and 1,10,+10,+10 are considered identical.

Examples

The following example uses the -*code* canned specification to set Tabs to the settings required by the IBM assembler, that is, columns 1, 10, 16, 36, 72.

castle% **tabs -a**

The following example uses the -*n* repetitive specification, where *n* is 8, to set Tabs every eight positions, that is, 1+(1*8), 1+(2*8),..., which evaluates to columns 9, 17,....

castle% **tabs -8**

The following example uses the *n1,n2,* ... arbitrary specification to set Tabs at columns 1, 8, and 36.

castle% **tabs 1,8,36**

The following example uses the --*file* file specification to set Tabs, using the first line of $HOME/fspec.list/att4425 (see fspec(4)).

castle% **tabs --$HOME/fspec.list/att4425**

Environment Variables

See environ(5) for descriptions of the following environment variables that affect the execution of tabs: LC_CTYPE, LC_MESSAGES, and NLSPATH.

TERM   Determine the terminal type. If this variable is unset or null and if you do not specify the -T option, use terminal type ansi+tabs.

Exit Status

0	Successful completion.
>0	An error occurred.

Attributes

See `attributes`(5) for descriptions of the following attributes:

Attribute Type	Attribute Value
Availability	SUNWcsu
CSI	Enabled

See Also

expand(1), newform(1), pr(1), stty(1), tput(1), fspec(4), terminfo(4), attributes(5), environ(5), term(5)

tail — Look at the Last Part of a File

Synopsis

```
/usr/bin/tail [+number [lbcr]][file]
/usr/bin/tail [-lbcr][file]
/usr/bin/tail [+number [lbcf]][file]
/usr/bin/tail [-lbcf][file]
/usr/xpg4/bin/tail [-f | -r][-c number | -n number][file]
/usr/xpg4/bin/tail [+number [l | b | c][f]][file]
/usr/xpg4/bin/tail [+number [l][f | r]][file]
```

Description

Use the `tail` command to look at the end of a file. By default, the last 10 lines are displayed. You can change the number of lines displayed by using the `-n number` option to specify the number of lines to be displayed. If you do not specify a file name, the standard input is used.

Lines are displayed to standard output beginning at a point in the file indicated by the `-c number`, `-n number`, or `±number` options (if you specify `+number`, the display begins at distance `number` from the beginning; if you specify `-number`, the count is done from the end of the input; if `number` is null, the value 10 is assumed). `number` is counted in units of lines or bytes according to the `-c` or `-n` options. Alternatively, you can append l, b, or c to the `number` to specify the count in lines, blocks, or bytes. When you specify no units, counting is by lines.

> **Note** — Piped tails relative to the end of the file are stored in a buffer and thus are limited in length. Various kinds of anomalous behavior can happen with character special files.

Options

The following options are supported for both /usr/bin/tail and /usr/xpg4/bin/tail. The -r and -f options are mutually exclusive. If you specify both, the -f option is ignored.

-b	Display units of blocks.
-c	Display units of bytes.
-f	If the input file is not a pipe, do not terminate after the line of the input file has been displayed; instead, enter an endless loop and sleep for a second, then try to read and display further records from the input file. You can use this option to monitor the growth of a file that is being written by some other process.
-l	Display units of lines.
-r	Display lines from the specified starting point in the file in reverse order. The default is to display the entire file in reverse order.

/usr/xpg4/bin/tail

The following options are supported for /usr/xpg4/bin/tail only.

-c *number*   Specify *number* as a decimal integer whose sign affects the location in the file, measured in bytes, to begin the display.

+	Start the display relative to the beginning of the file.
-	Start the display relative to the end of the file.
none	Start the display relative to the end of the file.
	The origin for counting is 1; that is, -c +1 represents the first byte of the file, -c -1 the last.

-n *number*   Equivalent to -c *number*, except measure the starting location in the file in lines instead of bytes. The origin for counting is 1; that is, -n +1 represents the first byte of the file, -n -1 the last.

Operands

file   A path name of an input file. If you specify no file operands, use the standard input.

Usage

See largefile(5) for the description of the behavior of tail when encountering files greater than or equal to 2 Gbytes (2**31 bytes).

Examples

The following command displays the last 10 lines of the file /var/adm/sulog followed by any lines that are appended to the file between the time you initiate tail and the time you kill it.

```
# tail -f /var/adm/sulog
SU 04/04 15:13 + pts/6 winsor-root
SU 04/04 17:25 + pts/6 winsor-root
SU 04/05 12:46 + pts/6 winsor-root
SU 04/05 12:48 + pts/6 winsor-root
SU 04/05 17:41 + pts/6 winsor-root
SU 04/06 09:46 + pts/3 winsor-root
SU 04/06 18:22 + pts/6 winsor-root
SU 04/07 08:56 + pts/6 winsor-root
SU 04/07 13:41 + pts/3 winsor-root
SU 04/07 16:17 + pts/6 winsor-root
SU 04/07 16:17 + pts/3 winsor-root
SU 04/07 16:17 + pts/3 winsor-root
SU 04/07 16:17 + pts/3 winsor-root
SU 04/07 16:18 + pts/3 winsor-root
^C#
```

The following example displays the last 15 bytes of the file /var/adm/sulog followed by any lines that are appended to it between the time you initiate tail and the time you kill it.

```
# tail -15cf /var/adm/sulog
/3 winsor-root
SU 04/07 16:22 + pts/5 winsor-root
SU 04/07 16:23 + pts/5 winsor-root
SU 04/07 16:24 + pts/5 winsor-root
^C#
```

The following example displays the contents of the file kookaburra-2 in reverse order.

```
castle% tail -r kookaburra-2
    8  Leave some there for me.
    7  Stop, kookaburra, stop, kookaburra
    6  Eating all the gumdrops he can see.
    5  Kookaburra sits in the old gum tree

    4  Gay your life must be
    3  Laugh, kookaburra, laugh, kookaburra
    2  Merry merry king of the bush is he.
    1  Kookaburra sits in the old gum tree
castle%
```

Environment Variables

See environ(5) for descriptions of the following environment variables that affect the execution of tail: LC_CTYPE, LC_MESSAGES, and NLSPATH.

Exit Status

0	Successful completion.
>0	An error occurred.

Attributes

See `attributes`(5) for descriptions of the following attributes:

/usr/bin/tail

Attribute Type	Attribute Value
Availability	SUNWcsu
CSI	Enabled

/usr/xpg4/bin/tail

Attribute Type	Attribute Value
Availability	SUNWxcu4
CSI	Enabled

See Also

`cat(1)`, `head(1)`, `more(1)`, `pg(1)`, `dd(1M)`, `attributes(5)`, `environ(5)`, `largefile(5)`, `XPG4(5)`

talk — Talk to Another User

Synopsis

```
/usr/bin/talk address [terminal]
```

Description

The `talk` command is a two-way, screen-oriented communication program. When you first invoke it, `talk` sends a message similar to the following to the specified address.

```
Message from TalkDaemon@ her-system at time...
 talk: connection requested by your-address
 talk: respond with: talk your-address
```

At this point, the recipient of the message can reply by typing:

```
talk your-address
```

Once communication is established, the two parties can type simultaneously with their output displayed in separate regions of the screen. Characters are processed as follows.

- The alert character alerts the recipient's terminal.
- Control-L refreshes the sender's screen regions.
- The erase and kill characters affect the sender's terminal in the manner described by the `termios(3)` interface.
- The interrupt or end-of-file characters terminate the local `talk` command. Once the `talk` session has been terminated on one side, the other side of the `talk` session is notified that the `talk` session has been terminated and is able to do nothing except exit.
- Typing characters from the print or space `LC_CTYPE` classifications sends those characters to the recipient's terminal.
- When and only when the `stty iexten` local mode is enabled, additional special control characters and multibyte or single-byte characters are processed as printable characters if their wide-character equivalents are printable.
- Typing other nonprintable characters writes them to the recipient's terminal as follows: control characters appear as a caret (`^`) followed by the appropriate ASCII character, and characters with the high-order bit set appear in "meta" notation. For example, `\003` is displayed as `^C` and `\372` as `M-z`.

You can grant or deny permission to be a recipient of a `talk` message with the `mesg(1)` command. However, a user's privilege can further constrain the domain of accessibility of other users' terminals. Certain commands, such as `pr(1)`, disallow messages to prevent interference with their output. `talk` fails when the user lacks the appropriate privileges to perform the requested action.

Certain block-mode terminals do not have all the capabilities necessary to support the simultaneous exchange of messages required for `talk`. When this type of exchange cannot be supported on such terminals, the implementation may support an exchange with reduced levels of simultaneous interaction or it may report an error describing the terminal-related deficiency.

Note — Typing Control-L redraws the screen, whereas the erase, kill, and word-kill characters work in `talk` as normal. To exit, type an interrupt character; `talk` then moves the cursor to the bottom of the screen and restores the terminal to its previous state.

Operands

<table>
<tr><td>address</td><td>Specify the recipient of the talk session. One form of address is the username, as returned by the who(1) command. If you want to talk to someone on your own system, then username is the person's login name. If you want to talk to a user on another host, then username is one of the following forms.</td></tr>
</table>

                    host!user

                    host.user

                    host:user

                    user@host (preferred)

<table>
<tr><td>terminal</td><td>If the recipient is logged in more than once, you can use terminal to indicate the appropriate terminal name. If you do not specify terminal, display the talk message on one or more accessible terminals in use by the recipient. The format of terminal is the same as that returned by who.</td></tr>
</table>

Environment Variables

See environ(5) for descriptions of the following environment variables that affect the execution of talk: LC_CTYPE, LC_MESSAGES, and NLSPATH.

<table>
<tr><td>TERM</td><td>Determine the name of the invoker's terminal type. If this variable is unset or null, use an unspecified terminal type.</td></tr>
</table>

Exit Status

<table>
<tr><td>0</td><td>Successful completion.</td></tr>
<tr><td>>0</td><td>An error occurred, or talk was invoked on a terminal incapable of supporting it.</td></tr>
</table>

Files

<table>
<tr><td>/etc/hosts</td><td>Host name database.</td></tr>
<tr><td>/var/adm/utmp</td><td></td></tr>
<tr><td></td><td>User and accounting information for talk.</td></tr>
</table>

Attributes

See attributes(5) for descriptions of the following attributes:

Attribute Type	Attribute Value
Availability	SUNWcsu

See Also
```
mail(1), mesg(1), pr(1), stty(1), who(1), write(1), termios(3),
attributes(5), environ(5)
```

tar — Create Tape Archives and Add or Extract Files

Synopsis
```
/usr/bin/tarc[bBeEfFhiklnopPqvwX[0-7]][block][tarfile][exclude-file] New!
   { -I include-file | -C directory file | file }...
/usr/bin/tar r [bBeEfFhiklnqvw [0-7]][block]                         New!
   { -I include-file | -C directory file | file }...
/usr/bin/tar t [BefFhiklnqvX [0-7]][tarfile][exclude-file]
   { -I include-file | file }...
/usr/bin/tar u [bBeEfFhiklnqvw [0-7]][block][tarfile] file...        New!
tar x [BefFhiklmnopqvwX [0-7]][tarfile][exclude-file][file...]
```

Description
Use the `tar` command to copy files and directory subtrees to a single tape. The advantages of the `tar` command are that it is available on most UNIX operating systems and that public domain versions are readily available. The disadvantages of the `tar` command are that `tar` is not aware of file-system boundaries, full path-name length cannot exceed 255 characters, it does not copy empty directories or special files such as device files, and it cannot be used to create multiple tape volumes.

The `tar` command archives and extracts files to and from a single file called a *tarfile*. A tarfile is usually a magnetic tape but it can be any file. You control `tar` with the key argument, which is a string of characters containing exactly one function letter—c (create), r (replace), t (table of contents), u (update), or x (extract)—and zero or more function modifiers (letters or digits), depending on the function letter used. The key string contains no space characters. Function modifier arguments are listed on the command line in the same order as their corresponding function modifiers appear in the key string.

The `-I include-file`, `-C directory file`, and `file` arguments specify which files or directories are to be archived or extracted. In all cases, appearance of a directory name refers to the files and (recursively) subdirectories of that directory. Arguments appearing within braces ({}) indicate that you must specify one of the arguments.

Notes
You cannot access the *n*-th occurrence of a file.

Tape errors are handled ungracefully.

When the Volume Management daemon is running, accesses to diskette devices through the conventional device names (for example, /dev/rdiskette) may not succeed. See vold(1M) for further details.

The tar archive format allows UIDs and GIDs up to 2097151 to be stored in the archive header. Files with UIDs and GIDs greater than this value are archived with the UID and GID of 60001 (nobody).

New! If you create an archive that contains files whose names are created by processes running in multiple locales, use a single locale with a full 8-bit codeset (for example, the en_US locale) both to create the archive and to extract files from it.

Options

-I *include-file*

> Open *include-file* containing a list of files, one per line, and treat as if each file appeared separately on the command line. Be careful of trailing white spaces. When you also specify excluded files (see the X function modifier), they take precedence over all included files. If a file is specified in both the *exclude-file* and the *include-file* (or on the command line), exclude it.

-C *directory file*

> Perform a change directory (see cd(1)) operation on *directory* and perform the c (create) or r (replace) operation on *file*. Use short relative path names for *file*. If *file* is dot (.), archive all files in *directory*. This option enables archiving files from multiple directories not related by a close common parent.

Operands

file

> A path name of a regular file or directory to be archived (when you specify the c, r, or u functions), extracted (x) ,or listed (t). When *file* is the path name of a directory, apply the action to all of the files and (recursively) subdirectories of that directory. The directory portion of file (see dirname(1)) cannot exceed 155 characters. The file-name portion (see basename(1)) cannot exceed 100 characters.

New!

> When you archive a file and do not specify the E function modifier, the file name cannot exceed 256 characters. In addition, it must be possible to split the name between parent directory names so that the prefix is no longer than 155 characters and the name is no longer than 100 characters. With the E function modifier, you can specify a name of up to PATH_MAX characters.

For example, you cannot archive a file whose basename is longer than 100 characters without using the E function modifier. You could archive a file whose directory portion is 200 characters and whose basename is 50 characters without using the E function modifier if the directory name contains a slash somewhere in character positions 151-156.

New!

Function Letters

Specify the function portion of the key with one of the following letters.

c Create by writing at the beginning of *tarfile* instead of at the end.

r Replace by writing the named files at the end of *tarfile*.

t List the table of contents of the specified files each time they occur in *tarfile*. If you specify no file argument, list the names of all files in *tarfile*. With the v function modifier, display additional information for the specified files.

u Update by writing the named files at the end of *tarfile* if they are not already in *tarfile* or if they have been modified since last written to that tarfile. An update can be rather slow. You cannot update a tarfile created on a 5.x system on a 4.x system.

x Extract or restore the named files from the tarfile and write them to the directory specified in *tarfile* relative to the current directory. Use the relative path names of files and directories to be extracted. If a named file matches a directory whose contents have been written to *tarfile*, extract this directory recursively. If possible, restore the owner, modification time, and mode; otherwise, you must be superuser to restore owner.

Only superuser can extract character-special and block-special devices (created by mknod(1M). If you specify no file argument, extract the entire content of *tarfile*. If *tarfile* contains several files with the same name, write each file to the appropriate directory, overwriting the previous one. You cannot use file-name substitution wild-cards for extracting files from the archive; instead, use a command of the following form.

```
tar xvf... /dev/rmt/0 `tar tf... /dev/rmt/0 | grep
'pattern'`
```

When extracting tapes created with the r or u functions, directory modification times may not be set correctly. These same functions cannot be used with many tape drives because of tape drive limitations such as the absence of backspace or append capabilities.

When you use the r, u, or x functions or the X function modifier, the named files must match exactly the corresponding files in *tarfile*. For example, to extract ./thisfile, you must specify ./thisfile, and not thisfile. The t function displays how each file was archived.

Function Modifiers

You can use the characters below in conjunction with the letter that selects the desired function.

b   Blocking Factor. Use when reading or writing to raw magnetic archives (see f). The block argument specifies the number of 512-byte tape blocks to be included in each read or write operation performed on *tarfile*. The minimum is 1, the default is 20. The maximum value is a function of the amount of memory available and the blocking requirements of the specific tape device involved. (See mtio(7I) for details.)

When a tape archive is being read, its actual blocking factor is automatically detected provided that it is less than or equal to the nominal blocking factor (the value of the block argument, or the default value if you do not specify the b modifier). If the actual blocking factor is greater than the nominal blocking factor, a read error results.

B   Block. Force tar to perform multiple reads (if necessary) to read exactly enough bytes to fill a block. This function modifier enables tar to work across the Ethernet because pipes and sockets return partial blocks even when more data is coming. When reading from standard input, -, the B function modifier is selected by default to ensure that tar can recover from short reads.

e   Error. Exit immediately with a positive exit status if any unexpected errors occur. The SYSV3 environment variable overrides the default behavior.

E   Write *tarfile* with extended headers. (Used with c, r, or u options; ignored with t or x options.) When *tarfile* is written with extended headers, maintain the modification time with a granularity of microseconds instead of seconds. In addition, support file names no longer than PATH_MAX characters that could not be archived without E and file sizes greater than 8 gigabytes. Require the E function modifier whenever archiving larger files, files with longer names, files whose UID/GID exceeds 2097151, or if you want time granularity of microseconds.

f   File. Use the *tarfile* argument as the name of the tarfile. If you specify f, do not search /etc/default/tar. If you omit f, use the device indicated by the TAPE environment variable if set; otherwise, use the default values defined in /etc/default/tar. If the name of the tarfile is -, write to the standard output or read from the standard input, whichever is appropriate. You can use `tar` as the head or tail of a pipeline. You can also use `tar` to move hierarchies with the command:

```
% cd fromdir; tar cf - .  |  (cd todir; tar xfBp -)
```

F   With one F argument, exclude all directories named SCCS and RCS from *tarfile*. With two arguments, FF, exclude all directories named SCCS and RCS, all files with .o as their suffix, and all files named errs, core, and a.out. The SYSV3 environment variable overrides the default behavior.

h   Follow symbolic links as if they were normal files or directories. Normally, `tar` does not follow symbolic links.

i   Ignore directory checksum errors.

k *size*   Use the *size* argument as the size of an archive in kilobytes. This option is useful when the archive is intended for a fixed-size device such as diskettes. Large files are then split across volumes if they do not fit in the specified size.

l   Link. Output error message if unable to resolve all links to the files being archived. If you do not specify l, print no error messages.

m   Modify. Set the modification time of the file as the time of extraction. This function modifier is valid only with the x function.

n   Specify that the file being read is not a tape device. Reading of the archive is faster because `tar` can randomly seek around the archive.

o   Ownership. Assign to extracted files the user and group identifiers of the user running the program instead of those on *tarfile*. This behavior is the default for users other than root. If you do not set the o function modifier and the user is root, the extracted files take on the group and user identifiers of the files on *tarfile* (see chown(1) for more information). The o function modifier is valid only with the x function.

p   Restore the named files to their original modes and ACLs if applicable, ignoring the present umask(1). This behavior is the default if you invoke p as superuser with the x function letter. If superuser, also extract SETUID and sticky bit information and restore files with their original owners and permissions instead of being owned by root. When you use this function modifier with the c function, create ACLs in *tarfile* along with other information. Errors occur when a tarfile with ACLs is extracted by previous versions of `tar`.

P   Suppress the addition of a trailing / on directory entries in the archive.

q	Stop after extracting the first occurrence of the named file. tar normally continues reading the archive after finding an occurrence of a file.
v	Verbose. Output the name of each file preceded by the function letter. With the t function, v provides additional information about the tarfile entries. The listing is similar to the format produced by the -l option of the ls(1) command.
w	What. Output the action to be taken and the name of the file, then await confirmation. If the response is affirmative, perform the action; otherwise, do not perform the action. You cannot use this function modifier with the t function.
X	Exclude. Use the exclude-file argument as a file containing a list of relative path names for files (or directories) to be excluded from tarfile when using the functions c, x, or t. Be careful of trailing white spaces. You can use multiple X arguments with one exclude-file per argument. In the case where you also specify included files (see -I include-file option), the excluded files take precedence over all included files. If you specify a file in both the exclude-file and the include-file (or on the command line), exclude it.
[0-7]	Select an alternative drive on which the tape is mounted. The default entries are specified in /etc/default/tar. If you specify no digit or f function modifier, the default is the entry in /etc/default/tar with digit 0.

Usage

See largefile(5) for the description of the behavior of tar when encountering files greater than or equal to 2 Gbytes (2**31 bytes).

The automatic determination of the actual blocking factor can be fooled when reading from a pipe or a socket (see the B function modifier).

1/4-inch streaming tape has an inherent blocking factor of one 512-byte block. You can read or write to it with any blocking factor.

The B function modifier works for archives on disk files and block special devices, among others, but it is intended principally for tape devices.

New!   For information on tar header format, see archives(4).

Examples

The following example uses tar to create an archive of your home directory on a tape mounted on drive /dev/rmt/0.

```
castle% cd
castle% tar cvf /dev/rmt/0 .
messages from tar
```

The c function letter means create the archive; the v function modifier outputs messages explaining what tar is doing; the f function modifier indicates the specified tarfile (/dev/rmt/0 in this example). The dot (.) at the end of the command line means the current directory and is the argument of the f function modifier.

The following example displays the table of contents of the tarfile. The output for the POSIX locale is shown.

```
castle% tar tvf /dev/rmt/0
rw-r--r-- 1677/40 2123  Mar  7 18:15 1999     ./test.c...
castle%
```

The columns have the following meanings.

- Column 1 is the access permissions to ./test.c.
- Column 2 is the user ID/group ID of ./test.c.
- Column 3 is the size of ./test.c in bytes.
- Column 4 is the modification date of ./test.c. When the LC_TIME category is not set to the POSIX locale, a different format and date order field can be used.
- Column 5 is the name of ./test.c.

The following example extracts files from the archive.

```
castle% tar xvf /dev/rmt/0
messages from tar
castle%
```

If a tape has multiple archive files, each is separated from the following one by an end-of-file marker. To have tar read the first and second archives from a tape with multiple archives on it, you must use the nonrewinding version of the tape device name with the f function modifier, as shown in the following example. The first command reads the first archive on the tape; the second command reads the second archive.

```
castle% tar xvfp /dev/rmt/0n
messages from tar
castle% tar xvfp /dev/rmt/0n
messages from tar
castle%
```

> **Note** — In some earlier releases, the above scenario did not work correctly and intervention with mt(1) between tar invocations was required. To emulate the old behavior, use the nonrewind device name containing the letter b for BSD behavior. See the "Close Operations" section of the mtio(7I) manual page.

The following example archives files from /usr/include and from /etc to default tape drive 0.

```
castle% tar c -C /usr include -C /etc .
```

The table of contents from the resulting *tarfile* would produce output like

```
include/
include/a.out.h
```

and all the other files in /usr/include...

```
./chown
```

and all the other files in /etc.

The following example extracts all files in the include directory

```
castle% tar xv include
x include/, 0 bytes, 0 tape blocks
```

and all files under include...

The following example uses tar to transfer files across the Ethernet. First, you archive files from the local system (castle) to a tape on a remote system (host).

```
castle% tar cvfb - 20 files | rsh host dd of=/dev/rmt/0 obs=20b
messages from tar
castle%
```

The previous example creates a *tarfile* with the c key letter, asks for verbose output from tar with the v function modifier, specifies the name of the output *tarfile* with the f function modifier (the standard output is where the *tarfile* appears, as indicated by the – sign), and uses the b function modifier to specify the blocksize (20). If you want to change the blocksize, you must change the blocksize arguments both on the tar command and on the dd command.

The following example uses tar to retrieve files from a tape on the remote system back to the local system.

```
castle% rsh -n host dd if=/dev/rmt/0 bs=20b |tar xvBfb - 20 files
messages from tar
castle%
```

The previous example extracts from the tarfile with the x key letter, asks for verbose output from tar with the v function modifier, tells tar it is reading from a pipe with the B function modifier, specifies the name of the input tarfile with the f function modifier (the standard input is where the tarfile appears, as indicated by the – sign), and specifies the blocksize (20) with the b function modifier.

The following example creates an archive of the home directory on /dev/rmt/0 with an actual blocking factor of 19.

```
castle% tar cvfb /dev/rmt/0 19 $HOME
```

The following example recognizes the archive's actual blocking factor without using the b function modifier.

```
castle% tar tvf /dev/rmt/0
tar: blocksize = 19
. . .
```

The following example recognizes the archive's actual blocking factor, using a larger nominal blocking factor.

```
castle% tar tvf /dev/rmt/0 30
tar: blocksize = 19
. . .
```

The following example tries to recognize the archive's actual blocking factor, using a nominal blocking factor that is too small.

```
castle% tar tvf /dev/rmt/0 10
tar: tape read error
```

Environment Variables

SYSV3   Override the default behavior of tar and provide compatibility with INTERACTIVE UNIX systems and SCO UNIX installation scripts. Do not use this environment variable in new scripts; it is intended for compatibility purposes only. When set, the following options behave differently.

-F *filename*   Use *filename* to obtain a list of command-line switches and files on which to operate.

-e   Prevent files from being split across volumes. If there is insufficient room on one volume, prompt for a new volume. If the file does not fit on the new volume, exit with an error.

See environ(5) for descriptions of the following environment variables that affect the execution of tar: LC_CTYPE, LC_MESSAGES, LC_TIME, TZ, and NLSPATH.

Exit Status

0   Successful completion.

>0   An error occurred.

Files

```
/dev/rmt/[0-7][b][n]
/dev/rmt/[0-7]l[b][n]
/dev/rmt/[0-7]m[b][n]
```

```
/dev/rmt/[0-7]h[b][n]

/dev/rmt/[0-7]u[b][n]

/dev/rmt/[0-7]c[b][n]
```

/etc/default/tar Settings may look like this:

```
                archive0=/dev/rmt/0

                archive1=/dev/rmt/0n

                archive2=/dev/rmt/1

                archive3=/dev/rmt/1n

                archive4=/dev/rmt/0

                archive5=/dev/rmt/0n

                archive6=/dev/rmt/1

                archive7=/dev/rmt/1n
```

/tmp/tar*

Attributes

See attributes(5) for descriptions of the following attributes:

Attribute Type	Attribute Value
Availability	SUNWcsu
CSI	Enabled

See Also

ar(1), basename(1), cd(1), chown(1), cpio(1), csh(1), dirname(1), ls(1), mt(1), pax(1), setfacl(1), umask(1), mknod(1M), vold(1M), attributes(5), environ(5), largefile(5), mtio(7I)

Diagnostics

Diagnostic messages are output for bad key characters and tape read/write errors and for insufficient memory to hold the link tables.

tbl — Format Tables for nroff or troff

Synopsis

/usr/bin/tbl [-me][-mm][-ms] [*filename*] . . .

Description

The `tbl` command is a preprocessor for formatting tables for `nroff`(1) or `troff`(1). A table is a rectangular arrangement of entries. Using the right commands, you can create multicolumn tables and enclose them in boxes. The `tbl` command automatically produces the correct column positioning. The input file names are copied to the standard output, except that lines between `.TS` (table start) and `.TE` (table end) command lines are assumed to describe tables and are reformatted.

If you specify no arguments, `tbl` reads the standard input, so you can use `tbl` as a filter. When you use `tbl` with `eqn`(1) or `neqn`, put the `tbl` command first to minimize the volume of data passed through pipes.

You define the structure of a table by specifying global options, described below, as a comma-separated list on the second line of a table.

Option	Description
center	Center the table on the page.
expand	Expand the table width to the current line length.
box	Draw a box around the entire table.
doublebox	Draw a double-line box around the entire table.
allbox	Enclose each cell in the table in a box.
tab(x)	Use the character x as the data separator.
linesize(n)	
	Set all lines in n point type.

Within the table structure, you can specify formats for column entries as described in the following table.

Code	Result
^	Expand entry from previous row to this row.
a	Indent characters from left alignment by one em.
c	Center data.
l	Left-justify data.
n	Align numbers by decimal points or unit places.
r	Right-justify data.
s	Straddle columns by extending data in previous column to this column.
t	Span vertically with text on top of the column

Options

−me	Copy the −me macro package to the front of the output file.
−mm	Copy the −mm macro package to the front of the output file.
−ms	Copy the −ms macro package to the front of the output file.

Examples

In the following example of tbl content, the at sign (@) represents a Tab that should be typed as an actual Tab character in the input file.

```
.TS
c s s
c c s
c c c
l n n.
Household Population
Town@Households
@Number@Size
Bedminster@789@3.26
Bernards Twp.@3087@3.74
Bernardsville@2018@3.30
Bound Brook@3425@3.04
Branchburg@1644@3.49
.TE
```

```
yields
```

```
Household Population
Town          Households Number     Size
  Bedminster         789    3.26
  Bernards Twp.     3087    3.74
  Bernardsville    2018    3.30
  Bound Brook      3425    3.04
  Branchburg       1644    3.49
```

Files

/usr/share/lib/tmac/e

    −me **macros.**

/usr/share/lib/tmac/m

    −mm **macros.**

/usr/share/lib/tmac/s

    −ms **macros.**

Attributes

See attributes(5) for descriptions of the following attributes:

Attribute Type	Attribute Value
Availability	SUNWdoc

See Also

eqn(1), nroff(1), troff(1), attributes(5)

tcopy — Copy a Magnetic Tape

Synopsis

/usr/bin/tcopy *source* [*destination*]

Description

Use the tcopy command to copy the magnetic tape mounted on the tape drive specified by the *source* argument. The only assumption made about the contents of a tape is that there are two tape marks at the end.

When you specify only a source drive, tcopy scans the tape and displays information about the sizes of records and tape files. If you specify a destination, tcopy copies the source tape onto the destination tape, with blocking preserved. As it copies, tcopy produces the same output as it does when only scanning a tape.

Note — tcopy runs only on systems supporting an associated set of ioctl(2) requests.

Attributes

See attributes(5) for descriptions of the following attributes:

Attribute Type	Attribute Value
Availability	SUNWesu

See Also

mt(1), ioctl(2), attributes(5)

tee — Replicate the Standard Output

Synopsis

```
/usr/bin/tee [-ai][file...]
```

Description

The tee command is analogous to a tee joint in plumbing that splits an incoming stream of water. tee splits standard input into two or more output streams, sending one to standard output and the others to files you specify on the command line.

   You can use the tee command to monitor a command to make sure it is doing what you want or to save an intermediate step in a pipeline sequence. tee does not buffer its output. The options determine if the specified files are overwritten or appended to.

Options

-a   Append the output to the files instead of overwriting them.

-i   Ignore interrupts.

Operands

file   A path name of an output file. You can process at least 13 file
            operands.

Examples

The following example uses the file command to display information about files in the current directory and also saves a copy of the information in a file named filetypes.

```
castle% file * | tee filetypes
085XDOCS.zip:   data
Appletviewer.rs:      rasterfile, 511 x 180 x 8 standard format image
Mail:           directory
bibliography:   ascii text
core:         ELF 32-bit MSB core file SPARC Version 1, from 'srchtxt'
examples:       ascii text
find.zip:       ZIP archive
kookaburra-1:   ascii text
kookaburra-2:   ascii text
olddir:         directory
program.c:      c program text
tbltest:        [nt]roff, tbl, or eqn input text
temp:           data
xaa:            English text
castle%
```

The following example writes sar data into a file named /tmp/sardata and also displays the data to standard output. If you look in /tmp, you'll also see a file named sardata.

```
# sar | tee /tmp/sardata

SunOS sun1 5.7 Generic sun4m    04/15/99

06:23:33    %usr    %sys    %wio    %idle
06:23:38      1       2       0       97
06:23:43      2       2       0       96
06:23:48      0       2       0       98
06:23:53     16       3       0       81
06:23:58      5       2       0       93
06:24:03      5       3       0       92
06:24:08      2       2       0       96
06:24:13      4       2       0       93
06:24:18      4       4       1       91
06:24:23      2       2       0       96

Average       4       2       0       93
#
```

If you want to append to a file instead of overwriting the contents, use the -a option.

Usage

See largefile(5) for the description of the behavior of tee when encountering files greater than or equal to 2 Gbytes (2**31 bytes).

Environment Variables

See environ(5) for descriptions of the following environment variables that affect the execution of tee: LC_CTYPE, LC_MESSAGES, and NLSPATH.

Exit Status

0	The standard input was successfully copied to all output files.
>0	The number of files that could not be opened or whose status could not be obtained.

Attributes

See attributes(5) for descriptions of the following attributes:

Attribute Type	**Attribute Value**
Availability	SUNWcsu
CSI	Enabled

See Also
```
cat(1), attributes(5), environ(5), largefile(5),
```

---

tek — Graphics Filters for Various Plotters

Synopsis
```
/usr/bin/plot [-Tterminal]
```

Description
See tplot(1).

---

telnet — User Interface to a Remote System, Using the TELNET Protocol

Synopsis
```
/usr/bin/telnet [-8ELcdr][-e escape-char][-l user][-n tracefile]
    [host [port]]
```

Description
Use the telnet command to remotely log in to a system running some other operating system or a different version of UNIX. telnet communicates with another host, using the TELNET protocol. If you invoke telnet without arguments, it enters command mode and displays the telnet> prompt. In this mode, it accepts and executes its associated commands. (See "telnet Commands" on page 1326.) If you invoke telnet with arguments, it performs an open command with those arguments.

Once a connection has been opened, telnet enters input mode. In this mode, text typed is sent to the remote host. The input mode entered depends on what the remote system supports. The three input modes are:

- *Line mode*: Character processing is done on the local system under the control of the remote system. When input editing or character echoing is to be disabled, the remote system relays that information. The remote system also relays changes to any special characters that happen on the remote system so that they can take effect on the local system.

- *Character-at-a-time mode*: Most text typed is immediately sent to the remote host for processing.

- *Old-line-by-line mode*: All text is echoed locally, and (normally) only completed lines are sent to the remote host. You can use the "local echo character" (initially, ^E) to turn off and on the local echo. (Use this feature mostly to enter passwords without the password being echoed.)

Note — In "old line by line" mode, or LINEMODE, the terminal's end-of-file character is recognized (and sent to the remote system) only when it is the first character on a line.

If the line mode option is enabled or if the localchars toggle is true (the default in "old line by line" mode), your quit, intr, and flush characters are trapped locally and sent as TELNET protocol sequences to the remote side. If "line mode" has ever been enabled, then your susp and eof are also sent as TELNET protocol sequences. quit is then sent as a TELNET ABORT instead of BREAK. The toggle autoflush and toggle autosynch options flush subsequent output to the terminal (until the remote host acknowledges the TELNET sequence) and flush previous terminal input, in the case of quit and intr.

While connected to a remote host, you can enter telnet command mode by typing the telnet escape character (initially ^]). When in command mode, the normal terminal editing conventions are available. Pressing Return at the telnet command prompt exits command mode.

Options

-8	Specify an 8-bit data path. Negotiating the BINARY option is attempted for both input and output.
-c	Disable the reading of the user's telnetrc file. (See the toggle skiprc command.)
-d	Set the initial value of the debug toggle to true.
-e *escape-char*	Set the initial escape character to *escape-char*. *escape-char* can also be a two-character sequence consisting of ^ followed by one character. If the second character is ?, select the DEL character. Otherwise convert the second character to a control character and use it as the escape character. If the escape character is the null string (that is, -e ' '), disable it.
-E	Stop any character from being recognized as an escape character.
-l *user*	When connecting to a remote system that understands the ENVIRON option, send *user* to the remote system as the value for the variable USER.
-L	Specify an 8-bit data path on output. This negotiates the BINARY option on output.

-n *tracefile*

> Open *tracefile* for recording trace information. See the set
> tracefile command.

-r

> Specify a user interface similar to rlogin. In this mode, set the
> escape character to the tilde (~) character unless modified by the
> -e option. The rlogin escape character is recognized only when it
> is preceded by a Return. In this mode, you must still precede a
> telnet command with the telnet escape character, normally ^].
> You can also follow the rlogin escape character by . \r or ^z, like
> rlogin(1), to close or suspend the connection. This option is an
> uncommitted interface and may change in the future.

Usage

telnet Commands

The commands described in this section are available with telnet. You need to
type only enough of each command to uniquely identify it. (This is also true for
arguments to the mode, set, toggle, unset, environ, and display
commands.)

close

> Close any open TELNET session and exit telnet. An end-of-file (in
> command mode) also closes a session and exits.

display [*argument*...]

> Display all or some of the set and toggle values (see toggle
> arguments).

environ *arguments*...

> Use the environ command to manipulate variables that can be sent
> through the ENVIRON option. Take the initial set of variables from
> your environment. Only export the DISPLAY and PRINTER variables
> by default. Valid arguments for the environ command are as
> follows.

define *variable value*

> > Define *variable* to have a value of *value*.
> > Automatically export any variables defined by this
> > command. You can enclose *value* in single or double
> > quotes so that you can include Tabs and spaces.

export *variable*

> > Mark the variable to be exported to the remote side.

list

> > List the current set of environment variables. Send
> > those marked with an asterisk (*) automatically.
> > Send other variables only if explicitly requested.

undefine *variable*

> Remove *variable* from the list of environment variables. Export *variable*.

unexport *variable*

> Mark the variable to not be exported unless explicitly requested by the remote side.

? Print help information for the environ command.

logout   Send the telnet logout option to the remote side. This command is similar to a close command. However, nothing happens if the remote side does not support the logout option. If the remote side does support the logout option, this command should close the remote side of the TELNET connection. If the remote side also supports the concept of suspending a user's session for later reattachment, the logout argument indicates that the remote side should terminate the session immediately.

mode *type*   The remote host is asked for permission to go into the requested mode. If the remote host is capable of entering that mode, enter the requested mode. *type* is one of the following.

character   Disable the LINEMODE option, or, if the remote side does not understand the LINEMODE option, enter "character at a time" mode.

edit (-edit)

> Try to enable (disable) the EDIT mode of the LINEMODE option. The LINEMODE option must be enabled.

isig (-isig)

> Try to enable (disable) the TRAPSIG mode of the LINEMODE option. The LINEMODE option must enabled.

line   Enable the LINEMODE option, or, if the remote side does not understand the LINEMODE option, try to enter "old line by line" mode.

litecho (-litecho)

> Try to enable (disable) the LIT_ECHO mode of the LINEMODE option. The LINEMODE option must be enabled.

softtabs (-softtabs)

> Try to enable (disable) the SOFT_TAB mode of the LINEMODE option. The LINEMODE option must be enabled.

? Print help information for the mode command.

```
open [-l user] host [port]
```
> Open a connection to the named `host`. If you specify no port number, `telnet` tries to contact a TELNET server at the default port. The host specification can be either a host name (see `hosts(4)`) or an Internet address specified in dot notation (see `inet(7P)`). The `-l` option passes `user` as the value of the ENVIRON variable USER to the remote system.

`quit`   Same as `close`.

`send` *arguments*

> Send one or more special character sequences to the remote host. You can specify one or more of the following arguments.

`abort`	Send the ABORT (abort process) sequence.
`ao`	Send the AO (abort output) sequence to flush all output from the remote system to your terminal.
`ayt`	Send the AYT (are you there) sequence. The remote system may or may not respond.
`brk or` `break`	Send the BRK (break) sequence, which may have significance to the remote system.

```
do option
dont option
will option
wont option
```
> Send the indicated protocol option negotiation. *option* can be the text name of the protocol option or the number corresponding to the option. The command is silently ignored if the indicated option negotiation is not valid in the current state. If you specify the `help` or `?` option, list known option names. This command is useful mostly for unusual debugging situations.

`ec`	Send the EC (erase character) sequence to erase the last character entered.
`el`	Send the EL (erase line) sequence to erase the line currently being entered on the remote system.
`eof`	Send the EOF (end-of-file) sequence.
`eor`	Send the EOR (end-of-record) sequence.
`escape`	Send the current `telnet` escape character (initially `^]`).
`ga`	Send the GA (go ahead) sequence, which probably has no significance for the remote system.

getstatus	If the remote side supports the STATUS command, getstatus sends the subnegotiation to request that the server send its current option status.
ip	Send the IP (interrupt process) sequence to abort the currently running process on the remote system.
nop	Send the NOP (no operation) sequence.
susp	Send the SUSP (suspend process) sequence.
synch	Send the SYNCH sequence to discard all previously typed but not yet read input on the remote system. This sequence is sent as TCP urgent data and may not work if the remote system is a 4.2 BSD system. If it does not work, a lowercase r may be echoed on the terminal.
?	Print help information for the send command.

set *argument* [*value*]

unset *argument*

Set any one of a number of telnet variables to a specific value. The special value off turns off the function associated with the variable. You can interrogate the values of variables with the display command. If you omit *value*, take the value to be true or on. If you use the unset form, take the value to be false or off. You can specify the following variables.

ayt	Send an AYT sequence to the remote host when in localchars mode or LINEMODE is enabled and you type the status character. The initial value for ayt is the terminal status character.
echo	Set the value (initially, ^E) that "old line by line" mode uses to toggle between local echoing of entered characters for normal processing and suppressed echoing of entered characters such as a password. Note that on some remote systems, you have to turn off echo manually when in "old line by line" mode.
eof	When you enter the eof character as the first character on a line, send the eof character to the remote system when operating in "old line by line" mode. Take the initial value of eof to be the terminal eof character.
erase	Send an ES sequence to the remote system when in localchars mode and operating in "character at a time" mode. Take the initial value for the erase character to be the terminal erase character.
escape	Set the telnet escape character (initially, ^]) that enters telnet command mode when connected to a remote system.

flushoutput	Send an AO sequence to the remote host when in localchars mode and you type the flushoutput character. Take the initial value for the flush character to be the terminal flush character.
forw1 forw2	Forward partial lines to the remote system when operating in LINEMODE (or "old line by line" mode) and you type the forw1 or forw2 character. The initial values for the forwarding characters come from the terminal eol and eol2 characters.
interrupt	Set the interrupt sequence that is sent to the remote host when in localchars mode (see toggle localchars) and you type the interrupt character. Take the initial value for the interrupt character to be the terminal intr character.
kill	Send an EL sequence to the remote system when telnet is in localchars mode, operating in "character at a time" mode, and you type the kill sequence. Take the initial value for the kill character to be the terminal kill character.
lnext	Assume the lnext character is the terminal lnext character when operating in LINEMODE or "old line by line" mode. Take the initial value for the lnext character to be the terminal lnext character.
quit	Send a BRK sequence to the remote host when in localchars mode and you type the quit character. Take the initial value for the quit character to be the terminal quit character.
reprint	Assume the reprint character is the terminal's reprint character when operating in LINEMODE or "old line by line" mode. Take the initial value for reprint to be the terminal reprint character.
rlogin	Set the rlogin escape character. Ignore the normal telnet escape character unless it is preceded by this character at the beginning of a line. Close the connection when the rlogin character followed by a . is at the beginning of a line. When followed by a ^z, suspend the telnet command. The initial state is to disable the rlogin escape character.
start	If the TOGGLE-FLOW-CONTROL option has been enabled, take the start character to be the terminal start character. Take the initial value for the kill character to be the terminal start character.

stop	If the TOGGLE-FLOW-CONTROL option has been enabled, take the stop character to be the terminal stop character. Take the initial value for the kill character to be the terminal stop character.
susp	Send a SUSP sequence to the remote host when in localchars mode or LINEMODE is enabled and you type the suspend character. Take the initial value for the suspend character to be the terminal suspend character.
tracefile	Write the output to this file when the netdata or the debug option is true. If it is set to -, then write the tracing information to standard output (the default).
worderase	If operating in LINEMODE or "old line by line" mode, take this character to be the terminal worderase character. Take the initial value for the worderase character to be the terminal worderase character.
?	Display the legal set and unset commands.

slc *state*   Set or change the state of special characters when the LINEMODE option has been enabled. Special characters are characters that get mapped to TELNET command sequences (like ip and quit) or line-editing characters (like erase and kill). By default, export the local special characters.

check	Verify the settings for the current special characters. The remote side is requested to send all the current special character settings. If there are any discrepancies with the local side, switch the local settings to the remote values.
export	Switch to the local defaults for the special characters. The local default characters are those of the local terminal at the time telnet was started.
import	Switch to the remote defaults for the special characters. The remote default characters are those of the remote system at the time when the TELNET connection was established.
?	Print help information for the slc command.

toggle *arguments*...

Toggle between true and false the various flags that control how telnet responds to events. You can specify more than one argument. You can interrogate the state of these flags with the display command. Valid arguments are as follows.

autoflush   If `autoflush` and `localchars` are both `true`, then when the `ao`, `intr`, or `quit` characters are recognized (and transformed into TELNET sequences; see `set` for details), refuse to display any data on your terminal until the remote system acknowledges (using a TELNET Timing Mark option) that it has processed those TELNET sequences. The initial value for this toggle is `true` if you have not done an `stty noflsh`. Otherwise, the value is `false` (see `stty(1)`).

autosynch   If `autosynch` and `localchars` are both `true`, then when you type either the `interrupt` or `quit` characters (see `set` for descriptions of `interrupt` and `quit`), send the resulting TELNET sequence followed by the `SYNCH` sequence. This procedure should throw away all previously typed input on the remote system until both of the TELNET sequences have been read and acted on. The initial value is `false`.

binary   Enable or disable the `BINARY` option on both input and output.

crlf   Determine how Returns are sent. If the value is `true`, then send Returns as CR/LF. If the value is `false`, then send Returns as CRnull. The initial value is `false`.

crmod   Toggle Return mode. When this mode is enabled, most Return characters received from the remote host are mapped into a Return followed by a linefeed. This mode does not affect those characters you type, only those received from the remote host. This mode is useful only for remote hosts that send Return but never send linefeed. The initial value is `false`.

debug   Toggle socket level debugging (only available to the superuser). The initial value is `false`.

inbinary   Enable or disable the `BINARY` option on input.

localchars   If `true`, then recognize the `flush`, `interrupt`, `quit`, `erase`, and `kill` characters (see `set`) locally and transform them into the appropriate TELNET control sequences `ao`, `ip`, `brk`, `ec`, and `el` (see `send`). The initial value for this toggle is `true` in "old line by line" mode and `false` in "character at a time" mode. When the `LINEMODE` option is enabled, ignore the value of `localchars` and assume it is always `true`. If `LINEMODE` has ever been enabled, then `quit` is sent as `abort`, and `eof` and `suspend` are sent as `eof` and `susp` (see `send`).

	`netdata`	Toggle the display of all network data (in hexadecimal format). The initial value is `false`.
	`options`	Toggle the display of some internal TELNET protocol processing (having to do with `telnet` options). The initial value is `false`.
	`outbinary`	Enable or disable the `BINARY` option on output.
	`prettydump`	When the `netdata` toggle is enabled, if `prettydump` is enabled, format the output from the `netdata` command in a more user-readable format. Put spaces between each character in the output. The beginning of any TELNET escape sequence is preceded by an asterisk (`*`) to aid in locating it.
	`skiprc`	When `true`, skip the reading of the `.telnetrc` file in your home directory when connections are opened. The initial value is `false`.
	`termdata`	Toggle the display of all terminal data (in hexadecimal format). The initial value is `false`.
	`?`	Display the legal toggle commands.
`status`		Show the current status of `telnet`, including the peer you are connected to and the current mode.
`z`		Suspend `telnet`. This command works only when you are using a shell that supports job control, such as `sh(1)`.

`? [command]`

Get help. With no arguments, print a help summary. If you specify *command*, print the help information for just that command.

Files

`$HOME/.telnetrc`

Commands to be executed before initiating a `telnet` session.

`/etc/nologin`

Message displayed to users trying to log in during system shutdown.

Attributes

See `attributes`(5) for descriptions of the following attributes:

Attribute Type	Attribute Value
Availability	SUNWcsu

See Also

rlogin(1), sh(1), stty(1), hosts(4), nologin(4), telnetrc(4), attributes(5), inet(7P)

Diagnostics

NO LOGINS: System going down in *N* minutes

> The system is in the process of being shut down and logins have been disabled.

test — Evaluate Conditions

Synopsis

/usr/bin/test [*condition*]
[*condition*]

sh, ksh
test *condition*
[*condition*]

Description

See if(1).

tftp — Trivial File Transfer Program

Synopsis

/usr/bin/tftp [*host*]

Description

The tftp command is the user interface to the Internet TFTP (Trivial File Transfer Protocol) that uses the User Datagram Protocol (UDP) instead of the Transmission Control Protocol (TCP) used by ftp. Use tftp when you have no login on the remote system and you want to transfer files that are publicly readable. Because tftp does not authenticate users, it is insecure. Because there is no user login or validation within the TFTP protocol, many remote sites restrict file access in various ways. Approved methods for file access are specific to each site and therefore cannot be documented here.

tftp communicates with the remote system when needed and does not run an interactive session with a remote host.

You can specify the remote host on the command line, in which case tftp uses *host* as the default host for future transfers (see the connect command).

Note — The default transfer mode is ascii. This default differs from pre-SunOS 4.0 and pre-4.3 BSD systems, so you must take explicit action when transferring non-ASCII binary files such as executable commands.

Usage

Once tftp is running, it issues the tftp> prompt and recognizes the following commands.

Commands

connect *host-name* [*port*]

> Set the host (and optionally port) for transfers. Unlike FTP, the TFTP protocol does not maintain connections between transfers; thus, the connect command does not actually create a connection but merely remembers what host is to be used for transfers. You do not have to use the connect command; you can specify the remote host as part of the get or put commands.

mode *transfer-mode*

> Set the mode for transfers; *transfer-mode* can be either ascii or binary. The default is ascii.

put *filename*
put *localfile remotefile*
put *filename1 filename2... filenameN remote-directory*

> Transfer a file or a set of files to the specified remote file or directory. The destination can be in one of two forms: a file name on the remote host if the host has already been specified or a string of the following form to specify both a host and file name at the same time.

> *host*:*filename*

> If you use the latter form, the specified host becomes the default for future transfers. If you use the *remote-directory* form, the remote host is assumed to be running the UNIX system. Files can be written only if they already exist and are publicly writable (see in.tftpd(1M)).

get *filename*
get *remotename localname*
get *filename1 filename2 filename3... filenameN*

> Get a file or set of files from the specified remote sources. The source can be in one of two forms: a file name on the remote host if

the host has already been specified or a string of the following form to specify both a host and file name at the same time.

`host:filename`

If you use the latter form, the last host specified becomes the default for future transfers. When using the `get` command to transfer multiple files from a remote host, you must specify three or more files. If you specify two files, the second file is used as a local file.

quit
: Exit `tftp`. An end-of-file also exits.

verbose
: Toggle verbose mode.

trace
: Toggle packet tracing.

status
: Show current status.

rexmt *retransmission-timeout*
: Set the per-packet retransmission timeout in seconds.

timeout *total-transmission-timeout*
: Set the total transmission timeout in seconds.

ascii
: Shorthand for `mode ascii`.

binary
: Shorthand for `mode binary`.

? [*command-name...*]
: Print help information.

Attributes

See `attributes`(5) for descriptions of the following attributes:

Attribute Type	Attribute Value
Availability	SUNWcsu

See Also

`attributes(5)`

time — Time a Simple Command

Synopsis

`/usr/bin/time [-p]` *command* [*argument...*]

Description

Use the time command to compute the time it takes a command to execute. time writes a message to standard error that lists timing statistics for *command* and the optional *arguments*. The message includes the following information.

- The elapsed (real) time between invocation of *command* and its termination.
- The user CPU time, equivalent to the sum of the tms_utime and tms_cutime fields returned by the times(2) function for the process in which *command* is executed.
- The system CPU time, equivalent to the sum of the tms_stime and tms_cstime fields returned by the times() function for the process in which *command* is executed.
- When time is used as part of a pipeline, the times reported are unspecified except when it is the sole command within a grouping command in that pipeline. For example, the following commands are unspecified.

  ```
  time a | b | c
  a | b | time c
  ```

- The following commands report on commands a and c.

  ```
  { time a } | b | c
  a | b | (time c)
  ```

Note — When you run the time command on a multiprocessor system, the total of the values printed for user and sys can exceed real because, on a multiprocessor system, it is possible to divide the task among the various processors.

When the command being timed is interrupted, the timing values displayed may not always be accurate.

Options

-p   Write the timing output to standard error in the following format.

real %f\nuser %f\nsys %f\n real-seconds, user-seconds, system-seconds

Operands

command   The name of the command to be invoked.

argument   Any string to be supplied as an argument when invoking *command*.

Usage

The time command returns exit status 127 if an error occurs so that applications can distinguish "failure to find a command" from "invoked command exited with an error indication." The value 127 was chosen because it is not commonly used for other meanings; most commands use small values for normal error conditions, and the values above 128 can be confused with termination because of receipt of a signal. The value 126 was chosen in a similar manner to indicate that the command could be found but not invoked.

Examples

If you want to apply time to pipelines or lists of commands, you can do so by putting pipelines and command lists in a single file. You can then invoke this file as a command, and the time applies to everything in the file.

Alternatively, you can use the following command to apply time to a complex command.

```
castle% time sh -c 'complex-command-line'
```

The following two examples show the differences between the csh version of time and the version in /usr/bin/time. These examples use the C shell.

```
castle# time find / -name core -print
/export/home/winsor/core
1.0u 13.0s 1:11 19% 0+0k 0+0io 0pf+0w
castle# /usr/bin/time find / -name core -print
/export/home/winsor/core

real        1:10.2
user           1.0
sys           13.5
castle#
```

See csh(1) for an explanation of the format of time output.

Environment Variables

See environ(5) for descriptions of the following environment variables that affect the execution of time: LC_CTYPE, LC_MESSAGES, LC_NUMERIC, NLSPATH, and PATH.

Exit Status

If *command* is invoked, the exit status of time is the exit status of *command*; otherwise, the time command exits with one of the following values.

1-125	An error occurred in the time command.
126	*command* was found but could not be invoked.
127	*command* could not be found.

Attributes

See attributes(5) for descriptions of the following attributes:

Attribute Type	Attribute Value
Availability	SUNWcsu

See Also

csh(1), shell_builtins(1), timex(1), times(2), attributes(5), environ(5)

Bugs

Elapsed time is accurate to the second, whereas the CPU times are measured to the 100th second. Thus, the sum of the CPU times can be up to a second larger than the elapsed time.

---

times — Shell Built-in Function to Report Time Use of the Current Shell

Synopsis

sh

times

ksh

*

times

Description

Bourne Shell

Print the accumulated user and system times for processes run from the shell.

Korn Shell

Print the accumulated user and system times for the shell and for processes run from the shell.

ksh(1) commands that are preceded by one or two asterisks (*) are treated specially in the following ways.

1. Variable assignment lists preceding the command remain in effect when the command completes.

2. I/O redirections are processed after variable assignments.

3. Errors abort a script that contains them.

4. Words following a command preceded by ** that are in the format of a

variable assignment are expanded with the same rules as a variable assignment. This means that tilde substitution is performed after the equal sign and that word splitting and file-name generation are not performed.

Attributes

See attributes(5) for descriptions of the following attributes:

Attribute Type	Attribute Value
Availability	SUNWcsu

See Also

ksh(1), sh(1), time(1), attributes(5)

timex — Time a Command; Report Process Data and System Activity

Synopsis

/usr/bin/timex [-o][-p [-fhkmrt]][-s] command

Description

The timex command, provided as part of the sar package, provides better diagnostic information than does the time command, especially for shell scripts that spawn child processes. By default, timex provides the same real, user, and sys times as the time command. In addition, it provides additional options to display the process accounting data (-p), the disk block use (-o), and total system activity data (-s) if the process accounting software is installed.

The timex command displays its results in seconds to standard error.

Note — Process records associated with *command* are selected from the accounting file /var/adm/pacct by inference because process genealogy is not available. Background processes having the same user ID, terminal ID, and execution time window are spuriously included.

Options

-o   Report the total number of blocks read or written and total characters transferred by *command* and all its children. This option works only if the process accounting software is installed.

-p   List process accounting records for *command* and all its children.
            This option works only if the process accounting software is
            installed. Suboptions f, h, k, m, r, and t modify the data items
            reported.

   -f   Print the fork(2) or exec(2) flag and system exit status
            columns in the output.

   -h   Instead of mean memory size, show the fraction of total
            available CPU time consumed by the process during its
            execution. This "hog factor" is computed as (total CPU
            time)/(elapsed time).

   -k   Instead of memory size, show total kcore minutes.

   -m   Show mean core size (the default).

   -r   Show CPU factor (user time/(system time + user time).

   -t   Show separate system and user CPU times. Always
            report the number of blocks read or written and the
            number of characters transferred.

-s   Report total system activity (not just that because of *command*) that
            occurred during the execution interval of *command*. Report all the
            data items listed in sar(1).

Examples

The following is a simple example of using timex.

```
castle% timex -ops sleep 60
```

The following example measures a terminal session of arbitrary complexity
by timing a subshell.

```
castle% timex -opskmt sh
session commands
EOT
```

Attributes

See attributes(5) for descriptions of the following attributes:

Attribute Type	Attribute Value
Availability	SUNWaccu

See Also

sar(1), time(1), times(2), attributes(5)

tip — Connect to Remote System

Synopsis

```
/usr/bin/tip [-v][-speed-entry] {hostname | phone-number | device}
```

Description

Use the tip command to establish a full-duplex terminal connection to a remote host. Once you establish the connection, a remote session using tip behaves like an interactive session on a local terminal.

The /etc/remote file contains entries describing remote systems and line speeds used by tip.

Each host has a default baud rate for the connection or you can specify a speed with the -speed-entry command-line argument.

When you specify phone-number, tip looks in the remote file for an entry of the following form.

```
tip -speed-entry
```

When it finds such an entry, tip sets the connection speed accordingly. If it finds no such entry, tip interprets -speed-entry as if it is a system name, resulting in an error message.

If you omit -speed-entry, tip uses the tip0 entry to set a speed for the connection.

When you specify device, tip tries to open that device but does so using the access privileges of the user instead of the usual tip access privileges (setuid uucp). You must have read/write access to the device. The tip command interprets any character string beginning with the slash character (/) as a device name.

When establishing the connection, tip sends a connection message to the remote system. You can find the default value for this message in the remote file.

When tip tries to connect to a remote system, it opens the associated device with an exclusive-open ioctl(2) call. Thus, only one user at a time can access a device. This restriction prevents multiple processes from sampling the terminal line. In addition, tip honors the locking protocol used by uucp(1C).

When tip starts up, it reads commands from the .tiprc file in your home directory.

Options

-v   Display commands from the .tiprc file as they are executed.

Usage

Typed characters are normally transmitted directly to the remote system (which also does the echoing).

Any time that `tip` prompts for an argument (for example, during setup of a file transfer) you can edit the typed line with the standard erase and kill characters. A `null` line in response to a prompt or an interrupt aborts the dialogue and returns you to the remote system.

Commands

A tilde (~) as the first character of a line acts as an escape signal that directs `tip` to perform some special action. `tip` recognizes the following escape sequences.

~^D ~.	Drop the connection and exit (you may still be logged in on the remote system).
~c [*name*]	Change directory to *name*. (No argument implies change to your home directory.)
~!	Escape to an interactive shell on the local system. (Exiting the shell returns you to `tip`.)
~>	Copy file from local to remote.
~<	Copy file from remote to local.
~p *from* [*to*]	Send a file to a remote host running the UNIX system. When you use the `put` command, the remote system runs the command string `cat > ` *to* while `tip` sends it the *from* file. If you do not specify the *to* file, use the *from* file name. This command is actually a UNIX-system-specific version of the ~> command.
~t *from* [*to*]	Take a file from a remote host running the UNIX system. As in the `put` command, the *to* file defaults to the *from* file name if you do not specify it. The remote host executes the command string `cat ` *from*`; echo ^A` to send the file to `tip`.
~|	Pipe the output from a remote command to a local process. The shell processes the command string sent to the local system.
~C	Connect a program to the remote system. The shell processes the command string sent to the program. The program inherits file descriptors 0 as remote line input, 1 as remote line output, and 2 as `tty` standard error.
~$	Pipe the output from a local process to the remote host. The shell processes the command string sent to the local system.
~#	Send a BREAK to the remote system.
~s	Set a variable (see the discussion below).

~^Z	Stop tip (only available when run under a shell, such as the C shell, that supports job control).
~^Y	Stop only the "local side" of tip (only available when run under a shell, such as the C shell, that supports job control); leave running the "remote side" of tip, the side that displays output from the remote host.
~?	Get a summary of the tilde escapes.

Copying files requires some cooperation on the part of the remote host. When you use a ~> or ~< escape to send a file, tip prompts for a file name (to be transmitted or received) and a command to be sent to the remote system in case the file is being transferred from the remote system. While tip is transferring a file, the number of lines transferred is continuously displayed on the screen. You can abort a file transfer with an interrupt.

Auto-Call Units

You can use tip to dial up remote systems using a number of auto-call units (ACUs). When the remote system description contains the du capability, tip uses the call unit (cu), ACU type (at), and phone numbers (pn) supplied. Normally, tip displays verbose messages as it dials.

Depending on the type of auto-dialer being used to establish a connection, the remote host can have garbage characters sent to it on connection. You should never assume that the first characters typed to the foreign host are the first ones presented to it. The recommended practice is to immediately type a kill character on establishing a connection (most UNIX systems support either @ or Control-U as the initial kill character).

tip currently supports the Ventel MD-212+ and DC Hayes-compatible modems.

When tip initializes a Hayes-compatible modem for dialing, it sets the modem to auto-answer. Normally, after the conversation is complete, tip drops DTR, which hangs up the modem.

Most modems can be configured so that when DTR drops, they reinitialize themselves to a preprogrammed state. You can use this feature to reset the modem and disable auto-answer.

Additionally, it is possible to start the phone number with a Hayes S command so that you can configure the modem before dialing. For example, to disable auto-answer, set up all the phone numbers in /etc/remote by using something like pn=S0=0DT5551212. The S0=0 disables auto-answer.

Remote Host Description

Descriptions of remote hosts are normally located in the systemwide file /etc/remote. However, you can maintain personal description files (and phone numbers) by defining and exporting the REMOTE shell variable. The remote file must be readable by tip, but you can maintain a secondary file describing phone numbers readable only by you. This secondary phone number file is /etc/phones unless the shell variable PHONES is defined and exported. The phone number file contains lines of the following form.

```
system-name phone-number
```

Each phone number found for a system is tried until either a connection is established or an end-of-file is reached. Phone numbers are constructed from 0123456789-=*, where the = and * indicate to wait for a second dial tone (ACU dependent).

tip Internal Variables

tip maintains a set of variables that are used in normal operation. Some of these variables are read-only to normal users (root is allowed to change anything of interest). You can display and set variables with the ~s escape. The syntax for variables is patterned after vi(1) and mail(1). Supplying all as an argument to the ~s escape displays all variables that you can read. Alternatively, you can request display of a particular variable by attaching a ? to the end. For example, ~s escape? displays the current escape character.

Variables are numeric (num), string (str), character (char), or Boolean (bool) values. You set Boolean variables merely by specifying their name. You can reset them by prepending a ! to the name. You set other variable types by appending an = and the value. The entire assignment must not have any blanks in it. You can use a single set command to interrogate as well as to set a number of variables.

Variables can be initialized at runtime by putting set commands (without the ~s prefix) in a .tiprc file in your home directory. The -v option displays the sets as they are made. You can precede comments in the .tiprc file with a #.

Finally, you must either completely specify the variable names or use an abbreviation. The following list details those variables known to tip.

beautify	(bool) Discard unprintable characters when a session is being scripted; abbreviated be. If the nb capability is present, initially set beautify to off; otherwise, initially set beautify to on.
baudrate	(num) The baud rate at which the connection was established; abbreviated ba. If you specified a baud rate on the command line, initially set baudrate to the specified value; otherwise, if the br capability is present, initially set baudrate to the value of that capability; otherwise, set baudrate to 300 baud. Once tip has been started, only superuser can change baudrate.
dialtimeout	(num) When dialing a phone number, the time (in seconds) to wait for a connection to be established; abbreviated dial. Initially set dialtimeout to 60 seconds. Only superuser can change this value.
disconnect	(str) The string to send to the remote host to disconnect from it; abbreviated di. If the di capability is present, initially set disconnect to the value of that capability; otherwise, set disconnect to a null string ("").

echocheck (bool) Synchronize with the remote host during file transfer by waiting for the echo of the last character transmitted; abbreviated ec. If the ec capability is present, initially set echocheck to on; otherwise, initially set echocheck to off.

eofread (str) The set of characters that signify an end-of-transmission during a ~< file transfer command; abbreviated eofr. If the ie capability is present, initially set eofread to the value of that capability; otherwise, set eofread to a null string (" ").

eofwrite (str) The string sent to indicate end-of-transmission during a ~> file transfer command; abbreviated eofw. If the oe capability is present, initially set eofread to the value of that capability; otherwise, set eofread to a null string (" ").

eol (str) The set of characters that indicate an end-of-line. tip recognizes escape characters only after an end-of-line. If the el capability is present, initially set eol to the value of that capability; otherwise, set eol to a null string (" ").

escape (char) The command prefix (escape) character; abbreviated es. If the es capability is present, initially set escape to the value of that capability; otherwise, set escape to ~.

etimeout (num) The amount of time, in seconds, that tip should wait for the echo-check response when echocheck is set; abbreviated et. If the et capability is present, initially set etimeout to the value of that capability; otherwise, set etimeout to 10 seconds.

exceptions (str) The set of characters that should not be discarded because of the beautification switch; abbreviated ex. If the ex capability is present, initially set exceptions to the value of that capability; otherwise, set exceptions to \t\n\f\b.

force (char) The character used to force literal data transmission; abbreviated fo. If the fo capability is present, initially set force to the value of that capability; otherwise, set force to \377 (which disables it).

framesize (num) The amount of data (in bytes) to buffer between file-system writes when receiving files; abbreviated fr. If the fs capability is present, initially set framesize to the value of that capability; otherwise, set framesize to 1024.

halfduplex (bool) Do local echoing because the host is halfduplex; abbreviated hdx. If the hd capability is present, initially set halfduplex to on; otherwise, initially set halfduplex to off.

hardwareflow

(bool) Do hardware flow control; abbreviated hf. If the hf capability is present, initially set hardwareflow to on; otherwise, initially set hardwareflow to off.

host	(str) The name of the host to which you are connected; abbreviated ho. Set host permanently to the name given on the command line or in the HOST environment variable.
localecho	(bool) A synonym for halfduplex; abbreviated le.
log	(str) The name of the file used to log information about outgoing phone calls. Initially set log to /var/adm/aculog. log can be inspected or changed only by superuser.
parity	(str) The parity to be generated and checked when talking to the remote host; abbreviated par. The possible values are:

none> zero	Parity is not checked on input and the parity bit is set to 0 on output.
one	Parity is not checked on input and the parity bit is set to 1 on output.
even	Even parity is checked for on input and generated on output.
odd	Odd parity is checked for on input and generated on output.

If the pa capability is present, initially set parity to the value of that capability; otherwise, set parity to none.

phones	The file used to find hidden phone numbers. If the environment variable PHONES is set, set phones to the value of PHONES; otherwise, set phones to /etc/phones. You cannot change the value of phones from within tip.
prompt	(char) The character that indicates an end-of-line on the remote host; abbreviated pr. Use this value to synchronize during data transfers. The count of lines transferred during a file transfer command is based on receipt of this character. If the pr capability is present, initially set prompt to the value of that capability; otherwise, set prompt to \n.
raise	(bool) Uppercase mapping mode; abbreviated ra. When this mode is enabled, map all lowercase letters to upper case for transmission to the remote system. If the ra capability is present, initially set raise to on; otherwise, initially set raise to off.
raisechar	(char) The input character used to toggle uppercase mapping mode; abbreviated rc. If the rc capability is present, initially set raisechar to the value of that capability; otherwise, set raisechar to \377 (which disables it).
rawftp	(bool) Send all characters during file transfers; do not filter nonprintable characters, and do not do translations like \n to \r. Abbreviated raw. If the rw capability is present, initially set rawftp to on; otherwise, initially set rawftp to off.

record (str) The name of the file used to record a session script; abbreviated `rec`. If the `re` capability is present, initially set `record` to the value of that capability; otherwise, set `record` to `tip.record`.

remote The file used to find descriptions of remote systems. If the environment variable `REMOTE` is set, set `remote` to the value of `REMOTE`; otherwise, set `remote` to `/etc/remote`. You cannot change the value of `remote` from within `tip`.

script (bool) Session scripting mode; abbreviated `sc`. When `script` is on, record everything transmitted by the remote system in the script record file specified in `record`. If the `beautify` switch is on, include only printable ASCII characters in the script file (those characters between `040` and `0177`). Use the variable `exceptions` to indicate characters that are an exception to the normal beautification rules. If the `sc` capability is present, initially set `script` to on; otherwise, initially set `script` to off.

tabexpand (bool) Expand Tab characters to space characters during file transfers; abbreviated `tab`. When `tabexpand` is on, expand each Tab to eight space characters. If the `tb` capability is present, initially set `tabexpand` to on; otherwise, initially set `tabexpand` to off.

tandem (bool) Use XON/XOFF flow control to limit the rate that data is sent by the remote host; abbreviated `ta`. If the `nt` capability is present, initially set `tandem` to off; otherwise, initially set `tandem` to on.

verbose (bool) Verbose mode; abbreviated `verb`; When `verbose` mode is enabled, print messages while dialing, show the current number of lines transferred during a file transfer operations, and more. If the `nv` capability is present, initially set `verbose` to off; otherwise, initially set `verbose` to on.

SHELL (str) The name of the shell to use for the `~!` command; default value is `/bin/sh`; otherwise, take the value from the environment.

HOME (str) The home directory to use for the `~c` command; take the default value from the environment.

Examples

The following example shows the dialog used to transfer files.

```
castle% tip monet
[connected]
...(assume we are talking to a UNIX system)...
ucbmonet login: sam
Password:
monet% cat > sylvester.c
~> Filename: sylvester.c
32 lines transferred in 1 minute 3 seconds
monet%
monet% ~< Filename: reply.c
List command for remote host: cat reply.c
65 lines transferred in 2 minutes
```

```
monet%
...(or, equivalently)...
monet% ~p sylvester.c
...(actually echoes as ~[put] sylvester.c)...
32 lines transferred in 1 minute 3 seconds
monet%
monet% ~t reply.c
...(actually echoes as ~[take] reply.c)...
65 lines transferred in 2 minutes
monet%
...(to print a file locally)...
monet% ~|Local command: pr -h sylvester.c | lpr
List command for remote host: cat sylvester.c
monet% ~^D
[EOT]
...(back on the local system)...
```

Environment Variables

The following environment variables are read by `tip`.

REMOTE	The location of the `remote` file.
PHONES	The location of the file containing private phone numbers.
HOST	A default host to connect to.
HOME	User's login directory (for `chdir`s).
SHELL	The shell to fork on a ~! escape.

Files

`/etc/phones`

`/etc/remote`

`/var/spool/locks/LCK ..*`

> Lock file to avoid conflicts with UUCP.

`/var/adm/aculog`

> File used to log outgoing calls.

`~/.tiprc`   Initialization file.

Attributes

See `attributes`(5) for descriptions of the following attributes:

Attribute Type	Attribute Value
Availability	SUNWcsu

See Also

    mail(1), vi(1), cu(1C), uucp(1C), ioctl(2), attributes(5)

Bugs

Two additional variables, chardelay and linedelay, are currently not
implemented.

tnfdump — Convert Binary Trace Normal Form (TNF) File to ASCII

Synopsis

    /usr/bin/tnfdump [-r] tnf-file...

Description

Use the tnfdump command to convert the specified binary Trace Normal Form
(TNF) trace files to ASCII. You can use the ASCII output to do performance
analysis. The default mode (without the -r option) prints all the event records
(that were generated by TNF_PROBE(3X)) and the event descriptor records only.
It also orders the events by time.

Options

    -r   Do a raw conversion of TNF to ASCII. Translate the output as a
literal translation of the binary TNF file and include all the
records in the file. This output is useful only if you have a good
understanding of TNF.

Examples

The following example converts the file /tmp/trace-2130 into ASCII use. The
output uses very long lines; they are wrapped in this example.

```
castle% tnfdump /tmp/trace-2130
probe      tnf_name: "inloop" tnf_string: "keys cookie main loop;file
   cookie2.c;line 50;sunw%debug in the loop"
probe      tnf_name: "end" tnf_string: "keys cookie main end;file
   cookie2.c;line 41;sunw%debug exiting program"
--------------- ---------------- ----- ----- ---------- ---
Elapsed (ms)      Delta (ms)   PID LWPID    TID    CPU Probe Name
   Data / Description . . .
------ --- ------------------------ ------------------------
0.000000        0.000000  8792    1     0       -    inloop
   loop_count: 0 total_iterations:  0
0.339000        0.339000  8792    1     0       -    inloop
   loop_count: 1 total_iterations:  1
0.350500        0.011500  8792    1     0       -    inloop
```

```
    loop_count: 2 total_iterations: 2
0.359500          0.009000 8792     1      0          -   inloop
    loop_count: 3 total_iterations: 3
0.369500          0.010000 8792     1      0          -   inloop
    loop_count: 4 total_iterations: 4
        7775.969500      7775.600000 8792   1      0          -   inloop
    loop_count: 0 total_iterations: 5
        7776.016000      0.046500 8792   1      0          -   inloop
    loop_count: 1 total_iterations: 6
        7776.025000      0.009000 8792   1      0          -   inloop
    loop_count: 2 total_iterations: 7
        7776.034000      0.009000 8792   1      0          -   inloop
    loop_count: 3 total_iterations: 8
        7776.043000      0.009000 8792   1      0          -   inloop
    loop_count: 4 total_iterations: 9
        7776.052000      0.009000 8792   1      0          -   inloop
    loop_count: 5 total_iterations: 10
        7776.061000      0.009000 8792   1      0          -   inloop
    loop_count: 6 total_iterations: 11
        9475.979500      1699.918500 8792   1      0          -   end
    node_struct: { type: node_tnf cur_sum: 9

    max_cnt: 12 }
```

A description is included for all probes that are encountered during execution. The description is one per line prefixed by the keyword `probe`. The name of the probe is in double quotes after the keyword `tnf_name`. The description of this probe is in double quotes after the keyword `tnf_string`.

A heading is printed after all the descriptions of the probes are printed. The first column shows the elapsed time in milliseconds since the first event. The second column shows the elapsed time in milliseconds since the previous event. The next four columns are the process ID, LWP ID, thread ID, and CPU number. The next column is the name of the probe that generated this event. You can match the probe name to the probe description explained above. The last column is the data that the event contains, formatted as `arg_name_n` (see TNF_PROBE(3X)) followed by a colon and the value of that argument. The format of the value depends on its type. `tnf_opaque` arguments are printed in hexadecimal, all other integers are printed in decimal, strings are printed in double quotes, and user-defined records are enclosed in braces { }. The first field of a user-defined record indicates its TNF type (see TNF_DECLARE_RECORD(3X)), and the rest of the fields are the members of the record.

A – in any column indicates that there is no data for that particular column.

The following example does a raw conversion of the file `/tmp/trace-4000` into ASCII.

```
castle% tnfdump -r /tmp/trace-4000
0x10e00    : {
tnf_tag 0x109c0      tnf_block_header
      generation 1
    bytes_valid 320
        A_lock 0
```

```
            B_lock 0
        next_block 0x0
}
0x10e10    : {
tnf_tag 0x10010    probe1
     tnf_tag_arg 0x10e24     <tnf_sched_rec>
      time_delta 128
      test_ulong 4294967295
       test_long -1
}

0x10e24    : {
tnf_tag 0x10cf4    tnf_sched_rec
             tid 0
           lwpid 1
             pid 13568
       time_base 277077875828500
}
0x10e3c    : {
tnf_tag 0x11010    probe2
     tnf_tag_arg 0x10e24     <tnf_sched_rec>
      time_delta 735500
        test_str 0x10e48     "string1"
}
0x10e48    : {
tnf_tag 0x1072c    tnf_string
   tnf_self_size 16
           chars "string1"
}
    0x10e58    : {
        tnf_tag 0x110ec     probe3
     tnf_tag_arg 0x10e24     <tnf_sched_rec>
      time_delta 868000
   test_ulonglong 18446744073709551615
   test_longlong -1
      test_float 3.142857
}
    ...
    ...
    ...
    0x110ec    : {
        tnf_tag 0x10030     tnf_probe_type
   tnf_tag_code 42
        tnf_name 0x1110c      "probe3"
  tnf_properties 0x1111c     <tnf_properties>
  tnf_slot_types 0x11130     <tnf_slot_types>
   tnf_type_size 32
  tnf_slot_names 0x111c4     <tnf_slot_names>
     tnf_string 0x11268      "keys targdebug main;file targdebug.c;line
   61;"
}
    0x1110c    : {
        tnf_tag 0x10068     tnf_name
   tnf_self_size 16
```

```
            chars "probe3"
   }
       0x1111c   : {
             tnf_tag 0x100b4      tnf_properties
       tnf_self_size 20
                   0 0x101a0      tnf_tagged
                   1 0x101c4      tnf_struct
                   2 0x10b84      tnf_tag_arg
   }
       0x11130   : {
             tnf_tag 0x10210      tnf_slot_types
       tnf_self_size 28
                   0 0x10bd0      tnf_probe_event
                   1 0x10c20      tnf_time_delta
                   2 0x1114c      tnf_uint64
                   3 0x10d54      tnf_int64
                   4 0x11188      tnf_float32
   }
```

The first number is the file offset of the record. The record is enclosed in braces { }. The first column in a record is the slot name (for records whose fields do not have names, it is the type name). The second column in the record is the value of that slot if it is a scalar (only scalars that are of type tnf_opaque are printed in hexadecimal) or the offset of the record if it is a reference to another record.

The third column in a record is optional. It does not exist for scalar slots of records. If it exists, the third column is a type name with or without angle brackets or a string in double quotes. Unadorned names indicate a reference to the named metatag record (that is, a reference to a record with that name in the tnf_name field). Type names in angle brackets indicate a reference to a record that is an instance of that type (that is, a reference to a record with that name in the tnf_tag field). The content of strings are printed in double quotes at the reference site.

For records that are arrays, their array elements follow the header slots and are numbered 0, 1, 2,..., except strings where the string is written as the chars (pseudonym) slot.

For records that are events (generated by TNF_PROBE(3X)), the second field has a slot name of tnf_tag_arg, which is a reference to the schedule record. Schedule records describe more information about the event, such as the thread ID, process ID, and the time_base. You can add the time_delta of an event to the time_base of the schedule record of that event reference to give an absolute time. This time is expressed as nanoseconds since some arbitrary time in the past (see gethrtime(3C)).

Exit Status

tnfdump returns 0 on successful exit.

Attributes

See `attributes`(5) for descriptions of the following attributes:

Attribute Type	**Attribute Value**
Availability	SUNWtnfd

See Also

`prex(1)`, `gethrtime(3C)`, `TNF_DECLARE_RECORD(3X)`, `TNF_PROBE(3X)`,
`tnf_process_disable(3X)`, `attributes(5)`

---

tnfxtract — Extract Kernel Probes Output into a Trace File

Synopsis

`/usr/bin/tnfxtract [-d dumpfile -n namelist] tnf_file`

Description

The `tnfxtract` command collects kernel trace output from an in-core buffer in the Solaris kernel or from the memory image of a crashed system and generates a binary Trace Normal Form (TNF) trace file like those produced directly by user programs being traced.

You must specify both or neither of the `-d` and `-n` options. If you specify neither, trace output is extracted from the running kernel. If you specify both, the `-d` argument names the file containing the (crashed) system memory image, and the `-n` argument names the file containing the symbol table for the system memory image.

The TNF trace file produced is exactly the same size as the in-core buffer; it is essentially a snapshot of that buffer. It is legal to run `tnfxtract` while kernel tracing is active, that is, while the in-core buffer is being written. `tnfxtract` ensures that the output file it generates is low-level consistent, that is, that only whole probes are written out and that internal data structures in the buffer are not corrupted because the buffer is being concurrently written.

The TNF trace file generated is suitable as input to `tnfdump(1)`, which generates an ASCII file.

Options

`-d dumpfile`

        Use `dumpfile` as the system memory image, instead of the running kernel image. The `dumpfile` is normally the path name of a file generated by the `savecore` command.

-n *namelist*

> Use *namelist* as the file containing the symbol table information for the given *dumpfile*.

Operands

tnf-file   Specify the output file generated by tnfxtract based on kernel trace output from an in-core buffer in the Solaris kernel.

Examples

The following example probes from the running kernel into ktrace.out.

```
castle% tnfxtract ktrace.out
```

The following example probes from a kernel crash dump into ktrace.out.

```
castle%tnfxtract-d/var/crash/`uname-n`/vmcore.0-n/var/crash/`uname
    -n`/unix.0 ktrace.out
```

Exit Status

0   Successful completion.

>0   An error occurred.

Attributes

See attributes(5) for descriptions of the following attributes:

Attribute Type	Attribute Value
Availability	SUNWtnfc

See Also

prex(1), tnfdump(1), savecore(1M), tnf_kernel_probes(4), attributes(5)

touch — Change File Access and Modification Times

Synopsis

```
/usr/bin/touch [-acm] [-r ref-file | -t time] file...
/usr/bin/touch [-acm] date-time] file...
/usr/bin/settime [-f ref-file] file...
```

New!

Description

Use the `touch` command to change access and modification times of files. If the file does not already exist, it is created.

You can specify the time used by `-t time`, by the corresponding time fields of the file referenced by `-r ref-file`, or by the `date-time` operand. If you specify none of these options, `touch` uses the current time (the value returned by the `time(2)` function).

If you specify neither the `-a` nor `-m` options, `touch` updates both the modification and access times.

New! The `settime` command is equivalent to `touch -c`.

Note — Users familiar with the BSD environment should note that, for the `touch` command, the `-f` option is accepted but ignored. The `-f` option is not needed because `touch` succeeds for all files owned by the user regardless of the permissions on the files.

Options

The `touch` command has the following options.

-a
: Change the access time of `file`. Do not change the modification time unless you also specify `-m`.

-c
: Do not create a specified file if it does not exist. Do not write any diagnostic messages concerning this condition.

-m
: Change the modification time of `file`. Do not change the access time unless you also specify `-a`.

-r ref-file
: Use the corresponding times of an existing file named by `ref-file` instead of the current time.

-t time
: Use the specified time instead of the current time. `time` is a decimal number of the form `[[CC]YY]MMDDhhmm[.SS]`, where each two-digit pair represents the following:

  MM
  : The month of the year [01-12].

  DD
  : The day of the month [01-31].

  hh
  : The hour of the day [00-23].

  mm
  : The minute of the hour [00-59].

  CC
  : The first two digits of the year.

  YY
  : The second two digits of the year.

  SS
  : The second of the minute [00-61].

  The range for *SS* is [00-61] instead of [00-59] because of leap seconds. If *SS* is 60 or 61 and the resulting time, as affected by the TZ environment variable, does not refer to a leap second, the resulting time is one or two seconds after a time where *SS* is 59. If you do not specify *SS*, assume it is 0.

Both *CC* and *YY* are optional. If you specify neither, assume the current year. If you specify *YY* but not *CC*, derive it as follows.

If *YY* is: *CC* becomes:

69-99   19

00-38   20

39-68   ERROR

The resulting time is affected by the value of the TZ environment variable. If the resulting time value precedes the Epoch, exit immediately with an error status. The range of valid times is the Epoch to January 18, 2038.

The settime command can use the optional -f *ref-time* option to reference the corresponding times from an existing file.

New!

Operands

file   A path name of a file whose times are to be modified.

date-time Use the specified *date-time* instead of the current time. *date-time* is a decimal number of the following form.

MMDDhhmm[*YY*]

where each two-digit pair represents the following:

MM   The month of the year [01-12].

DD   The day of the month [01-31].

hh   The hour of the day [00-23].

mm   The minute of the hour [00-59].

YY   The second two digits of the year.

             YY is optional. If you omit it , assume the current year. If you specify *YY*, derive the year as follows.

YY	Corresponding Year
69-99	1969-1999
00-38	2000-2038
39-68	ERROR

If you specify no -f option, no -t option, at least two operands, and the first operand is an 8- or 10-digit decimal integer, assume the first operand is a *date-time* operand; otherwise, assume the first operand is a *file* operand.

Examples

The following example shows the modification time for the file kookaburra-1 and changes the access and modification times to the current date and time.

```
castle% ls -l kookaburra-1
-rw-r--r--   1 winsor    staff        264 Feb 20 16:12 kookaburra-1
castle% touch kookaburra-1
castle% ls -l kookaburra-1
-rw-r--r--   1 winsor    staff        264 Apr  9 13:59 kookaburra-1
castle%
```

Usage

See largefile(5) for the description of the behavior of touch when encountering files greater than or equal to 2 Gbytes (2**31 bytes).

Environment Variables

See environ(5) for descriptions of the following environment variables that affect the execution of touch: LC_MESSAGES, NLSPATH, and TZ.

Exit Status

0	touch executed successfully and all requested changes were made.
>0	An error occurred. touch returns the number of files for which it could not successfully modify the times.

Attributes

See attributes(5) for descriptions of the following attributes:

Attribute Type	Attribute Value
Availability	SUNWcsu
CSI	Enabled

See Also

time(2), attributes(5), environ(5), largefile(5)

tplot, t300, t300s, t4014, t450, tek, ver — Graphics Filters for Terminal Output of Various Plotters

Synopsis

```
/usr/bin/tplot [-Tterminal]
```

Description

The `tplot` command reads plotting instructions from the standard input and produces plotting instructions suitable for a particular terminal on the standard output.

If you specify no terminal, the environment variable TERM is used. The default terminal is `tek`.

Environment Variables

Except for `ver`, you can use the following terminal types with `lpr -g` (see `lpr(1B)`) to produce plotted output.

`300`	DASI 300 or GSI terminal (Diablo® mechanism).
`300s` | `300S`	DASI 300s terminal (Diablo mechanism).
`450`	DASI Hyterm 450 terminal (Diablo mechanism).
`4014` | `tek`	Tektronix® 4014 and 4015 storage scope with Enhanced Graphics Module. (Use 4013 for Tektronix 4014 or 4015 without the Enhanced Graphics Module).
`ver`	Versatec® D1200A printer-plotter. The output is scan-converted and suitable input to `lpr -v`.

Files

```
/usr/lib/t300
/usr/lib/t300s
/usr/lib/t4014
/usr/lib/t450
/usr/lib/tek
/usr/lib/vplot
```

Attributes

See `attributes(5)` for descriptions of the following attributes:

Attribute Type	Attribute Value
Availability	SUNWcsu

See Also

`lp(1)`, `vi(1)`, `attributes(5)`

tput — Initialize a Terminal or Query terminfo Database

Synopsis

```
/usr/bin/tput [-Ttype] capname [parm...]
/usr/bin/tput -S <<
```

Description

The tput command uses the terminfo database to make the values of terminal-dependent capabilities and information available to the shell (see sh(1)); to clear, initialize, or reset the terminal; or to return the long name of the requested terminal type. tput outputs a string if the capability attribute (*capname*) is of type string or outputs an integer if the attribute is of type integer. If the attribute is of type boolean, tput simply sets the exit status (0 for true if the terminal has the capability, 1 for false if it does not) and produces no output. Before using a value returned on standard output, you should test the exit status to be sure it is 0 ($?, see sh(1)).

Options

-T*type* Indicate the type of terminal. Normally, you do not need to use this option because the default is taken from the environment variable TERM. If you specify -T, then do not reference the shell variables LINES and COLUMNS and the layer size.

-S Allow more than one capability per invocation of tput. You must pass the capabilities to tput from the standard input instead of from the command line. Only one *capname* is allowed per line. The -S option changes the meaning of the 0 and 1 Boolean and string exit statuses.

Operands

capname Indicate the capability attribute from the terminfo database. See terminfo(4) for a complete list of capabilities and the *capname* associated with each. The following strings are supported as operands by the implementation in the C locale.

clear Display the clear-screen sequence.

init If the terminfo database is present and an entry for your terminal exists (see -T*type*), the following occurs.

- If present, output the terminal's initialization strings (is1, is2, is3, if, iprog).

- Set any delays (for instance, newline) specified in the entry in the tty driver,

- Turn on or off Tabs expansion according to the specification in the entry.

- If Tabs are not expanded, set standard Tabs (every 8 spaces).

If an entry does not contain the information needed for any of the above four activities, silently skip that activity.

reset   Instead of putting out initialization strings, output the terminal's reset strings if present (rs1, rs2, rs3, rf). If the reset strings are not present but initialization strings are, output the initialization strings. Otherwise, reset acts identically to init.

longname   If the terminfo database is present and an entry for your terminal exists (see -Ttype), then output the long name of the terminal. The long name is the last name in the first line of the terminal description in the terminfo database (see term(5)).

parm   If the attribute is a string that takes parameters, instantiate the parm argument into the string. Pass an all-numeric argument to the attribute as a number.

Examples

The following example initializes the terminal according to the type of terminal in the environment variable TERM.

```
castle% tput init
castle%
```

This command should be included in everyone's .profile after the environment variable TERM has been exported, as illustrated in the profile(4) manual page.

The following example resets an AT&T 5620 terminal, overriding the type of terminal in the environment variable TERM.

```
castle% tput -T5620 reset
castle%
```

The following example sends the sequence to move the cursor to row 0, column 0 (the upper-left corner of the screen, usually known as the home cursor position).

```
castle% tput cup 0 0
castle%
```

The following example echoes the clear-screen sequence for the current terminal.

```
castle% tput clear
castle%
```

The following example prints the number of columns for the current terminal.

```
castle% tput cols
94
castle%
```

The following example prints the number of columns for the 450 terminal.

```
castle% tput -T450 cols
132
castle%
```

The following example sets the shell variables bold (to begin standout mode sequence) and offbold (to end standout mode sequence) for the current terminal, followed by a prompt.

```
$ bold=`tput smso`
$ offbold=`tput rmso`
$ echo "${bold}Please type your name: ${offbold}\c"
```

The following example sets the exit status to indicate whether the current terminal is a hardcopy terminal.

```
castle% tput hc
castle%
```

The following example sends the sequence to move the cursor to row 23, column 4.

```
castle% tput cup 23 4
castle%
```

The following example prints the long name from the terminfo database for the type of terminal specified in the environment variable TERM.

```
castle% tput longname
CDE terminal emulator
castle%
```

The following example shows tput processing several capabilities in one invocation. It clears the screen, moves the cursor to position 10, 10, and turns on bold (extra bright) mode. Terminate the list with an exclamation mark (!) on a line by itself.

```
$ tput -S <<!
> clear
> cup 10 10
> bold
> !
$
```

Environment Variables

See environ(5) for descriptions of the following environment variables that affect the execution of tput: LC_CTYPE, LC_MESSAGES, and NLSPATH.

TERM	Determine the terminal type. If this variable is unset or null and if you did not specify the -T option, use an unspecified default terminal type.

Exit Status

0	If *capname* is of type boolean and you did not specify -S, return true.
	If *capname* is of type string and you did not specify -S, indicate *capname* is defined for this terminal type.
	If *capname* is of type boolean or string and you specified -S, indicate that all lines were successful.
	If *capname* is of type integer.
	If the requested string was written successfully.
1	If *capname* is of type boolean and you did not specify -S, return false.
	If *capname* is of type string and you did not specify -S, indicate that *capname* is not defined for this terminal type.
2	Usage error.
3	No information is available about the specified terminal type.
4	The specified operand is invalid.
>4	An error occurred.
-1	If *capname* is a numeric variable that is not specified in the terminfo database; for instance, tput -T450 lines and tput -T2621 xmc.

Files

/usr/include/curses.h	
	curses(3X) header.
/usr/include/term.h	
	terminfo header.
/usr/lib/tabset/*	
	Tab settings for some terminals in a format appropriate to be output to the terminal (escape sequences that set margins and Tabs); for more information, see the "Tabs and Initialization" section of terminfo(4).

```
/usr/share/lib/terminfo/?/*
```
Compiled terminal description database.

Attributes

See attributes(5) for descriptions of the following attributes:

Attribute Type	Attribute Value
Availability	SUNWcsu

See Also

clear(1), stty(1), tabs(1), profile(4), terminfo(4), attributes(5), environ(5)

tr — Translate Characters

Synopsis

```
/usr/bin/tr [-cs] string1 string2
/usr/bin/tr -s|-d [-c] string1
/usr/bin/tr -ds [-c] string1 string2
/usr/bin/xpg4/tr [-cs] string1 string2
/usr/bin/xpg4/tr -s|-d [-c] string1
/usr/bin/xpg4/tr -ds [-c] string1 string2
```

Description

Use the tr (translate) command to substitute one set of strings for another in a file or to remove specified characters from a file. The tr command is one of the few common UNIX commands that does not enable you to specify a file name as an argument. Instead, you must use the < redirection symbol.

The tr command can translate any number of characters. Usually, you give tr an input list of characters, specified as *string1*, followed by an output list of characters, specified as *string2*. tr replaces every instance of a character in *string1* with the corresponding character in *string2*.

The options specified and the *string1* and *string2* operands control translations that occur while copying characters and single-character collating elements.

> **Note** — Unlike some previous versions, the tr command correctly processes null characters in its input stream. You can strip null characters by using tr -d '\000'.

Options

-c	Complement the set of characters specified by *string1*.
-d	Delete all occurrences of input characters that are specified by *string1*.
-s	Replace instances of repeated characters with a single character.

When you do not specify the -d option:

- Each input character found in the array specified by *string1* is replaced by the character in the same relative position in the array specified by *string2*. When the array specified by *string2* is shorter that the one specified by *string1*, the results are unspecified.

- If you specify the -c option, the complements of the characters specified by *string1* (the set of all characters in the current character set, as defined by the current setting of LC_CTYPE, except for those actually specified in the *string1* operand) are placed in the array in ascending collation sequence as defined by the current setting of LC_COLLATE.

- Because the order in which characters specified by character class expressions or equivalence class expressions is undefined, you should only use such expressions if you intend to map several characters into one. An exception is case conversion, as described below.

When you specify the -d option:

- Input characters found in the array specified by *string1* are deleted.

- When you specify the -c option with -d, all characters except those specified by *string1* are deleted. The contents of *string2* are ignored unless you also specify the -s option.

- You cannot use the same string for both the -d and the -s options; when you specify both options, both *string1* (used for deletion) and *string2* (used for squeezing) are required.

- When you specify the -s option, then after any deletions or translations have taken place, repeated sequences of the same character are replaced by one occurrence of the same character if the character is found in the array specified by the last operand. If the last operand contains a character class, such as tr -s '[:space:]', the last operand's array contains all of the characters in that character class. However, in a case conversion, as described below, such as tr -s '[:upper:]' '[:lower:]', the last operand's array contains only those characters defined as the second characters in each of the toupper or tolower character pairs, as appropriate. (See toupper(3C) and tolower(3C)).

- An empty string used for *string1* or *string2* produces undefined results.

Operands

string1 *string2*	Translation control strings. Each string represents a set of characters to be converted into an array of characters used for the translation.

The operands *string1* and *string2* (if specified) define two arrays of characters. You can use the constructs in the following list to specify characters or single-character collating elements. If any of the constructs result in multicharacter collating elements, tr excludes, without a diagnostic, those multicharacter elements from the resulting array.

character	Any character not described by one of the conventions below represents itself.
octal	You can use octal sequences to represent characters with specific coded values. An octal sequence consists of a backslash followed by the longest sequence of one-, two- or three-octal-digit characters (01234567). The sequence puts the character whose encoding is represented by the one-, two- or three-digit octal integer into the array. Multibyte characters require multiple, concatenated escape sequences of this type, including the leading \\ for each byte.
character	

The backslash-escape sequences \\a, \\b, \\f, \\n, \\r, \\t, and \\v are supported. The results of using any character other than an octal digit following the backslash are unspecified.

c-c (/usr/xpg4/bin/tr) [*c-c*] (/usr/bin/tr)	

Specify the range of collating elements between the range endpoints, inclusive, as defined by the current setting of the LC_COLLATE locale category. The starting endpoint must precede the second endpoint in the current collation order. Put the characters or collating elements in the range in the array in ascending collation sequence.

[:*class*:]	Represent all characters belonging to the defined character *class*, as defined by the current setting of the LC_CTYPE locale category. The following character class names are accepted when specified in *string1*: alnum alpha blank cntrl digit graph lower print punct upper space xdigit.

In addition, character class expressions of the form [:*name*:] are recognized in those locales where the name keyword has been given a charclass definition in the LC_CTYPE category.

When you specify both the -d and -s options, any of the character class names are accepted in *string2*. Otherwise, only character class names lower or upper are valid in *string2* and then only if the corresponding character class upper and lower is specified in the same relative position in *string1*. Such a specification is interpreted as a request for case conversion. When

[:lower:] appears in *string1* and [:upper:] appears in *string2*, the arrays contain the characters from the toupper mapping in the LC_CTYPE category of the current locale. When [:upper:] appears in *string1* and [:lower:] appears in *string2*, the arrays contain the characters from the tolower mapping in the LC_CTYPE category of the current locale. The first character from each mapping pair is in the array for *string1*, and the second character from each mapping pair is in the array for *string2* in the same relative position.

Except for case conversion, the characters specified by a character class expression are placed in the array in an unspecified order.

If the name specified for *class* does not define a valid character class in the current locale, the behavior is undefined.

[=*equiv*=]   Represent all characters or collating elements belonging to the same equivalence class as *equiv*, as defined by the current setting of the LC_COLLATE locale category. An equivalence class expression is allowed only in *string1* or in *string2* when it is being used by the combined -d and -s options. Put the characters belonging to the equivalence class in the array in an unspecified order.

[*x**n]   Represent *n* repeated occurrences of the character *x*. Because this expression is used to map multiple characters to one character, it is valid only when it occurs in *string2*. If you omit *n* or it is 0, interpret it as large enough to extend the *string2*-based sequence to the length of the *string1*-based sequence. If *n* has a leading 0, interpret it as an octal value. Otherwise, interpret it as a decimal value.

Usage

See largefile(5) for the description of the behavior of tr when encountering files greater than or equal to 2 Gbytes (2**31 bytes).

Examples

The following example converts all colons in the passwd file to Tabs. Notice that you enclose the Tab character in single quotes to prevent the shell from treating it as white space. In this example, the Tab character is represented as the word Tab. When you type the command line, simply press the Tab key. Also notice that you use the < redirection symbol to specify the file name to use as input to the tr command.

```
castle% tr : 'Tab' < passwd
root     x     0     1     Super-User         /          /sbin/sh
daemon   x     1     1                /
bin      x     2     2                /usr/bin
sys      x     3     3                /
adm      x     4     4     Admin      /var/adm
lp       x     71    8     Line Printer Admin       /usr/spool/lp
uucp     x     5     5     uucp Admin       /usr/lib/uucp
nuucp    x     9     9     uucp Admin       /var/spool/uucppublic
```

```
      /usr/lib/uucp/uucico
listen  x       37      4       Network Admin    /usr/net/nls
nobody  x       60001   60001   Nobody   /
noaccess        x       60002   60002   No Access User   /
nobody4 x       65534   65534   SunOS 4.x Nobody         /
winsor  x       1001    10              /export/home/winsor     /bin/csh
ray     x       1002    10              /export/home/ray        /bin/csh
des     x       1003    10              /esport/home/des        /bin/csh
rob     x       1004    10              /export/home/rob        /bin/csh
castle%
```

The following example creates a list of all words in kookaburra-1, one per line, in kook.out, where a word is taken to be a maximal string of letters.

```
castle% tr -cs "[:alpha:]" "[\n*]" < kookaburra-1 > kook.out
castle% cat kook.out
Kookaburra
sits
in
the
old
gum
tree
Merry
merry
king
of
the
bush
is
he
...(More lines not shown here)
castle%
```

The following example translates all lowercase characters in file1 to upper case and writes the results to standard output.

```
castle% tr "[:lower:]" "[:upper:]" < kookaburra-1
KOOKABURRA SITS IN THE OLD GUM TREE
MERRY MERRY KING OF THE BUSH IS HE.
LAUGH, KOOKABURRA, LAUGH, KOOKABURRA
GAY YOUR LIFE MUST BE

KOOKABURRA SITS IN THE OLD GUM TREE
EATING ALL THE GUMDROPS HE CAN SEE.
STOP, KOOKABURRA, STOP, KOOKABURRA
LEAVE SOME THERE FOR ME.
castle%
```

> **Note** — The caveat expressed in the corresponding example in
> XPG3(5) is no longer in effect. This case conversion is now a special
> case that uses the `tolower` and `toupper` classifications, ensuring
> that proper mapping is accomplished when the locale is correctly
> defined.

The following example uses an equivalence class to identify accented
variants of the base character e in `file1`, which are stripped of diacritical
marks and written to `file2`.

```
castle% tr "[=e=]" e <file1 >file2
castle%
```

Environment Variables

See `environ`(5) for descriptions of the following environment variables that
affect the execution of `tr`: LC_COLLATE, LC_CTYPE, LC_MESSAGES, and
NLSPATH.

Exit Status

0	All input was processed successfully.
>0	An error occurred.

Attributes

See `attributes`(5) for descriptions of the following attributes:

/usr/bin/tr

Attribute Type	Attribute Value
Availability	SUNWcsu
CSI	Enabled

/usr/xpg4/bin/tr

Attribute Type	Attribute Value
Availability	SUNWxcu4
CSI	Enabled

See Also

ed(1), sed(1), sh(1), tolower(3C), toupper(3C), ascii(5), attributes(5),
environ(5), largefile(5), XPG4(5)

trap, onintr — Shell Built-in Functions to Respond to Hardware Signals

Synopsis

sh

```
trap [argument n [n2...]]
```

csh

```
onintr [-| label]
```

ksh

```
*
trap [arg sig [sig2...]]
```

Description

Use the built-in shell `trap` and `onintr` commands in shell scripts to specify a sequence of commands to be executed when your shell script receives an interrupt signal.

Bourne Shell

The `trap` command argument is read and executed when the shell receives numeric or symbolic signal(s) (*n*).

> **Note** — *argument* is scanned once when the trap is set and once when the trap is taken.

Trap commands are executed in order of signal number or corresponding symbolic names. Any attempt to set a trap on a signal that was ignored on entry to the current shell is ineffective. An attempt to trap on signal 11 (memory fault) produces an error. If you do not specify *argument*, all trap(s) *n* are reset to their original values. If *argument* is a null string, this signal is ignored by the shell and by the commands it invokes. If *n* is 0, the command *argument* is executed on exit from the shell. The `trap` command with no arguments prints a list of commands associated with each signal number.

C Shell

The `onintr` command controls the action of the shell on interrupts. With no arguments, `onintr` restores the default action of the shell on interrupts. (The shell terminates shell scripts and returns to the terminal command input level). With the – argument, the shell ignores all interrupts. With a `label` argument, the shell executes a `goto` label when an interrupt is received or a child process terminates because it was interrupted.

Korn Shell

`trap` uses *arg* as a command to be read and executed when the shell receives signal(s) *sig*.

Note — *arg* is scanned once when the trap is set and once when the trap is taken.

You can specify each *sig* as a number or as the name of the signal. `trap` commands are executed in order of signal number. Any attempt to set a trap on a signal that was ignored on entry to the current shell is ineffective. If you omit *arg* or it is -, then the trap(s) for each *sig* are reset to their original values. If *arg* is null (the empty string " "), then this signal is ignored by the shell and by the commands it invokes. If *sig* is ERR, then *arg* is executed whenever a command has a non-zero exit status. If *sig* is DEBUG, then *arg* is executed after each command. If *sig* is 0 or EXIT for a trap set outside any function, then the command *arg* is executed on exit from the shell. The `trap` command with no arguments prints a list of commands associated with each signal number.

ksh(1) commands that are preceded by one or two asterisks (*) are treated specially in the following ways.

1. Variable assignment lists preceding the command remain in effect when the command completes.

2. I/O redirections are processed after variable assignments.

3. Errors abort a script that contains them.

4. Words following a command preceded by ** that are in the format of a variable assignment are expanded with the same rules as a variable assignment. This means that tilde substitution is performed after the equal sign and that word splitting and file-name generation are not performed.

Attributes

See attributes(5) for descriptions of the following attributes:

Attribute Type	Attribute Value
Availability	SUNWcsu

See Also

csh(1), exit(1), ksh(1), sh(1), attributes(5)

---

troff — Typeset or Format Documents

Synopsis

```
/usr/bin/troff [-a][-f][-Fdir][-i][-mname][-nN][-olist][-raN]
    [-sN][-Tdest][-uN][-z][filename]...
```

Description

The `troff` command is a programming language designed to manipulate text and drive an output device. You create text with a text editor such as `vi` or `emacs`, including `troff` formatting commands and macros within the text to produce an ASCII file that contains both the form and the contents of the document. Then you use the `troff` command to format or compile the program to produce the final output.

If you specify no *filename* argument, `troff` reads standard input. A dash (-) as a file name indicates that standard input should be read at that point in the list of input files.

The output of `troff` is usually piped through dpost(1) to create a printable PostScript file.

Notes

New!

Previous documentation incorrectly described the numeric register `yr` as being the "Last two digits of current year". `yr` is, in actuality, the number of years since 1900. To correctly obtain the last two digits of the current year through the year 2099, you can include the following definition of string register `yy` in a document to display a two-digit year. Note that you can substitute any other available one- or two-character register name for `yy`.

```
.\" definition of new string register yy--last two digits of year
.\" use yr (# of years since 1900) if it is < 100
.ie \n(yr<100 .ds yy \n(yr
.el \{          .\" else, subtract 100 from yr, store in ny
.nr ny \n(yr-100
.ie \n(ny>9 \{   .\" use ny if it is two digits
.ds yy \n(ny
.\" remove temporary number register ny
.rr ny \}
.el \{.ds yy 0
.\" if ny is one digit, append it to 0
.as yy \n(ny
.rr ny \} \}
```

`troff` is not 8-bit clean because it is, by design, based on 7-bit ASCII.

Options

You can specify the following options in any order, but they all must appear before the first file name.

`-a`	Send an ASCII approximation of formatted output to standard output.
`-f`	Do not print a trailer after the final page of output or relinquish the postprocessor control of the device.
`-Fdir`	Search directory *dir* for font width or terminal tables instead of searching the system default directory.
`-i`	Read standard input after all input files are exhausted.

-m*name*	Prepend the macro file /usr/share/lib/tmac/*name* to the input file names. Note that most references to macro packages include the leading m as part of the name. The man(5) macros reside in /usr/share/lib/tmac/. You can change the macro directory by setting the TROFFMACS environment variable to a specific path. Be certain to include the trailing / at the end of the path.
-n*N*	Number the first generated page *N*.
-o*list*	Print only pages whose page numbers appear in the comma-separated list of numbers and ranges. A range *N–M* means pages *N* through *M*, an initial *–N* means from the beginning to page *N*, and a final *N–* means from *N* to the end.
-q	Quiet mode in nroff; ignored in troff.
-ra*N*	Set register a (one-character names only) to *N*.
-s*N*	Stop the phototypesetter every *N* pages. On some devices, troff produces a trailer so you can change cassettes; resume by pressing the typesetter's start button.
-T*dest*	Prepare output for typesetter *dest*. The following values can be supplied for *dest*.

	post	A PostScript printer (the default). You must pipe the output through dpost(1) before it is sent to the PostScript printer to get the proper output.
	aps	Autologic® APS-5.

-u*N*	Set the bold factor for the font mounted in position 3 to *N*. If *N* is missing, then set the bold factor to 0.
-z	Suppress formatted output. Output only diagnostic messages and messages output using the .tm request.

Operands

filename	The file containing text to be processed by troff.

Examples

The following example shows how to print an input text file, mytext, coded with formatting requests and macros. The input file contains equations and tables and must go through the tbl(1) and eqn(1) preprocessors before it is formatted by troff with ms macros, processed by dpost(1), and printed by lp(1).

```
castle% tbl mytext | eqn | troff -ms | dpost | lp
```

Files

/tmp/trtmp Temporary file.

/usr/share/lib/tmac/*

Standard macro files.

/usr/lib/font/*

Font width tables for alternate mounted troff fonts.

/usr/share/lib/nterm/*

Terminal driving tables for nroff.

Attributes

See attributes(5) for descriptions of the following attributes:

Attribute Type	Attribute Value
Availability	SUNWdoc

See Also

checknr(1), col(1), dpost(1), eqn(1), lp(1), man(1), nroff(1), tbl(1), attributes(5), man(5), me(5), ms(5)

true, false — Provide Truth Values

Synopsis

/usr/bin/true
/usr/bin/false

Description

true does nothing, successfully. false does nothing, unsuccessfully. They are typically used in a shell script sh as:

```
while true
  do
    command
  done
```

which executes *command* forever.

Exit Status

true   0.

false   A non-zero value.

Attributes

See `attributes`(5) for descriptions of the following attributes:

Attribute Type	Attribute Value
Availability	SUNWcsu

See Also

`sh(1)`, `attributes(5)`

truss — Trace System Calls and Signals

Synopsis

```
/usr/bin/truss [-fcaeildD][- [tTvx][!]syscall,...]                    New!
    [-s [!]signal,...][-mM [!]fault,...]  [- [rw][!]fd,...]
    [- [uU][!][lib,...:[:][!]func,...][-o outfile] command | -p pid
```

Description

The `truss` command executes the specified command and produces a trace of
the system calls it performs, the signals it receives, and the system faults it
incurs. Each line of the trace output reports either the fault or signal name or
the system call name with its arguments and return value(s). System call
arguments are displayed symbolically when possible, using defines from
relevant system headers; for any path-name pointer argument, the pointed-to
string is displayed. Error returns are reported, using the error code names
described in `intro(2)`.

Optionally (see the –u option), `truss` also produces an entry/exit trace of   New!
user-level function calls executed by the traced process, that indicates nesting.

Notes

Some of the system calls described in Section 2 differ from the actual operating
system interfaces. Do not be surprised by minor deviations of the trace output
from the descriptions in Section 2.

Every system fault (except a page fault) results in the posting of a signal to
the lightweight process that incurred the fault. A report of a received signal

immediately follows each report of a system fault (except a page fault) unless that signal is being blocked.

The operating system enforces certain security restrictions on the tracing of processes. In particular, any command whose object file (a.out) cannot be read by a user cannot be traced by that user; setuid and setgid commands can be traced only by superuser. Unless run by superuser, truss loses control of any process that performs an exec() of a set ID or unreadable object file; such processes continue normally though independently of truss from the point of the exec().

To avoid collisions with other controlling processes, truss does not trace a process that it detects is being controlled by another process via the /proc interface. This allows truss to be applied to proc(4)-based debuggers as well as to another instance of itself.

The trace output contains Tab characters under the assumption that standard Tab stops are set every eight positions.

The trace output for multiple processes or for a multithreaded process (one that contains more than one lightweight process) is not produced in strict time order. For example, a read() on a pipe may be reported before the corresponding write(). For any one lightweight process (a traditional process contains only one), the output is strictly time-ordered.

Not all possible structures passed in all possible system calls are displayed under the -v option.

Options

For those options that take a *list* argument, you can use the name all as a shorthand to specify all possible members of the list. If the list begins with a !, the meaning of the option is negated (for example, exclude instead of trace). You can specify multiple occurrences of the same option. For the same name in a list, subsequent options (those to the right) override previous ones (those to the left).

-a   Show the argument strings that are passed in each exec() system call.

-c   Count traced system calls, faults, and signals instead of displaying the trace line-by-line. Produce a summary report after the traced command terminates or when truss is interrupted. If you also specify -f, include all traced system calls, faults, and signals for child processes in the counts.

New!   -d   Include a timestamp on each line of trace output. The timestamp is a field containing *seconds.fraction* at the start of a line. This value represents a time in seconds relative to the beginning of the trace. The first line of the trace output shows the base time from which the individual timestamps are measured, both as seconds since the Epoch (see time(2)) and as a date string (see ctime(3C) and date(1)). Report the times that the event in question occurred. For all system calls, the event is the completion of the system call, not the start of the system call.

-D   Include a time delta on each line of trace output. The value is a field containing *seconds.fraction* that represents the elapsed time for the LWP that incurred the event since the last reported event incurred by that LWP. Specifically, for system calls, this value is not the time spent within the system call.

-e   Show the environment strings that are passed in each exec() system call.

-f   Follow all children created by fork() or vfork() and include their signals, faults, and system calls in the trace output. Normally, only the first-level command or process is traced. Include the process ID with each line of trace output to indicate which process executed the system call or received the signal.

-i   Do not display interruptible sleeping system calls. Certain system calls, such as open() and read() on terminal devices or pipes can sleep for indefinite periods and are interruptible. Normally, truss reports such sleeping system calls if they remain asleep for more than one second. The system call is reported again a second time when it completes. The -i option reports such system calls only once, when they complete.

-l   Include the ID of the responsible lightweight process with each line of trace output. If you also specify -f, include both the process ID and the lightweight process ID.

-m [!]*fault*,...

     Specify system faults to trace or exclude. Trace those system faults specified in the comma-separated list. You can specify faults by name or number (see <sys/fault.h>). If the list begins with a not symbol (!), exclude the specified faults from the trace output. Default is -mall -m!fltpage.

-M [!]*fault*,...

     Show machine faults that stop the process. Add the specified faults to the set specified by -m. If one of the specified faults is incurred, leave the process stopped and abandoned (see the -T option). Default is -M!all.

-o *outfile*   Specify file to be used for the trace output. By default, the output goes to standard error.

-p *pid*   Interpret the arguments to truss as a list of process IDs for existing processes (see ps(1)) instead of as a command to be executed. truss takes control of each process and begins tracing it, provided that the user ID and group ID of the process match those of the user or that the user is superuser. You can also specify processes by their names in the /proc directory, for example, /proc/12345.

-r [!]*fd*, ...

Show the full contents of the I/O buffer for each read() on any of the specified file descriptors. Format the output 32 bytes per line, and show each byte as an ASCII character (preceded by one blank) or as a 2-character, C-language escape sequence for control characters such as horizontal Tab (\t) and newline (\n). If ASCII interpretation is not possible, show the byte in 2-character hexadecimal representation. Show the first 12 bytes of the I/O buffer for each traced read() even in the absence of -r. Default is -r!all.

-s [!]*signal*, ...

Specify signals to trace or exclude. Trace those signals specified in the comma-separated list. Report the receipt of each specified signal even if the signal is being ignored (not blocked). (Blocked signals are not received until they are unblocked.) You can specify signals by name or number (see <sys/signal.h>). If the list begins with a not symbol (!), exclude the specified signals from the trace output. Default is -sall.

-t [!]*syscall*, ...

Trace those system calls specified in the comma-separated list. If the list begins with a not symbol (!), exclude the specified system calls from the trace output. Default is -tall.

New!   -T [!]*syscall*, ...

Show system calls that stop the process. Add the specified system calls to the set specified by -t. If one of the specified system calls is encountered, leave the process stopped and abandoned. That is, release the process and exit, but leave the process in the stopped state at completion of the system call in question. You can apply a debugger, other process inspection tool, or truss (with the same or different options to continue tracing) to the stopped process. The default is -T!all.

You cannot restart a process left stopped in this way by using kill -CONT because the process stopped on an event of interest via /proc, not by the default action of a stopping signal. See signal(5)). You can use the prun(1) command described in proc(1) to set the stopped process running again.

New!   -u [!]*lib*, ... : [:] [!]*func*, ...

Specify user-level function call tracing. Specify *lib*, ... as a comma-separated list of dynamic library names excluding the .so.n suffix. Specify *func*, ... as a comma-separated list of function names. In both cases, the names can include name-matching metacharacters *, ?, [] with the same meanings as those of sh but as applied to the library/function namespaces, not to files. An empty library or function list defaults to *, that is, trace all libraries or functions in a library. A leading ! on either list specifies an exclusion list, names of libraries or functions not to be traced. Excluding a library excludes all functions in that library; ignore any function list following a library exclusion list.

A single : separating the library list from the function list means trace calls into the libraries from outside the libraries but omit calls made to functions in a library from other functions in the same library. A double : : means trace all calls, regardless of origin.

Library patterns do not patch either the executable file or the dynamic linker unless there is an exact match (1* does not match ld.so.1). To trace functions in either of these objects, you must specify the names exactly, as in truss -u a.out -u ld....Use a.out as the literal name for this purpose. It does not stand for the name of the executable file. Tracing a.out function calls implies all calls (default is : :).

You can specify multiple -u options, and they are honored left to right. If the process is linked with -lthread, the ID of the thread that performed the function call is included in the trace output for the call. truss searches the dynamic symbol table in each library to find function names and also searches the standard symbol table if it has not been stripped.

-U [!]*lib*,...:[:][!]*func*,...   *New!*

Specify user-level function calls that stop the process. Add the specified functions to the set specified by -u. If one of the specified functions is called, leave the process stopped and abandoned (see the -T option).

-v [!]*syscall*,...

Display the contents of any structures passed by address to the specified system calls (if traced). Show input values as well as values returned by the operating system. For any field used as both input and output, show only the output value. Default is -v!all.

-w [!]*fd*,...

Show the contents of the I/O buffer for each write() on any of the specified file descriptors (see -r). Default is -w!all.

-x [!]*syscall*,...

Display the arguments to the specified system calls (if traced) in raw form, usually hexadecimal, instead of symbolically. This option is for unredeemed hackers who must see the raw bits to be happy. Default is -x!all.

See intro(2) for system call names accepted by the -t, -v, and -x options. System call numbers are also accepted.

If you use truss to initiate and trace a specified command and if you use the -o option or if standard error is redirected to a nonterminal file, then truss runs with hangup, interrupt, and quit signals ignored. This behavior facilitates tracing of interactive programs that catch interrupt and quit signals from the terminal.

If the trace output remains directed to the terminal or if existing processes are traced (the -p option), then truss responds to hangup, interrupt, and quit signals by releasing all traced processes and exiting. This behavior enables you to terminate excessive trace output and to release previously existing processes. Released processes continue normally as though they had never been touched.

Usage

See largefile(5) for the description of the behavior of truss when encountering files greater than or equal to 2 Gbytes (2**31 bytes).

Examples

The following example shows the first few lines of a trace of the find(1) command on a terminal.

```
castle% truss find . -print >find.out
execve("/usr/bin/find", 0xEFFFF53C, 0xEFFFF54C)  argc = 3
open("/dev/zero", O_RDONLY)                      = 3
mmap(0x00000000,4096,PROT_READ|PROT_WRITE|PROT_EXEC,MAP_PRIVATE,3,
   0) = 0xEF7C0000
open("/usr/lib/libc.so.1", O_RDONLY)             = 4
fstat(4, 0xEFFFF0D4)                             = 0
mmap(0x00000000, 4096, PROT_READ|PROT_EXEC, MAP_PRIVATE, 4, 0) =
   0xEF7B0000
mmap(0x00000000, 761856, PROT_READ|PROT_EXEC, MAP_PRIVATE, 4, 0) =
   0xEF6C0000
munmap(0xEF762000, 61440)                        = 0
mmap(0xEF771000, 29252, PROT_READ|PROT_WRITE|PROT_EXEC,
   MAP_PRIVATE|MAP_FIXED, 4, 659456) = 0xEF771000
mmap(0xEF779000, 2968, PROT_READ|PROT_WRITE|PROT_EXEC,
   MAP_PRIVATE|MAP_FIXED, 3, 0) = 0xEF779000
close(4)                                         = 0
open("/usr/lib/libdl.so.1", O_RDONLY)            = 4
fstat(4, 0xEFFFF0D4)                             = 0
mmap(0xEF7B0000,4096,PROT_READ|PROT_EXEC,MAP_PRIVATE|MAP_FIXED,4,0)
   = 0xEF7B0000
close(4)                                         = 0
... (More information not shown)
```

The following example shows the first few lines of a trace of the open, close, read, and write system calls.

```
castle% truss -t open,close,read,write find . -print >find.out
open("/dev/zero", O_RDONLY)                          = 3
open("/usr/lib/libc.so.1", O_RDONLY)                 = 4
close(4)                                             = 0
open("/usr/lib/libdl.so.1", O_RDONLY)                = 4
close(4)                                             = 0
open("/usr/platform/SUNW,SPARCstation-10/lib/libc_psr.so.1"Q_RDONLY)
  Err#2 ENOENT
close(3)                                             = 0
open64("./../", O_RDONLY|O_NDELAY)                   = 3
close(3)                                             = 0
```
... (*More information not shown*)

The following example produces a trace of the `spell`(1) command in the file `truss.out`.

```
castle% truss -f -o truss.out spell kookaburra-1
Kookaburra
kookaburra
castle% more truss.out
455:    execve("/usr/bin/spell", 0xEFFFF524, 0xEFFFF534)  argc = 3
455:    open("/dev/zero", O_RDONLY)                    = 3
455:    mmap(0x00000000, 4096, PROT_READ|PROT_WRITE|PROT_EXEC,
  MAP_PRIVATE, 3, 0
) = 0xEF7C0000
455:    open("/usr/lib/libsocket.so.1", O_RDONLY)      = 4
455:    fstat(4, 0xEFFFF0BC)                           = 0
455:  mmap(0x00000000, 4096, PROT_READ|PROT_EXEC, MAP_PRIVATE, 4, 0) =
  0xEF7B0
000
455:  mmap(0x00000000, 102400, PROT_READ|PROT_EXEC, MAP_PRIVATE, 4, 0)
  = 0xEF7
90000
455:    munmap(0xEF798000, 61440)                      = 0
455:    mmap(0xEF7A7000, 6977, PROT_READ|PROT_WRITE|PROT_EXEC,
  MAP_PRIVATE|MAP_F
IXED, 4, 28672) = 0xEF7A7000
```
... (*More information not shown*)

`spell` is a shell script, so you need the `-f` option to trace not only the shell but also the processes created by the shell. (The `spell` script runs a pipeline of eight concurrent processes.)

Note — When tracing more than one process, `truss` runs as one controlling process for each process being traced. In the `spell` command example, `spell` itself uses 9 process slots, one for the shell and 8 for the 8-member pipeline, while `truss` adds another 9 processes, for a total of 18.

New!

In the following (boring) example, 97 percent of the output reports `lseek()`, `read()`, and `write()` system calls.

```
$ truss nroff -mm document >nroff.out
```

You can use the following command to abbreviate the output.

```
$ truss -t !lseek,read,write nroff -mm document >nroff.out
```

New!   The following example traces all user-level calls made to any function in the
C library from outside the C library.

```
$ truss -u libc...
```

The following example includes calls made to functions in the C library from
within the C library itself.

```
example$ truss -u libc::...
```

The following example traces all user-level calls made to any library other
than the C library.

```
$ truss -u '*' -u !libc...
```

The following example traces all user-level calls to functions in the printf
and scanf family contained in the C library.

```
$ truss -u 'libc:*printf,*scanf'...
```

The following example traces every user-level function call from anywhere to
anywhere.

```
$ truss -u a.out -u ld:: -u ::...
```

The following example verbosely traces the system call activity of process #1,
init(1M) (if you are superuser).

```
# truss -p -v all 1
```

Interrupting truss returns init to normal operation.

Files

/proc/*nnnnn*

>   Process files.

/proc/*processID*

Attributes

See attributes(5) for descriptions of the following attributes:

Attribute Type	Attribute Value
Availability	SUNWtoo

See Also

intro(2), proc(4), attributes(5), largefile(5)

---

tset, reset — Establish or Restore Terminal Characteristics

Synopsis

```
/usr/ucb/tset [-InQrs][-ec][-kc][-m [port -ID [baudrate] :
    type]...][type]
/usr/ucb/reset [-][-ec][-I][-kc][-n][-Q][-r][-s][-m [indent]
    [test baudrate]: type]... [type]
```

Description

The tset command sets up your terminal, typically when you first log in. It does terminal-dependent processing such as setting erase and kill characters, setting or resetting delays, sending any sequences needed to properly initialize the terminal, and the like. tset first determines the type of terminal involved and then does necessary initializations and mode settings. If a port is not wired permanently to a specific terminal (not hardwired), it is given an appropriate generic identifier such as dialup.

The reset command clears the terminal settings by turning off CBREAK and RAW modes, output delays, and parity checking; turns on newline translation, echo, and Tab expansion; and restores undefined special characters to their default state. It then sets the modes as usual, based on the terminal type (which probably overrides some of the above). See stty(1) for more information. You can use all arguments to tset with reset. reset also uses rs= and rf= to reset the initialization string and file. This feature is useful after a program dies and leaves the terminal in a peculiar state. Often in this situation, characters do not echo as you type them. You may have to type linefeed reset linefeed because Return may not work.

When you specify no arguments, tset reads the terminal type from the TERM environment variable, reinitializes the terminal, and performs initialization of mode, environment, and other options at login time to determine the terminal type and to set up terminal modes.

When you use tset in a startup script (.profile for sh(1) users or .login for csh(1) users), it is desirable to give information about the type of terminal you usually use on ports that are not hardwired. Any of the alternate generic names given in the file /etc/termcap are possible identifiers. Refer to the -m option below for more information. If no mapping applies and you specify a final type option on the command line not preceded with a -m, then that type is used.

It is usually desirable to return the terminal type, as finally determined by tset, and information about the terminal's capabilities, to a shell's environment. You can do so with the -, -s, or -S options.

For the Bourne shell, put the following command in your `.profile` file.

```
eval `tset -s options...`
```

For the C shell, put the following commands in your `.login` file.

```
set noglob
eval `tset -s options...`
unset noglob
```

With the C shell, it is also convenient to include the following alias in your `.cshrc` file.

```
alias ts 'eval `tset -s \!*`'
```

This alias also allows the following command to be invoked at any time to set the terminal and environment.

```
ts 2621
```

You cannot get this aliasing effect with a Bourne shell script because shell scripts cannot set the environment of their parent. If a process could set its parent's environment, none of this nonsense would be necessary in the first place.

Once the terminal type is known, `tset` sets the terminal driver mode. This process normally involves sending an initialization sequence to the terminal, setting the single character erase (and optionally the line-kill (full line erase)) characters, and setting special character delays. Tab and newline expansion are turned off during transmission of the terminal initialization sequence.

On terminals that can backspace but not overstrike (such as a CRT) and when the erase character is #, the erase character is changed as if you had used `-e`.

Notes

The `tset` command is one of the first commands you must master when getting started on a UNIX system. Unfortunately, it is one of the most complex, largely because of the extra effort you must go through to set the environment of the login shell. Something needs to be done to make all this simpler; either the `login` program should do the setup, a default shell alias should be made, or a way to set the environment of the parent should exist.

This program cannot intuit personal choices for erase, interrupt, and line-kill characters, so it leaves these set to the local system standards.

It could well be argued that the shell should be responsible for ensuring that the terminal remains in a sane state; this would eliminate the need for the `reset` program.

Options

    –   Output the name of the terminal on the standard output. This information is intended to be captured by the shell and placed in the TERM environment variable.

    -e*c*   Set the erase character to be the named character *c* on all terminals. Default is the backspace key on the keyboard, usually ^H (Control-H). You can either type the character *c* directly or enter it by using the circumflex-character notation used here.

    -i*c*   Set the interrupt character to be the named character *c* on all terminals. Default is ^C (Control-C). You can either type the character *c* directly or enter it by using the circumflex-character notation used here.

    -I   Suppress transmitting terminal-initialization strings.

    -k*c*   Set the line-kill character to be the named character *c* on all terminals. Default is ^U (Control-U). The kill character is left alone if you do not specify -k. You can specify control characters by prefixing the alphabetical character with a circumflex (as in Control-U) instead of entering the actual control key itself. This syntax enables you to specify control keys that are currently assigned.

-m [*port-ID* [*baudrate*] : *type*]...

            Specify (map) a terminal type when connected to a generic port (such as dialup or plugboard) identified by *port-ID*. You can use the *baudrate* argument to check the baud rate of the port and set the terminal type accordingly. The target rate is prefixed by any combination of the following operators to specify the conditions under which the mapping is made.

    >   Greater than.

    @   Equal or at.

    <   Less than.

    !   It is not the case that. (Negates the above operators.)

    ?   Prompt for the terminal type. If no response is given, then *type* is selected by default.

In the following example, the terminal type is set to adm3a if the port is a dialup with a speed greater than 300 or to dw2 if the port is a dialup at 300 baud or less. In the third case, the question mark preceding the terminal type indicates that you are to verify the type desired. A null response indicates that the named type is correct. Otherwise, your response is taken to be the type desired.

```
tset -m 'dialup>300:adm3a' -m
'dialup:dw2' -m \
'plugboard:?adm3a'
```

To prevent interpretation as metacharacters, enclose the entire argument to –m in single quotes. When using the C shell, precede exclamation points by a backslash (\).

–n   Specify that the new tty driver modes should be initialized for this terminal. Probably useless because stty new is the default.

–Q   Suppress printing the Erase set to and Kill set to messages.

–r   In addition to other actions, report the terminal type.

–s   Output commands to set and export TERM. This option can be used with

```
set noglob
eval `tset -s...`
unset noglob
```

to bring the terminal information into the environment. Doing so makes programs such as vi(1) start faster. If the SHELL environment variable ends with csh, output C shell commands; otherwise, output Bourne shell commands.

Examples

These examples all use the dash (–) option. A typical use of tset in a .profile or .login also uses the –e and –k options, and often the –n or –Q options as well. These options have been omitted here to keep the examples short.

To select a 2621, you might put the following sequence of commands in your .login file (or .profile for Bourne shell users).

```
set noglob
eval `tset -s 2621`
unset noglob
```

If you have a switch that connects to various ports (making it impractical to identify which port you may be connected to) and use various terminals from time to time, you can select from among those terminals according to the speed or baud rate. In the example below, tset prompts you for a terminal type if the baud rate is greater than 1200 (say, 9600 for a terminal connected by an RS-232 line), and uses a Wyse® 50 by default. If the baud rate is less than or equal to 1200, tset selects a 2621. Note the placement of the question mark and the quotes to protect the > and ? from interpretation by the shell.

```
set noglob
eval `tset -s -m 'switch>1200:?wy' -m 'switch<=1200:2621'`
unset noglob
```

The following entry is appropriate if you always dial up, always at the same baud rate, on many different kinds of terminals, and the terminal you use most often is an adm3a.

```
set noglob
eval `tset -s ?adm3a`
unset noglob
```

If you want to make the selection based only on the baud rate, you might use the following settings.

```
set noglob
eval `tset -s -m '>1200:wy' 2621`
unset noglob
```

The following example quietly sets the erase character to backspace and sets kill to Control-U. If the port is switched, tset selects a Concept™ 100 for speeds less than or equal to 1200 and otherwise asks for the terminal type (the default in this case is a Wyse 50). If the port is a direct dialup, tset selects Concept 100 as the terminal type. If login is over the ARPANET, the terminal type selected is a Datamedia® 2500 terminal or emulator. Note the backslash escaping the newline at the end of the first line.

```
set noglob
eval `tset -e -k^U -Q -s -m 'switch<=1200:concept100' -m \
   'switch:?wy' -m dialup:concept100 -m arpanet:dm2500`
unset noglob
```

Files

```
.login

.profile

/etc/termcap
```

Attributes

See attributes(5) for descriptions of the following attributes:

Attribute Type	Attribute Value
Availability	SUNWscpu

See Also

```
csh(1), sh(1), stty(1), vi(1), attributes(5), environ(5)
```

tsort — Topological Sort

Synopsis

```
/usr/ccs/bin/tsort [file]
```

Description

The `tsort` command produces on the standard output a totally ordered list of items consistent with a partial ordering of items mentioned in the input file.

The input consists of pairs of items (nonempty strings) separated by blanks. Pairs of different items indicate ordering. Pairs of identical items indicate presence, but not ordering.

Operands

`file`   A path name of a text file to order. If you specify no `file` operand, use the standard input.

Examples

The following command sorts the characters you type between the first and second EOF.

```
castle% tsort <<EOF
a b c c d e
g g
f g e f
EOF
a
b
c
d
e
f
g
castle%
```

Environment Variables

See `environ`(5) for descriptions of the following environment variables that affect the execution of `tsort`: LC_CTYPE, LC_MESSAGES, and NLSPATH.

Exit Status

0   Successful completion.

>0   An error occurred.

Attributes

See `attributes`(5) for descriptions of the following attributes:

Attribute Type	Attribute Value
Availability	SUNWbtool

See Also

    lorder(1), attributes(5), environ(5)

Diagnostics

    Odd data: The input file contains an odd number of fields.

---

tty — Return User's Terminal Name

Synopsis

    /usr/bin/tty [-l][-s]

Description

The tty command writes to the standard output the name of the terminal that is open as standard input. The name that is used is equivalent to the string that would be returned by the ttyname(3C) function.

Options

-l   Print the synchronous line number to which the user's terminal is connected if it is on an active synchronous line.

-s   Inhibit printing of the terminal path name; enables you to test just the exit status. The -s option is useful only if you want the exit status. It does not rely on the ability to form a valid path name. Portable applications should use test -t.

Examples

The following example shows the output of the tty command from two separate terminal windows.

```
castle% tty
/dev/pts/4
castle% tty
/dev/pts/5
castle%
```

Environment Variables

See environ(5) for descriptions of the following environment variables that affect the execution of tty: LC_CTYPE, LC_MESSAGES, and NLSPATH.

Exit Status

0	Standard input is a terminal.
1	Standard input is not a terminal.
>1	An error occurred.

Attributes

See `attributes`(5) for descriptions of the following attributes:

Attribute Type	Attribute Value
Availability	SUNWcsu
CSI	Enabled

See Also

`isatty(3C)`, `ttyname(3C)`, `attributes(5)`, `environ(5)`

Diagnostics

`not on an active synchronous line`

> The standard input is not a synchronous terminal, and you specified `-l`.

`not a tty` The standard input is not a terminal, and you did not specify `-s`.

type — Write a Description of Command Type

Synopsis

`/usr/bin/type name...`

Description

The `type` command indicates how each *name* operand would be interpreted if used as a command. `type` displays information about each operand, identifying the operand as a shell built-in, function, alias, hashed command, or keyword, and can display the path name of the operand where applicable.

The shell built-in version of `type` is similar to the `type` command.

Operands

name   A name to be interpreted.

Examples

The following example shows the output for the tty, who, and whence commands.

```
castle% type tty
tty is /bin/tty
castle% type who
who is a tracked alias for /bin/who
castle% type whence
whence is a shell builtin
castle%
```

Environment Variables

See environ(5) for descriptions of the following environment variables that affect the execution of type: LC_CTYPE, LC_MESSAGES, and NLSPATH.

PATH   Determine the location of name.

Exit Status

0   Successful completion.

>0   An error occurred.

Attributes

See attributes(5) for descriptions of the following attributes:

Attribute Type	Attribute Value
Availability	SUNWcsu

See Also

typeset(1), attributes(5), environ(5)

typeset, whence — Shell Built-in Command to Get/Set Attributes and Values for Shell Variables and Functions

Synopsis

```
**
typeset [± HLRZfilrtux[n]] [name[=value] ]...
whence [-pv] name...
```

Description

The `typeset` built-in command sets attributes and values for shell variables and functions. When you invoke `typeset` inside a function, a new instance of the variable's name is created. The variable's value and type are restored when the function completes. You can specify the following attributes.

`-f`	Specify that names refer to function names instead of variable names. No assignments can be made, and the only other valid options are `-t`, `-u`, and `-x`. The `-t` option turns on execution tracing for this function. The `-u` option marks this function undefined. Search the `FPATH` variable to find the function definition when the function is referenced. The `-x` option enables the function definition to remain in effect across shell procedures invoked by *name*.
`-H`	Provide UNIX to host-name file mapping on non-UNIX systems.
`-i`	Specify *parameter* as an integer to make arithmetic faster. If n is non-zero, it defines the output arithmetic base; otherwise, use the first assignment to determine the output base.
`-l`	Convert all uppercase characters to lowercase characters. Turn off the uppercase `-u` option.
`-L`	Left-justify and remove leading blanks from *value*. If n is non-zero, it defines the width of the field; otherwise, use the width of the first assignment to determine its value. When the variable is assigned to, it is filled on the right with blanks or truncated, if necessary, to fit into the field. Leading zeros are removed if you also specify the `-Z` option. The `-R` option is turned off.
`-r`	Mark the given names read-only. You cannot change these names by subsequent assignment.
`-R`	Right-justify and fill with leading blanks. If n is non-zero, it defines the width of the field; otherwise, determine it by the width of the value of first assignment. The field is filled on the left with blanks or truncated from the end if the variable is reassigned. The `-L` option is turned off.
`-t`	Tag the variables. Tags are user definable and have no special meaning to the shell.
`-u`	Convert all lowercase characters to uppercase characters. Turn off the lowercase `-l` option.
`-x`	Mark the given names for automatic export to the environment of subsequently executed commands.
`-Z`	Right-justify and fill with leading zeros if the first nonblank character is a digit and you have not specified the `-L` option. If n is non-zero, it defines the width of the field; otherwise, use the width of the first assignment to determine the value.

You cannot specify the `-i` option along with `-R`, `-L`, `-Z`, or `-f`.

Using + instead of – turns these options off. If you specify no *name* arguments but do specify options, a list of names (and optionally the values) of the variables that have these options set is printed. (Using + instead of – keeps the values from being printed.) If you specify no names or options, the names and attributes of all variables are printed.

For each name, whence indicates how it would be interpreted if used as a command name.

-p	Do a path search for *name* even if *name* is an alias, a function, or a reserved word.
-v	Produce a more verbose report.

ksh(1) commands that are preceded by one or two asterisks (*) are treated specially in the following ways.

1. Variable assignment lists preceding the command remain in effect when the command completes.
2. I/O redirections are processed after variable assignments.
3. Errors abort a script that contains them.
4. Words following a command preceded by ** that are in the format of a variable assignment are expanded with the same rules as a variable assignment. This means that tilde substitution is performed after the equal sign and that word splitting and file-name generation are not performed.

Attributes

See attributes(5) for descriptions of the following attributes:

Attribute Type	Attribute Value
Availability	SUNWcsu

See Also

ksh(1), set(1) sh(1), attributes(5)

U

---

u3b, u3b2, u3b5, u3b15, u370 — Get Processor Type Truth
Value

Synopsis

```
/usr/bin/u3b
/usr/bin/u3b2
/usr/bin/u3b5
/usr/bin/u3b15
/usr/bin/u370
```

Description

See machid(1).

---

ucblinks — Add /dev Entries for SunOS 4.x Compatibility

Synopsis

```
/usr/ucb/ucblinks [-e rulebase][-r rootdir]
```

Description

ucblinks creates symbolic links under the /dev directory for devices with SunOS 5.x names that differ from their SunOS 4.x names. Where possible, these symbolic links point to the device's SunOS 5.x name instead of to the actual /devices entry.

ucblinks does not remove unneeded compatibility links; you must remove these by hand.

After any new SunOS 5.x links have been created, you should call ucblinks each time the system is reconfiguration-booted because the reconfiguration may have resulted in more compatibility names being needed.

In releases before SunOS 5.4, ucblinks used a nawk rule-base to construct the SunOS 4.x compatible names. ucblinks no longer uses nawk for the default operation, although you can still specify nawk rule-bases with the -e option. You can find the nawk rule-base equivalent to the SunOS 5.4 default operation in /usr/ucblib/ucblinks.awk.

Options

-e *rulebase*

Specify *rulebase* as the file containing nawk(1) pattern-action statements.

-r *rootdir*

Specify *rootdir* as the directory under which dev and devices are found, instead of the standard root directory /.

Files

/usr/ucblib/ucblinks.awk

Sample rule-base for compatibility links.

Attributes

See attributes(5) for descriptions of the following attributes:

Attribute Type	Attribute Value
Availability	SUNWscpu

See Also

devlinks(1M), disks(1M), ports(1M), tapes(1M), attributes(5)

ul — Underline Text on Terminal Display

Synopsis

```
/usr/bin/ul [-i][-t terminal][filename...]
```

Description

ul reads the named file names (or the standard input if you specify no file names) and, using the environment variable TERM, determines how to translate underscores to the sequence that indicates underlining for your terminal. ul uses the /usr/share/lib/terminfo entry to determine the appropriate sequences for underlining. If the terminal is incapable of underlining but is capable of a standout mode, that mode is used instead. If the terminal can overstrike or handle underlining automatically, ul degenerates to cat(1). If the terminal cannot underline, underlining is ignored.

Bugs

nroff usually generates a series of backspaces and underlines intermixed with the text to indicate underlining. ul tries to optimize the backward motion.

Options

-i   Indicate underlining by a separate line containing appropriate dashes (-); this option is useful when you want to look at the underlining that is present in an nroff(1) output stream on a CRT-terminal.

-t terminal

Override the terminal kind specified in the environment. If the terminal cannot underline, ignore underlining. If the terminal name is not found, do no underlining.

Exit Status

ul returns exit code 1 if the file specified is not found.

Files

```
/usr/share/lib/terminfo/*
```

Attributes

See attributes(5) for descriptions of the following attributes:

Attribute Type	Attribute Value
Availability	SUNWdoc

See Also

cat(1), man(1), nroff(1), attributes(5)

ulimit, unlimit — Set or Get Shell Limitations on System Resources

Synopsis

/usr/bin/ulimit [-f] [*blocks*]

sh

ulimit [-[HS] [a | cdfnstv]]
ulimit [-[HS]] c | d | f | n | s | t | v]] *limit*

csh

unlimit [-h] [*resource*]

ksh

ulimit [-HSacdfnstv] [*limit*]

Description

See limit(1).

umask — Get or Set the File Mode Creation Mask

Synopsis

/usr/bin/umask [-S] [*mask*]

sh, csh

umask [*ooo*]

ksh

umask [-S] [*mask*]

Description

When you create a file or directory, the default file permissions assigned to the file or directory are controlled by the user mask. You set the user mask with the umask command in a user initialization file such as /etc/profile or .cshrc. You can display the current value of the user mask by typing umask and pressing Return.

You set the user mask with a three-digit octal value such as 022. The first digit sets permissions for the user, the second for the group, the third for others. To set the umask to 022, type

```
umask 022
```

File permissions of 666 grant read and write permission to the user, group, and others. Directory permissions of 777 grant read, write, and execute permissions to the user, group, and others. The value assigned by umask is subtracted from these values. To determine the umask value you want to set, subtract the value of the permissions you want from 666 (for a file) or 777 (for a directory). The remainder is the value to use with the umask command. For example, suppose you want to change the default mode for files to 644 (rw-r--r--). The difference between 666 and 644 is 022, which is the value to use as an argument to the umask command.

Setting the umask value denies permissions in the same way that the chmod command grants them. For example, while the chmod 022 command grants write permission to group and others, umask 022 denies write permission for group and others.

/usr/bin/umask

The umask command sets the file-mode creation mask of the current shell execution environment to the value specified by the *mask* operand. This mask affects the initial value of the file permission bits of subsequently created files. If umask is called in a subshell or separate command execution environment, such as one of the following,

```
(umask 002)
nohup umask ...
find . -exec umask ...
```

it does not affect the file-mode creation mask of the caller's environment. For this reason, you cannot use /usr/bin/umask to change the umask in an ongoing session. Its usefulness is limited to checking the caller's umask. To change the umask of an ongoing session, use one of the shell built-ins.

If you do not specify the *mask* operand, the umask command displays to standard output the value of the invoking process file-mode creation mask.

Bourne and C Shells

Set the user file-mode creation mask to *ooo*. The three octal digits refer to read/write/execute permissions for owner, group, and other (see chmod(1), chmod(2), and umask(2)). The value of each specified digit is subtracted from the corresponding digit specified by the system for the creation of a file (see creat(2)). For example, umask 022 removes write permission for group and other (files normally created with mode 777 become mode 755; files created with mode 666 become mode 644).

- If you omit *ooo*, the current value of the mask is displayed.
- umask is recognized and executed by the shell.
- To automatically set the permissions on created files or directories, you can include umask in your .profile for the Bourne shell (see profile(4) or in your .cshrc file for the C shell. These initialization files are invoked at login.

Korn Shell

Set the user file-mode creation mask to *mask*. *mask* can either be an octal number or a symbolic value as described in chmod(1). If you omit *mask*, the current value of the mask is printed.

Options

-S   Specify *mask* as a symbolic argument.

The default output style is unspecified but is recognized on a subsequent invocation of umask on the same system as a *mask* operand to restore the previous file-mode creation mask.

Operands

mask   A string specifying the new file-mode creation mask. The string is treated in the same way as the *mode* operand described in the chmod(1) manual page.

For a *symbolic-mode* value, the new value of the file-mode creation mask is the logical complement of the file permission bits portion of the file mode specified by the *symbolic-mode* string.

In a *symbolic-mode* value, the permissions characters + and – are interpreted relative to the current file-mode creation mask; + clears the indicated permissions in the mask; – sets the bits of the indicated permissions in the mask.

The interpretation of mode values that specify file mode bits other than the file permission bits is unspecified.

The file-mode creation mask is set to the resulting numeric value.

The default output of a prior invocation of umask on the same system with no operand is also recognized as a *mask* operand. The use of an operand obtained in this way is not obsolescent, even if it is an octal number.

Output

When you specify no *mask* arguments, the umask command writes a message to standard output that can later be used as a umask *mask* operand.

If you specify -S for /usr/bin/umask, the output is displayed in symbolic format, as shown in the following example.

```
castle% /usr/bin/umask -S
u=rwx,g=rx,o=rx
castle%
```

The three values are combinations of letters from the set r, w, x; the presence of a letter indicates that the corresponding bit is clear in the file-mode creation mask. The symbolic syntax in the previous example is equivalent to an octal umask of 022.

```
castle% /usr/bin/umask
022
castle%
```

If you specify a *mask* operand, no output is written to standard output.

Examples

Either of the following commands sets the mode mask so that subsequently created files have their S_IWOTH (others) bit cleared.

```
umask a=rx,ug+w
umask 002
```

After setting the mode mask with either of the above commands, you can use the umask command to display the current value of the mode mask.

```
castle% ksh
$ umask 002
$ umask
02
$ umask -S
u=rwx,g=rwx,o=rx
$
```

Note — The output format is unspecified, but historical implementations use the obsolescent octal integer mode format.

You can then use either of these outputs as the mask operand to a subsequent invocation of the umask command.

Assuming the mode mask is set as above, the following command sets the mode mask so that subsequently created files have their S_IWGRP (group) and S_IWOTH (others) bits cleared.

```
$ umask g-w
$ umask
022
$
```

The following command sets the mode mask so that subsequently created files have all their write bits cleared.

```
$ umask -- -w
$ umask
0222
$
```

Note — You must precede mask operands r, w, x, or anything beginning with a dash (-) with two dashes (--) to prevent them from being interpreted as an option.

Environment Variables

See environ(5) for descriptions of the following environment variables that affect the execution of umask: LC_CTYPE, LC_MESSAGES, and NLSPATH.

Exit Status

0	The file-mode creation mask was successfully changed, or no mask operand was supplied.
>0	An error occurred.

Attributes

See attributes(5) for descriptions of the following attributes:

Attribute Type	Attribute Value
Availability	SUNWcsu

See Also

chmod(1), csh(1), ksh(1), sh(1), chmod(2), creat(2), umask(2), profile(4), attributes(5), environ(5)

---

unalias — Remove Command Pseudonyms

Synopsis

```
/usr/bin/unalias alias-name ...
/usr/bin/unalias -a
```

csh
```
unalias pattern
```

ksh
```
unalias name...
```

Description

See alias(1).

---

uname — Print Name of Current System

Synopsis

```
/usr/bin/uname [-aimnprsvX]
/usr/bin/uname [-S system-name]
```

Description

The uname command prints information about the current system on the standard output.

By default, the uname command with no options displays only the name of the current operating system, as shown in the following example.

```
castle% uname
SunOS
castle%
```

When you specify options, symbols representing one or more system characteristics are written to the standard output. The options print selected information returned by uname(2), sysinfo(2), or both.

Independent software vendors (ISVs) and others who need to determine detailed characteristics of the platform on which their software is either being installed or executed should use the uname command.

To determine the operating system name and release level, use uname -sr. To determine only the operating system release level, use uname -r.

> **Note** — Operating system release levels are not guaranteed to be in *x.y* format (such as 5.5, 5.6, 5.7); future releases could be in the *x.y.z* format (such as 5.3.1, 5.3.2, 5.4.1).

In SunOS 4.x releases, the arch command was often used to obtain information similar to that obtained with the uname command. The arch command output sun4 was often incorrectly interpreted to signify a SunOS SPARC system. If hardware platform information is desired, use uname -sp.

The arch -k and uname -m commands return equivalent values; however, the use of either of these commands by third-party programs is discouraged, as is the use of the arch command in general. To determine the system's Instruction Set Architecture (ISA or processor type), use uname with the -p option.

Options

-a	Print basic information currently available from the system.
-i	Print the name of the hardware implementation (platform).
-m	Print the system hardware name (class). Use of this option is discouraged; use uname -p instead.
-n	Print the node name (the node name is the name by which the system is known to a communications network).
-p	Print the current host ISA or processor type.
-r	Print the operating system release level.
-s	Print the name of the operating system (the default).
-v	Print the operating system version.
-X	Print expanded system information, one information element per line, as expected by SCO UNIX. The displayed information includes:

- System name, node, release, version, system, and number of CPUs.
- BusType, Serial, and Users (set to "unknown" in Solaris).
- OEM# and Origin# (set to 0 and 1, respectively).

-S *system-name*

Change the node name by specifying a *system-name* argument. The *system-name* argument is restricted to SYS_NMLN characters. SYS_NMLN is an implementation specific value defined in <sys/utsname.h>. Only superuser can change the node name.

Examples

The following example displays the operating system name and release level, separated by a space.

```
castle% uname -sr
SunOS 5.7
castle%
```

The following example displays basic information currently known about the system.

```
castle% uname -a
SunOS castle 5.7 Generic sun4m sparc SUNW,SPARCstation-10
castle%
```

The seven items listed include the operating system name, node name, operating system release level, kernel ID, system hardware name, current processor type, and platform name.

The following example uses the -X option to display extended system information.

```
castle% uname -X
System = SunOS
Node = castle
Release = 5.7
KernelID = Generic
Machine = sun4m
BusType = <unknown>
Serial = <unknown>
Users = <unknown>
OEM# = 0
Origin# = 1
NumCPU = 1

castle%
```

Environment Variables

SYSV3 Use to override the default behavior of uname to enable some INTERACTIVE UNIX systems and SCO UNIX programs and scripts to work properly. Many scripts use uname to determine the OS type or the version of the OS to ensure software is compatible with that OS. Setting SYSV3 to an empty string makes uname print the following default values:

nodename nodename 3.2 2 i386

You can also modify the individual elements that uname displays by setting SYSV3 in the following format:

os,sysname,node,rel,ver,mach

os	Operating system (IUS or SCO).
sysname	System name.
node	Node name as displayed by the -n option.
rel	Release level as displayed by the -r option.
ver	Version number as displayed by the -v option.
mach	Machine name as displayed by -m option.

Do not put spaces between the elements. If you omit an element, the current system value is used.

See environ(5) for descriptions of the following environment variables that affect the execution of uname: LC_CTYPE, LC_MESSAGES, and NLSPATH.

Exit Status

0	Successful completion.
>0	An error occurred.

Attributes

See attributes(5) for descriptions of the following attributes:

Attribute Type	Attribute Value
Availability	SUNWcsu

See Also

New! arch(1), isalist(1), sysinfo(2), uname(2), attributes(5), environ(5)

---

uncompress — Uncompress or Display Expanded Files

Synopsis

/usr/bin/uncompress [-cfv] [*file...*]

Description

See compress(1).

---

unexpand — Convert Space Characters to Tabs

Synopsis

/usr/bin/unexpand [-a] [-t *tablist*] [*file...*]

Description

See expand(1).

---

unget — Undo a Previous Get of an SCCS File

Synopsis

/usr/ccs/bin/unget [-ns] [-r*sid*] s.*filename* ...

Description

See sscs-unget(1).

unhash — Evaluate the Internal Hash Table of the Contents of Directories

Synopsis

csh
unhash

Description

See hash(1).

unifdef — Resolve and Remove ifdef'd Lines from C Program Source

Synopsis

/usr/ccs/bin/unifdef [-clt] [-Dname] [-Uname] [-iDname] [-iUname] ...
    [*filename*]

Description

unifdef removes ifdef'd lines from a file while otherwise leaving the file alone. It is smart enough to deal with the nested ifdefs, comments, and the single and double quotes of C syntax, but it does not do any inclusion or interpretation of macros. Neither does it strip out comments, although it recognizes and ignores them. You specify which symbols you want defined with -D options and which you want undefined with -U options. Lines within those ifdefs are copied to the output or removed, as appropriate. Any ifdef, ifndef, else, and endif lines associated with file name are also removed.

    ifdefs involving symbols you do not specify are untouched and copied out along with their associated ifdef, else, and endif lines.

    If an ifdefX is nested inside another ifdefX, the inside ifdef is treated as if it is an unrecognized symbol. If the same symbol appears in more than one argument, only the first occurrence is significant.

    unifdef copies its output to the standard output and takes its input from the standard input if you specify no *filename* argument.

Options

-c	Complement the normal operation. Retain lines that would have been removed or blanked, and vice versa.
-l	Replace removed lines with blank lines.

-t	Plain text option. Refrain from attempting to recognize comments and single and double quotes.
-D*name*	Specify which symbols you want defined with *name*.
-U*name*	Specify which symbols you want undefined with *name*.
-iD*name*	Ignore but print lines associated with the defined symbol *name*. If you use ifdefs to delimit non-C lines, such as comments or code that is under construction, then you must tell unifdef which symbols are used for that purpose so that it does not try to parse for quotes and comments within them.
-iU*name*	Ignore, but print lines associated with the undefined symbol *name*.

Exit Status

0	Success.
1	Problems encountered.

Attributes

See attributes(5) for descriptions of the following attributes:

Attribute Type	Attribute Value
Availability	SUNWbtool

See Also

diff(1), attributes(5)

Diagnostics

Premature EOF

Inappropriate else or endif.

uniq — Report or Filter Out Repeated Lines in a File

Synopsis

```
/usr/bin/uniq[-c|-d|-u] [-ffields] [-schars] [input-file[output-file]]
/usr/bin/uniq [-c|-d|-u] [-n] [+m] [input-file [output-file]]
```

Description

The uniq command produces a list of the unique lines in a file by filtering or removing repeated lines. It is usually used with files that have first been sorted with the sort(1) command.

uniq reads an input file, compares adjacent lines, and writes one copy of each input line on the output. The second and succeeding copies of repeated adjacent input lines are not written.

Repeated lines in the input are not detected if they are not adjacent.

Options

-c	Precede each output line with a count of the number of times the line occurred in the input.
-d	Suppress the writing of lines that are not repeated in the input.
-f *fields*	Ignore the first *fields* on each input line when doing comparisons, where *fields* is a positive decimal integer. A field is the maximal string matched by the basic regular expression:
	`[[:blank:]]*[^[:blank:]]*`
	If *fields* specifies more fields than appear on an input line, use a null string for comparison.
-s *chars*	Ignore the first *chars* characters when doing comparisons, where *chars* is a positive decimal integer. If specified in conjunction with the -f option, ignore the first *chars* characters after the first *fields*. If *chars* specifies more characters than remain on an input line, use a null string for comparison.
-u	Suppress the writing of lines that are repeated in the input.
-n	Equivalent to -f *fields* with *fields* set to *n*.
+m	Equivalent to -s *chars* with *chars* set to *m*.

Operands

input-file	A path name of the input file. If you do not specify *input-file* or if the *input-file* is -, use the standard input.
output-file	A path name of the output file. If you do not specify *output-file*, use the standard output. The results are unspecified if the file named by *output-file* is the file named by *input-file*.

Examples

The following example lists the contents of the uniq.test file and outputs a copy of the repeated lines.

```
castle% cat uniq.test
This is a test.
This is a test.
```

```
TEST.
Computer.
TEST.
TEST.
Software.
castle% uniq -d uniq.test
This is a test.
TEST.
castle%
```

The following example outputs just those lines that are not repeated in the uniq.test file.

```
castle% uniq -u uniq.test
TEST.
Computer.
Software.
castle%
```

The following example precedes each line with a count of the number of times each line occurred in the file.

```
castle% uniq -c uniq.test
2 This is a test.
1 TEST.
1 Computer.
2 TEST.
1 Software.
castle%
```

The following example uses the sort command to sort the file kookaburra-1 and pipes the output to the uniq -c command. You need to sort the file first because uniq does not match discontiguous lines.

```
castle% sort kookaburra-1 | uniq -c
   1
   1 Eating all the gumdrops he can see.
   1 Gay your life must be
   2 Kookaburra sits in the old gum tree
   1 Laugh, kookaburra, laugh, kookaburra
   1 Leave some there for me.
   1 Merry merry king of the bush is he.
   1 Stop, kookaburra, stop, kookaburra
castle%
```

Environment Variables

See environ(5) for descriptions of the following environment variables that affect the execution of uniq: LC_CTYPE, LC_MESSAGES, and NLSPATH.

Exit Status

0	Successful completion.
>0	An error occurred.

Attributes

See attributes(5) for descriptions of the following attributes:

Attribute Type	Attribute Value
Availability	SUNWesu
CSI	Enabled

See Also

comm(1), pack(1), pcat(1), sort(1), uncompress(1), attributes(5), environ(5)

units — Convert Quantities Expressed in Standard Scales to Other Units

Synopsis

/usr/bin/units

Description

units converts quantities expressed in various standard scales to their equivalents in other scales. It works interactively in the following way. Type units to start the command. A you have: prompt is displayed. Type the first standard scale and press Return. A you want: prompt is displayed. Type the second standard scale and press Return. The results are displayed as shown in the following examples.

```
castle% units
you have: inch
you want: cm
        * 2.540000e+00
        / 3.937008e-01
you have: 15 lbs force/in2
you want: atm
        * 1.020689e+00
        / 9.797299e-01
you have: 3 teaspoon
you want: tablespoon
        * 1.000000e+00
        / 1.000000e+00
```

```
you have: 45 liters
you want: gallons
        * 1.188774e+01
        / 8.412026e-02
you have: 12 gallons
you want: liters
        * 4.542494e+01
        / 2.201434e-02
you have: ^D
castle%
```

To exit, type Control-D or Control-C.

Specify a quantity as a multiplicative combination of units optionally preceded by a numeric multiplier. Indicate powers by suffixed positive integers, division by the usual sign.

`units` only does multiplicative scale changes; thus, it can convert Kelvin to Rankine, but not Celsius to Fahrenheit. Most familiar units, abbreviations, and metric prefixes are recognized, together with a generous leavening of exotica and a few constants of nature including the following.

pi	Ratio of circumference to diameter.
c	Speed of light.
e	Charge on an electron.
g	Acceleration of gravity.
force	Same as g.
mole	Avogadro's number.
water	Pressure head per unit height of water.
au	Astronomical unit.

Pound is not recognized as a unit of mass, though `lb` is. Compound names are run together, (for example, `lightyear`). British units that differ from their U.S. counterparts are prefixed thus: `brgallon`. For a complete list of units, type:

```
castle% cat /usr/share/lib/unittab
```

Files

/usr/share/lib/unittab

Attributes

See attributes(5) for descriptions of the following attributes:

Attribute Type	Attribute Value
Availability	SUNWesu

See Also

attributes(5)

---

unix2dos — Convert Text File from ISO Format to DOS Format

Synopsis

/usr/bin/unix2dos [-ascii][-iso][-7] *originalfile convertedfile*

Description

unix2dos converts ISO standard characters to the corresponding characters in the DOS extended character set.

You can invoke this command from either DOS or SunOS. However, the file names must conform to the conventions of the environment in which you invoke the command.

If the original file and the converted file are the same, unix2dos rewrites the original file after converting it.

Options

-ascii	Add Returns and convert end-of-file characters in SunOS format text files to conform to DOS requirements.
-iso	Convert ISO standard characters to the corresponding character in the DOS extended character set (the default).
-7	Convert 8-bit SunOS characters to 7-bit DOS characters.

Attributes

See attributes(5) for descriptions of the following attributes:

Attribute Type	**Attribute Value**
Availability	SUNWesu

See Also

dos2unix(1), attributes(5)

Diagnostics

File *filename* not found, or no read permission

The input file you specified does not exist, or you do not have read permission (check with the SunOS command ls -l).

```
Bad output filename filename, or no write permission
```
> The output file you specified is either invalid, or you do not have write permission for that file or the directory that contains it. Check also that the drive or diskette is not write protected.

```
Error while writing to temporary file
```
> An error occurred while converting your file, possibly because there is not enough space on the current drive.Check the amount of space on the current drive, using the DIR command. Also, be certain that the default diskette or drive is write enabled (not write protected). Note that when this error occurs, the original file remains intact.

```
Could not rename tmpfile to filename.
Translated tmpfile name = filename.
```
> The program could not perform the final step in converting your file. Your converted file is stored under the name indicated on the second line of this message.

unlimit — Set or Get Shell System Resource Limitations

Synopsis

csh
```
unlimit [-h][resource]
```

Description

See limit(1).

unpack — Compress and Expand Files

Synopsis
```
/usr/bin/unpack file ...
```

Description

See pack(1).

unset, unsetenv — Shell Built-in Functions to Determine Environment Variable Characteristics

Synopsis

sh
unset [*name* ...]

csh
unset *pattern*
unsetenv *variable*

ksh
unset [-f] *name* ...

Description
See set(1).

until — Shell Built-in Functions to Execute Actions Until Conditions Are Evaluated True

Synopsis

sh, ksh
until [*conditions*]; do *actions* ; done

Description
See while(1).

unzip — List, Test, and Extract Compressed Files from a Zip Archive

Synopsis
/usr/bin/unzip[-Z] [-cflptTuvz[abBCjnLoMqsVX$]]*file*[.zip] [*file*(s)...]
   [- x *xfile*(s)...] [-d *exdir*]

Description

unzip lists, tests, or extracts files from a ZIP archive. The default behavior (with no options) is to extract all files from the specified ZIP archive into the current directory (and subdirectories below it). You can use a companion program, zip (available from http://www.cdrom.com/pub/infozip/) to creates ZIP archives. Both programs are compatible with archives created by PKWARE's PKZIP and PKUNZIP for MS-DOS, but in many cases the program options or default behaviors differ.

Arguments

file[.zip]   Path of the ZIP archive(s). If you specify a wild-card for *file*, process each matching file in an order determined by the operating system (or file system). Only the file name can be a wild-card; the path itself cannot. Wild-card expressions are similar to UNIX egrep(1) (regular) expressions and can contain:

   *   Match a sequence of zero or more characters.

   ?   Match exactly one character.

   [...]   Match any single character found inside the brackets; specify ranges with a beginning character, a dash, and an ending character. If an exclamation point (!) or a caret (^) follows the left bracket, then the range of characters within the brackets is complemented (that is, anything except the characters inside the brackets is considered a match).

   Be sure to quote any character that might otherwise be interpreted or modified by the operating system, particularly under UNIX and VMS. If no matches are found, assume a literal file name; if that also fails, append the suffix .zip. Note that self-extracting ZIP files are supported, as with any other ZIP archive; just specify the .exe suffix (if any) explicitly.

[*file*(s)]   An optional, space-separated list of archive items to be processed. (VMS versions compiled with VMSCLI defined must delimit files with commas instead. See -v.) You can use regular expressions (wild-cards) to match multiple items. Be sure to quote expressions that would otherwise be expanded or modified by the operating system.

[-x *xfile*(s)]

   An optional list of archive items to be excluded from processing. Because wild-card characters match directory separators (/), you can use this option to exclude any files that are in subdirectories. For example,
   unzip foo *.[ch] -x */*

extracts all C source files in the main directory, but none in any subdirectories. Without the -x option, extract all C source files in all directories within the file.

[-d *exdir*] An optional directory to which to extract files. By default, all files and subdirectories are recreated in the current directory; the -d option enables you to extract into an arbitrary directory (assuming you have permission to write to the directory). This option need not appear at the end of the command line; it is also accepted before the file specification (with the normal options), immediately after the file specification, or between the file(s) and the -x option. You can concatenate the option and directory without any white space between them, but note that this may suppress normal shell behavior. In particular, -d ~ (tilde) is expanded by UNIX C shells into the name of the user's home directory, but -d~ is treated as a literal subdirectory ~ of the current directory.

Options

Note — To support obsolete hardware, the unzip usage screen is limited to 22 or 23 lines. Consider the usage message as a reminder of only the basic unzip syntax instead of as an exhaustive list of all possible options.

The following example shows the unzip usage screen.

```
castle% unzip
UnZip 5.32 of 3 November 1997, by Info-ZIP.  Maintained by Greg Roelofs.  Send
bug reports to the authors at Zip-Bugs@lists.wku.edu; see README for details.

Usage: unzip [-Z] [-opts[modifiers]] file[.zip] [list] [-x xlist] [-d exdir]
  Default action is to extract files in list, except those in xlist, to exdir;
  file[.zip] may be a wildcard.  -Z => ZipInfo mode ("unzip -Z" for usage).

  -p  extract files to pipe, no messages      -l  list files (short format)
  -f  freshen existing files, create none     -t  test compressed archive data
  -u  update files, create if necessary       -z  display archive comment
  -x  exclude files that follow (in xlist)    -d  extract files into exdir

modifiers:                                    -q  quiet mode (-qq => quieter)
  -n  never overwrite existing files          -a  auto-convert any text files
  -o  overwrite files WITHOUT prompting        -aa treat ALL files as text
  -j  junk paths (do not make directories)    -v  be verbose/print version info
  -C  match filenames case-insensitively      -L  make (some) names lowercase
  -X  restore UID/GID info                     -V  retain VMS version numbers
                                              -M  pipe through "more" pager
Examples (see unzip.doc for more info):
  unzip data1 -x joe   => extract all files except joe from zipfile data1.zip
  unzip -p foo | more  => send contents of foo.zip via pipe into program more
  unzip -fo foo ReadMe => quietly replace existing ReadMe if archive file newer
castle%
```

The exhaustive list of options is shown below.

-A Print extended help for the DLL programming interface (API) (OS/2, UNIX DLL).

-c Extract files to standard output. This option is similar to the -p option, except print the name of each file as it is extracted. Allow the -a option. Automatically perform ASCII-EBCDIC conversion if appropriate. This option is not listed in the unzip usage screen.

-f Freshen existing files; that is, extract only those files that already exist on disk and that are newer than the disk copies. By default unzip queries before overwriting, but you can use the -o option to suppress the queries. Note that under many operating systems, the TZ (time zone) environment variable must be set correctly for -f and -u to work properly (under UNIX the variable is usually set automatically). TZ must be set to resolve the differences between DOS-format file times (always local time) and UNIX-format times (always in GMT/UTC). A typical TZ value is PST8PDT (U.S. Pacific time with automatic adjustment for standard or daylight saving time).

-l List archive files (short format). Print the names, uncompressed file sizes, modification dates and times of the specified files, and totals for all files specified. If UnZip was compiled with OS2_EAS defined, the -l option also lists columns for the sizes of stored OS/2 extended attributes (EAs) and OS/2 access control lists (ACLs). In addition, display the zip file comment and individual file comments (if any). If a file was archived from a single-case file system (for example, the old MS-DOS FAT file system) and you specify the -L option, convert the file name to lower case and prefixed it with a caret (^).

-p Extract files to pipe (standard output). Send nothing but the file data to standard output and always extract the files in binary format just as they are stored (no conversions).

-t Test archive files. Extract each specified file in memory, and compare the cyclic redundancy check (CRC, an enhanced checksum) of the expanded file with the original file's stored CRC value.

-T Set the timestamp on the archive(s) to that of the newest file in each one. This option corresponds to the zip -go option except that you can use it on wild-card files (for example, unzip -T *.zip) and it is much faster. (Most operating systems.)

-u Update existing files and create new ones if needed. This option performs the same function as the -f option, extracting (with query) files that are newer than those with the same name on disk. In addition, extract those files that do not already exist on disk. See -f for information on setting the time zone properly.

-v   Be verbose or print diagnostic version information. This option behaves as both an option and a modifier.

As an option -v has two purposes: when you specify a file with no other options, list archive files verbosely, adding to the basic -l information the compression method, compressed size, compression ratio, and 32-bit CRC. When you specify no file (that is, the complete command is simply unzip -v), print a diagnostic screen. In addition to the normal header with release date and version, list the home Info-ZIP ftp site and where to find a list of other ftp and non-ftp sites, the target operating system for which it was compiled, (possibly) the hardware on which it was compiled, the compiler and version used, and the compilation date. Also list any special compilation options that might affect the program's operation and any options stored in environment variables that might do the same.

As a modifier, the -v option is used with other options (such as -t) to produce more verbose or debugging output. This feature is not yet fully implemented but will be in future releases.

-z   Display only the archive comment.

-Z   If the first option on the command line is -Z, interpret the remaining options as zipinfo(1) options.

Modifiers

-a   Convert text files. Automatically extract files identified by zip as text files (those with the t label in zipinfo listings), converting line endings, end-of-file characters, and the character set itself as necessary. (For example, UNIX files use linefeeds (LFs) for end-of-line (EOL) and have no end-of-file (EOF) marker. Macintosh uses Returns (CRs) for EOLs. Most PC operating systems use CR+LF for EOLs and Control-Z for EOF. IBM mainframes and the Michigan Terminal System use EBCDIC instead of the more common ASCII character set, and NT supports Unicode.) Note that zip identification of text files is by no means perfect; some text files may actually be binary, and vice versa. unzip, therefore, prints [text] or [binary] as a visual check for each file it extracts when you specify the -a option. Doubling the option (-aa) forces all files to be extracted as text regardless of the supposed file type. Without the -a option, extract all files exactly as they are stored (as binary files).

-b   Treat all files as binary (no text conversions). This option is a shortcut for ---a (non-VMS).

-b   Autoconvert binary files (see -a) to fixed-length, 512-byte record format. Doubling the option (-bb) forces all files to be extracted in this format (VMS).

-B   Save a backup copy of each overwritten file with a tilde appended (for example, rename the old copy of foo to foo~). This option is similar to the default behavior of emacs(1) in many locations. (UNIX only and only if compiled with UNIXBACKUP defined.)

-C   Match file names case insensitively. Because some file systems are fully case sensitive (notably those under the UNIX operating system) and because both ZIP archives and unzip itself are portable across platforms, the default behavior is to match both wild-card and literal file names case sensitively. That is, specifying makefile on the command line only matches makefile in the archive, not Makefile or MAKEFILE (and similarly for wild-card specifications). Because this behavior does not match that of many other operating/file systems (for example, OS/2 HPFS, which preserves mixed case but is not sensitive to it), you can use the -C option to force all file name matches to be case insensitive. In the example above, all three files then match makefile (or make*, or similar). The -C option affects files in both the normal-file list and the excluded-file list (xlist).

-j   Junk paths. Do not recreate the archive's directory structure. Deposit all files in the extraction directory (by default, the current one).

-L   Convert to lower case any file name originating on an uppercase-only operating system or file system. (This was the default behavior in releases before 5.11. The new default behavior is identical to the old behavior with the -U option, which is now obsolete and will be removed in a future release.) Depending on the archiver, store files archived under single-case file systems (such as VMS and old MS-DOS FAT) as all uppercase names. The default behavior can be ugly or inconvenient when extracting to a case-preserving file system such as OS/2 HPFS or a case-sensitive one such as UNIX. By default, unzip lists and extracts file names exactly as they are stored (excepting truncation, conversion of unsupported characters, and so on).

-M   Pipe all output through an internal pager similar to the UNIX more(1) command. At the end of a screen of output, pause with a --More-- prompt. You can view the next screen by pressing the Enter (Return) key or the space bar. You can quit unzip with the q key and, on some systems, the Enter/Return key. Unlike UNIX more(1), unzip does not allow you to search forward or edit. Also, unzip doesn't notice if long lines wrap at the edge of the screen, effectively resulting in the printing of two or more lines or that some text scrolls off the top of the screen before being viewed. On some systems, the number of available lines on the screen is not detected, in which case unzip assumes the height is 24 lines.

-n	Never overwrite existing files. If a file already exists, skip the extraction of that file without prompting. By default, unzip queries before extracting any file that already exists; you can choose to overwrite only the current file, overwrite all files, skip extraction of the current file, skip extraction of all existing files, or rename the current file.
-N	Extract file comments as Amiga file notes. Create file comments with the -c option of zip, or with the -N option of the Amiga port of zip, which stores file notes as comments (Amiga).
-o	Overwrite existing files without prompting. This option is dangerous, so use it with care. (Under OS/2, you must often use it with -f as the only way to overwrite directory EAs.)
q	Use quiet mode.
V	Retain VMS version numbers.
X	Restore UID/GID information.

Environment Variables

The default environment variable name is UNZIP for all operating systems except VMS. For VMS systems, the environment variable name is UNZIP_OPTS because the symbol used to install unzip as a foreign command would otherwise be confused with the environment variable. For compatibility with zip, UNZIPOPT is also accepted (don't ask). If both UNZIP and UNZIPOPT are defined, UNZIP takes precedence. You can use the unzip diagnostic option (-v with no file name) to check the values of all possible unzip and zipinfo environment variables, as shown in the following example.

```
castle% unzip -v
UnZip 5.32 of 3 November 1997, by Info-ZIP.  Maintained by Greg Roelofs.  Send
bug reports to the authors at Zip-Bugs@lists.wku.edu; see README for details.

Latest sources and executables are at ftp://ftp.cdrom.com/pub/infozip/ , as of
above date; see http://www.cdrom.com/pub/infozip/UnZip.html for other sites.

Compiled with cc for Unix (Sun SPARC/Solaris) on Sep 10 1998.

UnZip special compilation options:
        COPYRIGHT_CLEAN (PKZIP 0.9x unreducing method not supported)
        LZW_CLEAN (PKZIP/Zip 1.x unshrinking method not supported)
        TIMESTAMP
        USE_EF_UT_TIME

UnZip and ZipInfo environment options:
           UNZIP:  [none]
        UNZIPOPT:  [none]
         ZIPINFO:  [none]
      ZIPINFOOPT:  [none]
castle%
```

Set the time zone variable (TZ) according to the local time zone so that the -f and -u options operate correctly. This variable may also be needed to correctly set timestamps on extracted files. Under Windows 95/NT, unzip should know the correct time zone even if TZ is unset, assuming the time zone is correctly set in the Control Panel.

You can modify the unzip default behavior by putting options in the UNZIP environment variable. You can use any option; however, this feature is probably most useful with the following modifiers to perform the following modifications:

- Autoconvert text files by default (-a).
- Convert file names from uppercase systems to lower case (-L).
- Match names case insensitively (-C).
- Make unzip quieter (-q).
- Always overwrite or never overwrite files as they are extracted (-o or -n).

For example, to make unzip act as quietly as possible, reporting only errors, you could use one of the following commands:

UNZIP=-qq; export UNZIP	UNIX Bourne shell.
setenv UNZIP -qq	UNIX C shell.
set UNZIP=-qq	OS/2 or MS-DOS.
define UNZIP_OPTS "-qq"	VMS (quotes for lower case).

Environment options are just like any other command-line options except that they are effectively the first options on the command line. To override an environment option, you can use the minus operator to remove it. For example, to override one of the quiet-flags in the example above, use the following command.

```
castle% unzip --q[other-options] file
```

The first dash is the normal switch character, and the second is a minus sign acting on the q option. Thus. the effect is to cancel one quantum of quietness. To cancel both quiet options, you can use two (or more) minuses.

```
castle% unzip -t--q file
castle% unzip ---qt file
```

The two commands are equivalent. This syntax may seem awkward or confusing, but it is reasonably intuitive. After the first dash, any other dashes signify a negative option. This syntax is consistent with the behavior of the nice(1) command.

Decryption

Encrypted archives are fully supported by Info-ZIP software, but because of U.S. export restrictions, the encryption and decryption sources are not packaged with the regular unzip and zip distributions. Because the sources were written by Europeans, however, they are freely available at sites throughout the world; see

`http://www.cdrom.com/pub/infozip/doc/WHERE`

or the WHERE file in any Info-ZIP source or binary distribution for locations both inside and outside the United States.

Because of the separate distribution, not all compiled versions of unzip support decryption. To check a version for crypt support, either try to test or extract an encrypted archive or check the unzip diagnostic screen (see the -v option) for [decryption] as one of the special compilation options.

You can use the -P option to supply a password on the command line, but at a cost in security. The preferred decryption method is simply to extract normally; if a file is encrypted, unzip prompts for the password without echoing what is typed. unzip continues to use the same password as long as it appears to be valid, by testing a 12-byte header on each file. The correct password always checks out against the header, but there is a 1-in-256 chance that an incorrect password may also work. (This is a security feature of the PKWARE zipfile format; it helps prevent brute-force attacks that might otherwise gain a speed advantage by testing only the header.) When you give an incorrect password that passes the header test anyway, either an incorrect CRC is generated for the extracted data or unzip fails during the extraction because the decrypted bytes do not constitute a valid compressed data stream.

If the first password fails the header check on some file, unzip prompts for another password, and so on until all files are extracted. If you do not know the password, press Return or Enter as a signal to skip all further prompting. Thereafter, only unencrypted files in the archive(s) are extracted. (In fact, that's not quite true; older versions of zip and zipcloak allowed null passwords, so unzip checks each encrypted file to see if the null password works. This may result in false positives and extraction errors, as noted above.)

Archives encrypted with 8-bit passwords (for example, passwords with accented European characters) may not be portable across systems and/or other archivers. This problem stems from the use of multiple encoding methods for such characters, including Latin-1 (ISO 8859-1) and OEM code page 850. DOS PKZIP 2.04g uses the OEM code page; Windows PKZIP 2.50 uses Latin-1 (and is therefore incompatible with DOS PKZIP); Info-ZIP uses the OEM code page on DOS, OS/2, and Win3.x ports but Latin-1 everywhere else; and Nico Mak's WinZip 6.x does not permit 8-bit passwords at all. UnZip 5.3 tries to use the default Latin-1 character set first, followed by the alternate one (OEM code page) to test passwords. On EBCDIC systems, if both of these character sets fail, EBCDIC encoding is tested as a last resort. (Because there are no known archivers that encrypt using EBCDIC encoding, EBCDIC is not tested on non-EBCDIC systems.) ISO character encodings other than Latin-1 are not supported.

Bugs

Multipart archives are not yet supported, except in conjunction with zip. To fix the problem, concatenate all parts in order and then perform zip -F on the concatenated archive. This problem will definitely be corrected in the next major release.

Archives read from standard input are not yet supported, except with funzip, and then you can extract only the first item in the archive.

Archives encrypted with 8-bit passwords (that is, passwords with accented European characters) may not be portable across systems and/or other archivers.

Dates, times, and permissions of stored directories are not restored except under UNIX.

[MS-DOS] When extracting or testing files from an archive on a defective diskette, if you choose the Fail option from the DOS Abort, Retry, Fail? message, older versions of unzip may hang the system, requiring a reboot. This problem appears to be fixed. You can use Control-C (or Control-Break) to terminate unzip.

Under DEC Ultrix, unzip sometimes fails on long files (bad CRC, not always reproducible). This problem was apparently because of either a hardware bug (cache memory) or an operating system bug (improper handling of page faults?). Because Ultrix has been abandoned in favor of Digital UNIX (OSF/1), this bug may no longer be an issue.

[UNIX] UNIX special files such as FIFO buffers (named pipes), block devices, and character devices are not restored even if they are somehow represented in the file, nor are hard-linked files relinked. Basically, the only file types restored by unzip are regular files, directories, and symbolic (soft) links.

[OS/2] Extended attributes for existing directories are updated only if you specify the -o (overwrite all) option. This is a limitation of the operating system; because only directories have a creation time associated with them, unzip has no way to determine whether the stored attributes are newer or older than those on disk. In practice, you may need to take a two pass approach: first unpack the archive normally (with or without freshening/updating existing files), then overwrite just the directory entries (for example, unzip -o foo */).

[VMS] When extracting to another directory, only the [.foo] syntax is accepted for the -d option; the simple UNIX foo syntax is silently ignored (as is the less common VMS foo.dir syntax).

[VMS] When the file being extracted already exists, unzip queries only permit skipping, overwriting, or renaming. The overwrite choice creates a new version of the file; the old version is not overwritten or deleted.

Examples

The following example extracts all items in the archive letters.zip into the current directory and subdirectories below it, creating any subdirectories as necessary.

```
castle% unzip letters
Archive:  letters.zip
  inflating: letters.rtf
castle%
```

The following example extracts all items in `letters.zip` into the current directory.

```
castle% unzip -j letters
Archive:  letters.zip
  inflating: letters.rtf
castle%
```

The following example tests `letters.zip`, printing a summary message indicating whether the archive is OK.

```
castle% unzip -tq letters
No errors detected in compressed data of letters.zip.
castle%
```

The following example tests all zip files in the current directory, printing only the summaries.

```
castle% unzip -tq \*.zip
No errors detected in compressed data of letters.zip.
castle%
```

Note — The backslash before the asterisk is required only if the shell expands wild-cards, as in UNIX. You can use double quotes instead.

The following example extracts to standard output all files in `letters.zip` whose names end in `.rtf`, autoconverting to the local end-of-line convention and piping the output into `more(1)`.

```
castle% unzip -ca letters \*.rtf | more
Archive:  letters.zip
  inflating: letters.rtf              [text]
{\rtf1\mac\ansicpg10000\uc1
  \deff0\deflang1033\deflangfe1033{\upr{\fonttbl{\f0\fn
il\fcharset256\fprq2{\*\panose 02020603050405020304}Times New
  Roman;}{\f6\fnil\fc
harset256\fprq2{\*\panose 02000500000000000000}Courier;}
}{\*\ud{\fonttbl{\f0\fnil\fcharset256\fprq2{\*\panose
  02020603050405020304}Times
New Roman;}{\f6\fnil\fcharset256\fprq2{\*\panose
  02000500000000000000}Courier;}}}
}{\colortbl;\red0\green0\blue0;\red0\green0\blue255;\red0\green255\blue255;
\red0\green255\blue0;\red255\green0\blue255;\red255\green0\blue0;\red255\green2
  55
... (More text not shown)
castle%
```

The following example extracts the binary file `paper1.dvi` to standard output and pipes it to a printing program.

```
castle% unzip -p articles paper1.dvi | lp
request id is seachild-3 (standard input)
castle%
```

The following example extracts all FORTRAN and C source files—`*.f`, `*.c`, `*.h`, and `Makefile`—into the `/tmp` directory.

```
castle% unzip source.zip "*.[fch]" Makefile -d /tmp
```

Note — The double quotes are needed only in UNIX and only if globbing is turned on.

The following example extracts all FORTRAN and C source files, regardless of case (that is, both `*.c` and `*.C`, and any `makefile`, `Makefile`, `MAKEFILE`, or similar capitalization form).

```
castle% unzip -C source.zip "*.[fch]" makefile -d /tmp
```

The following example extracts all FORTRAN and C source files, regardless of case (that is, both `*.c` and `*.C`, and any `makefile`, `Makefile`, `MAKEFILE`, or similar form), converts any uppercase MS-DOS or VMS names to lower case, and converts the line endings of all of the files to the local standard (without respect to any files that might be marked binary).

```
castle% unzip -aaCL source.zip "*.[fch]" makefile -d /tmp
```

The following example extracts only newer versions of the files already in the current directory, without querying.

```
castle% unzip -fo sources
```

Note — Be careful of unzipping in one time zone a file that was created in another time zone. ZIP archives other than those created by `Zip` 2.1 or later contain no time zone information, and a newer file from an Eastern time zone may, in fact, be older.

The following example extracts newer versions of the files already in the current directory and creates any files not already there (same caveat as for the previous example).

```
castle% unzip -uo sources
```

In the following five examples, assume that `UNZIP` or `UNZIP_OPTS` is set to `-q`. The following example does a single quiet listing.

```
castle% setenv UNZIP -qq
castle% unzip -l letters.zip
  20038  02-18-99  08:44   letters.rtf
castle%
```

The following example does a double quiet listing.

```
castle% setenv UNZIP -qq
castle% unzip -ql letters.zip
  20038  02-18-99  08:44    letters.rtf
castle%
```

Note — You generally don't need to add the `.zip` suffix.

Use any of the following three commands to do a standard listing. The extra dashes are ignored.

```
castle% unzip --ql file.zip
castle% unzip -l-q file.zip
castle% unzip -l--q file.zip
```

To `unzip` more than one archive file using the asterisk metacharacter, you must escape it by preceding it with a backslash. The following example unzips three archives that start with the characters `085`.

```
castle% unzip 085\*
Archive:   085XDOCS.ZIP
  inflating: 085X01.DOC
  inflating: 085X02.DOC
  inflating: 085X03~1.DOC
  inflating: 085X042.DOC
  inflating: 085X08R.DOC
  inflating: 085X09E.RTF

Archive:   085XFILE.ZIP
  inflating: 085X05.DOC

Archive:   085XINTR.ZIP
  inflating: 085X06.DOC
  inflating: 085X07.RTF

3 archives were successfully processed.
castle%
```

Tips

It is worth getting in the habit of testing your `zip` archives. To test them, you may find it useful to define an alias such as the following.

```
alias tt unzip -tq
```

You can then simply type `tt` *file* to test an archive, something that is worth doing. With luck, `unzip` reports `No errors detected in compressed data of zipfile.zip`.

It is also useful to set the `UNZIP` environment variable to `-aLC`. You can set your `ZIPINFO` variable to `-z`.

Exit Status

The exit status (or error level) approximates the exit codes defined by PKWARE and takes on the following values, except under VMS.

0	Normal; no errors or warnings detected.
1	One or more warning errors were encountered, but processing completed successfully. This status includes files where one or more files were skipped because of unsupported compression methods or encryption with an unknown password.
2	A generic error in the file format was detected. Processing may have completed successfully; some broken files created by other archivers have simple workarounds.
3	A severe error in the file format was detected. Processing probably failed immediately.
4	Unable to allocate memory for one or more buffers during program initialization.
5	Unable to allocate memory or unable to obtain a TTY to read the decryption password(s).
6	Unable to allocate memory during decompression to disk.
7	Unable to allocate memory during memory decompression.
8	[Currently not used.]
9	The specified files were not found.
10	Invalid options were specified on the command line.
11	No matching files were found.
50	The disk is (or was) full during extraction.
51	The end of the ZIP archive was encountered prematurely.
80	You aborted unzip prematurely with Control-C (or equivalent).
81	Testing or extraction of one or more files failed because of unsupported compression methods or unsupported decryption.
82	No files were found because of bad decryption password(s). If even one file is successfully processed, however, the exit status is 1.

VMS interprets standard UNIX (or PC) return values as other, scarier-looking things, so unzip instead maps them into VMS-style status codes. The current mapping is as follows:

1 (success)	Normal exit.
0x7fff0001	Warning errors.
(0x7fff000? + 16*normal_unzip_exit_status)	
	All other errors, where the ? is 2 (error) for unzip values 2, 9-11, and 80-82, and 4 (fatal error) for the remaining ones (3-8, 50, 51).

In addition, a compilation option expands on this behavior: defining `RETURN_CODES` results in a human-readable explanation of what the error status means.

See Also
`zipinfo(1)`

URL
The Info-ZIP home page is currently at
`http://www.cdrom.com/pub/infozip/`

Copyright
Distributed with permission from Info-ZIP. Please see
`http://www.cdrom.com/pub/infozip/doc/COPYING` for copyright information.

Authors
The primary Info-ZIP authors (current semi-active members of the Zip-Bugs work group) are: Greg "Cave Newt" Roelofs (`UnZip`); Onno van der Linden (`Zip`); Jean-Loup Gailly (compression); Mark Adler (decompression, `fUnZip`); Christian Spieler (VMS, MS-DOS, Windows 95, NT, shared code, general `Zip` and `UnZip` integration and optimization); Mike White (Windows GUI, Windows DLLs); Kai Uwe Rommel (OS/2); Paul Kienitz (Amiga, Windows 95); Chris Herborth (BeOS, QNX, Atari); Jonathan Hudson (SMS/QDOS); Sergio Monesi (Acorn RISC OS); Harald Denker (Atari, MVS); John Bush (Solaris, Amiga); Hunter Goatley (VMS); Steve Salisbury (Windows 95, NT); Steve Miller (Windows CE GUI), Johnny Lee (MS-DOS, Windows 95, NT); and Dave Smith (Tandem NSK). The author of the original `unzip` code on which Info-ZIP is based is Samuel H. Smith; Carl Mascott did the first UNIX port; and David P. Kirschbaum organized and led Info-ZIP in its early days, with Keith Petersen hosting the original mailing list at WSMR-SimTel20. The full list of contributors to `UnZip` has grown quite large; please refer to the `CONTRIBS` file in the `UnZip` source distribution for a relatively complete version.

Versions

`v1.2`	15 Mar 89	Samuel H. Smith.
`v2.0`	9 Sep 89	Samuel H. Smith.
`v2.x`	Fall 1989	Many Usenet contributors.
`v3.0`	1 May 90	Info-ZIP (DPK, consolidator).
`v3.1`	15 Aug 90	Info-ZIP (DPK, consolidator).
`v4.0`	1 Dec 90	Info-ZIP (GRR, maintainer).
`v4.1`	12 May 91	Info-ZIP.

v4.2	20 Mar 92	Info-ZIP (Zip-Bugs subgroup, GRR).
v5.0	21 Aug 92	Info-ZIP (Zip-Bugs subgroup, GRR).
v5.01	15 Jan 93	Info-ZIP (Zip-Bugs subgroup, GRR).
v5.1	7 Feb 94	Info-ZIP (Zip-Bugs subgroup, GRR).
v5.11	2 Aug 94	Info-ZIP (Zip-Bugs subgroup, GRR).
v5.12	28 Aug 94	Info-ZIP (Zip-Bugs subgroup, GRR).
v5.2	30 Apr 96	Info-ZIP (Zip-Bugs subgroup, GRR).
v5.3	22 Apr 97	Info-ZIP (Zip-Bugs subgroup, GRR).
v5.31	31 May 97	Info-ZIP (Zip-Bugs subgroup, GRR).
v5.32	3 Nov 97	Info-ZIP (Zip-Bugs subgroup, GRR).

uptime — Show How Long a System Has Been Up

Synopsis

```
/usr/bin/uptime
```

Description

The uptime command prints the current time, the length of time the system has been up, and the average number of jobs in the run queue over the last 1, 5, and 15 minutes. It is, essentially, the first line of a w(1) command.

Note — You can use the who -b command to display the time the system was last booted.

Example

The following example shows the output of uptime.

```
castle% uptime
10:47am up 27 day(s), 50 mins, 1 user, load average: 0.18, 0.26, 0.20
castle%
```

Attributes

See attributes(5) for descriptions of the following attributes:

Attribute Type	Attribute Value
Availability	SUNWcsu

See Also

w(1), who(1), whodo(1M), attributes(5)

---

users — Display a Compact List of Logged-In Users

Synopsis

/usr/ucb/users [*filename*]

Description

users lists the login names of the users currently on the system in a compact, one-line format. Specifying *filename* tells users where to find its information; by default, it checks /var/adm/utmp.

The users command is equivalent to typing who -q.

Examples

The following example shows that four users are logged in to the system castle.

```
castle% users
winsor ray des rob
castle%
```

Files

/var/adm/utmp

Attributes

See attributes(5) for descriptions of the following attributes:

Attribute Type	Attribute Value
Availability	SUNWscpu

See Also

who(1), attributes(5)

uucp, uulog, uuname — UNIX-to-UNIX System Copy

Synopsis
```
/usr/bin/uucp [-c | -C][-d | -f][-ggrade][-jmr][-nuser][-sfile]
   [-xdebug-level] source-file source-file
/usr/bin/uulog[-ssys][-source-file][-x][-source-filedestination-file
/usr/bin/uuname [-c|-l]
```

Description
The uucp (UNIX-to-UNIX copy) suite of commands is part of a data communications subsystem that enables you to transfer ASCII and binary files between systems, control execution of commands, queue jobs for later transfer, and automatically retry when transfer fails. The complete uucp suite of commands includes user commands and functions, security features, logging and debugging tools, and a number of data transfer protocols. This section describes the uucp, uulog, and uuname commands.

uucp

uucp copies files named by the *source-file* arguments to the location specified by the *destination-file* argument.

uulog

uulog queries a log file of uucp or uuxqt transactions in file /var/uucp/.Log/uucico/system or /var/uucp/.Log/uuxqt/system.

uuname

uuname lists the names of systems known to uucp.

Notes
For security reasons, the domain of remotely accessible files may be severely restricted. You probably cannot access files by path name; ask a responsible person on the remote system to send them to you. For the same reasons, you probably cannot send files to arbitrary path names. As distributed, the remotely accessible files are those whose names begin /var/spool/uucppublic (equivalent to ~/).

All files received by uucp are owned by uucp.

Protected files and files that are in protected directories that are owned by the requester can be sent by uucp. However, if the requester is root and the directory is not searchable by other or the file is not readable by other, the request fails.

Strings that are passed to remote systems may not be evaluated in the same locale as the one in use by the process that invoked uucp on the local system.

Configuration files must be treated as C- (or POSIX-) locale text files.

Options

uucp

-c	Do not copy local file to the spool directory for transfer to the remote system (default).
-C	Force the copy of local files to the spool directory for transfer.
-d	Make all necessary directories for the file copy (default).
-f	Do not make intermediate directories for the file copy.
-g*grade*	Specify the grade as a single letter, number, or a string of alphanumeric characters defining a service grade. Use the uuglist command to determine whether it is appropriate to use the single letter, number, or a string of alphanumeric characters as a service grade. The output from the uuglist command is a list of service grades that are available or a message that says to use a single letter or number as a grade of service.
-j	Print the uucp job identification string on standard output. This job identification can be used by uustat to obtain the status of a uucp job or to terminate a uucp job. The uucp job is valid as long as the job remains queued on the local system.
-m	Send mail to the requester when the copy is complete. The -m option works only when sending files or receiving a single file. Receiving multiple files specified by special shell characters ?, &, and [. . .] does not activate the -m option.
-n*user*	Notify user on the remote system that a file was sent.
-r	Do not start the file transfer, just queue the job.
-s*file*	Report status of the transfer to *file*. This option is accepted for compatibility but is ignored because it is insecure.
-x*debug-level*	
	Produce debugging output on standard output. *debug-level* is a number between 0 and 9; as it increases to 9, show more detailed debugging information. This option may not be available on all systems.

uulog
The following options print logging information.

-s*sys*	Print information about file transfer work involving system *sys*.
-f*system*	Do a tail -f of the file transfer log for *system*. (You must press the Break key to exit this function.)

Other options you can use in conjunction with the above options are:

-x	Look in the uuxqt log file for the given system.
-*number*	Execute a tail command of *number* lines.

uuname

-c	Display the names of systems known to cu. The two lists are the same unless your system is using different Systems files for cu and uucp. See the Sysfiles file.
-l	Display the local system name.

Operands

The source file name may be a path name on your system or may have the form:

system-name!pathname

where *system-name* is taken from a list of system names that uucp knows about. *source-file* is restricted to no more than one *system-name*. The destination *system-name* can also include a list of system names such as

system-name!system-name!...!system-name!pathname

With this syntax, uucp tries to send the file to the destination, using the specified route. Take care to ensure that intermediate nodes in the route are willing to forward information.

Note — The forwarding of files through other systems may not be compatible with the previous version of uucp. If you use forwarding, all systems in the route must have compatible versions of uucp.

For C shell, surround the ! character with single quotes (`'`), or precede it with a backslash (\).

The shell metacharacters ?, * and [...] appearing in *pathname* are expanded on the appropriate system.

Path names can be one of the following:

- An absolute path name.
- A path name preceded by ~*user* where *user* is a login name on the specified system and is replaced by that user's login directory.
- A path name preceded by ~/*destination* where *destination* is appended to /var/spool/uucppublic.

Note — This destination is treated as a file name unless you are transferring more than one file with this request or the destination is already a directory. To ensure that the destination is a directory, follow it with a slash (/). For example ~/dan/ as the destination creates the directory /var/spool/uucppublic/dan if it does not exist and puts the requested file(s) in that directory). Anything else is prefixed by the current directory.

If the result is an erroneous path name for the remote system, the copy fails. If the *destination-file* is a directory, the last part of the *source-file* name is used.

Invoking uucp with shell wild-card characters as the remote *source-file* invokes the uux(1C) command to execute the uucp command on the remote system. The remote uucp command spools the files on the remote system. After the first session terminates, if the remote system is configured to transfer the spooled files to the local system, the remote system initiates a call and sends the files; otherwise, the user must "call" the remote system to transfer the files from the spool directory to the local system. This call can be done manually with Uutry(1M) or as a side effect of another uux(1C) or uucp call.

Note that the local system must have permission to execute the uucp command on the remote system so that the remote system can send the spooled files.

uucp removes execute permissions across the transmission and gives 0666 read and write permissions (see chmod(2)).

Environment Variables

See environ(5) for descriptions of the following environment variables that affect the execution of uucp: LC_COLLATE, LC_CTYPE, LC_MESSAGES, LC_TIME, TZ, and NLSPATH.

Exit Status

0   Successful completion.

>0   An error occurred.

Files

/bin/uu*   uucp commands.

/etc/uucp/* Other data files.

/var/spool/uucp

             Spool directories.

/usr/lib/uucp/*

             Other program files.

/var/spool/uucppublic/*

             Public directory for receiving and sending.

Attributes

See attributes(5) for descriptions of the following attributes:

Attribute Type	Attribute Value
Availability	SUNWbnuu

See Also

mail(1), uuglist(1C), uustat(1C), uux(1C), Uutry(1M), uuxqt(1M), chmod(2), attributes(5)

---

uuencode, uudecode — Encode or Decode a Binary File

Synopsis

/usr/bin/uuencode [*source-file*] *decode-pathname*
/usr/bin/uudecode [-p] *encoded-file*

Description

Use the uuencode/uudecode commands to convert between ASCII and binary data.

Warning — If you run uuencode then run uudecode on a file in the same directory, you will overwrite the original file.

---

uuencode

uuencode converts a binary file into an encoded representation that you can send using mail(1). It encodes the contents of *source-file* or the standard input if you specify no *source-file* argument. The *decode-pathname* argument is required. The *decode-pathname* is included in the encoded file header as the name of the file where uudecode puts the binary (decoded) data. uuencode also includes the permission modes of *source-file*, (except setuid, setgid, and sticky bits), so that *decode-pathname* is recreated with those same permission modes.

Note — Because the encoded file's size is expanded by 35 percent (3 bytes become 4, plus control information) it takes longer to transmit than the equivalent binary file.

---

uudecode

uudecode reads an *encoded-file*, strips off any leading and trailing lines added by mailer programs, and recreates the original binary data with the file name and the mode specified in the header.

The encoded file is an ordinary, portable, character-set text file; you can edit it with any text editor. It is best to change only the mode or *decode-pathname* in the header to avoid corrupting the decoded binary.

Note — The user on the remote system who is invoking uudecode (typically uucp) must have write permission on the file specified in the *decode-pathname* operand.

Options

uudecode

-p   Decode *encoded-file* and send it to standard output. This option
                enables you to use uudecode in a pipeline.

Operands

uuencode

decode-pathname

                The path name of the file where the uudecode command puts the
                decoded file. If there are characters in *decode-pathname* that are
                not in the portable file-name character set, the results are
                unspecified.

source-file

                A path name of the file to be encoded.

uudecode

encoded-file

                The path name of a file containing the output of uuencode.

Usage

See largefile(5) for the description of the behavior of uuencode and
uudecode when encountering files greater than or equal to 2 Gbytes (2**31
bytes).

Environment Variables

See environ(5) for descriptions of the following environment variables that
affect the execution of uuencode and uudecode: LC_CTYPE, LC_MESSAGES,
and NLSPATH.

Output

The standard output is a text file (encoded in the character set of the current
locale) that begins with the line

"begin%s%s\n", <mode>, decode_pathname

and ends with the line

end\n

In both cases, the lines have no preceding or trailing blank characters.
    The algorithm that is used for lines in between begin and end takes three
octets as input and writes four characters of output by splitting the input at
six-bit intervals into four octets, containing data in the lower six bits only.

These octets are converted to characters by adding a value of 0x20 to each octet so that each octet is in the range 0x20-0x5f. It is then assumed to represent a printable character. Each octet is translated into the corresponding character codes for the codeset in use in the current locale. (For example, the octet 0x41, representing A, is translated to A in the current codeset, such as 0xc1 if it is EBCDIC.)

Where the bits of two octets are combined, the least significant bits of the first octet are shifted left and combined with the most significant bits of the second octet shifted right. Thus, the three octets A, B, C are converted into the four octets:

```
0x20 + (( A >> 2) & 0x3F)
0x20 + (((A << 4) ((B >> 4) & 0xF)) & 0x3F)
0x20 + (((B << 2) ((C >> 6) & 0x3)) & 0x3F)
0x20 + (( C) & 0x3F)
```

These octets are then translated into the local character set.

Each encoded line contains a length character, equal to the number of characters to be decoded plus 0x20 translated to the local character set as described above, followed by the encoded characters. The maximum number of octets to be encoded on each line is 45.

Exit Status

| 0 | Successful completion. |
| >0 | An error occurred. |

Attributes

See attributes(5) for descriptions of the following attributes:

Attribute Type	Attribute Value
Availability	SUNWesu

See Also

mail(1), mailx(1), uucp(1C), uux(1C), attributes(5), largefile(5)

uuglist — Print the List of Available Service Grades

Synopsis

/usr/bin/uuglist [-u]

Description

A system may provide several grades of service for uucp commands. Each grade receives different priorities from the UUCP system. You can use the uuglist command to display a list of service grades that are available on the system to use with the -g option of uucp(1C) and uux(1C), as shown in the following example.

```
castle% uuglist -u
high
low
medium
castle%
```

Options

-u   List the names of the service grades that the user is allowed to use with the -g option of the uucp and uux commands.

Files

/etc/uucp/Grades

Contains the list of service grades.

Attributes

See attributes(5) for descriptions of the following attributes:

Attribute Type	Attribute Value
Availability	SUNWbnuu

See Also

uucp(1C), uux(1C), attributes(5)

---

uulog, uuname — UNIX-to-UNIX System Copy

Synopsis

```
/usr/bin/uulog [-ssys] [-fsystem] [-x] [-number] system
/usr/bin/uuname [-c|-l]
```

Description

See uucp(1).

uupick — Public UNIX-to-UNIX System File Copy

Synopsis
```
/usr/bin/uupick [-ssystem]
```

Description
See uuto(1).

uustat — uucp Status Inquiry and Job Control

Synopsis
```
/usr/bin/uustat [-m] | [-p] | [-q] | [-kjobid [-n]] | [-rjobid [-n]]
/usr/bin/uustat [-a][-ssystem [-j]][-uuser][-Sqric]
/usr/bin/uustat -tsystem [-c][-dnumber]
```

Description
uustat functions in the following three areas:

- Displays the general status of, or cancels, previously specified uucp commands.
- Provides remote system performance information, such as average transfer rates or average queue times.
- Provides general, remote system-specific and user-specific status of uucp connections to other systems.

Note — After the user has issued the uucp request, if the file to be transferred is moved, is deleted, or was not copied to the spool directory (-C option) when the uucp request was made, uustat reports a file size of -99999. This job eventually fails because the file(s) to be transferred cannot be found.

Options

General Status
The following options obtain general status of, or cancel, previously specified uucp commands.

-a   List all jobs in queue.

-j	List the total number of jobs displayed. You can use this option with the -a or the -s option.
-k*jobid*	Kill the uucp request whose job identification is *jobid*. The killed uucp request must belong to the user issuing the uustat command unless the user is the superuser or uucp administrator. If the superuser or the uucp administrator kills the job, send e-mail to the user.
-m	Report the status of accessibility of all systems.
-n	Suppress all standard output, but not standard error. Use this option with the -k and -r options.
-p	Execute the command ps -flp for all the process IDs that are in the lock files.
-q	List the jobs queued for each system. If a status file exists for the system, report its date, time, and status information. If a number appears in parentheses next to the number of C or X files, it is the age in days of the oldest C./X. file for that system. The Retry field represents the number of hours until the next possible call. The Count is the number of failure attempts. Note that for systems with a moderate number of outstanding jobs, this command can take 30 seconds or more of real time to execute. An example of the output produced by the -q option is:

```
eagle 3C 04/07-11:07 NO DEVICES AVAILABLE

mh3bs3 2C 07/07-10:42 SUCCESSFUL
```

	This output indicates the number of command files that are waiting for each system. Each command file may have zero or more files to be sent (zero means to call the system and see if work is to be done). The date and time refer to the previous interaction with the system, followed by the status of the interaction.
-r*jobid*	Rejuvenate *jobid*. Touch the files associated with *jobid* so that their modification time is set to the current time. This adjustment prevents the cleanup daemon from deleting the job until the job modification time reaches the limit imposed by the daemon.

Remote System Status
The following options provide remote system performance information such as average transfer rates or average queue times. You can use the -c and -d options only with the -t option.

-c	Calculate average queue time. With no -c option, calculate the average transfer. For example, the command

```
castle% uustat -teagle -d50 -c
```

produces output in the following format:

```
average queue time to eagle for last 50 minutes:
5 seconds
```

The same command without the `-c` parameter produces output in the following format:

```
average transfer rate with eagle for last 50 minutes:
2000.88 bytes/sec
```

-d*number*   Specify *number* in minutes to override the 60-minute default used for calculations. These calculations are based on information contained in the optional performance log and therefore may not be available. Calculations can be made only from the time that the performance log was last cleaned up.

-t*system*   Report the average transfer rate or average queue time for the past 60 minutes for the remote system.

User- or System-Specific Status

The following options provide general, remote-system-specific and user-specific status of uucp connections to other systems. You can specify either or both of the following options with uustat. You can use the `-j` option with the `-s` option to list the total number of jobs displayed.

-s*system*   Report the status of all uucp requests for remote system *system*.

-u*user*   Report the status of all uucp requests issued by *user*.

Output for both the `-s` and `-u` options has the following format:

```
eagleN1bd7  4/07-11:07  S  eagle  dan  522      /home/dan/A

eagleC1bd8  4/07-11:07  S  eagle  dan  59       D.3b2a12ce4924
4/07-11:07  S  eagle  dan  rmail  mike
```

The first field is the job ID of the job followed by the date/time. The next field is an S if the job is sending a file or an R if the job is requesting a file. The next field is the system where the file is to be transferred, followed by the user ID of the user who queued the job. The next field contains the size of the file or, in the case of a remote execution, the name of the command. In this example, rmail is the command used for remote mail. When this field contains the size, the file name is also shown. The file name can either be the name given by the user or an internal name (for example, D.3b2a1ce4924) that is created for data files associated with remote executions (rmail in this example).

-S*qric*   Report the job state.

    q   Queued jobs. The transfer has not started.

    r   Running jobs. The transfer has begun.

    i   Interrupted jobs. The transfer began but was terminated before the file was completely transferred.

    c   Completed jobs. The job successfully transferred.

You can use the parameters in any combination, but you must specify at least one parameter. You can also use the `-S` option with `-s` and `-u` options. The output for this option is exactly like the output for `-s` and `-u`, except that the job states are appended as the last output word. Output for a completed job has the following format:

```
eagleC1bd3 completed
```

When you specify no options, `uustat` writes to standard output the status of all `uucp` requests issued by the current user.

Environment Variables

See `environ`(5) for descriptions of the following environment variables that affect the execution of `uustat`: `LC_CTYPE`, `LC_MESSAGES`, `LC_TIME`, `TZ`, and `NLSPATH`.

Exit Status

0	Successful completion.
>0	An error occurred.

Files

`/var/spool/uucp/*`

> Spool directories.

`/var/uucp/.Admin/account`

> Accounting log.

`/var/uucp/.Admin/perflog`

> Performance log.

Attributes

See `attributes`(5) for descriptions of the following attributes:

Attribute Type	Attribute Value
Availability	SUNWbnuu

See Also

`uucp(1C)`, `attributes(5)`

Diagnostics

The `-t` option produces no message when the data needed for the calculations is not being recorded.

uuto, uupick — Public UNIX-to-UNIX System File Copy

Synopsis
```
/usr/bin/uuto [-mp] source-file...destination
/usr/bin/uupick [-ssystem]
```

Description

uuto

uuto sends *source-file* to *destination*. uuto uses uucp(1C) to send files; it allows the local system to control the file access. A *source-file* name is a path name on your system. Destination has the form:

```
system[!system] ... !user
```

where *system* is taken from a list of system names that uucp knows about. *user* is the login name of someone on the specified system.

The files (or subtrees if you specify directories) are sent to PUBDIR on *system*, where PUBDIR is a public directory defined in the uucp source. By default, this directory is /var/spool/uucppublic. Specifically, the files are sent to

```
PUBDIR/receive/user/mysystem/files.
```

The recipient is notified by mail(1) of the arrival of files.

Note — To send files that begin with a dot (for instance, .profile), you must include the dot. For example, the following file names are correct:

```
.profile.prof*  .profil?
```

The following file names are incorrect:

```
*prof*  ?profile
```

---

uupick

uupick accepts or rejects the files transmitted to the user. Specifically, uupick searches PUBDIR for files destined for the user. For each entry (file or directory) found, the following message is printed on standard output:

```
from system sysname: [file file-name][dir dirname] ?
```

uupick then reads a line from standard input to determine the disposition of the file.

newline   Go to next entry.

d	Delete the entry.
m [*dir*]	Move the entry to named directory *dir*. If you do not specify *dir* as a complete path name (in which $HOME is legitimate), assume a destination relative to the current directory. If you specify no destination, the default is the current directory.
a [*dir*]	Same as m above, except move all the files sent from *system*.
p	Print the content of the file.
q	Stop.
EOT (control-d)	
	Same as q.
!*command*	Escape to the shell to do *command*.
*	Print a command summary.

Options

uuto

-m	Send mail to the sender when the copy is complete.
-p	Copy the source file into the spool directory before transmission.

uupick

-s system	Search the PUBDIR only for files sent from system.

Operands

destination

A string of the form:

system-name!*user*

where *system-name* is taken from a list of system names that uucp knows about; see uuname. The *user* argument is the login name of someone on the specified system. The *system-name* destination can also be a list of names such as

system-name!*system-name*!...!*system-name*!*user*

in which case, try to send the file via the specified route to the destination. Take care to ensure that intermediate nodes in the route are willing to forward information.

source-file

A path name of a file on the local system to be copied to destination.

Environment Variables

See environ(5) for descriptions of the following environment variables that affect the execution of uuto and uupick: LC_TYPE, LC_MESSAGES, and NLSPATH.

Exit Status

0	Successful completion.
>0	An error occurred.

Files

PUBDIR   /var/spool/uucppublic public directory.

Attributes

See attributes(5) for descriptions of the following attributes:

Attribute Type	Attribute Value
Availability	SUNWbnuu

See Also

mail(1), uucp(1C), uustat(1C), uux(1C), uucleanup(1M), attributes(5)

uux — UNIX-to-UNIX System Command Execution

Synopsis

```
/usr/bin/uux [-] [-bcCjnprz] [-aname] [-ggrade] [-sfilename] [-xdebug-level]
    command-string
```

Description

uux gathers zero or more files from various systems, executes a command on a specified system, and then sends standard output to a file on a specified system.

Note — For security reasons, most installations limit the list of commands executable on behalf of an incoming request from uux, permitting only the receipt of mail (see mail(1)). Remote execution permissions are defined in /etc/uucp/Permissions.

The command-string is made up of one or more arguments that look like a shell command line, except that you can prefix the command and file names with system-name!. A null system-name is interpreted as the local system.

File names can be one of the following:

- An absolute path name.
- A path name preceded by ~*xxx*, where *xxx* is a login name on the specified system and is replaced by that user's login directory.

Anything else is prefixed by the current directory.

For example, the following command gets the `filename1` and `filename2` files from the `sys1` and `sys2` systems, executes a `diff(1)` command, and puts the results in `filename.diff` in the local `PUBDIR/dan/` directory.

```
castle% uux "!diff sys1!/home/dan/filename1sys2!/a4/dan/filename2 >
!~/dan/filename.diff"
```

`PUBDIR` is a public directory defined in the `uucp` source. By default, this directory is `/var/spool/uucppublic`.

`uux` tries to get all appropriate files to the specified system where they are processed. For files that are output files, escape the file name by using parentheses. For example, the following command gets `/usr/filename` from system b and sends it to system a, performs a `cut` command on that file, and sends the result of the `cut` command to system c.

```
castle% uux "a!cut -f1 b!/usr/filename >c!/usr/filename"
```

`uux` notifies you if the requested command on the remote system is disallowed. You can turn off this notification with the -n option. The response comes by mail from the remote system.

The following restrictions apply to the shell pipeline processed by `uux`.

- Quote any special shell characters, such as <, >, ;, | either by quoting the entire command string or by quoting the special characters as individual arguments.
- In gathering files from different systems, `uux` does not perform path-name expansion. Thus, a request such as `uux "c89 remsys!~/*.c"` would try to copy the file named literally `*.c` to the local system.
- Only the first command of a shell pipeline can have a *system-name*!. All other commands are executed on the system of the first command.
- The use of the shell metacharacter * probably does not do what you want it to do.
- The shell tokens << and >> are not implemented.
- You cannot use the redirection operators >>, <<, >| or >&.
- You cannot use the reserved word ! at the head of the pipeline to modify the exit status.
- Alias substitution is not performed.

Notes

The execution of commands on remote systems takes place in an execution directory known to the uucp system.

All files required for the execution are put into this directory unless they already reside on that system. Therefore, the simple file name (without path or system reference) must be unique within the uux request. The following command does *not* work.

```
castle% uux "a!diff b!/home/dan/xyz c!/home/dan/xyz >!xyz.diff"
```

But the following command does work if diff is a permitted command.

```
castle% uux "a!diff a!/home/dan/xyz c!/home/dan/xyz > !xyz.diff"
```

Protected files and files that are in protected directories that are owned by the requester can be sent in commands using uux. However, the requests fail if the requester is root and the directory is not searchable by other.

Options

–	Specify that *command-string* comes from standard input.
-a*name*	Use *name* as the user job identification replacing the initiator user ID. (Return notification to the user ID name.)
-b	Return whatever standard input was provided to the uux command if the exit status is non-zero.
-c	Do not copy local file to the spool directory for transfer to the remote system (default).
-C	Force the copy of local files to the spool directory for transfer.
-g*grade*	Specify *grade* as a single letter, number, or a string of alphanumeric characters defining a service grade. Use the uuglist(1C) command to determine whether it is appropriate to use the single letter, number, or a string of alphanumeric characters as a service grade. The output from the uuglist command is a list of service grades that are available or a message that says to use a single letter or number as a grade of service.
-j	Output the job ID string on the standard output, which is the job identification. uustat(1C) can use this job identification to obtain the status or terminate a job.
-n	Do not notify the user if the command fails.
-p	Same as –. Specify that *command-string* comes from standard input.
-r	Queue the job but do not start the file transfer.
-s*filename*	Report status of the transfer in *filename*. This option is accepted for compatibility but is ignored because it is insecure.

-xdebug-level

> Produce debugging output on the standard output. Specify *debug-level* as a number between 0 and 9; as it increases to 9, show more detailed debugging information.

-z   Send success notification to the user.

Environment Variables

See environ(5) for descriptions of the following environment variables that affect the execution of uux: LC_CTYPE, LC_MESSAGES, and NLSPATH.

Exit Status

0   Successful completion.

>0   An error occurred.

Files

/etc/uucp/*

> Other data and programs.

/etc/uucp/Permissions

> Remote execution permissions.

/usr/lib/uucp/*

> Other programs.

/var/spool/uucp

> Spool directories.

Attributes

See attributes(5) for descriptions of the following attributes:

Attribute Type	Attribute Value
Availability	SUNWbnuu

See Also

cut(1), mail(1), uucp(1C), uuglist(1C), uustat(1C), attributes(5)

V

vacation — Reply to Mail Automatically

Synopsis
```
/usr/bin/vacation [-I]
/usr/bin/vacation [-j][-a alias][-tN] username
```

Description
vacation automatically replies to incoming e-mail. It uses the `.forward` file in your home directory to automatically forward the message in `.vacation.msg` to any user who sends you an e-mail message while the vacation program is activated. It also uses the `.vacation.pag` and `.vacation.dir` files in your home directory to store a list of senders.

No vacation message is sent in the following cases:

- When the `To:` or the `Cc:` line does not list the users to whom the original message was sent or one of a number of aliases for them.
- When the initial `From:` line includes the string `-REQUEST@` or if the header includes a `Precedence: bulk` or `Precedence: junk` line.
- When mail is received from `postmaster`.
- When mail is received from `Mailer-Daemon`.

Setting Up vacation

vacation provides an interactive program that you can use to set up the basic vacation configuration.

The interactive program automatically creates the following files in your home directory.

~/.vacation.msg

> Contains the message that is sent in response to incoming mail.

~/.forward Contains a line of the following form that is used to forward the message in the .vacation.msg file.

> *username*, "|/usr/bin/vacation *username*"

~/.vacation.pag
~/.vacation.dir

> Contains a list of senders when vacation is enabled.

To set up vacation, type the command with no arguments. If there is no .vacation.msg file in your home directory, vacation creates it with a default message and starts an editor that you can use to modify the message. If there is an existing .vacation.msg file in your home directory, vacation asks you if you want to edit it.

vacation uses the VISUAL or EDITOR environment variable to determine which editor to invoke. If neither environment variable is set, vacation uses vi(1) as the editor.

The following example sets up vacation, using the default .vacation.msg file that already exists in the home directory.

```
castle% vacation
This program can be used to answer your mail automatically
when you go away on vacation.
You have a message file in /export/home/winsor/.vacation.msg.
Would you like to see it? y
From: winsor (via the vacation program)
Subject: away from my mail

I will not be reading my mail for a while.
Your mail regarding "$SUBJECT" will be read when I return.
Would you like to edit it? n
To enable the vacation feature a ".forward" file is created.
Would you like to enable the vacation feature? y
Vacation feature ENABLED. Please remember to turn it off when
you get back from vacation. Bon voyage.
castle%
```

When vacation is enabled, the mailer sends a copy of an incoming message to *username* and pipes another copy into vacation.

Disabling vacation

The presence of the .forward file determines whether vacation is enabled or disabled. To disable vacation, remove the .forward file or move it to a new name.

You can use the vacation program to disable vacation. If a .forward file is present in your home directory, you are asked whether you want to remove it to disable vacation and end the installation.

Existing .vacation.msg, .vacation.pag, and .vacation.dir files are not affected.

The following example uses the vacation command to disable vacation.

```
castle% vacation
This program can be used to answer your mail automatically
when you go away on vacation.
You have a message file in /export/home/winsor/.vacation.msg.
Would you like to see it? n
Would you like to edit it? n
You have a .forward file in your home directory containing:
 \winsor, "|/usr/bin/vacation winsor"
Would you like to remove it and disable the vacation feature? y
Back to normal reception of mail.
castle%
```

Options

-I   Clear the .vacation.pag and .vacation.dir files. If you do not specify the -I flag and provide a *username* argument, vacation reads the first line from the standard input (for a From: line, no colon). If absent, it produces an error message.

Use the following configuration options in the .forward file, not on the command line. For example, *username*, "|/usr/bin/vacation -t1m *username*" repeats replies to the sender every minute.

-a *alias*   Indicate that *alias* is one of the valid aliases for the user running vacation so that mail addressed to that alias generates a reply.

-j   Do not check whether the recipient appears in the To: or the Cc: line.

-t*N*   Change the interval between repeat replies to the same sender. The default is 1 week. A trailing s, m, h, d, or w scales *N* to seconds, minutes, hours, days, or weeks.

Usage

The ~/.vacation.msg file should include a header with at least a Subject: line. It should not include a From: or a To: line. For example:

```
Subject: I am on vacation
I am on vacation until March 8. If you have an urgent issue, please
  contact my manager.
--Janice
```

If you include the string $SUBJECT in the `.vacation.msg` file, it is replaced with the subject of the original message when the reply is sent. For example, the following `.vacation.msg` file includes the subject of the message in the reply.

```
Subject: I am on vacation
I am on vacation until March 8.
I will read your mail regarding "$SUBJECT" when I return. If you have an
  urgent issue, please contact my manager.
--Janice
```

Files

`~/.forward`

> Contains a line of the following format that is used to forward the message in the `.vacation.msg` file.
>
> `\`*username*`, "|/usr/bin/vacation` *username*`"`

`~/.vacation.msg`

> Contains the message that is sent in response to incoming mail.

`~/.vacation.pag`

> Stores a list of senders when `vacation` is enabled. You cannot view this file directly with a text editor.

`~/.vacation.dir`

> Stores a list of senders when `vacation` is enabled. You cannot view this file directly with a text editor.

Attributes

See `attributes`(5) for descriptions of the following attributes:

Attribute Type	Attribute Value
Availability	SUNWcsu

See Also

`vi`(1), `sendmail`(1M), `dbm`(3B), `aliases`(4), `attributes`(5)

val — Validate an SCCS File

Synopsis
```
/usr/ccs/bin/val -
/usr/ccs/bin/val [-s][-m name][-rsid][-y type] s.filename ...
```

Description
See sccs-val(1).

vax — Get Processor Type Truth Value

Synopsis
```
/usr/bin/vax
```

Description
See machid(1).

vc — Version Control

Synopsis
```
/usr/ccs/bin/vc [-a][-t][-cchar][-s][keyword=value... keyword=value]
```

Description

> **Note** — This command is obsolete and will be removed in the next release.

The vc command copies lines from the standard input to the standard output, using arguments and control statements from the standard input. In a copy operation, user-declared keywords can be replaced by their string value when they appear in plain text and/or control statements.

The copying of lines from the standard input to the standard output is conditional, based on tests (in control statements) of keyword values specified in control statements or as vc command arguments.

A control statement is a single line beginning with a control character, except as modified by the -t key letter. The default control character is colon (:)

except as modified by the -c key letter. Input lines beginning with a backslash (\) followed by a control character are not control lines and are copied to the standard output with the backslash removed. Lines beginning with a backslash followed by a noncontrol character are copied in their entirety.

A keyword is composed of nine or fewer alphanumerics; the first must be alphabetic. A value is any ASCII string that can be created with ed; a numeric value is an unsigned string of digits. Keyword values may not contain blanks or Tabs.

Keywords are replaced by values whenever a keyword surrounded by control characters is encountered on a version control statement. The -a key letter forces replacement of keywords in all lines of text. You can include an uninterpreted control character in a value by preceding it with \. If a literal \ is desired, then you must precede it with \.

Options

-a   Force replacement of keywords surrounded by control characters with their assigned value in all text lines and not just in vc statements.

-c*char*   Specify a control character to be used in place of the colon (:) default.

-s   Silence warning messages (not error) that are normally printed on the diagnostic output.

-t   Ignore all characters from the beginning of a line up to and including the first Tab character for the purpose of detecting a control statement. If a control statement is found, discard all characters up to and including the Tab.

     vc recognizes the following version control statements.

:asg *keyword=value*

          Assign values to keywords. An asg statement overrides the assignment for the corresponding keyword on the vc command line and all previous asg statements for that keyword. Keywords that are declared but are not assigned values have null values.

:dcl *keyword[, ..., keyword]*

          Declare keywords. All keywords must be declared.

:if *condition*

...

:end   Skip lines of the standard input. If *condition* is true, copy all lines between the if statement and the matching end statement to the standard output. If *condition* is false, discard all intervening lines, including control statements. Note that intervening if statements and matching end statements are recognized solely for the purpose of maintaining the proper if-end matching.

The syntax of a *condition* is:

```
cond   ::= ["not"] <or>
or     ::= <and> | <and> "|" <or>
and    ::= <exp> | <exp> "&" <and>
exp    ::= "(" <or> ")" | <value> <op> <value>
op     ::= "=" | "!=" | "<" | ">"
value  ::= <arbitrary ASCII string> | <numeric string>
```

The available operators and their meanings are:

=	Equal.
!=	Not equal.
&	AND.
|	OR.
>	Greater than.
<	Less than.
()	Used for logical groupings.

You can use not only immediately after an if. When not is present, it inverts the value of the entire condition.

> and < operate only on unsigned integer values (for example, : 012 > 12 is false). All other operators take strings as arguments (for example, : 012 != 12 is true).

The precedence of the operators (from highest to lowest) is:

- = != > < All of equal precedence.

- &

- |

You can use parentheses to alter the order of precedence.

Separate values from operators or parentheses by at least one blank or Tab.

::*text*	Replace keywords on lines that are copied to the standard output. Remove the two leading control characters and replace keywords surrounded by control characters in *text* with their value before copying the line to the output file. This action is independent of the -a key letter.
:on :off	Turn on or off keyword replacement on all lines.
:ctl *char*	Change the control character to *char*.
:msg *message*	Print *message* on the diagnostic output.
:err *message*	Print *message* followed by ERROR: err statement on line ... (915) on the diagnostic output. Halt execution, and return an exit code of 1.

Attributes

See attributes(5) for descriptions of the following attributes:

Attribute Type	Attribute Value
Availability	SUNWsprot

See Also

ed(1), attributes(5)

---

vedit — Screen-Oriented Visual Display Editor Based on ex

Synopsis

Synopsis

New! /usr/bin/vedit [- | -s] [-l] [-L] [-R] [-r [*filename*]] [-S] [-t *tag*] [-v] [-V]
[-x] [-wn] [-C] [+*command* | -c *command*] *filename*...

New! /usr/xpg4/bin/vedit [- | -s] [-l] [-L] [-R] [-r [*filename*]] [-S] [-t *tag*]
[-v] [-V] [-x] [-wn] [-C] [+*command* | -c *command*] *filename*...

New! /usr/bin/vedit [- | -s] [-l] [-L] [-R] [-r [*filename*]] [-t *tag*] [-v] [-V]
[-x] [-wn] [-C] [+*command* | -c *command*] *filename*...

New! /usr/xpg4/bin/vedit [- | -s] [-l] [-L] [-R] [-r [*filename*]] [-t *tag*]
[-v] [-V] [-x] [-wn] [-C] [+*command* | -c *command*] *filename*...

Description

See vi(1).

---

ver — Graphics Filters for Various Plotters

Synopsis

/usr/bin/tplot [-T*terminal*]

Description

See tplot(1).

vgrind — Format Program Listings

Synopsis

```
/usr/bin/vgrind [-2fntwWx][-d defs-file][-h header][-llanguage]
    [-sn][-opagelist][-Pprinter] [-Toutput-device] filename...
```

Description

vgrind formats the program sources named by the *filename* arguments, using troff(1). Comments are in italics, keywords in bold, and as each function is encountered, its name is listed on the page margin.

vgrind runs in two basic modes, filter mode or regular mode. In filter mode, vgrind acts as a filter in a manner similar to tbl(1). The standard input is passed directly to the standard output except for lines bracketed by the following troff-like macros:

.vS   Start processing.

.vE   End processing.

These lines are formatted as described above. The output from this filter can be passed to troff for output. There need be no particular ordering with eqn(1) or tbl(1).

In regular mode, vgrind accepts input file names, processes them, and passes them to troff for output. If you specify no file name or if you specify - as the argument, vgrind reads from the standard input (default if you specify -f).

In both modes, vgrind does not convert any lines beginning with a decimal point.

Bugs

vgrind assumes that a certain programming style is followed.

C   Precede function names on a line only with space, Tab, or an asterisk. The parenthesized arguments must also be on the same line.

FORTRAN   Put function names on the same line as the keywords function or subroutine.

MLisp   Do not put function names on the same line as the preceding *defun*.

Model   Put function names on the same line as the keyword *is beginproc*.

Pascal   Put function names on the same line as the keywords function or procedure.

If you do not follow these conventions, the indexing and marginal, function-name comment mechanisms fail.

More generally, arbitrary formatting styles for programs mostly look bad. The use of space characters to align source code fails miserably. This result is somewhat inevitable because the fonts vgrind uses are of variable width. Use Tab characters if you plan to use vgrind on your program.

The mechanism of ctags(1) in recognizing functions should be used here.

The -w option is a kludge, but there is no other way to achieve the desired effect.

The macros defined in tmac.vgrind do not coexist gracefully with those of other macro packages, making filter mode difficult to use effectively.

vgrind does not process certain special characters in csh(1) scripts correctly.

The tmac.vgrind formatting macros wire in the page height and width used in two-column mode, effectively making two-column output useless for paper sizes other than the standard American size of 8.5 by 11 inches. For other paper sizes, you need to edit the size values given in tmac.vgrind. A better solution is to create a troff output device specification intended specifically for landscape output and record size information there.

Options

The syntax of options with arguments is important. Some options require a space between the option name and the argument, while those that do not have a space cannot tolerate one.

-2	Produce two-column output. Change the default point size to 8 (as if you specified the -s8 option). Arrange for output in landscape mode by supplying the -L flag to the formatter and changing the page height and width accordingly.
-d *defs-file*	Specify an alternate language definitions file (default is /usr/lib/vgrindefs).
-f	Force filter mode.
-h *header*	Specify a header to appear in the center of every output page.
-l*language*	Specify the language to use. The languages currently known are:

	-lsh	Bourne shell
	-lc	C (the default)
	-lc++	C++
	-lcsh	C shell
	-lml	Emacs MLISP
	-lf	FORTRAN
	-lI	Icon
	-li	ISP
	-lLDL	LDL

-lm	Model
-lp	Pascal
-lr	Ratfor

-n   Do not make keywords boldface.

-s*n*   Specify a point size to use on output (exactly the same as the argument of a `troff` `.ps` point size request).

-w   Consider Tab characters to be spaced four columns apart instead of the usual eight.

-x   Output the index file in a pretty format. The index file itself is produced whenever you run `vgrind` with a file called `index` present in the current directory. You can then run off the index of function definitions by specifying `vgrind -x` *index-file*.

> `vgrind` passes the following options to the formatter specified by the `TROFF` environment variable.

-o*pagelist*   Print only those pages whose page numbers appear in the comma-separated *pagelist* of numbers and ranges. A range *N-M* means pages *N* through *M*, an initial *-N* means from the beginning to page *N*, and a final *N-* means from *N* to the end.

-P*printer*   Send output to the named *printer*.

-t   Send formatted text to the standard output. Similar to the same option in `troff`.

-T*output-device*

     Format output for the specified *output-device*.

-W   Force output to the (wide) Versatec printer instead of the (narrow) Varian printer.

Operands

filename   Name of the program source to be processed by `vgrind`. Use a dash (–) to specify the standard input.

New!

Environment Variables

In regular mode, `vgrind` feeds its intermediate output to the text formatter given by the value of the `TROFF` environment variable or to `troff` if the `TROFF` variable is not defined in the environment. This mechanism allows for local variations in `troff`'s name.

Files

`index`   File where source for index is created.

`/usr/lib/vgrindefs`

     Language descriptions.

/usr/lib/vfontedpr

Preprocessor.

/usr/share/lib/tmac/tmac.vgrind

Macro package.

Attributes

See attributes(5) for descriptions of the following attributes:

Attribute Type	Attribute Value
Availability	SUNWdoc

See Also

New!   csh(1), ctags(1), eqn(1), tbl(1), troff(1), attributes(5), vgrinddefs(5)

vi, view, vedit — Screen-Oriented Visual Display Editor Based on ex

Synopsis

New!   /usr/bin/vi [- | -s] [-l] [-L] [-R] [-r [*filename*]] [-S] [-t *tag*] [-v] [-V]
          [-x] [-w*n*] [-C] [+*command* | -c *command*] *filename*...

New!   /usr/bin/view [- | -s] [-l] [-L] [-R] [-r [*filename*]] [-S] [-t *tag*] [-v] [-V]
          [-x] [-wn] [-C] [+*command* | -c *command*] *filename*...

New!   /usr/bin/vedit [- | -s] [-l] [-L] [-R] [-r [*filename*]] [-S] [-t *tag*] [-v] [-V]
          [-x] [-wn] [-C] [+*command* | -c *command*] *filename*...

New!   /usr/xpg4/bin/vi [-|-s] [-l] [-L] [-R] [-r[*filename*]] [-S] [-t*tag*] [-v] [-V]
          [-x] [-wn] [-C] [+*command* | -c *command*] *filename*...

New!   /usr/xpg4/bin/view [- | -s] [-l] [-L] [-R] [-r [*filename*]] [-S] [-t *tag*]
          [-v] [-V] [-x] [-wn] [-C] [+*command* | -c *command*] *filename*...

New!   /usr/xpg4/bin/vedit [- | -s] [-l] [-L] [-R] [-r [*filename*]] [-S] [-t *tag*]
          [-v] [-V] [-x] [-wn] [-C] [+*command* | -c *command*] *filename*...

Description

vi (visual) is a display-oriented text editor based on the underlying ex line
editor. You can use the command mode of ex from within vi, and you can use
the command mode of vi from within ex. The visual commands are described
on this manual page. Refer to the ex(1) manual page for information about all
ex line editor commands and about how to set options such as automatically
numbering lines and automatically starting a new output line when you press
Return

When using `vi`, changes you make to the file are reflected in what you see on your terminal screen. The position of the cursor on the screen indicates the position within the file.

The `view` invocation is the same as `vi` except that the read-only flag is set.

The `vedit` invocation is intended for beginners. It is the same as `vi` except that the `report` flag is set to 1, the `showmode` and `novice` flags are set, and `magic` is turned off. These preset defaults make it easier to learn `vi`.

Notes

Tampering with entries in `/usr/share/lib/terminfo/?/*` or `/usr/share/lib/terminfo/?/*` (for example, changing or removing an entry) can affect programs such as `vi` that expect the entry to be present and correct. In particular, removing the `dumb` terminal may cause unexpected problems.

Software Tabs using `^T` work only immediately after an autoindent.

Left and right shifts on intelligent terminals do not make use of insert and delete character operations in the terminal.

The standard Solaris version of `vi` will be replaced by the POSIX.2-conforming version (see `standards(5)`) in the future. Scripts that use the `ex` family of addressing and features should use the `/usr/xpg4/bin` version of these commands.

Options

`- | -s`	Suppress all interactive user feedback. This option is useful when processing editor scripts.
`-C`	Same as the `-x` option except simulate the `C` command of `ex`. The `C` command is like the `X` command of `ex`, except that all text read in is assumed to have been encrypted.
`-l`	Set up for editing LISP programs.
`-L`	List the name of all files saved as the result of an editor or system crash.
`-r filename`	Edit `filename` after an editor or system crash. (Recover the version of `filename` that was in the buffer when the crash occurred.) The `file too large to recover with -r option` message that you may see when you load a file indicates that the file can be edited and saved successfully, but if the editing session is lost, recovery of the file is not possible with the `-r` option.
`-R`	Set the read-only flag to prevent accidental overwriting of the file.

New! −S	Use in conjunction with the −t *tag* option to tell `vi` not to sort the tags file. If the binary search (which relies on a sorted tag file for *tag*) fails to find it, do a much slower, linear search. Because the linear search is slow, for large files, ensure that the `tags` files are sorted instead of using this option. Creation of `tags` files normally produces sorted `tags` files. See `ctags`(1) for more information on tags files.
−t *tag*	Edit the file containing *tag* and position the editor at its definition.
−v	Start up in display editing state using `vi`. You can achieve the same effect by simply typing the `vi` command itself.
−V	Echo input to standard error when `ex` commands are read by means of standard input. This option is useful when processing `ex` commands within shell scripts.
−w*n*	Set the default window size to *n*. This option is useful when using the editor over a slow-speed line.
−x	Simulate the X command of `ex` and prompt for a key. The key is used to encrypt and decrypt text, using the algorithm of the `crypt` command. The X command makes an educated guess to determine whether text read in is encrypted. The temporary buffer file is also encrypted, using a transformed version of the key that you type in for the −x option.
+*command* | −c *command*	
	Begin editing by executing the specified editor command (usually a search or positioning command).

Note — Although they continue to be supported, two options have been replaced in the documentation by options that follow the Command Syntax Standard (see `intro`(1)). A −r option that is not followed by an argument has been replaced by −L, and +*command* has been replaced by −c *command*.

/usr/xpg4/bin/vi
If you use both the −t *tag* and the −c *command* options, the −t *tag* is processed first. That is, the file containing the tag is selected by −t and then the command is executed.

Operands

filename	A file to be edited.

Command Summary

vi Modes

Command	Normal and initial mode. Other modes return to command mode on completion. Use ESC (Escape) to cancel a partial command.
Input	Enter by setting any of the following options: a A i I o O c C s S R. You can then type arbitrary text. You usually exit input mode with an ESC character or, abnormally, with an interrupt.
Last line	Read input for : / ? or !. Terminate by pressing Return. An interrupt cancels termination.

Sample Commands

In the descriptions, CR stands for Return and ESC stands for the escape key.

`<- |?v |?^ ->`	
	Arrow keys move the cursor.
`h j k l`	Same as arrow keys.
`itextESC`	Insert text.
`cwnewESC`	Change word to *new*.
`easESC`	Pluralize word (end of word; append *s*; escape from input state).
`x`	Delete a character.
`dw`	Delete a word.
`dd`	Delete a line.
`3dd`	Delete three lines.
`u`	Undo previous change.
`ZZ`	Save changes and exit.
`:q!CR`	Discard changes and quit.
`/textCR`	Search for *text*.
`^U ^D`	Scroll up or down.
`:cmdCR`	Any *ex* or *ed* command.

Counts Before vi Commands

You can type numbers as a prefix to some commands. Numbers are interpreted in one of these ways.

`z G |`	Line/column number.
`^D ^U`	Scroll amount.
most of the rest	
	Repeat effect.

Interrupting, Canceling

ESC	End insert or incomplete command.
DEL	Delete or rub out interrupts.

Manipulating Files

ZZ	If file modified, write and exit; otherwise, exit.
:wCR	Write back changes.
:w!CR	Forced write if permission originally not valid.
:qCR	Quit.
:q!CR	Quit, discard changes.
:e *name*CR	Edit file *name*.
:e!CR	Reedit, discard changes.
:e + *name*CR	Edit starting at end of file *name*.
:e +*n*CR	Edit starting at line *n*.
:e #CR	Edit alternate file.
:e! #CR	Edit alternate file, discard changes.
:w *name*CR	Write file *name*.
:w! *name*CR	Overwrite file *name*.
:shCR	Run shell, then return.
:!*cmd*CR	Run *cmd*, then return.
:nCR	Edit next file in *arglist*.
:n *args*CR	Specify new *arglist*.
^G	Show current file and line.
:ta *tag*CR	Position cursor to *tag*.

In general, you can type any ex or ed command (such as substitute or global) preceded by a colon and followed by a Return.

Positioning Within File

^F	Forward screen.
^B	Backward screen.
^D	Scroll down half screen.
^U	Scroll up half screen.
*n*G	Go to the beginning of the specified line (end default), where *n* is a line number.
/*pat*	Next line matching *pat*.
?*pat*	Previous line matching *pat*.

n	Repeat last / or ? command.
N	Reverse last / or ? command.
/pat/+n	n-th line after pat.
?pat?-n	n-th line before pat.
]]	Next section/function.
[[	Previous section/function.
(	Beginning of sentence.
)	End of sentence.
{	Beginning of paragraph.
}	End of paragraph.
%	Find matching ( ) or { }.

Adjusting the Screen

^L	Clear and redraw window.
^R	Clear and redraw window if ^L is -> key.
zCR	Redraw screen with current line at top of window.
z-CR	Redraw screen with current line at bottom of window.
z.CR	Redraw screen with current line at center of window.
/pat/z-CR	Move pat line to bottom of window.
zn.CR	Use n-line window.
^E	Scroll window down one line.
^Y	Scroll window up one line.

Marking and Returning

``	Move cursor to previous context.
' '	Move cursor to first nonwhite space in line.
mx	Mark current position with the ASCII lowercase letter x.
`x	Move cursor to mark x.
'x	Move cursor to first nonwhite space in line marked by x.

Line Positioning

H	Top line on screen.
L	Last line on screen.
M	Middle line on screen.
+	Next line, at first nonwhite.
-	Previous line, at first nonwhite.

CR	Return, same as +.
`|?v or j`	Next line, same column.
`|?^ or k`	Previous line, same column.

Character Positioning

^	First nonwhite space character.
0	Beginning of line.
$	End of line.
l or ->	Forward.
h or <-	Backward.
^H	Same as <- (backspace).
space	Same as -> (space).
f*x*	Find next *x*.
F*x*	Find previous *x*.
t*x*	Move to character prior to next *x*.
T*x*	Move to character following previous *x*.
;	Repeat last f, F, t, or T.
,	Repeat inverse of last f, F, t, or T.
n|	Move to column *n*.
%	Find matching ( ) or { }.

Words, Sentences, Paragraphs

w	Forward a word.
b	Back a word.
e	End of word.
)	To next sentence.
}	To next paragraph.
(	Back a sentence.
{	Back a paragraph.
W	Forward a blank-delimited word.
B	Back a blank-delimited word.
E	End of a blank-delimited word.

Corrections During Insert

| ^H | Erase last character (backspace). |
| ^W | Erase last word. |

`erase`	Your erase character, same as `^H` (backspace).
`kill`	Your kill character, erase this line of input.
`\`	Quote your erase and kill characters.
`ESC`	End insert, back to command mode.
`CTRL-C`	Interrupt, suspend insert mode.
`^D`	Backtab one character. Reset left margin of autoindent.
`^^D`	Caret (`^`) followed by Control-D (`^D`). Backtab to beginning of line; do not reset left margin of autoindent.
`0^D`	Backtab to beginning of line. Reset left margin of autoindent.
`^V`	Quote nonprintable character.

Insert and Replace

`a`	Append after cursor.
`A`	Append at end of line.
`i`	Insert before cursor.
`I`	Insert before first nonblank.
`o`	Open line below.
`O`	Open above.
`rx`	Replace single char with *x*.
`RtextESC`	Replace characters.

Operators

Operators are followed by a cursor motion and affect all text that would have been moved over. For example, because `w` moves over a word, `dw` deletes the word that would be moved over. Double the operator (for example, `dd`) to affect entire lines.

`d`	Delete.
`c`	Change.
`y`	Yank lines to buffer.
`<`	Left- shift.
`>`	Right-shift.
`!`	Filter through command.

Miscellaneous Operations

`C`	Change rest of line (`c$`).
`D`	Delete rest of line (`d$`).
`s`	Substitute characters (`c1`).

S	Substitute lines (cc).
J	Join lines.
x	Delete characters (dl).
X	Delete characters before cursor (dh).
Y	Yank lines (yy).

Yank and Put

Put inserts the text most recently deleted or yanked; however, if a buffer is named (using the ASCII lowercase letters a–z), the text in that buffer is put instead.

3yy	Yank three lines.
3yl	Yank three characters.
p	Put back text after cursor.
P	Put back text before cursor.
"xp	Put from buffer x.
"xy	Yank to buffer x.
"xd	Delete into buffer x.

Undo, Redo, Retrieve

u	Undo last change.
U	Restore current line.
.	Repeat last change.
"dp	Retrieve d-th last delete.

Usage

See largefile(5) for the description of the behavior of vi and view when encountering files greater than or equal to 2 Gbytes (2**31 bytes).

Environment Variables

See environ(5) for descriptions of the following environment variables that affect the execution of vi: LC_CTYPE, LC_TIME, LC_MESSAGES, and NLSPATH.

The editing environment defaults to certain configuration options. When you initiate an editing session, vi tries to read the EXINIT environment variable. If it exists, the editor uses the values defined in EXINIT; otherwise, it uses the values set in $HOME/.exrc. If $HOME/.exrc does not exist, the default values are used.

To use a copy of .exrc located in the current directory other than $HOME, set the exrc option in EXINIT or $HOME/.exrc. You can turn off options set in EXINIT in a local .exrc only if exrc is set in EXINIT or $HOME/.exrc.

Files

/var/tmp   Default directory where temporary work files are placed. You can change the default with the directory option (see the ex(1) set command).

/usr/share/lib/terminfo/?/*

    Compiled terminal description database /usr/lib/.COREterm/?/*. Subset of compiled terminal description database.

Attributes

See attributes(5) for descriptions of the following attributes:

/usr/bin/vi, /usr/bin/view, /usr/bin/vedit

Attribute Type	Attribute Value
Availability	SUNWcsu
CSI	Not enabled

/usr/xpg4/bin/vi, /usr/xpg4/bin/view, /usr/xpg4/bin/vedit

Attribute Type	Attribute Value
Availability	SUNWxcu4
CSI	Enabled

See Also

ctags(1), ed(1), edit(1), ex(1), intro(1), attributes(5), environ(5), *New!*
largefile(5), standards(5)
    Solaris Advanced User's Guide

Author

vi and ex were developed by The University of California, Berkeley California, Computer Science Division, Department of Electrical Engineering and Computer Science.

view — Screen-Oriented Visual Display Editor Based on ex

Synopsis

```
/usr/bin/view [- | -s][-l][-L][-R][-r [filename]][-S][-t tag]
     [-v][-V][-x][-wn][-C]
```
```
/usr/xpg4/bin/view [- | -s][-l][-L][-R] [-r [filename]][-S][-t tag]
     [-v][-V][-x][-wn][-C][+command | -c command] filename...
```
```
/usr/bin/view [- | -s][-l][-L][-R][-r [filename]] [-t tag][-v][-V]
     [-x][-wn][-C] [+command | -c command] filename...
```
```
/usr/xpg4/bin/view [-|-s][-l][-L][-R][-r [filename]][-t tag][-v][-V]
     [-x][-wn] [-C][+command | -c command] filename...
```

Description

See vi(1).

vipw — Edit the Password File

Synopsis

```
/usr/ucb/vipw
```

Description

vipw edits the passwd file while setting the appropriate locks and does any necessary processing after the password file is unlocked. If the password file is already being edited, you are told to try again later. The vi(1) editor is used unless the environment variable VISUAL or EDITOR indicates an alternate editor.

vipw performs a number of consistency checks on the password entry for root and does not allow a password file with a "mangled" root entry to be installed. It also checks the /etc/shells file to verify the login shell for root.

Files

/etc/ptmp

/etc/shells

Attributes

See attributes(5) for descriptions of the following attributes:

Attribute Type	Attribute Value
Availability	SUNWscpu

See Also

passwd(1), vi(1), passwd(4), attributes(5)

---

volcancel — Cancel Request for Removable Media Not Currently in Drive

Synopsis

/usr/lib/vold/volcancel [-n][*volume*]

Description

volcancel cancels a request to access a particular diskette or CD-ROM file system. This command is useful when the removable media containing the file system is not currently in the drive.

Use the path /vol/rdsk/*name_of_volume* to specify the volume. If called without a volume name to cancel, volcancel checks whether Volume Management is running.

Options

-n   Display the nickname to the device name translation table.

Examples

The following example cancels a request to access an unnamed CD-ROM.

```
castle% /usr/lib/vold/volcancel vol/rdsk/unnamed_cdrom
```

You can use the volcancel command to check if Volume Management is running. In the following example, Volume Management is running.

```
castle% /usr/lib/vold/volcancel
castle%
```

In the following example, Volume Management is not running and the message `volume management is not running` is displayed.

```
castle% /usr/lib/vold/volcancel
/usr/lib/vold/volcancel: volume management is not running
castle%
```

Attributes

See `attributes`(5) for descriptions of the following attributes:

Attribute Type	Attribute Value
Availability	SUNWvolu

See Also

```
volcheck(1), volmissing(1), rmmount(1M), vold(1M), rmmount.conf(4),
vold.conf(4), attributes(5), volfs(7FS)
```

volcheck — Check for Media in a Drive

Synopsis

```
/usr/bin/volcheck [-v] [-i secs] [-t secs] pathname
```

Description

The `volcheck` command tells Volume Management to look at each `dev/`*pathname* in sequence and determine if new media has been inserted in the drive.

The default action is for `volcheck` to run on all checkable media managed by Volume Management.

Warning — Because of a hardware limitation in many diskette drives, checking for media results in mechanical action in the diskette drive. Continuous polling of the diskette drive wears out the drive. It is recommended that you poll the drive only during periods of high use.

Options

`-i secs`   Set the frequency of device checking to *secs* seconds. The default is 2 seconds. The minimum frequency is 1 second.

-t *secs*	Check the named device(s) for the next *secs* seconds. The maximum number of seconds allowed is 28800, which is 8 hours. You specify the frequency of checking with -i. There is no default total time.
-v	Verbose.

Operands

pathname	The path name of a media device.

Examples

The following example asks Volume Management to examine the diskette drive for new media.

```
castle% volcheck -v /dev/diskette
/dev/diskette has media
castle%
```

The following example asks Volume Management to check in the background for a diskette in the diskette drive every 2 seconds for 600 seconds (10 minutes).

```
castle% volcheck -i 2 -t 600 /dev/diskette1 &
```

Description

/dev/volctl

Volume Management control port.

Attributes

See attributes(5) for descriptions of the following attributes:

Attribute Type	Attribute Value
Availability	SUNWvolu

See Also

eject(1), volcancel(1), volmissing(1) rmmount(1M), vold(1M), rmmount.conf(4), vold.conf(4), attributes(5), volfs(7FS)

volmissing — Notify User That Volume Requested Is Not in the CD-ROM or Diskette Drive

Synopsis

    /usr/lib/vold/volmissing [-c][-p][-s][-m alias]

Description

volmissing informs you when a requested volume is not available. Depending on the specified option, you are notified through your console window, syslogd(1M), or with an e-mail message.

volmissing -p is the default action taken by vold(1M), the Volume Management daemon, when it needs to notify you that the requested volume is not available. If you want to change this default, modify the /etc/vold.conf file. See vold.conf(4).

You can change the notification method for your system by editing the vold.conf configuration file and providing a new option for volmissing in the notify entry under the Events category.

Options

-c   Send a message to the console requesting the volume be inserted. To end the notification without inserting the requested volume, use volcancel(1).

-m alias   Send an e-mail message to the specified mail alias about the missing volume.

-p   All volmissing events are handled through a GUI, provided a window system is running on the console. If you specify this option and no window system is running, all messages go to the system console.

-s   Send one message to the syslogd(1M).

Files

/etc/vold.conf

                Volume Management daemon configuration file. Directs the Volume Management daemon to control certain devices and takes action when specific criteria are met.

/usr/lib/vold/volmissing_popup

                Pop-up used when the -p option is supplied and a window system is running.

Attributes

See `attributes`(5) for descriptions of the following attributes:

Attribute Type	Attribute Value
Availability	SUNWvolu

See Also

volcancel(1), volcheck(1), rmmount(1M), syslogd(1M), vold(1M), rmmount.conf(4), vold.conf(4), attributes(5), volfs(7FS)

---

volrmmount — Call rmmount to Mount or Unmount Media

Synopsis

```
/usr/bin/volrmmount [-i|-e][name | nickname]
/usr/bin/volrmmount [-d]
```

Description

volrmmount calls rmmount(1M) to simulate insertion (-i) or ejection (-e) of media. Simulating insertion often means that rmmount mounts the media. Conversely, simulating ejection often means that rmmount unmounts the media. However, these actions can vary, depending on the rmmount configuration and media type (see rmmount.conf(4)).

For example, if you use the default /etc/rmmount.conf and insert a music CD, it won't be mounted. However, you can configure rmmount so that it calls workman whenever you insert a music CD.

The volrmmount command enables you to override Volume Management's usual handling of media.

Note — Volume Management (vold) must be running before you can use this command.

Options

-i	Simulate insertion of the specified media by calling rmmount.
-e	Simulate ejection of the specified media by calling rmmount.
-d	Display the name of the default device for volrmmount to handle. This device is used if you supply no *name* or *nickname*.

Operands

name   The name that Volume Management recognizes as the device's name. See volfs(7FS).

nickname   A shortened version of the device's name.

The following list shows the recognized nicknames:

Nickname	Path
fd	/dev/rdiskette
fd0	/dev/rdiskette
fd1	/dev/rdiskette1
diskette	/dev/rdiskette
diskette0	/dev/rdiskette0
diskette1	/dev/rdiskette1
rdiskette	/dev/rdiskette
rdiskette0	/dev/rdiskette0
rdiskette1	/dev/rdiskette1
floppy	/dev/rdiskette
floppy0	/dev/rdiskette0
floppy1	/dev/rdiskette1

Examples

When Volume Management finds a diskette that contains a file system, it calls rmmount to mount it. If you want to run tar(1) or cpio(1) on that diskette, it must first be unmounted.

The following example unmounts the diskette.

```
castle% volrmmount -e floppy0
castle%
```

After volrmmount unmounts the diskette, if you want to remount it (instead of ejecting it and reinserting it), use the following command.

```
castle% volrmmount -i floppy0
castle%
```

Note — If you are using a named diskette, you can use its name in place of floppy0.

Description

/dev/volctl   Volume Management control port.

Attributes

See attributes(5) for descriptions of the following attributes:

Attribute Type	Attribute Value
Availability	SUNWvolu

See Also

cpio(1), eject(1), tar(1), rmmount(1M), vold(1M), rmmount.conf(4), attributes(5), volfs(7FS)

---

vplot — Graphics Filters for Various Plotters

Synopsis

/usr/ucb/plot [-T*terminal*]

Description

See plot(1).

W

w — Display Information About Currently Logged-in Users

Synopsis
```
/usr/bin/w [-hlsuw] [user]
```

Description
The w command displays a summary of the current activity on the system, including what each user is doing. The heading line shows the current time, the length of time the system has been up, the number of users logged into the system, and the average number of jobs in the run queue over the last 1, 5, and 15 minutes. w is a combination of who, uptime, and ps -a.

The fields displayed are the user's login name, the name of the TTY the user is on, the time of day the user logged on (in hours:minutes), the idle time (that is, the number of minutes since the user last typed anything in hours:minutes), the CPU time used by all processes and their children on that terminal (in minutes:seconds), the CPU time used by the currently active processes (in minutes:seconds), and the name and arguments of the current process.

Notes
The notion of the current process is unclear. The current algorithm is the highest-numbered process on the terminal that is not ignoring interrupts or, if there is none, the highest-numbered process on the terminal. This algorithm fails, for example, in critical sections of programs like the shell and editor or

when faulty programs running in the background fork and fail to ignore interrupts. In cases where no process can be found, w prints -.

The CPU time is only an estimate; in particular, if someone leaves a background process running after logging out, the person currently on that terminal is charged with the time.

Background processes are not shown, even though they account for much of the load on the system.

Sometimes processes, typically those in the background, are printed with null or garbled arguments. In these cases, the name of the command is printed in parentheses.

w does not know about the conventions for detecting background jobs. It sometimes finds a background job instead of the right one.

Options

-h	Suppress the heading.
-l	Produce a long form of output (the default).
-s	Produce a short form of output. The short form abbreviates the TTY, omits the login time, CPU times, and the arguments to commands.
-u	Produce the heading line that shows the current time, the length of time the system has been up, the number of users logged in to the system, and the average number of jobs in the run queue over the last 1, 5, and 15 minutes.
-w	Produce a long form of output (same as the default).

Operands

user	Specify the name of a user for whom login information is displayed.

Examples

The following example uses the w command with no option to display a summary of current system activity.

```
castle% w
  2:47pm  up 58 min(s),  1 user,  load average: 0.08, 0.05, 0.04
User       tty            login@  idle   JCPU   PCPU   what
winsor    console        1:52pm    55      3           /usr/dt/bin/sdt_shell
   -c unseten
winsor    pts/3          1:53pm     1                  csh
winsor    pts/4          1:53pm     1                  /bin/csh
winsor    pts/5          1:53pm    54                  /bin/csh
winsor    pts/6          1:53pm            13          w
castle%
```

Environment Variables

See `environ`(5) for descriptions of the following environment variables that affect the execution of w: LC_CTYPE, LC_MESSAGES and LC_TIME.

Files

/var/adm/utmp

> User and accounting information.

Attributes

See `attributes`(5) for descriptions of the following attributes:

Attribute Type	Attribute Value
Availability	SUNWcsu

See Also

ps(1), who(1), whodo(1M), utmp(4), attributes(5), environ(5)

wait — Await Process Completion

Synopsis

sh
wait [*pid*]

/bin/jsh, /bin/ksh, /usr/xpg4/bin/sh
wait [*pid*]
wait [*%job-id* ...]

/bin/csh
wait

Description

When writing shell scripts, occasionally it is important to be able to run simultaneous processes and wait for their conclusion before proceeding with other commands. The `wait` command provides shells with some of the job control features. It waits for all background processes to complete and reports their exit status.

The shell itself executes `wait` without creating a new process. If you get the error message `cannot fork, too many processes`, try using the `wait` command to clean up your background processes. If this doesn't help, the system process table is probably full or you have too many active foreground processes. (There is a limit to the number of process IDs associated with your login and to the number the system can track.)

New! Not all the processes of a pipeline with three or more stages are children of the shell and, thus, they cannot be waited for.

Bourne and Job Control Shells

New! The `wait` command waits for a background process whose process ID is *pid* and reports its exit status. If you omit *pid*, all the shell's currently active background processes are waited for and the return code is 0. `wait` accepts a job identifier when job control is enabled (`jsh`), and you precede the *job-id* argument with a percent sign (`%`).

New! If *pid* is not an active process ID, the `wait` command returns immediately and the exit status is 0.

C Shell

Wait for your background processes.

Korn Shell

When the shell starts an asynchronous list, the process ID of the last command in each element of the asynchronous list becomes known in the current shell execution environment.

If you invoke the `wait` command with no operands, the command waits until all process IDs known to the invoking shell have terminated and have exited with an exit status of 0.

If you specify one or more *pid* operands that represent known process IDs, the `wait` command waits until all of them have terminated. If you specify one or more *pid* operands that represent unknown process IDs, `wait` treats them as if they were known process IDs that exited with exit status 127. The exit status returned by the `wait` command is the exit status of the process requested by the last *pid* or *job-id* operand.

The known process IDs are applicable only for invocations of `wait` in the current shell execution environment.

Operands

New!   *pid*   The unsigned decimal integer process ID of a command to be waited for.

New!   *job-id*   A job control job ID that identifies a background process group to be waited for. The job ID notation is applicable only for invocations of `wait` in the current shell execution environment and only on systems that support the job control options.

Usage

On most implementations, `wait` is a shell built-in command. If you call `wait` in a subshell or separate command execution environment, such as one of the following, it returns immediately because there are no known process IDs to wait for in those environments.

```
(wait)
nohup wait ...
find . -exec wait ... \;
```

Examples

Although the exact value used when a process is terminated by a signal is
unspecified, if it is known that a signal terminated a process, a script can still
reliably figure out which signal is using kill. The following example uses a
script to identify the exit status.

```
sleep 1000&
pid=$!
kill -kill $pid
wait $pid
echo $pid was terminated by a SIG$(kill -l $?) signal.
```

For /bin/ksh and /usr/xpg4/bin/sh, if you run the following sequence of
commands in less than 31 seconds, wait returns the exit status of the second
sleep in the pipeline.

```
$ sleep 257 | sleep 31 &
[1]     450
$ jobs -l %%
[1] + 450          Running              sleep 257 | sleep 31 &
$ wait %%
$ [1] -  Done                 sleep 257 | sleep 31 &
$ ksh: wait: no such job
$
```

/bin/csh, however, reports the status of both jobs, as shown below.

```
castle% sleep 257 | sleep 31 &
[2] 442 443
castle% jobs -l
[1]   -   433 Running            sleep 257 |
          434 Done               sleep 31
[2]   +   442 Running            sleep 257 |
          443                     sleep 31
castle% wait
[2]     Done          sleep 257 | sleep 31
[1]   + Done          sleep 257 | sleep 31
castle%
```

Environment Variables

See environ(5) for descriptions of the following environment variables that
affect the execution of wait: LC_CTYPE, LC_MESSAGES, and NLSPATH.

Attributes

See attributes(5) for descriptions of the following attributes:

Attribute Type	Attribute Value
Availability	SUNWcsu

See Also

csh(1), jobs(1), ksh(1), sh(1), attributes(5)

wc — Display a Count of Lines, Words, and Characters in a File

Synopsis

/usr/bin/wc [-c | -m | -C] [-lw] [*file*...]

Description

Use the wc command to display a count of the lines, words, and characters in a file. The wc command reads one or more input files and, by default, writes the number of newline characters, words, and bytes contained in each input file to the standard output.

The command also writes a total count for all named files if you specify more than one input file.

wc considers a word to be a non-zero-length string of characters delimited by white space such as space or Tab (see iswspace(3C) or isspace(3C)).

Options

-c	Count bytes.
-m	Count characters.
-C	Same as -m.
-l	Count lines.
-w	Count words delimited by white space characters or newline characters. Delimiting characters are Extended Unix Code (EUC) characters from any code set defined by iswspace().

If you specify no option, the default is -lwc (count lines, words, and bytes.)

Operands

file   A path name of an input file. If you specify no file operands, use the standard input.

Examples

The following example uses the wc command with no options to display the number of lines, words, and characters in the file kookaburra-1.

```
castle% wc kookaburra-1
      9      47     264 kookaburra-1
castle%
```

The kookaburra-1 file contains 9 lines, 47 words, and 264 characters.
The following example uses the wc command to display a count for all of the files in the directory that start with kook.

```
castle% wc kook*
      9      47     264 kookaburra-1
      9      47     264 kookaburra-2
     18      94     528 total
castle%
```

Usage

See largefile(5) for the description of the behavior of wc when encountering files greater than or equal to 2 Gbytes (2**31 bytes).

Environment Variables

See environ(5) for descriptions of the following environment variables that affect the execution of wc: LC_CTYPE, LC_MESSAGES, and NLSPATH.

Exit Status

0   Successful completion.

>0   An error occurred.

Attributes

See attributes(5) for descriptions of the following attributes:

Attribute Type	Attribute Value
Availability	SUNWcsu
CSI	Enabled

See Also

cksum(1), isspace(3C), iswalpha(3C), iswspace(3C), setlocale(3C), attributes(5), environ(5), largefile(5)

what — Extract SCCS Version Information from a File

Synopsis

```
/usr/ccs/bin/what [-s] filename ...
```

Description

Use the what command to print identification strings for Source Code Control System (SCCS) files. The what command searches each file name for occurrences of the pattern @(#) that the SCCS get command (see sccs-get(1)) substitutes for the %Z% ID keyword and prints what follows up to a ", >, newline, \, or null character.

Options

-s   Stop after the first occurrence of the pattern.

Examples

For example, if a C program in file program.c contains the line

```
char sccsid[] = "@(#)identification information";
```

and program.c is compiled to yield program.o and a.out, the following command lists the string following the @(#).

```
castle% what program.c program.o a.out
program.c:
        identification information
program.o:
        identification information
a.out:  identification information
castle%
```

Attributes

See attributes(5) for descriptions of the following attributes:

Attribute Type	Attribute Value
Availability	SUNWsprot

See Also

sccs(1), sccs-admin(1), sccs-cdc(1), sccs-comb(1), sccs-delta(1), sccs-get(1), sccs-help(1), sccs-prs(1), sccs-prt(1), sccs-rmdel(1), sccs-sact(1), sccs-sccsdiff(1), sccs-unget(1), sccs-val(1), sccs-file(4), attributes(5)

Programming Utilities Guide

Diagnostics

Use the SCCS `help` command for explanations (see `sccs-help(1)`).

Bugs

There is a remote possibility that `what` could find a spurious occurrence of the `@(#)` pattern.

whatis — Display a One-Line Summary About a Command

Synopsis

```
/usr/bin/whatis command...
```

Description

Some commands are listed in more than one section of the manual pages. You can find the section number(s) for a manual page with the `whatis` command. `whatis` looks up a given command and displays the header line from the manual section. You can then run the man(1) command to get more information. If the line starts `name(section)` ..., you can type `man -s section-number` to view its documentation.

`whatis` is actually just the `-f` option to the man(1) command.

> **Note —** `whatis` uses the `/usr/share/man/windex` database that you can create with the catman(1M) command. If the `windex` database does not exist, `whatis` fails. To use the catman(1M) command to set up manual pages, become superuser, type `catman n`, and press Return, where *n* is the number of the section you want to set up.

Examples

The following example lists the header line for the `ed` manual page.

```
castle% whatis ed
ed                 ed (1)             - text editor
```

The following example uses the `whatis` command to list all of the manual pages for the `chown` command.

```
castle% whatis chown
chown              chown (1)          - change file ownership
chown              chown (1b)         - change owner
chown              chown (1m)         - change owner
chown              chown (2)          - change owner and group of a file
castle%
```

To display the manual page for a specific section, type
`man -s section-number command.`

Files

`/usr/share/man/windex`
> Table of contents and keyword database.

Attributes

See `attributes`(5) for descriptions of the following attributes:

Attribute Type	Attribute Value
Availability	SUNWdoc
CSI	Enabled

See Also

`apropos(1)`, `man(1)`, `catman(1M)`, `attributes(5)`

whence — Shell Built-in Function to Get/Set Shell Variable and Function Attributes and Values

Synopsis

`whence [-pv] name ...`

Description

See `typeset(1)`.

whereis — Locate the Binary, Source, and Manual Page Files for a Command

Synopsis

`/usr/ucb/whereis [-bmsu] [-BMS directory... -f] filename...`

Description

`whereis` locates source binary and manual sections for specified files. The supplied names are first stripped of leading path-name components and any (single) trailing extension of the form .ext, for example, .c. Prefixes of s. resulting from use of source code control are also stripped. whereis then tries to locate the desired program in a list of standard places:

```
/usr/bin
/usr/bin
/usr/5bin
/usr/games
/usr/hosts
/usr/include
/usr/local
/usr/etc
/usr/lib
/usr/share/man
/usr/src
/usr/ucb
```

Options

-b	Search only for binaries.
-m	Search only for manual sections.
-s	Search only for sources.
-u	Search for unusual sources. A file is unusual if it does not have one entry of each requested type. Thus, whereis -m -u * asks for those files in the current directory that have no documentation.
-B	Change or otherwise limit the places whereis searches for binaries.
-M	Change or otherwise limit the places whereis searches for manual sections.
-S	Change or otherwise limit the places whereis searches for sources.
-f	Terminate the last directory list and signal the start of file names. You must use this option with any of the -B, -M, or -S options.

Examples

The following example finds the location of all files named libc.

```
castle% whereis libc
libc: /usr/lib/libc.so /usr/lib/libc2.so /usr/lib/libc2.a
  /usr/lib/libc.a
castle%
```

The following example finds all files in /usr/ucb with source in /usr/src/cmd that are not documented in /usr/share/man/man1.

```
castle% cd /usr/ucb
castle% whereis -u -M /usr/share/man/man1 -S /usr/src/cmd -f *
Mail: /usr/ucb/Mail
aedplot: /usr/ucb/aedplot
```

```
arch: /usr/bin/arch /usr/ucb/arch
atoplot: /usr/ucb/atoplot
basename: /usr/bin/basename /usr/ucb/basename
bgplot: /usr/ucb/bgplot
biff: /usr/ucb/biff
cc: /usr/ucb/cc
chown: /usr/bin/chown /usr/ucb/chown
clear: /usr/bin/clear /usr/ucb/clear
... (More lines not listed)
castle%
```

Files

/usr/src/*

/usr/{doc,man}/*

/etc, /usr/{lib,bin,ucb,old,new,local}

Attributes

See attributes(5) for descriptions of the following attributes:

Attribute Type	Attribute Value
Availability	SUNWscpu

See Also

chdir(2), attributes(5)

Bugs

Because whereis uses chdir(2) to run faster, you must specify full path names with the -M, -S, or -B options; that is, path names must begin with a slash (/).

---

which — Locate a Command; Display Its Path Name or Alias

Synopsis

/usr/bin/which [*filename*] ...

Description

which takes a list of names and looks for the files that would be executed had these names been given as commands. Each argument is expanded if it is aliased and is searched for along the user's path. Both aliases and path are taken from the user's .cshrc file.

> **Note** — `which` is not a shell built-in command; it is the UNIX command, `/usr/bin/which`.

Bugs

Only aliases and paths from `~/.cshrc` are used; importing from the current environment is not attempted. The `which` command must be executed by csh(1) because only `csh` knows about aliases.

To compensate for `~/.cshrc` files in which aliases depend on the prompt variable being set, `which` sets this variable to null. If the `~/.cshrc` produces output or prompts for input when prompt is set, `which` may produce some strange results.

Examples

In the following example, the `which` command cannot locate the `whence` command. Instead, it displays the search path that it used to try and locate the command.

```
castle% which whence
no whence in /usr/openwin/bin /usr/dt/bin /bin /usr/bin /usr/sbin
   /usr/ucb /etc /usr/proc/bin /opt/hpnp/bin /usr/local/games
   /usr/ccs/bin .
castle%
```

In the following examples, the `which` command displays the location of the `which` and `whereis` commands.

```
castle% which which
/bin/which
castle% which whereis
/usr/ucb/whereis
castle%
```

Files

`~/.cshrc`   Source of aliases and path values.

`/bin/which`

Attributes

See attributes(5) for descriptions of the following attributes:

Attribute Type	Attribute Value
Availability	SUNWcsu

See Also

csh(1), attributes(5)

Diagnostics

A diagnostic is given for names that are aliased to more than a single word or if an executable file with the argument name was not found in the path.

while — Shell Built-in Function to Execute Conditional Actions

Synopsis

sh, ksh
```
while [ conditions ]; do actions ; done
```

csh
```
while ( conditions )
... # do actions
end
```

Description

You can use loops to control the flow of execution in a script. A loop is an iterative mechanism that repeats a sequence of instructions until a predetermined condition is met. A `while` loop repeatedly executes a group of commands within the body of the loop until the test condition in the expression is no longer true. In other words, the `while` loop says, "While the expression is true, execute these commands."

sh, ksh

A `while` command repeatedly executes the `while` conditions and, if the exit status of the last command in the conditions list is 0, executes the do `actions`; otherwise the loop terminates. If no commands in the do `actions` are executed, then the `while` command returns a 0 exit status. You can use `until` in place of `while` to negate the loop termination test.

> **Note —** Both the Bourne shell, `sh`, and the Korn shell, `ksh`, can use the semicolon and the Return interchangeably in their syntax of the `if`, `for`, and `while` built-in commands.

csh

While `conditions` is `true` (evaluates to non-zero), the `while` command repeats `actions` between the `while` and the matching end statement. The `while` and end must appear alone on their input lines. If the shell input is from a terminal, it prompts for commands with a question mark until you enter the end command and then performs the commands in the loop.

Loop Interrupts

You can use the built-in `continue` command to terminate the execution of the current iteration of a `while` or `until` loop and the built-in `break` command to terminate execution of a `while` or `until` command.

Examples

In the following examples, you are repeatedly prompted for a name of a file to be located until you choose to finish the execution by entering an empty line.

sh, ksh

```
filename=anything
while [ $filename ]
   do
   echo "file?"
   read filename       # read from terminal
   find . -name $filename -print
done
```

The brackets surrounding $`filename` are needed for evaluation. (See the `test` built-in command in the `if`(1) manual page.) Additionally, a blank space must separate each bracket from any characters within.

csh

```
set filename = anything
while ( "$filename" != "" )
     echo "file?"
     set filename = $<       # read from terminal
     find . -name $filename -print
end
```

Attributes

See `attributes`(5) for descriptions of the following attributes:

Attribute Type	Attribute Value
Availability	SUNWcsu

See Also

`break`(1), `csh`(1), `if`(1), `ksh`(1), `sh`(1), `attributes`(5)

who — Report Who Is on the System

Synopsis

```
/usr/bin/who [-abdHlmpqrstTu][file]
/usr/bin/who -q [-n x][file]
/usr/bin/who am i
/usr/bin/who am I

/usr/xpg4/bin/who [-abdHlmpqrtTu][file]
/usr/xpg4/bin/who -q [-n x][file]
/usr/xpg4/bin/who -s [-bdHlmpqrtu][file]
/usr/xpg4/bin/who am i
/usr/xpg4/bin/who am I
```

Description

The who command displays information about the current status of the system. It can list the user's name, terminal line, login time, elapsed time since activity occurred on the line, and the process ID of the command interpreter (shell) for each current UNIX system user. It examines the /var/adm/utmp file to obtain its information. If you specify *file*, that file (which must be in utmp(4) format) is examined. Usually, *file* is /var/adm/wtmp, which contains a history of all logins since the file was last created.

The general format for output is as follows:

name [*state*] *line time* [*idle*][*pid*][*comment*][*exit*]

where:

name	User's login name.
state	Capability of writing to the terminal.
line	Name of the line found in /dev.
time	Time since user's login.
idle	Time elapsed since the user's last activity.
pid	User's process ID.
comment	Comment line in inittab(4).
exit	Exit status for dead processes.

Note — After a shutdown to the single-user state, who returns a prompt. Because /var/adm/utmp is updated at login time and there is no login in single-user state, who cannot report accurately on this state. who am i, however, returns the correct information.

Options

-a	Process /var/adm/utmp or the named file with -b, -d, -l, -p, -r, -t, -T, and -u options turned on.
-b	Indicate the time and date of the last reboot.
-d	Display all processes that have expired and not been respawned by init. The EXIT field for dead processes contains the termination and exit values (as returned by wait(3B)) of the dead process. This information can be useful in determining why a process terminated.
-H	Output column headings above the regular output.
-l	List only those lines on which the system is waiting for someone to log in. The NAME field is LOGIN in such cases. Other fields are the same as for user entries except that the STATE field does not exist.
-m	Output only information about the current terminal.
-n *x*	Take a numeric argument, *x*, which specifies the number of users to display per line. *x* must be at least 1. You can use the -n option only with -q.
-p	List any other process that is currently active and has been previously spawned by init. The NAME field is the name of the program executed by init as found in /sbin/inittab. The STATE, LINE, and IDLE fields have no meaning. The COMMENT field shows the ID field of the line from /sbin/inittab that spawned this process. See inittab(4).
-q	Display only the names and the number of users currently logged on. Ignore all other options.
-r	Indicate the current run level of the init process.
-s	List only the NAME, LINE, and TIME fields (the default).

/usr/bin/who

-T	Same as the -s option, except also write the STATE, IDLE, PID, and COMMENT, fields. STATE is one of the following characters:

+	Allow write access to other users.
–	Deny write access to other users.
?	Cannot determine the terminal write access state.

/usr/xpg4/bin/who

-T	Same as the -s option, except also write the STATE field. STATE is one of the characters listed under the /usr/bin/who version of this option. If you use the -u option with -T, add the idle time to the end of the previous format.

-t   Indicate the last change to the system clock (using the date
            command) by root. See su(1M) and date(1).

-u   List only those users who are currently logged in. The name is the
            user's login name. The LINE is the name of the line as found in the
            directory /dev. The TIME is the time that the user logged in. The
            IDLE column contains the number of hours and minutes since
            activity last occurred on that particular line. A dot (.) indicates
            that the terminal has seen activity in the last minute and is
            therefore current. If more than twenty-four hours have elapsed or
            the line has not been used since boot time, mark the entry as old.
            The IDLE field is useful when trying to determine whether a
            person is working at the terminal. The PID is the process ID of the
            user's shell. The COMMENT is the comment field associated with this
            line as found in /sbin/inittab (see inittab(4)). The COMMENT
            field can contain information such as where the terminal is
            located, the telephone number of the data set, and type of terminal
            if hardwired.

Operands

am i   In the C locale, limit the output to describing the invoking user,
am I   equivalent to the -m option. You must separate the am and i or I
            arguments with a space.

file   Specify a path name of a file to substitute for the database of
            logged-on users that who uses by default.

Environment Variables

See environ(5) for descriptions of the following environment variables that
affect the execution of who: LC_CTYPE, LC_MESSAGES, LC_TIME, and NLSPATH.

Exit Status

0   Successful completion.

>0   An error occurred.

Files

/sbin/inittab

            Script for init.

/var/adm/utmp

            Current user and accounting information.

/var/adm/wtmp

            Historic user and accounting information.

Attributes

See attributes(5) for descriptions of the following attributes:

/usr/bin/who

Attribute Type	Attribute Value
Availability	SUNWcsu

/usr/xpg4/bin/who

Attribute Type	Attribute Value
Availability	SUNWxcu4

See Also

date(1), login(1), mesg(1), init(1M), su(1M), wait(3B), inittab(4), utmp(4), attributes(5), environ(5), XPG4(5)

whoami — Display the Effective Current User Name

Synopsis

/usr/ucb/whoami

Description

whoami displays the login name corresponding to the current effective user ID. If you have used su to temporarily adopt another user identity, whoami reports the login name associated with that user ID. whoami gets its information from the geteuid and getpwuid library routines (see getuid(2) and getpwnam(3C)).

Examples

The following examples show the current effective user ID. Because root does not have /usr/ucbt in the search path, the full path name is required to execute the command as root.

```
castle% whoami
winsor
castle% su
# whoami
whoami: not found
# /usr/ucb/whoami
root
# exit
castle% su ray
```

```
castle% whoami
ray
castle%
```

Files

/etc/passwd

User name database.

Attributes

See attributes(5) for descriptions of the following attributes:

Attribute Type	Attribute Value
Availability	SUNWscpu

See Also

who(1), su(1M), getuid(2), getpwnam(3C), attributes(5)

whocalls — Report on the Calls to a Specific Procedure

Synopsis

```
/usr/ccs/bin/whocalls whocalls [-l wholib] funcname
    executable [executable arguments ...]
```

Description

The whocalls command is based on the Link-Auditing library that permits the tracking of a given function call. See *Linker and Libraries Guide* for more information. The executable is run as normal. Each time the procedure *funcname* is called, both the arguments to that procedure and a stack trace are displayed on standard output.

Options

-l *wholib*   Specify an alternate who.so Link-Auditing library to use.

Examples

This examples tracks the calls to printf() made by a simple hello_world program.

```
castle% whocalls printf hello
printf(0x106e4, 0xef625310, 0xef621ba8)
```

```
hello:main+0x10
hello:_start+0x5c
hello
castle%
```

Attributes

See attributes(5) for descriptions of the following attributes:

Attribute Type	Attribute Value
Availability	SUNWtoo

See Also

ld.so.1(1), sotruss(1), attributes(5)
Linker and Libraries Guide

whois — Internet User Name Directory Service

Synopsis

/usr/bin/whois [-h *host*] *identifier*

Description

whois searches for an Internet directory entry for an *identifier* that is
either a name, such as Smith, or a handle, such as SRI-NIC.
  The following characters preceding the identifier can modify the search.

.	Force a name-only search.
!	Force a handle-only search.
*	Search for a group or organization entry. The entire membership list of the group is displayed with the record.

You can, of course, use an exclamation point and an asterisk, or a period and
asterisk together.

Options

-h *host*   Specify the name of the host to search.

Operands

identifier Specify a name, such as Smith, or a handle, such as SRI-NIC to
search for in an Internet directory

Examples

The following command looks for the name or handle `Smith`.

```
castle% whois Smith
```

The following command looks only for the handle `SRI-NIC`.

```
castle% whois !SRI-NIC
```

The following command looks only for the name `John Smith`.

```
castle% whois .Smith, John
```

Adding . . . to the name or handle argument matches anything from that point; that is, `ZU. . .` matches `ZUL`, `ZUM`, and so on.

Attributes

See `attributes`(5) for descriptions of the following attributes:

Attribute Type	Attribute Value
Availability	SUNWcsu

See Also

```
attributes(5)
```

---

write — Write to Another User

Synopsis

```
/usr/bin/write user [terminal]
```

Description

You can use the `write` command to send a message to the terminal of an individual user. When a windowing system such as CDE or OpenWindows is used, each window is considered a separate login. If the user is logged in more than once, the message is directed to the console window.

The `write` command reads lines from standard input and writes them to the terminal of another user. When first invoked, it writes the following message to the user.

```
Message from sender-login-id (sending-terminal)
 [date]...
```

When write has successfully completed the connection, the sender's terminal is alerted twice to indicate that what the sender is typing is being written to the recipient's terminal.

The recipient can reply by typing

```
write sender-login-id [sending-terminal]
```

on receipt of the initial message. Whenever a line of input as delimited by a newline, end-of-file, or end-of-line special character is accumulated while in input mode, the accumulated data is written on the other user's terminal. Characters are processed as follows.

- The alert character writes the alert character to the recipient's terminal.
- The erase and kill characters affect the sender's terminal in the manner described by the termios(3) interface.
- The interrupt or end-of-file characters write an appropriate message (EOT\n in the C locale) to the recipient's terminal and exit.
- Characters from LC_CTYPE classifications are sent to the recipient's terminal.
- Only when the stty iexten local mode is enabled, additional special control characters and multibyte or single-byte characters are processed as printable characters if their wide-character equivalents are printable.
- Other nonprintable characters are written to the recipient's terminal as follows: control characters appear as a ^ followed by the appropriate ASCII character, and characters with the high-order bit set appear in meta notation (M-*char*. For example, \003 is displayed as ^C and \372 as M-z.

To write to a user who is logged in more than once, you can use the *terminal* argument to indicate which terminal to write to; otherwise, the recipient's terminal is the first writable instance of the user found in /usr/adm/utmp, and the following informational message is written to the sender's standard output, indicating which terminal was chosen:

```
user is logged on more than one place.
You are connected to terminal.
Other locations are: terminal.
```

You can deny or grant permission to be a recipient of a write message with the mesg command. However, a user's privilege may further constrain the domain of accessibility of other users' terminals. The write command fails when the user lacks the appropriate privileges to perform the requested action.

If you use the character ! at the beginning of a line, write calls the shell to execute the rest of the line as a command.

write runs setgid() (see setuid(2)) to the group ID tty to gain write permission on other user's terminals.

The following protocol is suggested for using `write`: when you first write to another user, wait for him to write back before starting to send. Each person should end a message with a distinctive signal (such as, `(o)` for over) so that the other person knows when to reply. The signal `(oo)` (for over and out) is suggested when conversation is to be terminated.

You can also redirect a message from a file with the `write` command by using the following syntax:

```
write username < filename
```

Operands

user	Login name of the person to whom the message is written. This operand must be of the form returned by the who(1) command.
terminal	Terminal identification in the same format provided by the who command.

Environment Variables

See `environ`(5) for descriptions of the following environment variables that affect the execution of `write`: `LC_CTYPE`, `LC_MESSAGES`, and `NLSPATH`.

Exit Status

0	Successful completion.
>0	The addressed user is not logged on or the addressed user denies permission.

Files

`/var/adm/utmp`

> User and accounting information for write.

`/usr/bin/sh`

> Bourne shell executable file.

Attributes

See `attributes`(5) for descriptions of the following attributes:

Attribute Type	Attribute Value
Availability	SUNWcsu
CSI	Enabled

See Also

`mail(1)`, `mesg(1)`, `pr(1)`, `sh(1)`, `talk(1)`, `who(1)`, `setuid(2)`, `termios(3)`, `attributes(5)`, `environ(5)`

Diagnostics

`user is not logged on`

> The person you are trying to write to is not logged on.

`Permission denied`

> The person you are trying to write to denies that permission (with `mesg`).

`Warning: cannot respond, set mesg -y`

> Your terminal is set to `mesg` n and the recipient cannot respond to you.

`Can no longer write to user`

> The recipient has denied permission (`mesg` n) after you had started writing.

xargs — Construct Argument Lists and Invoke Command

Synopsis

```
/usr/bin/xargs [-t][-p][-e[eofstr]][-E eofstr][-I replstr]
    [-i[replstr]][-L number][-l[number]][-n number [-x]]
    [-s size][command [argument...]]
```

Description

The xargs command is a shell programming tool that enables you to use the output of one command to define the arguments for another. The xargs command constructs a command line consisting of the specified *command* and *argument* operands followed by as many arguments read in sequence from standard input as fit in the length and number constraints specified by the options. The xargs command then invokes the constructed command line and waits for its completion. This sequence is repeated until an end-of-file condition is detected on standard input or an invocation of a constructed command line returns an exit status of 255.

Separate arguments to the standard input by unquoted blank characters, unescaped blank characters, or newline characters. You can quote a string of zero or more non-double-quote (") and non-newline characters by enclosing them in double quotes. You can quote a string of zero or more nonapostrophe (') and non-newline characters by enclosing them in apostrophes. You can escape any unquoted character by preceding it with a backslash (\). The command is

1507

executed one or more times until the end-of-file is reached. If the command tries to read from its standard input, the results are unspecified.

The generated command-line length is the sum of the size in bytes of the command name and each argument treated as strings, including a null byte terminator for each of these strings. The xargs command limits the command-line length so that when the command line is invoked, the combined argument and environment lists do not exceed {ARG_MAX}-2048 bytes. Within this constraint, if you specify neither the -n nor the -s option, the default command-line length is at least {LINE_MAX}.

Options

-e[*eofstr*] Use *eofstr* as the logical end-of-file string. Underscore (_) is assumed for the logical EOF string if you use neither -e nor -E. When you omit the -*eofstr* option-argument, disable the logical EOF string capability and take underscores literally. Read standard input until either end-of-file or the logical EOF string is encountered.

-E *eofstr* Specify a logical end-of-file string to replace the default underscore. Read the standard input until either end-of-file or the logical EOF string is encountered.

-i[*replstr*] Equivalent to -I *replstr*. The string {} is assumed for *replstr* if you omit the option-argument.

-I *replstr* Execute *command* for each line from standard input, taking the entire line as a single argument, inserting it in argument s for each occurrence of *replstr*. You can use a maximum of five arguments in *argument*, each containing one or more instances of *replstr*. Ignore any blank characters at the beginning of each line. Constructed arguments cannot grow larger than 255 bytes. Option -x is forced on. The -I and -i options are mutually exclusive; the last one specified takes effect.

-l[*number*] If you omit *number*, 1 is assumed. Option -x is forced on. Equivalent to -L *number*.

-L *number* Execute the command for each nonempty *number* lines of arguments from standard input. The last invocation of *command* is with fewer lines of arguments if fewer than *number* remain. Consider a line to end with the first newline character unless the last character of the line is a blank character; a trailing blank character signals continuation to the next nonempty line, inclusive. The -L, -l, and -n options are mutually exclusive; the last one specified takes effect.

-n *number* Invoke *command*, using as many standard input arguments as possible up to a maximum of *number* (a positive decimal integer) arguments. Fewer arguments are used if:

- The command-line length accumulated exceeds the size specified by the -s option (or {LINE_MAX} if there is no -s option).

- The last iteration has fewer than *number*, but not 0, operands remaining.

-p   Prompt whether to execute *command* at each invocation. Turn on trace mode (-t) to write the command instance to be executed, followed by a prompt to standard error. An affirmative response (specific to the user's locale) read from /dev/tty executes the command; otherwise, skip that particular invocation of *command*.

-s *size*   Invoke *command*, using as many standard input arguments as possible and yielding a command-line length less than *size* (a positive decimal integer) bytes. Fewer arguments are used if:

- The total number of arguments exceeds that specified by the -n option.

- The total number of lines exceeds that specified by the -L option.

- End-of-file is encountered on standard input before *size* bytes accumulate.

Support values of *size* up to at least {LINE_MAX} bytes, provided that the specified constraints are met. You can give a value larger than that supported by the implementation or exceeding the specified constraints; xargs uses the largest value it supports within the constraints.

-t   Enable trace mode. Write each generated command line to standard error just before invocation.

-x   Terminate if a command line containing *number* arguments (see the -n option) or number lines (see the -L option) do not fit in the implied or specified *size* (see the -s option above).

Operands

command   The name of the command to be invoked, found by search path using the PATH environment variable; see environ(5). If you omit *command*, the default is the echo(1) command. If the *command* operand names any of the special built-in commands in shell_builtins(1), the results are undefined.

argument   An initial option or operand for the invocation of *command*.

Usage

The 255 exit status enables a command being used by xargs to tell xargs to terminate if it knows no further invocations using the current data stream will succeed. Thus, *command* should explicitly exit with an appropriate value to avoid accidentally returning with 255.

Input is parsed as lines; blank characters separate arguments. If xargs is used to bundle output of commands like find *dir* -print or ls into commands to be executed, unexpected results are likely if file names contain any blank characters or newline characters. You can fix this problem by using find to call a script that converts each file found into a quoted string that is then piped to xargs.

> **Note** — The quoting rules used by xargs are not the same as in the shell. They were not made consistent here because existing applications depend on the current rules and the shell syntax is not fully compatible with it. An easy rule that you can use to transform any string into a quoted form that xargs interprets correctly is to precede each character in the string with a backslash (\\).

On implementations with a large value for {ARG_MAX}, xargs may produce command lines longer than {LINE_MAX}. For invocation of commands, this is not a problem. If xargs is being used to create a text file, you should explicitly set the maximum command-line length with the -s option.

The xargs command returns exit status 127 if an error occurs so that applications can distinguish "failure to find a command" from "invoked command exited with an error indication." The value 127 was chosen because it is not commonly used for other meanings; most commands use small values for "normal" error conditions, and the values above 128 can be confused with termination because of receipt of a signal. The value 126 was chosen in a similar manner to indicate that the command could be found, but not invoked.

Examples

The following example moves all files from directory $1 to directory $2 and echoes each mv command just before doing it.

```
ls $1 | xargs -I {} -t mv $1/{} $2/{}
```

The following example combines the output of the parenthesized commands onto one line, which is then written to the end of file log.

```
(logname; date; printf "%s\n" "$0 $*") | xargs >>log
```

The following command invokes diff with successive pairs of arguments originally typed as command-line arguments (assuming there are no embedded blank characters in the elements of the original argument list).

```
printf "%s\n" "$*" | xargs -n 2 -x diff
```

In the following example, the user is asked which files in the current directory are to be archived. The files are archived into arch either one at a time (for the first example) or many at a time (for the second example).

```
castle% ls | xargs -p -L 1 ar -r arch
ar -r arch Mail?...y
```

```
ar: creating arch
ar -r arch SOLD515.PKG?...y
ar -r arch catman.man?...y
ar -r arch examples?...y
castle%

castle% ls | xargs -p -L 1 | xargs ar -r arch
/usr/bin/echo Mail?...y
/usr/bin/echo SOLD515.PKG?...y
/usr/bin/echo arch?...y
/usr/bin/echo catman.man?...y
/usr/bin/echo examples?...y
castle%
```

The following command executes with successive pairs of arguments originally typed as command-line arguments.

```
echo $* | xargs -n 2 diff
```

Environment Variables

See environ(5) for descriptions of the following environment variables that affect the execution of xargs: LC_COLLATE, LC_CTYPE, LC_MESSAGES, NLSPATH, and PATH.

Exit Status

0	All invocations returned exit status 0.
1-125	A command line meeting the specified requirements could not be assembled, one or more of the invocations of the command returned a non-zero exit status, or some other error occurred.
126	The command specified by *command* was found but could not be invoked.
127	The command specified by *command* could not be found.

If a command line meeting the specified requirements cannot be assembled, the command cannot be invoked, an invocation of the command is terminated by a signal, or an invocation of the command exits with exit status 255, then the xargs command writes a diagnostic message and exits without processing any remaining input.

Attributes

See attributes(5) for descriptions of the following attributes:

Attribute Type	Attribute Value
Availability	SUNWcsu
CSI	Enabled

See Also

```
echo(1), shell_builtins(1), attributes(5), environ(5)
```

xgettext — Extract gettext Call Strings from C Programs

Synopsis

```
/usr/bin/xgettext [-ns][-a [-x exclude-file]][-c comment-tag]
    [-d default-domain] [-j][-m prefix][-M suffix][-p pathname]
    - | filename ...
/usr/bin/xgettext -h
```

Description

Use the xgettext command to automate the creation of portable message files
(.po). A .po file contains copies of C strings that are found in ANSI C source
code in *filename* or the standard input if you specify - on the command line.
You can use the .po file as input to the msgfmt(1) command, which produces a
binary form of the message file that can be used by an application during
runtime.

xgettext writes *msgid* strings from gettext(3C) calls in *filename* to the
default output file messages.po. You can change the default output file name
with the -d option. *msgid* strings in dgettext() calls are written to the
output file *domainname*.po, where *domainname* is the first parameter to the
dgettext() call.

By default, xgettext creates a .po file in the current working directory,
and each entry is in the same order the strings are extracted from *filename*s.
When you specify the -p option, the .po file is created in the *pathname*
directory. Any existing .po file is overwritten.

Duplicate *msgid*s are written to the .po file as comment lines. When you
specify the -s option, the .po file is sorted by the *msgid* string and all
duplicated *msgid*s are removed. All *msgstr* directives in the .po file are
empty unless you use the -m option.

> **Note** — xgettext is not able to extract cast strings, for example,
> ANSI C casts of literal strings to (const char *). This feature is
> unnecessary anyway because the prototypes in <libintl.h>
> already specify this type.

Options

-a   Extract all strings, not just those found in gettext(3C) and
                   dgettext() calls. Create only one .po file.

-c *comment-tag*

                   Add the comment block beginning with *comment-tag* as the first
                   token of the comment block to the output .po file as # delimited
                   comments. For multiple domains, xgettext directs comments
                   and messages to the prevailing text domain.

-d *default-domain*

                   Rename default output file from messages.po to
                   default-domain.po.

-h   Print a help message on the standard output.

-j   Join messages with existing message files. If a .po file does not
                   exist, create it. If a .po file exists, append new messages.
                   Comment out any duplicate *msgids* in the resulting .po file.
                   Ignore domain directives in the existing .po file. Results are not
                   guaranteed if the existing message file has been edited.

-m *prefix*   Fill in the *msgstr* with *prefix*. This *option* is useful for
                   debugging. To make *msgstr* identical to *msgid*, use an empty
                   string (" ") for *prefix*.

-M *suffix*   Fill in the *msgstr* with *suffix*. This option is useful for
                   debugging.

-n   Add comment lines to the output file, indicating file name and line
                   number in the source file where each extracted string is
                   encountered. These lines appear before each *msgid* in the
                   following format:

                   #
                   # File: *filename*, line: *line-number*

-p *pathname* Specify the directory where the output files are placed. This option
                   overrides the current working directory.

-s   Generate output sorted by *msgids* with all duplicate *msgids*
                   removed.

-x *exclude-file*

                   Specify a .po file that contains a list of *msgids* that are not to be
                   extracted from the input files. The format of *exclude-file* is
                   identical to the .po file. However, use only the *msgid* directive line
                   in *exclude-file*. Ignore all other lines. You can use the -x option
                   only with the -a option.

Attributes

See attributes(5) for descriptions of the following attributes:

Attribute Type	Attribute Value
Availability	SUNWloc

See Also

msgfmt(1), gettext(3C), attributes(5)

---

xstr — Extract Strings from C Programs

Synopsis

```
/usr/bin/xstr -c filename [-v][-l array]
/usr/bin/xstr [-l array]
/usr/bin/xstr filename [-v][-l array]
```

Description

xstr maintains a file called strings into which a large program hashes strings in component parts. These strings are replaced with references to this common area. This approach implements shared constant strings, which are most useful if they are also read-only.

The following command extracts the strings from the C source in filename, replacing string references by expressions of the form &xstr[number] for some number.

```
castle% xstr -c filename
```

An appropriate declaration of xstr is prepended to the file. The resulting C text is placed in the file x.c to then be compiled. The strings from this file are placed in the strings database if they are not there already. Repeated strings and strings that are suffixes of existing strings do not change the database.

After all components of a large program have been compiled, you can create a file declaring the common xstr space called xs.c with a command of the following form.

```
castle% xstr
```

You should then compile the resulting xs.c file and load it with the rest of the program. If possible, make the array read-only (shared) to save space and overhead for swapping.

You can also use `xstr` on a single file. The following command creates files `x.c` and `xs.c` as before without using or affecting any `strings` files in the same directory.

```
castle% xstr filename
```

It can be useful to run `xstr` after the C preprocessor if any macro definitions yield strings or if there is conditional code that contains strings which may not, in fact, be needed. `xstr` reads from the standard input when you specify the - argument. The following examples show an appropriate command sequence for running `xstr` after the C preprocessor.

```
castle% cc -E name.c | xstr -c -
castle% cc -c x.c
castle% mv x.o name.o
```

`xstr` does not touch the file strings unless new items are added; thus, make(1S) can avoid remaking `xs.o` unless truly necessary.

Notes

Be aware that `xstr` indiscriminately replaces all strings with expressions of the form `&xstr[number]` regardless of the way the original C code might have used the string. For example, you will encounter a problem with code that uses `sizeof()` to determine the length of a literal string because `xstr` replaces the literal string with a pointer that most likely has a different size than the string. To circumvent this problem:

- Use `strlen()` instead of `sizeof()`. Note that `sizeof()` returns the size of the array including the null byte at the end, whereas `strlen()` does not count the null byte. The equivalent of `sizeof("xxx")` really is `(strlen("xxx"))+1`.

- Use `#define` for operands of `sizeof()` and use the `define` version. `xstr` ignores `#define` statements. Make sure you run `xstr` on `filename` before you run it on the preprocessor.

You will also encounter a problem when declaring an initialized character array of the following form.

```
char x[] = "xxx";
```

`xstr` replaces `xxx` with an expression of the following form.

```
&xstr[number]
```

which does not compile. To circumvent this problem, use `static char *x = "xxx"` instead of `static char x[] = "xxx"`.

Options

-c *filename*

        Take C source text from *filename*.

-v   Display a progress report indicating where new or duplicate strings are found.

-l *array*   Specify the named array in program references to abstracted strings. The default array name is xstr.

Files

Strings   Database of strings.

x.c   Massaged C source.

xs.c   C source for definition of array "xstr*(rq.

/tmp/xs*   Temporary file when xstr file name doesn't touch strings.

Attributes

See attributes(5) for descriptions of the following attributes:

Attribute Type	Attribute Value
Availability	SUNWcsu

See Also

make(1S), attributes(5)

Bugs

If a string is a suffix of another string in the database and the shorter string is seen first by *xstr,* both strings are placed in the database when just placing the longer one there would suffice.

Y

---

yacc — Yet Another Compiler-Compiler

Synopsis

```
/usr/ccs/bin/yacc [-dltVv][-b file-prefix]
    [-Q [y|n]][-P parser][-p sym-prefix] file
```

Description

The yacc command is a fourth-generation development tool that, together with the lex(1) command, enables you to perform lexical analysis and development by describing how an application should act instead of specifying what it should do.

The yacc command converts a context-free grammar into a set of tables for a simple automaton that executes an LALR(1) parsing algorithm. LALR (lookahead LR) parsing is a less powerful variant of LR parsing that produces much smaller parsing tables. The grammar can find LR grammars ambiguous. You can use specified precedence rules to break ambiguities.

You must compile the y.tab.c output file with the C compiler to produce a yyparse() function. You must then load this program with the yylex() lexical analyzer program, as well as with main() and the yyerror() error handling routine. You must supply these routines. The lex(1) command is useful for creating lexical analyzers usable by yacc.

To use the yacc command to generate a parser, specify a grammar file that describes the input data stream and what the parser is to do with the data.

The grammar file includes rules described in the input structure, the code to be invoked when these rules are recognized, and a subroutine to do the basic input.

Two adjacent double percent signs (%%) separate each section of the grammar file. To make the file easier to read, put the %% on a line by themselves. A complete grammar file has the following structure.

```
declarations
%%
rules
%%
programs
```

The declarations section can be empty. If you omit the programs section, also omit the second set of %%. The smallest yacc grammar file has the following structure.

```
%%
rules
```

yacc ignores blanks, Tabs, and newline characters in the grammar files. You can use these characters to make the file easier to read. You should not, however, use blanks, Tabs, or newlines in names or reserved symbols.

yacc uses the information in the grammar file to generate a parser that controls the input process. This parser calls an input subroutine (the lexical analyzer) to pick up the tokens from the input stream. The parser organizes the tokens, using the structure rules from the grammar file. When the parser recognizes one of the grammar rules, it executes the action from the user code suppled for that rule. Actions return values and use the values returned by other actions.

Note — Because file names are fixed, only one yacc process can be active in a given directory at a given time.

Options

-b *file-prefix*

> Use *file-prefix* instead of y as the prefix for all output files. The y.tab.c code file, the y.tab.h header file (created when you specify -d), and the y.output description file (created when you specify -v) are changed to *file-prefix*.tab.c, *file-prefix*.tab.h, and *file-prefix*.output.

-d

> Generate the y.tab.h file with the #define statements that associate the yacc user-assigned token codes with the user-declared token names. This association enables source files other than y.tab.c to access the token codes.

-l   Specify that the code produced in `y.tab.c` does not contain any
                `#line` constructs. Use this option only after you fully debug the
                grammar and the associated actions.

-P *parser*   Specify the parser of your choice instead of
                `/usr/ccs/bin/yaccpar`. For example, you can specify:

                castle% **yacc -P ~/myparser parser.y**

-p *sym-prefix*

                Use *sym-prefix* instead of yy as the prefix for all external
                names produced by yacc. The names affected include the
                functions `yyparse()`, `yylex()`, `yyerror()`, and the variables
                `yylval`, `yychar`, and `yydebug`. (In the remainder of this section,
                the six symbols cited are referenced with their default names
                only as a notational convenience.) Local names may also be
                affected by the -p option; however, the -p option does not affect
                `#define` symbols generated by yacc.

-Q[y|n]   Put the version stamping information in `y.tab.c`. This option
                enables you to know what version of yacc built the file. The -Qn
                option (the default) writes no version information.

-t   Compile runtime debugging code by default. The size and
                execution time of a program produced without the runtime
                debugging code is smaller and slightly faster. Runtime
                debugging code is always generated in `y.tab.c` under
                conditional compilation control. By default, this code is not
                included when `y.tab.c` is compiled. The runtime debugging
                code is always under the control of YYDEBUG, a preprocessor
                symbol. If YYDEBUG has a non-zero value, include the debugging
                code. If its value is 0, do not include the code.

-V   Print on the standard error output the version information for
                yacc.

-v   Prepare the file `y.output`, which contains a description of the
                parsing tables and a report on conflicts generated by ambiguities
                in the grammar.

Operands

file   A path name of a file containing instructions for which a parser is
                to be created.

Examples

Access to the yacc library is obtained with library search operands to cc. The
following example uses the yacc library `main`.

castle% **cc y.tab.c -ly**

Both the `lex` library and the `yacc` library contain `main`. The following example accesses the `yacc main` and ensures that the `yacc` library is searched first so that its `main` is used.

example% **cc y.tab.c lex.yy.c -ly -ll**

The historical `yacc` libraries have contained two simple functions that are normally coded by the application programmer. These library functions are similar to the following code.

```
#include <locale.h>
int main(void)
{
    extern int yyparse();
    setlocale(LC_ALL, "");
    /* If the following parser is one created by lex, the
       application must be careful to ensure that LC_CTYPE
       and LC_COLLATE are set to the POSIX locale.   */
    (void) yyparse();
    return (0);
}

    #include <stdio.h>
    int yyerror(const char *msg)
{

    (void) fprintf(stderr, "%s\n", msg);
    return (0);
}
```

The following example draws `yacc` rules from the `grammar.y` file and puts the output in `y.tab.c`.

castle% **yacc grammar.y**

The following example draws `yacc` rules from the `grammar.y` file and puts the output in `y.tab.c`. It also produces the `y.tab.h` file, which would contain C-style `#define` statements for each of the tokens defined in the `grammar.y` file.

castle% **yacc -d grammar.y**

Environment Variables

See `environ(5)` for descriptions of the following environment variables that affect the execution of `yacc`: LC_CTYPE, LC_MESSAGES, and NLSPATH.

`yacc` can handle characters from Extended Unix Code (EUC) primary and supplementary code sets as one-token symbols. EUC codes can be only single-character quoted terminal symbols. `yacc` expects `yylex()` to return a wide-character (`wchar_t`) value for these one-token symbols.

Exit Status

0	Successful completion.
>0	An error occurred.

Files

y.output	State transitions of the generated parser.
y.tab.c	Source code of the generated parser.
y.tab.h	Header file for the generated parser.
yacc.acts	Temporary file.
yacc.debug	Temporary file.
yacc.tmp	Temporary file.
yaccpar	Parser prototype for C programs.

Attributes

See attributes(5) for descriptions of the following attributes:

Attribute Type	Attribute Value
Availability	SUNWbtool

See Also

lex(1), cc(1B), attributes(5), environ(5)
   Programming Utilities Guide

Diagnostics

The number of reduce-reduce and shift-reduce conflicts is reported on the standard error output. You can find a more detailed report in the y.output file. Similarly, if some rules are not reachable from the start symbol, this instance is also reported.

ypcat — Print Values in an NIS Database

Synopsis

    /usr/bin/ypcat [-kx][-d ypdomain] mname

Description

The ypcat command prints out values in the NIS name service map specified
by *mname*, which may be either a map name or a map nickname. Because
ypcat uses the NIS network services, you need not specify an NIS server.
   Refer to ypfiles(4) for an overview of the NIS name service.

Options

    -d ypdomain

                      Specify a domain other than the default domain.

    -k   Display the keys for those maps in which the values are null or
                      the key is not part of the value. None of the maps derived from
                      files that have an ASCII version in /etc fall into this class.

    -x   Display map nicknames.

Examples

The following example shows the output for the ypcat -x command on a
system that is not on an NIS+ network.

```
castle% ypcat -x
Use "passwd"    for map "passwd.byname"
Use "group"     for map "group.byname"
Use "networks"  for map "networks.byaddr"
Use "hosts"     for map "hosts.byname"
Use "protocols" for map "protocols.bynumber"
Use "services"  for map "services.byname"
Use "aliases"   for map "mail.aliases"
Use "ethers"    for map "ethers.byname"
castle%
```

Attributes

See attributes(5) for descriptions of the following attributes:

Attribute Type	Attribute Value
Availability	SUNWnisu

See Also
```
ypmatch(1), ypfiles(4), attributes(5)
```

ypmatch — Print the Value of Keys from an NIS Map

Synopsis
```
/usr/bin/ypmatch [-k][-t][-d domain] key [key...] mname
ypmatch -x
```

Description
ypmatch prints the values associated with one or more keys from the NIS name services map specified by *mname*, which may be either a map name or a map nickname.

You can specify multiple keys. All keys are searched for in the same map. The keys must be the same case and length. No pattern matching is available. If a key is not matched, a diagnostic message is displayed.

Note — ypmatch fails with an RCP error message on yp operations if enough file descriptors are not available. If this problem occurs, increase the number of file descriptors.

New!

Options

-d *domain*	Specify a domain other than the default domain.
-k	Before printing the value of a key, print the key itself, followed by a colon (:).
-t	Inhibit map nickname translation.
-x	Display the map nickname table. This option lists the nicknames (*mnames*) the command knows and indicates the map name associated with each nickname.

Operands

mname	The NIS name services map.	*New!*

Exit Status

New!

0	Successful operation.
1	An error occurred.

Attributes

See attributes(5) for descriptions of the following attributes:

Attribute Type	Attribute Value
Availability	SUNWnisu

See Also

ypcat(1), ypfiles(4), attributes(5)

yppasswd — Change Your Network Password in the NIS Database

Synopsis

/usr/bin/yppasswd [*username*]

Description

> **Note** — The use of yppasswd is discouraged, as it is now only a
> link to the passwd(1) command, which you should use instead. Use
> passwd(1) with the -r nis option to achieve the same results, and
> be consistent across all available name services.

yppasswd changes the network password associated with the user *username*
in the Network Information Service (NIS+) database. If the user has done a
keylogin(1) and a publickey/secretkey pair exists for the user in the NIS
publickey.byname map, yppasswd also reencrypts the secret key with the
new password. The NIS password may be different from your local one. Use
passwd(1) to change the password information on the local machine, and
nispasswd(1) to change the password information stored in Network
Information Service Plus, Version 3 (NIS+).

yppasswd prompts for the old NIS password and then for the new one. You
must type in the old password correctly for the change to take effect. You must
type the new password twice for verification.

New passwords must be at least four characters long if they use a
sufficiently rich alphabet, and at least six characters long if monocase. These
rules are relaxed if you are insistent enough. Only the owner of the user name
or the superuser can change a password; superuser on the root master is not
prompted for the old password and does not need to follow password
construction requirements.

The NIS password daemon, rpc.yppasswdd, must be running on your NIS
server for the new password to take effect.

> **Warning** — Even after you have successfully changed your
> password using this command, the subsequent login(1) using the
> new password is successful only if your password and shadow
> information is obtained from NIS. (See getpwnam(3C),
> getspnam(3C), and nsswitch.conf(4).)

Attributes

See attributes(5) for descriptions of the following attributes:

Attribute Type	Attribute Value
Availability	SUNWcsu

See Also

keylogin(1), login(1), nispasswd(1), passwd(1), getpwnam(3C),
getspnam(3C), secure_rpc(3N), nsswitch.conf(4), attributes(5)

Bugs

The update protocol passes all the information to the server in one RPC call
without ever looking at it. Thus, if you type your old password incorrectly, you
are not notified until after you have entered your new password.

ypwhich — Return Name of NIS Server of Map Master

Synopsis

/usr/bin/ypwhich [-d *domain*][[-t] -m [*mname*] | [-V*n*] *hostname*]
/usr/bin/ypwhich -x

Description

ypwhich returns the name of the NIS server that supplies the NIS name
services to an NIS client or that is the master for a map. If invoked without
arguments, ypwhich gives the NIS server for the local system. If you specify
hostname, that system is queried to find out which NIS master it is using.

Refer to ypfiles(4) for an overview of the NIS name services.

Options

-d *domain*	Use *domain* instead of the default domain.
-m *mname*	Find the master NIS server for a map. You cannot specify a host name with -m. *mname* can be a map name or a nickname for a map. When you omit *mname*, produce a list of available maps.
-t	Inhibit map nickname translation.
-x	Display the map nickname translation table.
-V*n*	Version of ypbind, V3 is the default.

Attributes

See attributes(5) for descriptions of the following attributes:

Attribute Type	Attribute Value
Availability	SUNWnisu

See Also

ypfiles(4), attributes(5)

Z

Z

zcat — Compress, Uncompress Files or Display Expanded Files

Synopsis
```
/usr/bin/zcat [file...]
```

Description
See compress(1).

zipinfo — List Detailed Information About a Zip Archive   *New!*

Synopsis
```
/usr/bin/zipinfo[-12smlvhMtTz]file[.zip][file(s)...][-x xfile(s)...]
/usr/bin/unzip -Z [-12smlvhMtTz] file[.zip] [file(s)...]
   [-x xfile(s)...]
```

Description

> **Note** — zipinfo is the same program as unzip (under UNIX, a link to it); on some systems, however, zipinfo support may have been omitted when unzip was compiled.

zipinfo lists technical information about files in a ZIP archive. Such information includes file access permissions, encryption status, type of compression, version, and operating or file system of compressing program. The default behavior (specifying *file* with no options) is to list single-line entries for each file in the archive, with header and totals lines providing summary information for the entire archive. The format is a cross between UNIX ls -l and unzip -v output, as shown in the following example.

```
castle% zipinfo 085XDOCS
Archive:   085XDOCS.zip    106272 bytes    4 files
-rw-a--     2.0 fat    76800 t- defN 18-Aug-98 21:55 085X01.DOC
-rw-a--     2.0 fat    67072 b- defN 22-Aug-98 01:39 085X02.DOC
-rw-a--     2.0 fat    95232 t- defN 31-Aug-98 20:29 085X042.DOC
-rw-a--     2.0 fat    63488 t- defN  4-Oct-98 20:24 085X04E.DOC
4 files, 302592 bytes uncompressed, 105858 bytes compressed:  65.0%
castle%
```

> **Note** — You may find it convenient to define an ii alias for zipinfo on systems that allow aliases. On other systems you can copy and rename the executable, create a link, or create a command file with the name ii. The ii usage parallels the common ll alias for long listings in UNIX. The similarity between the outputs of the two commands was intentional.

Arguments

file[.zip]   Path of the ZIP archive(s). If you specify a wild-card for *file*, process each matching file in an order determined by the operating system (or file system). Only the file name can be a wild-card; the path itself cannot. Wild-card expressions are similar to UNIX egrep(1) (regular) expressions and may contain:

     `*`   Match a sequence of zero or more characters

     `?`   Match exactly one character

     `[...]`   Match any single character found inside the brackets; specify ranges with a beginning character, a hyphen, and an ending character. If an exclamation point (!) or a caret (^) follows the left bracket, then the range of characters within the brackets is complemented (that is, anything except the characters inside the brackets is considered a match).

Be sure to quote any character that might otherwise be interpreted or modified by the operating system, particularly under UNIX and VMS. If no matches are found, assume a literal file name; and if that also fails, append the suffix `.zip`. Note that self-extracting ZIP files are supported, as with any other ZIP archive; just specify the `.exe` suffix (if any).

`[file(s)]`   An optional, space-separated list of archive members to be processed. (For VMS versions compiled with VMSCLI defined, delimit files with commas instead. See `-v`.) You can use regular expressions (wild-cards) to match multiple members. Again, be sure to quote expressions that would otherwise be expanded or modified by the operating system.

`[-x xfile(s)]`

An optional list of archive members to be excluded from processing.

Options

`-1`   List file names only, one per line. This option excludes all others. Never print headers, totals lines, or file comments. This option is intended for use in UNIX shell scripts.

`-2`   List file names only, one per line, and display headers (`-h`), totals lines (`-t`), and file comments (`-z`). This option can be useful in cases where the stored file names are particularly long.

`-s`   List file information in short UNIX `ls -l` format (the default).

`-m`   List file information in medium UNIX `ls -l` format. Identical to the `-s` output, except also list the compression factor expressed as a percentage.

`-l`   List file information in long UNIX `ls -l` format. Identical to the `-m` output except express the compressed size (in bytes) instead of the compression ratio.

`-v`   List file information in verbose, multipage format.

`-h`   List header line. Print the archive name, actual size (in bytes), and total number of files.

`-M`   Pipe all output through an internal pager similar to the UNIX `more(1)` command. At the end of a screen of output, pause with a `--More--` prompt. To view the next screen, you press the Enter (Return) key or the space bar. You can quit `zipinfo` with the `q` key and, on some systems, with the Enter/Return key. Unlike UNIX `more(1)`, `zipinfo` does not allow you to search forward or edit. `zipinfo` does not notice if long lines wrap at the edge of the screen, effectively resulting in the printing of two or more lines. Some text may scroll off the top of the screen before being viewed.

On some systems, the number of available lines on the screen is not detected, in which case zipinfo assumes the height is 24 lines.

-t   List the number of files, their uncompressed and compressed total sizes, and their overall compression factor. Alternatively, list the values for the entire archive if only the totals line is printed Note that the total compressed (data) size never matches the actual file size because the latter includes all of the internal file headers in addition to the compressed data.

-T   Print the file dates and times in a sortable decimal format (*yymmdd.hhmmss*). The default date format is a more standard, human-readable version with abbreviated month names.

-z   Include the archive comment (if any) in the listing.

-Z   If the first option on the command line is -Z, interpret the remaining options as zipinfo(1) options.

Note — When you use the -h or -t options by themselves or with each other, they override any default listings of files in the archive. Only the header and/or totals lines are displayed. This behavior is useful when you use zipinfo with a wild-card file specification; the contents of all files are then summarized with a single command.

Detailed Description

zipinfo has a number of modes and its behavior can be difficult to fathom if you aren't familiar with the UNIX ls(1) command. The default behavior is to list files in the format shown below.

```
-rw-rws---  1.9 unx   2802 t- defX 11-Aug-91 13:48 perms.2660
```

This example is for a ZIP file generated on a UNIX system.Because it comes from UNIX, the file permissions at the beginning of the line in this example are printed in UNIX format.

The second and third fields indicate that the file was zipped under UNIX with version 1.9 of zip. The fourth field shows the uncompressed file size (2802 in this example).

The fifth field consists of two characters, either of which can have several values. The first character may be either t or b, indicating that zipinfo believes the file to be text or binary. If the file is encrypted, the letters are capitalized. The second character can display four values, depending on whether there is an extended local header and/or an extra field associated with the file. (The values are fully explained in PKWARE's APPNOTE.TXT but are basically analogous to programs in ANSI C—that is, they provide a standard way to include nonstandard information in the archive.)

Values for the second character are summarized below.

-	Neither the header nor the extra field exists.
1	The file has an extended local header but no extra field.
x	The file has an extra field but no extended local header.
X	The file has an extra field and an extended local header.

Thus, the file in this example is (probably) a text file, is not encrypted, and has neither an extra field nor an extended local header associated with it.

The sixth field indicates the compression method and possible submethod used. Six methods are known at present:

- Storing (no compression).
- Reducing.
- Shrinking.
- Imploding.
- Tokenizing (never publicly released).
- Deflating.

In addition, there are four levels of reducing (1 through 4); four types of imploding (4K or 8K sliding dictionary, and 2 or 3 Shannon-Fano trees); and four levels of deflating (superfast, fast, normal, maximum compression). `zipinfo` represents these methods and their submethods as follows: `stor`; `re:1`, `re.2`, etc.; `shrk`; `i4:2`, `i8:3`, etc.; `tokn`; and `defS`, `defF`, `defN`, and `defX`.

The last three fields contain the modification date and time of the file and its name. The case of the file name is respected so that files that come from MS-DOS `PKZIP` are always capitalized. If the file was zipped with a stored directory name, that name is also displayed as part of the file name.

The following example is an encrypted binary file with an extra field. The file attributes in the first field are listed in VMS format.

```
RWD,R,R    0.9 vms     168 Bx shrk  9-Aug-91 19:15 perms.0644
```

Extra fields are used for various purposes (see discussion of the -v option) including the storage of VMS file attributes, which is presumably the case here. Some other possibilities for the host file system include OS/2 or NT with High Performance File System (HPFS), MS-DOS, OS/2, or NT with File Allocation Table (FAT) file system, and Macintosh. These are denoted as follows:

```
-rw-a--    1.0 hpf    5358 Tl i4:3  4-Dec-91 11:33 longfilename.hpfs
-r--ahs    1.1 fat    4096 b- i4:2 14-Jul-91 12:58 EA DATA. SF
--w-------  1.0 mac   17357 bx i8:2  4-May-92 04:02 unzip.macr
```

File attributes in the first two cases are indicated in a UNIX-like format, with seven subfields that specify the following information.

1. The file is a directory.
2. The file is readable (always `true`).

3. The file is writable.

4. The file is executable (guessed on the basis of the extension—`.exe`, `.com`, `.bat`, `.cmd`, or `.btm`).

5. The file has its archive bit set.

6. The file is hidden.

7. The file is a system file.

Interpretation of Macintosh file attributes is unreliable because some Macintosh archivers don't store any attributes in the archive.

The medium and long listings are almost identical to the short format except that they add information on file compression. The medium format lists the file compression factor as a percentage, indicating the amount of space that has been removed. In the following example, the file has been compressed by more than a factor of five; the compressed data are only 19 percent of the original size.

```
-rw-rws---  1.5 unx    2802 t- 81% defX 11-Aug-91 13:48 perms.2660
```

The long format shows the compressed file's size in bytes, as shown in the following example.

```
-rw-rws---  1.5 unx    2802 t-    538 defX 11-Aug-91 13:48 perms.2660
```

You can add the `-T` option to change the file date and time to decimal format, as shown below.

```
-rw-rws---  1.5 unx    2802 t-    538 defX 910811.134804 perms.2660
```

Note that because of limitations in the MS-DOS format used to store file times, the seconds field is always rounded to the nearest even second. For UNIX files, this is expected to change in the next major releases of `zip` and `unzip(1)`.

In addition to individual file information, a default file listing also includes header and totals lines, as shown in the following example.

```
Archive:  OS2.zip    5453 bytes    5 files
,,rw,        1.0 hpf      730 b- i4:3 26-Jun-92 23:40 Contents
,,rw,        1.0 hpf     3710 b- i4:3 26-Jun-92 23:33 makefile.os2
,,rw,        1.0 hpf     8753 b- i8:3 26-Jun-92 15:29 os2unzip.c
,,rw,        1.0 hpf       98 b- stor 21-Aug-91 15:34 unzip.def
,,rw,        1.0 hpf       95 b- stor 21-Aug-91 17:51 zipinfo.def
5 files, 13386 bytes uncompressed, 4951 bytes compressed: 63.0%
```

The header line shows the name of the archive, its total size, and the total number of files. The totals line shows the number of files listed, their total uncompressed size, and their total compressed size (not including any of `zip`'s internal overhead). If, however, you specify one or more file(s), the header and totals lines are not listed. This behavior is also similar to that of the UNIX `ls -l` command. You can override this behavior by specifying the `-h` and `-t` options. When you specify the `-h` or `-t` options, you must also specify the listing format; for example, `zipinfo -htl find.zip`. If you do not specify a listing format with `-h`, `-t`, or `-ht`, only the specified lines are listed.

The verbose listing is mostly self-explanatory. It also lists file comments, if any, and the type and number of bytes in any stored extra fields. Currently known types of extra fields include PKWARE's authentication (`AV`) information; OS/2 extended attributes; VMS file system information, both PKWARE and Info-ZIP versions; Macintosh resource forks; Acorn/Archimedes SparkFS information; and so on.

> **Note** — In the case of OS/2 extended attributes—perhaps the most common use of file extra fields—the size of the stored EAs as reported by `zipinfo` may not match the number given by OS/2's `dir` command: OS/2 always reports the number of bytes required in 16-bit format, whereas `zipinfo` always reports the 32-bit storage.

Environment Options

Modifying the `zipinfo` default behavior with options in an environment variable can be a bit complicated to explain because `zipinfo` tries to handle various defaults in an intuitive, yet UNIX-like, manner. (Try not to laugh.) `zipinfo` has three priority levels of options.

- Default options.
- Environment options, which can override or add to the defaults.
- Explicit options specified on the command line, which can override or add to either of the above.

The default variable names are `ZIPINFO_OPTS` for VMS (where the symbol used to install `zipinfo` as a foreign command would otherwise be confused with the environment variable) and `ZIPINFO` for all other operating systems. For compatibility with `zip`, `ZIPINFOOPT` is also accepted (don't ask). If you define both `ZIPINFO` and `ZIPINFOOPT`, `ZIPINFO` takes precedence. You can use the `unzip` diagnostic option (`-v` with no file name) to check the values of all four possible `unzip` and `zipinfo` environment variables.

The default listing format corresponds roughly to the `zipinfo -hst` command (except when you specify individual files). If you prefer the long format listing (`-l`) you can change the default by using the `ZIPINFO` environment variable, as shown below.

```
ZIPINFO=-l; export ZIPINFO
```
        UNIX Bourne shell

```
setenv ZIPINFO -l
```
        UNIX C shell

```
set ZIPINFO=-l
```
        OS/2 or MS-DOS

```
define ZIPINFO_OPTS "-l"
```
        VMS (quotes for lower case)

    You can also specify negative options to override defaults. Precede the
undesired option with one or more dashes. If, for example, you don't like the
totals line, you can specify -l-t or --tl options. The first dash is the regular
switch character, but the second one is always interpreted as a minus sign. This
dual use of dashes may seem a little awkward, but it's reasonably intuitive.
After the first dash, any other dashes signify a negative option. This syntax is
consistent with the behavior of the UNIX nice(1) command.

Bugs

    As with unzip, the zipinfo -M (more) option is overly simplistic in its
handling of screen output. It fails to detect the wrapping of long lines and may
scroll lines at the top of the screen before they are read. zipinfo should detect
and treat each occurrence of line wrap as one additional line printed, which
requires knowledge of both the screen width and height. In addition, zipinfo
should detect the true screen geometry on all systems.
    The multiple listing formats are unnecessarily complex and should be
simplified. (That is not to say that they will be.)

Examples

    The following example displays a basic, short-format listing of the complete
contents of the 085XDOCS.ZIP archive, with both header and totals lines.

```
castle% zipinfo 085XDOCS
Archive:   085XDOCS.zip   106272 bytes   4 files
-rw-a--     2.0 fat    76800 t- defN 18-Aug-98 21:55 085X01.DOC
-rw-a--     2.0 fat    67072 b- defN 22-Aug-98 01:39 085X02.DOC
-rw-a--     2.0 fat    95232 t- defN 31-Aug-98 20:29 085X042.DOC
-rw-a--     2.0 fat    63488 t- defN  4-Oct-98 20:24 085X04E.DOC
4 files, 302592 bytes uncompressed, 105858 bytes compressed:  65.0%
castle%
```

    The following example displays a basic, long-format listing (not verbose),
including header and totals lines.

```
castle% zipinfo -l 085XDOCS
Archive:   085XDOCS.ZIP   106272 bytes   4 files
-rw-a--     2.0 fat    76800 t-    28048 defN 18-Aug-98 21:55 085X01.DOC
-rw-a--     2.0 fat    67072 b-    24492 defN 22-Aug-98 01:39 085X02.DOC
-rw-a--     2.0 fat    95232 t-    30592 defN 31-Aug-98 20:29 085X042.DOC
-rw-a--     2.0 fat    63488 t-    22726 defN  4-Oct-98 20:24 085X04E.DOC
4 files, 302592 bytes uncompressed, 105858 bytes compressed:  65.0%
castle%
```

The following example lists the complete contents of the archive without header and totals lines.

```
castle% zipinfo --h-t 085XDOCS
-rw-a--    2.0 fat    76800 t- defN 18-Aug-98 21:55 085X01.DOC
-rw-a--    2.0 fat    67072 b- defN 22-Aug-98 01:39 085X02.DOC
-rw-a--    2.0 fat    95232 t- defN 31-Aug-98 20:29 085X042.DOC
-rw-a--    2.0 fat    63488 t- defN  4-Oct-98 20:24 085X04E.DOC
castle%
```

The following example produces the same result as the previous one, using a different syntax. The backslash is required only if the shell would otherwise expand the * wild-card. Alternatively, you can enclose the * in double quotes.

```
castle% zipinfo 085XDOCS \*
-rw-a--    2.0 fat    76800 t- defN 18-Aug-98 21:55 085X01.DOC
-rw-a--    2.0 fat    67072 b- defN 22-Aug-98 01:39 085X02.DOC
-rw-a--    2.0 fat    95232 t- defN 31-Aug-98 20:29 085X042.DOC
-rw-a--    2.0 fat    63488 t- defN  4-Oct-98 20:24 085X04E.DOC
castle%
```

The following example uses the ZIPINFO environment variable to turn off the totals line.

```
castle% setenv ZIPINFO --t
castle% zipinfo 085XDOCS
Archive:   085XDOCS.zip    106272 bytes    4 files
-rw-a--    2.0 fat    76800 t- defN 18-Aug-98 21:55 085X01.DOC
-rw-a--    2.0 fat    67072 b- defN 22-Aug-98 01:39 085X02.DOC
-rw-a--    2.0 fat    95232 t- defN 31-Aug-98 20:29 085X042.DOC
-rw-a--    2.0 fat    63488 t- defN  4-Oct-98 20:24 085X04E.DOC
castle%
```

The following examples show how to display the full, short-format listing when the environment variable is set to turn off the totals line. Note that you must explicitly specify the -s option because the -t option by itself implies that only the totals line is to be printed:

```
castle% setenv ZIPINFO --t
castle% zipinfo -t 085XDOCS
4 files, 302592 bytes uncompressed, 105858 bytes compressed:  65.0%
castle% zipinfo -st 085XDOCS
Archive:   085XDOCS.zip    106272 bytes    4 files
-rw-a--    2.0 fat    76800 t- defN 18-Aug-98 21:55 085X01.DOC
-rw-a--    2.0 fat    67072 b- defN 22-Aug-98 01:39 085X02.DOC
-rw-a--    2.0 fat    95232 t- defN 31-Aug-98 20:29 085X042.DOC
-rw-a--    2.0 fat    63488 t- defN  4-Oct-98 20:24 085X04E.DOC
4 files, 302592 bytes uncompressed, 105858 bytes compressed:  65.0%
castle%
```

The -s option, like -m and -l, includes header and totals lines by default, unless you specify otherwise. Because the environment variable specified no totals lines, and that setting has a higher precedence than the default behavior of -s, you must use an explicit -t option to produce the full listing. Because nothing was indicated about the header, the -s option is sufficient.

The following example lists information in medium format about a single file within the archive.

```
castle% zipinfo -m 085XDOCS 085X01.DOC
-rw-a--    2.0 fat    76800 t- 64% defN 18-Aug-98 21:55 085X01.DOC
castle%
```

When you specify any individual file with any of the format options, zipinfo displays only the single line of information about the requested file, regardless of the default specifications for header and totals lines. You can, of course, add the t or h option to the command.

The following example displays the first screen of information about the zip archive, using the verbose option and piping the output through the more(1) command.

```
castle% zipinfo -v 085XDOCS | more
Archive:  085XDOCS.zip   106272 bytes    4 files

End-of-central-directory record:
-------------------------------

    Actual offset of end-of-central-dir record:    106250 (00019F0Ah)
    Expected offset of end-of-central-dir record:  106250 (00019F0Ah)
    (based on the length of the central directory and its expected offset)

    This zipfile constitutes the sole disk of a single-part archive; its
    central directory contains 4 entries.  The central directory is 226
    (000000E2h) bytes long, and its (expected) offset in bytes from the
    beginning of the zipfile is 106024 (00019E28h).

    There is no zipfile comment.

Central directory entry #0:
---------------------------

    085X01.DOC

    offset of local header from start of archive:    4 (00000004h) bytes
    file system or operating system of origin:       MS-DOS, OS/2 or NT
    FAT
    version of encoding software:                    2.0
    minimum file system compatibility required:      MS-DOS, OS/2 or NT
    FAT
    minimum software version required to extract:    2.0
    compression method:                              deflated
    compression sub-type (deflation):                normal
    file security status:                            not encrypted
    extended local header:                           no
    file last modified on (DOS date/time):           1998 Aug 18 21:55:14
    32-bit CRC value (hex):                          dcd30c5e
    compressed size:                                 28048 bytes
```

```
        uncompressed size:                                    76800 bytes
        length of filename:                                   10 characters
    --More--
```

The following example shows the most-recently modified files in the archive
by using the -T option in conjunction with the sort(1) and tail(1) commands.

```
castle% zipinfo  -T 085XDOCS | sort -n +6 | tail -15
Archive:  085XDOCS.zip     106272 bytes    4 files
-rw-a--     2.0 fat     76800 t- defN 19980818.215514 085X01.DOC
-rw-a--     2.0 fat     67072 b- defN 19980822.013946 085X02.DOC
-rw-a--     2.0 fat     95232 t- defN 19980831.202906 085X042.DOC
-rw-a--     2.0 fat     63488 t- defN 19981004.202402 085X04E.DOC
castle%
```

The -n option to sort(1) sorts numerically instead of in ASCII order. The +6
option sorts on the sixth field after the first one (that is, the seventh field). This
count assumes the default short format listing; if you use -m or -l, the proper
sort(1) option is +7. The tail(1) command filters out all but the last 15 lines
of the listing. Future releases of zipinfo may incorporate date/time and file
name sorting as built-in options.

To display information for a list of files using the asterisk metacharacter, you
must escape it by preceding it with a backslash. The following example shows
information about three zip archives.

```
castle% zipinfo \*.ZIP
Archive:  085XDOCS.ZIP     145051 bytes     6 files
-rw-a--     2.0 fat     76800 t- defN 18-Aug-98 21:55 085X01.DOC
-rw-a--     2.0 fat     67072 b- defN 22-Aug-98 01:39 085X02.DOC
-rw-a--     2.0 fat     80384 b- defN 24-Sep-98 18:40 085X03~1.DOC
-rw-a--     2.0 fat     95232 t- defN 31-Aug-98 20:29 085X042.DOC
-rw-a--     2.0 fat     50688 b- defN  8-Jan-99 09:48 085X08R.DOC
-rw-a--     2.0 fat     73238 t- defN 18-Dec-98 14:18 085X09E.RTF
6 files, 443414 bytes uncompressed, 144439 bytes compressed:  67.4%

Archive:  085XFILE.ZIP    30716 bytes     1 file
-rw-a--     2.0 fat     95232 t- defN 31-Aug-98 20:29 085X042.DOC
1 file, 95232 bytes uncompressed, 30592 bytes compressed:  67.9%

Archive:  085XINTR.ZIP    43319 bytes     2 files
-rw-a--     2.0 fat     76800 t- defN 18-Aug-98 21:55 085X01.DOC
-rw-a--     2.0 fat     73238 t- defN 18-Dec-98 14:18 085X09E.RTF
2 files, 150038 bytes uncompressed, 43099 bytes compressed:  71.3%

3 archives were successfully processed.
castle%
```

See Also

```
ls(1), unzip(1)
```

URL

The Info-ZIP home page is currently at
`http://www.cdrom.com/pub/infozip/`

Copyright

Distributed with permission from Info-ZIP. Please see
`http://www.cdrom.com/pub/infozip/doc/COPYING` for copyright
information.

Author

Greg "Cave Newt" Roelofs. `ZipInfo` contains pattern matching code by Mark
Adler and fixes/improvements by many others. Please refer to the `CONTRIBS`
file in the `UnZip` source distribution for a more complete list.

SUBJECT INDEX

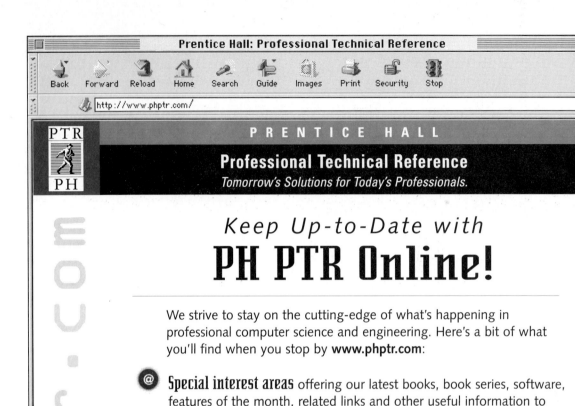